THE LAW OF BUSINESS TORTS AND UNFAIR COMPETITION

CASES, MATERIALS, AND PROBLEMS

■ ■ ■

Colin P. Marks

Professor of Law
St. Mary's University School of Law

Douglas K. Moll

Beirne, Maynard & Parsons, L.L.P. Professor of Law
University of Houston Law Center

AMERICAN CASEBOOK SERIES®

American Casebook Series is a trademark registered in the U.S. Patent and Trademark Office.

© 2016 LEG, Inc. d/b/a West Academic
    444 Cedar Street, Suite 700
    St. Paul, MN 55101
    1-877-888-1330

West, West Academic Publishing, and West Academic are trademarks of West Publishing Corporation, used under license.

Printed in the United States of America

ISBN: 978-0-314-27786-2

To my mother and father, who have always supported me in all my endeavors, and to my wife Jill and children Savy-Jo and George, who make me happy every day.

—CPM

To Stefanie, Asher, Samara, Daisy, and Gatsby, who make it all fun.

—DKM

PREFACE

This book is a comprehensive study of the law of business torts and unfair competition. A few features deserve specific mention. First, by design, the book provides comprehensive notes and questions that generally appear at the end of each principal case or excerpt. The notes and questions are intended to raise issues that we believe are important to an understanding of the materials. Second, a substantial number of problems are included to raise critical issues, to facilitate comprehension, and to present opportunities for students to apply concepts and doctrines to various factual settings. Finally, the accompanying statutory supplement contains all of the Restatement, uniform act, and other statutory provisions that are cited in the book.

We have used a number of stylistic conventions in the preparation of this book. Ellipses indicate textual omissions in cases and materials. Citations and footnotes, however, are usually omitted with no indication. Any footnotes that remain in cases and materials retain their original numbers. Square brackets typically identify author-added text, while letter footnotes identify author-added footnotes.

We would like to thank several people for their assistance in the preparation of this book: the librarians at the University of Houston Law Center; Professor Marks' research assistants at St. Mary's Law School, including Tapas Agarwal, Jared Anderson, Cheryl Auster, Kwenje Banda, John Bray, Rene DeLaO, Allison Ellis, Jennifer Fields, Kimberly Graves, Isaac Ta, Sanjeev Kumar, Sarah Minter, Randall Ordones, Reid Renken, Dena Richardson, and David Thomas; and the wonderful folks at West Academic Publishing.

COLIN P. MARKS
DOUGLAS K. MOLL

January 1, 2016

SUMMARY OF CONTENTS

TABLE OF CONTENTS

TABLE OF CASES

The principal cases are in bold type.

THE LAW OF
BUSINESS TORTS AND
UNFAIR COMPETITION

CASES, MATERIALS, AND PROBLEMS

INTRODUCTION

■ ■ ■

What are business torts? The typical first-year Torts class focuses on torts that cause personal injury and property damage. While there is usually some discussion of economic losses (e.g., an accident victim's lost wages or medical expenses), the discussion of such losses is generally incidental to the primary focus on the physical harm sustained by the victim. Business torts have a different focus. Such torts often cause "pure economic loss"—i.e., economic harm without any accompanying personal injury or property damage. For example, in a fraudulent investment scheme, the victim loses money, but rarely suffers bodily harm or property damage. Think of a business tort, therefore, as tortious conduct that primarily harms a plaintiff's wallet rather than his person or things.[a]

What is unfair competition? Unfair competition is an umbrella term used to describe "an array of legal actions addressing methods of competition that improperly interfere with the legitimate commercial interests of other sellers in the marketplace." RESTATEMENT (THIRD) OF UNFAIR COMPETITION (1995) (foreword). Examples of unfair competition actions include claims for deceptive marketing, trademark infringement, and theft of trade secrets. Each of these claims seeks a remedy for conduct that allegedly constitutes an inappropriate method of competing in the marketplace. Although unfair competition is used in this book primarily as a generic term to describe the various causes of action discussed in Part Two of the book, many states retain unfair competition as a "catch-all" cause of action of its own. In other words, if a defendant inappropriately competes in a manner that has not yet been recognized by existing causes of action, a catch-all unfair competition claim could be used to challenge the conduct. *See id.* § 1(a) (allowing a plaintiff to recover for deceptive marketing, trademark infringement, appropriation of trade secrets, and for "other acts or practices . . . determined to be actionable as an unfair method of competition, taking into account the nature of the conduct and its likely effect on both the person seeking relief and the public").

Why study business torts and unfair competition together? Business torts and unfair competition are similar in a number of ways. First, like business torts, unfair competition practices generally result in pure

---

[a] There are, of course, exceptions. For example, if a landlord fraudulently misrepresents that an apartment complex is safe to a prospective tenant, the misrepresentation may result in personal injury if the tenant is assaulted. The misrepresentation may also result in property damage if the tenant's personal property is stolen or otherwise harmed.

1

economic loss. Thus, both areas provide a nice counterpoint to the personal injury and property damage coverage of a standard introductory Torts course. Second, both areas form the core of a typical non-personal injury civil litigation practice. A commercial (i.e., business) litigator, in other words, frequently handles lawsuits involving business torts and unfair competition. As a result, knowledge of these topics is essential for any litigator wishing to have a practice broader than personal injury disputes.[b] Third, business torts and unfair competition are thematically related in that both areas reflect the type of conduct that society considers permissible (and impermissible) in a business context. Their collective law regulates the conduct of business transactions and seeks to promote fairness and competition.

Because of these similarities, the line between what is considered a business tort and what is considered unfair competition is not entirely clear. Do not let this trouble you. The terms have substantial overlap[c] and, for our purposes, the distinction is not important. In this book, we divide the material into Part One on business torts and Part Two on unfair competition based on two general criteria. First, business torts are largely governed by common law, while unfair competition practices are mostly regulated by statute. In general, therefore, the material in Part One of the book focuses on causes of action whose governing principles are provided by the common law, while the material in Part Two of the book focuses on causes of action whose governing principles are provided (at least partially) by statute.[d] Second, much of the business torts material in Part One of the book is the subject of the Third Restatement of Torts, while much of the unfair competition material in Part Two of the book is the subject of the Third Restatement of Unfair Competition. *See* RESTATEMENT (THIRD) OF TORTS: LIABILITY FOR ECONOMIC HARM (Tentative Draft No. 1, Apr. 4, 2012); RESTATEMENT (THIRD) OF TORTS: LIABILITY FOR ECONOMIC HARM (Tentative Draft No. 2, Apr. 7, 2014);

---

[b] *Cf.* Jay M. Feinman, *Teaching Economic Torts*, 95 KY. L.J. 893, 893–94 (2006–07) ("In practice, disputes involving economic torts are expanding as a mainstay of civil litigation practice, both because of the apparently infinite capacity of businesses to engage in questionable and dispute-generating behavior and because of the entrepreneurship of lawyers as the profitability of personal injury litigation declines due to the success of the tort reform movement in contracting the rights of victims of personal injuries.").

[c] *See, e.g.*, DAN B. DOBBS, THE LAW OF TORTS § 457, at 1300 (2000) (stating that "[u]nfair competition is a general term that includes deceptive trade practices, acts such as trademark infringement, and appropriation of trade values," and noting that "[a]ll of these are torts under common law rules"). The fact that unfair competition practices were once included in the Restatement of Torts is further evidence of the overlap between business torts and unfair competition. *See* RESTATEMENT (THIRD) OF UNFAIR COMPETITION (1995) (foreword) ("The subject of unfair competition was to have been addressed in the Restatement, Second, of Torts, as it had been in the original Restatement of Torts. However, it was eventually decided that the law of unfair competition had evolved to the point that it was no longer appropriate to treat it as a subcategory of the law of Torts.").

[d] Once again, this is true "in general" and not as an absolute matter. For example, as you will learn, many state unfair competition actions are governed by common law principles and not by statute. Nevertheless, we discuss these actions in Part Two of the book.

RESTATEMENT (THIRD) OF UNFAIR COMPETITION (1995). Thus, the subject matter of these Restatements has guided, to some extent, the division of topics in this book.[e]

As mentioned, Part One of the book covers business torts. This Part addresses the economic loss rule between non-contracting parties (Chapter 1); misrepresentation, including fraud, negligent misrepresentation, and innocent misrepresentation (Chapter 2); tortious interference with economic relations, including intentional interference with existing contract and prospective contract (Chapter 3); breach of fiduciary duty (Chapter 4); bad faith breach of contract, including insurance (Chapter 5); and the economic loss rule between contracting parties (Chapter 6). These Chapters focus primarily on principles articulated by the Second and Third Restatements of Torts. *See* RESTATEMENT (SECOND) OF TORTS (1977); RESTATEMENT (THIRD) OF TORTS: LIABILITY FOR ECONOMIC HARM (Tentative Draft No. 1, Apr. 4, 2012); RESTATEMENT (THIRD) OF TORTS: LIABILITY FOR ECONOMIC HARM (Tentative Draft No. 2, Apr. 7, 2014). The American Law Institute—an association of lawyers, academics, and judges—author the Restatements and, like all Restatements, their text and comments represent an effort to capture the law as developed by the courts. Keep in mind that the Restatements are influential and are persuasive to many courts, but they are not binding.

A major theme in Part One of the book involves the boundary between the law of tort and the law of contract. Tort claims are often more attractive to plaintiffs than contract claims because of the potential for punitive and mental anguish damages in tort. Contract law generally prohibits such recoveries. *See* RESTATEMENT (SECOND) OF CONTRACTS §§ 353, 355 (1981). Tort claims between contracting parties, however, can undermine the bargain that the parties struck. As you will learn, therefore, the law has developed limitations on when contracting parties are permitted to assert tort claims against one another.

Part Two of the book covers unfair competition. This Part addresses deceptive marketing (Chapter 7); commercial disparagement, including injurious falsehood (Chapter 8); misappropriation (Chapter 9); trade secrets (Chapter 10); trademark infringement (Chapter 11); antitrust (Chapter 12); and civil RICO (Chapter 13). These Chapters focus on common law and statutory principles articulated by various sources, including (among others) the Third Restatement of Unfair Competition, the Lanham Act, the Uniform Trade Secrets Act, and the Sherman Act.

---

[e] A notable exception involves injurious falsehood, which is slated to be part of the Third Restatement of Torts. *See* RESTATEMENT (THIRD) OF TORTS: LIABILITY FOR ECONOMIC HARM (Tentative Draft No. 1, Apr. 4, 2012) (prospective table of contents). This book includes injurious falsehood in Part Two on the theory that the topic is substantially related to the unfair competition material on commercial disparagement.

See RESTATEMENT (THIRD) OF UNFAIR COMPETITION (1995); Lanham Act, 15 U.S.C. §§ 1051–1141n; UNIF. TRADE SECRETS ACT §§ 1–12 (1985); Sherman Act, 15 U.S.C. §§ 1–7.

The major themes in Part Two of the book are the virtues of competition and the role of the law in regulating competitive behavior. If competition is valued, why not encourage competition to any extent? What considerations might justify limiting the types of conduct that count as permissible competition? *See generally* RESTATEMENT (THIRD) OF UNFAIR COMPETITION § 1 cmt. a (1995) ("The freedom to engage in business and to compete for the patronage of prospective customers is a fundamental premise of the free enterprise system.... The freedom to compete necessarily contemplates the probability of harm to the commercial relations of other participants in the market.... Liability is imposed under this Section, and under this Restatement generally, only in connection with harm resulting from particular methods of competition determined to be unfair.").

As a final note, it is highly unlikely that your professor will have time to assign every Chapter in the book. This should not worry you, as the book has been designed to allow picking and choosing among materials. Depending upon the length of your course and the particular focus of your professor, your class may cover only some of the Chapters in Parts One and Two, or perhaps omit a Part in its entirety. Regardless of what is covered, the information should be useful to you in understanding the important role that business torts and unfair competition actions play in our civil litigation system.

PART ONE

BUSINESS TORTS

∎ ∎ ∎

CHAPTER 1

THE ECONOMIC LOSS RULE (I)

■ ■ ■

As mentioned in the Introduction, business torts often cause "pure economic loss"—i.e., economic harm without any accompanying personal injury or property damage. The policy considerations surrounding pure economic loss and whether (and when) it should be legally compensable are different from those surrounding injuries to person and property, as illustrated by the materials below.

STATE OF LOUISIANA V. M/V TESTBANK
752 F.2d 1019 (5th Cir. 1985)

Before CLARK, CHIEF JUDGE, WISDOM, GEE, RUBIN, REAVLEY, POLITZ, RANDALL, TATE, JOHNSON, WILLIAMS, GARWOOD, JOLLY, HIGGINBOTHAM, DAVIS and HILL, CIRCUIT JUDGES.

PATRICK E. HIGGINBOTHAM, CIRCUIT JUDGE:

We are asked to abandon physical damage to a proprietary interest as a prerequisite to recovery for economic loss in cases of unintentional maritime tort. We decline the invitation.

I

In the early evening of July 22, 1980, the M/V SEA DANIEL, an inbound bulk carrier, and the M/V TESTBANK, an outbound container ship, collided at approximately mile forty-one of the Mississippi River Gulf outlet. At impact, a white haze enveloped the ships until carried away by prevailing winds, and containers aboard TESTBANK were damaged and lost overboard. The white haze proved to be hydrobromic acid and the contents of the containers which went overboard proved to be approximately twelve tons of pentachlorophenol, PCP, assertedly the largest such spill in United States history. The United States Coast Guard closed the outlet to navigation until August 10, 1980 and all fishing, shrimping, and related activity was temporarily suspended in the outlet and four hundred square miles of surrounding marsh and waterways.

Forty-one lawsuits were filed and consolidated before the same judge in the Eastern District of Louisiana. These suits presented claims of shipping interests, marina and boat rental operators, wholesale and retail seafood enterprises not actually engaged in fishing, seafood restaurants, tackle and bait shops, and recreational fishermen. They proffered an assortment of liability theories, including maritime tort, private actions pursuant to various sections of the Rivers & Harbors Appropriation Act of 1899 and rights of action under Louisiana law. . . .

Defendants moved for summary judgment as to all claims for economic loss unaccompanied by physical damage to property. The district court granted the requested summary judgment as to all such claims except those asserted by commercial oystermen, shrimpers, crabbers and fishermen who had been making a commercial use of the embargoed waters. . . .

On appeal a panel of this court affirmed, concluding that claims for economic loss unaccompanied by physical damage to a proprietary interest were not recoverable in maritime tort. 728 F.2d 748 (5th Cir.1984). The panel, as did the district court, pointed to the doctrine of *Robins Dry Dock & Repair Co. v. Flint*, 275 U.S. 303 (1927), and its development in this circuit. Judge Wisdom specially concurred, agreeing that the denial of these claims was required by precedent, but urging reexamination en banc. We then took the case en banc for that purpose. After extensive additional briefs and oral argument, we are unpersuaded that we ought to drop physical damage to a proprietary interest as a prerequisite to recovery for economic loss. To the contrary, our reexamination of the history and central purpose of this pragmatic restriction on the doctrine of foreseeability heightens our commitment to it. Ultimately we conclude that without this limitation foreseeability loses much of its ability to function as a rule of law.

. . . .

III

The meaning of *Robins Dry Dock v. Flint*, 275 U.S. 303 (1927) (Holmes, J.) is the flag all litigants here seek to capture. We turn first to that case and to its historical setting.

Robins broke no new ground but instead applied a principle, then settled both in the United States and England, which refused recovery for negligent interference with "contractual rights." Stated more broadly, the prevailing rule denied a plaintiff recovery for economic loss if that loss resulted from physical damage to property in which he had no proprietary interest. *See, e.g., Byrd v. English*, 117 Ga. 191, 43 S.E. 419 (1903); *Cattle v. Stockton Waterworks Co.*, 10 Q.B. 453, 457 (C.A.1875). *See also* James, *Limitations on Liability for Economic Loss Caused by Negligence: A Pragmatic Appraisal*, 25 Vand.L.Rev. 43, 44–46 (1972) (discussing history of the rule). Professor James explains this limitation on recovery of pure economic loss: "The explanation . . . is a pragmatic one: the physical consequences of negligence usually have been limited, but the indirect economic repercussions of negligence may be far wider, indeed virtually open-ended." James, *supra*, at 45.

Decisions such as *Stockton* illustrate the application of this pragmatic limitation on the doctrine of foreseeability. The defendant negligently caused its pipes to leak, thereby increasing the plaintiff's cost in performing its contract to dig a tunnel. The British court, writing fifty-two years before *Robins*, denied the plaintiff's claim. The court explained that if recovery were not contained, then in cases such as *Rylands v. Fletcher*, 1 L.R.–Ex. 265 (1866), the defendant would be liable not only to the owner of the mine and its workers "but also to . . . every workman and person employed in the mine, who in consequence of its stoppage made less wages than he would otherwise have done." *Id.* at 457.

–1–

In *Robins*, the time charterer of a steamship sued for profits lost when the defendant dry dock negligently damaged the vessel's propeller. The propeller had to be replaced, thus extending by two weeks the time the vessel was laid up in dry dock, and it was for the loss of use of the vessel for that period that the charterer sued. The Supreme Court denied recovery to the charterer, noting:

> . . . no authority need be cited to show that, as a general rule, at least, a tort to the person or property of one man does not make the tort-feasor liable to another merely because the injured person was under a contract with that other unknown to the doer of the wrong. (citation omitted). The law does not spread its protection so far.

275 U.S. at 309. . . .

–2–

The principle that there could be no recovery for economic loss absent physical injury to a proprietary interest was not only well established when *Robins Dry Dock* was decided, but was remarkably resilient as well. Its strength is demonstrated by the circumstance that *Robins Dry Dock* came ten years after Judge Cardozo's shattering of privity in *MacPherson v. Buick Motor Co.*, 217 N.Y. 382, 111 N.E. 1050 (1916). *See also Glanzer v. Shepard*, 233 N.Y. 236, 135 N.E. 275 (1922). Indeed this limit on liability stood against a sea of change in the tort law. Retention of this conspicuous bright-line rule in the face of the reforms brought by the increased influence of the school of legal realism is strong testament both to the rule's utility and to the absence of a more "conceptually pure" substitute. The push to delete the restrictions on recovery for economic loss lost its support and by the early 1940's had failed. *See* W. Prosser, *Law of Torts* § 129, at 938–940 (4th ed. 1971). In sum, it is an old sword that plaintiffs have here picked up.

–3–

Plaintiffs would confine *Robins* to losses suffered for inability to perform contracts between a plaintiff and others, categorizing the tort as a species of interference with contract. When seen in the historical context described above, however, it is apparent that *Robins Dry Dock* represents more than a limit on recovery for interference with contractual rights. Apart from what it represented and certainly apart from what it became, its literal holding was not so restricted. If a time charterer's relationship to its negligently injured vessel is too remote, other claimants without even the connection of a contract are even more remote.

It is true that in *Robins* the lower courts had sustained recovery on contract principles, but the Supreme Court pushed the steamship company's contract arguments aside and directly addressed its effort to recover in tort. . . . The language and the cases the *Robins* Court pointed to as "good statement[s]" of the principle make plain that the charterer failed to recover its delay claims from the dry dock because the Court believed them to be too remote. Notably, although the dry dock company did not know of the charter party when it damaged the propeller, delay losses by users of the vessel were certainly foreseeable. Thus *Robins* was a pragmatic limitation imposed by the Court upon the tort doctrine of foreseeability.

In a sense, every claim of economic injury rests in some measure on an interference with contract or prospective advantage. It was only in this sense that profits were lost in *Byrd v. English* when the electrical power to plaintiff's printing plant was cut off. The printing company's contractual right to receive power was interfered with, and in turn, its ability to print for its customers was impinged. That the printing company had a contract with the power company did not make more remote the relationship between its loss of profits and the tortious acts. To the contrary, the contract reduced this remoteness by defining an orbit of predictable injury smaller than if there were no contract between the power company and the printer. When the loss is economic rather than physical, that the loss caused a breach of contract or denied an expectancy is of no moment. If a plaintiff connected to the damaged chattels by contract cannot recover, others more remotely situated are foreclosed *a fortiori*. Indisputably, the *Robins Dry Dock* principle is not as easily contained as plaintiff would have it. . . .

–4–

This circuit has consistently refused to allow recovery for economic loss absent physical damage to a proprietary interest. . . .

. . . .

In sum, the decisions of courts in other circuits convince us that *Robins Dry Dock* is both a widely used and necessary limitation on recovery for economic losses.... The courts [have] made plain that restrictions on the concept of foreseeability ought to be imposed where recovery is sought for pure economic losses.

. . . .

IV

Plaintiffs urge that the requirement of physical injury to a proprietary interest is arbitrary, unfair, and illogical, as it denies recovery for foreseeable injury caused by negligent acts. At its bottom the argument is that questions of remoteness ought to be left to the trier of fact. Ultimately the question becomes who ought to decide—judge or jury—and whether there will be a rule beyond the jacket of a given case. The plaintiffs contend that the "problem" need not be separately addressed, but instead should be handled by "traditional" principles of tort law. Putting the problem of which doctrine is the traditional one aside, their rhetorical questions are flawed in several respects.

Those who would delete the requirement of physical damage have no rule or principle to substitute. Their approach fails to recognize limits upon the adjudicating ability of courts. We do not mean just the ability to supply a judgment; prerequisite to this adjudicatory function are preexisting rules, whether the creature of courts or legislatures. Courts can decide cases without preexisting normative guidance but the result becomes less judicial and more the product of a managerial, legislative or negotiated function.

Review of the foreseeable consequences of the collision of the SEA DANIEL and TESTBANK demonstrates the wave upon wave of successive economic consequences and the managerial role plaintiffs would have us assume. The vessel delayed in St. Louis may be unable to fulfill its obligation to haul from Memphis, to the injury of the shipper, to the injury of the buyers, to the injury of their customers. Plaintiffs concede, as do all who attack the requirement of physical damage, that a line would need to be drawn—somewhere on the other side, each plaintiff would say in turn, of its recovery. Plaintiffs advocate not only that the lines be drawn elsewhere but also that they be drawn on an ad hoc and discrete basis. The result would be that no determinable measure of the limit of foreseeability would precede the decision on liability. We are told that when the claim is too remote, or too tenuous, recovery will be denied. Presumably then, as among all plaintiffs suffering foreseeable economic loss, recovery will turn on a judge or jury's decision. There will be no rationale for the differing results save the "judgment" of the trier of fact. Concededly, it can "decide" all the claims presented, and with comparative if not absolute ease. The point is not that such a process cannot be administered but rather that its judgments would be much less the products of a determinable rule of law. In this important sense, the resulting decisions would be judicial products only in their draw upon judicial resources.

The bright line rule of damage to a proprietary interest, as most, has the virtue of predictability with the vice of creating results in cases at its edge that are said to be "unjust" or "unfair." Plaintiffs point to seemingly perverse results, where claims the rule allows and those it disallows are juxtaposed—such as vessels striking a dock, causing minor but recoverable damage, then lurching athwart a channel causing great but unrecoverable economic loss. The answer is that when lines are drawn sufficiently sharp in their definitional edges to be reasonable and predictable, such differing results are the inevitable result—indeed, decisions are the desired product. But there is more. The line drawing sought by plaintiffs is no less arbitrary because the line drawing appears only in the outcome—as one claimant is found too remote and another is allowed to recover. The true difference is that plaintiffs' approach would mask the results. The present rule would be more candid, and in addition, by making results more predictable, serves a normative function. It operates as a rule of law and allows a court to adjudicate rather than manage.[12]

V

That the rule is identifiable and will predict outcomes in advance of the ultimate decision about recovery enables it to play additional roles. Here we agree with plaintiffs that economic analysis, even at the rudimentary level of jurists, is helpful both in the identification of such roles and the essaying of how the roles play. Thus it is suggested that placing all the consequence of its error on the maritime industry will enhance its incentive for safety. While correct, as far as such analysis goes, such *in terrorem* benefits have an optimal level. Presumably, when the cost of an unsafe condition exceeds its utility there is an incentive to change. As the costs of an accident become increasing multiples of its utility, however, there is a point at which greater accident costs lose meaning, and the incentive curve flattens. When the accident costs are added in large but unknowable amounts the value of the exercise is diminished.

With a disaster inflicting large and reverberating injuries through the economy, as here, we believe the more important economic inquiry is

---

[12] Fuller, *The Forms and Limits of Adjudication*, 92 Harv.L.Rev. 353, 396 (1978). This case illustrates how our technocratic tradition masks a deep difference in attitudes toward the roles of a judiciary. The difference between the majority and dissenting opinions is far more than a choice between competing maritime rules. The majority is driven by the principle of self ordering and modesty for the judicial role; the dissent accepts a role of management which can strain the limits of adjudication.

that of relative cost of administration, and in maritime matters administration quickly involves insurance. Those economic losses not recoverable under the present rule for lack of physical damage to a proprietary interest are the subject of first party or loss insurance. The rule change would work a shift to the more costly liability system of third party insurance. For the same reasons that courts have imposed limits on the concept of foreseeability, liability insurance might not be readily obtainable for the types of losses asserted here. As Professor James has noted, "[s]erious practical problems face insurers in handling insurance against potentially wide, open-ended liability. From an insurer's point of view it is not practical to cover, without limit, a liability that may reach catastrophic proportions, or to fix a reasonable premium on a risk that does not lend itself to actuarial measurement." James, *supra*, at 53. By contrast, first party insurance is feasible for many of the economic losses claimed here. Each businessman who might be affected by a disruption of river traffic or by a halt in fishing activities can protect against that eventuality at a relatively low cost since his own potential losses are finite and readily discernible. Thus, to the extent that economic analysis informs our decision here, we think that it favors retention of the present rule.

VI

. . . .

Plaintiffs seek to avoid the *Robins* rule by characterizing their claims as damages caused by a public nuisance. They suggest that when a defendant unreasonably interferes with public rights by obstructing navigation or negligently polluting a waterway he creates a public nuisance for which recovery is available to all who have sustained "particular damages." As defined at common law such damages are those which are substantially greater than the presumed-at-law damages suffered by the general public as a result of the nuisance. *See generally Restatement (Second) of Torts* §§ 821B, 821C (1977); Prosser, *Private Action For Public Nuisance,* 52 Va.L.Rev. 997 (1966). Characterizing the problem as one of public nuisance, however, does not immediately solve the problems with plaintiffs' damage claims for pure economic losses. As Dean Prosser has explained, "courts have not always found it at all easy to determine what is sufficient 'particular damage' to support [a] private action [for a public nuisance], and some rather fine lines have been drawn in the decisions." W. Prosser, *Law of Torts* § 88 (4th ed. 1971). In drawing such lines today we are unconvinced that we should abandon the physical damage limitation as a prerequisite to recovery for economic loss.

The problem in public nuisance theory of determining when private damages are sufficiently distinct from those suffered by the general public so as to justify recovery is as difficult, if not more so, as determining which foreseeable damages are too remote to justify recovery in negligence. In each case it is a matter of degree, and in each case lines must be drawn. With economic losses such as the ones claimed here the problem is to determine who among an entire community that has been commercially affected by an accident has sustained a pecuniary loss so great as to justify distinguishing his losses from similar losses suffered by others. Given the difficulty of this task, we see no jurisprudential advantage in permitting the use of nuisance theory to skirt the *Robins* rule.

Were we to allow plaintiffs recovery for their losses under a public nuisance theory we would permit recovery for injury to the type of interest that, as we have already explained, we have consistently declined to protect. Nuisance, as Dean Prosser has explained, is not a separate tort subject to rules of its own but instead is a type of damage. W. Prosser, *Law of Torts* § 87 (4th ed. 1971). Our decisions under *Robins* have emphasized the nature of the interest harmed rather than the theory of recovery. As we noted in *Dick Meyers Towing*, "[r]ephrasing the claim as a public nuisance claim does not change its essential character." [*Dick Meyers Towing Serv., Inc. v. United States*, 577 F.2d 1023, 1025 n.4 (5th Cir. 1978)]. Thus we conclude that plaintiffs may not recover for pure economic losses under a public nuisance theory in maritime tort.

. . . .

VII

In conclusion, having reexamined the history and central purpose of the doctrine of *Robins Dry Dock* as developed in this circuit, we remain committed to its teaching. Denying recovery for pure economic losses is a pragmatic limitation on the doctrine of foreseeability, a limitation we find to be both workable and useful. . . .

Accordingly, the decision of the district court granting summary judgment to defendants on all claims for economic losses unaccompanied by physical damage to property is AFFIRMED.

GEE, CIRCUIT JUDGE, with whom CLARK, CHIEF JUDGE, joins, concurring:

. . . .

If the rule which Judge Wisdom espouses were one written in stone, I would be the first to enforce it by whatever means and procedures, inadequate or no, were available. That is not the question. The question is whether we should *ourselves adopt* such a rule and then proceed to apply it. My answer is that since I do not believe we are capable of administering such a procedure justly, we should not set ourselves the task. Nor am I so clear as my dissenting brethren seem to be about where the high ground lies in these premises. Extending theories of liability may not always be the more moral course, especially in such a case as this, where the extension, in the course of awarding damages to unnumbered claimants for injuries that are unavoidably speculative, may well visit destruction on enterprise after enterprise, with the consequent loss of employment and productive capacity which that entails.

WISDOM, CIRCUIT JUDGE, with whom ALVIN B. RUBIN, POLITZ, TATE, and JOHNSON, CIRCUIT JUDGES, join, dissenting.

Robins is the Tar Baby of tort law in this circuit. And the brier-patch is far away. This Court's application of *Robins* is out of step with contemporary tort doctrine, works substantial injustice on innocent victims, and is unsupported by the considerations that justified the Supreme Court's 1927 decision.

Robins was a tort case grounded on a contract. Whatever the justification for the original holding, this Court's requirement of physical injury as a condition to recovery is an unwarranted step backwards in torts jurisprudence. The resulting bar for claims of economic loss unaccompanied by any physical damage conflicts with conventional tort principles of foreseeability and proximate cause. I would analyze the plaintiffs' claims under these principles, using the "particular damage" requirement of public nuisance law as an additional means of limiting claims. Although this approach requires a case-by-case analysis, it comports with the fundamental idea of fairness that innocent plaintiffs should receive compensation and negligent defendants should bear the cost of their tortious acts. Such a result is worth the additional costs of adjudicating these claims, and this rule of liability appears to be more economically efficient. Finally, this result would relieve courts of the necessity of manufacturing exceptions totally inconsistent with the expanded *Robins* rule of requiring physical injury as a prerequisite to recovery.

. . . .

Whatever the pragmatic justification for the original holding in *Robins,* the majority has extended the case beyond the warrant of clear necessity in requiring *a physical injury* for a recovery of economic loss in cases such as the one before the court. *Robins* prevented plaintiffs who were neither proximately nor foreseeably injured by a tortious act or product from recovering solely by claiming a contract with the injured party. The wisdom of this rule is apparent. This rule, however, has been expanded now to bar recovery by plaintiffs who would be allowed to recover if judged under conventional principles of foreseeability and proximate cause.

. . . .

Robins held only that if a defendant's negligence injures party *A*, and the plaintiff suffers loss of expected income or profits because it had a contract with *A*, then the plaintiff has no cause of action based on the defendant's negligence.

. . . It is a long step from *Robins* to a rule that requires *physical damage* as a prerequisite to recovery in maritime tort. The majority believes that the plaintiff's lack of any contractual connection with an injured party, taken with the *Robins* rule, forecloses liability: "If a plaintiff connected to the damaged chattels by contract cannot recover, others more remotely situated are foreclosed *a fortiori*." This conclusion follows readily from the reasoning that if uninjured contracting parties are barred from recovery, and if contracting parties have a closer legal relationship than non-contracting parties, then a party who is not physically injured and who does not have a contractual relation to the damage is surely barred.

This argument would be sound in instances where the plaintiff suffered no loss *but for a contract* with the injured party. We would measure a plaintiff's connection to the tortfeasor by the only line connecting them, the contract, and disallow the claim under *Robins*. In the instant case, however, some of the plaintiffs suffered damages whether or not they had a contractual connection with a party physically injured by the tortfeasor. These plaintiffs do not need to rely on a contract to link them to the tort: The collision proximately caused their losses, and those losses were foreseeable. These plaintiffs are therefore freed from the *Robins* rule concerning the recovery of those who suffer economic loss because of an injury to a party with whom they have contracted.

. . . .

One cannot deny that *Robins*'s policy of limiting the set of plaintiffs who can recover for a person's negligence and damage to physical property provides a "bright line" for demarcating the boundary between recovery and nonrecovery. Physical harm suggests a proximate relation between the act and the interference. At bottom, however, the requirement of a tangible injury is artificial because it does not comport with accepted principles of tort law. Mrs. Palsgraf, although physically injured, could not recover. Many other plaintiffs, although physically uninjured, can recover.

The inapplicability of *Robins* to plaintiffs who have been proximately and foreseeably injured by the collision illustrates the fundamental weakness of founding a rule of recovery in tort upon *Robins*. Conventional tort principles do not apply in *Robins* because the connection between the plaintiff and the tort was a contract, not a tortious act or a defective product. In cases where the parties have suffered losses only because they are parts of a chain of contracting parties, only one of whom was physically injured, *Robins* provides a bright-line rule to limit claims. Whatever the justification for this rule in its original context, however, we should not extend it to instances where the parties are not linked merely in a contractual chain. Instead, we should allow recovery in instances where each of the parties alleges a loss that occurred outside this contractual chain, where each injured party, isolated from another injured party, can assert an injury that is cognizable when judged by our usual rules of proximate cause and foreseeability.[25] There is only one justification for the requirement of physical injury: If *Robins* establishes a policy of restricting the type of plaintiff who can recover for a defendant's negligence, physical property damage furnishes an easily discernible boundary between recovery and nonrecovery.

With deference to the majority, I suggest, notwithstanding their well reasoned opinion, that the utility derived from having a "bright line" boundary does not outweigh the disutility caused by the limitation on recovery imposed by the physical-damage requirement. *Robins* and its progeny represent a wide departure from the usual tort doctrines of foreseeability and proximate cause. Those doctrines, as refined in the law of public nuisance, provide a rule of recovery that compensates innocent plaintiffs and holds the defendants liable for much of the harm proximately caused by their negligence.

III. AN ALTERNATE RULE OF RECOVERY

Rather than limiting recovery under an automatic application of a physical damage requirement, I would analyze the plaintiffs' claims under the conventional tort principles of negligence, foreseeability, and proximate causation. I would confine *Robins* to the "factual contours" of that case: A plaintiff's claim may be barred only if the claim is derived solely through contract with an injured party. The majority's primary criticism of this approach to a determination of liability is that it is potentially open ended. Yet, there are well-established tort principles to limit liability for a widely-suffered harm. Under the contemporary law of public nuisance, courts compensate "particularly" damaged plaintiffs for harms suffered from a wide-ranging tort, but deny recovery to more generally damaged parties. Those parties who are foreseeably and proximately injured by an oil spill or closure of a navigable river, for example, and who can also prove damages that are beyond the general

---

[25] A recent article asserts that applications of *Robins* only appear to have created the requirement for physical injury. Rizzo, *A Theory of Economic Loss in the Law of Torts*, 11 J.Legal Stud. 281 (1982). Professor Rizzo has as his central hypothesis that courts' allowance or denial of recovery for economic loss can be explained by the absence or presence of the opportunity to reallocate losses contractually. According to Professor Rizzo, courts have established a rule that, by denying recovery in certain types of situations, will encourage contracts of indemnity between the physically injured party and those suffering pure economic harm. Similarly, courts permit recovery when it would be difficult or impossible for the parties to form such an indemnity contract. This rule, in turn, reduces litigation costs. . . .

economic dislocation that attends such disasters should recover whether or not they had contractual dealings with others who were also damaged by the tortious act. The limitation imposed by "particular" damages, together with refined notions of proximate cause and foreseeability, provides a workable scheme of liability that is in step with the rest of tort law, compensates innocent plaintiffs, and imposes the costs of harm on those who caused it.

. . . .

IV. ADVANTAGES OF THE ALTERNATE RULE OF RECOVERY

The advantages of this alternate rule of recovery are that it compensates damaged plaintiffs, imposes the cost of damages upon those who have caused the harm, is consistent with economic principles of modern tort law, and frees courts from the necessity of creating a piecemeal quilt of exceptions to avoid the harsh effects of the *Robins* rule.

. . . If tort law fails to compensate plaintiffs or to impose the cost of damages on those who caused the harm, it should be under a warrant clear of necessity. When a rule of law, once extended, leads to inequitable results and creates principles of recovery that are at odds with the great weight of tort jurisprudence, then that rule of law merits scrutiny. A strict application of the extension denies recovery to many plaintiffs who should be awarded damages. Conventional tort principles of foreseeability, proximate causation, and "particular" damages would avoid such unfairness.

It is true that application of foreseeability and proximate causation would necessitate case-by-case adjudication. But I have a more optimistic assessment of courts' ability to undertake such adjudication than the majority.[38] Certainly such an inquiry would be no different from our daily task of weighing such claims in other tort cases.

The majority opinion also states that the *Robins* rule, being free from the vagaries of factual findings in a case-by-case determination, serves an important normative function because it is more predictable and more "candid." Normative values would also be served, however, by eliminating a broad categorical rule that is insensitive to equitable and social policy concerns that would support allowing the plaintiffs' claims in many

---

[38] The majority criticizes foreseeability because it necessitates a case-by-case determination of liability. But this criticism of "foreseeability" as the criterion for judgment applies with equal force to well-established tort law for physical injury. The unquestioned concepts of foreseeability and proximate cause as established in *Palsgraf* and its progeny are open to the same condemnation that the majority makes of a rule of liability that would abandon *Robins*. . . . The majority opinion favors a bright line rule, as opposed to a case-by-case determination of liability, because it enables courts to "adjudicate" rather than to "manage." A bright line rule such as the one the majority proposes, however, requires no adjudication whatsoever. Judges need merely to preside over a self-executing system of limited liability where recovery is predicated upon an easily determined physical injury. The application of such a rule, rather than a case-by-case determination, seems more "management" than adjudication.

individual cases. In assessing "normative concerns," the courts' compass should be a sense of fairness and equity, both of which are better served by allowing plaintiffs to present their claims under usual tort standards. It is not clear, moreover, that a jury's finding of negligence in a case-by-case determination is "less the product of a determinable rule of law" when the finder of fact is guided in its determination by rules of law. The jury's finding of liability in this case would be no more "lawless" than a finding of proximate cause, foreseeability, and particular damages in a physical damage case.

. . . The economic arguments regarding allocation of loss that purportedly favor the *Robins* rule of nonliability are not as clear to me as they appear to be to the majority. It is true that denial of recovery may effectively spread the loss over the victims. It is not certain, however, that victims are generally better insurers against the risk of loss caused by tortious acts having widespread consequences. Although the victims do possess greater knowledge of their circumstances and their potential damages, we do not know whether insurance against these types of losses is readily available to the businesses that may be affected. We do know that insurance against this kind of loss is already available for shippers. Imposition of liability upon the shippers helps ensure that the potential tortfeasor faces incentives to take the proper care. The majority's point is well taken that the incentives to avoid accidents do not increase once potential losses pass a certain measure of enormity. But in truth we have no idea what this measure is: Absent hard data, I would rather err on the side of receiving little additional benefit from imposing additional quanta of liability than err by adhering to *Robins'* inequitable rule and bar victims' recovery on the mistaken belief that a "marginal incentive curve" was flat, or nearly so. If a loss must be borne, it is no worse if a "merely" negligent defendant bears the loss than an innocent plaintiff absorb the damages.

V. CONCLUSION

The *Robins* approach restricts liability more severely than the policies behind limitations on liability require and imposes the cost of the accident on the victim, who is usually not in a superior position to obtain insurance to cover this loss. I would apply a rule of recovery based on conventional tort principles of proximate cause and foreseeability and limit eligibility only by the requirement that a claimant prove "particular" damages.

ALVIN B. RUBIN, CIRCUIT JUDGE, with whom WISDOM, POLITZ and TATE, CIRCUIT JUDGES, join, dissenting.

. . . .

Robins should not be extended beyond its actual holding and should not be applied in cases like this, for the result is a denial of recompense to innocent persons who have suffered a real injury as a result of someone else's fault. We should not flinch from redressing injury because Congress has been indifferent to the problem.

NOTES & QUESTIONS

(1) *Testbank* sets forth the general rule that, in actions for unintentional torts, a plaintiff cannot recover for economic loss in the absence of personal injury to the plaintiff or damage to the plaintiff's property. *See* RESTATEMENT (THIRD) OF TORTS: LIABILITY FOR ECONOMIC HARM §§ 1(a), 2 (Tentative Draft No. 1, Apr. 4, 2012) (stating that "[a]n actor has no general duty to avoid the unintentional infliction of economic loss on another," and defining "economic loss" as "pecuniary damage not arising from injury to the plaintiff's person or from physical harm to the plaintiff's property"). A number of courts refer to this principle as the "economic loss rule." *See, e.g., LAN/STV & STV, Inc. v. Martin K. Eby Constr. Co.*, 435 S.W.3d 234, 235 (Tex. 2014) ("In actions for unintentional torts, the common law has long restricted recovery of purely economic damages unaccompanied by injury to the plaintiff or his property—a doctrine we have referred to as the economic loss rule.").

(2) What policy arguments are raised by the *Testbank* majority in support of retaining the economic loss rule? In thinking about this question, consider the following observations:

> An economic loss or injury, as the term is used here, means a financial loss not arising from injury to the plaintiff's person or from physical harm to the plaintiff's property. Economic injuries may be no less important than injuries of other kinds; a pure but severe economic loss might well be worse for a plaintiff than a more modest personal injury, and the difference between economic loss in itself and economic loss resulting from property damage may be negligible from the victim's standpoint. For several reasons, however, courts impose tort liability for economic loss more selectively than liability for other types of harms.

> *(1). Indeterminate and disproportionate liability.* Economic losses proliferate more easily than losses of other kinds. Physical forces that cause injury ordinarily spend themselves in predictable ways; their exact courses may be hard to predict, but their lifespan and power to harm are limited. A badly driven car threatens physical harm only to others nearby. Economic harm is not self-limiting in this way. A single negligent utterance can cause economic loss to thousands of people who rely on it, those losses may produce additional losses to those who were relying on the first round of victims, and so on. Consequences of this sort may be at least generally foreseeable to the person who commits the negligent act. Defendants in such cases thus might face liabilities that are indeterminate and out of proportion to their culpability. Those

liabilities may in turn create an exaggerated pressure to avoid an activity altogether.

(2). Deference to contract. Risks of economic loss tend to be especially well suited to allocation by contract. First, economic injuries caused by negligence often result from a decision by the victim to rely on a defendant's words or acts when entering some sort of transaction—an investment in a company, the purchase of a house, and so forth. A potential plaintiff making such a decision has a full chance to consider how to manage the risks involved, whether by inspecting the item or investment, obtaining insurance against the risk of disappointment, or making a contract that assigns the risk of loss to someone else. Second, money is a complete remedy for an economic injury. Insurance benefits, indemnification by agreement, or other replacements of money payments are just as good as the money lost in a transaction that turns out badly. This fungibility makes those other ways of managing risk—insurance, indemnity, and the like—more attractive than they might be to a party facing a prospect of personal injury.

Those same points often will make it hard for a court to know what allocation of responsibility for economic loss would best serve the interests of the parties to a risky situation. A contract that settles responsibility for such a risk will therefore be preferable in most cases to a judicial assignment of liability after harm is done. The contract will better reflect the preferences of the parties and help prevent the need for speculation and litigation later. Contracts also are governed by a body of commercial law that has been developed to address economic loss, and thus will often be better suited for that task than the law of torts. In short, contracts to manage the risk of economic loss are more often possible, and more often desirable, than contracts to manage risks of other types of injury. As a result, courts . . . often restrict the role of tort law in . . . circumstances in which protection by contract is available.

RESTATEMENT (THIRD) OF TORTS: LIABILITY FOR ECONOMIC HARM § 1 cmt. c (Tentative Draft No. 1, Apr. 4, 2012).

(3) Despite the implication from *Testbank*, the economic loss rule is neither limited to the maritime setting, nor is it restricted to large-scale accidents. *See, e.g., Coastal Conduit & Ditching, Inc. v. Noram Energy Corp.,* 29 S.W.3d 282, 283–84, 287–88 (Tex. App. 2000) (noting that the rule has been adopted "in non-admiralty contexts by other jurisdictions," and applying the rule to prevent a plaintiff excavation company from recovering in negligence for its economic losses (increased overhead and other expenses) caused by the defendant failing to mark or mismarking its underground gas lines). Indeed, the Third Restatement makes clear that the *Testbank* rule is broader than the factual setting of *Testbank* itself. Section 1 of the Third Restatement generically asserts that "[a]n actor has no general duty to avoid

the unintentional infliction of economic loss on another," and several illustrations apply the rule to bar a plaintiff's recovery in situations not involving large-scale accidents. *See* RESTATEMENT (THIRD) OF TORTS: LIABILITY FOR ECONOMIC HARM § 1(a) & illus. 3–5 (Tentative Draft No. 1, Apr. 4, 2012). Similarly, § 7 of the Third Restatement broadly states that "a claimant cannot recover for economic loss caused by (a) unintentional injury to another person; or (b) unintentional injury to property in which the claimant has no proprietary interest."

(4) Business torts usually avoid the application of the economic loss rule set forth in *Testbank*. Although business torts typically involve pure economic loss, many of the torts are intentional in nature (e.g., fraud, interference with existing contract, interference with prospective contract), which places them outside the scope of the rule. Moreover, many jurisdictions allow certain negligence-related torts to proceed, such as professional malpractice and negligent misrepresentation. Thus, the *Testbank* rule tends to preclude only general negligence and strict liability actions that seek recovery for pure economic loss. *See, e.g.*, William Powers, Jr. & Margaret Niver, *Negligence, Breach of Contract, and the "Economic Loss" Rule*, 23 TEX. TECH L. REV. 477, 480 n.13 (1992) ("Moreover, the 'economic loss' rule is applicable, if at all, only in negligence and strict products liability. It does not preclude recovery for pure economic loss in cases involving fraud, negligent misrepresentation, or intentional interference with contract."); *see also* RESTATEMENT (THIRD) OF TORTS: LIABILITY FOR ECONOMIC HARM § 1(b) & cmt. d (Tentative Draft No. 1, Apr. 4, 2012) (noting that "[d]uties to avoid the unintentional infliction of economic loss are recognized in the circumstances set forth in [the subsequent sections of the chapter]," which include professional negligence and negligent misrepresentation).

(5) In actuality, the rule of *Testbank* reflects only one strand of the economic loss rule. Consider the following observations:

> Two quite different types of cases implicate the economic loss rule. In the first type, represented by *Testbank* . . . , the plaintiff and defendant are strangers (that is, they do not have a contractual relationship). One rationale for precluding recovery of pure economic loss in these cases is a fear that the purely economic consequences of a defendant's negligence are not limited by the normal tort limit on the scope of a negligent defendant's liability, foreseeability on a case-by-case basis. Another rationale is that plaintiffs are in a better position than defendants to evaluate their own susceptibility to pure economic loss and protect against the economic loss through first-party insurance. . . .

>   . . . .

> In the second type of case, the plaintiff and the defendant are not strangers. They either have a contractual relationship, or if they are not in technical privity of contract, they are at least indirect parties to a market transaction. A rationale for precluding recovery

of pure economic damages in these cases is that the bargaining process, and therefore contract law, is a better method of assigning economic risks than are the socially imposed norms of tort law. This does not mean that we should give the parties unlimited power to assign risks of economic loss. Rather, it merely means that we should decide such questions using the tools of contract law, including the appropriate rules about privity of contract, third-party beneficiaries and unconscionability.

Many of the cases of this second type have involved strict products liability claims, where an additional reason exists for precluding recovery of pure economic loss. If courts permitted plaintiffs to recover under strict products liability for pure economic loss caused by poor performance of the product, they could be accused of impinging on the domain of the warranty provisions of the Uniform Commercial Code (the "Code"). Strict products liability and warranty are similar in that they require proof of a defect but, at least nominally, they do not require proof of the defendant's fault. It would be problematic to have a tort theory similar to warranty that is not bound by the other requirements of the Code, such as privity, notice, disclaimers, and remedy limitations. . . . Thus, courts seemingly have been compelled to carve out a core of "economic" disputes to keep strict products liability from displacing the Code entirely.

William Powers, Jr. & Margaret Niver, *Negligence, Breach of Contract, and the "Economic Loss" Rule*, 23 TEX. TECH L. REV. 477, 481–83 (1992).

As mentioned, business torts usually avoid the application of the "stranger" strand of the economic loss rule. The relationship between business torts and the "nonstranger" strand of the rule will be discussed in Chapter 6.

CHAPTER 2

MISREPRESENTATION

■ ■ ■

Misrepresentation refers to a collection of related torts that all address liability for economic harm caused by a plaintiff's justifiable reliance upon a defendant's material misstatements. Most often, such misstatements cause the plaintiff to enter into a bargain or other transaction that does not turn out how the plaintiff expected. Liability may be based on the defendant's intent to deceive (the tort of "fraud" or "deceit"), his negligence (the tort of "negligent misrepresentation"), or upon a policy requiring the defendant to be strictly liable for his inaccurate statements (the tort of "innocent misrepresentation"). Each of these misrepresentation torts will be discussed in the materials below.

A. INTENTIONAL MISREPRESENTATION (FRAUD)

The tort of fraud (also known as "deceit," or referred to imprecisely as "misrepresentation") has existed for hundreds of years. In *Neurosurgery and Spine Surgery, S.C. v. Goldman*, 790 N.E.2d 925 (Ill. App. Ct. 2003), the court described the historical origins of the tort and the modern context in which it typically arises:

> We begin our discussion by noting that the tort of fraudulent misrepresentation is often surrounded by unnecessary confusion, because misrepresentations themselves often play large roles in a variety of other torts. For instance, an untrue assertion may be at the heart of an action for false imprisonment, conversion, or trespass to land. A misrepresentation is the essence of torts such as defamation, interference with contractual relations, and malicious prosecution. A malicious, outrageous lie may even give rise to a cause of action for intentional infliction of emotional distress. In summary, a great number of causes of action stem from misrepresentations.
>
> However, not every misrepresentation gives rise to a cause of action for fraudulent misrepresentation. The origin of fraudulent misrepresentation lies in the common law action of deceit, which was a very narrow tort. See *Pasley v. Freeman*, 100 Eng. Rep. 450 (K.B.1789); *Derry v. Peek*, 14 A.C. 337 (H.L.1888). Prior to the eighteenth century, recovery on the action of deceit was not available unless the misrepresentation was part of some

contractual dealing between the parties. Then, in 1789, in *Pasley*, it was held that one who fraudulently induced a third party to extend credit to a person known to be untrustworthy was liable to the defrauded party. Deceit, as a distinct tort, thus came into being, independent of any contractual relationship.

In 1889, in *Peek*, deceit became the tort we today refer to as fraudulent misrepresentation. In *Peek*, the directors of a tramway company issued a prospectus to induce the public to subscribe for stock; the prospectus contained the following unqualified statement: "[T]he company has the right to use steam or mechanical motive power instead of horses * * *." In fact, however, the company had no such right inasmuch as the government permitted the use of steam as a motive power only if the company first obtained governmental consent and the company had never obtained such consent. Peek, a stockholder who had purchased shares on the faith of the prospectus, brought an action for deceit. The court concluded that the defendants had honestly believed the statement to be true, although they had no reasonable grounds for any such belief. It was held that the action could not be maintained, since nothing more than negligence was shown.

Historically, the torts of deceit and fraudulent misrepresentation have been limited to cases involving business or financial transactions between parties, right down to the first recorded cases, *Pasley* and *Peek*. See W. Prosser, Torts § 105 (4th ed.1971); see also *Johnson v. State*, 447 P.2d 352, 365 (1968) (holding that the tort of fraudulent misrepresentation applies only to interferences with financial or commercial interests). The United States Supreme Court has similarly observed:

> "[M]any familiar forms of * * * conduct may be said to involve an element of 'misrepresentation,' in the generic sense of that word, but '[s]o far as misrepresentation has been treated as giving rise in and of itself to a distinct cause of action in tort, it has been identified with the common law action of deceit,' and has been confined 'very largely to the invasion of interests of a financial or commercial character, in the course of business dealings.' " *United States v. Neustadt,* 366 U.S. 696, 711 n. 26 (1961), quoting W. Prosser, Torts § 85, at 702–03 (1941).

The tort of fraudulent misrepresentation has also historically been limited to cases where a plaintiff has suffered a pecuniary harm. See W. Prosser, Torts, § 105 (4th ed.1971); see also Restatement (Second) of Torts § 531 (1976) (defining damages only in terms of pecuniary loss). Where a plaintiff has sustained physical harm, recovery will lie in one of the above other tortious actions. See E. Kionka, Torts 268 (2d ed.1993). Indeed, fraudulent misrepresentation is purely an economic tort under which one may recover only monetary damages. *McConkey v. AON Corp.*, 354 N.J.Super. 25, 59, 804 A.2d 572, 593 (2002) (holding that damages in a fraudulent misrepresentation action are limited to those that are pecuniary); *Jourdain v. Dineen,* 527 A.2d 1304, 1307 (Me.1987) (holding that pecuniary damages are essential to a fraudulent misrepresentation cause of action).

> "Although the invasion of an economic interest by tort or by contract breach will often cause the plaintiff personal distress, the interest ordinarily protected in such cases is purely an economic interest. . . . Accordingly the usual rule is that the plaintiff must show pecuniary loss in misrepresentation cases and the damages are limited to such pecuniary loss, with no recovery for emotional distress." D. Dobbs, Remedies § 9.2(4), at 559–60 (2d ed.1993).

> While no court has yet specifically declined to extend fraudulent misrepresentation to noncommercial situations or to damages for physical harm, there is little occasion to depart from the historical trend that our predecessor courts have created because other nominate tort actions have provided adequate remedies. See W. Keeton, Prosser & Keeton on Torts §§ 105 through 110 (5th ed.1984). Simply put, fraudulent misrepresentation has emerged as a tort distinct from the general milieu of negligent and intentional wrongs and applies only to interferences with financial or commercial interests where a party suffers some pecuniary loss.

Goldman, 790 N.E.2d at 931–33.

As *Goldman* indicates, the tort of fraud is typically concerned only with pecuniary loss in business or commercial settings—i.e., misrepresentations in commercial transactions that result in financial harm without causing injury to person or property. While some of the statements in *Goldman* suggest that the tort of fraud is *never* associated with physical harm, that assertion is too strong, as there is authority indicating that a fraud action may be maintained when misrepresentations result in bodily injury or property damage. *See, e.g., O'Hara v. Western Seven Trees Corp.*, 142 Cal. Rptr. 487, 489, 492 (Ct. App. 1977) (allowing a plaintiff who was raped to bring a fraud cause of action against the owners of an apartment complex alleged to have "knowingly misrepresented the safety and security of the complex with the intent to induce appellant to rent an apartment"); *id.* at 491 ("An action [of fraud] may be maintained to recover for physical harm proximately caused by a defendant's deceit."); *B.N. v. K.K.*, 538 A.2d 1175, 1176, 1182–84 (Md. 1988) (allowing a fraud claim by a plaintiff who alleged that the defendant concealed the existence of his genital herpes and transmitted the disease to her via sexual intercourse); RESTATEMENT (SECOND) OF TORTS § 557A & cmt. a (1977) ("The rule here stated permits a tort action of deceit to be maintained, when there is physical harm to person, land or chattels of a person who justifiably relies on [a fraudulent misrepresentation]."). Similarly, there is authority allowing a fraud action to be maintained in a non-commercial setting. *See, e.g., B.N.*, 538 A.2d at 1182 ("It is true that this tort [fraud] is usually applied in a business setting, or to one in which some pecuniary loss is claimed. Obviously, this [sexual transmission of herpes] is not that kind of case. But a business setting and pecuniary loss are not necessarily required."); W. PAGE KEETON ET AL., PROSSER AND KEETON ON TORTS § 105, at 726 (5th ed. 1984) (citing cases where a fraud action was allowed "for tricking the plaintiff into an invalid marriage or marriage with one who is physically unfit, or for inducing the plaintiff to leave a husband, or to incur criminal penalties"). Nevertheless, *Goldman* accurately captures the typical scope of the fraud action—pecuniary loss in the business or commercial setting—and it is this typical scope that is the focus of the materials in this Section.

While the elements of the common-law fraud action may differ slightly among jurisdictions, the courts generally agree that the plaintiff must establish the following: (1) a false, material representation was made; (2) when made, the speaker knew or believed that the representation was false, or recklessly asserted it without any knowledge of its truth (the "scienter" requirement); (3) the speaker made the representation with the intent to induce the plaintiff to act or to refrain from acting; (4) the plaintiff justifiably relied upon the representation; (5) the plaintiff suffered injury resulting from such reliance. *See, e.g., Goldman*, 790 N.E.2d at 933; *Trenholm v. Ratliff*, 646 S.W.2d 927, 930 (Tex. 1983); *see also* RESTATEMENT (SECOND) OF TORTS § 525 (1977) (stating similar elements); RESTATEMENT (THIRD) OF TORTS: LIABILITY FOR ECONOMIC HARM § 9 (Tentative Draft No. 2, Apr. 7, 2014) (same).

NOTES & QUESTIONS

(1) The cause of action for fraud often has a heightened pleading requirement. For example, Rule 9(b) of the Federal Rules of Civil Procedure requires a complaint alleging fraud to state "the circumstances constituting fraud . . . with particularity." Most states have a similar requirement. *See, e.g., John Doe 1 v. Archdiocese of Milwaukee*, 734 N.W.2d 827, 839–40 (Wis. 2007) (noting that a Wisconsin statute "pertaining to pleadings for fraud,

states [that] 'the circumstances constituting fraud or mistake shall be stated with particularity.' We have interpreted this statute to require that 'allegations of fraud must specify the particular individuals involved, where and when misrepresentations occurred, and to whom misrepresentations were made.' ").

(2) Some jurisdictions also elevate the evidentiary standard that a plaintiff must satisfy in a fraud action. Rather than the usual civil standard of "more likely than not" or "preponderance of the evidence," some jurisdictions require the plaintiff to satisfy a higher "clear and convincing evidence" standard. *See, e.g., In re Marriage of Cutler*, 588 N.W.2d 425, 430 (Iowa 1999) ("Proving fraud is a difficult task. A plaintiff must prove several factors by clear and convincing evidence, including (1) misrepresentation or failure to disclose when under a legal duty to do so, (2) materiality, (3) scienter, (4) intent to deceive, (5) justifiable reliance, and (6) resulting injury or damage.").

1. MISREPRESENTATIONS AND OMISSIONS

LINDBERG CADILLAC CO. V. ARON

371 S.W.2d 651 (Mo. Ct. App. 1963)

WOLFE, JUDGE.

This is an action in fraud in which the defendant is charged by the plaintiff with concealing defects in an automobile which he traded to plaintiff in part payment of the purchase price of a new car which the plaintiff sold to him. The trial was to the court, which found for the plaintiff. . . . After an unavailing motion for a new trial, the defendant appealed.

The plaintiff company was engaged in the sale of automobiles. Its business was located in the City of St. Louis. The defendant was in the vending machine business in St. Louis. He had some trucks and a Cadillac and Imperial automobiles which he used in connection with his business.

He decided to trade in his 1957 Imperial on another Cadillac. In June of 1959 the Imperial was brought into the plaintiff's place of business and was appraised by the sales manager in charge of such work. He examined the automobile and appraised its value to be $2,165 at that time. No deal was made then because the parties were unable to reach a trade-in figure that was agreeable to both.

In the month of October, 1959, during a cold spell, the coolant in the Imperial froze. The car was taken to a filling station which Aron, the defendant, patronized. According to the testimony of the filling station operator, defendant told him that the motor had frozen and he wanted it checked to see if it had cracked. The filling station operator thawed out the motor and placed the car on a grease rack to check it over. He testified that he found two cracks on each side of the motor block. He said that he told Aron, the defendant, that the block was cracked. He estimated the cost of a new block to be in the neighborhood of four or five hundred dollars. He told Aron that he could put a 'K and W sealer' in the cracks, but that it would be 'strictly temporary.' He also suggested that if the car was to be traded in, the cracks filled with the sealer could be covered with Permatex, which would conceal the filled cracks. Permatex is a gasket sealer and could serve no purpose other than to conceal the filled cracks in the motor block. He said that Aron told him to do this work, and that he did a 'pretty smooth job' and that the Permatex concealed the cracks.

About the 20th of November, 1959, Aron drove the Imperial into the Lindberg Cadillac Company's service department for appraisal as a trade-in. It was there about half an hour, and he then drove it away. Aron had not driven the Imperial after the crack sealer was put in until the time he drove it to the plaintiff's place of business for the purpose of a trade-in. Defendant Aron testified that he discussed the condition of the Imperial in plaintiff's office when they were attempting to close the deal. He said that they agreed that it needed floor mats, that the motor was leaking oil and needed repair, and that the fenders needed fixing. He did not tell either the salesman or the sales manager about the cracked block. Thus the car which had been appraised in June was reappraised on November 20, and an agreement was eventually reached to allow $2,290 for the Imperial on the purchase price of a new Cadillac. . . .

The sales manager for the plaintiff company, who made the appraisal of the car, drove it for a few minutes on November 20. He checked the heat gauge to see if it was overheating. This would normally disclose a cracked motor block. He also checked for water leaks, and found none. After the appraisal and sale, the car was reconditioned in the normal course of business for sale. This usually took about 30 days.

On December 21, the Imperial as reconditioned was sold for $2,476.08. The purchaser returned the next day and complained that it was overheating. The car was taken to the plaintiff's shop to verify the purchaser's complaint. It was found that the motor block had the cracks in it, and the plaintiff refunded to the purchaser the money he had paid for the car. The plaintiff then sold the Imperial, known to the buyer to have a cracked motor block, for $1,200.

The defendant, testifying in his own behalf, said that he did not know what a motor block was. He said that when the Imperial was frozen, he took it to the filling station because they were supposed to have put anti-freeze in the radiator. He testified that the station attendant said that he would take care of what was wrong, and kept the car for about a day. The attendant said nothing to him about the cracked motor block. He said that after he was informed of the cracked block by the plaintiff, he never went to the filling station attendant about the matter nor had any communication with him in relation to it. Defendant also testified that he had been sentenced to three and one-half years for counterfeiting cigarette tax stamps, and at the time of trial he was on probation for a period of seven years.

As stated, the court found for the plaintiff . . . and the defendant appealed.

The first point he raises is that the appellant failed to make a prima facie showing of fraud, and that the court should have found for the defendant. The appellant asserts in support of this that he made no misrepresentation. . . .

We have in the facts before us more than a failure to speak. There is also a positive fraudulent concealment. In the case of Jones v. West Side Buick Auto Co., 93 S.W.2d 1083, decided by this court, we have before us facts quite similar in effect to those here under consideration. There a fraudulent seller turned back the speedometer in the car sold to 22,400 miles, when the car had in fact been driven 48,800 miles. There was no verbal or written representation by the seller, but the buyer, relying upon the mileage registered on the speedometer, purchased the car. We held that the buyer had been defrauded by the deception, stating: ' * * * a representation is not confined to words or positive assertions; it may consist as well of deeds, acts, or artifices of a nature calculated to mislead another and thereby to allow the fraud-feasor to obtain an undue advantage over him.' The acts of the defendant as stated above were designed to, and did, defraud the plaintiff, and there is no merit to the contention that a case in fraud was not made.

We find no error present, and the judgment is affirmed.

NOTES & QUESTIONS

(1) Are words necessary to establish a misrepresentation? What was the substance of the misrepresentation made by the defendant in *Lindberg*? How was the misrepresentation made?

(2) According to the Restatement, what action or conduct will suffice to establish a misrepresentation? *See* RESTATEMENT (SECOND) OF TORTS §§ 525 cmt. b, 550 (1977); RESTATEMENT (THIRD) OF TORTS: LIABILITY FOR ECONOMIC HARM § 9 cmt. c (Tentative Draft No. 2, Apr. 7, 2014).

(3) A, selling an apartment building to B, informs B that the apartments are all rented to tenants at $200 a month. This is true, but A does not inform B of A's knowledge that the $200 rent has not been approved by the local rent control authorities, and that without this approval it is illegal. B buys the apartment house, believing that the $200 rent is legal and

that he can continue to collect it. Has A made a misrepresentation? *See* RESTATEMENT (SECOND) OF TORTS § 529 (1977); RESTATEMENT (THIRD) OF TORTS: LIABILITY FOR ECONOMIC HARM § 9 cmt. c (Tentative Draft No. 2, Apr. 7, 2014).

(4) The tort of fraud is concerned only with misrepresentations that are material. According to the Second Restatement, a matter is material if "(a) a reasonable man would attach importance to its existence or nonexistence in determining his choice of action in the transaction in question; or (b) the maker of the representation knows or has reason to know that its recipient regards or is likely to regard the matter as important in determining his choice of action, although a reasonable man would not so regard it." *See* RESTATEMENT (SECOND) OF TORTS § 538 (1977). Simply put, a matter is material if a reasonable person would consider it important or if the defendant knows that the plaintiff would consider it important. *See also* RESTATEMENT (THIRD) OF TORTS: LIABILITY FOR ECONOMIC HARM § 9 cmt. d (Tentative Draft No. 2, Apr. 7, 2014) ("A misrepresentation is material if a reasonable person would give weight to it in deciding whether to enter into the relevant transaction, or if the defendant knew that the plaintiff would give it weight (whether reasonably or not). The question, in effect, is whether the defendant knew or should have known that the misrepresentation would matter to the plaintiff.").

(5) Statements of opinion, representations about a person's intentions, and assertions regarding law can all constitute fraudulent misrepresentations in certain circumstances. *See, e.g.,* RESTATEMENT (SECOND) OF TORTS § 525 & cmts. c–d (1977); RESTATEMENT (THIRD) OF TORTS: LIABILITY FOR ECONOMIC HARM § 9 (Tentative Draft No. 2, Apr. 7, 2014). These issues will be explored in greater detail in Section A(5) below.

SWINTON V. WHITINSVILLE SAVINGS BANK

42 N.E.2d 808 (Mass. 1942)

QUA, JUSTICE.

The declaration alleges that on or about September 12, 1938, the defendant sold the plaintiff a house in Newton to be occupied by the plaintiff and his family as a dwelling; that at the time of the sale the house 'was infested with termites, an insect that is most dangerous and destructive to buildings'; that the defendant knew the house was so infested; that the plaintiff could not readily observe this condition upon inspection; that 'knowing the internal destruction that these insects were creating in said house,' the defendant falsely and fraudulently concealed from the plaintiff its true condition; that the plaintiff at the time of his purchase had no knowledge of the termites, exercised due care thereafter, and learned of them about August 30, 1940; and that, because of the destruction that was being done and the dangerous condition that was being created by the termites, the plaintiff was put to great expense for repairs and for the installation of termite control in order to prevent the loss and destruction of said house.

There is no allegation of any false statement or representation, or of the uttering of a half truth which may be tantamount to a falsehood. There is no intimation that the defendant by any means prevented the plaintiff from acquiring information as to the condition of the house. There is nothing to show any fiduciary relation between the parties, or that the plaintiff stood in a position of confidence toward or dependence upon the defendant. So far as appears the parties made a business deal at arm's length. The charge is concealment and nothing more; and it is concealment in the simple sense of mere failure to reveal, with nothing to show any peculiar duty to speak. The characterization of the concealment as false and fraudulent of course adds nothing in the absence of further allegations of fact.

If this defendant is liable on this declaration every seller is liable who fails to disclose any nonapparent defect known to him in the subject of the sale which materially reduces its value and which the buyer fails to discover. Similarly it would seem that every buyer would be liable who fails to disclose any nonapparent virtue known to him in the subject of the purchase which materially enhances its value and of which the seller is ignorant. The law has not yet, we believe, reached the point of imposing upon the frailties of human nature a standard so idealistic as this. That the particular case here stated by the plaintiff possesses a certain appeal to the moral sense is scarcely to be denied. Probably the reason is to be found in the facts that the infestation of buildings by termites has not been common in Massachusetts and constitutes a concealed risk against which buyers are off their guard. But the law cannot provide special rules for termites and can hardly attempt to determine liability according to the varying probabilities of the existence and discovery of different possible defects in the subjects of trade. The rule of nonliability for bare nondisclosure has been stated and followed by this court. . . . It is adopted in the American Law Institute's Restatement of Torts, § 551.

The order sustaining the demurrer is affirmed, and judgment is to be entered for the defendant.

NOTES & QUESTIONS

(1) *Swinton* reflects the traditional common-law rule that silence is not fraudulent unless there is a duty to disclose, and there is no duty to disclose merely because the other party would find the information to be beneficial. *See, e.g.*, RESTATEMENT (SECOND) OF TORTS § 551 & cmt. a (1977); RESTATEMENT (THIRD) OF TORTS: LIABILITY FOR ECONOMIC HARM § 13 (Tentative Draft No. 2, Apr. 7, 2014). As a matter of policy, is this rule a sensible one? *Cf.* W. PAGE KEETON ET AL., PROSSER AND KEETON ON TORTS § 106, at 737 (5th ed. 1984) ("[The rule] finds proper application in cases

where the fact undisclosed is patent, or the plaintiff has equal opportunities for obtaining information which he may be expected to utilize, or the defendant has no reason to think that he is acting under any misapprehension.").

(2) This traditional rule of non-liability for silence has become subject to several important exceptions. In general, there is a duty to speak before the transaction is consummated when (a) the parties are in a fiduciary or similar relationship of trust and confidence; (b) the speaker has uttered a misleading half-truth; (c) the speaker has learned that a previous statement is untrue or misleading, even though it was true or believed to be true when made; and (d) the speaker has made a statement with no expectation that it will be acted upon, but has subsequently learned that another is about to act in reliance on it in a transaction with the speaker. *See, e.g.*, RESTATEMENT (SECOND) OF TORTS § 551(2)(a)–(d) (1977). As a matter of policy, do these exceptions make sense? *See also* RESTATEMENT (THIRD) OF TORTS: LIABILITY FOR ECONOMIC HARM § 13(a)–(b) (Tentative Draft No. 2, Apr. 7, 2014) (describing situations where an actor has a duty to speak).

(3) The Second Restatement also provides that a party to a business transaction has a duty to disclose "facts basic to the transaction, if he knows that the other is about to enter into [the transaction] under a mistake as to them, and that the other, because of the relationship between them, the customs of the trade or other objective circumstances, would reasonably expect a disclosure of those facts." RESTATEMENT (SECOND) OF TORTS § 551(2)(e) (1977); *see also* RESTATEMENT (THIRD) OF TORTS: LIABILITY FOR ECONOMIC HARM § 13(c) (Tentative Draft No. 2, Apr. 7, 2014) (substantially the same). When should this exception be applicable? Consider the following case:

GRIFFITH V. BYERS CONSTRUCTION CO.
510 P.2d 198 (Kan. 1973)

FROMME, JUSTICE:

The purchasers of new homes in Woodlawn East Addition, City of Wichita, Kansas, brought separate actions for damages because of the saline condition of the soil of their homesites. These actions were filed on alternative theories, [including] fraud in the concealment of a material matter. The actions were brought against the developer. This appeal is from an order granting summary judgments in favor of the developer, Byers Construction Co. of Kansas, Inc. (Byers).

The petitions allege that Byers developed and advertised the addition as a choice residential area. Prior to the time of development the addition was part of an abandoned oil field which contained salt water disposal areas which Byers knew or should have known would not sustain vegetation because of the saline content of the soil. It was alleged that Byers graded and developed the whole addition for homesites in such a manner that it became impossible for a purchaser to discover the presence of these salt areas. It further appears from allegations in the petitions and testimony in depositions that each of the plaintiffs selected a homesite which was located within a salt water disposal area. After houses were constructed attempts to landscape the homesites failed. Grass, shrubs and trees were planted and died because of the saline content of the soil.

. . . .

These additional allegations or facts, gleaned from the pleadings and depositions, should be noted. The purchase of the homesites and the construction of the homes was handled in this manner. Each prospective homeowner contracted with a separate building contractor to construct a home on a homesite to be chosen by the owner. The homesites in Woodlawn East Addition were advertised by the developer and considered to be in a restricted residential area developed for choice homes. Each prospective homeowner picked out a homesite without personally consulting the developer Byers but each was influenced by billboard advertising and by the general reputation of the area. When a homesite was chosen the respective building contractor then purchased the lot. The contractors obtained warranty deeds from Byers. When the houses were completed in accordance with specifications titles were transferred and the homeowners then received deeds to the improved homesites. No inquiry was made and no assurance was given by Byers on soil fertility.

The facts of this case appear to be unique [because], although many cases can be found on a vendor-builder's liability for the sale of a defective home, no cases are cited and we find none which discuss a developer's liability for defects arising from sterility of soil. The saline content of the soil of these homesites does not affect the structural qualities of the homes. The allegations of the petitions and deposition testimony indicate that landscaping is either impossible or highly expensive.

. . . .

Our next inquiry is directed to the claims based on fraud. The trial court held as a matter of law no claims for fraud could be maintained because of lack of privity between the developer and these appellants. The residential lots were sold to the builders who in turn constructed the houses and then deeded the improved lots to the appellants.

. . . .

The allegations of fraud appear to be viable issues for trial if nondisclosure of a known material defect in the lots constitutes actionable fraud as to the appellants.

This court has held that the purchaser may recover on the theory of fraud from a vendor-builder for nondisclosure of defects. In Jenkins v. McCormick, 184 Kan. 842, 339 P.2d 8, it is stated:

> "Where a vendor has knowledge of a defect in property which is not within the fair and reasonable reach of the vendee and which he could not discover by the exercise of reasonable diligence, the silence and failure of the vendor to disclose the defect in the property constitutes actionable fraudulent concealment."

This *Jenkins* rule approximates that stated in Restatement, Second, Torts, § 551 (Ten. Draft No. 12, 1966):

> "(1) One who fails to disclose to another a thing which he knows may justifiably induce the other to act or refrain from acting in a business transaction is subject to the same liability to the other as though he had represented the nonexistence of the matter which he has failed to disclose, if, but only if, he is under a duty to the other to exercise reasonable care to disclose the matter in question.

> "(2) One party to a business transaction is under a duty to disclose to the other before the transaction is consummated. . . .

> "(e) Facts basic to the transaction, if he knows that the other is about to enter into the transaction under a mistake as to such facts, and that the other, because of the relationship between them, the customs in the trade, or other objective circumstances, would reasonably expect a disclosure of such facts."

A similar rule has been recognized in other states. See Bethlahmy v. Bechtel, 91 Idaho 55, 415 P.2d 698, where a drainage ditch underlay a garage and was not disclosed to the purchaser. See also Buist v. C. Dudley DeVelbiss Corp., 182 Cal.App.2d 325, 6 Cal.Rptr. 259; Cohen v. Vivian, 141 Colo. 443, 349 P.2d 366, where there was a failure by vendors to disclose that the homes sold were built on filled land and subsidence of the land damaged plaintiffs' homes. . . . We see no reason why the rule in *Jenkins* should not be extended in the present case to a developer of residential lots.

The appellee Byers next contends, without agency, there can be no privity and without privity there can be no duty to disclose. Here, of course, appellants never dealt with the appellee, Byers. The duty to disclose the saline nature of the soil must extend to appellants if their fraud claims are to be upheld. However, the doctrine of privity provides no defense to appellee Byers if appellants were within a class of persons appellee intended to reach. Liability for misrepresentation is not necessarily limited to the person with whom the misrepresenter deals. The rule is embodied in Restatement, Second, Torts, s 531 (Ten. Draft No. 10, 1964):

> "One who makes a fraudulent misrepresentation is subject to liability for pecuniary loss

> "(a) To the persons or class of persons whom he intends or has reason to expect to act or to refrain from action in reliance upon the misrepresentation; and

> "(b) For pecuniary loss suffered by them through their reliance in the type of transaction in which he intends or has reason to expect their conduct to be influenced."

Liability may exist in a situation similar to that of the present case without a specific finding of agency. In Massei v. Lettunich, 248 Cal.App.2d 68, 56 Cal.Rptr. 232, Lettunich owned hillside property and in the course of laying out lot plans for a residential subdivision had the land filled. An engineering firm advised him regarding the depth to which the foundation should be laid to insure safety. Without informing a builder of the engineering report or that the land had been filled, Lettunich sold the land to the builder. Massei and others purchased homes from the builder and were damaged when the filled dirt subsided. The court found that the ultimate purchasers could recover from Lettunich because of the nondisclosure. In the opinion it was stated:

> "The contention of Lettunich that he had no contact with appellants and that therefore it was impossible for him to be guilty of deceit toward them is without merit. 'The law is well settled that representations made to one person with intention that they will be repeated to another and acted upon by him and which are repeated and acted upon to his injury gives the person so acting the same right to relief as if the representations had been made to him directly.' (Citations omitted.) No reason appears why this same rule should not be applicable to nondisclosures as well as misrepresentations. The jury could easily have found that Lettunich, in failing to disclose to the [builder] that the lots had been filled, did so because he was fearful that the prospective purchasers would in turn learn that fact and be dissuaded. . . ." (p. 73, 56 Cal.Rptr. p. 235).

. . . .

Under the alleged facts of our present case, accepting the same in the light most favorable to the appellants, we must assume the appellee, Byers, had knowledge of the saline content of the soil of the lots it placed on the market. After the grading and development of the area this material defect in the lots was not within the fair and reasonable reach of the vendees, as they could not discover this latent defect by the exercise of reasonable care. The silence of the appellee, Byers, and its failure to disclose this defect in the soil condition to the purchasers could constitute actionable fraudulent concealment under the rule in Jenkins v. McCormick, supra. One who makes a fraudulent misrepresentation or concealment is subject to liability for pecuniary loss to the persons or class of persons whom he intends or has reason to expect to act or to refrain from action in reliance upon the misrepresentation or concealment.

Of course, the fraudulent concealment to be actionable has to be material to the transaction. A matter is material if it is one to which a reasonable man would attach importance in determining his choice of action in the transaction in question. (Restatement, Second, Torts, s 538 (Ten. Draft No. 10, 1964).) There is little doubt in this case a prospective purchaser of a residential building site would consider the soil condition a material factor in choosing a lot on which to build his home. It materially affected the value and acceptability of the homesite.

As to privity we do not believe it is important to categorize its existence under a particular legal theory. Suffice it to say the appellants were in that class of persons desiring building lots in a choice residential area whom appellee intended and had reason to expect would purchase and build their homes. The fact that title was first taken in the names of the builders did not change the identity of those who would be ultimately affected by any fraudulent misrepresentations or nondisclosure of material defects in the lots. The building contractors were acting on behalf of their respective purchasers as a conduit or temporary way station for the legal title which, it was understood, would pass on completion of the homes to the appellants. There is no lack of privity in this case which would prevent causes of action based on fraud, and, in this, the district court erred in entering summary judgments for the appellee, Byers.

. . . .

[T]he order of the district court entering summary judgment in favor of the appellee is . . . reversed as to the alternative claims based on fraud, and these cases are remanded with instructions to proceed in accordance with the views expressed herein.

NOTES & QUESTIONS

(1) What constitutes a basic fact, and when would it be reasonable to expect disclosure of such a fact? *See* RESTATEMENT (SECOND) OF TORTS § 551(2)(e) & cmts. j–l (1977); RESTATEMENT (THIRD) OF TORTS: LIABILITY FOR ECONOMIC HARM § 13(c) & cmt. d (Tentative Draft No. 2, Apr. 7, 2014). Consider the following observations:

[T]here has been a rather amorphous tendency on the part of most courts in recent years to find a duty of disclosure when the circumstances are such that the failure to disclose something would violate a standard requiring conformity to what the ordinary ethical person would have disclosed. . . . Some factors of importance are as follows: (1) The difference in the degree of intelligence of the parties to the transaction. This is simply because the community sense of justice demands it; (2) The relation that the parties bear to each other; (3) The manner in which the information is acquired. Information which affects the value of the subject matter of a contract may have been acquired by chance, by effort, or by an illegal act. It makes a difference on the ethical equality of non-disclosure; (4) The nature of the fact not disclosed. In contracts of sale of real property, if the vendor conceals an intrinsic defect not discoverable by reasonable care, there is a much greater likelihood of the existence of a duty to disclose the non-discoverable and intrinsic defect than there would be to disclose something extrinsic likely to affect market value; (5) The general class to which the person who is concealing the information belongs. It is much more likely that a seller will be required to disclose information than a purchaser; (6) The nature of the contract itself. In releases, and contracts of insurance, practically all material facts must be disclosed; (7) The importance of the fact not disclosed; (8) Any conduct of the person not disclosing something to prevent discovery.

W. PAGE KEETON ET AL., PROSSER AND KEETON ON TORTS § 106, at 739 (5th ed. 1984).

(2)   Can *Griffith* be explained as a § 551(2)(e) (or § 13(c)) case? If so, how? Is there an alternative basis for a fraud finding that is not premised on the developer's silence? *See* RESTATEMENT (SECOND) OF TORTS § 550 (1977); RESTATEMENT (THIRD) OF TORTS: LIABILITY FOR ECONOMIC HARM § 9 cmt. c (Tentative Draft No. 2, Apr. 7, 2014).

(3)   The *Griffith* court noted that the *"Jenkins* rule approximates that stated in Restatement, Second, Torts, § 551[(2)(e)]." Do you agree? How are the *Jenkins* rule and § 551(2)(e) alike? How are they different?

(4)   In *Blaine v. J.E. Jones Construction Co.*, 841 S.W.2d 703 (Mo. Ct. App. 1992), the plaintiffs purchased homes from J.E. Jones Construction Company ("Jones")—the company that developed the subdivision and built their homes. The plaintiffs claimed that Jones failed to disclose its intent to build a nearby apartment complex in the subdivision, and that such failure constituted fraud. The court disagreed:

> For the purpose of our discussion, we have assumed, without deciding, that the Jones Company did intend to build apartments when plaintiffs purchased their homes; therefore, it did have superior knowledge of this fact. Nonetheless, we still find it had no duty to disclose that fact.

First, there is no indication that any party's intelligence was superior to another. Plaintiffs were college educated. Second, the parties did not bear any special relation to each other beyond their status as buyer and seller. There was no evidence that a confidential relationship of any sort developed between the parties or that the parties were in a fiduciary relationship, such as executor and beneficiary of an estate, or attorney and client. The existence of such a relationship makes it more likely that a duty to disclose would be found. However, here the transactions at issue were the normal arm's length sales of homes.

Third, the nature of the fact not disclosed is an extrinsic fact, not an intrinsic defect. In sales contracts, if the vendor conceals an intrinsic defect not discoverable by reasonable care, there is a greater likelihood that a duty to disclose will be found than if the fact is something extrinsic to the property likely to affect market value. The intent to build apartments in the future is not a defect in plaintiffs' houses which is not discoverable by reasonable care; rather, the intent is a fact that normally can be ascertained by reasonable inquiry. . . .

Fourth, the contract is an arm's length sales contract for property, it is not a release or contract of insurance where arguably, all material facts must be disclosed. Fifth, the concealer in this case is a seller. A seller is more likely to have a duty to disclose than a buyer.

The sixth factor is the importance or materiality of the fact not disclosed. Admittedly, a developer's intent to build apartments on nearby property could have an effect on a reasonable buyer's decision to buy a house, and, thus, intent is an important fact. However, the significance of this fact is lessened by its extrinsic nature. The fact may affect the market value of the house, but is not a defect in the house itself. Moreover, the Jones Company's intent to build apartments was a decision about the use of land zoned multi-family which could have changed at any time. The actual layout of the multi-family buildings in fact did change from the time of the original [filing with the county] to the actual constructed buildings. Furthermore, a developer could reasonably expect that a potential buyer would inquire about the zoning of his and nearby undeveloped property, as well as potential uses for the undeveloped property.

. . . .

Finally, the seventh factor is the respective knowledge of the parties of the fact and their means of acquiring this knowledge. There is no question in this case that the existence of multi-family zoning and a proposed layout of the multi-family buildings were a part of the public record. Plaintiffs and potential buyers had access to the information, and indeed plaintiff Ronck did get zoning information from St. Louis County. Admittedly, the multi-family buildings were not designated as any particular type of multi-family building. Such a designation was not required by St. Louis County.

Here, again, however, the public disclosure of zoning for multi-family units puts a reasonable purchaser of a house in close proximity on notice to inquire about the type of multi-family units to be built. Indeed, plaintiffs here testified they made this inquiry.

The fact the Jones Company or its agent allegedly responded with false representations may be the factual basis for fraud based upon false representation. It is not, however, a factual basis for nor relevant to the imposition of a naked duty to disclose on the Jones Company. . . .

It is clear then that the respective knowledge of each party and the means of acquiring . . . this knowledge was not unbalanced or unfair. The zoning information was available and within the reasonable reach of the plaintiffs. It is true that public record of an undisclosed fact may not necessarily negate a party's duty to disclose; however, reasonable availability of the fact to the party claiming fraudulent disclosure still remains a factor in the analysis.

Quite simply, the undisclosed fact in this case, the Jones Company's intent, should not trigger a duty to disclose. The undisclosed fact was not an intrinsic defect not discoverable by reasonable care; rather, it was, under plaintiffs' chosen theory, an extrinsic fact which was discoverable by reasonable inquiry.

A developer in the marketplace should not be saddled with the duty to disclose that, as one of the available options under multi-family zoning, he intends to build apartments. The Jones Company, as any other developer, could assume, quite sensibly and rationally, that a buyer would check the public record or ask the developer or its agent to acquire information about the zoning of his and nearby property. It is not unreasonable for an innocent developer with no intent to deceive to believe that the disclosure of multi-family zoning is sufficient notice to a rational buyer of a house near a then undeveloped multi-family zone.

Id. at 708–09. Is the result in *Blaine* consistent with the result in *Griffith*?

(5)   The *Griffith* court acknowledged that the homeowners "never dealt with the appellee, Byers." How then were they proper plaintiffs in a fraud lawsuit against Byers? *See* RESTATEMENT (SECOND) OF TORTS § 531 (1977); RESTATEMENT (THIRD) OF TORTS: LIABILITY FOR ECONOMIC HARM § 12 cmt. b (Tentative Draft No. 2, Apr. 7, 2014).

(6)   With respect to the buyer's nondisclosure, consider the following:

. . . . A person may with perfect honesty and propriety use for his own advantage the superior knowledge of property he desires to purchase that has been acquired by skill, energy, vigilance, and other legitimate means, [a]nd in the ordinary business and commercial affairs of the world he is not under any legal obligation to disclose to the person he is trading with the reasons that influenced him to desire the property or his views as to its value, or the sources of information at his disposal. Nor need he disclose the knowledge that he has concerning the circumstances or condition that may depreciate or enhance its value. If any other rule were adopted, it would have a depressing tendency on trade and commerce by removing the incentive to speculation and profit that lies at the foundation of almost every business venture. Every purchaser of land or other property of value buys it because he believes he can make a profit on the investment, or because he needs it in his business or for some purpose of his own; and he is not required to explain the reasons that induce him to make the purchase, or give to the seller any information concerning the purpose to which he intends to put the property.

Hays v. Meyers, 107 S.W. 287, 288 (Ky. 1908); *see also* DAN B. DOBBS, THE LAW OF TORTS § 481, at 1376 (2000) ("It has been generally thought that buyers are under no duty to disclose material facts to sellers. The leading case on the point held that the buyer was not required to disclose market factors (that peace had been declared) [*see Laidlaw v. Organ*, 15 U.S. (2 Wheat.) 178 (1817)], but some other authority has gone on to say that the buyer need not disclose facts about the very property being purchased either. [*See Harrell v. Powell*, 106 S.E.2d 160 (N.C. 1958).] A fiduciary buyer, like a fiduciary seller, must make full disclosure of material facts.").

PROBLEM 2.1

If the facts of *Swinton* occurred today, what would be the result?

2. SCIENTER

RECEIVABLES PURCHASING CO. v. ENGINEERING & PROFESSIONAL SERVICES, INC.
510 F.3d 840 (8th Cir. 2008)

ARNOLD, CIRCUIT JUDGE.

Receivables Purchasing Company, Inc., sued Engineering and Professional Services, Inc., (EPS) for fraud. . . . The district court granted summary judgment in favor of EPS. . . . We . . . reverse and remand for further proceedings on the fraud claim.

I.

EPS was the general contractor on a construction project for which RJS Utility Construction, Inc., (RJS) was a subcontractor. Receivables bought the rights to certain invoices that RJS sent EPS for work that RJS asserted that it had performed. Receivables produced evidence that before it bought each invoice it had called EPS's project manager, Richard D. Getts, Jr., to confirm that the work had been completed and that EPS had approved the invoice for payment. Receivables also adduced proof that during each of these conversations, Mr. Getts stated that the invoice had been approved for payment. EPS eventually refused to pay four of the invoices according to the terms of its original contract with RJS because of problems with the work that RJS performed. . . . Receivables filed suit against EPS, claiming that . . . Mr. Getts's representations were fraudulent.

. . . .

III.

We turn now to the fraud claim. The district court granted summary judgment, stating initially that a plaintiff in a fraud claim must prove that the defendant "knew or should have known that the representation was false." It then set out a different standard, saying that Receivables was required to "set forth evidence showing that Getts knew the representations he was making to Plaintiff were false." Finally, the court, returning to its earlier standard, concluded that "no evidence creates a genuine issue of material fact regarding whether Getts, at the time he represented to Plaintiff that the invoices would be paid, knew or should have known that the invoices were not going to be paid." After reviewing the Arkansas cases, we have concluded that a somewhat different standard from either of these applies here.

In *Bomar v. Moser*, 369 Ark. 123, 131 (2007), the Supreme Court of Arkansas held that a cause of action for fraud consists of five elements. The *Bomar* court described the three elements at issue in this case as follows: "knowledge that the representation is false or that there is insufficient evidence upon which to make the representation" (the scienter element), "intent to induce action or inaction in reliance upon the representation," and "justifiable reliance on the representation." *Id.*; *see also Delanno, Inc. v. Peace,* 366 Ark. 542, 545, 237 S.W.3d 81 (2006).

Though the simple and clear definition of scienter laid out in *Bomar* has been frequently repeated in the Arkansas case law, it has, at least in recent times, often been coupled with an inconsistent idea. The Arkansas Supreme Court appears to have begun this trend in 1997: After stating that "[r]epresentations are considered fraudulent when the one making them either knows them to be false or, not knowing, asserts them to be true," it immediately added that a "grant of summary judgment on a claim of misrepresentation is appropriate when a plaintiff does not produce specific facts that the defendant knew his representations were false." *O'Mara v. Dykema*, 942 S.W.2d 854, 858, 328 Ark. 310, 317 (1997) (internal citation omitted). The Arkansas courts have continued to repeat these inconsistent standards side by side. *See, e.g., Morris v. Rush,* 69 S.W.3d 876, 880, 77 Ark.App. 11, 17 (2002). The standards are incompatible because these cases say first that a defendant does not need to be aware that his representations were false and then say that he does.

The Arkansas law regarding negligent misrepresentation provides us with some guidance in determining which of these competing principles the Arkansas Supreme Court would likely adopt. Unlike some jurisdictions, *see, e.g., Federal Land Bank Ass'n of Tyler v. Sloane,* 825 S.W.2d 439, 442 (Tex.1991); *Chapman v. Rideout,* 568 A.2d 829, 830 (Me.1990), Arkansas has refused to recognize the common-law tort of negligent misrepresentation, *South County, Inc. v. First Western Loan Co.,* 871 S.W.2d 325, 326, 315 Ark. 722, 726 (1994). The primary difference between the tort of fraud and the tort of negligent misrepresentation is that the latter does not require scienter: Fraud is an intentional tort, which requires scienter, but negligent misrepresentation is an unintentional tort, which does not. Thus, a defendant will be liable for negligent misrepresentation when he "fails to exercise reasonable care or competence in obtaining or communicating the information." Restatement (Second) of Torts § 552(1). The question in a negligent misrepresentation claim is merely whether the defendant "should have known" that the representation was false, regardless of what the defendant actually knew.

While there are various logical bases for the Arkansas Supreme Court's decision that liability does not attach to negligent misrepresentations, we think it unlikely that that court would reject liability for knowingly ignorant misrepresentations. Knowingly false misrepresentations and knowingly ignorant misrepresentations are both acts to which the common law normally attaches liability, *see* Restatement (Second) of Torts § 526, and the older Arkansas cases were clear that liability attached to both. *See e.g. Fausett & Co. v. Bullard,* 229 S.W.2d 490, 491, 217 Ark. 176, 178–79 (1950); *Laney-Payne Farm Loan Co. v. Greenhaw,* 9 S.W.2d 19, 20–21, 177 Ark. 589 (1928). Making a representation without knowing that it is true may not be as blameworthy as making a representation knowing that it is false, but a defendant is morally culpable in both instances. It would therefore be odd if the Arkansas Supreme Court rejected liability for all misrepresentations where the defendant didn't have full knowledge that he or she was asserting an untruth. . . . Victims of damaging and intentional misrepresentations would be without a remedy in circumstances in which other jurisdictions would sustain a claim. *See* Restatement (Second) of Torts § 526.

We therefore believe that the Arkansas Supreme Court would hold that liability for fraud attaches in cases where a defendant lacked knowledge that his or her representation was false but did not know whether it was true or not. The district court's statement that Receivables had to show that Mr. Getts knew that the representation was false is thus incorrect, and its reference to the "should-have-known" standard for the scienter requirement was inappropriate in this case because that standard would relate only to a claim for negligent misrepresentation. Applying the correct principle, we hold, for reasons that follow, that a genuine issue of material fact exists as to whether Mr. Getts had the requisite scienter when he made the representation that Receivables asserts he made.

EPS has made much of the fact that Ralph Lewis, the president of Receivables, admitted that he was unsure of what Mr. Getts knew when he (Mr. Getts) made the representations that Mr. Lewis attributed to him. When asked if he was contending that Mr. Getts knew that his representations were false, Mr. Lewis replied, "I can't answer that. I don't know what his thoughts were." Mr. Lewis's position on Mr. Getts's state of mind was made clear later in the deposition when he was questioned along the same lines and said, "Mr. Getz [sic] should have known. He was the superintendent on the job." Brent Lewis, Receivables's other principal officer, made similar statements in his deposition. By itself, this testimony would tend to make out a claim only for negligent misrepresentation, which, as we have said, is not recognized in Arkansas.

But "it is not necessary that fraud be shown by direct evidence or positive testimony. Circumstantial evidence can provide a basis for the jury to infer fraud where . . . the circumstances are inconsistent with honest intent." *Stine v. Sanders*, 987 S.W.2d 289, 293 n.3 (1999) (citing *Pacini v. Haven,* 105 S.W.2d 85, 194 Ark. 31 (1937)). Receivables produced proof that Mr. Getts had a motive to induce Receivables to purchase the invoices: Mr. Getts admitted in a deposition that he knew that RJS was dependent on Receivables's financing to continue working. Furthermore, when asked in the same deposition, "When you signed off on the invoices why didn't you put that [the work] was accomplished rather than approved?", Mr. Getts stated that he was signing the invoices as "approved" solely for the benefit of RJS so that it could continue to receive financing and that he did not consider the posited distinction. Given Mr. Getts's position as project manager responsible for the RJS work, this evidence gives rise to a reasonable inference that he was at least unaware of whether his representations that the invoices were, in fact, approved and would be paid were true or false.

EPS also maintains that Receivables has failed to create a genuine issue of material fact as to whether EPS intended to induce reliance and whether Receivables's reliance was justified. We need address these points only briefly. As for the first, the motive that Mr. Getts had to induce Receivables to purchase the invoices is by itself sufficient to create a genuine issue of material fact as to whether EPS intended to induce reliance. Regarding the second, the *prima facie* reasonableness of relying on the representations of a project manager that his company would pay for work represented by a particular invoice is at least sufficient to create a genuine issue of material fact as to whether Receivables's reliance was justified. Genuine issues of material fact thus exist on the fraud claim.

IV.

Accordingly, we . . . reverse the judgment for EPS on the fraud claim and remand for further proceedings on that claim.

NOTES & QUESTIONS

(1) The *Receivables* court uses the terms "knowingly false misrepresentations" and "knowingly ignorant misrepresentations." What is a knowingly false misrepresentation? What is a knowingly ignorant misrepresentation?

(2) Did Mr. Getts know that his "approved for payment" statements were false? If not, shouldn't the fraud claim have been dismissed?

(3) Many courts capture the notion that scienter includes knowingly false representations and knowingly ignorant representations by stating that fraud can be found when the speaker knows that his statement is false or when he makes the statement with "reckless indifference as to its truth." *Powell v. D.C. Hous. Auth.*, 818 A.2d 188, 197–98 (D.C. 2003); *see also* RESTATEMENT (SECOND) OF TORTS § 526 cmt. e (1977) ("In order that a misrepresentation may be fraudulent it is not necessary that the maker know the matter is not as represented. Indeed, it is not necessary that he should even believe this to be so. It is enough that being conscious that he has neither knowledge nor belief in the existence of the matter he chooses to assert it as a fact. Indeed, since knowledge implies a firm conviction, a misrepresentation of a fact so made as to assert that the maker knows it, is fraudulent if he is conscious that he has merely a belief in its existence and recognizes that there is a chance, more or less great, that the fact may not be as it is represented. This is often expressed by saying that fraud is proved if it is shown that a false representation has been made without belief in its truth or recklessly, careless of whether it is true or false."). In the leading 19th century decision of *Derry v. Peek*, 14 App. Cas. 337 (H.L. 1889)—a decision that was highly influential upon American courts—Lord Herschell defined the scienter requirement in a similar manner:

> [F]raud is proved when it is shown that a false representation has been made (1) knowingly, or (2) without belief in its truth, or (3)

recklessly, careless whether it be true or false. Although I have treated the second and third as distinct cases, I think the third is but an instance of the second, for one who makes a statement under such circumstances can have no real belief in the truth of what he states. To prevent a false statement being fraudulent, there must, I think, always be an honest belief in its truth. And this probably covers the whole ground, for one who knowingly alleges that which is false, has obviously no such honest belief.

Id. at 374.

(4) Would knowingly false representations and knowingly ignorant representations satisfy the scienter requirement of the Restatement? *See* RESTATEMENT (SECOND) OF TORTS § 526 (1977); RESTATEMENT (THIRD) OF TORTS: LIABILITY FOR ECONOMIC HARM § 10 (Tentative Draft No. 2, Apr. 7, 2014).

(5) The unreasonableness of a defendant's belief that a statement is true may be strong circumstantial evidence that the defendant does not actually hold the belief. *See, e.g., Stromberger v. 3M Co.,* 990 F.2d 974, 978 (7th Cir. 1993) ("No doubt some statements are so outlandish that no one in his right mind could think them true when he said them, and then intent to defraud could be inferred from the statement itself."); *Derry,* 14 App. Cas. at 375–76 ("I can conceive of many cases where the fact that an alleged belief was destitute of all reasonable foundation would suffice of itself to convince the Court that it was not really entertained, and that the representation was a fraudulent one."); *see also* RESTATEMENT (SECOND) OF TORTS § 526 cmt. d (1977) ("The fact that the misrepresentation is one that a man of ordinary care and intelligence in the maker's situation would have recognized as false is not enough to impose liability upon the maker for a fraudulent misrepresentation under the rule stated in this Section, but it is evidence from which his lack of honest belief may be inferred.").

(6) A motive to injure or harm is not a required element of the tort of fraud. If scienter is established, the defendant can be liable even if he meant no harm or simply intended to do a favor for the plaintiff. The presence of a motive to injure or harm, however, is often relevant to the issue of punitive damages.

PROBLEM 2.2

Abby has owned a house for two years. Bob is interested in purchasing the house. Abby tells Bob that "the roof was replaced three years ago," but it turns out that this statement is untrue. Consider whether scienter is established under (a) § 526 of the Second Restatement and (b) *Derry v. Peek* in each of the following circumstances:

(1) When Abby made the statement, she knew that it was false.

(2) When Abby made the statement, she believed that it was false.

(3)   When Abby made the statement, she neither knew that it was false nor believed that it was false. She knew that the roof had been replaced, but she had no idea when the replacement had occurred.

(4)   When Abby made the statement, she believed that it was true. But she does not know for sure whether the replacement occurred three years ago.

(5)   Now assume that Abby changes the wording of her statement. Instead of stating definitively that "the roof was replaced three years ago," Abby states "I *believe* that the roof was replaced three years ago." Abby does in fact believe this. Abby knows, however, that Bob will assume that her statement is based upon Abby's personal conversations with the former owner of the house; indeed, Bob asked about the roof when he and Abby were discussing what the former owner told her about his maintenance of the home. In fact, Abby had no personal conversations with the former owner about the roof. Instead, Abby has simply heard from some neighbors who she considers reliable that the roof was replaced three years ago.

3.   INTENT TO INDUCE RELIANCE

ERNST & YOUNG, L.L.P. v. PACIFIC MUTUAL LIFE INSURANCE CO.
51 S.W.3d 573 (Tex. 2001)

JUSTICE O'NEILL delivered the opinion of the Court.

In this case, we must decide the scope of an accounting firm's liability for making fraudulent misrepresentations in an audit report.[a] Specifically, we consider whether the intent-to-induce-reliance element of a fraud claim requires a direct relationship between the alleged fraudfeasor and a specific known person—commonly referred to in this context as "privity." The court of appeals followed the *Restatement (Second) of Torts* section 531, which does not require privity and recognizes liability when an alleged fraudfeasor "has reason to expect" a person's or class of persons' reliance on the misrepresentations. Concluding that the plaintiff-investor raised a fact issue on this element, the court of appeals reversed the trial court's summary judgment for the accounting firm. Although we need not decide whether to adopt *Restatement* section 531, we conclude that section 531's reason-to-expect standard is consistent with our fraud jurisprudence. But we agree with the accounting firm that the court of appeals misapplied that standard in this case. We hold that the accounting firm established as a matter of law

---

[a]   For some background on the auditing process, see Section B(1) of this Chapter.

that it had no reason to expect the investor's reliance on the audit report in the transaction at issue, and because the investor's remaining claims were premised on the fraud claim the trial court properly granted summary judgment in the accounting firm's favor. Accordingly, we reverse the court of appeals' judgment and render judgment that the investor take nothing.

I.   Background

At the center of this litigation is a series of notes that InterFirst Corporation issued in 1982 and Pacific Mutual Life Insurance Company purchased in 1987 after InterFirst merged with RepublicBank Corporation. Pacific claims that in purchasing the InterFirst notes it relied on an Ernst & Young audit report that confirmed RepublicBank's financial strength. When RepublicBank filed for bankruptcy shortly after the merger and the InterFirst notes became virtually worthless, Pacific sued Ernst & Young for fraudulent misrepresentation. Before addressing Ernst & Young's potential fraud liability, we review the underlying transaction and the context in which the alleged misrepresentations were made.

In 1982, InterFirst issued a series of notes scheduled to mature in 1989. By 1986, InterFirst was in financial difficulty and it began to negotiate a merger with RepublicBank, which appeared at the time to be a stronger, more profitable bank. Ernst & Young audited RepublicBank's financial statements for the year ending December 31, 1986, and gave an unqualified opinion that those statements fairly presented the bank's financial position. RepublicBank incorporated Ernst & Young's audit report and the audited financial statement in the 1986 annual report it made to its shareholders and the Form 10–K it filed with the Securities and Exchange Commission.

The banks merged in June 1987. RepublicBank offered several securities as part of the merger, including notes and two classes of stock in the merged entity. Together with InterFirst, RepublicBank issued a Joint Proxy and Prospectus soliciting their respective shareholders' proxies to approve the merger. The Joint Proxy and Prospectus also discussed the common stock and one series of preferred stock to be issued in connection with the merger. To promote another series of preferred stock and capital notes, RepublicBank issued two other prospectuses. These two prospectuses incorporated by reference the Joint Proxy and Prospectus. All three prospectuses incorporated RepublicBank's 1986 Form 10–K, which contained the audited financial statements and Ernst & Young's audit opinion. These documents were also incorporated by reference in a section of the prospectuses entitled "Experts," which stated that the RepublicBank financials were incorporated "in reliance upon [the audit] report and upon the authority of [Ernst & Young] as experts in auditing and accounting." Finally, RepublicBank included the three prospectuses in the Form S–3 registration statements filed with the SEC to register the securities described in the prospectuses. Ernst & Young consented to including its audit opinion and the financial information that had been the subject of its report in the prospectuses and to having its name mentioned in the "Experts" section.

The underwriters who were seeking buyers for the merger-related securities contacted Pacific. At the time, Pacific was considering whether to purchase the 1982 InterFirst notes. It was initially reluctant to do so because of its experience with other InterFirst notes purchased some years earlier, which it had placed on its problem asset list due to InterFirst's poor financial condition. But after reviewing public information relating to the merger, including the merger prospectuses and newspaper articles, Pacific decided that the InterFirst notes were a good investment because they would be backed by the merged bank. Pacific bought $415,725 of the 1982 InterFirst notes one month after the merger, and then bought nearly $8 million more a few months later. Pacific did not buy any securities offered in the three prospectuses.

Shortly after Pacific completed buying the InterFirst notes, the merged entity, First RepublicBank Corporation, disclosed serious financial problems with its real-estate portfolio and filed for bankruptcy. Alleging that it had been misled by fraudulent representations in the three prospectuses, Pacific sued Ernst & Young, among others. Pacific alleged that Ernst & Young's audit opinion contained misrepresentations, including statements that the audit complied with generally accepted auditing standards ("GAAS") and that the financial statements "fairly presented" RepublicBank's financial position as of December 31, 1986. Pacific alleged that the financial statements did not accurately reflect RepublicBank's financial condition and actually understated RepublicBank's real-estate liabilities. Pacific further alleged that Ernst & Young violated GAAS standards, including the auditor's standard of independence. Ernst & Young allegedly violated the independence standard by failing to disclose that, at the time Ernst & Young issued its opinion, several of its partners had significant outstanding RepublicBank loans.

Ernst & Young moved for summary judgment based in part upon affidavits asserting that Ernst & Young did not specifically intend for Pacific to rely on representations made in the 1986 audit report when making its decision to buy the InterFirst notes. Pacific responded and filed a cross-motion for partial summary judgment claiming that, as a matter of law, Ernst & Young intended to induce its reliance. . . .

To defeat Ernst & Young's motion, Pacific produced two experts' affidavits and an affidavit from Larry Card, a Pacific vice-president who had overseen the InterFirst note purchases. All three affidavits state that it is a commonly known and accepted practice in the financial industry for investors like Pacific to rely on representations about an entity contained in SEC filings, whether the investor is purchasing the specific security being offered or another investment the entity backs.

The trial court granted Ernst & Young's summary judgment motion and denied Pacific's cross-motion as moot. Pacific appealed, and the court of appeals reversed the summary judgment. It held that there were fact issues on each element of Pacific's common-law fraud claim. . . . In concluding that a fact issue existed on Ernst & Young's intent, the court of appeals applied section 531 of the *Restatement*, which provides:

> One who makes a fraudulent misrepresentation is subject to liability to the persons or class of persons whom he intends or *has reason to expect* to act or to refrain from action in reliance upon the misrepresentation, for pecuniary loss suffered by them through their justifiable reliance in the type of transaction in which he intends or has reason to expect their conduct to be influenced.

RESTATEMENT (SECOND) OF TORTS § 531 (1977) (emphasis added). The court held that Pacific's three affidavits created a fact issue on whether Ernst & Young had "reason to expect" that an institutional investor like Pacific would rely on its representations about RepublicBank's financial strength in purchasing securities issued by InterFirst before the banks merged. We granted Ernst & Young's petition for review to examine the intent element of Pacific's fraud claim.

II. Fraud

As the summary judgment movant, Ernst & Young has the burden to establish, as a matter of law, that there are no material fact issues concerning one or more of the essential elements of Pacific's claims. When reviewing a summary judgment, we assume that all evidence favorable to the nonmovant is true. We indulge every reasonable inference and resolve any doubts in the nonmovant's favor.

To prevail on its fraud claim, Pacific must prove that: (1) Ernst & Young made a material representation that was false; (2) it knew the representation was false or made it recklessly as a positive assertion without any knowledge of its truth; (3) it intended to induce Pacific to act upon the representation; and (4) Pacific actually and justifiably relied upon the representation and thereby suffered injury. *See Trenholm v. Ratcliff*, 646 S.W.2d 927, 930 (Tex.1983). Ernst & Young's summary judgment motion sought to negate each of these elements, but its argument here concerns only the third and fourth elements. Specifically, Ernst & Young contends that it did not intend to induce Pacific's reliance on its audit report and, in any event, Pacific's reliance was not justifiable.

The court of appeals applied the *Restatement's* "reason-to-expect" standard; that is, Pacific could establish fraud's intent element by showing that Ernst & Young had "reason to expect" that institutional investors like Pacific would rely on Ernst & Young's audit opinion when evaluating securities that the audited entity backs. Ernst & Young claims the court of appeals erred because Texas law requires Pacific to demonstrate a direct intent to specifically induce Pacific's reliance in order to maintain its fraud claim. In other words, Ernst & Young asserted that Pacific must show that Ernst & Young, in auditing RepublicBank's 1986 financial statements, specifically intended to induce Pacific to buy the InterFirst notes. Ernst & Young likens the direct-intent requirement to the doctrine of "privity," which requires a direct relationship between the alleged fraudfeasor and a specific known person. Ernst & Young contends that the *Restatement's* reason-to-expect standard is incompatible with Texas law in this regard. We disagree.

A. Intent

Our fraud jurisprudence has traditionally focused not on whether a misrepresentation is directly transmitted to a known person alleged to be in privity with the fraudfeasor, but on whether the misrepresentation was intended to reach a third person and induce reliance. *See, e.g., Gainesville Nat'l Bank v. Bamberger,* 77 Tex. 48, 13 S.W. 959 (1890). In *Bamberger,* for example, a firm made statements to an agency regarding its financial status and solvency, and subscribers to that agency relied upon those statements in extending credit to the firm. We held that a fraud cause of action exists "[i]f the false representations be made with a view of reaching the third person to whom it is repeated, and for the purpose of influencing him." *Id.* at 960–61 (citations omitted). Similarly, we allowed a third-party bonding company to sue an accounting firm based on its fraudulent report prepared for a school district, stating

> [W]here a party makes a false representation to another with the intent or knowledge that it should be exhibited or repeated to a third party for the purpose of deceiving him, the third party, if so deceived to his injury, can maintain an action in tort against the party making the false statement for the damages resulting from the fraud.

American Indem. Co. v. Ernst & Ernst, 106 S.W.2d 763, 765 (Tex.Civ.App.—Waco 1937, writ ref'd). Thus, we have held that a misrepresentation made through an intermediary is actionable if it is intended to influence a third person's conduct.

Ernst & Young relies on *Westcliff Co. v. Wall,* 267 S.W.2d 544 (1954), for the proposition that there must be privity between the alleged fraudfeasor and the person he intends to influence. But there we focused on what the defendant knew and could therefore have intended, not on whether the parties were in privity. We held that the defendant who had made misrepresentations about some property to a potential buyer in the presence of a Mr. Wall, who was with the buyer, was not liable to Wall for fraud when Wall relied on the statements in buying the property instead. Although we noted that the defendant was not a party to the transaction because he did not own the property that Wall bought, our holding was based on what the defendant knew. We reasoned that, because there was no evidence that the defendant knew Wall was interested in the property, the defendant could not have intended to induce Wall's reliance.

Under *Restatement* section 531, a person who makes a misrepresentation is liable to the person or class of persons the maker intends or "has reason to expect" will act in reliance upon the misrepresentation. Our jurisprudence, which focuses on the defendant's knowledge and intent to induce reliance, is consistent with the *Restatement* and with the law in other jurisdictions that have considered the issue. Those jurisdictions have either explicitly followed section 531 or adopted its approach.

Ernst & Young claims that the *Restatement's* reason-to-expect language creates a foreseeability standard for fraud that is contrary to Texas's specific intent requirement and is more akin to a "knew or should have known" negligence standard. According to Ernst & Young, Texas jurisprudence has always required an actual purpose or desire to induce reliance, thus precluding liability if a defendant has a reason to expect reliance but no desire or purpose to bring it about.

While it is true that Texas courts have not used the words "reason to expect" when discussing fraud's intent element, a defendant who acts with knowledge that a result will follow is considered to intend the result. *See generally Formosa Plastics Corp. v. Presidio Eng'rs & Contractors, Inc.*, 960 S.W.2d 41, 48–49 (holding that evidence the defendant knew the plaintiff would rely on its representations supported fraud finding); *cf. Reed Tool Co. v. Copelin*, 689 S.W.2d 404, 406 (Tex.1985) (holding that to establish intentional conduct " 'the known danger must cease to become only a foreseeable risk which an ordinary, reasonable, prudent person would avoid (ordinary negligence), and become a substantial certainty.' " (quoting *VerBouwens v. Hamm Wood Prods.*, 334 N.W.2d 874, 876 (S.D.1983))). Thus, Texas jurisprudence is entirely consistent with section 531's reason-to-expect standard, which requires a degree of certainty that goes beyond mere foreseeability. *See Geernaert v. Mitchell*, 31 Cal.App.4th 601, 37 Cal.Rptr.2d 483, 487 (1995); *see also Blue Bell, Inc. v. Peat, Marwick, Mitchell & Co.*, 715 S.W.2d 408, 415 (Tex.App.—Dallas 1986, writ ref'd n.r.e.) (holding that evidence on whether accountants "should have known" plaintiff would rely on combined financial statements does not satisfy Texas fraud law's intent-to-induce-reliance element, which requires more than mere foreseeability).

The *Restatement's* comments further illustrate the narrow scope of the reason-to-expect standard and foreclose the potential for "unlimited liability" that Ernst & Young decries. Even an obvious risk that a misrepresentation might be repeated to a third party is not enough to satisfy the reason-to-expect standard; rather, the alleged fraudfeasor must "have information that would lead a reasonable man to conclude that there is *an especial likelihood* that it will reach those persons *and will influence their conduct.*" RESTATEMENT (SECOND) OF TORTS § 531 cmt. d (1977) (emphasis added). Section 531 also applies a similar-transaction requirement that further circumscribes that section's scope and offers additional guidance in applying the reason-to-expect standard. It is not enough that a defendant intends or has reason to expect that its representation will reach and be relied upon by one who receives it. The plaintiff must have incurred pecuniary loss "in the type of transaction in which [the maker of the representation] intends or has reason to expect [the plaintiff's] conduct to be influenced." RESTATEMENT (SECOND) OF TORTS § 531 (1977). Though the transaction sued upon need not be identical to that the defendant contemplates, it must have the same essential character: "It may differ in matters of detail or in extent, unless these differences are so great as to amount to a change in the essential character of the transaction." *Id.* § 531 cmt. g. In sum, the reason-to-expect standard requires more than mere foreseeability; the claimant's reliance must be "especially likely" and justifiable, and the transaction sued upon must be the type the defendant contemplated. Thus, while we need not presently decide whether to adopt section 531, the reason-to-expect standard's reach is not as broad as Ernst & Young claims and adequately protects a defendant from unlimited liability without requiring privity.

We conclude that section 531's reason-to-expect standard comports with our jurisprudence and does not expand the parameters of common-law fraud in Texas as Ernst & Young claims. We disapprove of *Kanon v. Methodist Hospital,* 9 S.W.3d 365, 372 (Tex.App.—Houston [14th Dist.] 1999, no pet.), to the extent it suggests that Texas law requires privity to establish fraud. But we agree with Ernst & Young that the court of appeals incorrectly applied the reason-to-expect standard to the summary-judgment proof.

B. Reason to Expect

Pacific offered affidavits from an employee and two experts to show that Ernst & Young had reason to expect that Pacific would rely on the RepublicBank audit opinion when deciding to purchase the InterFirst notes. Victor Moore, a certified public accountant, testified that Ernst & Young "knew" that investors in all securities backed by First Republic, the merged entity, would rely upon the information in the audit report. Larry Card, a Pacific executive vice-president, testified that it was "known and expected" by public accounting firms like Ernst & Young that documents like the prospectuses and proxy materials at issue here are widely disseminated throughout the investment community and investors rely upon information from these materials when evaluating investments in securities the subject entity backs. Finally, Alan Coleman, former dean of Southern Methodist University's Edwin L. Cox School of Business, testified that investors like Pacific commonly rely on representations made in SEC-filed documents in evaluating securities backed by an entity. He also testified that Ernst & Young's contention that it did not intend Pacific to rely on the audit report in buying the InterFirst notes was contrary to commonly accepted and firmly established practices in the investment community. The court of appeals concluded that this evidence raised a fact issue on whether Ernst & Young had "reason to expect" Pacific's reliance on the audit report in deciding to buy the InterFirst notes. We disagree.

Pacific's affidavits speak in terms of what is commonly "known" or "expected" in the investment community. But even an obvious risk that a third person will rely on a representation is not enough to impose liability. *See* RESTATEMENT (SECOND) OF TORTS § 531 cmt. d (1977). General industry practice or knowledge may establish a basis for foreseeability to show negligence, but it is not probative of fraudulent intent. To prove that an alleged fraudfeasor had reason to expect reliance,

> [t]he maker of the misrepresentation *must have information* that would lead a reasonable man to conclude that there is *an especial likelihood* that it will reach those persons and will influence their conduct. There must be something in the situation *known to the maker* that would lead a reasonable man to govern his conduct on the assumption that this will occur. *If he has the information*, the maker is subject to liability under the rule stated here.

Id. (emphasis added). The generalized industry practice or understanding the affidavits describe is insufficient to show that Ernst & Young possessed information of an especial likelihood that investors like Pacific would rely on Ernst & Young's statements in the merger-related prospectuses in purchasing securities InterFirst had issued years earlier.

Pacific argues that, even without the affidavits, the SEC documents were filed under statutes designed to protect investors like Pacific; accordingly, *Restatement* section 536 affords a presumption that Ernst & Young had reason to expect Pacific's reliance on the filed documents. RESTATEMENT (SECOND) OF TORTS § 536 (1977). Section 536 provides:

> If a statute requires information to be ... filed ... for the protection of a particular class of persons, one who makes a fraudulent misrepresentation in so doing is subject to liability to

the persons for pecuniary loss suffered through their justifiable reliance upon the misrepresentation in a transaction of the kind in which the statute is intended to protect them.

Under this section, one who complies with a statutory filing requirement is presumed to have reason to expect that the information will reach and influence the class of persons the statute is designed to protect. *Id.* cmt. c. In determining the protected class, the focus is on the statute's purpose rather than the person furnishing the information. *Id.* cmt. d.

Pacific claims that it relied on all publicly available information about RepublicBank, including its Form S–3 registrations and Form 10–K. A Form S–3 is filed under regulations issued pursuant to the Securities Act of 1933, which mandates delivery of a prospectus to an investor upon the distribution of securities. A Form 10–K is filed pursuant to the Securities Exchange Act of 1934, which mandates periodic filing of disclosure documents. These and other federal securities regulations emerged in the aftermath of the 1929 market crash and were generally designed to protect investors. Pacific points to the federal securities acts' enforcement mechanism, Rule 10b–5, and claims that it is a member of the investing public these regulations were designed to protect; therefore, *Restatement* section 536 presumes Ernst & Young had reason to expect Pacific's reliance on the SEC-filed documents. But section 536 cannot be applied so broadly.

According to the *Restatement,* the general purpose behind a statute requiring a corporation to publicly report its financial condition is to make the information available to all those who consider it important in determining their course of action "in any type of transaction with the corporation in question." RESTATEMENT (SECOND) OF TORTS § 536 cmt. e (1977). But Pacific's purchase of the InterFirst notes was not a transaction with RepublicBank or with the proposed merger entity described in the offerings that incorporated the SEC filings. While section 536's presumption might apply to purchasers of securities in the merged entity or to RepublicBank shareholders who relied on the filed information in voting to approve the merger, which we do not decide, we cannot say its reach extends to open-market purchases of unrelated securities.

Moreover, unlike section 531, which is compatible with Texas fraud jurisprudence, section 536 has no counterpart in Texas common law and other courts have rarely applied it. Because section 536 effectively alleviates a claimant's burden to show intent to induce reliance in fraud actions, it should be applied narrowly if at all. Investors already have remedies for securities violations under Rule 10b–5 and other federal and state securities laws. Indeed, this case was originally filed in federal court as a Rule 10b–5 action, but was dismissed because the statute of limitations had run. Because these and other remedies are available to protect investors, we are reluctant to apply section 536's presumption and subject market participants to liability for fraud damages to an almost limitless class of potential plaintiffs.

In sum, we hold that, because Ernst & Young negated the intent-to-induce-reliance element of Pacific's fraud claim, the trial court properly granted summary judgment in Ernst & Young's favor. And because summary judgment was proper on this basis, we need not consider Ernst & Young's alternative argument that Pacific's reliance was not justifiable. . . .

. . . .

IV. Conclusion

We conclude that Ernst & Young is entitled to summary judgment on Pacific's fraud claim because it negated the intent element of the claim as a matter of law by establishing that it did not have reason to expect Pacific would rely on the audit report when it bought the InterFirst notes. . . . We therefore reverse the court of appeals' judgment and render judgment for Ernst & Young.

NOTES & QUESTIONS

(1)   Why was privity lacking between Ernst & Young and Pacific? Does the Restatement require privity? *See* RESTATEMENT (SECOND) OF TORTS §§ 531, 533 (1977); RESTATEMENT (THIRD) OF TORTS: LIABILITY FOR ECONOMIC HARM § 12 cmt. b (Tentative Draft No. 2, Apr. 7, 2014).

(2)   Section 531 of the Second Restatement indicates that a defendant can be liable to persons or classes of persons "whom he intends or has reason to expect" to rely upon the misrepresentation. *See also* RESTATEMENT (THIRD) OF TORTS: LIABILITY FOR ECONOMIC HARM § 12 cmt. b (Tentative Draft No. 2, Apr. 7, 2014) (discussing the same concepts). The "intends" part of the clause would seemingly cover liability to persons or classes of persons (1) whose reliance is desired by the defendant, and (2) whose reliance is believed by the defendant to be substantially certain to result, even if not desired. *See* RESTATEMENT (SECOND) OF TORTS § 8A & cmt. b (1977); *id.* § 531 cmt. c. What then does the "reason to expect" part of the clause cover?

(3)   The court's opinion focuses on the "reason to expect" language. Is there an argument that Ernst & Young *intended* to induce Pacific's reliance?

(4)   Why was the "generalized industry practice or understanding" described in the affidavits insufficient to satisfy the "reason to expect" language?

(5)   Why was § 536 of the Second Restatement insufficient to satisfy the "reason to expect" language?

(6) Consider § 532 of the Second Restatement. Would that section have been helpful to Pacific?

(7) Does the approach of § 531 of the Second Restatement seem sensible? Why shouldn't those who make fraudulent misrepresentations be liable to anyone whose reliance is foreseeable? *See also* RESTATEMENT (THIRD) OF TORTS: LIABILITY FOR ECONOMIC HARM § 12 cmt. b (Tentative Draft No. 2, Apr. 7, 2014) (discussing the same concepts).

(8) Keep in mind that § 531 also requires the plaintiff to rely "in the type of transaction" that the defendant intends or has reason to expect to influence. Thus, even if the plaintiff is a person whose reliance the defendant intends or has reason to expect to induce, the defendant will not be liable if the transaction that occurred was substantially different from the transaction contemplated by the defendant. *See* RESTATEMENT (SECOND) OF TORTS § 531 cmt. g (1977) ("This does not mean that the transaction into which the plaintiff enters must be identical with that contemplated by the defendant. It may differ in matters of detail or in extent, unless these differences are so great as to amount to a change in the essential character of the transaction."); *see also* RESTATEMENT (THIRD) OF TORTS: LIABILITY FOR ECONOMIC HARM § 12 cmt. b (Tentative Draft No. 2, Apr. 7, 2014) ("The same general principles apply to the types of decisions affected by the defendant's statements: liability extends to transactions of the kind the defendant meant to influence by the fraudulent statement, or had reason to believe would be influenced by it.").

PROBLEM 2.3

Able, a certified public accountant, fraudulently certifies an erroneous balance sheet for B Company. Able is informed that B Company intends to exhibit the balance sheet to one or more of a group of banks or other lenders or investors for the purpose of obtaining a loan. Able does not know the specific identity of any of the persons B Company may decide to approach. B Company exhibits the balance sheet to C Company, who, in reliance upon it, makes a loan to B Company, and as a result suffers pecuniary loss.

(a) Is Able subject to liability to C Company? Why? *See* RESTATEMENT (SECOND) OF TORTS § 531 (1977); RESTATEMENT (THIRD) OF TORTS: LIABILITY FOR ECONOMIC HARM § 12 cmt. b (Tentative Draft No. 2, Apr. 7, 2014).

(b) Assume that Able was *not* informed that B Company intended to exhibit the balance sheet to a group of banks or other lenders or investors for the purpose of obtaining a loan. Through general industry practice, however, Able knows that certified balance sheets are commonly shown to such audiences for the purpose of obtaining a loan. B Company exhibits the balance sheet to C Company, who, in reliance upon it, makes a loan to B Company, and as a result suffers pecuniary loss. Is Able subject to liability to C Company? Why? *See* RESTATEMENT (SECOND) OF TORTS § 531 (1977); RESTATEMENT (THIRD) OF TORTS: LIABILITY FOR ECONOMIC HARM § 12 cmt. b (Tentative Draft No. 2, Apr. 7, 2014).

4. RELIANCE

WILLIAMS V. RANK & SON BUICK, INC.

170 N.W.2d 807 (Wis. 1969)

HANLEY, JUSTICE.

[On March 19, 1968, respondent and his brother went to appellant's used car lot where they examined a 1964 Chrysler Imperial automobile. While doing so, they were approached by a salesman who permitted them to take the car for a test run. They drove the car for approximately one and one-half hours before returning the car to the appellant's lot. During that time they tested the car's general handling as well as its radio and power windows. According to the respondent, however, it was not until several days after he had purchased the car that he discovered that the knobs marked 'AIR' were for ventilation and that the car was not air-conditioned.

At trial, the respondent testified that while examining the car he discussed its equipment with the salesman and was told that it was air-conditioned. He also testified that he relied upon both this representation and an advertisement that indicated that the car had "factory air conditioning."

The appellant's salesman denied making any representations concerning air conditioning and testified that the only equipment discussed with the respondent was the car's vinyl roof. An examination of the record discloses that the advertisement introduced into evidence was dated March 21, 1968, whereas the sales contract signed by both parties was dated March 19, 1968.

Upon these facts, the trial court found that the respondent had proven fraud on the part of the appellant and awarded him $150 in damages. The appellant appeals from a circuit court order affirming that judgment.]

Finding of Fraud.

This court has consistently held that the party alleging fraud has the burden of proving it by clear and convincing evidence and that factual findings of the trial court will not be upset unless contrary to the great weight and clear preponderance of the evidence. Based upon these principles it is this court's duty on this appeal to determine if all the elements of fraud have been properly established.

In order to establish that a representation was fraudulent one must establish, first, that the statement of fact is untrue; second, that it was made with intent to defraud and for the purpose of inducing the other party to act upon it; and third, that he did in fact rely upon it and was thereby induced to act, to his injury or damage.

As to the first element there is no question that the advertisement and the alleged oral representation of the salesman were false. The automobile in question was simply not equipped with air conditioning.

Some argument, however, has been raised as to whether there was any intent on the part of the appellant to defraud the respondent. In regard to the advertisement, the respondent argues that the very highlighting of the words "FACTORY AIR CONDITIONING" evinces an intent to defraud. Although this argument is quite unpersuasive in light of the consistency with which such highlighting is used in today's automobile advertising, it is "possible" to draw such an inference.

. . . .

In regard to the alleged oral misrepresentations of the appellant's salesman, there is, of course, conflict in testimony. Despite denial by the salesman, however, there is sufficient evidence upon which the trial court could find that such statements were made and that they were made with intent to defraud the respondent.

Appellant's counsel argues that there was no reliance by the respondent and that therefore there was no fraud. The record indicates that the only advertisement introduced into evidence was one which appeared in the *Milwaukee Journal* on March 21, 1968. On direct examination the respondent testified that in response to the ad he went to the appellant's used car lot on March 21, 1968. On cross-examination, however, he testified that he had read the contract and that the space for the date of the contract had been filled in prior to his signing. Clearly, the respondent purchased the car on the date of the contract—March 19, 1968.

The appellant argues that no reliance could possibly have been placed upon the ad because it did not appear in the newspaper until two days after the automobile was purchased. It is thus contended that the respondent seized upon the error in the ad to seek a reduction in the price previously paid for the automobile.

The respondent, on the other hand, argues that since he saw the ad before purchasing the car the ad must have run for several days prior to the purchase and cites Madison v. Geier (1965), 135 N.W.2d 761:

> "The inferences to be drawn from the observable facts (are) for the trial court, and unless they are inherently impossible or unreasonable they should be accepted on appeal. * * *"

We cannot accept respondent's reasoning and are of the opinion that to infer that the ad ran prior to March 19, 1968, is unreasonable. Such evidence is certainly not clear and convincing. Had the ad in fact been placed prior to March 19, 1968, it would have been a simple matter to have introduced such ad, rather than resort to the strained logic now urged upon this court.

Although the respondent has not established reliance upon the advertisement by clear and convincing evidence, there is ample evidence to warrant the trial court's finding that the oral misrepresentation of the appellant's salesman was in fact made. In response to his attorney's question as to whether the car was represented as having certain features, the respondent answered, "Oh, yes, that it was full power and air conditioning and everything, and that Chrysler was a nice car, it was, and all that kind of jazz." He then added that he had purchased the car "Mainly because it was a Chrysler Imperial and that it had air conditioning."

Despite denials by the salesman, the trial court, having had an opportunity to view the witnesses, apparently determined that the respondent's testimony was more credible than that of the salesman.

The question of reliance is another matter. Many previous decisions of this court have held that one cannot justifiably rely upon obviously false statements. In Jacobsen v. Whitely (1909), 120 N.W. 285, 286, the court said:

> " * * * It is an unsavory defense for a man who by false statements, induces another to act to assert that if the latter had disbelieved him he would not have been injured. * * * Nevertheless courts will refuse to act for the relief of one claiming to have been misled by another's statements who blindly acts in disregard of knowledge of their falsity or with such opportunity that by the exercise of ordinary observation, not necessarily by search, he would have known. He may not close his eyes to what is obviously discoverable by him. * * * "

It is apparent that the obviousness of a statement's falsity vitiates reliance since no one can rely upon a known falsity. Were the rule otherwise a person would be free to enter into a contract with no intent to perform under the contract unless it ultimately proved profitable. On the other hand, a party who makes an inadvertent slip of the tongue or pencil would continually lose the benefit of the contract.

The question is thus whether the statement's falsity could have been detected by ordinary observation. Whether the falsity of a statement could have been discovered through ordinary care is to be determined in light of the intelligence and experience of the misled individual. Also to be considered is the relationship between the parties.

In several cases this court has held that the above factors negated the opportunity to inspect and the obviousness of the statement's falsity.

In the instant case, however, no such negating factors exist. The respondent specifically testified that, being a high school graduate, he was capable of both reading and writing. It is also fair to assume that he possessed a degree of business acumen in that he and his brother operated their own business. No fiduciary relationship existed between the parties. They dealt with each other at arms' length. The appellant made no effort to interfere with the respondent's examination of the car, but, on the contrary, allowed him to take the car from the premises for a period of one and one-half hours.

Although the obviousness of a statement's falsity is a question of fact, this court has decided some such questions as a matter of law. . . .

In the instant case the respondent had ample opportunity to determine whether the car was air-conditioned. He had examined the car on the lot and had been allowed to remove the car from the lot unaccompanied by a salesman for a period of approximately one and one-half hours. This customers were normally not allowed to do.

No great search was required to disclose the absence of the air conditioning unit since a mere flip of a knob was all that was necessary. If air conditioning was, as stated by the respondent, the main reason he purchased the car, it is doubtful that he would not try the air conditioner.

"It seems plain that, whether the representation in question was made, the (respondent) failed to exercise that care for (his) own protection which was easily within (his) power to exercise, and, under all the circumstances, (he) was not justified in relying upon such a representation, if made." Acme Chair & M.C. Co. v. Northern C. Co., 243 N.W. at p. 418.

We conclude that as a matter of law the respondent under the facts and circumstances was not justified in relying upon the oral representation of the salesman. This is an action brought in fraud and not an action for a breach of warranty.

. . . .

Order reversed.

WILKIE, JUSTICE (dissenting).

At a time when there is so much emphasis on consumer protection, the majority, in effect, revitalizes the old *caveat emptor* doctrine without specifically mentioning it.

The majority opinion holds that the respondent could not, as a matter of law, have relied on the representation that there was air conditioning in the car since such representation was obviously false.

While the majority concedes that the "statement's falsity is a question of fact" it states that "this court has decided some such questions as a matter of law."

. . . .

In the instant case the respondent was an individual bargaining with a large car dealership. There is no evidence to show that the respondent was familiar with auto air-conditioning systems. The false advertisement said that the air-conditioning unit in the car was factory equipment. Thus, it can be inferred that there would be no box-type unit under the dashboard which would be readily apparent upon entering the car. Presumably, a factory equipped unit would be housed under the hood of the car. Similarly, the fact that the car was purchased in March rather than in the midst of a heat wave would tend to reduce the significance of respondent's failure to test the air conditioning before purchase.

. . . .

Here, I would hold that the falsity of the representation was not so obvious that it could be held as a matter of law that the respondent had no right to rely on it. It was for the finder of fact and by finding reliance the trial court, by implication, found respondent had a right to rely thereon. That finding is not against the great weight and clear preponderance of the evidence. I would affirm.

NOTES & QUESTIONS

(1) According to § 537 of the Second Restatement, a plaintiff can recover pecuniary loss resulting from a fraudulent misrepresentation only if "he relies on the misrepresentation in acting or refraining from action" and if "his reliance is justifiable." Notice, therefore, that there are two components to the reliance requirement: (1) the plaintiff must establish that he in fact relied upon the misrepresentation (subjective reliance), and (2) the plaintiff must establish that his subjective reliance was "justifiable"—i.e., his reliance was, in some sense, reasonable (objective reliance). *See also id.* § 548 (noting that "[t]he maker of a fraudulent misrepresentation is not liable to one who does not rely upon its truth"). Did the *Williams* court conclude that the respondent lacked subjective reliance, objective reliance, or both? *See also* RESTATEMENT (THIRD) OF TORTS: LIABILITY FOR ECONOMIC HARM § 11 (Tentative Draft No. 2, Apr. 7, 2014) (addressing reliance).

(2) Is the analysis in *Williams* consistent with §§ 540–541 of the Second Restatement?

(3) Section 538(1) of the Second Restatement indicates that "[r]eliance upon a fraudulent misrepresentation is not justifiable unless the matter misrepresented is material." *See also id.* § 538(2) (defining materiality); Section A(1) (discussing materiality in the "Notes & Questions" after *Lindberg*). If a reasonable man would not regard a matter as important in

determining his choice of action, can the matter be material? For example, assume that A knows that B is a devout believer in astrology. In an effort to persuade B to purchase stock in a corporation, A fraudulently tells B that the horoscopes of the officers of the company all indicate that the company will be successful in the next year. Is that misrepresentation material? *See* RESTATEMENT (SECOND) OF TORTS § 538(2)(b) (1977); *see also* RESTATEMENT (THIRD) OF TORTS: LIABILITY FOR ECONOMIC HARM § 9 cmt. d (Tentative Draft No. 2, Apr. 7, 2014) (discussing materiality).

(4) In light of the above notes, is there any difference between "justifiable" reliance and "reasonable" reliance? Are there situations where we might say that a plaintiff's reliance is justifiable, but unreasonable? *See* RESTATEMENT (SECOND) OF TORTS § 545A cmt. b (1977) (discussing the relationship between justifiable reliance and unreasonable conduct).

(5) Section 540 of the Second Restatement indicates that a fraud plaintiff does not have to make an investigation into the truth of a fraudulent statement. Nevertheless, if there are "red flags" that would put a reasonable person on notice of a statement's falsity, a court may reject a claim of justifiable reliance on the ground that it was unreasonable to proceed in the face of such warning signs without an investigation. *See, e.g., Schlaifer Nance & Co. v. Estate of Warhol*, 119 F.3d 91, 98–99 (2d Cir. 1997) ("Circumstances may be so suspicious as to suggest to a reasonably prudent plaintiff that the defendants' representations may be false, and that the plaintiff cannot reasonably rely on those representations, but rather must 'make additional inquiry to determine their accuracy.' . . . The Estate's actions, the Agreement, and other circumstances should have raised more than one eyebrow, compelling SNC's officers or employees to investigate the extent of the Estate's control over Warhol's works."). Are these "red flag" cases inconsistent with § 540?

(6) If a plaintiff does investigate the truth of a fraudulent statement and chooses nevertheless to enter into the transaction, what significance should be given to the investigation? *See* RESTATEMENT (SECOND) OF TORTS §§ 546–547 (1977). Does § 547 stand for the proposition that an investigation by the plaintiff defeats the fraud claim because it shows that the plaintiff relied on his own investigation and not the defendant's misrepresentation?

(7) In discussing reliance in a silence case, the Supreme Court of California stated: "[I]t is not logically impossible to prove reliance on an omission. One need only prove that, had the omitted information been disclosed one would have been aware of it and behaved differently." *Mirkin v. Wasserman*, 858 P.2d 568, 574 (Cal. 1993); *see also Buckland v. Threshold Enters.*, 66 Cal. Rptr. 3d 543, 549–50 (Ct. App. 2007) ("Claims for fraud by omission are also subject to the requirement of actual reliance. . . . Because these claims do not involve affirmative misrepresentations, we conclude that actual reliance for the purpose of fraud by omission occurs only when the plaintiff reposes confidence in the *material completeness* of the defendant's representations, and acts upon this confidence."); *Schlumberger Tech. Corp.*

v. Swanson, 959 S.W.2d 171, 181 (Tex. 1997) ("The Swansons assert that the jury's verdict must be sustained because reliance is not an element of a claim for fraud by non-disclosure. We disagree. Reliance is an element of fraud. Fraud by non-disclosure is simply a subcategory of fraud because, where a party has a duty to disclose, the non-disclosure may be as misleading as a positive misrepresentation of facts.").

(8) Contributory negligence is not a defense to fraud. *See* RESTATEMENT (SECOND) OF TORTS § 545A (1977). The plaintiff's unreasonable conduct, therefore, cannot be asserted as an affirmative defense. (In general, even in comparative negligence states, the plaintiff's negligence does not reduce or preclude recovery in an action for intentional wrongdoing. *Cf.* RESTATEMENT (THIRD) OF TORTS: LIABILITY FOR ECONOMIC HARM § 11 cmt. d (Tentative Draft No. 2, Apr. 7, 2014) (noting that "[p]rinciples of comparative negligence do not apply to a claim of fraud")). Keep in mind, however, that the same unreasonable conduct might be used to rebut the justifiable reliance element of the plaintiff's prima facie case. Thus, although the plaintiff's unreasonable conduct cannot be used as an affirmative defense, it may be used to defeat the plaintiff's claim.

5. STATEMENTS OF OPINION, LAW, AND INTENTION

a. Opinion

Statements of opinion present special difficulties in fraud actions. Many courts explicitly assert that an action for fraud must be premised on a misrepresentation of fact and not a mere statement of opinion. *See, e.g., Saxby v. Southern Land Co.*, 63 S.E. 423, 424 (Va. 1909) ("It is well settled that a misrepresentation, the falsity of which will afford ground for an action for damages, must be of an existing fact, and not the mere expression of an opinion."). The rationale for this assertion has been explained as follows: "[Expressions of opinion] are not fraudulent in law, because . . . they do not ordinarily deceive or mislead. Statements which are vague and indefinite in their nature and terms, or are merely loose, conjectural or exaggerated, go for nothing, though they may not be true, for a man is not justified in placing reliance upon them. An indefinite representation ought to put the person to whom it is made on inquiry." *Id.*

This oft-repeated assertion, however, is misleading. First, it wrongly suggests that a statement of opinion cannot be viewed as a statement of fact. At a minimum, a statement of opinion is a statement of at least one fact—the fact that it is the speaker's opinion. *See* RESTATEMENT (SECOND) OF TORTS § 525 cmt. d (1977); RESTATEMENT (THIRD) OF TORTS: LIABILITY FOR ECONOMIC HARM § 14 cmt. a (Tentative Draft No. 2, Apr. 7, 2014). Moreover, an opinion may be interpreted as conveying other implied facts, such as the fact that the speaker has sufficient information to justify his opinion. *See* RESTATEMENT (SECOND) OF TORTS § 539 (1977); RESTATEMENT (THIRD) OF TORTS: LIABILITY FOR ECONOMIC HARM § 14 cmt. a (Tentative Draft No. 2, Apr. 7, 2014). Second, the assertion is an overstatement, as courts have allowed a misleading statement of opinion to serve as the basis of a fraud action in various circumstances where a plaintiff's reliance has been viewed as justifiable. *See* RESTATEMENT (SECOND) OF TORTS §§ 542–543 (1977); RESTATEMENT (THIRD) OF TORTS: LIABILITY FOR ECONOMIC HARM § 14 (Tentative Draft No. 2, Apr. 7, 2014). Thus, as one authority concluded: "It is more correct to say . . . that a statement of opinion is a representation of a fact, but of an immaterial fact, on which the law will not permit the opposing party to rely. When, for any reason, such reliance is regarded as reasonable and permissible, a misstatement of opinion may be a sufficient basis for relief." W. PAGE KEETON ET AL., PROSSER AND KEETON ON TORTS § 109, at 755 (5th ed. 1984); *see also Vulcan Metals Co. v. Simmons Mfg. Co.*, 248 F. 853, 856 (2d Cir. 1918) ("An opinion is a fact, and it may be a very relevant fact; the expression of an opinion is the assertion of a belief, and any rule which condones the expression of a consciously false opinion condones a consciously false statement of fact. When the parties are so situated that the buyer may reasonably rely upon the expression of the seller's opinion, it is no excuse to give a false one.").

HANBERRY V. HEARST CORP.
81 Cal. Rptr. 519 (Ct. App. 1969)

AULT, ASSOCIATE JUSTICE, PRO TEM.

. . . .

The basic facts upon which appellant relies are repleaded in each of the causes of action under consideration. She alleges she purchased a pair of shoes on March 30, 1966 at a retail store owned and operated by the defendant Akron; the shoes had been imported and distributed to Akron by the defendant Victor B. Handal & Bros., Inc.; the shoes were defective in manufacture and design and had a low co-efficient of friction on vinyl and certain other floor coverings commonly used in this area and were slippery and unsafe when worn on such floor coverings; she was unaware of the defect and in wearing the shoes on the same day she purchased them, she stepped on the vinyl floor of her kitchen, slipped, fell and sustained severe personal injuries.

Appellant further alleges respondent Hearst publishes a monthly magazine known as Good Housekeeping in which products, including the shoes she purchased, were advertised as meeting the "Good Housekeeping's Consumers' Guaranty Seal." With respect to this seal the magazine stated: "This is Good Housekeeping's Consumers' Guaranty" and "We satisfy ourselves that products advertised in Good Housekeeping are good ones and that the advertising claims made for them in our magazine are truthful." The seal itself contained the promise, "If the product or performance is defective, Good Housekeeping guarantees replacement or refund to consumer."

Appellant alleges further she had frequently read Good Housekeeping Magazine "and believed the products bearing the seal had been examined, tested and inspected by defendant and were good and safe for the use intended"; prior to purchasing the shoes she had seen an advertisement of them, either in Good Housekeeping Magazine or in a newspaper and placed by defendant Handal which incorporated the contents of the Good Housekeeping endorsement; [the] Good Housekeeping seal was affixed to the shoes and the container for the shoes with Hearst's consent; Hearst was paid for the advertising of the shoes which appeared [in] its magazine and for the use of its seal; appellant relied upon respondent's representation and seal and purchased the shoes because of them. Appellant further alleges Hearst made no examination, test or investigation of the shoes, or a sample thereof, or if such tests were made they were done in a careless and negligent manner and that Hearst's issuance of its seal and certification as to the shoes was not warranted by the information it possessed.

In the second and eighth causes of action, appellant seeks to recover on the theory of negligent misrepresentation. . . .

The basic question presented on this appeal is whether one who endorses a product for his own economic gain, and for the purpose of encouraging and inducing the public to buy it, may be liable to a purchaser who, relying on the endorsement, buys the product and is injured because it is defective and not as represented in the endorsement. We conclude such liability may exist and a cause of action has been pleaded in the instant case. In arriving at this conclusion, we are influenced more by public policy than by whether such cause of action can be comfortably fitted into one of the law's traditional categories of liability.

Appellant's third amended complaint alleges facts which support her argument [that] respondent Hearst is not just a publisher of a magazine which accepts and publishes advertisements from manufacturers and retailers of consumer products. To enhance the value of its magazine as an advertising medium, [and] to compete more favorably in the advertising market, it offers to those whose products meet such standards as it may impose and who choose to purchase its services, the "Good Housekeeping Consumers' Guaranty Seal" and its certification, "We have satisfied ourselves the products and services advertised in Good Housekeeping are good ones and the advertising claims made for them in our magazine are truthful."

Respondent's endorsement and approval of a product is not confined to the pages of its own magazine. It permits the manufacturer or retailer of a product which has been approved by Good Housekeeping Magazine to advertise that fact in other advertising media and permits its seal to appear in such ads and to be attached to the product itself. While the device used by respondent enhances the value of Good Housekeeping Magazine for advertising purposes, it does so because its seal and certification tend to induce and encourage consumers to purchase products advertised in the magazine . . . which bear that seal and certification. Implicit in the seal and certification is the representation [that] respondent has taken reasonable steps to make an independent examination of the product endorsed, with some degree of expertise, and found it satisfactory. Since the very purpose of respondent's seal and certification is to induce consumers to purchase products so endorsed, it is foreseeable certain consumers will do so, relying upon respondent's representations concerning them, in some instances, even more than upon statements made by the retailer, manufacturer or distributor.

Having voluntarily involved itself into the marketing process, having in effect loaned its reputation to promote and induce the sale of a given product, the question arises whether respondent can escape liability for injury which results when the product is defective and not as represented by its endorsement. In voluntarily assuming this business relationship, we think respondent Hearst has placed itself in the position where public policy imposes upon it the duty to use ordinary care in the issuance of its seal and certification of quality so that members of the consuming public who rely on its endorsement are not unreasonably exposed to the risk of harm.

The fact [that] Hearst is not in privity of contract with those who, relying on its endorsement, purchase the products it endorses, does not mean it is relieved from the responsibility to exercise ordinary care toward them.

. . . .

We believe appellant has set forth sufficient facts . . . to establish for pleading purposes [that] respondent Hearst had a duty to exercise ordinary care in issuing its seal and its certification [that] it had satisfied itself the shoes were 'good ones.' In both the second and eighth cause of action of the complaint under consideration, appellant has alleged respondent extended its certification and permitted the use of its seal in connection with the shoes she purchased without test, inspection or examination of the shoes, or a sample thereof, or if it tested, inspected or examined, it did so in a careless and negligent manner which did not reveal their dangerous and defective condition. If either of the alternative allegations is true, respondent violated its duty of care to the appellant and the issuance of its seal and certification with respect to the shoes under that circumstance would amount to a negligent misrepresentation.

. . . .

Hearst urges its representation [that] the shoes were "good ones" was a mere statement of opinion, not a statement of a material fact, and therefore not actionable. Since the very purpose of the seal and its certification [that] the shoes were "good ones" was to induce and encourage members of the public to buy the shoes, respondent is in poor position to argue its endorsement cannot legally be considered as the inducing factor in bringing about their sale. Respondent was not the seller or manufacturer of the shoes; it held itself out as a disinterested third party which had examined the shoes, found them satisfactory, and gave its endorsement. By the very procedure and method it used, respondent represented to the public [that] it possessed superior knowledge and special information concerning the product it endorsed. Under such circumstance, respondent may be liable for negligent representations of either fact or opinion. (See Restatement of the Law of Torts, vol. 3, section 543.)

Respondent argues no basis for liability has been shown because, "It is a matter of common knowledge that brand new soles on brand new shoes have a tendency of being slick and slippery until the shoes have been worn sufficiently long thereafter." The argument may well have merit, but it is one addressed properly to the trier of fact. The case is presented to us in the pleading context. We are unwilling to hold as a matter of law that liability will not attach under any circumstance based upon a defectively designed shoe. Whether a material used in the soles of shoes is so slick and slippery as to create an unreasonable and foreseeable risk of injury, and whether the buyer of such a shoe who is injured should anticipate the condition under existing circumstances, are questions of fact which cannot be decided at the pleading stage.

. . . .

The judgment of dismissal is . . . reversed as to the second and eighth causes of action (negligent misrepresentation).

NOTES & QUESTIONS

(1) According to the Second Restatement, what is an opinion? *See* RESTATEMENT (SECOND) OF TORTS § 538A (1977). What is the rationale for the general assertion that an action for fraud cannot be premised on a mere statement of opinion?

(2) Isn't Hearst's statement that the shoes were "good ones" an opinion? If so, why is the misrepresentation claim allowed to proceed? *See* RESTATEMENT (SECOND) OF TORTS §§ 539, 543 (1977); RESTATEMENT (THIRD) OF TORTS: LIABILITY FOR ECONOMIC HARM § 14 (Tentative Draft No. 2, Apr. 7, 2014).

PRESIDIO ENTERPRISES, INC. V. WARNER BROS. DISTRIBUTING CORP.

784 F.2d 674 (5th Cir. 1986)

GOLDBERG, CIRCUIT JUDGE:

The distinctly unsettling thought of angry "killer bees" terrorizing an unsuspecting Texas town lies at the heart of this case. Appellant Warner Bros. thought it could turn this idea into a "chilling, riveting, harrowing, cinematic experience," and spent $10 million trying to do so. Appellee Presidio Enterprises was apparently similarly affected, for it agreed to pay Warner $65,000 for the right to show the film, sight unseen, at two of its theatres in Austin, Texas. To make a long story short, the film was a flop. Stung by this turn of events, Presidio flew enraged into federal court, where it somehow managed to persuade a judge and jury that it had been tricked into purchasing a defective product and could collect damages. . . . We reverse.

. . . .

I.   FACTUAL AND PROCEDURAL BACKGROUND

Plaintiffs-appellees Presidio Enterprises et al. ("Presidio") are experienced film exhibitors who own and successfully operate five movie theatres (with a total of 18 screens); their operations in Austin, Texas, date back to 1973. Defendant-appellant Warner Bros. Distributing Corporation ("Warner") is a major motion picture distributor; it licenses exhibitors to show films under copyright.

In late 1977 Warner was completing filming of a movie entitled *The Swarm*, which concerned an invasion of Texas by "killer bees" from South America. *The Swarm* was based on a best-selling novel by Arthur Herzog and was directed by Irwin Allen, who had an Oscar award to his credit and had recently produced two enormously successful "disaster" films, *The Poseidon Adventure* and *The Towering Inferno*. The cast of *The Swarm* included such well known stars as Michael Caine, Richard Chamberlain, Olivia de Havilland, Patty Duke Astin, Henry Fonda, Ben Johnson, Slim Pickens, Katharine Ross, and Richard Widmark. The production budget for *The Swarm* was about $10,000,000.

The Swarm was scheduled for release in July, 1978. As is the practice with such productions, Warner began advertising the film to potential exhibitors far in advance of the release date. In August, 1977, Warner sent Presidio and other exhibitors a brochure that read as follows:

August 22, 1977

Dear Mr. Exhibitor:

"THE SWARM" IS COMING!

Today, shooting started at Warner Bros. on your blockbuster for the summer of '78.

"THE SWARM" IS COMING!

From the man who brought you the stunning successes of "THE POSEIDON ADVENTURE" and "THE TOWERING INFERNO" now comes what we hope to be the greatest adventure-survival movie of all time.

"THE SWARM" IS COMING!

After more than two years of preparation, that master showman, Irwin Allen, combines terror, suspense and startling performances in an eleven million dollar spectacular intended for audiences of all ages.

"THE SWARM" IS COMING!

Starring Michael Caine, Katharine Ross, Richard Widmark, Olivia de Havilland, Ben Johnson, Lee Grant, Patty Duke Astin, Slim Pickens, Bradford Dillman, and Henry Fonda as Dr. Krim, this will be the most "want-to-see" movie of the year.

"THE SWARM" IS COMING AND AVAILABLE July 14, 1978!

Sincerely,

/s/Terry Semel

. . . .

In December, 1977, Warner sent Presidio and other exhibitors a second brochure [and a letter soliciting exhibition bids. The language used in these materials was similar to the language in the first brochure.]

In effect, Presidio was being invited to bid for the exhibition rights to the film sight unseen. This practice, known as "blind bidding," is relatively common in the film industry. It apparently makes economic sense for both distributors and exhibitors to reserve theatres and films far in advance of the important Christmas and summer viewing seasons. Distributors want to be sure their films are solidly booked before they set in motion their expensive advertising campaigns (in this case, Warner spent over $4,000,000 advertising *The Swarm*), and exhibitors want to be sure they have promising films to show during periods of peak attendance. At any rate, *The Swarm* was blind bid, and Presidio knew that it was being invited to bid on a film that would not be complete or available for viewing until months later.[3]

In its bid letter Warner suggested a minimum "guarantee" of $35,000 for *The Swarm*.[4] The "guarantee" is a fixed minimum amount to be paid in advance to the distributor, whatever the film grosses; if it grosses more than the guarantee, the exhibitor may also (depending on the contractual terms that have been worked out) have to pay a percentage of receipts over and above the guarantee. Presidio responded with bids of $35,000 and $30,000 as the guarantees for eight-week runs at two of its theatres;[5] its remaining terms closely mirrored those suggested by Warner. . . .

The Swarm opened as scheduled on July 14, 1978. It was not a big success. The film ran for only five weeks at one of Presidio's theatres, and four weeks at the other. Presidio calculated that, after subtracting the guarantees and operating expenses from box office revenues, it had sustained a loss of $56,056.69.

Instead of accepting this result as an unsuccessful business venture, Presidio brought suit against Warner in federal district court, alleging common law fraud and negligent misrepresentation. . . .

II. EXPRESSIONS OF OPINION

The first obstacle in Presidio's path is the rule that expressions of opinion are not actionable. This is a wise and sound principle that is deeply embedded in the common law. Opinions and beliefs reside in an inner sphere of human personality and subjectivity that lies beyond the reach of the law and is not subject to its sanctions. In the criminal law, for example, it may be useful for investigative purposes to ascribe "motives" to suspects; and the *mens rea* or "guilty mind" makes overt actions blameworthy; but these subjective states are themselves not considered criminal as such. Similarly, actions for fraud or misrepresentation must be based on objective statements of fact, not expressions of personal opinion. The law wisely declines to tread in the latter area because, in some deep sense, "everyone is entitled to his own opinion." . . .

A statement of fact is one that (1) admits of being adjudged true or false in a way that (2) admits of empirical verification. The statements complained of by Presidio fail on both counts.

---

[3] Before making its bid Presidio also had the benefit of advice from a paid consultant in Hollywood, Mr. Jim Leroy, an "experienced film buyer" with "very close ties to the motion picture community." Mr. Leroy pointed out problems with *The Swarm* and advised "Don't go out on it." [Transcript] at 636. (" 'Don't go out on it' means don't sell the farm and family jewels and everything to buy this picture. . . ." *Id*.).

[4] This was not a particularly high suggested guarantee. By comparison, other films offered around that time had the following suggested guarantees: *Goin' South*—$60,000 (blind bid by Paramount Pictures); *Grease*—$60,000 (blind bid by Paramount); *Damien-Omen II*—$80,000 (Twentieth Century-Fox); *The Deep*—$85,000 (blind bid by Columbia Pictures).

[5] These were not top-dollar bids. During the same season Presidio bid $55,000 for *Revenge of the Pink Panther* and $50,000 for *Jaws II*.

We turn first to the brochure of August 22, 1977. Here Warner announces that " 'THE SWARM' IS COMING!" and that "Today, shooting started at Warner Bros." on the film, assertions that Presidio does not dispute. It is probably also indisputable that Warner "hope[d]" *The Swarm* would be "the greatest adventure-survival movie of all time." But then Mr. Semel goes on to term the film "your blockbuster for the summer of '78," and states that "this will be the most 'want-to-see' movie of the year." These assertions are disputable, but they are not statements of fact for two reasons: (1) they turn on vague, essentially [un]definable terms; (2) they are predictions.

If we interpret Mr. Semel's phrase "your blockbuster for the summer of '78" as implying a statement of the form, "This film will be a blockbuster in the summer of '78," we encounter the problem of vagueness with the term "blockbuster." What does it mean? According to *Webster's New World Dictionary of the American Language* (College ed. 1966), a blockbuster is "a large bomb that is dropped from an airplane and can demolish an entire city block." *Id.* at 157. *Webster's Seventh New Collegiate Dictionary* (1965) elaborates that the term can be used of "something or someone notably effective or violent," *id.* at 91, and the *American Heritage Dictionary of the English Language* (1976) adds that it may refer to "Anything of devastating effect," *id.* at 142. We would be hard pressed to deny that *The Swarm* might qualify as a "blockbuster" under one or more of these definitions. Even Charles Chick, president of Presidio, seems unsure as to the meaning of the term; on direct examination he testified as follows: "By 'blockbuster,' I guess they mean it's going to do good box office business, be an important box office picture." A party complaining about the fraudulent and misleading use of language should, at the very least, know what he is complaining about. The term "blockbuster" is inherently vague; it can mean just about whatever Terry Semel wants it to, and that is probably why he used it.

Even if we interpret Mr. Semel's assertion in the way Presidio prefers, we still encounter the problem that it is a prediction, not a statement of fact. Assuming, *arguendo,* that Mr. Semel is saying something to the effect that "*The Swarm* will be far more profitable than your average summer of '78 film"—would *that* be a statement of fact? Does it admit of being adjudged true or false? Can it be empirically verified? We answer "no" on all counts.

A prediction, or statement about the future, is essentially an expression of opinion.[11] When the weatherman says "It will rain tomorrow," he comes closest to making a verifiable statement of fact by

---

[11] *See* Prosser & Keeton, *The Law of Torts*, ch. 18 § 109, at 762 (5th ed. 1984) ("Ordinarily a prediction as to events to occur in the future is to be regarded as a statement of opinion only, on which the adverse party has no right to rely. It was said very early that 'one cannot warrant a thing which will happen in the future,' . . . .") (footnote omitted).

correcting himself and rephrasing as follows: "I think (or: it is my opinion) that it will rain tomorrow." Another possible rephrasing is: "The readings on my instruments are now the way they usually are when rain is coming." (The first statement is a factual report on the weatherman's state of mind; the second is a factual report on the state of his instruments. Both can be empirically verified.) The weatherman does not know whether it will in fact rain tomorrow. No one does. Thus no one knows whether the statement is true or false; perhaps it would be better to say that it is *neither true nor false*. A statement about the future can be verified only in the future; but then, of course, it is no longer a statement about the future as such. When tomorrow finally comes, and it is indeed raining, one no longer says "It will rain tomorrow" but rather "It is now raining." *That* statement can be empirically verified as true or disconfirmed as false.

Complaining that a film *turned out* to be a flop six months after binding, "non-cancellable" bids on it were accepted is like suing the weatherman because rain spoiled a picnic when he predicted fair skies. When Terry Semel says "this will be the most 'want-to-see' movie of the year," he is, quite literally, speaking in the grand tradition of those who do not know what they are talking about, unless we understand him to be giving a report on the present state of his mind (*e.g.,* "I think (or: it is my opinion) that this will be the most 'want-to-see' movie of the year"), or on the state of predictive information at his disposal (*e.g.,* "I have reliable surveys on hand, and they indicate that folks will be swarming on to my movie next summer"). Under the first interpretation, the assertion is an explicit expression of personal opinion that is not actionable at law; the second interpretation goes far beyond any plausible reading of the brochure.

Our analysis of the December, 1977, brochure and bid letter is similar. The film is still a "blockbuster," but now it is also a "giant spectacular," "one of the greatest adventure-survival movies of all time," and a "chilling, riveting, harrowing, cinematic experience" that "promises to be Irwin Allen's biggest and best to date." We have difficulty discerning a single verifiable, factual claim in this excited welter of salesmen's hoopla. Presidio is perhaps on strongest ground in questioning whether *The Swarm* could possibly "promise" to be Irwin Allen's "biggest and best" in December, 1977, but even if Mr. Semel had made the stronger claim that "It *is* Irwin Allen's biggest and best to date," the law provides no guidance for the assessment of this claim. "Biggest" in what sense? (*The Oxford English Dictionary* (1971) lists more than a dozen). *Cf.* Tr. at 425 ("Q. Does 'big' and 'it's big' mean big box office? A. Yes, it *could* mean that.") (Testimony of Charles Chick) (emphasis added). "Best" for whom or for what purpose? If aesthetic evaluation were our task, we certainly could not simply assume that the "best" films were those that generated the highest box-office revenues; indeed, the converse relationship seems more likely. Fortunately, aesthetic evaluation is not our task, so we can note without discomfiture that the same film could find its way into a *New York Times* listing of the 10 Best Movies of the Year as well as a book on *The Fifty Worst Movies of All Time*.[15] Here, as elsewhere in the realm of opinion, one man's meat is another man's poison.

III. SPECIAL KNOWLEDGE, AND "PUFFERY"

Presidio's main argument on appeal seems to be that, even if the statements it complains of are expressions of opinion, a "special knowledge" exception to the opinion rule makes them actionable. . . . We have serious reservations about this argument because: (1) Warner's representations are salesmen's "puffery," which reasonable people do not take seriously; (2) Presidio's executives were experienced, professional film exhibitors who could not reasonably have relied on Warner's puffery; (3) the record amply supports Warner's contentions that its alleged "special knowledge," in the form of marketing surveys and sneak previews, was useful solely for purposes of improving the as yet incomplete film and planning advertising strategies for it; and, (4) in any event, the jury found, by special interrogatories, that Warner's failure to disclose whatever special knowledge it had was not a proximate or producing cause of Presidio's damages.

Presidio cites the *Restatement (Second) of Torts* §§ 539, 542 (1977), in support of its "special knowledge" argument. But Presidio inadvertently neglects to call our attention to several highly relevant comments to the *Restatement* sections it cites. These comments indicate that the "special knowledge" exception is inapplicable where the opinion relied on is clearly salesmen's puffery. In explaining section 539, "Representation of Opinion Implying Justifying Facts," the *Restatement* comment elaborates:

> The habit of vendors to exaggerate the advantages of the bargain that they are offering to make is a well recognized fact. An intending purchaser may not be justified in relying upon his vendor's statement of the value, quality or other advantages of a thing that he is intending to sell as carrying with it any assurance that the thing is such as to justify a reasonable man in praising it so highly.

§ 539, Comment on Subsection (2). Similarly, the *Restatement* amplifies its discussion of "Opinion of Adverse Party" in section 542 with the following qualifying comment:

> [T]he purchaser of an ordinary commodity is not justified in relying upon the vendor's opinion of its quality or worth. For example, one who is purchasing a horse from a dealer is not

---

[15] The film was *Last Year at Marienbad*.

justified in relying upon the dealer's opinion, although the latter has a greater experience in judging the effect of the factors which determine its value.

    e. *This is true particularly of loose general statements made by sellers in commending their wares, which are commonly known as "puffing," or "sales talk."* It is common knowledge and may always be assumed that any seller will express a favorable opinion concerning what he has to sell; and when he praises it in general terms, without specific content or reference to facts, buyers are expected to and do understand that they are not entitled to rely literally upon the words. "Such statements, like the claims of campaign managers before election, are rather designed to allay the suspicion which would attend their absence than to be understood as having any relation to objective truth." [Learned Hand, C.J., in *Vulcan Metals v. Simmons Mfg. Co.,* (2 Cir.1918) 248 Fed. 853, 856.]

    Thus no action lies against a dealer who describes the automobile he is selling as a "dandy," a "bearcat," a "good little car," and a "sweet job," or as "the pride of our line," or "the best in the American market."

§ 542, Comments d–e (emphasis added). The "special knowledge" exception applies typically to the opinions of specialized experts—such as jewelers, lawyers, physicians, scientists, and dealers in antiques—where their opinions are based on concrete, specific information and objective, verifiable facts. *See Restatement* § 542, comment f.

Presidio's claim that its experienced executives were hoodwinked by Warner's extravagant puffery has a distinctly hollow ring to it. The claim is facially implausible in light of the fact that Warner, all puffing aside, suggested only a relatively modest guarantee for the film, *see* note 4 *supra;* Presidio responded with what its own executives testified was only "a good medium-range bid." As noted previously, Presidio's actual bids for several other films the same year were far higher than its bids for *The Swarm, see* note 5 *supra*, which was supposed to be "the greatest adventure-survival movie of all time." Apparently, neither side in this case let puffery interfere with its sound business judgments. . . . Another Presidio executive testified that *The Swarm*'s promotional material did not even reach "the high water mark for puffery."[21] It was no doubt for reasons of this sort that Presidio did not rely solely on Warner's representations concerning *The Swarm* but instead got the opinion of a

---

[21] Presidio was apparently so accustomed to dealing with film promoters' hyperbole that it even had a special stamp made up with which it could imprint the word "bullshit" on the more flagrantly offending documents. . . .

paid consultant in Hollywood, whose advice was: "Don't go out on it." *See* note 3 *supra*. And, in fact, Presidio did not "go out on it". . . .

As it happens, a not insubstantial "jurisprudence of puffery" has developed in the area of film licensing and distribution. It is instructive to compare the present case with the strikingly similar "Doctor Dolittle Case," *Twentieth Century-Fox Distributing Corp. v. Lakeside Theatres, Inc.,* 267 So.2d 225 (La.App.), *cert. denied and judgment aff'd.,* 263 La. 365, 268 So.2d 257 (1972). There, Twentieth Century-Fox, another major film producer and distributor, had described *Doctor Dolittle* to exhibitors as a "blockbuster" of "road show" quality. Like *The Swarm, Doctor Dolittle* was a flop. Lakeside, a disgruntled exhibitor, charged that Fox had misrepresented the quality of the picture. The court firmly rejected that argument as follows:

> While the record confirms that Fox's salesman stated to Mr. Cobb that "Doctor Dolittle" should be a "blockbuster," this is merely an opinion statement on the film's money making potential. Such an obvious speculative projection is not a misrepresentation of a material fact sufficient to constitute fraud. . . .

Id. at 229. The court added that "It is difficult to accept that Mr. Cobb, a man with 38 years' experience in the movie industry who obviously is aware of the uncertainty of public reaction, would blindly enter a contract based on the laudatory statements of a salesman." *Id.* Likewise, in *Penfield v. Bennett Film Laboratories,* 4 Cal.App.2d 306, 40 P.2d 587 (1935), the court held that a producer's statements to the effect that what he had seen of a film was "very good" and that it would be successful "if the balance was as good as that" were not actionable, "uncertainties as to actors, purchasers, and public taste being matters of general knowledge." *Id.* at 587; *see also Dawn Associates v. Links,* 203 U.S.P.Q. 831, 835 (N.D.Ill.1978) (use of the phrase "Horror Classic" is "mere 'puffing' ").

Holmes remarked of the opinion and puffery rule almost a century ago that "The rule of law is hardly to be regretted, when it is considered how easily and insensibly words of hope or expectation are converted by an interested memory into statements of quality and value, when the expectation has been disappointed." *Deming v. Darling,* 148 Mass. 504, 20 N.E. 107, 108–09 (1889). The rule is particularly appropriate in the film industry, which is a risky and unpredictable business even in the best of times, and one where promoters deal more in hopes, dreams, and images than in the more mundane widgets purveyed elsewhere. Terry Semel, Warner's General Sales Manager at the time of *The Swarm's* release, testified on this point as follows:

> I never talk, nor do my colleagues ever talk, to other professional[s] about a comedy. We talk about a hilarious comedy

or a very funny comedy. We never talk about a love story. We talk about a very tender, very moving, very emotional, tearful love story. We never talk about a war story. We talk about the greatest story ever told. We never—do not describe our business in shorthand to each other as if we were selling toaster ovens. . . .

. . . .

Our contemporary jurisprudence is in the process of eroding a number of common law asseverations, but *caveat emptor* has not yet been entirely replaced in our vocabulary by *caveat venditor*. The motion picture industry is entitled to the same license of hyperbole, exaggeration, bombasticism, and flamboyance that the makers of toothpaste and other commodities enjoy in advertising their products. The law recognizes that a vendor is allowed some latitude in claiming merits for his wares by way of an opinion rather than an absolute guarantee, so long as he hews to the line of rectitude in matters of fact. Opinions are not only the lifestyle of democracy, they are the brag in advertising that has made for the wide dissemination of products that otherwise would never have reached the households of our citizens. If we were to accept the thesis set forth by appellees, the advertising industry would have to be liquidated in short order.

. . . .

V.   CONCLUSION

The nub of Presidio's case is its charge of misrepresentation. Presidio must show that (1) Warner misrepresented its film; and (2) that Warner's misrepresentations were the cause of Presidio's injury. We conclude on the basis of the foregoing analysis that Warner's representations concerning its film *The Swarm* are not actionable as a matter of law. . . .

Accordingly, we set aside the verdict, vacate the judgment, and direct the district court to dismiss Presidio's complaint.

NOTES & QUESTIONS

(1)   "The term 'puffing' was first used to describe the practice of illegally bidding up prices at an auction. The person who was paid secretly by the seller to bid up the prices was called a puffer." M. Neil Browne, Kathleen M.S. Hale, and Maureen Cosgrove, *Legal Tolerance Toward the Business Lie and the Puffery Defense: The Questionable Assumptions Of Contract Law*, 37 S. ILL. U. L.J. 69, 70–71 (2012).

(2)   What is meant by the term "puffing" today? Why isn't puffing actionable? *See* RESTATEMENT (SECOND) OF TORTS § 542 cmt. e (1977); RESTATEMENT (THIRD) OF TORTS: LIABILITY FOR ECONOMIC HARM § 9 cmt. d (Tentative Draft No. 2, Apr. 7, 2014); *cf. Vulcan Metals Co. v. Simmons Mfg.*

Co., 248 F. 853, 856 (2d Cir. 1918) ("There are some kinds of talk which no sensible man takes seriously, and if he does he suffers from his credulity. If we were all scrupulously honest, it would not be so; but, as it is, neither party usually believes what the seller says about his own opinions, and each knows it. Such statements, like the claims of campaign managers before election, are rather designed to allay the suspicion which would attend their absence than to be understood as having any relation to objective truth."). Puffing is discussed further in the deceptive marketing materials. *See* Chapter 7, Section B(2).

(3)   Were the statements made by Warner puffing? Why? If Warner had made the following statements, would they constitute non-actionable puffing or actionable misrepresentations: (a) "This film is a cinematic tour de force." (b) "This film has an impressive budget." (c) "This film has not yet been rated by the Motion Picture Association of America." (d) "Test audiences have had favorable impressions of this film."

(4)   As a general matter, a person's reliance upon the opinion of an adverse party is not viewed by the law as justifiable. Why? Section 542 of the Second Restatement reflects this general proposition, but it also lists "exceptions" where reliance on the opinion of an adverse party may be viewed as justifiable. *See also* RESTATEMENT (THIRD) OF TORTS: LIABILITY FOR ECONOMIC HARM § 14 (Tentative Draft No. 2, Apr. 7, 2014) (addressing when false statements of opinion may result in liability).

(a)   Consider the "special knowledge" exception in § 542(a). Why was Presidio unable to take advantage of it? Wouldn't this exception apply to almost all transactions between merchants and consumers, as the merchant typically has greater knowledge about the product than the ordinary buyer? *See* RESTATEMENT (SECOND) OF TORTS § 542 cmts. d, f (1977).

(b)   Consider § 542(b). Why should a fiduciary relationship between the adverse party and the "recipient" make reliance justifiable?

(c)   Consider § 542(c), (d). What factual circumstances might implicate these provisions? *See id.* § 542 cmts. h, i.

(5)   In *Hanberry*, Hearst opined that the shoes were "good ones." The statement was actionable. In *Presidio*, Warner opined (not precisely, but in effect) that the film was a "great one." The statement was not actionable. Are these results consistent?

(6)   Courts often state that a fraud claim must be predicated on a statement of existing fact and not on a prediction about the future. *See, e.g., McElrath v. Electric Inv. Co.*, 131 N.W. 380, 381 (Minn. 1911) ("[A]s a general rule . . . false representations, upon which fraud may be predicated, must be of existing facts, and cannot consist of mere promises or conjectures as to future acts or events."). This statement is simply a variant of the oft-repeated (and misleading) assertion that an action for fraud must be premised on a

misrepresentation of fact and not on a mere statement of opinion. After all, as the *Presidio* court notes, a prediction is merely a type of opinion—an opinion as to what will happen in the future. Thus, the rules that govern when opinions can serve as the basis of a fraud claim, *see* RESTATEMENT (SECOND) OF TORTS §§ 539, 542–543 (1977); RESTATEMENT (THIRD) OF TORTS: LIABILITY FOR ECONOMIC HARM § 14 (Tentative Draft No. 2, Apr. 7, 2014), are applicable to predictions as well.

b. Law

NAGASHIMA V. BUSCK
541 So. 2d 783 (Fla. Dist. Ct. App. 1989)

RIVKIND, LEONARD, ASSOCIATE JUDGE.

The trial court denied appellant an opportunity to amend his multiple count complaint and dismissed it with prejudice.

Appellant/buyer is appealing the dismissal of count III for fraud and count IV for reformation of the terms of a consummated contract of purchase and sale of a multi-family building.

It appears from the record that the trial judge dismissed the fraud count on the ground that the alleged fraud was based upon a material misrepresentation of law instead of fact and, therefore, was not actionable. The reformation count was dismissed because the underlying cause of action for fraud was dismissed.

Appellee/seller sold appellant a multi-family building which consisted of three rental units. The seller had clearly marked each unit with a separate number. The sales contract represented that the building was a "free standing three unit building," and the seller allegedly made oral representations, relied upon by the buyer, that the property complied with all municipal ordinances.

The building, in fact, was zoned for a duplex, not a triplex, and the buyer has since been required to modify the structure to comply with applicable zoning laws. The buyer complains that the costs of modification and resulting diminution in value were directly attributable to the knowing deceit of the seller and constitutes actionable fraud.

It has long been the law in Florida that misrepresentations of law or matters of law such as zoning representations cannot form the basis for a tort action in fraud. *Marks v. Fields*, 160 Fla. 789, 36 So.2d 612 (1948). We acknowledged this rule in *Nantell v. Lim-Wick Construction Co.*, 228

So.2d 634 (Fla. 4th DCA 1969), and clearly held that misrepresentations of fact were actionable while those of law generally were not.[2]

The modern trend in the law seems to be moving away from the rigid fact/law distinction enunciated in *Marks* and *Nantell*. RESTATEMENT (SECOND) OF TORTS § 525 (1979), permits recovery for fraud where one makes a misrepresentation of law for the purpose of inducing another to act and the other's action in reliance causes pecuniary loss. Comment (b) to section 525 defines "misrepresentation" as not only words spoken or written, but any other conduct which amounts to an assertion not in accordance with the truth. RESTATEMENT (SECOND) OF TORTS § 545 . . . permits recovery if the misrepresentation as to a matter of law includes an express or implied misrepresentation of fact.

The modern view expressed by the Restatement, which is in conflict with *Marks*, has not been addressed by our supreme court. We are not at liberty to adopt the Restatement view. Thus, we are bound by *Marks* and *Nantell* and, therefore, consider the allegations of appellant's complaint in light of those authorities.[3]

Though *Marks* is devoid of facts, we find nothing in that opinion to suggest that the supreme court intended an unscrupulous seller to profit from the fact that his factual material misrepresentations were placed under an umbrella of protection by his material misrepresentations as to the law.

We hold that the appellee's misrepresentations were primarily those of fact and as such, the appellant's complaint properly stated a cause of action for fraud.

Accordingly, we reverse the trial court's dismissal of counts III and IV and remand this cause for further proceedings in accordance herewith.

. . . .

NOTES & QUESTIONS

(1) As noted in *Nagashima*, the traditional common-law view was that misrepresentations of law could not form the basis of a fraud claim. Thus, statements such as "this lot is zoned for commercial use" or "this house was built in compliance with local building codes" were not actionable. The justification for this view has been explained as follows:

> Statements of law likewise are commonly said to be mere assertions of opinion, which are insufficient as a basis for deceit. . . .

---

[2] This court in *Zuckerman-Vernon Corp. v. Rosen*, 361 So.2d 804 (Fla. 4th DCA 1978), permitted recovery for fraud against a real estate broker who misrepresented the status of zoning to a vendee. *Rosen* did not address *Marks* and appears to be in conflict.

[3] We note that the facts of this case fall classically within the Restatement sections herein described and we observe that the time may be at hand to abandon the artificial fact/law distinction and recast *Marks* in conformity with those authorities.

In explanation, two reasons have been repeated, sometimes in the same decision: first, that every man is presumed to know the law, and hence the plaintiff cannot be heard to say that he reasonably believed the statement made to him; and second, that no man, at least without special training, can be expected to know the law, and so the plaintiff must have understood that the defendant was giving him nothing more than an opinion. The contradiction is sufficiently obvious. . . . The general rule seems to have arisen rather out of a deliberate policy requiring the parties to a bargain to deal at arm's length with respect to the law, and not to rely upon one another.

W. PAGE KEETON ET AL., PROSSER AND KEETON ON TORTS § 109, at 758–59 (5th ed. 1984).

(2) What was the alleged misrepresentation in *Nagashima*? Would it be actionable under the traditional common-law view? Would it be actionable under § 545 of the Second Restatement? *See also* RESTATEMENT (THIRD) OF TORTS: LIABILITY FOR ECONOMIC HARM § 14 cmt. c (Tentative Draft No. 2, Apr. 7, 2014) (discussing statements of law).

(3) As *Nagashima* suggests, the modern view of the Restatement on misrepresentations of law has largely displaced the traditional common-law view. Consider the following observations:

The present tendency is strongly in favor of eliminating the distinction between law and fact as "useless duffle of an older and more arbitrary day," and recognizing that a statement as to the law, like a statement as to anything else, may be intended and understood either as one of fact or one of opinion only, according to the circumstances of the case. Most courts still render lip service to the older rule, but they have been inclined whenever possible to find statements of fact "implied" in representations as to the law. Thus, an assertion that a company has the legal right to do business in a state carries an assurance that it has, as a matter of fact, been duly qualified; a representation that certain lands may be obtained by patent free from mineral reservations amounts to saying that the government does not classify them as mineral lands; and statements as to the title of land, the priority of a particular lien, or the validity of a note, as well as many similar legal conclusions, have been held to convey similar implications of fact. Since it is obvious that representations of law almost never are made in such a vacuum that supporting facts are not to be "implied," it would seem that very little can be left of the "general rule" in the face of a series of such decisions.

W. PAGE KEETON ET AL., PROSSER AND KEETON ON TORTS § 109, at 759–60 (5th ed. 1984).

c. Intention

SPOLJARIC V. PERCIVAL TOURS, INC.

708 S.W.2d 432 (Tex. 1986)

MCGEE, JUSTICE.

This is a fraudulent misrepresentation case. Ralph Spoljaric sued his former employer for breach of a promise to implement a bonus plan. The trial court rendered judgment for Spoljaric and in an unpublished opinion the court of appeals reversed that judgment and rendered judgment for Percival Tours. The principal question before us is whether there is some evidence to support the jury's finding that the employer did not intend to implement a bonus plan at the time he promised to do so. Because we hold there is some evidence to support the jury's finding, we reverse the judgment of the court of appeals and remand the cause to that court for further consideration.

In March, 1978, Ralph W. Spoljaric negotiated with Jessie L. Upchurch, president of Percival Tours, Inc., for Spoljaric's employment with Percival. The parties entered into a written two-year employment contract. Spoljaric took the position of vice president of finance and accountancy at an annual salary of $42,000 per year.

Toward the end of the two-year contract, Spoljaric began to make plans for his future. He made contacts in New York and initiated talks with Upchurch for a new employment contract. In December, 1979, Spoljaric and Upchurch met. Upchurch offered Spoljaric a salary of $50,000 per year to remain with Percival Tours but refused to enter into a second written contract. Spoljaric declined this offer.

The two met the next day, and Spoljaric counter-offered for a salary of $70,000 without a written contract. Upchurch agreed to the higher salary. The two also discussed Spoljaric's increased responsibilities to the company due to the resignation of Mario Balestrieri, executive vice president of operations.

Approximately two weeks later, a third meeting was held between Spoljaric, Upchurch, and Balestrieri. Balestrieri agreed to stay with Percival at the same terms as Spoljaric. A bonus plan was also discussed. Under the proposed plan, Spoljaric and Balestrieri would be paid a 5 percent bonus on any improvement over Percival's net operating loss of 2 million dollars. The bonus would be paid when the company realized a profit. Upchurch instructed Spoljaric to formalize a plan in writing.

It took almost two months for Spoljaric to draft a bonus plan. He gave the draft to Upchurch for his approval. Because Upchurch objected to certain parts, he instructed his corporate secretary, G. Lisle, to draft an alternate provision dealing with the voluntary termination of executive officers. Lisle drafted the requested provision and Upchurch approved the amended bonus plan. However, the record is silent whether Spoljaric ever saw the new amended bonus plan. Spoljaric and Balestrieri made several inquiries over the next eight months about the status of the proposed bonus plan. Upchurch told them that his New York lawyers were reviewing the plan.

In October, 1980, Percival Tours purchased Jackson Travel Agency, Inc., and Jackson Tours. A press release announced that Robert Jackson would thereafter serve as the president and chief operating officer of Percival Tours. Spoljaric read the press release and believed that Jackson had taken his position.

On October 9, 1980, Spoljaric talked to Jackson concerning his position with Percival Tours and the proposed bonus arrangement. Jackson told Spoljaric that he had no knowledge of either. At Spoljaric's request, Jackson approached Upchurch with the original bonus plan draft. Upchurch read it and said that he had no intention of signing it. When Jackson related this to Spoljaric, Spoljaric walked off the job.

Spoljaric brought suit against Percival Tours, Inc., Upchurch Corporation, and Jessie L. Upchurch for breach of oral contract and fraudulent misrepresentation. In answer to issues, the jury found that (1) Upchurch promised Spoljaric that a bonus plan would be implemented to pay Spoljaric a bonus for improvements in Percival's financial condition, (2) this representation was false, (3) when this representation was made, Upchurch did not intend to keep the promise, (4) Spoljaric justifiably relied on this representation to his detriment, and (5) Upchurch breached the oral contract to pay Spoljaric a bonus. The jury awarded Spoljaric $30,000 in actual damages and $750,000 in punitive damages for fraudulent misrepresentation. The trial court directed a remittitur of $690,000 of the punitive damages. Spoljaric remitted this amount under protest, and the trial court rendered judgment on the balance of the jury findings.

Upchurch appealed. The court of appeals reversed and rendered, holding there was no evidence to support the jury's finding that Upchurch did not intend to implement a bonus plan and there was factually insufficient evidence to uphold the oral contract. The court of appeals did not reach Spoljaric's cross-point concerning remittitur.

Spoljaric contends there is legally sufficient evidence to support the jury's finding that Upchurch did not intend to keep his promise to set up a bonus plan. In reviewing a legal sufficiency point, this court will consider the record as a whole, viewing the evidence and inferences most favorable to the jury verdict and disregarding all other evidence and inferences.

A promise to do an act in the future is actionable fraud when made with the intention, design and purpose of deceiving, and with no intention of performing the act. *Stanfield v. O'Boyle,* 462 S.W.2d 270, 272 (Tex.1971); *Turner v. Biscoe,* 141 Tex. 197, 199, 171 S.W.2d 118, 119 (Tex.Comm'n App.1943, opinion adopted). While a party's intent is determined at the time the party made the representation, it may be inferred from the party's subsequent acts after the representation is made. Intent is a fact question uniquely within the realm of the trier of fact because it so depends upon the credibility of the witnesses and the weight to be given to their testimony.

Failure to perform, standing alone, is no evidence of the promissor's intent not to perform when the promise was made. However, that fact is a circumstance to be considered with other facts to establish intent. Since intent to defraud is not susceptible to direct proof, it invariably must be proven by circumstantial evidence. "Slight circumstantial evidence" of fraud, when considered with the breach of promise to perform, is sufficient to support a finding of fraudulent intent.

Courts have held a party's denial that he ever made a promise is a factor showing no intent to perform when he made the promise. *Stone v. Williams,* 358 S.W.2d 151, 155 (Tex.Civ.App.—Houston 1962, writ ref'd n.r.e.). *See also O'Boyle,* 462 S.W.2d at 272. (Denial of a promise coupled with failure to perform the promise is some evidence of fraudulent intent). No pretense of performance by the defendant has also been held to be a factor showing lack of intent.

The record shows that Upchurch agreed to implement a bonus plan when he was faced with the prospect of losing two executive vice-presidents, Spoljaric and Balestrieri. Viewing this evidence and the inferences therefrom in support of the jury verdict, it is fair to say the jury reasonably believed Upchurch used the bonus plan as an inducement to keep Spoljaric and Balestrieri from leaving the agency.

Spoljaric, Balestrieri, and Upchurch tacitly agreed to parts of a bonus plan in December, 1979; but, no plan was implemented by October, 1980, the date Spoljaric left the agency. Eight months passed from the time Spoljaric gave Upchurch a draft of the bonus plan for his approval. Over this period, Spoljaric and Balestrieri made inquiries whether Upchurch was going to approve the proposed plan. Upchurch told them that his New York lawyers were reviewing it. This testimony conflicts with Lisle's testimony that Upchurch had approved an "amended" plan shortly after receiving Spoljaric's draft of a bonus plan. Upchurch had a duty to tell Spoljaric and Balestrieri that he had approved an amended plan. When the particular circumstances impose on a person a duty to speak and he deliberately remains silent, his silence is equivalent to a false representation. *Smith v. National Resort Communities, Inc.,* 585 S.W.2d

655, 658 (Tex.1979). These circumstances are consistent with Upchurch's lack of intent to keep his promise and no pretense of implementing a bonus plan.

The record shows that Upchurch refused to give Spoljaric a written employment contract after Spoljaric's first contract expired, while he gave written contracts to Jackson and other employees in similar positions. Conversely, Upchurch insisted on a written bonus plan over an oral agreement to its terms. The jury could have inferred that Upchurch's course of conduct in agreeing to a bonus plan when faced with the prospect of losing Spoljaric and Balestrieri and the inconsistency of Upchurch's insistence on an *oral* employment contract and on a *written* bonus plan is circumstantial evidence that Upchurch never intended to implement a bonus plan. This inference is strengthened by Upchurch's testimony at trial that his other bonus plans were "all being honored to the letter."

There is testimony that can be construed as a denial by Upchurch of his promise to implement a bonus plan. Robert Jackson testified that the day Spoljaric left, Spoljaric asked him to inquire whether Upchurch had approved a bonus plan. Jackson approached Upchurch and handed a copy of Spoljaric's proposed bonus plan to Upchurch, who read it and said, "I have no intention of signing this." This testimony is inconsistent with the fact that Upchurch approved an "amended" plan many months earlier. Upchurch's failure to explain his unequivocal statement that he had approved an amended bonus plan is indicative of Upchurch's intent not to implement a bonus plan.

Considering all of the circumstantial evidence of Upchurch's lack of intent in conjunction with Upchurch's failure to keep his promise, we hold that a fact issue of Upchurch's intent was raised sufficient to submit the issue to the jury and that there is some evidence to support the jury's answer.

Spoljaric asserts that there is legally sufficient evidence to support the jury's award of punitive damages for fraudulent misrepresentation. A finding of intent to harm or conscious indifference to the rights of others will support an award of exemplary damages. *Trenholm v. Ratcliff*, 646 S.W.2d 927, 933 (Tex.1983). In *Trenholm*, this court held that a fraudulent inducement was enough to support at least a finding of conscious indifference. *Id.* Our holding of some evidence to support Upchurch's intent to induce Spoljaric by a false representation is some evidence of conscious indifference. Therefore, there is some evidence to support a jury award of punitive damages.

. . . .

The judgment of the court of appeals is reversed and the cause is remanded to that court for further consideration.

NOTES & QUESTIONS

(1) The *Spoljaric* court states that "[a] promise to do an act in the future is actionable fraud when made . . . with no intention of performing the act." *Spoljaric* is consistent with § 530 of the Second Restatement, which similarly states that "[a] representation of the maker's own intention to do or not to do a particular thing is fraudulent if he does not have that intention." *See also id.* § 544 (noting that "the recipient of a fraudulent misrepresentation of intention is justified in relying upon it if the existence of the intention is material and the recipient has reason to believe that it will be carried out"); RESTATEMENT (THIRD) OF TORTS: LIABILITY FOR ECONOMIC HARM § 15 (Tentative Draft No. 2, Apr. 7, 2014) ("A statement of a speaker's intention to perform a promise is a fraudulent misrepresentation if the intention does not exist at the time the statement is made.").

(2) The rule of *Spoljaric* and § 530 is often implicated when parties have entered into a contract with one another. As the Second Restatement explains: "The rule stated in this Section finds common application when the maker misrepresents his intention to perform an agreement made with the recipient. The intention to perform the agreement may be expressed but it is normally merely to be implied from the making of the agreement. Since a promise necessarily carries with it the implied assertion of an intention to perform[,] it follows that a promise made without such an intention is fraudulent. . . ." RESTATEMENT (SECOND) OF TORTS § 530 cmt. c (1977); *see also* RESTATEMENT (THIRD) OF TORTS: LIABILITY FOR ECONOMIC HARM § 15 cmt. b (Tentative Draft No. 2, Apr. 7, 2014) ("Ordinarily, a contract itself will suffice as a representation of the defendant's intent to perform; a party who signs a contract presumptively represents, at least by implication, an intent to do what the contract requires.").

Assume that the defendant enters into a contract with the plaintiff and then subsequently breaches by failing to perform. Under the rule of *Spoljaric* and § 530, are these facts alone sufficient to establish fraud? *See* RESTATEMENT (SECOND) OF TORTS § 530 cmts. c–d (1977); RESTATEMENT (THIRD) OF TORTS: LIABILITY FOR ECONOMIC HARM § 15 cmt. b (Tentative Draft No. 2, Apr. 7, 2014).

(3) In *Spoljaric*, Upchurch failed to keep his promise to implement a bonus plan. Why was this fraudulent? What evidence suggested that this was more than a simple breach of contract claim—i.e., more than a promise made by a defendant, but not ultimately kept?

(4) Why would a plaintiff harmed by a broken promise ever need to claim fraud? Wouldn't a breach of contract action be sufficient? *See* RESTATEMENT (SECOND) OF TORTS § 530 cmt. c (1977); RESTATEMENT (THIRD) OF TORTS: LIABILITY FOR ECONOMIC HARM § 15 cmts. a, c (Tentative Draft No. 2, Apr. 7, 2014); *cf. Burgdorfer v. Thielemann*, 55 P.2d 1122, 1124–25 (Or. 1936) ("The precise objection which defendant makes is that the alleged promise could not have been performed within one year and, therefore, to be enforceable [under the statute of frauds] it must have been reduced to writing

and signed by the party sought to be charged. . . . We think that, in an action for deceit, this provision of the statute does not have the effect of rendering inadmissible testimony of an oral promise made with the fraudulent intent on the part of the promisor at the time the promise was made not to fulfill or perform the same. One of the reasons leading to this conclusion is that the purpose of such oral testimony is not to establish an agreement, but to prove fraud. The gist of the fraud consists in the false representation of the existence of an intention which in truth and in fact has no existence.").

PROBLEM 2.4

Pat buys a home in a brand-new subdivision. Before buying, Pat asked the developer if a swimming pool and exercise facility would be built for the common use of the owners. The developer assured Pat that such facilities were planned and would be ready for use in approximately a year. Eighteen months have passed and construction of the facilities has not begun. The developer has recently told Pat that "we will build the facilities if we can," but Pat is not hopeful in light of the delay and rumors that the developer has longstanding financial difficulties. Pat has checked his purchase contract and there are no representations in it about the developer constructing or otherwise providing a pool and exercise area for residents.

If Pat sues the developer for fraud, what specific evidence would be helpful to him? *See* RESTATEMENT (SECOND) OF TORTS § 530 cmt. d (1977); RESTATEMENT (THIRD) OF TORTS: LIABILITY FOR ECONOMIC HARM § 15 cmt. b (Tentative Draft No. 2, Apr. 7, 2014).

6.   DAMAGES

FORMOSA PLASTICS CORP. V. PRESIDIO ENGINEERS & CONTRACTORS, INC.
960 S.W.2d 41 (Tex. 1998)

ABBOTT, JUSTICE, delivered the opinion of the Court, in which PHILLIPS, CHIEF JUSTICE, GONZALEZ, HECHT, ENOCH, OWEN and HANKINSON, JUSTICES, join.

. . . .

I

In 1989, Formosa Plastics Corporation began a large construction "expansion project" at its facility in Point Comfort, Texas. Presidio Engineers and Contractors, Inc. received an "Invitation to Bid" from Formosa on that part of the project requiring the construction of 300 concrete foundations. The invitation was accompanied by a bid package containing technical drawings, specifications, general information, and a sample contract. The bid package also contained certain representations about the foundation job. These representations included that (1) Presidio would arrange and be responsible for the scheduling, ordering, and delivery of all materials, including those paid for by Formosa; (2) work was to progress continually from commencement to completion; and (3) the job was scheduled to commence on July 16, 1990, and be completed 90 days later, on October 15, 1990.

Presidio's president, Bob Burnette, testified that he relied on these representations in preparing Presidio's bid. Because the bid package provided that the contractor would be responsible for all weather and other unknown delays, he added another 30 days to his estimate of the job's scheduled completion date. He submitted a bid on behalf of Presidio in the amount of $600,000. Because Presidio submitted the lowest bid, Formosa awarded Presidio the contract.

The job was not completed in 120 days. Rather, the job took over eight months to complete, more than twice Burnette's estimate and almost three times the scheduled time provided in the bid package. The delays caused Presidio to incur substantial additional costs that were not anticipated when Presidio submitted its bid.

Presidio asserted a claim under paragraph 17 of the parties' contract, which provided that Formosa was liable for all delay damages within the "control of the owner." Formosa countered that, while it may have been liable for some of the delays, it was not responsible for all of the delays and losses asserted by Presidio. Because the parties were not able to resolve their dispute, Presidio sued Formosa for ... fraudulent inducement of contract and fraudulent performance of contract claims based on representations made by Formosa that Presidio discovered were false after commencing performance of the contract. Formosa counterclaimed for breach of contract, urging that Presidio had not properly completed some of its work.

Presidio presented evidence to the jury that Formosa had an intentional, premeditated scheme to defraud the contractors working on its expansion project. Under this scheme, Formosa enticed contractors to make low bids by making misrepresentations in the bid package regarding scheduling, delivery of materials, and responsibility for delay damages. Jack Lin, the director of Formosa's civil department, admitted that Formosa acted deceptively by representing in the bid package that the contractors would have the ability to schedule the delivery of concrete when in truth Formosa had secretly decided to set up its own delivery schedule in order to save money. Formosa also scheduled multiple contractors, doing mutually exclusive work, to be in the same area at the same time. For instance, Formosa scheduled another contractor to install underground pipe in Presidio's work area at the same time that Presidio was supposed to be pouring foundations. Thomas Pena, Formosa's inspector, admitted that Formosa knew that contractors would be working right on top of each other, but this information was not passed on to the contractors. Of course, once the contractors were on the job, they would realize that, due to such unexpected delays caused by Formosa, their bids were inadequate. But when the contractors requested delay damages under the contract, Formosa would rely on its superior economic position and offer the contractors far less than the full and fair value of the delay damages. In fact, Ron Robichaux, head of Formosa's contract administration division, testified that Formosa, in an effort to lower costs, would utilize its economic superiority to string contractors along and force them to settle. Robichaux added that "if [a contractor] continued to complain then [Formosa] would take the contract from him and make sure he loses his money." Under this scheme, Formosa allegedly stood to save millions of dollars on its $1.5 billion expansion project.

The jury found that Formosa defrauded Presidio and awarded Presidio $1.5 million. . . . Based on its findings that Formosa's fraud . . . [was] done willfully, wantonly, intentionally, or with conscious indifference to the rights of Presidio, the jury further awarded Presidio $10 million as exemplary damages. . . . On the other hand, the jury also concluded that Presidio did not fully comply with the contract, causing Formosa $107,000 in damages.

The trial court suggested a remittitur reducing the tort damages to $700,000 . . . which Presidio accepted. [T]he trial court rendered a judgment in favor of Presidio for $700,000 in actual damages, $10 million in punitive damages, prejudgment interest, attorney's fees, and costs. The damages caused by Presidio's breach of contract were offset against the judgment.

Formosa appealed the judgment to the court of appeals, which affirmed the judgment of the trial court. We granted Formosa's application for writ of error. . . .

. . . .

III

A fraud cause of action requires "a material misrepresentation, which was false, and which was either known to be false when made or was asserted without knowledge of its truth, which was intended to be acted upon, which was relied upon, and which caused injury." *Sears, Roebuck & Co. v. Meadows,* 877 S.W.2d 281, 282 (Tex.1994). A promise of future performance constitutes an actionable misrepresentation if the promise was made with no intention of performing at the time it was made. However, the mere failure to perform a contract is not evidence of fraud. Rather, Presidio had to present evidence that Formosa made representations with the intent to deceive and with no intention of performing as represented. Moreover, the evidence presented must be relevant to Formosa's intent at the time the representation was made.

. . . .

We conclude that Presidio presented legally sufficient evidence that Formosa made representations with no intention of performing as represented in order to induce Presidio to enter into this contract at a low bid price. . . .

Formosa contends, however, that the award of $700,000 in fraud damages to Presidio is excessive as a matter of law. Presidio counters that the damage award is supported by Burnette's testimony that, if he had been told the truth about the project, he "would have bid in the neighborhood of $1,300,000" to perform the contract, and that that amount was a reasonable and necessary cost for doing the work. Presidio maintains that, by subtracting the amount they were paid on the contract, $600,000, from the $1,300,000 reasonable and necessary cost for doing the work, there is legally sufficient evidence to support the damage award of $700,000. But Formosa objected at trial to this testimony on the basis that it was both speculative and an improper measure of damages. Formosa argued again in its motion for new trial that the damages awarded were excessive because Burnette's testimony was speculative and based on an improper measure of damages. Formosa re-urges these complaints to this Court.

Texas recognizes two measures of direct damages for common-law fraud: the out-of-pocket measure and the benefit-of-the-bargain measure.[1] The out-of-pocket measure computes the difference between the value paid and the value received, while the benefit-of-the-bargain measure computes the difference between the value as represented and the value received.

The out-of-pocket measure allows the injured party "to recover the *actual injury* suffered measured by 'the difference between the value of that which he has *parted with,* and the value of that which he has received.'" [*Leyendecker & Assocs., Inc. v. Wechter,* 683 S.W.2d 369, 373 (Tex.1984) (quoting *George v. Hesse,* 100 Tex. 44, 93 S.W. 107 (1906) (emphasis added))]; *see also Morriss-Buick Co. v. Pondrom,* 131 Tex. 98, 113 S.W.2d 889, 890 (1938) (because out-of-pocket fraud damages are intended to provide actual compensation for the injury rather than profit, the proper measure of damages is the difference between the value of what was parted with and what was received). Burnette's testimony regarding what he would have bid if he had known the truth is not the proper measure of out-of-pocket damages. Burnette computed his $1.3

---

[1] When properly pleaded and proved, consequential damages that are foreseeable and directly traceable to the fraud and result from it might be recoverable. It is possible that, in the proper case, consequential damages could include foreseeable profits from other business opportunities lost as a result of the fraudulent misrepresentation. Presidio makes no argument in this case that the $700,000 damage award is supported by legally sufficient evidence of any consequential damages it suffered as a result of Formosa's fraud.

million bid by taking the total amount Presidio spent on the labor, materials, supplies, and equipment used on the job, $831,000, divided by the original expected cost of the job, $370,000, multiplied by his actual bid of $600,000. He also performed an alternative calculation that reached a similar result by dividing the 264 days the job actually took by the 134 days the job should have taken multiplied by his actual bid of $600,000. Basically, both of these methods multiplied the actual bid price of $600,000, which included a profit margin on the job, by a ratio comparing what actually occurred to what was anticipated. Thus, both of these calculations incorporated expected lost profits on a bargain that was never made. But the out-of-pocket measure only compensates for actual injuries a party sustains through parting with something, not loss of profits on a bid not made, and a profit never realized, in a hypothetical bargain never struck. Thus, the $1.3 million hypothetical bid less the $600,000 actually received is not probative of Presidio's out-of-pocket loss. The proper out-of-pocket calculation of damages, based on Burnette's testimony, was $831,000 less the amount he actually received, $600,000, for damages of $231,000.

Burnette's testimony regarding the $1.3 million hypothetical bid is also not probative evidence of benefit-of-the-bargain damages. Under the benefit-of-the-bargain measure, lost profits on the bargain may be recovered if such damages are proved with reasonable certainty. *See* RESTATEMENT (SECOND) OF TORTS § 549(2) (1977) ("The recipient of a fraudulent misrepresentation in a business transaction is also entitled to recover additional damages sufficient to give him the benefit of his contract with the maker, if these damages are proved with reasonable certainty."). But, while a benefit-of-the-bargain measure can include lost profits, it only compensates for the profits that would have been made if the bargain had been performed as promised. Accordingly, the proper calculation of benefit-of-the-bargain damages is Presidio's anticipated profit on the $600,000 bid plus the actual cost of the job less the amount actually paid by Formosa. Based on Burnette's testimony, Presidio's benefit-of-the-bargain damages are not $700,000, but rather $461,000 (bid price of $600,000 less original expected cost of $370,000 for profit of $230,000, plus $831,000 actual cost less $600,000 actually paid).

Burnette calculated his hypothetical $1.3 million bid by multiplying his $600,000 bid, including his anticipated profit, by a factor of about 2.2. However, this doubling of Presidio's bid is entirely speculative because there is no evidence that Presidio would have been awarded the project if it had made a $1.3 million bid. In fact, if any inference could be drawn, it would lead to the opposite conclusion because two of the three other bids Formosa received were lower than $1.3 million. Burnette's testimony as to what he would have bid had he known the truth simply does not establish the benefit of any bargain made with Formosa. It is not based on the expenses incurred and profits lost on this contract because of Formosa's representations, but rather is based on an entirely hypothetical, speculative bargain that was never struck and would not have been consummated. This testimony is therefore not legally sufficient evidence supporting an award of $700,000 in damages.[3]

We accordingly hold that there is no probative evidence supporting the entire amount of damages awarded by the judgment. There is, however, clearly legally sufficient evidence that Presidio suffered some damages as a result of Formosa's fraud; in fact, Burnette's testimony, while it does not support a damage award of $700,000, does support an out-of-pocket damage award of $231,000 or a benefit-of-the-bargain damage award of $461,000. But, because the issue of damages was contested by Formosa, we cannot render judgment in favor of Presidio for a lesser dollar amount. Instead, because there is no legally sufficient evidence to support the entire amount of damages, but there is some evidence of the correct measure of damages, we reverse the judgment of the court of appeals and remand the cause for a new trial. . . .

NOTES & QUESTIONS

(1)   What is Presidio's argument for a damages award of $700,000? Why does the *Formosa* court reject it? Can you explain why the court concludes that the evidence supports "an out-of-pocket damage award of $231,000 or a benefit-of-the-bargain damage award of $461,000"?

(2)   Consider the following observations:

> The American courts are divided over two standards of measurement. One of these, the so-called "out of pocket" rule, looks to the loss which the plaintiff has suffered in the transaction, and gives him the difference between the value of what he has parted with and the value of what he has received. If what he received was worth what he paid for it, he has not been damaged, and there can be no recovery. This rule is followed in deceit actions by the English courts, and by a minority of perhaps a dozen American jurisdictions. . . . The other measurement, called the "loss-of-bargain" rule, gives the plaintiff the benefit of what he was promised, and allows recovery of the difference between the actual value of what he has received and the value that it would have had if it had been as represented. . . . It has been adopted by some two-

---

[3]   . . . . This Court has repeatedly recognized that determining whether lost profits have been proved with reasonable certainty is a fact-intensive determination dependent upon the circumstances of a particular case. When a review of the surrounding circumstances establishes that the profits are not reasonably certain, there is no evidence to support the lost profits award. In this case, we are merely considering all of Burnette's testimony, while indulging all reasonable inferences in Presidio's favor, to conclude that it does not constitute legally sufficient evidence of $700,000 in actual damages because it is speculative and based on an improper measure of damages.

thirds of the courts which have considered the question in actions of deceit. . . . Few courts have followed either rule with entire consistency. . . .

W. PAGE KEETON ET AL., PROSSER AND KEETON ON TORTS § 110, at 767–68 (5th ed. 1984). In the more recent THE LAW OF TORTS, Professor Dobbs observes that "[m]ost courts . . . now permit the plaintiff to recover the loss of bargain, or choose the measure they deem best to fit the facts, or say with the Restatement that the plaintiff can recover under either loss of bargain or out of pocket, at her option." DAN B. DOBBS, THE LAW OF TORTS § 483, at 1380–81 (2000).

(3) The Second Restatement explicitly allows the plaintiff to choose between out of pocket damages or benefit of the bargain damages. *See* RESTATEMENT (SECOND) OF TORTS § 549 & cmt. h (1977). What would motivate a plaintiff to choose one measure over another? Consider the following examples:

(a) Price paid $10,000; value of property purchased $8,000; value as represented $12,000.

(b) Price paid $10,000; value of property purchased $10,000; value as represented $12,000.

(c) Price paid $10,000; value of property purchased $5,000; value as represented $8,000.

(d) An owner of valuable property (worth $500,000) is induced to sell it for less than its value (sale price of $50,000) by a misrepresentation that the property has defects that make it practically worthless.

Out of pocket damages may also be chosen in situations where it is difficult to prove with reasonable certainty what a bargain was worth. In such circumstances, out of pocket losses may be a more reliable measure of damages. *See id.* § 549 cmt. g ("[T]here are many cases in which the value that the plaintiff would have received if the bargain made with him had been performed cannot be proved with any satisfactory degree of certainty, because it must necessarily turn upon the estimated value of something non-existent and never in fact received. In this case the benefit-of-the-bargain harm to the plaintiff becomes mere speculation, and ordinary rules of the law of damages preclude the award."). Finally, in some cases, the victim of a misrepresentation never entered into a contract. In such disputes, benefit of the bargain damages make little sense. *See also* RESTATEMENT (THIRD) OF TORTS: LIABILITY FOR ECONOMIC HARM § 9 cmt. b (Tentative Draft No. 2, Apr. 7, 2014) (expressing a preference for out of pocket damages for fraud).

(4) Benefit of the bargain damages are often determined by the cost of repair. For example, in *Hinkle v. Rockville Motor Co.*, 278 A.2d 42 (Md. 1971), the plaintiff purchased an automobile that was represented to be new, but which actually had been involved in an accident and had over 2,000 miles on it. The plaintiff failed to present evidence on the actual value of the

automobile at the time of sale. Nevertheless, he did present evidence that "the effects of the accident could be remedied and the car returned to new car condition by the expenditure of $800 for repairs." The court noted that the "evidence in regard to the cost of necessary repairs demonstrated the existence of damages and provided an adequate measure upon which they could be predicated." *Id.* at 43, 48. Can you explain why the cost of repair is consistent with a benefit of the bargain measurement of damages?

(5) In *Wallis v. Ford Motor Co.*, 208 S.W.3d 153 (Ark. 2005), a class action lawsuit was brought against Ford for common-law fraud and other claims. The plaintiff asserted that Ford knowingly concealed a dangerous rollover design defect in its 1991–2001 Ford Explorers, and that the "cover up of the inherent design problems . . . led millions of consumers to purchase or lease Ford Explorers at prices far in excess of the values which would have been assigned to such vehicles had these dangers been disclosed." Significantly, the plaintiff "[did] not allege any personal injury or property damage caused by the design defect, nor [did] he allege that the Explorer malfunctioned in any way." Instead, "his entire damage claim rest[ed] on the assertion that the design defect 'substantially diminished' the value of the Explorer."

The Supreme Court of Arkansas held that the fraud claim did not survive a motion to dismiss. As the court observed:

> [I]n a misrepresentation or a fraud case . . . the cause of action rests solely on the premise that a party *did not* receive the benefit of his or her bargain. In order to prove the . . . claim, a party must show that the product delivered was not in fact what was promised. . . . Here, there is no allegation in the complaint that the Ford Explorer has not, to date, been exactly what Wallis bargained for; that is, he does not allege that the vehicle has actually malfunctioned or that the defect has manifested itself.

> Moreover, numerous other jurisdictions have refused to award benefit-of-the-bargain damages when there is no allegation that the product received was not the bargained-for product.

> Despite the fact that some jurisdictions have concluded that the "diminution in value" of a product alone is enough to succeed on a common-law fraud claim, we decline to adopt this principle. According to our well-settled case law, common-law fraud claims not resulting in injury are not actionable. Accordingly, we hold that [a] common-law fraud claim for an allegedly defective vehicle is insufficient to survive a Rule 12(b)(6) motion to dismiss where the only injury alleged is a diminution in value of the vehicle.

Id. at 154–55, 159. Do you agree with the result in *Wallis*? Isn't it true that the value of the Explorer has been diminished to the extent that the public now recognizes the model as having a propensity for defects, even if those defects have not yet manifest themselves in a particular Explorer? Stated more simply, doesn't the risk of a future defect create a present loss of value?

(6) Principles of proximate causation apply to damages sought in a fraud action. *See* RESTATEMENT (SECOND) OF TORTS § 548A (1977); RESTATEMENT (THIRD) OF TORTS: LIABILITY FOR ECONOMIC HARM § 12 (Tentative Draft No. 2, Apr. 7, 2014). As one court explained:

> We begin our analysis by noting that this is a fraud case, *i.e.,* a case involving an intentional tort. Our past cases have referred to proximate cause (or "proximate injury") as one of nine elements of a claim for tortious fraud. Although our more recent cases have employed a more abbreviated list of the elements of fraud, *see, e.g., Riley Hill General Contractor v. Tandy Corp.,* 303 Or. 390, 405, 737 P.2d 595 (1987) (listing five elements), we agree that some notion of proximate cause is subsumed under the last element in that abbreviated list: "Damage to the plaintiff, *resulting from* [the plaintiff's] reliance [on defendant's representation]." *Id.* (emphasis added).

> The question, then, is whether that notion of proximate cause or proximate injury is equivalent to the concept of "reasonable foreseeability," as we have used that phrase in cases [involving negligence]. We are persuaded that it is.

> Courts have noted that, when an intentional tort is involved, the range of legal causation can be quite broad.... Still, the historical references to "proximate injury" as an element of fraud indicates that courts also recognize that there is *some* limitation on the consequences for which a perpetrator of an intentional fraud may be held liable. A requirement that any claimed damages be foreseeable appropriately recognizes that the scope of liability for an intentional, fraudulent misrepresentation depends on the nature of the misrepresentation, the audience to whom the misrepresentation was directed, and the nature of the action or forbearance, intended or negligent, that the misrepresentation justifiably induced. *Restatement (Second) of Torts* § 548A (1977) incorporates that requirement:

>> "A fraudulent misrepresentation is a legal cause of a pecuniary loss resulting from action or inaction in reliance upon it *if, but only if, the loss might reasonably be expected to result from the reliance.*"

> (Emphasis added.) Comments to that *Restatement* section make the same point even more clearly:

>> "a. * * * In general, the misrepresentation is a legal cause only of those pecuniary losses that are within the foreseeable risk of harm that it creates."

Knepper v. Brown, 195 P.3d 383, 387–88 (Or. 2008).

(7)   Consequential damages can also be recovered in an action for fraud. *See, e.g.,* RESTATEMENT (SECOND) OF TORTS § 549(1)(b) (1977). As the Second Restatement explains:

> Although the most usual form of financial loss caused by participation in a financial transaction induced by a fraudulent misrepresentation is the lessened value of the subject matter due to its falsity, the loss may result from a purchaser's use of the article for a purpose for which it would be appropriate if the representation were true but for which it is in fact harmfully inappropriate. So, too, it may be the expense to which he has gone in preparation for a use of the article for which it would have been appropriate if the representation had been true.

> These "indirect" or "consequential" damages resulting from the misrepresentation are recoverable if the misrepresentation is a legal cause of them, as stated in § 548A. This means that they must be of a kind that might reasonably be expected to result from reliance upon the misrepresentation.

Id. § 549 cmt. d. In short, to be recoverable, consequential damages must be foreseeable, *see id.* § 548A, and must be established with reasonable certainty.

(8)   Can mental anguish damages be recovered in a fraud action? Courts have reached different results. *Compare Cornell v. Wunschel,* 408 N.W.2d 369, 382 (Iowa 1987) ("One of the keys to an award of damages for fraudulent misrepresentation is that the party committing the fraud could have contemplated the claimed damage as a consequence of the fraud at the time the misrepresentation was made. Damages for mental distress are not ordinarily contemplated in a business transaction; thus, few courts have recognized their availability as an element of fraud damages."), *with Kilduff v. Adams, Inc.,* 593 A.2d 478, 484 (Conn. 1991) ("Although several courts have denied recovery for mental distress in a fraud action on the ground that damages in such an action are solely intended to compensate the plaintiff for pecuniary loss . . . we concur with those jurisdictions that allow the recovery of emotional damages that are the natural and proximate result of fraud."), *and Osbourne v. Capital City Mortg. Corp.,* 667 A.2d 1321, 1328 (D.C. 1995) ("We hold that, upon proof of intentional misrepresentation, a plaintiff may recover 'emotional damages that are the natural and proximate result' of the defendant's conduct. While the underlying dispute here is contractual in nature, defendants are alleged to have committed an intentional tort when they misrepresented the payoff amount of the note. Whether or not the tort was committed in a contractual context is not dispositive; mental suffering is a 'natural and proximate' consequence of intentional fraud and should be a compensable injury.").

(9)   As in *Formosa,* a plaintiff may be able to recover punitive damages for fraud. *See, e.g., Rogers v. Alexander,* 244 S.W.3d 370, 380, 388 (Tex. App. 2007) (concluding that "[defendants'] fraud was established by clear and

convincing evidence such that an [$850,000] award of punitive damages was appropriate"); *Follo v. Florindo*, 970 A.2d 1230, 1245 (Vt. 2009) (noting that "our cases indicate that when defendants have been found liable for common-law fraud, it is proper to put the issue of punitive damages to the jury"); *State v. Berger*, 567 S.E.2d 265, 278 n.8 (W. Va. 2002) ("A plaintiff who proves common-law fraud may recover punitive damages."); *see also* TEX. CIV. PRAC. & REM. CODE § 41.003 ("[E]xemplary damages may be awarded only if the claimant proves by clear and convincing evidence that the harm with respect to which the claimant seeks recovery of exemplary damages results from: (1) fraud; (2) malice; or (3) gross negligence."). Keep in mind that the amount of punitive damages may be limited by statute. *See, e.g.*, TEX. CIV. PRAC. & REM. CODE § 41.008(b) ("Exemplary damages awarded against a defendant may not exceed an amount equal to the greater of: (1)(A) two times the amount of economic damages; plus (B) an amount equal to any noneconomic damages found by the jury, not to exceed $750,000; or (2) $200,000.").

(10) A defrauded plaintiff may rescind the transaction. In general, rescission "undoes" the transaction by obligating the plaintiff to return what he has received from the defendant, and by allowing the plaintiff to recover what he has transferred to the defendant. Along with rescission, fraud also gives the plaintiff a claim in restitution as necessary to avoid unjust enrichment. *See, e.g.*, RESTATEMENT (THIRD) OF RESTITUTION & UNJUST ENRICHMENT §§ 13(1), 51, 54 (2011).

B. NEGLIGENT MISREPRESENTATION

In general, negligent misrepresentations that cause physical injury are actionable under the same principles that govern ordinary negligence. *See, e.g.*, RESTATEMENT (SECOND) OF TORTS § 311 (1977). For example, gesturing that it is safe to pass on a highway when it is not, or telling someone that a ladder is strong enough to stand on when it is in poor condition, could impose negligence liability on the speaker if he failed to exercise reasonable care in making the representation. *See id.* § 311 illus. 1–9 (providing examples). The separate tort of negligent misrepresentation, however, focuses on negligent misrepresentations that cause pure economic loss. This separate tort, and its corresponding emphasis on economic injury, is the subject of the materials in this Section.

The tort of negligent misrepresentation shares many of the same elements as the tort of fraud. There must be a false, material misrepresentation, the plaintiff must have justifiably relied, and the plaintiff must suffer injury resulting from such reliance. The primary differences between the two causes of action involve the defendant's state of mind (negligence rather than scienter) and the correspondingly narrower scope of liability for the less-culpable, negligence-based tort.

1. SCOPE OF LIABILITY

The scope of liability for negligent misrepresentation has generated a considerable amount of litigation. Who can sue, in other words, for negligent misrepresentation? Many of the judicial precedents involve accountants who are sued for negligently misrepresenting the financial health of a business in the course of an audit that they were hired to conduct. These lawsuits are typically brought not by the accountant's client, but instead by third-party investors or lenders (i.e., persons not in a contractual relationship with the accountant) who allegedly relied on misstatements in the audit report. Given that audit reports are often circulated widely in the financial community to a vast number of investors and lenders, the potential exposure for accountants is significant.

Because so many of the relevant precedents involve third-party suits against accountants, some background on the auditing process is useful:

> Although certified public accountants (CPA's) perform a variety of services for their clients, their primary function, which is the one that most frequently generates lawsuits against them by third persons, is financial auditing. An audit is a verification of the financial statements of an entity through an examination of the underlying accounting records and supporting evidence. In an audit engagement, an accountant reviews financial statements prepared by a client and issues an opinion stating whether such statements fairly represent the financial status of the audited entity.

> In a typical audit, a CPA firm may verify the existence of tangible assets, observe business activities, and confirm account balances and mathematical computations. It might also examine sample transactions or records to ascertain the accuracy of the client company's financial and accounting systems. For example, auditors often select transactions recorded in the company's books to determine whether the recorded entries are supported by underlying data (vouching). Or, approaching the problem from the opposite perspective, an auditor might choose particular items of data to trace through the client's accounting and bookkeeping process to determine whether the data have been properly recorded and accounted for (tracing).

> For practical reasons of time and cost, an audit rarely, if ever, examines every accounting transaction in the records of a business. The planning and execution of an audit therefore require a high degree of professional skill and judgment. Initially, the CPA firm plans the audit by surveying the client's business operations and accounting systems and making

preliminary decisions as to the scope of the audit and what methods and procedures will be used. The firm then evaluates the internal financial control systems of the client and performs compliance tests to determine whether they are functioning properly. Transactions and data are sampled, vouched for, and traced. Throughout the audit process, results are examined and procedures are reevaluated and modified to reflect discoveries made by the auditors. For example, if the auditor discovers weaknesses in the internal control system of the client, the auditor must plan additional audit procedures which will satisfy himself that the internal control weaknesses have not caused any material misrepresentations in the financial statements.

The end product of an audit is the audit report or opinion. The report is generally expressed in a letter addressed to the client. The body of the report refers to the specific client-prepared financial statements which are attached. In the case of the so-called "unqualified report" . . . two paragraphs are relatively standard.

In a scope paragraph, the CPA firm asserts that it has examined the accompanying financial statements in accordance with GAAS [Generally Accepted Auditing Standards]. . . .

. . . .

In an opinion paragraph, the audit report generally states the CPA firm's opinion that the audited financial statements, taken as a whole, are in conformity with GAAP [Generally Accepted Accounting Principles] and present fairly in all material respects the financial position, results of operations, and changes in financial position of the client in the relevant periods.

. . . . Like GAAS, GAAP include broad statements of accounting principles amounting to aspirational norms as well as more specific guidelines and illustrations.

In addition to or in place of the standardized statements in an audit report, the auditing CPA firm may also qualify its opinion, noting exceptions or matters in the financial statements not in conformity with GAAP or significant uncertainties which might affect a fair evaluation of the statements. The report may also contain a disclaimer stating the accountant's inability to express any opinion about the statements or an adverse opinion that the statements do not fairly present the financial position of the client in conformity with GAAP.

> . . . [A]udits may be commissioned by clients for different purposes. Nonetheless, audits of financial statements and the resulting audit reports are very frequently (if not almost universally) used by businesses to establish the financial credibility of their enterprises in the perceptions of outside persons, e.g., existing and prospective investors, financial institutions, and others who extend credit to an enterprise or make risk-oriented decisions based on its economic viability. The unqualified audit report of a CPA firm, particularly one of the "Big Six," is often an admission ticket to venture capital markets—a necessary condition precedent to attracting the kind and level of outside funds essential to the client's financial growth and survival. As one commentator summarizes: "In the first instance, this unqualified opinion serves as an assurance to the client that its own perception of its financial health is valid and that its accounting systems are reliable. The audit, however, frequently plays a second major role: it assists the client in convincing third parties that it is safe to extend credit or invest in the client."

Bily v. Arthur Young & Co., 834 P.2d 745, 749–51 (Cal. 1992).

CREDIT ALLIANCE CORP. V. ARTHUR ANDERSEN & CO.

483 N.E.2d 110 (N.Y. 1985)

JASEN, JUDGE.

The critical issue common to these two appeals is whether an accountant may be held liable, absent privity of contract, to a party who relies to his detriment upon a negligently prepared financial report and, if so, within what limits does that liability extend.

I

In *Credit Alliance Corp. v. Andersen & Co.* ("*Credit Alliance*"), plaintiffs are major financial service companies engaged primarily in financing the purchase of capital equipment through installment sales or leasing agreements. Defendant, Arthur Andersen & Co. ("Andersen"), is a national accounting firm. Plaintiffs' complaint and affidavit allege that prior to 1978, plaintiffs had provided financing to L.B. Smith, Inc. of Virginia ("Smith"), a capital intensive enterprise that regularly required financing. During 1978, plaintiffs advised Smith that as a condition to extending additional major financing, they would insist upon examining an audited financial statement. Accordingly, Smith provided plaintiffs with its consolidated financial statements, covering both itself and its subsidiaries, "For The Years Ended December 31, 1977 and 1976" (the "1977 statements"). These statements contained an auditor's report prepared by Andersen stating that it had examined the statements in accordance with generally accepted auditing standards ("GAAS") and found them to reflect fairly the financial position of Smith in conformity with generally accepted accounting principles ("GAAP"). In reliance upon the 1977 statements, plaintiffs provided substantial amounts in financing to Smith through various extensions of credit. Thereafter, in 1979, as a precondition to continued financing, plaintiffs requested and received from Smith the consolidated financial statements "For The Years Ended February 28, 1979 and December 31, 1977" (the "1979 statements"). Again, Andersen's report vouched for its examination of the financial statements and the financial position of Smith reflected therein. Relying upon these certified statements, plaintiffs provided additional substantial financing to Smith.

It is alleged that both statements overstated Smith's assets, net worth and general financial health, and that Andersen failed to conduct investigations in accordance with proper auditing standards, thereby failing to discover Smith's precarious financial condition and the serious possibility that Smith would be unable to survive as a going concern. Indeed, in 1980, Smith filed a petition for bankruptcy. By that time, Smith had already defaulted on several millions of dollars of obligations to plaintiffs.

In August 1981, plaintiffs commenced this suit for damages lost on its outstanding loans to Smith, claiming both negligence and fraud by Andersen in the preparation of its audit reports. The complaint alleges that Andersen knew, should have known or was on notice that the 1977 and 1979 certified statements were being utilized by Smith to induce companies such as plaintiffs to make credit available to Smith. The complaint further states that Andersen knew, should have known or was on notice that the certified statements were being shown to plaintiffs for such a purpose. It is also alleged that Andersen knew or recklessly disregarded facts which indicated that the 1977 and 1979 statements were misleading.

On Andersen's motion to dismiss the complaint, Special Term initially held the negligence cause of action to be barred by the Statute of Limitations, but denied the motion with regard to the claim for fraud. On reargument, the court reversed its dismissal of the negligence cause of action and denied Andersen's motion in its entirety. On appeal, the Appellate Division affirmed the order below, holding, in part, that despite the absence of contractual privity between the parties, plaintiffs were members of a limited class whose reliance upon the financial statements should have been specifically foreseen by defendants. The court concluded that plaintiffs fell within the exception to the general rule that requires privity to maintain an action against an accountant for negligence. Two Justices dissented on the ground that the rule requiring privity has been repeatedly reaffirmed by this court and mandates dismissal of the action for negligence.

The Appellate Division granted Andersen's motion for leave to appeal to this court and certified the following question: "Was the order of the Supreme Court, as affirmed by this Court, properly made?" Because the allegations in plaintiffs' complaint and affidavit fail to set forth either a relationship of contractual privity with Andersen or a relationship sufficiently intimate to be equated with privity, the first cause of action should be dismissed. Further, inasmuch as plaintiffs' second cause of action, sounding in fraud, comprises mere conclusory allegations, it also should be dismissed. Accordingly, in *Credit Alliance,* we now reverse and answer the certified question in the negative.

In *European Am. Bank & Trust Co. v. Strauhs & Kaye ("European American"),* the complaint, together with the affidavit in opposition to the motion to dismiss, alleges that plaintiff, European American Bank and Trust Company ("EAB"), made substantial loans to Majestic Electro Industries and certain of its subsidiaries (collectively, "Majestic Electro") in March 1979 pursuant to their written agreements. Several months later, EAB partially financed Majestic Electro's acquisition of Brite Lite Lamps Corp. by again advancing substantial funds.

Beginning in 1979, and continuing thereafter at all relevant times, Majestic Electro retained defendant Strauhs & Kaye ("S & K"), an accounting partnership rendering services in this State, to audit its financial records in accordance with GAAS and to report its findings in conformity with GAAP. During the course of its lending relationship with Majestic Electro, EAB relied upon the interim and year-end financial reports prepared by S & K to determine the maximum amounts it was willing to lend. From 1979 through 1982, S & K allegedly, *inter alia,* overstated Majestic Electro's inventory and accounts receivable, and failed to disclose the inadequacy of Majestic Electro's internal recordkeeping and inventory control.

When, in December 1982, a Majestic Electro subsidiary defaulted on its loan agreement, EAB caused the subsidiary's inventory, in which it had a security interest, to be liquidated. It was then that EAB allegedly began to discover that S & K's reports had seriously exaggerated the financial solvency of Majestic Electro. Indeed, between the time the complaint was filed and the submission of papers upon the motion to dismiss, Majestic Electro filed a petition in bankruptcy. EAB suffered substantial losses from the loans remaining unpaid.

EAB commenced this action in May 1983, seeking damages for those losses allegedly resulting from its reliance upon S & K's reports. EAB specifically alleges negligence in that S & K, in performing auditing and accounting services for Majestic Electro, at all relevant times knew that

EAB was Majestic Electro's principal lender, was familiar with the terms of the lending relationship, and was fully aware that EAB was relying on the financial statements and inventory valuations certified by S & K. Moreover, it is alleged that representatives of EAB and S & K were in direct communication, both oral and written, during the entire course of the lending relationship between EAB and Majestic Electro, and, indeed, that representatives of EAB and S & K met together throughout this time to discuss S & K's evaluation of Majestic Electro's inventory and accounts receivable and EAB's reliance thereon. The complaint also alleges a second cause of action, merely adding that defendants were "grossly negligent or recklessly indifferent" in performing professional services and that EAB was damaged as a result.

On S & K's motion, Special Term dismissed the complaint holding that, absent a contractual relationship between the parties or an allegation of fraud, the complaint failed to state a cause of action. On appeal, the Appellate Division unanimously reversed and reinstated the complaint in its entirety. Focusing on the direct communications between the parties, the court held that contractual privity was not a prerequisite to liability inasmuch as S & K specifically knew that their reports would be relied upon by EAB for a particular purpose.

The Appellate Division granted S & K's motion for leave to appeal to this court and certified the following question: "Was the order of this Court, which reversed the order of the Supreme Court, properly made?" Because EAB's complaint and affidavit posit a direct nexus between the parties, to wit: the direct communications between them concerning EAB's intended reliance upon S & K's financial evaluation of Majestic Electro, the causes of action for negligence and for gross negligence or reckless indifference are adequately alleged. Accordingly, in *European American,* we now affirm and answer the certified question in the affirmative.

II

In the seminal case of *Ultramares Corp. v. Touche,* 255 N.Y. 170, 174 N.E. 441, this court, speaking through the opinion of Chief Judge Cardozo more than 50 years ago, disallowed a cause of action in negligence against a public accounting firm for inaccurately prepared financial statements which were relied upon by a plaintiff having no contractual privity with the accountants. This court distinguished its holding from *Glanzer v. Shepard,* 233 N.Y. 236, 135 N.E. 275, a case decided in an opinion also written by Cardozo nine years earlier. We explained that in *Glanzer,* an action in negligence against public weighers had been permitted, despite the absence of a contract between the parties, because the plaintiff's intended reliance, on the information *directly transmitted* by the weighers, created a bond so closely approaching privity that it was, in practical effect, virtually indistinguishable therefrom. This court has subsequently reaffirmed its holding in *Ultramares* which has been, and continues to be, much discussed and analyzed by the commentators and by the courts of other jurisdictions. These appeals now provide us with the opportunity to reexamine and delineate the principles enunciated in both *Ultramares* and *Glanzer*. Inasmuch as we believe that a relationship "so close as to approach that of privity" remains valid as the predicate for imposing liability upon accountants to noncontractual parties for the negligent preparation of financial reports, we restate and elaborate upon our adherence to that standard today.

. . . .

Although accountants might be held liable in fraud to nonprivy parties who were intended to rely upon the accountants' misrepresentations, we noted that "[a] different question develops when we ask whether they owed a duty to these to make [their reports] without negligence." (*Ultramares Corp. v. Touche, supra*, 255 N.Y., at p. 179, 174 N.E. 441.) Disputing the wisdom of extending the duty of care of accountants to anyone who might foreseeably rely upon their financial reports, Cardozo, speaking for this court, remarked: "If liability for negligence exists, a thoughtless slip or blunder, the failure to detect a theft or forgery beneath the cover of deceptive entries, may expose accountants to a liability in an indeterminate amount for an indeterminate time to an indeterminate class. The hazards of a business conducted on these terms are so extreme as to enkindle doubt whether a flaw may not exist in the implication of a duty that exposes to these consequences." (*Id.,* at pp. 179–180, 174 N.E. 441.)

In *Ultramares*, the accountants had prepared a certified balance sheet for their client to whom they provided 32 copies. The client, in turn, gave one to the plaintiff company. The latter, relying upon the misinformation contained in the balance sheet, made loans to the accountants' client who, only months later, was declared bankrupt. This court, refusing to extend the accountants' liability for negligence to their client's lender, with whom they had no contractual privity, noted that the accountants had prepared a report on behalf of their client to be exhibited generally to "banks, creditors, stockholders, purchasers or sellers, *according to the needs of the occasion*." (225 N.Y. at pp. 173–174, 174 N.E. 441 [emphasis added].) In reciting the facts, we emphasized that: "*Nothing was said as to the persons to whom these [copies] would be shown or the extent or number of the transactions in which they would be used.* In particular there was no mention of the plaintiff, a corporation doing business chiefly as a factor, which till then had never made advances to the [accountants' client], though it had sold merchandise in small amounts. The range of the transactions in which a certificate of audit might be expected to play a part was as indefinite and wide as the possibilities of the business that was mirrored in the summary." (*Id.,* at p. 174, 174 N.E. 441 [emphasis added].)

The accountants' report was primarily intended as a convenient instrumentality for the client's use in developing its business. "[O]nly incidentally or collaterally" was it expected to assist those to whom the client "might exhibit it thereafter." (*Id.,* at p. 183, 174 N.E. 441.) Under such circumstances, permitting recovery by parties such as the plaintiff company would have been to impose a duty upon accountants "enforce[able] by any member of an indeterminate class of creditors, present and prospective, known and unknown." (*Id.,* at p. 184, 174 N.E. 441.)

By sharp contrast, the facts underlying *Glanzer* bespoke an affirmative assumption of a duty of care to a specific party, for a specific purpose, regardless of whether there was a contractual relationship. There, a seller of beans employed the defendants who were engaged in business as public weighers. Pursuant to instructions, the weighers furnished one copy of the weight certificate to their employer, the seller, and another to the prospective buyer. In reliance upon the inaccurately certified weight, the buyer purchased beans from the seller and, thereby, suffered a loss.

Explaining the imposition upon the weighers of a "noncontractual" duty of care to the buyer, this court held: "We think the law imposes a duty toward buyer as well as seller in the situation here disclosed. The [buyer's] use of the certificates was *not an indirect or collateral consequence* of the action of the weighers. It was a consequence which, to the weighers' knowledge, was the *end and aim of the transaction.* [The seller] ordered, but [the buyer was] to use. The defendants held themselves out to the public as skilled and careful in their calling. They knew that the beans had been sold, and that on the faith of their certificate payment would be made. *They sent a copy to the [buyer] for the very purpose of inducing action.* All this they admit. In such circumstances, assumption of the task of weighing was the assumption of a duty to weigh carefully for the benefit of all whose conduct was to be governed. We do not need to state the duty in terms of contract or of privity. Growing out of a contract, it has nonetheless an origin not exclusively contractual. Given the contract and the relation, the duty is imposed by law (cf. *MacPherson v. Buick Motor Co.,* 217 N.Y. 382, 390 [111 N.E. 1050])." (233 N.Y. at pp. 238–239, 135 N.E. 275 [emphasis added].)

The critical distinctions between the two cases were highlighted in *Ultramares,* where we explained: "In *Glanzer v. Shepard* * * * [the certificate of weight], which was made out in duplicate, one copy to the seller and the other to the buyer, *recites that it was made by order of the* *former for the use of the latter* * * * Here was something more than the rendition of a service in the expectation that the one who ordered the certificate would use it thereafter in the operations of his business as occasion might require. Here was a case where *the transmission of the certificate to another was* not merely one possibility among many, but [was] *the 'end and aim of the transaction,'* as certain and immediate and deliberately willed as if a husband were to order a gown to be delivered to his wife, or a telegraph company, contracting with the sender of a message, were to telegraph it wrongly to the damage of the person expected to receive it * * * The *intimacy of the resulting nexus* is attested by the fact that after stating the case in terms of legal duty, we went on to point out that * * * we could reach the same result by stating it in terms of contract * * * The bond was *so close as to approach that of privity, if not completely one with it.* Not so in the case at hand [i.e., *Ultramares*]. No one would be likely to urge that there was a contractual relation, *or even one approaching it*, at the root of any duty that was owing from the [accountants] now before us to the indeterminate class of persons who, presently or in the future, might deal with the [accountants' client] in reliance on the audit. In a word, the service rendered by the defendant in *Glanzer v. Shepard* was primarily for the information of a third person, *in effect, if not in name, a party to the contract*, and only incidentally for that of the formal promisee." (*Ultramares Corp. v. Touche, supra*, 255 N.Y., at pp. 182–183, 174 N.E. 441 [emphasis added].)

Several years subsequent to the decision in *Ultramares,* this court reiterated the requirement for a "contractual relationship or its equivalent," and more recently, in *White v. Guarente*, 43 N.Y.2d 356, 401 N.Y.S.2d 474, 372 N.E.2d 315, such an equivalent was presented for our consideration. There, the accountants had contracted with a limited partnership to perform an audit and prepare the partnership's tax returns. The nature and purpose of the contract, to satisfy the requirement in the partnership agreement for an audit, made it clear that the accountants' services were obtained to benefit the members of the partnership who, like plaintiff, a limited partner, were necessarily dependent upon the audit to prepare their own tax returns. After outlining the principles articulated in *Ultramares* and *Glanzer*, this court observed that: "[T]his plaintiff seeks redress, not as a mere member of the public, but as one of a settled and particularized class among the members of which the report would be circulated *for the specific purpose of fulfilling the limited partnership agreed upon arrangement.*" (43 N.Y.2d, at p. 363, 401 N.Y.S.2d 474, 372 N.E.2d 315 [emphasis added].) Because the accountants knew that a limited partner would have to rely upon the audit and tax returns of the partnership, and inasmuch as this was within the specific contemplation of the accounting retainer, we held that, "at least on the facts here, an accountant's liability may be so imposed." (*Id.,* at p. 358, 401 N.Y.S.2d 474, 372 N.E.2d 315.) The resulting relationship between the accountants and the limited partner was clearly one "approach[ing] that of privity, if not completely one with it." (*Ultramares Corp. v. Touche, supra*, 255 N.Y. at p. 183, 174 N.E. 441.)

Upon examination of *Ultramares* and *Glanzer* and our recent affirmation of their holdings in *White*, certain criteria may be gleaned. Before accountants may be held liable in negligence to noncontractual parties who rely to their detriment on inaccurate financial reports, certain prerequisites must be satisfied: (1) the accountants must have been aware that the financial reports were to be used for a particular purpose or purposes; (2) in the furtherance of which a known party or parties was intended to rely; and (3) there must have been some conduct on the part of the accountants linking them to that party or parties, which evinces the accountants' understanding of that party or parties' reliance. While these criteria permit some flexibility in the application of the doctrine of privity to accountants' liability, they do not represent a departure from the principles articulated in *Ultramares, Glanzer* and *White*, but, rather, they are intended to preserve the wisdom and policy set forth therein.

. . . .

III

In the appeals we decide today, application of the foregoing principles presents little difficulty. In *Credit Alliance*, the facts as alleged by plaintiffs fail to demonstrate the existence of a relationship between the parties sufficiently approaching privity. Though the complaint and supporting affidavit do allege that Andersen specifically knew, should have known or was on notice that plaintiffs were being shown the reports by Smith, Andersen's client, in order to induce their reliance thereon, nevertheless, there is no adequate allegation of either a particular purpose for the reports' preparation or the prerequisite conduct on the part of the accountants. While the allegations state that Smith sought to induce plaintiffs to extend credit, no claim is made that Andersen was being employed to prepare the reports with that particular purpose in mind. Moreover, there is no allegation that Andersen had any direct dealings with plaintiffs, had specifically agreed with Smith to prepare the report for plaintiffs' use or according to plaintiffs' requirements, or had specifically agreed with Smith to provide plaintiffs with a copy or actually did so. Indeed, there is simply no allegation of any word or action on the part of Andersen directed to plaintiffs, or anything contained in Andersen's retainer agreement with Smith which provided the necessary link between them.

By sharp contrast, in *European American*, the facts as alleged by EAB clearly show that S & K was well aware that a primary, if not the exclusive, *end and aim* of auditing its client, Majestic Electro, was to provide EAB with the financial information it required. The prerequisites for the cause of action in negligence, as well as in gross negligence, are fully satisfied. Not only is it alleged, as in *Credit Alliance*, that the accountants knew the identity of the specific nonprivy party who would be relying upon the audit reports, but additionally, the complaint and affidavit here allege both the accountants' awareness of a particular purpose for their services and certain conduct on their part creating an unmistakable relationship with the reliant plaintiff. It is unambiguously claimed that the parties remained in direct communication, both orally and in writing, and, indeed, met together throughout the course of EAB's lending relationship with Majestic Electro, for the very purpose of discussing the latter's financial condition and EAB's need for S & K's evaluation. Moreover, it is alleged that S & K made repeated representations personally to representatives of EAB, on these occasions, concerning the value of Majestic Electro's assets. It cannot be gainsaid that the relationship thus created between the parties was the practical equivalent of privity. The parties' direct communications and personal meetings resulted in a nexus between them sufficiently approaching privity under the principles of *Ultramares, Glanzer* and *White* to permit EAB's causes of action.

Finally, disposition of the second cause of action alleged in *Credit Alliance* need not detain us long. The cause of action for fraud repeats the allegations for the negligence cause of action and merely adds a claim that Andersen recklessly disregarded facts which would have apprised it that its reports were misleading or that Andersen had actual knowledge that such was the case. This single allegation of scienter, without additional detail concerning the facts constituting the alleged fraud, is insufficient under the special pleading standards required under CPLR 3016(b), and, consequently, the cause of action should have been dismissed.

Accordingly, in *Credit Alliance* both causes of action should be dismissed, the order of the Appellate Division reversed, with costs, and the certified question answered in the negative. In *European American*, the order of the Appellate Division should be affirmed, with costs, and the certified question answered in the affirmative.

NOTES & QUESTIONS

(1) In *Ultramares Corp. v. Touche*, Chief Judge Cardozo refused to allow a plaintiff to sue an accounting firm for negligence based upon inaccurately prepared financial statements when the plaintiff was not in contractual privity with the firm. What was Cardozo's concern about permitting such negligence claims? Consider an accounting firm who is retained to audit the financial statements of AT&T to satisfy the Securities &

Exchange Commission's requirement of audited financial statements for public companies.

(2) The *Credit Alliance* court announced the following "test" for when parties not in contractual privity with the defendant may sue for negligent misrepresentation:

> Before accountants may be held liable in negligence to noncontractual parties who rely to their detriment on inaccurate financial reports, certain prerequisites must be satisfied: (1) the accountants must have been aware that the financial reports were to be used for a particular purpose or purposes; (2) in the furtherance of which a known party or parties was intended to rely; and (3) there must have been some conduct on the part of the accountants linking them to that party or parties, which evinces the accountants' understanding of that party or parties' reliance.

How would you describe the intent of this test? In other words, what is it trying to accomplish? Does the test satisfy Cardozo's concern?

(3) What is the independent function of the third element of the *Credit Alliance* test? If the defendant accountant knows the purpose of the financial reports, and knows the party who will be using the financial reports for that purpose, why is there a need for "linking conduct" between the accountant and the known party? What sort of conduct would satisfy this third element?

(4) In *Security Pacific Business Credit, Inc. v. Peat Marwick Main & Co.*, 597 N.E.2d 1080 (N.Y. 1992), Top Brass, a retailer, hired Main Hurdman ("Main"), a predecessor of the defendant accounting firm, to audit its 1984 financial statements. Main issued an unqualified audit report, and Security Pacific ("SPBC") allegedly loaned funds to Top Brass in reliance on the report. When Top Brass filed for bankruptcy, SPBC sued the defendant (as Main's successor) for negligently misrepresenting Top Brass' financial condition.

SPBC primarily relied on an unsolicited telephone call that it made to Main's audit partner to establish the "linking conduct" aspect of the *Credit Alliance* test. The call, allegedly made at the suggestion of Top Brass officers, was to discuss the draft audit report that SPBC had received from Top Brass. In the call, SPBC purportedly told the audit partner that it would be relying on the audit, and the partner generally reported that Main was comfortable with its unqualified opinion. *See id.* at 1081–83. Nevertheless, the Court of Appeals concluded that the telephone call did not establish a sufficient connection between SPBC and Main:

> The fact pattern of *European American* [discussed in *Credit Alliance*] offers a cogent contrasting illustration. There, the accountants had multiple, direct and substantive communications and personal meetings with the relying lender during the entire course of the lending relationship. Here, SPBC's claimed relationship to Main Hurdman, "sufficiently approaching privity,"

rises or falls essentially on the single unsolicited phone call. We conclude that the relationship fails to connect because Main Hurdman's partner's responses to SPBC's inquiries in that single call placed after the audit field work was completed were, viewed even in the most favorable light plaintiff places on them, "limited to generalities that nothing untoward had been uncovered in the course of the audit and that an unqualified opinion would issue, certifying the tentative draft which plaintiff had received from Top Brass itself" (*Security Pac. Business Credit v. Peat Marwick Main & Co.,* 165 A.D.2d 622, 626, 569 N.Y.S.2d 57). SPBC's efforts to elevate these facts to the critical rank and linking relationship akin to privity, as our precedents require, are unavailing. SPBC cannot unilaterally create such an extraordinary obligation, imposing negligence liability of significant commercial dimension and consequences by merely interposing and announcing its reliance in this fashion.

Moreover, no sufficient *conduct* appears in this record evidencing a relationship between SPBC and the accountants, which *Credit Alliance* contemplates. In this respect, the dissent would substantially extend *Credit Alliance* by allowing *any* conduct by the accountants to result in a potential for liability. This plainly is not what *Credit Alliance* and its related precedents effected. As the Supreme Court observed in granting defendant's motion for summary judgment in this case, "if a lender can secure possible loan recourse against a borrower's auditor by the simple act of calling the auditor before advancing a loan and announcing reliance on the auditor's opinion, then every lender's due diligence list will in the future mandate such a telephone call. For the small price of a phone call, the bank would in effect acquire additional loan protection [by] placing the auditor in the role of an insurer or guarantor of loans extended to [its] clients." The facile acquisition of deep pocket surety coverage, with no opportunity for actuarial assessment and self-protection, by the party sought to be charged, at the mere cost of a telephone call by the lender, is a bargain premium rate indeed. This, too, was surely not within the ambit of liability promulgated and recognized in *Credit Alliance.*

As exemplified in many of this Court's precedents, in contradistinction to plaintiff's allegations here, no claim is made and no evidence is tendered that Main Hurdman was retained to prepare the audit report for the purpose of inducing SPBC to extend credit to Top Brass, or that Main Hurdman ever specifically agreed with Top Brass to prepare the report for SPBC's use or according to SPBC's requirements. While those features are not exclusive prerequisites to satisfy the *Credit Alliance* analysis, they provide confident and significant foundational support, which this Court has previously recognized and, therefore, appropriately now considers in deciding this case.

Also, there is no evidence that Main Hurdman shaped its 1984 audit opinion to meet any needs of SPBC. Neither is there any claim or proof that Main Hurdman directly supplied SPBC with a copy of the audit report or opinion or ever agreed to do so. Indeed, the record shows that Main Hurdman's client, Top Brass, sent SPBC the [final] report only after it was publicly filed with the SEC. Similarly, the audit engagement letter between Top Brass and Main Hurdman does not mention SPBC or provide or suggest the necessary link to SPBC. To be sure also, there is no claim that Main Hurdman was aware that "*a* [emphasis added] primary, if not the exclusive, *end and aim* [emphasis in original] of auditing its client [Top Brass] was to provide [SPBC] with the financial information it required." . . . In fact, the record indicates that the primary, if not exclusive, end and aim of the Main Hurdman audit was for use in Top Brass's audit report as required by Federal law for a publicly held company. . . . In sum, Main Hurdman's audit work was clearly for the benefit of its client, Top Brass, as a "convenient instrumentality for use in the development of [its] business, and only incidentally or collaterally for the use of those to whom [Top Brass] might exhibit it thereafter" (*Ultramares Corp. v. Touche*, 255 N.Y., at 183, 174 N.E. 441; *cf.*, *Glanzer v. Shepard*, 233 N.Y. 236, 135 N.E. 275).

Security Pacific, 597 N.E.2d at 1085–87.

Does *Security Pacific* suggest that an unsolicited telephone call can *never* be sufficient linking conduct between a plaintiff third party and a defendant accountant? What if, for example, the telephone call had taken place before Main had committed to the engagement? (In the actual case, Main's engagement letter was dated August 20, 1984; its audit field work was conducted from August 20 to September 12–13, 1984; it sent a draft audit report to Top Brass (and Top Brass forwarded the draft to SPBC) on September 13, 1984; and it issued its final audit report to Top Brass on September 26, 1984. The telephone call allegedly took place after September 13 but before September 17, 1984.)

(5) Why are negligent misrepresentation lawsuits against accountants typically brought by third parties and not by the accountant's client? At least part of the explanation is that the client is often the initial wrongdoer. The client usually prepares the financial statements that the accountant is auditing, and the client may intentionally misrepresent the financial position of the company. While the accountant may fail to discover the misrepresentation, the misrepresentation itself originated with the client. *Cf. Bily v. Arthur Young & Co.*, 834 P.2d 745, 762 (Cal. 1992) ("An auditor is a watchdog, not a bloodhound. As a matter of commercial reality, audits are performed in a client-controlled environment. The client typically prepares its

own financial statements; it has direct control over and assumes primary responsibility for their contents. The client engages the auditor, pays for the audit, and communicates with audit personnel throughout the engagement. Because the auditor cannot in the time available become an expert in the client's business and record-keeping systems, the client necessarily furnishes the information base for the audit."). In short, the client typically does not sue over a problem that it knowingly created. Moreover, the accountant's negligence may benefit the client by making the client's financial position look better. As a result, the client may not directly suffer damages in the same way that a third party might when lending or investing in reliance on an audit report. Finally, in some jurisdictions, a client's negligent misrepresentation claim against its accountant would be barred by the economic loss rule. *See* Chapter 6; *see also* RESTATEMENT (THIRD) OF TORTS: LIABILITY FOR ECONOMIC HARM § 5(5) (Tentative Draft No. 1, Apr. 4, 2012) ("This Section does not recognize liability for negligent misrepresentation made in the course of negotiating or performing a contract between the parties."); *id.* § 6(4) (substantially the same).

On a related note, given that the client is often the initial wrongdoer, why isn't the client the primary target in the third party's lawsuit? As one court explained: "The client, its promoters, and its managers have generally left the scene, headed in most cases for government-supervised liquidation or the bankruptcy court. The auditor has now assumed center stage as the remaining solvent defendant and is [often] faced with a claim for all sums of money ever loaned to or invested in the client." *Bily*, 834 P.2d at 763.

(6) Regardless of how a court resolves the scope of liability issue, a successful negligent misrepresentation claim requires proof of negligence. An accountant's failure to detect an irregularity in its client's financial information does not necessarily mean that the accountant was negligent. After all, for practical reasons of time and cost, an accountant in a typical audit reviews only a sample of the client's financial and other business transactions. Failing to examine all of the client's transactions, in other words, is not unreasonable. Moreover, a client's fraud in the preparation of financial statements may be sophisticated and very difficult to discover, even for an accountant who is conducting an audit with reasonable care.

CITIZENS STATE BANK V. TIMM, SCHMIDT & CO.
335 N.W.2d 361 (Wis. 1983)

DAY, JUSTICE.

This is a review of an unpublished decision of the court of appeals which affirmed a judgment and order of the Circuit Court for Portage County, Honorable Fred A. Fink, Judge. The judgment granted the respondents', Timm, Schmidt & Company and General Casualty Company, (hereinafter Timm) motion for summary judgment dismissing

Citizens State Bank (hereinafter Citizens) negligence cause of action in this accountant malpractice case. . . .

The issue considered on review is: May an accountant be held liable for the negligent preparation of an audit report to a third party not in privity who relies on the report?

We conclude that an accountant may be held liable to a third party not in privity for the negligent preparation of an audit report under the principles of Wisconsin negligence law. We also conclude that the information in the record raises a material issue of fact so that the summary judgment motion was improperly granted. We reverse the decision of the court of appeals and remand the case to the trial court for a trial on the negligence cause of action.

From the record, the following facts appear to be undisputed.

Timm is an accounting firm in Stevens Point. For the years 1973–1976, Timm employees prepared financial statements for Clintonville Fire Apparatus, Inc. (hereinafter CFA). These financial statements included: a comparative statement of financial condition, a statement of yearly income, a statement of retained income and a statement of changes in financial position. In addition, for each year except 1973, Timm sent an opinion letter to CFA which stated [that] the financial statements fairly presented the financial condition of CFA and that the statements were prepared in accordance with generally accepted accounting principles.

In November, 1975, CFA obtained a $300,000 loan from Citizens. The loan was guaranteed by the Small Business Administration, a federal agency (hereinafter SBA). Citizens made the loan to CFA after reviewing the financial statements which Timm had prepared. Additional loans, apparently not SBA guaranteed, were made by Citizens to CFA in 1976. By the end of 1976, CFA had a total outstanding indebtedness to Citizens of approximately $380,000.

In early 1977, during the course of preparing CFA's financial statement for 1976, Timm employees discovered that the 1974 and 1975 financial statements contained a number of material errors totalling over $400,000 once all period adjustments were made.

Once these errors were corrected and Citizens, as a creditor of CFA, was informed by Timm of the errors, Citizens called all of its loans due. As a result, CFA went into receivership and was ultimately liquidated and dissolved. As of the date the complaint was filed, the amount outstanding on Citizens' loans to CFA was $152,214.44.

Citizens filed an action against Timm and its malpractice insurance company on September 14, 1979, seeking to recover $152,214.44, the amount due on its loans to CFA.

Timm answered in October, 1979. On March 25, 1980, Timm filed a motion for summary judgment on the grounds that the pleadings and affidavits it submitted with its motion raised no issue of material fact and showed Timm was entitled to judgment as a matter of law. The affidavits submitted with the motion came from every member of the Timm firm who had worked on the CFA account. Each affidavit stated that the affiant had no knowledge, until after the fact, that CFA intended to or had obtained any loans from Citizens. The affidavit of Elmer Timm, president of the firm, also stated that he was never informed by any person that any audit report prepared by his firm for CFA would be used by any lender for the purpose of determining whether or not to make a loan to CFA.

Citizens submitted a number of affidavits in opposition to the motion for summary judgment. The affidavit of Den E. Hood, a certified public accountant, stated that he had examined the audit procedures used by Timm employees in preparing the 1974 and 1975 financial reports. Hood concluded after examining the procedures that the audit examinations had not been conducted in accordance with generally accepted auditing standards. He also concluded that had such standards been complied with, the material errors in the 1974 and 1975 statements should have been discovered and corrected prior to the issuance of each statement.

Citizens also submitted affidavits from its president, Gerald Beier, and a transcript of part of a deposition taken from Elmer Timm. Beier's affidavit contains a reference to a letter in Citizens' files from an employee of SBA "which indicated that they were waiting for more financial information from the accountants for CFA before approving and guaranteeing the loan to CFA, which was ultimately made by [Citizens'] in November of 1975." Beier also stated that Citizens' loans to CFA were made in reliance upon financial statements which had been prepared by Timm. The Elmer Timm deposition includes testimony showing that he knew the audited statement his firm prepared for CFA for the year ending in 1974 would be used by CFA to receive a guarantee on a loan through SBA. In the deposition however, there is a statement suggesting that he misspoke and actually intended to refer to the statement his firm had prepared for the year ending December 31, 1973, instead of 1974.

Citizens also filed two affidavits from John Dando, CFA's president. The first was filed on October 8, 1980 and was considered by the trial judge in his original decision. That affidavit recited that Dando believed Timm was aware that statements its employees prepared would be submitted to SBA and that audited statements were a requirement of SBA loans.

Dando's second affidavit was not filed until October 28, 1980. . . .

In that affidavit, Dando stated that Timm was "told that as soon as the third quarter [1975] statement was finished, it would be personally picked up at [Timm's] office and taken directly to Citizens State Bank in order to expedite the loan application."

. . . .

The question on review is whether accountants may be held liable for the negligent preparation of an audit report to a third party not in privity who relies on the report.

This is a question of first impression in this state. However, the issue has received wide consideration in both courts and law journals.

Accountants have long been held not liable for their negligence to relying third parties not in privity under an application of Judge Cardozo's decision in *Ultramares v. Touche,* 255 N.Y. 170, 174 N.E. 441 (1931). . . .

. . . .

In this state, although the liability of accountants to third parties not in privity has not been examined, the liability of an attorney to one not in privity was recently examined in *Auric v. Continental Casualty Co.,* 111 Wis.2d 507, 331 N.W.2d 325 (1983). This court concluded that an attorney may be held liable to a will beneficiary not in privity for the attorney's negligence in supervising the execution of a will. Part of the rationale for this decision was that the imposition of liability would make attorneys more careful in the execution of their responsibilities to their clients.

That rationale is applicable here. Unless liability is imposed, third parties who rely upon the accuracy of the financial statements will not be protected. Unless an accountant can be held liable to a relying third party, this negligence will go undeterred.

There are additional policy reasons to allow the imposition of liability. If relying third parties, such as creditors, are not allowed to recover, the cost of credit to the general public will increase because creditors will either have to absorb the costs of bad loans made in reliance on faulty information or hire independent accountants to verify the information received. Accountants may spread the risk through the use of liability insurance.

We conclude that the absence of privity alone should not bar negligence actions by relying third parties against accountants.

Although the absence of privity does not bar this action, the question remains as to the extent of an accountant's liability to injured third parties. . . .

. . . .

The fundamental principle of Wisconsin negligence law is that a tortfeasor is fully liable for all foreseeable consequences of his act except as those consequences are limited by policy factors. . . .

We conclude that accountants' liability to third parties should be determined under the accepted principles of Wisconsin negligence law. According to these principles, a finding of non-liability will be made only if there is a strong public policy requiring such a finding. Liability will be imposed on these accountants for the foreseeable injuries resulting from their negligent acts unless, under the facts of this particular case, as a matter of policy to be decided by the court, recovery is denied on grounds of public policy. This Court has set out a number of public policy reasons for not imposing liability despite a finding of negligence causing injury:

> "(1) The injury is too remote from the negligence; or (2) the injury is too wholly out of proportion to the culpability of the negligent tort-feasor; or (3) in retrospect it appears too highly extraordinary that the negligence should have brought about the harm; or (4) because allowance of recovery would place too unreasonable a burden on the negligent tort-feasor; or (5) because allowance of recovery would be too likely to open the way for fraudulent claims; or (6) allowance of recovery would enter a field that has no sensible or just stopping point."

Although in some cases this court has decided at the motion-to-dismiss stage that policy factors preclude the imposition of liability for negligent acts, it has generally been found to be better practice to have a full factual resolution before evaluating the public policy considerations involved.

In this case we conclude that a determination of the public policy questions should be made after the facts of this case have been fully explored at trial. The question of the proper scope of these accountants' liabilities to the third party bank cannot be determined upon the information contained in the record. A full factual resolution is necessary before it can be said that public policy precludes Timm's liability for its allegedly negligent conduct.

The pleadings, affidavits and other information in the record before this court do not establish that Timm was entitled as a matter of law to summary judgment. Under the accepted principles of Wisconsin negligence law, Timm could be liable to Citizens if Timm's actions were the cause of Citizens' injuries and if the injuries were reasonably foreseeable unless public policy precluded recovery.

Timm's affidavits do not dispute that Citizen's reliance upon the financial statements led to the making of the loans and ultimately to the losses which were incurred. Each affidavit recites that Timm employees had no knowledge that the financial statements would actually be used by

CFA to apply for a new bank loan or to increase existing loan indebtedness. However, the affidavit of Elmer Timm stated that "as a certified public accountant, I know that audited statements are used for many purposes and that it is common for them to be supplied to lenders and creditors, and other persons."

These affidavits and other information contained in the record do not dispose of the issue of whether it was foreseeable that a negligently prepared financial statement could cause harm to Citizens.

Therefore, Timm having failed to establish a *prima facie* case for summary judgment, we conclude the trial judge erred in granting the motion for summary judgment.

Decision of the court of appeals is reversed and cause remanded to the trial court for further proceedings not inconsistent with this opinion.

NOTES & QUESTIONS

(1) The *Citizens* court concludes that "[u]nder the accepted principles of Wisconsin negligence law, Timm could be liable to Citizens if Timm's actions were the cause of Citizens' injuries and if the injuries were reasonably foreseeable unless public policy precluded recovery." This "foreseeability" approach is very much a minority position, as only a few courts have adopted it. *See, e.g., Touche Ross & Co. v. Commercial Union Ins. Co.*, 514 So. 2d 315, 322 (Miss. 1987); *H. Rosenblum, Inc. v. Adler*, 461 A.2d 138, 153 (N.J. 1983). It should be noted that the *Rosenblum* decision has been effectively overruled by statute. *See* N.J. STAT. 2A:53A–25 (adopting an approach similar to *Credit Alliance*, but limited to negligent misrepresentation claims against accountants).

(2) What policy arguments does the *Citizens* court make in support of its foreseeability approach? Do you agree with them? In thinking about these questions, consider the following:

> In contrast to the "presumptively powerless consumer" in product liability cases, the third party in an audit negligence case has other options—he or she can "privately order" the risk of inaccurate financial reporting by contractual arrangements with the client. For example, a third party might expend its own resources to verify the client's financial statements or selected portions of them that were particularly material to its transaction with the client. Or it might commission its own audit or investigation, thus establishing privity between itself and an auditor or investigator to whom it could look for protection. . . .

> As a matter of economic and social policy, third parties should be encouraged to rely on their own prudence, diligence, and contracting power, as well as other informational tools. This kind of self-reliance promotes sound investment and credit practices and

discourages the careless use of monetary resources. If, instead, third parties are simply permitted to recover from the auditor for mistakes in the client's financial statements, the auditor becomes, in effect, an insurer of not only the financial statements, but of bad loans and investments in general.

. . . Courts and commentators advocating auditor negligence liability to third parties also predict that such liability might deter auditor mistakes, promote more careful audits, and result in a more efficient spreading of the risk of inaccurate financial statements. . . .

We are not directed to any empirical data supporting these prognostications. From our review of the cases and commentary, we doubt that a significant and desirable improvement in audit care would result from an expanded rule of liability. Indeed, deleterious economic effects appear at least as likely to occur.

In view of the inherent dependence of the auditor on the client and the labor-intensive nature of auditing, we doubt whether audits can be done in ways that would yield significantly greater accuracy without disadvantages. Auditors may rationally respond to increased liability by simply reducing audit services in fledgling industries where the business failure rate is high, reasoning that they will inevitably be singled out and sued when their client goes into bankruptcy regardless of the care or detail of their audits. . . . Consistent with this reasoning, the economic result of unlimited negligence liability could just as easily be an increase in the cost and decrease in the availability of audits and audit reports with no compensating improvement in overall audit quality.

In light of the relationships between auditor, client, and third party, and the relative sophistication of third parties who lend and invest based on audit reports, it might also be doubted whether auditors are the most efficient absorbers of the losses from inaccuracies in financial information. Investors and creditors can limit the impact of losses by diversifying investments and loan portfolios. They effectively constitute a "broad social base upon which the costs of accounting errors can be spread." In the audit liability context, no reason appears to favor the alleged tortfeasor over the alleged victim as an effective distributor of loss.

Bily v. Arthur Young & Co., 834 P.2d 745, 765–66 (Cal. 1992).

(3) How does the *Citizens* foreseeability approach compare to the *Credit Alliance* framework? Suppose that the Timm affidavits were the only evidence before the court. Would Citizens have been permitted to sue Timm under the foreseeability approach (ignoring the public policy factors)? What about under *Credit Alliance*? Now consider the evidence provided by Citizens as well. Do your answers change?

(4) As a result of the "public policy reasons for not imposing liability," the *Citizens* foreseeability approach and the *Credit Alliance* framework may, in practice, produce similar outcomes. That is, while a foreseeability approach surely risks "liability in an indeterminate amount for an indeterminate time to an indeterminate class" (particularly when dealing with audit reports for public companies that may be relied upon by a vast number of lenders and investors), a court can always extinguish liability to foreseeable (but not "known") third parties by invoking the public policy factors. For example, liability could be extinguished on the grounds that "allowance of recovery would enter a field that has no sensible or just stopping point," "because allowance of recovery would place too unreasonable a burden on the negligent tort-feasor," or because "the injury is too wholly out of proportion to the culpability of the negligent tort-feasor." Thus, while *Citizens* is frequently cited as an example of a broad foreseeability approach—one that purportedly differs in material respects from more restrictive approaches to third-party liability—the actual scope of liability imposed by such an approach will depend on how frequently courts invoke the public policy factors to limit exposure.

ELLIS V. GRANT THORNTON LLP
530 F.3d 280 (4th Cir. 2008)

HAMILTON, SENIOR CIRCUIT JUDGE:

The principal issue presented in this appeal is whether Grant Thornton LLP (Grant Thornton), an accounting firm retained by First National Bank of Keystone (Keystone), in response to an investigation by the Office of the Comptroller of the Currency (OCC) into Keystone's banking activities, owed a duty of care under the West Virginia law of negligent misrepresentation to Gary Ellis, who allegedly relied on oral statements made by Stan Quay (Quay), a Grant Thornton partner, and a Grant Thornton audit report of Keystone's 1998 financial statements in deciding to accept the job as president of Keystone. We hold that Grant Thornton owed Ellis no such duty under West Virginia law. Accordingly, we reverse the judgment of the district court, which found in favor of Ellis on his negligent misrepresentation claim against Grant Thornton.

I

In late June 1999, the OCC began to intensify its ongoing investigation into Keystone's banking activities. The OCC's investigation revealed that Keystone's books overstated the value of the loans Keystone owned by over $515 million. Based on these overstatements, Keystone was declared insolvent and was closed on September 1, 1999. . . . This case concerns Ellis, who took the job as president of Keystone in April 1999. According to Ellis, he took the position only because he relied on negligent misrepresentations made by Quay and made by Grant Thornton in the audit report.

A

Prior to 1992, Keystone was a small community bank providing banking services to clients located primarily in McDowell County, West Virginia. Before its collapse, Keystone was a national banking association within the Federal Reserve System, the deposits of which were insured by the FDIC.

In 1992, Keystone began to engage in an investment strategy that involved the securitization of high risk mortgage loans. Between 1992 and 1998, Keystone originated nineteen securitizations. In general, Keystone would acquire Federal Housing Authority or high loan to value real estate mortgage loans from around the United States, pool a group of these loans, and sell interests in the pool through underwriters to investors. The pooled loans were serviced by third-party loan servicers, including companies like Advanta and Compu-Link. Keystone retained residual interests (residuals) in each loan securitization. The residuals were subordinated securities that would receive payments only after all expenses were paid and all investors in each securitization pool were paid. Thus, Keystone stood to profit from a securitization only after everyone else was paid in full. The residuals were assigned a value that was carried on the books of Keystone as an asset. Over time, the residual valuations came to represent a significant portion of Keystone's book value.

From 1993 until 1998, when the last loan securitization was completed, the size and frequency of these transactions expanded from about $33 million to approximately $565 million for the last one in September 1998. All told, Keystone acquired and securitized over 120,000 loans with a total value in excess of $2.6 billion.

The loan securitization business appeared to be quite profitable. On paper, Keystone's assets grew from $107 million in 1992 to over $1.1 billion in 1999. In reality, however, the securitization program proved highly unprofitable. Due to the risky nature of many of the underlying mortgage loans, the failure rate was excessive. As a result, the residual interests retained by Keystone proved highly speculative and, in actuality, they did not perform well.

Keystone's valuation of the residuals was greater than their market value. J. Knox McConnell, Keystone's largest shareholder until his death, Terry Church (Church), another Keystone director, and others concealed the failure of the securitizations by falsifying Keystone's books. Bogus entries and documents hid the true financial condition of Keystone from the bank's directors, shareholders, depositors, and federal regulators.

Keystone's irregular bank records drew the attention of the OCC, which began an investigation into Keystone's banking activities. This investigation revealed major errors in Keystone's accounting records that financially jeopardized Keystone. In May 1998, the OCC required Keystone to enter into an agreement obligating Keystone to take specific steps to improve its regulatory posture and financial condition. This agreement required Keystone to, among other things, retain a nationally recognized independent accounting firm "to perform an audit of the Bank's mortgage banking operations and determine the appropriateness of the Bank's accounting for purchased loans and all securitizations." In August 1998, Keystone retained Grant Thornton as its outside auditor.

Under the agreement between Grant Thornton and Keystone, Grant Thornton was to, among other things, perform for Keystone, in accordance with Generally Accepted Auditing Standards (GAAS), an audit of Keystone's consolidated financial statements as of December 31, 1998. Quay was the lead Grant Thornton partner on the Keystone audit. Susan Buenger (Buenger), a junior manager, performed substantial work on the audit as well.

Grant Thornton performed the audit on Keystone's 1998 financial statements. Keystone's 1998 financial statements reflected ownership of more than $515 million in loans that it did not own. Due to negligence on the part of both Quay and Buenger, Grant Thornton's audit did not uncover the $515 million discrepancy.[1] In fact, on March 24, 1999, Quay presented several members and prospective members of Keystone's board and Keystone's shareholders with draft copies of Keystone's 1998 financial statements and told them that Keystone was going to get an unqualified or "clean" audit opinion on its 1998 financial statements. At the shareholders meeting the next day, Quay also distributed copies of Keystone's financial statements. At that time, Quay reiterated that Keystone was going to get a clean audit opinion on its 1998 financial statements.

On April 19, 1999, even though Keystone was, in fact, insolvent as of the end of 1998, Grant Thornton issued and delivered to Keystone's board its audit opinion stating that Keystone's financial statements were fairly stated in accordance with the GAAP and reflecting a shareholder's equity of $184 million. The intent of the report was plainly stated on the first page of the report: "This report is intended for the information and use of the Board of Directors and Management of The First National Bank of Keystone and its regulatory agencies and should not be used by third parties for any other purpose."

---

[1] Grant Thornton does not challenge the district court's finding of negligence in this appeal, electing to assume, for the sake of argument, that Quay and Buenger were negligent in preparing the audit and making any statements concerning the soundness of Keystone's financial condition. Given Grant Thornton's position, we, too, will assume, without deciding, that Quay and Buenger were negligent in preparing the audit and making any statements concerning the soundness of Keystone's financial condition.

The audited financial statements provided by Quay to the board on April 19, 1999 were substantially the same as the financial statements Quay had provided board members and shareholders in March 1999. Based on Grant Thornton's audit report, Keystone's board continued to declare dividends and operate the bank.

B

In 1984, Gary Ellis was President of the Bank of Dunbar. The Bank of Dunbar was later merged into United National Bank (United) at which time Ellis joined the management team at United, eventually becoming its president. From the time of the merger with the Bank of Dunbar until the time Ellis left United, United more than doubled in size. In 1998, United merged with George Mason Bankshares of Virginia. In the spring of 1999, following the merger, Ellis voluntarily began looking for employment outside United. Ellis had dealt with Keystone in the past, and, on March 19, 1999, Billie Cherry (Cherry), chairman of Keystone's board, called Ellis and invited Ellis to attend Keystone's annual shareholders meeting on March 25, 1999. During the call, Cherry suggested that Ellis should consider becoming president of Keystone.

Ellis was not fired or told to leave United, had no deadline for leaving United, and could have remained at United rather than leaving for the Keystone position. Ellis attended Keystone's board meeting on March 24, 1999, at which the board granted Ellis' request to review, upon the signing of a confidentiality agreement, the financial condition of the bank. Although it is not clear from the record whether a confidentiality agreement was signed, the Keystone board permitted Ellis to discuss the financial condition of the bank with Quay and other Keystone insiders with the understanding that the information be kept confidential. Consequently, following the Keystone board meeting on March 24, 1999, Ellis met Quay and two other outside directors at a bar at the Fincastle Country Club. Quay spoke with Ellis and the two outside directors because Keystone did not have a chief financial officer, thus making Quay the only person capable of going over the financial statements with the others. At the country club, Quay told Ellis and the two outside directors that Keystone was going to receive a "clean [audit] opinion." Ellis also attended the March 25, 1999 shareholders' meeting at which Quay informed the group that Grant Thornton was going to give Keystone a clean audit opinion for 1998. On March 30, 1999, Ellis visited Keystone. During this visit, Quay told Ellis once again that Keystone would receive a clean audit opinion for 1998.

On April 2, 1999, Ellis met with his attorneys to draft a proposed employment agreement with Keystone. During the first two weeks of April 1999, Ellis met with Church and others regarding their expectations for him. It was decided that Ellis would be responsible for the "banking" business at Keystone as opposed to the mortgage loan securitizations. On April 19, 1999, at a Keystone board meeting, Ellis reviewed Grant Thornton's final audit report on Keystone for 1998. The board voted to approve Ellis' hiring as president of Keystone. Ellis officially resigned from United by letter dated April 20, 1999. Ellis' employment contract was signed on April 26, 1999. According to Ellis, he relied on Grant Thornton's audit, which was consistent with Quay's earlier March 1999 statements that Grant Thornton was going to issue a clean audit opinion for 1998, in deciding to accept the job as president of Keystone.

C

After being named as a defendant in the *Gariety v. Grant Thornton, LLP* securities class action, Ellis filed a cross-claim against Grant Thornton for negligent misrepresentation under West Virginia law in which he sought to recover damages in the form of lost earnings. The district court . . . ruled in favor of Ellis on his negligent misrepresentation claim and found that he was entitled to $2,419,233 in damages. The district court found that, in accepting the job as president of Keystone, "Ellis relied on the financial statements Quay gave him," "Quay's oral representations," and the Grant Thornton audit report. The district court also found that "Quay intended and knew that Ellis would rely on his statements." In view of these findings of fact, the district court concluded that Grant Thornton, as the auditor of Keystone, was liable to Ellis under the West Virginia law of negligent misrepresentation, citing *First National Bank of Bluefield v. Crawford*, 182 W.Va. 107, 386 S.E.2d 310 (1989), because Grant Thornton (through Quay's oral statements and the audit report) made negligent misrepresentations concerning the financial condition of Keystone knowing that Ellis would receive and rely upon those representations in making his decision to accept or reject employment with Keystone. . . .

II

. . . .

As a federal court sitting in diversity, we have an obligation to apply the jurisprudence of West Virginia's highest court, the Supreme Court of Appeals of West Virginia. *Wells v. Liddy*, 186 F.3d 505, 527–28 (4th Cir.1999). In a situation where the state's highest court has spoken neither directly nor indirectly on the particular issue before us, we are called upon to predict how that court would rule if presented with the issue. In this case, we are called upon to predict whether, under the facts of this case, Grant Thornton owed Ellis a duty of care under the West Virginia law of misrepresentation.

In *Bank of Bluefield*, the Supreme Court of Appeals of West Virginia addressed the question of whether the lack of privity of contract between an accountant and a bank was a complete defense to the bank's suit against the accountant for professional negligence in preparing a financial statement. The court answered that question in the negative. . . .

In resolving the issue before it, the court in *Bank of Bluefield* discussed the four approaches to resolving the question of under what circumstances an accountant can be liable to third parties for a negligent misrepresentation. The first of these approaches was announced in *Ultramares Corp. v. Touche*, 174 N.E. 441 (1931), which held that negligence actions were only permitted by parties in privity of contract or in a situation so close as to approach that of privity. The second approach was also developed by the New York Court of Appeals, which slightly modified the *Ultramares Corp.* approach in 1985. *See Credit Alliance Corp. v. Arthur Andersen & Co.*, 483 N.E.2d 110 (1985) (relaxing the strict *Ultramares Corp.* privity doctrine by requiring a relationship "sufficiently approaching privity").[4] The third approach is set forth in § 552 of the Restatement (Second) of Torts. Under this approach, a person or a limited class of persons who the auditor can foresee as parties who will (and do) rely upon financial statements are allowed to recover. Restatement (Second) of Torts § 552(1)–(2). The fourth approach is the reasonably foreseeable approach, which permits all parties who are reasonably foreseeable recipients of financial statements for business purposes to recover as long as they rely on the statements for those business purposes.[5]

After summarizing these four approaches, the court in *Bank of Bluefield* adopted the Restatement § 552 approach for West Virginia, finding that the rule stated therein was "more appropriate because it imposes a standard of care only to known users who will actually be relying on the information provided by the accountant." 386 S.E.2d at 313; *see also id.* at 310 Syllabus of the Court ("In the absence of privity of contract, an accountant is liable for the negligent preparation of a financial report only to those he knows will be receiving and relying on

---

[4] . . . . The *Credit Alliance Corp.* approach is often referred to as the "near-privity" approach.

[5] Although it is sometimes difficult to discern the differences between the four approaches, appropriate lines can be drawn between the restrictive *Ultramares Corp.*, *Credit Alliance Corp.*, and Restatement approaches and the nonrestrictive foreseeability approach. For example, although the Restatement's approach expands liability to a larger potential class of third parties than do the *Ultramares Corp.* and *Credit Alliance Corp.* approaches, it does not extend liability beyond an identified third party, a known third party, or third parties who enter into the same type of transaction as originally contemplated. In other words, under the *Ultramares Corp.* and *Credit Alliance Corp.* approaches, "the precise identity of the informational consumer [must] be foreseen by the auditor," [*First Nat'l Bank of Commerce v. Monco Agency, Inc.*, 911 F.2d 1053, 1059 (5th Cir. 1990)], but, under the Restatement approach, the precise "informational consumer" need not be known, *id.*; rather the Restatement approach "contemplates identification of a narrow group, not necessarily the specific membership within that group." *Id.* Moreover, unlike the foreseeability approach, the Restatement approach does not extend to "every reasonably foreseeable consumer of financial information." *Id.* at 1060.

the report."). In view of the court's adoption of the Restatement approach in *Bank of Bluefield,* the court answered the certified question—was privity a defense—in the negative. Consequently, other than the adoption of the Restatement approach, the *Bank of Bluefield* court gave no further meaningful guidance concerning under what circumstances an accountant can be liable to third parties for negligent misrepresentations under § 552.

Restatement (Second) of Torts § 552 provides in relevant part:

(1) One who, in the course of his business, profession or employment, or in any other transaction in which he has a pecuniary interest, supplies false information for the guidance of others in their business transactions, is subject to liability for pecuniary loss caused to them by their justifiable reliance upon the information, if he fails to exercise reasonable care or competence in obtaining or communicating the information.

[T]he liability stated in Subsection (1) is limited to loss suffered

(a) by the person or one of a limited group of persons for whose benefit and guidance he intends to supply the information or knows that the recipient intends to supply it; and

(b) through reliance upon it in a transaction that he intends the information to influence or knows that the recipient so intends or in a substantially similar transaction.

Restatement (Second) of Torts § 552(1)–(2). The Restatement approach is deliberately restrictive to encourage the free flow of commercial information. *See id.* § 552, cmt. ("By limiting the liability for negligence of a supplier of information to be used in commercial transactions to cases in which he manifests an intent to supply the information for the sort of use in which the plaintiff's loss occurs, the law promotes the important social policy of encouraging the flow of commercial information upon which the operation of the economy rests."). It also seeks to protect suppliers of commercial information from liability in instances in which they oblige themselves to provide information but the terms of the obligation are unknown to them. *See id.* ("A user of commercial information cannot reasonably expect its maker to have undertaken to satisfy this obligation unless the terms of the obligation were known to him.").

Although the West Virginia Supreme Court of Appeals in *Bank of Bluefield* did not set forth what must be proven by an injured third party proceeding under § 552 against an accountant for the accountant's negligent misrepresentations, other courts have set forth six elements that essentially track the language of the Restatement. *See, e.g., N. Am. Specialty Ins. Co. v. Lapalme,* 258 F.3d 35, 41–42 (1st Cir.2001) (setting forth six elements). Under this authority, a finding of liability requires the injured party to prove (1) inaccurate information, (2) negligently supplied, (3) in the course of an accountant's professional endeavors, (4) to a third person or limited group of third persons for whose benefit and guidance the accountant actually intends or knows will receive the information, (5) for a transaction (or for a substantially similar transaction) that the accountant actually intends to influence or knows that the recipient so intends, (6) with the result that the third party justifiably relies on such misinformation to his detriment. The third party has the burden of proving each of these elements. Moreover, the accountant's "actual knowledge . . . should be ascertained at the time the audit report or financial statement is issued." *Id.* at 39, 42.

In this case, the record simply is devoid of evidence suggesting that Ellis proved the fourth, fifth, and sixth elements. With regard to the fourth element, it is clear that Ellis failed to show that Grant Thornton knew (or intended) that potential employees, like Ellis, were intended to receive the audit report for their benefit and guidance. The audit report was delivered to the board of directors of Keystone. The audit report plainly states that the audit report was *not* intended for use by third parties. Rather, the audit report was prepared for the benefit of Keystone and the OCC, which is entirely consistent with the agreements between Keystone and the OCC and between Keystone and Grant Thornton. Thus, Ellis, or any other potential employee, was not a member of any limited group of persons for whose benefit the audit report was prepared.

Perhaps recognizing the tenuousness of relying on the audit report itself, especially since he signed his employment contract a week after the audit report was issued to the board, Ellis relies heavily on Quay's statements in March 1999 indicating that Grant Thornton was going to give Keystone a clean audit opinion. Of course, reliance on Quay's statements improves the position of Ellis, as Quay's statements did not include a disclaimer. However, the Restatement approach instructs that we should assess cases in light of "[t]he ordinary practices and attitudes of the business world." Restatement (Second) of Torts § 552, cmt. j. Viewed in this light, it is clear that Grant Thornton was Keystone's auditor and was hired to conduct an audit for the benefit of Keystone and the OCC. Grant Thornton was not hired to go over with each potential employee the soundness of Keystone's financial condition. Indeed, throughout most of the course of the audit report's preparation, Ellis was an unknown, unidentified potential employee of Keystone. Grant Thornton was not aware of the existence of the potential employment transaction between Ellis and Keystone until *after* Grant Thornton reached its decision to give Keystone a clean audit opinion. If the scope of the audit involved potential employees, one would expect at least some knowledge on the part of Grant Thornton *before* they formed their audit opinion.

Moreover, Quay first informed the board of directors on March 24, 1999 that Grant Thornton was going to give Keystone a clean audit opinion. Thus, the clean audit opinion information was disclosed for the benefit of Keystone's board and not potential employees such as Ellis. Ellis' attempt at turning Quay's clean audit opinion statements into ones for his benefit, by virtue of his meetings with Quay, ignores the business reality that Grant Thornton was hired and performed the audit for the benefit of Keystone and the OCC. It also ignores the fact that any release of information to Ellis was done at the behest of Keystone, not Grant Thornton. There is no evidence in the record to support the conclusion that Ellis was a member of any limited group of persons for whose benefit Quay's statements were made.

Our conclusion concerning the fourth element is buttressed by Illustration 10 in § 552. That illustration provides:

> A, an independent public accountant, is retained by B Company to conduct an annual audit of the customary scope for the corporation and to furnish his opinion on the corporation's financial statements. A is not informed of any intended use of the financial statements; but A knows that the financial statements, accompanied by an auditor's opinion, are customarily used in a wide variety of financial transactions by the corporation and that they may be relied upon by lenders, investors, shareholders, creditors, purchasers and the like, in numerous possible kinds of transactions. In fact B Company uses the financial statements and accompanying auditor's opinion to obtain a loan from X Bank. Because of A's negligence, he issues an unqualifiedly favorable opinion upon a balance sheet that materially misstates the financial position of B Company, and through reliance upon it X Bank suffers pecuniary loss. A is not liable to X bank.

Id. § 552, cmt. h, illus. 10. Illustration 10, we believe, is materially indistinguishable from our case. Like the accountant in the illustration, Grant Thornton was not aware of an intended use of its audit opinion beyond the customary business planning use of an audit opinion by a corporation such as Keystone and the use by the OCC for oversight, as it was hired "to conduct an annual audit of the customary scope for [Keystone] and to furnish [its] opinion on [Keystone's] financial statements." *Id.* Indeed, Grant Thornton was not aware that any potential employee of Keystone was going to base their decision to seek employment with Keystone on the outcome of the audit. Rather, in performing its audit function, Grant Thornton was aware that its audit opinion and any statements made leading up to the issuance of the audit opinion *may* be relied upon by shareholders, investors, and perhaps potential employees such as Ellis. However, more than a tenuous awareness of this sort is required to impose liability on Grant Thornton. To hold otherwise would transform the Restatement approach into the foreseeability approach, which the court in *Bank of Bluefield* clearly rejected. Ellis was required to show that Grant Thornton knew that its audit opinion would be used by Keystone to assist potential employees in making their decision concerning whether to come to work for Keystone. The record simply does not demonstrate that Ellis made such a showing.

With regard to the fifth element's substantiality requirement, we examine two questions. First, we examine, from the accountant's standpoint, what risks he reasonably perceived he was undertaking when he delivered the challenged report or financial statement. If the accountant is unaware of a potential risk, then liability cannot attach. Next, we make an objective comparison between the transaction to which the accountant had actual knowledge and the transaction that in fact occurred. This comparison cannot be hypertechnical, but, rather, must be conducted in light of customary business world practices and attitudes. Restatement (Second) of Torts § 552, cmt. j. "The goal of this inquiry is to determine whether the two transactions share essentially the same character. If so, the actual transaction is substantially similar to the contemplated transaction (and, therefore, liability-inducing)." *Lapalme*, 258 F.3d at 41.

When Grant Thornton issued its audit report, it was not assuming the risk that third parties would rely on the report. As noted above, the report itself states that it is not to be used by third parties. To the extent that Ellis relied on Quay's statements, it cannot be said that Grant Thornton was assuming the risk of being liable for Ellis' future lost earnings. The audit opinion was formed by the time Quay met with Ellis, and Quay was simply repeating information that was earlier disclosed to the Keystone board in his presence.

With regard to the objective comparison, the liability of the maker of a negligent misrepresentation extends "to all transactions of the type or kind that the maker intends or has reason to expect." Restatement (Second) of Torts § 552, cmt. j. For example, "independent public accountants who negligently make an audit of books of a corporation, which they are told is to be used only for the purpose of obtaining a particular line of banking credit, are not subject to liability to a wholesale merchant whom the corporation induces to supply it with goods on credit by showing him the financial statements and the accountant's opinion." *Id.* Moreover, an accountant who negligently conducts an audit for A corporation knowing that A corporation is going to show the audit to B corporation as a basis for the extension of credit from B corporation is not liable to B corporation if B corporation buys a controlling interest in A corporation in reliance upon the audit. *Id.* § 552, cmt. j, illus. 14. Thus, when the character of the transaction materially changes, there is no liability. *See Lapalme*, 258 F.3d at 44 ("Even if the change involves a new transaction, rather than merely a modification of the earlier (known) transaction, the accounting firm might still be held liable if the identity of the third party is unchanged, the type of transaction pretty much the same, and the firm's exposure relatively constant.").

Here, Grant Thornton was hired to conduct an audit of Keystone. It was aware at the time it was hired and during the auditing process that the audit was being done for the benefit of Keystone and the OCC. It was not aware during this process that its audit was being performed for the benefit of potential employees of Keystone. Indeed, there simply is no evidence in the record that Grant Thornton cared one way or the other who Keystone hired or whether Ellis became president of Keystone. In fact, Ellis was not even on the radar screen until *after* Grant Thornton concluded that it was going to issue Keystone a clean audit opinion. Moreover, any release of information to Ellis was done at the behest of Keystone, not Grant Thornton. This fact further suggests that Grant Thornton never intended to deviate from its standard auditing functions. In short, to find the fifth element satisfied, we would have to materially change the transaction from an audit undertaken to benefit Keystone and the OCC to one intended to benefit potential employees of Keystone. Such a material change to the nature of the transaction is prohibited under the Restatement approach.

Ellis fares no better on the sixth element. Unquestionably, given that the audit report stated that it was not intended for use by third parties, Ellis could not justifiably rely on the audit report in signing his employment contract with Keystone. With regard to Quay's oral assurances, likewise, Ellis could not justifiably rely on those statements. First, Ellis was aware at the time he signed his employment contract that the audit report was not to be used by third parties. A person as sophisticated and experienced in the banking business as Ellis is, he knew he could not justifiably rely on Quay's statements when the report itself stated otherwise. Moreover, as previously noted, Quay's statements concerning the clean audit opinion were offered by Quay to the board and the shareholders to apprise the board and the OCC of Keystone's financial condition. They were not offered to induce individuals to accept employment with Keystone. As such, it is difficult to discern how an individual as sophisticated and experienced as Ellis would justifiably rely on this information in accepting a job at Keystone.

III

For the reasons stated herein, the judgment of the district court is reversed.

NOTES & QUESTIONS

(1) Why did Ellis' claim fail under § 552 of the Second Restatement? How would Ellis have fared under *Credit Alliance*? Under the foreseeability approach? Can you articulate the differences between these three approaches?

(2) How would you describe the purpose of § 552? In other words, what is the section trying to accomplish? *See also* RESTATEMENT (THIRD) OF TORTS: LIABILITY FOR ECONOMIC HARM §§ 5–6 (Tentative Draft No. 1, Apr. 4, 2012) (addressing negligent misrepresentation).

(3) Section 552(2)(a) states that if a defendant "knows that the recipient intends to supply" the defendant's information to a third party, the defendant can be liable to that third party. Similarly, § 552(2)(b) indicates that such liability extends to transactions that the defendant "knows" the recipient intends to influence. *See also* RESTATEMENT (THIRD) OF TORTS: LIABILITY FOR ECONOMIC HARM §§ 5(2), 6(2) (Tentative Draft No. 1, Apr. 4, 2012) (setting forth similar provisions).

(a) According to the *Ellis* court, at what point in time should the defendant's knowledge be measured for purposes of these standards? Given what § 552 is trying to accomplish, does this seem sensible?

(b) Are these standards inquiring into the defendant's "actual knowledge" (i.e., what the defendant knew), the defendant's "constructive knowledge" (i.e., what the defendant should have known), or both? In *First National Bank of Commerce v. Monco Agency Inc.*, 911 F.2d 1053 (5th Cir. 1990), the court rejected an argument that constructive knowledge was sufficient for § 552: "Anything less than actual knowledge, in fact, would extend liability to the bounds of 'reasonable foreseeability,' similar to that in New Jersey. . . . We conclude, therefore, that the Restatement requires *actual* knowledge on the part of accountants of the limited—though unnamed—group of potential lenders that will rely upon the inaccurate 1980 audit, as well as actual knowledge of the particular financial transaction that such information is designed to influence." *Id.* at 1062. Does the *Ellis* court agree with this "actual knowledge" conclusion?

(c) Is a defendant's general knowledge of how its information is customarily used sufficient to meet these standards? *See* RESTATEMENT (SECOND) OF TORTS § 552 cmt. h & illus. 10, 12 (1977).

(d) Do these standards inquire into what a "reasonable person" would have known?

(4) Section 552 is only applicable to a defendant who provides false information "in the course of his business, profession or employment, or in any other transaction in which he has a pecuniary interest." Can you give some examples of transactions in which the defendant has a "pecuniary interest"? *See id.* § 552 cmts. c–d; RESTATEMENT (THIRD) OF TORTS: LIABILITY FOR ECONOMIC HARM § 5 cmt. c (Tentative Draft No. 1, Apr. 4, 2012).

(5) What constitutes a "limited group" of persons under § 552(2)(a)? If an accountant were told that his audit report would be shown to "banks," would that count as a limited group? What if the accountant were told that his report would be shown to "investors"? Would that count? *See* RESTATEMENT (SECOND) OF TORTS § 552 cmt. h & illus. 5–7 (1977); RESTATEMENT (THIRD) OF TORTS: LIABILITY FOR ECONOMIC HARM § 5 cmts. f–g & illus. 6–8, 10–11 (Tentative Draft No. 1, Apr. 4, 2012).

(6) Under § 552(2)(b), a defendant's liability for negligent misrepresentation extends to a transaction that he intends to influence or to a substantially similar transaction. It also extends to a transaction that he knows the recipient intends to influence or to a substantially similar transaction. For examples of substantially similar (and not substantially similar) transactions, see § 552 comment j and illustrations 13–15. *See also* RESTATEMENT (THIRD) OF TORTS: LIABILITY FOR ECONOMIC HARM §§ 5(2)(b), 6(2)(b) (Tentative Draft No. 1, Apr. 4, 2012) (setting forth similar provisions).

(7) The scope of liability for negligence torts is typically narrower than the scope of liability for intentional torts because reduced culpability on the part of the defendant justifies a lesser exposure to liability. *See, e.g.*, RESTATEMENT (SECOND) OF TORTS § 552 cmt. a (1977) ("The liability stated in this Section is likewise more restricted than that for fraudulent misrepresentation stated in § 531. When there is no intent to deceive but only good faith coupled with negligence, the fault of the maker of the misrepresentation is sufficiently less to justify a narrower responsibility for its consequences."). Reexamine § 531 (fraud) and § 552 (negligent misrepresentation) of the Second Restatement. Can you explain how § 552 results in a lesser exposure to liability? *See also* RESTATEMENT (THIRD) OF TORTS: LIABILITY FOR ECONOMIC HARM § 12 (Tentative Draft No. 2, Apr. 7, 2014) (addressing the scope of liability for fraud); RESTATEMENT (THIRD) OF TORTS: LIABILITY FOR ECONOMIC HARM §§ 5–6 (Tentative Draft No. 1, Apr. 4, 2012) (addressing negligent misrepresentation).

(8) Although much of the material in this Section has focused on the liability of accountants, keep in mind that negligent misrepresentation claims have been recognized against many other types of defendants. *See, e.g.*, *Ossining Union Free Sch. Dist. v. Anderson LaRocca Anderson*, 539 N.E.2d 91, 92, 95–96 (N.Y. 1989) (architects and engineers); *id.* at 94–95 ("It is true that in many of the cases involving claims for negligent misrepresentation, the defendants are accountants. . . . But while the rule has been developed in

the context of cases involving accountants, it reflects our concern for fixing an appropriate ambit of duty, and there is no reason for excepting from it defendants other than accountants who fall within the narrow circumstances we have delineated."); *McCamish, Martin, Brown & Loeffler v. F.E. Appling Interests*, 991 S.W.2d 787, 791 (Tex. 1999) ("We perceive no reason why section 552 should not apply to attorneys."); *id.* (noting that "[c]ourts applying Texas law have recognized a section 552 cause of action against other professionals as well," and citing cases involving an auditor, a physician, a real estate broker, a securities placement agent, a surveyor, and a title insurer); *see also* RESTATEMENT (SECOND) OF TORTS § 552 (1977) (providing illustrations involving defendants other than accountants); RESTATEMENT (THIRD) OF TORTS: LIABILITY FOR ECONOMIC HARM §§ 5–6 (Tentative Draft No. 1, Apr. 4, 2012) (same).

(9) Can business adversaries negotiating at arm's length sue each other for negligent misrepresentation? In *Onita Pacific Corp. v. Bronson Trustees*, 843 P.2d 890 (Or. 1992), the court refused to allow such a claim:

> . . . . [W]e conclude that, in arm's-length negotiations, economic losses arising from a negligent misrepresentation are not actionable. This conclusion is in accord with the opinions of some commentators. Professors Harper, James, and Gray have noted the desirability of limiting the class of persons to whom the duty of care is owed in the context of negligent misrepresentations causing economic losses.
>
> > "On the whole, as indicated above, courts have provided a remedy for negligent misrepresentation principally against those who advise in an essentially nonadversarial capacity. As against sellers and other presumed antagonists, on the other hand, the tendency of most courts has instead been either to rely on deceit with the requirement of scienter, however expanded, or to shift (by analogy to restitution or warranty) to strict liability * * *." 2 Harper, James & Gray, The Law of Torts 412–13, § 7.6 (2d ed 1986).
>
> Similarly, Professor Alfred Hill distinguishes between misrepresentations made by an adversary in a sales transaction and by one who holds out to the general public that he or she supplies information and has noted:
>
> > "The situation is different in the case of 'antagonists.' When the aggrieved person is a buyer, who does not complain of the negligent performance of a service but rather of misrepresentation by a seller inducing the making of a contract, the conceptual mold has been different from the inception of modern contract law: the options have been to sue on the contract or to sue in deceit, without a middle ground consisting of actionable negligence." Hill, *Damages for Innocent Misrepresentation*, 73 Colum L Rev 679, 688 (1973).

Hill also states that allowing recovery for negligent misrepresentations made in the bargaining process would undermine the law of contracts, especially rules of law concerning written contracts. *Id.* at 717–18.

. . . .

On the other hand, Prosser and Keeton argue that "there would seem to be very little justification for not extending liability to all parties and agents to a bargaining transaction for making misrepresentations negligently." Prosser & Keeton, Torts 745, § 107 (5th ed. 1984). However, they do not explain or support that assertion; they merely state it. Prosser and Keeton do acknowledge that most courts have restricted liability for negligent misrepresentations causing pecuniary losses by "limit[ing] the group of persons to whom the defendant may be liable, short of the foreseeability of possible harm." *Ibid.* Further, the situations that they describe involve suppliers of information, as distinct from parties in bargaining transactions. . . .

Our conclusion also is consistent with Restatement (Second) of Torts § 552. The text of section 552 and the comments and illustrations thereto suggest that the editors, in using the words "[o]ne who, in the course of his business, profession or employment, or in any other transaction in which he has a pecuniary interest, supplies false information for the guidance of others in their business transactions," had in mind relationships other than the relationship between persons negotiating at arm's length. The comments provide no illustrations dealing with business adversaries in the commercial sense. . . .

We read Restatement section 552 as consistent with the rule that this court has adopted for negligence actions for the recovery of economic losses, *viz.,* nongratuitous suppliers of information owe a duty to their clients or employers or to intended third-party beneficiaries of their contractual, professional, or employment relationship to exercise reasonable care to avoid misrepresenting facts. In the case at bar, defendants and their representative did not owe any duty to plaintiffs during the negotiations by virtue of a contractual, professional, or employment relationship or as a result of any fiduciary or similar relationship implied in the law. Here, the relationship was adversarial. In an arm's-length negotiation, a negligent misrepresentation is not actionable. Hence, plaintiffs cannot maintain their claim for negligent misrepresentation against defendants.

Onita, 843 P.2d at 897–99.

Do you agree that the *Onita* conclusion is consistent with § 552 of the Second Restatement? As a matter of policy, why should we allow business adversaries negotiating at arm's length to make negligent misrepresentations to one another? *See also* RESTATEMENT (THIRD) OF TORTS: LIABILITY FOR ECONOMIC HARM § 5(5) (Tentative Draft No. 1, Apr. 4, 2012) (refusing to recognize liability for negligent misrepresentations "made in the course of negotiating or performing a contract between the parties").

(10) Silence can serve as the basis of a fraud claim, *see* Section A(1), but can it similarly serve as the basis of a negligent misrepresentation claim? Under the Second Restatement, the word choice of § 552(1) would seem to preclude silence claims, as liability is imposed only on one who "supplies false information." "Supplies" suggests an affirmative act rather than nondisclosure. With respect to liability for fraud, however, § 525 also uses the affirmative-sounding language of "makes a misrepresentation," but no one doubts that § 551 brings silence within the purview of this language. In fact, § 551 effectively states that a failure to disclose a matter should be treated as equivalent to an affirmative representation of the nonexistence of the matter. One could argue that § 551 should have a similar effect on the affirmative language of § 552. After all, the text of § 551 is not limited to fraud claims, and even the placement of the section suggests that it is not limited to fraud claims (i.e., in the Second Restatement's table of contents, § 551 is not in the "Fraudulent Misrepresentation (Deceit)" topic, but is instead in the "Concealment and Nondisclosure" topic). *But see* RESTATEMENT (THIRD) OF TORTS: LIABILITY FOR ECONOMIC HARM § 5 cmt. e (Tentative Draft No. 1, Apr. 4, 2012) ("A failure to speak, by itself, does not create liability under this [negligent misrepresentation] Section.").

The case law on silence-based negligent misrepresentation claims is divided. *Compare Wengert v. Thomas L. Meyer, Inc.*, 152 S.W.3d 379, 382 (Mo. Ct. App. 2004) ("Fraudulent misrepresentation and negligent misrepresentation can arise from a person's affirmative misrepresentations or from passive nondisclosure."), *with Eberts v. Goderstad*, 569 F.3d 757, 765 (7th Cir. 2009) ("Negligent misrepresentation by nondisclosure is a claim of questionable heritage and has been soundly rejected in some jurisdictions.").

(11) In certain circumstances, an opinion can serve as the basis of a fraud claim. *See* Section A(5). In the same circumstances, can an opinion serve as the basis of a negligent misrepresentation claim? On the one hand, the number of negligent misrepresentation cases allowing claims against accountants for their audit opinions suggests an affirmative answer to the question (at least with respect to opinions of persons who purport to have special knowledge of the matter). In addition, the comments to § 552 of the Second Restatement clearly indicate that opinions are covered, and several illustrations are premised on opinions. *See, e.g.*, RESTATEMENT (SECOND) OF TORTS § 552 cmt. b (1977) ("The rule stated in this Section applies not only to information given as to the existence of facts but also to an opinion given upon facts equally well known to both the supplier and the recipient."); *id.* cmt. e ("When the information consists of an opinion upon facts supplied by the recipient or otherwise known to him, the recipient is entitled to expect a careful consideration of the facts and competence in arriving at an intelligent

judgment."); *id.* § 552 illus. 5, 10–11, 14; *see also* RESTATEMENT (THIRD) OF TORTS: LIABILITY FOR ECONOMIC HARM § 5 cmt. d (Tentative Draft No. 1, Apr. 4, 2012) (stating that opinions may serve as the basis of a negligent misrepresentation claim in certain circumstances).

On the other hand, the Second Restatement sections addressing opinions (§§ 539, 542–543) only discuss fraudulent misrepresentations and not negligent ones. This creates some uncertainty as to whether the sections were meant to apply to negligent misrepresentations. Moreover, some courts state unequivocally that opinions cannot serve as the basis for negligent misrepresentation claims (although courts misleadingly make similar unequivocal statements in fraud disputes as well). *See, e.g., Sain v. Cedar Rapids Cmty. Sch. Dist.*, 626 N.W.2d 115, 127 (Iowa 2001) ("Additionally, we observe that the tort [negligent misrepresentation] applies only to false information and does not apply to personal opinions or statements of future intent."); *Birt v. Wells Fargo Home Mortg., Inc.*, 75 P.3d 640, 657–58 (Wyo. 2003) ("The gist of the district court's reasoning, which is correct, is that negligent misrepresentation does not apply to misrepresentations of future intent or to statements of opinion. The tort of negligent misrepresentation, as defined by Restatement (Second) of Torts [§ 552], applies only to misrepresentations of facts.").

(12) Can a misrepresentation of intention serve as the basis of a negligent misrepresentation claim? *Cf.* Section A(5) (discussing a misrepresentation of intention as the basis of a fraud claim). From a Second Restatement standpoint, there is nothing in § 552 that would seem to prevent misrepresentations of intention from being actionable (assuming that the requirements of § 552 are otherwise satisfied). Nevertheless, the text of § 530 only applies to fraud claims, and some of the comments to § 530 suggest that a negligent misrepresentation of intent claim was not contemplated. *See* RESTATEMENT (SECOND) OF TORTS § 530 cmt. b (1977) ("To be actionable the statement of the maker's own intention must be fraudulent, which is to say that he must in fact not have the intention stated. . . . If the recipient wishes to have legal assurance that the intention honestly entertained will be carried out, he must see that it is expressed in the form of an enforceable contract, and his action must be on the contract."). As the prior note indicates, some courts have concluded that the tort of negligent misrepresentation does not apply to misrepresentations of intent. When a rationale is given for this conclusion, it is often something along the following lines: "Indeed, the extension of negligent misrepresentation to situations involving future intentions would endow every breach of contract with a potential tort claim for negligent promise." *Birt v. Wells Fargo Home Mortg., Inc.*, 75 P.3d 640, 658 (Wyo. 2003); *see also* RESTATEMENT (THIRD) OF TORTS: LIABILITY FOR ECONOMIC HARM § 5(5) (Tentative Draft No. 1, Apr. 4, 2012) (refusing to recognize liability for negligent misrepresentations "made in the course of negotiating or performing a contract between the parties").

PROBLEM 2.5

Able is an independent public accountant. He is retained by B Corporation to conduct an annual audit for the corporation and to furnish an opinion on the corporation's financial statements. Able is not informed of any intended use for the audited financial statements, but Able knows that a corporation's audited financial statements are customarily used in a wide variety of financial transactions. Able also knows that lenders and investors frequently rely on audited financial statements in deciding whether to commit capital to the corporation. After performing the audit, Able issues an unqualified report opining that B Corporation's financial statements present fairly in all material respects the financial position of the company.

B Corporation uses the audited financial statements to obtain a $100 million loan from X Bank. Unfortunately, the statements materially misrepresent the financial position of B Corporation, and Able negligently failed to discover the misrepresentation. X Bank relies on the audited financial statements in deciding to make the loan, and it suffers pecuniary loss when B Corporation ultimately files for bankruptcy.

(a) X Bank sues Able for negligent misrepresentation. What result under § 552 of the Second Restatement? Under § 5 of the Third Restatement?

(b) Consider the following modification: before Able was retained, B Corporation told Able that his audit would be used to procure a "bank loan" for approximately $50 million. When X Bank sues for negligent misrepresentation, what result? *See* RESTATEMENT (SECOND) OF TORTS § 552(2) (1977); *id.* § 552 cmt. h & illus. 5–7, cmt. j & illus. 13–15; RESTATEMENT (THIRD) OF TORTS: LIABILITY FOR ECONOMIC HARM § 5(2) (Tentative Draft No. 1, Apr. 4, 2012); *id.* § 5 cmt. g & illus. 10–11.

(c) Consider a different modification: before Able was retained, B Corporation told Able that his audit would be used to procure as much "investment" in the company's shares as possible. India relied on the audited financial statements in deciding to make a $250,000 investment in the company before it filed for bankruptcy. When India sues for negligent misrepresentation, what result? *See* RESTATEMENT (SECOND) OF TORTS § 552(2) (1977); *id.* § 552 cmt. h; RESTATEMENT (THIRD) OF TORTS: LIABILITY FOR ECONOMIC HARM § 5(2) (Tentative Draft No. 1, Apr. 4, 2012); *id.* § 5 cmt. f & illus. 6–8.

(d) What if Able's conduct had risen to the level of fraud instead of negligence? Would Able have been liable under the above scenarios? *See* RESTATEMENT (SECOND) OF TORTS § 531 (1977); RESTATEMENT (THIRD) OF TORTS: LIABILITY FOR ECONOMIC HARM § 12 cmt. b (Tentative Draft No. 2, Apr. 7, 2014).

2. DAMAGES

FEDERAL LAND BANK ASS'N V. SLOANE

825 S.W.2d 439 (Tex. 1991)

GONZALEZ, JUSTICE.

. . . .

In early 1986, William, Lettie, and Robert Sloane had been out of the business of raising chickens for two years when they learned they could get a contract from Pilgrim's Pride to raise broilers for the company on the condition that they build new chicken houses on their farm.[1] On March 7, 1986, the Sloanes applied for a $141,000 loan from the Federal Land Bank Association of Tyler. During the application process, the Sloanes obtained an estimate of $105,000 for the costs of necessary equipment and the construction of two chicken houses. They also obtained a letter from Pilgrim's Pride stating that the company agreed to "feed out broilers" for the Sloanes once the houses were constructed according to specifications provided by Pilgrim's Pride. The Sloanes subsequently sent the construction estimate and the letter from Pilgrim's Pride to their loan officer at the bank.

Approximately a month after the Sloanes had applied for the loan, the loan officer informed them that the bank's board had approved the loan, and that the Sloanes could go ahead with site preparation work. The contractor hired by the Sloanes to build the new chicken houses contacted the bank's loan officer to see if he should begin construction, notwithstanding the pending nature of the loan. The loan officer said that there was "no problem," and that "there was not any reason for them not to continue at that point." (The bank officer disputes these statements; however, the jury resolved this issue in the Sloanes' favor, and the bank subsequently did not challenge on appeal the legal or factual sufficiency of the evidence supporting the fact).

In June 1986, the Sloanes had one of their old chicken houses demolished, and they paid approximately $9,000 for further site preparation. As the work progressed they supplied the bank with receipts. In August, 1986, the Sloanes received a letter from the bank denying their loan application, giving as reasons the fact that they failed to include two outstanding debts on their application, and that they incurred additional liability for a car purchase while the loan was being

---

[1] A Pilgrim's Pride representative testified at trial that the company enters into contracts with its growers for an indefinite term, each party having the right to terminate upon 30 days' notice. Pursuant to the contract the company delivers the chicks and feed to the grower, and after a certain amount of time, pays a fee based on the amount of weight the chickens have gained.

processed.[2] The Sloanes subsequently failed to obtain other financing. They then sued the bank alleging that the loan officer had negligently misrepresented that the bank would approve their loan application. Their claims included the financial and property damages suffered in preparing to build the chicken houses, the loss of the Pilgrim's Pride contract, and the mental anguish caused by the bank's allegedly negligent conduct.[3]

The case was tried before a jury which found that: (1) the bank negligently misrepresented to the Sloanes that the bank had approved their loan application; (2) the Sloanes justifiably relied on such misrepresentation; and (3) reliance upon such misrepresentation caused the Sloanes pecuniary loss. The jury assessed damages against the bank amounting to $26,500 for past and future monetary losses other than lost profits, $28,500 for past and future lost profits, and $15,000 for mental anguish.

The trial court rendered an $81,974.48 judgment for the Sloanes, which included $11,974.48 in prejudgment interest. The court of appeals subsequently held that there was no evidence of lost profits and certain other expenditures, and thus the court affirmed the balance of the judgment after reformation. . . .

. . . .

The Sloanes claim that the bank has a duty to use reasonable care whenever it provides information to its customers or potential customers, and that the bank breached this duty when it allegedly encouraged the Sloanes to incur expenses in reliance on the information related to their loan application. The Sloanes further allege that the bank misrepresented an existing fact rather than a promise of future conduct. Both the bank and the Sloanes rely on RESTATEMENT (SECOND) OF TORTS § 552 (1977) to define the scope of this duty. We agree with the Restatement's definition, as have several courts of appeal that have previously considered this question.

The elements of a cause of action for the breach of this duty are: (1) the representation is made by a defendant in the course of his business,

---

[2]   The Sloanes concede that the bank acted reasonably in denying their request for the loan.

[3]   The petition states:

"More particularly, Plaintiffs expended approximately $15,000.00 in site preparation work for construction of the broiler houses, which were never built, and which has further resulted in a reduction in the value of their property because of the resulting damage to their hay pastures. Plaintiffs were further deprived of the opportunity to enter into a contract with Pilgrim's Pride Corporation for the feeding of broiler chickens, as a result of which they would in all reasonable probability have realized the profits of approximately $12,000.00 per year for at least five (5) years. Plaintiffs further suffered mental anguish and emotional distress and upset as the result of Defendant's negligent conduct, all to their damage in the total sum of ONE HUNDRED THOUSAND ($100,000.00) DOLLARS, for which they come now and sue."

or in a transaction in which he has a pecuniary interest; (2) the defendant supplies "false information" for the guidance of others in their business; (3) the defendant did not exercise reasonable care or competence in obtaining or communicating the information; and (4) the plaintiff suffers pecuniary loss by justifiably relying on the representation. Issues substantially conforming to these elements were submitted to the jury, which returned a verdict favorable to the Sloanes. The bank makes no challenge to the sufficiency of the evidence of liability, so the remaining issue is what damages are available for this tort.

DAMAGES

The Restatement provides damages for this tort as follows:

(1) The damages recoverable for a negligent misrepresentation are those necessary to compensate the plaintiff for the pecuniary loss to him of which the misrepresentation is legal cause, including

> (a) the difference between the value of what he has received in the transaction and its purchase price or other value given for it; and

> (b) pecuniary loss suffered otherwise as a consequence of the plaintiff's reliance upon the misrepresentation.

(2) the damages recoverable for a negligent misrepresentation do not include the benefit of the plaintiff's contract with the defendant.

RESTATEMENT (SECOND) OF TORTS § 552B (1977).

While the Sloanes adopt the Restatement's terminology to support the basic elements of their cause of action, they reject the language of Restatement section 552B which limits damages to pecuniary loss alone. Specifically, the Sloanes argue that this court should allow them damages for mental anguish. The Restatement advances several policy reasons for limiting damages, including a lower degree of fault indicated by a less culpable mental state and the need to keep liability proportional to risk. RESTATEMENT (SECOND) OF TORTS § 552, comment a. There has been no trend to reject the pecuniary loss rule in what is essentially a commercial tort. We decline to extend damages beyond those limits provided in Restatement section 552B.

The Sloanes complain that they should receive damages for the profits they anticipated from the Pilgrim's Pride contract. As discussed above, Restatement (Second) section 552B allows for damages suffered in reliance upon negligent misrepresentation, but not for the failure to obtain the benefit of the bargain. Restatement (Second) §§ 552B(1)(a) & (2). The Sloanes would not have received the contract regardless of whether the misrepresentation was made. Under the legal theory of this section of the Restatement, they should not, therefore, receive the benefit of a bargain that would never have taken place. The sole reason the Sloanes did not get the Pilgrim's Pride contract is because the bank did not give them the loan money to build acceptable chicken houses. The Sloanes' claim to these damages is impermissibly predicated on giving them the benefit of the loan.

For the foregoing reasons, we reverse the judgment of the court of appeals insofar as it includes an award for mental anguish. In all other respects, the judgment of the court of appeals is affirmed. We remand this cause to the trial court for rendition of judgment for $11,427.03 for past pecuniary losses other than lost profits, plus prejudgment interest.

. . . .

NOTES & QUESTIONS

(1) Consider § 549 and § 552B of the Second Restatement. How does the measure of damages for fraud compare to the measure of damages for negligent misrepresentation? *See also* RESTATEMENT (THIRD) OF TORTS: LIABILITY FOR ECONOMIC HARM § 9 cmt. b (Tentative Draft No. 2, Apr. 7, 2014) (discussing damages for fraud); RESTATEMENT (THIRD) OF TORTS: LIABILITY FOR ECONOMIC HARM § 5 cmt. l (Tentative Draft No. 1, Apr. 4, 2012) (discussing damages for negligent misrepresentation).

(2) The Sloanes ultimately received damages for "past pecuniary losses other than lost profits," which presumably included compensation for the construction expenses incurred before the loan was denied. Under § 552B of the Second Restatement, would these sums have been awarded under subsection (1)(a) or (1)(b)? *See also* RESTATEMENT (THIRD) OF TORTS: LIABILITY FOR ECONOMIC HARM § 5 cmt. l (Tentative Draft No. 1, Apr. 4, 2012) (discussing damages for negligent misrepresentation).

(3) Why were the Sloanes unable to recover damages for the profits anticipated from the Pilgrim's Pride contract? What if the Sloanes would have received a loan from another bank if the negligent misrepresentation had not been made? (In other words, what if the misrepresentation delayed the Sloanes from looking for another lender until it was too late?) Would they then have been able to recover the anticipated profits from the Pilgrim's Pride contract?

(4) The court in *Sloane* denied mental anguish damages on the grounds that § 552B only allows recovery for "pecuniary" losses. This refusal to allow mental anguish damages in negligent misrepresentation claims is consistent with the position of most (but not all) other courts. *See, e.g., Crowley v. Global Realty, Inc.,* 474 A.2d 1056, 1058 (N.H. 1984) (denying recovery for mental distress); *Pearson v. Simmonds Precision Prods., Inc.,* 624 A.2d 1134, 1137 (Vt. 1993) (same). *But see Dousson v. S. Cent. Bell,* 429 So. 2d 466, 468–69

(La. Ct. App. 1983) (allowing the recovery of mental anguish damages in a negligent misrepresentation claim).

(5)   Given that negligent misrepresentation is a species of negligence, it is not surprising that authorities typically conclude that contributory or comparative negligence (depending upon the law of the jurisdiction) may be raised as a defense to a negligent misrepresentation claim. *See, e.g.,* RESTATEMENT (SECOND) OF TORTS § 552A (1977) ("The recipient of a negligent misrepresentation is barred from recovery for pecuniary loss suffered in reliance upon it if he is negligent in so relying."); RESTATEMENT (THIRD) OF TORTS: LIABILITY FOR ECONOMIC HARM § 5(4) (Tentative Draft No. 1, Apr. 4, 2012) ("A plaintiff's recovery under this [negligent misrepresentation] Section is subject to the same principles of comparative responsibility that apply to other claims of negligence."); *id.* § 6(3) (substantially the same); *see also Florenzano v. Olson*, 387 N.W.2d 168, 176 (Minn. 1986) ("We agree with these commentators and with the majority of states that have considered the issue. . . . We hold that the principles of comparative responsibility apply to negligent misrepresentation. . . .").

C. INNOCENT MISREPRESENTATION

There are many legal theories of relief based upon innocent misrepresentation. For example, under contract law, if a defendant's representation can be characterized as a warranty, damages can be recovered for breach of warranty regardless of the defendant's fault. *See, e.g.,* U.C.C. § 2–313 (allowing for the creation of express warranties); *id.* § 2–714 (stating the measure of damages for breach of warranty). The law of restitution also provides relief by allowing a plaintiff to rescind a transfer that was induced by a material misrepresentation, even if the misrepresentation was innocently made. *See, e.g.,* RESTATEMENT (THIRD) OF RESTITUTION AND UNJUST ENRICHMENT § 13(1) & cmt. c (2011) (noting that "a transfer induced by innocent misrepresentation is subject to rescission only if the misrepresentation was material"). Finally, in some states, consumer protection or related statutes provide relief for innocent misrepresentation. *See, e.g., Gennari v. Weichert Co. Realtors*, 691 A.2d 350, 365 (N.J. 1997) ("Throughout its history, the [New Jersey Consumer Fraud] Act has protected consumers from deception and fraud, even when committed in good faith. . . . One who makes an affirmative misrepresentation is liable even in the absence of knowledge of the falsity of the misrepresentation, negligence, or the intent to deceive.").

Recovery in *tort* for innocent misrepresentation, however, is very much a minority position. Although some courts purport to adopt such an action, the language used to describe the claim often sounds like negligent misrepresentation or fraud. *See, e.g., Richard v. A. Waldman and Sons, Inc.*, 232 A.2d 307, 309 (Conn. 1967) ("An innocent misrepresentation may be actionable if the declarant has the means of knowing, ought to know, or has the duty of knowing the truth."); *Schurmann v. Neau*, 624 N.W.2d 157, 161 (Wis. Ct. App. 2000) (stating that, for innocent misrepresentation, the representation must be made on the defendant's "personal knowledge or under circumstances in which he necessarily ought to have known the truth or untruth of the statement"). Further, as one commentator suggests: "Perhaps many of the cases using broad strict liability language do not entirely mean it. Some, for example, are merely rescission cases. . . . Some others have used the broad language of strict liability merely in dicta, and in still others the court may have adopted the broad rule of liability without realizing that it imposed strict liability, and certainly without giving a reason for strict liability." DAN B. DOBBS, THE LAW OF TORTS § 473, at 1354–55 (2000). In short, one can question whether some of the purported authority for the tort of innocent misrepresentation actually supports such a claim.

Section 552C of the Second Restatement does provide a tort cause of action for innocent misrepresentation "in a sale, rental or exchange transaction." The misrepresentation must be "of a material fact" and made "for the purpose of inducing [a person] to act or to refrain from acting in reliance upon it." Liability is imposed "for pecuniary loss caused to [the person] by [the person's] justifiable reliance upon the misrepresentation." *Id.* § 552C(1). Due to the strict liability nature of the claim, consequential and benefit of the bargain damages are unavailable; instead, damages are limited to "the difference between the value of what [the person] has parted with and the value of what [the person] has received in the transaction." *Id.* § 552C(2) & cmt. f.

NOTES & QUESTIONS

(1) Given that claims for breach of warranty and rescission are often available for innocent misrepresentation, why would a plaintiff ever desire to bring a tort action? What advantages, in other words, does a tort action for innocent misrepresentation provide? *See id.* § 552C cmt. b.

(2) Under the law of products liability, an innocent misrepresentation about a product that causes personal injury or property damage is actionable. *See, e.g.*, RESTATEMENT (THIRD) OF TORTS: PRODUCTS LIABILITY § 9 (1998) ("One engaged in the business of selling or otherwise distributing products who, in connection with the sale of a product, makes a fraudulent, negligent, or innocent misrepresentation of material fact concerning the product is subject to liability for harm to persons or property caused by the misrepresentation.").

(3) Outside of the products liability context, the Third Restatement rejects a tort action for innocent misrepresentation—primarily on the ground that the economic loss rule between contracting parties would preclude such an action. *See* RESTATEMENT (THIRD) OF TORTS: LIABILITY FOR ECONOMIC HARM § 3 cmt. d (Tentative Draft No. 1, Apr. 4, 2012) (rejecting the approach

of § 552C of the Second Restatement); *see also* Chapter 6 (discussing the economic loss rule between contracting parties).

CHAPTER 3

TORTIOUS INTERFERENCE WITH ECONOMIC RELATIONS

■ ■ ■

Tortious interference with economic relations is a general term that encompasses two related (but distinct) torts: (1) intentional interference with existing contract, and (2) intentional interference with a relationship that is likely to lead to a contract (often referred to as intentional interference with "prospective contract" or "prospective advantage"). Most states recognize both torts, and they are frequently asserted in commercial disputes.

A. INTENTIONAL INTERFERENCE WITH EXISTING CONTRACT

1. INTERFERING WITH PERFORMANCE OWED TO THE PLAINTIFF

LUMLEY V. GYE
118 Eng. Rep. 749 (Q.B. 1853)

[The declaration alleged that Lumley, the proprietor of the Queen's Theatre, and Johanna Wagner, a well-known opera singer, entered into a contract for Wagner to perform for three months at Lumley's theater. The defendant, Gye, was the owner of a rival theater who knew about the Lumley-Wagner agreement and wished to procure Wagner's services for himself. According to the declaration, Gye, "whilst the agreement was in full force, and before the expiration of the period for which Miss Wagner was engaged, wrongfully and maliciously enticed and procured Miss Wagner to refuse to sing or perform at [Lumley's] theatre, and to depart from and abandon her contract with the plaintiff and all service thereunder, whereby Miss Wagner wrongfully, during the full period of the engagement, refused and made default in performing at the theatre." Lumley claimed damages arising from Wagner's refusal to perform. The defendant demurred.]

ERLE J.

The question raised upon this demurrer is, [w]hether an action will lie by the proprietor of a theatre against a person who maliciously procures an entire abandonment of a contract to perform exclusively at that theatre for a certain time; whereby damage was sustained? And it seems to me that it will. The authorities are numerous and uniform, that an action will lie by a master against a person who procures that a servant should unlawfully leave his service. The principle involved in these cases comprises the present; for, there, the right of action in the master arises from the wrongful act of the defendant in procuring that the person hired should break his contract, by putting an end to the relation of employer and employed; and the present case is the same. If it is objected that this class of actions for procuring a breach of contract of hiring rests upon no principle, and ought not to be extended beyond the cases heretofore decided, and that, as those have related to contracts respecting trade, manufactures or household service, and not to performance at a theatre, therefore they are no authority for an action in respect of a contract for such performance; the answer appears to me to be, that the class of cases referred to rests upon the principle that the procurement of the violation of the right is a cause of action, and that, when this principle is applied to a violation of a right arising upon a contract of hiring, the nature of the service contracted for is immaterial. It is clear that the procurement of the violation of a right is a cause of action in all instances where the violation is an actionable wrong, as in violations of a right to property, whether real or personal, or to personal security: he who procures the wrong is a joint wrong-doer, and may be sued, either alone or jointly with the agent, in the appropriate action for the wrong complained of. . . . He who maliciously procures . . . damage to another by violation of his right ought to be made to indemnify; and that, whether he procures an actionable wrong or a breach of contract. . . . The remedy on the contract may be inadequate, as where the measures of damages is restricted; . . . or, in the case of the non-delivery of the goods, the disappointment may lead to a heavy forfeiture under a contract to complete a work within a time, but the measure of damages against the vendor of the goods for non-delivery may be only the difference between the contract price and the market value of the goods in question at the time of the breach. In such cases, he who procures the damage maliciously might justly be made responsible beyond the liability of the contractor.

With respect to the objection that the contracting party had not begun the performance of the contract, I do not think it a tenable ground of defence. The procurement of the breach of the contract may be equally injurious, whether the service has begun or not, and in my judgment ought to be equally actionable, as the relation of employer and employed is constituted by the contract alone, and no act of service is necessary thereto.

The result is that there ought to be, in my opinion, judgment for the plaintiff.

NOTES & QUESTIONS

(1) "The doctrine thus announced [in *Lumley*], that intentional interference with a contract may be an actionable tort, was received at first with hesitation or disapproval, but it was reaffirmed nearly thirty years later in England, and then by degrees was extended, first to cover contracts other than those for personal services, and later to include interferences in which no ill-will was to be found on the part of the defendant. The present English law gives it full acceptance, as to all intentional interferences with any type of contract. The American courts were reluctant to accept the doctrine in the beginning, and a few of them rejected it outright as applied to interference with relations other than that of master and servant. Such decisions have for the most part been overruled, and the tort is now recognized virtually everywhere as to any contract, regardless of its character." W. PAGE KEETON ET AL., PROSSER AND KEETON ON TORTS § 129, at 980–81 (5th ed. 1984).

(2) How did Gye cause Wagner to breach her contract with Lumley? Did he assault her or kidnap her to prevent her from performing? Did he defraud her? *See* RESTATEMENT (SECOND) OF TORTS § 766 cmt. c (1979).

(3) Was it necessary for Lumley to sue Gye? Couldn't Lumley have been made whole simply by suing Wagner for breach of contract? Can you think of circumstances where a plaintiff in a similar situation would *not* be made whole by suing for breach of contract?

(4) Section 766 of the Second Restatement recognizes the tort of intentional interference with existing contract: "One who intentionally and improperly interferes with the performance of a contract (except a contract to marry) between another and a third person by inducing or otherwise causing the third person not to perform the contract, is subject to liability to the other for the pecuniary loss resulting to the other from the failure of the third person to perform the contract." Would the facts of *Lumley* satisfy § 766?

(5) Some authorities contend that the threat of a § 766 interference claim is beneficial because it encourages voluntary bargaining transactions between the third party and the promisee. That is, if Gye desires Wagner's services when she is under contract to Lumley, Gye will need to bargain with Lumley. If Gye approaches Wagner directly, he risks Lumley bringing a § 766 lawsuit against him. As one court explained:

> . . . . In the § 766 inducement case, the effect of tort liability is to encourage voluntary transactions. If an "inducer" wishes to receive a promisee's promised advantage, then the inducer must bargain directly with the promisee. This "bargain-forcing" aspect of inducement liability protects the security of transactions, reduces

monitoring costs, encourages consensual rearrangements of contractual obligations, and avoids the negotiation and litigation costs that arise where an inducer causes a promisor to breach its contract with its promisee.

Windsor Securities, Inc. v. Hartford Life Ins. Co., 986 F.2d 655, 661 (3d Cir. 1993).

(6) As the prior note suggests, doesn't the tort of intentional interference with existing contract impede efficient breaches? In thinking about this question, consider the following background:

> . . . [F]rom an economic perspective, a refusal to perform a particular promise may not only be defensible but desirable. If *X* and *Y* exchange promises and *X* later discovers that the future exchange to which he has agreed will be detrimental rather than beneficial to him, *X* may breach the contract so made by the exchange of promises. If *X*'s refusal to perform his promise is accompanied by sufficient compensation to *Y*, the result may be economically efficient, whereas a legal insistence that *X*'s promise be performed would be inefficient. "Efficiency" may be viewed as the utilization of economic resources in such a fashion that "value"— human satisfaction as measured by aggregate consumer willingness to pay for resources—is maximized. Normally, a refusal to perform a future exchange will result in loss to the non-breaching party that must be compensated to fulfill the expectations of that party. Thus if *X* agrees to supply 1,000 tape recorders to *Y*, a refusal by *X* to perform will require *Y* to seek an alternative supplier of the recorders. If *Y* must pay a higher price, the difference between the contract price and the higher (substitute purchase) price will make *Y* whole in terms of fulfilling *Y*'s reasonable expectations.

> However, assume that *X* has agreed to deliver the 1,000 recorders of a particular brand with a peculiar feature to *Y* at $200 per unit. Before the future exchange is to be performed, *Z* requires 1,000 recorders with the peculiar feature of the models *X* has promised to sell to *Y*. *X* has no more of these or any other recorders. Since *Y* has no interest in the peculiar feature, *Y* can purchase substitute recorders that will serve him at least as well as *X*'s recorders at $210 per unit. However, no substitutes would satisfy the needs of *Z*. *Z* is willing to pay *X* $220 per unit. If *X* refuses to perform his promise to *Y*, *Y* may be compensated by a $10,000 payment from *X*. Having received $220 per unit from *Z*, *X* receives a net of $10,000 more than he would have received from *Y* though *Y*, again, has been compensated. Thus *Y* is made whole, *X* receives expected value, and *Z* is satisfied. Not only are the parties better off, the society in which the parties live is also better off in terms of efficiency or value maximization. This situation is often described as one of "efficient breach" of contract. This economic analysis is

consistent with the fundamental concept of contract remedies, i.e., to compensate the injured party by placing him in the position he would have occupied had the contract been performed. The protection of the injured party's expectation interest provides an incentive for the other party to breach *only* if the gain from the breach (notwithstanding compensation to the injured party) is greater than the gain from contract performance.

JOHN E. MURRAY, JR., MURRAY ON CONTRACTS § 6, at 14–15 (3d ed. 1990); *see also* Lillian R. BeVier, *Reconsidering Inducement*, 76 VA. L. REV. 877, 877–78 (1990) ("If Promisor regards herself as worse off performing the contract than she would be paying damages, the law of contract remedies seems to encourage her to breach and pay. The structure of that law has been convincingly interpreted to hold that a fully compensated breach of contract can be socially productive because it can, among other things, cost-effectively move resources from lower to higher valued uses.").

Assuming that Z knows about the X–Y contract, won't the interference tort deter Z from approaching X (because Z would fear being sued by Y for interference)? Doesn't that diminish the likelihood that this efficient breach will occur? *See* RESTATEMENT (SECOND) OF TORTS § 774A & cmt. a (1979) (noting that compensatory damages (including damages for emotional distress) and punitive damages can be recovered for interference with existing contract).

(7)   In one of the more well-known disputes in American civil litigation, Pennzoil Company sued Texaco, Inc. for tortious interference with its existing contract to purchase control of Getty Oil Company. Pennzoil argued that after it had reached a contractual agreement with Getty, Texaco interfered by inducing Getty to breach the contract in favor of a more lucrative offer from Texaco. In response, Texaco contended that at the time its offer was made, Pennzoil had, at most, merely a prospective contractual interest in Getty.

The jury found for Pennzoil and awarded the staggering sum of $7.53 billion in compensatory damages and $3 billion in punitive damages. On appeal, the judgment was affirmed, but the punitive damages award was reduced to $1 billion. *See Texaco, Inc. v. Pennzoil, Co.*, 729 S.W.2d 768 (Tex. App. 1987). After Texaco filed for bankruptcy and appealed to the United States Supreme Court, the parties agreed to settle the dispute for $3 billion.

(8)   Although intentional interference with existing contract (or prospective contract) is actionable, negligent interference is typically not. *See, e.g.*, RESTATEMENT (SECOND) OF TORTS § 766C (1979); RESTATEMENT (THIRD) OF TORTS: LIABILITY FOR ECONOMIC HARM § 7 (Tentative Draft No. 2, Apr. 7, 2014).

PROBLEM 3.1

(a)   Able hires Baker as an at-will employee (meaning, in general, that Baker can be fired at any time for any reason). After two years of employment, Carter uses fraud to convince Able to terminate Baker (Carter hates Baker, and her defrauding of Able is motivated purely by spite towards Baker.) Will Baker's suit against Carter for intentional interference with existing contract be successful? *See* RESTATEMENT (SECOND) OF TORTS § 766 cmt. g (1979).

(b)   Able enters into an oral contract with Baker to sell Baker a parcel of land. (Assume that the oral contract clearly violates the applicable statute of frauds.) Carter threatens to physically harm Able if Able does not sell the land to her (Carter) instead. As a result, Able sells the land to Carter. Will Baker's suit against Carter for intentional interference with existing contract be successful? *See id.* § 766 cmt. f.

(c)   Able enters into a contract with Baker whereby Able will be paid to murder Baker's wife. Carter persuades Able to refuse to perform. Will Baker's suit against Carter for intentional interference with existing contract be successful? (Assume that Baker is, in fact, stupid enough to bring this claim.) *See id.* §§ 766 cmts. e–f, 774.

KNIGHT ENTERPRISES V. BEARD

2004 WL 60323 (Mich. Ct. App. 2004)

PER CURIAM.

Plaintiff, Knight Enterprises, Inc., appeals as of right from the trial court's grant of a directed verdict in favor of defendants, Mark Beard and M & L Petroleum, Inc. . . . We affirm.

This case involves the question of whether a petroleum distributor (defendants Beard and M & L Petroleum Inc.) can be liable to another petroleum distributor (plaintiff Knight) for tortious interference with contractual relations when the defendants delivered fuel to plaintiff's customers at those customer's requests.

Beard is the president of M & L Petroleum, a Michigan corporation that is in the business of the wholesale and transportation of gasoline. Beard obtains his gasoline product from Primcor, Peerless Distributing, or unbranded Marathon suppliers. Beard also hauls product for Peerless, a wholesale distributor, and purchases product from Peerless so that he may supply the product to his own customers. Beard testified that distributors haul different products into their own branded stations every day. Beard indicated that if a station called his company and requested delivery, he assumed that they had the right to do so and that he would sell gasoline to that station. Station owners with CITGO signs contact Beard and make inquiries on defendants' price for gasoline. Some of the station owners contact defendants because of their cheaper price for gasoline, and other station owners contact defendants because the station is out of product and cannot otherwise obtain delivery of the product.

Beard denied contacting, inducing, or coercing any of plaintiff's customer stations to purchase gasoline from him. Beard also denied soliciting any of the accounts, and indicated that the station owners contacted defendants. Beard admitted he knew of the contracts between plaintiff and Pars Petro and Jefferson Petro (two stations defendant delivered fuel to), but denied having any knowledge of any other contracts between plaintiff and other stations. At trial, plaintiff conceded that they had no evidence to suggest that defendants had made any contacts or solicitations with its customers. Plaintiff also admitted that there was no evidence to suggest that defendants told plaintiff's customers to stop purchasing fuel from plaintiff.

Knight Enterprises has a franchise agreement or contract with CITGO to use the brand identification in order to obtain dealer customers, who Knight then enters into contracts with in order to supply them with petroleum products. According to Knight, one is not qualified to deliver product to a location if there is a major brand identification and that seller does not have a formal agreement with that location.

Knight also testified that most major oil companies operate directly with their own distributors, and will occasionally have a surplus of product that they sell as unbranded gasoline. Unbranded gasoline products may be three to five cents per gallon cheaper than branded products. Knight testified that there are three reasons that a station owner or dealer would call defendant for delivery of gasoline: (1) economic; (2) the station owner could not obtain deliveries from plaintiff because of credit problems; and (3) the station owner is incompetent in planning deliveries for the station.

Additionally, Knight testified that the solicitation was based on defendants' price for unbranded surplus gasoline. Knight insisted that defendants' inducement was economic, because defendants purchased unbranded gasoline at a certain price and then would sell it to a branded location at a better economical price. Regarding Jefferson [Petro], Knight testified that defendants' continued relationship with the station along with defendants' offer to sell the gasoline at a lower price was evidence of defendants' solicitation. Knight further testified that [Beard's] . . . "practice of . . . selling product to locations that have a branded sign is the proof that he solicited something." Knight believed that if defendants sold gasoline to a station owner cheaper than the stations could buy the product from plaintiff, this was inducement for the station owner to purchase product from defendants instead of plaintiff.

On August 3, 2001, the jury returned with a verdict. The jury found in favor of plaintiff on the tortious interference with a contractual relationship claim, and determined that plaintiff's lost net profit was

$225,027.15. . . . However, as noted, after the verdict was rendered the trial court granted defendants a directed verdict. . . .

. . . .

Plaintiff next argues that the trial court erred in granting defendants' motion for directed verdict because plaintiff was not required to prove active solicitation by defendants. . . .

In order to establish a claim for tortious interference with a contractual relationship, a plaintiff must demonstrate the following: "(1) a contract, (2) a breach, and (3) an unjustified instigation of the breach by the defendant." *Mahrle v. Danke*, 549 NW2d 56 (1996). Regarding the third element, "one who alleges tortious interference with a contractual . . . relationship must allege the intentional doing of a per se wrongful act or the doing of a lawful act with malice and unjustified in law for the purpose of invading the contractual rights or business relationship of another." [*CMI Int'l Inc v. Interment Int'l Corp.*, 649 NW2d 808 (2002).] This Court has further held that a person is not liable for tortious interference with a contract if legitimate personal or business interests motivate him or her.

"A wrongful act per se is an act that is inherently wrongful or an act that can never be justified under any circumstances." *Prysak v. R L Polk Co*, 483 NW2d 629 (1992). If the plaintiff relies on the second theory to demonstrate a claim for tortious interference with a contractual relationship, i.e., the intentional doing of a lawful act done with malice and unjustified in law, the plaintiff "necessarily must demonstrate, with specificity, affirmative acts by the interferer which corroborate the unlawful purpose of the interference." *Feldman v. Green*, 360 NW2d 881 (1984). As shown below, in this case plaintiff alleged that defendants interfered with plaintiff's contracts by offering fuel at a low price. Because such conduct is not wrongful per se, plaintiff was required to prove that defendants took affirmative acts to interfere with plaintiff's contracts. This plaintiff failed to do.

In *Wilkinson v. Powe*, 1 NW2d 539 (1942), the Michigan Supreme Court addressed, in detail, the tort of the intentional procurement of a breach of contract.[5] In *Wilkinson*, the Court addressed the issue of . . . the defendants' acts of writing letters to farmers indicating that they would not accept deliveries of milk from trucks that did not belong to defendants. The Court in *Wilkinson* found:

> If the defendants in the instant case had merely refused to accept further delivery of milk by plaintiff, they would have been clearly within their legal rights, although this would have

---

[5] The tort "intentional procurement of a breach of contract" is the same tort now called tortious interference with contractual relations.

resulted in a breach of contract between plaintiff and the farmers. But defendants did more. Their letters of May 29th and June 1st show active solicitation of a breach of the contract and their refusal to accept delivery of milk was merely another step in bringing about the breach.

In *Bahr v. Miller Brothers Creamery*, 112 NW2d 463 (1961), the Supreme Court reiterated the principle that in order for a defendant to be held liable for the intentional procurement of a breach of contract between the plaintiff and another, there must be some evidence of inducement of a third party to break their contract with the plaintiff.

In adopting its position, the *Bahr* Court relied on *Imperial Ice Co v. Rossier*, 112 P.2d 631 (1941), which held that a party may not, under the guise of competition, actively and affirmatively induce the breach of a competitor's contract in order to secure an economic advantage over that competitor. Quoting *Imperial Ice,* the *Bahr* Court held that the mere selling of a product to a person under contract with another is not the active inducement to breach a contract required to sustain the tort:

> "Had defendants merely sold ice to Coker without actively inducing him to violate his contract, his distribution of the ice in the forbidden territory in violation of his contract would not then have rendered defendants liable. They may carry on their business of selling ice as usual without incurring liability for breaches of contract by their customers. *It is necessary to prove that they intentionally and actively induced the breach.*"

The *Bahr* Court indicated that in the cases finding liability for such conduct, there was proof or accepted allegations of active solicitation and instigation of the breach on the part of the defendants. In *Bahr,* the Court indicated that there was no testimony from which it could be asserted or inferred that the corporate defendant approached, solicited, or induced a breach of the contract between the third party and the plaintiff, and further noted that the evidence presented demonstrated that the approach was made from the "other direction" or from the third party. Specifically, the Court stated the following:

> Plaintiff's reliance on these cases is misplaced. They do clearly hold that a cause of action is available where a defendant has induced a third party to break a contract with plaintiff. But in each case there was proof (or accepted allegations) of active solicitation and instigation of the breach on the part of the defendants. And in each case the court qualified its holding by stating that had the defendants not been the instigators, they would not have been liable.

> There is no testimony in this record from which it can be asserted or inferred that the corporate defendant approached,

solicited or induced the breach of contract by the individual defendants. On the contrary, the approach appears to have been made wholly from the other direction. . . .

Similarly, and contrary to plaintiff's argument on appeal, the Restatement of Torts supports this position. Regarding claims of "inducement by offer of better terms," the Restatement provides:

> Another method of inducing B to sever his business relations with C is to offer B a better bargain than that which he has with C. Here, . . . a nice question of fact is presented. A's freedom to conduct his business in the usual manner, to advertise his goods, to extol their qualities, to fix their prices and to sell them is not restricted by the fact that B has agreed to buy similar goods from C. Even though A knows of B's contract with C, he may nevertheless send his regular advertising to B and may solicit business in the normal course. This conduct *does not constitute inducement of the breach of contract.* The illustration below is a case of solicitation that does constitute inducement.
>
> Illustration:
>
> 3.   A writes to B: "I know you are under contract to buy these goods from C. Therefore I can offer you a special price way below my cost. If you accept this offer, you can break your contract with C, pay him something in settl11ement and still make money. I am confident that you will find it more satisfactory to deal with me than with C." As a result of this letter, B breaks his contract with C. A has induced the breach.

[RESTATEMENT (SECOND) OF TORTS § 766 cmt. m (1979).]

As noted throughout this opinion, Knight unequivocally testified that the alleged inducement from defendants was stating a low fuel price in response to the customer's inquiry. This is not an unlawful act per se. Therefore, in accordance with Michigan law and the Restatement of Torts, plaintiff was required to prove that defendant took an affirmative act to induce the customers to break the exclusive contract with plaintiff. Indeed, in *Hutton v. Roberts*, 451 NW2d 536 (1989) we held, after examining *Wilkinson* and *Feldman, supra:*

> Consistent with the case law discussed above, *it is instead necessary to show some active solicitation or encouragement of a breach of an already existing contract,* accompanied by and corroborative of a malicious, unjustified purpose to inflict injury. *The act of* making an offer or of *accepting an offer of another in violation of the other's contractual obligations is, by itself, not enough.*

Plaintiff has simply failed to present any evidence whatsoever demonstrating that defendants' conduct induced or otherwise caused[6] the station owners to breach their contracts with plaintiff. Plaintiff admitted that defendants never contacted plaintiff's customers, but only gave the pricing in response to the customers unsolicited inquiries. This evidence is insufficient, as a matter of law, to sustain the tort of tortious interference with contractual relations. Thus, the trial court properly granted defendants' motion for directed verdict.[7]

NOTES & QUESTIONS

(1)   Assume that § 766 of the Second Restatement governed the dispute in *Knight*. Can you explain why, in § 766 terms, the defendants prevailed? *See* RESTATEMENT (SECOND) OF TORTS § 766 cmts. m–n (1979).

(2)   Assume that Johanna Wagner contacted Gye and stated "I would like to sing at your theater from January–March." Gye knows that Wagner is under contract to sing at Lumley's theater from January–March; nevertheless, he makes an offer with better terms than Wagner has with Lumley. Wagner accepts and breaches her contract with Lumley. What result under § 766 when Lumley sues Gye for interference with the Wagner contract? *See id.* § 766 cmts. m–n.

PROBLEM 3.2

(a)   Assume that defendants Beard and M & L Petroleum Inc. send out regular advertisements to service station operators in the area discussing the products that they have available for sale. The defendants are aware that some of the operators receiving the advertisements have already contracted to purchase similar products from Knight. As a result of the advertising, some of the operators breach their contracts with Knight and purchase the products from defendants instead. What result under § 766 when Knight sues the defendants for interference with the operators' contracts? *See id.* § 766 cmt. m.

---

[6]   Indeed, as stated in the Restatement, there must be some conduct that induces or otherwise causes one to breach a contract with the plaintiff. The Restatement indicates that conduct that induces refers to situations where one party causes another party to choose one course of conduct rather than another, while "otherwise causing" refers to situations where one party leaves the other party no choice but to breach their contact with another party. [RESTATEMENT (SECOND) OF TORTS § 766 cmt. h (1979).] Neither of these situations applies to the instant case where it was the station owner's own choice to breach their contracts with plaintiff in order to obtain fuel from defendants.

[7]   *Bonelli v. Volkswagen of America, Inc,* 421 NW2d 213 (1988) is distinguishable from the case at bar. In *Bonelli,* there was ample evidence presented to demonstrate the defendants' active conduct in inducing or causing a breach or termination of the plaintiff's business relationship. . . . Thus, in *Bonelli,* there was evidence that the defendants unilaterally and knowingly appropriated to themselves the benefits of the plaintiff's exclusive contractual rights. Here, however, as previously stated, there was no evidence that defendants engaged in any conduct that began the station owner's breach. Instead, defendants merely operated the business, and it was the station owners that initiated contact with defendants regarding their price of gasoline, and the station owners that requested deliveries of the product.

(b)   Reconsider the facts of (a) above. Assume further that, along with their regular advertisements, defendants send additional discounts and other promotional information to Knight's largest customer, Ajax, even though defendants know that Ajax is under contract to purchase from Knight. These additional discounts and other promotional information are sent only to Ajax and not to any other service station operator. As a result of this material, Ajax breaches its contract with Knight and purchases the products from defendants instead. What result under § 766 when Knight sues the defendants for interference with the Ajax contract? *See id.* § 766 cmt. m.

(c)   Assume that Customer has purchased raw materials from Supplier for years. Upon hearing that Supplier has entered into a contract with Enemy, Customer ceases to buy from Supplier. When Supplier asks Customer why the purchases have ceased, Customer responds that the reason is Supplier's contract with Enemy. Supplier then breaks the contract with Enemy to regain Customer's business. What result under § 766 when Enemy sues Customer for interference with the Enemy-Supplier contract? *See id.* § 766 cmt. l.

(d)   Assume instead that, upon hearing that Supplier has entered into a contract with Enemy, Customer calls Supplier and states that he will no longer purchase any raw materials from Supplier unless Supplier stops doing business with Enemy. Supplier then breaks the contract with Enemy to maintain the relationship with Customer. What result under § 766 when Enemy sues Customer for interference with the Enemy-Supplier contract? *See id.* § 766 cmt. l.

2.   INTERFERING WITH THE PLAINTIFF'S PERFORMANCE

NESLER V. FISHER & CO.
452 N.W.2d 191 (Iowa 1990)

LARSON, JUSTICE.

Ferd Nesler sued Fisher and Company, Inc., and Plastic Center, Inc., for interference with existing ... contracts ... based on Restatement (Second) of Torts [section] 766A. ... He recovered compensatory damages of $576,476 and punitive damages of $100,000; however, the district court granted the defendants' motion for judgment notwithstanding the verdict on the ground of insufficient evidence on the key elements of his claims. We reverse and remand.

In our review of a trial court ruling on a motion for judgment notwithstanding the verdict, the question is whether the evidence, when viewed in the light most favorable to the plaintiff, was sufficient to generate a jury question.

When viewed in that light, the evidence reveals the following events. In 1981, Nesler purchased a building in downtown Dubuque for the purpose of renovation and leasing to commercial and governmental tenants. His plan was to syndicate the building by selling shares to investors at a profit and to later manage the building for a fee. Within a year, Nesler received tentative commitments from several county agencies to relocate their offices to the refurbished building, which was to be called Nesler Centre. These commitments were subject to the approval of the Dubuque County Board of Supervisors.

Louis Pfohl, an attorney in New York City and an owner of substantial property in Dubuque, was president of the defendant corporations, which owned space previously leased to the county. After learning that the board of supervisors was considering the approval of relocation of the county offices to the Nesler Centre, Pfohl dropped his rental to a figure below what Nesler had offered.

The board of supervisors, in October 1982, approved the proposed move. Twelve county agencies, all of which had either been occupants of buildings owned by the defendants or interested in leasing from them, decided to locate at the Nesler Centre. Pfohl, angry at the action by the board of supervisors, predicted that Nesler would not complete his renovation on time and offered to bet each of the supervisors $1000 on it. Pfohl also stated that Nesler would "pay" for taking his tenants.

Shortly after the board's approval of the office relocations, Pfohl sued the board, claiming that it was required by law to accept his rental bid, which was slightly lower than Nesler's. The action was summarily dismissed by the trial court, and Pfohl's corporations appealed. We ruled [in 1985] that the statutory requirements for accepting low bids did not apply to rentals.

There was substantial evidence that Pfohl began a strategy of repeated trips to the Nesler Centre, then under reconstruction, and to the city building department for the purpose of pressuring the building inspector to take action against the project. The effect was to impede the progress of the restoration of Nesler Centre.

There was also evidence that Pfohl persuaded one of his tenants, Handicapped Persons, Inc., to file a lawsuit against Nesler and several government agencies to challenge the failure of the Nesler Centre to provide adequate handicapped access. Pfohl's attorney brought the action on behalf of Handicapped Persons without charge to it. This case, which was the only work that Pfohl's attorney had ever done for Handicapped Persons, was dismissed on the pleadings. The jury could infer that the suit was encouraged, and paid for, by the defendants.

Throughout all of this time, local news media reported on the inspections and the alleged building code violations. People in the community began to express doubts about the Nesler Centre and about the problems Nesler was having in completing the project. Nesler claims the effect of this was to undermine confidence in his project, leading to his failure to finance it through a bank loan or syndication.

Nesler alleged that, had it not been for the interruptions caused by Pfohl, the project would have been substantially completed on time. He testified that, prior to the problems he experienced over the Nesler Centre, he had been a successful real estate developer and had never experienced problems with syndicating or financing similar projects.

Potential investors told Nesler that they were concerned about [Pfohl's] lawsuit against the county board of supervisors and [the possibility that Nesler] would lose his tenants. Investors were also concerned about the Handicapped Persons suit, fearing that an adverse result might affect the income for the project.

The Dubuque Bank and Trust, which had loaned Nesler $450,000 for the project in March of 1983, refused to provide further financing when his plan to syndicate ran into problems. The bank told Nesler that it was because of the lawsuits. When potential investors and the bank withdrew from the project, Nesler had no alternative but to deed his equity in the Nesler Centre to the bank. As a result, he claims he lost a substantial amount of money that he would have obtained on its sale, that he lost potential management fees, and that he suffered severe emotional distress. The jury apparently agreed.

I.   *The Judgment Notwithstanding the Verdict.*

In granting the defendants' motion for judgment notwithstanding the verdict, the district court stated: "The court has been most reluctant to grant this motion, because it is convinced, as was the jury, that the defendants, acting through their president [Pfohl], were clearly motivated by an intention to harm plaintiff in some way." Despite this reluctance, the judgment for the plaintiff was set aside.

A.   *Interference with existing contracts.* We first address the judgment notwithstanding the verdict on Nesler's claim for interference with an existing contract under Restatement (Second) of Torts section 766A. Nesler had two types of existing contracts as to which he claimed interference: his contract to purchase the building and his lease agreements with future tenants. In setting aside Nesler's judgment on this claim, the court observed that Nesler had introduced no evidence of interference because the owners of the building which Nesler was buying on contract . . . and the potential tenants of the Nesler Centre were still willing to perform, even after the acts of the defendants had occurred.

Nesler contends that this was error because his claim was based on intentional interference with *his* ability to perform, not the ability of the other contract parties, *i.e.,* the sellers under Nesler's land contract and the potential lessees of Nesler Centre. Nesler contends that the court's ruling shows that it confused Restatement section 766A, on which his claim was based, with section 766, which is not involved.

Restatement (Second) of Torts section 766 provides:

> One who intentionally and improperly interferes with the performance of a contract (except a contract to marry) between another and a third person by inducing or otherwise causing the *third person* not to perform the contract, is subject to liability to the other for the pecuniary loss resulting to the other from the failure of the *third person* to perform the contract.

(Emphasis added.) Section 766A of the Restatement applies to different parties. It provides:

> One who intentionally and improperly interferes with the performance of a contract (except a contract to marry) between another and a third person, by preventing *the other* [here Nesler] from performing the contract or causing his performance to be more expensive or burdensome, is subject to liability to the other for the pecuniary loss resulting to him.

(Emphasis added.)

The court apparently had section 766A in mind when it charged the jury, in Instruction 11, that "the interference [claimed] prevented *Nesler* from performing the contract to buy the Nesler Centre and caused Nesler to lose the benefit of the leases of space in the Nesler Centre." (Emphasis added.)

Also, Nesler's evidence was aimed at liability under section 766A, not section 766. His evidence was that, by reason of the actions of Pfohl and his corporations, *Nesler* was prevented from completing payment on the contract for the purchase of the building, on which he still owed a substantial amount, and from completing the contracts with his potential lessees. He did not show, or even contend, that the contract sellers or his potential lessees were prevented from performance.

In this case, there was substantial evidence that the defendants' actions, including the lawsuits, the building department inspections, the publicity, and the resulting loss of investor and bank confidence prevented Nesler's own performance of the contract and lease agreements. This is the gist of an action under section 766A. It is immaterial in a claim under section 766A whether other parties were prevented from performance. The Restatement explains the distinction:

> This Section [766A] is concerned only with the actor's intentional interference with the plaintiff's performance of his

own contract, either by preventing that performance or making it more expensive or burdensome. It is to be contrasted with § 766, which states the rule for the actor's intentional interference with a third person's performance of his existing contract with the plaintiff.

Restatement (Second) of Torts § 766A, comment *a*.

Because there was substantial evidence of interference with Nesler's own performance, it was error to enter a judgment notwithstanding the verdict.

. . . .

NOTES & QUESTIONS

(1)   Consider § 766A of the Second Restatement. How does it differ from § 766?

(2)   Why was a § 766 claim unavailable in *Nesler*? Why was a § 766A claim available in *Nesler*? Was Nesler's § 766A claim based on the defendants' "preventing [Nesler] from performing the contract" or "causing [Nesler's] performance to be more expensive or burdensome"?

(3)   What sorts of conduct can make the performance of a contract more "expensive or burdensome"? The Second Restatement gives the following example: "Thus if the plaintiff is under a contract to keep a highway in repair, a defendant who intentionally inflicts additional expense upon him by damaging the highway is subject to liability under this Section." *Id.* § 766A cmt. g. Further examples might include depriving the plaintiff of needed supplies or labor, such that performance can only occur with higher-priced substitutes; causing a delay in the plaintiff's ability to complete a transaction through groundless assertions of contractual or other rights; or making it more difficult for the plaintiff to get to the place of performance.

(4)   Not all courts recognize a claim under § 766A. In *Price v. Sorrell*, 784 P.2d 614 (Wyo. 1989), for example, the court declined to adopt § 766A even though it had previously adopted § 766 and § 766B:

> The difference between §§ 766 and 766A is substantial and significant. Where § 766 requires non-performance which includes a breach of the contract for liability to attach, § 766A requires, not a breach or non-performance, but only that performance became more expensive and burdensome. We are convinced that such an element of proof is too speculative and subject to abuse to provide a meaningful basis for a cause of action. The breach or non-performance of a contract, or the loss of a prospective contractual relation, is a reasonably bright line that reduces the potential for abuse of the causes of action defined by §§ 766 and 766B.

Id. at 615–16; *see also St. Louis Convention & Visitors Comm'n v. Nat'l Football League*, 154 F.3d 851, 865 (8th Cir. 1998) ("CVC contends, however, that the NFL can be liable for tortious interference even without a breach if it caused the performance of the contract to be more burdensome and expensive, citing Restatement (Second) of Torts, § 766A. CVC points to no Missouri authority which has recognized this theory, and a federal court ruling on a point of state law is obligated to follow the law as announced by that state's highest court. To adopt CVC's theory would be contrary to the Missouri requirement that a plaintiff prove that the defendant induce a breach of contract.").

What does the *Price* court mean when it states that the "more expensive or burdensome" requirement is "too speculative and subject to abuse"? The court does not explain itself, but consider the observations of one commentator:

> Interference torts are always formulated broadly, but the rule in § 766A may be broader than many courts will accept. Given that wrongfulness of interference lies in the eye of the beholder and that interference is intentional if the defendant is substantially certain that it will result from his acts, thousands of acts could intentionally interfere with the plaintiff's contract relations by making the contract more difficult to perform. Even the bus driver who sleeps late one morning might be intentionally interfering with his passengers' performance of their employment contracts. No court would hold the driver liable, but that merely shows that liability can not well be based upon the logic of § 766A.

DAN B. DOBBS, THE LAW OF TORTS § 448, at 1270 (2000).

(5) Some courts have criticized § 766A on different grounds. While the threat of a § 766 interference claim may be beneficial because it encourages voluntary bargaining transactions between the third party and the promisee (see note 5 after *Lumley*), that benefit is absent from a § 766A claim:

> However, in the § 766A "hindrance" case, this "bargain-forcing" justification appears absent. Imposition of liability under this theory does not encourage the third party to bargain with the promisee. In cases where a third-party's conduct "burdens" but does not prevent the plaintiff-promisor's performance, plaintiff's performance is rendered more expensive. The question becomes not whether plaintiff will perform but rather at what cost. This dispute does not involve the promisee.

Windsor Securities, Inc. v. Hartford Life Ins. Co., 986 F.2d 655, 661–62 (3d Cir. 1993).

Moreover, because § 766A claims will frequently involve independently tortious conduct against the plaintiff, the need for a distinct interference action has been questioned:

> In cases where plaintiff's performance is prevented, the third party's actions are directed at the plaintiff-promisor. Yet where the defendant prevents plaintiff's performance, plaintiff will

presumably not be a willing participant. Generally, such cases will involve force, fraud, or other independently actionable conduct; adverse effects on contract rights will become an element of damages subject only to the usual limitations of causation, mitigation, and reasonable certainty. As Professor Prosser points out,

> *[t]he bulk of the cases involving interference as distinct from inducement involve ... physical interference with person or property and also involve the commission of some independent tort*, as where the defendant interferes with the plaintiff's rights by converting goods to which the plaintiff was entitled under the contract, or commits an injurious falsehood of the kind sometimes called slander of title. Methods tortious in themselves are of course unjustified and liability is appropriately imposed where the plaintiff's contract rights are invaded by violence, threats and intimidation, defamation, misrepresentation, unfair competition, bribery and the like. Constitutional violations have been put in the same category. *Thus in many cases interference with contract is not so much a theory of liability in itself as it is an element of damage resulting from the commission of some other tort, or the breach of some other contract.*

W. Page Keeton et al., *Prosser and Keeton on the Law of Torts* § 129, at 992 (5th ed. 1984) (footnotes omitted) (emphasis added).

Thus, in non-inducement cases, expanding the tortious interference principle to recognize a § 766A "hindrance" cause of action may duplicate protection already afforded through tort and contract. But duplication comes at a cost. It risks chilling socially valuable conduct and creates new liability of uncertain dimensions. Some commentators have criticized the amorphous nature of the tortious interference principle, warning that its expansion is ill-conceived, threatening both fairness and efficiency. These concerns counsel some caution in expanding tortious interference liability.

Windsor Securities, 986 F.2d at 662–63.

Does this latter criticism apply to the facts of *Nesler*? That is, in *Nesler*, did the § 766A claim "duplicate protection already afforded through tort and contract"?

B. INTENTIONAL INTERFERENCE WITH PROSPECTIVE CONTRACT

DELLA PENNA V. TOYOTA MOTOR SALES, U.S.A., INC.

902 P.2d 740 (Cal. 1995)

ARABIAN, JUSTICE.

We granted review to reexamine, in light of divergent rulings from the Court of Appeal and a doctrinal evolution among other state high courts, the elements of the tort variously known as interference with "prospective economic advantage," "prospective contractual relations," or "prospective economic relations," and the allocation of the burdens of proof between the parties to such an action. We conclude that those Court of Appeal opinions requiring proof of a so-called "wrongful act" as a component of the cause of action, and allocating the burden of proving it to the plaintiff, are the better reasoned decisions; we accordingly adopt that analysis as our own, disapproving language in prior opinions of this court to the contrary. Such a requirement, incorporating the views of several other jurisdictions, much of the Restatement Second of Torts, the better reasoned decisions of the Court of Appeal, and the views of leading academic authorities, sensibly redresses the balance between providing a remedy for predatory economic behavior and keeping legitimate business competition outside litigative bounds. We do not in this case, however, go beyond approving the requirement of a showing of wrongfulness as part of the plaintiff's case; the case, if any, to be made for adopting refinements to that element of the tort—requiring the plaintiff to prove, for example, that the defendant's conduct amounted to an independently tortious act, or was a species of anticompetitive behavior proscribed by positive law, or was motivated by unalloyed malice—can be considered on another day, and in another case.

In this case, after the trial court modified the standard jury instruction to require the plaintiff automobile dealer to show that defendant Toyota's interference with his business relationships was "wrongful," the jury returned a verdict for Toyota. The Court of Appeal reversed the ensuing judgment and ordered a new trial on the ground that plaintiff's burden of proof did not encompass proof of a "wrongful" act and that the modified jury instruction was therefore erroneous. Given our conclusion that the plaintiff's burden *does* include proof that the defendant's conduct was wrongful by some measure other than an interference with the plaintiff's interest itself, we now reverse the Court of Appeal and direct that the judgment of the trial court be affirmed.

I

John Della Penna, an automobile wholesaler doing business as Pacific Motors, brought this action for damages against Toyota Motor Sales, U.S.A., Inc., and its Lexus division, alleging that certain business conduct of defendants both violated provisions of the Cartwright Act, California's state antitrust statute (Bus. & Prof.Code, § 16700 et seq.), and constituted an intentional interference with his economic relations. The impetus for Della Penna's suit arose out of the 1989 introduction into the American luxury car market of Toyota's Lexus automobile. Prior to introducing the Lexus, the evidence at trial showed, both the manufacturer, Toyota Motor Corporation, and defendant, the American distributor, had been concerned at the possibility that a resale market might develop for the Lexus in Japan. Even though the car was manufactured in Japan, Toyota's marketing strategy was to bar the vehicle's sale on the Japanese domestic market until after the American roll-out; even then, sales in Japan would only be under a different brand name, the "Celsior." Fearing that auto wholesalers in the United States might re-export Lexus models back to Japan for resale, and concerned that, with production and the availability of Lexus models in the American market limited, re-exports would jeopardize its fledgling network of American Lexus dealers, Toyota inserted in its dealership agreements a "no export" clause, providing that the dealer was "authorized to sell [Lexus automobiles] only to customers located in the United States. [Dealer] agrees that it will not sell [Lexus automobiles] for resale or use outside the United States. [Dealer] agrees to abide by any export policy established by [distributor]."

Following the introduction into the American market, it soon became apparent that some domestic Lexus units were being diverted for foreign sales, principally to Japan. To counter this effect, Toyota managers wrote to their retail dealers, reminding them of the "no-export" policy and explaining that exports for foreign resale could jeopardize the supply of Lexus automobiles available for the United States market. In addition, Toyota compiled a list of "offenders"—dealers and others believed by Toyota to be involved heavily in the developing Lexus foreign resale market—which it distributed to Lexus dealers in the United States. American Lexus dealers were also warned that doing business with those whose names appeared on the "offenders" list might lead to a series of graduated sanctions, from reducing a dealer's allocation to possible reevaluation of the dealer's franchise agreement.

During the years 1989 and 1990, plaintiff Della Penna did a profitable business as an auto wholesaler purchasing Lexus automobiles, chiefly from the Lexus of Stevens Creek retail outlet, at near retail price and exporting them to Japan for resale. By late 1990, however, plaintiff's sources began to dry up, primarily as a result of the "offenders list."

Stevens Creek ceased selling models to plaintiff; gradually other sources declined to sell to him as well.

In February 1991, plaintiff filed this lawsuit against Toyota Motors, U.S.A., Inc., alleging . . . interference with his economic relationship with Lexus retail dealers. . . . [At trial, the interference] action went to the jury . . . under the standard [Book of Approved Jury Instructions ("BAJI")] applicable to such claims with one significant exception. At the request of defendant and over plaintiff's objection, the trial judge modified BAJI No. 7.82—the basic instruction identifying the elements of the tort and indicating the burden of proof—to require plaintiff to prove that defendant's alleged interfering conduct was "wrongful."[1]

The jury returned a divided verdict, nine to three, in favor of Toyota. After Della Penna's motion for a new trial was denied, he appealed. In an unpublished disposition, the Court of Appeal unanimously reversed the trial court's judgment, ruling that a plaintiff alleging intentional interference with economic relations is not required to establish "wrongfulness" as an element of its prima facie case, and that it was prejudicial error for the trial court to have read the jury an amended instruction to that effect. The Court of Appeal remanded the case to the trial court for a new trial; we then granted Toyota's petition for review and now reverse.

II

A

Although legal historians have traced the origins of the so-called "interference torts" as far back as the Roman law, the proximate historical impetus for their modern development lay in mid-19th century English common law. The opinion of the Queen's Bench in *Lumley v. Gye* (1853) 2 El. & Bl. 216, a case that has become a standard in torts casebooks, is widely cited as the origin of the two torts—interference with contract and its sibling, interference with prospective economic relations[2]—in the form in which they have come down to us. The plaintiff

---

[1] The standard instruction governing "intentional interference with prospective economic advantage," BAJI No. 7.82, describes the essential elements of the claim as (1) an economic relationship between the plaintiff and another, "containing a probable future economic benefit or advantage to plaintiff," (2) defendant's knowledge of the existence of the relationship, (3) that defendant "intentionally engaged in acts or conduct designed to interfere with or disrupt" the relationship, (4) actual disruption, and (5) damage to the plaintiff as a result of defendant's acts. The modification sought by defendant and adopted by the trial court consisted [of] adding the word "wrongful" in element (3) between the words "in" and "acts." The trial court also read to the jury *plaintiff's* special jury instruction defining the "wrongful acts" required to support liability as conduct "outside the realm of legitimate business transactions. . . . Wrongfulness may lie in the method used or by virtue of an improper motive."

[2] Throughout this opinion, in an effort to avoid both cumbersome locutions and clumsy acronyms ("IIPEA"), we use the phrase "interference with economic relations" to refer to the tort generally known as "intentional interference with prospective contractual or economic relations" and to distinguish it from the cognate form, "intentional interference with *contract*."

owned the Queen's Theatre, at which operas were presented. He contracted for the services of a soprano, Johanna Wagner, to perform in various entertainments between April 15 and July 15, with the stipulation that Miss Wagner would not perform elsewhere during that time without his permission.

In an action on the case, the theater owner alleged that Gye, the owner of a rival theater, knowing of the Wagner-Lumley agreement, "maliciously" interfered with the contract by "enticing" Wagner to abandon her agreement with Lumley and appear at Gye's theater. Gye's demurrer to the complaint was overruled by the trial court, a ruling that was affirmed by the justices of the Queen's Bench on the then somewhat novel grounds that (1) "enticing" someone to leave his or her employment was not limited to disrupting the relationship between master and servant but applied to a "dramatic artiste" such as Miss Wagner, and (2) "wrongfully and maliciously, or, which is the same thing, with notice, interrupt[ing]" a personal service contract, regardless of the means the defendant employed, was an actionable wrong.

The opinion in *Lumley* dealt, of course, with conduct intended to induce the *breach* of an *existing* contract, not conduct intended to prevent or persuade others *not to contract* with the plaintiff. That such an interference with *prospective* economic relations might itself be tortious was confirmed by the Queen's Bench over the next 40 years. In *Temperton v. Russell* (1893) 1 Q.B. 715 (*Temperton*), a labor union, embroiled in a dispute with a firm of builders, announced what today would be called a secondary boycott, intended to force a resolution of the union's grievances by pressuring suppliers of the builder to cease furnishing him construction materials. A failure to comply with the union's boycott demands, suppliers were warned, would result in union pressure on those who bought *their* supplies not to deal with *them*.

One such supplier of the builder, Temperton, sued the union's leadership, alleging that his business had been injured by breaches of supply contracts and the refusal of others to do business with him, all as a result of the union's threats. A unanimous Queen's Bench upheld the jury's verdict for the plaintiff, reasoning in part on the authority of *Lumley v. Gye,* that in the words of Lord Esher, the Master of the Rolls, "the distinction . . . between the claim for inducing persons to break contracts already entered into . . . and . . . inducing persons not to enter into contracts . . . can [not] prevail."

"There was the same wrongful intent in both cases, wrongful because malicious," Lord Esher wrote. "There was the same kind of injury to the plaintiff. It seems rather a fine distinction to say that, where a defendant maliciously induces a person not to carry out a contract already made with the plaintiff and so injures the plaintiff, it is actionable, but where he injures the plaintiff by maliciously preventing a person from entering into a contract with the plaintiff, which he would otherwise have entered into, it is not actionable."

As a number of courts and commentators have observed, the keystone of the liability imposed in *Lumley* and *Temperton*, to judge from the opinions of the justices, appears to have been the "malicious" intent of a defendant in enticing an employee to breach her contract with the plaintiff, and damaging the business of one who refused to cooperate with the union in achieving its bargaining aims. While some have doubted whether the use of the word "malicious" amounted to anything more than an intent to commit an act, knowing it would harm the plaintiff, Dean Keeton, assessing the state of the tort as late as 1984, remarked that "[w]ith intent to interfere as the usual basis of the action, the cases have turned almost entirely upon the defendant's motive or purpose and the means by which he has sought to accomplish it. As in the cases of interference with contract, any manner of intentional invasion of the plaintiff's interests may be sufficient if the purpose is not a proper one." (Prosser and Keeton on Torts (5th ed. 1984) Interference with Prospective Advantage, § 130, p. 1009.)

It was, legal historians have suggested, this early accent on the defendant's "intentionality" that was responsible for allying the interference torts with their remote relatives, intentional torts of a quite different order—battery, for example, or false imprisonment. More than one account of the rise of the tort has relied on Lord Bowen's statement in an interference with contract case that "intentionally to do that which is calculated in the ordinary course of events to damage, and which does, in fact, damage another in that person's property or trade, is actionable if done without just cause or excuse." (*Mogul Steamship Co. v. McGregor, Gow & Co.* (1889) 23 Q.B.D. 598, 613.)

One consequence of this superficial kinship was the assimilation to the interference torts of the pleading and burden of proof requirements of the "true" intentional torts: the requirement that the plaintiff need only allege a so-called "prima facie tort" by showing the defendant's awareness of the economic relation, a deliberate interference with it, and the plaintiff's resulting injury. By this account of the matter—the traditional view of the torts and the one adopted by the first Restatement of Torts—the burden then passed to the defendant to demonstrate that its conduct was *privileged*, that is, "justified" by a recognized defense such as the protection of others or, more likely in this context, the defendant's own competitive business interests.

These and related features of the economic relations tort and the requirements surrounding its proof and defense led, however, to calls for a reexamination and reform as early as the 1920's. Tracing the origins and the current status of the two interference torts in 1923, Francis Sayre concluded that "a somewhat uncertain law has resulted. [¶] ... [¶] ... Courts still punctiliously repeat the well-known formula which requires 'malice,' or 'without just cause' ... as one of the requirements of the tort; but there has been such a lack of agreement as to what constitutes 'malice' or 'absence of justification' that such words are becoming little more than empty phrases.... Is it not time to formulate the problem of what these worn phrases mean?" (Sayre, *Inducing Breach of Contract*, 36 Harv.L.Rev. at pp. 672, 674–675.) The nature of the wrong itself seemed to many unduly vague, inviting suit and hampering the presentation of coherent defenses. More critically in the view of others, the procedural effects of applying the prima facie tort principle to what is essentially a business context led to even more untoward consequences.

Because the plaintiff's initial burden of proof was such a slender one, amounting to no more than showing the defendant's conscious act and plaintiff's economic injury, critics argued that legitimate business competition could lead to time consuming and expensive lawsuits (not to speak of potential liability) by a rival, based on conduct that was regarded by the commercial world as both commonplace and appropriate. The "black letter" rules of the Restatement of Torts surrounding the elements and proof of the tort, some complained, might even suggest to "foreign lawyers reading the Restatement as an original matter [that] the whole competitive order of American industry is prima facie illegal." (Statement of Professor Carl Auerbach at ALI Proceedings, quoted in Perlman, *Interference with Contract and Other Economic Expectancies: A Clash of Tort and Contract Doctrine* (1982) 49 U.Chi.L.Rev. 61, 79, fn. 89; see also Myers, *The Differing Treatment of Efficiency and Competition in Antitrust and Tortious Interference Law* (1993) 77 Minn.L.Rev. 1097, 1122 ["In an economic system founded upon the principle of free competition, competitors should not be liable in tort for seeking a legitimate business advantage."].)

Calls for a reformulation of both the elements and the means of establishing the economic relations tort reached a height around the time the Restatement Second of Torts was being prepared for publication and are reflected in its departures from its predecessor's version. Acknowledging criticism, the American Law Institute discarded the prima facie tort requirement of the first Restatement. A new provision, section 766B, required that the defendant's conduct be "improper," and adopted a multifactor "balancing" approach, identifying seven factors for the trier of fact to weigh in determining a defendant's liability. The Restatement Second of Torts, however, declined to take a position on the issue of which of the parties bore the burden of proof, relying on the "considerable disagreement on who has the burden of pleading and proving certain matters" and the observation that "the law in this area has not fully congealed but is still in a formative stage." In addition, the Restatement Second provided that a defendant might escape liability by showing that his conduct was justifiable and did *not* include the use of "wrongful means." (*Id.*, §§ 768–771.)

B

In the meantime, however, an increasing number of state high courts had traveled well beyond the Second Restatement's reforms by redefining and otherwise recasting the elements of the economic relations tort and the burdens surrounding its proof and defenses. In *Top Service Body Shop, Inc. v. Allstate Ins. Co.* (1978) 283 Or. 201, 582 P.2d 1365 (*Top Service*), the Oregon Supreme Court, assessing this "most fluid and rapidly growing tort," noted that "efforts to consolidate both recognized and unsettled lines of development into a general theory of 'tortious interference' have brought to the surface the difficulties of defining the elements of so general a tort without sweeping within its terms a wide variety of socially very different conduct."

Recognizing the force of these criticisms, the court went on to hold in *Top Service* that a claim of interference with economic relations "is made out when interference resulting in injury to another is *wrongful by some measure beyond the fact of the interference itself.* Defendant's liability may arise from improper motives or from the use of improper means. They may be wrongful by reason of a statute or other regulation, or a recognized rule of common law, or perhaps an established standard of a trade or profession. No question of privilege arises unless the interference would be wrongful but for the privilege; it becomes an issue *only if the acts charged would be tortious on the part of an unprivileged defendant.*"

Four years later, the views of the Oregon Supreme Court in *Top Service* were adopted by the Utah Supreme Court. In *Leigh Furniture and Carpet Co. v. Isom* (Utah 1982) 657 P.2d 293, that court underlined the same concerns that had moved the Oregon Supreme Court in *Top Service:* "The problem with the prima facie tort approach is that basing liability on a mere showing that defendant intentionally interfered with plaintiff's prospective economic relations makes actionable all sorts of contemporary examples of otherwise legitimate persuasion, such as efforts to persuade others not to . . . engage in certain activities, or deal with certain entities. The major issue in the controversy—justification for the defendant's conduct—is left to be resolved on the affirmative defense of privilege. In short, the prima facie approach to the tort of interference with prospective economic relations requires too little of the plaintiff."

The Utah Supreme Court went on, however, to reject the alternative, multifactor approach adopted by the Second Restatement: "We concur in the *Restatement (Second)*'s rejection of the prima facie tort approach because it leaves too much uncertainty about the requirements for a recognized privilege and the defendant's burden of pleading and proving these and other matters. But we also reject the *Restatement (Second)*'s definition of the tort because of its complexity. We seek a better alternative." That alternative, the court concluded, was the one advanced by the Oregon Supreme Court in *Top Service*, a "middle ground" that requires "the plaintiff to allege and prove more than the prima facie tort, but not to negate all defenses of privilege."

Over the past decade or so, close to a majority of the high courts of American jurisdictions have imported into the economic relations tort variations on the *Top Service* line of reasoning, explicitly approving a rule that requires the plaintiff in such a suit to plead and prove the alleged interference was either "wrongful," "improper," "illegal," "independently tortious" or some variant on these formulations. . . .

III

In California, the development of the economic relations tort has paralleled its evolution in other jurisdictions. . . .

. . . .

These developments, of course, closely reflect a nearly concurrent change in views both within the American Law Institute and in other jurisdictions. In the face of those twin lines of development, we are thus presented with the opportunity to consider whether to expressly reconstruct the formal elements of the interference with economic relations tort to achieve a closer alignment with the practice of the trial courts, emerging views within the Court of Appeal, the rulings of many other state high courts, and the critiques of leading commentators. We believe that we should.

IV

In searching for a means to recast the elements of the economic relations tort and allocate the associated burdens of proof, we are guided by an overmastering concern articulated by high courts of other jurisdictions and legal commentators: The need to draw and enforce a sharpened distinction between claims for the tortious disruption of an *existing* contract and claims that a *prospective* contractual or economic relationship has been interfered with by the defendant. Many of the cases do in fact acknowledge a greater array of justificatory defenses against claims of interference with prospective relations. Still, in our view and that of several other courts and commentators, the notion that the two torts are analytically unitary and derive from a common principle sacrifices practical wisdom to theoretical insight, promoting the idea that the interests invaded are of nearly equal dignity. They are not.

The courts provide a damage remedy against third party conduct intended to disrupt an existing contract precisely because the exchange of promises resulting in such a formally cemented economic relationship is deemed worthy of protection from interference by a stranger to the agreement. Economic relationships short of contractual, however, should stand on a different legal footing as far as the potential for tort liability is reckoned. Because ours is a culture firmly wedded to the social rewards of commercial contests, the law usually takes care to draw lines of legal liability in a way that maximizes areas of competition free of legal penalties.

A doctrine that blurs the analytical line between interference with an existing business contract and interference with commercial relations *less* than contractual is one that invites both uncertainty in conduct and unpredictability of its legal effect. The notion that inducing the breach of an existing contract is simply a subevent of the "more inclusive" class of acts that interfere with economic relations, while perhaps theoretically unobjectionable, has been mischievous as a practical matter. Our courts should, in short, firmly distinguish the two kinds of business contexts, bringing a greater solicitude to those relationships that have ripened into agreements, while recognizing that relationships short of that subsist in a zone where the rewards and risks of competition are dominant.

Beyond that, we need not tread today. It is sufficient to dispose of the issue before us in this case by holding that a plaintiff seeking to recover for alleged interference with prospective economic relations has the burden of pleading and proving that the defendant's interference was wrongful "by some measure beyond the fact of the interference itself." (*Top Service, supra,* 582 P.2d at p. 1371.) It follows that the trial court did not commit error when it modified BAJI No. 7.82 to require the jury to find that defendant's interference was "wrongful." And because the instruction defining "wrongful conduct" given the jury by the trial court was offered by plaintiff himself, we have no occasion to review its sufficiency in this case. The question of whether additional refinements to the plaintiff's pleading and proof burdens merit adoption by California courts—questions embracing the precise scope of "wrongfulness," or whether a "disinterested malevolence," in Justice Holmes's words (*American Bank & Trust Co. v. Federal Reserve Bank* (1921) 256 U.S. 350, 358) is an actionable interference in itself, or whether the underlying policy justification for the tort, the efficient allocation of social resources, justifies including as actionable conduct that is recognized as anticompetitive under established state and federal positive law—are matters that can await another day and a more appropriate case.

CONCLUSION

We hold that a plaintiff seeking to recover for an alleged interference with prospective contractual or economic relations must plead and prove as part of its case-in-chief that the defendant not only knowingly interfered with the plaintiff's expectancy, but engaged in conduct that was wrongful by some legal measure other than the fact of interference itself. The judgment of the Court of Appeal is reversed and the cause is remanded with directions to affirm the judgment of the trial court.

NOTES & QUESTIONS

(1) "Lumley v. Gye and the succeeding cases laid emphasis upon the existence of the contract. . . . The subsequent development of the law has extended the principle to interference with advantageous economic relations even where they have not been cemented by contract, and the liability for inducing breach of contract now is regarded as merely one instance of protection against such unjustified interference." W. PAGE KEETON ET AL., PROSSER AND KEETON ON TORTS § 129, at 981 (5th ed. 1984).

(2) Section 766B of the Second Restatement recognizes the tort of intentional interference with prospective contract: "One who intentionally and improperly interferes with another's prospective contractual relation (except a contract to marry) is subject to liability to the other for the pecuniary harm resulting from loss of the benefits of the relation, whether the interference consists of (a) inducing or otherwise causing a third person not to enter into or continue the prospective relation or (b) preventing the other from acquiring or continuing the prospective relation." Do the facts of *Della Penna* fall within the scope of § 766B?

(3) As mentioned in *Della Penna*, in the ALI proceedings surrounding the tortious interference provisions, Professor Auerbach opined that "foreign lawyers reading the Restatement as an original matter would find it astounding that the whole competitive order of American industry is prima facie illegal." What does this statement mean? How does it relate to the statement in *Della Penna* that "the plaintiff's initial burden of proof was such a slender one"? How does the *Della Penna* court resolve these concerns? *See also* RESTATEMENT (SECOND) OF TORTS § 768 (1979) (discussing competition).

(4) Suppose the *Della Penna* court was considering the elements of a tortious interference with *existing* contract claim. Do you think the court would similarly rule that the plaintiff "has the burden of pleading and proving that the interference was wrongful by some measure beyond the fact of the interference itself"?

(5) The jury instruction cited in *Della Penna* stated that interference with a relationship "containing a probable future economic benefit or advantage to plaintiff" was an element of an intentional interference with prospective contract claim. Many articulations of the tort expressly include a similar element, and even if not express, such an element is presumably implied in the definition of a prospective contract. *See, e.g., Nathanson v. Medical College of Pennsylvania*, 926 F.2d 1368, 1392 (3d Cir. 1991) ("In order to prove the existence of a prospective contractual relationship, [the plaintiff] must show that there was a 'reasonable probability' that she would have entered into a contract. . . ."); *Suprise v. DeKock*, 84 S.W.3d 378, 382

(Tex. App. 2002) ("The law does not require absolute certainty that a prospective contract would have been made were it not for the interference; it must reasonably appear so, in view of all of the circumstances."); *see also Thompson Coal Co. v. Pike Coal Co.*, 412 A.2d 466, 471 (Pa. 1979) ("Defining a 'prospective contractual relation' is admittedly problematic. To a certain extent, the term has an evasive quality, eluding precise definition. It is something less than a contractual right, something more than a mere hope.").

(6)   Unlike § 766A, the language of § 766B does not include liability for making the realization of a prospective contract more expensive or burdensome. Nevertheless, some courts have extended liability to cover such circumstances. *See, e.g., Kelly-Springfield Tire Co. v. D'Ambro*, 596 A.2d 867, 871 (Pa. Super. Ct. 1991) ("It also was not fatal to appellant's cause of action [for tortious interference with prospective business relations] that an agreement for the sale of the warehouse property was ultimately reached with National Life Insurance Company. The complaint contains averments that a resale was unnecessarily delayed by the interference of D'Ambro and Stradley, Ronon and that actual damage was caused thereby. This was sufficient.").

(7)   Although the interference torts typically address contractual relationships (either existing or prospective), there are cases extending the tortious interference doctrine to other forms of advantageous economic relations. *See, e.g., Harmon v. Harmon*, 404 A.2d 1020, 1023 (Me. 1979) (involving interference with the plaintiff's expected inheritance under his mother's will: "If the law protects a person from interference with an opportunity to receive a benefit by entering into contractual relations in the future, the same protection should be accorded to a person's opportunity to receive a benefit as a prospective legatee. The uncertainty attendant upon the expectancy is equivalent."); *id.* at 1024 ("We conclude that where a person can prove that, but for the tortious interference of another, he would in all likelihood have received a gift or a specific profit from a transaction, he is entitled to recover for the damages thereby done to him."); *Longo v. Reilly*, 114 A.2d 302, 305–06 (N.J. Super. Ct. App. Div. 1955) (involving interference with the plaintiff's election bid for union secretary); *see also* RESTATEMENT (SECOND) OF TORTS § 774B (1979) ("One who by fraud, duress or other tortious means intentionally prevents another from receiving from a third person an inheritance or gift that he would otherwise have received is subject to liability to the other for loss of the inheritance or gift.").

C. ESTABLISHING "IMPROPER" INTERFERENCE

LEIGH FURNITURE & CARPET CO. v. ISOM
657 P.2d 293 (Utah 1982)

OAKS, JUSTICE.

In 1970, Leigh Furniture and Carpet Co., a corporation, sold a furniture business in St. George to T. Richard Isom on a contract specifying a $20,000 down payment for immediate possession, with the balance of $60,000 at $500 per month plus interest for ten years.

In 1975, when the contract balance was $27,000, Leigh Furniture (hereafter "the Leigh Corporation") brought this action against Isom to repossess the business, terminate his interest under the contract, and obtain a deficiency judgment for any sums due after liquidation. Isom denied that he was in default under the agreement, alleged his tender and the Leigh Corporation's refusal to accept the sum due under the contract, and counterclaimed for $100,000 damages caused when the Corporation intentionally and maliciously forced him out of business and into bankruptcy. Isom also sought punitive damages.

The jury found for Isom in all respects, including compensatory damages of $65,000 and punitive damages of $35,000 on his counterclaim. The district court denied the Leigh Corporation's motion for judgment notwithstanding the verdict, which challenged the legal and evidentiary basis for the verdict on the counterclaim. However, the court reduced the punitive damages to $13,000, and, upon Isom's accepting that remittitur, also denied the Corporation's motion for a new trial on the amount of punitive damages. Judgment was thereupon entered on the verdict against the Leigh Corporation (reduced as to punitive damages). The Corporation took this appeal. . . .

The issues on this appeal are exclusively concerned with Isom's recovery on the counterclaim. They are: (1) whether Utah has a cause of action for intentional interference with prospective economic relations; and, if so, (2) whether that tort was proved on the facts of this case. . . .

I.   THE FACTS

. . . .

Leigh Furniture, a closely held family corporation, operated a main store in Cedar City and branch stores in Kanab and St. George. The principal owner and chief executive officer was W.S. "Dub" Leigh (hereafter "Leigh"). In 1969, Leigh decided to sell the St. George store. He contacted T. Richard Isom ("Isom"), a Utah native then living in Washington State but desirous of returning to Utah, as a possible buyer. Discussions ensued, and Isom moved to St. George and began working as an employee in the Leigh store. On May 14, 1970, Isom signed the contract to buy the St. George store from the Leigh Corporation. Isom agreed to maintain the inventory, together with cash and accounts receivable, at a level of at least $60,000, and to provide the Leigh Corporation with an inventory each quarter and a financial statement each month.

In the same document, the Leigh Corporation leased Isom the parking lot and the first floor of the building containing the store, but expressly retained the second floor of the building, which consisted of 17 apartments the Corporation had leased to others. As monthly rental, Isom agreed to pay 3% of his gross sales for the previous month, with a minimum of $500 per month the first year and $600 per month thereafter. The lease term was ten years, with an option to renew for an additional ten years.

The contract also granted Isom an option to purchase the entire building, including the upstairs apartments, exercisable once he had paid the $60,000 balance on his contract. The option price was to be determined at the time of exercise by a committee of three appraisers, one to be appointed by each party and a third to be chosen by the other two.

Finally, the contract provided that if Isom defaulted in payment or performance of any term and the default remained uncured for 60 days, the Leigh Corporation could cancel the agreement, repossess the merchandise and real property, and retain all payments and rents as liquidated damages.

For one year, relations between the contracting parties were peaceful, but in June and July of 1971, Leigh began to complain about the contract and to state that he wanted to sell the entire building but prospective buyers would not purchase it subject to Isom's long-term lease and option to buy. In a letter to Isom, Leigh complained that Isom was in default on his payments and was allowing his inventory to drop below $60,000. (Isom was behind in his payments at that time but was within the 60-day grace period in the contract and therefore was not in default.) At that same time, Leigh visited Isom in the store, verbally attacking him while he was with a customer and causing the customer to leave the store.

Beginning in July, 1971, Leigh, his wife, and the Corporation's bookkeeper, acting as the Leigh Corporation's agents, began a continuous pattern of visiting Isom at least once a week while he was working in his store, questioning him concerning his operation of the business, and making demands and accusations. In addition to the visits, Leigh wrote defendant letters criticizing various aspects of the business. In one week in the summer of 1971, Isom received four letters from Leigh, his wife, and his bookkeeper complaining about the furnace, the heat, and the delay in receiving the monthly financial statements. All of this conduct on Leigh's part had the cumulative effect of demoralizing and upsetting Isom and his employees, reducing their productivity, and impairing their ability to deal with the public and to conduct their business. [This type of conduct continued over the next few years. Leigh repeatedly interfered with Isom's business operations and customer relations, made unreasonable and contradictory demands on the business, and filed two groundless lawsuits against Isom. On several occasions, Leigh reiterated his regret at having granted Isom a long-term lease and stated that he wanted to get the property back.]

. . . .

On February 24, 1975, without notifying Isom of any default, Leigh filed the complaint in this case, seeking to repossess the premises and terminate Isom's interest under the contract. Three days later, unaware that the complaint had been filed, Isom tendered to Leigh the $27,000 balance due. He requested that Leigh give a receipt for the payment [and] appoint an appraiser to facilitate his exercise of the purchase option. . . .

. . . . Leigh never responded to Isom's tender of the remaining $27,000 . . . nor would he permit a sale of the property for its appraised value of $130,000. When confronted by Isom's attorney and accused of being recalcitrant so that Isom's business would fail and Leigh could reacquire the business and property, Leigh made no denial.

. . . . Isom declared bankruptcy shortly thereafter. . . . The record further indicates that through bankruptcy proceedings, the Leigh Corporation, as secured party, finally achieved its goal of reacquiring the business, including inventory, accounts receivable, and the leased premises.

II. INTERFERENCE WITH CONTRACT

Leigh Furniture first contends that Isom's recovery cannot be sustained as an interference with contract because the evidence showed no conduct which "intentionally and improperly interferes with the performance of a contract . . . between another and a third person by inducing or otherwise causing the third person not to perform the contract." *Restatement (Second) of Torts* § 766 (1979). In this case, the only contract in evidence was the contract between Isom and the Leigh Corporation. It is settled that one party to a contract cannot be liable for the tort of interference with contract for inducing a breach by himself or the other contracting party. [Having] failed to prove a cause of action for intentional interference with contract, we cannot sustain the verdict on that theory.

However, the right of action for interference with a specific contract is but one instance, rather than the total class, of protections against wrongful interference with advantageous economic relations. We therefore proceed to consider whether the jury's verdict for Isom can be sustained on the basis of the related tort of interference with prospective economic relations.

. . . .

III. INTERFERENCE WITH PROSPECTIVE ECONOMIC RELATIONS

A.   History and Elements of the Tort

The tort of intentional interference with prospective economic relations reaches beyond protection of an interest in an existing contract and protects a party's interest in prospective relationships of economic advantage not yet reduced to a formal contract (and perhaps not expected to be). Although previously faced with arguments or circumstances presenting the issue, we have never expressly resolved the question of whether Utah recognizes this tort. We now resolve that question, in the affirmative.

The plethora of decided cases and abundant literature on the tort of intentional interference with prospective economic relations has been helpful in our consideration. In summarizing the history of this tort, the *Restatement (Second) of Torts*, ch. 37, "Interference with Contract or Prospective Contractual Relation" (1979), observes that its elements are a curious blend of the principles of liability for intentional torts (in which the plaintiff proves a prima facie case of liability, subject to the defendant's proof of justification) and for negligent torts (in which the plaintiff must prove liability based on the interplay of various factors). The disagreement and confusion incident to this blend of intentional and negligent tort principles has produced two different approaches to the definition of this tort.

Influenced by the model of the intentional tort, many jurisdictions and the first *Restatement of Torts* define the tort of intentional interference with prospective economic relations as a prima facie tort, subject to proof of privilege as an affirmative defense. To recover, the plaintiff need only prove a prima facie case of liability, *i.e.*, that the defendant intentionally interfered with his prospective economic relations and caused him injury. As with other intentional torts, the burden of going forward then shifts to the defendant to demonstrate as an affirmative defense that under the circumstances his conduct, otherwise culpable, was justified and therefore privileged. . . .

The problem with the prima facie-tort approach is that basing liability on a mere showing that defendant intentionally interfered with plaintiff's prospective economic relations makes actionable all sorts of contemporary examples of otherwise legitimate persuasion, such as efforts to persuade others not to eat certain foods, use certain substances, engage in certain activities, or deal with certain entities. The major issue in the controversy—justification for the defendant's conduct—is left to be resolved on the affirmative defense of privilege. In short, the prima facie approach to the tort of interference with prospective economic relations requires too little of the plaintiff.

Under the second approach, which is modeled after other negligent torts, the plaintiff must prove liability based on the interplay of various factors. The *Restatement (Second) of Torts* now defines an actionable interference with prospective economic relations as an interference that is both "intentional" and "improper." *Id.* at § 766B. Under this approach, the trier of fact must determine whether the defendant's interference was "improper" by balancing and counterbalancing seven factors, including the interferor's motive, the nature of his conduct and interests, and the nature of the interests with which he has interfered. *Id.* at § 767. In those jurisdictions which have followed the negligence model, the plaintiff bears the burden of proving that in view of all of these factors the defendant's interference was improper. This obviously imposes a very significant burden on the plaintiff and magnifies the difficulty of resolving some contested issues on the pleadings. So far as we have been able to discover, only four states have specifically adopted the *Restatement (Second)* definition of the elements of this tort, though others have apparently applied some portion of the *Restatement* formulation in their own definitions.

In short, there is no generally acknowledged or satisfactory majority position on the definition of the elements of the tort of intentional interference with prospective economic relations. In its historical review, the *Restatement (Second) of Torts* states that "the law in this area has not fully congealed but is still in a formative stage" so that the "several forms of the tort . . . are often not distinguished by the courts, and cases have been cited among them somewhat indiscriminately." *Id.*, Introductory Note to ch. 37 at 5. We concur in the *Restatement (Second)*'s rejection of the prima facie tort approach because it leaves too much uncertainty about the requirements for a recognized privilege and the defendant's burden of pleading and proving these and other matters. *Id.* But we also reject the *Restatement (Second)*'s definition of the tort because of its complexity. We seek a better alternative.

Oregon has outlined a middle ground by defining the tort of interference with prospective economic relations so as to require the plaintiff to allege and prove more than the prima facie tort, but not to negate all defenses of privilege. Privileges remain as affirmative defenses. This approach originated with Justice Linde's opinion in *Top Service Body Shop, Inc. v. Allstate Insurance Co.,* 283 Or. 201, 582 P.2d 1365 (1978). After summarizing the history of this tort and specifically refusing to require a plaintiff to prove that the interference was "improper" under the balancing-of-factors approach specified in the *Restatement (Second)*, the court defined the cause of action for "wrongful interference with economic relationships" as follows:

> Either the pursuit of an improper objective of harming plaintiff or the use of wrongful means that in fact cause injury to plaintiff's contractual or business relationships may give rise to a tort claim for those injuries. . . . In summary, such a claim is made out when interference resulting in injury to another is wrongful by some measure beyond the fact of the interference itself. Defendant's liability may arise from improper motives or from the use of improper means.

Top Service Body Shop, Inc., 582 P.2d at 1368, 1371. A subsequent decision of that court [*Straube v. Larson,* 287 Or. 357, 361, 600 P.2d 371, 374 (1979)] restated and elaborated what the plaintiff must prove, as follows:

> In *Top Service* we decided that the defendant's improper intent, motive or purpose to interfere was a necessary element of the plaintiff's case, rather than a lack thereof being a matter of justification or privilege to be asserted as a defense by defendant. Thus, to be entitled to go to a jury, plaintiff must not only prove that defendant intentionally interfered with his business relationship but also that defendant had a duty of non-interference; *i.e.,* that he interfered for an improper purpose rather than for a legitimate one, or that defendant used improper means which resulted in injury to plaintiff.

We recognize a common-law cause of action for intentional interference with prospective economic relations, and adopt the Oregon definition of this tort. Under this definition, in order to recover damages, the plaintiff must prove (1) that the defendant intentionally interfered with the plaintiff's existing or potential economic relations, (2) for an improper purpose or by improper means, (3) causing injury to the plaintiff. Privilege is an affirmative defense, which does not become an issue unless "the acts charged would be tortious on the part of an unprivileged defendant." *Top Service Body Shop, Inc.,* 283 Or. at 210, 582 P.2d at 1371.

. . . .

C. Evidence of Intentional Interference and Causation

Reviewing the record, we conclude that there was sufficient evidence to sustain the jury's verdict against the Leigh Corporation for intentional interference with prospective economic relations that caused injury to Isom.

There was ample evidence that Isom had business relationships with various customers, suppliers, and potential business associates, and that Leigh, the former owner of the business, understood the value of those relationships. There was also substantial competent evidence that the Corporation, through Leigh, his wife, and his bookkeeper, intentionally interfered with and caused a termination of some of those relationships (actual or potential). Their frequent visits to Isom's store during business hours to confront him, question him, and make demands and inquiries regarding the manner in which he was conducting his business repeatedly interrupted sales activities, caused his customers to comment and complain, and more than once caused a customer to leave the store. Driving away an individual's existing or potential customers is the archetypical injury this cause of action was devised to remedy.

Other actions by which the Leigh Corporation imposed heavy demands on Isom's time and financial resources to the detriment of his ability to attract and retain customers and conduct the other activities of his business included: numerous letters of complaint, Leigh's demand for an audit of Isom's books and inventory during the busy holiday season, his continued threats to cancel the contract and sell the building and business to another buyer, his refusal to pay the contracted share of the heating bills or the cost of repairing the furnace and the store's broken window, his refusal of the tendered payment of the balance due under the contract, and his suit for repossession, termination, and injunction. Leigh's refusals also prevented Isom from consummating potentially advantageous business associations with [prospective partners], all experienced retailers able to contribute expertise and additional capital to Isom's business.

Taken in isolation, each of the foregoing interferences with Isom's business might be justified as an overly zealous attempt to protect the Corporation's interests under its contract of sale. As such, none would establish the intentional interference element of this tort, though some might give rise to a cause of action for breach of specific provisions in the contract or of the duty of good faith performance which inheres in every contractual relation. Even in small groups, these acts might be explained as merely instances of aggressive or abrasive—though not illegal or tortious—tactics, excesses that occur in contractual and commercial relationships. But in total and in cumulative effect, as a course of action extending over a period of three and one-half years and culminating in the failure of Isom's business, the Leigh Corporation's acts cross the threshold beyond what is incidental and justifiable to what is tortious. The Corporation's acts provide sufficient evidence to establish two of the elements in the definition of this tort: an intentional interference with present or prospective economic relations that caused injury to the plaintiff.

Focusing on the issue of causation, the Leigh Corporation argues that Isom's losses resulted from his inadequate working capital or from his unilateral decision to close his store immediately after being served with the complaint and to file for bankruptcy shortly thereafter. These arguments are unavailing because there was substantial evidence of causation to support the jury's verdict. For example, the jury could have found that the initiation of this lawsuit was but another instance of the Corporation's ongoing pattern of harassment, which made it impossible for Isom to continue to operate his business with any anticipation of success or profit. The parties had reached an impasse: Leigh had refused to accept Isom's tender of payment in full and had refused to permit Isom to exercise his option to purchase the building or to associate himself with experienced partners. Upon being served with the complaint, Isom could reasonably have concluded that the Corporation's interference and harassment would continue to thwart his commercial efforts for the foreseeable future. . . .

The evidence was also sufficient to support the verdict under the requirement that the intentional interference with prospective economic relations (in this case, Isom's relations with his customers, suppliers, and potential business associates) must have been for an improper purpose or by the use of improper means. These two alternatives are discussed in the next two sections.

D.   Improper Purpose

The alternative of improper purpose (or motive, intent, or objective) will support a cause of action for intentional interference with prospective economic relations even where the defendant's means were proper. In the context of the related tort of interference with contract, *Prosser* had this to say about improper purpose:

> Since *Lumley v. Gye* there has been general agreement that a purely "malicious" motive, in the sense of spite and a desire to do harm to the plaintiff for its own sake, will make the defendant liable for interference with a contract. The same is true of a mere officious intermeddling for no other reason than a desire to interfere. On the other hand, in the few cases in which the question has arisen, it has been held that where the defendant has a proper purpose in view, the addition of ill will toward the plaintiff will not defeat his privilege. It may be suggested that here, as in the case of mixed motives in the exercise of a privilege in defamation and malicious prosecution, the court may well *look to the predominant purpose underlying the defendant's conduct.* [Citations omitted; emphasis added.]

W. Prosser, *Handbook of the Law of Torts* § 129 at 943 (4th ed. 1971).

Because it requires that the improper purpose predominate, this alternative takes the long view of the defendant's conduct, allowing objectionable short-run purposes to be eclipsed by legitimate long-range economic motivation. Otherwise, much competitive commercial activity, such as a businessman's efforts to forestall a competitor in order to further his own long-range economic interests, could become tortious. In the rough and tumble of the marketplace, competitors inevitably damage one another in the struggle for personal advantage. The law offers no remedy for those damages—even if intentional—because they are an inevitable byproduct of competition. Problems inherent in proving motivation or purpose make it prudent for commercial conduct to be regulated for the most part by the improper means alternative, which typically requires only a showing of particular conduct.

The alternative of improper purpose will be satisfied where it can be shown that the actor's predominant purpose was to injure the plaintiff.

. . . .

As noted earlier, there is substantial evidence that the Leigh Corporation deliberately injured Isom's economic relations. But that injury was not an end in itself. It was an intermediate step toward achieving the long-range financial goal of profitably reselling the building free of Isom's interest. Because that economic interest seems to have been controlling, we must conclude that the evidence in this case would not support a jury finding that the Corporation's predominant purpose was to injure or ruin Isom's business merely for the sake of injury alone.

. . . .

E.   Improper Means

The alternative requirement of improper means is satisfied where the means used to interfere with a party's economic relations are contrary to law, such as violations of statutes, regulations, or recognized common-law rules. Such acts are illegal or tortious in themselves and hence are clearly "improper" means of interference, unless those means consist of constitutionally protected activity, like the exercise of First Amendment rights. "Commonly included among improper means are violence, threats or other intimidation, deceit or misrepresentation, bribery, unfounded litigation, defamation, or disparaging falsehood." *Top Service Body Shop, Inc.,* 582 P.2d at 1371 & n.11. Means may also be improper or wrongful because they violate "an established standard of a trade or profession." *Id.* at 1371.

By forcing Isom to defend what appear to have been two groundless lawsuits, the Leigh Corporation was clearly employing an improper means of interference with Isom's business. Such use of civil litigation as a weapon to damage another's business, besides being an intolerable waste of judicial resources, may give rise to independent causes of action in tort for abuse of process and malicious prosecution. The jury's verdict can therefore be sustained on the ground that the Leigh Corporation intentionally interfered with Isom's economic relations by improper means.

There is also another basis for affirming that verdict on the basis of improper means.

A deliberate breach of contract, even where employed to secure economic advantage, is not, by itself, an "improper means." Because the law remedies breaches of contract with damages calculated to give the aggrieved party the benefit of the bargain, there is no need for an additional remedy in tort (unless the defendant's conduct would constitute a tort independent of the contract).

Neither a deliberate breach of contract nor an immediate purpose to inflict injury which does not predominate over a legitimate economic end will, by itself, satisfy this element of the tort. However, they may do so in combination. This is so because contract damages provide an insufficient remedy for a breach prompted by an immediate purpose to injure, and that purpose does not enjoy the same legal immunity in the context of contract relations as it does in the competitive marketplace. As a result, a breach of contract committed for the immediate purpose of injur[ing] the other contracting party is an improper means that will satisfy this element of the cause of action for intentional interference with economic relations.

Two cases illustrate how breach of contract (or lease), when done with a purpose to injure, satisfy this element of the tort. In both cases, the defendant committed a breach not just to obtain relief from its obligation under the contract or lease (for which contract damages would have made the plaintiff whole), but to achieve a larger advantage by injuring the plaintiff in a manner not compensable merely by contract damages. In both cases, the defendant ruined the plaintiff's business by its breach, and in both cases the plaintiff was given substantial damages for the tort of interference with prospective economic relations.

In *Buxbom v. Smith,* 145 P.2d 305 (1944), a retail grocery chain contracted with the plaintiff to publish and distribute a "shopping news." In order to do so, the plaintiff abandoned his printing customers and expanded his distribution organization. After becoming the plaintiff's sole customer and acquiring complete knowledge of his business, the retailer deliberately breached its contract in order to ruin the plaintiff's business by cutting off the work required to sustain it and then hired his employees. The California Supreme Court affirmed a verdict for the plaintiff, awarding damages for breach of contract and additional damages for "tortious interference with his business" in order to give him "complete recompense for his combined injuries. . . ." *Id.* at 310. The gravamen of the tort, the court explained, was the defendant's breaching its contract with plaintiff as a means of acquiring plaintiff's employees:

> Although defendant's conduct may not have been tortious if he had merely broken the contract and subsequently decided to hire plaintiff's employees, an additional factor is present in this case. From the evidence the trial court could reasonably infer that *the breach, at the time it was made, was intended as a means of facilitating defendant's hiring of plaintiff's employees.* A breach of contract is a wrong and in itself actionable. It is also wrongful when *intentionally utilized as the means of depriving plaintiff of his employees,* and, in our opinion, constitutes an unfair method of interference with advantageous relations within the rule set forth above. [Emphasis added.]

Id. at 311.

In *Cherberg v. Peoples National Bank of Washington*, 564 P.2d 1137 (1977), a lessor deliberately breached its duty to repair a structurally unsound wall on the leased premises in order to destroy the restaurant business of a lessee who had leased a portion of the premises. The lessor's purpose was to retake the entire building as soon as possible, demolish the structure, and erect a more profitable building. The jury gave a verdict of $42,000 against the lessor. Apart from the $3,100 damages for breach of the lease (economic losses from temporary closure of the restaurant business), this verdict represented a recovery of damages for inconvenience, discomfort, and mental anguish for "the tort of intentional interference with business expectancies." The Washington Supreme Court sustained the verdict in an opinion that squarely relies on the combination of improper means and improper purpose in defendant's deliberate breach for the purpose of injuring the plaintiff.

After reviewing cases holding that a breach of covenants may also give rise to liability in tort, the court summarized:

> It appears to be the general view that, in those instances in which the conduct of the breaching party indicates a motive to destroy some interest of the adverse party, a tort action may lie and items of damage not available in contract actions will be allowed.

Id. at 1143. The court then acknowledged the "separate line of cases" holding that a breach of duty under a contract or a lease does not constitute an independent tort even where it interferes with the injured party's business relations. The court explained as follows:

> The distinguishing feature between the two lines of cases would seem to be whether the interference with business

relations was a mere incidental consequence of the breach or a motive or purpose therefor.

Id. In *Cherberg,* the court found that the defendant had breached its lease and interfered with the plaintiff's business not for the "privileged" reason of escaping from an unsatisfactory return on its investment in the leased premises (upon payment of contract damages), but for the impermissible purpose of injuring the tenant in order to secure an advantage beyond the scope of the lease:

> There is, instead, evidence in the record from which the jury could have inferred the lessor used the condition of the wall as a means to oust the petitioners and gain possession of the leased premises in order that the lessor might put those premises to a different and perhaps considerably more profitable use. *Proof of a breach based upon such a motive* demonstrates a failure to make a good faith effort to meet obligations under the lease and *may give rise to liability in tort.* [Emphasis added.]

Id. at 1143–44.

. . . .

In the case at bar, the Leigh Corporation breached its contract in various ways.

It breached its implied duty to exercise all of its rights under the contract reasonably and in good faith. Leigh's unexplained refusal to approve Isom's prospective business partners without consideration of their merits indicates an absence of good faith and provides evidence that the Corporation's breach was intended to deprive Isom's business of additional capital and valuable expertise which . . . Leigh himself had repeatedly urged Isom to acquire. . . . In addition, Leigh, his wife, and his bookkeeper continually interrupted sales activities with their visits, letters, threats, and demands, causing customers to comment and complain and sometimes to leave. Although the contract entitled the Corporation, as lessor and secured party, to reasonable supervision of Isom's business, the jury had sufficient evidence to conclude that this conduct constituted an unreasonable exercise of contract rights and/or was done in bad faith for the purpose of injuring Isom's business relations.

The Corporation also breached its contractual duty by refusing Isom's tender of the balance of the purchase price and by refusing to appoint an appraiser to establish a price for the sale of the entire building, thereby preventing Isom from exercising his purchase option. There is evidence of Leigh's purpose in the fact that he openly regretted his contract with Isom and frequently expressed his desire to "get Richard out" of the business and building. Furthermore, he continually contacted prospective buyers for the building, even approaching two of Isom's employees for this purpose.

All of the above provide substantial evidence from which the jury could have concluded that the Corporation breached its express and implied contractual duties for the purpose of ruining Isom's business and obtaining possession of the building in order to sell it more profitably elsewhere. By themselves, the Corporation's breaches would not satisfy the requirement of "improper means," but they could do so when coupled with the improper purpose of injuring Isom. In combination, a breach of contract and an intent to injure satisfy the improper means requirement for the cause of action for intentional interference with prospective economic relations.

F.   Summary

In defining the tort of intentional interference with prospective economic relations, we reject the two extremes of the prima facie tort and the balancing-of-factors approach. Instead, we adopt the Oregon definition, under which the plaintiff must prove that the intentional interference with existing or potential economic relations that caused injury to the plaintiff was done for an improper purpose or by improper means. . . .

To satisfy the alternative of improper purpose, the defendant's purpose to injure the plaintiff must predominate over all other purposes, including the long-range purpose of achieving some personal economic gain. Under this definition, the evidence is insufficient to justify a verdict against Leigh Corporation on the basis of improper purpose. Improper means refers primarily to actions that are contrary to law, such as violations of statutes, regulations, or recognized common-law rules. The Leigh Corporation's pursuit of two groundless lawsuits against Isom was an improper means. A deliberate breach of contract for the purpose of injuring the contracting party is also an improper means, and there is also sufficient evidence to sustain the jury's verdict on that basis.

. . . .

[T]he judgment on the verdict for defendant Isom is affirmed. . . .

NOTES & QUESTIONS

(1) Why does the *Leigh Furniture* court reject Isom's claim that Leigh Furniture interfered with the existing Isom-Leigh Furniture contract? *Cf.* RESTATEMENT (SECOND) OF TORTS § 766 (1979) (addressing interference with the performance of a contract "between another and a third person").

(2) The *Leigh Furniture* court requires the plaintiff in an "interference with prospective economic relations" claim to establish that the interference was "for an improper purpose or by improper means." What does the court

mean by "improper purpose"? What does the court mean by "improper means"? Did Isom establish an improper purpose, an improper means, or both?

(3) Are there problems with allowing impropriety to be established through improper purpose or motive? Consider the following observations:

[Another] reason for the common law's near-incoherence on the tort of intentional interference with prospective economic advantage may be discovered in its focus on the interfering party's motive, that is, *why* he seeks whatever it is that he seeks through his interference, and on his moral character as revealed thereby.

. . . .

It may be hard for a trier of fact to discern the interfering party's motive because of factors peculiar to the latter. That is true when the interfering party is an individual: a person's mind and heart typically reveal themselves and conceal themselves at one and the same time. It is truer still when the interfering party is a group of individuals: many minds and hearts are then involved, and they cannot simply be added up. And, of course, it is truest when the interfering party is a corporation or similar entity: the "mind" and "heart" of such a one is purely fictive.

. . . .

The untoward results of the focus on the interfering party's motive may present themselves in individual cases in the form of arbitrary and capricious outcomes. In matters in which the trier of fact believes it has discerned good motive or at least persuades itself it has, an interfering party who has both engaged in objectively bad conduct and produced objectively bad consequences may evade liability for injury. By contrast, in matters in which it adopts a contrary view, an interfering party who has neither engaged in such conduct nor produced such consequences may be made to pay for what is simply *damnum absque injuria*. In a word, much may depend on mere appearances and perceptions and on nothing more.

Such untoward results, however, will not confine themselves to individual cases but will spread generally to deter what should be encouraged and also to encourage what should be deterred. The example of the interfering party who has both engaged in objectively bad conduct and produced objectively bad consequences, but has nevertheless evaded liability, may lure others to follow in his steps, and thereby cause detriment to society as a whole. Conversely, the example of the interfering party who has neither engaged in such conduct nor produced such consequences, but has still been made to pay, may serve to turn aside others, and thereby deny the community the benefit of good acts and good effects or at least the freedom to do as one chooses when he does no injury.

Moreover, the example of both may lead to further social costs, as "properly motivated actors" take "precautions . . . to avoid liability" that they should not be exposed to and actors otherwise motivated fabricate schemes to escape responsibility that they deserve.

Della Penna v. Toyota Motor Sales, U.S.A., Inc., 902 P.2d 740, 757, 759–60 (Cal. 1995) (Mosk, J., concurring); *see also Texas Beef Cattle Co. v. Green*, 921 S.W.2d 203, 211 (Tex. 1996) ("Improper motives cannot transform lawful actions into actionable torts. 'Whatever a man has a legal right to do, he may do with impunity, regardless of motive, and if in exercising his legal right in a legal way damage results to another, no cause of action arises against him because of a bad motive in exercising the right.' "); *Pratt v. Prodata, Inc.*, 885 P.2d 786, 789 n.3 (Utah 1994) (". . . *Leigh*'s improper-purpose test creates a trap for the wary and unwary alike: business practices that are found to be 'proper means' by a finder of fact and may otherwise be regarded as wholly legitimate under our capitalistic economic system may be recast through a jury's unguided exercise of its moral judgment into examples of spite or malice. For example, the enforcement of a binding, valid contractual noncompete provision can result in liability under *Leigh* merely upon a jury finding of some ill-defined 'improper purpose.' For these reasons, the author of this opinion thinks *Leigh*'s improper-purpose test should be revisited and recast to minimize its potential for misuse.").

(4)   Under *Leigh Furniture*, a "deliberate breach of contract . . . is not, by itself, an 'improper means.' " When a deliberate breach is coupled with a purpose to injure the contracting party, however, it is an improper means. What is the court's rationale for this distinction? Doesn't such a conclusion interfere with the concept of efficient breach? *Cf.* 3 E. ALLAN FARNSWORTH, CONTRACTS § 12.8, at 194–95 (2d ed. 1990) ("Most courts have not infringed on the freedom to keep or to break a contract traditionally afforded a party by the common law and endorsed by the notion of efficient breach.").

(5)   As opposed to the approach in *Leigh Furniture*, a number of courts permit impropriety to be established only through improper means. For example, in *Wal-Mart Stores, Inc. v. Sturges*, 52 S.W.3d 711 (Tex. 2001), the court observed:

> . . . [W]e conclude that to establish liability for interference with a prospective contractual or business relation the plaintiff must prove that it was harmed by the defendant's conduct that was either independently tortious or unlawful. By "independently tortious" we mean conduct that would violate some other recognized tort duty. We must explain this at greater length, but by way of example, a defendant who threatened a customer with bodily harm if he did business with the plaintiff would be liable for interference because his conduct toward the customer—assault—was independently tortious, while a defendant who competed legally for the customer's business would not be liable for interference. Thus defined, an action for interference with a prospective contractual or

business relation provides a remedy for injurious conduct that other tort actions might not reach (in the example above, the plaintiff could not sue for assault), but only for conduct that is already recognized to be wrongful under the common law or by statute.

. . . .

We therefore hold that to recover for tortious interference with a prospective business relation a plaintiff must prove that the defendant's conduct was independently tortious or wrongful. By independently tortious we do not mean that the plaintiff must be able to prove an independent tort. Rather, we mean only that the plaintiff must prove that the defendant's conduct would be actionable under a recognized tort. Thus, for example, a plaintiff may recover for tortious interference from a defendant who makes fraudulent statements about the plaintiff to a third person without proving that the third person was actually defrauded. If, on the other hand, the defendant's statements are not intended to deceive . . . then they are not actionable. Likewise, a plaintiff may recover for tortious interference from a defendant who threatens a person with physical harm if he does business with the plaintiff. The plaintiff need prove only that the defendant's conduct toward the prospective customer would constitute assault. Also, a plaintiff could recover for tortious interference by showing an illegal boycott, although a plaintiff could not recover against a defendant whose persuasion of others not to deal with the plaintiff was lawful. Conduct that is merely "sharp" or unfair is not actionable and cannot be the basis for an action for tortious interference with prospective relations, and we disapprove of cases that suggest the contrary. These examples are not exhaustive, but they illustrate what conduct can constitute tortious interference with prospective relations.

The concepts of justification and privilege are subsumed in the plaintiff's proof, except insofar as they may be defenses to the wrongfulness of the alleged conduct. For example, a statement made against the plaintiff, though defamatory, may be protected by a complete or qualified privilege. Justification and privilege are defenses in a claim for tortious interference with prospective relations only to the extent that they are defenses to the independent tortiousness of the defendant's conduct. Otherwise, the plaintiff need not prove that the defendant's conduct was not justified or privileged, nor can a defendant assert such defenses.

Id. at 713, 726–27; *see also Speakers of Sport, Inc. v. ProServ, Inc.*, 178 F.3d 862, 867 (7th Cir. 1999) ("We agree . . . that the tort of interference with business relationships should be confined to cases in which the defendant employed unlawful means to stiff a competitor. . . .").

(6)   The approach of the Second Restatement to impropriety involves a multi-factor balancing test that considers the following: (a) the nature of the actor's conduct, (b) the actor's motive, (c) the interests of the other with which the actor's conduct interferes, (d) the interests sought to be advanced by the actor, (e) the social interest in protecting the freedom of action of the actor and the contractual interests of the other, (f) the proximity or remoteness of the actor's conduct to the interference, and (g) the relations between the parties. *See* RESTATEMENT (SECOND) OF TORTS § 767 (1979).

PROBLEM 3.3

Acme Co. is a large supplier of fuel with thousands of customers nationwide. Baker is a former executive of Acme who left the company on bad terms and started his own fuel supply business. Baker operates on a much smaller scale than Acme in a geographic area that Acme has historically avoided. Nevertheless, Acme begins to actively solicit Baker's existing customers (who are not under any contracts with Baker) and it offers them various lawful promotions and price discounts. Many of these customers stop doing business with Baker and start doing business with Acme.

Baker sues Acme for intentional interference with prospective contract. At trial, Acme board minutes are introduced indicating that Acme's conduct was motivated partially by the desire to expand its business into new geographic areas, but primarily because the board members despised Baker and wished to financially injure him. What result under *Leigh Furniture*? Under § 768 of the Second Restatement? Under Texas law (see *Texas Beef Cattle* in note (3) and *Sturges* in note (5))?

RICHARDSON V. LA RANCHERITA, INC.

159 Cal. Rptr. 285 (Ct. App. 1979)

WIENER, ASSOCIATE JUSTICE.

Defendants La Rancherita of La Jolla, Inc. (La Rancherita) and Louis Martinez (Martinez) appeal from the judgment awarding damages to plaintiffs based on the tort of intentional interference with a contractual relationship. The factual setting of this case—the commercial dealings between a landlord and tenant—requires the drawing of the line between sophisticated negotiations necessary to strike a better deal and economic constraints on those negotiations imposed by the tort of inducing breach of contract. We affirm the judgment.

Factual and Procedural Background

. . . .

In 1971, plaintiff Breg, a California corporation (Breg), negotiated for the purchase of all fixtures, equipment and liquor license of a restaurant in La Jolla. Through Basilio Martinez acting on behalf of the lessor, La Rancherita, the former tenants' interest in the original lease dated April

1, 1954, was assigned to Breg on terms contained in an addendum dated April 6, 1971. Breg lost money every year. In mid-December 1973, with shareholder approval, Breg signed escrow instructions for the sale of the assets of its restaurant to Norman Bomze (Bomze). The contract was contingent upon Breg obtaining the consent of the lessor to the assignment of the lease. The transaction between Breg and Bomze had been carefully structured as a sale of assets for, among other reasons, Breg's shareholders wished to retain the carry-forward tax loss of their subchapter "S" corporation. La Rancherita refused to consent to assignment of a lease to Bomze, relying on the paragraph of the lease which provided:

> "That the Lessees shall pay the Lessors said rent in the manner hereinbefore specified, and shall not let or underlet the whole or any part of said premises, nor sell or assign this lease, either voluntarily or by operation of law, nor allow said property to be occupied by anyone contrary to the terms hereof, without the written consent of the Lessors."

La Rancherita indicated through counsel and Martinez they were not attempting to "kill the deal," but only wanted to renegotiate the lease on terms which would include increased rent, shared use of an adjoining parking lot, and a cost of living escalation provision. Bomze rejected the proposed terms. Bomze and Breg decided to revise their agreement to by-pass the need for La Rancherita's consent to the assignment. The shareholders of Breg agreed to sell their corporate stock to Bomze; Breg would continue as tenant under the lease and addendum.

La Rancherita, upon being informed of the new agreement, continued its position that its consent was still necessary. In a letter to Breg's lawyer, counsel for La Rancherita stated the sale of stock, after a refusal to consent to a sale of assets, was merely a change of form to circumvent the consent provision of the lease. Counsel for both parties had reviewed and analyzed *Ser-Bye Corp. v. C.P. & G. Markets* (1947) 78 Cal.App.2d 915, 179 P.2d 342, which involved a similar legal question and had reached different conclusions. The sale of the stock originally set to close on January 31, 1974, was postponed solely as a result of La Rancherita's actions in threatening a forfeiture of the lease. The sale finally closed on March 3, 1974.

The complaint filed by Breg and its shareholders on February 21, 1974, sought declaratory relief to determine whether a transfer of the Breg stock constituted an assignment of Breg's lease, thereby necessitating La Rancherita's consent plus damages for intentional interference with the contract between Breg and Bomze for the sale of stock. Before trial, plaintiffs' motion for partial summary judgment was granted on their first cause of action—the court finding the lessor's consent was not required. After a court trial, damages of $7,233.06 were awarded for the losses plaintiffs sustained during the period from January 31 to March 3, 1974.

The Granting of Plaintiffs' Motion for Partial Summary Judgment Was Proper

. . . .

The lease provision in dispute prohibits occupancy by anyone contrary to its terms without the written consent of the lessor. Other than the issue of consent to the assignment, neither party has argued that occupancy by Breg with new shareholders violated the lease in any other respect. The lease itself did not provide that an individual was responsible for rent or liable for the performance of any other provision. The parties, at the time of their negotiations, were apparently satisfied with a corporation as lessee, making no provision to the contrary. Thus the court was asked to bar the transfer of shares of common stock in a valid corporation, permissible under corporate law, solely because of a lease provision prohibiting assignment of the lease, but containing no restraints on transfer of stock ownership. The court, under these circumstances, declined to do so, recognizing the separateness of the corporate form and properly granted plaintiffs' motion for partial summary judgment. (See *Ser-Bye Corp. v. C.P. & G. Markets*, supra, 78 Cal.App.2d at pp. 920–921, 179 P.2d 342.)

Defendants' Conduct Was Not Justified; It Constituted the Intentional Tort of Inducing Breach of Contract

. . . . To recover for inducing breach of contract, a plaintiff must establish (1) the existence of a valid contract; (2) the defendant had knowledge of the contract and intended to induce its breach; (3) the contract was in fact breached by the third party; (4) the breach was proximately caused by defendant's unjustified and wrongful conduct; and (5) that the foregoing resulted in damage to plaintiff.

Defendants' arguments rest on the premise that their actions were justified. They contend their conduct was not done solely to damage plaintiffs, for they were motivated by the good faith belief based on their lawyers' advice that their consent to the assignment of the lease was required. Withholding their consent pending negotiations with the prospective tenant to improve their financial interest was thus proper.

The test of whether there is justification for conduct which induces a breach of contract turns on a balancing of the social and private importance of the objective advanced by the interference against the importance of the interest interfered with, considering all the circumstances including the nature of the actor's conduct and the relationship between the parties. (See also Rest., 2d Torts, s 767.)

In harmony with the general guidelines of the test for justification is the narrow protection afforded to a party where (1) he has a legally protected interest, (2) in good faith threatens to protect it, and (3) the threat is to protect it by appropriate means. (Rest., 2d Torts, s 773.) . . .

The financial interest which defendants sought to protect included their right to continue to receive rent and to demand compliance with the essential terms of their lease. The determinative question thus becomes whether their claim was asserted in good faith. Or, phrased differently in the context of this case, was there any reasonable basis, either factually or legally, for their counsel to believe their distinguishing of the *Ser-Bye* case had merit.

Ser-Bye Corp. v. C.P. & G. Markets, supra, 78 Cal.App.2d 915, 179 P.2d 342, involved a lease provision prohibiting assignment similar to the one in the case before us. In affirming a judgment on the pleadings in an unlawful detainer action in favor of the corporate lessee, the court held the sale of stock of the corporation did not constitute an assignment to void the lease.

The language in paragraph First of the La Rancherita lease consisting of the phrase, ". . . nor allow said property to be occupied by anyone contrary to the terms hereof, . . ." does not help defendants' argument. As we have stated previously, the quoted words do not reflect an intent that any change in stock ownership requires the lessor's consent. Rather, the language reasonably interpreted simply provides the premises shall be occupied in accordance with all the terms of the lease.

Defendants have also placed reliance in the criticism of *Ser-Bye* in 3 Witkin, Summary of California Law (8th ed. 1973), as further support for the reasonableness [and] good faith of their legal position. Witkin's comment involves his concern with the apparent inadequate consideration given by the *Ser-Bye* court of the rule which requires "disregard(ing) the corporate entity when it is used to circumvent an obligation." At no time, either at summary judgment or at trial, did defendants suggest there were any factual questions relating to the alter ego of Breg or that any of Breg's shareholders had guaranteed Breg's rental obligation. . . .

Factual issues including elements which bear on "good faith" were properly before the trial court. There was ample evidence for the court to find that defendants' concern with the assignment of the lease was only incidental to their predominant motive of terminating the existing lease to obtain a new lease upon more favorable terms to themselves. Defendants made no effort to inquire into the financial condition of the successor stockholders or their intended method of operation. They restricted their negotiations to increasing their financial return and not to preserve their interest as lessor. The record is devoid of any evidence that defendants believed their leasehold interest was threatened by the new owners. The court was justified in finding that "(t)he transaction as ultimately consummated was clearly within the parameters of the *Ser-Bye* case. . . ."

Something other than sincerity and an honest conviction by a party in his position is required before justification for his conduct on the grounds of "good faith" can be established. There must be an objective basis for the belief which requires more than reliance on counsel.[1] It is the opinion of counsel that must be examined, recognizing that creative and conscientious lawyers should be given every opportunity to challenge outmoded precedent to permit constructive development of the law. However, to merely equate reliance on an attorney's advice with "good faith" is to shield those parties from liability who seek and obtain counsel. To create such a blanket rule of immunity is unwarranted.

Judgment affirmed.

COLOGNE, ACTING P. J., concurs.

STANIFORTH, ASSOCIATE JUSTICE, dissenting.

I respectfully dissent.

The trial court, in granting the challenged partial summary judgment . . . failed to discern a multitude of factual issues that precluded granting of the summary judgment. . . .

. . . .

. . . . The *Ser-Bye* decision is neither good law nor applicable factually to the situation at bar. *Ser-Bye* involved a judgment on the pleadings in an unlawful detainer action in favor of the corporate lessee. The *Ser-Bye* pleadings charged that the lease contained a covenant to the effect that the lease would not "assign the leasehold estate . . . without the written consent of the plaintiff first obtained." Here, factually to the contrary, the covenant in dispute provides not only against assignment of the lease without written consent, but prohibits occupancy by anyone contrary to the terms thereof without the written consent of the lessor. Thus, the critical language here was not in any way involved in *Ser-Bye*. Further, from the face of the lease provisions, as well as from the hot contentions made by the parties, different meanings are in fact to be found and can be reasonably argued from these words. Thus, *Ser-Bye* is factually inapplicable.

. . . . Here, the lessor is required to respond in damages because he had the temerity to contend and on basis of sound legal advice which

---

[1]   Counsel for defendants did not cast their professional advice in concrete. Martinez quite candidly testified that he understood he was taking a gamble that everybody had the feeling that the lawsuit could go either way.

sustained him in his contention that the attempted assignment was in violation of express terms of the lease prohibiting assignment or a change in occupancy without written consent. The proposed opinion offers no case, no scholarly authority to indicate that in these conceded factual circumstances the landlord does not have a right, a legally protected interest in making a good faith attempt to enforce the express terms of his lease. Certainly a lessor may protect an express right reserved to him in his lease by refusing to accede to the lessee's attempt to subvert that right by resorting to a legal fiction. *Ser-Bye*, supra, does not involve a question of damages for an intentional interference with a contractual relationship but rather involved an action for unlawful detainer. If *Ser-Bye* is good law . . . wholly different public policy considerations are present here. We have not yet reached a state in this society where either a landlord or tenant may not advance a position in good faith as regards an interpretation of a document between them. There is a right and a duty upon the part of the landlord or tenant if they in good faith believe that the other party is breaching their lease to maintain that position [and] to defend it stoutly.

. . . . The conceded facts here establish justification. The lessor's motives for asserting his legal rights are totally irrelevant.

. . . .

I would reverse and remand the cause with directions to dismiss proceedings.

NOTES & QUESTIONS

(1) Is the plaintiff in *La Rancherita* bringing a claim under § 766, § 766A, or § 766B of the Second Restatement?

(2) The *La Rancherita* court cites § 773 of the Second Restatement in its analysis. That section provides a defense for parties who assert legal rights and interfere with an existing or prospective contract as a result. Section 773 requires, in part, that a defendant "assert[ ] in good faith a legally protected interest of his own," and that the defendant "believe[ ] that his interest may otherwise be impaired or destroyed by the performance of the contract or transaction."

Why didn't La Rancherita prevail under the language of § 773? Is motive relevant to § 773?

(3) Some courts have distinguished between correct and mistaken assertions of legal rights. For example, in *Texas Beef Cattle Company v. Green*, 921 S.W.2d 203 (Tex. 1996), the court described the "justification defense" as follows:

. . . [T]he justification defense is based on either the exercise of (1) one's own legal rights or (2) a good-faith claim to a colorable legal right, even though that claim ultimately proves to be mistaken. Thus, if the trial court finds as a matter of law that the defendant had a legal right to interfere with a contract, then the defendant has conclusively established the justification defense, and the motivation behind assertion of that right is irrelevant. Improper motives cannot transform lawful actions into actionable torts. " 'Whatever a man has a legal right to do, he may do with impunity, regardless of motive, and if in exercising his legal right in a legal way damage results to another, no cause of action arises against him because of a bad motive in exercising the right.' " *Montgomery v. Phillips Petroleum Co.*, 49 S.W.2d 967, 972 (Tex.Civ.App.— Amarillo 1932, writ ref'd).

On the other hand, if the defendant cannot establish such a legal right as a matter of law, it may nevertheless prevail on its justification defense if: (1) the trial court determines that the defendant interfered while exercising a colorable right, and (2) the jury finds that, although mistaken, the defendant exercised that colorable legal right in good faith. . . . A jury question is presented only when the court decides that although no legal right to interfere exists, the defendant has nevertheless produced evidence of a good faith, albeit mistaken, belief in a colorable legal right.

Id. at 211; *see also Calvillo v. Gonzalez*, 922 S.W.2d 928, 929 (Tex. 1996) (noting the "recent holding that, in a tortious interference case, a defendant's motivation behind the assertion of a legal right is irrelevant since the right conclusively establishes the justification defense," and stating that "[g]ood faith is not a relevant factor in determining justification if the defendant acts to assert a legal right").

(4) If the *Texas Beef* framework had governed the dispute in *La Rancherita*, what result? Is *Texas Beef* consistent with § 773 of the Second Restatement?

WALNUT STREET ASSOCIATES, INC. V. BROKERAGE CONCEPTS, INC.

20 A.3d 468 (Pa. 2011)

CHIEF JUSTICE CASTILLE.

We consider whether Restatement (Second) of Torts § 772(a) applies in Pennsylvania to preclude an action for tortious interference with contractual relations where it is undisputed that the defendant's interfering statements were truthful. We hold that Section 772(a) is applicable, and we affirm the decision of the Superior Court.

Appellant, Walnut Street Associates ("WSA"), provides insurance brokerage services and assists employers in obtaining health insurance for their employees. Since the 1980s, WSA was the broker of record for health insurance provided to employees of Procacci Brothers Sales Corporation ("Procacci"). Appellee, Brokerage Concepts, Inc. ("BCI"), is a third party administrator of employee benefit plans. In 1994, at the recommendation of WSA, Procacci retained BCI as administrator of its insurance plans, and BCI paid commissions to WSA based on premiums paid by Procacci.

In 2005, Procacci requested that BCI lower costs, but BCI would not meet Procacci's proposal. Procacci then notified BCI that it would be moving its business to another third-party administrator. Shortly thereafter, BCI's employee Kimberly Macrone wrote a letter to Procacci asking it to reconsider its decision, and in the process advising Procacci of the amount of compensation WSA had been receiving as broker of record. The amount was apparently higher than Procacci believed WSA had been earning, but there is no dispute that Macrone's statements about WSA's compensation were true. As a result of Macrone's letter, Procacci terminated its longstanding contractual relationship with WSA.

WSA then filed this action against BCI and Macrone. . . . WSA alleged that BCI had tortiously interfered with the WSA/Procacci contractual relationship by disclosing the amount of WSA's compensation. In its answer and new matter, BCI alleged, *inter alia*, that it could not be held liable for tortious interference because the information it provided to Procacci was truthful, or otherwise justified and privileged, and not confidential. The parties went to trial on the tortious interference claim. At the charging conference, BCI requested a jury instruction on truthfulness as a defense pursuant to Section 772(a), but the court denied it. Instead, the court's instruction on tortious interference tracked two other Restatement provisions, Restatement (Second) of Torts §§ 766 and 767. The jury, so charged, specifically found that BCI had intentionally and improperly interfered with the WSA/Procacci contract, caused Procacci to terminate that contract, and awarded WSA $330,000 in damages. After its post-trial motion was denied, BCI filed an appeal to Superior Court.

The Superior Court reversed, holding that Macrone's truthful statements to Procacci regarding WSA's compensation could not support a claim for tortious interference with contractual relations. The court relied on Restatement Section 772(a), which, as noted above, provides that one who intentionally causes a third person not to perform a contract with another does not interfere improperly with the other's contractual relation by giving the third person truthful information. Because Macrone's statements to Procacci about WSA's compensation were true, the court held as a matter of law that BCI's interference with the WSA/Procacci contract was not actionable as tortious interference, and remanded for entry of judgment notwithstanding the verdict in favor of BCI. In doing so, the Superior Court predicted that this Court would adopt and apply Section 772(a) under these circumstances, and noted that "the courts of sister jurisdictions have nearly universally adopted" it.

. . . .

In *Adler Barish* . . . this Court acknowledged a well-established cause of action for intentional, improper interference with existing contractual relations. " '[T]he common law has recognized an action in tort for an intentional, unprivileged interference with contractual relations. It is generally recognized that one has the right to pursue his business relations or employment free from interference on the part of other persons except where such interference is justified or constitutes an exercise of an absolute right.' " *Adler Barish*, 393 A.2d at 1182 (quoting from *Birl*, 167 A.2d at 474). The Court explained that "[s]ince *Birl*, we have repeatedly looked to the Restatement as authority for the elements of a cause of action for intentional interference with existing contract relations." *Id.* at 1182 n.13. The Court further recognized that it "constantly seeks to harmonize common law rules, principles, and doctrines with modern perceptions of societal needs and responsibilities," and since the American Law Institute, which publishes the Restatements, makes a "continuing effort to provide the judicial system orderly and accurate restatements of the common law," it is "appropriate to analyze this case in light of the approach fashioned by Restatement (Second)." *Id.* at 1183.

. . . .

Ours is a free society where citizens may freely interact and exchange information. Tortious interference, as a basis for civil liability, does not operate to burden such interactions, but rather, to attach a reasonable consequence when the defendant's intentional interference was "improper." The term is addressed in several sections of the Restatement (Second) of Torts. In *Adler Barish*, this Court looked to Section 767. . . . After analyzing the facts of that case under Section 767, the Court concluded that the former associates' contact with clients of their former employer—clients who had open, active cases being handled by that firm—"unduly suggested a course of action" for them, "unfairly prejudiced" Adler Barish, and thus was improper. The former associates had even used the potential fees from these Adler Barish clients' active cases as collateral for obtaining a line of bank credit for their new firm. We noted that "[n]o public interest is served in condoning use of confidential information which has these effects." *Id.* at 1185. As BCI accurately notes, the *Adler Barish* Court did not consider Section 772(a), which had not yet been published, nor the specific proposition for which it stands. . . .

Together with Sections 766 and 767, Section 772 is now part of a larger scheme of Second Restatement provisions regarding tortious interference with contractual relations, and further defines the core concept of "improper" interference. Indeed, commentary appended to Section 767 provides that "Sections 769–773 deal with other special situations in which application of the factors enumerated in this Section [767] have produced more clearly identifiable decisional patterns. The specific applications in these Sections [769–773] therefore **supplant the generalization** expressed in this Section." RESTATEMENT (SECOND) OF TORTS § 767, cmt. a (emphasis added). This is not an extraordinary proposition; this is the manner in which the law often progresses. As general principles are tested in practice, more specific and accurate paradigms arise. Indeed, the commentary indicates that in situations where a Section 772(a) truthfulness defense is raised against claims of tortious interference, analysis of the general factors enumerated in Section 767 is not necessary. The commentary further supports this conclusion by recognizing that there are some situations where "the process of weighing the conflicting factors set forth in this Section has already been performed by the courts. . . . When this has been accomplished and the scope of the more or less crystallized rule or privilege has been indicated by the decisions, the responsibility in the particular case is simply to apply it to the facts involved; and there is no need to go through the balancing process afresh. Some of the situations in which this development has occurred are stated in §§ 769–773." *See* RESTATEMENT (SECOND) OF TORTS § 767, cmt. j (determination of whether actor's conduct is improper or not).

We do not view Section 772(a) as intending to alter the traditional understanding of the tort; as the Second Restatement makes clear, the elaborations are a product of experience and refinement. It is true that this Court has not yet expressly "adopted" Restatement (Second) of Torts § 772(a); nor have we rejected it. However, the Court did rely on the precursor to Section 772(b) to shield defendants from a tortious interference claim where they gave advice to their employer about another employee. And, even earlier, this Court recognized the countervailing proposition that a "groundless" allegation or a "misrepresentation" would indeed support an action for interference with contractual relations. Our focus on fraudulent and groundless actions suggests a recognition of the relevance of truth in assessing the proper application of the tort.

. . . . Now that Restatement (Second) of Torts § 772(a) is squarely before us, we hold that the Superior Court properly determined that Section 772(a) should apply, and that it controls under the facts of this case.

There is no dispute that BCI's employee Macrone intentionally imparted information about WSA's compensation to Procacci, when Procacci was seeking lower employee health insurance costs, and that the information was truthful. As a result of its learning that truth, Procacci fired WSA as insurance broker of record. The question is whether BCI's intentional interference with the Procacci/WSA contract was improper, and thus actionable. The jury found that the interference was improper, but only after being instructed on the Section 767 factors. The parties do not dispute that, if the trial court had deemed Section 772(a) applicable as BCI advocated, BCI would have been entitled to judgment as a matter of law. In our view, the Superior Court properly determined that Section 772(a)—the more specific Restatement provision regarding truthful disclosures—was available to BCI, rather than the more general Section 767 factors, exclusively.

As we have noted, Section 772 addresses a particular, recurring subclass of cases involving the construction of what may be deemed to be "improper" (and hence actionable) interference with contractual relations. Section 772 provides that it is not improper interference if the defendant is merely giving the third person: "(a) truthful information, or (b) honest advice within the scope of a request for the advice." The comments to Section 772 amplify the meaning of subsection (a):

> *a.*   This Section is a special application of the general test for determining whether an interference with an existing or prospective contractual relation is improper or not, as stated in §§ 766–766B and 767. Comments to those Sections may be relevant here.

> *b.   Truthful information.* **There is of course no liability for interference with a contract or with a prospective contractual relation on the part of one who merely gives truthful information to another. The interference in this instance is clearly not improper.** This is true even though the facts are marshaled in such a way that they speak for themselves and the person to whom the information is given immediately recognizes them as a reason for breaking his contract or refusing to deal with another. It is also true whether or not the information is requested. Compare § 581A, on the effect of truth in an action for defamation.

RESTATEMENT (SECOND) OF TORTS § 772, cmts. a–b (emphasis added).

Of course, the fact that the Second Restatement contains this refinement, and explicitly provides that the conveyance of truthful information is not "improper" interference, is not reason alone for this Court to "adopt" the provision, or to deem it a proper statement of Pennsylvania law. We adopt the provision, instead, because we believe the formulation is consistent with the very nature of the tort, and with

Pennsylvania law.[13] And, in this instance, we need not belabor the reasons why we believe that the elaboration is a proper understanding of what comprises improper conduct. The Restatement commentary we have set forth above amply explains why the conveyance of truthful information cannot reasonably be deemed to be "improper" interference. It would be strange, indeed, to deem disclosures of mere truth to be actionable. Those who would shield their contracting partners from non-privileged information that might affect those partners' business decisions properly run a risk that speech in the form of a truth, when disclosed, might imperil the relationship. Application of these precepts to the facts in this case leads us to hold as a matter of law that BCI's truthful statement to Procacci about WSA was not an improper interference, and cannot, on its own, support a claim for tortious interference with contractual relations.

. . . .

Order affirmed.

NOTES & QUESTIONS

(1) In *Walnut Street*, BCI prevailed under § 772 because the information that its employee provided was truthful. The jury, however, found that the interference was improper under § 767. What is the relationship between § 767 and § 772? Why does the court effectively conclude that § 772 trumps § 767? *See* RESTATEMENT (SECOND) OF TORTS § 767 cmts. a, j (1979).

(2) Why might the jury have concluded that a truthful statement was improper under § 767? In thinking about this question, consider the following:

> When BCI refused to meet the reduced cost proposal for the union program, PBS [Procacci] decided to move that plan so it could save $14.65 per person in administrative fees (a saving of over $137,000 per year). Once the client notified BCI that it had terminated BCI as the union plan TPA [third-party administrator] and it was too late to save that relationship, BCI acted intentionally and tortiously to destroy the 25 year business relationship between WSA and PBS. BCI sent a letter to PBS guised as "informative" but clearly intended to anger PBS' human resources manager (George Brack) by placing the blame for BCI's less than competitive rates on the compensation it was paying to WSA for both the union and non-union plans. Knowing PBS' desire to save on administrative fees, BCI disclosed WSA's per person share of the fees. Although correctly stating the share (but omitting other relevant

---

[13] As stated by the Superior Court in its opinion, and by BCI in its brief, courts in a majority of states have held that an action for tortious interference may not be based on truthful statements.

information), its disclosure caused PBS to terminate its relationship with WSA. The letter worked exactly as it was intended. WSA was immediately fired as PBS' Broker of Record for both the union and non-union plans.

As further evidence of BCI's motive and intent, BCI then stopped payment on WSA's commission check containing the payments due to WSA for the PBS account for the previous month (February) and refused to pay WSA commissions earned in March, 2005.

Plaintiff's Memorandum of Law in Opposition to Defendants' Motion for Summary Judgment and in Support of Cross-Motion for Summary Judgment, 2006 WL 6416321 (Aug. 2, 2006); *see also Walnut Street Assocs. v. Brokerage Concepts, Inc.,* No. 2626, 2008 WL 4176752, at *4 (Pa. Ct. of Common Pleas Aug. 6, 2008) ("Defendant Macrone testified that at the time she wrote the letter, she knew that her firm had been terminated and that Procacci was bound to another contract with Loomis Company. This knowledge was evident in the letter she had written Procacci. The facts demonstrated that disclosure of [Plaintiff's] compensation was intended to harm Plaintiff rather than to legitimately revive the union account.").

(3) A truth "privilege" under § 772 is not universally recognized. In *Pratt v. Prodata, Inc.,* 885 P.2d 786 (Utah 1994), the Utah Department of Transportation terminated Pratt, a computer programmer, based on information provided by Pratt's former employer (Prodata). The jury found that Prodata did not make any false statements. Nevertheless, the jury concluded that tortious interference occurred because Prodata acted with an improper purpose—i.e., its primary motivation was hostility and ill will towards Pratt. *See id.* at 786–88. In affirming the jury verdict, the Supreme Court of Utah rejected Prodata's § 772(a) argument:

> Finally, we reject defendants' assertion that under *Leigh* a judgment for intentional interference with economic relations cannot be based on the transmission of truthful information. . . .

> Defendants' reliance on section 772(a) is misplaced. As our decision in *Leigh* makes clear, this court has rejected the various Restatement formulations of the tort of intentional interference with economic relations. Under *Leigh,* "the alternative of improper purpose (or motive, intent, or objective) will support a cause of action for intentional interference with prospective economic relations *even where the defendant's means were proper.*" Because we explicitly rejected the Restatement versions of the tort in *Leigh* and because liability may attach under *Leigh* even where a defendant's means were proper, we reject defendants' call to adopt truthfulness as an absolute defense to the tort of intentional interference with prospective economic relations.

Id. at 790.

(4)   Does § 772(a) change the result in *Lumley v. Gye*? Assume that Gye induced Wagner to breach her contract with Lumley by truthfully telling her "I will pay you twice what Lumley is paying you." Isn't that statement "truthful information," and doesn't it result in no liability for Gye? *Compare* RESTATEMENT (SECOND) OF TORTS § 772(a) (1979), *with id.* § 766 cmt. m, *and id.* § 768(2).

(5)   In *J.D. Edwards & Co. v. Podany*, 168 F.3d 1020 (7th Cir. 1999), Judge Posner discussed the "honest advice" provision of § 772(b):

> . . . .   The only issue is whether the jury was justified in rejecting, en route to awarding the plaintiff $2.3 million in damages, the defense to inducing breach of contract that is called the "consultant's privilege," or more commonly the privilege of "honest advice." This is the privilege of a consultant, or other advisor, to offer good-faith advice to a client without fear of liability should the client act on that advice to the harm of a third person, in this case the plaintiff.
>
> The privilege resembles the rule in defamation law that where there is a duty to speak, a defamatory utterance, if made in good faith and not disseminated any further than necessary, is privileged. A consultant is hired to give advice. Often the advice is painful, because firms frequently turn to consultants when they are in trouble or when they want to do something that hurts and want to spread the blame a bit. The consultant's advice may lead to downsizing, layoffs, outsourcing, and countless other perturbations, including, as here, contractual terminations. It would cast quite a large, dark cloud over the consulting business if consultants could be hauled into court for having given advice that in hindsight could be characterized as having been ill-advised, ill-informed, or otherwise negligent. The consultant's privilege cuts off this possibility. But it is not absolute. It is a qualified privilege, like qualified immunity as distinct from absolute immunity in the law of public officers' torts.
>
> It is qualified in two ways. First, it is limited to advice given within the scope of the consultant's engagement. *Restatement, supra,* § 772(b) and comment d. If a consultant hired to advise the client, a fast-food chain, on selecting a new telephone system suggested that the client terminate its fast-food franchisee in Oshkosh because the franchisee was serving soggy doughnuts, and the suggestion was adopted, the consultant could not set up the consultant's privilege in defense of the franchisee's suit for interference with contract. Not having been hired to advise on the client's franchise system, the consultant would have no contractual duty to render frank and fearless (or indeed any) advice on the subject.

Second, if the consultant does not give honest advice—if he uses his engagement to hurt other people exclusively for his own benefit (or out of dislike of his victim) rather than for the benefit of his client—he forfeits the privilege. If solely to feather his own nest, and without believing that (or caring whether) he is helping his client, he causes the client to break a contract to the detriment of the other party to the contract, he is liable for inducing the breach.

Id. at 1022–23.

In *Podany*, there was evidence suggesting that a consultant (Podany) recommended that a client (SNE) replace software so that Podany could "land himself a lucrative job with SNE's parent as director of information services." The court observed:

If Podany was simply a fool, and got SNE to replace [the former] software with [the new software] because he ignorantly believed that the latter really was superior for SNE's needs even though it lacked a configurator, he and his employer would be sheltered from liability by the consultant's privilege. They would be, indeed, securely within the core of the privilege. But if Podany's only object was to enrich himself . . . the privilege is forfeited. . . .

In pointing to Podany's motives, we do not make the mistake of confusing bad faith with greed. A consultant might be in consulting purely for the money, but as long as he made his money by offering honest advice within the scope of his employment, his private motives would be irrelevant. *Restatement, supra,* § 772 comment c. It is when a consultant decides to make money by rendering dishonest advice (or going outside the terms of his engagement) that he loses the protection of privilege and assumes the usual liabilities.

Podany denied any such ulterior motive. But his credibility was impeached, and the jury was not required to believe him. His lack of credibility, like pretext in a discrimination case, combined with circumstantial evidence to justify the jury in finding bad faith.

Id. at 1024–25.

(6)   As discussed, § 772 (truth and honest advice) and § 773 (asserting legally protected interests) of the Second Restatement both provide "defenses" or "privileges" to intentional interference claims by stating that conduct within their scope does not constitute improper interference. Another such defense is the competition privilege in § 768, which protects persons in certain circumstances from liability for competitive conduct. As one court observed:

One recognized "just cause for damaging another in his [or her] business is competition." Thus, interference with another's contract or business relations in the name of competition is improper only if the means used are, in themselves, improper. *See Goldman,* 150 Md. at 684, 133 A. at 846, in which we said:

"Iron sharpeneth iron" is ancient wisdom, and the law is in accord in favoring free competition, since ordinarily it is essential to the general welfare of society, notwithstanding competition is not altruistic but is fundamentally the play of interest against interest, and so involves the interference of the successful competitor in the matter of their common rivalry. Competition is the state in which men live and is not a tort, unless the nature of the method employed is not justified by public policy, and so supplies the condition to constitute a legal wrong.

Macklin v. Robert Logan Assocs., 639 A.2d 112, 119 (Md. 1994).

Does § 768 protect defendants from claims under § 766, § 766A, and § 766B? Is interference with an existing terminable-at-will contract protected by § 768? Does motive have any role in a § 768 analysis? *See also* RESTATEMENT (SECOND) OF TORTS §§ 766 cmt. g, 766B cmt. c (1979). (Note: For additional defenses/privileges, please see the Problem below.)

PROBLEM 3.4

(a)   Able is a 10% shareholder in XYZ, Inc.—a small closely held corporation. The corporation is very close to hiring Betty as its new CEO. Able knows Betty and thinks that the company would do poorly under her risky management style. He also despises Betty because she broke off a personal relationship with him some years ago. He contacts the board of directors of XYZ and strongly lobbies the individual directors to not hire Betty. As a result of Able's efforts, the board does not extend an offer. If Betty sues Able for intentional interference with her prospective employment contract with XYZ, what result? What if Able was not a shareholder, but was instead an XYZ vendor who the current CEO had used for years to supply XYZ with copy machines? *See* RESTATEMENT (SECOND) OF TORTS § 769 (1979).

(b)   Frank has a twenty-five year old daughter named Delilah. Delilah enters into a contract for the purchase of a parcel of real estate located near an industrial plant. Frank believes that the purchase is a financial disaster for his daughter. Without being asked for his advice, he tells Delilah that he thinks she has made a mistake, and he persuades her to breach the contract. The seller sues Frank for intentional interference with his existing contract with Delilah. What result? Does it matter if Frank acted with mixed motives—i.e., partially because of his concern for Delilah's finances, but partially because he knows the seller, despises him, and wishes to cause him harm? *See id.* § 770.

(c)   Able owns an ice cream shop in the Marksville mall (as well as several other ice cream shops around town). Before the prior movie theater operator in the mall went out of business, Able generated a significant amount of revenue on Monday afternoons and evenings from patrons exiting a movie. Unfortunately, the new movie theater operator has a policy of keeping the business closed on Mondays. Despite pleas from Able and other merchants in the mall, the new operator has refused to change its policy. As a result of these events, Able has developed ill will towards the operator, and he informs the operator that he will start "playing hardball" to make the operator change his policy.

Baker is a supplier of snack foods (including candy, popcorn, and frozen treats) to local stores in Marksville. Able is one of Baker's best customers because Able regularly purchases large quantities of high-priced, premium ice cream from Baker. Able tells Baker that he will decrease his purchases from Baker dramatically unless Baker stops providing popcorn to the new movie theater operator in the mall. Baker ceases its periodic sales of popcorn to the theater, and the theater is unable to procure another reliable source of popcorn. The theater operator sues Able for intentional interference with prospective contract. What result? *See id.* § 771.

D. THE LIABILITY OF AGENTS

HOLLOWAY V. SKINNER
898 S.W.2d 793 (Tex. 1995)

CORNYN, JUSTICE, delivered the opinion of the Court, in which PHILLIPS, CHIEF JUSTICE, GONZALEZ, JUSTICE, GAMMAGE, JUSTICE, and SPECTOR, JUSTICE, join.

In this case, we consider whether Graham Holloway, the president, director, and largest shareholder of Holligan, Inc. (the Corporation), can be held liable for tortiously interfering with a contract between the Corporation and a third party. Rick Skinner and Alvin Ord's, Inc. (collectively, Skinner), sued Holloway for, among other things, tortious interference with a contract between the Corporation and Skinner. The trial court rendered judgment on the jury's verdict against Holloway on the tortious interference claim. The court of appeals affirmed. Because Skinner presented no evidence that Holloway, *in his personal capacity*, willfully or intentionally interfered with the contract, we reverse the judgment of the court of appeals and render judgment that Skinner take nothing.

Skinner previously owned a sandwich shop franchise, Alvin Ord's. In 1981, Holloway and his father-in-law, Tom Culligan, approached Skinner about purchasing the franchise. Rather than negotiating an outright purchase, the parties settled upon a plan of joint ownership and agreed to form a corporation, Holligan, Inc., to control their holdings. Skinner contributed to the Corporation his company-owned Alvin Ord's stores, franchise agreements, the Alvin Ord's trade name, and trade secrets. Holloway and Culligan contributed their management services and additional capital. As part of this agreement, Skinner received a $63,000 promissory note from the Corporation, a six percent royalty on gross receipts from Alvin Ord's stores, stock, and a managerial position in the Corporation.[1] Holloway served as the Corporation's president.

Between 1981 and 1984, the Corporation failed to make some payments due under the note and royalty agreement. In 1984, Skinner left his position at the Corporation because of a deteriorating personal relationship with Holloway. The Corporation defaulted entirely on its obligations to him in July 1985.

Skinner successfully sued the Corporation for breach of its obligations under the note and royalty agreement, but the Corporation filed for bankruptcy, and that judgment remains unsatisfied. Skinner then filed the suit against Holloway, claiming, among other things, that he tortiously interfered with the note and royalty agreement by inducing the Corporation to default on its obligations. In accord with the jury's verdict, the trial court rendered judgment against Holloway on the tortious interference claim. The court of appeals affirmed, holding that Holloway's status as a corporate agent did not bar Skinner's claim of tortious interference with the Corporation's contract, that some evidence supported the jury's finding that Holloway induced a breach of the contract, and that Holloway had not conclusively [established] that his conduct was legally justified.

I.

Texas jurisprudence has long recognized that a party to a contract has a cause of action for tortious interference against any third person (a stranger to the contract) who wrongly induces another contracting party to breach the contract. By definition, the person who induces the breach cannot be a contracting party. Were we to recognize the tortious interference claim when this identity of interest exists, any party who breaches a contract could be said to have induced his own breach and would therefore be liable for tortious interference. Such logic would convert every breach of contract claim into a tort claim. In most cases, however, this qualification is not an issue because the alleged tortfeasor is clearly a stranger to the contract.

Here, the act of interference was allegedly committed by an individual who was also the lawful representative of the contracting party. Such a case tests the limits of the general rule barring tortious interference claims when the inducing and the breaching party are one and the same. The inducement and the breach were allegedly committed when the same person was functioning in distinctly different legal capacities.

---

[1]   During the negotiations, Skinner unsuccessfully attempted to obtain personal guarantees from Holloway and Culligan on the Corporation's obligations to Skinner.

Corporations, by their very nature, cannot function without human agents. As a general rule, the actions of a corporate agent on behalf of the corporation are deemed the corporation's acts. For this reason, we have held that "an officer or director [of a corporation] may not be held liable in damages for inducing the corporation to violate a contractual obligation, provided that the officer or director acts in good faith and believes that what he does is for the best interest of the corporation." *Maxey v. Citizen's Nat'l Bank*, 507 S.W.2d 722, 726 (Tex.1974). "Even the officers and directors of an ordinary corporation, while acting as such, are not personally liable even though they recommend a breach of a valid contract." *Id.* at 725 (quoting *Russell v. Edgewood Indep. Sch. Dist.*, 406 S.W.2d 249, 252 (Tex.Civ.App.—San Antonio 1966, writ ref'd n.r.e.)). The reason for this rule has been explained as follows:

> Doing business through corporate structures is a recognized and necessary incident of business life. A party is usually able to abandon a disadvantageous but valid contract and be responsible for breach of contract only. Corporations would substantially be prevented from similarly abandoning disadvantageous but valid contracts, and from securing related business advice, if the officers and employees who advised and carried out the breach had to run the risk of personal responsibility in an action for personal interference with the contract.

Wampler v. Palmerton, 439 P.2d 601, 606 (1968). Based on this same rationale, we have emphasized that "a clear distinction should be maintained between individual liability as distinguished from that of the corporate employer." *See Maxey*, 507 S.W.2d at 726.

The elements of a cause of action for tortious interference with a contract are: (1) the existence of a contract subject to interference, (2) the occurrence of an act of interference that was willful and intentional, (3) the act was a proximate cause of the plaintiff's damage, and (4) actual damage or loss occurred. The second element of this cause of action is of particular importance when the defendant serves the dual roles of the corporate agent and the third party who allegedly induces the corporation's breach. To establish a prima facie case under such circumstances, the alleged act of interference must be performed in furtherance of the defendant's personal interests so as to preserve the logically necessary rule that a party cannot tortiously interfere with its own contract.

We hold that to meet this burden in a case of this nature, the plaintiff must show that the defendant acted in a fashion so contrary to the corporation's best interests that his actions could only have been motivated by personal interests.[3] Inasmuch as it is the duty of corporate officers to protect the interests of the corporation, the mere existence of a personal stake in the outcome, especially when any personal benefit is derivative of the improved financial condition of the corporation or consists of the continued entitlement to draw a salary, cannot alone constitute proof that the defendant committed an act of willful or intentional interference. *[S]ee also Welch v. Bancorp Management Advisors, Inc.*, 675 P.2d 172, 178 (1983) (holding that even a corporate agent's "mixed motives" to benefit himself as well as the corporation are insufficient to establish liability). Were this not the rule, virtually every failure to pay a corporate debt would constitute a prima facie case of tortious interference against the corporate officer who decided not to pay the debt.

. . . .

Much of the argument in this appeal has concentrated on the legal effect of Holloway's corporate role. Holloway asserts that a corporate representative who controls the corporation cannot interfere with the corporation's contracts because the representative is legally indistinguishable from the corporation. The record establishes, however, that Holloway personally owned only forty percent of the stock in the Corporation. Skinner argues that this lack of complete identity of interests between the Corporation and Holloway permits the jury to infer that Holloway interfered with the contract in question.

This argument primarily addresses the first element of tortious interference: whether there was a contract subject to interference. When there is a complete identity of interests, there can be no interference as a matter of law. Here, however, because Holloway's interests as a minority shareholder and those of the Corporation are not of necessity identical, we hold that Holloway could have acted in a manner that served his interests at the expense of the other shareholders. Thus, the contract at issue here was subject to interference, despite the substantial alignment of his interests with those of the Corporation.

In his concurring opinion, JUSTICE HECHT states that Holloway's authority to act on behalf of the Corporation is the dispositive inquiry. We disagree. JUSTICE HECHT'S view represents a substantial departure from Texas law and would effectively abrogate the tortious interference cause of action and confer blanket immunity anytime an agent acts within the scope of the agent's general authority and regardless of whether the agent is exclusively pursuing his personal interests. In this case, Skinner does

---

[3] Our holding today is consistent with the standard we enunciated in *Maxey*: that to prevail the defendant must act in good faith and believe the act to be in the best interest of the corporation. *Maxey*, 507 S.W.2d at 726. If the defendant acts in a fashion so contrary to the corporation's best interests that his actions could only have been motivated by personal interests, he by definition does not act in good faith.

not even claim that Holloway was not authorized by the Corporation to perform all of the actions of which Skinner complains. Still, we can conceive of other scenarios in which a corporate agent, while acting within the scope of his general authority, might pursue purely selfish interests in inducing a breach of the corporation's contract. An agent's interests and those of the corporation are not always monolithic, especially when, as here, the agent is a minority shareholder. Accordingly, we reject a "scope of authority" test and hold that the ultimate issue in a case of this nature is whether the corporation's agent acted in a manner so contrary to the corporation's interests that the agent could only have been motivated by personal interest.

The alignment of Holloway's interests with those of the Corporation is also relevant to the second element of tortious interference: whether the agent of the corporation committed a willful and intentional act of interference. The plaintiff must prove more than the fact that the defendant benefitted from the breach. The plaintiff must prove that the defendant acted willfully or intentionally to serve the defendant's personal interests at the expense of the corporation. In this case, to support the jury's finding of tortious interference, there must be evidence that Holloway personally benefitted from decisions that were inconsistent with his duty to the Corporation, and that were directly connected to the Corporation's decision not to pay Skinner.

The testimony at trial, as well as audit reports and bankruptcy records, establish the following uncontroverted facts. The Corporation suffered severe cash flow problems and had current liabilities that far exceeded its current assets at the time the breach occurred. These financial difficulties caused the Corporation to fall behind on its royalty payments to Skinner during the period from 1981 to 1984, and to cease making payments altogether in 1985. The salary paid to Holloway was originally $36,000, but was reduced to $24,000 prior to 1984 due to cash flow problems. During the 1984–85 fiscal year, Holloway raised his salary to $33,750. During the next year, his salary was increased to $45,000. The increase in Holloway's salary was offset by decreases in other salaries paid as the Corporation trimmed the size of its work force, and there is no evidence that these actions were unreasonable. Holloway further testified that, in his capacity as a corporate officer, he was required to prioritize between competing claims because the Corporation had insufficient cash flow to meet all obligations when they came due.

On this record, we conclude that there is no evidence that the decision to breach the contract was so contrary to the Corporation's best interests that it could only have been motivated by the pursuit of Holloway's personal interests. As we have already noted, a personal benefit limited to the continued entitlement to draw a salary or derivative of the improved financial condition of the corporation does not raise a triable issue of fact in this type of tortious interference case.

Because Skinner failed to introduce any evidence tending to prove that Holloway committed an act that was so contrary to the Corporation's best interests that it could only have been motivated by the pursuit of his personal interests, there is no evidence that Holloway tortiously interfered with Skinner's contractual rights with the Corporation. Accordingly, we reverse the judgment of the court of appeals and render judgment that Skinner take nothing on his tortious interference claim.

HECHT, JUSTICE, joined by OWEN, JUSTICE, filed an opinion concurring in the judgment only.

The rule the Court adopts today exposes all agents, including corporate officers, directors and employees, to increased personal liability for the decisions they make on behalf of their principals. Even when an employer, corporation or other principal authorizes its agent to act on its behalf with a third party, the Court holds that the agent personally—not just the principal—may be liable to the third party. While the Court correctly relieves the corporate officer in this case of the judgment against him, it enlarges the threat of liability to all others in his position. The better rule, in my view, is that an agent is liable to a third party for tortious interference with a contract between that party and the agent's principal if the agent's conduct exceeded his authority.

. . . .

As the Court recognizes, a person cannot interfere with his own contract. When a person is authorized to act for another, his action[s] are the other's. In my view, an agent authorized to cause his principal to terminate a contract should not be liable for tortious interference when that decision turns out to be in the agent's best interests and not the principal's; he should be liable only if he acted outside his authority. The Court seems to fear that this rule would shield agents in circumstances when they should not be free of responsibility, but it cannot even imagine a single example. If there are any, they certainly do not raise the same threats as are raised by the flaws in the Court's rule.

. . . .

For these reasons I believe it is important that an action for tortious interference against an agent be limited to circumstances in which the agent has transgressed his authority. The Court's broader rule is, in my view, prone to mischief. Accordingly, I concur only in the Court's judgment.

ENOCH, JUSTICE, concurring in the judgment.

. . . .

To the extent that JUSTICE HECHT concludes that the issue in this case is whether the action of the agent was within the scope and authority granted to it by its principal, I agree. But, I cannot agree that the scope of authority is merely a question of whether an act is explicitly authorized. Our cases have recognized that an agent must exercise corporate authority in *good faith* in order to be treated as the principal. *See Maxey v. Citizens National Bank*, 507 S.W.2d 722, 726 (Tex.1974) (an officer is not liable for inducing the corporation to breach a contract provided that the officer acts in good faith and believes what he does is for the best interest of the corporation). This good faith requirement forces this Court to recognize that lack of authority may be shown where an agent acts so contrary to the corporation's best interests that his actions could only be motivated by personal interests. Because JUSTICE HECHT does not recognize the role of good faith in the agency inquiry, I cannot join his concurrence. Therefore, I concur in the Court's judgment and write separately.

. . . .

[Dissenting opinion of JUSTICE HIGHTOWER omitted.]

NOTES & QUESTIONS

(1) *Holloway* involved a suit by one party (Skinner) against another party (Holloway) for interference with an existing contract between Skinner and a third person (Holligan, Inc.). Doesn't this three-party setting fit the typical pattern of an interference claim? What is the conceptual problem that the court is wrestling with?

(2) The *Holloway* court stated that "the plaintiff must show that the defendant acted in a fashion so contrary to the corporation's best interests that his actions could only have been motivated by personal interests." How does this requirement address the conceptual problem that you identified above? Given that Holloway clearly had a personal interest in preserving sufficient corporate funds to pay his salary, why wasn't this requirement met?

(3) How would Justice Hecht reformulate the majority's rule? Is there much difference between the two approaches? *Cf.* RESTATEMENT (THIRD) OF AGENCY § 2.02 cmt. e (2006) ("An agent does not have actual authority to do an act if the agent does not reasonably believe that the principal has consented to its commission.").

(4) In the subsequent decision of *Powell Industries, Inc. v. Allen*, 985 S.W.2d 455 (Tex. 1998), Thomas Powell, president and chief executive officer of Powell Industries, Inc., asked Corbett Allen, the company's chief financial officer, to have the company pay $3,000 for Powell's personal accounting

services. Allen refused the request, claiming that it would be illegal for him to pay the invoice, and he complained to others about Powell's behavior. At a special board meeting convened less than a week later, Allen presented his grievances against Powell and questioned Powell's ability to serve as CEO. In response, the board allegedly voted to keep Powell as CEO and granted authority to Powell "to take such action as he deemed necessary where the Corbett Allen affair [is] concerned." The next day, Powell fired Allen. *See id.* at 456.

Allen sued Powell for intentionally interfering with Allen's employment contract with Powell Industries. The court cited the *Holloway* framework, and then further observed:

> In addition, when determining whether an agent acted against the corporation's interests, we consider the corporation's evaluation of the agent's actions. A corporation is a better judge of its own best interests than a jury or court. A principal's complaint about its agent's actions is not conclusive of whether the agent acted against the principal's best interests. However, if a corporation does not complain about its agent's actions, then the agent cannot be held to have acted contrary to the corporation's interests.
>
> .... According to Allen's version of the facts, Allen presented his case at a board meeting, telling the directors about Powell's demands.... Even under Allen's version of the facts, the board had an opportunity to complain of Powell's actions and chose not to do so. Therefore, Powell cannot be held to have acted contrary to Powell Industries' interests.

Id. at 457. Given *Holloway* and *Powell Industries*, do you think it is likely that, under Texas law, a plaintiff's interference claim against an agent will succeed?

(5) Other courts follow approaches similar to those mentioned in *Holloway*. For example, in *Nordling v. Northern States Power Co.*, 478 N.W.2d 498 (Minn. 1991), the court adopted a "scope of authority" framework, although it held that actions predominantly motivated by ill will would not merit protection:

> .... The general rule is that a party cannot interfere with its own contract. If a corporation's officer or agent acting pursuant to his company duties terminates or causes to be terminated an employee, the actions are those of the corporation; the employee's dispute is with the company employer for breach of contract, not the agent individually for a tort. To allow the officer or agent to be sued and to be personally liable would chill corporate personnel from performing their duties and would be contrary to the limited liability accorded incorporation. Nevertheless ... a corporate officer or agent may be liable for tortious contract interference if he or she acts outside the scope of his or her duties.

It is not always easy to determine when a corporate officer or agent's actions are outside the scope of his company responsibilities, *i.e.*, when he is engaged in a personal vendetta or excursion. Particularly is this true in a job termination case where the officer's duties include the evaluation and supervision of the plaintiff employee's performance or the power to participate in the corporate decision to terminate or otherwise discipline the plaintiff.

. . . .

In this case the contract interfered with is an employment contract and the alleged interferer is employed by the same employer. It becomes important, therefore, to determine first the scope of the defendant officer or agent's duties with respect to the plaintiff employee's employment. Conceivably, there may be instances where the defendant officer or agent's conduct is decidedly outside the scope of his duties. The more common situation, we think, is when the defendant's conduct is subject to conflicting inferences. In this situation, the defendant's motive becomes critical. While motive or malice is only one factor to consider in determining whether a defendant officer or agent is acting outside the scope of his duties in dealing with the plaintiff employee, it can be the critical factor. . . .

. . . .

[W]e conclude that a company officer, agent or employee is privileged to interfere with or cause a breach of another employee's employment contract with the company, if that person acts in good faith, whether competently or not, believing that his actions are in furtherance of the company's business. This privilege may be lost, however, if the defendant's actions are predominantly motivated by malice and bad faith, that is, by personal ill-will, spite, hostility, or a deliberate intent to harm the plaintiff employee.

Id. at 505–07; *see also McGanty v. Staudenraus*, 901 P.2d 841, 846 (Or. 1995) ("[I]t follows that, when an employee is acting in the scope of the employee's employment, the employee is acting as the employer, and not as an independent entity. Accordingly, when an employee is acting within the scope of the employee's employment, and the employer, as a result, breaches a contract with another party, that employee is not a third party for the tort of intentional interference with economic relations.").

(6) How would the *Holloway* dispute be resolved under the Second Restatement? *See* RESTATEMENT (SECOND) OF TORTS §§ 766, 770 (1979).

CHAPTER 4

BREACH OF FIDUCIARY DUTY

■ ■ ■

Who is a fiduciary? Broadly speaking, a fiduciary is a person "who appear[s] to accept, expressly or impliedly, an obligation to act in a position of trust or confidence for the benefit of another or who [has] accepted a status or relationship understood to entail such an obligation, generating the beneficiary's justifiable expectations of loyalty." 3 DAN B. DOBBS ET AL., THE LAW OF TORTS § 697, at 749 (2d ed. 2011); *see also* RESTATEMENT (SECOND) OF TORTS § 874 cmt. a (1979) ("A fiduciary relation exists between two persons when one of them is under a duty to act for or to give advice for the benefit of another upon matters within the scope of the relation."). Courts often speak of two types of fiduciary relationships. First, "formal" fiduciary relationships are those that have categorically been held, as a matter of law, to be fiduciary in nature. Common examples of formal fiduciary relationships include the relationship of an attorney to his client, an agent to his principal, a partner to his fellow partner, and a trustee to his beneficiary.[a] Second, "informal" fiduciary relationships (also referred to as "confidential" relationships) are those that may arise on the facts of particular disputes based on a relationship of trust and confidence between the parties. *See, e.g.,* 3 DOBBS ET AL., *supra,* § 697, at 753 ("Apart from formalized or categorical fiduciary relationships, other fiduciary obligations may arise on the facts of particular cases where the plaintiff reposes special trust and confidence in the defendant and the defendant gives the appearance of tacitly accepting that trust and hence his fiduciary role.").

What duties do fiduciaries owe? Breach of fiduciary duty is a powerful cause of action for plaintiffs because fiduciaries owe very strict obligations to their beneficiaries. In general, because fiduciaries act for the benefit of other persons, they owe duties of care and loyalty to those persons. The duty of care requires the fiduciary to act with the care, competence, and diligence normally exercised by fiduciaries in similar circumstances. The duty of loyalty requires the fiduciary to act solely in the best interests of the beneficiary. This includes (at least traditionally) the fiduciary's obligations to avoid conflicts of interest, to disclose all

---

[a] These fiduciary relationships are often not reciprocal. For example, an attorney owes a fiduciary duty to his client, but the client does not owe a fiduciary duty to his attorney. Similarly, while an agent owes a fiduciary duty to his principal, the principal does not owe a fiduciary duty to his agent.

material information, and to put the beneficiary's interests ahead of his own. As an example of the potency of the breach of fiduciary duty action, consider the onerous obligations of a fiduciary as set forth in this Texas pattern jury charge:

Did [Defendant] comply with his fiduciary duty to [Plaintiff]?

. . . [Defendant] owed [Plaintiff] a fiduciary duty. To prove he complied with his duty, [Defendant] must show:

a.   the transaction[s] in question [was/were] fair and equitable to [Plaintiff];

b.   [Defendant] made reasonable use of the confidence that [Plaintiff] placed in him;

c.   [Defendant] acted in the utmost good faith and exercised the most scrupulous honesty toward [Plaintiff];

d.   [Defendant] placed the interests of [Plaintiff] before his own, did not use the advantage of his position to gain any benefit for himself at the expense of [Plaintiff], and did not place himself in any position where his self-interest might conflict with his obligations as a fiduciary; and

e.   [Defendant] fully and fairly disclosed all important information to [Plaintiff] concerning the transaction[s].

STATE BAR OF TEXAS, TEXAS PATTERN JURY CHARGES PJC 104.2 (2012) (italics omitted).

What remedies exist for breach of fiduciary duty? A breach of fiduciary duty is a tort. As a consequence, a plaintiff may recover compensatory damages and, in egregious cases, punitive damages. Equitable remedies are also available, including injunctions, rescission, restitution of payments made to the fiduciary, disgorgement of the fiduciary's profits in a particular transaction, or any other equitable remedy deemed appropriate by the court.

As mentioned, fiduciary relationships may be formal (established as a matter of law in a categorical fashion) or informal (established as a matter of fact in a particular case). It is always easier for a plaintiff to assert a formal fiduciary relationship, if available, because no proof is required other than evidence that the parties' relationship falls into one of the established categories. If a formal fiduciary relationship does not exist, however, how can a plaintiff demonstrate an informal fiduciary relationship? What evidence, in other words, will suffice to establish the requisite relationship of trust and confidence between the parties? The following case addresses these questions.

CRIM TRUCK & TRACTOR CO. V. NAVISTAR INT'L TRANSP. CORP.

823 S.W.2d 591 (Tex. 1992)

CORNYN, JUSTICE.

. . . .

This case presents the question of whether there is evidence of a confidential relationship, giving rise to a fiduciary duty, between the parties to a franchise agreement. Plaintiffs are the franchisee, Crim Truck and Tractor Company, Travis Crim and Tim Farley (the Crims). The defendant is the franchisor, Navistar International Transportation Corporation (Navistar), formerly known as International Harvester Corporation. The trial court rendered judgment for the Crims based on jury findings of breach of contract, breach of fiduciary duty and fraud. The court of appeals found no evidence of a confidential relationship which would give rise to a fiduciary duty. The court of appeals also found no evidence of an actionable misrepresentation, an essential element of the Crims' fraud cause of action. The court of appeals, however, found some evidence that Navistar breached its contract with the Crims, but reversed the trial court's judgment because of insufficient evidence to support the damages awarded by the jury on that theory. Consequently, the court remanded the case for a new trial on the contract issues. Because we also find no evidence of a confidential relationship, or of an actionable misrepresentation, we affirm the judgment of the court of appeals.

Crim Truck and Tractor's relationship with Navistar's predecessor, International Harvester, began in 1943. The parties enjoyed a mutually beneficial working relationship for years before reducing their agreement to writing in 1958. The written agreement was amended in 1964 and again in 1979. The 1979 revision of the franchise agreement, at issue here, allows the Crims to terminate the franchise at will. However, Navistar could not unilaterally terminate the franchise unless the Crims breached any of eleven conditions of the contract. The contract, furthermore, grants the Crims a reasonable opportunity to cure any claimed breach.

The sometimes stormy[2] relationship between the parties further deteriorated in September 1983. In 1983 Navistar decided to establish a

---

[2] Although both Travis Crim and Tim Farley testified to a generally cordial relationship between the parties, Travis Crim testified that Navistar's predecessor, International Harvester, had threatened termination of the franchise agreement on at least two prior occasions. The first occasion was in 1962, when Travis Crim's father was still running the dealership. This resulted in an exchange of letters threatening legal action between the parties' attorneys. The last occasion, prior to termination of the franchise agreement, occurred in 1976. At that time, International Harvester decided not to renew the Crims' franchise agreement. The parties continued to do business under the terms of the expired contract. At the urging of an International Harvester manager, the contract at issue was executed three years later.

nationwide dealer communications network to share computerized information between Navistar and all of its dealers. This system was designed to facilitate distribution of supplies among dealers, and the provision of warranty and repair services to customers. Navistar called a meeting of all of its dealers in September 1983 to introduce the dealer communications network system. The Crims declined to send a representative to this meeting.

Thereafter, Navistar asked its dealers to sign and return a sales and service agreement that obligated them to purchase the computer equipment required to implement the dealer communications network system. The Crims elected not to sign the contract. In October 1984, Navistar notified the Crims that it considered participation in the dealer communications network mandatory. Navistar also informed the Crims that it considered them to be in anticipatory breach of the contract, but gave them an opportunity to cure the alleged breach by signing and returning the sales and service agreement by November 26, 1984. The Crims never signed and returned the contract.

Finally, on December 10, 1984, Navistar reiterated its intention to terminate the franchise agreement effective April 1, 1985. Once again the Crims were given an opportunity to sign and return the sales and service agreement before the effective date and avoid termination. Because the Crims did not comply with Navistar's repeated requests, the franchise was terminated April 1, 1985.

Thereafter, the Crims brought this suit seeking damages for breach of contract, breach of fiduciary duty and fraud. [They] alleged loss of past and future profits, diminution of the value of the business, loss of investment, mental anguish, and exemplary damages. The trial court rendered judgment in favor of the Crims in accordance with the jury's verdict. Navistar appealed.

Historically, we have recognized that certain relationships give rise to a "fiduciary" duty as a matter of law. *See, e.g., Kinzbach Tool Co. v. Corbett-Wallace Corp.,* 138 Tex. 565, 160 S.W.2d 509, 513 (1942) (principal/agent); *Johnson v. Peckham,* 132 Tex. 148, 120 S.W.2d 786, 787 (1938) (partners). More recently, we have also categorized certain relationships as "special relationships," giving rise to a tort duty of good faith and fair dealing. *See, e.g., Aranda v. Insurance Co. of N. Am.,* 748 S.W.2d 210, 212–13 (Tex.1988); *Arnold v. National County Mut. Fire Ins. Co.,* 725 S.W.2d 165, 167 (Tex.1987). Although a fiduciary duty encompasses at the very minimum a duty of good faith and fair dealing, the converse is not true. The duty of good faith and fair dealing merely requires the parties to "deal fairly" with one another and does not encompass the often more onerous burden that requires a party to place the interest of the other party before his own, often attributed to a fiduciary duty.

We have also recognized that certain informal relationships may give rise to a fiduciary duty. Such informal fiduciary relationships have also been termed "confidential relationships" and may arise "where one person trusts in and relies upon another, whether the relation is a moral, social, domestic or merely personal one." *Fitz-Gerald v. Hull*, 150 Tex. 39, 237 S.W.2d 256, 261 (1951). Because not every relationship involving a high degree of trust and confidence rises to the stature of a formal fiduciary relationship, the law recognizes the existence of confidential relationships in those cases "in which influence has been acquired and abused, in which confidence has been reposed and betrayed." *Texas Bank & Trust Co. v. Moore*, 595 S.W.2d 502, 507 (Tex.1980). The existence of a confidential relationship is usually a question of fact. . . .

The Crims concede that *not every* franchise agreement creates a fiduciary relationship. But, they argue that the facts here prove a confidential relationship giving rise to an informal fiduciary relationship, imposing the duty on Navistar, not just to seek its own economic interests, but to put the Crims' interests before its own.[4]

But, this argument clashes with the rule that a party to a contract is free to pursue its own interests, even if it results in a breach of that contract, without incurring tort liability. *See Amoco Production Co. v. Alexander*, 622 S.W.2d 563, 571 (Tex.1981). The fact that one businessman trusts another, and relies upon his promise to perform a contract, does not rise to a confidential relationship. Every contract includes an element of confidence and trust that each party will faithfully perform his obligation under the contract.[5] Neither is the fact that the

---

[4]   The trial court submitted the question of the existence of a confidential relationship in terms of a fiduciary duty. The jury was instructed that:

> [a] "fiduciary duty" arises from a confidential relationship or when a relationship of trust is placed by one in another and the one relies on and acts on the representations of the other. Where this relationship of confidence or trust exists, a duty rests on the party in whom the confidence or trust is placed, in entering into any transaction with the other, to make a full disclosure of the other's rights in the transaction and a full disclosure of all material facts which might affect the other's decision whether to enter the transaction and to refrain from abusing the confidence or trust by obtaining an advantage to himself at the expense of the confiding or trusting party.

The jury was then asked in special question 3 as to whether a "fiduciary relationship" existed between the Crims and Navistar. If they answered special question 3 affirmatively, the jury was then asked whether Navistar had breached its "fiduciary duty" to the Crims "in connection with the termination of [the Crims'] franchise" in special question 4. Conditioned upon an affirmative response to question 4, special question 5 inquired as to whether the breach of fiduciary duty by Navistar was "made consciously and willfully, or with gross indifference and reckless disregard" for the Crims' rights. Navistar objected to this submission on the grounds that "as a matter of law, there is no fiduciary relationship" between the parties and "there is no evidence that there is or was a fiduciary relationship" between the parties.

[5]   The majority of other jurisdictions have rejected the imposition of general fiduciary duties on the franchise relationship. Several of those jurisdictions that have rejected imposition of general fiduciary duties in this context have also recognized that fiduciary duties may

relationship has been a cordial one, of long duration, evidence of a confidential relationship.[6] *See Thigpen*, 363 S.W.2d at 253.

Travis Crim testified that he believed the relationship with Navistar was one of mutual trust and confidence. However, "mere subjective trust alone is not enough to transform arms-length dealing into a fiduciary relationship." *Thigpen*, 363 S.W.2d at 253. Further, the Crims point to language in the contract which they claim articulates a special trust and confidence between these parties beyond that ordinarily found in a contract.[7] We are unpersuaded that this language was ever intended to inject an element of personal trust and confidence above and beyond that which is ordinarily contemplated by parties to contracts of this type.

As a general rule, all contracts are assignable. An exception to this rule is that a contract that relies on the personal trust, confidence, skill, character or credit of the parties, may not be assigned without the consent of the parties. "Rights arising out of a contract cannot be transferred if they involve a relation of personal confidence such that the party whose agreement conferred those rights must have intended them to be exercised only by him in whom he actually confided." [*Moore v. Mohon*, 514 S.W.2d 508, 513 (Tex. Civ. App.—Waco 1974, no writ).] The Crims' reliance on the cited contract language as evidence of a confidential relationship is misplaced. Such "boiler plate" language is

---

independently arise because of the nature of the relationship of the parties without regard to the underlying contract between the parties. Others have recognized an implied contractual duty of good faith and fair dealing in franchise agreements arising out of a general duty of good faith and fair dealing implied in all contracts. We, however, have specifically rejected the implication of a general duty of good faith and fair dealing in all contracts. In any event, a breach of this contractual duty of good faith and fair dealing gives rise only to a cause of action for breach of contract and does not give rise to an independent tort cause of action.

[6]　The dissent in the court of appeals cites testimony from Travis Crim that "he and his father had always done the things requested by the Franchisor. . . ." The record reveals that the Crims followed the requests made by the franchisor on two occasions. The first instance occurred in 1947, when the elder Crim moved the dealership location and built a prototype building suggested by International Harvester. Travis Crim testified that the building and land remained the property of his family. Additionally, several years earlier the Crims purchased computer software recommended by International Harvester. We find nothing extraordinary about these requests in the context of the franchise agreement. But, this is not evidence of a confidential relationship.

The dissent also points to the fact that Navistar's predecessor had held out the Crims as an excellent dealership with whom they hoped to continue a long and fruitful relationship. This is based on events that occurred in 1947 during the "grand opening" of the new dealership facility. On that occasion, International Harvester purchased an ad in an area newspaper congratulating the Crims on their new building and complimenting them on their performance. Likewise, this one occurrence thirty-eight years prior to termination of the franchise agreement is no evidence of a confidential relationship.

[7]　The "General Provisions" section of the contract between the parties contains paragraph 34, which beside a margin notation of "Parties Bound, Effect of Partial Invalidity and Assignment" (emphasis supplied), provides in part:

> This is a personal agreement, involving mutual confidence and trust, and it may not be assigned by either party without the written consent of the other party, except that [Navistar] may, however, assign the agreement to any of its subsidiary or affiliated corporations, without the consent of the [Crims].

designed to give the parties some degree of control over with whom they do business, and nothing more. This language was obviously intended to render the franchise agreement unilaterally unassignable.

Alternatively, the Crims urge us, at the very minimum, to impose a common law fiduciary duty on franchisors in the termination of franchise agreements. However, we find imposition of a common law duty unnecessary under the current statutory scheme controlling this aspect of the franchise relationship. In the most recent amendments to the Texas Motor Vehicle Commission Code, the Legislature has undertaken to regulate many aspects of the relationship at issue here. *See* Tex.Rev.Civ.Stat.Ann. art. 4413(36) § 5.02 (Vernon Supp.1991).[9] Wrongful termination of a motor vehicle dealership franchise agreement is now governed by the Texas Motor Vehicle Commission Code. A person who has sustained damages as a result of a violation of these provisions may bring suit under the Texas Deceptive Trade Practices–Consumer Protection Act. Tex.Rev.Civ.Stat.Ann. art. 4413(36) § 6.06 (Vernon Supp.1991). Additionally, since 1956, Congress has imposed a duty of good faith in terminating automobile franchise agreements. 15 U.S.C. §§ 1221–1225 (1988). The federal statute is designed to supplement state common law and statutory rights and duties. *Id.* § 1225. We see no good reason to add to the existing regulatory scheme by implication of a common law fiduciary duty.

The Crims, in their cross-points in this court, argue that the damages awarded by the jury for mental anguish, loss of investment and as punitive damages are supported by the jury's findings on the fraud issues, as well as breach of fiduciary duty. The court of appeals found no evidence of a misrepresentation, observing that the only misrepresentations claimed are the terms of the contract themselves. We agree with the court of appeals.

As a general rule, the failure to perform the terms of a contract is a breach of contract, not a tort. However, when one party enters into a contract with no intention of performing, that misrepresentation may give rise to an action in fraud. But, a party's failure to perform a contract, standing alone, is no evidence of that party's intent not to perform at the time the contract was made. A review of this record reveals that there is no evidence that Navistar did not intend to perform the terms of the contract at the time it was made in 1979.

For these reasons, we affirm the judgment of the court of appeals remanding the case to the trial court for a new trial only on the contract and related damage issues.

---

[9] Those portions of the amendments regulating franchise termination or nonrenewal became effective June 16, 1989, and thus are inapplicable to the termination in the present case which occurred April 1, 1985 and the suit subsequently filed based thereon in 1987.

MAUZY, JUSTICE, dissenting.

. . . .

Once again wrongfully disregarding a jury verdict, the court has rejected vital protection for Texas businesses. Ignoring a long-standing contract and the circumstances surrounding it, the court abandons motor vehicle dealers and other small businesses across the state to the whims of powerful franchisors. These massive enterprises are invited to enter our state and abuse local businesses without fear of reproach from Texas courts. Today's decision leaves Texas franchisees with less protection than they would have in virtually any other jurisdiction.

This court has long recognized that "where one person trusts in and relies upon another," the relationship between the two may give rise to a fiduciary duty. *Fitz-Gerald v. Hull*, 150 Tex. 39, 237 S.W.2d 256, 261 (1951). As the court notes today, the existence of an informal fiduciary relationship, or "confidential" relationship, is usually a question of fact. What sort of evidence, then, might tend to establish a confidential relationship?

—the fact that one businessman trusts another, and relies upon his promise to perform a contract? No, the court says today; one may trust another implicitly, and stake a lifetime of earnings on the other's promise, but that is still no evidence of a confidential relationship.

—the fact that the relationship has been a cordial one, of long duration? No, says the court; businesses might interact on the best of terms for a century, but that would still not be any evidence of trust and confidence.

—express contractual language stating that the relationship is one involving mutual confidence and trust? No, says the court; regardless of what the parties thought, that language indicates only unassignability, which has nothing to do with trust and confidence.

To reach these bizarre conclusions, the court misrepresents important precedents, and then misapplies them to the facts of this case. The court relies heavily on *Thigpen v. Locke*, 363 S.W.2d 247 (Tex.1962), to establish that nothing in the present case suggests the existence of a confidential relationship. In that case, though, the court was careful to limit the scope of its holding:

> All we hold is that [plaintiffs] do not testify to facts—other than their own subjective feelings—which show that their relationship with [defendant] was anything more than a debtor-creditor relationship.

363 S.W.2d at 253. At the time of the conveyance disputed in *Thigpen*, the parties had known each other for less than four years. Nonetheless, the

court cites *Thigpen,* 363 S.W.2d at 253, for the proposition that "the fact that the relationship has been a cordial one, *of long duration,* [is not] evidence of a confidential relationship." I challenge anyone to find anything on the referenced page that supports the proposition for which it is cited.

Similarly, the court misrepresents the import of *Consolidated Gas & Equipment Co. v. Thompson,* 405 S.W.2d 333, 336 (Tex.1966). The court relies on that case without even referring to its reasoning. The *Thompson* opinion does not indicate the duration of the parties' relationship; rather, it cites *Thigpen* and other cases, and then explains them as follows:

> Our holdings above cited are to the effect that for a constructive trust to arise there must be a fiduciary relationship before, and apart from, the agreement made the basis of the suit. Such is our holding here.[b]

405 S.W.2d at 336. The court's failure today to explain *Thompson* is understandable: the parties in the present case had a relationship of trust and confidence for fifteen years before the franchise agreement made the basis of this suit.

The court then explains away some of the contract's most important language. Parties may agree, in writing, that their relationship is one of mutual confidence; but even so, the court decides, they don't really mean it. Offering no authority for disregarding such language, the court also disregards longstanding rules that a contract should be construed in accordance with its plain language, and that a writing is construed most strictly against its author. By simply dismissing this language as "obviously intended to render the franchise agreement unilaterally unassignable," the court misses an equally obvious point: the unassignability of the agreement plainly indicates a confidential relationship. If there were no trust and confidence involved, why would a party care whether the agreement was assignable? A nonassignability clause may not conclusively establish the existence of a confidential relationship; but surely it is some evidence of trust and confidence. *See Carter Equip. Co. v. John Deere Indus. Equip. Co.,* 681 F.2d 386, 391 (5th

---

[b] In a later decision, the Supreme Court of Texas made this point more generally: "To impose an informal fiduciary duty in a business transaction, the special relationship of trust and confidence must exist prior to, and apart from, the agreement made the basis of the suit." *Associated Indem. Corp. v. CAT Contracting, Inc.,* 964 S.W.2d 276, 288 (Tex. 1998). The court also noted that an "arms-length transaction entered into for the parties' mutual benefit" is insufficient to establish this pre-existing relationship of trust and confidence. *Id.; see also Meyer v. Cathey,* 167 S.W.3d 327, 331 (Tex. 2005) ("To impose an informal fiduciary duty in a business transaction, the special relationship of trust and confidence must exist prior to, and apart from, the agreement made the basis of the suit. Here, there is no evidence of such a preexisting relationship between Meyer and Cathey. The court of appeals' reliance on Meyer's and Cathey's work on prior projects is misplaced. These earlier projects were arms-length transactions entered into for the parties' mutual benefit, and thus do not establish a basis for a fiduciary relationship.").

Cir.1982) ("[T]he nature of the agreement between the parties may provide evidence that a fiduciary relationship exists.").

The Crims presented a wealth of evidence indicating that their forty-three-year relationship with Navistar was, in fact, one of trust and confidence. After a fifteen-year relationship based solely on trust—the parties working together without any written contract—the Crims continued to trust their franchisor, and to do its bidding. Travis Crim testified that he maintained his faith in Navistar partly because of the franchise provision that "[t]his is a personal agreement involving mutual confidence and trust. . . ."; without which language, Crim testified, he would not have signed the franchise agreement. After the Crims built a prototype building in a new location at Navistar's direction, Navistar placed a newspaper ad describing this structure as a symbol of "good faith and permanency in the progressive community of Henderson, Texas." Tim Farley testified that the termination of the franchise agreement by Navistar "broke" his "trust in them." Dick Ettle, a Navistar Area Sales Manager, testified that he did not recall the Crims ever refusing to do anything that he asked of them. Travis Crim testified that the Crims carried every line of Navistar product offered to them.

After hearing all of the evidence, the jury determined that a fiduciary relationship existed between Navistar and the Crims. In reviewing that determination on a no evidence point of error, this court must consider only the evidence and inferences tending to support the jury verdict, and disregard all evidence to the contrary. When there is more than a scintilla of evidence, an appellate court may not overturn the jury's finding on a no evidence point of error.

The court today fails to give due consideration to the evidence supporting the jury verdict; indeed, the court does not even bother to mention much of that evidence. The court simply presents selected facts, assigning weight to those according to its own inclinations. In doing so, the court assumes for itself the job which the trial court properly assigned to twelve jurors. I would uphold the jury's finding of a fiduciary relationship.

    . . . .

Other courts throughout the nation have recognized the immense power wielded by franchisors, and have developed their law so as to afford some protection to franchisees. *See Atlantic Richfield Co. v. Razumic*, 480 Pa. 366, 390 A.2d 736, 742 (1978) ("The weight of commentary has argued in favor of judicial recognition that the nature of a franchise agreement imposes a duty upon franchisors not to act arbitrarily in terminating the franchise agreement.") A number of courts have held that obligations of good faith and fair dealing prevent a franchisor from terminating a franchise agreement without cause. Other courts have held that a franchise relationship may give rise to fiduciary duties in the context of dealership termination.

To make its decision seem within the mainstream of American case law, the court cites the foregoing cases and others for a proposition no one disputes: "The majority of other jurisdictions have rejected the imposition of general fiduciary duties on the franchise relationship." As the court itself recognizes, the Crims do not suggest that this court impose general fiduciary duties on the franchise relationship. Rather, the Crims argue that the evidence in this case supports the conclusion that a confidential relationship existed, and alternatively that a fiduciary relationship should be recognized where a franchisor has wrongfully terminated the franchise agreement. Both of those arguments are consistent with every one of the cases the court cites.

In contrast, the court's decision today is fundamentally at odds with most of the cases it cites, at least insofar as the court completely rejects the Crims' arguments. For instance, in *Carter Equip. Co. v. John Deere Indus. Equip. Co.,* 681 F.2d 386 (5th Cir.1982), the court recognized that relationships like the one at issue here may be fiduciary in nature.[2] Moreover, of the cases the court cites as rejecting a general fiduciary duty, none reject such a duty in the context of franchise termination; in fact, those that address the issue actually recognize such a duty. Most state courts addressing the issue have done the same.

. . . .

In addressing whether to impose a fiduciary duty on franchisors in the termination of franchise agreements, the court finds "no good reason

---

[2] In addition to the goals of the parties and the requisite need for trust or confidence in one another, the nature of the agreement between the parties may provide evidence that a fiduciary relationship exists. If the franchisor has power to control the franchisee, there is an increased likelihood that a fiduciary relationship exists, since trust or confidence necessarily must flow from the controlled or dominated party. As a result, the power, authority, and bargaining position of *both* the franchisor and franchisee becomes critical.

["Here, there is ample evidence of Navistar's . . . exclusive control over its franchisees. The 1979 franchise agreement contains the following provisions which, individually and collectively, show the imbalance in bargaining power: (1) Navistar may add or eliminate truck models without incurring liability to the Crims. (2) Navistar has unilateral control over what orders it will accept from the Crims. (3) Only under very limited circumstances can the Crims cancel their order for products from Navistar. (4) Navistar can retroactively modify the price and the terms of an order from the Crims *after* the Crims have placed the order. . . . (6) Navistar has the right to add the cost of company advertising to the Crims' prices. (7) Navistar expressly reserves the right to compete with the Crims for major sales accounts in the Crims' own designated trade areas. (8) Navistar reserves the right to change the specifications and design of any product and requires the Crims to accept that modified product in fulfillment of existing orders. (9) The Crims are not allowed to change the location of their retail establishment without Navistar's approval. (10) Navistar controls the content and quality of the Crims' advertising activities. . . . (13) The Crims must provide a service center and a building to sell and service Navistar's products. . . . (14) The Crims must, at their own risk and expense, hire and train service, sales, and accounting personnel to service and sell Navistar's products. Travis Crim testified that he had no input on the wording of the franchise agreement. He stated that 'We either signed it, or we did not have a contract.' "]

to add to the existing regulatory scheme by implication of a common law fiduciary duty." The court notes that after June 16, 1989, the wrongful termination of a motor vehicle dealership franchise agreement is governed by the Texas Motor Vehicle Commission Code (TMVCC). Since this suit was filed before that time, the Crims did not have the benefit of this statutory remedy. Moreover, the legislature's treatment of the franchise relationship hardly requires this court to blind itself to [the] nature of that relationship. *Compare Arnott v. American Oil Co.,* 609 F.2d at 883 ("[F]urther indication of the fiduciary nature of a franchise relationship is found in the recent surge of general franchise legislation.").

The court would also have the Crims believe that they could have been aided by the Automobile Dealers' Day in Court Act (ADDCA), 15 U.S.C. §§ 1221–1225 (1988), in which Congress has imposed a duty of good faith in terminating automobile franchise agreements. Case law under the ADDCA, however, holds that the Act does not protect the dealer from mere "arbitrary" or bad faith conduct. Coercion or intimidation is needed to show a lack of good faith under the Code's stricter definition of "good faith."

The termination in this case was arbitrary. Rex Templeton, Finance Planning Manager for Navistar, testified that not all dealers who failed to sign the agreement to purchase the new computer system were terminated. In fact, there is no specific evidence in the record of this case of any other dealer of Navistar products being terminated for failure to purchase the computer system except for the Crims. Virgil Nelson, a retired Navistar Contracts Manager, testified at trial, a full three years after the Crims were terminated for not agreeing to purchase the computer system, that Navistar still had not provided its dealers with the forms necessary for the dealers to use the computers to order inventory and products. Both Nelson and Templeton, as well as Navistar dealer Al Pliler, testified that Navistar still had dealers using the same written forms that the Crims were using when terminated in 1985. Nelson testified that fifty percent of the dealers were not using the computer system to place orders.

The Crims did not plead coercion or intimidation. On the contrary, the Crims contended and proved to the jury that this action was a wrongful termination by Navistar. Thus, there is no evidence in the record to suggest that the Crims could have availed themselves of the protections provided by the ADDCA. The fact that Congress eventually recognized, by enactment of legislation, the same disparity of bargaining power that gives rise to this action is twisted by the court to justify its inequitable result. Although the Crims can in no way utilize ADDCA, the court relies on it to reject their claim.

Because the court today fails completely to give due recognition to imbalances of power in business relationships, I strongly dissent. I would reverse the judgment of the court of appeals and remand this cause to that court for consideration of the factual insufficiency points.

DOGGETT and GAMMAGE, JJ., join in this dissenting opinion.

NOTES & QUESTIONS

(1) Were the Crims asserting a "formal" or "informal" fiduciary relationship between themselves and Navistar? What evidence did the Crims introduce to establish this relationship? Why was that evidence insufficient?

(2) The *Crim Truck* court noted the "onerous burden that requires a [fiduciary] to place the interest of the other party before his own." *See also Zastrow v. Journal Communications, Inc.*, 718 N.W.2d 51, 59 (Wis. 2006) ("A consistent facet of a fiduciary duty is the constraint on the fiduciary's discretion to act in his own self-interest because by accepting the obligation of a fiduciary he consciously sets another's interests before his own."). Is that obligation to act selflessly consistent with the relationship between the Crims and Navistar? Is such an obligation consistent with the relationship between most contracting parties?

(3) As *Crim Truck* suggests, not every relationship involving trust and confidence between the parties rises to the level of an informal fiduciary (or confidential) relationship. Precise rules suggesting that such a relationship exists are difficult to articulate. *Cf. Texas Bank and Trust Co. v. Moore*, 595 S.W.2d 502, 508 (Tex. 1980) (noting that "the circumstances out of which a fiduciary relationship will be said to arise are not subject to hard and fast lines"); GEORGE G. BOGERT ET AL., THE LAW OF TRUSTS AND TRUSTEES § 482 (3d ed. 2009) ("Equity has never bound itself by any hard and fast definition of the phrase 'confidential relation' and has not listed the necessary elements for such a relationship to exist but rather has reserved discretion to apply the doctrine whenever it believes that a suitable occasion has arisen."). In general, a court will find that an informal fiduciary relationship exists only in egregious circumstances where the plaintiff reposes a significant amount of trust and confidence in the defendant, and the defendant appears to accept that trust. As one commentator observed:

> . . . . In determining whether a fiduciary relation exists because of special confidence reposed, courts will consider evidence bearing on the plaintiff's reasonable expectations based on the defendant's apparent acceptance of the plaintiff's confidence and his own fiduciary responsibility. Broadly stated, factors include the course of the parties' prior relationship over time, the defendant's evident allegiances, the inability of the putative beneficiary to protect herself and analogies to the recognized categories of fiduciaries. . . . The unequal position of the parties is an important factor—a

variation on the idea that the plaintiff is unable to protect herself or her property.

3 DAN B. DOBBS ET AL., THE LAW OF TORTS § 697, at 754 (2d ed. 2011); *cf.* Gillespie v. Seymour, 796 P.2d 1060, 1063 (Kan. Ct. App. 1990), *rev'd in part on other grounds*, 823 P.2d 782 (Kan. 1991) ("A fiduciary relationship requires confidence of one in another and a certain inequity or dependence arising from weakness of age, mental strength, business intelligence, knowledge of facts involved, or other conditions which give one an advantage over the other."). *See generally First Nat'l Bank of Meeker v. Theos*, 794 P.2d 1055, 1061 (Colo. App. 1990) ("[A] confidential relationship may arise if: (1) one party has taken steps to induce another to believe that it can safely rely on the first party's judgment or advice; (2) one person has gained the confidence of the other and purports to act or advise with the other's interest in mind; or (3) the parties' relationship is such that one is induced to relax the care and vigilance one ordinarily would exercise in dealing with a stranger.").

For examples of decisions finding that an informal fiduciary relationship existed, see *Nelson v. Dodge*, 68 A.2d 51, 55–58 (R.I. 1949) (involving a religious leader who convinced a member of her church that the member needed to sell all of his assets and give the proceeds to her); *Dixon v. Dixon*, 608 S.E.2d 849, 853–54 (S.C. 2005) (involving an elderly mother who gave her son partial control over her affairs, made her bank accounts available to him, and signed documents that he prepared without reviewing them); *Buxcel v. First Fidelity Bank*, 601 N.W.2d 593, 595, 597–98 (S.D. 1999) (involving a bank who convinced a customer/borrower to take out a Small Business Administration loan to purchase a failing grocery store).

(4) Do family members owe fiduciary duties to one another? In general, courts have not characterized family as a formal fiduciary relationship. *See, e.g., Francois v. Francois*, 599 F.2d 1286, 1292 (3d Cir. 1979) (observing that "[t]he marital relation does not automatically give rise to a confidential relation"); *In re Kieras*, 521 N.E.2d 263, 280 (Ill. App. Ct. 1988) ("However, the relationship between parent and child is not fiduciary as a matter of law."); *Simpson v. Dailey*, 496 A.2d 126, 128 (R.I. 1985) (stating that "[a] family relationship, of itself, does not create a fiduciary relationship"); *Texas Bank and Trust Co. v. Moore*, 595 S.W.2d 502, 508 (Tex. 1980) (noting that "the relationship of Mrs. Littell and Moore[—]that of aunt and nephew[—]together with Moore's assistance to Mrs. Littell, do not, standing alone, establish a fiduciary relationship"). There are some decisions—often older decisions—to the contrary. *See, e.g., Putnam v. Putnam*, 150 So. 2d 209, 213 (Ala. 1963) ("The marriage of the complainant and the respondent . . . created between them a relationship of confidence and trust, exacting the utmost good faith in their dealing with each other."). In addition, a statute may change the result. *See, e.g.*, CAL. FAM. CODE § 721(b) (stating that "in transactions between themselves, spouses are subject to the general rules governing fiduciary relationships that control the actions of persons occupying confidential relations with each other.").

With respect to an informal fiduciary relationship, a family connection can be evidence of the requisite relationship of trust and confidence between the parties. Once again, however, the mere existence of family ties is typically insufficient. *See, e.g., Francois*, 599 F.2d at 1292 ("The marital relation does not automatically give rise to a confidential relation, but it 'arises when one party places confidence in the other with a resulting superiority and influence on the other side.' Thus, each marriage must be examined on its own facts to determine if a confidential relation exists."); *Liapis v. Dist. Ct.*, 282 P.3d 733, 738 (Nev. 2012) (stating that "although a fiduciary relationship 'is particularly likely to exist when there is a family relationship,' '[a] family relationship, of itself, does not create a fiduciary relationship' unless it is established by additional facts"); *Dixon v. Dixon*, 608 S.E.2d 849, 853 (S.C. 2005) ("Although this Court has declined to hold that a familial relationship, alone, is sufficient evidence of a confidential relationship, a familial relationship certainly *supports* an argument that a confidential relationship exists."); *cf. Mendenhall v. Judy*, 671 N.W.2d 452, 455 (Iowa 2003) (noting that a confidential relationship "is particularly likely to exist where there is a family relationship"); RESTATEMENT (SECOND) OF TORTS § 551 cmt. f (1977) (noting that "members of the same family normally stand in a fiduciary relation to one another, although it is of course obvious that the fact that two men are brothers does not establish [a] relation of trust and confidence when they have become estranged").

(5)   A fiduciary's wrongdoing may not constitute a breach of fiduciary duty if it falls outside the scope of the particular fiduciary obligation. For example, "[a] lawyer, who is a fiduciary to his client, might negligently drive his automobile, causing physical harm to his client, but that would ordinarily not show a breach of fiduciary duty, which relates to loyalty to the client, not to good driving." 3 DOBBS ET AL., *supra*, § 699, at 762 n.20.

(6)   As mentioned, breach of fiduciary duty is a powerful cause of action for plaintiffs because fiduciaries owe very strict obligations to their beneficiaries. Moreover, when a fiduciary's compliance with his obligations is challenged, courts in many situations will impose the burden of proof upon the fiduciary himself. *See, e.g., Cadle Co. v. D'Addario*, 844 A.2d 836, 847 (Conn. 2004) ("The superior position of the fiduciary or dominant party affords him great opportunity for abuse of the confidence reposed in him. . . . Once a [fiduciary] relationship is found to exist, the burden of proving fair dealing properly shifts to the fiduciary."). For plaintiffs, this potential burden shift is another attractive aspect of the breach of fiduciary duty cause of action.

(7)   Persons who aid and abet violations of fiduciary duties are generally subject to liability as well. *See, e.g.*, RESTATEMENT (SECOND) OF TORTS § 874 cmt. c (1979) ("A person who knowingly assists a fiduciary in committing a breach of trust is himself guilty of tortious conduct and is subject to liability for the harm thereby caused." (citing *id.* § 876)).

(8) The *Crim Truck* court observed that it had "categorized certain relationships as 'special relationships,' giving rise to a tort duty of good faith and fair dealing." The court then distinguished this good faith duty from a fiduciary duty: "Although a fiduciary duty encompasses at the very minimum a duty of good faith and fair dealing, the converse is not true. The duty of good faith and fair dealing merely requires the parties to 'deal fairly' with one another and does not encompass the often more onerous burden that requires a party to place the interest of the other party before his own, often attributed to a fiduciary duty." For more on the duty of good faith and fair dealing, see Chapter 5.

CHAPTER 5

BAD FAITH BREACH OF CONTRACT: INSURANCE AND BEYOND

■ ■ ■

As a general rule, a mere breach of contract does not give rise to liability in tort. Whether the defendant breaches intentionally, negligently, or innocently makes no difference—the defendant is ordinarily liable in contract, but not in tort. As one court observed:

> . . . . Whereas an intentional tort is seen as reprehensible— the deliberate or reckless harming of another—the intentional breach of contract has come to be viewed as a morally neutral act, as exemplified in Justice Holmes's remark that "[t]he duty to keep a contract at common law means a prediction that you must pay damages if you do not keep it—and nothing else." (Holmes, The Path of the Law (1897) 10 Harv.L.Rev. 457, 462.) This amoral view is supported by the economic insight that an intentional breach of contract may create a net benefit to society. The efficient breach of contract occurs when the gain to the breaching party exceeds the loss to the party suffering the breach, allowing the movement of resources to their more optimal use. Contract law must be careful "not to exceed compensatory damages if it doesn't want to deter efficient breaches."

Freeman & Mills, Inc. v. Belcher Oil Co., 900 P.2d 669, 682 (Cal. 1995) (Mosk, J., concurring and dissenting).

In limited circumstances, however, tort liability has been imposed for "bad faith" breaches of contract. Insurance disputes are a well-established example, but courts have also addressed tort liability in other contractual contexts (e.g., employment). What constitutes a bad faith breach of contract? Why is it considered tortious in some contexts, but not in others? These questions and related issues will be explored in the materials below.

A. INSURANCE

1. THE DUTY TO DEFEND AND THE DUTY TO INDEMNIFY

NORTH STAR MUTUAL INSURANCE CO. v. R.W.
431 N.W.2d 138 (Minn. Ct. App. 1988)

FOLEY, JUDGE.

This appeal is from a summary judgment granted in favor of respondent North Star Insurance Company after it had brought a declaratory judgment action against appellant T.F. to determine whether T.F.'s homeowner's insurance policy provided coverage for the negligent transmission of herpes through voluntary consensual sexual intercourse. We reverse and remand for trial.

FACTS

T.F. was insured under a homeowner's policy issued by North Star effective July 9, 1983 through July 9, 1984. In May of 1984, T.F. and R.W., both adults, voluntarily engaged in sexual intercourse at T.F.'s home. Later that month, R.W. was diagnosed as having genital herpes. R.W. claims that T.F. negligently transmitted herpes to her through their sexual intercourse. T.F. acknowledges that after R.W. asked him to submit to a medical exam, he learned that he [had] herpes. He affirmatively asserts, however, that he did not know that he had herpes at the time that the couple engaged in intercourse.

The complaint specifically alleges that the actions of T.F. were *negligent* and *not intentional*. T.F. tendered the defense to North Star which declined coverage and subsequently commenced a declaratory judgment action. The trial court granted summary judgment in favor of North Star dismissing the complaint.

ISSUES

1. Is the negligent transmission of herpes through voluntary consensual sexual intercourse an accidental occurrence under the homeowner's policy issued by North Star that requires North Star to defend the underlying action?

2. When an adult insured engages in voluntary consensual sexual intercourse with an adult partner that results in the transmission of a sexual disease, must intent to injure be inferred as a matter of law where there exists a material issue of fact as to whether the disease was negligently transmitted?

3. Is the duty to defend a claim of negligent transmission of a sexual disease under a homeowner's policy contrary to public policy?

ANALYSIS

. . . .

1. The issue of whether an insurance company, under the terms of a homeowner's policy, has a duty to defend its insured in a claim of negligent transmission of herpes through voluntary consensual sexual intercourse is one of first impression in Minnesota.

It is well established however, that if any claim is made against an insured which could result in liability for covered damages, the insurer has a duty to defend. Additionally, the Minnesota Supreme Court has held:

> If any part of the claim is *arguably* within the scope of coverage afforded by the policy, the insurer should defend and reserve its right[a] to contest coverage based on facts developed at trial.

Brown v. State Automobile & Casualty Underwriters, 293 N.W.2d 822, 825–26 (Minn.1980) (emphasis added).

Examination of North Star's Policy Provisions

A. *Definition of Bodily Injury*

Bodily injury is defined as "bodily harm, sickness or *disease* to a person including required care, loss of services, and death resulting therefrom." (Emphasis added.) It was conceded at oral argument that herpes is a disease. The language in the policy is clear. Herpes is a disease, and is not specifically excluded from the policy.

B. *Liability Provision*

Under *Coverage L, Personal Liability,* the policy provides in part:

> We pay, up to our limit of liability, all sums for which any insured is legally liable because of bodily injury or property damage caused by an occurrence to which this coverage applies.

> We will defend any suit seeking damages, provided the suit resulted from bodily injury or property damage not excluded under this coverage.

(Emphasis omitted.)

Occurrence is defined in the policy as "an accident, including continuous or repeated exposure to substantially similar conditions." An "accident" is not defined in the policy but has been defined in Minnesota in the landmark case of *Hauenstein v. St. Paul-Mercury Indemnity Co.,* 242 Minn. 354, 65 N.W.2d 122 (1954), as follows:

---

[a] A reservation of rights "means that the insurer reserves the right to later contest coverage in the event a judgment is entered against the insured or the lawsuit is settled on terms involving payment to the plaintiff." ROBERT H. JERRY, II & DOUGLAS R. RICHMOND, UNDERSTANDING INSURANCE LAW § 112[e], at 876 (4th ed. 2007).

Accident, as a source and cause of damage to property, within the terms of an accident policy, is an unexpected, unforeseen, or undesigned happening or consequence from either a known or an unknown cause.

Id. at 358–59, 65 N.W.2d at 126.

Here, T.F. contends that he did not know that he had herpes, and therefore the transmission of herpes to R.W. was an accident. Contrarily, North Star argues that the transmission of a sexual disease is *never* an accident, and the disease does not occur without *wrongful sexual conduct.* Our role on appeal is not to measure moral conduct but to determine if, under the facts stated, the duty to defend is required of North Star.

Only one other jurisdiction has considered this issue. In *State Farm Fire and Casualty Co. v. Irene S. (Anonymous)*, 138 A.D.2d 589, 526 N.Y.S.2d 171 (1988), the plaintiff in the underlying action alleged that the defendant had intentionally assaulted and raped her with the intent of transmitting genital herpes. The defendant was covered by a homeowner's policy with language similar to that involved here. There, the New York court held that the defendant had set forth a meritorious defense in that if he proved that the damages sustained by the plaintiff were unintended, the injuries would be covered by the policy, and recognized that at the least, the insurer was obligated to defend in the underlying action, although a decision on the insurer's ultimate responsibility would have to await the trial itself. The court also recognized that

it is not legally impossible to find accidental results flowing from intentional causes, i.e., that the resulting damage was unintended although the original act or acts leading to the damages were intentional.

Id. at 591, 526 N.Y.S.2d at 173 (citations omitted).

We agree with the reasoning of the New York court. Here, T.F. contends that he did not know that he had herpes on the date that the couple had sexual intercourse. The claim is based in negligence principles. Accordingly, we hold that this is a material issue of fact for a jury to decide. Until this fact question is answered, we hold that the claim is arguably within the scope of coverage, and therefore North Star must defend T.F. in the underlying action. We observe that the duty to defend is broader than the duty to pay, and the obligation to defend is not synonymous with coverage.

2.   North Star next contends that as a matter of law, the intentional acts exclusion should apply. The specific provision provides in part:

1. *Exclusions that Apply to Both Personal Liability and Medical Payments to Others*—This policy does not apply to liability:

. . . .

h. caused intentionally by or at the direction of any *insured;*

(Emphasis in original.)

North Star argues that intent to injure is inferred as a matter of law when the insured engages in sexual misconduct even though the claim is based on negligence. To support this argument, North Star cites . . . Minnesota cases. None of these cases supports North Star's argument that we should infer intent to injure upon the facts here. North Star relies on the following cases.

Fireman's Fund Insurance Co. v. Hill, 314 N.W.2d 834 (Minn.1982). Hill and his wife were foster parents. Hill had been arrested for criminal sexual conduct with a foster child. He engaged in sexual conduct with another boy for 15 months. Hill asserted that he did not intend to harm the boy. The court found that the nature of his conduct was such that an intention to inflict injury could be inferred as a matter of law. Before the abused boy was placed with Hill, the welfare department had confronted Hill with allegations that he had sexually assaulted other foster children. Hill knew that the welfare department viewed his conduct as detrimental to the boy. A psychiatrist testified that if Hill had been confronted with and warned of his activities with other children before having contact with the boy, then he must have realized that his sexual play with him was not in the boy's best interest. The court held that [these] facts give rise to an inference of intent to inflict injury.

Horace Mann Insurance Co. v. Independent School District No. 656, 355 N.W.2d 413 (Minn.1984). Phillips, a counselor/basketball coach for Independent School District No. 656, allegedly had sexual contact with R.L.E., a high school student who played on the girls basketball team. Phillips became aware of R.L.E.'s history of drug use and began counseling her. She alleged that he inflicted several sexual contacts upon her during counseling with him and while on the basketball team. After the first alleged contact, she began to exhibit emotional problems more severe than those previously experienced with her drug problems. Since 1979 she experienced severe psychological illness and has required hospitalization on numerous occasions for suicidal tendencies, depression and anorexia. Her medical expenses as of 1983 were approximately $90,000. The court inferred intent to injure from the nature of the acts, *nonconsensual sexual contact with a minor.*

. . . .

Here, North Star is asking us to infer intent as a matter of law in a negligence case involving consenting adults. We decline to do so. . . .

3. North Star argues that it is against public policy to allow coverage here. North Star asserts in support of its position that Minnesota has not recognized a cause of action in tort for the transmission of sexual disease through sexual intercourse. We have, however, recently recognized a cause of action for the fraudulent and negligent transmission of sexual diseases, and in making that decision, we have outlined several important public policy considerations in support of that decision. *See R.A.P. v. B.J.P.*, 428 N.W.2d 103, 106 (Minn.Ct.App.1988) ("Minnesota courts have long recognized that the preservation of public health is a matter of great public importance. Legal duties and rules must therefore be designed, whenever possible, to help prevent the spread of dangerous, communicable diseases.")

Next, North Star argues that financial responsibility for sexual misconduct should not be spread among insureds through insurance. We find no merit in this argument. An insurance company can adjust and rewrite its policies to create more specific terms and exclusions. North Star could specifically exclude coverage to policy holders for the transmission of sexual diseases.

Accordingly, we hold that North Star's duty to defend T.F. pursuant to the terms of his homeowner's policy is not contrary to public policy.

DECISION

The decision of the trial court is reversed and remanded for trial of the underlying action. Viewed in the light most favorable to T.F., we hold that North Star's duty to defend T.F. in that action is arguably within the scope of coverage afforded by North Star's policy. The duty to indemnify, however, shall be deferred until a trial on the merits in the underlying action.

NOTES & QUESTIONS

(1) In insurance disputes, it is important to understand the distinction between "first party" insurance and "third party" insurance. First-party insurance is a contract involving an insurer's promise to pay an insured when the insured himself suffers a loss. Property insurance and health insurance are examples of first-party insurance. By contrast, third-party insurance is a contract involving an insurer's promise to pay a third party when the insured's actions have resulted in liability to the third party. This protection may involve defending the insured in a lawsuit, paying or settling a claim against the insured, or a combination of both. Liability insurance is third-party insurance.

In *North Star*, T.F. was insured under a homeowner's policy. Do you think the policy provided any first-party insurance? Did it provide any third-party insurance?

(2) An insurance policy will have language setting forth the coverage of the policy (the "insuring language"). For example, in *North Star*, the insuring language provided: "We pay, up to our limit of liability, all sums for which any insured is legally liable because of bodily injury or property damage caused by an occurrence to which this coverage applies." It is generally the insured's burden to prove that a claim is encompassed by the insuring language of the policy.

The policy will also contain exclusions that allow the insurer to control its risk by providing more precisely tailored coverage. As an example, most standard liability policies contain an exclusion for intentional harm caused by the insured. Indeed, in *North Star*, the policy excluded "liability . . . caused intentionally by or at the direction of any insured." Unlike the insuring language, it is generally the insurer's burden to prove that a policy exclusion is applicable.

Would insureds be better off in a world without exclusions? Not necessarily. Exclusions allow the insurer to create differentiated risk pools and to correspondingly offer less expensive policies to insureds who do not need protection from particular risks:

> . . . [I]nsureds rationally would seek full protection for all types of liability that might in fact be imposed on the individual despite the precautions that the individual realistically expects to take. For instance, the individual would wish for protection against liability resulting from slip-and-fall injuries, premises defects, and the like because he would realize that such liability is still possible even after cost-justified and realistic precautions on his part. Yet he would be willing to agree to exclusions for categories of liability that clearly will never attach to him. For instance, the insured would agree to an exclusion for liability resulting from the sale or manufacture of products, since the individual faces no real risk of being found liable as a product supplier or manufacturer and will welcome paying a lower premium for insurance that excludes such coverage. And the individual who never drinks alcohol, never keeps it on the premises, and never serves it at parties or dinners might agree to an exclusion for liabilities arising out of the serving of alcohol from the home, because he can be fairly certain that he will not be found liable in such a case.

Ellen S. Pryor, *The Stories We Tell: Intentional Harm and the Quest for Insurance Funding*, 75 TEX. L. REV. 1721, 1741 (1997).

Is an exclusion for intentional harm desirable for the insurer? Why? What about for the insured?

(3)   Under most standard liability insurance policies, the insurer owes a duty to defend and a duty to indemnify. How are these duties different? Consider the following:

> An insurer's duty to defend a lawsuit against its insured is both separate and distinct from the insurer's duty to indemnify its insured for liability that is imposed against the insured after trial. In liability insurance policies generally, an insurer assumes both the duty to indemnify the insured, that is, to pay all covered claims and judgments against [the] insured,[b] and the duty to defend any lawsuit brought against [the] insured that alleges and seeks damages for an event potentially covered by the policy, even if groundless, false or fraudulent.
>
> The duty to defend is likewise broader than the duty to indemnify. Accordingly, the insurer has a duty to defend an insured against a lawsuit based merely on the potential of liability under a policy, despite the fact that the insurer could eventually be determined to have no duty to indemnify the insured. Further, because the duty to defend is broader than an insurer's duty to indemnify, if a court determines that there is no duty to defend, the insurer will not have a duty to indemnify.

STEVEN PLITT ET AL., 14 COUCH ON INSURANCE § 200:3 (3d ed. 2015).

(4)   Not surprisingly, the test for when the duty to defend is triggered is different from the test for when the duty to indemnify is triggered. As one commentator observed:

> . . . . The initial test for deciding the duty to defend is the eight-corners rule [the petition's "four corners" and the policy's "four corners"]: the insurer must provide a defense when the plaintiff's pleadings make allegations that, if true, would create liability that is covered by the policy. In addition, in most jurisdictions the insurer also has a duty to defend if it becomes aware of information that potentially brings the claim within coverage. If the complaint alleges one covered claim, then the insurer must defend even if other claims are outside the policy.
>
> Suppose, for instance, that the tort plaintiff alleges that the insured owned an apartment building and that negligent security at the apartment caused the plaintiff's injury. In fact, the insured did not own or have anything to do with the building. The insurer nonetheless has a duty to defend. The plaintiff's pleading contains

---

[b]   Under an indemnity policy, the insurer promises to reimburse the insured, up to the policy limits, for any loss that the insured suffers as a result of a covered risk. The insurer's liability under such a policy technically does not arise until a judgment has been obtained and the insured has paid it. Under a liability policy, the insurer becomes liable immediately upon the entry of judgment against the insured. Under either form of policy, the obligation of the insurer to pay is referred to as the duty to "indemnify," even though the insurer may be paying the insured's obligation directly rather than reimbursing the insured.

allegations that, if true—we must assume the insured did own the building—would establish liability that is covered under the policy—negligence-based liability for bodily harm. This example illustrates why it makes perfect sense to assume the truth of the plaintiff's liability-related allegations when determining the duty to defend. Otherwise, insurers could avoid defending meritless lawsuits. And most of us, of course, want litigation insurance against both legitimate and meritless claims.

The duty to pay, by contrast, is not based on what the plaintiff alleges, but instead on the relevant facts as ultimately adjudicated. Suppose that the liability policy contains an exclusion for liabilities arising out of business-related uses of the insured's property. The tort plaintiff alleges a negligently caused slip-and-fall injury on the insured's premises, the insurer provides a defense, the tort plaintiff obtains a judgment, the insurer refuses to pay the judgment, and the insured sues the insurer for breach of the duty to pay. Whether the insurer breached the duty to pay will turn on an adjudication of how the property was being used.

Pryor, *supra*, at 1730–31; *see also* PLITT ET AL., *supra*, §§ 200:11, 200:12 ("An insurer's duty to defend is expansive and arises when any part of the claim is potentially or arguably within the scope of the policy's coverage, even if the allegations of the suit are false, fraudulent, or groundless. . . . When there is doubt as to whether claims potentially fall within policy coverage, any doubt or ambiguity in coverage is generally resolved in favor of the insured.").

Does it make sense that the duty to defend is based on the plaintiff's allegations, while the duty to indemnify is based on adjudicated facts? Why?

(5) What test does the *North Star* court announce for whether the duty to defend is triggered? Why does the court conclude that the test was satisfied?

(6) Did the *North Star* court resolve the duty to indemnify? If not, what remains to be determined?

(7) Assume that North Star now realizes that its homeowners' policies may cover at least some tort judgments for negligently transmitted sexual diseases. How might North Star address that risk in the future?

(8) The insurer's breach of its duty to defend is generally viewed as a breach of contract. Indeed, the typical measure of damages for breach of the duty to defend is contractual in nature, as it includes the costs and reasonable attorney's fees incurred by the insured in defending himself, plus any consequential damages suffered by the insured as a result of the insurer's breach. *See* ALAN D. WINDT, 1 INSURANCE CLAIMS AND DISPUTES § 4:33 (6th ed. 2015); *see also* ROBERT H. JERRY, II & DOUGLAS R. RICHMOND, UNDERSTANDING INSURANCE LAW § 111[h], at 851 (4th ed. 2007) ("Because the duty to defend is a contract duty, an insured can recover compensatory damages for the insurer's breach of its duty to defend."). A breach of the duty

to defend does not ordinarily result in the insurer's liability for an excess judgment against the insured. *See, e.g.*, JERRY & RICHMOND, *supra*, § 111[h][2], at 853 (stating that "[p]resumably the attorney hired by the insured will provide the same quality of representation as the attorney that the insurer would have provided," observing that "[i]f this is so, the amount of the judgment in the underlying action against the insured should be the same, regardless of who provides the insured's defense," and concluding that "[t]herefore, it cannot be said that the insurer's refusal to defend the insured is the cause of any excess judgment," but noting that courts have found exceptions to this rule).

With respect to the duty to indemnify, "[b]ecause the insurer's duty to pay proceeds is created by an express promise set forth in the language of the policy, an action for breach of the duty to pay proceeds sounds in contract." JERRY & RICHMOND, *supra*, § 99[a][1], at 737. That statement is slightly misleading, however, as an unreasonable (or worse) refusal to pay gives rise to a tort action in many jurisdictions. *See* WINDT, *supra*, § 6:40 ("Under certain circumstances, however, the insurer's wrongful refusal to indemnify can give rise to a cause of action in tort, in which event the insurer may have additional liability. An insurer has a duty to act in good faith and fairly in handling an insured's claim. When, therefore, it breaches that duty, in some states by unreasonably withholding payments due under the policy, in others by recklessly withholding payments, and in still others by withholding payments in bad faith, the insurer's conduct will be deemed to give rise to a cause of action in tort."). The rationale for this tort characterization will be discussed in later materials. *See* Section A(3) (discussing the duty of good faith and fair dealing).

(9) Liability insurance policies often state that the insurer has the "right and duty" to defend the insured. This language and related terms are typically interpreted to mean that the insurer has a right to control the defense:

> .... Primary insurance policies, such as the standard commercial general liability policy ("the CGL policy"), give the company "the right and duty to defend any 'suit' " in which a claim for a covered loss is asserted against the insured. The CGL policy also entitles the company to "investigate and settle any claim or 'suit' at [the company's] discretion." It imposes a variety of general and specific duties on the insured to cooperate with the company and to refrain from meddling in the defense. And it establishes that the insured may not settle a claim without the company's consent, except at the insured's own expense. These contract provisions are generally interpreted as granting the company plenary and exclusive control of the defense. Ordinarily, the company can select counsel to defend the insured, discharge appointed counsel and name a replacement without the insured's consent, bargain with appointed counsel over fees, monitor counsel and direct litigation strategy, require counsel to inform the company of settlement

demands and procedural developments, direct counsel to initiate settlement discussions, settle claims without an insured's consent and decline to settle claims over an insured's objection, and file appeals.

Charles Silver, *Does Insurance Defense Counsel Represent the Company or the Insured?*, 72 TEX. L. REV. 1583, 1594–95 (1994).

Why would the insurer want the right to control the defense? Is this good for the insured? Consider the following:

> .... Why would a company want the right to defend and demand exclusive control of defense and settlement decisions? The reasons usually given for the right—the need to defeat unwarranted claims, the desire to minimize outlays on valid claims, and the need to prevent collusion between claimants and insureds—emphasize the value the company derives from the right to defend. However, it is important to see that the insured also benefits from the rule of exclusive company control. The insured is protected by the company's financial resources, expertise, and efficiency in dealing with claims, and by its risk-neutrality, bureaucratic structure, reputation, bargaining skill, and ability to select and monitor defense counsel, all of which enable the company to react to claims better than the insured. . . .

> Insureds are likely to find it particularly difficult to select, bargain with, and monitor defense counsel. Most insureds participate in litigation infrequently. Often, they cannot tell bad lawyers from good ones, and they cannot distinguish bad lawyering from bad luck. By contrast, insurance companies are archetypal repeat players in litigation. They see the same kinds of claims over and over. They form long-term relationships with lawyers that encourage lawyers to act responsively, cooperatively, and economically. And they can often tell the difference between misconduct and misfortune. Given a company's relative advantages, both parties profit by giving the company exclusive control over defense counsel.

Id. at 1595–98.

(10) Should an insurer's right to control the defense be affected by a conflict of interest between the insurer and the insured over defense strategy? A conflict of interest does not exist simply because the insurer and the insured have differing views as to the insured's potential liability. After all, the parties still have a common interest in defense counsel providing a vigorous defense and, ideally, achieving a complete victory.

Suppose that the plaintiff in *North Star*, however, had sued for both intentional misconduct and for negligence. Assume further that North Star had a duty to defend, and that it hired a lawyer to represent the insured, T.F. In this situation, North Star's interests would conflict with T.F.'s interests with respect to how T.F.'s defense is handled. Both North Star and T.F. would, of course, prefer that the plaintiff lose. If the plaintiff prevails, however, North Star would prefer a judgment based on intentional misconduct (which will likely preclude coverage), while T.F. would prefer a judgment based on negligence. The prevailing rule is that, when such a conflict exists, the insurer must relinquish control over the defense and pay for independent counsel to represent the insured.

(11) The potential availability of insurance can cause plaintiffs to "underlitigate" their tort claims. Underlitigation has been defined as "the plaintiff's choice to plead and prove negligence rather than or in addition to intentional tort theories when, absent insurance considerations, the plaintiff would either frame the case solely as an intentional tort claim or emphasize the intentional tort claim." Pryor, *supra*, at 1722. Professor Pryor has explained the rationale for underlitigating as follows:

> It is not hard to find the basic reason for underlitigating. Most standard liability policies that insure against the risk of bodily harm and property damage do not insure against liabilities resulting from harms that the insured intentionally causes. If a defendant has insufficient noninsurance assets to satisfy the potential tort judgment, then plaintiffs, quite naturally, will have an incentive to evade an intentional-harm exclusion. Underlitigating, as I will explain, offers some opportunities for evasion.
>
> . . . .
>
> . . . . Why then would it ever be in the tort plaintiff's interest to plead a suit in a way that invoked a defense when insurance coverage is questionable? One would suppose that plaintiffs' lawyers welcome the duty to pay but are not thrilled at the prospect of a defense funded and directed by an insurer—a skilled repeat litigation player. For several reasons, however, triggering the duty to defend could enhance the possibility that insurance funding will be available for some or all of the value of the tort claim.
>
> The first reason is the most obvious. If an insurer finds itself obligated to defend, it may rationally take account of those defense costs in calculating the settlement value of the case. This will be true even when the insurer doubts it will have any obligation to indemnify if the tort plaintiff were to prevail. Suppose that a liability policy has limits of $100,000 and that the insurer calculates the plaintiff's chances of success at fifty percent with expected damages of $200,000, so that the expected value of the outcome against the insured is $100,000. Suppose the chances that the insurer will have to pay that amount are only two percent; thus, the insurer's expected indemnity payment is only $2000. Yet the insurer must defend the lawsuit, and it anticipates that the costs of defense will equal $120,000. The tort plaintiff submits a settlement

"demand" of $100,000. The insurer could rationally accept the demand.

A second reason relates to the extracontractual "duty to settle" that most jurisdictions impose on insurers that are providing a defense for the insured. As described by scholars and courts, an insurer has a conflict of interest with its insured when faced with a within-the-limits settlement demand from the tort plaintiff. Thus, virtually all jurisdictions impose an extracontractual obligation that the insurer adhere to some standard of care in responding to the settlement demand. One typical formulation of the standard is that the insurer must evaluate the offer as would a reasonable insurer under a policy with no limits. An insurer that breaches this duty will be liable for the full amount of the judgment, not just the amount of the judgment within policy limits.

In cases of questionable coverage—including cases in which the intentional harm exclusion might apply—the duty to settle may give some settlement value even to claims of doubtful coverage. . . .

Third, the plaintiff could plead in a way that triggers the duty to defend, hoping the insurer will erroneously decide it has no duty to defend. In some jurisdictions, an incorrect denial of the duty to defend will "estop" the insurer from contesting the duty to pay. That is, even if the insurer has an airtight defense against the duty to pay, a wrong call on the duty to defend will create a duty to pay at least the sum within the coverage limits—and possibly the judgment amount in excess of policy limits.

Fourth, if the insurer wrongfully denies a defense, in some jurisdictions the insurer may be liable for extracontractual damages under either tort or unfair-claims-practices statutes. Although such a claim will not create coverage, it still may have considerable value.

Fifth, if the insurer chooses to defend but then fails fully to "reserve rights" to contest coverage, most jurisdictions will estop the carrier from contesting its duty to pay if the failure to reserve rights actually or presumptively harmed the insured. Once again, knowledgeable plaintiffs' lawyers realize that certain missteps on the carrier's part may lead to a duty to pay when otherwise that duty is unlikely.

If an insurer makes any of the missteps just noted, the insurer will be liable to the insured either for the judgment amount or for some sum representing the damage that the insurer's action has inflicted on the insured. Thus, an insurer that otherwise owes no indemnity coverage will now owe something to the insured, creating a source of funding for a tort judgment that otherwise would not be collectible. Tort plaintiffs thus have reason to plead in a way that triggers the duty to defend when: (1) the duty to pay is questionable and (2) the tort defendant is unlikely to have the means to satisfy the tort judgment from noninsurance assets.

Id. at 1725–26, 1731–35.

(12) A plaintiff's attempt to underlitigate can occur at the pleading stage and beyond:

> Underpleading is perhaps the most important tactic for triggering the duty to defend in cases of questionable coverage. A complaint that alleges only intentional tort theories—or in some jurisdictions, only facts showing intentional harm—often will not trigger a duty to defend because the plaintiff's allegations, even if successful, would not lie within the coverage of the policy. But, if the plaintiff adds a negligence theory or negligence-related facts, the complaint may trigger the duty to defend.

> Triggering this duty, in turn, can help the plaintiff access insurance funds even in cases of questionable coverage for all the reasons noted above. . . .

> Underlitigating also presents some benefits for the plaintiff after the pleading stage. Before explaining these, however, it is important to understand why the plaintiff's underlitigating efforts usually will not, by themselves, lead to coverage. One might suppose that the plaintiff could plead negligence, submit only negligence to the jury, and therefore likely receive a finding from the jury grounded in negligence—a liability finding covered under the policy.

> But this simple route to coverage usually is unavailable to the tort plaintiff. If the plaintiff pleads negligence rather than, or in addition to, intentional conduct, the insurer that hopes to escape coverage on the grounds of intentional conduct generally should relinquish control of the defense even though it still must fund it. The carrier, in other words, should provide independent counsel to the insured. This is because the negligence-intentional conduct issue creates a conflict of interest between the insurer and the insured over how the defense in the underlying tort suit is conducted. Under proper application of collateral estoppel principles, a negligence-based judgment in the tort suit should not have collateral estoppel effect on the lawsuit between the insurer and insured over whether the intentional-injury exclusion applies. Thus, prevailing on a negligence theory in the underlying tort suit should not by itself do much to create access to insurance funding.

> Still, tort plaintiffs have several reasons to underlitigate the underlying tort suit. First, the collateral estoppel principles just set out are not the rule in all jurisdictions and may remain unclear in some. Plaintiffs in these jurisdictions might plausibly perceive potential collateral estoppel benefits from underlitigating.

Second, even when the collateral estoppel principles control, plaintiffs will wish to keep the negligence theory alive. If the pleading is amended to omit negligence, the insurer's duty to defend may be at an end, basically closing the various routes to insurance funding. Third, discovery and proof adduced in the underlying trial might be admissible in the coverage suit. Thus, the plaintiff will have reason to shape the evidence in the underlying tort suit in a way that makes a nonintent finding in the coverage suit more likely. Fourth, even if a finding of negligence in the tort suit will not create coverage, a finding of intentional conduct may defeat coverage. Thus, the plaintiff has an incentive to avoid such a finding.

Pryor, *supra*, at 1735–37.

Should we care about underlitigation? Does it cause any harm? Did underlitigation happen in *North Star*?

2. THE DUTY TO SETTLE

CRISCI v. SECURITY INSURANCE COMPANY
426 P.2d 173 (Cal. 1967)

PETERS, JUSTICE.

In an action against The Security Insurance Company of New Haven, Connecticut, the trial court awarded Rosina Crisci $91,000 (plus interest) because she suffered a judgment in a personal injury action after Security, her insurer, refused to settle the claim. Mrs. Crisci was also awarded $25,000 for mental suffering. Security has appealed.

June DiMare and her husband were tenants in an apartment building owned by Rosina Crisci. Mrs. DiMare was descending the apartment's outside wooden staircase when a tread gave way. She fell through the resulting opening up to her waist and was left hanging 15 feet above the ground. Mrs. DiMare suffered physical injuries and developed a very severe psychosis. In a suit brought against Mrs. Crisci the DiMares alleged that the step broke because Mrs. Crisci was negligent in inspecting and maintaining the stairs. They contended that Mrs. DiMare's mental condition was caused by the accident, and they asked for $400,000 as compensation for physical and mental injuries and medical expenses.

Mrs. Crisci had $10,000 of insurance coverage under a general liability policy issued by Security. The policy obligated Security to defend the suit against Mrs. Crisci and authorized the company to make any settlement it deemed expedient.[1] Security hired an experienced lawyer,

---

[1] Mrs. Crisci's own attorney, Mr. Pardini, was consulted by the counsel for the insurance company, but Mr. Pardini did not direct or control either settlement negotiations or the defense of Mrs. DiMare's suit.

Mr. Healy, to handle the case. Both he and defendant's claims manager believed that unless evidence was discovered showing that Mrs. DiMare had a prior mental illness, a jury would probably find that the accident precipitated Mrs. DiMare's psychosis. And both men believed that if the jury felt that the fall triggered the psychosis, a verdict of not less than $100,000 would be returned.

An extensive search turned up no evidence that Mrs. DiMare had any prior mental abnormality. As a teenager Mrs. DiMare had been in a Washington mental hospital, but only to have an abortion. Both Mrs. DiMare and Mrs. Crisci found psychiatrists who would testify that the accident caused Mrs. DiMare's illness, and the insurance company knew of this testimony. Among those who felt the psychosis was not related to the accident were the doctors at the state mental hospital where Mrs. DiMare had been committed following the accident. All the psychiatrists agreed, however, that a psychosis could be triggered by a sudden fear of falling to one's death.

The exact chronology of settlement offers is not established by the record. However, by the time the DiMares' attorney reduced his settlement demands to $10,000, Security had doctors prepared to support its position and was only willing to pay $3,000 for Mrs. DiMare's physical injuries. Security was unwilling to pay one cent for the possibility of a plaintiff's verdict on the mental illness issue. This conclusion was based on the assumption that the jury would believe all of the defendant's psychiatric evidence and none of the plaintiff's. Security also rejected a $9,000 settlement demand at a time when Mrs. Crisci offered to pay $2,500 of the settlement.

A jury awarded Mrs. DiMare $100,000 and her husband $1,000. After an appeal the insurance company paid $10,000 of this amount, the amount of its policy. The DiMares then sought to collect the balance from Mrs. Crisci. A settlement was arranged by which the DiMares received $22,000, a 40 percent interest in Mrs. Crisci's claim to a particular piece of property, and an assignment of Mrs. Crisci's cause of action against Security. Mrs. Crisci, an immigrant widow of 70, became indigent. She worked as a babysitter, and her grandchildren paid her rent. The change in her financial condition was accompanied by a decline in physical health, hysteria, and suicide attempts. Mrs. Crisci then brought this action.

The liability of an insurer in excess of its policy limits for failure to accept a settlement offer within those limits was considered by this court in Comunale v. Traders & General Ins. Co., 328 P.2d 198. It was there reasoned that in every contract, including policies of insurance, there is an implied covenant of good faith and fair dealing that neither party will do anything which will injure the right of the other to receive the benefits of the agreement; that it is common knowledge that one of the usual methods by which an insured receives protection under a liability insurance policy is by settlement of claims without litigation; that the implied obligation of good faith and fair dealing requires the insurer to settle in an appropriate case although the express terms of the policy do not impose the duty; that in determining whether to settle the insurer must give the interests of the insured at least as much consideration as it gives to its own interests; and that when "there is great risk of a recovery beyond the policy limits so that the most reasonable manner of disposing of the claim is a settlement which can be made within those limits, a consideration in good faith of the insured's interest requires the insurer to settle the claim." (328 P.2d at p. 201.)

In determining whether an insurer has given consideration to the interests of the insured, the test is whether a prudent insurer without policy limits would have accepted the settlement offer.

Several cases, in considering the liability of the insurer, contain language to the effect that bad faith is the equivalent of dishonesty, fraud, and concealment. Obviously a showing that the insurer has been guilty of actual dishonesty, fraud, or concealment is relevant to the determination whether it has given consideration to the insured's interest in considering a settlement offer within the policy limits. The language used in the cases, however, should not be understood as meaning that in the absence of evidence establishing actual dishonesty, fraud, or concealment no recovery may be had for a judgment in excess of the policy limits. Comunale v. Traders & General Ins. Co., supra, 328 P.2d 198, makes it clear that liability based [on] an implied covenant exists whenever the insurer refuses to settle in an appropriate case and that liability may exist when the insurer unwarrantedly refuses an offered settlement where the most reasonable manner of disposing of the claim is by accepting the settlement. Liability is imposed not for a bad faith breach of the contract but for failure to meet the duty to accept reasonable settlements, a duty included within the implied covenant of good faith and fair dealing. Moreover, examination of the balance of [other] opinions makes it abundantly clear that recovery may be based on unwarranted rejection of a reasonable settlement offer and that the absence of evidence, circumstantial or direct, showing actual dishonesty, fraud, or concealment is not fatal to the cause of action.

Amicus curiae argues that, whenever an insurer receives an offer to settle within the policy limits and rejects it, the insurer should be liable in every case for the amount of any final judgment whether or not within the policy limits. As we have seen, the duty of the insurer to consider the insured's interest in settlement offers within the policy limits arises from an implied covenant in the contract, and ordinarily contract duties are strictly enforced and not subject to a standard of reasonableness.

Obviously, it will always be in the insured's interest to settle within the policy limits when there is any danger, however slight, of a judgment in excess of those limits. Accordingly the rejection of a settlement within the limits where there is any danger of a judgment in excess of the limits can be justified, if at all, only on the basis of interests of the insurer, and, in light of the common knowledge that settlement is one of the usual methods by which an insured receives protection under a liability policy, it may not be unreasonable for an insured who purchases a policy with limits to believe that a sum of money equal to the limits is available and will be used so as to avoid liability on his part with regard to any covered accident. In view of such expectation an insurer should not be permitted to further its own interests by rejecting opportunities to settle within the policy limits unless it is also willing to absorb losses which may result from its failure to settle.

The proposed rule is a simple one to apply and avoids the burdens of a determination whether a settlement offer within the policy limits was reasonable. The proposed rule would also eliminate the danger that an insurer, faced with a settlement offer at or near the policy limits, will reject it and gamble with the insured's money to further its own interests. Moreover, it is not entirely clear that the proposed rule would place a burden on insurers substantially greater than that which is present under existing law. The size of the judgment recovered in the personal injury action when it exceeds the policy limits, although not conclusive, furnishes an inference that the value of the claim is the equivalent of the amount of the judgment and that acceptance of an offer within those limits was the most reasonable method of dealing with the claim.

Finally, and most importantly, there is more than a small amount of elementary justice in a rule that would require that, in this situation where the insurer's and insured's interests necessarily conflict, the insurer, which may reap the benefits of its determination not to settle, should also suffer the detriments of its decision. On the basis of these and other considerations, a number of commentators have urged that the insurer should be liable for any resulting judgment where it refuses to settle within the policy limits.

We need not, however, here determine whether there might be some countervailing considerations precluding adoption of the proposed rule because, under Comunale v. Traders & General Ins. Co., supra, 328 P.2d 198, and the cases following it, the evidence is clearly sufficient to support the determination that Security breached its duty to consider the interests of Mrs. Crisci in proposed settlements. Both Security's attorney and its claims manager agreed that if Mrs. DiMare won an award for her psychosis, that award would be at least $100,000. Security attempts to justify its rejection of a settlement by contending that it believed Mrs. DiMare had no chance of winning on the mental suffering issue. That belief in the circumstances present could be found to be unreasonable. Security was putting blind faith in the power of its psychiatrists to convince the jury when it knew that the accident could have caused the psychosis, that its agents had told it that without evidence of prior mental defects a jury was likely to believe the fall precipitated the psychosis, and that Mrs. DiMare had reputable psychiatrists on her side. Further, the company had been told by a psychiatrist that in a group of 24 psychiatrists, 12 could be found to support each side.

The trial court found that defendant "knew that there was a considerable risk of substantial recovery beyond said policy limits" and that "the defendant did not give as much consideration to the financial interests of its said insured as it gave to its own interests." That is all that was required. The award of $91,000 must therefore be affirmed.

We must next determine the propriety of the award to Mrs. Crisci of $25,000 for her mental suffering. In Comunale v. Traders & General Ins. Co., supra, 328 P.2d 198, 203, it was held that an action of the type involved here sounds in both contract and tort and that "where a case sounds both in contract and tort the plaintiff will ordinarily have freedom of election between an action of tort and one of contract. An exception to this rule is made in suits for personal injury caused by negligence, where the tort character of the action is considered to prevail (citations), but no such exception is applied in cases, like the present one, which relate to financial damage (citations)."[3] Although this rule was applied in Comunale with regard to a statute of limitations, the rule is also applicable in determining liability. Insofar as language in Critz v. Farmers Ins. Group, 41 Cal.Rptr. 401 [(Ct. App. 1964)], might be interpreted as providing that the action for wrongful refusal to settle sounds solely in contract, it is disapproved.

Fundamental in our jurisprudence is the principle that for every wrong there is a remedy and that an injured party should be compensated for all damage proximately caused by the wrongdoer. Although we recognize exceptions from these fundamental principles, no departure should be sanctioned unless there is a strong necessity therefor.

The general rule of damages in tort is that the injured party may recover for all detriment caused whether it could have been anticipated or not. In accordance with the general rule, it is settled in this state that mental suffering constitutes an aggravation of damages when it naturally ensues from the act complained of, and in this connection mental suffering includes nervousness, grief, anxiety, worry, shock, humiliation and indignity as well as physical pain. The commonest example of the award of damages for mental suffering in addition to other damages is

---

[3] . . . . *Comunale* expressly recognizes that "wrongful refusal to settle has generally been treated as a tort." (328 P.2d at p. 203.)

probably where the plaintiff suffers personal injuries in addition to mental distress as a result of either negligent or intentional misconduct by the defendant. Such awards are not confined to cases where the mental suffering award was in addition to an award for personal injuries; damages for mental distress have also been awarded in cases where the tortious conduct was an interference with property rights without any personal injuries apart from the mental distress.

We are satisfied that a plaintiff who as a result of a defendant's tortious conduct loses his property and suffers mental distress may recover not only for the pecuniary loss but also for his mental distress. No substantial reason exists to distinguish the cases which have permitted recovery for mental distress in actions for invasion of property rights. The principal reason for limiting recovery of damages for mental distress is that to permit recovery of such damages would open the door to fictitious claims, to recovery for mere bad manners, and to litigation in the field of trivialities. Obviously, where, as here, the claim is actionable and has resulted in substantial damages apart from those due to mental distress, the danger of fictitious claims is reduced, and we are not here concerned with mere bad manners or trivialities but tortious conduct resulting in substantial invasions of clearly protected interests.

Recovery of damages for mental suffering in the instant case does not mean that in every case of breach of contract the injured party may recover such damages. Here the breach also constitutes a tort. Moreover, plaintiff did not seek by the contract involved here to obtain a commercial advantage but to protect herself against the risks of accidental losses, including the mental distress which might follow from the losses. Among the considerations in purchasing liability insurance, as insurers are well aware, is the peace of mind and security it will provide in the event of an accidental loss, and recovery of damages for mental suffering has been permitted for breach of contracts which directly concern the comfort, happiness or personal esteem of one of the parties.

It is not claimed that plaintiff's mental distress was not caused by defendant's refusal to settle or that the damages awarded were excessive in the light of plaintiff's substantial suffering.

The judgment is affirmed.

NOTES & QUESTIONS

(1) As mentioned in the "Notes & Questions" after *North Star*, language in most liability insurance policies is typically interpreted to mean that the insurer has a right to control the defense, including a right to control settlement of a claim against the insured. For example, policies usually indicate that the insured may not settle a claim without the insurer's consent, except at the insured's own expense.

(2) In *Crisci*, did the policy expressly impose a duty to settle appropriate claims upon the insurer? If not, what is the source of the duty to settle found by the court?

(3) Unlike *Crisci*, some courts conclude that the duty to settle arises out a fiduciary relationship between the insurer and the insured. For example, in *Beck v. Farmers Insurance Exchange*, 701 P.2d 795 (Utah 1985), the Supreme Court of Utah observed:

> . . . . In a third-party situation, the insurer controls the disposition of claims against its insured, who relinquishes any right to negotiate on his own behalf. An insurer's failure to act in good faith exposes its insured to a judgment and personal liability in excess of the policy limits. In essence, the contract itself creates a fiduciary relationship because of the trust and reliance placed in the insurer by its insured. The insured is wholly dependent upon the insurer to see that, in dealing with claims by third parties, the insured's best interests are protected. In addition, when dealing with third parties, the insurer acts as an agent for the insured with respect to the disputed claim. Wholly apart from the contractual obligations undertaken by the parties, the law imposes upon all agents a fiduciary obligation to their principals with respect to matters falling within the scope of their agency.

Id. at 799–800; *cf. G.A. Stowers Furniture Co. v. Am. Indem. Co.*, 15 S.W.2d 544, 547 (Tex. Comm'n App. 1929) ("[T]he indemnity company had the right to take complete and exclusive control of the suit against the assured, and the assured was absolutely prohibited from making any settlement, except at his own expense, or to interfere in any negotiations for settlement or legal proceeding without the consent of the company; the company reserved the right to settle any such claim or suit brought against the assured. Certainly, where an insurance company makes such a contract; it, by the very terms of the contract, assumed the responsibility to act as the exclusive and absolute agent of the assured in all matters pertaining to the questions in litigation. . . .").

(4) Why do courts impose a duty to settle upon insurers? Consider first how settlement demands are evaluated when no insurance is involved:

> Assume that Paul Plaintiff, a guest of homeowner Donna Defendant, slips, falls, and files a lawsuit against Defendant seeking $200,000 in damages for his injuries. In theory, Defendant's potential liability is $200,000, but as a practical matter, Defendant's ability to file for bankruptcy may limit her liability to the value of her assets. Let us assume Defendant has $100,000 in assets. How will Defendant respond to a settlement demand from Plaintiff—that is, to a proposal that the lawsuit be dismissed in return for Defendant's payment of a fixed sum of money (say, $50,000) to Plaintiff?

Most economic theories of litigation suggest that Defendant will compare Plaintiff's demand to what Defendant expects will be the costs of going to trial. Defendant's trial costs include the expected judgment if Defendant loses multiplied by the expected probability of loss, as well as the additional attorneys' fees and litigation expenses incurred by Defendant through trial.... If Defendant is risk-neutral, expects to pay $20,000 in fees and expenses to try her case, foresees an 80% chance of a plaintiff's verdict at trial, and expects judgment if Plaintiff wins will be $40,000, then her expected trial costs are $52,000 (or (.8) ($40,000) + $20,000). Accordingly, she would rationally accept Plaintiff's $50,000 settlement demand.

Kent D. Syverud, *The Duty to Settle*, 76 VA. L. REV. 1113, 1128–29 (1990).

Now assume that the defendant in the above fact pattern has a liability insurance policy with a $100,000 limit. The plaintiff makes a settlement demand for $100,000. Will the insurer want to settle at that amount or proceed to trial? What about the insured?

Now consider a starker example: assume the same liability insurance policy with a $100,000 limit. Assume further that there is a 90% chance of a plaintiff's verdict at trial, an expected judgment of $200,000 if plaintiff wins, and the same $20,000 in litigation costs. The plaintiff makes a settlement demand for $100,000. Will the insurer want to settle at that amount? Will the insured?

(5)   In *Crisci*, was there a need for a duty to settle? Was there a conflict of interest between the insurer (Security) and the insured (Mrs. Crisci)?

(6)   What standards do courts use to determine whether the duty to settle has been breached? Consider the following:

Many courts have described the insurer's obligation by reference to the concept of "good faith and fair dealing." Under this test, if the insurer acts in good faith and deals fairly when responding to a settlement offer, the insurer has complied with its duty to settle. Bad faith conduct is more than making a mistake in judgment or failing to predict correctly the outcome of the litigation between plaintiff and insured. Rather, bad faith connotes some sort of intentional, reckless, or otherwise improper disregard of the legitimate interests and expectations of the insured in the circumstances. . . .

Another test often found in the reported cases, although not as frequently as the "good faith" test, is the "due care" standard. Under the due care test, if the insurer is not negligent in deciding to [reject] a settlement offer within the policy limits, the insurer has fulfilled its duty. This test, which draws heavily from tort law, asks whether the insurer's conduct conforms with what is expected of a reasonable insurer in the same circumstances. This test implies that a mere "accident" in the outcome of the plaintiff's suit against the insured does not establish the insurer's breach of its obligation to the insured. Hindsight alone is not enough to hold the insurer liable. Whether any practical distinction exists between the good faith and due care tests is not readily apparent. . . .

Various other formulations exist for the amount of deference the insurer should give the insured's interests when responding to a settlement offer. These tests are best understood as efforts by courts to give more content to the elusive concepts of "good faith," "due care," and "reasonableness." Some courts have stated that the insurer must give "equal consideration" to the insured's interests. This test gives little guidance to insurers; at what point the insurer has given ample consideration to the insured's interests such that it can be said that the insurer is acting with "equal" regard for the insured is not capable of easy measurement. Other courts have stated that the insurer must give paramount weight to the insured's interests, even at the expense of its own. When the insurer's deference to the insured's interests has moved to a level that can be described as "paramount weight" is also difficult to ascertain.

If the "good faith" and "due care" tests coalesce, and if one agrees that the differences among these tests and the other formulations are subtle, it is fair to describe all of these assorted tests under the label of the "reasonable-offer" test. Under this test, the issue is simply whether an insurer under a policy with no limits would accept the offer; in fact, a number of courts have articulated the insurer's duty to settle in virtually identical language. . . .

The reasonable-offer test is premised on the assumption that some settlement offers should be accepted by an insurer and others should be rejected. Thus, for the insurer to fulfill the duty to settle, the insurer must give appropriate deference to the insured's interests. This test contemplates that the insurer can permissibly reject some settlement offers, even if it turns out in hindsight that the insured would have been better served by accepting the offer. Thus, a judgment against the insured in excess of the settlement offer, or in excess of the policy limits, does not automatically mean that the insurer has breached the duty to settle.

ROBERT H. JERRY, II & DOUGLAS R. RICHMOND, UNDERSTANDING INSURANCE LAW § 112[b][1], at 868–70 (4th ed. 2007).

(7) Under these various standards, what factors are relevant to determining whether a breach of the duty to settle has occurred? In *Commercial Union Insurance Co. v. Liberty Mutual Insurance Co.*, 393 N.W.2d 161 (Mich. 1986), the court provided the following list:

. . . . Among the factors which the factfinder may take into account, together with all other evidence in deciding whether or not the defendant acted in bad faith are:

1) failure to keep the insured fully informed of all developments in the claim or suit that could reasonably affect the interests of the insured,

2) failure to inform the insured of all settlement offers that do not fall within the policy limits,

3) failure to solicit a settlement offer or initiate settlement negotiations when warranted under the circumstances,

4) failure to accept a reasonable compromise offer of settlement when the facts of the case or claim indicate obvious liability and serious injury,

5) rejection of a reasonable offer of settlement within the policy limits,

6) undue delay in accepting a reasonable offer to settle a potentially dangerous case within the policy limits where the verdict potential is high,

7) an attempt by the insurer to coerce or obtain an involuntary contribution from the insured in order to settle within the policy limits,

8) failure to make a proper investigation of the claim prior to refusing an offer of settlement within the policy limits,

9) disregarding the advice or recommendations of an adjuster or attorney,

10) serious and recurrent negligence by the insurer,

11) refusal to settle a case within the policy limits following an excessive verdict when the chances of reversal on appeal are slight or doubtful, and

12) failure to take an appeal following a verdict in excess of the policy limits where there are reasonable grounds for such an appeal, especially where trial counsel so recommended.

In applying any factors, it is inappropriate in reviewing the conduct of the insurer to utilize "20–20 hindsight vision." The conduct under scrutiny must be considered in light of the circumstances existing at the time. A microscopic examination, years after the fact, made with the luxury of actually knowing the outcome of the original proceeding is not appropriate. It must be remembered that if bad faith exists in a given situation, it arose upon the occurrence of the acts in question; bad faith does not arise at some later date as a result of an unsuccessful day in court.

Id. at 165–66; *see also* JERRY & RICHMOND, *supra*, § 112[d], at 875 ("No precise formula exists for what kinds of insurer conduct constitute breach of the duty to settle."); *id.* § 112[b][2], at 870 ("Although the [reasonable offer] test allows any factor relevant to the reasonableness of the insurer's conduct to be considered, the test's flexibility is a recipe for inconsistent and unpredictable results.").

(8) What standard did the *Crisci* court adopt for determining whether the duty to settle had been breached? Compare it to the standard proposed by the amicus curiae: "[W]henever an insurer receives an offer to settle within the policy limits and rejects it, the insurer should be liable in every case for the amount of any final judgment whether or not within the policy limits." Which standard do you prefer?

(9) Like *Crisci*, most jurisdictions conclude that a tort claim exists for breach of the duty to settle. Given the source of the duty found by the *Crisci* court, does this tort conclusion make sense? Is a tort claim necessary to fully protect the insured? *See, e.g.*, RESTATEMENT (SECOND) OF CONTRACTS § 353 (1981) ("Recovery for emotional disturbance will be excluded unless the breach also caused bodily harm or the contract or the breach is of such a kind that serious emotional disturbance was a particularly likely result."). Is there any downside to subjecting insurers to tort liability?

3. THE DUTY OF GOOD FAITH

UNIVERSE LIFE INSURANCE CO. v. GILES
950 S.W.2d 48 (Tex. 1997)

SPECTOR, JUSTICE, announced the judgment of the Court and delivered an opinion in which CORNYN, BAKER and ABBOTT, JUSTICES, join.

The two issues in this case are whether any evidence supports an insured's judgment against her health insurer for breach of the duty of good faith and fair dealing, and whether any evidence supports a punitive damages award. . . . The court of appeals reduced the amount of punitive damages awarded the insured and otherwise affirmed the judgment. We reverse the punitive damages award but affirm the court of appeals' judgment in other respects.

A majority of the Court—eight Justices—agrees that an insurer violates its duty of good faith and fair dealing by denying or delaying payment of a claim if the insurer knew or should have known that it was reasonably clear that the claim was covered. Our fundamental disagreement concerns who should decide that issue. Those joining Justice Hecht's concurrence would take the resolution of bad-faith disputes away from the juries that have been deciding bad faith cases for more than a decade. However, a majority of the Court—the four Justices joining this opinion and Justice Enoch—continues to believe that whether an insurer breached its duty of good faith and fair dealing remains a fact question. Nothing we have seen persuades us that juries are unsuited to decide whether an insurer breached its duty of good faith and fair dealing.

I.

Ida Mae Giles, age 61, underwent heart bypass surgery about three months after she obtained health insurance from The Universe Life Insurance Company. Universe denied Giles's claim for payment of her medical bills on the ground that the policy did not cover her heart condition because she had received treatment for it before Universe issued the policy. Universe based its denial on four alleged facts. First, Giles's hospital records stated that she had had a two- or three-year history of recurrent chest pain. Second, the same records stated that she had a positive history of heart disease. Third, other medical records reflected that for years before the policy issued Giles had been treated with Mevacor and Lorelco, two drugs used to lower blood cholesterol. Fourth, Giles's medical records indicated that she suffered from atherosclerosis, a condition that must have developed over several years.

When Giles learned why Universe had denied coverage, she asked two of her physicians to write to Universe to clarify her medical records. The physician whose notes stated that Giles had suffered chest pain for some years explained that the statement resulted from a transcription error, and that in fact, Giles had suffered chest pain for only two or three *weeks* before her surgery—the entire time being after her insurance policy issued. The physician who had prescribed Mevacor and Lorelco explained that he had given them to Giles for hypercholesteremia, not for hypertension or heart problems. The medical record indicating that Giles had a positive history of heart disease actually stated that Giles "has never had any history of heart problems. . . . She has a positive history of heart disease with a mother who recently had coronary artery bypass grafting. . . . She does not smoke, has no history of hypertension or diabetes, but has had an elevated cholesterol in the past. . . ." Taken in context, the "positive history" appears to refer to family history. It thus became quite clear that Giles was not treated for heart problems until a few weeks before surgery, after the policy issued, and that the policy covered her claim.

Universe never questioned Giles's physicians' credibility in clarifying her medical history and never insinuated that they misstated her history to help her with her insurance claim. Nevertheless, Universe persisted in denying Giles's claim until it received a letter from her attorney, about ten months after the surgery, demanding payment of Giles's medical bills of $51,086.10 (less her $1,000 deductible) and $1,500 attorney fees.

Several weeks later Universe paid medical bills totaling $48,074.51, but it refused to pay about $2,000 of charges it considered unreasonable, and it refused to pay any attorney fees.

Giles then sued Universe and two related companies, AIA Insurance, Inc., which sold polices underwritten by Universe, and AIA Services Corporation, which owned the other two (hereafter collectively referred to as "Universe"). After a jury trial, the district court rendered judgment for Giles on a verdict that Universe had breached its duty of good faith and fair dealing and assessed $75,000 damages for mental anguish and $500,000 punitive damages. The court of appeals held that section 41.007 of the Civil Practice and Remedies Code limited punitive damages to the greater of $200,000 or four times actual damages, and reduced that award to $300,000. In all other respects the court of appeals affirmed the district court's judgment.

In this Court, Universe contends that no evidence supports either the bad-faith finding or the punitive damages award. We address each of these contentions in turn. . . .

. . . .

II.

[Under Texas law, "[a]n insurer has a duty to deal fairly and in good faith with its insured in the processing and payment of claims." *Republic Ins. Co. v. Stoker*, 903 S.W.2d 338, 340 (Tex.1995).] An insurer breaches its duty of good faith and fair dealing when "the insurer had no reasonable basis for denying or delaying payment of [a] claim, and [the insurer] knew or should have known that fact." *Transportation Ins. Co. v. Moriel*, 879 S.W.2d 10, 18 (Tex.1994). . . .

III.

. . . .

This Court first recognized the tort [for breach of the duty of good faith and fair dealing] more than ten years ago. *Arnold v. National County Mut. Fire Ins. Co.*, 725 S.W.2d 165 (Tex.1987). We did so because

> [i]n the insurance context a special relationship arises out of the parties' unequal bargaining power and the nature of insurance contracts which would allow unscrupulous insurers to take advantage of their insureds' misfortunes in bargaining for settlement or resolution of claims. . . . An insurance company has exclusive control over the evaluation, processing and denial of claims.

Id. at 167. Before we recognized the tort,

> [c]ontract law served as the exclusive theory on which policyholders could recover from an insurer for the bad faith

handling of claims. Although a policyholder may have successfully proved that an insurer wrongfully denied benefits, damages were limited to the amount due under the policy, plus interest. The policyholder was prevented from recovering damages for emotional distress or economic loss caused by the deprivation of policy benefits. Punitive damages also were unavailable to deter insurers from wrongfully or even fraudulently denying claims. Therefore, insurers had nothing to lose by wrongfully denying claims or coercing unfair settlements.

James A. McGuire & Kristin Dodge McMahon, *Issues for Excess Insurer Counsel in Bad Faith and Excess Liability Cases*, 62 DEF. COUNS. J. 337, 337 (1995) (citations omitted).

The consequences of a covered loss on the insured and the insurer are often dramatically different. Accordingly, we imposed the tort duty recognizing that insureds who encounter losses they believe to be covered will often be particularly vulnerable to an insurer's arbitrary or unscrupulous conduct. *See Lyons* [*v. Millers Casualty Ins. Co.*, 866 S.W.2d 597, 600 (Tex.1993)] (referring to the insurer's "disproportionately favorable bargaining posture in the claims handling process"). People generally buy insurance to protect against risks that they cannot easily afford to pay. When an insurer unreasonably denies a claim, an insured who has suffered a loss that should rightfully be covered may reluctantly choose to drop the claim rather than suffer the emotional and financial burden of litigation. Even insureds who go so far as to hire a lawyer may often be inclined to settle for only a part of their contract damages due to financial stress or other pressures stemming from the loss.

We are in the mainstream in recognizing a bad-faith tort in the context of first-party claims. At least twenty-four states have done the same. At least five other state supreme courts have allowed recovery of extra-contractual damages without recognizing the tort. Only four state courts of last resort have rejected a tort of bad faith in first-party insurance cases.

The bad-faith tort has, as Justice Hecht's concurring opinion points out, been criticized. The criticism has focused in large part upon the extra-contractual damages that may be recovered:

[T]he new tort remedy, although necessary in some form, now shows signs of being too oppressive on an industry whose financial vitality and efficiency are essential to social well-being. Multimillion dollar awards for wrongfully denying claims not only are unnecessary to correct the situation, but such awards, which often have a windfall nature, may raise the cost of insurance for the vast numbers of insureds who are not mistreated and may do great harm to the risk-transfer-and-distribution mechanism in our society by making insurance so expensive that it can no longer be purchased like a household commodity.

Roger C. Henderson, *The Tort of Bad Faith in First-Party Insurance Transactions: Refining the Standard of Culpability and Reformulating the Remedies by Statute*, 26 U. MICH. J.L. REF. 1, 32 (1992) (citations omitted). This concern is obviously legitimate; we have long-recognized that the insurance industry is peculiarly affected with a public interest. We do not believe, however, that it justifies eliminating the cause of action. Even the tort's most outspoken critics recognize that "some measures were needed to redress the legitimate complaints of insureds. . . ." Henderson, 26 U. MICH. J.L. REF. at 31–32. And one commentator recently noted that changes in Texas law have gone far to constrain past excesses that may have adversely affected the insurance industry.

Moreover, this Court has carefully defined the conditions under which plaintiffs may recover the two primary forms of extra-contractual damages most common in bad faith cases, punitive and mental anguish damages. We have recognized that even if an insurer is liable for bad faith, a plaintiff may not recover punitive damages on that basis alone. Instead, "[o]nly when accompanied by malicious, intentional, fraudulent, or grossly negligent conduct does bad faith justify punitive damages." [*Moriel*, 879 S.W.2d at 18.] The plaintiff in a bad faith case must therefore prove that "the insurer was actually aware that its action would probably result in extraordinary harm not ordinarily associated with breach of contract or bad faith denial of a claim—such as death, grievous physical injury, or financial ruin." *Id.* at 24. This relatively stringent standard of proof ensures that punitive damages will ordinarily be available only in exceptional cases.

Similarly, concerned with the subjective nature of mental anguish damages, we have admonished courts to closely scrutinize such awards. In most cases, plaintiffs may not recover mental anguish damages unless they introduce "direct evidence of the nature, duration, and severity of their mental anguish, thus establishing a substantial disruption in the plaintiffs' daily routine." [*Parkway Co. v. Woodruff*, 901 S.W.2d 434, 444 (Tex.1995).] This standard ensures that fact-finders are provided "with adequate details to assess mental anguish claims." *Id.* In the context of bad faith actions, mental anguish damages will be limited to those cases in which the denial or delay in payment of a claim has seriously disrupted the insured's life.

Accordingly, we believe the better approach is to clarify the "no reasonable basis" standard for the tort rather than to abandon an established and widely recognized cause of action.

IV.

In *Aranda* [*v. Insurance Co. of N. Am.*, 748 S.W.2d 210 (Tex.1988)], we attempted to articulate a standard for recovery that balanced the remedial purposes of the bad-faith tort against the carrier's right to deny invalid or questionable claims. . . .

In clarifying the tort, we look first to other jurisdictions that recognize a bad faith cause of action. Of these jurisdictions, the majority will not impose liability so long as the coverage issue is "fairly debatable." William T. Barker & Paul E.B. Glad, *Use of Summary Judgment in Defense of Bad Faith Actions Involving First-Party Insurance,* 30 TORT & INS. L.J. 49, 52 (1994). The highest courts of at least sixteen different states impose liability for bad faith under some variant of this standard.

Although the standard has the benefit of being fairly widespread, we reject it. . . . [I]n many jurisdictions the term is virtually synonymous with our present no-reasonable-basis standard. . . .

The Legislature's recent amendment of Article 21.21, section 4 of the Insurance Code suggests a more workable approach. In 1995, the Legislature amended Article 21.21, Section 4, of the Insurance Code to define unfair insurance settlement practices. The amendment provides in part:

> Sec. 4.   The following are hereby defined as unfair methods of competition and unfair and deceptive acts or practices in the business of insurance:
>
> * * * * * *
>
> (10) Unfair Settlement Practices. (a) Engaging in any of the following unfair settlement practices with respect to a claim by an insured or beneficiary:
>
> * * * * * *
>
> (ii) failing to attempt in good faith to effectuate a prompt, fair, and equitable settlement of a claim with respect to which the insurer's liability has become reasonably clear. . . .

TEX. INS.CODE art. 21.21, § 4(10)(a)(ii). Section 16 of Article 21.21 gives a private right of action for violations of Section 4(10)(a)(ii). In section 4(10)(a)(ii), the Legislature has drawn a line that defines when an insurer's denial or delay in paying an insurance claim is no longer merely erroneous but in bad faith.

Although section 4(10)(a)(ii) does not, by its terms, govern common-law bad-faith actions, we believe that the standard it establishes will prove workable in such actions. Adopting this standard has several advantages. . . . [T]his solution unifies the common law and statutory standards for bad faith. The "reasonably clear" standard also allows for a factual inquiry that trial courts can easily and intelligently craft into a jury charge.[4]

The standard has the further advantage of familiarity. The Legislature first included section 4(10)(a)(ii) in the laundry list of claims available to private litigants under section 16 of Article 21.21 in 1995. But the Insurance Code has prohibited insurers from engaging in the conduct now described in section 4(10)(a)(ii) since 1973. Thus, we impose no new requirements upon insurers by applying the standard to the common law bad faith cause of action.

The "reasonably clear" standard recasts the liability standard in positive terms, rather than the current negative formulation.[5] Under this standard, an insurer will be liable if the insurer knew or should have known that it was reasonably clear that the claim was covered.

V.

However, we reject the suggestion that whether an insurer's liability has become reasonably clear presents a question of law for the court rather than a fact issue for the jury. . . .

We have long recognized that the Texas Constitution confers an exceptionally broad jury trial right upon litigants. And we have warned that courts must not lightly deprive our people of this right by taking an issue away from the jury. A court may be entitled to decide an issue as a matter of law when there is no conflict in the evidence, but when there is evidence on either side, the issue is a fact question. Justice Hecht's concurring opinion identifies no circumstances that make a jury unsuited to decide whether an insurer has denied or delayed payment of a claim after its liability has become reasonably clear.[6] We therefore hold that whether an insurer acted in bad faith because it denied or delayed payment of a claim after its liability became reasonably clear is a question for the fact-finder.

VI.

The trial court submitted this case under the "no reasonable basis" standard. Under either that standard or the "reasonably clear" standard, however, there is some evidence to support the jury's finding that Universe acted in bad faith. Universe explains its reasons for continuing to deny Giles's claim in its petition in this Court as follows:

---

[4] However, we reject the suggestion in Justice Hecht's concurrence that section 4 of Article 21.21 preempts the common-law bad-faith tort.

[5] An insurer will not escape liability merely by failing to investigate a claim so that it can contend that liability was never reasonably clear. Instead, we reaffirm that an insurance company may also breach its duty of good faith and fair dealing by failing to reasonably investigate a claim.

[6] Furthermore, the contention that we should treat the issue as one of law radically departs from a wealth of caselaw holding that reasonableness is ordinarily a question of fact.

> The denial of the claim as a pre-existing condition was justified because the undisputed medical records revealed that Mrs. Giles had "a positive history of heart disease," that she had probably suffered a heart attack that was caused by atherosclerotic cardiovascular disease, that the atherosclerotic cardiovascular disease was an illness that had been medically treated with Mevacor, and that she had received treatment for this illness within the twelve months preceding the issuance of the policy. The Mevacor and Lorelco that were prescribed as a treatment for an illness that was later positively diagnosed as atherosclerosis, constitutes medical care or treatment within the exclusionary language of the policy.

Giles's medical records do not say that she had "a positive history of heart disease"; they say she had "a positive history of heart disease *with a mother who recently had coronary artery bypass grafting*." Two sentences before, the same record states: "She [Giles] has never had any history of heart problems." The medical records do not reflect that Giles was treated for heart disease before her insurance coverage became effective. While she had been treated for high cholesterol for some time, Universe points to no evidence that such treatment was tantamount to treatment for heart disease. In fact, all the evidence was to the contrary.

From the medical records, it should have been reasonably clear to Universe that Giles's claim should be paid. Universe does not argue that the records were unreliable; to the contrary, Universe relied on them. Nor is there evidence of any need for further investigation after Giles's physicians wrote to Universe. Giles's physicians clarified her medical records within four months of her surgery. Coverage of the claim was reasonably clear by then, yet Universe continued to deny coverage for an additional seven months. The jury could have logically concluded that Universe denied Giles's claim without a reasonable basis and that its purported reliance on Giles's medical records was a mere pretext. Applying the traditional standard of no-evidence review, we conclude that some evidence supports the jury's finding that Universe was liable for bad faith.

VII.

Universe also complains that there is no evidence to support the punitive damages awarded. . . .

In *Moriel*, we held that punitive damages can be awarded for bad faith only when an insurer was actually aware that its actions involved an extreme risk—that is, a high probability of serious harm, such as death, grievous physical injury, or financial ruin—to its insured and was nevertheless consciously indifferent to its insured's rights, safety, or welfare. Giles argues that this standard should not apply in this case because *Moriel* was decided after the parties tried this case. But *Moriel* only "clarif[ied] the standards governing the imposition of punitive damages in the context of bad faith insurance litigation." Accordingly, *Moriel* applies in this case.

The record reflects that medical care providers repeatedly asked Giles about payment of her bills. Although Giles testified that these inquiries caused her great distress, there is no evidence of the type of risk required for punitive damages. Though Universe may have been aware of Giles's distress, there is no evidence that Universe's claims decision was likely to cause any extreme risk to Giles.

Accordingly, we hold that there is no evidence to support the punitive damages award.

. . . .

HECHT, JUSTICE, joined by PHILLIPS, CHIEF JUSTICE, GONZALEZ and OWEN, JUSTICES, concurring in the judgment.

. . . .

. . . . Replacing the "no reasonable basis" standard of common-law bad-faith insurance liability with the more recently enacted "reasonably clear" statutory bad-faith standard simplifies the law but does nothing to clarify what bad faith means. . . .

JUSTICE SPECTOR's vaunting of an altered standard as a solution to the bad-faith dilemma is betrayed by her alternative position, advanced with equal force and straight face, that no change is really necessary because no significant damages can be recovered for bad faith. Bad-faith liability is no longer a problem, JUSTICE SPECTOR's opinion assures, because the Court has tightened the standards for awarding mental anguish and punitive damages, and these are most of the damages in bad-faith cases. If bad faith really afforded no significant recovery of damages, one could wonder why the cause of action should exist at all, but one's effort would be better spent trying to understand what JUSTICE SPECTOR thinks is significant. *Simmons* [a case pending before the Texas Supreme Court] involves awards of $200,000 in mental anguish and $2 million in punitive damages on a policy claim of $75,000. *Dal-Worth* [another case pending before the Texas Supreme Court] involves an $11.5 million punitive damages award on a policy claim of several thousand dollars. Even in today's "enlightened" view of damage awards, such sums are hardly insignificant.

. . . .

I would define bad faith as unscrupulous, arbitrary conduct and make the standard one of law as it is in many other instances, such as: whether an action under the Deceptive Trade Practices Act was groundless and brought in bad faith; whether a writing is ambiguous; whether a provision is conspicuous in a document; whether a person had probable cause for prosecuting charges; and whether language is defamatory. I would impose liability for intentional or reckless conduct on the part of an insurer but not merely for negligence or mistakes.

I

A

Since about the turn of the century courts throughout the country have imposed a duty on insurers to consider their insureds' interests in settling liability claims against their insureds. Texas did so in *G. A. Stowers Furniture Co. v. American Indemnity Co.,* 15 S.W.2d 544 (Tex. Comm'n App.1929, holding approved). An action for breach of the *Stowers* duty affords the remedy of extra-contractual damages to an insured who suffers a judgment in excess of coverage because of the insurer's wrongful failure to accept a settlement offer within policy limits. Absent such a duty, an insurer has little incentive to settle a claim against its insured because its risk is limited to the amount of coverage. Breach of the duty is usually characterized as a tort—either negligence, as in Texas, or bad faith. Because the duty arises in the context of a claim by a third party against the insured, the cases are usually referred to as third-party cases. Although important differences in the breadth of the duty have emerged among American jurisdictions, liability in third-party cases in this State and elsewhere is "a relatively mature, stable, and complete body of law." [STEPHEN S. ASHLEY, BAD FAITH ACTIONS, LIABILITY AND DAMAGES § 5.01 (1992).]

So-called first-party cases involve claims by insureds for policy benefits for their own damages rather than indemnity for injuries to third parties. Courts have been more reluctant to impose a tort duty on insurers to settle first-party claims. For one thing, an insurer's and an insured's interests are not aligned when the insured is claiming on his own behalf as they are or should be in third-party cases where insurer and insured face a common opponent. While insurers are obliged to pay valid claims promptly, they are entitled to challenge claims they believe may be invalid. Indeed, from a competitive viewpoint, an insurer must pay only valid claims and must deny invalid claims to keep premiums to customers at a minimum. In a third-party case, both the insurer and the insured have a common interest in challenging a third-party's claim. But in a first-party case, an insurer's interest in challenging the claim directly conflicts with the insured's interest in making the claim.

For another thing, insureds already have a remedy against their insurers by suit for breach of contract. Although this remedy does not ordinarily include consequential damages because of the rule of *Hadley v. Baxendale,* 9 Exch. 341, 354 (1854), or mental anguish damages, and thus does not always fully compensate an insured wrongfully deprived of benefits, it is

> just plain wrong to say "[w]ithout a cause of action for breach of the duty of good faith and fair dealing . . . insurers [can] . . . arbitrarily den[y] coverage . . . with no more penalty than interest on the amount owed." [*Union Bankers Ins. Co. v. Shelton*, 889 S.W.2d 278, 283 (Tex.1994) (citing *Arnold v. National County Mut. Fire Ins. Co.*, 725 S.W.2d 165, 167 (Tex.1987))]. This statement is no more true today than it was when it first was made. To the contrary, even if an insurer that denies a claim prevails at trial, it must pay the costs of its own defense. If the insured prevails, the insurer must pay not only prejudgment interest, but also the insured's reasonable attorneys' fees. TEX. CIV. PRAC. & REM.CODE §§ 38.001–38.006 (Vernon 1986). . . . Further, an insurer may face statutory penalties for improper claims handling. *See, e.g.,* TEX. INS.CODE ANN. arts. 21.21, 21.55 (Vernon 1981 & Supp.1994). Liability for such additional sums, over and above policy benefits, may reasonably be expected to deter even "repeat-players" in litigation, like insurance carriers, from arbitrarily denying benefits under a policy.

Shelton, 889 S.W.2d at 286–287 (Cornyn, J., joined by Gonzalez and Hecht, JJ., concurring and dissenting).

Moreover, it is far from clear whether giving insureds a tort action does not create more problems than it solves. If the threat of liability is too great, insurers are discouraged from denying any claims, even those it suspects may be fraudulent.

> This danger is doubly troubling in light of recent fears that insurance fraud is rampant. Although its exact magnitude is difficult to ascertain for obvious reasons, various estimates suggest that excess medical claims alone may add over $100 per year to the average cost of auto insurance for each customer, that about 10 percent of all auto insurance claims are fraudulent, that property/casualty insurance fraud may amount to about $20 billion annually, that health care fraud may be as much as $100 billion annually, and that workers' compensation fraud may account for as much as 25 percent of all claims. It has even been suggested that insurance fraud is second only to illegal drug trafficking in the amount of illicit revenue that it generates for perpetrators. The potential joint returns to insurance companies and honest policyholders from reductions in fraud thus appear to be quite considerable across the board. If

reasonable efforts to reduce fraud can become "bad faith" down the road, however, insurers may simply give up on them.

Alan O. Sykes, *"Bad Faith" Breach of Contract by First-Party Insurers,* 25 J. LEGAL STUD. 405, 434–435 (1996) (footnotes omitted).

> In one of the few formal studies conducted, Massachusetts found that 32 percent of the total number of claims studied contained an element of fraud. An Insurance Research Council study estimates that 36 percent of all bodily injury liability claims appear to involve fraud or buildup. It is generally conceded by industry experts that 10 to 25 percent of all property-casualty claims are fraudulent.

Edward L. Schrenk & Jonathon B. Palmquist, *Fraud and Its Effects on the Insurance Industry,* 64 DEF. COUNS. J. 23, 24 (1997) (footnotes omitted). If an insurer is to remain in business, compensation to bad-faith claimants, like policy benefits, must ultimately come from premiums paid by policyholders.

Still, courts have felt strong pressures to discourage unscrupulous insurers from taking advantage of their superior bargaining position to delay adjustment of claims and force insureds to accept less than they are entitled to. Consequently, most jurisdictions have recognized a tort of bad-faith in first-party insurance cases. The first court of last resort to do so was the California Supreme Court in *Gruenberg v. Aetna Insurance Co.,* 510 P.2d 1032 (1973). Since then at least twenty-five other state supreme courts have recognized the tort in such cases.

. . . .

Despite fairly widespread adoption of the tort, two principal arguments continue to be made for rejecting altogether the tort of bad faith in first-party insurance cases.

First, most scholars have argued that contract law should provide all redress for an insurer's wrongful denial of its insureds' claims. Reflecting on the adoption of the bad-faith tort in Texas, Professor Mark Gergen writes:

> Opening the door to tort claims in contract, with their lure of emotional and exemplary damages, creates a crush of claims as plaintiffs and their lawyers attempt to cash in. Trial judges vary in how closely they police the door, and juries sometimes award extraordinary damages in what seem to be run-of-the-mill contract cases. While the Texas appellate courts have policed this particular door between contract and tort fairly closely (they limited the tort to the area of insurance, and only a few cases have upheld large exemplary damage awards when an insurer made what seemed a good faith mistake in denying a claim), the

opinions are ill-reasoned because the ways in which the tort's boundaries are defined defy reasoned analysis. The huge stakes in bad faith cases and its flimsy doctrinal garb make this a particularly volatile area of the law.

[Mark Gergen, *A Cautionary Tale About Contractual Good Faith in Texas*, 72 TEX. L. REV. 1235, 1236 (1994).] The argument for a contract remedy rather than a tort aims mostly at the difference in available damages and the uncertainty in determining extracontractual damages like mental anguish and punitive damages.

Second, the argument is made with increasing force that a bad-faith tort does more harm than good. Even scholars who accept the need for some remedy in tort are troubled by developments in bad-faith law:

The need for a tort remedy for insurers' predatory or unscrupulous claims practices is well-recognized. But plaintiffs' attorneys today strive to manipulate insurers into extracontractual and punitive exposure. Increasingly, plaintiffs groundlessly allege insurance companies' bad faith in attempts to win the judicial lottery. . . . There now exists a nightmarish extracontractual insurance culture.

[Douglas R. Richmond, *An Overview of Insurance Bad Faith Law and Litigation*, 25 SETON HALL L.REV. 74, 76 (1994) (footnotes and text omitted) [hereinafter Richmond I]]. Professor Sykes writes:

Insurers may at times employ lamentable tactics to reduce their payments under first-party insurance policies, primarily by exploiting the delay inherent in the civil litigation process to induce a needy insured to settle for less than the amount that the contract promises. The prospect of tort remedies at the end of the litigation process can make such tactics unprofitable and thus serve a potentially valuable function. Yet we must be alert to the danger that the remedy may be worse than the problem— a fact that may explain the absence of greater market response to it. Nevertheless, one cannot rule out the possibility that the courts can step in constructively when an insurer knowingly refuses to make good on its clear obligations.

Unfortunately, however, the courts seem to find tortious conduct on the part of insurers who have bona fide disputes with their policyholders over the terms of the policy or over factual issues essential to the insured's right to recover. The ability of the courts to identify opportunistic behavior in such cases is very much in doubt, and the distinct possibility arises that bad faith doctrine here does little to police misconduct while doing much to cause uneconomic increases in the premiums that policyholders must pay.

Sykes, *supra*, at 443.

. . . .

While such arguments cannot be ignored, reversing course has its own problems. Bad faith has come to be accepted as a cause of action and is being litigated in a great many cases. The cause of action is currently recognized in about half the states; only a handful of jurisdictions have rejected it. And as virtually every legal commentator concedes, there should be some remedy for insurers' abuse of the claims process. But if the tort is to exist, it must be defined.

B

"The term 'bad faith' . . . is not self-defining, nor has it historically been a recognized independent basis of culpability in tort law. It has come to mean different things to different courts. Consequently, its use has caused definitional problems from the outset." [Roger C. Henderson, *The Tort of Bad Faith in First-Party Insurance Transactions After Two Decades*, 37 ARIZ. L.REV. 1153, 1156 (1995) (footnotes omitted) [hereinafter Henderson I]].

As in many jurisdictions, the tort of bad faith in Texas has two elements: "that the insurer had no reasonable basis for denying or delaying payment of the claim, and that it knew or should have known that fact." *Transportation Ins. Co. v. Moriel*, 879 S.W.2d 10, 18 (Tex.1994). Thus, the touchstone of bad-faith liability—or more precisely, a breach of the duty of good faith and fair dealing—is unreasonableness in processing insurance claims. The measure of reasonableness is not clear. It is the courts' duty to provide clarity because the existence and scope of a legal duty are questions of law. The courts have failed to define the scope of the duty.

. . . .

. . . [T]he purpose of the duty of good faith and fair dealing is to discourage "unscrupulous insurers [from taking] advantage of their insureds' misfortunes in bargaining for settlement or resolution of claims." *Arnold*, 725 S.W.2d at 167. The duty is also to prevent insurers from acting arbitrarily. *Arnold*, 725 S.W.2d at 167. "Unscrupulous," "arbitrary," and "taking advantage" are not synonyms for negligence. They require, not merely misfeasance, but malfeasance.

The distinction between the unreasonableness standard for bad faith and the unreasonableness standard in other liability contexts is significant, and the confusion of the two concepts accounts for much of the present difficulty with the bad-faith tort. Defining bad faith as a failure to use ordinary care is simply unworkable.

. . . .

But if bad faith is not negligence, what is it? The failure to define clear liability standards for a bad-faith tort has caused many problems. One is that insurers cannot anticipate what circumstances will risk liability and avoid them. . . . It is fundamentally unfair for the law to impose liability without defining what conduct is culpable precisely enough for it to be avoided.

Another problem with not defining bad faith is that it encourages the allegation in every case.

> Unfortunately, insurance bad faith litigation has gotten out of hand. When courts initially recognized bad faith as an independent tort they anticipated that such claims would be rare. In fact, they should be. By and large insurers process a vast amount of claims in an ethical and responsible manner. But now, almost every first-party action for an insurer's breach of contract includes a bad faith count, and liability insurers are deliberately "set up" for bad faith claims.

Richmond I, *supra,* at 140 (footnotes omitted). Commentators refer to bad-faith actions as "the judicial equivalent of the Wheel of Fortune," and a "lottery." There is always a chance it will pay off. But inclusion of a bad-faith allegation in every first-party insurance case distorts not only the litigation system but the insurance industry itself.

> I am inclined to think that a bad-faith count is included in most claims against insurers in jurisdictions that recognize the tort. We must assume that the count adds a premium to whatever value the claim has, and this suggests that the overall, system-wide cost of recognizing the tort of bad faith may be large, even if insurers are now able to better identify and redistribute these costs.

Robert H. Jerry, II, *The Wrong Side of the Mountain: A Comment on Bad Faith's Unnatural History*, 72 TEX. L.REV. 1317, 1343 (1994). Bad-faith allegations not only make cases more expensive to settle, "[t]he addition of a claim of uncertain value in a dispute makes settlement less likely and thus increases litigation costs." Gergen, *supra*, at 1252–1253.

Still another problem with an undefined bad-faith tort is the effect on policyholders and the public who never have a claim.

> There is no doubt that the tort of bad faith has had and will continue to have a terrific impact on first-party insurers. In practically every lawsuit that is filed against an insurer providing first-party benefits there is a count seeking consequential and punitive damages, in addition to policy benefits. This development has significant implications for insurers and how they do business.

Henderson I, *supra*, at 1182. Bad-faith liability "enriches a few at the expense of many with significant transaction costs." Gergen, *supra*, at 1250. Without principles and limits, a bad-faith tort does more harm than good.

> In the context of insurance claims practices, it is clear that some measures were needed to redress the legitimate complaints of insureds, but now it appears that the balance may have been tipped too far in their favor by unduly exposing insurers to extra-contractual damages. The judicial filling of the vacuum left by the legislative and administrative processes was justified when it was made; real abuses by insurers need to be identified and corrected. Nevertheless, the new tort remedy, although necessary in some form, now shows signs of being too oppressive on an industry whose financial vitality and efficiency are essential to social well-being. Multimillion dollar awards for wrongfully denying claims not only are unnecessary to correct the situation, but such awards, which often have a windfall nature, may raise the cost of insurance for the vast numbers of insureds who are not mistreated and may do great harm to the risk-transfer-and-distribution mechanism in our society by making insurance so expensive that it can no longer be purchased like a household commodity. There is a point at which potential insureds will either elect reduced coverage or forgo purchases or other activities because of insurance costs. This negative impact certainly could extend to and affect the standard of living for individuals if too much of their income must be spent on premiums that spread the cost of awards for extra-contractual damages and the related expenses of defending against such claims, in addition to covering the primary risks insured against.

[Roger C. Henderson, *The Tort of Bad Faith in First-Party Insurance Transactions: Refining the Standard of Culpability and Reformulating the Remedies by Statute*, 26 U. MICH. J.L. REF. 1, 31–32 (1992) (footnote omitted) [hereinafter Henderson II]].

. . . .

C

Like many courts, our principal reason for adopting the bad-faith tort was to discourage "unscrupulous insurers [from taking] advantage of their insureds' misfortunes in bargaining for settlement or resolution of claims." *Arnold*, 725 S.W.2d at 167.

It is not unscrupulous for an insurer to deny or delay payment of a claim about which there is a bona fide dispute. We have never intended that an insurer should be liable for tort damages simply for denying a claim in error, even if the insurer was negligent. To the contrary, we promised at the tort's inception that "carriers will maintain the right to deny invalid or questionable claims and will not be subject to liability for an erroneous denial of a claim." *Aranda*, 748 S.W.2d at 213. We have reiterated the promise in several cases.

> In other words, if the insurer has denied what is later determined to be a valid claim under the contract of insurance, the insurer must respond in actual damages up to the policy limits. But as long as the insurer has a reasonable basis to deny or delay payment of the claim, even if that basis is eventually determined by the factfinder to be erroneous, the insurer is not liable for the tort of bad faith.

Lyons, 866 S.W.2d at 600.

> Evidence that merely shows a bona fide dispute about the insurer's liability on the contract does not rise to the level of bad faith. . . . Nor is bad faith established if the evidence shows the insurer was merely incorrect about the factual basis for its denial of the claim, or about the proper construction of the policy. . . . A simple disagreement among experts about whether the cause of the loss is one covered by the policy will not support a judgment for bad faith.

Moriel, 879 S.W.2d at 17–18.

> "[This] bona fide dispute rule" is nothing more than a shorthand notation for the observation that the parties to an insurance contract will sometimes have a good faith disagreement about coverage. Under such circumstances, the parties may require a court to interpret policy language for them, or a jury to resolve factual disputes. Simply because the parties go to court does not raise an issue of the insurer's bad faith.

Id. at 18 n.8.

In theory, what protects an insurer from bad-faith liability for simply denying a claim erroneously is the first element of the tort—no reasonable basis. This is true in most other jurisdictions that have recognized a bad-faith tort. An early first-party bad-faith case, *Anderson v. Continental Insurance Co.,* 85 Wis.2d 675, 271 N.W.2d 368, 376–377 (1978), stated what seems intuitive, that insurers have a reasonable basis for challenging claims that are "fairly debatable" and thus cannot be liable for bad faith for doing so. Bad faith does not extend to all errors in judgment. An insurer has the "right to be wrong."

. . . .

II

The second element of bad faith is that an insurer "knew or should have known" that it had no reasonable basis for denying or delaying payment of a claim. The Court has not been precise in stating what mental state an insurer must have for bad faith.

. . . .

Bad-faith liability should not . . . extend to negligence—an insurer's failure to pay a claim as an ordinarily prudent insurer would. For one thing, it is not clear what the standard of ordinary care would be. As Professor Gergen argues, the decision to pay claims usually involves a number of variables which are difficult to evaluate. Payment of even a small claim is often important to an insured, but there are practical limits to the time and resources an insurer can expend in investigating a claim. For another thing, even if a negligence standard could practicably be determined, insurers should be permitted some margin of error before suffering extra-contractual damages. "Insureds do make inaccurate, groundless, and even fraudulent claims and insurers need some margin of error within which to operate, but this margin should not extend into the area of conduct described as reckless under the Restatement of Torts." Henderson II, *supra*, at 54.

I would hold that "knew or should have known" in the second element of bad faith requires intentional or reckless conduct as defined in the Restatement. This appears to be the rule in a majority of jurisdictions. . . .

III

. . . .

I agree with the other Members of the Court that Universe Life had no basis for delaying payment of Giles' claim but that there was no evidence supporting an award of punitive damages. Accordingly, I concur in the Court's judgment.

. . . .

NOTES & QUESTIONS

(1) What is the relationship between the duty to settle and the duty of good faith? The duties differ with respect to the settings in which they are invoked. The duty to settle arises in the third-party insurance context, while the duty of good faith typically arises in the first-party insurance context. Nevertheless, the duties are similar in that they are both means by which courts regulate the insurer-insured relationship. Indeed, the duty to settle has been characterized as bad faith breach of contract in third-party insurance cases, while the duty of good faith has been characterized as bad faith breach of contract in first-party insurance disputes. *See, e.g.*, ROBERT H.

JERRY, II & DOUGLAS R. RICHMOND, UNDERSTANDING INSURANCE LAW § 25G, at 176–84 (4th ed. 2007); 3 DAN B. DOBBS ET AL., THE LAW OF TORTS §§ 701–702, at 767–74 (2d ed. 2011). In *Gruenberg v. Aetna Insurance Co.,* 510 P.2d 1032 (Cal. 1973), the Supreme Court of California similarly linked the two duties:

> . . . . The duty of an insurer to deal fairly and in good faith with its insured is governed by our decisions in Crisci v. Security Ins. Co. (1967) 426 P.2d 173, and Comunale v. Traders & General Ins. Co. (1958) 328 P.2d 198. We explained that this duty, the breach of which sounds in both contract and tort, is imposed because "(t)here is an implied covenant of good faith and fair dealing in every contract (including insurance policies) that neither party will do anything which will injure the right of the other to receive the benefits of the agreement."

> . . . . In those two cases, we considered the duty of the insurer to act in good faith and fairly in handling the claims of third persons against the insured, described as a "duty to accept reasonable settlements"; in the case before us we consider the duty of an insurer to act in good faith and fairly in handling the claim of an insured, namely a duty not to withhold unreasonably payments due under a policy. These are merely two different aspects of the same duty. . . . It is the obligation, deemed to be imposed by the law, under which the insurer must act fairly and in good faith in discharging its contractual responsibilities. Where in so doing, it fails to deal fairly and in good faith with its insured by refusing, without proper cause, to compensate its insured for a loss covered by the policy, such conduct may give rise to a cause of action in tort for breach of an implied covenant of good faith and fair dealing.

> . . . .

> It is manifest that a common legal principle underlies all of the foregoing decisions; namely, that in every insurance contract there is an implied covenant of good faith and fair dealing. The duty to so act is imminent in the contract whether the company is attending to the claims of third persons against the insured or the claims of the insured itself. Accordingly, when the insurer unreasonably and in bad faith withholds payment of the claim of its insured, it is subject to liability in tort.

Id. at 1036–38.

(2) What standards do courts use to determine whether the duty of good faith has been breached? Consider the following:

> Although judicial formulations of what constitutes bad faith vary widely, the weight of authority favors what is commonly called the "fairly debatable" standard. One court explained this standard as follows:

This "fairly debatable" standard is premised on the idea that when an insurer denies coverage with a reasonable basis to believe that no coverage exists, it is not guilty of bad faith even if the insurer is later held to have been wrong. "The rationale for this legal principle is based upon the potential in terrorem effect of bad faith litigation upon the insurer." "An insurer should have the right to litigate a claim when it feels there is a question of law or fact which needs to be decided before it in good faith is required to pay the claimant." In order to impose "bad faith" liability, the insured must demonstrate that no debatable reasons existed for denial of the benefits available under the policy.

Many courts require in addition to the objective element of "absence of a reasonable basis for denying the claim" proof that the insurer "knew or had reason to know that its denial was without reasonable basis," which is in the nature of a subjective test. . . . Under this standard, the insurer as a matter of law cannot be held liable for bad faith if "an objectively reasonable basis for denying the [insured's] claim exists." It is also common for courts to ratchet up the evidentiary standard that the plaintiff must hurdle in order to prevail, such as, for example, by requiring proof of bad faith by "substantial evidence" or "clear and convincing evidence."

Other courts have articulated in a variety of ways the idea that "something more" is needed than mere nonperformance of the insurer's contractual duties. For example, it has been said that mere negligence on the part of the insurer is usually not enough to constitute bad faith. Resolving good faith doubts about a claim against the insured is not bad faith, even if a court subsequently determines that the insurer's denial was erroneous. Negligence combined with something else (such as the insurer's awareness at some point while handling the claim that the claim was probably covered) is sometimes enough to constitute bad faith; this may amount to a "gross negligence" or "reckless disregard" standard. One court stated that "bad faith requires an extraordinary showing of disingenuous or dishonest failure to carry out a contract." Another said that bad faith is "affirmative misconduct, without good faith defense, in a malicious, dishonest, or oppressive attempt to avoid liability." . . .

JERRY & RICHMOND, *supra*, § 25G[d][2], at 186–87.

(3) A range of insurer conduct has been found to constitute a breach of the duty of good faith:

. . . . For example, failure to handle a claim in a manner that would alleviate the insured's hardship without impairing the insurer's interests in circumstances where the insurer is aware of the insured's dire straits may constitute bad faith. Making "low ball" offers of settlement to an insured in the first-party setting when the insurer's own claims adjustment shows the insured's claim to have more value may be bad faith. Intentional denial of a claim known to be valid is classic bad faith. Systematically canceling insurance policies whenever claims are submitted without determining whether there are good grounds to do so is bad faith.

Id. at 188–89; *see also Beck v. Farmers Ins. Exch.*, 701 P.2d 795, 801 (Utah 1985) ("[W]e conclude that the implied obligation of good faith performance contemplates, at the very least, that the insurer will diligently investigate the facts to enable it to determine whether a claim is valid, will fairly evaluate the claim, and will thereafter act promptly and reasonably in rejecting or settling the claim. The duty of good faith also requires the insurer to 'deal with laymen as laymen and not as experts in the subtleties of law and underwriting' and to refrain from actions that will injure the insured's ability to obtain the benefits of the contract.").

(4) What standard did the *Giles* court articulate for determining whether a breach of the duty of good faith had occurred? Why did the court believe that the standard had been met?

(5) When an insurer acts improperly in the processing or payment of an insured's claim, it is clearly a breach of the insurance contract. Why, however, is it a tort in most jurisdictions? What rationales for and against tort liability are discussed in *Giles*? Do you agree with the tort characterization? As part of your analysis, consider the following:

> . . . [W]e cannot agree with the *Gruenberg* court that the considerations which compel the recognition of a tort cause of action in a third-party context are present in the first-party situation. . . .
>
> . . . [I]n *Lyon v. Hartford Accident and Indemnity Co.*, we held that a tort cause of action did not arise in a first-party insurance contract situation because the relationship between the insurer and its insured is fundamentally different than in a third-party context:
>
>> In the [third-party] situation, the insurer must act in good faith and be as zealous in protecting the interests of the insured as it would be in regard to its own. In the [first-party] situation, the insured and the insurer are, in effect and practically speaking, adversaries.
>
> This distinction is of no small consequence. In a third-party situation . . . the contract itself creates a fiduciary relationship because of the trust and reliance placed in the insurer by its insured. The insured is wholly dependent upon the insurer to see that, in dealing with claims by third parties, the insured's best interests are protected. In addition, when dealing with third parties, the insurer acts as an agent for the insured with respect to the disputed claim. . . .

In the first-party situation, on the other hand, the reasons for finding a fiduciary relationship and imposing a corresponding duty are absent. No relationship of trust and reliance is created by the contract; it simply obligates the insurer to pay claims submitted by the insured in accordance with the contract. Furthermore, none of the indicia of agency are present.

Beck v. Farmers Ins. Exch., 701 P.2d 795, 799–800 (Utah 1985).

(6) In many jurisdictions, statutes exist that authorize a court to award attorney's fees, costs, or penalties to an insured who prevails in an action against an insurer for misconduct in the payment or processing of a claim. The statutes are intended to benefit the insured by increasing the insurer's liability and correspondingly deterring (ideally) the insurer's misbehavior. For example, "to the extent an insurer decides to deny a first-party claim under the reasoning that even if the insurer loses at trial the damages will be no greater than what the insurer would have paid if it had performed under the contract, the prospect that the successful insured will recover attorney's fees reduces the insurer's incentive to engage in this kind of behavior." JERRY & RICHMOND, *supra*, § 25G[d][3], at 189–90.

Does the existence of such statutes provide an argument against tort liability for breach of the duty of good faith?

B. EMPLOYMENT

FOLEY V. INTERACTIVE DATA CORP.
765 P.2d 373 (Cal. 1988)

LUCAS, CHIEF JUSTICE.

After Interactive Data Corporation (defendant) fired plaintiff Daniel D. Foley, an executive employee, he filed this action seeking compensatory and punitive damages for wrongful discharge. In his second amended complaint, plaintiff asserted . . . a cause of action alleging a tortious breach of the implied covenant of good faith and fair dealing. The trial court sustained a demurrer without leave to amend, and entered judgment for defendant.

The Court of Appeal affirmed. . . .

We will hold that . . . the covenant of good faith and fair dealing applies to employment contracts and that breach of the covenant may give rise to contract but not tort damages.

FACTS

. . . .

According to the complaint, plaintiff is a former employee of defendant, a wholly owned subsidiary of Chase Manhattan Bank that markets computer-based decision-support services. Defendant hired plaintiff in June 1976 as an assistant product manager at a starting salary of $18,500. As a condition of employment defendant required plaintiff to sign a "Confidential and Proprietary Information Agreement" whereby he promised not to engage in certain competition with defendant for one year after the termination of his employment for any reason. . . . It did not state any limitation on the grounds for which plaintiff's employment could be terminated.

Over the next six years and nine months, plaintiff received a steady series of salary increases, promotions, bonuses, awards and superior performance evaluations. In 1979 defendant named him consultant manager of the year and in 1981 promoted him to branch manager of its Los Angeles office. His annual salary rose to $56,164 and he received an additional $6,762 merit bonus two days before his discharge in March 1983. He alleges defendant's officers made repeated oral assurances of job security so long as his performance remained adequate.

Plaintiff also alleged that during his employment, defendant maintained written "Termination Guidelines" that set forth express grounds for discharge and a mandatory seven-step pretermination procedure. Plaintiff understood that these guidelines applied not only to employees under plaintiff's supervision, but to him as well. On the basis of these representations, plaintiff alleged that he reasonably believed defendant would not discharge him except for good cause, and therefore he refrained from accepting or pursuing other job opportunities.

The event that led to plaintiff's discharge was a private conversation in January 1983 with his former supervisor, vice president Richard Earnest. During the previous year defendant had hired Robert Kuhne and subsequently named Kuhne to replace Earnest as plaintiff's immediate supervisor. Plaintiff learned that Kuhne was currently under investigation by the Federal Bureau of Investigation for embezzlement from his former employer, Bank of America. Plaintiff reported what he knew about Kuhne to Earnest, because he was "worried about working for Kuhne and having him in a supervisory position . . . in view of Kuhne's suspected criminal conduct." Plaintiff asserted he "made this disclosure in the interest and for the benefit of his employer," allegedly because he believed that because defendant and its parent do business with the financial community on a confidential basis, the company would have a legitimate interest in knowing about a high executive's alleged prior criminal conduct.

In response, Earnest allegedly told plaintiff not to discuss "rumors" and to "forget what he heard" about Kuhne's past. In early March, Kuhne informed plaintiff that defendant had decided to replace him for "performance reasons" and that he could transfer to a position in another division in Waltham, Massachusetts. Plaintiff was told that if he did not accept a transfer, he might be demoted but not fired. One week later, in Waltham, Earnest informed plaintiff he was not doing a good job, and six days later, he notified plaintiff he could continue as branch manager if he "agreed to go on a 'performance plan.' Plaintiff asserts he agreed to consider such an arrangement." The next day, when Kuhne met with plaintiff, purportedly to present him with a written "performance plan" proposal, Kuhne instead informed plaintiff he had the choice of resigning or being fired. Kuhne offered neither a performance plan nor an option to transfer to another position.

. . . .

III. BREACH OF THE IMPLIED COVENANT OF GOOD FAITH AND FAIR DEALING

We turn now to plaintiff's cause of action for tortious breach of the implied covenant of good faith and fair dealing. . . . [P]laintiff asserts we should recognize tort remedies for such a breach in the context of employment termination.

The distinction between tort and contract is well grounded in common law, and divergent objectives underlie the remedies created in the two areas. Whereas contract actions are created to enforce the intentions of the parties to the agreement, tort law is primarily designed to vindicate "social policy." (Prosser, Law of Torts (4th ed. 1971) p. 613.) The covenant of good faith and fair dealing was developed in the contract arena and is aimed at making effective the agreement's promises. Plaintiff asks that we find that the breach of the implied covenant in employment contracts also gives rise to an action seeking an award of tort damages.

In this instance, where an extension of tort remedies is sought for a duty whose breach previously has been compensable by contractual remedies, it is helpful to consider certain principles relevant to contract law. First, predictability about the cost of contractual relationships plays an important role in our commercial system. Moreover, "Courts traditionally have awarded damages for breach of contract to compensate the aggrieved party rather than to punish the breaching party." (Note, *"Contort": Tortious Breach of the Implied Covenant of Good Faith and Fair Dealing in Noninsurance, Commercial Contracts—Its Existence and Desirability* (1985) 60 Notre Dame L.Rev. 510, 526, & fn. 94, citing Rest.2d Contracts, § 355, com. a ["The purpose[ ] of awarding contract damages is to compensate the injured party"].)[25] With these concepts in

---

[25] At times certain breaches of contract have been deemed economically desirable. As the reporter's notes to Restatement Second of Contracts, chapter 16, section 344 et seq., pages 101–102, state, "a breach of contract will result in a gain in 'economic efficiency' if the party contemplating breach evaluates his gains at a higher figure than the value that the other party

mind, we turn to analyze the role of the implied covenant of good faith and fair dealing and the propriety of the extension of remedies urged by plaintiff.

"Every contract imposes upon each party a duty of good faith and fair dealing in its performance and its enforcement." (Rest.2d Contracts, § 205.) This duty has been recognized in the majority of American jurisdictions, the Restatement, and the Uniform Commercial Code. Because the covenant is a contract term, however, compensation for its breach has almost always been limited to contract rather than tort remedies. As to the scope of the covenant, " '[t]he precise nature and extent of the duty imposed by such an implied promise will depend on the contractual purposes.' " (*Egan v. Mutual of Omaha Ins. Co.* (1979) 620 P.2d 141.) Initially, the concept of a duty of good faith developed in contract law as "a kind of 'safety valve' to which judges may turn to fill gaps and qualify or limit rights and duties otherwise arising under rules of law and specific contract language." (Summers, *The General Duty of Good Faith—Its Recognition and Conceptualization* (1982) 67 Cornell L.Rev. 810, 812, fn. omitted; see also Burton, [*Breach of Contract and the Common Law Duty to Perform in Good Faith* (1980)] 94 Harv.L.Rev. 369, 371 ["the courts employ the good faith doctrine to effectuate the intentions of parties, or to protect their reasonable expectations" (fn. omitted)].) As a contract concept, breach of the duty led to imposition of contract damages determined by the nature of the breach and standard contract principles.

An exception to this general rule has developed in the context of insurance contracts where, for a variety of policy reasons, courts have held that breach of the implied covenant will provide the basis for an action in tort. California has a well-developed judicial history addressing this exception. In *Comunale v. Traders & General Ins. Co.* (1958) 328 P.2d 198, we stated, "There is an implied covenant of good faith and fair dealing in every contract that neither party will do anything which will injure the right of the other to receive the benefits of the agreement." Thereafter, in *Crisci v. Security Ins. Co.* (1967) 426 P.2d 173, for the first time we permitted an insured to recover in tort for emotional damages caused by the insurer's breach of the implied covenant. We explained in *Gruenberg v. Aetna Ins. Co.* (1973) 510 P.2d 1032, that "[t]he duty [to comport with the implied covenant of good faith and fair dealing] is imminent in the contract whether the company is attending [on the insured's behalf] to the claims of third persons against the insured or the claims of the insured itself. Accordingly, when the insurer unreasonably and in bad faith withholds payment of the claim of its insured, it is subject to liability in tort."

---

puts on his losses, and this will be so if the party contemplating breach will gain enough from the breach to have a net benefit even though he compensates the other party for his resulting loss."

In *Egan v. Mutual of Omaha Ins. Co.*, 620 P.2d 141, we described some of the bases for permitting tort recovery for breach of the implied covenant in the insurance context. "The insured in a contract like the one before us does not seek to obtain a commercial advantage by purchasing the policy—rather, he seeks protection against calamity." (Id.) Thus, "As one commentary has noted, 'The insurers' obligations are . . . rooted in their status as purveyors of a vital service labeled quasi-public in nature. Suppliers of services affected with a public interest must take the public's interest seriously, where necessary placing it before their interest in maximizing gains and limiting disbursements. . . . [A]s a supplier of a public service rather than a manufactured product, the obligations of insurers go beyond meeting reasonable expectations of coverage. The obligations of good faith and fair dealing encompass qualities of decency and humanity inherent in the responsibilities of a fiduciary.' . . . (Goodman & Seaton, *Foreword: Ripe for Decision, Internal Workings and Current Concerns of the California Supreme Court* (1974) 62 Cal.L.Rev. 309, 346–347.)" (620 P.2d 141.)

In addition, the *Egan* court emphasized that "the relationship of insurer and insured is inherently unbalanced: the adhesive nature of insurance contracts places the insurer in a superior bargaining position." (620 P.2d 141.) This emphasis on the "special relationship" of insurer and insured has been echoed in arguments and analysis in subsequent scholarly commentary and cases which urge the availability of tort remedies in the employment context.

The first California appellate case to permit tort recovery in the employment context was *Cleary* [v. American Airlines, Inc. (1980) 168 Cal.Rptr. 722]. To support its holding that tort as well as contract damages were appropriate to compensate for a breach of the implied covenant, the *Cleary* court relied on insurance cases without engaging in comparative analysis of insurance and employment relationships and without inquiring into whether the insurance cases' departure from established principles of contract law should generally be subject to expansion.

Similarly, *Cleary's* discussion of two previous California employment cases was insufficient. It found a "hint" in *Coats v. General Motors Corp.* (1934) 39 P.2d 838, to support the proposition that "on occasion, it may be incumbent upon an employer to demonstrate *good faith* in terminating an employee" but failed to acknowledge that in *Coats*, the employee sought recovery of only contract damages. Next, the *Cleary* court placed undue reliance on dictum in this court's *Tameny* [v. Atlantic Richfield Co. (1980) 610 P.2d 1330)] decision, which suggested that tort remedies might be available when an employer breaches the implied covenant of good faith and fair dealing. The qualified *Tameny* dictum was based exclusively on precedent in insurance cases from this state, and two out-of-state employment cases. The out-of-state cases included *Monge v. Beebe Rubber Company* (1974) 316 A.2d 549, in which the court permitted an action for wrongful discharge but limited the plaintiff's recovery to contract damages, specifically excluding recovery for mental distress. Moreover, the New Hampshire Supreme Court thereafter confined *Monge* to cases in which the employer's actions contravene public policy. In the second case, *Fortune v. National Cash Register Co.* (1977) 364 N.E.2d 1251, 1256, the court created a right of action based on breach of the implied covenant, but limited recovery to benefits the employee had already earned under the contract. Subsequent Massachusetts cases have pursued the same limited course.

In fact, although Justice Broussard asserts that the weight of authority is in favor of granting a tort remedy, the clear majority of jurisdictions have either expressly rejected the notion of tort damages for breach of the implied covenant in employment cases or impliedly done so by rejecting any application of the covenant in such a context.

Both the *Tameny* dictum and *Cleary* failed to recognize that imposing *tort* liability for breach of the implied covenant was unprecedented in the employment area. The *Tameny* court expressly found it unnecessary to venture into the area of the implied covenant more completely and only briefly touched on the subject. The *Cleary* court erred in its uncritical reliance on insurance law and its casual extension of *Tameny* to find tort damages recoverable in the case before it.

Dictum in *Seaman's Direct Buying Service, Inc. v. Standard Oil Co.* (1984) 686 P.2d 1158 also is not helpful. There, the court focused on a standard commercial contract. We stated, "[w]hile the proposition that the law implies a covenant of good faith and fair dealing in all contracts is well established, the proposition advanced by Seaman's—that breach of the covenant always gives rise to an action in tort—is not so clear." We also observed that the propriety of a tort action for breach of the implied covenant in the insurance context was based on the "special relationship" of insurer and insured, and continued, "No doubt there are other relationships with similar characteristics and deserving of similar legal treatment." In a footnote to the last statement, we referred to *Tameny,* observing that there "this court intimated that breach of the covenant of good faith and fair dealing in the employment relationship might give rise to tort remedies. That relationship has some of the same characteristics as the relationship between insurer and insured." This allusion to the potential for extending tort remedies for breach of the implied covenant was tentative at best.[27]

---

[27] Contrary to Justice Broussard's suggestion, our statements in *Seaman's* were far from a definitive signal of approval for a tort remedy for breach of the covenant in employment cases. If anything, the reference highlighted the fact that this question remained to be decided by this court.

Most of the other Court of Appeal cases following *Cleary* suffer from similar failures comprehensively to consider the implications of their holdings. These opinions either merely refused to find a breach of the implied covenant on the facts of the case, or relied uncritically on *Cleary* or the dicta in *Tameny* and *Seaman's*. . . .

. . . .

In our view, the underlying problem in the line of cases relied on by plaintiff lies in the decisions' uncritical incorporation of the insurance model into the employment context, without careful consideration of the fundamental policies underlying the development of tort and contract law in general or of significant differences between the insurer/insured and employer/employee relationships. When a court enforces the implied covenant it is in essence acting to protect "the interest in having promises performed" (Prosser, Law of Torts (4th ed. 1971) p. 613)—the traditional realm of a contract action—rather than to protect some general duty to society which the law places on an employer without regard to the substance of its contractual obligations to its employee. Thus, in *Tameny*, 610 P.2d 1330, as we have explained, the court was careful to draw a distinction between "ex delicto" and "ex contractu" obligations. An allegation of breach of the implied covenant of good faith and fair dealing is an allegation of breach of an "ex contractu" obligation, namely one arising out of the contract itself. The covenant of good faith is read into contracts in order to protect the express covenants or promises of the contract, not to protect some general public policy interest not directly tied to the contract's purposes. The insurance cases thus were a major departure from traditional principles of contract law. We must, therefore, consider with great care claims that extension of the exceptional approach taken in those cases is automatically appropriate if certain hallmarks and similarities can be adduced in another contract setting. With this emphasis on the historical purposes of the covenant of good faith and fair dealing in mind, we turn to consider the bases upon which extension of the insurance model to the employment sphere has been urged.

The "special relationship" test gleaned from the insurance context has been suggested as a model for determining the appropriateness of permitting tort remedies for breach of the implied covenant [in] the employment context. One commentary has observed, "[j]ust as the law of contracts fails to provide adequate principles for construing the terms of an insurance policy, the substantial body of law uniquely applicable to insurance contracts is practically irrelevant to commercially oriented contracts. . . . These [unique] features characteristic of the insurance contract make it particularly susceptible to public policy considerations." (Louderback & Jurika, *Standards for Limiting the Tort of Bad Faith Breach of Contract* (1982) 16 U.S.F.L.Rev. 187, 200–201, fns. omitted.) These commentators assert that tort remedies for breach of the covenant should not be extended across the board in the commercial context, but that, nonetheless, public policy considerations suggest extending the tort remedy if certain salient factors are present. "The tort of bad faith should be applied to commercial contracts only if four of the features characteristic of insurance bad faith actions are present. The features are: (1) one of the parties to the contract enjoys a superior bargaining position to the extent that it is able to dictate the terms of the contract; (2) the purpose of the weaker party in entering into the contract is not primarily to profit but rather to secure an essential service or product, financial security or peace of mind; (3) the relationship of the parties is such that the weaker party places its trust and confidence in the larger entity; and (4) there is conduct on the part of the defendant indicating an intent to frustrate the weaker party's enjoyment of the contract rights." (Id., at p. 227.) The discussion of these elements includes an assumption that a tort remedy should be recognized in employment relationships within the stated limitations.

Others argue that the employment context is not sufficiently analogous to that of insurance to warrant recognition of the right to tort recovery. (See, e.g., Miller & Estes, 16 U.C. Davis L.Rev. 65, 90–91; Note, *Defining Torts*, 34 Stan.L.Rev. at pp. 164–167.) They contend that (1) inequality in bargaining power is not a universal characteristic of employment contracts, standardized forms are often not used, and there is often room for bargaining as to special conditions; (2) employers do not owe similar fiduciary duties to employees who are themselves agents of the employer and obligated to act in the employer's interests; and (3) unlike insurance companies, employers are not "quasi-public entities" and they "seldom have government-like functions, and do not serve primarily, if at all, to spread losses across society." (Note, *Defining Torts*, supra, 34 Stan.L.Rev. at pp. 165–167; Miller & Estes, supra, 16 U.C.Davis L.Rev. at p. 91.)

In contrast to those concentrating on the match between insurance and employment relationships, yet another article suggests, "The fundamental flaw in the 'special relationship' test is that it is illusory. It provides a label to hang on a result but not a principled basis for decision. . . . The qualifying contracts cannot be identified until the issue has been litigated, which is too late." (Putz & Klippen, 21 U.S.F.L.Rev. at p. 478–479.) The authors assert that " 'public interest, adhesion and fiduciary responsibility,' are not sufficiently precise to provide a basis for reliable prediction." (Id., at p. 479, fn. omitted.) Instead, they assert that, "While the 'special relationship' test purports to be only a modest extension of the tort of bad faith beyond insurance and employment, it opens the way for pleading a tort cause of action in nearly every contract case, leaving it ultimately to a jury to decide whether or not the parties had a 'special relationship.' " (Id., at p. 480, fn. omitted.) Extension of the test to employment cases would similarly leave the door open to such a claim in every termination case, and readers are cautioned not to infer "that the authors support extension of tort liability beyond insurance through use of the 'special relationship' test." (Id., at p. 461, fn. 163.)

. . . .

After review of the various commentators, and independent consideration of the similarities between the two areas, we are not convinced that a "special relationship" analogous to that between insurer and insured should be deemed to exist in the usual employment relationship which would warrant recognition of a tort action for breach of the implied covenant. Even if we were to assume that the special relationship model is an appropriate one to follow in determining whether to expand tort recovery, a breach in the employment context does not place the employee in the same economic dilemma that an insured faces when an insurer in bad faith refuses to pay a claim or to accept a settlement offer within policy limits. When an insurer takes such actions, the insured cannot turn to the marketplace to find another insurance company willing to pay for the loss already incurred. The wrongfully terminated employee, on the other hand, can (and must, in order to mitigate damages) make reasonable efforts to seek alternative employment. Moreover, the role of the employer differs from that of the "quasi-public" insurance company with whom individuals contract specifically in order to obtain protection from potential specified economic harm. The employer does not similarly "sell" protection to its employees; it is not providing a public service. Nor do we find convincing the idea that the employee is necessarily seeking a different kind of financial security than those entering a typical commercial contract. If a small dealer contracts for goods from a large supplier, and those goods are vital to the small dealer's business, a breach by the supplier may have financial significance for individuals employed by the dealer or to the dealer himself. Permitting only contract damages in such a situation has ramifications no different from a similar limitation in the direct employer-employee relationship.

Finally, there is a fundamental difference between insurance and employment relationships. In the insurance relationship, the insurer's and insured's interest[s] are financially at odds. If the insurer pays a claim, it diminishes its fiscal resources. The insured of course has paid for protection and expects to have its losses recompensed. When a claim is paid, money shifts from insurer to insured, or, if appropriate, to a third party claimant.

Putting aside already specifically barred improper motives for termination which may be based on both economic and noneconomic considerations,[30] as a general rule it is to the employer's economic benefit to retain good employees. The interests of employer and employee are most frequently in alignment. If there is a job to be done, the employer must still pay someone to do it. This is not to say that there may never be a "bad motive" for discharge not otherwise covered by law. Nevertheless, in terms of abstract employment relationships as contrasted with abstract insurance relationships, there is less inherent relevant tension between the interests of employers and employees than exists between that of insurers and insureds. Thus the need to place disincentives on an employer's conduct in addition to those already imposed by law simply does not rise to the same level as that created by the conflicting interests at stake in the insurance context. Nor is this to say that the Legislature would have no basis for affording employees additional protections. It is, however, to say that the need to extend the special relationship model in the form of judicially created relief of the kind sought here is less compelling.

We therefore conclude that the employment relationship is not sufficiently similar to that of insurer and insured to warrant judicial extension of the proposed additional tort remedies in view of the countervailing concerns about economic policy and stability, the traditional separation of tort and contract law, and finally, the numerous protections against improper terminations already afforded employees.

. . . .

As we have reiterated, the employment relationship is fundamentally contractual, and several factors combine to persuade us that in the absence of legislative direction to the contrary contractual remedies should remain the sole available relief for breaches of the implied covenant of good faith and fair dealing in the employment context. Initially, predictability of the consequences of actions related to employment contracts is important to commercial stability.[33] In order to

---

[30] In the employment relationship, the employer is already barred by law from, and the employee can obtain relief for, discriminatory discharges based on age, sex, race, and religion. Similarly, the employee is protected from discrimination based on the exercise of rights under the workers' compensation laws or for engaging in union activities. He can gain relief if he is terminated in order for the employer to avoid payment of certain benefits. The employee may sue in tort for discharges based on breaches of public policy.

[33] The generally predictable and circumscribed damages available for breaches of contract reflect the importance of this value in the commercial context. In the employment context specifically, Professor Gould observes, "[t]he cost of lawsuits that respond to a discharge, as measured by jury awards and settlements, has also increased geometrically and is beginning to draw concern from the business community.... [T]he awards [in California wrongful termination suits] *actually exceeded settlement demands* by the employees' lawyers by 187 percent." (Gould, *Stemming the Tide*, 13 Emp.Rel.L.J. at pp. 405–406, fns. omitted, italics in original; see also Note, *Protecting At Will Employees*, 93 Harv.L.Rev. 1816, 1834, 1835 ["employers may fear that imposition of liability threatens the fundamental prerogatives of management: to control the workplace and to retain only the best-qualified employees;" "[a]nother concern is that the threat of increased liability will impair firms' ability to respond flexibly to changing economic conditions"].)

achieve such stability, it is also important that employers not be unduly deprived of discretion to dismiss an employee by the fear that doing so will give rise to potential tort recovery in every case.

Moreover, it would be difficult if not impossible to formulate a rule that would assure that only "deserving" cases give rise to tort relief. Professor Summers, in his seminal article, described the term "good faith" as used in the duty of good faith imposed in contract law and the Uniform Commercial Code, as an "excluder" phrase which is "without general meaning (or meanings) of its own and serves to exclude a wide range of heterogenous forms of bad faith. In a particular context the phrase takes on specific meaning, but usually this is only by way of contrast with the specific form of bad faith actually or hypothetically ruled out." (Summers, *"Good Faith" in General Contract Law and the Sales Provisions of the Uniform Commercial Code* (1968) 54 Va.L.Rev. 195, 201, fn. omitted.) In a tort action based on an employee's discharge, it is highly likely that each case would involve a dispute as to material facts regarding the subjective intentions of the employer. As a result, these actions could rarely be disposed of at the demurrer or summary judgment stage.

. . . .

Review of [various lower court] formulations [e.g., "If, however, the existence of good cause for discharge is asserted by the employer without probable cause and in bad faith, that is, without a good faith belief that good cause for discharge in fact exists, the employer has tortiously attempted to deprive the employee of the benefits of the agreement, and an action for breach of the implied covenant of good faith and fair dealing will lie"] reveals that ultimately they require nothing "unusual" about the breach: under the approaches of those courts, an ordinary contract breach might give rise to a bad faith action. Resolution of the ensuing inquiry into the employer's motives has been difficult to predict and demonstrates the imprecision of the standards thus far formulated. This situation undermines the statutory mandate that neither compensatory tort damages nor exemplary damages are available in an action arising from the breach of a contract obligation. (Civ.Code, §§ 3333, 3294.) Adoption of tests such as those formulated by the Court of Appeal would result in the anomalous result that henceforth the implied covenant in an employment contract would enjoy protection far greater than that afforded to express and implied-in-fact promises, the breach of which gives rise to an action for contract damages only.[39]

---

[39] Moreover, with regard to an at-will employment relationship, breach of the implied covenant cannot logically be based on a claim that a discharge was made without good cause. If such an interpretation applied, then all at-will contracts would be transmuted into contracts requiring good cause for termination. . . . This is not to say that the Legislature could not impose such a requirement in every employment contract. It has not done so, however, and the implied covenant should not be read as uniformly imposing such a contractual term. Thus, in *Wagenseller v. Scottsdale Memorial Hosp.*, 710 P.2d at page 1040, the court properly stressed,

. . . . If the covenant is implied in every contract, but its breach does not in every contract give rise to tort damages, attempts to define when tort damages are appropriate simply by interjecting a requirement of "bad faith" do nothing to limit the potential reach of tort remedies or to differentiate between those cases properly and traditionally compensable by contract damages and those in which tort damages should flow. Virtually any firing (indeed any breach of a contract term in any context) could provide the basis for a pleading alleging the discharge was in bad faith under the cited standards.

Finally, and of primary significance, we believe that focus on available contract remedies offers the most appropriate method of expanding available relief for wrongful terminations. The expansion of tort remedies in the employment context has potentially enormous consequences for the stability of the business community.

We are not unmindful of the legitimate concerns of employees who fear arbitrary and improper discharges that may have a devastating effect on their economic and social status. Nor are we unaware of or unsympathetic to claims that contract remedies for breaches of contract are insufficient because they do not fully compensate due to their failure to include attorney fees and their restrictions on foreseeable damages. These defects, however, exist generally in contract situations. As discussed above, the variety of possible courses to remedy the problem is well demonstrated in the literature and include[s] increased contract damages, provision for award of attorney fees, establishment of arbitration or other speedier and less expensive dispute resolution, or the tort remedies (the scope of which is also subject to dispute) sought by plaintiff here.

The diversity of possible solutions demonstrates the confusion that occurs when we look outside the realm of contract law in attempting to fashion remedies for a breach of a contract provision. As noted, numerous legislative provisions have imposed obligations on parties to contracts which vindicate significant social policies extraneous to the contract itself. As Justice Kaus observed in his concurring and dissenting opinion in *White v. Western Title Ins. Co.* (1985) 710 P.2d 309, "our experience in *Seaman's* surely tells us that there are real problems in applying the substitute remedy of a tort recovery—with or without punitive damages— outside the insurance area. In other words, I believe that under all the circumstances, the problem is one for the Legislature. . . ."

"[w]hat cannot be said is that one of the agreed benefits to the at-will employee is a guarantee of continued employment or tenure." Because the implied covenant protects only the parties' right to receive the benefit of their agreement, and, in an at-will relationship there is no agreement to terminate only for good cause, the implied covenant standing alone cannot be read to impose such a duty. (See ibid.)

CONCLUSION

.... [A]s to [plaintiff's] cause of action for tortious breach of the implied covenant of good faith and fair dealing, we hold that tort remedies are not available for breach of the implied covenant in an employment contract to employees who allege they have been discharged in violation of the covenant.

. . . .

BROUSSARD, JUSTICE, concurring and dissenting.

. . . .

2. Analogy to the cases upholding a tort cause of action for bad faith breach of a contract of insurance justifies a tort action for bad faith discharge of an employee.

The majority deride the prior cases for their uncritical incorporation of the insurance model into the employment context without considering the significant differences between the insurer-insured and employer-employee relationships. But when we consider the differences noted by the majority, we find that they are not significant at all.

The majority find one fundamental difference between insurance and employment relationships: "[i]f an insurer pays a claim, it diminishes its fiscal resources ... [while] as a general rule it is to the employer's economic benefit to retain good employees." But their comparison is not between insurers and employers, but between short-sighted insurers and far-sighted employers. In the short run, the insurer saves money by not paying claims, and the employer by not paying wages. (If the work cannot be deferred, he can hire less experienced but cheaper help.) In the long run, an insurer that never paid claims would be out of business, and an employer that always fired experienced help would not be much better off. Thus if we examine insurers and employers with the same lens, the difference the majority find[s] fundamental simply disappears.

But the majority's analysis leaves a lingering trace, for it betrays their misunderstanding of the problem. We need not be concerned about insurers that never pay claims or employers that fire all experienced help—the marketplace will take care of them. The concern is with the insurer or employer that acts arbitrarily some of the time—and can get away with it unless threatened with damages that, unlike traditional contract damages, exceed the short-term profit.[5]

---

[5] Consider, for example, the case of *K Mart Corp. v. Ponsock* (Nev.1987) 732 P.2d 1364. Ponsock was a forklift driver with 10 years longevity, whose pension would vest in another 6 months. He discovered that the battery cover on his forklift needed painting. Finding a damaged (and thus unsaleable) can of spray paint, he used it to paint the forklift. Although other forklifts had been painted in a similar manner without any action against the employee in question, Ponsock was fired for "defacing" company property and "stealing" a can of paint. When he attempted to explain his conduct, he was excluded from the premises. After a long period of

The majority also point to some nonfundamental distinctions between the insurer-insured and the employer-employee relationships. They argue that the discharged employee may be able to mitigate damages while the insured generally cannot. But as we all know, in many cases the discharged worker cannot mitigate damages. As Justice Kaufman asks, "What market is there for the factory worker laid-off after 25 years of labor in the same plant, or for the middle-aged executive fired after 25 years with the same firm?" (Con. and dis. opn. at p. 415 of 765 P.2d.) The ability of some persons to mitigate damages is no reason to deny a cause of action to those unable to mitigate them.

It is next suggested that the employer, unlike the insurer, is not performing a "public service." I fail to understand the significance of the statement. Employment is even more important to the community than insurance; most people value their jobs more than their insurance policies. The public interest in deterring arbitrary breach of employment contracts is, I suggest, at least equal to that in deterring arbitrary breach of insurance contracts.

Finally, the majority reject the idea that an employee is like an insured because both contract for financial security. A business, they point out, may also seek financial security. They put the case of a business contracting to secure a reliable source of supply. But what emerges from the majority's analysis is three propositions: a) that insureds *generally* buy insurance policies for financial security; (b) that employees *generally* seek financial security in their employment; (c) that businesses *occasionally* contract for financial security. These propositions should lead the majority to conclude that the employment contract is more analogous to an insurance contract than to a commercial contract.

The majority are focusing upon the exceptions, not upon the general rule. If we must argue analogies, the question is not whether the employment contract differs from an insurance contract in one particular respect, or resembles a commercial contract in another. It is whether, as a whole, the contract of employment more closely resembles an insurance contract or an ordinary commercial contract. The answer is clear. The principal reason we permit tort damages for breach of the covenant of good faith and fair dealing in an insurance contract is that persons do not generally purchase insurance to obtain a commercial advantage, but to

---

unemployment, he finally obtained a job as a laborer at half his previous wage with no benefits. This income was inadequate to meet mortgage payments, and Ponsock was forced to sell his home at a loss.

Traditional contract damages would not compensate Ponsock for the loss incurred on the sale of a home, or for emotional suffering. In addition, such damages would do nothing to deter further arbitrary actions. The employer would be required to compensate Ponsock for the difference between his prior wage and his present wage, but since Ponsock could be replaced by a lower wage worker whose pension would not vest for many years, the employer might profit from his wrong.

secure the peace of mind and security it will provide in protecting against accidental loss. That reason applies equally to the employer-employee relationship. A man or a woman usually does not enter into employment solely for the money; a job is status, reputation, a way of defining one's self-worth and worth in the community. It is also essential to financial security, offering assurance of future income needed to repay present debts and meet future obligations. Without a secure job a worker frequently cannot obtain a retirement pension, and often lacks access to affordable medical insurance. In short, "in a modern industrialized economy employment is central to one's existence and dignity." (Gould, *The Idea of the Job as Property in Contemporary America: The Legal and Collective Bargaining Framework*, 1986 B.Y.U.L.Rev. 885, 892.)[6]

Because workers value their jobs as more than merely a source of money, contract damages, if limited to loss of income, are inadequate. Again the analogy to the insurance cases is close. Explaining the basis for tort damages in insurance cases, *Wallis v. Superior Court*, 207 Cal.Rptr. 123 [(Ct. App. 1984)], said that "[m]oney damages paid pursuant to a judgment years after . . . do not remedy the harm suffered . . . , namely the immediate inability to support oneself and its attendant horrors"— language which applies equally to a suit for wrongful discharge. As summarized in Miller & Estes, *Recent Judicial Limitations On the Right to Discharge: A California Trilogy* (1982) 16 U.C. Davis L.Rev. 65, 90–91, insureds and employees both depend on the contracts "for their security, well-being, and peace of mind. If insurance companies or employers act in bad faith, the consequences can be very severe, indeed much greater than those that result from a breach of contract."

In contrast, commercial contracts, generally speaking, are negotiated between parties of more nearly equal bargaining strength, and are entered into for purpose of profit. Breach entails only lost profits, and often a market exists in which the damaged party can cover its loss. I conclude that past decisions were justified in analogizing the relationship between employer and employee to that between insurer and insured, and in distinguishing both from commercial contracts for the sale of goods and services.

. . . .

---

[6] A second significant similarity is that both insurance contracts and employment contracts arise from a context of disparity of bargaining power. Numerous cases have noted this disparity in insurance cases; it has led to the adoption of a general rule that insurance contracts are construed against the insurer. There are fewer cases in the employment context, but here the principle is embodied in a statutory finding that "the individual unorganized worker is helpless to exercise actual liberty of contract and to protect his freedom of labor, and thereby to obtain acceptable terms and conditions of employment." (Lab.Code, § 923.)

KAUFMAN, JUSTICE, concurring and dissenting.

. . . .

First, the majority asserts that a breach in the employment context "does not place the employee in the same economic dilemma that an insured faces" because the insured "cannot turn to the marketplace," while an employee presumably may "seek alternative employment." Next, the majority argues that an employer, unlike an insurance company, does not sell economic "protection." The majority also rejects the insurance analogy because an employee, unlike an insured, allegedly does not seek a "different kind of financial security than those entering a typical commercial contract." Finally, the majority asserts that insurance and employment contracts differ "fundamental[ly]" because the insured's and insurer's interests are "financially at odds," while the employer's and employee's interests allegedly are "most frequently in alignment."

Such conclusions, in my view, expose an unrealistic if not mythical conception of the employment relationship. They also reveal a misplaced reluctance to define the minimal standards of decency required to govern that relationship. The delineation of such standards is not, as the majority strongly implies, judicial legislation, but rather constitutes this court's fundamental obligation.

It is, at best, naive to believe that the availability of the "marketplace," or that a supposed "alignment of interests," renders the employment relationship less special or less subject to abuse than the relationship between insurer and insured. Indeed, I can think of no relationship in which one party, the employee, places more reliance upon the other, is more dependent upon the other, or is more vulnerable to abuse by the other, than the relationship between employer and employee. And, ironically, the relative imbalance of economic power between employer and employee tends to increase rather than diminish the longer that relationship continues. Whatever bargaining strength and marketability the employee may have at the moment of hiring, diminishes rapidly thereafter. Marketplace? What market is there for the factory worker laid-off after 25 years of labor in the same plant, or for the middle-aged executive fired after 25 years with the same firm?

Financial security? Can anyone seriously dispute that employment is generally sought, at least in part, for financial security and all that that implies: food on the table, shelter, clothing, medical care, education for one's children. Clearly, no action for breach of the covenant of good faith and fair dealing will lie *unless* it has first been proved that, expressly or by implication, the employer has given the employee a reasonable expectation of continued employment so long as the employee performs satisfactorily. And that expectation constitutes a far greater and graver security interest than any which inheres in the insurance context. Most of us can live without insurance. Few of us could live without a job.

Peace of mind? One's work obviously involves more than just earning a living. It defines for many people their identity, their sense of self-worth, their sense of belonging. The wrongful and malicious destruction of one's employment is far more certain to result in serious emotional distress than any wrongful denial of an insurance claim.

If everything this court has written concerning the relation between insurer and insured has any deeper meaning; if we have created a living principle based upon justice, reason and common sense and not merely a fixed, narrow and idiosyncratic rule of law, then we must acknowledge the irresistible logic and equity of extending that principle to the employment relationship. We can reasonably do no less.

. . . .

NOTES & QUESTIONS

(1) The business of insurance is often described as "affected with a public interest" and providing a service that is "quasi-public" in nature. Such characterizations were historically used to justify government regulation of rates and other aspects of insurance. In *German Alliance Insurance Co. v. Lewis*, 233 U.S. 389 (1914), the United States Supreme Court discussed the basis for such characterizations in the context of fire insurance:

> . . . . "The underlying principle is that business of certain kinds hold such a peculiar relation to the public interest that there is superinduced upon it the right of public regulation." Is the business of insurance within the principle? . . .

> A contract for fire insurance is one for indemnity against loss, and is personal. The admission, however, does not take us far in the solution of the question presented. Its personal character certainly does not of itself preclude regulation, for there are many examples of government regulation of personal contracts, and in the statutes of every state in the Union superintendence and control over the business of insurance are exercised, varying in details and extent. . . .

> Those regulations exhibit it to be the conception of the lawmaking bodies of the country without exception that the business of insurance so far affects the public welfare as to invoke and require governmental regulation. A conception so general cannot be without cause. The universal sense of a people cannot be accidental; its persistence saves it from the charge of unconsidered impulse, and its estimate of insurance certainly has substantial basis. Accidental fires are inevitable and the extent of loss very great. The effect of insurance—indeed, it has been said to be its

fundamental object—is to distribute the loss over as wide an area as possible. In other words, the loss is spread over the country, the disaster to an individual is shared by many, the disaster to a community shared by other communities; great catastrophes are thereby lessened, and, it may be, repaired. In assimilation of insurance to a tax, the companies have been said to be the mere machinery by which the inevitable losses by fire are distributed so as to fall as lightly as possible on the public at large, the body of the insured, not the companies, paying the tax. Their efficiency, therefore, and solvency, are of great concern. The other objects, direct and indirect, of insurance, we need not mention. Indeed, it may be enough to say, without stating other effects of insurance, that a large part of the country's wealth, subject to uncertainty of loss through fire, is protected by insurance. This demonstrates the interest of the public in it, and we need not dispute with the economists that this is the result of the "substitution of certain for uncertain loss," or the diffusion of positive loss over a large group of persons, as we have already said to be certainly one of its effects. We can see, therefore, how it has come to be considered a matter of public concern to regulate it, and, governmental insurance has its advocates and even examples. Contracts of insurance, therefore, have greater public consequence than contracts between individuals to do or not to do a particular thing whose effect stops with the individuals. We may say in passing that when the effect goes beyond that, there are many examples of regulation.

. . . .

. . . . To the contention that the business is private we have opposed the conception of the public interest. We have shown that the business of insurance has very definite characteristics, with a reach of influence and consequence beyond and different from that of the ordinary businesses of the commercial world, to pursue which a greater liberty may be asserted. The transactions of the latter are independent and individual, terminating in their effect with the instances. The contracts of insurance may be said to be interdependent. They cannot be regarded singly, or isolatedly, and the effect of their relation is to create a fund of assurance and credit, the companies becoming the depositories of the money of the insured, possessing great power thereby, and charged with great responsibility. How necessary their solvency is, is manifest. On the other hand, to the insured, insurance is an asset, a basis of credit. It is practically a necessity to business activity and enterprise. It is, therefore, essentially different from ordinary commercial transactions, and, as we have seen, according to the sense of the world from the earliest times,—certainly the sense of the modern world,—is of the greatest public concern. It is therefore within the principle we have announced.

.... And both by the expression of the principle and the citation of the examples we have tried to confine our decision to the regulation of the business of insurance, it having, become "clothed with a public interest," and therefore subject "to be controlled by the public for the common good."

Id. at 411–16; *see also* 2 GALE ENCYCLOPEDIA OF AMERICAN LAW 197 (3d ed. 2011) ("What constitutes a business affected with a public interest varies from state to state. Three classes of businesses have been traditionally regarded as affected with a public interest: (1) those carried on pursuant to a public grant or privilege imposing a duty of making available essential services demanded by the public, such as common carriers and public utilities; (2) occupations considered from the earliest times in common law to be exceptional, such as the operation of inns or cabs; and (3) businesses that although not public at their inception have become such by devoting their activities to a public use, such as insurance companies and banks. A business affected with a public interest remains the property of its owner, but the community is considered to have such a stake in its operation that it becomes subject to public regulation to the extent of that interest.").

(2)   Is the employer-employee relationship sufficiently analogous to the insurer-insured relationship to warrant a tort action for bad faith termination of employment? What arguments are made by the various opinions in *Foley*?

(3)   If an implied covenant of good faith and fair dealing were recognized in the employment context, what would it mean? Consider the following observations:

.... In general, the employment at will doctrine provides an employer with the discretion to terminate an employee with or without just cause, so long as there is no agreement requiring cause-based terminations or specifying the term of employment. The doctrine is often justified on the ground that an employer needs unimpeded discretion to manage its workforce and to remain competitive. As a result of the employment at will doctrine, courts largely avoid inquiring into the propriety of an employee's discharge, and employer decisions to terminate are typically upheld.

....

.... In the employment context ... courts tend to disfavor the covenant of good faith and fair dealing "primarily on the theory that the doctrine of employment at will, under which an employer can discharge an employee for any reason, even a bad one, is inherently inconsistent with an implied covenant of good faith and fair dealing." MARK A. ROTHSTEIN & LANCE LIEBMAN, CASES AND MATERIALS ON EMPLOYMENT LAW 931 (3d ed. 1994). Indeed, commentators indicate that the covenant has not gained widespread acceptance in the employment context.

When the covenant is applied to the employment context, it generally does not create job security through a "just cause" or "good cause" [termination] requirement. Instead, it is used to prevent employers from depriving employees of previously earned benefits. *See, e.g.*, Wagenseller v. Scottsdale Memorial Hosp., 710 P.2d 1025, 1040 (Ariz. 1985) (recognizing an implied covenant but noting that it does not require a "good cause" termination: "The covenant does not protect the employee from a 'no cause' termination because tenure was never a benefit inherent in the at-will agreement."); *id.* ("The covenant does protect an employee from a discharge based on an employer's desire to avoid the payment of benefits already earned by the employee.").

DOUGLAS K. MOLL & ROBERT A. RAGAZZO, CLOSELY HELD CORPORATIONS § 7.01[B][3], at 7–14, 7–15, 7–17 n.50 (LexisNexis 2014).

(4) 3 DAN B. DOBBS ET AL., THE LAW OF TORTS § 703, at 775–76 (2d ed. 2011):

.... Most decisions have now rejected the whole idea that employers of at-will employees can be liable in tort for a termination in bad faith or for bad motives alone. ...

.... With the independent claim for bad faith breach largely eliminated from the tort repertoire, the claim of tortious wrongful discharge is now commonly predicated upon a specific and identifiable public policy that would be undermined if the employer were free to take adverse action against the employee who acts in accord with that policy. Examples include cases in which the employer fires the at-will employee for refusing to engage in illegal conduct, for performing a public duty, for blowing the whistle on the employer's illegal conduct, or for asserting her rights, as where she claims workers' compensation benefits for an employment injury or for merely exercis[ing] her free speech rights. Some cases have held that an employer who discriminates on the basis of race or gender by discharging an employee violates public policy as declared by statute and is thus liable for the wrongful discharge. ...

(5) The franchisor-franchisee relationship has also been the subject of judicial inquiry. As with employment, courts have wrestled with the question of whether the franchisor-franchisee relationship is sufficiently analogous to the insurer-insured relationship to warrant a tort action for bad faith termination of a franchise. In *Crim Truck & Tractor Co. v. Navistar International Transportation Corp.*, 823 S.W.2d 591 (Tex. 1992), the Supreme Court of Texas refused to impose a tort duty of good faith on franchise agreements:

.... In the most recent amendments to the Texas Motor Vehicle Commission Code, the Legislature has undertaken to regulate many aspects of the relationship at issue here. *See*

Tex.Rev.Civ.Stat.Ann. art. 4413(36) § 5.02 (Vernon Supp.1991). Wrongful termination of a motor vehicle dealership franchise agreement is now governed by the Texas Motor Vehicle Commission Code. A person who has sustained damages as a result of a violation of these provisions may bring suit under the Texas Deceptive Trade Practices–Consumer Protection Act. Tex.Rev.Civ.Stat.Ann. art. 4413(36) § 6.06 (Vernon Supp.1991). Additionally, since 1956, Congress has imposed a duty of good faith in terminating automobile franchise agreements. 15 U.S.C. §§ 1221–1225 (1988). The federal statute is designed to supplement state common law and statutory rights and duties. *Id.* § 1225. . . .

Amici Curiae, Texas Automobile Dealers Association, National Automobile Dealers Association, and Southwest Association (the Associations), urge us to engraft a tort duty of good faith and fair dealing into all franchise agreements. They contend that the franchisee/franchisor relationship should be deemed a special relationship because of the franchisor's disproportionate bargaining power and control inherent in the typical franchise agreement. We disagree. We find no evidence in this case that the franchisor exerted control over its franchisee's business comparable to that exerted by an insurer over its insured's claim. The Associations argue that significant abuse of power and control by franchisors will go unredressed unless a common law duty of good faith and fair dealing is engrafted into franchise agreements by law. Under the current statutory scheme in effect today these concerns are unfounded.

Id. at 596 & n.8.

C. ORDINARY COMMERCIAL CONTRACTS

SEAMAN'S DIRECT BUYING SERVICE, INC. v. STANDARD OIL CO.
686 P.2d 1158 (Cal. 1984)

Before BIRD, C.J., and MOSK, KAUS, BROUSSARD, REYNOSO and GRODIN, JJ.

This case, which arises out of a complex factual setting, presents three issues for decision. . . . (3) May a plaintiff recover in tort for breach of an implied covenant of good faith and fair dealing in a noninsurance, commercial contract?

I.

Plaintiff, Seaman's Direct Buying Service, Inc. (Seaman's), is a close corporation composed of three shareholders. During the late 1960's and early 1970's, Seaman's operated as a ship chandler, i.e., a dealer in ship supplies and equipment, in the City of Eureka (City). By 1970, Seaman's business encompassed a number of activities including acting as a "general contractor" for incoming vessels, i.e., refurbishing their supplies, selling tax-free goods for off-shore use, and managing a small marine fueling station as the consignee of Mobil Oil Company (Mobil).

Around this time, the City decided to condemn the decrepit waterfront area where Seaman's was located for development into a modern marina. To this end, it sought funds from the federal Economic Development Agency (EDA). Seaman's saw the redevelopment as a way to expand and modernize its operations. Accordingly, the company approached the City with a plan to lease a large portion of the new marina. Seaman's planned to use some of the area for its own operations and to profitably sublet the remainder.

In early 1971, Seaman's and the City signed an initial lease for a relatively small area, with the understanding that the lease could be renegotiated to include the larger area that Seaman's wanted. The renegotiation was conditioned on Seaman's providing evidence of financial responsibility to both the EDA and the City's bonding consultants.

A major element of Seaman's planned expansion, and the key to approval of the larger lease, was Seaman's operation of a marine fuel dealership with modernized fueling equipment. To secure such a dealership, Seaman's opened negotiations with several oil companies, but soon narrowed the field to Mobil and the defendant here, Standard Oil of California (Standard).

While negotiations with both companies were progressing, the City began pressuring Seaman's for a final decision on the marina lease. The City's bonding consultants demanded written evidence of a binding agreement with an oil supplier before they would approve leasing the larger area to Seaman's.

Upon reaching a tentative agreement with Standard, Seaman's requested evidence of that agreement—"something that would be binding on both parties"—to show to the City. In response, Standard sent a "letter of intent" setting forth the terms of negotiation. However, the letter explicitly provided that the terms were not binding. Since Seaman's needed a binding commitment, it continued to negotiate with Mobil.

Finally, Seaman's and Standard reached an agreement on all major points. Upon Seaman's repeated requests for an instrument evidencing a binding commitment, Standard, on October 11, 1972, wrote a letter setting forth the terms of the agreement. In the letter, Standard proposed (1) to sign a Chevron Marine Dealer agreement with Seaman's for an initial term of 10 years; (2) to advance Seaman's the cost of the new fueling facilities, or up to $75,000, which sum was to be amortized over the life of the agreement at the rate of one cent per gallon of oil; (3) to provide a 4.5 cent discount per gallon off the posted price of fuel; and (4) to sign an agreement providing for Standard's right to cure in case of default by Seaman's.

The letter concluded "this offer is subject to our mutual agreement on the specific wording of contracts to be drawn, endorsement and/or approval by governmental offices involved, and continued approval of Seaman's credit status at the time the agreements are to go into effect.[1] If this approach and proposal meets with your approval, *we would appreciate your acknowledgement and acceptance of these terms by signing and returning two copies of this letter.* We can then proceed further with the drafting of the final agreements. . . ." (Emphasis added.) The letter was signed by an agent of Standard and—under the legend, *"we accept and agree to the terms and conditions stated herein"*—by an agent of Seaman's. (Emphasis added.)

According to Seaman's, the signing of this letter was a momentous occasion. One of those present suggested, "Well, shouldn't we have souvenir pens here and I will exchange pens," as "when the President signs a bill into law." Standard's representative exclaimed that it was "going to be great doing business with [Seaman's]" and that the agreement was a "feather in his cap." One of the parties declared, "We finally have a contract" and "we're on our way."

Seaman's immediately presented the letter to the City and shortly thereafter signed a 40-year lease for the entire area it sought in the marina. Seaman's also ended negotiations with Mobil after informing them that a contract had been signed with Standard.

Conditions in the oil industry soon changed, however. By the end of 1972, what had been a "buyer's market" had become a "seller's market." As a result, in January of 1973, Standard adopted a "no new business" policy. During 1973, Standard and Seaman's signed a temporary marine dealership agreement designed to supply Seaman's with the fuel it needed while the new marina was under construction. The marine dealership agreement contemplated in the October 11, 1972, letter, however, was never signed.

In November of 1973, a federal program mandating the allocation of petroleum products among existing customers went into effect. By letter dated November 20, 1973, Standard told Seaman's that the new federal "regulations require suppliers to supply those purchasers to whom they sold during [the base period of 1972]. Our records disclose that we did not supply diesel fuel to you at any time during 1972. . . . [¶] Under the

---

[1] Internal memoranda indicate that Standard contemplated using nonapproval of Seaman's credit as an excuse to justify nonperformance should the terms of the agreement later prove unfavorable.

circumstances, we will not be able to go forward with the financing we [have] been discussing. In the event the mandatory program is withdrawn and our supply situation improves, we would, of course, be pleased to again discuss supplying your needs."

In telephone calls and personal meetings with Seaman's, Standard indicated that the new federal regulations were the *only* barrier to the contract. "[I]f it wasn't for the [federal agency], . . . [Standard] would be willing to go ahead with the contract. . . ." "If [Seaman's could] get the federal government to change that order so that Standard could supply [Seaman's] with fuel [Standard] would be very happy. . . ." Standard even supplied Seaman's with the forms necessary to seek a supply authorization from the federal agency and helped fill them out.

As a result of these efforts, a supply order was issued on February 4, 1974. Standard responded by changing its position. The company contended now that no binding agreement with Seaman's had ever been reached. Therefore, Standard decided to appeal the order "[b]ecause [it] did not want to take on any new business." When Seaman's learned of the appeal, it twice wrote to Standard requesting an explanation. None was forthcoming. Standard's federal appeal was successful. Internal memoranda reveal Standard's reaction to this result: "[g]reat!!" "We are recommending to other div[isions] that they follow your example."

Seaman's then appealed and this decision was, in turn, reversed. The new decision provided that an order "direct[ing] [Standard] to fulfill supply obligations to Seaman's" would be issued upon the filing of a copy of a court decree that a valid contract existed between the parties under state law.

Seaman's asked Standard to stipulate to the existence of a contract, explaining that it could not continue in operation throughout the time that a trial would take. In reply, Standard's representative laughed and said, "See you in court." Seaman's testified that if Standard had cooperated, Seaman's would have borrowed funds to remain in business until 1976 when the new marina opened.

Seaman's discontinued operations in early 1975. Soon thereafter, the company filed suit against Standard, charging Standard with breach of contract, fraud, breach of the implied covenant of good faith and fair dealing, and interference with Seaman's contractual relationship with the City. The case was tried before a jury which returned a verdict for Seaman's on all but the fraud cause of action. For breach of contract, the jury awarded compensatory damages of $397,050. For tortious breach of the implied covenant of good faith and fair dealing, they awarded $397,050 in compensatory damages and $11,058,810 in punitive damages. Finally, for intentional interference with an advantageous business relationship, the jury set compensatory damages at $1,588,200 and punitive damages at $11,058,810.

Standard moved for a new trial, charging, inter alia, that the damages were excessive as a matter of law. The trial court conditionally granted the motion unless Seaman's consented to a reduction of punitive damages on the interference count to $6 million and on the good faith count to $1 million. Seaman's consented to the reduction, and judgment was entered accordingly. Standard appeals from the judgment. Seaman's has filed a cross-appeal.

. . . .

IV.

The principal issue raised by this appeal is whether, and under what circumstances, a breach of the implied covenant of good faith and fair dealing in a commercial contract may give rise to an action in tort. Standard contends that a tort action for breach of the implied covenant has always been, and should continue to be, limited to cases where the underlying contract is one of insurance. Seaman's, pointing to several recent cases decided by this court and the Courts of Appeal, challenges this contention. A brief review of the development of the tort is in order.

It is well settled that, in California, the law implies in *every* contract a covenant of good faith and fair dealing. *Crisci v. Security Ins. Co.* (1967) 426 P.2d 173 ["*in every contract*, including policies of insurance, there is an implied covenant of good faith and fair dealing . . ." (emphasis added)]. Broadly stated, that covenant requires that neither party do anything which will deprive the other of the benefits of the agreement.

California courts have recognized the existence of this covenant, and enforced it, in cases involving a wide variety of contracts. Courts have provided contract remedies for breach of the covenant in such diverse contracts as agreements to make mutual wills, agreements to sell real property, employee incentive contracts, leases, and contracts to provide utility services.

In the seminal cases of *Comunale v. Traders & General Ins. Co.*, 328 P.2d 198, and *Crisci v. Security Ins. Co., supra,* 426 P.2d 173, this court held that a breach of the covenant of good faith and fair dealing by an insurance carrier may give rise to a cause of action in tort as well as in contract.

While the proposition that the law implies a covenant of good faith and fair dealing in all contracts is well established, the proposition advanced by Seaman's—that breach of the covenant always gives rise to an action in tort—is not so clear. In holding that a tort action is available for breach of the covenant in an insurance contract, we have emphasized the "special relationship" between insurer and insured, characterized by elements of public interest, adhesion, and fiduciary responsibility. (*Egan v. Mutual of Omaha Ins. Co.*, 620 P.2d 141 [(Cal. 1979)].) No doubt there are other relationships with similar characteristics and deserving of similar legal treatment.[6]

When we move from such special relationships to consideration of the tort remedy in the context of the ordinary commercial contract, we move into largely uncharted and potentially dangerous waters. Here, parties of roughly equal bargaining power are free to shape the contours of their agreement and to include provisions for attorney fees and liquidated damages in the event of breach. They may not be permitted to disclaim the covenant of good faith but they are free, within reasonable limits at least, to agree upon the standards by which application of the covenant is to be measured. In such contracts, it may be difficult to distinguish between breach of the covenant and breach of contract, and there is the risk that interjecting tort remedies will intrude upon the expectations of the parties. This is not to say that tort remedies have no place in such a commercial context, but that it is wise to proceed with caution in determining their scope and application.

For the purposes of this case it is unnecessary to decide the broad question which Seaman's poses. Indeed, it is not even necessary to predicate liability on a breach of the implied covenant. It is sufficient to recognize that a party to a contract may incur tort remedies when, in addition to breaching the contract, it seeks to shield itself from liability by denying, in bad faith and without probable cause, that the contract exists.

It has been held that a party to a contract may be subject to tort liability, including punitive damages, if he coerces the other party to pay more than is due under the contract terms through the threat of a lawsuit, made " 'without probable cause and with no belief in the existence of the cause of action.' " (*Adams v. Crater Well Drilling, Inc.* (1976) 556 P.2d 679, 681.) There is little difference, in principle, between a contracting party obtaining excess payment in such manner, and a contracting party seeking to avoid all liability on a meritorious contract claim by adopting a "stonewall" position ("see you in court") without probable cause and with no belief in the existence of a defense. Such conduct goes beyond the mere breach of contract. It offends accepted notions of business ethics. Acceptance of tort remedies in such a situation is not likely to intrude upon the bargaining relationship or upset reasonable expectations of the contracting parties.

Turning to the facts of this case, the jury was instructed that "where a binding contract [has] been agreed upon, the law implies a covenant

---

[6] In *Tameny v. Atlantic Richfield Co.* (1980) 610 P.2d 1330, this court intimated that breach of the covenant of good faith and fair dealing in the employment relationship might give rise to tort remedies. That relationship has some of the same characteristics as the relationship between insurer and insured.

that neither party will deny the existence of a contract, since doing so violates the legal prohibition against doing anything to prevent realization of the promises of the performance of the contract."

According to Standard, this instruction erroneously allowed the jury to hold Standard liable if it found that Standard denied the existence of a valid contract, regardless of whether that denial was in good or bad faith.

Of course, "it is not a tort for a contractual obligor to dispute his liability under [a] contract" (*Sawyer v. Bank of America* (1978), 145 Cal.Rptr. 623) if the dispute is honest and undertaken in good faith. Similarly, it is not a tort for one party to deny, in good faith, the existence of a binding contract.

Since Standard's denial of the existence of a binding contract would not have been tortious if made in good faith, the trial court erred in failing to so instruct the jury. It is then necessary to decide whether this error requires that the judgment be reversed.

. . . .

In this case, there is a considerable degree of conflict in the evidence on the issue of whether Standard denied the existence of a contract in bad faith. On the one hand, the record contains evidence from which the jury could have inferred that Standard acted in bad faith and without a reasonable belief in its position when it denied the existence of a binding contract. The timing of the denials and the circumstances in which they were made would support the conclusion that Standard was cynically attempting to avoid *both* performance *and* liability for nonperformance of contractual obligations which it privately recognized to be binding.

On the other hand, Standard offered conflicting evidence from which the jury could have concluded that it acted in good faith. Standard argued strenuously that it never viewed the October 11, 1972, document as a binding contract since it believed that the document did not contain essential elements and, therefore, failed to satisfy the statute of frauds. . . .

. . . .

"Where it seems probable that the jury's verdict may have been based on the erroneous instruction prejudice appears and this court 'should not speculate upon the basis of the verdict.'" (*Robinson v. Cable*, 359 P.2d 929; *Henderson v. Harnischfeger Corp.*, 527 P.2d 353.) Here, it seems probable that the jury may have imposed liability on Standard as a result of the trial court's failure to instruct as to the bad faith requirement. Accordingly, the judgment in favor of Seaman's for breach of the duty of good faith and fair dealing must be reversed.

V.

. . . . The judgment for . . . breach of the duty of good faith and fair dealing is reversed with directions to conduct further proceedings consistent with this opinion.

BIRD, CHIEF JUSTICE, concurring and dissenting.

. . . . A contracting party should not be able to deny the existence of a valid contract in order to shield itself from liability for breach of that contract. Today, the court holds that an action will lie in tort against such conduct. However, it refuses to acknowledge that its holding is compelled by this court's past decisions analyzing the scope of the implied covenant of good faith and fair dealing. This court should not continue to retreat from its own decisional authority in this area.

. . . I believe that this court should forthrightly recognize the principle that, under certain circumstances, a breach of contract may support a tort cause of action for breach of implied covenant.

I.

. . . .

Past cases which have recognized a tort cause of action for breach of the covenant emphasize "reasonableness." . . .

. . . . The standard of good faith conduct that emerges from these decisions is that both contracting parties must act reasonably in light of the justified expectations of the other.

. . . .

Certain expectations derive from assumptions so basic to the very notion of a contract that they are shared by virtually all contracting parties. Foremost among these is the expectation that a breaching party will compensate the other party for losses caused by the breaching party's failure to perform. The availability of contract damages, in turn, supports the equally fundamental assumption that breach is a foreseeable and, in most situations, acceptable possibility.

Indeed, the assumption that parties may breach at will, risking only contract damages, is one of the cornerstones of contract law. "[I]t is not the policy of the law to compel adherence to contracts, but only to require each party to choose between performing in accordance with the contract and compensating the other party for injury resulting from a failure to perform. This view contains an important economic insight. In many cases it is uneconomical to induce the completion of the contract after it has been breached." (Posner, Economic Analysis of Law (1972) p. 55.) In most commercial contracts, recognition of this economic reality leads the parties to accept the possibility of breach, particularly since their right to recover contract damages provides adequate protection.

For example, one party to a contract may decide to breach if it concludes that the market will bring a higher price for its product than that set forth in the contract. In commercial contracts, the risk of such a breach is widely recognized and generally accepted. "[I]ntentional, willful, selfishly induced breach[es] of contract [are] often an anticipated, expected and encouraged reality of commercial life." (Diamond, *The Tort of Bad Faith Breach of Contract: When, If At All, Should It Be Extended Beyond Insurance Transactions?* (1981) 64 Marq.L.Rev. 425, 438.)

When the breaching party acts in bad faith to shield itself entirely from liability for contract damages, however, the duty of good faith and fair dealing is violated. Keeton, *Liability Insurance and Responsibility for Settlement* (1954) 67 Harv.L.Rev. 1136, 1139, fn. 6 [bad faith is frequently defined as "the intentional disregard of the financial interests of the (other contracting party) in the hope of escaping . . . full responsibility. . . ."].)

This type of conduct violates the nonbreaching party's justified expectation that it will be able to recover damages for its losses in the event of a breach. That expectation must be protected. Otherwise, the acceptance of the possibility of breach by the contracting parties and by society as a whole may be seriously undermined.

There is no danger that permitting tort recovery for bad faith denial of the existence of a valid commercial contract will make every breach of contract a tort. . . . [T]he vast majority of contract breaches in the commercial context do *not* involve this type of bad faith conduct.

   . . . .

It is a well-established principle of law that the parties' reasonable expectations should govern the determination of what conduct constitutes a tortious breach of the implied covenant of good faith and fair dealing. Application of that principle is fully warranted here. The duty of good faith and fair dealing was violated because a party attempted to avoid all liability for a contract breach by denying, in bad faith, the very existence of the contract. Such conduct violates the nearly universal expectation that the injured party will be compensated for losses caused by the breaching party's failure to perform. This tort remedy was recognized by this court in its earlier decisions involving the implied covenant of good faith and fair dealing. Those decisions should be the basis for the holding here.

NOTES & QUESTIONS

(1) Suppose that a defendant denies that he is liable under a contract with the plaintiff. The basis for the denial is a dispute over the meaning of a key provision of the contract. Does the *Seaman's* tort apply to these facts? Should it?

(2) In *Oki America, Inc. v. Microtech International, Inc.*, 872 F.2d 312 (9th Cir. 1989), the court confronted a *Seaman's* claim for bad faith denial of the existence of a contract. The court noted that "the elements of this tort are: (1) the denial of the existence of a contract (2) in bad faith, and (3) without probable cause." In a concurring opinion, Judge Kozinski expressed his frustration with the *Seaman's* action:

> Nowhere but in the Cloud Cuckooland of modern tort theory could a case like this have been concocted. One large corporation is complaining that another obstinately refused to acknowledge they had a contract. For this shocking misconduct it is demanding millions of dollars in punitive damages. I suppose we will next be seeing lawsuits seeking punitive damages for maliciously refusing to return telephone calls or adopting a condescending tone in interoffice memos. Not every slight, nor even every wrong, ought to have a tort remedy. The intrusion of courts into every aspect of life, and particularly into every type of business relationship, generates serious costs and uncertainties, trivializes the law, and denies individuals and businesses the autonomy of adjusting mutual rights and responsibilities through voluntary contractual agreement.

> In inventing the tort of bad faith denial of a contract, *Seaman's Direct Buying Serv., Inc. v. Standard Oil Co.*, 686 P.2d 1158 (1984), the California Supreme Court has created a cause of action so nebulous in outline and so unpredictable in application that it more resembles a brick thrown from a third story window than a rule of law. *Seaman's* gives nary a hint as to how to distinguish a bad faith denial that a contract exists, from a dispute over contract terms, from a permissible attempt to rescind a contract, or from "a loosely worded disclaimer of continued contractual responsibility." *Quigley v. Pet, Inc.*, 208 Cal.Rptr. 394 (1984).

> Small wonder: It is impossible to draw a principled distinction between a tortious denial of a contract's existence and a permissible denial of liability under the terms of the contract. The test—if one can call it such—seems to be whether the conduct "offends accepted notions of business ethics." *Seaman's*, 686 P.2d 1158. This gives judges license to rely on their gut feelings in distinguishing between a squabble and a tort. As a result, both the commercial world and the courts are needlessly burdened: The parties are hamstrung in developing binding agreements by the absence of clear legal principles; overburdened courts must adjudicate disputes that are incapable of settlement because no one can predict how—or even by what standard—they will be decided.

> *Seaman's* throws kerosene on the litigation bonfire by holding out the allure of punitive damages, a golden carrot that entices into court parties who might otherwise be inclined to resolve their differences. . . .

This tortification of contract law—the tendency of contract disputes to metastasize into torts—gives rise to a new form of entrepreneurship: investment in tort causes of action. "If Pennzoil won $11 billion from Texaco, why not me?" That thought must cross the minds of many enterprising lawyers and businessmen. A claim such as "defined" by *Seaman's* is a particularly attractive investment vehicle: The potential rewards are large, the rules nebulous, and the parties unconstrained by such annoying technicalities as the language of the contract to which they once agreed. . . .

. . . .

The eagerness of judges to expand the horizons of tort liability is symptomatic of a more insidious disease: the novel belief that any problem can be ameliorated if only a court gets involved. Not so. Courts are slow, clumsy, heavy-handed institutions, ill-suited to oversee the negotiations between corporations, to determine what compromises a manufacturer and a retailer should make in closing a mutually profitable deal, or to evaluate whether an export-import consortium is developing new markets in accordance with the standards of the business community.

Moreover, because litigation is costly, time consuming and risky, judicial meddling in many business deals imposes onerous burdens. It wasn't so long ago that being sued (or suing) was an unthinkable event for many small and medium-sized businesses. Today, legal expenses are a standard and often uncontrollable item in every business's budget, diverting resources from more productive areas of entrepreneurship. Nor can commercial enterprises be expected to flourish in a legal atmosphere where every move, every innovation, every business decision must be hedged against the risk of exotic new causes of action and incalculable damages.

Perhaps most troubling, the willingness of courts to subordinate voluntary contractual arrangements to their own sense of public policy and proper business decorum deprives individuals of an important measure of freedom. The right to enter into contracts—to adjust one's legal relationships by mutual agreement with other free individuals—was unknown through much of history and is unknown even today in many parts of the world. Like other aspects of personal autonomy, it is too easily smothered by government officials eager to tell us what's best for us. The recent tendency of judges to insinuate tort causes of action into relationships traditionally governed by contract is just such overreaching. It must be viewed with no less suspicion because the government officials in question happen to wear robes.

Id. at 314–16 (Kozinski, J., concurring).

(3) Even without the *Seaman's* decision, a party's bad faith denial of the existence of a contract may contribute to a tort finding. *See, e.g., Spoljaric v. Percival Tours, Inc.*, 708 S.W.2d 432, 434–35 (Tex. 1986) ("A promise to do an act in the future is actionable fraud when made with the intention, design and purpose of deceiving, and with no intention of performing the act. While a party's intent is determined at the time the party made the representation, it may be inferred from the party's subsequent acts after the representation is made.... Courts have held [that] a party's denial that he ever made a promise is a factor showing no intent to perform when he made the promise.").

FREEMAN & MILLS, INC. v. BELCHER OIL CO.
900 P.2d 669 (Cal. 1995)

LUCAS, CHIEF JUSTICE.

We granted review in this case to resolve some of the widespread confusion that has arisen regarding the application of our opinion in *Seaman's Direct Buying Service, Inc. v. Standard Oil Co.* (1984) 686 P.2d 1158 (*Seaman's*). We held in that case that a tort cause of action might lie "when, in addition to breaching the contract, [defendant] seeks to shield itself from liability by denying, in bad faith and without probable cause, that the contract exists."

In the present case, the Court of Appeal reversed judgment for plaintiff and remanded the case for a limited retrial, but also suggested that "it is time for the Supreme Court to reexamine the tort of 'bad faith denial of contract.' " We agree, and proceed to do so here. . . .

In light of certain developments occurring subsequent to *Seaman's* that call into question its continued validity, we find it appropriate to reexamine that decision. As will appear, we have concluded that the *Seaman's* court incorrectly recognized a tort cause of action based on the defendant's bad faith denial of the existence of a contract between the parties. That holding has been widely criticized by legal scholars, has caused considerable confusion among lower courts, and has been rejected by the courts of several other jurisdictions. These critics convincingly argue that the *Seaman's* decision is confusing and ambiguous, analytically flawed, and promotes questionable policy. After careful review of all the foregoing considerations, we conclude that our *Seaman's* holding should be overruled.

I.   Facts

We first review the underlying facts, taken largely from the Court of Appeal opinion herein. In June 1987, defendant Belcher Oil Company retained the law firm of Morgan, Lewis & Bockius (Morgan) to defend it in a Florida lawsuit. Pursuant to a letter of understanding signed by Belcher Oil's general counsel (William Dunker) and a Morgan partner

(Donald Smaltz), Belcher Oil was to pay for costs incurred on its behalf, including fees for accountants. In February 1988, after first obtaining Dunker's express authorization, Smaltz hired plaintiff, the accounting firm of Freeman & Mills, Incorporated, to provide a financial analysis and litigation support for Belcher Oil in the Florida lawsuit.

In March, an engagement letter was signed by both Morgan and Freeman & Mills. At about this time, William Dunker left Belcher Oil and was replaced by Neil Bowman. In April 1988, Bowman became dissatisfied with Morgan's efforts and the lawyers were discharged. Bowman asked Morgan for a summary of the work performed by Freeman & Mills and, at the same time, directed Smaltz to have Freeman & Mills stop their work for Belcher Oil. Smaltz did as he was asked. Freeman & Mills's final statement was for $70,042.50 in fees, plus $7,495.63 for costs, a total of $77,538.13.

Freeman & Mills billed Morgan, but no payment was forthcoming. Freeman & Mills then billed Belcher Oil directly and, for about a year, sent monthly statements and regularly called Bowman about the bill, but no payment was forthcoming. In August 1989, Smaltz finally told Freeman & Mills that Belcher Oil refused to pay their bill. Freeman & Mills then wrote to Bowman asking that the matter be resolved. In September 1989, Bowman responded, complaining that Belcher Oil had not been consulted about the extent of Freeman & Mills's services and suggesting Freeman & Mills should look to Morgan for payment of whatever amounts were claimed due.

Ultimately, Freeman & Mills filed this action against Belcher Oil, alleging (in its second amended complaint) causes of action for breach of contract, "bad faith denial of contract," and quantum meruit. Belcher Oil answered and the case was presented to a jury in a bifurcated trial, with punitive damages reserved for the second phase. According to the evidence presented during the first phase, the amount owed to Freeman & Mills (as indicated on their statements) was $77,538.13.

The jury returned its first phase verdict. On Freeman & Mills's breach of contract claim, the jury found that Belcher Oil had authorized Morgan to retain Freeman & Mills on Belcher Oil's behalf, that Freeman & Mills had performed its obligations under the contract, that Belcher Oil had breached the contract, and that the amount of damages suffered by Freeman & Mills was $25,000. The jury also answered affirmatively the questions about whether Belcher Oil had denied the existence of the contract and had acted with oppression, fraud, or malice. Thereafter, the jury returned its verdict awarding $477,538.13 in punitive damages and judgment was entered consistent with the jury's verdicts.

In three post-trial motions, Freeman & Mills asked for orders (1) "correcting" the jury's verdicts and the court's judgment to reflect compensatory damages of $77,538.13 and punitive damages of $425,000 (on the ground that the jury's questions showed this was its true intent); (2) awarding attorney fees as sanctions for the litigation tactics of Belcher Oil's attorneys; and (3) awarding prejudgment interest on the compensatory damage award. Over Belcher Oil's opposition, all three motions were granted—but with some changes in the course of correcting the judgment—by giving Freeman & Mills $131,614.93 in compensatory damages (the $25,000 actually awarded by the jury, plus the $77,538.13 included in the punitive damage award, plus $29,076.80 for prejudgment interest), and $400,000 (not $425,000 as requested) in punitive damages.

Belcher Oil appealed from the "corrected" judgment. Freeman & Mills cross-appealed from a mid-trial order denying its request to amend its complaint to add a cause of action for fraud, an issue not presently before us. The Court of Appeal majority, finding no "special relationship" between the parties to justify a tort theory of recovery under *Seaman's*, reversed the judgment and remanded the case to the trial court for a retrial limited to the issue of damages under plaintiff's breach of contract cause of action. (The Court of Appeal dissenting justice would have sustained the tort cause of action and remanded for retrial of the damage issue as to both causes of action.) As will appear, we affirm the judgment of the Court of Appeal, concluding that a tort recovery is unavailable in this case.

. . . .

III. Stare Decisis

Before examining various recent developments pertinent to our reconsideration of *Seaman's,* we briefly review certain well-established principles governing the respect we confer upon prior opinions of this court. These principles were summarized in [*Moradi-Shalal v. Fireman's Fund Ins. Cos.,* 758 P.2d 58 (Cal. 1988)], as follows:

> ". . . It is, of course, a fundamental jurisprudential policy that prior applicable precedent usually must be followed even though the case, if considered anew, might be decided differently by the current justices. This policy, known as the doctrine of stare decisis, 'is based on the assumption that certainty, predictability and stability in the law are the major objectives of the legal system; i.e., that parties should be able to regulate their conduct and enter into relationships with reasonable assurance of the governing rules of law.' (9 Witkin, Cal.Procedure (3d ed. 1985) Appeal, § 758, at p. 726, and see cases cited.)

> "It is likewise well established, however, that the foregoing policy is sufficiently flexible to permit this court to reconsider, and ultimately to depart from, its own prior precedent in an

appropriate case. As we stated in *Cianci v. Superior Court* (1985) 710 P.2d 375, '[a]lthough the doctrine [stare decisis] does indeed serve important values, it nevertheless should not shield court-created error from correction.' In *Anderson,* Justice Mosk noted the need for flexibility in applying stare decisis, stating, 'This is especially so when, as here, the error [in the prior opinion] is related to a "matter of continuing concern" to the community at large.'

"*Anderson* also recognized that reexamination of precedent may become necessary when subsequent developments indicate an earlier decision was unsound, or has become ripe for reconsideration."

As we explain below, developments occurring subsequent to the *Seaman's* decision convince us that it was incorrectly decided, that it has generated unnecessary confusion, costly litigation, and inequitable results, and that it will continue to produce such effects unless and until we overrule it.

IV. Subsequent Developments

A.   California Supreme Court Decisions—Subsequent opinions of this court indicate a continuing reluctance, originally reflected in *Seaman's* itself, to authorize tort recovery for noninsurance contract breaches.

In *Foley v. Interactive Data Corp.* (1988) 765 P.2d 373 (*Foley*), we considered the availability of tort damages for the wrongful termination of a discharged employee. Declining to rely on dictum in *Seaman's* regarding the possible availability of tort remedies for breach of the implied covenant of good faith and fair dealing (hereafter the implied covenant) in the employment context, we refused to afford such remedies for the essentially contractual claim of breach of the implied covenant arising in that context.

In reaching our conclusion in *Foley,* we relied in part on certain basic principles relevant to contract law, including the need for "predictability about the cost of contractual relationships," and the purpose of contract damages to compensate the injured party rather than punish the breaching party. Focusing on the implied covenant, we observed that, with the exception of insurance contracts, "[b]ecause the covenant is a contract term . . . compensation for its breach has almost always been limited to contract rather than tort remedies."

We acknowledged in *Foley* that "[t]he insurance cases . . . were a major departure from traditional principles of contract law," and we stressed that the courts should take "great care" before extending "the exceptional approach taken in those cases" to "another contract setting."

We concluded that "the employment relationship is not sufficiently similar to that of insurer and insured to warrant judicial extension of the proposed additional tort remedies. . . ."

Thereafter, in *Hunter v. Up-Right, Inc.* (1993) 864 P.2d 88 (Hunter), we held that *Foley's* analysis would preclude recovery of tort damages for employer misrepresentations made to induce termination of employment. In the course of our analysis, and without mentioning *Seaman's*, we nonetheless confirmed that, with the exception of insurance contracts, remedies for breach of the implied covenant "have almost always been limited to contract damages."

We reasoned in *Hunter* that the defendant's misrepresentations were "merely the means to the end desired by the employer, i.e., termination of employment. They cannot serve as a predicate for tort damages. . . ." Similar analysis would apply to a defendant's denial of the existence of the underlying contract. Although such "stonewalling" conduct may have been intended to terminate the contractual relationship, there is no logical reason why it should serve as a predicate for tort damages.

Most recently, in *Applied Equipment Corp. v. Litton Saudi Arabia Ltd.* (1994) 869 P.2d 454, we held that a contracting party may not be held liable in tort for conspiring with another to interfere with his own contract. We reiterated the important differences between contract and tort theories of recovery, stating that "[c]onduct amounting to a breach of contract becomes tortious only when it also violates an independent duty arising from principles of tort law," and that "the law generally does not distinguish between good and bad motives for breaching a contract." We noted that limiting contract breach damages to those within the reasonably foreseeable contemplation of the parties when the contract was formed "serves to encourage contractual relations and commercial activity by enabling parties to estimate in advance the financial risks of their enterprise."

Our decisions in *Foley, Hunter*, and *Applied Equipment* each contains language that strongly suggests courts should limit tort recovery in contract breach situations to the insurance area, at least in the absence of violation of an independent duty arising from principles of tort law other than denial of the existence of, or liability under, the breached contract. (See also *White v. Western Title Ins. Co.* (1985) 710 P.2d 309 (conc. and dis. opn. of Kaus, J.) [observing that "our experience in *Seaman's* surely tells us that there are real problems in applying the substitute remedy of a tort recovery—with or without punitive damages—outside the insurance area," and urging a legislative solution].)

B. Court of Appeal Decisions—Subsequent decisions of the Courts of Appeal have encountered considerable difficulty in applying our *Seaman's* decision. As one recent commentary stated, "The *Seaman's* tort has generated confusion among California courts. Consequently, in recent decisions, almost every court offers a different interpretation of the tort." (Comment, *California's Detortification of Contract law: Is the Seaman's Tort Dead?* (1992) 26 Loyola L.A.L.Rev. 213, 223 (hereafter Detortification Comment).)

Without analyzing the particular facts of each case, it is sufficient to observe that our *Seaman's* holding has presented the lower courts with a number of unanswered questions, and that these courts have reached varying, and often inconsistent, conclusions in response. (See, e.g., *Harris v. Atlantic Richfield Co.* (1993) 17 Cal.Rptr.2d 649 (hereafter *Harris*) [reviewing cases and noting criticism of *Seaman's* for "singling out" one type of bad faith contract breach for tort damages]; *DuBarry Internat., Inc. v. Southwest Forest Industries, Inc.* (1991) 282 Cal.Rptr. 181 (hereafter *DuBarry*) [reviewing conflicting cases and holding *Seaman's* requires actual denial of contract's existence rather than mere denial of contract *liability*]; *Copesky v. Superior Court* (1991) 280 Cal.Rptr. 338 [general review of cases]; *Careau & Co. v. Security Pacific Business Credit, Inc.* (1990) 272 Cal.Rptr. 387 (hereafter *Careau*) [acknowledging "confusion and uncertainty" generated by *Seaman's*]; *Lynch & Freytag v. Cooper* (1990) 267 Cal.Rptr. 189 (hereafter *Lynch & Freytag*) [ruling *Seaman's* inapplicable to denials of contract existence set forth in pleadings]; *Okun v. Morton* (1988) 250 Cal.Rptr. 220 (hereafter *Okun*) [concluding that *Seaman's* tort is based on breach of implied covenant]; *Multiplex Ins. Agency, Inc. v. California Life Ins. Co.* (1987) 235 Cal.Rptr. 12 (hereafter *Multiplex*) [extending *Seaman's* to bad faith denial of *liability*]; *Koehrer v. Superior Court* (1986) 226 Cal.Rptr. 820 [extending *Seaman's* to bad faith attempt to deprive employee of contractual benefits]; *Quigley v. Pet, Inc.* (1984) 208 Cal.Rptr. 394 [noting uncertainties presented by *Seaman's,* including its application to bad faith disputes over contractual "terms and performance"]; *Wallis v. Superior Court* (1984) 207 Cal.Rptr. 123 [interpreting *Seaman's* as allowing tort action for breach of implied covenant in noninsurance cases].)

Several of the foregoing cases criticize our *Seaman's* holding, raise doubts as to its continued viability, or urge our reconsideration of that decision. (See *Harris, supra,* 17 Cal.Rptr.2d 649 [noting criticism and declining to extend *Seaman's* tort to contract breaches in violation of public policy]; *Careau, supra,* 272 Cal.Rptr. 387 ["unfortunate" that *Seaman's* failed to explain or justify why tort liability could be imposed for bad faith denial of contract existence but not for bad faith assertion of other defenses]; *Lynch & Freytag, supra,* 267 Cal.Rptr. 189 (maj. opn.) [observing that "The contours of this new tort have perplexed the appellate courts almost from the day *Seaman's* was filed."], [197] (conc. opn. of Woods (Fred), J.) [stating that "[t]he general viability of *Seaman's* in view of *Foley* appears to be tenuous at best"]; *Okun, supra,* 250 Cal.Rptr. 220 ["we are of the view—as are many others—that the whole concept of tort liability in bad faith commercial litigation needs to be reexamined"].)

As these cases indicate, much confusion and conflict has arisen regarding the scope and application of our *Seaman's* holding. For example, does the *Seaman's* tort derive from breach of the implied covenant or from some other independent tort duty? Does the *Seaman's* tort extend to a bad faith *denial of liability* under a contract, as well as denial of its existence? Is a "special relationship" between the contracting parties a prerequisite to a *Seaman's* action?

The foregoing "special relationship" conflict extends to the present case, for as previously noted, the Court of Appeal herein concluded that the *Seaman's* tort requires a showing of a special relationship between the parties. As the Court of Appeal stated, "Whatever need there may be to provide special remedies to cover special relationships, there is no similar need in routine business cases. For this reason, we believe our colleagues in Division Two were correct when they interpreted *Seaman's* narrowly, limiting the tort of bad faith denial of contract to the situations where, in addition to whatever other elements may be required (which depends on which case is cited), there is (1) a special relationship and (2) conduct extraneous to the contract (as there was in *Seaman's*). . . ."

Confusion and conflict alone might not justify a decision to abrogate *Seaman's,* for we could attempt to resolve all the uncertainties engendered by that decision. But there are additional considerations that convince us to forgo that predictably Herculean effort. Many of the pertinent Court of Appeal decisions recognize compelling *policy* reasons supporting the preclusion of tort remedies for contractual breaches outside the insurance context.

For example, in *DuBarry, supra,* 282 Cal.Rptr. 181, the court refused to extend the *Seaman's* tort to bad faith *defenses* to contract claims. The court explained that, "If the rule were otherwise, then any party attempting to defend a disputed contract claim would risk, at the very least, exposure to the imposition of tort damages and an expensive and time-consuming expansion of the litigation into an inquiry as to the motives and state of mind of the breaching party. The distinction between tort and contract actions, and their purposefully different measures of damages, would be blurred if not erased. The insult to commercial predictability and certainty would only be exceeded by the increased burden on the already overworked judicial system." Many of these considerations are equally applicable to the *Seaman's* tort itself.

Similarly, in *Harris, supra,* 17 Cal.Rptr.2d 649, the Court of Appeal denied a tort recovery for bad faith contract breach in violation of public policy. The court elaborated on the applicable policy considerations as follows: "The traditional goal of contract remedies is compensation of the promisee for the loss resulting from the breach, not compulsion of the promisor to perform his promises. Therefore, 'willful' breaches have not been distinguished from other breaches. The restrictions on contract remedies serve purposes not found in tort law. They protect the parties' freedom to bargain over special risks and they promote contract formation by limiting liability to the value of the promise. This encourages efficient breaches, resulting in increased production of goods and services at lower cost to society. Because of these overriding policy considerations, the California Supreme Court has proceeded with caution in carving out exceptions to the traditional contract remedy restrictions."

The *Harris* court set forth as reasons for denying tort recovery in contract breach cases (1) the different objectives underlying the remedies for tort and contract breach, (2) the importance of predictability in assuring commercial stability in contractual dealings, (3) the potential for converting every contract breach into a tort, with accompanying punitive damage recovery, and (4) the preference for legislative action in affording appropriate remedies.

As we shall see, the foregoing policy considerations fully support our decision to overrule *Seaman's* rather than attempt to clarify its uncertain boundaries. . . .

C. Criticism by Courts of Other Jurisdictions

We decided *Seaman's* in 1984. Since then, courts of other jurisdictions have either criticized or declined to follow our *Seaman's* analysis. Of all the states, only Montana has recognized the tort of bad faith in typical arm's length commercial contracts, and recently even that state has qualified the tort by requiring a showing of a special relationship between the contracting parties. (See *Story v. Bozeman* (1990) 791 P.2d 767, 776.)

Ninth Circuit Judge Kozinski expressed his candid criticism of *Seaman's* in a concurring opinion in *Oki America, Inc. v. Microtech Intern., Inc.* (9th Cir.1989) 872 F.2d 312, 314–317 (*Oki America*). Among other criticism, Judge Kozinski found the *Seaman's* holding unduly imprecise and confusing. As he stated, "It is impossible to draw a principled distinction between a tortious denial of a contract's existence and a permissible denial of liability under the terms of the contract. The test ... seems to be whether the conduct 'offends accepted notions of business ethics.' This gives judges license to rely on their gut feelings in distinguishing between a squabble and a tort. As a result, both the commercial world and the courts are needlessly burdened. . . ."

Judge Kozinski also mentioned the substantial costs associated with *Seaman's* litigation, and the resulting interference with contractual relationships. "Perhaps most troubling, the willingness of courts to subordinate voluntary contractual arrangements to their own sense of public policy and proper business decorum deprives individuals of an important measure of freedom. The right to enter into contracts—to adjust one's legal relationships by mutual agreement [ ] is too easily smothered by government [officials] eager to tell us what's best for us." Judge Kozinski concluded by observing that "*Seaman's* is a prime candidate for reconsideration."

Similarly, in *Air-Sea Forwarders, Inc. v. Air Asia Co., Ltd.*, 880 F.2d at pages 184–185 [(9th Cir. 1989)], Judge Hall observed that *Seaman's* "ambiguous" holding had caused widespread confusion among the lower courts. As Judge Hall stated, "Indeed, the *Seaman's* court's failure to explain *why* it was not necessary to predicate its holding on the implied covenant of good faith and fair dealing, or to *justify* the dramatically greater liability for the bad faith denial of the existence of a contract as compared to the bad faith dispute of a contract's terms, undoubtedly spawned the confusion in the appellate division cases discussed *infra*."

Other federal courts have found similar difficulty interpreting and applying *Seaman's*. Thus, in *Elxsi v. Kukje America Corp.* (N.D.Cal.1987) 672 F.Supp. 1294, 1296, Judge Aguilar observed that "The major difficulty confronting jurists and commentators trying to understand and apply *Seaman's* is the faithful interpretation of the ... passage [condemning "stonewalling" "without probable cause and with no belief in the existence of a defense"]. The initial sentence . . . states that the new tort is denial of the *existence of a contract*, while the subsequent passage describes denial of the *existence of liability*. Ultimately, the dilemma involves determining whether the subsequent passage is definitional or descriptive."

As we stated in *Moradi-Shalal, supra,* 758 P.2d 58, in which we were faced with a similar tide of critical or contrary authority from other jurisdictions regarding one of our prior decisions, "[a]lthough holdings from other states are not controlling, and we remain free to steer a contrary course, nonetheless the near unanimity of agreement ... indicates we should question the advisability of continued allegiance to our minority approach."

D. Scholarly Criticism

Scholarly commentary on *Seaman's* also has been generally critical of our *Seaman's* holding and underlying analysis. (See, e.g., Ashley, Bad Faith Actions; Liability and Damages (1994) § 11.08, at p. 28 [the *Seaman's* court, in creating a new tort of "stonewalling" based on "inapposite" authority, "can only be described as out of balance," having "lost touch with the traditions of contract law"]; Putz & Klippen, *Commercial Bad Faith: Attorney Fees—Not Tort Liability—is the Remedy* for *"Stonewalling"* (1987) 21 U.S.F.L.Rev. 419, 459 (hereafter Putz & Klippen) [finding "no rational way" to distinguish denial of contract existence from other denials of liability]; Sebert, *Punitive and Nonpecuniary Damages in Actions Based Upon Contract: Toward Achieving the Objective of Full Compensation* (1986) 33 U.C.L.A.L.Rev. 1565, 1640–1641 (hereafter Sebert) [stating that *Seaman's* is an "unhappy compromise" that is "both troubling and likely to be mischievous" by creating a "meaningless distinction" between denial of contract existence and other breaches]; Snyderman, *What's So Good About Good Faith? The Good Faith Performance Obligation in Commercial Lending* (1988) 55 U.Chi.L.Rev. 1335, 1363 (hereafter Snyderman) [stating that *Seaman's* "represents a potentially disastrous expansion of the bad faith tort into the commercial realm"]; Wallenstein, *Breach of the Implied Covenant of Good Faith and Fair Dealing in Commercial Contracts: A Wrong in Search of a Remedy* (1988–1989) 20 U.West L.A.L.Rev. 113, 124 ["With the advent of *Seaman's*, the root causes of the confusion surrounding the implied covenant in commercial contracts began to emerge"]; Comment, *The Role of Good Faith in Lender Liability Suits: Rising Star or Fading Gadfly* (1989) 31 Ariz.L.Rev. 939, 953 (hereafter Arizona Comment) [stating that *Seaman's* created an "undefined new source of liability" that will have the effect of "deter(ring) zealous advocacy"]; Comment, *Extending the Bad Faith Tort Doctrine to General Commercial Contracts* (1985) 65 B.U.L.Rev. 355, 376 (hereafter Boston Comment) [observing that *Seaman's* failed to articulate a "generally applicable tort standard which would differentiate between mere breaches of contract and breaches of the tort duty of good faith and fair dealing"]; Comment, *Tort Remedies for Breach of Contract: The Expansion of Tortious Breach of the Implied Covenant of Good Faith and Fair Dealing into the Commercial Realm* (1986) 86 Colum.L.Rev. 377, 401 (hereafter Columbia Comment) [finding "no principled distinction" between denial of a contract's existence, and denial that certain parts or terms exist, and concluding that *Seaman's* ultimate result "will be to expose commercial parties to tort-level damages whenever a party refuses to perform under the contract"]; Comment, *Bad Faith Lenders* (1989) 60 Colo.L.Rev. 417, 427 [*Seaman's* disclaimer of reliance on implied covenant is inconsistent with imposition of liability for bad faith denial of contract's existence]; Comment, *Lender Liability for Breach of the Obligation of Good Faith Performance* (1987) 36 Emory L.J. 917, 960 [*Seaman's* award of tort damages for contract breach is "troublesome" and "easy to misinterpret"]; Comment, *Seaman's Direct Buying Service, Inc. v. Standard Oil Co.: Tortious Breach of the Covenant of Good Faith and Fair Dealing in a Noninsurance Commercial Contract Case* (1986) 71 Iowa L.Rev. 893, 898 ["*Seaman's* leaves attorneys to guess whether their commercial client's conduct is merely healthy capitalistic competition or manifest bad faith."]; Detortification Comment, *supra*, 26 Loyola

L.A.L.Rev. at p. 239 ["A growing distaste for the *Seaman's* tort among the California appellate districts, in the Ninth Circuit and in other states mandates that the California Supreme Court . . . overrule *Seaman's*"]; Comment, *Sailing the Uncharted Seas of Bad Faith: Seaman's Direct Buying Services, Inc. v. Standard Oil Co.* (1985) 69 Minn.L.Rev. 1161, 1175 (hereafter Minnesota Comment) [observing that *Seaman's* failure to distinguish its new tort from breaches of implied covenant of good faith "exacerbated the confusion" in the area].)

Many of the foregoing articles and commentaries observe that the *Seaman's* decision, being unclear and subject to multiple interpretations, has resulted in widespread confusion among the lower courts. (E.g., Snyderman, *supra,* 55 U.Chi.L.Rev. at p. 1363 [*Seaman's* tort could be applied in all contract breach cases, resulting in "complete subversion of the expectation damages standard"]; Sebert, *supra,* at pp. 1640–1641 [decision is "troubling" because it "singles out one particular type of breach for sanction—the bad faith denial of the existence of a contract"]; Detortification Comment, *supra,* 26 Loyola L.A.L.Rev. at p. 223 ["The *Seaman's* tort has generated confusion among California courts. Consequently, in recent decisions, almost every court offers a different interpretation of the tort. The one similarity . . . is that every court appears to limit the tort's application."].)

Additionally, several of these commentaries emphasize the extreme difficulty courts experience in distinguishing between tortious denial of a contract's existence and permissible denial of *liability* under the terms of the contract. Further confusion concerns the quantum of proof required to establish a denial of the existence of the contract and, as previously discussed, whether or not proof is required of a "special relationship" between the contracting parties.

The foregoing commentaries raise a wide variety of additional criticisms that support reconsideration of the *Seaman's* decision, including widespread confusion among judges and juries in applying its holding, inappropriately excessive damage awards, overcrowded court dockets and speculative litigation, delay and complication of ordinary contract breach claims, deterrence of contract formation, and restraint on zealous advocacy. As one article observes, *Seaman's* created "intolerable uncertainty" and constitutes a "dangerous misstep" that this court should "promptly correct." (Putz & Klippen, *supra,* 21 U.S.F.L.Rev. at p. 499.)

As we stated in *Moradi-Shalal, supra,* 758 P.2d 58, "the breadth of the criticism . . . is disturbing and, like the flood of contrary decisions of other state courts, is pertinent to our determination whether or not to reconsider that decision."

V. Seaman's Should be Overruled

As previously indicated, the *Seaman's* decision has generated uniform confusion and uncertainty regarding its scope and application, and widespread doubt about the necessity or desirability of its holding. These doubts and criticisms, express or implied, in decisions from this state and from other state and federal courts, echoed by the generally adverse scholarly comment[ary] cited above, convince us that *Seaman's* should be overruled in favor of a general rule precluding tort recovery for noninsurance contract breach, at least in the absence of violation of "an independent duty arising from principles of tort law" (*Applied Equipment Corp. v. Litton Saudi Arabia Ltd., supra*, 869 P.2d 454) other than the bad faith denial of the existence of, or liability under, the breached contract.

As set forth above, the critics stress, among other factors favoring *Seaman's* abrogation, the confusion and uncertainty accompanying the decision, the need for stability and predictability in commercial affairs, the potential for excessive tort damages, and the preference for legislative rather than judicial action in this area.

Even if we were unimpressed by the nearly unanimous criticism leveled at *Seaman's*, on reconsideration the analytical defects in the opinion have become apparent. It seems anomalous to characterize as "tortious" the bad faith denial of the existence of a contract, while treating as "contractual" the bad faith denial of liability or responsibility under an acknowledged contract. In both cases, the breaching party has acted in bad faith and, accordingly, has presumably committed acts offensive to "accepted notions of business ethics." Yet to include bad faith denials of liability within *Seaman's* scope could potentially convert every contract breach into a tort. Nor would limiting *Seaman's* tort to incidents involving "stonewalling" adequately narrow its potential scope. Such conduct by the breaching party, essentially telling the promisee, "See you in court," could incidentally accompany *every* breach of contract.

For all the foregoing reasons, we conclude that *Seaman's* should be overruled. We emphasize that nothing in this opinion should be read as affecting the existing precedent governing enforcement of the implied covenant in insurance cases. Further, nothing we say here would prevent the Legislature from creating additional civil remedies for noninsurance contract breach, including such measures as providing litigation costs and attorney fees in certain aggravated cases, or assessing increased compensatory damages covering lost profits and other losses attributable to the breach, as well as restoration of the *Seaman's* holding if the Legislature deems that course appropriate. Thus far, however, the Legislature has not manifested an intent either to expand contract breach recovery or to provide tort damages for ordinary contract breach.

[VI.] Conclusion

The judgment of the Court of Appeal, reversing the trial court's judgment in plaintiff's favor and remanding the case for a retrial limited to the issue of damages under plaintiff's breach of contract cause of action, and for judgment in favor of defendant on plaintiff's bad faith denial of contract cause of action, is affirmed.

. . . .

MOSK, JUSTICE, concurring and dissenting.

I concur in the judgment. I disagree, however, with the majority's conclusion that *Seaman's Direct Buying Service, Inc. v. Standard Oil Co.* (1984) 686 P.2d 1158 (*Seaman's*) was wrongly decided. Although in retrospect I believe its holding was too broad, our task, both for the sake of sound public policy and stare decisis, is to clarify rather than repudiate that holding.

The majority would displace *Seaman's* with "a general rule precluding tort recovery for noninsurance contract breach, at least in the absence of violation of 'an independent duty arising from principles of tort law' [citation] other than the bad faith denial of the existence of, or liability under, the breached contract." I agree that the bad faith denial of the existence of a contract or contractual liability, *alone,* cannot give rise to tort liability. I agree as well with the tautological proposition that a breach of contract is made tortious only when some "independent duty arising from tort law" is violated.

In my view, however, this "independent duty arising from tort law" can originate from torts other than those traditionally recognized at common law. There are some types of intentionally tortious behavior unique to the contractual setting that do not fit into conventional tort categories. Allowing for the possibility of tort causes of action outside conventional categories is consistent with the malleable and continuously evolving nature of the tort law. " 'The law of torts is anything but static, and the limits of its development are never set. When it becomes clear that the plaintiff's interests are entitled to legal protection against the conduct of the defendant, the mere fact that the claim is novel will not of itself operate as a bar to the remedy.' " (*Soldano v. O'Daniels* (1983) 190 Cal.Rptr. 310, quoting Prosser on Torts (4th ed. 1971) pp. 3–4.)

Seaman's should be viewed within the context of this common law tradition of innovation. When *Seaman's* is understood in light of its facts, it stands for the proposition, in my view, that a contract action may also sound in tort when the breach of contract is intentional and in bad faith, *and* is aggravated by certain particularly egregious forms of intentionally injurious activity. Because, as will be explained, there is no such tortious activity in the present case, I concur in the majority's disposition.

. . . .

I.

. . . .

It is . . . true that public policy does not always favor a limitation on damages for *intentional* breaches of contract. The notion that society gains from an efficient breach must be qualified by the recognition that many intentional breaches are not efficient. (See *Patton v. Mid-Continent Systems, Inc.* (7th Cir.1988) 841 F.2d 742, 751 (hereafter *Patton*).) As Judge Posner explained in *Patton, supra*, 841 F.2d at page 751: "Not all breaches of contract are involuntary or otherwise efficient. Some are opportunistic; the promisor wants the benefit of the bargain without bearing the agreed-upon costs, and exploits the inadequacies of purely compensatory remedies (the major inadequacies being that pre-and post-judgment interest rates are frequently below market levels when the risk of nonpayment is taken into account and that the winning party cannot recover . . . attorney's fees)." Commentators have also pointed to other "inadequacies of purely compensatory remedies" that encourage inefficient breaches (i.e. breaches that result in greater losses to the promisee than gains for the promisor): the lack of emotional distress damages, even when such damages are the probable result of the breach, and the restriction of consequential damages to those in the contemplation of the parties at the time the contract was formed.

In addition to fully compensating contract plaintiffs and discouraging inefficient breaches, the imposition of tort remedies for certain intentional breaches of contract serves to punish and deter business practices that constitute distinct social wrongs independent of the breach. For example, we permit the plaintiff to recover exemplary damages in cases in which the breached contract was induced through promissory fraud, even though the plaintiff has incurred the same loss whether the contract was fraudulently induced or not. Our determination to allow the plaintiff to sue for fraud and to potentially recover exemplary damages is not justified by the plaintiff's greater loss, but by the fact that the breach of a fraudulently induced contract is a significantly greater wrong, from society's standpoint, than an ordinary breach. "We are aware of the danger of grafting tort liability on what ordinarily should be a breach of contract action. . . . However, no public policy is served by permitting a party who never intended to fulfill his obligations to fraudulently induce another to enter into an agreement." (*Las Palmas Associates v. Las Palmas Center Associates* (1991) 1 Cal.Rptr.2d 301.)

As the above illustrate, the rationale for limiting actions for intentional breaches of contract to contract remedies—that such limitation promotes commercial stability and predictability and hence advances commerce—is not invariably a compelling one. Breaches accompanied by deception or infliction of intentional harm may be so disruptive of commerce and so reprehensible in themselves that the value of deterring such actions through the tort system outweighs the marginal loss in the predictability of damages that may result. But in imposing tort duties to deter intentionally harmful acts among contracting parties, courts must be cautious not to fashion remedies which overdeter the illegitimate and as a result chill legitimate activities. Thus, courts should be careful to apply tort remedies only when the conduct in question is so clear in its deviation from socially useful business practices that the effect of enforcing such tort duties will be, as in the case of fraud, to aid rather than discourage commerce.

As observed above, not all tortious breaches of contract arise from conventional torts. Numerous courts have recognized types of intentionally tortious activity that occur exclusively or distinctively within the context of a contractual relationship. The most familiar type of tortious breach of contract in this state is that of the insurer, whose unreasonable failure to settle or resolve a claim has been held to violate the covenant of good faith and fair dealing. Tort liability is imposed primarily because of the distinctive characteristics of the insurance contract: the fiduciary nature of the relationship, the fact that the insurer offers a type of quasi-public service that provides financial security and peace of mind, and the fact that the insurance contract is generally one of adhesion. In these cases, the special relationship between insurer and insured supports the elevation of the covenant of good faith and fair dealing, a covenant implied by law in every contract and generally used as an aid to contract interpretation, into a tort duty.

Because the good faith covenant is so broad and all-pervasive, this court and others have been reluctant to expand recognition of the action for tortious breach of the covenant beyond the insurance context. (See *Foley, supra,* 765 P.2d 373 [no special relationship in the employment context]; but see *id.* at pp. [402], [412], [418] (separate conc. and dis. opns. of Broussard, J., Kaufman, J., and Mosk, J.).) Unfortunately, the preoccupation of California courts with limiting the potentially enormous scope of this tort has diverted attention away from the useful task of identifying *specific practices* employed by contracting parties that merit the imposition of tort remedies. . . .

. . . .

A . . . tortious intentional breach has been found when the *consequences* of the breach are especially injurious to the party suffering the breach, and the breaching party intentionally or knowingly inflicts such injury. Cases of this type have generally occurred outside the commercial context, involving manifestly unequal contracting parties and contracts concerning matters of vital personal significance, in which great mental anguish or personal hardship are the probable result of the breach. In these cases, courts have permitted substantial awards of emotional distress damages and/or punitive damages, both as a means of providing extra sanctions for a defendant engaging in intentionally injurious activities against vulnerable parties, and as a way of fully compensating plaintiffs for types of injury that are neither readily [amenable] to mitigation nor generally recoverable as contract damages. For example, in *K-Mart Corp. v. Ponsock* (Nev.1987) 732 P.2d 1364, 1370, disapproved on other grounds by *Ingersoll-Rand Co. v. McClendon* (1990) 498 U.S. 133, 137, the Nevada Supreme Court allowed a $50,000 award of punitive damages to stand when an employer discharged a long-term employee on a fabricated charge for the purpose of defeating the latter's contractual entitlement to retirement benefits. (See also *Ainsworth v. Franklin County Cheese Corp.* (1991) 592 A.2d 871, 871, 874–875 [punitive damages permitted when a defendant/employer discharged on pretext of good cause the plaintiff/employee in order to extricate itself from the obligation to pay severance benefits].)

In other cases of this type, an intentional breach of a warranty of habitability by a landlord or building contractor has given rise to substantial emotional distress or punitive damages awards. For example, Missouri courts recognize that a wrongful eviction will sound in tort as well as contract. (*Ladeas v. Carter* (Mo.Ct.App.1992) 845 S.W.2d 45, 52; see also *Emden v. Vitz* (1948) 198 P.2d 696 [wrongful eviction accompanied by verbal abuse sounds in tort]; *Hilder v. St. Peter* (1984) 478 A.2d 202, 210 [punitive damages permitted against a landlord who, "after receiving notice of a defect, fails to repair the facility that is essential to the health and safety of his or her tenant"]; *B & M Homes, Inc. v. Hogan* (Ala.1979) 376 So.2d 667, 671–672 [substantial emotional distress damages award against contractor who refused to repair construction defects leading to great personal discomfort]; *Ducote v. Arnold* (La.Ct.App.1982) 416 So.2d 180, 183–185 [damages for mental anguish permitted for breach of home remodeling contract].) The New Mexico Supreme Court, in *Romero v. Mervyn's* (1989) 784 P.2d 992, 999–1001, citing *Seaman's* with approval, upheld a punitive damage award against a department store, which had entered into an oral agreement to pay the medical expenses of a customer accidentally injured on its premises, and then reneged on its agreement.

The principle that certain contractual interests of vulnerable parties deserve greater protection than ordinary contract damages would otherwise provide has led our Legislature to authorize special sanctions for various types of intentional breaches. For example, one who is the victim of an intentional breach of warranty of consumer goods may recover twice the amount of actual damages (Civ.Code, § 1794, subd. (c)) and treble damages may be awarded to a retail seller who is injured by "willful or repeated" warranty violations (*id., § 1794.1, subd. (a)*). Labor Code section 206 provides for treble damages for the willful failure to pay wages after the Labor Commissioner determines the wages are owing. But the fact that the Legislature has acted in some instances to afford these special protections does not mean that it has preempted the courts from exercising their traditional role of fashioning appropriate tort remedies for various kinds of intentionally injurious conduct.

In sum, the above cited cases show that an intentional breach of contract may be found to be tortious when the breaching party exhibits an extreme disregard for the contractual rights of the other party, either knowingly harming the vital interests of a promisee so as to create substantial mental distress or personal hardship, or else employing coercion or dishonesty to cause the promisee to forego its contractual rights. These cases illustrate the recognition by a number of jurisdictions that an intentional breach of contract outside the insurance context, and not accompanied by any conventional tortious behavior such as promissory fraud, may nonetheless be deemed tortious when accompanied by these kinds of aggravating circumstances.

With this in mind, I next reconsider the *Seaman's* case.

II.

. . . .

Seaman's was correct, in my view, in refusing to rely on the general breach of the covenant of good faith and fair dealing as a justification for imposing tort remedies, and instead seeking to identify specific practices used by Standard that violated "accepted notions of business ethics." *Seaman's* wisely recognized that courts do not have to choose between the wholesale transformation of a breach of the implied good faith covenant into a tort and the complete refusal to recognize a cause of action for tortious breach of contract. In retrospect, however, *Seaman's* holding appears to be both overly broad and overly narrow. It was overly narrow because, as numerous authorities cited by the majority point out, there is no logical reason to distinguish between the tort of "bad faith denial of the existence of a contract" and "bad faith denial of liability under a contract." The former is but a subspecies of the latter. Both forms of bad faith are equally reprehensible on the defendant's part and equally injurious to plaintiff.

Seaman's was overly broad because, for a number of reasons, it appears to have been unwise to impose tort liability for *all* breaches that involve bad faith denial of a contract or liability under the contract. Although the bad faith denial of contractual liability may be ethically inexcusable, we should hesitate to categorically impose tort liability on such activity for fear it may overly deter legitimate activities that we wish to permit or encourage. Specifically, the bad faith denial of the existence of a contract consists of two actions on the defendant's part that do not, taken individually, give rise to tort liability: First, the defendant intentionally breaches its contract. As discussed above, because of our notions of efficient breach and the freedom of the marketplace, we have generally not considered an intentional breach tortious.

Second, the defendant asserts a bad faith defense to liability under the contract—or, more precisely, *threatens* to assert such a defense. We have consistently refused to recognize a tort of "malicious defense" that would be equivalent to that of malicious prosecution. The refusal to recognize such a tort "protect[s] the right of a defendant, involuntarily haled into court, to conduct a vigorous defense." (*Bertero v. National General Corp.* (1974) 529 P.2d 608.) Instead, the Legislature has fashioned a more limited punishment to fit the "crime" of bad faith defense to a civil action: the awarding of attorney fees and other reasonable expenses incurred by a party to litigation as the result of another's bad faith actions "that are frivolous or solely intended to cause unnecessary delay." (Code Civ.Proc., § 128.5, subd. (a).) So too, the proper remedy to deter intentional breaches that are combined with bad faith denials of liability is to consistently award attorney fees to the plaintiffs as a sanction. But if a bad faith defense is not a tortious act, then the threat of such defense, as occurred in *Seaman's,* also cannot be considered tortious.

Seaman's was nonetheless correctly decided, in my view, on narrower grounds than bad faith denial of the contract's existence. As discussed above, a number of cases allow tort damages for an intentional breach which the breaching party knows will probably result in significant emotional distress or personal hardship. In the commercial sphere, we do not as a rule permit such recovery for personal distress—the frustrations that attend breached contracts, unreliable suppliers, and the like are part of the realities of commerce. Society expects the business enterprise to go to the marketplace to seek substitutes to mitigate its losses, and to seek contract damages for those losses that cannot be mitigated. But there are some commercial cases in which the harm intentionally inflicted on an enterprise cannot be mitigated, and in which ordinary contract damages are insufficient compensation. *Seaman's* is such a case. In *Seaman's,* because of the unusual combination of market forces and government regulation set in motion by the 1973 oil embargo, Standard's conduct had a significance beyond the ordinary breach: its practical effect was to shut *Seaman's* out of the oil market entirely, forcing it out of business. In other words, Standard intentionally breached its contract with Seaman's with the knowledge that the breach would result in Seaman's demise. Having thus breached its contract with blithe disregard for the severe and, under these rare circumstances, unmitigatable injury it caused Seaman's, Standard was justly subject to tort damages.

In sum, I would permit an action for tortious breach of contract in a commercial setting when a party intentionally breaches a contractual obligation with neither probable cause nor belief that the obligation does *not* exist, *and* when the party intends or knows that the breach will result in severe consequential damages to the other party that are not readily subject to mitigation, and such harm in fact occurs. . . . A breach should not be considered tortious if the court determines that it was justified by avoidance of some substantial, unforeseen cost on the part of the breaching party, even if such cost does not excuse that party's nonperformance. Nor should a tortious breach under these circumstances be recognized if it is clear that the party suffering the harm voluntarily accepted that risk under the contract. But the intentional or knowing infliction of severe consequential damages on a business enterprise through the unjustified, bad faith breach of a contract is reprehensible and costly both for the party suffering the breach and for society as a whole, and is therefore appropriately sanctioned through the tort system.

III.

The present case, on the other hand, is essentially a billing dispute between two commercial entities. Belcher Oil Company claimed, apparently in bad faith and without probable cause, that it had no contractual agreement with Freeman & Mills. That is, Belcher Oil not only intentionally breached its contract, but then asserted a bad faith defense to its liability. As explained above, the solution which the Legislature has devised for this kind of transgression is the awarding of the other party's attorney fees, and this is precisely what occurred—Freeman & Mills was awarded $212,891 in attorney fees pursuant to Code of Civil Procedure sections 128.5 and 2033, subdivision (c). To permit the award of punitive damages in addition to this sum would upset the legislative balance established in the litigation sanctions statutes and make tortious actions—intentional breach of contract and the assertion of a bad faith defense—which we have consistently held not to be tortious.

On this basis, I concur in the majority's disposition in favor of Belcher Oil on the bad faith denial of contract cause of action.

NOTES & QUESTIONS

(1) Why did the *Freeman & Mills* court overrule *Seaman's*? Do you agree with Justice Mosk that, instead of repudiating the *Seaman's* tort, it would have been preferable to limit the tort to "when a party intentionally breaches a contractual obligation with neither probable cause nor belief that the obligation does *not* exist, *and* when the party intends or knows that the breach will result in severe consequential damages to the other party that are not readily subject to mitigation, and such harm in fact occurs"?

(2)   3 DAN B. DOBBS ET AL., THE LAW OF TORTS § 700, at 765 (2d ed. 2011):

> . . . . For a brief period, several cases supported tort liability for bad faith breach of contract. Tort liability for bad faith breach is still possible in certain insurance bad faith cases, but the tort approach to bad faith breach in ordinary commercial contracts has now been forsaken in the states that adopted it. The general rule today is that the defendant who is guilty of a bad faith breach of contract—that is, guilty of breaching the implied covenant of good faith and fair dealing—is generally liable only in contract, not in tort.

CHAPTER 6

THE ECONOMIC LOSS RULE (II)

■ ■ ■

In Chapter 1, the "stranger" strand of the economic loss rule was discussed. As between parties lacking a contractual relationship, a plaintiff cannot recover for unintentionally caused economic loss in the absence of personal injury to the plaintiff or damage to the plaintiff's property. Business torts usually avoid the application of this strand of the economic loss rule.

This Chapter discusses a different fact pattern where the parties to a tort action are also in a contractual relationship. In such "nonstranger" cases, is a tort recovery for pure economic loss permissible? As in the stranger context, do business torts avoid the application of any restrictive doctrine? These questions will be discussed in the materials below.

TOWN OF ALMA v. AZCO CONSTRUCTION, INC.
10 P.3d 1256 (Colo. 2000)

JUSTICE RICE delivered the Opinion of the Court.

We issued a writ of certiorari to review the court of appeals' judgment in *Town of Alma v. AZCO Constr., Inc.*, 985 P.2d 56 (Colo.App.1999). The Town of Alma, joined by several individual town residents, filed suit against AZCO Construction, Inc. ("AZCO"), asserting claims for breach of contract, breach of the implied warranty of sound workmanship, and negligence. . . .

I. FACTS AND PROCEDURAL HISTORY

Petitioners' amended complaint alleged the following facts. On October 28, 1992, the town and AZCO entered into a contract for the construction of improvements to Petitioners' water distribution system. The contract called for AZCO to install new water mains, and to tie those water mains to existing water service lines which served residential properties in the town. Pursuant to the contract, AZCO agreed to furnish all labor, equipment, and materials for the connection of the existing water service lines with the new water mains. The contract contained two separate warranty provisions. Section 29.1 of the contract, titled "GUARANTEE," provided, "[AZCO] shall guarantee all materials and equipment furnished and WORK performed for a period of one (1) year from the date of SUBSTANTIAL COMPLETION. [AZCO] warrants and guarantees . . . that the completed system is free from all defects due to faulty materials or workmanship. . . ." In addition, section 3.3.1 of the "Special Conditions" attached to the contract, titled "MAINTENANCE AND GUARANTY," provided, "[AZCO] hereby guarantees that the entire work constructed by [it] under the contract will fully meet all requirements of the contract as to quality of workmanship and materials. . . . [AZCO] hereby agrees to make at [its] own expense, any repairs or replacement made necessary by defects in materials or workmanship supplied by [it] that become evident within one year after the date of final payment. . . ."

In 1993, AZCO installed 115 flared fittings for the water service line connections. In June 1995, Petitioners discovered leaks in three water service line connections that AZCO installed pursuant to the contract. AZCO repaired those three leaks under the one-year warranty provision of the contract. In November 1995 and June 1996, additional leaks in water service line connections were discovered but AZCO refused to repair these leaks on the basis that the one-year warranty provision had expired. The leaks were repaired at the expense of individual town residents.

Petitioners filed suit against AZCO on November 27, 1996, asserting claims for breach of contract, breach of the implied warranty of sound workmanship, negligence per se, and negligence. Two more leaks were discovered in June 1997, after Petitioners had filed their original complaint against AZCO, and AZCO again refused to repair the leaks. Petitioners subsequently filed an amended complaint seeking damages for the cost to repair or replace every water service line connection installed or repaired by AZCO.

Petitioners voluntarily dismissed their negligence per se claim and AZCO moved to dismiss the breach of implied warranty of sound workmanship and negligence claims. The trial court granted AZCO's motion to dismiss these claims and the case proceeded to trial on the breach of contract claim only, with the jury returning a verdict for AZCO on this claim. . . .

Petitioners appealed the trial court's dismissal of its breach of implied warranty of sound workmanship and negligence claims. . . . The court of appeals affirmed the trial court's dismissal of Petitioners' claims. . . . In affirming the dismissal of Petitioners' negligence claim, the court of appeals relied on the economic loss rule and stated that "[t]o hold otherwise would permit the non-breaching party to avoid the contractual limitation of remedy." *Town of Alma*, 985 P.2d at 57.

We granted certiorari to review the dismissal of Petitioners' negligence claim. . . .

II. ANALYSIS

This case, along with *Grynberg v. Agri Tech, Inc.*, 10 P.3d 1267 (Colo. 2000), presents an opportunity for us to address the status of the economic loss rule in Colorado. The rule has been applied by our court of appeals in various contexts to bar tort claims. As this is a matter of first impression, our analysis encompasses an examination of the development of the rule in other jurisdictions, as well as a discussion of the principles and rationale underlying the rule.

. . . .

B. Origins of the Economic Loss Rule

Broadly speaking, the economic loss rule is intended to maintain the boundary between contract law and tort law. Although these two areas of law traditionally occupy discrete spheres of legal practice, the distinction between the two blurs. This becomes problematic when, as in this case, a commercial buyer seeks to use a tort theory to recover damages for a defective product.

The economic loss rule emerged largely from the development of products liability jurisprudence. As courts abandoned the requirement for privity in contract, the doctrine of strict liability in warranty developed with the leading case of *Henningsen v. Bloomfield Motors, Inc.*, 32 N.J. 358, 161 A.2d 69 (1960). The *Henningsen* court held that an automobile manufacturer and a dealer were liable to the automobile purchaser's wife, who was driving the car when she was injured, on a theory of implied warranty of safety. *See id.* at 84. The *Henningsen* decision was quickly followed by a flood of cases from other jurisdictions extending the implied warranty theory to many other products. *See* W. Page Keeton et al., *Prosser and Keeton on the Law of Torts* § 97, at 690 (5th ed.1984) [hereinafter *Prosser and Keeton*]. The use of the implied warranty theory, however, generated numerous difficulties as courts struggled to apply contract rules to implied warranty cases. Courts proceeded on the assumption that contract rules must apply because these were "warranty" actions, though there was often no contract involved. *See id.* at 690–91.

In response to the difficulties of attempting to apply contract rules to products liability cases in the absence of a contract, courts moved away from the implied warranty theory of recovery and adopted a strict liability in tort theory. A tort theory based on the dangerousness of conduct was considered more appropriate and more adaptable than a contract theory because the policy reasons courts were supplying to justify the imposition of strict liability go far beyond any conventional contract notions. *See id.* at 692. The California Supreme Court led the way with its decision in *Greenman v. Yuba Power Products, Inc.*, 377 P.2d 897, 900 (1963) (holding a manufacturer strictly liable in tort for injury to plaintiff caused by defective power tool), and the American Law Institute followed with the final adoption of section 402A[6] of the Second Restatement of Torts the following year. *See id.* at 694.

As courts made the shift to employing tort law for these products liability cases, a need developed to prevent tort law from "swallowing" the law of contracts. After paving the road to allow tort theories to proceed in products liability cases, the California Supreme Court, in *Seely v. White Motor Co.,* 403 P.2d 145 (1965), was the first to adopt the economic loss rule and to recognize the importance of limiting the use of tort theories. In *Seely,* the plaintiff purchased a truck manufactured by White Motor Company ("White") for use in his business and the truck subsequently overturned when the brakes failed. The plaintiff was not injured but he sued White for damages for the repair of the truck as well as damages to recover the purchase price and the lost profits in his business. The California Supreme Court refused to allow the plaintiff to use a strict liability in tort theory to recover damages for the purchase price and for the profits lost in his business. The court explained the rationale for limiting tort recovery in these situations:

> The distinction that the law has drawn between tort recovery for physical injuries and warranty recovery for economic loss is not arbitrary and does not rest on the "luck" of one plaintiff in having an accident causing physical injury. The distinction rests, rather, on an understanding of the nature of the responsibility a manufacturer must undertake in distributing his products. He can appropriately be held liable for physical injuries caused by defects by requiring his goods to match a standard of safety in terms of conditions that create unreasonable risks of harm. He cannot be held liable for the level of performance of his products in the consumer's business unless he agrees that the product was designed to meet the consumer's demands. A consumer should not be charged at the will of the manufacturer with bearing the risk of physical injury when he buys a product on the market. He can, however, be fairly charged with the risk that the product

---

[6]   Section 402A provides:

§ 402A SPECIAL LIABILITY OF SELLER OF PRODUCT FOR PHYSICAL HARM TO USER OR CONSUMER

(1) One who sells any product in a defective condition unreasonably dangerous to the user or consumer or to his property is subject to liability for physical harm thereby caused to the ultimate user or consumer, or to his property, if

    (a) the seller is engaged in the business of selling such a product, and

    (b) it is expected to and does reach the user or consumer without substantial change in the condition in which it is sold.

(2) The rule stated in Subsection (1) applies although

    (a) the seller has exercised all possible care in the preparation and sale of his product, and

    (b) the user or consumer has not bought the product from or entered into any contractual relation with the seller.

will not match his economic expectations unless the manufacturer agrees that it will. *Even in actions for negligence, a manufacturer's liability is limited to damages for physical injuries and there is no recovery for economic loss alone.*

Seely, 403 P.2d at 151 (emphasis added). From this final statement, the economic loss rule was born.

. . . .

Subsequent to the *Seely* decision, many jurisdictions adopted a form of the economic loss rule. The United States Supreme Court adopted a version of the rule in *East River Steamship Corp. v. Transamerica Delaval, Inc.*, 476 U.S. 858, 106 S.Ct. 2295, 90 L.Ed.2d 865 (1986). In *East River*, charter operators of oil supertankers sued the manufacturer of turbines used for ship propulsion after the turbines malfunctioned, seeking damages for the cost of repairing the turbines and for income lost while the ships were out of service. The suit originally contained both contract and tort claims but the contract claims were subsequently dropped because of a statute of limitations defense, leaving only the tort claims. The Court held that although admiralty law incorporated products liability principles, there was no cause of action in tort, under either negligence or strict liability, for damage caused when a product malfunctions and causes purely economic loss through damage to the product itself. In reaching its holding, the Court cited *Seely* and discussed the factors weighing against tort liability:

> When a product injures only itself the reasons for imposing a tort duty are weak and those for leaving the party to its contractual remedies are strong. . . . Losses like these can be insured [through warranties]. . . . The increased cost to the public that would result from holding a manufacturer liable in tort for injury to the product itself is not justified.

Id. at 871–72. The Court continued by explaining how contract law is designed to account for the costs and risks of a product's nonperformance:

> Contract law, and the law of warranty in particular, is well suited to commercial controversies of the sort involved in this case because the parties may set the terms of their own agreements. The manufacturer can restrict its liability, within limits, by disclaiming warranties or limiting remedies. In exchange, the purchaser pays less for the product. Since a commercial situation generally does not involve large disparities in bargaining power, we see no reason to intrude into the parties' allocation of the risk.

Id. at 872–73. As discussed in more detail below, this principle that parties must be able to confidently allocate their risks and costs in a bargaining situation underlies the necessity for the economic loss rule.

    . . . .

C. Rationale Underlying the Economic Loss Rule

Although originally born from products liability law, the application of the economic loss rule is broader, because it serves to maintain a distinction between contract and tort law. The essential difference between a tort obligation and a contract obligation is the source of the duties of the parties.

Tort obligations generally arise from duties imposed by law. Tort law is designed to protect all citizens from the risk of physical harm to their persons or to their property. These duties are imposed by law without regard to any agreement or contract.

In contrast, contract obligations arise from promises made between parties. Contract law is intended to enforce the expectancy interests created by the parties' promises so that they can allocate risks and costs during their bargaining. Limiting tort liability when a contract exists between parties is appropriate because a product's potential nonperformance can be adequately addressed by rational economic actors bargaining at arms length to shape the terms of the contract. For example, a buyer may demand additional warranties on a product while agreeing to pay a higher price, or the same buyer may choose to assume a higher level of risk that a product will not perform properly by accepting a more limited warranty in exchange for a lower product price. Limiting the availability of tort remedies in these situations holds parties to the terms of their bargain. In this way, the law serves to encourage parties to confidently allocate risks and costs during their bargaining without fear that unanticipated liability may arise in the future, effectively negating the parties' efforts to build these cost considerations into the contract. The economic loss rule thus serves to ensure predictability in commercial transactions.

The key to determining the availability of a contract or tort action lies in determining the source of the duty that forms the basis of the action.[8] We find the following discussion by the South Carolina Supreme Court informative:

> The question, thus, is not whether the damages are physical or economic. Rather the question of whether the plaintiff may maintain an action in tort for purely economic loss turns on the

---

[8]   As such, we believe that a more accurate designation of what is commonly termed the "economic loss rule" would be the "independent duty rule." However, for the sake of consistency, we will continue to refer to it as the economic loss rule.

determination of the source of the duty [the] plaintiff claims the defendant owed. A breach of a duty which arises under the provisions of a contract between the parties must be redressed under contract, and a tort action will not lie. A breach of a duty *arising independently* of any contract duties between the parties, however, may support a tort action.

Tommy L. Griffin Plumbing & Heating Co. v. Jordan, Jones & Goulding, Inc., 463 S.E.2d 85, 88 (1995) (emphasis added).

Determining when a contract action will lie and when a tort action will lie requires maintaining this distinction in the sources of the respective obligations. The phrase "economic loss rule"[9] necessarily implies that the focus of the inquiry under its analysis is on the type of damages suffered by the aggrieved party. However, the relationship between the type of damages suffered and the availability of a tort action is inexact at best. Examining the type of damages suffered may assist in determining the source of the duty underlying the action (e.g., most actions for lost profits are based on breaches of contractual duties while most actions involving physical injuries to persons are based on common law duties of care). However, some torts are expressly designed to remedy pure economic loss (e.g., professional negligence, fraud, and breach of fiduciary duty). It is here that substantial confusion arises from the use of the term "economic loss rule."

This confusion can be avoided, however, by maintaining the focus on the source of the duty alleged to have been violated. For example, we have recognized that some special relationships by their nature automatically trigger an independent duty of care that supports a tort action even when the parties have entered into a contractual relationship. *See, e.g., Bebo Constr. Co. v. Mattox & O'Brien, P.C.*, 990 P.2d 78, 83 (Colo.1999) (attorney-client relationship creates independent duty of care); *Greenberg v. Perkins*, 845 P.2d 530, 534 (Colo.1993) (physician-patient relationship creates independent duty of care, as does physician's independent medical examination of non-patient); *Farmers Group, Inc. v. Trimble*, 691 P.2d 1138, 1141–42 (Colo.1984) (quasi-fiduciary nature of insurer-insured relationship creates independent duty of care). We have also recognized that certain common law claims that sound in tort and are expressly designed to remedy economic loss may exist independent of a breach of contract claim. *See Brody v. Bock*, 897 P.2d 769, 776 (Colo.1995) (common law fraud claim is based on violation of a duty independent of contract); *Keller v. A.O. Smith Harvestore Prods., Inc.*, 819 P.2d 69, 73 (Colo.1991) (negligent misrepresentation is a tort claim based "not on principles of contractual obligation but on principles of duty and reasonable conduct.").

---

[9]   While the economic loss rule serves today to maintain the distinction between contract and tort law, its continued designation as the "economic loss" rule is merely an unfortunate carry-over from its origins in products liability jurisprudence.

In these situations where we have recognized the existence of a duty *independent* of any contractual obligations, the economic loss rule has no application and does not bar a plaintiff's tort claim because the claim is based on a recognized independent duty of care and thus does not fall within the scope of the rule.

D.   A Workable Economic Loss Rule: The Focus on Duty

We believe the principles underlying the rule, as discussed above, serve an important role and should be observed and applied in Colorado jurisprudence.[11] In recognition of its importance, we undertake here to formulate its content.

We have previously recognized a court's duty to determine, at the outset of a lawsuit, the type of duty that has allegedly been breached. In *Taco Bell v. Lannon* we described the court's function as such:

> The question of whether a defendant owes a plaintiff a duty to act to avoid injury is a question of law to be determined by the court. The court determines, as a matter of law, the existence and scope of the duty[;] that is, whether the plaintiff's interest that has been infringed by the conduct of the defendant is entitled to legal protection.

744 P.2d 43, 46 (Colo.1987) (internal quotation marks omitted, citations omitted).

Consistent with this duty analysis, we now expressly adopt the economic loss rule. We hold that a party suffering only economic loss from the breach of an express or implied contractual duty may not assert a tort claim for such a breach absent an independent duty of care under tort law.[12] Economic loss is defined generally as damages other than physical harm to persons or property.

---

[11] A trial judge observed the following after presiding over a case involving duplicative contract and tort claims:

> Ambiguity in the law breeds a multiplicity of claims, which breeds a geometrically increased multiplicity of motions, which results in fees and expenses disproportionate to the amount in controversy. . . . The distinction between tort and contract is important. The distinction determines the measure of damages, the applicable statute of limitations and whether procedural prerequisites such as certificates of review must be followed.

Stephen Phillips, *Tort or Contract: A History of Ambiguity and Uncertainty,* 21 The Colorado Lawyer 241, 241 (1992); *see also Prosser and Keeton* § 92, at 655 ("The availability of both kinds of liability for precisely the same kind of harm has brought about confusion and unnecessary complexity. It is to be hoped that eventually the availability of both theories tort and contract for the same kind of loss . . . will be reduced in order to simplify the law and reduce the costs of litigation.").

[12] The scope of this rule includes third-party contract beneficiaries who may have a cause of action for breach of contractual duties. "A basic rule of contract law is that 'a person not a party to an express contract may bring an action on such contract if the parties to the agreement intended to benefit the non-party, provided that the benefit claim is a direct and not merely an incidental benefit of the contract.' " *Jefferson County Sch. Dist. No. R–1 v. Shorey,* 826 P.2d 830, 843 (Colo.1992) (*quoting E.B. Roberts Constr. Co. v. Concrete Contractors, Inc.,* 704 P.2d 859, 865

E. Application of the Rule

Turning to the facts before us, the contract in the instant case expressly assigned a duty of care to AZCO in the installation of the water system [and] it was this contractual duty that AZCO allegedly breached. The provisions contained within the contract demonstrate that AZCO guaranteed its workmanship when it installed the water system. Section 29.1 of the Contract, titled "GUARANTEE," provided, "[AZCO] shall guarantee all materials and equipment furnished *and WORK performed* for a period of one (1) year. . . . [AZCO] warrants and guarantees . . . that the completed system is free from all defects due to faulty materials *or workmanship*." (Emphasis added.) In addition, section 3.3.1 of the "Special Conditions" attached to the contract, titled "MAINTENANCE AND GUARANTY," provided, "[AZCO] hereby guarantees that the entire work constructed by [it] under the contract will fully meet all requirements of the contract as to *quality of workmanship* and materials. . . ." (Emphasis added.) These contractual provisions demonstrate that AZCO expressly assumed the duty to guarantee its quality of workmanship and its materials when it undertook to install the water system. As such, Petitioners have failed to demonstrate that AZCO breached any duty independent of its contractual obligations.

Moreover, the [Petitioners] are only seeking damages for the cost of repair and replacement of the water lines that were the subject of the contract. Damages for the cost of repair and replacement of property that were the subject of the contract constitute economic loss damages that must be supported by an independent duty of care to be recoverable in a negligence action. As there is no independent duty to support Petitioners' negligence claim, the economic loss rule bars this claim. *See Sensenbrenner v. Rust, Orling & Neale, Architects, Inc.,* 236 Va. 419, 374 S.E.2d 55, 58 (1988) ("The effect of the failure of the substandard parts to meet the bargained-for level of quality was to cause a diminution in the value of the whole, measured by the cost of repair. This is a purely economic loss, for which the law of contracts provides the sole remedy.").

. . . .

III. CONCLUSION

In sum, we hold that the economic loss rule bars Petitioners' negligence claim against AZCO. . . . Therefore, we affirm the judgment of the court of appeals. . . .

(Colo.1985)). The individual residents alleged in the amended complaint: "Plaintiffs Shanks, Johnson, McManus, Greising, Davis and Roberts were intended to benefit directly from the improvement to the water system in the Town of Alma." In their briefs to us they argue that they may maintain their suit for negligence and as third-party beneficiaries at the same time to recover for their economic loss. We hold that the economic loss rule applies here to prohibit their duplicate claims under tort and contract theories.

NOTES & QUESTIONS

(1)   As the case discusses, the town of Alma had entered into a contract with AZCO for the construction of improvements to Alma's water distribution system. What is problematic about allowing Alma to assert a negligence claim against AZCO for AZCO's allegedly faulty work?

(2)   What "rule" does the court adopt for determining whether contractual parties will be permitted to assert tort claims against one another? How does this rule alleviate the problems that you identified in the prior note?

(3)   Why does Alma's negligence claim fail under the court's rule? Given that several water service line connections installed by AZCO were leaking, doesn't the dispute fall outside of the scope of the rule? *See* RESTATEMENT (THIRD) OF TORTS: LIABILITY FOR ECONOMIC HARM § 2 & cmt. b (Tentative Draft No. 1, Apr. 4, 2012).

(4)   Some courts determine whether contractual parties will be permitted to assert tort claims against one another based upon a "nature of the injury" test. For example, in *Jim Walter Homes v. Reed*, 711 S.W.2d 617 (Tex. 1986), the Supreme Court of Texas observed:

> The acts of a party may breach duties in tort or contract alone or simultaneously in both. The nature of the injury most often determines which duty or duties are breached. When the injury is only the economic loss to the subject of a contract itself the action sounds in contract alone. The Reeds' injury was that the house they were promised and paid for was not the house they received. This can only be characterized as a breach of contract. . . .

Id. at 618. Under this test, how would the dispute in *Town of Alma* have been resolved?

(5)   Are there problems with using a "nature of the injury" test to determine whether contractual parties can assert tort claims against one another? Consider a seller's contractual representation that a house is free of termites. At the time the representation is made, the seller knows that it is false. Under the test in *Jim Walter Homes*, can the buyer maintain a fraud action against the seller?

FORMOSA PLASTICS CORP. V. PRESIDIO ENGINEERS & CONTRACTORS, INC.

960 S.W.2d 41 (Tex. 1998)

ABBOTT, JUSTICE, delivered the opinion of the Court, in which PHILLIPS, CHIEF JUSTICE, GONZALEZ, HECHT, ENOCH, OWEN AND HANKINSON, JUSTICES, join.

. . . .

I

In 1989, Formosa Plastics Corporation began a large construction "expansion project" at its facility in Point Comfort, Texas. Presidio Engineers and Contractors, Inc. received an "Invitation to Bid" from Formosa on that part of the project requiring the construction of 300 concrete foundations. The invitation was accompanied by a bid package containing technical drawings, specifications, general information, and a sample contract. The bid package also contained certain representations about the foundation job. These representations included that (1) Presidio would arrange and be responsible for the scheduling, ordering, and delivery of all materials, including those paid for by Formosa; (2) work was to progress continually from commencement to completion; and (3) the job was scheduled to commence on July 16, 1990, and be completed 90 days later, on October 15, 1990.

Presidio's president, Bob Burnette, testified that he relied on these representations in preparing Presidio's bid. Because the bid package provided that the contractor would be responsible for all weather and other unknown delays, he added another 30 days to his estimate of the job's scheduled completion date. He submitted a bid on behalf of Presidio in the amount of $600,000. Because Presidio submitted the lowest bid, Formosa awarded Presidio the contract.

The job was not completed in 120 days. Rather, the job took over eight months to complete, more than twice Burnette's estimate and almost three times the scheduled time provided in the bid package. The delays caused Presidio to incur substantial additional costs that were not anticipated when Presidio submitted its bid.

Presidio asserted a claim under paragraph 17 of the parties' contract, which provided that Formosa was liable for all delay damages within the "control of the owner." Formosa countered that, while it may have been liable for some of the delays, it was not responsible for all of the delays and losses asserted by Presidio. Because the parties were not able to resolve their dispute, Presidio sued Formosa for breach of contract. . . . Presidio also brought fraudulent inducement of contract and fraudulent performance of contract claims based on representations made by Formosa that Presidio discovered were false after commencing performance of the contract. Formosa counterclaimed for breach of contract, urging that Presidio had not properly completed some of its work.

Presidio presented evidence to the jury that Formosa had an intentional, premeditated scheme to defraud the contractors working on its expansion project. Under this scheme, Formosa enticed contractors to make low bids by making misrepresentations in the bid package regarding scheduling, delivery of materials, and responsibility for delay damages. Jack Lin, the director of Formosa's civil department, admitted that Formosa acted deceptively by representing in the bid package that the contractors would have the ability to schedule the delivery of concrete when in truth Formosa had secretly decided to set up its own delivery schedule in order to save money. Formosa also scheduled multiple contractors, doing mutually exclusive work, to be in the same area at the same time. For instance, Formosa scheduled another contractor to install underground pipe in Presidio's work area at the same time that Presidio was supposed to be pouring foundations. Thomas Pena, Formosa's inspector, admitted that Formosa knew that contractors would be working right on top of each other, but this information was not passed on to the contractors. Of course, once the contractors were on the job, they would realize that, due to such unexpected delays caused by Formosa, their bids were inadequate. But when the contractors requested delay damages under the contract, Formosa would rely on its superior economic position and offer the contractors far less than the full and fair value of the delay damages. In fact, Ron Robichaux, head of Formosa's contract administration division, testified that Formosa, in an effort to lower costs, would utilize its economic superiority to string contractors along and force them to settle. Robichaux added that "if [a contractor] continued to complain then [Formosa] would take the contract from him and make sure he loses his money." Under this scheme, Formosa allegedly stood to save millions of dollars on its $1.5 billion expansion project.

The jury found that Formosa defrauded Presidio and awarded Presidio $1.5 million. . . . Based on its findings that Formosa's fraud . . . [was] done willfully, wantonly, intentionally, or with conscious indifference to the rights of Presidio, the jury further awarded Presidio $10 million as exemplary damages. Additionally, the jury found that Formosa breached its contract with Presidio, causing $1.267 million in damages. On the other hand, the jury also concluded that Presidio did not fully comply with the contract, causing Formosa $107,000 in damages.

The trial court suggested a remittitur reducing the tort damages to $700,000 and the contract damages to $467,000, which Presidio accepted. Based on Presidio's election to recover tort rather than contract damages, the trial court rendered a judgment in favor of Presidio for $700,000 in actual damages, $10 million in punitive damages, prejudgment interest, attorney's fees, and costs. The damages caused by Presidio's breach of contract were offset against the judgment.

Formosa appealed the judgment to the court of appeals, which affirmed the judgment of the trial court. We granted Formosa's application for writ of error to consider, among other things, whether Presidio has a viable fraud claim when it suffered only economic losses related to the performance and subject matter of the parties' contract. . . . We conclude that . . . Presidio has a viable fraud claim. . . .

II

Formosa asserts that Presidio's fraud claim cannot be maintained because "Presidio's losses were purely economic losses related to performance and the subject matter of the contract." Formosa contends that our decision in *Southwestern Bell Telephone Co. v. DeLanney,* 809 S.W.2d 493 (Tex.1991), compels us to examine the substance of Presidio's tort claim to determine whether the claim is, in reality, a re-packaged breach of contract claim. Formosa urges that, in making this determination, we should analyze the nature of the alleged injury, the source of the breached duty, and whether the loss or risk of loss is contractually contemplated by the parties. Presidio counters that a *DeLanney*-type analysis does not apply to fraud claims. For the reasons discussed below, we agree with Presidio.

A

Over the last fifty years, this Court has analyzed the distinction between torts and contracts from two different perspectives. At first, we merely analyzed the source of the duty in determining whether an action sounded in tort or contract. For instance, in *International Printing Pressmen & Assistants' Union v. Smith,* 198 S.W.2d 729, 735 (1946), this Court held that " 'an action in contract is for the breach of a duty arising out of a contract either express or implied, while an action in tort is for a breach of duty imposed by law.' " *Id.* (quoting 1 C.J.S. *Actions* § 44).

Later, we overlaid an analysis of the nature of the remedy sought by the plaintiff. In *Jim Walter Homes, Inc. v. Reed,* 711 S.W.2d 617 (Tex.1986), we recognized that, while the contractual relationship of the parties could create duties under both contract law and tort law, the "nature of the injury most often determines which duty or duties are breached. When the injury is only the economic loss to the subject of a contract itself, the action sounds in contract alone." *Id.* at 618. Because a mere breach of contract cannot support recovery of exemplary damages, and because the plaintiffs did not "prove a distinct tortious injury with actual damages," we rendered judgment that the plaintiffs take nothing on their exemplary damages claim. *Id.*

We analyzed both the source of the duty and the nature of the remedy in *DeLanney*. DeLanney asserted that Bell was negligent in failing to publish his Yellow Pages advertisement as promised. The trial court rendered judgment for DeLanney, and the court of appeals affirmed. This Court, however, held that the claim sounded in contract, not negligence, and accordingly rendered judgment in favor of Bell. We provided the following guidelines on distinguishing contract and tort causes of action:

> If the defendant's conduct—such as negligently burning down a house—would give rise to liability independent of the fact that a contract exists between the parties, the plaintiff's claim may also sound in tort. Conversely, if the defendant's conduct—such as failing to publish an advertisement—would give rise to liability only because it breaches the parties' agreement, the plaintiff's claim ordinarily sounds only in contract. In determining whether the plaintiff may recover on a tort theory, it is also instructive to examine the nature of the plaintiff's loss. When the only loss or damage is to the subject matter of the contract, the plaintiff's action is ordinarily on the contract.

DeLanney, 809 S.W.2d at 494. In applying these guidelines, we first determined that Bell's duty to publish DeLanney's advertisement arose solely from the contract. We then concluded that DeLanney's damages, lost profits, were only for the economic loss caused by Bell's failure to perform the contract. Thus, while DeLanney pleaded his action as one in negligence, he clearly sought to recover the benefit of his bargain with Bell such that Bell's failure to publish the advertisement was not a tort.

Most recently, in *Crawford v. Ace Sign, Inc.*, 917 S.W.2d 12, 13–14 (Tex.1996), we considered the intersection of the Deceptive Trade Practices Act and contract law. Ace Sign sued Bell for omission of a yellow pages advertisement, alleging negligence, DTPA misrepresentation, and breach of contract. Bell stipulated the contract breach, and was granted summary judgment on Ace Sign's DTPA and negligence claims. The court of appeals reversed the trial court's judgment on the DTPA claim, but this Court then reversed the court of appeals. We noted that, under *DeLanney*, we were to consider "both the source of the defendant's duty to act (whether it arose solely out of the contract or from some common-law duty) and the nature of the remedy sought by the plaintiff." *Id.* at 12. We then examined the relationship of the DTPA and contract law, concluding that an allegation of mere breach of contract, without more, does not violate the DTPA. We held that, because the alleged representations of Bell were simply representations that it would fulfill its contractual duty to publish the advertisement, and a mere failure to later perform a promise does not constitute misrepresentation, Crawford could only recover in contract.

B

Several appellate courts have considered the application of our decisions in *DeLanney* and *Reed* to fraudulent inducement claims. Some of these courts have concluded that these decisions mandate that tort damages are not recoverable for a fraudulent inducement claim unless the plaintiff suffers an injury that is distinct, separate, and independent from the economic losses recoverable under a breach of contract claim. The United States Court of Appeals for the Fifth Circuit has also adopted this view of Texas law. Other Texas appellate decisions, however, have rejected the application of *DeLanney* and *Reed* to preclude the recovery of tort damages for fraudulent inducement claims.

We too reject the application of *DeLanney* to preclude tort damages in fraud cases. Texas law has long imposed a duty to abstain from inducing another to enter into a contract through the use of fraudulent misrepresentations. As a rule, a party is not bound by a contract procured by fraud. Moreover, it is well established that the legal duty not to fraudulently procure a contract is separate and independent from the duties established by the contract itself. *See* [*Dallas Farm Mach. Co. v. Reaves*, 307 S.W.2d 233, 239 (1957)] (" '[T]he law long ago abandoned the position that a contract must be held sacred regardless of the fraud of one of the parties in procuring it.' ") (quoting *Bates v. Southgate*, 308 Mass. 170, 31 N.E.2d 551, 558 (1941)).

This Court has also repeatedly recognized that a fraud claim can be based on a promise made with no intention of performing, irrespective of whether the promise is later subsumed within a contract. For example, in *Crim Truck & Tractor Co. v. Navistar Int'l Transp. Corp.*, 823 S.W.2d 591, 597 (Tex.1992), we noted: "As a general rule, the failure to perform the terms of a contract is a breach of contract, not a tort. However, when one party enters into a contract with no intention of performing, that misrepresentation may give rise to an action in fraud." Similarly, in *Spoljaric v. Percival Tours, Inc.*, 708 S.W.2d 432, 434 (Tex.1986), we held that a fraud claim could be maintained, under the particular facts of that case, for the breach of an oral agreement to pay a bonus because a "promise to do an act in the future is actionable fraud when made with the intention, design and purpose of deceiving, and with no intention of performing the act."

Our prior decisions also clearly establish that tort damages are not precluded simply because a fraudulent representation causes only an economic loss. Almost 150 years ago, this Court held in *Graham v. Roder*, 5 Tex. 141, 149 (1849), that tort damages were recoverable based on the plaintiff's claim that he was fraudulently induced to exchange a promissory note for a tract of land. Although the damages sustained by the plaintiff were purely economic, we held that tort damages, including exemplary damages, were recoverable. Since *Graham*, this Court has continued to recognize the propriety of fraud claims sounding in tort despite the fact that the aggrieved party's losses were only economic losses. *See, e.g., Spoljaric*, 708 S.W.2d at 436; *International Bankers Life Ins. Co. v. Holloway*, 368 S.W.2d 567, 583 (Tex.1963); *cf.* TEX.CIV.PRAC. & REM.CODE § 41.003(a)(1) (expressly authorizing exemplary damages for fraud without making any exception based on the type of loss sustained by the injured party). Moreover, we have held in a similar context that tort damages were not precluded for a tortious interference with contract claim, notwithstanding the fact that the damages for the tort claim compensated for the same economic losses that were recoverable under a breach of contract claim. *American Nat'l Petroleum Co. v. Transcontinental Gas Pipe Line Corp.*, 798 S.W.2d 274, 278 (Tex.1990).

Accordingly, tort damages are recoverable for a fraudulent inducement claim irrespective of whether the fraudulent representations are later subsumed in a contract or whether the plaintiff only suffers an economic loss related to the subject matter of the contract. Allowing the recovery of fraud damages sounding in tort only when a plaintiff suffers an injury that is distinct from the economic losses recoverable under a breach of contract claim is inconsistent with this well-established law, and also ignores the fact that an independent legal duty, separate from the existence of the contract itself, precludes the use of fraud to induce a binding agreement. We therefore disapprove of ... appellate court opinions to the extent that they hold that tort damages cannot be recovered for a fraudulent inducement claim absent an injury that is distinct from any permissible contractual damages.... We instead conclude that, if a plaintiff presents legally sufficient evidence on each of the elements of a fraudulent inducement claim, any damages suffered as a result of the fraud sound in tort.

We thus conclude that Presidio has a viable fraud claim that it can assert against Formosa. However, this conclusion does not end our inquiry. We must also determine whether legally sufficient evidence supports the jury's fraud and damage findings.

III

A fraud cause of action requires "a material misrepresentation, which was false, and which was either known to be false when made or was asserted without knowledge of its truth, which was intended to be acted upon, which was relied upon, and which caused injury." *Sears, Roebuck & Co. v. Meadows,* 877 S.W.2d 281, 282 (Tex.1994). A promise of future performance constitutes an actionable misrepresentation if the promise was made with no intention of performing at the time it was made. However, the mere failure to perform a contract is not evidence of fraud.

Rather, Presidio had to present evidence that Formosa made representations with the intent to deceive and with no intention of performing as represented. Moreover, the evidence presented must be relevant to Formosa's intent at the time the representation was made.

Presidio alleges that Formosa made three representations that it never intended to keep in order to induce Presidio to enter into the contract. First, the bid package and contract represented that Presidio would "arrange the delivery schedule of [Formosa]-supplied material and be responsible for the delivery . . . of all materials (this includes material supplied by [Formosa])." Second, the bid package and the contract provided the job was scheduled to begin on July 16, 1990, and be completed on October 15, 1990, 90 days later. Third, paragraph 17 of the contract represented that Formosa would be responsible for the payment of any delay damages within its control.

. . . .

We conclude that Presidio presented legally sufficient evidence that Formosa made representations with no intention of performing as represented in order to induce Presidio to enter into this contract at a low bid price. In the bid package and the contract, Formosa represented that Presidio would have control of the delivery of the concrete necessary for the project. While Formosa argues that other more general provisions contained in the contract refute this representation, the contract and the bid package specifically and unequivocally provide that Presidio would "arrange the delivery schedule of [Formosa]-supplied material and be responsible for the delivery . . . of all materials." Further, even Formosa's own witnesses admitted that, under the plain language of the contract, Presidio had control over the scheduling and delivery of concrete. Accordingly, there is clearly sufficient evidence that this representation was in fact made by Formosa.

In contravention of this representation, Formosa decided, two weeks before the contract was signed, to take over the delivery of the concrete without informing Presidio. Jack Lin, Formosa's civil department director, testified that Formosa, in an effort to save money, decided to take over the concrete delivery and set up its own delivery schedule. However, Presidio was not informed of this change until after the contract was signed. Lin admitted that Formosa acted deceptively by taking over the concrete delivery and scheduling when the bid package expressly provided that the contractor would have control. He further admitted that Formosa knew that Presidio would rely on this representation in preparing its bid.

Presidio's president, Bob Burnette, testified that Presidio did in fact rely on this representation in preparing its bid. Burnette further testified that every concrete pour was delayed one-to-two days while Presidio waited for Formosa to obtain the requested concrete. Because Burnette did not calculate such delays into his bid, the actual cost of the project exceeded the contract price.

This testimony provides more than a scintilla of evidence supporting Presidio's contention that Formosa intentionally made representations that it never intended to keep in order to induce Presidio to enter into the contract at a low bid price and that Presidio relied on these misrepresentations to its detriment. Thus, legally sufficient evidence supports the jury's fraud finding. We need not consider whether any other representations Formosa allegedly made were fraudulent.

. . . .

In conclusion, we hold that, when a party fraudulently procures a contract by making a promise without any intent of keeping the promise in order to induce another into executing the contract, a tort cause of action for that fraud exists. Accordingly, Presidio has a viable fraud claim against Formosa even though it only seeks damages for economic losses related to the subject matter and performance of the contract between the parties. . . .

NOTES & QUESTIONS

(1) In the *DeLanney* decision cited by the court, the Supreme Court of Texas observed:

> If the defendant's conduct—such as negligently burning down a house—would give rise to liability independent of the fact that a contract exists between the parties, the plaintiff's claim may also sound in tort. Conversely, if the defendant's conduct—such as failing to publish an advertisement—would give rise to liability only because it breaches the parties' agreement, the plaintiff's claim ordinarily sounds only in contract.

Southwestern Bell Tel. Co. v. Delanney, 809 S.W.2d 493, 494 (Tex. 1991). Would Presidio's fraud claim have survived under this test?

(2) In *DeLanney*, the court further observed: "In determining whether the plaintiff may recover on a tort theory, it is also instructive to examine the nature of the plaintiff's loss. When the only loss or damage is to the subject matter of the contract, the plaintiff's action is ordinarily on the contract." *Id.* Would Presidio's fraud claim have survived under this test?

(3) What explains the court's conclusion in *Formosa*? Is the court stating that "duty" (focusing on the defendant's conduct) trumps "injury" (focusing on the nature of the plaintiff's loss)? Alternatively, can the conclusion be explained using a *Town of Alma*-like "protection of the bargain" rationale? Consider the following statement in the Reporter's Note to § 3 of the RESTATEMENT (THIRD) OF TORTS: LIABILITY FOR ECONOMIC HARM (Tentative Draft No. 1, Apr. 4, 2012): "Courts are also reluctant to conclude

that a contract allocated to the plaintiff the risk that the defendant was lying; they are more inclined to view fraud as an attack on the integrity of the bargaining process itself."

(4) In some jurisdictions, a distinction is drawn between claims for "fraud in the inducement of a contract" and claims for "fraud in the performance of a contract." While claims for fraud in the inducement are not barred by the economic loss rule, claims for fraud in the performance are precluded by the rule. For example, in *Huron Tool and Engineering Co. v. Precision Consulting Services, Inc.*, 532 N.W.2d 541 (Mich. Ct. App. 1995), the court stated the following:

> . . . [W]e decline to adopt defendants' position that the economic loss doctrine precludes *any* fraud claim. Fraud in the inducement presents a special situation where parties to a contract appear to negotiate freely—which normally would constitute grounds for invoking the economic loss doctrine—but where in fact the ability of one party to negotiate fair terms and make an informed decision is undermined by the other party's fraudulent behavior. In contrast, where the only misrepresentation by the dishonest party concerns the quality or character of the goods sold, the other party is still free to negotiate warranty and other terms to account for possible defects in the goods.

The distinction between fraud in the inducement and other kinds of fraud is the same as the distinction drawn by a New Jersey federal district court between fraud extraneous to the contract and fraud interwoven with the breach of contract. *Public Service Enterprise Group, Inc. v. Philadelphia Elec. Co.*, 722 F.Supp. 184, 201 (D.N.J., 1989). With respect to the latter kind of fraud, the misrepresentations relate to the breaching party's performance of the contract and do not give rise to an independent cause of action in tort[:]

> Such fraud is not extraneous to the contractual dispute among the parties, but is instead but another thread in the fabric of [the] plaintiffs' contract claim. . . . [It] is undergirded by factual allegations identical to those supporting their breach of contract counts. . . . This fraud did not induce the plaintiffs to enter into the original agreement nor did it induce them to enter into additional undertakings. It did not cause harm to the plaintiffs distinct from those caused by the breach of contract. . . . [*Id.*]

Huron Tool, 532 N.W.2d at 545. Do you agree with treating these claims differently under the economic loss rule?

D.S.A., INC. V. HILLSBORO INDEPENDENT SCHOOL DISTRICT

973 S.W.2d 662 (Tex. 1998)

PER CURIAM.

. . . .

The principal issue in this case is whether a party may recover benefit-of-the-bargain and punitive damages for negligent and grossly negligent misrepresentations made by the other party in pre-contractual negotiations. We conclude that such damages may not be recovered under either theory, and we reverse the judgment of the court of appeals.

This suit arises out of an elementary school construction project overseen by D.S.A., Inc. ("DSA"), a construction management firm, for the Hillsboro Independent School District ("HISD"). The school building, completed and occupied in the fall of 1987, suffered several severe defects. The roof was unable to withstand winds common to Hill County and was plagued with numerous leaks. Poor water drainage of the ground beneath and around the school caused the soil in the crawlspace to expand and buckle the sewage lines suspended beneath the floor joists. After HISD spent an additional $220,244.33 to repair these defects, it sued DSA for breach of contract, negligent and gross negligent misrepresentation, and DTPA violations in connection with DSA's contract to manage the construction of an elementary school.

The jury returned findings against DSA on three theories of recovery—breach of contract, negligent misrepresentation, and DTPA—and awarded HISD $220,661 in actual and $170,000 in exemplary damages plus attorneys' fees. The trial court rendered judgment on HISD's DTPA cause of action.

The court of appeals disposed of HISD's DTPA claims as barred by the statute of limitations. It held that DSA breached its supervisory duties under the contract, fulfillment of which might have protected HISD from defects and deficiencies in the roof and crawlspace of the building. It also held that during pre-contractual negotiations, DSA negligently misrepresented the functions it would perform and that it was grossly negligent in doing so. The court of appeals reduced actual damages by $416.67 but otherwise affirmed, based on HISD's grossly negligent misrepresentation claim.

On appeal, DSA argues that HISD's negligent misrepresentation claim sounds only in contract. The damages the jury awarded for negligent misrepresentation were identical to the damages it awarded for breach of contract, and HISD did not offer proof of any economic injury independent of contract damages. In response, HISD urges that being induced into the contract was itself an independent injury. Citing our opinion in *Formosa Plastics Corp. v. Presidio Engineers*, 960 S.W.2d 41,

46–47 (Tex.1998), HISD further argues that it could recover in tort for losses related to the subject matter of the contract because DSA had a legal duty, independent from its contractual duties, not to make misrepresentations to induce HISD into the contract.

Without deciding whether [DSA] breached a *legal* duty independent of its *contractual* duties, we conclude that HISD's negligent misrepresentation claim must fail for lack of any independent *injury*. The *Formosa* opinion's rejection of the independent injury requirement in fraudulent inducement claims does not extend to claims for negligent misrepresentation or negligent inducement. Unlike fraudulent inducement, the benefit of the bargain measure of damages is not available for a claim of negligent misrepresentation. In *Federal Land Bank Ass'n v. Sloane*, 825 S.W.2d 439, 442–43 (Tex.1991), we adopted the independent injury requirement of section 552B of the Restatement (Second) of Torts:

> (1) The damages recoverable for a negligent misrepresentation are those necessary to compensate the plaintiff for the pecuniary loss to him of which the misrepresentation is [a] legal cause, including:
>
> > (a) the difference between the value of what he has received in the transaction and its purchase price or other value given for it; and
> >
> > (b) pecuniary loss suffered otherwise as a consequence of the plaintiff's reliance upon the misrepresentation.
>
> (2) the damages recoverable for a negligent misrepresentation do not include the benefit of the plaintiff's contract with the defendant.

RESTATEMENT (SECOND) OF TORTS § 552B (1977). The rationale for fixing a narrower scope of liability for negligent misrepresentation than for fraudulent inducement "is to be found in the difference between the obligations of honesty and of care." *Id.* § 552 cmt. a. Negligent misrepresentation implicates only the duty of *care* in supplying commercial information; honesty or good faith is no defense, as it is to a claim for fraudulent misrepresentation. Repudiating the independent injury requirement for negligent misrepresentation claims would potentially convert every contract interpretation dispute into a negligent misrepresentation claim.

HISD did not meet its burden of proving the independent injury required under section 552 of the Restatement. HISD's theory of recovery and charge to the jury did not attempt any distinction between its out-of-pocket damages and the benefit of the bargain. See *Arthur Andersen & Co. v. Perry Equip. Corp.*, 945 S.W.2d 812, 817 (Tex.1997) (defining the out-of-pocket and benefit-of-the-bargain measures of recovery). Instead, by seeking recovery for its costs to replace the roof, repair the plumbing, and re-grade the parking lots, HISD in essence asked for the benefit of its bargain—in this case, the reasonable costs needed to bring the school up to the "bargained-for" standard. Consequently, HISD is not entitled to any recovery under the theory of negligent misrepresentation.

We also reject HISD's award of exemplary damages under its theory of gross negligence, whether evaluated as gross negligence in the breach of contract or gross negligence in the inducement of contract. We have already held that "[g]ross negligence in the breach of contract will not entitle an injured party to exemplary damages because even an intentional breach will not." *Jim Walter Homes, Inc. v. Reed,* 711 S.W.2d 617, 618 (Tex.1986). Neither HISD nor the court of appeals cites any Texas case recognizing a claim for gross negligence in the inducement of contract. Given the availability of a cause of action for fraudulent inducement, we fail to perceive any rationale for acknowledging a claim for grossly negligent inducement.

Moreover, the court of appeals erroneously sustained HISD's gross negligence recovery on the theory that DSA, by inducing HISD to build a school without adequate supervision, imposed an extreme risk of harm on third parties—the children who eventually occupied the building. A party may recover for negligent misrepresentations involving a risk of physical harm only if actual physical harm results. *See* RESTATEMENT (SECOND) OF TORTS § 311 (1965). As there is no evidence that any children were *actually* harmed or that any of the other hypothetical dangers the court of appeals cited actually materialized, HISD is not entitled to exemplary damages.

. . . .

DSA further asserts that there was no evidence that it breached its contract with respect to the roofing or foundation defects. We conclude that there was legally sufficient evidence that DSA neglected its contractual obligation to "endeavor to protect Owner against defects and deficiencies in the work."

Because there was no evidence to support HISD's recovery on its negligent inducement and gross negligence causes of action, the court of appeals erred in affirming recovery on those grounds. We conclude that the remaining issues raised by DSA are either resolved by our disposition of HISD's negligent inducement and gross negligence claims or are without merit. Accordingly . . . we reverse the judgment of the court of appeals and remand the case to the trial court to recalculate damages on HISD's contract cause of action.

NOTES & QUESTIONS

(1) In *Formosa*, the Supreme Court of Texas noted that "it is well established that a legal duty not to fraudulently procure a contract is separate and independent from the duties established by the contract itself." Because of this independent legal duty, the court upheld the plaintiff's fraud claim even though the plaintiff "only [sought] damages for economic losses related to the subject matter and performance of the contract between the parties." Is the result in *DSA* consistent with *Formosa*? With *Town of Alma*?

(2) The *DSA* court referred to "[t]he *Formosa* opinion's rejection of the independent injury requirement in fraudulent inducement claims." What was the "independent injury requirement" in *Formosa*? Is it the same requirement in *DSA*? If HISD had simply asked for out-of-pocket damages from the jury (and the jury had awarded them), would HISD have had an "independent injury"?

(3) As part of the rationale for its decision, the *DSA* court noted that "[r]epudiating the independent injury requirement for negligent misrepresentation claims would potentially convert every contract interpretation dispute into a negligent misrepresentation claim." Can you explain what the court means by this statement? What is the problem with potentially converting every contract interpretation dispute into a negligent misrepresentation claim?

PROBLEM 6.1

Consider § 3 of the RESTATEMENT (THIRD) OF TORTS: LIABILITY FOR ECONOMIC HARM (Tentative Draft No. 1, Apr. 4, 2012). Under that section, how would the disputes in *Town of Alma*, *Formosa*, and *DSA* have been resolved?

PART TWO

UNFAIR COMPETITION

∎ ∎ ∎

CHAPTER 7

DECEPTIVE MARKETING

■ ■ ■

In Part One of this book, we examined what we labeled the "business torts." In Part Two, we will examine the field of unfair competition. Under early common law, unfair competition was a limited concept. The typical case involved one party attempting to sell their goods while claiming the goods were that of another (a practice known as "palming off"). The term has expanded, evolving throughout the twentieth century, to now encompass a wide variety of torts. Indeed, in recognition of this fact, the American Law Institute drafted the Restatement (Third) of Unfair Competition, which was published in 1995. This was done recognizing that unfair competition had become a specialty all of its own.

Today, the term "unfair competition" encompasses a large number of causes of action, including deceptive marketing, intentional interference with contract, fraud, trademark infringement, and misappropriation of trade secret. You may note that some of these concepts have already been addressed in Part One of this book as business torts, and indeed, there is an inevitable amount of overlap with the materials covered in that Part, in particular with regard to intentional interference with contract. Similarly, topics from this Part of the book, such as commercial disparagement, could be included in the business torts portion. This fact should not discourage you—if anything, it shows how these topics are often related by unifying themes of what actions society will permit in a business context.

Indeed, we begin our chapter with a concept already discussed in the Tortious Interference with Economic Relations Chapter; where do we draw the line between unfair competition and the right to compete? We start with the Restatement of Unfair Competition § 1, which begins with a presumption that pure acts of competition are not actionable unless they fall into a category listed.

§ 1. General Principles

One who causes harm to the commercial relations of another by engaging in a business or trade is not subject to liability to the other for such harm unless:

(a) the harm results from acts or practices of the actor actionable by the other under the rules of this Restatement relating to:

(1) deceptive marketing, as specified in Chapter Two;

(2) infringement of trademarks and other indicia of identification, as specified in Chapter Three;

(3) appropriation of intangible trade values including trade secrets and the right of publicity, as specified in Chapter Four;

or from other acts or practices of the actor determined to be actionable as an unfair method of competition, taking into account the nature of the conduct and its likely effect on both the person seeking relief and the public; or

(b) the acts or practices of the actor are actionable by the other under federal or state statutes, international agreements, or general principles of common law apart from those considered in this Restatement.

From the phrasing and comments to this section, it is clear that the burden of proof is upon the one alleging injury. This burden is overcome when there is a violation of state or federal law (such as the Lanham Act) or if one of the Restatement sections dealing with deceptive marketing, misappropriation of trade secrets or trademarks, is violated. In this Chapter, we will focus on deceptive marketing under both state common law and federal law. We leave discussion of the latter two topics to Chapters 10 and 11. Also notice that there is a catch-all at the end of subsection (a) which states "or from other acts or practices of the actor determined to be actionable as an unfair method of competition, taking into account the nature of the conduct and its likely effect on both the person seeking relief and the public." This phrase was inserted recognizing that the law of unfair competition, like much of business torts, is constantly developing.

A. EARLY COMMON LAW

At early common law, the tort of unfair competition was severely limited, and was basically only recognized in instances in which a competitor falsely claimed to have goods from a particular geographic region (Champagne, for example, is meant to come from a particular region in France; otherwise, it is just sparkling wine). The early case that demonstrates this principle, *American Washboard v. Saginaw Manufacturing Co.*, 103 F. 281 (6th Cir. 1900), is mentioned in the following two cases.

In *American Washboard*, the plaintiff alleged that it was the only producer of an aluminum rubber-faced washboard. The plaintiff claimed that the defendant advertised that it also produced an aluminum rubber-faced washboard when, in fact, its washboard contained zinc. The court held that unless the defendant was passing off its own washboards as those of the plaintiff's, there was no cause of action. According to the court, if a cause of action were to exist, it was up to the legislature to create it.

Judge Hand sought to escape this harsh rule in *Ely-Norris*.

ELY-NORRIS SAFE CO. V. MOSLER SAFE CO.
7 F.2d 603 (2d Cir. 1925)

The jurisdiction of the District Court depended upon diverse citizenship and the suit was for unfair competition. The bill alleged that the plaintiff manufactured and sold safes under certain letters patent, which had as their distinctive feature an explosion chamber, designed for protection against burglars. Before the acts complained of, no one but the plaintiff had ever made or sold safes with such chambers, and, except for the defendant's infringement, the plaintiff has remained the only manufacturer and seller of such safes. By reason of the plaintiff's efforts the public has come to recognize the value of the explosion chamber and to wish to purchase safes containing them. Besides infringing the patent, the defendant has manufactured and sold safes without a chamber, but with a metal bank around the door, in the same place where the plaintiff put the chamber, and has falsely told its customers that this bank was employed to cover and close an explosion chamber. Customers have been thus led to buy safes upon the faith of the representation, who in fact wished to buy safes with explosion chambers, and would have done so, but for the deceit.

The bill prayed an injunction against selling safes with such metal bands, and against representing that any of its safes contained an explosion chamber. From the plaintiff's answers to interrogatories it appeared that all the defendant's safes bore the defendant's name and address, and were sold as its own. Furthermore, that the defendant never gave a customer reason to suppose that any safe sold by it was made by the plaintiff.

Before HOUGH, MANTON, AND HAND, CIRCUIT JUDGES.

HAND, CIRCUIT JUDGE (after stating the facts as above).

This case is not the same as that before Mr. Justice Bradley in *New York & Rosendale Co. v. Coplay Cement Co.*, 44 F. 277. The plaintiffs there manufactured cement at Rosendale, N.Y., but it did not appear that they were the only persons making cement at that place. There was no reason, therefore, to assume that a customer of the defendant, deceived as to the place of origin of the defendant's cement, and desiring to buy only such cement, would have bought of the plaintiffs. It resulted that the plaintiffs did not show any necessary loss of trade through the defendant's fraud upon its own customers. We agree that some of the language of the opinion goes further, but it was not necessary for the disposition of the case.

American Washboard Co. v. Saginaw Mfg. Co., 103 F. 281, was, however, a case in substance like that at bar, because there the plaintiff alleged that it had acquired the entire output of sheet aluminum suitable for washboards. It necessarily followed that the plaintiff had a practical monopoly of this metal for the articles in question, and from this it was a fair inference that any customer of the defendant, who was deceived into buying as an aluminum washboard one which was not such, was a presumptive customer of the plaintiff, who had therefore lost a bargain. This was held, however, not to constitute a private wrong, and so the bill was dismissed.

Furthermore, we do not agree with the plaintiff that cases like *Federal Trade Commission v. Winsted Hosiery Co.*, 258 U.S. 483, and our decision in *Royal Baking Powder Co. v. Federal Trade Commission*, 281 F. 744, are in his favor. These arose under the Federal Trade Commission Act where it is only necessary to show that the public interest has been affected. The defendant's customers in such cases had an undoubted grievance, and this was thought to be enough to justify the intervention of the Federal Trade Commission. It by no means follows from such decisions that a competing manufacturer has any cause of suit.

We must concede, therefore, that on the cases as they stand the law is with the defendant, and the especially high authority of the court which decided *American Washboard Co. v. Saginaw Mfg. Co., supra*, makes us hesitate to differ from their conclusion. Yet there is no part of the law which is more plastic than unfair competition, and what was not reckoned an actionable wrong 25 years ago may have become such today. We find it impossible to deny the strength of the plaintiff's case on the allegations of its bill. As we view it, the question is, as it always is in such cases, one of fact. While a competitor may, generally speaking, take away all the customers of another that he can, there are means which he must not use. One of these is deceit. The false use of another's name as maker or source of his own goods is deceit, of which the false use of geographical or descriptive terms is only one example. But we conceive that in the end the questions which arise are always two: Has the plaintiff in fact lost customers? And has he lost them by means which the law forbids? The false use of the plaintiff's name is only an instance in which each element is clearly shown.

In the case at bar the means are as plainly unlawful as in the usual case of palming off. It is as unlawful to lie about the quality of one's wares as about their maker; it equally subjects the seller to action by the buyer. Indeed, as to this the case of *Federal Trade Commission v. Winsted Hosiery Co., supra,* is flatly in point, if authority be needed. The reason, as we think, why such deceits have not been regarded as actionable by a competitor, depends only upon his inability to show any injury for which there is a known remedy. In an open market it is generally impossible to prove that a customer, whom the defendant has secured by falsely describing his goods, would have bought of the plaintiff, if the defendant had been truthful. Without that, the plaintiff, though aggrieved in company with other honest traders, cannot show any ascertainable loss. He may not recover at law, and the equitable remedy is concurrent. The law does not allow him to sue as a vicarious avenger of the defendant's customers.

But, if it be true that the plaintiff has a monopoly of the kind of wares concerned, and if to secure a customer the defendant must represent his own as of that kind, it is a fair inference that the customer wants those and those only. Had he not supposed that the defendant could supply him, presumably he would have gone to the plaintiff, who alone could. At least, if the plaintiff can prove that in fact he would, he shows a direct loss, measured by his profits on the putative sale. If a tradesman falsely foists on a customer a substitute for what the plaintiff alone can supply, it can scarcely be that the plaintiff is without remedy, if he can show that the customer would certainly have come to him, had the truth been told.

Yet that is in substance the situation which this bill presents. It says that the plaintiff alone could lawfully make such safes, and that the defendant has sold others to customers who asked for the patented kind. It can make no difference that the defendant sold them as its own. The sale by hypothesis depended upon the structure of the safes, not on their maker. To be satisfied, the customer must in fact have gone to the plaintiff, or the defendant must have infringed. Had he infringed, the plaintiff could have recovered his profit on the sale; had the customer gone to him, he would have made that profit. Any possibilities that the customers might not have gone to the plaintiff, had they been told the truth, are foreclosed by the allegation that the plaintiff in fact lost the sales. It seems to us merely a corollary of *Federal Trade Commission v. Winsted Hosiery Co., supra,* that, if this can be proved, a private suit will lie.

Decree reversed.

MOSLER SAFE CO. v. ELY-NORRIS SAFE CO.
273 U.S. 132 (1927)

MR. JUSTICE HOLMES delivered the opinion of the Court.

This is a bill in equity brought by a corporation of New Jersey against a corporation of New York alleging unfair competition. It was treated below as a suit by the only manufacturer of safes containing an explosion chamber for protection against burglars. It seeks an injunction against selling safes with a metal band around the door in the place where the plaintiff put the chamber, or falsely representing that the defendant's safes contain an explosion chamber. The plaintiff admitted that the defendant's safes bore the defendant's name and address and that the defendant never gave any customer reason to believe that its safes were of the plaintiff's make. The District Court, following *American Washboard Co. v. Saginaw Manufacturing Co.*, 103 F. 281, held that representations such as were sought to be enjoined did not give a private cause of action. The Circuit Court of Appeals held that if, as it took it to be alleged, the plaintiff had the monopoly of explosion chambers and the defendant falsely represented that its safes had such chambers, the plaintiff had a good case, and that since the decision above cited the law had grown more liberal in granting relief. It therefore reversed the decree below. *Ely Norris Safe Co. v. Mosler Safe Co.*, 7 F.2d 603. In view of the conflict between the Circuit Courts of Appeals a writ of certiorari was granted by this Court. [*Mosler Safe Co. v. Ely-Norris Safe Co.*,] 268 U.S. 684.

At the hearing below all attention seems to have been concentrated on the question passed upon and the forcibly stated reasons that induced this Court of Appeals to differ from that for the Sixth Circuit. But, upon a closer scrutiny of the bill than seems to have been invited before, it does not present that broad and interesting issue. The bill alleges that the plaintiff has a patent for an explosion chamber 'as described and claimed in said letters patent'; that it has the exclusive right to make and sell 'safes containing such an explosion chamber'; that no other safes containing 'such an explosion chamber' could be got in the United States before the defendant, as it is alleged, infringed the plaintiff's patent, for which alleged infringement a suit is pending. It then is alleged that the defendant is making and selling safes with a metal band around the door at substantially the same location as the explosion chamber of plaintiff's safes, and has represented to the public 'that the said metal band was employed to cover or close an explosion chamber' by reason of which 'the public has been led to purchase defendant's said safes as and for safes containing an explosion chamber, such as is manufactured and sold by the plaintiff herein.' It is alleged further that sometimes the defendant's safes have no explosion chamber under the band but are bought by those who want safes with a chamber and so the defendant has deprived the plaintiff of sales, competed unfairly and damaged the plaintiff's reputation. The plaintiff relies upon its patent suit for relief in respect of the sales of safes alleged to infringe its rights. It complains here only of false representations as to safes that do not infringe but that are sold as having explosion chambers although in fact they do not.

It is consistent with every allegation in the bill and the defendant in argument asserted it to be a fact, that there are other safes with explosion chambers beside that for which the plaintiff has a patent. The defendant is charged only with representing that its safes had an explosion chamber, which, so far as appears, it had a perfect right to do if the representation was true. If on the other hand the representation was false as it is alleged sometimes to have been, there is nothing to show that customers had they known the facts would have gone to the plaintiff rather than to other competitors in the market, or to lay a foundation for the claim for a loss of sales. The bill is so framed as to seem to invite the decision that was obtained from the Circuit Court of Appeals, but when scrutinized is seen to have so limited its statements as to exclude the right to complain.

Decree reversed.

NOTES & QUESTIONS

(1) Prior to Judge Hand's ruling, was a finding for the plaintiff supported by case law? How does Judge Hand justify his ruling?

(2) On appeal, Justice Holmes reverses Judge Hand—why? Is it because he disagrees with the "single-source" exception?

(3) In modern times, the single-source exception has largely fallen into disfavor because it is too narrow. (This is reflected in the RESTATEMENT (THIRD) OF UNFAIR COMPETITION (1995), which is discussed below.) In fact, there is a noticeable dearth of cases citing to the doctrine since 2000 (and even in the decades prior).

B. ELEMENTS OF FALSE ADVERTISING UNDER THE RESTATEMENT OF UNFAIR COMPETITION AND THE LANHAM ACT

The First Restatement of Torts accepted the "single-source" exception, but critics and commentators agreed that even with this exception in place, the rule of false advertising was too narrow. The Third Restatement of Unfair Competition recognizes a much broader scope of liability:

§ 2. Deceptive Marketing: General Principle

One who, in connection with the marketing of goods or services, makes a representation relating to the actor's own goods, services, or commercial activities that is likely to deceive or mislead prospective purchasers to the likely commercial detriment of another under the rule stated in § 3 is subject to liability to the other for the relief appropriate under the rules stated in §§ 35–37.

Section 2 is a broad recognition of liability in connection with misrepresentations about one's own goods. (Section 6 also recognizes a limited ability to sue for misrepresentations regarding selling another's goods second-hand and saying that they are new.) Section 2 departs, as does federal law under the Lanham Act, from the old common law rule with its narrow "single-source exception" and now permits a cause of action even when there is no intent to deceive.

Section 2 states that liability is to be determined based upon a finding that the statements are "likely to deceive or mislead prospective purchasers to the likely commercial detriment of another under the rule stated in § 3." Section 3 speaks to the materiality of the harm:

§ 3. Commercial Detriment Of Another

A representation is to the likely commercial detriment of another if:

(a) the representation is material, in that it is likely to affect the conduct of prospective purchasers; and

(b) there is a reasonable basis for believing that the representation has caused or is likely to cause a diversion of trade from the other or harm to the other's reputation or good will.

Section 3 requires only that a prospective purchaser's conduct is likely to be affected, and the comments to §§ 1 and 2 make clear that the burden of proof is on the plaintiff to demonstrate this. This standard differs from the common law approach seen in *Ely-Norris*, as the burden of proof is much lighter than it was under the single-source exception. As opposed to having to prove that it is the "single source", a plaintiff under § 3 only needs to show that a representation is "likely to influence prospective purchasers to some substantial degree." *See* RESTATEMENT (THIRD) OF UNFAIR COMPETITION § 3 cmt. b (1995).

The Restatement does not do away with reliance, however, and it is still a factor in a finding of liability. Also, the comments note that this is not a subjective test—so "puffing" or "puffery" is still a defense: "This Section does not subject the actor to liability, however, unless a significant number of prospective purchasers have or are likely to rely on the representation. If a reasonably prudent purchaser of the goods or services would not rely on the representation, the actor is not subject to liability in the absence of evidence establishing that the representation is nevertheless likely to be relied upon by a significant number of prospective purchasers." RESTATEMENT (THIRD) OF UNFAIR COMPETITION § 3 cmt. d (1995).[a]

It has been said that there is no federal law of unfair competition; however, many of the same claims brought under state common law doctrines can be brought in federal court under § 43 of the Lanham Act. *See* 15 U.S.C. § 1125 (2006). Though the Lanham Act is typically associated with trademark infringement, § 43 broadly provides for recovery in a number of false advertising situations regardless of the presence of a trademark or federal registration of a mark:

15 U.S.C. § 1125 [Lanham Act § 43(a)]. False designations of origin, false descriptions, and dilution forbidden

(a) Civil action

(1) Any person who, on or in connection with any goods or services, or any container for goods, uses in commerce any word, term, name, symbol, or device, or any combination thereof, or any false designation of origin, false or misleading description of fact, or false or misleading representation of fact, which—

(A) is likely to cause confusion, or to cause mistake, or to deceive as to the affiliation, connection, or association of such person with another person, or as to the origin, sponsorship, or approval of his or her goods, services, or commercial activities by another person, or

(B) in commercial advertising or promotion, misrepresents the nature, characteristics, qualities, or geographic origin of his or her or another person's goods, services, or commercial activities,

shall be liable in a civil action by any person who believes that he or she is or is likely to be damaged by such act.

As you can see, § 43(a)(1) is divided into two main subsections. Subsection (A) is sometimes referred to as the "trademark" provision because its scope is broad enough to enforce unregistered trademarks, a concept we discuss in more detail in Chapter 11. Subsection (A) also reaches deceptive marketing techniques such as passing off one's own goods as those of another, which we discuss below in Section C. Subsection (B) is the false advertising provision. Unlike subsection (A), it

---

[a]   The comments also address elements of standing and the role that intent to deceive plays in a cause of action. These issues will be addressed later in this Chapter.

requires that the false statements be made as part of commercial advertising.

While § 43 codifies much of the law of unfair competition, especially with regard to deceptive marketing, its language is limited. Section 43 is meant to be supplemental to state unfair competition causes of action and does not preempt state law. Furthermore, due to the limitations of the Commerce Clause, § 43 does not reach purely intrastate activities, though, given how much advertising is performed via the internet and television, this requirement can be met rather easily in a false advertising claim.

Note that the language of § 43 is broad enough to prohibit not just false advertising, but also advertising and representations that disparage another's products or business. In this regard, § 43 is broader than the Restatement of Unfair Competition, which does not address this area of law, but rather leaves the subject to the Restatement of Torts. We address this area of law in Chapter 8, but it is worth noting the overlap that business and product disparagement have with the law of false advertising. Indeed, as you will see, the elements of the causes of action are very similar.

Early courts read § 43 as a codification of the common law, and thus imported the single-source exception into the Lanham Act. Amendments to the act now make clear that no such limitation is to be placed on a § 43 claim. In this sense, § 43 is similar to the Restatement of Unfair Competition. Given its links to the common law, it is perhaps not surprising that the Lanham Act's materiality requirement incorporates a virtually identical rule as the Restatement of Unfair Competition.

The following two cases demonstrate two common types of deceptive marketing: false statements concerning product origin and false statements regarding the characteristics of the product itself. Both cases involve alleged violations of § 43 of the Lanham Act. As you read these cases, try to identify the elements at play and how these cases would be decided under the Restatement.

BLACK HILLS JEWELRY MANUFACTURING CO. V. GOLD RUSH, INC.
633 F.2d 746 (8th Cir. 1980)

Before BRIGHT, ROSS AND STEPHENSON, CIRCUIT JUDGES.

STEPHENSON, CIRCUIT JUDGE.

Plaintiffs-appellees are three South Dakota corporations located in the Black Hills area of South Dakota. They are in the business of manufacturing a certain design of gold jewelry which they market under the name "Black Hills Gold Jewelry." Appellees brought this action under section 43(a) of the Lanham Act, 15 U.S.C. § 1125(a), seeking injunctive relief against the use by defendants-appellants of the words "Black Hills Gold Jewelry" to describe jewelry of a style similar to that of appellees, but not manufactured in the Black Hills of South Dakota.

The district court, relying on 15 U.S.C. §§ 1125(a) and 1127, held that although appellees were not entitled to the exclusive use of the phrase "Black Hills Gold Jewelry," an injunction would issue prohibiting appellants from using the phrases "Black Hills Gold" or "Black Hills Gold Jewelry" to describe jewelry not made in the Black Hills of South Dakota. Appellants' major contentions on appeal are that: (1) The district court incorrectly held [appellees] could be afforded relief based on the existence of a common law unregistered certification mark; (2) the district court was clearly erroneous in several factual findings especially in finding that the phrase "Black Hills Gold Jewelry" was merely geographically descriptive and not a generic term for the design of the gold jewelry; (3) several evidentiary rulings by the district court were improper; and (4) the issuing of the injunction was improper. We affirm.

I.   BACKGROUND

Appellees are three separate, distinct, and independent companies that manufacture basically only one product, three-color gold jewelry in a grape and leaf design. All three appellees market their product as "Black Hills Gold Jewelry," sometimes preceded by their corporate name and the word "original" or "genuine." . . . All three companies can trace their beginnings back to one of the earliest manufacturers of "Black Hills Gold Jewelry," Mr. F. L. Thorpe.

Until recently, appellees were the only manufacturers of this design of jewelry who marketed it as "Black Hills Gold Jewelry," and their only place of manufacture was and is the Black Hills of South Dakota. Beginning sometime in 1977, other manufacturers and retailers began to market jewelry of this or a similar design as "Black Hills Gold Jewelry," although none of the jewelry was manufactured in the Black Hills.[2]

In 1978, appellant Gold Rush, Inc. began manufacturing three-color gold grape and leaf design jewelry in Bismarck, North Dakota and selling it as "Black Hills Gold Jewelry by Gold Rush." The other two appellants are retailers of "Black Hills Gold Jewelry." Appellant Herberger's purchased jewelry which was sold as "Black Hills Gold" from Gold Rush, Inc., and appellant LaBelle's purchased jewelry which was sold as "Black Hills Gold" from both Gold Rush, Inc. and Felco Jewel Industries, a manufacturer of jewelry located in Rio Rancho, New Mexico. Appellees brought suit in August 1979, against Gold Rush and later against the retailers. These suits were consolidated for trial.

---

[2]   Neither appellants nor appellees obtain all their gold in the Black Hills, and appellees are alleging a false designation of origin only as to the manufacturing of the gold jewelry.

[T]he district court made the following findings of fact which are relevant to this appeal:

> 20. In connection with its store located in Sioux Falls, South Dakota, Defendant Herberger's advertised in the Sioux Falls Argus Leader a sale of "Black Hills Gold Jewelry by Gold Rush" and included in said advertisement a picture of Mount Rushmore National Monument, which is located in the Black Hills of South Dakota.

> 21. Defendant LaBelle's has also run advertisements promoting the sale of so-called Black Hills Gold Jewelry in newspapers in Sioux Falls, South Dakota, Grand Forks, North Dakota and Rapid City, South Dakota. These advertisements have included pictures of Mount Rushmore National Monument, even though the jewelry advertised was manufactured in either Bismarck, North Dakota or Rio Rancho, New Mexico.

> 26. The consuming public generally considers the terms Black Hills Gold or Black Hills Gold Jewelry to refer to jewelry products manufactured in the Black Hills of South Dakota.

> 27. The actions of the Defendants in promoting and selling jewelry not manufactured in the Black Hills as Black Hills Gold or Black Hills Gold Jewelry has created the likelihood of consumer confusion as to the origin of products [labeled] as Black Hills Gold or Black Hills Gold Jewelry.

> . . . .

> 30. Plaintiffs have been reasonably diligent in taking action to protect the name Black Hills Gold Jewelry from use by manufacturers of similar products located outside the Black Hills of South Dakota.

> 31. Plaintiffs have not been guilty of unclean hands surrounding their attempts to protect their use of the terms Black Hills Gold and Black Hills Gold Jewelry.

> 32. Use of the terms Black Hills Gold or Black Hills Gold Jewelry will cause consumers to purchase products of the Defendants when they in fact wished to purchase a product manufactured in the Black Hills of South Dakota. This will enable the Defendants to wrongfully trade upon and profit from Plaintiff's reputation and good will and will result in business losses to Plaintiffs.

The district court granted appellees injunctive relief on what we view as two alternative holdings. The court first stated:

The statute (section 43(a) of the Lanham Act, 11 U.S.C. § 1125(a)) under which plaintiffs brought this action appears to continue this tradition of providing protection against outsiders for those using a geographical name. The statute prohibits a "false designation of origin," which would appear to prohibit a producer from [labeling] his product so as to make consumers believe it came from somewhere it did not.

The court also held that:

Another section of the Lanham Act (15 U.S.C. § 1127) deals with what is known as a certification mark. This section also appears to provide protection for a group of producers using a geographical name to designate their product.

[The court first addressed the certification mark issue and agreed with appellants that appellees were not entitled to the benefit of a certification mark.]

III. SECTION 43(a) OF THE LANHAM ACT

We disagree with appellants' argument that the district court relied solely on the existence of a common law unregistered certification mark to afford relief. The district court's Memorandum Opinion discusses in detail unfair competition under section 43(a) of the Lanham Act, 11 U.S.C. § 1125(a). It concluded that pre-Lanham Act cases established it was possible for a group of manufacturers to assert the right to a geographical designation without establishing secondary meaning[b] and a single source. The court also concluded that section 43(a) continued this tradition of providing protection against outsiders who use the same geographical designation.

It is our view that the Findings of Fact support a conclusion that appellees are entitled to injunctive relief under section 43(a) of the Lanham Act. We agree with the district court that several cases prior to the Lanham Act protected groups of plaintiffs-producers who asserted their right to the use of a geographical designation in a suit against other producers who did not manufacture their goods in said area but nevertheless used the geographical designation in their name or label. *See, e.g., Grand Rapids Furniture Co. v. Grand Rapids Furniture Co.*, 127 F.2d 245 (7th Cir. 1942).

Section 43(a) does not by its terms restrict the holdings of these cases. In fact section 43(a) obviates several requirements necessary under common law unfair competition. The "single source" rule has been held to be inapplicable to suits under section 43(a), and the "likely to be

---

[b] As we will learn in Chapter 11, normally marks that are merely descriptive must acquire what is known as "secondary meaning" in the eyes of the consuming public before trademark protection will attach.

damaged" provision obviates the necessity of proving actual diversion of trade. For these reasons it has been stated that section 43(a) creates a federal statutory tort sui generis and does not merely codify the common law principles of unfair competition. . . .

The plain meaning of the statute supports these views. Section 43(a) imposes civil liability upon "any person who shall * * * use in connection with any goods * * * a false designation of origin, or any false description or representation, including words or other symbols tending falsely to describe or represent the same." It gives a cause of action to "any person doing business in the locality falsely indicated as that of origin * * * or by any person who believes that he is or is likely to be damaged by the use of any such false description or representation." Clearly appellees fit this definition. As stated in the landmark case of *L'Aiglon Apparel v. Lana Lobell, Inc.*, 214 F.2d 649, 651:

> (H)owever similar to or different from pre-existing law, here is a provision of a federal statute which, with clarity and precision adequate for judicial administration, creates and defines rights and duties and provides for their vindication in the federal courts. For illuminating discussions of Section 43(a) and its relation to precedent law, *see* Callman, *False Advertising as a Competitive Tort*, 1948, 48 Col. L. Rev. 876, 877–886; Bunn, *The National Law of Unfair Competition*, 1949, 62 Harv. L. Rev. 987, 998–1000.

. . . .

Scotch Whiskey Ass'n v. Barton Distilling Co., 489 F.2d 809 (7th Cir. 1973), *aff'g* 338 F. Supp. 595 (N.D. Ill. 1971), a case similar to the case at bar, allowed recovery under section 43(a). In that case, two producers of Scotch whiskey and an association that promoted Scotch whiskey were granted an injunction against a third producer whose label indicated the product was Scotch whiskey, but whose product was in fact found to have ingredients not from Scotland. The district court found this to be a false designation of origin. The Seventh Circuit affirmed the finding of a section 43(a) violation and was apparently not troubled by any lack of secondary meaning or "single source." The court required nothing more than a showing that the designation was false and that defendant knew or should have known of the falsity. *Scotch Whiskey Ass'n*, 489 F.2d at 811. *See also Cmty. of Roquefort v. William Faehndrich, Inc.*, 198 F. Supp. 291 (S.D.N.Y. 1961), *aff'd*, 303 F.2d 494 (2d Cir. 1962).

IV. GENERICNESS

Appellants argue that even if recovery would be allowed based on the district court's Findings of Fact, nevertheless several of these Findings of Fact are clearly erroneous and therefore the injunction was still improper. Appellants' major contention on this point is that the district court was clearly erroneous in finding the phrase "Black Hills Gold Jewelry" to be geographically descriptive of the gold jewelry. They argue that the evidence at trial established that the phrase was a generic reference to three-color gold grape and leaf design jewelry no matter where it was manufactured.

If "Black Hills Gold Jewelry" was found to be a generic term, then it would be in the public domain for all to use. *Abercrombie & Fitch Co. v. Hunting World, Inc.*, 537 F.2d 4, 9 (2d Cir. 1976). Appellants rely principally on the discussions of genericness in *Kellogg Co. v. Nat'l Biscuit Co.*, 305 U.S. 111, 116 (1938) ("shredded wheat" held generic) and *Anti-Monopoly, Inc. v. General Mills Fun Grp.*, 611 F.2d 296 (9th Cir. 1979) (involving genericness of "MONOPOLY").

The evidence at trial in the present case was conflicting concerning whether the public generally considered "Black Hills Gold Jewelry" to mean gold jewelry manufactured only in the Black Hills, or instead three-color gold grape and leaf design jewelry wherever produced. The district court found the former to be established by the evidence. For "Black Hills Gold Jewelry" to be generic, it must be applied to three-color gold grape and leaf design jewelry wherever produced. *Cmty. of Roquefort v. William Faehndrich, Inc.*, *supra*, 198 F. Supp. at 293. Appellants point to no evidence, nor does the record indicate any evidence introduced at trial establishing that outside manufacturers and dealers referred to their jewelry of this type as "Black Hills Gold Jewelry" prior to approximately late 1977 or early 1978. Indeed, appellees point to several manufacturers of gold jewelry of a design similar to that of appellees which had not referred to their product as "Black Hills Gold."

Although some catalogue houses, dealers and manufacturers have used the term to describe three-color gold grape and leaf design jewelry manufactured outside the Black Hills since early 1978, this is not controlling.[5] The first time another manufacturer used the name "Black Hills Gold" (approximately three years prior to this litigation) the appellees complained to the Rhode Island firm which stopped the practice. The appellees brought this action when appellants openly began advertising their product as "Black Hills Gold Jewelry."

Evidence supporting the district court's finding that the term "Black Hills Gold Jewelry" is merely geographically descriptive included the fact appellees had advertised their product in a manner which utilized the history and folklore of the Black Hills of South Dakota. All gold jewelry sold as "Black Hills Gold" had been manufactured in the Black Hills for over one hundred years. Thus an association with the geographical area

---

[5]   In fact there was some indication at trial that the owner of Felco convinced catalogue houses that it was permissible to refer to any three-color gold grape and leaf design jewelry as "Black Hills Gold" because it merely described the design of the jewelry.

was established. That appellants had in mind using this favorable association is apparent from their advertisements prominently displaying Mount Rushmore, as well as using historical folklore of the Black Hills in their advertising. In examining all the evidence, we cannot say the district court's finding that the phrase "Black Hills Gold Jewelry" is merely geographically descriptive of origin . . . is clearly erroneous.

. . . .

VI. PROPRIETY OF INJUNCTION

Appellants argue that the injunction should not have issued because appellees did not show either irreparable harm or that money damages would be inadequate. They also argue the claim is barred by estoppel, laches, and acquiescence, and that the injunction is too broad.

It is our view that the injunction was proper. The district court found that there was a likelihood of confusion to consumers as to the origin of the products [labeled] as "Black Hills Gold" or "Black Hills Gold Jewelry." It found that appellees and their predecessors had made this high quality jewelry for over one hundred years and sold it as "Black Hills Gold Jewelry." It also found that appellants' use of the term would cause consumers who wished to purchase a product produced in the Black Hills to purchase appellants' product instead. It stated this would allow appellants to wrongfully profit from appellees' reputation and good will and result in business losses to appellees.

It is unlikely that appellees could show specific monetary damages, yet clearly under the district court's findings they have suffered injury. To obtain an injunction under section 43(a) appellees need only show that the falsities complained of had a tendency to deceive. A finding of tendency to deceive satisfies the requisite of irreparable harm. *See Ames Publ'g Co. v. Walker-Davis Publ'ns, Inc.*, 372 F. Supp. 1, 13 (E.D. Pa. 1974); Note, 25 DRAKE L. REV. 228, 236 (1975).[7]

---

[7]   (A) showing of a likelihood of confusion of consumers will usually result in proving the requisite likelihood of damage to the plaintiff-competitor. Thus, the prime test of liability under section 43(a) is closely analogous to, if not identical with, the likelihood-of-confusion test of federal and common-law trademark infringement and unfair competition.

Since section 43(a) was passed as a consumer protection statute, the courts are not reluctant to allow a commercial plaintiff to obtain an injunction even where the likelihood of pecuniary injury to the plaintiff may be slight. Thus, under section 43(a), Congressional policy appears to encourage commercial companies to act as the fabled "vicarious avenger" of consumer rights. An injunction, as opposed to money damages, is no windfall to the commercial plaintiff. An injunction protects both consumers and the commercial plaintiff from continuing acts of false advertising. The fact that section 43(a) was passed to protect consumers as well as competitors is illustrated by the rule that a likelihood of consumer confusion is sufficient for injunctive relief. An injunction protects the consumer from continued false advertising. Money damages, on the other hand, primarily aid only the competitor, and he is required to satisfy a higher standard of proof as to injury.

J. McCarthy, Trademarks & Unfair Competition § 27:5A at 250–51 (1973) (footnotes omitted).

We agree with the district court that appellees were reasonably diligent in taking action to protect the name "Black Hills Gold Jewelry." A Rhode Island firm which began using the term three years prior to this litigation stopped upon demand by the appellees. This action was brought eighteen months after appellants' first use and soon after appellants began openly advertising their jewelry as "Black Hills Gold" with pictures of Mount Rushmore in the ads. Appellants note appellees had not obtained a trademark, nor had they tried to obtain registration of a certification mark. This is not controlling in an action brought under section 43(a). *Bos. Prof'l Hockey Ass'n, Inc. v. Dall. Cap & Emblem Mfg., Inc.*, 510 F.2d 1004, 1010 (5th Cir. 1975), *cert. denied*, 423 U.S. 868, (1976); *Iding v. Anaston*, 266 F. Supp. 1015 (N.D. Ill. 1967); Comment, 58 Neb. L. Rev. 159, 161 (1979); Note, 25 Drake L. Rev. 228, 232 (1975). The district court's finding of due diligence is not clearly erroneous.

Appellants allege the injunction was too broad. However there was evidence that both appellees and appellants were selling their products in a large geographical region, and it is not necessary that actual confusion of consumers be shown. Appellants were found to have made a false designation of origin of their goods and were enjoined from continuing the deceptive practice. Such an injunction is proper under the circumstances.

Affirmed.

NOTES & QUESTIONS

(1) The defendants argued that the term "Black Hills Gold Jewelry" was generic in that it described merely the style of jewelry. How would a finding of genericness have helped the defendants? What evidence supported the parties' claims on this point?

(2) The court noted that there was conflicting evidence concerning the meaning of the term "Black Hills Gold Jewelry." In light of this conflicting evidence, do you agree with the court's decision to affirm?

(3) The court never explicitly states that the defendants' assertions regarding "Black Hills Gold Jewelry" must be material to be actionable. Nonetheless, it is a required element of a plaintiff's case. Can you articulate the standard for materiality from the case? How does this compare to the standard from the Restatement of Unfair Competition?

(4) In light of the court's decision, how would you advise the defendants to market their gold jewelry in the future?

(5) In an omitted portion of the opinion, the court addressed whether the appellees were entitled to the benefits of a certification mark:

> The Lanham Act defines a "certification mark" to be "any word, name, symbol, or device, or combination thereof . . . to certify regional or other origin, material, mode of manufacture, quality, accuracy, or other characteristics of a person's goods or services or

that work or labor on the goods or services was performed by a member of a union or other organization." Lanham Act § 45, 15 U.S.C. § 1127 (2006). In effect, a Certification Mark certifies the nature or origin of the goods or services to which it has been applied (it can also certify manufacture or provision of services by members of a union or other organization to certain standards). For example, Rochefort is used to certify that cheese bearing the mark "has been manufactured from sheep's milk only, and had been cured in the natural caves of the Community of Roquefort, Department of Aveyron, France, in accordance with the historic methods and usages of production, curing and development which have been in vogue there for a long period of years." *Community of Roquefort v. William Faehndrich, Inc.*, 303 F.2d 494, 496 (2d Cir. 1962). Regional certification marks are frequently challenged as being generic. The general rule is that a regional certification mark will not be deemed to be generic, unless it appears that it has lost its significance as an indication of regional origin for those goods (or the other aspect signifying origin that the Mark was identifying).

(6)   However, to obtain the protections of a certification mark under the Lanham Act, the mark must be registered and the one registering the mark cannot be the one who seeks to use or adopt the mark (for instance, it was the community of Roquefort that registered the mark in the above cited case). As the appellees Gold Rush were the ones who used the marks, they could not have registered the mark even if they had wanted to. There is some question as to whether a common law certification mark can be created without registration. *See* J. Thomas McCarthy, *McCarthy on Trademarks and Unfair Competition* § 19.90 (4th ed. 2011); *Florida v. Real Juices, Inc.*, 330 F. Supp. 428 (M.D. Fla. 1971) (recognizing an unregistered certification mark that was used to certify Florida citrus products). The Restatement of Unfair Competition takes the position that such certification marks can exist at common law. *See* RESTATEMENT (THIRD) OF UNFAIR COMPETITION § 11 (1995).

(7)   You may have noted that in the trial court's findings of fact, it found that the plaintiffs were not guilty of unclean hands. A plaintiff that is itself guilty of engaging in inequitable conduct may be subject to a defense of unclean hands. In *Hagen-Dazs, Inc. v. Frusen Gladje Ltd.*, 493 F. Supp. 73 (S.D.N.Y. 1980), the plaintiff sought to enjoin the defendant claiming that the defendant's trade dress was intended to give consumers the false impression that its ice cream was made in Sweden (when in fact it was made in the United States). The only problem: the plaintiff was itself guilty of attempting to package its ice cream to give the impression that it was of Scandinavian origin when it was in fact made domestically. *Id.* at 76. The court denied the relief sought. This defense is only available when the plaintiff's own conduct is both inequitable and involves the same subject matter that the plaintiff is complaining about.

CASHMERE & CAMEL HAIR MANUFACTURERS INSTITUTE V. SAKS FIFTH AVENUE

284 F.3d 302 (1st Cir. 2002)

TORRUELLA, CIRCUIT JUDGE.

Plaintiffs-appellants L.W. Packard & Co. ("Packard") and Cashmere & Camel Hair Manufacturers Institute (the "Institute") appeal from the district court's entry of partial summary judgment dismissing their false advertising claims under the Lanham Act, 15 U.S.C. § 1125(a), and Massachusetts state law. In particular, Packard challenges the dismissal of its claims for money damages, while the Institute argues that the district court erred in dismissing one of its claims for injunctive relief. Because we conclude that the district court relied on impermissible inferences in favor of the moving party in reaching its conclusions, we reverse and remand the case for action consistent with this opinion.

Background

The Institute is a trade association of cashmere manufacturers dedicated to preserving the name and reputation of cashmere as a specialty fiber. Packard is a member of the Institute and a manufacturer of cashmere and cashmere-blend fabric.

In 1993, defendant-appellee Harve Benard, Ltd. ("Harve Benard") began manufacturing a line of women's blazers that were labeled as containing 70 percent wool, 20 percent nylon, and 10 percent cashmere. Its labels also portrayed the blazers as "A Luxurious Blend of Cashmere and Wool," "Cashmere and Wool," or "Wool and Cashmere." Harve Benard sold large quantities of these cashmere-blend garments to retail customers, including defendants Saks Fifth Avenue ("Saks") and Filene's Basement.

In 1995, plaintiffs began purchasing random samples of the Harve Benard garments and giving them to Professor Kenneth Langley and Dr. Franz-Josef Wortmann, experts in the field of cashmere identification and textile analysis. After conducting separate tests on the samples, the experts independently concluded that, despite Harve Benard's labels to the contrary, the garments contained no cashmere.[2] In addition, Dr. Wortmann found that approximately 10 to 20% of the fibers in the Harve Benard garments were recycled—that is, reconstituted from the deconstructed and chemically-stripped remnants of previously used or woven garments.

Relying on their experts' findings, plaintiffs filed this suit in district court claiming that defendants falsely advertised their garments in violation of § 43(a) of the Lanham Act, 15 U.S.C. § 1125(a), the

---

[2] The experts found that, at most, the garments contained only trace levels (less than 0.1%) of cashmere.

Massachusetts Unfair and Deceptive Trade Practices Act, Mass. Gen. Laws ch. 93A, and the common law of unfair competition. More specifically, plaintiffs claim that the garments were mislabeled in two material respects: (1) the Harve Benard blazers contained significantly less than the 10% cashmere they were represented as having ("cashmere content claim"); and (2) any cashmere that the blazers did contain was not virgin, as the unqualified word "cashmere" on the label suggests, but recycled ("recycled cashmere claim").[3] Each plaintiff seeks a different form of relief for these alleged misrepresentations: whereas the Institute seeks a permanent injunction against any future mislabeling, Packard seeks monetary damages on the theory that it lost sales as a result of the manufacture and sale of the mislabeled garments.

The district court granted partial summary judgment in favor of defendants, dismissing both of Packard's claims for money damages and seemingly dismissing the Institute's request for injunctive relief on its recycled cashmere claim. . . .

Discussion

. . . .

II.

The Lanham Act prohibits false and misleading descriptions of products and services in interstate commerce. *See* 15 U.S.C. § 1125(a). The statute was designed to protect consumers and competitors from any duplicitous advertising or packaging which results in unfair competition. *See id.*

To prove a false advertising claim under the Lanham Act, a plaintiff must demonstrate that (1) the defendant made a false or misleading description of fact or representation of fact in a commercial advertisement about his own or another's product; (2) the misrepresentation is material, in that it is likely to influence the purchasing decision; (3) the misrepresentation actually deceives or has the tendency to deceive a substantial segment of its audience; (4) the defendant placed the false or misleading statement in interstate commerce; and (5) the plaintiff has been or is likely to be injured as a result of the misrepresentation, either by direct diversion of sales or by a lessening of goodwill associated with its products. *See Clorox Co. P.R. v. Proctor & Gamble Commercial Co.*, 228 F.3d 24, 33 n.6.

A plaintiff can succeed on a false advertising claim by proving either that the defendant's advertisement is literally false or implicitly false— that is, the advertisement is true or ambiguous yet misleading. *See id.* Where the advertisement is literally false, a violation may be established

---

[3]   After this suit was filed, Harve Benard agreed to label its 1996 and subsequent line of blazers as being made from recycled cashmere.

without evidence of consumer deception. *See id.*; *Balance Dynamics Corp. v. Schmitt Indus.*, 204 F.3d 683, 693 (6th Cir. 2000) (noting that when a statement is literally false, "a plaintiff need not demonstrate actual customer deception in order to obtain relief"). Where the advertisement is implicitly false, however, "an additional burden is placed upon the plaintiff to show that the advertisement . . . conveys a misleading message to the viewing public." *Clorox*, 228 F.3d at 33.[8]

In addition, this Court has recognized a difference in the burdens of proof between injunctive relief claims and monetary damages claims under the Lanham Act. In *Quabaug Rubber Co. v. Fabiano Shoe Co., Inc.*, 567 F.2d 154 (1st Cir. 1977), we held that whereas a showing that the defendant's activities are likely to cause confusion or to deceive customers is sufficient to warrant injunctive relief, a plaintiff seeking damages must show actual harm to its business. *See id.* at 160–61.[9]

With these elaborate and intricate statutory requirements in mind, we assess plaintiffs' claims to determine if there is enough competent evidence for a reasonable factfinder to conclude that they have satisfied their burdens of proof under the Lanham Act.

A. Concessions

For the purposes of this appeal, defendants concede that they have made a false or misleading statement of fact in describing their blazers. Defendants also concede that they placed these misrepresentations in interstate commerce.

B. Materiality

The materiality component of a false advertising claim requires a plaintiff to prove that the defendant's deception is "likely to influence the purchasing decision." *Clorox*, 228 F.3d at 33 n.6. One method of establishing materiality involves showing that the false or misleading statement relates to an "inherent quality or characteristic" of the product. *Nat'l Basketball Ass'n v. Motorola, Inc.*, 105 F.3d 841, 855 (2d Cir. 1997).[10]

---

[8] As discussed below, a plaintiff alleging an implied falsity claim, however, is relieved of the burden of demonstrating consumer deception when there is evidence that defendants intentionally deceived the consuming public. . . .

[9] Furthermore, unlike a plaintiff seeking injunctive relief who only has to show that the misrepresentation had the tendency to deceive, a plaintiff seeking monetary damages must show that consumers were actually deceived by the misrepresentation, unless he can avail himself of a presumption to that effect.

[10] Whether a misrepresentation is material has nothing to do with the nature of the relief sought or the defendant's intent. Rather, materiality focuses on whether the false or misleading statement is likely to make a difference to purchasers. Thus, even when a statement is literally false or has been made with the intent to deceive, materiality must be demonstrated in order to show that the misrepresentation had some influence on consumers.

On their first claim, plaintiffs argue that overstating the cashmere content of cashmere-blend blazers is material because the misrepresentation relates to an inherent characteristic of the product sold. Indeed, it seems obvious that cashmere is a basic ingredient of a cashmere-blend garment; without it, the product could not be deemed a cashmere-blend garment or compete in the cashmere-blend market. Thus, it seems reasonable to conclude that defendants' misrepresentation of the blazers' cashmere content is material because it relates to a characteristic that defines the product at issue, as well as the market in which it is sold.

Moreover, defendants prominently labeled their garments as "Cashmere and Wool," "A Luxurious Blend of Cashmere and Wool," "Cashmere Blend," or "Wool and Cashmere," and their garments were conspicuously advertised in stores and catalogues as "Cashmere Blazers." It seems reasonable to infer from defendants' aggressive marketing strategy highlighting the "cashmere" nature of the blazers that defendants themselves believed cashmere to be an inherent and important characteristic of the blazers.

With respect to their second claim, plaintiffs argue that defendants' misrepresentation of the recycled nature of their cashmere also relates to an inherent characteristic of the garments. To substantiate this point, plaintiffs offer the affidavit of Karl Spilhaus, the Institute's president, in which he explains:

> The process of recycling . . . involves the use of machinery to tear apart existing garments, during or after which they are subjected to a wet processing with the resulting wool fibers dried out, frequently carbonized (subjected to heat and sulphuric acid), and then re-used in the manufacture of other fabric.
>
> In the process of tearing apart existing garments, considerable damage is inevitably done to the fibers in those garments, and additional damage is also done by the acid or other chemical treatments applied to them during the recycling process. The result is that recycled fibers frequently have substantial surface damage to their scale structure which effects [sic] their ability to felt, or bind together, thereby effecting [sic] the ability of a recycled fiber fabric to hold together as well or as long as fibers which are being used in the fabric for the first time. Such fabric will be rougher to the touch and lack "handle," plushness or softness normally associated with quality woolen or cashmere products.

Given the degree to which recycled fibers affect the quality and characteristics of a garment, a rational factfinder could conclude that consumers, especially experienced ones like retail stores, would likely be influenced in their purchasing decisions by labeling that gave the false impression that the garments contained virgin cashmere.[11]

In fact, plaintiffs offer anecdotal evidence as corroboration for this very assertion. In January 1996, Saks, one of Harve Benard's largest customers, learned that the cashmere blazers it had purchased from Harve Benard might contain recycled cashmere. Shortly thereafter, Lynne Ronon, the merchandise manager at Saks, met with representatives of Harve Benard to inform them that Saks did not wish to sell garments containing recycled cashmere. After the meeting, Carole Sadler, the associate counsel for Saks, sent Harve Benard a letter restating Saks' position as set forth by Ronon: "Saks does not wish to sell jackets containing recycled cashmere."

Rather than viewing this anecdote as evidence of how an actual consumer's purchasing decision was influenced by the misrepresentation, defendants draw the opposite conclusion by focusing on Saks' ultimate purchasing decision. Notwithstanding its earlier position, Saks eventually decided to sell Harve Benard garments containing recycled cashmere. Moreover, Sadler testified that Saks' initial refusal to sell recycled cashmere garments was merely a strategic move on an issue "that could ripen into a negotiation or a renegotiation" between the parties.

The problem with defendants' rebuttal argument, however, is that it ignores what a rational juror could find after drawing all reasonable inferences in plaintiffs' favor. Saks' initial refusal to sell the recycled cashmere garments; Saks' belief that the matter could lead to a negotiation; and the actual negotiations that took place before Saks agreed to continue selling the garments are competent evidence from which a reasonable juror could conclude that the issue related to an inherent quality or characteristic of the garment. Indeed, it makes little sense that Saks and Harve Benard would spend so much time and effort resolving a matter they deemed immaterial.

Furthermore, it is important to reiterate, as the caselaw explicitly states, that plaintiffs are not required to present evidence that defendants' misrepresentation actually influenced consumers' purchasing decisions, but that it was *likely* to influence them. *See Clorox*, 228 F.3d at 33 n.6. Given the significant degree to which using recycled fibers adversely impacts the quality, texture, and characteristics of cashmere, and considering Saks' erratic behavior upon learning of the mislabeling, we find that plaintiffs have presented sufficient evidence to demonstrate that defendants' recycled cashmere misrepresentation was material.

---

[11] The relevant "consumers" are those groups of people to whom the advertisement was addressed. In this case, the relevant consumers include, but are not limited to, the retail stores that purchased Harve Benard garments instead of buying from Packard's garment manufacturer customers and individual purchasers.

C. Consumer Deception

The next element of a false advertising claim under the Lanham Act requires plaintiffs to demonstrate that the alleged misrepresentation deceived a substantial portion of the consuming public. *See Clorox*, 228 F.3d at 33 n.6.[12] Usually consumer deception is demonstrated through surveys, which establish that consumers were misled by the alleged misrepresentations. Plaintiff-appellant Packard argues, however, that it does not have to shoulder the burden of presenting this evidence because existing caselaw allows plaintiffs like it who allege claims that are literally false to avail themselves of a presumption of consumer deception. *See Castrol Inc. v. Pennzoil Co.*, 987 F.2d 939, 943 (3d Cir. 1993) (ruling that "a plaintiff must prove *either* literal falsity *or* consumer confusion, but not both"); *Johnson & Johnson v. GAC Int'l, Inc.*, 862 F.2d 975, 977 (2d Cir. 1988) ("When a . . . representation is literally or explicitly false, the court may grant relief without reference to the advertisement's impact on the buying public.").

In response, defendants recognize that a presumption of consumer deception is available to plaintiffs seeking injunctive relief for literal falsity claims; however, they argue that the presumption does not apply, without more, to plaintiffs seeking money damages for literal falsity claims.

Though there was once support for the assertion that consumer deception cannot be presumed simply because a plaintiff alleges a literal falsity claim for money damages . . . it has become the practice of most circuits to apply the presumption to all literal falsity claims. *See Pizza Hut, Inc. v. Papa John's Int'l, Inc.*, 227 F.3d 489, 497 (5th Cir. 2000) (holding, on a claim for damages and injunctive relief, that "when the statements of fact at issue are shown to be literally false, the plaintiff need not introduce evidence on the issue of the impact the statements had on consumers. . . . [However] [p]laintiffs looking to recover monetary damages for false or misleading advertising that is not literally false must prove actual deception"); *EFCO Corp. v. Symons Corp.*, 219 F.3d 734, 740 (8th Cir. 2000) (ruling, on a claim for damages, that "when an advertisement is literally false . . . the plaintiff need not prove that any of its customers were actually persuaded by the advertising"); *Balance*, 204 F.3d at 693 (noting that a presumption of consumer deception applies to a literal falsity claim for damages so long as there is other proof of marketplace damages); *B. Sanfield, Inc. v. Finlay Fine Jewelry Corp.*, 168 F.3d 967, 971 (7th Cir. 1999) (ruling, on a damages claim, that "[w]here the statement in question is actually false, then the plaintiff need not

---

[12] Since Packard is seeking monetary damages, it must demonstrate that consumers were actually deceived by the misrepresentations. Only plaintiffs seeking injunctive relief face the lesser burden of demonstrating a tendency to deceive.

show that the statement either actually deceived consumers or was likely to do so").

In fact, defendants' argument contradicts this Court's explicit pronouncements on the issue. In assessing whether a Lanham Act claim for injunctive relief and money damages had been properly dismissed, we stated, "If the advertisement is literally false, the court may grant relief without considering evidence of consumer reaction. In the absence of such literal falsity, an additional burden is placed upon plaintiff to show that the advertisement . . . conveys a misleading message to the viewing public." *Clorox*, 228 F.3d at 33 (internal citations omitted).

Moreover, applying a presumption of consumer deception to all literal falsity claims, irrespective of the type of relief sought, makes sense. When a plaintiff demonstrates that a defendant has made a material misrepresentation that is literally false, there is no need to burden the plaintiff with the onerous task of demonstrating how consumers perceive the advertising. . . . Common sense and practical experience tell us that we can presume, without reservation, that consumers have been deceived when a defendant has explicitly misrepresented a fact that relates to an inherent quality or characteristic of the article sold. To presume as much requires neither a leap of faith nor the creation of any new legal principle.[13]

Because defendants do not dispute that overstating cashmere content is a literal falsity claim, we apply a presumption of consumer deception in plaintiffs' favor on this claim. Based on this presumption, and defendants' failure to present evidence to rebut it, Packard has satisfied its burden of demonstrating consumer deception on its cashmere content claim.

Whether literal falsity is involved in plaintiffs' claim that defendants improperly labeled their goods as cashmere rather than recycled cashmere, however, is a contentious issue. Defendants argue that this claim is, by definition, one of implied falsity—that is, a representation that is literally true but in context becomes likely to mislead. *See Clorox*, 228 F.3d at 33 (defining an implied falsity claim as one in which the "advertisement, though explicitly true, nonetheless conveys a misleading message to the viewing public"). As further support for their argument, defendants offer a simple syllogism: all suits based on implied messages are implied falsity claims; since plaintiffs assert that the term "cashmere"

---

[13] Defendants also argue that before the presumption of consumer deception can apply to a literal falsity claim for damages, the plaintiff must demonstrate that the defendant intentionally deceived the consuming public. None of the five circuit cases cited supra, however, speaks of the intent to deceive as a prerequisite to applying a presumption of consumer deception on a literal falsity claim. As discussed in more detail below, the intent to deceive is an independent basis for triggering a presumption of consumer deception. See *William H. Morris Co. v. Group W, Inc.*, 66 F.3d 255, 258 (9th Cir. 1995) (ruling, on an implied falsity claim, that "[i]f [defendant] intentionally misled consumers, we would presume consumers were in fact deceived and [defendant] would have the burden of demonstrating otherwise").

on the garments' labels implicitly conveys the false message that the garments contain virgin cashmere, their claim must be one of implicit falsity.

We agree with defendants that normally a claim like plaintiffs', in which the representation at issue is literally true (the garments do contain cashmere as the label states) but is misleading in context (defendants failed to disclose that the cashmere is recycled), is evaluated as an implied falsity claim. *See id.* However, we disagree with defendants' assertion that all claims that rely on implied messages are necessarily implied falsity claims. In *Clorox*, this Court noted that "[a]lthough factfinders usually base literal falsity claims upon the explicit claims made by an advertisement, they may also consider any claims the advertisement conveys by 'necessary implication.'" *Id.* at 34–35. We explained that "[a] claim is conveyed by necessary implication when, considering the advertisement in its entirety, the audience would recognize the claim as readily as if it had been explicitly stated." *Id.* at 35.

After drawing all reasonable inferences in favor of the nonmoving party, a rational factfinder could conclude that plaintiffs' recycled cashmere claim is one of literal falsity. The Wool Products Labeling Act, 15 U.S.C. § 68 *et seq.*, requires recycled garments and fabrics, including cashmere, to be labeled as such. As a result, whenever a label represents that a garment contains the unqualified term "cashmere," the law requires that the garment contain only virgin cashmere. The Act, then, is essentially telling consumers that garments labeled "cashmere" can be presumed to be virgin cashmere "as if it had been explicitly stated." *Clorox*, 228 F.3d at 35. Plaintiffs also presented evidence demonstrating that experienced retailers, like Saks, were aware of the Act's requirements. Based on this evidence, we conclude that plaintiffs have presented sufficient evidence to demonstrate that consumers would view the term "virgin" as necessarily implicated when a garment was labeled "cashmere."

The district court rejected this argument because "[i]t is at least equally plausible to infer that Congress [in enacting the Wool Product Labeling Act] was concerned that it would be misleading for a seller to fail to distinguish between virgin and recycled cashmere, even though it would not be literally false to do so." The district court's argument, however, substitutes an irrelevant inquiry for the required analysis. Rather than assessing what consumers would necessarily infer from the unqualified term "cashmere" in light of the Act's requirements, the district court delved into issues of congressional intent and statutory interpretation. *See* [Johnson & Johnson * Merck Consumer Pharm. Co. v. Smithkline Beecham Corp., 960 F.2d 294, 297 (2d Cir. 1992)] ("The question in such cases is—what does the person to whom the advertisement is addressed find to be the message?"). Because the Act necessarily implies the term "virgin" anytime the unmodified word "cashmere" appears on a garment's label and experienced retailers, like Saks, were aware of the Act's requirements, we rule that plaintiffs' recycled cashmere claim can be reasonably seen as one of literal falsity. Therefore, plaintiffs may benefit from a presumption of consumer deception on this claim.

Even if plaintiffs' recycled cashmere claim did not involve literal falsity, plaintiffs would still be able to avail themselves of a presumption of consumer deception on alternative grounds. It is well established that if there is proof that a defendant intentionally set out to deceive or mislead consumers, a presumption arises that customers in fact have been deceived. *See Porous Media Corp. v. Pall Corp.*, 110 F.3d 1329, 1333 (8th Cir. 1997) (approving of a presumption of consumer deception upon a finding that defendant acted deliberately to deceive); *see also U-Haul Int'l, Inc. v. Jartran, Inc.*, 793 F.2d 1034, 1041 (9th Cir. 1986) (same).

As evidence of defendants' intentional mislabeling of the blazers' recycled cashmere, plaintiffs introduced a letter dated January 13, 1995, addressed to Harve Benard's president, Bernard Holtzman, from one of Harve Benard's testing laboratories. On the top of the letter, there is a handwritten note from "L. Pedell," an agent for Harve Benard, which states, "Also see note from mill below. This is an on-going saga." The note that Pedell is referring to reads, in pertinent part, "FOR YOUR INFO PLS NOTE MILL IS USING RECICLED CHASMERE [sic]." Despite receiving notice that its blazers were being made from recycled cashmere, Harve Benard continued to market its garments without any "recycled" designation, as required by law, until months after the commencement of this lawsuit in 1996. Thus, Harve Benard's unwillingness to comply with the law, despite being on notice of its violation, can be seen as an attempt deliberately to deceive the consuming public.

In response, defendants offer several factual and legal arguments, none of which we find persuasive. First, defendants argue that a presumption of consumer deception cannot be triggered on an implied falsity claim, even if there is evidence of an intent to deceive. Defendants' claim, however, is undermined by several circuit cases that have explicitly held otherwise. The justification for applying the presumption whenever there is evidence of intentional deception is perspicuous: "The expenditure by a competitor of substantial funds in an effort to deceive customers and influence their purchasing decisions justifies the existence of a presumption that consumers are, in fact, being deceived." *U-Haul*, 793 F.2d at 1041. This reasoning holds true regardless of whether the claim that plaintiffs allege involves an implied or literal falsity.

Second, defendants argue that the fact that an Italian mill stated that it was using recycled cashmere has little bearing on whether the mill was using cashmere that would be considered recycled under the definitions of the Wool Products Labeling Act. Defendants seem to misunderstand or underestimate the import of the letter. One of Harve Benard's mills informed the president of the company that its cashmere-blend garments contained recycled fabric. Rather than investigating the matter to determine whether Harve Benard was violating the law by not properly labeling its cashmere as "recycled," Harve Benard did nothing. It did not finally change the garments' labels until more than one year later when plaintiffs sought a temporary restraining order on the issue. One reasonable explanation, which a juror may choose to credit, for Harve Benard's refusal to investigate or act on the letter is that Harve Benard intended to deceive the consuming public about the recycled nature of its cashmere. *Cf. Amirmokri v. Balt. Gas & Elec. Co.*, 60 F.3d 1126, 1133 (4th Cir. 1995) (noting that intent may be inferred from a failure to act).

. . . .

With respect to the Institute's recycled cashmere claim for injunctive relief, the district court dismissed the claim because the Institute failed to demonstrate evidence of consumer deception. Because the foregoing analysis applies with equal force to the Institute's recycled cashmere claim, we rule that the Institute can avail itself of a presumption of consumer deception. Thus, the district court erred in granting defendants' motion for summary judgment on the Institute's recycled cashmere claim.

Nothing in this opinion, however, is meant to preclude defendants from rebutting the presumption of consumer deception at trial by showing that the labeling did not actually deceive consumers.

D. Causation and Damages

. . . .

In order to prove causation under § 1125(a) of the Lanham Act, the aggrieved party must demonstrate that the false advertisement actually harmed its business. "A precise showing is not required, and a diversion of sales, for example, would suffice." *Quabaug*, 567 F.2d at 161 (internal citations omitted).[16]

To satisfy this requirement, plaintiffs present two pieces of interrelated evidence. First, plaintiffs point to Harve Benard's purchase orders which demonstrate that Harve Benard was paying $5 per yard less for the fabric it was using to make its garments than Packard's

---

[16] Defendants at oral argument suggested that plaintiffs could not be damaged by Harve Benard's alleged mislabeling because the parties operate in different markets: whereas Harve Benard sells finished garments to retailers, Packard sells fabric to manufacturers. Defendants later conceded, however, that if Packard were to demonstrate that manufacturers refused to purchase its fabric because of defendants' false advertising and concomitant low prices, causation would be proved. Thus, the fact that the two parties are in different markets does not affect the analysis, so long as plaintiffs can prove the causal connection between the misrepresentations and the harm sustained.

customers, who were paying for legitimate 10% cashmere fabric. Next, plaintiffs offer uncontradicted evidence that Packard's customers actually reduced their purchases of Packard's cashmere-blend fabric because they could not compete with Harve Benard's lower-priced garments. Specifically, Peter Warshaw, a sales agent for Packard, testified that three of Packard's customers—Gilmore, RCM, and Perfect Petite— notified him that they could no longer purchase Packard's cashmere- blend fabric because Harve Benard's lower-priced garments were driving them out of the market. This evidence supports the plaintiffs' claim that Harve Benard's low prices caused Packard lost sales.

The critical question, then, is what enabled Harve Benard to lower its prices to the point that prospective competitors refused to purchase Packard fabric. Based on the evidence presented, a rational factfinder could reasonably infer that the substantial cost savings Harve Benard enjoyed from using non-cashmere or recycled cashmere fabric allowed Harve Benard to lower the price of its blazers, thereby preventing Packard's customers from competing in the market. Indeed, using inexpensive materials that are represented as something more valuable would generally create a substantial competitive advantage by undercutting competitors who correctly represent their products. *See* [Camel Hair & Cashmere Inst. Of Am. Inc. v. Associated Dry Goods Corp., 799 F.2d 6, 13 (1st Cir. 1986)] (approving the district court's commonsense "inference that the sale of cashmere-blend coats which overstated their cashmere content could cause a loss of sales of cashmere- blend coats which correctly stated their cashmere content"). This reasonable inference, to which plaintiffs are entitled at summary judgment, enables plaintiffs to demonstrate the causal link between the harm they suffered and defendants' misrepresentations.

In response, defendants argue that it is unreasonable to infer that Harve Benard's lower fabric costs translated into lower garment prices given that evidence in the record suggests otherwise. In his affidavit, Harve Benard's vice-president Harvey Schutzbank stated that Harve Benard's garment prices would have remained the same even if it had used the more expensive Packard fabric to manufacture its garments. Based on this evidence, Harve Benard claims it would still have enjoyed the same price advantage that prevented Packard's customers from competing in the market even if the garments had been properly labeled and manufactured with legitimate 10% cashmere fabric. In short, defendants cite Schutzbank's affidavit as proof that it was Harve Benard's low prices—not its mislabeling—that caused Packard's lost sales.

We agree with defendants that if they were to present undisputed evidence establishing that their garment prices would have remained the same even if they had used Packard fabric, it would be unreasonable to infer that Harve Benard's lower fabric costs translated into lower garment prices. However, plaintiffs present competent evidence which casts serious doubt on Schutzbank's testimony. Packard's president John Glidden testified to the relationship between fabric cost and garment price:

> Because Harve Benard was not putting the cashmere in the fabric, they had a tremendously reduced cost. . . . [T]he added expense of putting cashmere in a garment or in a fabric increases the garment's cost; and when [Packard] legitimately labeled [its] fabrics, [the fabrics] were too expensive for the marketplace which Harve Benard was selling to.

Moreover, Warshaw, who has years of experience working with garment manufacturers, testified that "Harve Benard had an unfair competitive advantage in fabric that is the major component of a garment. . . . *[B]y far and away the largest component of the total costs of a garment is the fabric.*" (emphasis added). He also testified to Harve Benard's comparative advantage:

> [T]he garment manufacturers that are available to compete with Harve Benard are savvy, smart, sharp manufacturers who have at their disposal cheap labor, cheap trim, cheap transportation. They have available to them the same range of possibilities for plugging in to a garment, except that if those sharp competitors use a Packard product that's $11.25, they're going to get blown out of the water by Harve Benard['s use of] inexpensive [ ] fabric.

After weighing all of this evidence, a rational jury could choose to discredit Schutzbank's affidavit, especially considering (1) the commonsense inference that a lower fabric cost translates into a price advantage; (2) the fact that Schutzbank does not provide any quantitative analysis to substantiate his bald assertion that the garments' prices would have remained the same even if Harve Benard were to have used the more expensive Packard fabric; (3) several "savvy, smart, sharp" garment manufacturers could not do what Harve Benard claims it can— that is, use Packard fabric and still keep its low prices; and (4) two of plaintiffs' witnesses assert that fabric cost has a substantial impact on garment price.

In the end, the parties present witnesses who hold inconsistent positions on a crucial issue of fact. Rather than weighing in on the matter, we conclude that this dispute is one which a jury is best suited to resolve.

III.

The district court dismissed plaintiffs' state law claims because it found that since plaintiffs were unable to satisfy the requirements of a

Lanham Act claim, they would not be able to prove their state law claims, as the two have overlapping requirements. Because the district court erred in concluding that plaintiffs' proof was insufficient to qualify for relief under the Lanham Act, we reverse its decision to dismiss plaintiffs' state law claims.

Conclusion

Based on the foregoing analysis, a reasonable factfinder could conclude that the defendants' material mislabeling of their garments deceived the consuming public, enabled defendants to lower their garment prices, and caused Packard to lose sales. For these reasons, we find summary judgment inappropriate, reverse the district court's judgment, and remand the case for action consistent with this opinion.

NOTES & QUESTIONS

(1)   What is the materiality standard under the Lanham Act and why did the *Cashmere* court find that it was met? In particular, why was the court not persuaded by the fact that Saks Fifth Avenue purchased the garments from Harve Bernard, Ltd. despite knowledge of the misrepresentation? What would the outcome have been under the Restatement of Unfair Competition § 3?

(2)   The court notes that one way to show materiality is to demonstrate that the false statement relates to an "inherent quality or characteristic of the product." This "inherent quality or characteristic" test is one developed by the Second Circuit. Some courts have made this an indispensable prerequisite, or *sine qua non*, of materiality, but amendments made to the language of the Lanham Act in 1988 have called into question the continued validity of this approach. In particular, § 43(a)(1)(A) now expressly encompasses misrepresentations relating to the actor's "commercial activities" in addition to misrepresentations relating to "goods" or "services." One commentator has opined that the fact that a representation goes to an inherent quality or characteristic merely creates a presumption of materiality. *See* R.J. Leighton, *Materiality and Puffing in Lanham Act False Advertising Cases: The Proofs, Presumptions and Pretexts*, 94 Trademark Rptr. 585, 594 (2004).

What do you think of the "inherent quality or characteristic" test as the test for whether a misrepresentation is material? Is such an approach consistent with the language of the Lanham Act § 43(a)? With the Restatement of Unfair Competition § 3?

(3)   An element of the plaintiff's case is to show consumer deception. How would you normally demonstrate consumer deception? How did the plaintiffs demonstrate it here?

(4)   A question left open by the consumer deception prong is how many persons need to have been deceived by the advertisement? Courts have

characterized the number required as needing to be "statistically significant," or "a substantial portion of the intended audience." *Johnson & Johnson-Merck Consumer Pharm. Co. v. Smithkline Beecham Corp.*, 960 F.2d 294 (2d Cir. 1992); *Johnson & Johnson-Merck Consumer Pharm. Co. v. Rhone-Polenc Rorer Pharm.*, 19 F.3d 125 (3d Cir. 1994). This does not mean a majority of consumers, but the standard is still a vague one, even with modifiers like "significant" and "substantial." Percentages of deceived respondents as low as 15% have been found sufficient to meet the burden of proof, *Novartis Cons. Health Inc. v. Johnson & Johnson-Merck Consumer Pharm. Co.*, 290 F.3d 578 (3d Cir. 2002), but 7.5% has been found insufficient. *Johnson & Johnson-Merck Consumer Pharm. Co. v. Rhone-Polenc Rorer Pharm.*, 19 F.3d 125, 134 & n.14 (3d Cir. 1994) (noting that 20% would likely be sufficient for other courts).

(5) Related to establishing that a substantial number of consumers have been deceived (or are likely to be deceived) is the validity of the tests used to establish deception. In evaluating the trustworthiness of consumer surveys, courts have considered a number of criteria such as: (1) was the "universe" (the population the poll aims to measure) properly defined, (2) was a representative sample of that universe selected, (3) were the questions asked of interviewees framed in a clear, precise, and non-leading manner, (4) were sound interview procedures followed by competent interviewers who had no knowledge of the litigation or the purpose for which the survey was conducted, (5) was the data gathered accurately reported, (6) was the data analyzed in accordance with accepted statistical principles and (7) was the objectivity of the entire process maintained. *See Schering Corp. v. Pfizer Inc.*, 189 F.3d 218, 224–25 (2d Cir. 1999); *see also Friends of Boundary Waters Wilderness v. Bosworth*, 437 F.3d 815, 825 (8th Cir. 2006); *Brokerage Concepts, Inc. v. U.S. Healthcare, Inc.*, 140 F.3d 494, 517 (3d Cir. 1998); *Jellibeans, Inc. v. Skating Clubs of Georgia, Inc.*, 716 F.2d 833, 846 (11th Cir. 1983).

(6) The court in *Cashmere* notes that the failure to disclose the recycled nature of the fabrics was one of literal falsity. How can an omission be a literally false claim?

(7) A mere failure to disclose does not normally trigger a violation of § 43(a) (but a half-truth, partially incorrect representation, or a statement that is untrue as a result of a failure to disclose a material fact is actionable). Indeed, a number of courts have refused to find that a failure to disclose something that is required under another federal law is actionable under the Lanham Act, particularly when the Food, Drug and Cosmetic Act (FDCA) is involved. *See Mylan Labs., Inc. v. Matkari*, 7 F.3d 1130, 1139 (4th Cir. 1993); *Sandoz Pharmaceuticals Corp. v. Richardson-Vicks, Inc.*, 902 F.2d 222, 231 (3d Cir. 1990); *see also All One God Faith, Inc. v. Hain Celestial Grp., Inc.*, No. C 09–03517 JF (HRL), 2009 WL 4907433 (N.D. Cal. 2009) (involving the U.S.D.A. & Organic Food Products Act). For instance, in *IQ Products Co. v. Pennzoil Products Co.*, 305 F.3d 368 (5th Cir. 2002), the plaintiffs alleged a violation of the Federal Hazardous Substances Act (FHSA) when a

competitor failed to label its product as "flammable" as required by the act, thus implying that the product was non-flammable. After noting that the FHSA does not provide for a private cause of action, the court refused to recognize a right of action under the Lanham Act. The court held:

> [T]he FHSA vests the [Consumer Product Safety Commission (CPSC)] with the authority to enforce federal labeling requirements. In this case, the CPSC was aware of [defendants'] alleged labeling deficiencies but took no action. As a result, [plaintiff] essentially seeks to enforce the labeling requirements of the FHSA—an action which the CPSC, the enforcing agency, declined to do. For these reasons, we conclude that the defendants' failure to label the product in keeping with FHSA regulations, even if true, does not constitute a false or misleading statement that is actionable under the Lanham Act.

Id. at 374. Based upon this reasoning, why did the court permit the omission claim of Packard and the Institute to go forward?

(8)   The court holds that both claims were literally false. If they were not literally false, would the plaintiffs' claims have been dismissed?

1.   LITERAL FALSITY, LITERALLY FALSE BY NECESSARY IMPLICATION, AND IMPLIED FALSITY

In the *Cashmere* case, we saw what are commonly listed as the elements of a Lanham Act false advertising claim: (1) a false statement of fact by the defendant in a commercial advertisement about its own or another's product; (2) the statement actually deceives or has a tendency to deceive a substantial segment of its audience; (3) the deception is material, in that it is likely to influence the purchasing decision; (4) the defendant placed the false or misleading statement in interstate commerce; and (5) the plaintiff has been or is likely to be injured as a result of the false statement.[c]

The first element of falsity can be difficult to establish and involves a two-step process. The court first determines what the message being conveyed by the advertisement is, and then decides whether the message is false. You may have noticed in *Cashmere* that the nature of the falsity was of particular importance as it affected the plaintiffs' burdens on the element of consumer deception. The *Cashmere* court identified three types of false or misleading statements: literally false statements, statements that are literally false by necessary implication, and implied false statements (sometimes referred to as literally true or ambiguous statements that are misleading). Differentiating statements that are literally false by necessary implication from those that are merely

---

[c]   The *Cashmere* court listed the materiality element before the consumer deception element, but many courts list them in the order set forth above.

impliedly false is no easy matter. In its explanation of the concept of literally false by necessary implication, the *Cashmere* court quoted *Clorox Co. P.R. v. Proctor & Gamble Comm. Co.*, 228 F.3d 24 (1st Cir. 2000). A fuller version of the quote from *Clorox* is enlightening on the subject:

> A claim is conveyed by necessary implication when, considering the advertisement in its entirety, the audience would recognize the claim as readily as if it had been explicitly stated. . . . This is not to say, however, that all messages implied by an advertisement will support a finding of literal falsity by a factfinder:
>
> > The greater the degree to which a message relies upon the viewer or consumer to integrate its components and draw the apparent conclusion, however, the less likely it is that a finding of literal falsity will be supported. Commercial claims that are implicit, attenuated, or merely suggestive usually cannot fairly be characterized as literally false.
>
> *United Indus. Corp.*, 140 F.3d at 1181. Similarly, a factfinder might conclude that the message conveyed by a particular advertisement remains so balanced between several plausible meanings that the claim made by the advertisement is too uncertain to serve as the basis of a literal falsity claim, though even in that case it could still form the basis for a claim that the advertisement is misleading.

Id. at 35.

NOTES & QUESTIONS

(1) Recall that the *Black Hills* case involved a claim that the manufacturers at issue were advertising their jewelry as "Black Hills Gold Jewelry," although it was not manufactured in the Black Hills region. Were the advertisements at issue in that case literally false, literally false by necessary implication, or literally true (or ambiguous) but misleading? How can you tell?

2. LITERAL FALSITY AND "PUFFERY"

A concept that is related to falsity, as well as to the elements of consumer deception and materiality, is "puffery." The Fifth Circuit, in the oft cited case of *Pizza Hut, Inc. v. Papa John's Int'l, Inc.*, 227 F.3d 489 (5th Cir. 2000), offered the following summary description of puffery:

> One form of non-actionable statements of general opinion under section 43(a) of the Lanham Act has been referred to as "puffery." Puffery has been discussed at some length by other circuits. The Third Circuit has described "puffing" as

"advertising that is not deceptive for no one would rely on its exaggerated claims." *U.S. Healthcare, Inc. v. Blue Cross of Greater Philadelphia*, 898 F.2d 914 (3d Cir.1990). Similarly, the Ninth Circuit has defined "puffing" as "exaggerated advertising, blustering and boasting upon which no reasonable buyer would rely and is not actionable under 43(a)." *Southland Sod Farms v. Stover Seed Co.*, 108 F.3d 1134, 1145 (9th Cir.1997).[6]

... A leading authority on unfair competition has defined "puffery" as an "exaggerated advertising, blustering, and boasting upon which no reasonable buyer would rely," or "a general claim of superiority over a comparative product that is so vague, it would be understood as a mere expression of opinion." 4 J. Thomas McCarthy, McCarthy on Trademark and Unfair Competition § 27.38 (4th ed.1996). Similarly, Prosser and Keeton on Torts defines "puffing" as "a seller's privilege to lie his head off, so long as he says nothing specific, on the theory that no reasonable man would believe him, or that no reasonable man would be influenced by such talk." W. Page Keeton, et al., Prosser and Keeton on the Law of Torts § 109, at 757 (5th ed.1984).

Drawing guidance from the writings of our sister circuits and the leading commentators, we think that non-actionable "puffery" comes in at least two possible forms: (1) an exaggerated, blustering, and boasting statement upon which no reasonable buyer would be justified in relying; or (2) a general claim of superiority over comparable products that is so vague that it can be understood as nothing more than a mere expression of opinion.

Id. at 496–97.

A claim by a seller that their product is "the best" often is held to be nonactionable puffery. This distinction is sometimes based upon the concept that the statement is one of opinion rather than fact, and therefore is not false or is not a false statement of fact as required by the Lanham Act. However, even statements of opinion can be transformed into false statements of fact if they imply a factual basis for their assertion. *See* Chapter 2 (discussing statements of opinion). Furthermore, the context in which an assertion is made can affect whether a statement is viewed as one of fact or opinion. The above quoted case offers a prime

---

[6] In the same vein, the Second Circuit has observed that "statements of opinion are generally not the basis for Lanham Act liability." Groden v. Random House, 61 F.3d 1045, 1051 (2d Cir.1995). When a statement is "obviously a statement of opinion," it cannot "reasonably be seen as stating or implying provable facts." Id. "The Lanham Act does not prohibit false statements generally. It prohibits only false or misleading description[s] or false or misleading representations of fact made about one's own or another's goods or services." Id. at 1052.

example of the role puffery can play in defense of a false advertising claim.

In *Pizza Hut*, a series of advertisements run by Papa John's (a pizza chain) were alleged to have violated the Lanham Act by use of the slogan "Better Ingredients ... Better Pizza." Some of the television ads, in addition to promoting the slogan, also compared specific ingredients used by Papa John's in making its pizza sauce and dough to ingredients used by competing chains. Rival pizza vendor Pizza Hut alleged that the slogan, in the context of the ads, was a false statement as there was no scientific evidence that the ingredients used by Papa John's had any discernible effect on the taste of the pizza. Operating under the above definition of puffery, the Fifth Circuit Court of Appeals first examined the slogan itself and found, in isolation, that the slogan "Better Ingredients ... Better Pizza" was mere non-actionable puffery that stated an opinion. However, when taken in the context of the sauce and dough comparisons, the court held that there was sufficient evidence to conclude that the ads were misleading:

> We agree that the message communicated by the slogan "Better Ingredients ... Better Pizza ..." is expanded and given additional meaning when it is used as the tag line in the misleading sauce and dough ads. The slogan, when used in combination with the comparison ads, gives consumers two fact-specific reasons why Papa John's ingredients are "better." Consequently, a reasonable consumer would understand the slogan, when considered in the context of the comparison ads, as conveying the following message: Papa John's uses "better ingredients," which produces a "better pizza" because Papa John's uses "fresh-pack" tomatoes, fresh dough, and filtered water. In short, Papa John's has given definition to the word "better." Thus, when the slogan is used in this context, it is no longer mere opinion, but rather takes on the characteristics of a statement of fact. When used in the context of the sauce and dough ads, the slogan is misleading for the same reasons we have earlier discussed in connection with the sauce and dough ads.

Id. at 501–02.

Despite this finding, the court went on to find that the slogan did not violate the Lanham Act, as there was no showing of either consumer deception or materiality.[d] This serves as a useful reminder that showing

---

[d]   The court's opinion is actually somewhat confusing on this point. The court makes reference to both the materiality and consumer deception elements in a way that seems to collapse them into one. We think it is more prudent for you to keep the elements separate—a statement could likely deceive consumers, but not affect the ultimate purchasing decision (and

a false or misleading statement of fact has been made is simply one element of a false advertising claim. This raises an interesting question—in what way is the concept of puffery tied to the element of consumer deception? Can a literally false statement be puffery because no reasonable consumer would ever be deceived? Conversely, can non-actionable puffery be transformed into a statement of fact if evidence shows that consumers are actually deceived? Consider these questions as you read the following case.

AMERICAN ITALIAN PASTA COMPANY V. NEW WORLD PASTA COMPANY

371 F.3d 387 (8th Cir. 2004)

RILEY, CIRCUIT JUDGE.

"America's Favorite Pasta"—Commercial puffery or factual claim?

American Italian Pasta Company (American) sued New World Pasta Company (New World), seeking a declaratory judgment that American's use of the phrase "America's Favorite Pasta" does not constitute false or misleading advertising under section 43(a) of the Lanham Act, 15 U.S.C. § 1125(a)(1)(B) (2000). New World counterclaimed, asserting American's use of "America's Favorite Pasta" violated the Lanham Act and many states' unfair competition laws. On summary judgment, the district court concluded American's use of "America's Favorite Pasta" did not violate the Lanham Act, dismissing New World's counterclaims and declining to exercise jurisdiction over New World's state law claims. We affirm.

I. BACKGROUND

From 1997 to 2000, American manufactured Mueller's brand (Mueller's) dried pasta for Best Foods. In the fall of 2000, American purchased Mueller's and assumed all packaging, distributing, pricing, and marketing for the brand. Since purchasing Mueller's, American has placed the phrase "America's Favorite Pasta" on Mueller's packaging. On various packages, the phrases "Quality Since 1867," "Made from 100% Semolina," or "Made with Semolina" accompany the phrase "America's Favorite Pasta." The packaging also contains a paragraph in which the phrase "America's Favorite Pasta" appears. The paragraph states (1) pasta lovers have enjoyed Mueller's pasta for 130 years; (2) claims Mueller's "pasta cooks to perfect tenderness every time," because Mueller's uses "100% pure semolina milled from the highest quality durum wheat;" and (3) encourages consumers to "[t]aste why Mueller's is America's favorite pasta."

---

thus not be material). Conversely, a false statement, if believed, might affect the purchasing decision, but be made in such a way that no consumer is deceived.

New World sent American a letter demanding American cease and desist using the phrase "America's Favorite Pasta." Consequently, American filed this suit, requesting a declaration that its use of the phrase "America's Favorite Pasta" does not constitute false or misleading advertising under the Lanham Act. In its federal counterclaim, New World asserted American's use of "America's Favorite Pasta" violated the Lanham Act. New World claims American's use of the phrase is false or misleading advertising, because, according to New World's consumer survey, the phrase conveys Mueller's is a national pasta brand or the nation's number one selling pasta. American and New World agree Barilla sells the most dried pasta in the United States and American's brands are regional.

American moved to dismiss New World's counterclaims, arguing the phrase "America's Favorite Pasta" constituted non-actionable puffery. New World resisted American's motion and filed a motion for partial summary judgment. The district court denied American's motion, concluding it would have to consider facts outside the pleadings to determine if the phrase "America's Favorite Pasta" constituted puffery. Two weeks later, the district court denied New World's motion for partial summary judgment, dismissed New World's Lanham Act counterclaim, and declined to exercise jurisdiction over New World's state law counterclaims. The district court concluded the phrase "America's Favorite Pasta" constitutes non-actionable puffery as a matter of law, and the phrase is not actionable under the Lanham Act. New World appeals, contending the phrase "America's Favorite Pasta" is not puffery, but is a deceptive factual claim.

II. DISCUSSION

. . . . A purpose of the Lanham Act is "to protect persons engaged in commerce against false advertising and unfair competition." *United Indus. Corp. v. Clorox Co.*, 140 F.3d 1175, 1179 (8th Cir. 1998). To establish a false or deceptively misleading advertising claim under section 43(a) of the Lanham Act, New World must establish:

> (1) a false statement of *fact* by [American on its packaging] about its own or another's product; (2) the statement actually deceived or has the tendency to deceive a substantial segment of its audience; (3) the deception is material, in that it is likely to influence the purchasing decision; (4) the defendant caused its false statement to enter interstate commerce; and (5) the plaintiff has been or is likely to be injured as a result of the false statement.

Id. at 1180 (emphasis added). The failure to establish any element of the prima facie case is fatal.

Under section 43(a), two categories of actionable statements exist: (1) literally false factual commercial claims; and (2) literally true or ambiguous factual claims "which implicitly convey a false impression, are misleading in context, or [are] likely to deceive consumers." *United Indus.*, 140 F.3d at 1180. Besides actionable statements, a category of non-actionable statements exists. *Id.* Many statements fall into this category, popularly known as puffery. *Id.* Puffery exists in two general forms: (1) exaggerated statements of bluster or boast upon which no reasonable consumer would rely; and (2) vague or highly subjective claims of product superiority, including bald assertions of superiority.

Juxtaposed to puffery is a factual claim. A factual claim is a statement that "(1) admits of being adjudged true or false in a way that (2) admits of empirical verification." [Pizza Hut, Inc. v. Papa John's Int'l, Inc., 227 F.3d 489, 496 (5th Cir. 2000).]. To be actionable, the statement must be a "specific and measurable claim, capable of being proved false or of being reasonably interpreted as a statement of objective fact." *Coastal Abstract Serv., Inc. v. First Am. Title Ins. Co.*, 173 F.3d 725, 731 (9th Cir. 1999). Generally, opinions are not actionable. *Coastal Abstract*, 173 F.3d at 731.

Puffery and statements of fact are mutually exclusive. If a statement is a specific, measurable claim or can be reasonably interpreted as being a factual claim, i.e., one capable of verification, the statement is one of fact. Conversely, if the statement is not specific and measurable, and cannot be reasonably interpreted as providing a benchmark by which the veracity of the statement can be ascertained, the statement constitutes puffery. Defining puffery broadly provides advertisers and manufacturers considerable leeway to craft their statements, allowing the free market to hold advertisers and manufacturers accountable for their statements, ensuring vigorous competition, and protecting legitimate commercial speech.

A. "America's Favorite Pasta" Standing Alone

The phrase "America's Favorite Pasta," standing alone, is not a statement of fact as a matter of law. The key term in the phrase "America's Favorite Pasta" is "favorite." Used in this context, "favorite" is defined as "markedly popular especially over an extended period of time." Webster's Third New International Dictionary 830 (unabridged 1961). Webster's definition of "favorite" begs the question of how "popular" is defined. In this context, "popular" is defined as "well liked or admired by a particular group or circle." *Id.* at 1766. By combining the term "favorite" with "America's," American claims Mueller's pasta has been well liked or admired over time by America, a non-definitive person.[5]

---

[5] We note the outcome of this case might be different if American claimed Mueller's pasta was the favorite pasta of a specific person or an identifiable group. Such a claim might be a

"America's Favorite Pasta" is not a specific, measurable claim and cannot be reasonably interpreted as an objective fact. "Well liked" and "admired" are entirely subjective and vague. Neither the words "well liked" nor "admired" provide an empirical benchmark by which the claim can be measured. "Well liked" and "admired" do not convey a quantifiable threshold in sheer number, percentage, or place in a series. A product may be well liked or admired, but the product may not dominate in sales or market share. For example, assume a consumer's favorite cut of meat is beef tenderloin. If we were to look at the sheer amount of beef tenderloin our hypothetical consumer buys relative to other cuts of meat, beef tenderloin may not have a sizable market share or account for a significant percentage of the amount of money spent on meat. Therefore, we could not accurately determine whether beef tenderloin was the consumer's favorite cut of beef based on those benchmarks. The fact is, the consumer may admire beef tenderloin and like it best among beef cuts, but beef tenderloin is too expensive for our consumer to eat often. Likewise, sales volume and total dollars spent on particular pasta brands in the United States may not uncover America's favorite pasta.

"America's Favorite Pasta" also does not imply Mueller's is a national brand. First, "America's" is vague, and "America's," as well as "America" and "American" used in a similar context, is a broad, general reference. Second, a brand, chain, or product could be America's favorite without being national. For example, an individual restaurant or restaurant chain may be America's favorite, but may be located only in one or a few states. Although the restaurant chain may not be available nationally, consumers may prefer the restaurant because of its quality of food, quality of service, atmosphere, or some other attribute. Because "America's Favorite" depends on numerous characteristics, many of which may be intrinsic, a product (be it a restaurant, grits, or pasta) need not be sold nationally to be America's favorite.

B. "America's Favorite Pasta" Viewed In Context

Having decided the phrase "America's Favorite Pasta," standing alone, is not a statement of fact, we consider whether the context in which the phrase is used by American transforms it into a statement of fact. *See Pizza Hut*, 227 F.3d at 495 n.5 (noting the context in which a statement appears can be used to determine if the statement is actionable under the Lanham Act). "America's Favorite Pasta" appears on Mueller's packaging in two places. First, Mueller's packaging contains the phrase "America's Favorite Pasta" in the following paragraph (Paragraph):

---

statement of fact. For example, the claim that Mueller's is Judge Michael Melloy's favorite pasta would not be puffery. Such a statement is a factual statement that could be verified by simply asking Judge Melloy which pasta brand is his favorite.

> For over 130 years, pasta lovers have enjoyed the great taste of Mueller's. Our pasta cooks to perfect tenderness every time because it's made from 100% pure semolina milled from the highest quality durum wheat. Taste why Mueller's is America's favorite pasta.

Second, "America's Favorite Pasta" appears directly above "Quality Since 1867" on some packaging, and directly above "Made from 100% Semolina" or "Made with Semolina" on other packaging (Phrases).

The Paragraph and the Phrases fail to transform "America's Favorite Pasta" into a statement of fact. The Paragraph does not suggest a benchmark by which the veracity of American's statement can be verified. The Paragraph generally declares the brand has existed for 130 years, Mueller's tastes great, cooks to perfect tenderness, and is manufactured from high quality grain. We assume, *arguendo,* the sentence "Taste why Mueller's is America's favorite pasta" incorporates the attributes listed in the Paragraph into American's claim. Two attributes listed in the Paragraph are subject to verification: Mueller's is made from 100% pure semolina, and the brand is more than 130 years old. New World does not contend these claims are false. The remaining attributes listed in the Paragraph are unquantifiable and subject to an individual's fancy.

Notwithstanding the incorporation of these claims into "America's Favorite Pasta," the unverifiable attributes attenuate verifiable, and accurate, claims. "Taste why Mueller's is America's favorite pasta" suggests all of the attributes listed in the Paragraph are the reason Mueller's is "America's Favorite Pasta" and suggests each carries equal weight. The unquantifiable attributes coupled with two verifiable attributes do not render the phrase "America's Favorite Pasta" subject to verification.

Similarly, the Phrases do not convey a benchmark for "America's Favorite Pasta." The term "quality" is vague, entirely subjective, and a bare assertion of product superiority. In the context used, "quality" means "inherent or intrinsic excellence of character or type" or "superiority in kind." Webster's Third New International Dictionary 1858 (unabridged 1961). The only portion of "Quality Since 1867" that can be verified is "Since 1867," but "Since 1867" does not provide a methodology or a reason why Mueller's is America's favorite. The words simply state, accurately, when the brand was founded. Likewise, while presenting factual claims, the phrases "Made from 100% Semolina" and "Made with Semolina" do not define a methodology by which to ascertain the veracity of American's claim that Mueller's is "America's Favorite Pasta." The two phrases simply, and correctly, list characteristics of the pasta.

C. Consumer Surveys

We now consider whether the results of New World's consumer survey transform the phrase "America's Favorite Pasta" into a specific, measurable claim. In its survey, New World asked consumers if the phrase "America's Favorite Pasta" conveyed a meaning. According to New World, thirty-three percent of those surveyed allegedly perceived the phrase "America's Favorite Pasta" to mean Mueller's is the number one brand. Fifty percent of those surveyed allegedly perceived the phrase "America's Favorite Pasta" to mean Mueller's is a national brand.

The Seventh Circuit confronted a similar question in *Mead Johnson & Co. v. Abbott Labs.*, 201 F.3d 883 (7th Cir. 2000), *opinion amended on denial of reh'g*, 209 F.3d 1032 (7th Cir. 2000). Having concluded the phrase "1st Choice of Doctors" conveyed more doctors prefer this product over its rivals, the Seventh Circuit considered whether a consumer survey can assign a different meaning to a phrase. *Id.* at 883–84. Mead Johnson's survey indicated consumers perceived the phrase "1st Choice of Doctors" to mean a majority of doctors. Concluding the district court erred in using the survey to assign such a meaning, the Seventh Circuit noted, "never before has survey research been used to determine the meaning of words, or to set the standard to which objectively verifiable claims must be held." *Id.* at 886. While acknowledging dictionaries are surveys by people who devote their entire lives to discovering the usage of words, the Seventh Circuit cogitated "[i]t would be a bad idea to replace the work of these professionals with the first impressions of people on the street." *Id.* The Seventh Circuit reasoned that using consumer surveys to determine the benchmark by which a claim is measured would remove otherwise useful words from products and would reduce ads and packaging to puffery. *Id.* at 886–87.

We agree with the Seventh Circuit. To allow a consumer survey to determine a claim's benchmark would subject any advertisement or promotional statement to numerous variables, often unpredictable, and would introduce even more uncertainty into the market place. A manufacturer or advertiser who expended significant resources to substantiate a statement or forge a puffing statement could be blind-sided by a consumer survey that defines the advertising statement differently, subjecting the advertiser or manufacturer to unintended liability for a wholly unanticipated claim the advertisement's plain language would not support. The resulting unpredictability could chill commercial speech, eliminating useful claims from packaging and advertisements. As the Seventh Circuit noted, the Lanham Act protects against misleading and false statements of fact, not misunderstood statements. *Id.* at 886.

III. CONCLUSION

For the foregoing reasons, we affirm.

NOTES & QUESTIONS

(1) In *Pizza Hut*, the court held that the phrase "Better Ingredients . . . Better Pizza," when taken in the context of the ingredient comparison, was an actionable statement. In *American Italian*, the court held that American's "100% Semolina" claim, in conjunction with the assertion of being "America's Favorite Pasta," was non-actionable puffery. Can you explain the different conclusions?

(2) In its opinion, the *American Italian* court made the following observations:

> Puffery and statements of fact are mutually exclusive. If a statement is a specific, measurable claim or can be reasonably interpreted as being a factual claim, i.e., one capable of verification, the statement is one of fact. Conversely, if the statement is not specific and measurable, and cannot be reasonably interpreted as providing a benchmark by which the veracity of the statement can be ascertained, the statement constitutes puffery.

Do you agree with these observations? Is it possible for an assertion to be a false statement of fact, yet still be puffery because it is so outrageous that no reasonable consumer could rely upon it?

(3) New World attempted to introduce evidence that the phrase "America's Favorite Pasta" was misleading by conducting its own consumer survey. Relying upon precedent from the Seventh Circuit, the court refused to consider the surveys. Given that one of the purposes of the Lanham Act is to protect consumers from false or misleading advertising, does this approach make sense? What justification is there for refusing to consider such evidence?

(4) In *American Italian*, the court did not reach the issue of falsity because it held the complained of language was puffery. What if the court had not reached this conclusion—how would the plaintiff then carry its burden to show that the ad was false? What if the ad had stated that Mueller's was "Voted America's Favorite Pasta," but still did not identify a more specific person or group? Assume that American based this claim on a survey with a very small test group from only two U.S. cities. Would this affect the outcome? What does adding the word "Voted" imply? What if it turned out that American had conducted no survey whatsoever to support the "Voted" claim? Should this affect the plaintiff's burden of proof on falsity?

(5) Although this was not an issue in the *American Italian* case, a frequent method of advertising is to make a claim that a manufacturer's product is more effective or superior in some fashion. Sometimes the bald assertion of superiority is held simply to be puffery. In comparative advertising, however, some courts have distinguished between bald assertions of superiority and claims of superiority that appear to draw upon tests, lowering the burden for establishing falsity in the test-based claims. In

United Industries Corp. v. Clorox Corp., 140 F.3d 1175 (8th Cir. 1998), the Eighth Circuit noted this distinction:

> We have recently distinguished between two types of comparative advertising claims brought under the Lanham Act: (1) "my product is better than yours" and (2) "tests prove that my product is better than yours." When challenging a claim of superiority that does not make express reference to testing, a plaintiff must prove that the defendant's claim of superiority is actually false, not simply unproven or unsubstantiated. Under a "tests prove" claim, in which a defendant has buttressed a claim of superiority by attributing it to the results of scientific testing, a plaintiff must prove only that the tests relied upon were not sufficiently reliable to permit one to conclude with reasonable certainty that they established the proposition for which they were cited. However, to ensure vigorous competition and to protect legitimate commercial speech, courts applying this standard should give advertisers a fair amount of leeway, at least in the absence of a clear intent to deceive or substantial consumer confusion.

Id. at 1181–82 (internal citations and quotations omitted).

Generally, it is not sufficient to merely show that an advertiser lacked substantiation for its claims; rather, the challenger has to affirmatively prove them false. However, if an ad claims its assertion is established through tests or surveys, then these are known as substantiation or "tests prove" ads (also referred to as establishment claims). If the challenged advertisement is an "establishment claim," a plaintiff need only "prove that these tests did not establish the proposition for which they were cited." *Johnson & Johnson Vision Care, Inc. v. 1–800 Contacts, Inc.*, 299 F.3d 1242, 1248 (11th Cir. 2002); RESTATEMENT (THIRD) OF UNFAIR COMPETITION § 2 cmt. d (1995).

(6) What justification is there for treating mere claims of superiority differently from substantiation or "tests prove" claims with regard to what the plaintiff must prove to establish falsity? *See BASF Corp. v. Old World Trading Co.*, 41 F.3d 1081, 1091 (7th Cir. 1994) ("[Because] the conditions under which a statement is true or false vary according to the statement at issue, a plaintiff's burden of proof may be satisfied in different ways with respect to different statements.").

PROBLEM 7.1

DE, Inc. has, for 20 years, organized a car and truck show in Houston, Texas called Autopalooza which is held every February. Though competitor shows exist, they are not annual events and Autopalooza has been by far the largest and most successful in Houston. Two of DE, Inc.'s employees, Phineas Flynn and Frank Fletcher, left DE, Inc. last year and decided to start up their own car and truck show called Monster Car & Truck Show. Phineas and Frank each had worked for DE, Inc. for over ten years and were an integral part of putting the Autopalooza shows together. They decided to hold their show in March, one month after Autopalooza. As part of their advertising, they hosted a website stating that Monster Car & Truck Show is "Houston's #1 Car & Truck Show," with over "20 years of successful car show experience."

DE, Inc. wishes to sue Phineas and Frank to enjoin the ads from making these claims. Are the claims made in the ads false? If so, are they literally false? What defenses might Phineas and Frank raise?

PROBLEM 7.2

(a) Terminite is a manufacturer of a wood treatment chemical known as T–1 which it distributes nationwide. T–1's purpose is to prevent termite infestations in wood treated with its product. Terminite sells its product for use on wood to be used in homes, commercial buildings, and fences.

A competitor of Terminite, Osmite, has been successfully marketing its own product, T–3, to the same target audience. Concerned over its loss of market share, Terminite sponsors a series of tests in which it located fence posts treated with T–3 and inspected them for termite damage. Terminite's tests revealed that of the 600 posts examined, 10 had evidence of termite damage. Based upon these results, Terminite began to send pamphlets to its target contractors (those who use or might use T–1 or T–3) stating that "recent tests show termite infestation in a significant number of wood samples treated with Osmite's T–3 chemical. Terminite's T–1 has shown no such ill effects. All users of T–3 should be aware of these results." If Osmite chooses to sue to enjoin the ads, how will it show that the ads are false?

(b) Assume that instead of the above-quoted language, Terminite states the following in its pamphlets: "Recent test results examining the efficacy of T–3 on treated wood have caused our company concerns over the safety and use of this product. In our opinion, these tests show that T–3 is not a sufficient or reliable termite treatment alternative to using Terminite's T–1." How would this change the falsity analysis?

C. OTHER FORMS OF DECEPTIVE MARKETING: PASSING-OFF AND REVERSE PASSING-OFF

Thus far, we have discussed false advertising in its most straightforward form: where a competitor makes a false statement about its own products. In *Black Hills*, the statement regarded the origin of the product. In *Cashmere*, the statement regarded the quality of the goods. We have not yet discussed, however, passing-off claims or reverse passing-off claims. These two additional forms of deceptive marketing[e] warrant separate treatment.

---

[e] We refer to these claims as deceptive marketing rather than false advertising because they fall under § 43(a)(1)(A), which, unlike § 43(a)(1)(B), does not require the misrepresentations to be made as part of a commercial advertising or promotion.

1. PASSING-OFF

Passing-off, simply put, is attempting to convince consumers that your product is actually someone else's. Think of the street vendor selling "Rolex" watches which are undoubtedly knock-offs. This is passing-off. It is easy to see why Rolex would want to prevent such activities, as the potential exists to divert sales of authentic Rolex watches. Moreover, the knock-off watches, which are of inferior quality, may hurt the Rolex image if consumers believe that the shoddy watches are genuine Rolex.

The language of § 43(a)(1)(A) of the Lanham Act regarding false designations of origin and affiliation encompass passing-off claims. The Restatement of Unfair Competition has similarly addressed the issue in § 4:

> § 4. Misrepresentations Relating To Source: Passing Off
>
> One is subject to liability to another under the rule stated in § 2 if, in connection with the marketing of goods or services, the actor makes a representation likely to deceive or mislead prospective purchasers by causing the mistaken belief that the actor's business is the business of the other, or that the actor is the agent, affiliate, or associate of the other, or that the goods or services that the actor markets are produced, sponsored, or approved by the other.

From the language of § 4, as well as the Lanham Act, it should be clear that liability is not simply limited to passing-off one's goods as those of another, but can also extend to false association of services or sponsorship. The following illustration from the comments to § 4 helps illustrate this point:

> 1. A and B are plumbing firms. A has a contract to provide plumbing services to the University of Nebraska. B falsely represents to prospective customers that it is the firm that does the plumbing work for the University. B is subject to liability to A.

PROBLEM 7.3

Monarch Cola is a national soda manufacturer and distributor. Hank's Hoagies and Grinders is a sandwich franchise located throughout the state of Arkansas that has purchased Monarch Cola brand sodas for its franchise's soda fountains for many years. About a year ago, Hank's decided to stop selling Monarch soda in favor of its own similar tasting brand of soda, Hankerin' Soda. Hank's placed signs all around its stores noting that they no longer sold Monarch Cola products and Hank's employees were instructed to inform customers who asked for Monarch Cola that they did not carry it.

Monarch Cola subsequently sends agents into Hank's shops to see if requests for Monarch Cola are met with the appropriate response. They find that in a significant number of instances, when customers ask for Monarch Cola, they are served Hankerin' Soda instead without being told of the change. Should Hank's be liable to Monarch Cola for passing-off? *See* RESTATEMENT (THIRD) OF UNFAIR COMPETITION § 4 cmt. d (1995).

As the Rolex example suggested, there is a strong tie between passing-off and trademark infringement. Indeed, § 43(a)(1)(A) is often pled in conjunction with a trademark infringement claim brought under § 32 of the Lanham Act (§ 32 covers registered trademarks while § 43 is broad enough to cover unregistered marks). Comment b to § 4 of the Restatement explains this relationship:

> The "passing off" held actionable at common law was frequently accomplished through the use of confusingly similar trade symbols, and during the 19th century this general principle of liability served as the genesis of the technical rules governing the validity and infringement of trademarks and the recognition of secondary meaning. See § 9, Comment d. . . . If a misrepresentation of source or sponsorship arises solely from the unauthorized use of a trademark or other indicia of identification, relief must be sought under the rules stated in [Chapter 3 governing the law of trademarks].

RESTATEMENT (THIRD) OF UNFAIR COMPETITION § 4 cmt. b (1995). Due to this relationship, we will forestall further discussion of passing-off under the Restatement and the Lanham Act until Chapter 11.

2. REVERSE PASSING-OFF

Given that passing-off is attempting to convince consumers that your product is actually someone else's, it does not take much intuition to guess what reverse passing-off entails. It is attempting to convince consumers that someone else's product is actually your own. Again, the language of the Lanham Act under § 43(a)(1)(A) reaches such claims. The Restatement of Unfair Competition has also addressed the claim in § 5:

> § 5. Misrepresentations Relating To Source: Reverse Passing Off
>
> One is subject to liability to another under the rule stated in § 2 if, in marketing goods or services manufactured, produced, or supplied by the other, the actor makes a representation likely to deceive or mislead prospective purchasers by causing the mistaken belief that the actor or a third person is the manufacturer, producer, or supplier of the goods or services if

the representation is to the likely commercial detriment of the other under the rule stated in § 3.

An obvious example of reverse passing-off would be if an artist, Art, was hired to paint a portrait for buyer, Bert. Upon completing the work, Bert resells it to an art gallery claiming it to be an original painting, not by Art, but by Bert himself. Based on the strength of the work, the gallery commissions Bert to complete more paintings for it. Art is understandably upset as he feels that if the gallery knew that he was the true artist, he would have received the subsequent commissions. This simplified hypothetical involves another area of law, copyright, and indeed many cases will implicate the Copyright Act rather than the Lanham Act. The key to knowing whether the Lanham Act applies centers around the use of the word "origin" in the Lanham Act, as discussed in the following seminal case.

DASTAR CORPORATION V. TWENTIETH CENTURY FOX FILM CORPORATION
539 U.S. 23 (2003)

JUSTICE SCALIA delivered the opinion of the Court.

In this case, we are asked to decide whether § 43(a) of the Lanham Act, 15 U.S.C. § 1125(a), prevents the unaccredited copying of a work, and if so, whether a court may double a profit award under § 1117(a), in order to deter future infringing conduct.

I

In 1948, three and a half years after the German surrender at Reims, General Dwight D. Eisenhower completed Crusade in Europe, his written account of the allied campaign in Europe during World War II. Doubleday published the book, registered it with the Copyright Office in 1948, and granted exclusive television rights to an affiliate of respondent Twentieth Century Fox Film Corporation (Fox). Fox, in turn, arranged for Time, Inc., to produce a television series, also called Crusade in Europe, based on the book, and Time assigned its copyright in the series to Fox. The television series, consisting of 26 episodes, was first broadcast in 1949. . . . In 1975, Doubleday renewed the copyright on the book. . . . Fox, however, did not renew the copyright on the Crusade television series, which expired in 1977, leaving the television series in the public domain.

In 1988, Fox reacquired the television rights in General Eisenhower's book, including the exclusive right to distribute the Crusade television series on video and to sublicense others to do so. Respondents SFM Entertainment and New Line Home Video, Inc., in turn, acquired from Fox the exclusive rights to distribute Crusade on video. SFM obtained the negatives of the original television series, restored them, and repackaged the series on videotape; New Line distributed the videotapes.

Enter petitioner Dastar. In 1995, Dastar decided to expand its product line from music compact discs to videos. Anticipating renewed interest in World War II on the 50th anniversary of the war's end, Dastar released a video set entitled World War II Campaigns in Europe. To make Campaigns, Dastar purchased eight beta cam tapes of the *original* version of the Crusade television series, which is in the public domain, copied them, and then edited the series. Dastar's Campaigns series is slightly more than half as long as the original Crusade television series. Dastar substituted a new opening sequence, credit page, and final closing for those of the Crusade television series; inserted new chapter-title sequences and narrated chapter introductions; moved the "recap" in the Crusade television series to the beginning and retitled it as a "preview"; and removed references to and images of the book. Dastar created new packaging for its Campaigns series and (as already noted) a new title.

Dastar manufactured and sold the Campaigns video set as its own product. The advertising states: "Produced and Distributed by: *Entertainment Distributing*" (which is owned by Dastar), and makes no reference to the Crusade television series. Similarly, the screen credits state "DASTAR CORP presents" and "an ENTERTAINMENT DISTRIBUTING Production," and list as executive producer, producer, and associate producer employees of Dastar. The Campaigns videos themselves also make no reference to the Crusade television series, New Line's Crusade videotapes, or the book. Dastar sells its Campaigns videos to Sam's Club, Costco, Best Buy, and other retailers and mail-order companies for $25 per set, substantially less than New Line's video set.

In 1998, respondents Fox, SFM, and New Line brought this action alleging that Dastar's sale of its Campaigns video set infringes Doubleday's copyright in General Eisenhower's book and, thus, their exclusive television rights in the book. Respondents later amended their complaint to add claims that Dastar's sale of Campaigns "without proper credit" to the Crusade television series constitutes "reverse passing off"[1] in violation of § 43(a) of the Lanham Act, 15 U.S.C. § 1125(a), and in violation of state unfair-competition law. On cross-motions for summary judgment, the District Court found for respondents on all three counts, treating its resolution of the Lanham Act claim as controlling on the state-law unfair-competition claim because "the ultimate test under both is whether the public is likely to be deceived or confused." The court awarded Dastar's profits to respondents and doubled them pursuant to

---

[1] Passing off (or palming off, as it is sometimes called) occurs when a producer misrepresents his own goods or services as someone else's. "Reverse passing off," as its name implies, is the opposite: The producer misrepresents someone else's goods or services as his own.

§ 35 of the Lanham Act, 15 U.S.C. § 1117(a), to deter future infringing conduct by petitioner.

The Court of Appeals for the Ninth Circuit affirmed the judgment for respondents on the Lanham Act claim, but reversed as to the copyright claim and remanded. (It said nothing with regard to the state-law claim.) With respect to the Lanham Act claim, the Court of Appeals reasoned that "Dastar copied substantially the entire *Crusade in Europe* series created by Twentieth Century Fox, labeled the resulting product with a different name and marketed it without attribution to Fox[, and] therefore committed a 'bodily appropriation' of Fox's series." It concluded that "Dastar's 'bodily appropriation' of Fox's original [television] series is sufficient to establish the reverse passing off."[2] The court also affirmed the District Court's award under the Lanham Act of twice Dastar's profits. We granted certiorari.

II

The Lanham Act was intended to make "actionable the deceptive and misleading use of marks," and "to protect persons engaged in . . . commerce against unfair competition." 15 U.S.C. § 1127. While much of the Lanham Act addresses the registration, use, and infringement of trademarks and related marks, § 43(a), 15 U.S.C. § 1125(a) is one of the few provisions that goes beyond trademark protection. As originally enacted, § 43(a) created a federal remedy against a person who used in commerce either "a false designation of origin, or any false description or representation" in connection with "any goods or services." As the Second Circuit accurately observed with regard to the original enactment, however—and as remains true after the 1988 revision—§ 43(a) "does not have boundless application as a remedy for unfair trade practices," *Alfred Dunhill, Ltd. v. Interstate Cigar Co.*, 499 F.2d 232, 237 (2d Cir. 1974). . . .

Although a case can be made that a proper reading of § 43(a), as originally enacted, would treat the word "origin" as referring only "to the geographic location in which the goods originated," the Courts of Appeals considering the issue, beginning with the Sixth Circuit, unanimously concluded that it "does not merely refer to geographical origin, but also to origin of source or manufacture," *Federal-Mogul-Bower Bearings, Inc. v. Azoff*, 313 F.2d 405, 408 (6th Cir. 1963), thereby creating a federal cause of action for traditional trademark infringement of unregistered marks. Moreover, every Circuit to consider the issue found § 43(a) broad enough to encompass reverse passing off. The Trademark Law Revision Act of

---

[2] As for the copyright claim, the Ninth Circuit held that the tax treatment General Eisenhower sought for his manuscript of the book created a triable issue as to whether he intended the book to be a work for hire, and thus as to whether Doubleday properly renewed the copyright in 1976. The copyright issue is still the subject of litigation, but is not before us. We express no opinion as to whether petitioner's product would infringe a valid copyright in General Eisenhower's book.

1988 made clear that § 43(a) covers origin of production as well as geographic origin. Its language is amply inclusive, moreover, of reverse passing off—if indeed it does not implicitly adopt the unanimous court-of-appeals jurisprudence on that subject. *See, e.g., ALPO Petfoods, Inc. v. Ralston Purina Co.*, 913 F.2d 958, 963–64, n.6 (D.C. 1990) (Thomas, J.).

Thus, as it comes to us, the gravamen of respondents' claim is that, in marketing and selling Campaigns as its own product without acknowledging its nearly wholesale reliance on the Crusade television series, Dastar has made a "false designation of origin, false or misleading description of fact, or false or misleading representation of fact, which . . . is likely to cause confusion . . . as to the origin . . . of his or her goods." § 43(a). That claim would undoubtedly be sustained if Dastar had bought some of New Line's Crusade videotapes and merely repackaged them as its own. Dastar's alleged wrongdoing, however, is vastly different: It took a creative work in the public domain—the Crusade television series—copied it, made modifications (arguably minor), and produced its very own series of videotapes. If "origin" refers only to the manufacturer or producer of the physical "goods" that are made available to the public (in this case the videotapes), Dastar was the origin. If, however, "origin" includes the creator of the underlying work that Dastar copied, then someone else (perhaps Fox) was the origin of Dastar's product. At bottom, we must decide what § 43(a)(1)(A) of the Lanham Act means by the "origin" of "goods."

III

The dictionary definition of "origin" is "[t]he fact or process of coming into being from a source," and "[t]hat from which anything primarily proceeds; source." Webster's New International Dictionary 1720–21 (2d ed. 1949). And the dictionary definition of "goods" (as relevant here) is "[w]ares; merchandise." *Id.* at 1079. We think the most natural understanding of the "origin" of "goods"—the source of wares—is the producer of the tangible product sold in the marketplace, in this case the physical Campaigns videotape sold by Dastar. The concept might be stretched . . . to include not only the actual producer, but also the trademark owner who commissioned or assumed responsibility for ("stood behind") production of the physical product. But as used in the Lanham Act, the phrase "origin of goods" is in our view incapable of connoting the person or entity that originated the ideas or communications that "goods" embody or contain. Such an extension would not only stretch the text, but it would be out of accord with the history and purpose of the Lanham Act and inconsistent with precedent.

Section 43(a) of the Lanham Act prohibits actions like trademark infringement that deceive consumers and impair a producer's goodwill. It forbids, for example, the Coca-Cola Company's passing off its product as

Pepsi-Cola or reverse passing off Pepsi-Cola as its product. But the brand-loyal consumer who prefers the drink that the Coca-Cola Company or PepsiCo sells, while he believes that that company produced (or at least stands behind the production of) that product, surely does not necessarily believe that that company was the "origin" of the drink in the sense that it was the very first to devise the formula. The consumer who buys a branded product does not automatically assume that the brand-name company is the same entity that came up with the idea for the product, or designed the product—and typically does not care whether it is. The words of the Lanham Act should not be stretched to cover matters that are typically of no consequence to purchasers.

It could be argued, perhaps, that the reality of purchaser concern is different for what might be called a communicative product—one that is valued not primarily for its physical qualities, such as a hammer, but for the intellectual content that it conveys, such as a book or, as here, a video. The purchaser of a novel is interested not merely, if at all, in the identity of the producer of the physical tome (the publisher), but also, and indeed primarily, in the identity of the creator of the story it conveys (the author). And the author, of course, has at least as much interest in avoiding passing off (or reverse passing off) of his creation as does the publisher. For such a communicative product (the argument goes) "origin of goods" in § 43(a) must be deemed to include not merely the producer of the physical item (the publishing house Farrar, Straus and Giroux, or the video producer Dastar) but also the creator of the content that the physical item conveys (the author Tom Wolfe, or—assertedly—respondents).

The problem with this argument according special treatment to communicative products is that it causes the Lanham Act to conflict with the law of copyright, which addresses that subject specifically. The right to copy, and to copy without attribution, once a copyright has expired, like "the right to make [an article whose patent has expired]—including the right to make it in precisely the shape it carried when patented—passes to the public." *Sears, Roebuck & Co. v. Stiffel Co.*, 376 U.S. 225, 230 (1964). "In general, unless an intellectual property right such as a patent or copyright protects an item, it will be subject to copying." *TrafFix Devices, Inc. v. Marketing Displays, Inc.*, 532 U.S. 23, 29 (2001). The rights of a patentee or copyright holder are part of a carefully crafted bargain, under which, once the patent or copyright monopoly has expired, the public may use the invention or work at will and without attribution. Thus, in construing the Lanham Act, we have been "careful to caution against misuse or over-extension" of trademark and related protections into areas traditionally occupied by patent or copyright. *TrafFix*, 532 U.S. at 29. "The Lanham Act," we have said, "does not exist to reward manufacturers for their innovation in creating a particular device; that is the purpose of the patent law and its period of exclusivity." *Id.* at 34. Federal trademark law has no necessary relation to invention or discovery, but rather, by preventing competitors from copying "a source-identifying mark," "reduce[s] the customer's costs of shopping and making purchasing decisions," and "helps assure a producer that it (and not an imitating competitor) will reap the financial, reputation-related rewards associated with a desirable product," *Qualitex Co. v. Jacobson Products Co.*, 514 U.S. 159, 163–64 (1995) (internal quotation marks and citation omitted). Assuming for the sake of argument that Dastar's representation of itself as the "Producer" of its videos amounted to a representation that it originated the creative work conveyed by the videos, allowing a cause of action under § 43(a) for that representation would create a species of mutant copyright law that limits the public's federal right to copy and to use expired copyrights.

. . . .

Reading "origin" in § 43(a) to require attribution of uncopyrighted materials would pose serious practical problems. Without a copyrighted work as the basepoint, the word "origin" has no discernable limits. A video of the MGM film Carmen Jones, after its copyright has expired, would presumably require attribution not just to MGM, but to Oscar Hammerstein II (who wrote the musical on which the film was based), to Georges Bizet (who wrote the opera on which the musical was based), and to Prosper Merimee (who wrote the novel on which the opera was based). In many cases, figuring out who is in the line of "origin" would be no simple task. Indeed, in the present case it is far from clear that respondents have that status. Neither SFM nor New Line had anything to do with the production of the Crusade television series—they merely were licensed to distribute the video version. While Fox might have a claim to being in the line of origin, its involvement with the creation of the television series was limited at best. Time, Inc., was the principal, if not the exclusive, creator, albeit under arrangement with Fox. And of course it was neither Fox nor Time, Inc., that shot the film used in the Crusade television series. Rather, that footage came from the United States Army, Navy, and Coast Guard, the British Ministry of Information and War Office, the National Film Board of Canada, and unidentified "Newsreel Pool Cameramen." If anyone has a claim to being the *original* creator of the material used in both the Crusade television series and the Campaigns videotapes, it would be those groups, rather than Fox. We do not think the Lanham Act requires this search for the source of the Nile and all its tributaries.

Another practical difficulty of adopting a special definition of "origin" for communicative products is that it places the manufacturers of those products in a difficult position. On the one hand, they would face Lanham Act liability for *failing* to credit the creator of a work on which their lawful copies are based; and on the other hand they could face Lanham Act liability for *crediting* the creator if that should be regarded as implying the creator's "sponsorship or approval" of the copy, 15 U.S.C. § 1125(a)(1)(A). In this case, for example, if Dastar had simply "copied [the television series] as Crusade in Europe and sold it as Crusade in Europe," without changing the title or packaging (including the original credits to Fox), it is hard to have confidence in respondents' assurance that they "would not be here on a Lanham Act cause of action," Tr. of Oral Arg. 35.

Finally, reading § 43(a) of the Lanham Act as creating a cause of action for, in effect, plagiarism—the use of otherwise unprotected works and inventions without attribution—would be hard to reconcile with our previous decisions. For example, in *Wal-Mart Stores, Inc. v. Samara Bros., Inc.*, 529 U.S. 205 (2000), we considered whether product-design trade dress can ever be inherently distinctive. Wal-Mart produced "knockoffs" of children's clothes designed and manufactured by Samara Brothers, containing only "minor modifications" of the original designs. *Id.* at 208. We concluded that the designs could not be protected under § 43(a) without a showing that they had acquired "secondary meaning," *id.* at 214, so that they "identify the source of the product rather than the product itself," *id.* at 211. This carefully considered limitation would be entirely pointless if the "original" producer could turn around and pursue a reverse-passing-off claim under exactly the same provision of the Lanham Act. Samara would merely have had to argue that it was the "origin" of the designs that Wal-Mart was selling as its own line. It was not, because "origin of goods" in the Lanham Act referred to the producer of the clothes, and not the producer of the (potentially) copyrightable or patentable designs that the clothes embodied.

Similarly under respondents' theory, the "origin of goods" provision of § 43(a) would have supported the suit that we rejected in *Bonito Boats*, 489 U.S. 141, where the defendants had used molds to duplicate the plaintiff's unpatented boat hulls (apparently without crediting the plaintiff). And it would have supported the suit we rejected in *TrafFix*, 532 U.S. 23: The plaintiff, whose patents on flexible road signs had expired, and who could not prevail on a trade-dress claim under § 43(a) because the features of the signs were functional, would have had a reverse-passing-off claim for unattributed copying of his design.

In sum, reading the phrase "origin of goods" in the Lanham Act in accordance with the Act's common-law foundations (which were *not* designed to protect originality or creativity), and in light of the copyright and patent laws (which *were*), we conclude that the phrase refers to the producer of the tangible goods that are offered for sale, and not to the author of any idea, concept, or communication embodied in those goods. To hold otherwise would be akin to finding that § 43(a) created a species of perpetual patent and copyright, which Congress may not do. *See Eldred v. Ashcroft*, 537 U.S. 186, 208 (2003).

The creative talent of the sort that lay behind the Campaigns videos is not left without protection. The original film footage used in the Crusade television series could have been copyrighted, as was copyrighted (as a compilation) the Crusade television series, even though it included material from the public domain. Had Fox renewed the copyright in the Crusade television series, it would have had an easy claim of copyright infringement. And respondents' contention that Campaigns infringes Doubleday's copyright in General Eisenhower's book is still a live question on remand. If, moreover, the producer of a video that substantially copied the Crusade series were, in advertising or promotion, to give purchasers the impression that the video was quite different from that series, then one or more of the respondents might have a cause of action—not for reverse passing off under the "confusion . . . as to the origin" provision of § 43(a)(1)(A), but for misrepresentation under the "misrepresents the nature, characteristics [or] qualities" provision of § 43(a)(1)(B). For merely saying it is the producer of the video, however, no Lanham Act liability attaches to Dastar.

* * *

Because we conclude that Dastar was the "origin" of the products it sold as its own, respondents cannot prevail on their Lanham Act claim. We thus have no occasion to consider whether the Lanham Act permitted an award of double petitioner's profits. The judgment of the Court of Appeals for the Ninth Circuit is reversed, and the case is remanded for further proceedings consistent with this opinion.

NOTES & QUESTIONS

(1)   Reconsider the hypothetical used to introduce this case. Would Art have a valid reverse passing-off claim against Bert under *Dastar*'s reading of § 43(a)(1)(A)?

(2)   What rationale(s), both policy-based and practical, does the Court offer for limiting the scope of the word "origin"?

(3)   In the penultimate paragraph of the case, the court notes that the plaintiffs may have had a case under § 43(a)(1)(B) had the factual circumstances been slightly different than alleged. Why would a claim exist under the changed facts? Couldn't the plaintiffs have brought such a claim under the facts they alleged? In other words, if the defendant Dastar had been advertising on the packages (either impliedly or explicitly) that it was the creator of the Campaigns DVD when in fact it was substantially lifted from another source (and indeed a competitor's source), would this not meet the standard for false advertising under § 43(a)(1)(B)?

(4) The scope of the *Dastar* opinion and whether its limits on authorship claims apply to § 43(a)(1)(B) is somewhat of an open question. A number of courts have held that the words "nature, characteristics, [or] qualities" in § 43(a)(1)(B) cannot be read to refer to authorship. *See Antidite Intern. Films, Inc. v. Bloomsbury Pub., PLC*, 467 F. Supp. 2d 394, 400 (S.D.N.Y. 2006) ("If authorship were a 'characteristic[ ]' or 'qualit[y]' of a work, then the very claim *Dastar* rejected under § 43(a)(1)(A) would have been available under § 43(a)(1)(B)."); *Baden Sports, Inc. v. Molten USA, Inc.*, 556 F.3d 1300, 1307 (Fed. Cir. 2009) (concluding that authorship is not a "nature, characteristic, [or] quality" as those terms are used in § 43(a)(1)(B)); *cf. Sybersound Records, Inc. v. UAV Corp.*, 517 F.3d 1137, 1144 (9th Cir. 2008) (holding that the "nature, characteristics, and qualities" language of § 43(a)(1)(B) does not refer to the licensing status of a copyrighted good because to hold otherwise would create overlap between the Copyright Act and the Lanham Act).

For instance, in *Lapine v. Seinfeld*, No. 08 Civ. 128 (LTS) (RLE), 2009 WL 2902584 (S.D.N.Y. 2010), Missy Chase Lapine sued Jessica Seinfeld (wife of comedian Jerry Seinfeld) and her publishers for copyright and trademark infringement as well as for a violation of § 43(a)(1)(B). Lapine had authored a book titled *The Sneaky Chef: Simple Strategies for Hiding Healthy Food in Kids' Favorite Meals*, which, as the title indicates, is a book on sneaking healthy foods, such as vegetables, into children's meals. Lapine's book came out, and in the same year, Seinfeld released her thematically similar book, *Deceptively Delicious: Simple Secrets to Get Your Kids Eating Good Food*. After reviewing and comparing the two books, the court dismissed the copyright claims, finding that the books were not substantially similar (as is required for a copyright infringement claim), and also dismissed the trademark claims. The court then turned to the § 43(a)(1)(B) claim that Seinfeld had taken Lapine's ideas and used them in her book without permission or attribution to the source of the ideas and work. Relying upon the *Dastar* limitation on the word "origin," the court held that § 43(a)(1)(B) did not apply to claims of failure to attribute authorship. *Id.* at 15. In reaching that conclusion, the court relied upon other courts which had held that, under *Dastar*, authorship is not a characteristic or quality.

At first blush, this limitation seems to make sense. After all, if a copyright claim doesn't exist under the Copyright Act, why should the Lanham Act provide one? But does *Dastar* really exclude all false claims of authorship under § 43(a)(1)(B)? Is a holding that authorship is not a "nature, characteristic, [or] quality" consistent with the reasoning in *Dastar* in all circumstances? This broad reading of *Dastar* is not universally accepted. Consider the following excerpt and hypothetical from Professor David Nimmer's article, *The Moral Imperative Against Academic Plagiarism (Without a Moral Right Against Reverse Passing Off)*, 54 DEPAUL L. REV. 1 (2004):

> The broad reading is that the opinion negates any regulation by the Lanham Act that is geared at works of authorship, rather than

being limited to the domain under review of reverse passing off. Under this interpretation, the tort of authorial passing off . . . as well as reverse passing off is no longer cognizable under federal law. The result would be that a publisher could hire a hack to write a potboiler and proceed to emblazon the resulting cover with the false legend "By John Grisham and Stephen King, in an unprecedented collaboration."

Id. at 43. Under the rationale of *Dastar*, do you think Professor Nimmer is correct? Is barring a cause of action under § 43(a)(1)(A) or (B) in the above hypothetical consistent with the policy and practical concerns articulated by the Court?

(5)   What would have been the result in *Dastar* under the Restatement § 5? Is *Dastar* consistent with § 5?

D. STANDING FOR FALSE ADVERTISING CLAIMS AND CONTRIBUTORY LIABILITY

1. PRUDENTIAL STANDING

An important concern for plaintiffs, under both the Lanham Act and in states that follow the Restatement, is who can sue, i.e., who has standing? A quick review of the language in § 43(a) of the Lanham Act reveals few limitations on who can actually sue for a violation of its provisions. By its terms, "any person who believes that he or she is or is likely to be damaged" is capable of suing. Thus, it would appear that the consumer on the street who believes a false advertisement and makes a purchase could sue for a violation of the Lanham Act. This is, however, not the case. Courts have read into the Lanham Act a limit on who can sue under the concept of prudential standing. This is a judicially created limit on who can sue under an act based upon what conduct the act is aimed at and which parties the act seeks to protect. In the false advertising area, courts have determined that § 43 of the Lanham Act is meant to protect commercial interests. Thus, consumers cannot sue for violations of the Lanham Act (although there are a number of state statutes that prohibit deceptive practices which do convey standing upon consumers—we discuss these below in Section E).

Although the federal courts agree that consumers cannot sue for violations of the Lanham Act, for many years there existed disagreement over what limits should be placed on parties with a commercial interest. Consider the following example. Brock's Menswear is the exclusive distributor of Venture Brand watches (manufactured by Venture Industries). Brock's competitor, Black Heart's Apparel, begins falsely advertising that it also sells Venture Brand watches, but the watches are actually cheap knock-offs. Brock's is the main competitor of Black Heart's, but is there any doubt that this false advertising will also harm Venture

Industries? Should the Lanham Act apply only to direct competitors, or can it also apply to those farther up (or down) the supply chain who are also injured by a false or misleading advertisement? Until 2014, the federal circuit courts were split over how to approach this problem. One approach, known as the "categorical" test, limited standing only to those persons in actual competition with each other. A second approach known as the "reasonable interest" test, looked to whether the plaintiff has some reasonable interest to be protected. Finally other courts adopted the "Conte Brothers" test, which was taken from the Third Circuit decision of *Conte Brothers Automotive, Inc. v. Quaker State-Slick 50, Inc.*, 165 F.3d 221 (3d Cir. 1998). That test considers five factors in weighing whether a plaintiff has standing. As you can see below, the Supreme Court was not satisfied with any of these tests (or with the label of "prudential standing").

LEXMARK INTERNATIONAL, INC. V. STATIC CONTROL COMPONENTS, INC.

134 S. Ct. 1377 (2014)

JUSTICE SCALIA delivered the opinion of the Court.

This case requires us to decide whether respondent, Static Control Components, Inc., may sue petitioner, Lexmark International, Inc., for false advertising under the Lanham Act, 15 U.S.C. § 1125(a).

I. Background

Lexmark manufactures and sells laser printers. It also sells toner cartridges for those printers (toner being the powdery ink that laser printers use to create images on paper). Lexmark designs its printers to work only with its own style of cartridges, and it therefore dominates the market for cartridges compatible with its printers. That market, however, is not devoid of competitors. Other businesses, called "remanufacturers," acquire used Lexmark toner cartridges, refurbish them, and sell them in competition with new and refurbished cartridges sold by Lexmark.

Lexmark would prefer that its customers return their empty cartridges to it for refurbishment and resale, rather than sell those cartridges to a remanufacturer. So Lexmark introduced what it called a "Prebate" program, which enabled customers to purchase new toner cartridges at a 20-percent discount if they would agree to return the cartridge to Lexmark once it was empty. Those terms were communicated to consumers through notices printed on the toner-cartridge boxes, which advised the consumer that opening the box would indicate assent to the terms—a practice commonly known as "shrinkwrap licensing," see, *e.g.,* *ProCD, Inc. v. Zeidenberg*, 86 F.3d 1447, 1449 (C.A.7 1996). To enforce the Prebate terms, Lexmark included a microchip in each Prebate cartridge that would disable the cartridge after it ran out of toner; for the cartridge to be used again, the microchip would have to be replaced by Lexmark.

Static Control is not itself a manufacturer or remanufacturer of toner cartridges. It is, rather, "the market leader [in] making and selling the components necessary to remanufacture Lexmark cartridges." 697 F.3d 387, 396 (C.A.6 2012) (case below). In addition to supplying remanufacturers with toner and various replacement parts, Static Control developed a microchip that could mimic the microchip in Lexmark's Prebate cartridges. By purchasing Static Control's microchips and using them to replace the Lexmark microchip, remanufacturers were able to refurbish and resell used Prebate cartridges.

Lexmark did not take kindly to that development. In 2002, it sued Static Control, alleging that Static Control's microchips violated both the Copyright Act of 1976, and the Digital Millennium Copyright Act. Static Control counterclaimed, alleging, among other things, violations of § 43(a) of the Lanham Act [for false advertising].

As relevant to its Lanham Act claim, Static Control alleged two types of false or misleading conduct by Lexmark. First, it alleged that through its Prebate program Lexmark "purposefully misleads end-users" to believe that they are legally bound by the Prebate terms and are thus required to return the Prebate-labeled cartridge to Lexmark after a single use. Second, it alleged that upon introducing the Prebate program, Lexmark "sent letters to most of the companies in the toner cartridge remanufacturing business" falsely advising those companies that it was illegal to sell refurbished Prebate cartridges and, in particular, that it was illegal to use Static Control's products to refurbish those cartridges. Static Control asserted that by those statements, Lexmark had materially misrepresented "the nature, characteristics, and qualities" of both its own products and Static Control's products. It further maintained that Lexmark's misrepresentations had "proximately caused and [we]re likely to cause injury to [Static Control] by diverting sales from [Static Control] to Lexmark," and had "substantially injured [its] business reputation" by "leading consumers and others in the trade to believe that [Static Control] is engaged in illegal conduct." Static Control sought treble damages, attorney's fees and costs, and injunctive relief.

The District Court granted Lexmark's motion to dismiss Static Control's Lanham Act claim. It held that Static Control lacked "prudential standing" to bring that claim, relying on a multifactor balancing test it attributed to *Associated Gen. Contractors of Cal., Inc. v. Carpenters*, 459 U.S. 519 (1983). The court emphasized that there were "more direct plaintiffs in the form of remanufacturers of Lexmark's cartridges"; that Static Control's injury was "remot[e]" because it was a mere "byproduct of the supposed manipulation of consumers' relationships with remanufacturers"; and that Lexmark's "alleged intent [was] to dry up spent cartridge supplies at the remanufacturing level, rather than at [Static Control]'s supply level, making remanufacturers Lexmark's alleged intended target."

The Sixth Circuit reversed the dismissal of Static Control's Lanham Act claim. 697 F.3d, at 423. Taking the lay of the land, it identified three competing approaches to determining whether a plaintiff has standing to sue under the Lanham Act. It observed that the Third, Fifth, Eighth, and Eleventh Circuits all refer to "antitrust standing or the [Associated General Contractors] factors in deciding Lanham Act standing," as the District Court had done. *Id.*, at 410 (citing *Conte Bros. Automotive, Inc. v. Quaker State-Slick 50, Inc.*, 165 F.3d 221, 233–234 (C.A.3 1998); *Procter & Gamble Co. v. Amway Corp.*, 242 F.3d 539, 562–563 (C.A.5 2001); *Gilbert/Robinson, Inc. v. Carrie Beverage-Missouri, Inc.*, 989 F.2d 985, 990–991 (C.A.8 1993); *Phoenix of Broward, Inc. v. McDonald's Corp.*, 489 F.3d 1156, 1162–1164 (C.A.11 2007)). By contrast, "[t]he Seventh, Ninth, and Tenth [Circuits] use a categorical test, permitting Lanham Act suits only by an actual competitor." 697 F.3d, at 410 (citing *L.S. Heath & Son, Inc. v. AT & T Information Systems, Inc.*, 9 F.3d 561, 575 (C.A.7 1993); *Waits* [*v. Frito-Lay, Inc.*, 978 F.2d 1093, 1108–1109 (C.A.9 1992)]; *Stanfield v. Osborne Industries, Inc.*, 52 F.3d 867, 873 (C.A.10 1995)). And the Second Circuit applies a " 'reasonable interest' approach," under which a Lanham Act plaintiff "has standing if the claimant can demonstrate '(1) a reasonable interest to be protected against the alleged false advertising and (2) a reasonable basis for believing that the interest is likely to be damaged by the alleged false advertising.' " 697 F.3d, at 410 (quoting *Famous Horse, Inc. v. 5th Avenue Photo Inc.*, 624 F.3d 106, 113 (C.A.2 2010)). The Sixth Circuit applied the Second Circuit's reasonable-interest test and concluded that Static Control had standing because it "alleged a cognizable interest in its business reputation and sales to remanufacturers and sufficiently alleged that th[o]se interests were harmed by Lexmark's statements to the remanufacturers that Static Control was engaging in illegal conduct." 697 F.3d, at 411.

We granted certiorari to decide the appropriate analytical framework for determining a party's standing to maintain an action for false advertising under the Lanham Act.[2]

II. "Prudential Standing"

The parties' briefs treat the question on which we granted certiorari as one of "prudential standing." Because we think that label misleading, we begin by clarifying the nature of the question at issue in this case.

---

[2] Other aspects of the parties' sprawling litigation, including Lexmark's claims under federal copyright and patent law and Static Control's claims under federal antitrust and North Carolina unfair-competition law, are not before us. Our review pertains only to Static Control's Lanham Act claim.

From Article III's limitation of the judicial power to resolving "Cases" and "Controversies," and the separation-of-powers principles underlying that limitation, we have deduced a set of requirements that together make up the "irreducible constitutional minimum of standing." *Lujan v. Defenders of Wildlife*, 504 U.S. 555, 560 (1992). The plaintiff must have suffered or be imminently threatened with a concrete and particularized "injury in fact" that is fairly traceable to the challenged action of the defendant and likely to be redressed by a favorable judicial decision. *Ibid.* Lexmark does not deny that Static Control's allegations of lost sales and damage to its business reputation give it standing under Article III to press its false-advertising claim, and we are satisfied that they do.

Although Static Control's claim thus presents a case or controversy that is properly within federal courts' Article III jurisdiction, Lexmark urges that we should decline to adjudicate Static Control's claim on grounds that are "prudential," rather than constitutional. That request is in some tension with our recent reaffirmation of the principle that "a federal court's 'obligation' to hear and decide" cases within its jurisdiction "is 'virtually unflagging.'" *Sprint Communications, Inc. v. Jacobs*, 571 U.S. ___, ___, 134 S.Ct. 584, 591 (2013) (quoting *Colorado River Water Conservation Dist. v. United States*, 424 U.S. 800, 817 (1976)). In recent decades, however, we have adverted to a "prudential" branch of standing, a doctrine not derived from Article III and "not exhaustively defined" but encompassing (we have said) at least three broad principles: " 'the general prohibition on a litigant's raising another person's legal rights, the rule barring adjudication of generalized grievances more appropriately addressed in the representative branches, and the requirement that a plaintiff's complaint fall within the zone of interests protected by the law invoked.' " *Elk Grove Unified School Dist. v. Newdow*, 542 U.S. 1, 12 (2004) (quoting *Allen v. Wright*, 468 U.S. 737, 751 (1984)).

Lexmark bases its "prudential standing" arguments chiefly on *Associated General Contractors*, but we did not describe our analysis in that case in those terms. Rather, we sought to "ascertain," as a matter of statutory interpretation, the "scope of the private remedy created by" Congress in § 4 of the Clayton Act, and the "class of persons who [could] maintain a private damages action under" that legislatively conferred cause of action. 459 U.S., at 529, 532. We held that the statute limited the class to plaintiffs whose injuries were proximately caused by a defendant's antitrust violations. *Id.*, at 532–533. Later decisions confirm that *Associated General Contractors* rested on statutory, not "prudential," considerations. See, *e.g., Holmes v. Securities Investor Protection Corporation*, 503 U.S. 258, 265–268 (1992) (relying on *Associated General Contractors* in finding a proximate-cause requirement in the cause of action created by the Racketeer Influenced and Corrupt Organizations Act (RICO), 18 U.S.C. § 1964(c)); *Anza v. Ideal Steel Supply Corp.*, 547

U.S. 451, 456 (2006) (affirming that *Holmes* "relied on a careful interpretation of § 1964(c)"). Lexmark's arguments thus do not deserve the "prudential" label.

Static Control, on the other hand, argues that we should measure its "prudential standing" by using the zone-of-interests test. Although we admittedly have placed that test under the "prudential" rubric in the past, see, *e.g., Elk Grove, supra,* at 12, it does not belong there any more than *Associated General Contractors* does. Whether a plaintiff comes within "the 'zone of interests' " is an issue that requires us to determine, using traditional tools of statutory interpretation, whether a legislatively conferred cause of action encompasses a particular plaintiff's claim. See *Steel Co. v. Citizens for Better Environment,* 523 U.S. 83, 97, and n. 2, (1998); *Clarke v. Securities Industry Assn.,* 479 U.S. 388, 394–395 (1987); *Holmes, supra,* at 288 (SCALIA, J., concurring in judgment). As Judge Silberman of the D.C. Circuit recently observed, " 'prudential standing' is a misnomer" as applied to the zone-of-interests analysis, which asks whether "this particular class of persons ha[s] a right to sue under this substantive statute." *Association of Battery Recyclers, Inc. v. EPA,* 716 F.3d 667, 675–676 (2013) (concurring opinion).

In sum, the question this case presents is whether Static Control falls within the class of plaintiffs whom Congress has authorized to sue under § 1125(a). In other words, we ask whether Static Control has a cause of action under the statute.[4] That question requires us to determine the meaning of the congressionally enacted provision creating a cause of action. In doing so, we apply traditional principles of statutory interpretation. We do not ask whether in our judgment Congress should have authorized Static Control's suit, but whether Congress in fact did so. Just as a court cannot apply its independent policy judgment to recognize a cause of action that Congress has denied, see *Alexander v. Sandoval,* 532 U.S. 275, 286–287 (2001), it cannot limit a cause of action that Congress has created merely because "prudence" dictates.

III.   Static Control's Right To Sue Under § 1125(a)

Thus, this case presents a straightforward question of statutory interpretation: Does the cause of action in § 1125(a) extend to plaintiffs like Static Control? The statute authorizes suit by "any person who believes that he or she is likely to be damaged" by a defendant's false advertising. § 1125(a)(1). Read literally, that broad language might suggest that an action is available to anyone who can satisfy the

---

[4]   We have on occasion referred to this inquiry as "statutory standing" and treated it as effectively jurisdictional. See, *e.g., Steel Co. v. Citizens for Better Environment,* 523 U.S. 83, 97, and n. 2 (1998). That label is an improvement over the language of "prudential standing," since it correctly places the focus on the statute. But it, too, is misleading, since "the absence of a valid (as opposed to arguable) cause of action does not implicate subject-matter jurisdiction, i.e., the court's statutory or constitutional power to adjudicate the case.' " *Verizon Md. Inc. v. Public Serv. Comm'n of Md.,* 535 U.S. 635, 642–643 (2002) (quoting *Steel Co., supra,* at 89).

minimum requirements of Article III. No party makes that argument, however, and the "unlikelihood that Congress meant to allow all factually injured plaintiffs to recover persuades us that [§ 1125(a)] should not get such an expansive reading." *Holmes*, 503 U.S., at 266, 112 S.Ct. 1311 (footnote omitted). We reach that conclusion in light of two relevant background principles already mentioned: zone of interests and proximate causality.

A. Zone of Interests

First, we presume that a statutory cause of action extends only to plaintiffs whose interests "fall within the zone of interests protected by the law invoked." *Allen*, 468 U.S., at 751. The modern "zone of interests" formulation originated in *Association of Data Processing Service Organizations, Inc. v. Camp*, 397 U.S. 150 (1970), as a limitation on the cause of action for judicial review conferred by the Administrative Procedure Act (APA). We have since made clear, however, that it applies to all statutorily created causes of action; that it is a "requirement of general application"; and that Congress is presumed to "legislat[e] against the background of" the zone-of-interests limitation, "which applies unless it is expressly negated." *Bennett v. Spear*, 520 U.S. 154, 163 (1997); see also *Holmes*, *supra*, at 287–288 (SCALIA, J., concurring in judgment). It is "perhaps more accurat[e]," though not very different as a practical matter, to say that the limitation always applies and is never negated, but that our analysis of certain statutes will show that they protect a more-than-usually "expan[sive]" range of interests. *Bennett*, *supra*, at 164. The zone-of-interests test is therefore an appropriate tool for determining who may invoke the cause of action in § 1125(a).[5]

We have said, in the APA context, that the test is not " 'especially demanding,' " *Match-E-Be-Nash-She-Wish Band of Pottawatomi Indians v. Patchak*, 567 U.S. ___, ___, 132 S.Ct. 2199, 2210, 183 L.Ed.2d 211 (2012). In that context we have often "conspicuously included the word 'arguably' in the test to indicate that the benefit of any doubt goes to the plaintiff," and have said that the test "forecloses suit only when a plaintiff's 'interests are so marginally related to or inconsistent with the purposes implicit in the statute that it cannot reasonably be assumed that' " Congress authorized that plaintiff to sue. *Id.*, at ___, 132 S.Ct., at 2210. That lenient approach is an appropriate means of preserving the

---

[5] Although we announced the modern zone-of-interests test in 1971, its roots lie in the common-law rule that a plaintiff may not recover under the law of negligence for injuries caused by violation of a statute unless the statute "is interpreted as designed to protect the class of persons in which the plaintiff is included, against the risk of the type of harm which has in fact occurred as a result of its violation." W. Keeton, D. Dobbs, R. Keeton, & D. Owen, Prosser and Keeton on Law of Torts § 36, pp. 229–230 (5th ed. 1984); see cases cited *id.*, at 222–227; *Gorris v. Scott*, [1874] 9 L.R. Exch. 125 (Eng.). Statutory causes of action are regularly interpreted to incorporate standard common-law limitations on civil liability—the zone-of-interests test no less than the requirement of proximate causation, see Part III–B, *infra*.

1

flexibility of the APA's omnibus judicial-review provision, which permits suit for violations of numerous statutes of varying character that do not themselves include causes of action for judicial review. "We have made clear, however, that the breadth of the zone of interests varies according to the provisions of law at issue, so that what comes within the zone of interests of a statute for purposes of obtaining judicial review of administrative action under the ' "generous review provisions" ' of the APA may not do so for other purposes." *Bennett, supra*, at 163 (quoting *Clarke*, 479 U.S., at 400, n. 16 in turn quoting *Data Processing, supra*, at 156).

Identifying the interests protected by the Lanham Act, however, requires no guesswork, since the Act includes an "unusual, and extraordinarily helpful," detailed statement of the statute's purposes. *H.B. Halicki Productions v. United Artists Communications, Inc.*, 812 F.2d 1213, 1214 (C.A.9 1987). Section 45 of the Act, codified at 15 U.S.C. § 1127, provides:

"The intent of this chapter is to regulate commerce within the control of Congress by making actionable the deceptive and misleading use of marks in such commerce; to protect registered marks used in such commerce from interference by State, or territorial legislation; to protect persons engaged in such commerce against unfair competition; to prevent fraud and deception in such commerce by the use of reproductions, copies, counterfeits, or colorable imitations of registered marks; and to provide rights and remedies stipulated by treaties and conventions respecting trademarks, trade names, and unfair competition entered into between the United States and foreign nations."

Most of the enumerated purposes are relevant to false-association cases; a typical false-advertising case will implicate only the Act's goal of "protect [ing] persons engaged in [commerce within the control of Congress] against unfair competition." Although "unfair competition" was a "plastic" concept at common law, *Ely-Norris Safe Co. v. Mosler Safe Co.*, 7 F.2d 603, 604 (C.A.2 1925) (L. Hand, J.), it was understood to be concerned with injuries to business reputation and present and future sales. See Rogers, Book Review, 39 Yale L.J. 297, 299 (1929); see generally 3 Restatement of Torts, ch. 35, Introductory Note, pp. 536–537 (1938).

We thus hold that to come within the zone of interests in a suit for false advertising under § 1125(a), a plaintiff must allege an injury to a commercial interest in reputation or sales. A consumer who is hoodwinked into purchasing a disappointing product may well have an injury-in-fact cognizable under Article III, but he cannot invoke the protection of the Lanham Act—a conclusion reached by every Circuit to consider the question. Even a business misled by a supplier into purchasing an inferior product is, like consumers generally, not under the Act's aegis.

B. Proximate Cause

Second, we generally presume that a statutory cause of action is limited to plaintiffs whose injuries are proximately caused by violations of the statute. For centuries, it has been "a well established principle of [the common] law, that in all cases of loss, we are to attribute it to the proximate cause, and not to any remote cause." *Waters v. Merchants' Louisville Ins. Co.*, 11 Pet. 213, 223, 9 L.Ed. 691 (1837); see *Holmes*, 503 U.S., at 287 (SCALIA, J., concurring in judgment). That venerable principle reflects the reality that "the judicial remedy cannot encompass every conceivable harm that can be traced to alleged wrongdoing." *Associated Gen. Contractors*, 459 U.S., at 536. Congress, we assume, is familiar with the common-law rule and does not mean to displace it sub silentio. We have thus construed federal causes of action in a variety of contexts to incorporate a requirement of proximate causation. See, *e.g.*, *Dura Pharmaceuticals, Inc. v. Broudo*, 544 U.S. 336, 346 (2005) (securities fraud); *Holmes, supra*, at 268–270 (RICO); *Associated Gen. Contractors, supra*, at 529–535 (Clayton Act). No party disputes that it is proper to read § 1125(a) as containing such a requirement, its broad language notwithstanding.

The proximate-cause inquiry is not easy to define, and over the years it has taken various forms; but courts have a great deal of experience applying it, and there is a wealth of precedent for them to draw upon in doing so. See *Exxon Co., U.S.A. v. Sofec, Inc.*, 517 U.S. 830, 838–839 (1996); *Pacific Operators Offshore, LLP v. Valladolid*, 565 U.S. ___, ___, 132 S.Ct. 680, 692–693, 181 L.Ed.2d 675 (2012) (SCALIA, J., concurring in part and concurring in judgment). Proximate-cause analysis is controlled by the nature of the statutory cause of action. The question it presents is whether the harm alleged has a sufficiently close connection to the conduct the statute prohibits.

Put differently, the proximate-cause requirement generally bars suits for alleged harm that is "too remote" from the defendant's unlawful conduct. That is ordinarily the case if the harm is purely derivative of "misfortunes visited upon a third person by the defendant's acts." *Holmes, supra*, at 268–269; see, *e.g.*, *Hemi Group, LLC v. City of New York*, 559 U.S. 1, 10–11 (2010). In a sense, of course, all commercial injuries from false advertising are derivative of those suffered by consumers who are deceived by the advertising; but since the Lanham Act authorizes suit only for commercial injuries, the intervening step of consumer deception is not fatal to the showing of proximate causation required by the statute. See *Harold H. Huggins Realty, Inc. v. FNC, Inc.*, 634 F.3d 787, 800–801 (C.A.5 2011). That is consistent with our recognition that under common-law principles, a plaintiff can be directly injured by a misrepresentation even where "a third party, and not the plaintiff, . . . relied on" it. *Bridge v. Phoenix Bond & Indemnity Co.*, 553 U.S. 639, 656 (2008).

We thus hold that a plaintiff suing under § 1125(a) ordinarily must show economic or reputational injury flowing directly from the deception wrought by the defendant's advertising; and that that occurs when deception of consumers causes them to withhold trade from the plaintiff. That showing is generally not made when the deception produces injuries to a fellow commercial actor that in turn affect the plaintiff. For example, while a competitor who is forced out of business by a defendant's false advertising generally will be able to sue for its losses, the same is not true of the competitor's landlord, its electric company, and other commercial parties who suffer merely as a result of the competitor's "inability to meet [its] financial obligations." *Anza*, 547 U.S., at 458.

C. Proposed Tests

At oral argument, Lexmark agreed that the zone of interests and proximate causation supply the relevant background limitations on suit under § 1125(a). See Tr. of Oral Arg. 4–5, 11–12, 17–18. But it urges us to adopt, as the optimal formulation of those principles, a multifactor balancing test derived from Associated General Contractors. In the alternative, it asks that we adopt a categorical test permitting only direct competitors to sue for false advertising. And although neither party urges adoption of the "reasonable interest" test applied below, several amici do so. While none of those tests is wholly without merit, we decline to adopt any of them. We hold instead that a direct application of the zone-of-interests test and the proximate-cause requirement supplies the relevant limits on who may sue.

The balancing test Lexmark advocates was first articulated by the Third Circuit in *Conte Bros.* and later adopted by several other Circuits. *Conte Bros.* identified five relevant considerations:

"(1) The nature of the plaintiff's alleged injury: Is the injury of a type that Congress sought to redress in providing a private remedy for violations of the [Lanham Act]?

"(2) The directness or indirectness of the asserted injury.

"(3) The proximity or remoteness of the party to the alleged injurious conduct.

"(4) The speculativeness of the damages claim.

"(5) The risk of duplicative damages or complexity in apportioning damages." 165 F.3d, at 233 (citations and internal quotation marks omitted).

This approach reflects a commendable effort to give content to an otherwise nebulous inquiry, but we think it slightly off the mark. The first factor can be read as requiring that the plaintiff's injury be within the relevant zone of interests and the second and third as requiring (somewhat redundantly) proximate causation; but it is not correct to treat those requirements, which must be met in every case, as mere factors to be weighed in a balance. And the fourth and fifth factors are themselves problematic. "[T]he difficulty that can arise when a court attempts to ascertain the damages caused by some remote action" is a "motivating principle" behind the proximate-cause requirement, *Anza, supra,* at 457–458; but potential difficulty in ascertaining and apportioning damages is not, as *Conte Bros.* might suggest, an independent basis for denying standing where it is adequately alleged that a defendant's conduct has proximately injured an interest of the plaintiff's that the statute protects. Even when a plaintiff cannot quantify its losses with sufficient certainty to recover damages, it may still be entitled to injunctive relief under § 1116(a) (assuming it can prove a likelihood of future injury) or disgorgement of the defendant's ill-gotten profits under § 1117(a). See *TrafficSchool.com, Inc. v. Edriver Inc.,* 653 F.3d 820, 831 (C.A.9 2011); *Johnson & Johnson v. Carter-Wallace, Inc.,* 631 F.2d 186, 190 (C.A.2 1980). Finally, experience has shown that the *Conte Bros.* approach, like other open-ended balancing tests, can yield unpredictable and at times arbitrary results. See, *e.g.,* Tushnet, Running the Gamut from A to B: Federal Trademark and False Advertising Law, 159 U. Pa. L.Rev. 1305, 1376–1379 (2011).

In contrast to the multifactor balancing approach, the direct-competitor test provides a bright-line rule; but it does so at the expense of distorting the statutory language. To be sure, a plaintiff who does not compete with the defendant will often have a harder time establishing proximate causation. But a rule categorically prohibiting all suits by noncompetitors would read too much into the Act's reference to "unfair competition" in § 1127. By the time the Lanham Act was adopted, the common-law tort of unfair competition was understood not to be limited to actions between competitors. One leading authority in the field wrote that "there need be no competition in unfair competition," just as "[t]here is no soda in soda water, no grapes in grape fruit, no bread in bread fruit, and a clothes horse is not a horse but is good enough to hang things on." Rogers, 39 Yale L. J., at 299; accord, *Vogue Co. v. Thompson-Hudson Co.,* 300 F. 509, 512 (C.A.6 1924); 1 H. Nims, The Law of Unfair Competition and Trade-Marks, p. vi (4th ed. 1947); 2 id., at 1194–1205. It is thus a mistake to infer that because the Lanham Act treats false advertising as a form of unfair competition, it can protect only the false-advertiser's direct competitors.

Finally, there is the "reasonable interest" test applied by the Sixth Circuit in this case. As typically formulated, it requires a commercial plaintiff to "demonstrate '(1) a reasonable interest to be protected against the alleged false advertising and (2) a reasonable basis for believing that the interest is likely to be damaged by the alleged false advertising.' " 697 F.3d, at 410 (quoting *Famous Horse*, 624 F.3d, at 113). A purely practical objection to the test is that it lends itself to widely divergent application. Indeed, its vague language can be understood as requiring only the bare minimum of Article III standing. The popularity of the multifactor balancing test reflects its appeal to courts tired of "grappl[ing] with defining" the " 'reasonable interest' " test "with greater precision." *Conte Bros.*, 165 F.3d, at 231. The theoretical difficulties with the test are even more substantial: The relevant question is not whether the plaintiff's interest is "reasonable," but whether it is one the Lanham Act protects; and not whether there is a "reasonable basis" for the plaintiff's claim of harm, but whether the harm alleged is proximately tied to the defendant's conduct. In short, we think the principles set forth above will provide clearer and more accurate guidance than the "reasonable interest" test.

IV. Application

Applying those principles to Static Control's false-advertising claim, we conclude that Static Control comes within the class of plaintiffs whom Congress authorized to sue under § 1125(a).

To begin, Static Control's alleged injuries—lost sales and damage to its business reputation—are injuries to precisely the sorts of commercial interests the Act protects. Static Control is suing not as a deceived consumer, but as a "perso[n] engaged in" "commerce within the control of Congress" whose position in the marketplace has been damaged by Lexmark's false advertising. § 1127. There is no doubt that it is within the zone of interests protected by the statute.

Static Control also sufficiently alleged that its injuries were proximately caused by Lexmark's misrepresentations. This case, it is true, does not present the "classic Lanham Act false-advertising claim" in which " 'one competito[r] directly injur[es] another by making false statements about his own goods [or the competitor's goods] and thus inducing customers to switch.' " *Harold H. Huggins Realty*, 634 F.3d, at 799, n. 24. But although diversion of sales to a direct competitor may be the paradigmatic direct injury from false advertising, it is not the only type of injury cognizable under § 1125(a). For at least two reasons, Static Control's allegations satisfy the requirement of proximate causation.

First, Static Control alleged that Lexmark disparaged its business and products by asserting that Static Control's business was illegal. See 697 F.3d, at 411, n. 10 (noting allegation that Lexmark "directly target[ed] Static Control" when it "falsely advertised that Static Control infringed Lexmark's patents"). When a defendant harms a plaintiff's reputation by casting aspersions on its business, the plaintiff's injury flows directly from the audience's belief in the disparaging statements. Courts have therefore afforded relief under § 1125(a) not only where a defendant denigrates a plaintiff's product by name, but also where the defendant damages the product's reputation by, for example, equating it with an inferior product. Traditional proximate-causation principles support those results: As we have observed, a defendant who " 'seeks to promote his own interests by telling a known falsehood to or about the plaintiff or his product' " may be said to have proximately caused the plaintiff's harm. *Bridge*, 553 U.S., at 657 (quoting Restatement (Second) of Torts § 870, Comment h (1977); emphasis added in *Bridge*).

The District Court emphasized that Lexmark and Static Control are not direct competitors. But when a party claims reputational injury from disparagement, competition is not required for proximate cause; and that is true even if the defendant's aim was to harm its immediate competitors, and the plaintiff merely suffered collateral damage. Consider two rival carmakers who purchase airbags for their cars from different third-party manufacturers. If the first carmaker, hoping to divert sales from the second, falsely proclaims that the airbags used by the second carmaker are defective, both the second carmaker and its airbag supplier may suffer reputational injury, and their sales may decline as a result. In those circumstances, there is no reason to regard either party's injury as derivative of the other's; each is directly and independently harmed by the attack on its merchandise.

In addition, Static Control adequately alleged proximate causation by alleging that it designed, manufactured, and sold microchips that both (1) were necessary for, and (2) had no other use than, refurbishing Lexmark toner cartridges. It follows from that allegation that any false advertising that reduced the remanufacturers' business necessarily injured Static Control as well. Taking Static Control's assertions at face value, there is likely to be something very close to a 1:1 relationship between the number of refurbished Prebate cartridges sold (or not sold) by the remanufacturers and the number of Prebate microchips sold (or not sold) by Static Control. "Where the injury alleged is so integral an aspect of the [violation] alleged, there can be no question" that proximate cause is satisfied. *Blue Shield of Va. v. McCready*, 457 U.S. 465, 479 (1982).

We understand this to be the thrust of both sides' allegations concerning Static Control's design and sale of specialized microchips for the specific purpose of enabling the remanufacture of Lexmark's Prebate cartridges.

To be sure, on this view, the causal chain linking Static Control's injuries to consumer confusion is not direct, but includes the intervening link of injury to the remanufacturers. Static Control's allegations therefore might not support standing under a strict application of the " ' "general tendency" ' " not to stretch proximate causation " ' "beyond the first step." ' " *Holmes*, 503 U.S., at 271. But the reason for that general tendency is that there ordinarily is a "discontinuity" between the injury to the direct victim and the injury to the indirect victim, so that the latter is not surely attributable to the former (and thus also to the defendant's conduct), but might instead have resulted from "any number of [other] reasons." *Anza*, 547 U.S., at 458–459. That is not the case here. Static Control's allegations suggest that if the remanufacturers sold 10,000 fewer refurbished cartridges because of Lexmark's false advertising, then it would follow more or less automatically that Static Control sold 10,000 fewer microchips for the same reason, without the need for any "speculative . . . proceedings" or "intricate, uncertain inquiries." *Id.*, at 459–460, 126 S.Ct. 1991. In these relatively unique circumstances, the remanufacturers are not "more immediate victim[s]" than Static Control. *Bridge*, *supra*, at 658.

Although we conclude that Static Control has alleged an adequate basis to proceed under § 1125(a), it cannot obtain relief without evidence of injury proximately caused by Lexmark's alleged misrepresentations. We hold only that Static Control is entitled to a chance to prove its case.

      * * *

To invoke the Lanham Act's cause of action for false advertising, a plaintiff must plead (and ultimately prove) an injury to a commercial interest in sales or business reputation proximately caused by the defendant's misrepresentations. Static Control has adequately pleaded both elements. The judgment of the Court of Appeals is affirmed.

It is so ordered.

NOTES & QUESTIONS

(1) Static Control alleged in its counterclaim that Lexmark violated the deceptive marketing provisions of the Lanham Act. Does it appear that Static Control has alleged all of the necessary elements of its deceptive marketing claim?

(2) Why does the Supreme Court take issue with the label "prudential standing"? Is this more than just a labeling problem?

(3) According to the Court, what was wrong with the existing standing tests that were being used by the various courts?

(4) The Court replaces the existing "prudential standing" tests with its own two-part inquiry: First, are the claimed injuries within the "zone of

interests" the Lanham Act was passed to address? Second, were the injuries proximately caused by the defendant's violation(s) of the Lanham Act?

How does a court go about determining whether these two inquiries have been met? Why were these two parts met in the *Lexmark* case? Is this two-part inquiry any more predictable than the tests the Court rejects?

(5)   One of the cases cited by the Court as utilizing the *Conte Bros.* test was *Phoenix of Broward, Inc. v. McDonald's Corp.*, 489 F.3d 1156 (11th Cir. 2007). That case involved a claim of false advertising brought by Burger King franchisees against McDonald's Corporation for advertisements regarding a contest which was tainted when an insider diverted some $20 million in prizes to his co-conspirators. Due to this diversion, the chances of winning one of the prizes were less than advertised. The Circuit Court affirmed dismissal of the franchisees claims under the *Conte Bros.* factors, finding that though factors 1 and 3 favored the franchisees (is the injury of a type that Congress sought to redress and the proximity of the party to the injurious conduct), factors 2, 4 and 5 justified the dismissal. With regard to the 2nd factor, the directness or indirectness of the asserted injury, the court was rather demanding of the plaintiffs at the dismissal stage:

> Phoenix essentially alleges that [McDonald's false advertisements] lured customers who would have eaten at Burger King (as opposed to one of numerous other fast food competitors), causing Burger King to lose sales ... but for this misrepresentation, these customers would have eaten at Burger King, even though the chances of winning one of the "rare" high-value prizes would have been minute had there been no theft, even though only "certain" high-value prizes were stolen, and even though these customers still had a fair and equal opportunity to win all of the other prizes. Accepting Phoenix's allegations as true, the causal chain linking McDonald's alleged misrepresentations about one aspect of its promotional games to a decrease in Burger King's sales is tenuous, to say the least.

The Court similarly was very demanding as to the speculativeness of the injury and the risk of duplicative damages. Noting that there were many competitors in the fast food market other than McDonald's and Burger King, the Eleventh Circuit said that the causal chain linking the alleged false advertising to a decrease in sales at Burger King's outlets was "tenuous, to say the least." How would the franchisees in *Phoenix of Broward* fared under the *Lexmark* standard?

(6)   Look at the language of the Restatement of Unfair Competition §§ 2–3. Do you see any similar limitations on what parties have standing to sue? What approach does the Restatement seem to favor? *See* RESTATEMENT (THIRD) OF UNFAIR COMPETITION § 3 cmt. f (1995).

2. CONTRIBUTORY LIABILITY OF MANUFACTURERS AND PUBLISHERS

Once a plaintiff has standing, a broader class of defendants may be sued for contributory liability. For instance, the Restatement of Unfair Competition allows for liability to attach to those who are not necessarily in direct competition with the plaintiff. This should have been apparent from the above discussion on standing—if a plaintiff need not be a direct competitor to bring suit, then obviously the defendant does not have to be a direct competitor. Section 3 speaks only in terms of the materiality of the representation and a reasonable basis for believing the representation will cause the plaintiff harm and thus does not limit the class of defendants to direct competitors. Liability can also extend to those who assist defendant in making false or misleading advertisements under a theory of contributory liability. This is provided for in §§ 7–8 of the Restatement, which extends contributory liability to the publishers of false or misleading advertising and for those who market goods to retailers who in turn engage in false advertising.

Although § 43(a)(1) of the Lanham Act does not address contributory liability, § 32 of the Lanham Act provides for a similar standard as § 7 of the Restatement. Further, the U.S. Supreme Court has long recognized contributory liability for trademark violations, *see Inwood Labs., Inc. v. Ives Labs., Inc.*, 456 U.S. 844, 854 (1982), and it has been extended to § 43. *See Procter & Gamble Co. v. Haugen*, 317 F.3d 1121, 1128–30 (10th Cir. 2003) (analyzing and rejecting a contributory liability claim in the alternative despite finding a failure to properly plead). Under the Lanham Act § 43, however, these claims are usually in relation to subsection (a)(1)(A) rather than (a)(1)(B). It is important to note that although publishers can be liable for contributory liability, innocent publishers are only subject to injunctive relief. *See* RESTATEMENT (THIRD) OF UNFAIR COMPETITION § 7(2) (1995); Lanham Act § 32, 15 U.S.C. § 1125 (2012).

PROBLEM 7.4

Sweet Creek Coffee Company roasts, grinds, packages, and distributes its coffee for use in coffee houses and restaurants nationwide. Yabbo's is a chain of coffee houses that operates in the Kansas City area (on both the Kansas and Missouri sides of the border). Recently, Yabbo's has been losing business to Big Kahuna's, a coffee house that specializes in Hawaiian Kona, which is coffee made exclusively from coffee beans grown in Hawaii (specifically grown on the slopes of Hualalai in the Kona District on the Big Island of Hawaii). Yabbo's would like to win back some of its customers by offering a Hawaiian Kona of its own. It approaches its distributor, Sweet Creek, about purchasing the coffee, but is shocked by the price tag. Sweet Creek's representative suggests instead that Yabbo's purchase its Special

Blend, at half the price, which, according to the representative, tastes similar to Hawaiian Kona. "Your customers won't be able to tell the difference in taste between our Special Blend and a Hawaiian Kona," he tells Yabbo's, "and I think some of our clients have actually secretly substituted it for Hawaiian Kona," he concludes with a wink.

Yabbo's moves forward with the blend and begins advertising in its stores and in the local paper, The Kansas City Star. The advertisements state the following: "Yabbo's now carries Hawaiian Kona! Come try it today!" Yabbo's sells the Special Blend as Hawaiian Kona for half the price charged by Big Kahuna's, and Big Kahuna's starts to lose customers.

Ultimately, Big Kahuna's learns the true origin of Yabbo's Hawaiian Kona and sues for false advertising. Big Kahuna's wishes to sue not just Yabbo's, but also Sweet Creek and the Kansas City Star for damages, injunctive relief, and a printed retraction. Can Big Kahuna's sue and obtain the relief it seeks from these two additional parties? *See* RESTATEMENT (THIRD) OF UNFAIR COMPETITION § 7 & cmts. a–b (1995); *id.* § 8 & cmts. b–c; Lanham Act § 32, 15 U.S.C. § 1125 (2012).

E. REMEDIES FOR FALSE ADVERTISING

The primary remedy sought in a deceptive marketing case is injunctive relief. Both the Restatement of Unfair Competition and the Lanham Act refer to the remedies available for trademark infringement for guidance on the issue of remedies. Injunctive relief is not the sole remedy. As noted in the *Cashmere* case, however, seeking monetary damages rather than injunctive relief will affect the plaintiff's burden of proof on its § 43(a) or common-law false advertising claim. As the *Cashmere* court noted in footnote 9 of its opinion, "unlike a plaintiff seeking injunctive relief who only has to show that the misrepresentation had the tendency to deceive, a plaintiff seeking monetary damages must show that consumers were actually deceived by the misrepresentation, unless he can avail himself of a presumption to that effect."

Along with affecting the consumer deception element, a party asking for monetary relief also bears a higher burden on causation. Again, you may have picked up on the court's language in the *Cashmere* decision, in which the court stated that a plaintiff seeking monetary damages must show *actual harm* to its business and a causal link between the defendant's actions and the damages. A plaintiff seeking only an injunction, on the other hand, has sufficiently met its burden once it has shown that there is a likelihood of harm (rather than having to show actual harm or damages). As comment a to the Restatement (Third) of Unfair Competition § 35 notes, "[f]requently, the harm is not reparable by an award of monetary relief because of the difficulty of proving the amount of loss and a causal connection with the defendant's wrongful conduct."

Section 34 of the Lanham Act provides the courts with the power to issue injunctive relief "according to the principles of equity and upon such terms as the court may deem reasonable . . . to prevent a violation under [§ 43]." When injunctive relief is sought, the primary goal is to protect both the plaintiff and the public from future harm. Fashioning an appropriate remedy can be a difficult task and is highly fact specific, as demonstrated by § 35(2) of the Restatement:

§ 35. Injunctions: Trademark   Infringement   and   Deceptive Marketing

. . . .

(2) The appropriateness and scope of injunctive relief depend upon a comparative appraisal of all the factors of the case, including the following primary factors:

    (a)   the nature of the interest to be protected;

    (b)   the nature and extent of the wrongful conduct;

    (c)   the relative adequacy to the plaintiff of an injunction and of other remedies;

    (d)   the relative harm likely to result to the legitimate interests of the defendant if an injunction is granted and to the legitimate interests of the plaintiff if an injunction is denied;

    (e)   the interests of third persons and of the public;

    (f)   any unreasonable delay by the plaintiff in bringing suit or otherwise asserting its rights;

    (g)   any related misconduct on the part of the plaintiff; and

    (h)   the practicality of framing and enforcing the injunction.

To demonstrate the difficulties that can be involved in fashioning an appropriate injunction, consider the following hypothetical: Gary Liu produces canned and frozen vegetables under the label DeLIUscious Veggies. As part of his marketing, he has been advertising his new line of "pesticide free" frozen vegetables, which the advertisements claim are grown without the use of any pesticides or insecticides. Unbeknownst to Gary, his producers in China have, in fact, been using pesticides on the vegetables they have been supplying to him—a fact Gary only becomes aware of when a competitor sues him for false advertising.

If the only advertising Gary has done involves television and print, simply enjoining him from running further advertisements with the false claim may be enough. However, what if Gary has been running these advertisements for many months and created goodwill and trust in his brand; should he also have to run corrective advertisements? What if, along with running advertisements, Gary's packaging prominently displayed the "pesticide free" claim? Should Gary have to issue a recall even though the vegetables are still safe to eat, or will simply placing a sticker on the products suffice (and what if, due to their frozen nature, the stickers easily fall off)? What if Gary knew that his producers were likely not shipping him pesticide-free vegetables, but he carried on with the advertisements anyway?

Obviously a number of factors can be, and are, considered by the court when issuing an injunction. The Restatement in § 35(2) has attempted to capture the various factors, but there is no mechanical way to predict how a court will weigh the factors or what injunction it will ultimately issue.

Under §§ 32 and 35 of the Lanham Act, a violation of § 43 makes a defendant liable for damages. The Restatement in § 36(2) lists four possible sources for determining damages:

(2) The pecuniary loss for which damages may be recovered under this Section includes:

(a) loss resulting to the plaintiff from sales or other revenues lost because of the actor's conduct;

(b) loss resulting from sales made by the plaintiff at prices that have been reasonably reduced because of the actor's conduct;

(c) harm to the market reputation of the plaintiff's goods, services, business, or trademark; and

(d) reasonable expenditures made by the plaintiff in order to prevent, correct, or mitigate the confusion or deception of prospective purchasers resulting from the actor's conduct.

Additionally, § 35 of the Lanham Act permits a court, in appropriate circumstances, to increase the award of actual damages by as much as three times the amount. Generally, under both the Lanham Act and the Restatement, the burden of proof is upon the plaintiff to show that it is entitled to damages and the amount. However, once the fact of damages has been proven, a court may be more forgiving of the degree of certainty it requires from the plaintiff in showing the exact amount. Relevant to this inquiry is the intent of the defendant and the relative clean hands of the plaintiff. Section 36(3) of the Restatement then lists a number of factors to be considered in awarding damages, including the intent of the parties.

Two additional remedies that may be sought are worth special mention. First, in certain circumstances, a plaintiff may be awarded the defendant's net profits instead of its own actual damages. Both § 35 of the

Lanham Act and § 37 of the Restatement provide for this option. The Restatement mentions two important limitations upon this remedy: "(a) the actor engaged in the conduct with the intention of causing confusion or deception; and (b) the award of profits is not prohibited by statute and is otherwise appropriate under the rule stated in Subsection (2)." Subsection (2) takes into account such factors as the degree of certainty that the actor benefitted from the unlawful conduct, the relative adequacy to the plaintiff of other remedies, including an award of damages, and the interests of the public in depriving the actor of unjust gains and discouraging unlawful conduct.

Second, the Lanham Act specifically provides that the prevailing party may be awarded reasonable attorney's fees. However, such fees are only to be awarded in "exceptional cases." This "exceptional cases" language has been interpreted to mean only in cases of deliberate infringement, or when the prosecution of the claim is in bad faith. The Restatement does not provide for attorney's fees as "[m]ost states do not provide for the recovery of attorney's fees in actions at common law." RESTATEMENT (THIRD) OF UNFAIR COMPETITION § 36 cmt. o (1995).

The case of *ALPO Petfoods, Inc. v. Ralston Purina Co.*, 913 F.2d 958 (D.C. Cir. 1990), demonstrates some of the obstacles inherent in awarding lost profits, attorney's fees, and injunctive relief. In *ALPO*, Ralston and ALPO sued each other for false advertising related to each party's claims about its puppy food brand. The district court found that each was liable and imposed injunctions on both parties. The district court also awarded ALPO $10.4 million in damages (which was deemed to be based upon Ralston's profits) and granted costs and attorney's fees to both sides.

On appeal, the D.C. Circuit overturned the award of damages. The court subscribed to the theory, held by many other courts, that awarding damages to a plaintiff based upon the defendant's profits (i.e., a disgorgement of profits) required a showing of willfulness or bad faith, which was lacking. Similarly, the court overturned the award of attorney's fees because the Lanham Act only permits such an award in "exceptional circumstances." As mentioned, although not defined in the Lanham Act, "exceptional circumstances" have been found when there is a finding of willfulness or "bad faith"—findings which were absent in this case. Finally, with regard to the injunction, the court upheld it as to both parties, but limited the scope as it applied to Ralston. The injunction issued by the district court was so broad as to require non-Ralston scientists to obtain court approval before publishing articles on Canine Hip Dysplasia ("CHD") (studies of which were at issue in the case). In addressing the scope of the injunction, the court stated:

> The law requires that courts closely tailor injunctions to the harm that they address. In enjoining Ralston, the district court

identified the harm redressed by the injunctions as deception of puppy food buyers and erosion of ALPO's business. Yet the prohibitory injunction, both as entered and, particularly, as implemented, suppresses more speech than protecting these interests requires. ALPO's false-advertising claim against Ralston involves a dispute over whether Ralston may commercially claim that Puppy Chow confers certain unproved health benefits [related to CHD]. Redressing the harm that these claims have caused in the puppy food market does not require that a court supervise all future debate on [a CHD-related theory].

Id. at 972.

The court, in remanding the case, did not leave the parties without guidance on damages that could still be available to them. In particular, the court noted that the parties could seek actual damages, including "profits lost by the plaintiff on sales actually diverted to the false advertiser," "profits lost by the plaintiff on sales made at prices reduced as a demonstrated result of the false advertising," "the costs of any completed advertising that actually and reasonably responds to the defendant's offending ads," and "quantifiable harm to the plaintiff's good will, to the extent that completed corrective advertising has not repaired that harm." *Id.* at 969. The parties took the court's advice, but as the next case demonstrates, issues remained even when pursuing these remedies.

ALPO PETFOODS, INC. V. RALSTON PURINA COMPANY
997 F.2d 949 (D.C. Cir. 1993)

D.H. GINSBURG, CIRCUIT JUDGE:

This case involves a dispute over the damages recoverable in an action for false advertising brought under the Lanham Act, 15 U.S.C. § 1125(a). ALPO Petfoods sued Ralston Purina and Ralston counter-claimed, each seeking damages for and injunctive relief against false advertising of the other's puppy food product. The district court found that both parties had advertised false claims in violation of the Lanham Act and enjoined both manufacturers from making similar claims in the future. *See ALPO Petfoods, Inc. v. Ralston Purina Co.*, 720 F. Supp. 194 (D.D.C. 1989) (*ALPO I*). The court awarded ALPO $10.4 million in damages but declined to award any damages to Ralston because its violations of the Lanham Act were so much more serious than ALPO's.

Ralston appealed that decision, which we affirmed with respect to liability but reversed and remanded with respect to the damage award. *See ALPO II*, 913 F.2d 958 (D.C. Cir. 1990). On remand, the district court heard testimony from an expert witness for each side and awarded ALPO $12,140,356 and Ralston $53,434 plus its attorneys' fees. *See ALPO III*,

778 F. Supp. 555 (D.D.C. 1991). Ralston now appeals that judgment. We affirm in part, reverse in part, and again remand the case for the district court to redetermine certain elements of ALPO's recovery.

I. Background

Ralston Purina's Puppy Chow is the long-standing leader in the puppy food market. ALPO entered that market in January 1985 when it introduced ALPO Puppy Food into selected states in the Northeast. The next year ALPO sued Ralston under the Lanham Act, challenging the truth of Ralston's advertised claim that Purina Puppy Chow could reduce the severity of canine hip dysplasia (CHD), a debilitating ailment in dogs. Ralston counterclaimed, challenging the truth of ALPO's advertised claims that veterinarians (1) prefer ALPO Puppy Food's formula over that of "the leading brand" (*i.e.,* Ralston) and (2) do so by a 2-to-1 margin.

Following a bench trial, the district court concluded that both Ralston and ALPO made false or misleading advertising claims in violation of the Lanham Act. The court awarded ALPO Ralston's profits, which it estimated at twice the amount that Ralston had spent on the CHD campaign, and awarded each side its attorneys' fees.

On appeal, this court held that it was not appropriate to award Ralston's profits to ALPO because, contrary to the district court's implicit finding, ALPO had not proven that Ralston had acted willfully or in bad faith. We remanded for the district court to award ALPO its actual damages and, if it were to enhance the award above that amount, to explain why the enhanced award is compensatory and not punitive.

On remand the district court refused to award either party the profits it claimed to have lost on sales diverted to the other, on the ground that any such award would be unduly speculative. The court then awarded ALPO damages in the amount of $12 million, comprised of (1) the cost it incurred for advertising responsive to Ralston's false claims, (2) the delay Ralston caused ALPO in achieving national distribution of ALPO Puppy Food (which it never did achieve), and (3) a 50% enhancement of the award intended roughly to compensate ALPO for profits lost on sales diverted to Ralston, the permanent distortion of the puppy food market caused by Ralston's false advertising, interest, and inflation. The court awarded Ralston (1) $53,434 for the cost of its advertising responsive to ALPO's false claims and (2) its attorneys' fees.

II. Analysis

Ralston now challenges the amount that the district court awarded to ALPO for the cost of responsive advertising, the entire award for the delay of ALPO's income stream from a national product rollout, and the 50% enhancement of those sums. Ralston also contests the court's refusal to award it any lost profits.

A. Responsive Advertising

The district court awarded ALPO approximately $3.6 million for the cost of its responsive advertising. *First,* Ralston argues that this award is improper because the advertisements for which ALPO was compensated were not specifically responsive to Ralston's false CHD claim. In fact, ALPO's campaign did not even mention Purina Puppy Chow by name.

Under the Lanham Act a party injured by false advertising may recover the cost of its own advertisements that "actually and reasonably respond[ed] to the defendant's offending ads." *ALPO II*, 913 F.2d at 969. Recovery is not limited, however, to advertisements that specifically address the false statements made by the defendant. If it were, then the price of recovery would be to give additional currency to the false claims. Where that did not completely defeat the purpose of the Act it would at least make the law a mighty poor remedy. (In the marketplace, it seems, the only thing worse than being talked about, as Oscar Wilde said of the salon, is not being talked about.) In this particular case, moreover, ALPO may not have been able to address the CHD claim at the outset of its responsive campaign, for it had no way of knowing as an initial matter that Ralston's claim was false.

To be sure, directly responsive advertising may be necessary in order to undo the harm where two products have become confused in the public mind as a result of a Lanham Act violation. Here, however, the claim is not that two products have become confused in the minds of consumers but rather that Ralston has falsely portrayed its Purina Puppy Chow as a superior product. In this circumstance, the purpose of the Lanham Act requires that ALPO be able to recover for the cost of the advertising campaign it initiated in response to the false CHD claim regardless of whether its advertising undertook expressly to rebut that claim.

Second, Ralston challenges the award for ALPO's responsive advertising on the ground that the evidence does not support the district court's finding that ALPO increased its spending on advertisements in response to Ralston's CHD campaign. According to Ralston, its false CHD campaign was only one of many factors that led ALPO to increase its advertising budget. While ALPO's witnesses could not state that the CHD campaign was the sole cause of its increased spending on advertising, they did clearly indicate that the increased spending was prompted in part by Ralston's CHD claims.

We [disagree with the proposition] that the party injured by a false advertising campaign be required to prove that the false advertisements were the sole reason for its responsive campaign. It is enough to show that, at the margin, the victim would not have undertaken the campaign but for the false ads. The inframarginal considerations taking it to the brink of that decision are as irrelevant to liability as are the reasons for which a man may have approached the cliff that a villain then pushed him off.

Third, Ralston attacks the district court's way of calculating the cost that ALPO incurred for responsive advertising. The court used ALPO's planned advertising budget for FY '86 as a baseline and assumed that ALPO's expenditures for FYs '86 and '87 would have been the same but for Purina's CHD campaign. The district court then subtracted what ALPO had planned to spend from what it actually spent for the two years, and treated the remainder as the cost of responding to Ralston's CHD campaign.

Ralston claims that for all its apparent precision the district court's approach is at bottom speculative. On the contrary, it seems to us that by using figures that ALPO had prepared in the ordinary course of business, the district court was able to start with an unusually solid foundation upon which to build its calculations. *See Am. Medical Imaging v. St. Paul Fire & Marine*, 949 F.2d 690, 694 (3rd Cir. 1991) ("[P]rojections . . . formulated in the regular course of business prior to the alleged loss may commend them to the trier of fact as more reliable than if they had been prepared after the fact for purposes of litigation.").

. . . .

Fifth, Ralston claims that the award should not stand because the amount ALPO spent on responsive advertisements was disproportionate to the amount Ralston spent on the CHD claims to which ALPO was responding. Ralston spent $2.2 million advertising its CHD claim in ALPO's marketing area; ALPO was awarded $3.6 million for responsive advertising. In view of the significance of Ralston's claims, however, it does not seem unreasonable for ALPO to have spent $3.6 million in order to rebut $2.2 million worth of false advertising; a consumer who heard the CHD claim would almost certainly conclude that Purina Puppy Chow was by far the superior product. Indeed, because Ralston's false claim was so bold and so specific, in comparison with which ALPO's reply was rather tepid and general, it stands to reason that ALPO's campaign may have been less persuasive dollar for dollar. In any event, ALPO's outspending Ralston by a ratio of little more than 1.5 to 1 is not so clearly disproportionate as to require any disallowance.

Sixth, The district court did not in fact award ALPO the full difference between its planned and its actual advertising expenditures, which came to $5.2 million. The court disallowed as unreasonable $1.6 million that ALPO had spent for a coupon campaign because "ALPO intentionally printed the false preference claim on a large number of its coupons." *I.e.*, some of ALPO's responsive advertising was itself false and in violation of the Lanham Act.

Ralston alleges that the $3.6 million awarded still compensates ALPO for some expenditures it made in order to advertise its false claims. Unfortunately, the district court did not address this claim other than as noted above, and we cannot resolve it on the present record. The district court found, in resolving Ralston's counterclaim, that ALPO did violate the Lanham Act. Over the relevant time period ALPO spent well in excess of $3.6 million on advertising, but ALPO may not have spent more than $3.6 million on non-false advertising. We cannot merely assume that the non-false advertisements run in FYs '86 and '87 were responsive to the CHD campaign (hence incremental and recoverable) while the false advertisements for which ALPO may not recover were part of the "baseline" expenditure (hence would have aired anyway and not recoverable). We must therefore remand this matter for the district court to determine in the first instance the percentage of ALPO's advertising expenses during the relevant period that were for false or misleading advertisements, and to reduce the $3.6 million award pro rata.

B. Delay of ALPO's Income Stream

Although the district court declined to speculate about the profits that either party lost on sales diverted to the other, the court did award ALPO the profits it lost due to the need, in view of Ralston's CHD campaign, to defer its national expansion. The court calculated ALPO's losses from the profits that ALPO had projected it would earn when it first decided to enter the national puppy food market. Early year losses and later year profits (projected into the indefinite future) were reduced to present value; the court then computed the present value of that same income stream assuming a five year delay in getting it started and awarded ALPO the difference, some $4.5 million.

Ralston argues that the delay in ALPO's receipt of income from a national rollout of ALPO Puppy Food is not a permissible category of damages, and is purely speculative. We disagree on both counts.

When we remanded this case earlier for the district court to recompute the damage award we noted that:

> [A]ctual damages under section 35(a) can include: profits lost by the plaintiff on sales actually diverted to the false advertiser, profits lost by the plaintiff on sales made at prices reduced as a demonstrated result of the false advertising, the costs of any completed advertising that actually and reasonably responds to the defendant's offending ads, and quantifiable harm to the plaintiff's good will, to the extent that completed corrective advertising has not repaired that harm.

ALPO II, 913 F.2d at 969. While we did not specifically itemize a delay in the receipt of a stream of income as a compensable category of damages, the district court correctly understood that our list of such categories was illustrative, not exhaustive. The statute itself suggests as much, for it specifically authorizes the court, if it finds that a recovery based upon profits would be inadequate, "in its discretion [to] enter judgment for such sum as the court should find to be just," and to award the plaintiff what is in effect the time value of its deferred profits is hardly an abuse of discretion.

Nor do we view the award as unduly uncertain. The district court found that ALPO would have expanded nationally but was stymied by Ralston's false advertisements. The court therefore looked at ALPO's projections, prepared in the ordinary course of business and on the basis of which it was prepared to risk its own capital, in order to estimate the profits that ALPO would have reaped from that expansion. ALPO was not certain to succeed, of course, but the question is who is to bear the now-hypothetical risk that it would fail? We answered that question when we remanded this case to the district court:

> When assessing actual damages, the court may take into account the difficulty of proving an exact amount of damages from false advertising, as well as the maxim that "the wrongdoer shall bear the risk of uncertainty which his own wrong has created."

913 F.2d at 969. That is what the district court has done—to Ralston's chagrin.

The district court erred, however, in refusing to reduce the award to reflect ALPO's alternative use of the funds it did not have to expend on a national rollout. In order to reflect economic reality, damages awarded in order to compensate for loss of a business opportunity should equal the plaintiff's "'opportunity cost,' or the return it could have made on an alternative investment" of the funds not spent on the foregone opportunity.

ALPO retained the use of the funds it would have spent on a national rollout; presumably it did not put the money under a mattress but obtained some (albeit a second best) return on that capital. That ALPO may in fact have spent some or all of the money on a responsive advertising campaign, as the district court found, is beside the point. The responsive campaign itself constituted, in effect, an alternative investment, the return on which is the prejudgment interest to which ALPO is entitled. *See generally Sands, Taylor & Wood Co. v. Quaker Oats Co.*, 978 F.2d 947, 963 (7th Cir. 1992) (award of prejudgment interest under Lanham Act); 26 U.S.C. § 6621 (provision for calculating interest award).

To award ALPO prejudgment interest without reducing the award made in compensation for the loss of the future income stream would be double counting. The district court should therefore reduce the award for deferral of ALPO's future income stream in order to reflect the return on capital it presumably received from alternative investments, using the prejudgment interest rate as a measure of that return.

C. Lost Profits

Ralston claims that it is entitled to recover its lost profits from ALPO. At trial, each side relied upon a regression analysis done by one of ALPO's experts in order to show the impact that the other side's advertising had on its sales. In *ALPO I* the district court inferred from this regression analysis that Ralston's advertising had a material effect upon ALPO's sales, thus warranting an award of damages under the Lanham Act. 720 F. Supp. at 209, *aff'd* 913 F.2d at 965. Ralston now argues that the district court abused its discretion when it declined to use the same data to calculate the profits that Ralston lost due to ALPO's diversion of sales by falsehoods.

We think the court reasonably found it could rely upon the regression to show the direction but not the magnitude of the effect that ALPO's advertisements had upon Ralston's profits. Ralston, however, presented no evidence with which the court could fill in the resulting gap. Therefore we affirm the court's refusal to award Ralston damages for profits lost on sales diverted to ALPO.

D. Enhancement

Section 35(a) of the Lanham Act authorizes the court to award up to three times a plaintiff's actual and proven damages so long as the result is compensatory, not punitive. The district court enhanced the award to ALPO by 50% in order to cover its lost profits (*i.e.,* on sales diverted from ALPO to Ralston), compensate ALPO for a permanent distortion in the market for puppy food, and for interest and inflation. Ralston says the enhancement is speculative, punitive, and an indirect attempt to award attorneys' fees to ALPO notwithstanding our earlier reversal of such an award.

The last allegation is as unworthy of counsel as it is unnecessary to Ralston's cause. An enhancement is appropriate to compensate a Lanham Act plaintiff only for such adverse effects as can neither be dismissed as speculative nor precisely calculated. Interest and inflation are not such elusive quanta. Lost profits and market distortion are, however, appropriate bases for the catch-all enhancement contemplated by § 35(a). We thus remand this aspect of the award to the district court to compute the precise amounts to be awarded for interest and the effect of inflation, and to reconsider such enhancement as may be appropriate solely in order to compensate ALPO for its lost profits on sales diverted to Ralston and the continuing distortion of the market owing to Ralston's false advertising.

III. Conclusion

We affirm the district court insofar as it awarded ALPO damages for a delay in income stream caused by Ralston's false advertising and refused to award Ralston lost profits on sales diverted by ALPO. We remand this matter for the court to reduce the award to ALPO for the cost of responsive advertising and to determine the amounts to be awarded for interest and inflation and reduce the enhancement in light thereof.

NOTES & QUESTIONS

(1) The court states that responsive advertising need not mention Ralston's CHD advertising to be recoverable. Why? What harm would result in requiring the responsive ad campaign to mention Ralston's advertisements?

(2) What is the reasoning for allowing a plaintiff to recover damages for responsive advertising? Recall that a plaintiff seeking monetary damages usually must show actual consumer confusion, but only a likelihood of confusion if the plaintiff is seeking an injunction. However, many courts only require a showing of a likelihood of confusion for a recovery of money spent on responsive advertising. *See Balance Dynamics Corp. v. Schmitt Indus.*, 204 F.3d 683, 692–93 (6th Cir. 2000) (stating that to recover loss control damages, plaintiffs must show that a violation of the Lanham Act occurred, and that (1) there was a likelihood of confusion or damages to sales, profits, or goodwill; (2) its damage control expenses are attributable to the violation (i.e., caused by the violation); and (3) its damage control efforts were reasonable under the circumstances and proportionate to the damage that was likely to occur). What justification is there for this lesser burden?

(3) Why does the court remand for a recalculation of the money spent on responsive advertising by ALPO? Based on the court's reasoning, why should ALPO recover any money at all? *See Ames Pub. Co. v. Walker-Davis Publications, Inc.*, 372 F. Supp. 1, 13–15 (E.D. Pa. 1974) (permitting a plaintiff to recover, despite unclean hands, in part because of the harm to the public that would result if recovery were denied).

(4) Although the court upholds the imposition of damages for the delay of ALPO's income stream from entering the national puppy food market, the court also remands the case to ensure that ALPO does not receive a double recovery. Why might a double recovery occur?

(5) According to the court, under what circumstances may an upward enhancement be imposed? Why was an upward enhancement appropriate in this case?

F. THE ROLE OF THE FTC AND "LITTLE FTC ACTS"

As noted in Section C above, consumers have no standing to sue under the Lanham Act and the Restatement. Nevertheless, two important avenues exist for protecting consumer interests in the absence of a suit by competitors: actions brought by the Federal Trade Commission ("FTC") under § 5 of the Federal Trade Commission Act ("FTCA"), and suits brought by consumers themselves under what have become known as "Little FTC Acts." Although a thorough coverage of each is beyond the scope of this text, we mention them here to give you some sense of other causes of action that may be asserted against a business engaged in deceptive marketing.

Congress first enacted the FTCA in 1914. Of particular importance, § 5 of the Act made "[u]nfair methods of competition" unlawful. The Act also created a new federal agency, the FTC, whose responsibilities would include investigating and prosecuting violations of the Act. Due to the "competition" language used in the original act, some courts construed the FTC's authority as limited to those cases involving injury to competitors. Thus, in 1938, Congress amended § 5 of the FTCA keeping the "[u]nfair methods of competition" language and adding that "unfair or deceptive acts or practices" were also unlawful.[f] As § 5 reads today, it prohibits not just activities "in commerce," but also activities "affecting commerce."

The FTC is a quasi-judicial body that administers the FTCA. It issues complaints and conducts hearings before administrative law judges. These decisions are reviewable by the full Commission (there are 5 commissioners), and further appeals may be heard by any federal circuit court of appeals. Typically the FTC seeks injunctive relief in the form of "cease and desist" letters, but it may seek other corrective actions, such as assessing civil penalties or having violators issue refunds.

The FTC's powers under the FTCA are great because the definition of "unfair methods of competition" has been construed broadly. The FTC has sought to challenge various types of conduct, including false and misleading use of trademarks, trade names, unsubstantiated product claims, testimonials, and even unfair credit practices and product disparagement claims. Furthermore, the FTC's grant of power authorizes it to bring federal antitrust actions. In short, § 5 grants the FTC the ability to challenge conduct which would often be actionable under the Lanham Act, as well as conduct that would fall outside of the Lanham Act's scope.

---

[f]   That same year, Congress added a new section, § 12, which defined the terms "unlawful" and "unfair or deceptive act or practice" with a particular focus on false advertising.

Although the FTC acts for the benefit of the public, there is no private right of action under the FTCA. If the FTC chooses not to pursue or challenge a particular practice, private parties or state attorneys general may still move forward under what have been dubbed "Little FTC Acts." These acts are state consumer protection statutes that typically prohibit a broad range of unfair or deceptive trade and business practices. Many are based upon the recommendations of the FTC, as found in its Unfair Trade Practices and Consumer Protection Act.

Although these statutes come from a common origin, it would be a mistake to assume that they offer little variation. For instance, some statutes provide a laundry list of specifically prohibited conduct while others do not. Some statutes provide that only consumers may sue, others also permit business consumers to sue, while still others permit business competitors to sue.[g] Some statutes place a greater emphasis on the role of intent, while others indicate that an intent to deceive is unnecessary for an action to lie. Some statutes even permit the imposition of punitive damages in certain cases. Despite these variations, common elements shared by many of these "Little FTC Acts" include the ability of plaintiffs to obtain damages in excess of their actual damages (typically treble damages in an appropriate case), the authorization of injunctive relief, and the recovery of attorney's fees.

---

[g] If you are wondering why a competitor might need the provisions of a "Little FTC Act" when the Lanham Act is available, consider the problems discussed above in Section C involving prudential standing as well as the requirement that the conduct affect interstate commerce.

CHAPTER 8

COMMERCIAL DISPARAGEMENT

■ ■ ■

We have just completed a review of the law of deceptive marketing, which, in essence, involves making false statements about one's own products or services. A closely related legal theory, and one that is often intertwined with deceptive marketing, is commercial disparagement, i.e., making or publishing disparaging statements about another's goods or services. Indeed, in the last chapter you may have noticed instances where the deceptive marketing also included disparaging remarks about a competitor. In this Chapter, we will examine commercial disparagement under both the common law and the Lanham Act (which is broadly worded to include disparagement claims). We also examine the similar but distinct concept of business defamation.

A. DISPARAGEMENT UNDER THE COMMON LAW GENERALLY

A cause of action for slander of title—i.e., for falsely claiming an ownership interest in property—has long been a part of the common law. The law eventually broadened to include liability for false statements concerning a plaintiff's products, and today, it includes any false statement that harms a plaintiff's pecuniary interest. *See* RESTATEMENT (SECOND) OF TORTS § 623A (1977). Unfortunately, courts have tended to use a variety of names for this cause of action, including "commercial disparagement," "product disparagement," "disparagement of property," "trade libel," and "injurious falsehood." For simplicity's sake, we will refer to the cause of action as commercial disparagement, but you should be aware of these variants as we move forward, and particularly as you read cases on the subject.

1. BUSINESS DISPARAGEMENT UNDER THE RESTATEMENT (SECOND) OF TORTS

The Restatement (Second) of Torts provides that a defendant may be liable to a plaintiff for publishing a false statement that is harmful to the plaintiff's pecuniary interest:

§ 623A. Liability For Publication Of Injurious Falsehood—General Principle

One who publishes a false statement harmful to the interests of another is subject to liability for pecuniary loss resulting to the other if

(a) he intends for publication of the statement to result in harm to interests of the other having a pecuniary value, or either recognizes or should recognize that it is likely to do so, and

(b) he knows that the statement is false or acts in reckless disregard of its truth or falsity.

Sections 624 and 626 specifically provide that a defendant may be liable for slander of title (calling into question the ownership rights of the plaintiff in land or other property) as well as for trade libel (disparaging the quality of the plaintiff's land or other property). Liability under § 623A is not limited to these two instances, however, and extends to any pecuniary harm resulting from disparaging the "interests" of the plaintiff. The following illustrations from § 623A are instructive on this point:

3. A, knowing his statement to be false, tells C that B has died. As a result C, who had intended to purchase goods from B, buys them elsewhere. A is subject to liability to B.

4. A, knowing his statement to be false, tells C that B, an importer of wood, does not deal in mahogany. As a result C, who had intended to buy mahogany from B, buys it elsewhere. A is subject to liability to B.

RESTATEMENT (SECOND) TORTS § 623A cmt. a (1977). Note how in each of the above illustrations, neither the title nor quality of property owned by the plaintiff is called into question, yet § 623A is broad enough to encompass both.

2. DISPARAGEMENT DISTINCT FROM DEFAMATION

It is tempting, given the nature of disparagement, to lump it together with the common law tort of defamation. After all, both causes of action involve the publication of false statements that affect the plaintiff. However, the two causes of action are, in fact, separate and evolved from completely different origins. This distinction is important as the causes of action protect different interests and carry different burdens of proof on key elements. Section 558 of the Restatement (Second) of Torts covers the defamation cause of action:

§ 558. Elements Stated

To create liability for defamation there must be:

(a) a false and defamatory statement concerning another;

(b) an unprivileged publication to a third party;

(c) fault amounting at least to negligence on the part of the publisher; and

(d) either actionability of the statement irrespective of special harm or the existence of special harm caused by the publication.

The primary distinction between a defamation action and a disparagement claim is not apparent from the text of this section unless we focus on the word "defamatory." A defamatory statement impugns the character or reputation of the plaintiff himself, whereas the sections on disparagement speak to harming the interests of the plaintiff, such as by calling into question the title or quality of the plaintiff's property. It may have occurred to you that some false statements may harm both the plaintiff's reputation and the interests of the plaintiff. For instance, a false allegation that a grocer has been selling non-organic fruits as "organic" harms both the reputation of the grocer in the community and the pecuniary interest of the grocer (assuming that the grocer can show a drop-off in sales). While it is possible that a false statement could be actionable as both defamation and disparagement, such cases are few and far between. Courts, in general, are reluctant to characterize a commercial disparagement cause of action as a defamation claim. The Eighth Circuit has utilized the following oft-cited test for when a commercial disparagement action can also be recognized as a defamation claim:

> [W]here the publication on its face is directed against the goods or product of a corporate vendor or manufacturer, it will not be held libelous per se as to the corporation, unless by fair construction and without the aid of extrinsic evidence it imputes to the corporation, fraud, deceit, dishonesty, or reprehensible conduct in its business in relation to said goods or product.

National Refining Co. v. Benzo Gas Motor Fuel Co., 20 F.2d 763, 771 (8th Cir. 1927). However, sometimes a case seems more properly characterized as defamation rather than disparagement. The next case may be such an example. As you read the case, note how the theory under which recovery is sought affects the plaintiff's burden of proof.

HURLBUT V. GULF ATLANTIC LIFE INSURANCE COMPANY

749 S.W.2d 762 (Tex. 1987)

CAMPBELL, JUSTICE.

Insurance agents C. Daniel Hurlbut and A.C. Hovater sued their former employer, Gulf Atlantic Insurance Company, its parent corporation, and several corporate officers for fraud, business disparagement, and tortious interference with contract rights. After a trial by jury, the trial court rendered judgment for actual and exemplary damages against all defendants. The court of appeals reversed the judgment of the trial court and rendered judgment that Hurlbut and Hovater take nothing, holding that all claims were barred by limitations. We reverse the judgment of the court of appeals and hold that a fact issue was raised regarding when Hurlbut and Hovater should have discovered defendants' fraud. Because the court of appeals additionally held that the great weight and preponderance of the evidence supported a finding that Hurlbut and Hovater should have discovered the fraud more than two years prior to filing suit, we remand the cause to the trial court for new trial.

FACTS

. . . .

In the spring of 1974, Hurlbut, Hovater and several officers of Gulf Atlantic met to discuss a new enterprise. At this meeting, representatives of Gulf Atlantic proposed that Hurlbut and Hovater form a partnership to serve as the administrator of a proposed health insurance trust which would sell and service group health insurance policies underwritten by Gulf Atlantic. Following this meeting, Hurlbut and Hovater returned to their home in Houston and formed "Agency Associates." Gulf Atlantic advanced funds to cover start-up costs. Gulf Atlantic also recommended an attorney to Hurlbut and Hovater to use in preparation of the trust documents. After the attorney had drafted the appropriate documents, they were signed by Hurlbut, Hovater and an officer of the bank Agency Associates intended to use as trustee of the premium trust account. The executed trust agreement was then returned to the attorney who Hurlbut and Hovater believed would, in conjunction with Gulf Atlantic, obtain state approval of the master policy.

In the late summer of 1974, Kenneth Thompson, an officer of Gulf Atlantic and Hurlbut and Hovater's primary contact with the company, instructed them to start selling group health insurance under the trust arrangement. When Hurlbut and Hovater inquired about the master policy, they were sent a copy of a proposed policy to be issued to the "West Texas Pipe Trades Health Insurance Trust" with the explanation that Agency Associates' master policy would be virtually identical. Hurlbut and Hovater sold the group health plan through the fall and winter of 1974. These sales were made without benefit of the master policy. Gulf Atlantic, however, continued to assure Hurlbut and Hovater that all was in order with the program and that the master policy would soon be provided.

Potential clients who were concerned regarding Agency Associates' inability to produce a master policy were referred to Gulf Atlantic by Hurlbut and Hovater. One such client placed a call to Gulf Atlantic in

December 1974. Thompson was unavailable so the caller talked with Gulf Atlantic's president, William Barnes, who denied that Gulf Atlantic was underwriting Agency Associates' group health insurance program. This client relayed his conversation to Hurlbut and also contacted the office of the Attorney General.

Hurlbut thereafter contacted Thompson who again reassured him that Gulf Atlantic was still underwriting the program. Hurlbut also contacted Jack Warner, vice president of Nationwide Corporation, the corporate parent of Gulf Atlantic. Warner had initially worked with Hurlbut and Hovater during the formative stages of Agency Associates. Warner also reassured Hurlbut and suggested a meeting between Barnes, Hurlbut and Hovater to straighten out the matter.

This meeting took place in Dallas at Gulf Atlantic's corporate offices on January 21, 1975. There Hurlbut and Hovater were surprised by the appearance of Bill Flanary, an assistant Attorney General assigned to investigate the group health insurance program being sold by Agency Associates. At this meeting Barnes told Flanary that Hurlbut and Hovater did not have authority to write group insurance for Gulf Atlantic through a trust plan.

Following this meeting, Hurlbut and Hovater accompanied Flanary to a local office of the Attorney General in Dallas and cooperated in the investigation. As a result of this investigation and those of local authorities as well, the assets of Agency Associates were placed in receivership, the insurance licenses of Hurlbut and Hovater were revoked and both civil and criminal charges were brought against them. Both Hurlbut and Hovater were arrested and jailed, lost their ability to make a living selling insurance and sustained other damage.

The motivation behind Gulf Atlantic's abandonment of its original arrangement with Hurlbut and Hovater is possibly explained by the difficulty it experienced in obtaining approval of the master policy for West Texas Pipe Trades Health Insurance Trust, the same policy previously provided to Hurlbut and Hovater with the explanation that theirs would be the same. Gulf Atlantic had some difficulty with the State Board of Insurance because it had authorized the sale of group health insurance prior to the approval of this master policy. Rather than acknowledge additional misconduct and complicity in the sales that Hurlbut and Hovater had made prior to issuance of a master policy, it is asserted that Gulf Atlantic decided to conceal its role by denying it had ever agreed to underwrite the program or obtain the state's approval of the master policy and thereby shift the entire responsibility to Hurlbut and Hovater.

On January 21, 1977, Hurlbut and Hovater filed suit against Gulf Atlantic and the other defendants seeking actual and exemplary damages alleging several theories of recovery including fraud, business disparagement and tortious interference with contract rights.

. . . .

BUSINESS DISPARAGEMENT AND TORTIOUS INTERFERENCE WITH CONTRACT RIGHTS

The plaintiffs also obtained favorable jury findings on their claims of business disparagement and tortious interference with contract. In analyzing these claims and the evidence supporting them, the court of appeals concluded that they were in essence a claim for slander and barred by the one year statute of limitations. TEX. REV. CIV. STAT. ANN. Art. 5524(1) (Vernon 1958). We find no reversible error in the judgment of the court of appeals as it pertains to these two claims.

The general elements of a claim for business disparagement are publication by the defendant of the disparaging words, falsity, malice, lack of privilege, and special damages. J. Fleming, *The Law of Torts* at 697–700 (5th ed. 1977); Annot., 74 A.L.R.3d 298, 301 (1976). The tort is part of the body of law concerned with the subject of interference with commercial or economic relations. The Restatement identifies the tort by the name "injurious falsehood" and notes its application "in cases of the disparagement of property in land, chattels, or intangible things or of their quality." Restatement (Second) of Torts § 623A, cmt. a (1977).

The court of appeals recognizes that an action for injurious falsehood or business disparagement is similar in many respects to an action for defamation. Both involve the imposition of liability for injury sustained through publications to third parties of a false statement affecting the plaintiff. The two torts, however, protect different interests. The action for defamation is to protect the personal reputation of the injured party, whereas the action for injurious falsehood or business disparagement is to protect the economic interests of the injured party against pecuniary loss.

More stringent requirements have always been imposed on the "plaintiff seeking to recover for injurious falsehood in three important respects—falsity of the statement, fault of the defendant and proof of damage." Restatement (Second) of Torts § 623A, cmt. g (1977). Regarding falsity, the common law presumed the defamatory statement to be false and truth was a defensive matter. The plaintiff in a business disparagement claim, however, must plead and prove the falsity of the statement as part of his cause of action. Regarding fault, the defendant in a defamation action was held strictly liable for his false statement whereas the defendant in an action for business disparagement or injurious falsehood is subject to liability "only if he knew of the falsity or acted with reckless disregard concerning it, or if he acted with ill will or intended to interfere in the economic interest of the plaintiff in an unprivileged fashion." *Id.* Finally regarding damages, the common law required plaintiff in a defamation action to prove special damages in only a limited number of situations, whereas pecuniary loss to the plaintiff must always be proved to establish a cause of action for business disparagement.

In the present case there is evidence to support findings that the statements of Gulf Atlantic were false and malicious in the sense that Gulf Atlantic knew them to be false. It is, however, with the element of special damages that the plaintiffs have some difficulty.

Proof of special damages is an essential part of the plaintiffs' cause of action for business disparagement. The requirement goes to the cause of action itself and requires that plaintiff "establish pecuniary loss that has been realized or liquidated as in the case of specific lost sales." W. Keeton, *Prosser and Keeton on the Law of Torts,* § 128 at 971 (5th ed. 1984). Furthermore, the communication must play a substantial part in inducing others not to deal with the plaintiff with the result that special damage, in the form of the loss of trade or other dealings, is established. *Id.* at 967; Restatement (Second) of Torts § 632 (1977).

Our examination of the record reveals no evidence of the direct, pecuniary loss necessary to satisfy the special damage element of a claim for business disparagement. The court of appeals found no evidence of special injury to the business, writing:

> No evidence was offered of damages resulting from loss of business expected from any particular customer or prospective customer to whom disparaging statements were made by defendants. The damages alleged and proved resulted only indirectly from the disparaging statements alleged, and more immediately from the receivership, the orders revoking their licenses, and their prosecution for misappropriation of insurance premiums.

In this regard we agree with the Court of Appeals that the damages proven were personal to the plaintiffs.

Similarly, the plaintiffs have not produced evidence supporting a claim for tortious interference with contract. As the court of appeals observed, plaintiffs did not allege or prove "any contract rights with which defendants interfered, other than Gulf Atlantic's own breach of contract with them and plaintiffs have asserted no claims for breach of contract." 696 S.W.2d at 100.

It is difficult to imagine a set of circumstances under which plaintiffs' theories of fraud and tortious interference with contract can co-exist. Although no specific contracts were proven, it was plaintiffs' testimony that any contract rights between their agency and the entities to which they were selling group health insurance were to be underwritten by Gulf

Atlantic. Hurlbut and Hovater were acting as agents for Gulf Atlantic and the economic benefits they expected from these contracts were to come from Gulf Atlantic in the form of commissions. Perhaps Gulf Atlantic breached its contract with plaintiffs when it refused to honor their agreement and perhaps Gulf Atlantic's conduct in the matter was fraudulent, but we see no evidence here supporting plaintiffs' claim that Gulf Atlantic tortiously interfered with any specific contract rights.

CONCLUSION

Although we agree with the court of appeals that the evidence developed in the present record suggests the submission of claims for fraud, and perhaps malicious prosecution and breach of contract, we do not foreclose any other theories which may on retrial find support in the evidence. The judgment of the court of appeals is reversed and the cause is remanded to the trial court for new trial.

NOTES & QUESTIONS

(1) Why did the plaintiffs fail to successfully make out a case for commercial disparagement? Would they have been more successful bringing a defamation claim (and if so, why didn't they do so)?

(2) What justification is there for requiring that a plaintiff prove more in a commercial disparagement claim than a defamation claim?

(3) The court indicates that the plaintiffs' claim that the defendants committed fraud upon them was inconsistent with their tortious interference with contract claim. Can you explain this inconsistency?

(4) It may have occurred to you that a claim for commercial disparagement could often give rise to a claim for intentional interference with existing or prospective contract. Indeed, the same facts often support both claims. As a result of this overlap, some courts have been unwilling to recognize the injurious falsehood cause of action. For instance, in *Kenney v. Hangar Prosthetics & Orthotics, Inc.*, 269 S.W.3d 866 (Ky. Ct. App. 2007), the court was faced with a plaintiff claiming a number of causes of action against his former employer, including breach of contract, defamation, and tortious interference with prospective business advantage. The plaintiff attempted to amend his complaint to include an injurious falsehood claim, but he was denied by the trial court. In affirming the trial court's denial, the *Kenney* court noted that an injurious falsehood claim was not recognized in Kentucky, as it was really just a form of intentional interference with economic relations. *Id.* at 873 (citing W. PAGE KEETON ET AL., PROSSER AND KEETON ON THE LAW OF TORTS § 128, at 964 (5th ed. 1984)).

Similarly, some courts have failed to recognize injurious falsehood as a separate tort on the ground that it is nothing more than a defamation claim. *See* DAN B. DOBBS ET AL., THE LAW OF TORTS § 656 (2d ed. 2012) (citing

Davita Inc. v. Nephrology Assocs., P.C., 253 F. Supp. 2d 1370, 1374–75 (S.D. Ga. 2003) (applying Georgia law)).

3. ELEMENTS OF DISPARAGEMENT

The *Hurlbut* opinion lists the elements of a commercial disparagement claim as "publication by the defendant of the disparaging words, falsity, malice, lack of privilege, and special damages." Although courts vary in how they articulate these elements, this listing is generally accurate. We address each element in turn below, save for lack of privilege, which is discussed last.

a. Publication by the Defendant of the Disparaging Words

The first element, publication by the defendant of disparaging words, has two parts: disparagement and publication. Section 629 of the Restatement (Second) of Torts defines a disparaging statement as follows:

§ 629. Disparagement Defined

A statement is disparaging if it is understood to cast doubt upon the quality of another's land, chattels or intangible things, or upon the existence or extent of his property in them, and

(a) the publisher intends the statement to cast the doubt, or

(b) the recipient's understanding of it as casting the doubt was reasonable.

Note that it is not enough to merely cast doubt; the defendant must also speak with the intent to cast doubt, or it must be reasonable for the recipient to have understood the statement as casting doubt.

With respect to publication, the law of disparagement is very broad, as it permits liability for either intentional or negligent publications. *See* RESTATEMENT (SECOND) OF TORTS § 630 (1977). Furthermore, disparagement makes actionable any publication, be it spoken, written, or communicated in some other manner, and the form taken does not necessarily affect the other elements of the claim (unlike defamation which makes some distinction between slander and libel).[a]

PROBLEM 8.1

In each of the situations below, identify whether there has been a publication of disparaging words. *See* RESTATEMENT (SECOND) OF TORTS § 629 & cmts. c–f; *id.* § 630 & cmts. a–b.

---

[a]   Libel, which generally refers to printed defamatory words, requires no showing of special damages for recovery. Slander, which generally refers to spoken defamatory words, requires a showing of special damages, and excuses such a showing only in a limited number of circumstances. *Compare* RESTATEMENT (SECOND) OF TORTS § 569 (1977), *with id.* § 570.

(a)   Maggie and Roscoe are neighbors with oceanfront property. Roscoe is selling his house. Maggie, who has designs to buy Roscoe's house herself, falsely tells people who look at the house that there is a public easement allowing people to cross the property to gain beach access. Maggie makes these statements in the hopes of deterring buyers and driving the price down so she can swoop in and purchase the property.

(b)   Assume the same facts as in (a), but now Maggie has no interest in buying Roscoe's house. One day, Dexter, a prospective buyer, comes to view Roscoe's house and sees Maggie outside gardening. He tells Maggie that he is interested in purchasing the house and asks if there are any easements on the property. Maggie replies that there is a pubic easement allowing beach access (Maggie assumes this is true because she frequently sees people cut through the property to get to the beach). Based on this information, Dexter does not pursue the purchase.

(c)   Assume the same facts as in (b), but instead of meeting on her own property, Maggie meets Dexter at a party. Maggie has no idea that Dexter is a possible buyer of Roscoe's house. During the course of the conversation, Maggie complains about the constant stream of people cutting across her neighbor's yard to get to the beach.

(d)   Assume the same facts as in (a), but instead of telling people there is an easement, Maggie files a lien in the county records claiming an easement on Roscoe's property in the hopes that this will cloud title to the property.

(e)   Cashton Hutcher is a famous celebrity and prolific Twitter user with one of the most followed feeds in the United States. One day, Cashton is denied access to one of L.A.'s hottest new restaurants, Derelicte. Angered by the perceived slight, Cashton writes a blistering review of Derelicte calling the food inedible and trashy.

(f)   Assume the same facts as in (e), except that instead of a famous celebrity, Cashton is an associate at a mid-size law firm. After being denied access to Derelicte, Cashton posts on his Facebook page that the place looked trashy.

b.   Falsity

Another element of a disparagement claim is that the disparaging comment is, in fact, false. Depending on your exposure to the tort of defamation, you may have read or heard that "truth is always a defense." However, this saying is misleading in the commercial disparagement area, as it misstates the burden. Recall from the *Hurlbut* case that the burden is upon the plaintiff to show falsity. Thus, while a truthful statement is not actionable, it is inaccurate to call truth a "defense." *See* RESTATEMENT (SECOND) OF TORTS § 651(1)(c) (1977).

The burden upon the plaintiff is not to show that its goods or services are perfect in every way, but merely to show that the specific statement at issue is false. *See* RESTATEMENT (SECOND) OF TORTS § 634 cmt. b (1977). Thus, if a car dealership accuses a competitor of rolling back the odometers on its used cars, the plaintiff dealership need only prove that it does not roll back the odometers (although the cars may have many other serious problems) to establish falsity.

Two concepts closely related to the element of falsity are the actionability of opinions and puffery. You may recall that we encountered these concepts in the Chapters on misrepresentation and deceptive marketing. In the commercial disparagement area, liability for opinions has come into question due to First Amendment concerns (which we cover more fully in Section C.3. below). Once, pure expressions of opinion were actionable under both defamation and disparagement law. The defamation rule has changed, and an expression of mere opinion is no longer actionable unless it also implies the existence of defamatory facts. A similar rule presumably applies to injurious falsehood, although it is unclear.

As for puffery, it is difficult to tell if this concept has its basis in the falsity of the statement, or in the relation of the statement to causation and injury. The Restatement (Second) of Torts has explicitly provided for a conditional privilege between competitors that speaks directly to the puffery concept:

§ 649.   Conditional Privilege Of Competitors

A competitor is conditionally privileged to make an unduly favorable comparison of the quality of his own land, chattels or other things, with the quality of the competing land, chattels or other things of a rival competitor, although he does not believe that his own things are superior to those of the rival competitor, if the comparison does not contain false assertions of specific unfavorable facts regarding the rival competitor's things.

The link to puffing is noted in comment c to § 649, which states:

. . . . These statements have a strong analogy to the 'sales talk' or 'puffing' that a vendor is permitted to indulge in without liability to a purchaser who alleges that he was thereby misled. In both cases the practice of vendors to make consciously exaggerated claims for their goods is so well known that little or no importance is attached to the statements. . . . If, however, [the defendant] goes further and makes a direct attack upon the quality of his competitor's things by stating specific unfavorable facts even though he does so to supply a reason for his claim that his own things are superior, he cannot successfully claim a privilege under the rule stated in this Section.

Thus, this section is consistent with our concepts of puffery previously discussed; the more vague the statement, the less actionable it is. Additional privileges available to a commercial disparagement defendant are discussed in more detail below.

c. Malice

The malice element of a disparagement cause of action does not necessarily mean malice in the sense that many would think. Usually the term "malice" invokes a sense of evil or ill will with regard to motive. Such is not the case (or at least not necessarily under the Restatement's view) when speaking of malice in a disparagement action. The Restatement § 623A(a) requires that the maker of the false statement intends "for publication of the statement to result in harm to interests of the other having a pecuniary value, or either recognizes or should recognize that it is likely to do so," and "knows that the statement is false or acts in reckless disregard of its truth or falsity." This is a two-step inquiry.

First, the publication must be made either with intent to harm (which is in-line with the ill will association) or simply recognition that the statement will or is likely going to cause harm. Note that this second way of meeting the first inquiry does not require evil motive, but simple recognition that the likely result is harm.

Similarly, the second inquiry asks if the statement is known to be false or is made with reckless disregard for the truth. This second inquiry is typically what is being referred to when courts mention the "malice" requirement. Thus, the Restatement does not necessarily appear to care about the motive or ill will of the defendant with regard to "malice." However, not all courts or jurisdictions limit the scope of this second inquiry so narrowly. As you read through the below case, consider how the court's malice standard compares to the Restatement's.

FASHION BOUTIQUE OF SHORT HILLS, INC. V. FENDI USA, INC.

1998 WL 259942 (S.D.N.Y. 1998)

CEDARBAUM, SENIOR J.

Defendants' earlier motion for summary judgment dismissing plaintiff's Lanham Act claims was granted. Defendants now move for summary judgment on plaintiff's two remaining common law claims, business slander and disparagement of goods. For the reasons that follow, the motion is granted in part and denied in part.

[From 1983 to July of 1991, Fashion Boutique operated a retail store in Short Hills, New Jersey, which sold only Fendi brand merchandise, including leather goods and furs. In August of 1988, Fashion Boutique and Fendi Diffusione entered into a written franchise agreement. The term of the franchise agreement was later extended, and limitations were placed on Fendi Diffusione's ability to sell Fendi products to certain retailers in New Jersey. Fashion Boutique purchased all of its goods from manufacturers within the Fendi organization and from affiliated licensees.

In 1989, Fendi Diffusione, through wholly owned subsidiaries, opened a store on Fifth Avenue in New York City. When the New York store opened, a list of Fendi boutiques was displayed at the entrance. Fashion Boutique's Short Hills store was not included on the list.

Fashion Boutique submitted declarations from fourteen people who visited the New York store before Fashion Boutique closed the Short Hills store. Four people were told that the Short Hills store sold a different line of Fendi products, although no reference was made to the quality of goods carried by the Short Hills store. Three of these people had come to the New York store for assistance with repairs of defective merchandise that had been purchased at the Short Hills store. Ten people were told that the Short Hills store carried a line of Fendi merchandise that was inferior to that carried by the New York store. Two people were told that the Short Hills store sold "fake" or "bogus" Fendi merchandise. One couple was told that the furs carried by the Short Hills store were old and not well made. Employees at the New York store encouraged three people to write letters to Fendi Stores complaining about the inferior goods sold at the Short Hills store. Fashion Boutique also submitted declarations from people who visited the New York store after Fashion Boutique closed, alleging similar comments were made.]

. . . .

Disparagement of Goods

An oral defamation directed at the quality of a business' goods or services is actionable not as slander, but as disparagement of goods. To establish such a claim, a plaintiff must prove falsehood, publication, malice, and special damages. See [Ruder & Finn, Inc. v. Seaboard Surety Co., 422 N.E.2d 518 (N.Y. 1981)] (distinguishing disparagement of goods claims from defamation claims).

To prove special damages, a plaintiff must identify actual pecuniary loss with particularity and establish that the disparaging statements caused the loss. See Kirby v. Wildenstein, 784 F. Supp. 1112, 1116 (S.D.N.Y. 1992) (pecuniary loss must be the natural and immediate consequence of the disparaging statements).

The parties agree that the malice element of disparagement of goods can be satisfied either by proof of common law malice or by proof of actual malice. Common law malice is spite or ill will. Actual malice is knowledge that the statement at issue is false or reckless disregard of whether it is false. Statements are made with actual malice if they are made with at least a high degree of awareness of their probable falsity, meaning that the speaker entertained serious doubts as to the truth of the publication. Common law malice focuses on the plaintiff's motive in publishing a falsehood, whereas actual malice focuses on the plaintiff's knowledge of the truth or falsity of the published defamatory statement. *Prozeralik v. Capital Cities Comm'ns., Inc.*, 626 N.E.2d 34 (N.Y. 1993).

As noted, the doctrine of respondeat superior applies to a slander claim. Defendants do not dispute that respondeat superior also applies to a claim for disparagement of goods, but rather argue that no issue of material fact exists as [to] whether the statements at issue were made with malice.

A material dispute of fact exists with regard to six claims of disparagement of goods. Amore, Bassett, Green, the Montalbanos, Ring, and Scheer all affirm that defendants' employees told them that plaintiff sold a line of goods inferior to the line sold at the Fendi store in New York. These customers also affirm that they stopped patronizing plaintiff's store because of these statements. *Cf. Payrolls & Tabulating, Inc. v. Sperry Rand Corp.*, 22 A.D.2d 595, 598 (holding that if special damages alleged are the loss of customers, persons who ceased to be customers must be named).

Furthermore, a reasonable juror could find that the statements to each of these customers were made with malice. Amore affirms that she went to the Fendi store in New York for repair of a handbag she had purchased at plaintiff's store. Defendants' customer service manager asked Amore where she had purchased her bag. When Amore told her, the manager "told me in a curt manner that she could not help me because [plaintiff's] store carried a completely different (and inferior) line of Fendi merchandise than the New York store." Amore never returned to either store again. Further, plaintiff asserts—and defendants do not dispute—that the statements to Amore were made by Joann Vernocchi. At her deposition, Vernocchi testified that the two stores did not sell "a different line of merchandise in terms of quality."

Bassett affirms that she was shopping in the Fendi store in New York and saw a handbag she wished to purchase. She asked a salesperson to write down the "style number" so that Bassett could order the handbag from plaintiff's store along with a garment bag she planned to order. The salesperson told Bassett "that would be a big mistake," because plaintiff's store sold a "franchise line" that was inferior to the "top Fendi line" sold in the New York store. When Bassett expressed disbelief, the salesperson "called over another salesperson who confirmed the first salesperson's story."

Green affirms that she was shopping in the Fendi store in New York when a salesperson approached her and asked her where she had purchased her handbag. When Green told her that Green had purchased the handbag at plaintiff's store, the salesperson responded that plaintiff's store sold a "lesser line" of Fendi products. The salesperson also asked Green to write a letter to Bruno D'Angelo to complain about plaintiff's store and "suggested" that Green " 'put more into the letter' in order to have a better effect." At that time, D'Angelo was the executive vice president of defendant Fendi USA, Inc. Previously, he had served as executive vice president of both Fendi USA, Inc. and Fendi Stores, Inc.

The Montalbanos affirm that the assistant manager of the Fendi store in New York urged them to write complaint letters about plaintiff's store even though the Montalbanos had expressed no complaints to the manager, and, in fact, had no complaints to express. Additionally, a fur salesman at the Fendi store in New York allegedly told the Montalbanos that plaintiff sold old furs. Plaintiff asserts—and defendants do not dispute—that the fur salesman at issue is Jack Cohen. At his deposition, Cohen stated that he had no knowledge of the age of plaintiff's furs.

Ring affirms that he was in the Fendi store in New York when a salesperson admired his briefcase and asked Ring where he had purchased it. When Ring told her that he had purchased it at plaintiff's store, she "immediately became upset," and told Ring, "If you bought it at the Fendi in Short Hills, it is not the *real* Fendi line." She then explained that plaintiff's store sold an inferior line of goods. Ring never returned to either store.

Scheer affirms that he and his wife brought a key case which they had purchased at plaintiff's store to the Fendi store in New York for repair. The Scheers were "very dissatisfied" with its "poor quality." The store manager told the Scheers that he could not repair the key case because they had purchased it at plaintiff's store, which sold an inferior line of Fendi merchandise. Scheer "could not understand" why the manager made his comments about plaintiff's store and concluded that the manager "appeared to be attempting to injure its reputation." Additionally, plaintiff asserts—and defendants do not dispute—that the statement to Scheer was made by Francesco Gittardi. At his deposition, Gittardi testified that the two stores sold "exactly" the same line of merchandise and denied that he had ever told a customer otherwise.

A rational jury could conclude that these alleged statements were gratuitous, unsolicited comments published with the intent to injure plaintiff, and, hence, that these statements were malicious. *Cf. Stukuls v. New York*, 366 N.E.2d 829 (N.Y. 1977) (in context of qualified privilege, to send question of malice to jury, statement must be consistent only with a desire to injure the plaintiff); *Herlihy v. Metrop. Museum of Art*, 214 A.D.2d 250, 259 (in context of qualified privilege, malice may be inferred from defendant's use of expressions beyond those necessary for the purpose of the privileged communication).

Given the discrepancy between the declarations submitted by Amore, the Montalbanos, and Scheer, and the deposition testimony of Vernocchi, Cohen, and Gittardi, plaintiff has also raised a genuine issue of material fact as to whether the statements made to Amore, the Montalbanos, and Scheer were made with actual malice. *See* [*Liberman v. Gelstein*, 605 N.E.2d 344 (N.Y. 1992)] (statements are made with actual malice if they are made with at least a high degree of awareness of their probable falsity).

Accordingly, there are genuine issues of disputed fact with respect to the statements to Amore, Bassett, Green, the Montalbanos, Ring, and Scheer.

The Remaining Statements

Defendants' motion for summary judgment is granted with respect to the remaining statements. A number of customers *were* allegedly told that the two stores sold a different line of goods, but not that plaintiff's goods were inferior. Another category of customers allegedly heard rumors about plaintiff's store. Summary judgment is granted as to these alleged statements. . . .

Lance, Mantel, Blomquist, and Parisi do not allege that they ceased patronizing plaintiff's store because of the statements made to them. Thus, plaintiff does not proffer evidence of the essential element of special damages. Accordingly, summary judgment is warranted on claims of disparagement of goods to those customers.

Summary judgment is also warranted as to other statements allegedly made to Lance and Mantel, because there is no assertion as to when the offending statements were published. If the alleged statement to Lance that her handbag was "fake" came after plaintiff's store closed, then this statement could neither have impugned plaintiff's integrity nor caused it damage. *See Dyer v. MacDougall*, 93 F. Supp. 484, 487 (E.D.N.Y. 1950) (to plead claim that oral statement tended to injure plaintiff in his profession, plaintiff must allege that he carried on the profession "at the time when the words complained of were published") (quoting *Shakun v. Sadinoff*, 272 A.D. 721). Similarly, both the falsity of the alleged statement to Mantel that plaintiff's store had a "very bad year" and "would not be there much longer," and the questions of whether plaintiff's integrity could have been impugned and whether plaintiff could have been damaged by the statement depend on the date of the statement in relation to the date on which plaintiff's store did in fact close. Without specifying the date of these statements, plaintiff does not show that it could withstand a trial motion to dismiss at the end of its case. The same reasoning warrants summary judgment with regard to the claims of the other customers who allegedly heard comments after plaintiff's store had closed. Indeed, plaintiff appears to concede that statements made after the store closed are significant not as claims of slander or disparagement, but only to "corroborate the widespread nature of the defamation and disparagement and to illustrate the malice."

. . . .

Conclusion

Material disputes of fact remain with respect to three claims of slander *per se* and six alleged statements disparaging goods. These claims were pleaded with enough specificity to give notice and to permit a defense. Accordingly, defendants' motion for summary judgment is denied as to these nine statements and granted with respect to the remainder of plaintiff's claims.

NOTES & QUESTIONS

(1) What is the standard articulated by the court for meeting the "malice" element? How does this standard compare to the Restatement's articulation in § 623A?

(2) Look back at the *Hurlbut* opinion. What standard does the Texas Supreme Court appear to adopt with regard to malice? You should note that while the approach in *Hurlbut* is contemplated by the Restatement, the ALI took no position on whether this approach was an appropriate substitute for the standard in § 623A. *See* RESTATEMENT (SECOND) OF TORTS § 623A (1977) (Caveats). The majority of courts appear to follow the Restatement's standard.

(3) What facts suggested malice in *Fashion Boutique*? Do you think the court would have reached a different result had it strictly followed the Restatement standard?

d. Special Damages

Under the law of defamation, an allegedly false and defamatory statement, negligently made and without privilege, is enough to incur damages regardless of whether special damages are proven. Re-read § 623A regarding commercial disparagement and note what is required in the first line—the publisher of the false statement is only subject to liability for "pecuniary loss resulting to the other." This is not an issue of just showing the amount of damages.[b] To succeed on a commercial

---

b   The terms "special damages" and "pecuniary loss" are often used interchangeably by the courts. Black's defines "special damages" as "[d]amages that are alleged to have been sustained in the circumstances of a particular wrong. To be awardable, special damages must be

disparagement claim, a plaintiff must prove a direct and causal connection between an identifiable pecuniary loss and the disparaging publication. The Restatement sets forth both the types of loss a publisher is liable for and how a plaintiff may establish such loss in § 633:

§ 633. Pecuniary Loss

(1) The pecuniary loss for which a publisher of injurious falsehood is subject to liability is restricted to

(a) the pecuniary loss that results directly and immediately from the effect of the conduct of third persons, including impairment of vendibility or value caused by disparagement, and

(b) the expense of measures reasonably necessary to counteract the publication, including litigation to remove the doubt cast upon vendibility or value by disparagement.

(2) This pecuniary loss may be established by

(a) proof of the conduct of specific persons, or

(b) proof that the loss has resulted from the conduct of a number of persons whom it is impossible to identify.

Courts vary with regard to the level of particularity by which damages must be shown. Recall in the *Hurlbut* decision above, the appellate court denied relief because no evidence was offered of "damages resulting from loss of business expected from any particular customer or prospective customer." This requirement that loss be shown through a specific customer is not universally accepted and is not necessarily consistent with the Restatement's view. *See* RESTATEMENT (SECOND) OF TORTS § 633 cmt. h (1977). The Restatement does not contemplate the recovery of consequential damages.

Given that special damages (or pecuniary loss to use the phrasing from the Restatement) is an element of the commercial disparagement cause of action, it should come as no surprise that damages are the most frequent remedy sought. Although injunctive relief is also a possibility, courts are generally reluctant to order injunctions. This is due in part to First Amendment concerns and the frequent overlap that occurs between defamation and disparagement. Nonetheless, in an appropriate case, injunctive relief may be issued.

PROBLEM 8.2

Roscoe Pet Food manufactures Roscoe's Canned Dog Grub. The product is successful and annual sales have been over $10,000,000 for the past three

---

specifically claimed and proved." BLACK'S LAW DICTIONARY, Damages–special damages (10TH ED. 2014).

years. At the beginning of this year, Dog Lover Magazine ran an article exposing the practices of many dog food manufacturers of using meat byproducts that had been exposed to bacteria, thus causing severe kidney failure and death in consuming dogs. The article named Roscoe Pet Food as one of the offending manufacturers, a fact that was false and based upon no investigation whatsoever. Following the publication of this article, Roscoe's sales plummeted to $3,000,000 for the year.

(a) Roscoe Pet Food sues for commercial disparagement. Assuming it has met the other elements of its cause of action, will it be able to establish special damages? Consider the *Hurlbut* opinion above and RESTATEMENT (SECOND) OF TORTS § 633 cmt. h (1977).

(b) Assume that prior to the publication, Roscoe Pet Food approached a group of venture capitalists regarding investing in the company to fund expansion into other pet food markets. This investment would have meant an additional $100,000,000 in working capital for the company. Upon publication of the article, the attorney representing the venture capitalists sent a letter to Roscoe Pet Food, informing them that in light of the information revealed in the Dog Lover Magazine article, the group was withdrawing from any further negotiations. Prior to this incident, the deal was in its final stages and was a "lock" according to many of the venture capitalists involved. Can Roscoe Pet Food recover for the lost investment? *See* RESTATEMENT (SECOND) OF TORTS § 633 cmt. i (1977).

(c) Assume that instead of expanding through investors, Roscoe Pet Supply approached Big Bank to make a large loan to fund the expansion. Prior to the dip in sales, the interest rate being discussed was a favorable 5%. However, due to the large dip in sales, the interest rate now being discussed is 8%. Assuming that Roscoe Pet Food goes forward with the loan, can it recover for this increase in the interest rate? *See* RESTATEMENT (SECOND) OF TORTS §§ 632, 633 & cmt. i (1977). What if it cannot move forward on the loan now at all? Should Roscoe Pet Food be able to recover?

e. Lack of Privilege

Although the *Hurlbut* court adopted lack of privilege as an element of a disparagement cause of action, privilege is an affirmative defense. The Restatement (Second) of Torts recognizes both absolute and conditional privileges, utilizing the same privileges available to a defendant in a defamation cause of action. *See* RESTATEMENT (SECOND) OF TORTS §§ 635, 646A (1977). Absolute privileges cover instances such as when the defendant has been granted consent by the plaintiff to publish the materials (§ 583), statements made to a spouse (§ 592), and various statements that relate to judicial and legislative proceedings (§§ 585–590A). The conditional privileges include situations in which the publisher of the disparaging information has done so to protect a sufficiently important interest of its own, a recipient or third party, or the public. *See id.* §§ 594–598. These privileges are labeled conditional because they can be lost if abused, such as when publication occurs with knowledge of the falsity of the statements or with reckless disregard for their truth. *See id.* §§ 599–601, 650A. The law of disparagement contains two conditional privileges, however, that are not subject to this abuse qualification. The first of these privileges is the one found in § 649 pertaining to the right of a competitor to make an unduly favorable comparison of its own goods, which has already been discussed above in Section A(3)(b). Because this privilege extends to statements of superiority not made with an honest belief, it is obviously not abused by the lack of honest belief in the superiority claim. The second privilege is found in § 647, which permits a publisher to assert that he, rather than the plaintiff, has a legal right to property. Such claims are privileged, despite being incorrect or unreasonable, so long as the claim is asserted in good faith (as judged subjectively). *See id.* § 647 cmts. b, d.

NOTES & QUESTIONS

(1)   Review the elements of a commercial disparagement cause of action. Given that malice is an element of such an action, what function do the conditional privileges serve? *Compare* RESTATEMENT (SECOND) OF TORTS § 623A (1977), *with id.* §§ 599–601, 650A.

B. FALSE STATEMENTS IN THE SALE OF ANOTHER'S GOODS

A claim that is related to commercial disparagement involves false statements in marketing another's goods. This claim encompasses, for example, a seller who makes misrepresentations about another's goods that he is selling. At first this may seem like an odd claim—after all, why would the original manufacturer or producer of the goods care about false statements that presumably help to sell its product (other than to worry about contributory liability)? To answer this, consider the example of a beer manufacturer who sends products to distributors with the understanding that beer that sits idle beyond its expiration date will not be sold. The manufacturer's reasoning is that beer sold past this expiration date can become stale and the taste may be altered. If distributors continue to sell the product to retailers as non-expired beer, the consuming public may receive stale beer and associate the resulting poor taste with the manufacturer's brand. Although a sale of the manufacturer's beer has occurred, the manufacturer would prefer not to have the sale than to lose goodwill and future sales due to an association with stale, poor tasting beer. The Third Restatement of Unfair Competition addresses this issue:

§ 6.   Misrepresentations In Marketing The Goods Or Services Of Another

> One is subject to liability to another under the rule stated in § 2 if, in marketing goods or services of which the other is truthfully identified as the manufacturer, producer, or supplier, the actor makes a representation relating to those goods or services that is likely to deceive or mislead prospective purchasers to the likely commercial detriment of the other under the rule stated in § 3.

The text and the comments note that this provision covers representations that are likely to deceive or mislead prospective purchasers with respect to a matter that relates to the goods or services, although the goods are truthfully identified as originating from another. The comments also provide examples that would encompass our beer manufacturer scenario and other similar situations. As one comment states: "The misrepresentations described in this Section are typically made in an attempt to sell goods that the actor has on hand and are thus generally laudatory rather than derogatory. A seller may assert, for example, that the goods are fresh when in fact they are stale or deteriorated, that they are the manufacturer's latest style or highest quality when in fact they are outdated or seconds, or that they are warranted by the manufacturer in respects that exceed the manufacturer's actual undertaking." RESTATEMENT (THIRD) OF UNFAIR COMPETITION § 6 cmt. b (1995). The language of the Lanham Act § 43(a) is also broad enough to encompass such claims, as it prohibits a person from falsely misrepresenting the "nature, characteristics [or] quality" of another's goods, services, or commercial activities.

C. BUSINESS DISPARAGEMENT UNDER THE LANHAM ACT

In this Section, we cover the topic of commercial disparagement through the lens of the Lanham Act. While false advertising under the Lanham Act focused upon false claims made about a party's own goods or services, disparagement focuses on false claims made about another's goods or services. Despite this difference, the elements of a false advertisement claim under the Lanham Act are identical to the elements of a disparagement claim under the Act. Recall that the elements of a false advertising claim under the Act are the following:

(1) A false statement of fact by the defendant in a commercial advertisement about its own product;

(2) The statement actually deceives or has a tendency to deceive a substantial segment of its audience;

(3) The deception is material, in that it is likely to influence the purchasing decision;

(4) The defendant placed the false or misleading statement in interstate commerce; and

(5) The plaintiff has been or is likely to be injured as a result of the false statement.

For a disparagement claim, we simply substitute "another's" for "its own" in the first element. Thus, much of the discussion of these elements from Chapter 7 is applicable in this area as well.

One part of the first element that we did not develop earlier is the requirement that the statement be made in a commercial advertisement. Although this is a requirement for both false advertising and disparagement claims under the Lanham Act (but not for the common law analogs), it tends to be more of an issue in the disparagement context.

In the following materials, after briefly exploring the development of the Lanham Act disparagement cause of action, we discuss how to determine whether the "in commercial advertising or promotion" element is met. We also explore First Amendment concerns that may arise in connection with a commercial disparagement claim. As to this last topic, it should be noted that although First Amendment concerns are also relevant to false advertising claims, they are implicated more frequently in disparagement actions.

1. DEVELOPMENT OF LIABILITY UNDER § 43(a)

For many years after the enactment of the Lanham Act, the tort of commercial disparagement was left exclusively to the common law. Prior to 1989, § 43 of the Lanham Act was interpreted purely as a false advertising statute and not as a prohibition on commercial disparagement. In fact, prior to the 1989 amendments, § 43(a) did not specifically contain language referring to "another person's" goods, services, or commercial activities. This change was a deliberate decision by Congress to prohibit commercial disparagement as part of a national policy of promoting fair competition. However, this expansion also brought First Amendment concerns over the chilling of free speech. Thus, the language of § 43(a)(1)(B) was limited to instances of commercial advertising or promotion.[c]

The federalization of commercial disparagement calls into question the extent to which the common law development of the tort should carry over to Lanham Act claims. This is particularly relevant to the issue of

---

[c] It was also limited to misrepresentations of fact (so as to exclude opinions that do not imply false facts). For an in-depth history of the development of the 1989 Amendments and their impact, see 5 MCCARTHY ON TRADEMARKS §§ 27:91–27:97 (4TH ED. 2015).

malice. Recall that the common law tort requires a showing of malice for recovery, but this element is absent from a § 43(a) claim. Indeed, malice is only relevant to the issue of damages (although it can also help excuse the burden of proof for a plaintiff on the issue of consumer deception). Absent a showing of malice, First Amendment concerns over the chilling effect of a lawsuit on free speech raise serious questions about the validity of the Lanham Act's disparagement action. As we will see, this issue is related to the commercial nature of the speech.

2.   COMMERCIAL ADVERTISING OR PROMOTION

An essential element of a § 43(a)(1)(B) Lanham Act claim is that the false statement be made "in [a] commercial advertising or promotion." Where the claim is made in a television or newspaper commercial, this element is easily met. However, issues can arise when the statements are made orally to select customers. This raises the question of what qualifies as a commercial advertising or promotion. The following case cites an oft-adopted standard and demonstrates the limits this phrase can place on a plaintiff's ability to bring suit under the Lanham Act.

FASHION BOUTIQUE OF SHORT HILLS, INC. V. FENDI USA, INC.

314 F.3d 48 (2d Cir. 2002)

JOHN M. WALKER, JR., CHIEF JUDGE.

Plaintiff-appellant Fashion Boutique of Short Hills, Inc. ("Fashion Boutique"), challenges a host of rulings by the United States District Court for the Southern District of New York (Miriam Goldman Cedarbaum, *District Judge*) during this lengthy litigation arising from the demise of its business. Fashion Boutique, formerly a seller of Fendi products, claims that its business was ruined by a campaign of disparagement conducted by a competing boutique, defendant-appellee Fendi Stores, Inc. ("Fendi Stores") and its parent company, defendant-appellee Fendi USA, Inc. ("Fendi USA") (collectively, "Fendi").

Fashion Boutique contends principally that the district court erred as follows: (1) by granting the motion for partial summary judgment in favor of Fendi, dismissing plaintiff's claims under the Lanham Act, *see Fashion Boutique of Short Hills, Inc. v. Fendi USA, Inc.*, 942 F. Supp. 209 (S.D.N.Y. 1996) ("*Fashion Boutique I*"); (2) by excluding plaintiff's expert testimony regarding the value of the lost business, *see Fashion Boutique of Short Hills, Inc. v. Fendi USA, Inc.*, 75 F. Supp. 2d 235 (S.D.N.Y. 1999) ("*Fashion Boutique III*"); and (3) by instructing the jury that general damages recoverable under New York law for slander were limited to the injury to its reputation in the minds of three individual customers.

For the following reasons, we affirm.

BACKGROUND

[This case flows from the same facts as the *Fashion Boutique* opinion excerpted earlier in this Chapter, but the issue here involves Fashion Boutique's Lanham Act claims. Fashion Boutique noticed a sharp decline in its sales after the opening of the defendants' New York store and was ultimately forced to close its retail operations. Fashion Boutique alleged that the precipitous fall in its sales was caused by a corporate policy carried out by Fendi to misrepresent the quality and authenticity of the products sold at Fashion Boutique. However, Fashion Boutique could not show that many of its customers heard disparaging statements first-hand at the defendants' Fifth Avenue store. Rather, it alleged that Fendi employees made misrepresentations to some customers at the Fifth Avenue store, these customers relayed the comments to others, and the false rumors were thus spread throughout Fashion Boutique's customer base of over 8,000 customers.

In challenging the district court's grant of partial summary judgment, Fashion Boutique relied primarily on reported conversations between Fendi personnel and nine undercover investigators hired to pose as shoppers and on declarations by forty Fashion Boutique customers. In none of the proffered interactions did employees at the Fifth Avenue store initiate conversations about Fashion Boutique. They commented on Fashion Boutique only after the customers mentioned plaintiff. For example, several customers who reported their conversations with Fendi employees went to the Fifth Avenue store seeking to repair or exchange products or were wearing Fendi products as they shopped at that store. After the customer informed Fendi personnel that the item had been bought at Fashion Boutique, the employee reacted by making critical comments about the quality of Fashion Boutique's merchandise and, on several occasions, refused to exchange or repair the product.

In particular, Fashion Boutique presented evidence that prior to its demise: Fendi personnel told some customers that Fashion Boutique carried an inferior, "department store" line of products or that Fashion Boutique sold "fake" or "bogus" merchandise; Fendi employees described Fashion Boutique's goods as a "different line" from that sold at the Fifth Avenue store; and Fendi employees made critical comments about Fashion Boutique's customer service. Fashion Boutique also presented evidence that other customers heard rumors to the same effect about Fashion Boutique. Fashion Boutique presented evidence that, after it closed, Fendi employees continued to make similar remarks to its customers.

To support its claim that this pattern was based on a policy of disparagement from Fendi, Fashion Boutique presented the deposition of Caroline Clarke, a former employee of Fendi USA, who stated that though her superiors never explicitly told her of a policy to disparage Fashion Boutique, she learned from speaking to managers and salespersons at Fendi Stores that salespersons followed a practice of disparaging the customer service at Fashion Boutique.

After carefully reviewing the evidence, the district judge found that a number of the alleged comments did not support Fashion Boutique's claim as the statements were not disparaging, were based upon inadmissible hearsay, were made after Fashion Boutique closed and thus not actionable under the Lanham Act or, because plaintiff and defendants were no longer competitors, were not relevant. The district court concluded that the remaining evidence of disparagement was insufficient to withstand a motion for summary judgment because it did not fall within the meaning of "commercial advertising or promotion" as set forth in the Lanham Act.]

On appeal, Fashion Boutique challenges principally the district court's grant of summary judgment on its Lanham Act claim, exclusion of its expert testimony, and the jury instructions with respect to general damages on its slander claims.

DISCUSSION

I. *Section 43(a) of the Lanham Act*

Fashion Boutique contends that the district court abused its discretion when it decided the summary judgment motion by not considering the rumor evidence, "different line" statements, and comments made after the close of the store. Fashion Boutique also argues that the district court erred in finding that Fendi's actions did not constitute "commercial advertising or promotion" under the Lanham Act. Specifically, Fashion Boutique maintains that its proof of several disparaging comments by defendants, together with evidence of rumors that plaintiff sold fake or inferior merchandise, falls into the category "commercial advertising or promotion."

. . . .

B. "Commercial Advertising or Promotion"

Section 43(a) of the Lanham Act provides that

> [a]ny person who . . . in commercial advertising or promotion, misrepresents the nature, characteristics, qualities, or geographic origin of his or her or another person's goods, services, or commercial activities, shall be liable in a civil action by any person who believes that he or she is likely to be damaged by such act.

15 U.S.C. § 1125(a)(1)(B). An important issue in this case is whether the allegedly disparaging statements by salespersons at the Fendi Fifth

Avenue store constituted "commercial advertising or promotion" within the meaning of Section 43(a).

The statute does not define the phrase "commercial advertising or promotion." In determining whether representations qualify as "commercial advertising or promotion," most courts have adopted the four-part test set forth in [*Gordon & Breach Sci. Publishers S.A. v. Am. Inst. of Physics*, 859 F. Supp. 1521, 1535–36 (S.D.N.Y. 1994) ("*Gordon & Breach I*")]. Under the test, in order to qualify as "commercial advertising or promotion," the contested representations must be "(1) commercial speech; (2) by a defendant who is in commercial competition with plaintiff; (3) for the purpose of influencing consumers to buy defendant's goods or services"; and, (4) although representations less formal than those made as part of a classic advertising campaign may suffice, they must be disseminated sufficiently to the relevant purchasing public. *See Gordon & Breach I*, 859 F. Supp. at 1535–36; *see also Proctor & Gamble Co. v. Haugen*, 222 F.3d 1262, 1273–74 (10th Cir. 2000) (adopting four-part test); *Coastal Abstract Serv., Inc. v. First Am. Title Ins. Co.*, 173 F.3d 725, 735 (9th Cir.1999) (same); *Seven-Up Co. v. Coca-Cola Co.*, 86 F.3d 1379, 1384 (5th Cir. 1996) (same).

In deciding whether to adopt this four-part test, we adhere to the ordinary rules of statutory construction and look first to the plain and ordinary meaning of statutory terms. Applying those rules to the terms "commercial advertising or promotion," we easily accept the first and third elements of the *Gordon & Breach* test that define the term "commercial" as referring to "commercial speech" that is made for the purpose of influencing the purchasing decisions of the consuming public. *See Gordon & Breach I*, 859 F. Supp. at 1536.

The precise meaning of "advertising or promotion" has been subject to various interpretations. *Compare Gordon & Breach Sci. Publishers S.A. v. Am. Inst. of Physics*, 905 F. Supp. 169, 182 (S.D.N.Y. 1995) (holding that "*any* promotional statement directed at actual or potential purchasers falls within the reach" of the Lanham Act), *and Mobius Mgmt. Sys., Inc. v. Fourth Dimension Software, Inc.*, 880 F. Supp. 1005, 1020–21 (S.D.N.Y. 1994) (holding that single letter addressed to one purchaser constitutes "advertising or promotion"); *with Garland Co. v. Ecology Roof Sys., Corp.*, 895 F. Supp. 274, 279 (D. Kan. 1995) (rejecting *Mobius* and holding that the Lanham Act is violated only where the misrepresentations are widely disseminated within the relevant purchasing public), *and Med. Graphics Corp. v. SensorMedics Corp.*, 872 F. Supp. 643, 650–51 (D. Minn. 1994). The statute's disjunctive wording compels us to give meanings to both "advertising" and "promotion" that do not render either term superfluous. We conclude that the distinction between advertising and promotion lies in the form of the representation. Although advertising is generally understood to consist of widespread communication through print or broadcast media, "promotion" may take other forms of publicity used in the relevant industry, such as displays at trade shows and sales presentations to buyers. *See, e.g., Seven-Up*, 86 F.3d at 1386 (finding sales presentation to a significant percentage of industry customers constitutes advertising under the Lanham Act).

The Seventh Circuit has recently limited the scope of the Lanham Act to advertising defined as "a form of promotion to anonymous recipients, as distinguished from face-to-face communication . . . [and] a subset of persuasion [that relies on] dissemination of prefabricated promotional material." *See First Health Group Corp. v. BCE Emergis Corp.*, 269 F.3d 800, 803 (7th Cir. 2001) (internal quotations omitted). The problem with the Seventh Circuit's focus on the term "advertising" is that it fails to define the term "promotion" in any meaningful way.

Although the Lanham Act encompasses more than the traditional advertising campaign, the language of the Act cannot be stretched so broadly as to encompass all commercial speech. The ordinary understanding of both "advertising" and "promotion" connotes activity designed to disseminate information to the public. Thus, the touchstone of whether a defendant's actions may be considered "commercial advertising or promotion" under the Lanham Act is that the contested representations are part of an organized campaign to penetrate the relevant market. Proof of widespread dissemination within the relevant industry is a normal concomitant of meeting this requirement. Thus, businesses harmed by isolated disparaging statements do not have redress under the Lanham Act; they must seek redress under state-law causes of action.

In determining whether a defendant's misrepresentations are designed to reach the public, we find the district court's proactive-reactive distinction instructive, but not necessarily dispositive. Although most reactive statements will doubtless consist of off-the-cuff comments that do not violate the Lanham Act because no broad dissemination is intended or effected, we leave open the possibility that a cause of action might exist where a defendant maintains a well-enforced policy to disparage its competitor each time it is mentioned by a customer, if such a policy of reactive disparagement successfully reaches a substantial number of the competitor's potential customers.

In sum, we adopt the first, third and fourth elements of the *Gordon & Breach* test. To decide this appeal, we need not decide whether [to adopt] the second element—that defendant and plaintiff be competitors. We note that the requirement is not set forth in the text of Section 43(a) and express no view on its soundness.

C.   Fashion Boutique's Lanham Act Claim

Based on the foregoing principles, we easily conclude that Fashion Boutique failed to put forward sufficient evidence that defendants' actions constituted "commercial advertising or promotion" under the Lanham Act.

Turning first to plaintiff's evidentiary claims, we believe that the district court did not abuse its discretion in excluding the evidence of rumors. Regardless of whether the rumor evidence was properly rejected as hearsay, the district court later decided, in any event, that its prejudicial effect outweighed its minimal probative value. We find no "manifest error" in this decision given the absence of proof connecting defendants to the rumors.

There is no evidence to suggest that the remaining statements were part of an organized campaign to penetrate the marketplace. Even including the "different line" statements, post-closing statements, and comments made to undercover investigators, Fashion Boutique has presented a total of twenty-seven oral statements regarding plaintiff's products in a marketplace of thousands of customers. Such evidence is insufficient to satisfy the requirement that representations be disseminated widely in order to constitute "commercial advertising or promotion" under the Lanham Act. *See Sports Unlimited* [*v. Lankford Enters., Inc.*, 275 F.3d 996, 1004–05 (10th Cir. 2002)] (finding evidence of dissemination of information to two customers, where plaintiff made up to 150 bids per year, insufficient to constitute "commercial advertising or promotion"). The Clark deposition was specifically limited to disparagement of the customer service at Fashion Boutique, as distinct from the products sold there, and there is nothing to suggest that the comments were anything more than individual reactions to particular customers' mention of Fashion Boutique.

. . . .

We have carefully considered appellant's remaining arguments and find them to lack merit.

CONCLUSION

For the foregoing reasons, we affirm the judgment of the district court.

NOTES & QUESTIONS

(1)   The court cites the often-adopted *Gordon & Breach* test for defining a "commercial advertising or promotion." Under this test, the contested representations must be:

(i)   Commercial speech;

(ii) By a defendant who is in commercial competition with plaintiff;

(iii) For the purpose of influencing consumers to buy defendant's goods or services; and

(iv) Although representations less formal than those made as part of a classic advertising campaign may suffice, they must be disseminated sufficiently to the relevant purchasing public.

On which of these factors does the court focus in affirming the district court?

(2) According to the court, what is the difference between advertising and promotion? Which was at issue in the case?

(3) What level of dissemination is required to qualify as "commercial advertising or promotion"? Should dissemination be to a majority of the consuming public? Who gets to decide the appropriate level? It should be noted that not all courts adopting the *Gordon & Breach* standard are equally demanding. *See, e.g., Seven-Up Co. v. Coca-Cola Co.,* 86 F.3d 1379 (5th Cir. 1996) (holding that a sales presentation made by Coca-Cola to eleven soft drink bottlers was a "commercial advertising or promotion" because the potential purchasers in the market were relatively limited such that "even a single promotional presentation to an individual purchaser may be enough to trigger protection"); *Mobius Mgmt. Sys., Inc. v. Fourth Dimension Software, Inc.,* 880 F. Supp. 1005, 1019 (S.D.N.Y. 1994) (finding, under the fourth prong of the *Gordon & Breach* test, that a letter to a single customer was an "advertising or promotion"); *Nat'l Artists Mgmt. Co., Inc. v. Weaving,* 769 F. Supp. 1224, 1235 (S.D.N.Y. 1991) (holding that a former employee's denigration of the plaintiff in telephone calls to persons who were both friends and professional contacts was actionable in the "theatre-booking industry," although the calls were not advertising or promotion in the usual sense of those words). *But see Am. Needle & Novelty, Inc. v. Drew Pearson Marketing, Inc.,* 820 F. Supp. 1072, 1077–78 (N.D. Ill. 1993) (relying upon dictionary definitions and finding that both "advertising" and "promotion" included connotations of public dissemination of information; thus, a single copy of a letter "addressed to a non-consuming licensor" did not fall under § 43(a)).

(4) The *Fashion Boutique* court did not address the second factor of the *Gordon & Breach* test. Can you see any reason why a court might not wish to adopt a requirement that, to qualify as a commercial advertisement or promotion, the defendant must be in commercial competition with the plaintiff?

3. FIRST AMENDMENT CONCERNS AND DISPARAGEMENT

The above case set forth the test used for determining whether a representation qualifies as "commercial advertising or promotion," but did not define the first requirement, i.e., that the representation involves "commercial speech." It would be tempting to assume that if speech qualifies as "advertising or promotion," it should automatically constitute commercial speech. However, a communication is not necessarily commercial speech for First Amendment purposes merely because it is contained in an advertisement. Also, recall that malice is not an element of a Lanham Act § 43(a) claim. This has important implications with regard to First Amendment concerns.

The distinction between commercial and noncommercial speech is critical to determining what level of protection the speech receives under U.S. Supreme Court precedent. Noncommercial speech, even if false, generally receives full First Amendment protection. This is qualified by the famous case of *New York Times v. Sullivan*, 376 U.S. 254 (1964), which added a scienter element to a defamation claimant's burden of proof in circumstances involving public figures. Specifically, the Supreme Court required a plaintiff to prove that the false statement at issue was made either with knowledge of its falsity, or with reckless disregard for the truth. (This scienter element is known as the "actual malice" requirement.) Although *New York Times* involved a defamation action rather than a disparagement claim, the Supreme Court has left open the possibility that the same actual malice requirement would apply to a commercial disparagement claim.

As opposed to noncommercial speech, commercial speech generally receives a lesser level of protection. It is protected only if truthful and, even then, is subject to some governmental regulation. In short, false commercial speech receives the least amount of First Amendment protection.

The Supreme Court has not yet determined whether the *New York Times* actual malice requirement applies to commercial disparagement claims. In the 1984 case of *Bose Corp. v. Consumers Union of the United States*, 466 U.S. 485 (1984), the Court applied the actual malice standard to deny Bose's (a manufacturer of speakers) recovery based on an allegedly disparaging article reviewing one of its products that was published in the defendant's magazine, "Consumer Reports." *Id.* at 513–14. However, the Court was not squarely faced with the issue of whether actual malice applied to disparagement claims. As the Court stated: "The Court of Appeals entertained some doubt concerning the ruling that the *New York Times* rule should be applied to a claim of product disparagement. . . . We express no view on that ruling. . . ." *Id.* at 513. The Court also did not have to decide the issue of whether a company offering goods for sale to the public qualifies as a public figure, as Bose did not contest such status. *Id.* at 492.

At the time of the *Bose* decision, the Lanham Act was not worded to include commercial disparagement claims. In 1989, amendments were added to § 43 that expanded the scope of the section's coverage to include commercial disparagement actions. Congress was concerned about the chilling effect that such an expansion could have on free speech, and it thus restricted the scope of the expansion to "commercial advertising or promotion." The remarks made by Representative Robert Kastenmeier of Wisconsin at the time are enlightening on this issue:

> To avoid legitimate constitutional challenge, it was necessary to carefully limit the reach of the subsection. Because section 43(a) will now provide a kind of commercial defamation action, the reach of the section specifically extends only to false and misleading speech that is encompassed within the "commercial speech" doctrine by the United States Supreme Court.... Thus ... innocent dissemination and communication of false and misleading advertising, including promotional material, by the media are excluded from the reach of section 43(a). For a defendant who is a member of the media to be found liable under section 43(a), the plaintiff must show that the defendant was not "innocent" under section 32(2) and, as noted, that state of mind must encompass the *New York Times v. Sullivan* standard.
>
> S. 1883 is limited in another important sense. It uses the word "commercial" to describe advertising or promotion for business purposes, whether conducted by for-profit or nonprofit organizations or individuals. Political advertising and promotion is political speech, and therefore not encompassed by the term "commercial."

Remarks of Rep. Kastenmeier on S. 1883, 134 Cong. Rec. 31850–52 (Oct. 19, 1988).

Although the intent of inserting the "commercial advertising or promotion" language seems clear, there is still no direct guidance from the Supreme Court on whether this will avert the Constitutional issue or what impact the status of the plaintiff will have (i.e., whether a public figure plaintiff is still held to the *New York Times* actual malice standard). Recall that, by the terms of § 43(a), a competitor may attack misleading commercial speech under § 43(a)(1)(B) without showing malice. If the Congressional intent is upheld, this means that a court's decision to classify speech as commercial may be pivotal.

U.S. HEALTHCARE, INC. V. BLUE CROSS OF GREATER PHILADELPHIA

898 F.2d 914 (3d Cir. 1990)

Before STAPLETON, SCIRICA, and COWEN, CIRCUIT JUDGES.

SCIRICA, CIRCUIT JUDGE.

U.S. Healthcare, Inc. and its subsidiaries, United States Health Care Systems of Pennsylvania, Inc. and Health Maintenance Organization of New Jersey, Inc. (collectively, "U.S. Healthcare"), appeal from the district court's post-trial entry of judgment in favor of Blue Cross of Philadelphia, its president David Markson, and Pennsylvania Blue Shield (collectively, "Blue Cross/Blue Shield"), directed under Fed. R. Civ. P. 50(b) on U.S. Healthcare's federal and pendent state law claims alleging violations of § 43(a) of the Lanham Act, 15 U.S.C. § 1125(a) (1982), commercial disparagement, defamation and tortious interference with contractual relations. Blue Cross/Blue Shield, in turn, appeals from the entry of judgment on the verdict in favor of U.S. Healthcare on Blue Cross/Blue Shield's counterclaims alleging the same causes of action brought by U.S. Healthcare. Additionally, Blue Cross/Blue Shield appeals the pre-trial dismissal of the abuse of process counts in its counterclaims. We will reverse the grant of the Rule 50(b) motions, the judgment on the verdict in favor of U.S. Healthcare on Blue Cross/Blue Shield's counterclaims and the dismissal of the counts on abuse of process.

I.

FACTS AND PROCEDURAL HISTORY

. . . .

For over fifty years, Blue Cross/Blue Shield operated as the largest health insurer in Southeastern Pennsylvania by offering "traditional" medical insurance coverage. Traditional insurance protects the subscriber from "major" medical expenses, with the insurer paying a negotiated amount based upon the services rendered, and the subscriber generally paying a deductible or some other amount. The subscriber has freedom in choosing hospitals and health care providers (i.e., doctors).

In the early 1970's, U.S. Healthcare began providing an alternative to traditional insurance in the form of a health maintenance organization, generically known as an "HMO." An HMO acts as both an insurer and a provider of specified services that are more comprehensive than those offered by traditional insurance. Generally, HMO subscribers choose a primary health care provider from the HMO network who coordinates their health care services and determines when hospital admission or treatment from a specialist is required. Usually, subscribers are not covered for services obtained without this permission or from providers outside this network. By 1986, U.S. Healthcare was the largest HMO in the area, claiming almost 600,000 members. During the same period, Blue Cross/Blue Shield experienced a loss in enrollment of over 1% per year, with a large number of those subscribers choosing HMO coverage over traditional insurance, and a majority of those defectors choosing a U.S. Healthcare company.

Blue Cross/Blue Shield considered a number of strategies to regain its market position, including the acquisition of its own HMO. In late 1985, in an admitted attempt to compete with HMO, Blue Cross/Blue Shield introduced a new product that it called "Personal Choice," known generically as a preferred provider organization or "PPO." PPO insurance provides subscribers with a "network" of health care providers and hospitals, and generally "covers" subscribers only for services obtained from the network providers and administered at the network hospitals. Subscribers must obtain permission to receive treatment from providers outside the network, and in such instances receive at most only partial coverage.

. . . . In July 1986, Blue Cross/Blue Shield launched what it termed a deliberately "aggressive and provocative" comparative advertising campaign calculated "to introduce and increase the attractiveness of its products"—in particular, Personal Choice—at the expense of HMO products. Blue Cross/Blue Shield's campaign, which included direct mailings, as well as television, radio and print advertisements, ran for about six months at a total cost of approximately $2.175 million. According to a Blue Cross memorandum . . . the campaign was designed specifically to "reduce the attractiveness of [HMO]."

The Blue Cross/Blue Shield advertising campaign consisted of eight different advertisements for the print media, seven different advertisements for television, three different advertisements for radio, and a direct mailing including a folding brochure. The eight print advertisements compare the features of HMO and Personal Choice. Seven of the eight represent that with HMO, the subscriber selects a "primary care physician" who, in turn, must give permission before HMO will provide coverage for examination by a specialist. (The eighth print advertisement simply states that with Personal Choice, the subscriber may be examined by a specialist whenever he chooses, without "permission."). After describing HMO's referral procedure, however, three of the eight print advertisements—as well as the brochure—say the following:

> You should also know that through a series of financial incentives, HMO encourages this doctor to handle as many patients as possible without referring to a specialist. When an HMO doctor does make a specialist referral, it could take money

directly out of his pocket. Make too many referrals, and he could find himself in trouble with HMO.[5]

One of the print advertisements and the brochure also feature a senior citizen under the banner heading "Your money or your life," juxtaposed with Blue Cross/Blue Shield's description of "The high cost of HMO Medicare."

[The television and radio advertisements generally followed this same pattern of comparing the virtues of PPO over HMO, claiming that HMO limited choice. However, one of the advertisements used by Blue Cross/Blue Shield, while following the same general format, was dramatically different from the others in that it appeared designed to play upon the fears of the consuming public. The commercial featured a grief-stricken woman who says, "The hospital my HMO sent me to just wasn't enough. It's my fault." The implication of the advertisement is that some tragedy has befallen the woman because of her choice of health care.

In response to this advertising campaign, U.S. Healthcare filed suit alleging commercial disparagement, defamation and tortious interference with contractual relations. In addition, the company embarked upon its own aggressive, comparative advertising blitz, which began sometime after the Blue Cross/Blue Shield campaign and ran until late February 1987, at a cost $1.255 million. U.S. Healthcare's campaign consisted of five different advertisements for the print media, four different television advertisements, and two different radio advertisements. Of these, two advertisements were adapted for all three media as a response to Blue Cross/Blue Shield's most serious criticisms.

The first of these multi-media advertisements were designed to counteract the Blue Cross/Blue Shield message that HMO doctors sacrificed quality of care for higher profit. The second multi-media advertisement addressed and explained HMO's practice of allowing examination by specialists only when the subscriber is referred by his primary care physician. However, U.S. Healthcare's responsive campaign did not just highlight the positive characteristics in its own product, but also featured "anti-Blue Cross" advertisements. Print advertisements explained that under Personal Choice, the number of hospitals available to the subscriber were limited and, moreover, that many Personal Choice doctors do not have admitting privileges at even those few hospitals. One of these advertisements ran under a banner heading of "When it Comes to Being Admitted to a Hospital, There's Something Personal Choice May Not Be Willing to Admit"; the other ran under a banner heading of "If You Really Look Into 'Personal Choice,' You Might Have a Better Name For It."

---

[5]   One of the print advertisements replaces the last sentence with the question, "How many doctors do you know who want to pay your doctor's bill?"

Two of U.S. Healthcare's television advertisements showed a person flipping through the Hospitals and Physicians Directory of Personal Choice, pointing out the "gray area" of physicians without admitting privileges. Another was an attempt to play upon the fears of the consuming public. As solemn music plays, the narrator lists the shortcomings of Personal Choice while the camera pans from a Personal Choice brochure resting on the pillow of a hospital bed to distraught family members standing at bedside. The advertisement closes with a pair of hands pulling a sheet over the Personal Choice brochure.]

After a fourteen-day trial, followed by eight days of deliberations, the jury announced it was deadlocked on all issues of liability and damages. The district court declared a mistrial and then, before excusing the jurors, invited them to share their thoughts on the case for the benefit of the lawyers. It became apparent that, with regard to the counterclaims, the jurors were not far from unanimity. Consequently, the district court sent the jury back to deliberate whether Blue Cross/Blue Shield could recover damages on its counterclaims. Only then did the jury return a verdict against Blue Cross/Blue Shield on its counterclaims. The district court thereafter entered judgment for U.S. Healthcare on the counterclaims and scheduled a new trial on U.S. Healthcare's own claims.

The case was never retried. Instead, Blue Cross/Blue Shield filed a motion under Fed. R. Civ. P. 50(b) requesting the court to direct entry of judgment in its favor, on the grounds that the advertisements were entitled to heightened constitutional protection under the First Amendment, and that U.S. Healthcare had not met the applicable standard of proof, set forth in *New York Times Co. v. Sullivan*, 376 U.S. 254 (1964). The district court granted the motion. *U.S. Healthcare, Inc. v. Blue Cross*, No. 86–6452, 1988 WL 21830 (E.D. Pa. Mar. 7, 1988). The court held that because the objects of the advertisements are "public figures," and because the matters in the advertisements are "community health issues of public concern," heightened constitutional protections attach to this speech. The court reasoned that the First Amendment limited the power of the state and of Congress to award damages resulting from the allegedly false and misleading advertisements. Accordingly, the district court held that in order to prevail on their respective claims of Lanham Act violation, commercial disparagement, defamation and tortious interference with contract, both parties were required to prove each claim by clear and convincing evidence: (1) that the other side published the advertisements with knowledge or with reckless disregard of their falsity, and (2) that the advertisements were false. Applying this standard of proof, the court concluded that "[a]lthough the jury could reasonably have concluded that both sides had proven falsity and actual malice by a preponderance of the evidence, neither side has presented clear and convincing evidence [of this]."

This appeal followed.

II.

THE ACTIONABLE CLAIMS AND COUNTERCLAIMS UNDER APPLICABLE SUBSTANTIVE FEDERAL AND STATE LAW

We note initially that federal law governs the substantive issues of the parties' Lanham Act claims, while Pennsylvania law governs the commercial disparagement, defamation and tortious interference with contract claims. Although the district court granted the Rule 50(b) motions on constitutional grounds, we must first determine whether the statements are actionable under the substantive law governing the case before addressing whether the First Amendment prohibits the imposition of liability, since a determination of the former may obviate the need to examine the latter. Furthermore, Blue Cross/Blue Shield argues that the "challenged advertisements are not actionable regardless of the standard of proof." Therefore, we turn to the federal and state substantive law governing the parties' claims to determine whether there might exist a genuine issue of material fact.

[The court recited the elements for each cause of action: Lanham Act § 43(a) violations, common law defamation, commercial disparagement, and tortious interference with contract. The court then concluded that although some of the advertisements were innocuous "puffing," others were actionable under various claims. In particular, the court found that Blue Cross/Blue Shield may have misrepresented its own product's qualities, that both parties' advertisements which described the competitor's plans may have given rise to commercial disparagement causes of action, and that both parties ran advertisements that were capable of defamatory meaning (in particular the "Distraught Woman" advertisement run by Blue Cross/Blue Shield and the "Critical Condition" commercial, run by U.S. Healthcare). In addition, the court found that to the extent these advertisements were unprivileged, were intended to interfere with existing or prospective contractual relations, and actually did interfere with such relations, an action could lie for tortious interference.]

III.

FIRST AMENDMENT PRINCIPLES AND THE STANDARD OF PROOF IN CLAIMS ARISING FROM A COMPARATIVE ADVERTISING CAMPAIGN

Having determined that some of the advertisements may be actionable under federal and state law, we must now consider whether the First Amendment affects the standard of proof. As we have already noted, the district court held that under *New York Times Co. v. Sullivan et seq.* each party must prove as to each claim, by clear and convincing evidence, that the other party acted with actual malice—that is, with knowledge that the advertisement was false or with reckless disregard of whether it was false or not. 376 U.S. 254, 279–80 (1964). In so holding, the court rejected U.S. Healthcare's argument that the advertisements were commercial speech and thereby entitled to less constitutional protection. The district court viewed the comparative advertising campaign giving rise to this litigation as a "dispute . . . about how best to deal with spiraling medical costs," and concluded that, "[t]o characterize the advertisements in this case as mere commercial speech ignores the fact that, at their core, they are instruments in a debate between two providers of public health care 'intimately involved in the resolution of important public questions.' "

In arguing that the district court erred in applying heightened evidentiary standards to any of its claims, U.S. Healthcare maintains that the *New York Times* standard is "not mandated where, as here, false commercial speech is at issue." In response, Blue Cross/Blue Shield contends that the principles set forth in the commercial speech doctrine are inapplicable to this case because the United States Supreme Court "views damage claims [brought by private citizens] and government restrictions of speech as requiring distinctly different analysis for First Amendment purposes."

A. *Background*

Distinguishing the Supreme Court's First Amendment jurisprudence is an express intention to "lay down broad rules of general application," rather than to allow balancing between competing values on a case-by-case basis, an approach that the Court fears would "lead to unpredictable results and uncertain expectations, and . . . render [its] duty to supervise the lower courts unmanageable." *Gertz v. Robert Welch, Inc.*, 418 U.S. 323, 343–44 (1974). In delineating the limits placed on state authority by the First Amendment, the Court has articulated two distinct lines of cases, one involving defamation and the other involving government regulation of commercial speech. We have found no decision by the Court considering a defamation action involving expression properly characterized as commercial speech.

Despite its intention to enunciate general rules, the Court has implicitly recognized the need for balancing when a novel issue arises. *See, e.g., Philadelphia Newspapers, Inc. v. Hepps*, 475 U.S. 767 (1986) (applying balancing test to determine whether private plaintiff or media defendant bears burden of proving falsity). Given the unique issue presented here, we believe it is necessary to evaluate the competing state and First Amendment interests. In taking this approach, we are mindful of the Supreme Court's admonition that nothing in *Gertz* "indicated that [the] same balance would be struck regardless of the type of speech involved." *Dun & Bradstreet, Inc. v. Greenmoss Builders, Inc.*, 472 U.S. 749, 756–57 (1985) (plurality opinion) (footnote omitted).

Our approach will proceed in light of the analytical framework of the defamation cases. We have found no comparable case, and the parties cite none. In what we believe is a matter of first impression, we are presented with the unique circumstance of allegedly defamatory statements made in the context of a comparative advertising campaign.

B. *Rules and Conceptual Framework*

Most speech is protected by the First Amendment. *Bose Corp. v. Consumers Union of U.S., Inc.*, 466 U.S. 485, 503 (1984). "Under the First Amendment there is no such thing as a false idea. However pernicious an opinion may seem, we depend for its correction not on the conscience of judges and juries but on the competition of other ideas." *Gertz*, 418 U.S. at 339–40 (footnote omitted). Even false statements of fact are insulated from liability in some situations.[15] *Hepps*, 475 U.S. at 778; *Gertz*, 418 U.S. at 340–41. As Judge Learned Hand put it, the First Amendment " 'presupposes that right conclusions are more likely to be gathered out of a multitude of tongues, than through any kind of authoritative selection.' " *New York Times Co. v. Sullivan*, 376 U.S. 254, 270 (1964) (quoting *United States v. Associated Press*, 52 F. Supp. 362, 372 (S.D.N.Y. 1943), *aff'd*, 326 U.S. 1 (1945)).

Although speech is generally protected, the Supreme Court has "long recognized that not all speech is of equal First Amendment importance. It is speech on 'matters of public concern' that is 'at the heart of the First Amendment's protection.' " *Dun & Bradstreet*, 472 U.S. at 758–59 (footnote and citations omitted). Such speech—unlike expression that is " 'no essential part of any exposition of ideas, and [is] of such slight social value as a step to truth that any benefit that may be derived from [it] is clearly outweighed by the social interest in order and morality,' " *Gertz*, 418 U.S. at 340 (quoting *Chaplinsky v. New Hampshire*, 315 U.S. 568, 572 (1942))—requires heightened constitutional protection in the defamation context.

Our brief review of the cases in this area must begin with *New York Times Co. v. Sullivan*, 376 U.S. 254 (1964). Since 1964, the Court has extended constitutional protection to defamatory criticism of public officials in their official capacity, unless those officials can demonstrate that the defamatory statement was made with "actual malice." *Id.* at

---

[15] In the context of government restriction of speech, false and misleading commercial speech have no First Amendment value. *Central Hudson Gas & Elec. Corp. v. Public Serv. Comm'n*, 447 U.S. 557, 563 (1980) ("[T]here can be no constitutional objection to the suppression of commercial messages that do not accurately inform the public about lawful activity[.]"). Similarly, in the context of defamation, false statements of fact have "no constitutional value." *Gertz*, 418 U.S. at 340. As we shall see, however, such speech sometimes warrants First Amendment protection in this context.

279–80. The issue was whether a paid advertisement soliciting funds to support civil rights demonstrations in the South and the defense of Dr. Martin Luther King against a perjury charge lost all constitutional protection because it contained libelous statements which a jury found to have impugned the reputation of the Commissioner of Public Affairs for Montgomery, Alabama. The Court framed the issue as public in nature, describing the advertisement as "an expression of grievance and protest on one of the major public issues of our time." *Id.* at 271. Against the background of the "profound national commitment to the principle that debate on public issues should be uninhibited, robust, and wide-open," *id.* at 270, the Court reasoned that traditional state libel laws "compelling the critic of official conduct to guarantee the truth of all his factual assertions"[16] would "dampen[ ] the vigor and limit[ ] the variety of public debate" by deterring true as well as false speech, *id.* at 279. Accordingly, after noting that "erroneous statement is inevitable in free debate," the Court decided "it must be protected if the freedoms of expression are to have the 'breathing space' that they 'need . . . to survive.' " *Id.* at 271–72 (citation omitted). The "actual malice" standard was adopted to serve this function.

Over the next two decades, the Court " 'struggle[d] . . . to define the proper accommodation between the law of defamation and the freedoms of speech and press protected by the First Amendment.' " *Hepps,* 475 U.S. at 768 (quoting *Gertz,* 418 U.S. at 325). During this period, the Court "varied its formulations of underlying policy and . . . first expanded, then shrunk the quantum of deference to First Amendment considerations." *Bruno & Stillman, Inc. v. Globe Newspaper Co.,* 633 F.2d 583, 587 (1st Cir. 1980). Nonetheless, at this stage, certain "black letter" rules have emerged. When the plaintiff is a public official or a "public figure" and the speech is of public concern, he must prove by clear and convincing evidence that the defamatory falsehood was made with "actual malice" by a media defendant. *See Gertz,* 418 U.S. at 335–37 & n.7. In such situations, the plaintiff must prove the falsity of the statements to prevail. When the plaintiff is a private figure but the speech involves a matter of "public concern," the states may define for themselves the appropriate standard of liability; however, they may not impose liability without fault, nor allow presumed or punitive damages without a showing of actual malice. In such instances, the plaintiff must prove the falsity of the speech to recover damages from a media defendant. In contrast, when the plaintiff is a private figure and the speech regards matters of "purely private concern," the plaintiff may prove presumed and punitive damages without a showing of "actual malice." *Dun & Bradstreet,* 472 U.S. at 761.

---

[16]   Under Alabama law, a defendant in a libel action could escape liability by proving the truth of the statements.

In arriving at these rules, the Court articulated the conceptual framework underlying its decisions. *New York Times*, the Court explained, represents an accommodation between the state interest in protecting the reputations of individuals and the First Amendment interest in safeguarding freedom of speech. *See Dun & Bradstreet*, 472 U.S. at 756–57; *Gertz*, 418 U.S. at 349.

In evaluating these competing interests, the Court has determined that the state has only a "limited" interest in compensating public persons for injury to reputation by defamatory statements, but has a "strong and legitimate" interest in compensating private persons for the same injury. *See Gertz*, 418 U.S. at 343 & 348–49. The Court has provided a two-fold explanation for the discrepancy in the extent of the state interests. First, because public officials and public figures enjoy "greater access to the channels of effective communication and hence have a more realistic opportunity to counteract false statements than private individuals," the states have a greater interest in protecting private persons whose relative lack of "self-help" remedies render them "more vulnerable to injury." *Id.* at 344. Second, the state has a stronger interest in protecting the reputations of private individuals because, unlike public persons, they have not voluntarily placed themselves in the public eye. *Id.* at 344–45.

On the other side of the coin, the "type of speech involved" also affects the way in which the "balance is struck," by varying the weight of the First Amendment interest. *Dun & Bradstreet*, 472 U.S. at 756–57. "[S]peech on 'matters of public concern' . . . is 'at the heart of the First Amendment's protection.'" *Dun & Bradstreet*, 472 U.S. at 758–59 (citations omitted). The Court has determined that "speech of private concern," such as a credit report for business, is of less First Amendment importance in the same way that utterances labeled "commercial speech" are "less central to the interests of the First Amendment," *id.* at 758 n.5.

C.   *Application of the Rules and Conceptual Framework*

At the outset, we note that it is of no consequence that the defendants (and counterclaim defendants) here are not members of the broadcast and print media. Although the Supreme Court has not finally settled whether "non-media" defendants should receive protections identical to those afforded "media" defendants, this court has so far declined to limit the protections of the *New York Times* standard to media defendants only.

In addition, we do not limit our consideration of the applicability of the *New York Times* standard to the parties' claims for defamation alone. The Supreme Court has already applied a similar analysis to other torts, such as intentional infliction of emotional distress, *Hustler Magazine, Inc.*

v. Falwell, 485 U.S. 46, 56 (1988), and "false light," *Time, Inc. v. Hill*, 385 U.S. 374, 390–91 (1967).

We next turn to assessing the relative weight of the First Amendment interests in this case. We recognize that traditional defamation analysis usually begins with an examination of the status of the plaintiff. Because of the facts presented, however, we shall first consider the content of the speech involved. . . . Our appraisal of these interests depends on whether the speech at issue can properly be characterized as commercial speech. "There is no longer any room to doubt that what has come to be known as 'commercial speech' is entitled to the protection of the First Amendment, albeit to protection somewhat less extensive than that afforded 'noncommercial speech.' " *Zauderer v. Office of Disciplinary Counsel*, 471 U.S. 626, 637 (1985). If the speech here is commercial speech, then it likely does not mandate heightened constitutional protection.

. . . .

In *Dun & Bradstreet*, the Court held that speech on matters of private concern, such as a credit report for business, receives less First Amendment protection than speech on matters of public concern. 472 U.S. at 757–59. More significantly for our purposes, the Court justified its decision to allow less protection for speech of private concern by drawing an analogy to the reduced First Amendment protection afforded commercial speech:

> This Court on many occasions has recognized that certain kinds of speech are less central to the interests of the First Amendment than others. . . . In the area of protected speech, the most prominent example of reduced protection for certain kinds of speech concerns commercial speech. Such speech, we have noted, occupies a "subordinate position in the scale of First Amendment values." *Ohralik v. Ohio State Bar Assn.*, 436 U.S. 447, 456 (1978). It also is more easily verifiable and less likely to be deterred by proper regulation. Accordingly, it may be regulated in ways that might be impermissible in the realm of noncommercial expression.

Similarly, the *New York Times* decision indicated that the importance of the First Amendment interests in defamation actions would be reduced in the commercial speech context. In that case, the Court considered the contention that "the constitutional guarantees of freedom of speech . . . are inapplicable here . . . because the allegedly libelous statements were published as part of a paid, 'commercial' advertisement." *New York Times*, 376 U.S. at 265. While the Court ultimately determined that the speech was properly characterized as an "editorial" rather than a "commercial" advertisement and therefore deserving of heightened constitutional protection, its analysis indicates that commercial speech, in a libel suit, would receive some, albeit less than heightened, constitutional protection.

Before proceeding further, we must consider what qualifies as "commercial speech." Since deciding *New York Times*, the Supreme Court has provided substantial guidance. Commercial speech may be broadly defined as expression related to the economic interests of the speaker and its audience, generally in the form of a commercial advertisement for the sale of goods and services. *See Bolger v. Youngs Drug Prods. Corp.*, 463 U.S. 60, 66–67 (1983). The Supreme Court has cited three factors to consider in deciding whether speech is commercial: (1) is the speech an advertisement; (2) does the speech refer to a specific product or service; and (3) does the speaker have an economic motivation for the speech. An affirmative answer to all three questions provides "strong support" for the conclusion that the speech is commercial. *Id.* at 67. Stated succinctly, the "commercial speech doctrine rests heavily on 'the common sense distinction between speech proposing a commercial transaction . . . and other varieties of speech.' " *Zauderer v. Office of Disciplinary Counsel*, 471 U.S. 626, 637 (1985) (quoting *Ohralik v. Ohio State Bar Ass'n*, 436 U.S. 447, 455–56 (1978)).

The Court has elaborated on the reasons why commercial speech receives less than heightened protection. First, commercial speech generally makes a different contribution to the exposition of ideas. *Compare Dun & Bradstreet*, 472 U.S. at 762 (holding private speech of reduced constitutional dimension partly because it was "solely in the individual interest of the speaker and its specific business audience) *with Central Hudson*, 447 U.S. at 561 (defining commercial speech as "expression related solely to the economic interests of the speaker and its audience"). In short, "[t]he First Amendment's concern for commercial speech is based on the informational function of advertising. . . ." *Central Hudson*, 447 U.S. at 563.

Second, commercial speech tends to be more durable than other types of speech. As the commercial speaker has an economic self-interest in dissemination, there is little likelihood of the speech being chilled by proper regulation. This attribute, the Court concluded, "may make it less necessary to tolerate inaccurate statements for fear of silencing the speaker." *Virginia Pharmacy Bd.*, 425 U.S. at 772 n.24; *see Dun & Bradstreet*, 472 U.S. at 758 n.5 (discussing durability "to show how many of the same concerns that argue in favor of reduced constitutional protection" in regulation of commercial speech actions apply to defamation actions involving private speech).

Third, commercial speakers have extensive knowledge of both their market and their own products. Consequently, they are uniquely situated to evaluate the truthfulness of their speech. *Central Hudson*, 447 U.S. at 564 n.6; *Bates*, 433 U.S. at 381; *see Virginia Pharmacy Bd.*, 425 U.S. at 772 n.24.

The fourth reason is extrinsic. "To require a parity of constitutional protection for commercial and noncommercial speech alike could invite dilution, simply by a leveling process, of the force of the [First] Amendment's guarantee with respect to the latter kind of speech." *Ohralik*, 436 U.S. at 456.

In this case, affirmative answers to all three prongs of the *Bolger* test provide "strong support" for our conclusion that the statements here are commercial in nature. First, there is no question that they are advertisements; they were disseminated as part of an expensive, professionally run promotional campaign.[25] Second, the speech specifically refers to a product; it touts the relative merits of Personal Choice (or U.S. Healthcare's HMO) over competing products. Third, the desire for revenue motivated the speech; the record contains abundant evidence that Blue Cross/Blue Shield launched the promotional campaign in order to recoup its share of the health insurance market. The trial testimony of Blue Cross/Blue Shield's president plainly states that the aggressive Personal Choice promotional campaign was developed for the express purpose of competing with HMOs. Moreover, Blue Cross/Blue Shield concedes that it developed a series of advertisements to introduce and increase the attractiveness of its products. Similarly, protection of its new market share motivated U.S. Healthcare's speech. In short, "common sense" informs us that the statements here propose a commercial transaction, and thus differ from other types of speech.

Even more importantly, we find it significant that the advertisements have all of the characteristics that the Supreme Court has identified in the commercial speech cases as making speech durable, not susceptible to "chill." Consequently, they do not require the heightened protection we extend to our most valuable forms of speech. Because the thrust of all of the advertisements is to convince the consuming public to bring its business to one of these health care giants rather than the other, there is no doubt that the advertisements were motivated by economic self-interest. Furthermore, given the size of the health care market in the Delaware Valley—Blue Shield virtually shouts about the hundreds of millions of dollars at stake—we believe it would have to be a cold day before these corporations would be chilled from speaking about the comparative merits of their products.

---

[25] That these are advertisements, while a fact that supports the conclusion they should receive less First Amendment protection under *Bolger*, is not by itself dispositive. Rather, the significance of speech as advertisement is that "advertising is the *sine qua non* of commercial profits." *Virginia Pharmacy Bd.*, 425 U.S. at 772 n.24.

In addition, these are advertisements for products and services in markets in which U.S. Healthcare and Blue Cross/Blue Shield deal—and, presumably, know more about than anyone else. The facts upon which the advertisements are based—comparative price, procedures, and services offered—are readily objectifiable. These advertisements were precisely calculated, developed over time and published only when the corporate speakers were ready. Consequently, the advertisements were unusually verifiable.

Finally, while the speech here does discuss costs and consequences of competing health insurance and health care delivery programs, some of the advertisements capable of defamatory meaning here add little information and even fewer ideas to the marketplace of health care thought.[26] The expression in these advertisements "differs markedly from ideological expression because it is confined to the promotion of specific . . . services." *Virginia Pharmacy Bd.*, 425 U.S. at 780. And to the extent that the advertisements are false statements of fact, of course, the speech has no constitutional value at all. *Central Hudson*, 447 U.S. at 563.

It is important to note that we do not have a situation in which a corporation addresses an issue of public concern involving a competitor, but does so with speech that is neither commercial nor chill resistant. We simply recognize here, as the Court has in a similar context, that "[a] company has the full panoply of protections available to its direct comments on public issues, so there is no reason for providing similar protection when such statements are made in the context of commercial transactions." *Bolger*, 463 U.S. at 68 (footnote omitted).

Despite these conclusive indications that the speech here is commercial in nature, Blue Cross/Blue Shield argues that the speech should be accorded heightened constitutional protection. Relying on *Bigelow v. Virginia*, 421 U.S. 809 (1975), it argues that speech which does more than "simply propose a commercial transaction" constitutes something more than commercial speech. Furthermore, it maintains that the "*Bigelow* standard" is applicable when the products are not merely linked to a public debate but are themselves "at the center of the public debate."[27] Blue Cross/Blue Shield concludes that its own advertisements

---

[26] We believe one such advertisement implicates important health care concerns. This advertisement suggests that HMO primary care physicians have a financial incentive to deny referrals to specialists. On the other hand, we believe the other advertisements capable of defamatory meaning make no such contribution. One portrays a woman grieving that the hospital to which HMO sent her was inadequate. The second, a "death" scene, shows a pair of hands pulling a hospital sheet over a personal choice brochure as a dirge plays. "There is simply no credible argument that this type of [advertisement] requires special protection to ensure that 'debate on public issues [will] be uninhibited, robust, and wide-open.'" *Dun & Bradstreet*, 472 U.S. at 762 (quoting *New York Times*, 376 U.S. at 270).

[27] In *Bigelow*, a newspaper editor published an abortion clinic's advertisement, which the state court determined violated a state criminal statute prohibiting dissemination of publications encouraging the processing of an abortion. The Supreme Court struck down the statute on First Amendment grounds, 421 U.S. at 818–22, stating that the advertisement could not be regulated

"educate[d] the public about the substantial differences among the[ ] available means for financing and delivering health care, thereby ensuring informed purchasing decisions" and rendering the advertisements non-commercial.

Notwithstanding Blue Cross/Blue Shields's call for application of the "*Bigelow* standard," we believe the *Central Hudson* decision, in which the Supreme Court expressly rejected such attempts to "blur further the line the Court has sought to draw in commercial speech cases," 447 U.S. at 563 n.5, represents the proper approach. *Central Hudson* prevents an advertiser from immunizing, in effect, otherwise defamatory speech— behind the actual malice standard afforded to core speech by the First Amendment—simply by reference to an issue of public concern.

In *Central Hudson*, the Court held that a regulation by a state public utility commission which prohibited an electric utility from advertising to promote the use of electricity constituted an improper regulation of commercial speech in violation of the First Amendment. In a concurring opinion, Justice Stevens maintained that the regulation at issue encompassed more than mere "commercial speech" because it would stifle, for example, advertising that promoted consumption of electricity by touting its environmental benefits, and thus would "curtail[ ] expression by an informed and interested group of persons of their point of view on questions relating to the production and consumption of electrical energy—questions frequently discussed and debated by our political leaders." 447 U.S. at 581 (Stevens, J., concurring). The *Central Hudson* majority was unconvinced:

> Apparently the [concurring] opinion would accord full First Amendment protection to all promotional advertising that includes claims "relating to . . . questions frequently discussed and debated by our political leaders." . . .

> Although this approach responds to the serious issues surrounding our national energy policy as raised in this case, we think it would blur further the line the Court has sought to draw in commercial speech cases. It would grant broad constitutional protection to any advertising that links a product to a current public debate. But many, if not most, products may be tied to public concerns with the environment, energy, economic policy, or *individual health and safety*. We rule today in *Consolidated Edison Co. v. Public Service Comm'n*, 447 U.S. 530 (1980), that utilities enjoy the full panoply of First Amendment protections for their direct comments on public issues.

---

as commercial speech because, "[v]iewed in its entirety, [it] conveyed information of potential interest and value to a diverse audience—not only to readers possibly in need of the services offered . . . ," *id.* at 822.

> *There is no reason for providing similar constitutional protection when such statements are made only in the context of commercial transactions.*

Central Hudson, 447 U.S. at 562 n.5 (emphasis added).

Similarly, in *Bolger*, the Court held "advertising which 'links a product to a current public debate' is not thereby entitled to the constitutional protection afforded noncommercial speech." *Bolger*, 463 U.S. at 68. Reasoned the Court: "Advertisers should not be permitted to immunize false or misleading product information from government regulation simply by including references to public issues." *Id.*

Finally, in *Zauderer*, the Supreme Court reiterated its holding that commercial advertisements do not qualify for heightened First Amendment protection simply because they include statements about issues of public debate and concern. Zauderer was a lawyer sanctioned by the disciplinary committee of the state supreme court for running deceptive newspaper advertisements for his services. Because some of the advertisements, which publicized the lawyer's willingness to represent women who had suffered injuries resulting from their use of the Dalkon Shield contraceptive device, contained statements regarding the legal rights of persons injured by the Dalkon Shield, the Supreme Court recognized that such statements "*in another context*, would be fully protected speech." 471 U.S. at 637 n.7 (emphasis added). "That this is so," the Court concluded, "does not alter the status of the advertisements as commercial speech." *Id.* The Court then restated its position that "advertising which 'links a product to a current public debate' is not thereby entitled to the constitutional protection afforded noncommercial speech." *Id.* (quoting *Central Hudson*, 447 U.S. at 563 n.5).

We find no principled distinction between the products in *Central Hudson* and those at issue here. Like the energy products advertised in *Central Hudson*, the products advertised here—health care insurance and delivery—are at the center of public debate. Consequently, while we agree that the quality, availability, and cost of health care are among the most important and debated issues of our time, these particular advertisements for specific health care products do not escape the commercial speech category. We conclude, as did the *Zauderer* Court, that whatever the precise boundaries of the "category of expression that may be termed commercial speech, . . . it is clear enough that the speech at issue in this case—advertising pure and simple—falls within those bounds." 471 U.S. at 637.

Therefore, while the speech here is protected by the First Amendment, we hold that the First Amendment requires no higher standard of liability than that mandated by the substantive law for each claim. The heightened protection of the actual malice standard is not "necessary to give adequate 'breathing space' to the freedoms protected by the First Amendment." *Hustler Magazine, Inc. v. Falwell*, 485 U.S. 46, 56 (1988).

Having concluded that the speech here is commercial speech that does not warrant heightened constitutional protection, we nonetheless proceed to consideration of the nature and weight of the state's interest in compensating individuals for injuries resulting from each of the distinct torts alleged. We have previously discussed the state and federal interests implicated. As we shall see in this case, however, traditional defamation analysis is not well suited to strike the proper balance between the state and federal interests and First Amendment values in the context of commercial speech.

In weighing the state interest, we must look to the status of the claimants. As we have noted, the Court has determined that the state has only a "limited" interest in compensating public persons for injury to reputation but has a "strong and legitimate" interest in compensating private persons for the same injury. *See Gertz*, 418 U.S. at 343[,] 348–49. Contending that the actual malice standard applies because a public figure is implicated, Blue Cross/Blue Shield argues that the following factors render U.S. Healthcare a "public figure": it has voluntarily exposed itself to public comment on the issues involved in this dispute; it is a contributor to the ongoing debate concerning health care insurance; it is among the nation's largest providers of HMO-type insurance coverage; it markets its products extensively and aggressively, and has a substantial annual advertising budget; and it frequently and consistently asserts the advantages of its method of health care financing and delivery, and has done so in advertisements, press releases, professional journals, newspapers, magazines and speeches before public assemblies. These activities, Blue Cross/Blue Shield submits, "constitute a voluntary effort to influence the consuming public." Similar statements can be made regarding Blue Cross/Blue Shield.

Gertz identified three classes of public figures: those who achieve such stature or notoriety that they are considered public figures in all contexts; those who become public figures involuntarily, but these are "exceedingly rare"; and those who are deemed public figures only within the context of a particular public dispute. *Id.* at 345. The Court defined the last group, limited purpose public figures, as individuals who voluntarily "thrust themselves to the forefront of particular public controversies in order to influence the resolution of the issues involved." *Id.*

At the outset, we note that "the classification of a [claimant] as a public or private figure is a question of law to be determined initially by the trial court and then carefully scrutinized by an appellate court."

Marcone v. Penthouse Int'l Magazine for Men, 754 F.2d 1072 (3d Cir. 1985) (citations omitted), *cert. denied,* 474 U.S. 864 (1985). Because neither claimant explicitly classified the other as a full purpose or involuntary public figure, the issue is whether either constitutes a limited purpose public figure.

Generally, two factors inform this determination. The first factor indicative of a claimant's status is his relative access to the media. Clearly, both parties have access to the media. Moreover, the magnitude of the advertising campaigns shows their ability to utilize it on a vast scale. While access to the media does not always make one a public figure for purposes of First Amendment analysis, the tremendous ability of these parties to advertise, indicating their lack of vulnerability, would support a finding that both are public figures.

The second factor is the manner in which the risk of defamation came upon them. Both companies, attempting to influence consumers' decisions, have thrust themselves into the controversy of who provides better value in health care delivery and insurance. Blue Cross/Blue Shield began the comparative advertising war with its pointed attacks on HMO. U.S. Healthcare, even before responding with its own comparative advertising, had used advertising to help establish itself as a leading provider of health care in the Delaware Valley. Consequently, by inviting comment and assuming the risk of unfair comment, both claimants resemble public figures.

Under traditional defamation analysis, the parties' considerable access to the media and their voluntary entry into a controversy are strong indicia that they are limited purpose public figures. Indeed, inflexible application of these factors would warrant a finding of public figure status and facilitate a finding of heightened constitutional protection. Nonetheless, we hold that these corporations are not public figures for the limited purpose of commenting on health care in this case.

As noted, *Gertz* defines the limited purpose public figure as one who has "thrust [himself] to the forefront of particular public controversies in order to influence the resolution of the issues involved." 418 U.S. at 345. Although some of the advertisements touch on matters of public concern, their central thrust is commercial. Thus, the parties have acted primarily to generate revenue by influencing customers, not to resolve "the issues involved."

While discerning motivations of the speaker is often difficult, we have a more fundamental reason for declining to find limited purpose public figure status in this case. The express analysis in *Gertz* is not helpful in the context of a comparative advertising war. Most products can be linked to a public issue. *See Central Hudson,* 447 U.S. at 563 n.5. And most advertisers—including both claimants here—seek out the media. Thus, it will always be true that such advertisers have voluntarily placed themselves in the public eye. It will be equally true that such advertisers have access to the media. Therefore, under the *Gertz* rationale, speech of public concern that implicates corporate advertisers—i.e., typical comparative advertising—will always be insulated behind the actual malice standard. We believe a corporation must do more than the claimants have done here to become a limited purpose public figure under *Gertz*.

In summary, we conclude that the speech at issue does not receive heightened protection under the First Amendment. Because this speech is chill-resistant, the *New York Times* standard is not, as we have noted, "necessary to give adequate 'breathing space' to the freedoms protected by the First Amendment." *Hustler Magazine, Inc. v. Falwell*, 485 U.S. 46, 56 (1988). Therefore, the standard of proof needed to establish the substantive claims is that applicable under federal and state law.

For these reasons, we hold that the district court erred in applying the *New York Times* standard to the claims in this case and in directing entry of judgment under Fed. R. Civ. P. 50(b). Accordingly, we will reverse the judgment of the district court and remand for proceedings consistent with this opinion.

. . . .

NOTES & QUESTIONS

(1) What is the standard for determining whether speech is "commercial speech"? What policy issues are relevant to this analysis and how did they apply to the statements in *U.S. Healthcare*?

(2) The court expressed an unwillingness to add a heightened level of protection to commercial speech that also implicated a public issue. Do you agree with the court's conclusion that the fact that the advertisements at issue involved health care was not enough to require heightened protection?

(3) Despite finding that the speech at issue was commercial, the court nonetheless continued to reflect upon whether the parties were public figures. What role did the commercial nature of the speech have on this analysis?

(4) As part of its opinion, the *U.S. Healthcare* court observed:

> At the outset, we note that it is of no consequence that the defendants (and counterclaim defendants) here are not members of the broadcast and print media. Although the Supreme Court has not finally settled whether "non-media" defendants should receive protections identical to those afforded "media" defendants, this court has so far declined to limit the protections of the *New York Times* standard to media defendants only.

Do you agree that the status of the defendants is "of no consequence"? For instance, what if, instead of suing over statements made as part of a competitive advertising campaign, Blue Cross/Blue Shield was suing a consulting firm hired by the state to make a recommendation about which plan to adopt for state employees? What if the recommendation revealed severe deficiencies in the hospital coverage of the "Personal Choice" plan? *See Kansas Bankers Sur. Co. v. Bahr Consultants, Inc.*, 69 F. Supp. 2d 1004, 1011–12 (E.D. Tenn. 1999) (holding that a consulting firm that did independent comparative analyses of insurance policies for the benefit of insurance buyers was not liable under the Lanham Act, as the statements did not qualify under the "commercial advertising or promotion" language).

(5)   The parties also brought a state common law action for commercial disparagement. What impact should First Amendment jurisprudence have on a common law disparagement claim?

(6)   In 2010, the United States Supreme Court sustained a challenge to a federal law prohibiting political speech during elections based on the speaker's corporate identity. *Citizens United v. Fed. Election Comm'n*, 558 U.S. 310 (2010). The Court held that First Amendment protection extended to corporations for political speech. In its analysis, the Court used the rationale that the press is made up of media companies which fall into the definition of corporations, and thus prohibitions on the political speech of corporations would result in a possible chilling effect on desirable political speech. The Court did not elaborate or discuss the lesser protections afforded by the First Amendment to commercial speech. Nevertheless, some commentators have argued that the natural trajectory of the decision is for the Court to do away with the "commercial speech doctrine" in the near future. *See* Tamara R. Piety, Commentary, *Citizens United and the Threat to the Regulatory State*, 109 MICH. L. REV. FIRST IMPRESSIONS 16, 16–17 (2010) (suggesting that the *Citizens United* decision is a sign that the Supreme Court may do away with the commercial speech doctrine in the near future, which would leave commercial and non-commercial speech with equivalent First Amendment protection); Darrel C. Menthe, *The Marketplace Metaphor and Commercial Speech Doctrine: Or How I Learned to Stop Worrying About and Love Citizens United*, 38 HASTINGS CONST. L.Q. 131, 135 (2010) (theorizing that the protection of the "marketplace of ideas" in *Citizens United* must necessarily lead to the end of the commercial speech doctrine).

Do you agree that *Citizens United* is a step towards rejection of the "commercial speech doctrine"? Alternatively, do you think the Court has created a narrow exception for equal First Amendment protection of commercial and non-commercial speech which is only applicable to political speech?

CHAPTER 9

MISAPPROPRIATION

■ ■ ■

A. THE COMMON LAW TORT OF MISAPPROPRIATION

The common law tort of misappropriation is not well-defined, nor even widely accepted. The Restatement of Unfair Competition § 38 limits its use to misappropriation of trade values, with specific reference to trade secrets, misappropriation of another's identity, and violations of copyright. The tort's origins, however, are much broader. The best way, perhaps, to summarize the tort is with reference to a quote from the *INS v. Associated Press* case below, in which Justice Pitney condemned attempts by competitors to "reap where [they had] not sown." But taken to its logical extension, this would prohibit all manner of activities without regard to what has been misappropriated. For instance, shouldn't a bar located near a sports arena be permitted to benefit from the increased patronage that comes with game days (and a successful team), although the bar has, in a sense, misappropriated the team's goodwill? Moreover, the tort runs afoul of many federally preempted areas of law, such as copyright and patent law. Due to these concerns, the courts that have been willing to recognize misappropriation as a general cause of action have done so cautiously.

B. THE ORIGINS OF THE TORT OF MISAPPROPRIATION

The seminal case on the tort of misappropriation is *INS v. Associated Press.* Copyright law at the time of the decision was not as developed as it is today, but the basic premise that underlies the perceived need for misappropriation is that information alone is not copyrightable (it is the original expression, selection, or arrangement of facts or ideas that is the subject of copyright protection). Although it is not clear from the facts below, the information being collected by the Associated Press involved World War I updates from Europe that the Associated Press apparently could access, but the INS could not due to foreign government prohibitions. Thus, if the INS was to report the news, it had to copy it from the Associated Press. The INS did just that, and then published the copied news in its West Coast papers. Due to the time difference between the East Coast and the West Coast, this erased any advantage the Associated Press gained by being the first to have the news.

INTERNATIONAL NEWS SERVICE V. ASSOCIATED PRESS
248 U.S. 215 (1918)

MR. JUSTICE PITNEY delivered the opinion of the Court.

The parties are competitors in the gathering and distribution of news and its publication for profit in newspapers throughout the United States. The Associated Press, which was complainant in the District Court, is a co-operative organization, incorporated under the Membership Corporations Law of the state of New York, its members being individuals who are either proprietors or representatives of about 950 daily newspapers published in all parts of the United States. That a corporation may be organized under that act for the purpose of gathering news for the use and benefit of its members and for publication in newspapers owned or represented by them, is recognized by an amendment enacted in 1901 (Laws N.Y. 1901, c. 436). Complainant gathers in all parts of the world, by means of various instrumentalities of its own, by exchange with its members, and by other appropriate means, news and intelligence of current and recent events of interest to newspaper readers and distributes it daily to its members for publication in their newspapers. The cost of the service, amounting approximately to $3,500,000 per annum, is assessed upon the members and becomes a part of their costs of operation, to be recouped, presumably with profit, through the publication of their several newspapers. Under complainant's by-laws each member agrees upon assuming membership that news received through complainant's service is received exclusively for publication in a particular newspaper, language, and place specified in the certificate of membership, that no other use of it shall be permitted, and that no member shall furnish or permit any one in his employ or connected with his newspaper to furnish any of complainant's news in advance of publication to any person not a member. And each member is required to gather the local news of his district and supply it to the Associated Press and to no one else.

Defendant is a corporation organized under the laws of the state of New Jersey, whose business is the gathering and selling of news to its customers and clients, consisting of newspapers published throughout the United States, under contracts by which they pay certain amounts at stated times for defendant's service. It has widespread news-gathering agencies; the cost of its operations amounts, it is said, to more than $2,000,000 per annum; and it serves about 400 newspapers located in the various cities of the United States and abroad, a few of which are represented, also, in the membership of the Associated Press.

The parties are in the keenest competition between themselves in the distribution of news throughout the United States; and so, as a rule, are the newspapers that they serve, in their several districts.

Complainant in its bill, defendant in its answer, have set forth in almost identical terms the rather obvious circumstances and conditions under which their business is conducted. The value of the service, and of the news furnished, depends upon the promptness of transmission, as well as upon the accuracy and impartiality of the news; it being essential that the news be transmitted to members or subscribers as early or earlier than similar information can be furnished to competing newspapers by other news services, and that the news furnished by each agency shall not be furnished to newspapers which do not contribute to the expense of gathering it. And further, to quote from the answer:

> 'Prompt knowledge and publication of worldwide news is essential to the conduct of a modern newspaper, and by reason of the enormous expense incident to the gathering and distribution of such news, the only practical way in which a proprietor of a newspaper can obtain the same is, either through co-operation with a considerable number of other newspaper proprietors in the work of collecting and distributing such news, and the equitable division with them of the expenses thereof, or by the purchase of such news from some existing agency engaged in that business.'

The bill was filed to restrain the pirating of complainant's news by defendant in three ways: First, by bribing employees of newspapers published by complainant's members to furnish Associated Press news to defendant before publication, for transmission by telegraph and telephone to defendant's clients for publication by them; second, by inducing Associated Press members to violate its by-laws and permit defendant to obtain news before publication; and, third, by copying news from bulletin boards and from early editions of complainant's newspapers and selling this, either bodily or after rewriting it, to defendant's customers.

The District Court, upon consideration of the bill and answer, with voluminous affidavits on both sides, granted a preliminary injunction under the first and second heads, but refused at that stage to restrain the systematic practice admittedly pursued by defendant, of taking news bodily from the bulletin boards and early editions of complainant's newspapers and selling it as its own. The court expressed itself as satisfied that this practice amounted to unfair trade, but as the legal question was one of first impression it considered that the allowance of an injunction should await the outcome of an appeal. Both parties having appealed, the Circuit Court of Appeals sustained the injunction order so far as it went, and upon complainant's appeal modified it and remanded the cause, with directions to issue an injunction also against any bodily taking of the words or substance of complainant's news until its commercial value as news had passed away. The present writ of certiorari was then allowed.

The only matter that has been argued before us is whether defendant may lawfully be restrained from appropriating news taken from bulletins issued by complainant or any of its members, or from newspapers published by them, for the purpose of selling it to defendant's clients. Complainant asserts that defendant's admitted course of conduct in this regard both violates complainant's property right in the news and constitutes unfair competition in business. And notwithstanding the case has proceeded only to the stage of a preliminary injunction, we have deemed it proper to consider the underlying questions, since they go to the very merits of the action and are presented upon facts that are not in dispute. As presented in argument, these questions are: (1) Whether there is any property in news; (2) Whether, if there be property in news collected for the purpose of being published, it survives the instant of its publication in the first newspaper to which it is communicated by the news-gatherer; and (3) whether defendant's admitted course of conduct in appropriating for commercial use matter taken from bulletins or early editions of Associated Press publications constitutes unfair competition in trade.

The federal jurisdiction was invoked because of diversity of citizenship, not upon the ground that the suit arose under the copyright or other laws of the United States. Complainant's news matter is not copyrighted. It is said that it could not, in practice, be copyrighted, because of the large number of dispatches that are sent daily; and, according to complainant's contention, news is not within the operation of the copyright act. Defendant, while apparently conceding this, nevertheless invokes the analogies of the law of literary property and copyright, insisting as its principal contention that, assuming complainant has a right of property in its news, it can be maintained (unless the copyright act be complied with) only by being kept secret and confidential, and that upon the publication with complainant's consent of uncopyrighted news of any of complainant's members in a newspaper or upon a bulletin board, the right of property is lost, and the subsequent use of the news by the public or by defendant for any purpose whatever becomes lawful.

. . . .

In considering the general question of property in news matter, it is necessary to recognize its dual character, distinguishing between the substance of the information and the particular form or collocation of words in which the writer has communicated it.

[The Court notes that although the literary quality of the news may be afforded protection under the copyright laws, the information contained in such articles is not subject to such protection. The framers of the Constitution did not intend to confer an exclusive right upon one who might happen to be the first to report a historic event.]

We need spend no time, however, upon the general question of property in news matter at common law, or the application of the copyright act, since it seems to us the case must turn upon the question of unfair competition in business. And, in our opinion, this does not depend upon any general right of property analogous to the common-law right of the proprietor of an unpublished work to prevent its publication without his consent; nor is it foreclosed by showing that the benefits of the copyright act have been waived. We are dealing here not with restrictions upon publication but with the very facilities and processes of publication. The peculiar value of news is in the spreading of it while it is fresh; and it is evident that a valuable property interest in the news, as news, cannot be maintained by keeping it secret. Besides, except for matters improperly disclosed, or published in breach of trust or confidence, or in violation of law, none of which is involved in this branch of the case, the news of current events may be regarded as common property. What we are concerned with is the business of making it known to the world, in which both parties to the present suit are engaged. That business consists in maintaining a prompt, sure, steady, and reliable service designed to place the daily events of the world at the breakfast table of the millions at a price that, while of trifling moment to each reader, is sufficient in the aggregate to afford compensation for the cost of gathering and distributing it, with the added profit so necessary as an incentive to effective action in the commercial world. The service thus performed for newspaper readers is not only innocent but extremely useful in itself, and indubitably constitutes a legitimate business. The parties are competitors in this field; and, on fundamental principles, applicable here as elsewhere, when the rights or privileges of the one are liable to conflict with those of the other, each party is under a duty so to conduct its own business as not unnecessarily or unfairly to injure that of the other.

Obviously, the question of what is unfair competition in business must be determined with particular reference to the character and circumstances of the business. The question here is not so much the rights of either party as against the public but their rights as between themselves. And, although we may and do assume that neither party has any remaining property interest as against the public in uncopyrighted news matter after the moment of its first publication, it by no means follows that there is no remaining property interest in it as between themselves. For, to both of them alike, news matter, however little susceptible of ownership or dominion in the absolute sense, is stock in trade, to be gathered at the cost of enterprise, organization, skill, labor, and money, and to be distributed and sold to those who will pay money for it, as for any other merchandise. Regarding the news, therefore, as but the material out of which both parties are seeking to make profits at the same time and in the same field, we hardly can fail to recognize that for this purpose, and as between them, it must be regarded as quasi property, irrespective of the rights of either as against the public.

In order to sustain the jurisdiction of equity over the controversy, we need not affirm any general and absolute property in the news as such. The rule that a court of equity concerns itself only in the protection of property rights treats any civil right of a pecuniary nature as a property right and the right to acquire property by honest labor or the conduct of a lawful business is as much entitled to protection as the right to guard property already acquired. It is this right that furnishes the basis of the jurisdiction in the ordinary case of unfair competition.

The question, whether one who has gathered general information or news at pains and expense for the purpose of subsequent publication through the press has such an interest in its publication as may be protected from interference, has been raised many times, although never, perhaps, in the precise form in which it is now presented.

. . . .

Not only do the acquisition and transmission of news require elaborate organization and a large expenditure of money, skill, and effort; not only has it an exchange value to the gatherer, dependent chiefly upon its novelty and freshness, the regularity of the service, its reputed reliability and thoroughness, and its adaptability to the public needs; but also, as is evident, the news has an exchange value to one who can misappropriate it.

The peculiar features of the case arise from the fact that, while novelty and freshness form so important an element in the success of the business, the very processes of distribution and publication necessarily occupy a good deal of time. Complainant's service, as well as defendant's, is a daily service to daily newspapers; most of the foreign news reaches this country at the Atlantic seaboard, principally at the city of New York, and because of this, and of time differentials due to the earth's rotation, the distribution of news matter throughout the country is principally from east to west; and, since in speed the telegraph and telephone easily outstrip the rotation of the earth, it is a simple matter for defendant to take complainant's news from bulletins or early editions of complainant's members in the eastern cities and at the mere cost of telegraphic transmission cause it to be published in western papers issued at least as early as those served by complainant. Besides this, and irrespective of time differentials, irregularities in telegraphic transmission on different lines, and the normal consumption of time in printing and distributing the newspaper, result in permitting pirated news to be placed in the hands of defendant's readers sometimes simultaneously with the service of competing Associated Press papers, occasionally even earlier.

Defendant insists that when, with the sanction and approval of complainant, and as the result of the use of its news for the very purpose for which it is distributed, a portion of complainant's members communicate it to the general public by posting it upon bulletin boards so that all may read, or by issuing it to newspapers and distributing it indiscriminately, complainant no longer has the right to control the use to be made of it; that when it thus reaches the light of day it becomes the common possession of all to whom it is accessible; and that any purchaser of a newspaper has the right to communicate the intelligence which it contains to anybody and for any purpose, even for the purpose of selling it for profit to newspapers published for profit in competition with complainant's members.

The fault in the reasoning lies in applying as a test the right of the complainant as against the public, instead of considering the rights of complainant and defendant, competitors in business, as between themselves. The right of the purchaser of a single newspaper to spread knowledge of its contents gratuitously, for any legitimate purpose not unreasonably interfering with complainant's right to make merchandise of it, may be admitted; but to transmit that news for commercial use, in competition with complainant—which is what defendant has done and seeks to justify—is a very different matter. In doing this defendant, by its very act, admits that it is taking material that has been acquired by complainant as the result of organization and the expenditure of labor, skill, and money, and which is salable by complainant for money, and that defendant in appropriating it and selling it as its own is endeavoring to reap where it has not sown, and by disposing of it to newspapers that are competitors of complainant's members is appropriating to itself the harvest of those who have sown. Stripped of all disguises, the process amounts to an unauthorized interference with the normal operation of complainant's legitimate business precisely at the point where the profit is to be reaped, in order to divert a material portion of the profit from those who have earned it to those who have not; with special advantage to defendant in the competition because of the fact that it is not burdened with any part of the expense of gathering the news. The transaction speaks for itself and a court of equity ought not to hesitate long in characterizing it as unfair competition in business.

The underlying principle is much the same as that which lies at the base of the equitable theory of consideration in the law of trusts—that he who has fairly paid the price should have the beneficial use of the property. Pom. Eq. Jur. § 981. It is no answer to say that complainant spends its money for that which is too fugitive or evanescent to be the subject of property. That might, and for the purposes of the discussion we are assuming that it would furnish an answer in a common-law controversy. But in a court of equity, where the question is one of unfair competition, if that which complainant has acquired fairly at substantial cost may be sold fairly at substantial profit, a competitor who is misappropriating it for the purpose of disposing of it to his own profit and to the disadvantage of complainant cannot be heard to say that it is too fugitive or evanescent to be regarded as property. It has all the attributes of property necessary for determining that a misappropriation of it by a competitor is unfair competition because contrary to good conscience.

The contention that the news is abandoned to the public for all purposes when published in the first newspaper is untenable. Abandonment is a question of intent, and the entire organization of the Associated Press negatives such a purpose. The cost of the service would be prohibited if the reward were to be so limited. No single newspaper, no small group of newspapers, could sustain the expenditure. Indeed, it is one of the most obvious results of defendant's theory that, by permitting indiscriminate publication by anybody and everybody for purposes of profit in competition with the news-gatherer, it would render publication profitless, or so little profitable as in effect to cut off the service by rendering the cost prohibitive in comparison with the return. The practical needs and requirements of the business are reflected in complainant's by-laws which have been referred to. Their effect is that publication by each member must be deemed not by any means an abandonment of the news to the world for any and all purposes, but a publication for limited purposes; for the benefit of the readers of the bulletin or the newspaper as such; not for the purpose of making merchandise of it as news, with the result of depriving complainant's other members of their reasonable opportunity to obtain just returns for their expenditures.

It is to be observed that the view we adopt does not result in giving to complainant the right to monopolize either the gathering or the distribution of the news, or, without complying with the copyright act, to prevent the reproduction of its news articles, but only postpones participation by complainant's competitor in the processes of distribution and reproduction of news that it has not gathered, and only to the extent necessary to prevent that competitor from reaping the fruits of complainant's efforts and expenditure, to the partial exclusion of complainant and in violation of the principle that underlies the maxim 'sic utere tuo,' etc.

. . . .

Besides the misappropriation, there are elements of imitation, of false pretense, in defendant's practices. The device of rewriting complainant's news articles, frequently resorted to, carries its own comment. The habitual failure to give credit to complainant for that which is taken is significant. Indeed, the entire system of appropriating complainant's news and transmitting it as a commercial product to defendant's clients and patrons amounts to a false representation to them and to their newspaper readers that the news transmitted is the result of defendant's own investigation in the field. But these elements, although accentuating the wrong, are not the essence of it. It is something more than the advantage of celebrity of which complainant is being deprived.

. . . .

The decree of the Circuit court of Appeals will be

Affirmed.

. . . .

MR. JUSTICE BRANDEIS, dissenting.

. . . . The sole question for our consideration is this: Was the International News Service properly enjoined from using, or causing to be used gainfully, news of which it acquired knowledge by lawful means (namely, by reading publicly posted bulletins or papers purchased by it in the open market) merely because the news had been originally gathered by the Associated Press and continued to be of value to some of its members, or because it did not reveal the source from which it was acquired?

. . . .

News is a report of recent occurrences. The business of the news agency is to gather systematically knowledge of such occurrences of interest and to distribute reports thereof. The Associated Press contended that knowledge so acquired is property, because it costs money and labor to produce and because it has value for which those who have it not are ready to pay; that it remains property and is entitled to protection as long as it has commercial value as news; and that to protect it effectively, the defendant must be enjoined from making, or causing to be made, any gainful use of it while it retains such value. An essential element of individual property is the legal right to exclude others from enjoying it. If the property is private, the right of exclusion may be absolute; if the property is affected with a public interest, the right of exclusion is qualified. But the fact that a product of the mind has cost its producer money and labor, and has a value for which others are willing to pay, is not sufficient to ensure to it this legal attribute of property. The general rule of law is, that the noblest of human productions—knowledge, truths ascertained, conceptions, and ideas—become, after voluntary communication to others, free as the air to common use. Upon these incorporeal productions the attribute of property is continued after such communication only in certain classes of cases where public policy has seemed to demand it. These exceptions are confined to productions which, in some degree, involve creation, invention, or discovery. But by no means all such are endowed with this attribute of property. The creations which are recognized as property by the common law are literary, dramatic, musical, and other artistic creations; and these have also protection under the copyright statutes. The inventions and discoveries upon which this attribute of property is conferred only by statute, are the few comprised within the patent law. There are also many other cases in which courts interfere to prevent curtailment of plaintiff's enjoyment of incorporal productions; and in which the right to relief is often called a property right, but is such only in a special sense. In those cases, the plaintiff has no absolute right to the protection of his production; he has merely the qualified right to be protected as against the defendant's acts, because of the special relation in which the latter stands or the wrongful method or means employed in acquiring the knowledge or the manner in which it is used. Protection of this character is afforded where the suit is based upon breach of contract or of trust or upon unfair competition.

The knowledge for which protection is sought in the case at bar is not of a kind upon which the law has heretofore conferred the attributes of property; nor is the manner of its acquisition or use nor the purpose to which it is applied, such as has heretofore been recognized as entitling a plaintiff to relief.

. . . .

That news is not property in the strict sense is illustrated by the case of Sports and General Press Agency, Ltd., v. 'Our Dogs' Publishing Co., Ltd., [1916] 2 K.B. 880, where the plaintiff, the assignee of the right to photograph the exhibits at a dog show, was refused an injunction against defendant who had also taken pictures of the show and was publishing them. The court said that, except in so far as the possession of the land occupied by the show enabled the proprietors to exclude people or permit them on condition that they agree not to take photographs (which condition was not imposed in that case), the proprietors had no exclusive right to photograph the show and could therefore grant no such right. And it was further stated that, at any rate, no matter what conditions might be imposed upon those entering the grounds, if the defendant had been on top of a house or in some position where he could photograph the show without interfering with the physical property of the plaintiff, the plaintiff would have no right to stop him. If, when the plaintiff creates the event recorded, he is not entitled to the exclusive first publication of the news (in that case a photograph) of the event, no reason can be shown why he should be accorded such protection as to events which he simply records and transmits to other parts of the world, though with great expenditure of time and money.

. . . .

Plaintiff further contended that defendant's practice constitutes unfair competition, because there is 'appropriation without cost to itself of values created by' the plaintiff; and it is upon this ground that the decision of this court appears to be based. To appropriate and use for profit, knowledge and ideas produced by other men, without making compensation or even acknowledgment, may be inconsistent with a finer sense of propriety; but, with the exceptions indicated above, the law has heretofore sanctioned the practice. Thus it was held that one may ordinarily make and sell anything in any form, may copy with exactness that which another has produced, or may otherwise use his ideas without his consent and without the payment of compensation, and yet not inflict a legal injury; and that ordinarily one is at perfect liberty to find out, if he can by lawful means, trade secrets of another, however valuable, and then use the knowledge so acquired gainfully, although it cost the original owner much in effort and in money to collect or produce.

. . . .

That competition is not unfair in a legal sense, merely because the profits gained are unearned, even if made at the expense of a rival, is shown by many cases besides those referred to above. He who follows the pioneer into a new market, or who engages in the manufacture of an article newly introduced by another, seeks profits due largely to the labor and expense of the first adventurer; but the law sanctions, indeed encourages, the pursuit. He who makes a city known through his product, must submit to sharing the resultant trade with others who, perhaps for that reason, locate there later.

. . . .

The means by which the International News Service obtains news gathered by the Associated Press is also clearly unobjectionable. It is taken from papers bought in the open market or from bulletins publicly posted. No breach of contract such as the court considered to exist in *Hitchman Coal & Coke Co. v. Mitchell*, 245 U.S. 229, 254; or of trust such as was present in Morison v. Moat, 9 Hare, 241; and neither fraud nor force is involved. The manner of use is likewise unobjectionable. No reference is made by word or by act to the Associated Press, either in transmitting the news to subscribers or by them in publishing it in their papers. Neither the International News Service nor its subscribers is gaining or seeking to gain in its business a benefit from the reputation of the Associated Press. They are merely using its product without making compensation. That they have a legal right to do, because the product is not property, and they do not stand in any relation to the Associated

Press, either of contract or of trust, which otherwise precludes such use. The argument is not advanced by characterizing such taking and use [as] a misappropriation.

It is also suggested that the fact that defendant does not refer to the Associated Press as the source of the news may furnish a basis for the relief. But the defendant and its subscribers, unlike members of the Associated Press, were under no contractual obligation to disclose the source of the news; and there is no rule of law requiring acknowledgment to be made where uncopyrighted matter is reproduced. The International News Service is said to mislead its subscribers into believing that the news transmitted was originally gathered by it and that they in turn mislead their readers. There is, in fact, no representation by either of any kind. Sources of information are sometimes given because required by contract; sometimes because naming the source gives authority to an otherwise incredible statement; and sometimes the source is named because the agency does not wish to take the responsibility itself of giving currency to the news. But no representation can properly be implied from omission to mention the source of information except that the International News Service is transmitting news which it believes to be credible.

. . . . The great development of agencies now furnishing country-wide distribution of news, the vastness of our territory, and improvements in the means of transmitting intelligence, have made it possible for a news agency or newspapers to obtain, without paying compensation, the fruit of another's efforts and to use news so obtained gainfully in competition with the original collector. The injustice of such action is obvious. But to give relief against it would involve more than the application of existing rules of law to new facts. It would require the making of a new rule in analogy to existing ones. The unwritten law possesses capacity for growth; and has often satisfied new demands for justice by invoking analogies or by expanding a rule or principle. This process has been in the main wisely applied and should not be discontinued. Where the problem is relatively simple, as it is apt to be when private interests only are involved, it generally proves adequate. But with the increasing complexity of society, the public interest tends to become omnipresent; and the problems presented by new demands for justice cease to be simple. Then the creation or recognition by courts of a new private right may work serious injury to the general public, unless the boundaries of the right are definitely established and wisely guarded. In order to reconcile the new private right with the public interest, it may be necessary to prescribe limitations and rules for its enjoyment; and also to provide administrative machinery for enforcing the rules. It is largely for this reason that, in the effort to meet the many new demands for justice incident to a rapidly changing civilization, resort to legislation has latterly been had with increasing frequency.

The rule for which the plaintiff contends would effect an important extension of property rights and a corresponding curtailment of the free use of knowledge and of ideas; and the facts of this case admonish us of the danger involved in recognizing such a property right in news, without imposing upon news-gatherers corresponding obligations.

. . . .

Courts are ill-equipped to make the investigations which should precede a determination of the limitations which should be set upon any property right in news or of the circumstances under which news gathered by a private agency should be deemed affected with a public interest. Courts would be powerless to prescribe the detailed regulations essential to full enjoyment of the rights conferred or to introduce the machinery required for enforcement of such regulations. Considerations such as these should lead us to decline to establish a new rule of law in the effort to redress a newly disclosed wrong, although the propriety of some remedy appears to be clear.

NOTES & QUESTIONS

(1)   Did the majority find that the Associated Press had a property right in the news? If not, what right was the misappropriation claim based upon?

(2)   INS argued that, once the information was made available to the public, the Associated Press no longer had the right to complain if others (whether a member of the public or a competitor) passed that information along. Why was the majority not persuaded by this argument?

(3)   The majority's opinion notes that the conduct of the INS was problematic in part due to the nature of transmitting the news from the East Coast to the West Coast and the time differentials involved. Is this still a concern in a modern internet-connected world?

(4)   Review § 1 and comment g of the Restatement of Unfair Competition. Is the Restatement approach consistent with the *INS* decision? *Compare* RESTATEMENT OF UNFAIR COMPETITION § 1(a) & cmt. g (1995), *with id.* § 38 cmts. b–c.

(5)   In support of his conclusion that the conduct of INS was not actionable, Justice Brandeis in his dissent cited to *Sports and General Press Agency, Ltd., v. 'Our Dogs' Publishing Co., Ltd.* Do you find this case supportive of Justice Brandeis' position, or is it distinguishable? Do you agree with Justice Brandeis' assertion that "[h]e who makes a city known through his product, must submit to sharing the resultant trade with others who, perhaps for that reason, locate there later"?

(6) Justice Brandeis admits that what INS has done results in an injustice, yet he still refuses to recognize a right to enjoin its actions. Why? What policy concerns are driving his dissent?

(7) Justice Holmes also dissented from the majority opinion, stating that "[w]hen an uncopyrighted combination of words is published there is no general right to forbid other people [from] repeating them—in other words there is no property in the combination or in the thoughts or facts that the words express." However, he posited that the claim of the Associated Press was better suited for another cause of action:

> If a given person is to be prohibited from making the use of words that his neighbors are free to make some other ground must be found. One such ground is vaguely expressed in the phrase unfair trade. . . . The ordinary case, I say, is palming off the defendant's product as the plaintiff's but the same evil may follow from the opposite falsehood—from saying whether in words or by implication that the plaintiff's product is the defendant's, and that, it seems to me, is what has happened here.

Reflecting upon some of the other causes of action discussed in previous Chapters, what claim has Justice Holmes described? Can you think of any other claims that the Associated Press might have asserted against the INS?

(8) You may find it interesting to know that the Associated Press has brought a claim similar to the one asserted in the above case as recently as 2009. In *Associated Press v. All Headline News Corp.*, 608 F. Supp. 2d 454 (S.D.N.Y. 2009), the Associated Press sued All Headline News Corp. ("AHN") for misappropriation. AHN did not engage in any original reporting, but instead hired individuals to find news stories on the internet, rewrite the text, or copy the stories in full for publication on the AHN website. Although many of the stories were based on the work of the Associated Press, AHN marketed itself as the original provider. The district court denied AHN's motion to dismiss based on the continued recognition of misappropriation as a valid cause of action under New York law.

C. MODERN DAY MISAPPROPRIATION: "HOT NEWS" CLAIMS

The continued validity of the misappropriation action under *INS* came into question after the Supreme Court's decision in *Erie Railroad v. Tompkins*, 304 U.S. 64 (1938), which abolished claims based upon any sort of federal common law in diversity cases. Furthermore, courts and commentators questioned whether such an action could survive the preemptive effect of the federal copyright and patent laws, which are often implicated in such cases. For example, absent a patent, ideas and innovations are generally unprotected from exploitation by others. In *Bonito Boats, Inc. v. Thunder Craft Boats, Inc.*, 489 U.S. 141, 156–57 (1989), the Supreme Court stated, with regard to patent protection, that "[a] state law that substantially interferes with the enjoyment of an unpatented utilitarian or design conception which has been freely disclosed by its author to the public at large impermissibly contravenes the ultimate goal of public disclosure and use which is the centerpiece of federal patent policy." Similarly, § 301 of the 1976 Copyright Act precludes recognition of a state law cause of action which protects rights "equivalent" to any of the exclusive rights of copyright recognized by the Act. See 17 U.S.C. § 301. Nonetheless, a number of states have continued to recognize misappropriation as a state common law theory of recovery. In such states, however, courts have often limited the misappropriation doctrine to so-called "hot news" cases, which mirror the facts of *INS*. Furthermore, as the next case demonstrates, preemption may remain an issue.

THE NATIONAL BASKETBALL ASSOCIATION V. MOTOROLA, INC.

105 F.3d 841 (2d Cir. 1997)

WINTER, CIRCUIT JUDGE:

Motorola, Inc. and Sports Team Analysis and Tracking Systems ("STATS") appeal from a permanent injunction entered by Judge Preska. The injunction concerns a handheld pager sold by Motorola and marketed under the name "SportsTrax," which displays updated information of professional basketball games in progress. The injunction prohibits appellants, absent authorization from the National Basketball Association and NBA Properties, Inc. (collectively the "NBA"), from transmitting scores or other data about NBA games in progress via the pagers, STATS's site on America On-Line's computer dial-up service, or "any equivalent means."

The crux of the dispute concerns the extent to which a state law "hot-news" misappropriation claim based on *International News Service v. Associated Press*, 248 U.S. 215 (1918) ("INS"), survives preemption by the federal Copyright Act and whether the NBA's claim fits within the surviving *INS*-type claims. We hold that a narrow "hot-news" exception does survive preemption. However, we also hold that appellants' transmission of "real-time" NBA game scores and information tabulated from television and radio broadcasts of games in progress does not constitute a misappropriation of "hot news" that is the property of the NBA.

. . . .

I. BACKGROUND

The facts are largely undisputed. Motorola manufactures and markets the SportsTrax paging device while STATS supplies the game information that is transmitted to the pagers. The product became available to the public in January 1996, at a retail price of about $200. SportsTrax's pager has an inch-and-a-half by inch-and-a-half screen and operates in four basic modes: "current," "statistics," "final scores" and "demonstration." It is the "current" mode that gives rise to the present dispute.[1] In that mode, SportsTrax displays the following information on NBA games in progress: (i) the teams playing; (ii) score changes; (iii) the team in possession of the ball; (iv) whether the team is in the free-throw bonus; (v) the quarter of the game; and (vi) time remaining in the quarter. The information is updated every two to three minutes, with more frequent updates near the end of the first half and the end of the game. There is a lag of approximately two or three minutes between events in the game itself and when the information appears on the pager screen.

SportsTrax's operation relies on a "data feed" supplied by STATS reporters who watch the games on television or listen to them on the radio. The reporters key into a personal computer changes in the score and other information such as successful and missed shots, fouls, and clock updates. The information is relayed by modem to STATS's host computer, which compiles, analyzes, and formats the data for retransmission. The information is then sent to a common carrier, which then sends it via satellite to various local FM radio networks that in turn emit the signal received by the individual SportsTrax pagers.

. . . .

The NBA's complaint asserted six claims for relief: (i) state law unfair competition by misappropriation; (ii) false advertising under Section 43(a) of the Lanham Act, 15 U.S.C. § 1125(a); (iii) false representation of origin under Section 43(a) of the Lanham Act; (iv) state and common law unfair competition by false advertising and false designation of origin; (v) federal copyright infringement; and (vi) unlawful interception of communications under the Communications Act of 1934, 47 U.S.C. § 605. Motorola counterclaimed, alleging that the NBA unlawfully interfered with Motorola's contractual relations with four individual NBA teams that had agreed to sponsor and advertise SportsTrax.

The district court dismissed all of the NBA's claims except the first—misappropriation under New York law. The court also dismissed

---

[1] The other three SportsTrax modes involve information that is far less contemporaneous than that provided in the "current" mode. In the "statistics" mode, the SportsTrax pager displays a variety of player and team statistics, such as field goal shooting percentages and top scorers. However, these are calculated only at half-time and when the game is over. In the "final scores" mode, the unit displays final scores from the previous day's games. In the "demonstration" mode, the unit merely simulates information shown during a hypothetical NBA game. The core issue in the instant matter is the dissemination of continuously-updated real-time NBA game information in the "current" mode. Because we conclude that the dissemination of such real-time information is lawful, the other modes need no further description or discussion.

Motorola's counterclaim. Finding Motorola and STATS liable for misappropriation, Judge Preska entered the permanent injunction, reserved the calculation of damages for subsequent proceedings, and stayed execution of the injunction pending appeal. Motorola and STATS appeal from the injunction, while NBA cross-appeals from the district court's dismissal of its Lanham Act false-advertising claim. The issues before us, therefore, are the state law misappropriation and Lanham Act claims.

II. THE STATE LAW MISAPPROPRIATION CLAIM

[The court first reviews the district court's conclusion that Motorola did not infringe NBA's copyright. The court noted that the Copyright Act distinguishes between the sporting event itself and the broadcast of the event, offering protection only as to the latter. As Motorola only conveyed information about the sporting events and did not re-broadcast the events, there was no copyright infringement.]

C. *The State-Law Misappropriation Claim*

The district court's injunction was based on its conclusion that, under New York law, defendants had unlawfully misappropriated the NBA's property rights in its games. The district court reached this conclusion by holding: (i) that the NBA's misappropriation claim relating to the underlying games was not preempted by Section 301 of the Copyright Act; and (ii) that, under New York common law, defendants had engaged in unlawful misappropriation. We disagree.

1. *Preemption Under the Copyright Act*

a) Summary

When Congress amended the Copyright Act in 1976, it provided for the preemption of state law claims that are interrelated with copyright claims in certain ways. Under 17 U.S.C. § 301, a state law claim is preempted when: (i) the state law claim seeks to vindicate "legal or equitable rights that are equivalent" to one of the bundle of exclusive rights already protected by copyright law under 17 U.S.C. § 106—styled the "general scope requirement"; and (ii) the particular work to which the state law claim is being applied falls within the type of works protected by the Copyright Act under Sections 102 and 103—styled the "subject matter requirement."

The district court concluded that the NBA's misappropriation claim was not preempted because, with respect to the underlying games, as opposed to the broadcasts, the subject matter requirement was not met. The court dubbed as "partial preemption" its separate analysis of misappropriation claims relating to the underlying games and misappropriation claims relating to broadcasts of those games. *Id.* at 1098, n. 24. The district court then relied on a series of older New York misappropriation cases involving radio broadcasts that considerably broadened *INS*. We hold that where the challenged copying or misappropriation relates in part to the copyrighted broadcasts of the games, the subject matter requirement is met as to both the broadcasts and the games. We therefore reject the partial preemption doctrine and its anomalous consequence that "it is possible for a plaintiff to assert claims both for infringement of its copyright in a broadcast and misappropriation of its rights in the underlying event." *Id.* We do find that a properly-narrowed INS "hot-news" misappropriation claim survives preemption because it fails the general scope requirement, but that the broader theory of the radio broadcast cases relied upon by the district court were preempted when Congress extended copyright protection to simultaneously-recorded broadcasts.

b)   "Partial Preemption" and the Subject Matter Requirement

The subject matter requirement is met when the work of authorship being copied or misappropriated "fall[s] within the ambit of copyright protection." *Harper & Row, Publishers, Inc. v. Nation Enter.*, 723 F.2d 195, 200 (1983), *rev'd on other grounds*, 471 U.S. 539 (1985). We believe that the subject matter requirement is met in the instant matter and that the concept of "partial preemption" is not consistent with Section 301 of the Copyright Act. Although game broadcasts are copyrightable while the underlying games are not, the Copyright Act should not be read to distinguish between the two when analyzing the preemption of a misappropriation claim based on copying or taking from the copyrightable work. We believe that:

> [O]nce a performance is reduced to tangible form, there is no distinction between the performance and the recording of the performance for the purposes of preemption under § 301(a). Thus, if a baseball game were not broadcast or were telecast without being recorded, the Players' performances similarly would not be fixed in tangible form and their rights of publicity would not be subject to preemption. By virtue of being videotaped, however, the Players' performances are fixed in tangible form, and any rights of publicity in their performances that are equivalent to the rights contained in the copyright of the telecast are preempted.

[*Baltimore Orioles, Inc. v. Major League Baseball Players Ass'n*, 805 F.2d 663, 675 (7th Cir. 1986) (citation omitted).]

Copyrightable material often contains uncopyrightable elements within it, but Section 301 preemption bars state law misappropriation claims with respect to uncopyrightable as well as copyrightable elements. . . .

Adoption of a partial preemption doctrine—preemption of claims based on misappropriation of broadcasts but no preemption of claims based on misappropriation of underlying facts—would expand significantly the reach of state law claims and render the preemption intended by Congress unworkable. It is often difficult or impossible to separate the fixed copyrightable work from the underlying uncopyrightable events or facts. Moreover, Congress, in extending copyright protection only to the broadcasts and not to the underlying events, intended that the latter be in the public domain. Partial preemption turns that intent on its head by allowing state law to vest exclusive rights in material that Congress intended to be in the public domain and to make unlawful conduct that Congress intended to allow. . . .

c)   The General Scope Requirement

Under the general scope requirement, Section 301 "preempts only those state law rights that 'may be abridged by an act which, in and of itself, would infringe one of the exclusive rights' provided by federal copyright law." *Computer Assoc. Int'l, Inc. v. Altai, Inc.*, 982 F.2d 693, 716 (2d Cir.1992) (quoting *Harper & Row*, 723 F.2d at 200). However, certain forms of commercial misappropriation otherwise within the general scope requirement will survive preemption if an "extra-element" test is met. As stated in *Altai*:

> But if an "extra element" is "required instead of or in addition to the acts of reproduction, performance, distribution or display, in order to constitute a state-created cause of action, then the right does not lie 'within the general scope of copyright,' and there is no preemption."

Id. (quoting 1 *Nimmer on Copyright* § 1.01[B] at 1–15).

. . . .

In *INS*, the plaintiff AP and defendant INS were "wire services" that sold news items to client newspapers. AP brought suit to prevent INS from selling facts and information lifted from AP sources to INS-affiliated newspapers. One method by which INS was able to use AP's news was to lift facts from AP news bulletins. Another method was to sell facts taken from just-published east coast AP newspapers to west coast INS newspapers whose editions had yet to appear. The Supreme Court held (prior to *Erie R. Co. v. Tompkins*, 304 U.S. 64 (1938)), that INS's use of AP's information was unlawful under federal common law. It characterized INS's conduct as

> amount[ing] to an unauthorized interference with the normal operation of complainant's legitimate business precisely at the point where the profit is to be reaped, in order to divert a

material portion of the profit from those who have earned it to those who have not; with special advantage to defendant in the competition because of the fact that it is not burdened with any part of the expense of gathering the news.

INS, 248 U.S. at 240.

. . . .

Our conclusion, therefore, is that only a narrow "hot-news" misappropriation claim survives preemption for actions concerning material within the realm of copyright.[6] *See also 1 McCarthy on Trademarks and Unfair Competition* (4th ed. 1996), § 10:69, at 10–134 (discussing *National Exhibition Co. v. Fass*, 133 N.Y.S.2d 379 (Sup.Ct.1954), [*Mut. Broad. Sys., Inc. v. Muzak Corp.*, 30 N.Y.S.2d 419 (Sup. Ct. 1941)], and other cases relied upon by NBA that pre-date the 1976 amendment to the Copyright Act and concluding that after the amendment, "state misappropriation law would be unnecessary and would be preempted: protection is solely under federal copyright").

In our view, the elements central to an *INS* claim are: (i) the plaintiff generates or collects information at some cost or expense, (ii) the value of the information is highly time-sensitive; (iii) the defendant's use of the information constitutes free-riding on the plaintiff's costly efforts to generate or collect it; (iv) the defendant's use of the information is in direct competition with a product or service offered by the plaintiff; (v) the ability of other parties to free-ride on the efforts of the plaintiff would so reduce the incentive to produce the product or service that its existence or quality would be substantially threatened.[8]

INS is not about ethics; it is about the protection of property rights in time-sensitive information so that the information will be made available

---

[6]   State law claims involving breach of fiduciary duties or trade-secret claims are not involved in this matter and are not addressed by this discussion. These claims are generally not preempted because they pass the "extra elements" test.

[8]   Some authorities have labeled this element as requiring direct competition between the defendant and the plaintiff in a primary market. "[I]n most of the small number of cases in which the misappropriation doctrine has been determinative, the defendant's appropriation, like that in INS, resulted in direct competition in the plaintiffs' primary market . . . Appeals to the misappropriation doctrine are almost always rejected when the appropriation does not intrude upon the plaintiff's primary market." *Restatement (Third) of Unfair Competition*, § 38 cmt. c, at 412–13; *see also National Football League v. Governor of State of Delaware*, 435 F.Supp. 1372 (D.Del.1977). In that case, the NFL sued Delaware over the state's lottery game which was based on NFL games. In dismissing the wrongful misappropriation claims, the court stated:

While courts have recognized that one has a right to one's own harvest, this proposition has not been construed to preclude others from profiting from demands for collateral services generated by the success of one's business venture.

Id. at 1378. The court also noted, "It is true that Delaware is thus making profits it would not make but for the existence of the NFL, but I find this difficult to distinguish from the multitude of charter bus companies who generate profit from servicing those of plaintiffs' fans who want to go to the stadium or, indeed, the sidewalk pop-corn salesman who services the crowd as it surges towards the gate." *Id.*

to the public by profit seeking entrepreneurs. If services like AP were not assured of property rights in the news they pay to collect, they would cease to collect it. The ability of their competitors to appropriate their product at only nominal cost and thereby to disseminate a competing product at a lower price would destroy the incentive to collect news in the first place. The newspaper-reading public would suffer because no one would have an incentive to collect "hot news."

We therefore find the extra elements—those in addition to the elements of copyright infringement—that allow a "hot-news" claim to survive preemption are: (i) the time-sensitive value of factual information, (ii) the free-riding by a defendant, and (iii) the threat to the very existence of the product or service provided by the plaintiff.

2. *The Legality of SportsTrax*

We conclude that Motorola and STATS have not engaged in unlawful misappropriation under the "hot-news" test set out above. To be sure, some of the elements of a "hot-news" *INS* claim are met. The information transmitted to SportsTrax is not precisely contemporaneous, but it is nevertheless time-sensitive. Also, the NBA does provide, or will shortly do so, information like that available through SportsTrax. It now offers a service called "Gamestats" that provides official play-by-play game sheets and half-time and final box scores within each arena. It also provides such information to the media in each arena. In the future, the NBA plans to enhance Gamestats so that it will be networked between the various arenas and will support a pager product analogous to SportsTrax. SportsTrax will of course directly compete with an enhanced Gamestats.

However, there are critical elements missing in the NBA's attempt to assert a "hot-news" INS-type claim. As framed by the NBA, their claim compresses and confuses three different informational products. The first product is generating the information by playing the games; the second product is transmitting live, full descriptions of those games; and the third product is collecting and retransmitting strictly factual information about the games. The first and second products are the NBA's primary business: producing basketball games for live attendance and licensing copyrighted broadcasts of those games. The collection and retransmission of strictly factual material about the games is a different product: e.g., box-scores in newspapers, summaries of statistics on television sports news, and real-time facts to be transmitted to pagers. In our view, the NBA has failed to show any competitive effect whatsoever from SportsTrax on the first and second products and a lack of any free-riding by SportsTrax on the third.

With regard to the NBA's primary products—producing basketball games with live attendance and licensing copyrighted broadcasts of those games—there is no evidence that anyone regards SportsTrax or the AOL site as a substitute for attending NBA games or watching them on television. In fact, Motorola markets SportsTrax as being designed "for those times when you cannot be at the arena, watch the game on TV, or listen to the radio. . ."

The NBA argues that the pager market is also relevant to a "hot-news" *INS*-type claim and that SportsTrax's future competition with Gamestats satisfies any missing element. We agree that there is a separate market for the real-time transmission of factual information to pagers or similar devices, such as STATS's AOL site. However, we disagree that SportsTrax is in any sense free-riding off Gamestats.

An indispensable element of an *INS* "hot-news" claim is free riding by a defendant on a plaintiff's product, enabling the defendant to produce a directly competitive product for less money because it has lower costs. SportsTrax is not such a product. The use of pagers to transmit real-time information about NBA games requires: (i) the collecting of facts about the games; (ii) the transmission of these facts on a network; (iii) the assembling of them by the particular service; and (iv) the transmission of them to pagers or an on-line computer site. Appellants are in no way free-riding on Gamestats. Motorola and STATS expend their own resources to collect purely factual information generated in NBA games to transmit to SportsTrax pagers. They have their own network and assemble and transmit data themselves.

To be sure, if appellants in the future were to collect facts from an enhanced Gamestats pager to retransmit them to SportsTrax pagers, that would constitute free-riding and might well cause Gamestats to be unprofitable because it had to bear costs to collect facts that SportsTrax did not. If the appropriation of facts from one pager to another pager service were allowed, transmission of current information on NBA games to pagers or similar devices would be substantially deterred because any potential transmitter would know that the first entrant would quickly encounter a lower cost competitor free-riding on the originator's transmissions.

However, that is not the case in the instant matter. SportsTrax and Gamestats are each bearing their own costs of collecting factual information on NBA games, and, if one produces a product that is cheaper or otherwise superior to the other, that producer will prevail in the marketplace. This is obviously not the situation against which *INS* was intended to prevent: the potential lack of any such product or service because of the anticipation of free-riding.

For the foregoing reasons, the NBA has not shown any damage to any of its products based on free-riding by Motorola and STATS, and the NBA's misappropriation claim based on New York law is preempted.

NOTES & QUESTIONS

(1) The district court found for the NBA, concluding that the NBA's misappropriation claim was only partially preempted. What is partial preemption and why does the Second Circuit reject this concept?

(2) The court finds that, despite being within the scope of the Copyright Act, state law claims can move forward if there exists an "extra element" in addition to, or instead of, the normal elements associated with copyright infringement. What extra elements exist in "hot news" claims? Why was the test announced by the court not met?

(3) In *Barclays Capital Inc. v. Theflyonthewall.com, Inc.*, 650 F.3d 876 (2d Cir. 2011), the Second Circuit re-examined its analysis under *NBA v. Motorola*. Barclays Capital, Merrill Lynch, and Morgan Stanley (collectively "The Firms") brought suit against Theflyonthewall.com ("Fly") for "hot news" misappropriation under New York law. Each Firm would develop market research about major publicly traded equity securities. Once compiled, the Firms would sell this research (along with recommendations on potential action) to clients who would act on the information. In producing this research, the Firms limited their disclosure and attempted to protect the information in a variety of ways—e.g., safeguarding passwords, forbidding clients from redistributing, etc. Despite their efforts, much of their research would leak and would be posted by online aggregators or reported as financial news. The Firms identified Fly as one of the more systematic unauthorized publishers. Evidence introduced at trial was compelling and demonstrated that the unauthorized redistribution was a major contributor to the decline in the resources that each Firm devoted to market research.

The district court applied the five-element test from *NBA* and found that Fly was liable for misappropriation. On appeal, the court engaged in a somewhat convoluted explanation of the rationale of *NBA*. The court stated that the five-part test in *NBA* articulated the elements of a "hot news" misappropriation claim, and the later three-part test articulated the "extra elements" needed to avoid preemption. However, the court went on to question the rationale of *NBA*: "The NBA panel decided the case before it, and we think that the law it thus made regarding 'hot news' preemption is, as we have tried to explain, determinative here. But the Court's various explanations of its five-part approach are not." It then reversed the district court based on what it viewed as a lack of free-riding:

> . . . the Firms' claim is not a so-called *INS*-type non-preempted claim because Fly is not, under *NBA*'s analysis, "free-riding." It is collecting, collating and disseminating factual information—the facts that Firms and others in the securities business have made recommendations with respect to the value of and the wisdom of purchasing or selling securities—and attributing the information to its source. The Firms are making the news; Fly, despite the Firms' understandable desire to protect their business model, is breaking it.

Id. at 902–03.

(4) What role should direct competition play in a misappropriation analysis? The *NBA* court noted in footnote 8 that direct competition in a primary market is typically a requirement of a misappropriation claim. In *U.S. Golf Association v. St. Andrews Systems, Data-Max, Inc.*, 749 F.2d 1028, 1035 (3d Cir. 1984), the USGA developed a mathematical formula for amateur golf players to determine their handicap. Data-Max developed and marketed small computers that were programmed to calculate a golfer's handicap based on USGA's equation. USGA brought a misappropriation claim under New Jersey law seeking to enjoin Data-Max's use of its handicapping formula The court looked at whether there was direct competition and concluded that there was not. The USGA was not involved in marketing the formula; it was simply promoting discussion. Data-Max, on the other hand, was involved in providing "instant handicaps." Because the two parties were not in direct competition, the court rejected the misappropriation claim.

Under very similar facts, however, an injunction barring the use of USGA's handicap formulas was upheld in *U.S. Golf Association v. Arroyo Software Corp.*, 69 Cal. App. 4th 607 (1999). Arroyo argued that USGA's claims should be collaterally estopped due to the Third Circuit's opinion in *St. Andrews*. The California Court of Appeal rejected this argument: "Collateral estoppel does not apply where there are changed conditions or new facts which did not exist at the time of the prior judgment, or where the previous decision was based on different substantive law." The court held that the factual circumstances were different, as the new formula was much more complex, involved the expenditure of millions of dollars, and was developed after the *St. Andrews* decision. The court also held that California substantive law was different from the New Jersey misappropriation claim at issue in *St. Andrews*:

> The elements of a claim for misappropriation under California law consist of the following: (a) the plaintiff invested substantial time, skill or money in developing its property; (b) the defendant appropriated and used the plaintiff's property at little or no cost to the defendant; (c) the defendant's appropriation and use of the plaintiff's property was without the authorization or consent of the plaintiff; and (d) the plaintiff can establish that it has been injured by the defendant's conduct. The principal basis for the decision of the Third Circuit in *St. Andrews* was the fact that New Jersey law required proof of direct competition between the plaintiff and the defendant as an essential element of any misappropriation claim. Under the California law applicable here, on the other hand, the essential elements of a misappropriation claim simply do not include any such requirement of proof of direct competition between the plaintiff and the defendant. Because California law does not require a showing of direct competition between the parties before conduct otherwise constituting misappropriation can be prohibited,

the trial court was correct in holding both that the issues decided under New Jersey law in *St. Andrews* were not identical to those arising under California law in this case, and that collateral estoppel does not preclude USGA's claims in this case.

Id. at 618–19.

(5)   As noted in the introduction to this Chapter, misappropriation is far from a uniformly accepted cause of action. The states of California, Connecticut, Colorado, Delaware, Hawaii, Illinois, Maryland, Missouri, New York, New Jersey, Texas, Pennsylvania, Washington, and Wisconsin recognize a general common law misappropriation claim. However, the Third Restatement of Unfair Competition rejects a general cause of action for misappropriation. *See* RESTATEMENT (THIRD) OF UNFAIR COMPETITION § 38 cmt. b (1995) ("The better approach . . . does not recognize a residual common law tort of misappropriation.").

(6)   Given that many jurisdictions do not recognize a misappropriation claim at all, and considering the difficulties involved in prevailing on such a claim when it is recognized, how is a party to protect the fruits of its labor from free-riders? One solution, discussed in a later Chapter, is through the law of trade secrets. However, a trade secret claim requires the information to not be publicly disseminated, which can pose problems for parties like the Associated Press. A better solution, therefore, may be through contract law.

In *ProCD, Inc. v. Zeidenberg*, 86 F.3d 1447 (7th Cir. 1996), an opinion known more for its discussion of what have been termed "rolling contracts," Judge Easterbrook found that a breach of contract claim was not preempted by federal copyright law. Matthew Zeidenberg entered a local retail store and bought ProCD's product, "Select Phone," which was a CD-ROM disk containing over 95,000,000 telephone listings compiled by ProCD. Inside the package was a user guide containing a "Single User License Agreement," which prohibited the purchaser from copying the software for non-personal use (the license would appear on most computer screens before the listings could be accessed). The license stated the following: "By using the discs and the listings licensed to you, you agree to be bound by the terms of this License. If you do not agree to the terms of this License, promptly return all copies of the software . . . to the place where you obtained it."

Zeidenberg soon realized that he could copy the information and make it available to the public himself. He subsequently incorporated under the name Silken Mountain Web Services, Inc. and purchased an updated version of Select Phone. ProCD sued to enjoin Zeidenberg, and the district court denied relief. The court concluded that the terms of the license were not part of the contract between Zeidenberg and ProCD. Alternatively, the court found that any breach of contract claim was preempted by the Copyright Act.

On appeal, the Seventh Circuit reversed and remanded. The court held that the contract was not formed in the store, but was instead consummated when Zeidenberg reviewed the terms of the license and proceeded to use the software. (This method of contract formation is often referred to as a "rolling" or "layered" contract.) In addition, the court held that contract claims were not preempted by the Copyright Act:

> But are rights created by contract "equivalent to any of the exclusive rights within the general scope of copyright"? Three courts of appeals have answered "no." *National Car Rental System, Inc. v. Computer Associates International, Inc.*, 991 F.2d 426, 433 (8th Cir.1993); *Taquino v. Teledyne Monarch Rubber*, 893 F.2d 1488, 1501 (5th Cir.1990); *Acorn Structures, Inc. v. Swantz*, 846 F.2d 923, 926 (4th Cir.1988). The district court disagreed with these decisions, 908 F.Supp. at 658, but we think them sound. Rights "equivalent to any of the exclusive rights within the general scope of copyright" are rights established by law—rights that restrict the options of persons who are strangers to the author. Copyright law forbids duplication, public performance, and so on, unless the person wishing to copy or perform the work gets permission; silence means a ban on copying. A copyright is a right against the world. Contracts, by contrast, generally affect only their parties; strangers may do as they please, so contracts do not create "exclusive rights."

ProCD, 86 F.3d at 1454. Could contract law have helped the NBA in its case against Motorola?

(7)   As we saw in the *NBA* decision, a misappropriation claim may be preempted by copyright law. In the landmark case of *Feist Publications, Inc. v. Rural Telephone Service Co.*, 499 U.S. 340 (1991), the Supreme Court rejected "sweat of the brow" as a valid basis for a cause of action for copyright infringement. Rural was a local telephone company that was required by Kansas state law to annually publish a telephone directory for its service area. Feist was a publisher in the business of publishing directories covering larger geographical areas. The companies were in competition for the advertising revenue from the directories. Unable to procure a license from Rural for its subscriber information, Feist decided to misappropriate the information from Rural's directory. Feist included the material in its own directory after sorting and verifying the information. Rural brought a copyright infringement action against Feist claiming that Feist had reproduced Rural's copyrighted material without authorization—material that Rural had invested substantial resources in creating.

The Supreme Court held that Rural's material was not original enough to be covered by copyright law. In so doing, the Court rejected "sweat of the brow" (substantial investments made by Rural in creating its directory) as a basis for a copyright infringement claim. The Court held that names, towns, and telephone numbers of Rural's subscribers were uncopyrightable facts, and these bits of information were not selected, coordinated, or arranged in an original way in Rural's directory. As a result, Rural's claim did not meet constitutional or statutory requirements for copyright protection. (It is worth noting that Rural did not raise a misappropriation claim.)

(8) A misappropriation action is generally filed in conjunction with other unfair competition claims. In *eBay, Inc. v. Bidder's Edge, Inc.*, 100 F. Supp. 2d 1058, 1063 (N.D. Cal. 2000), eBay filed for injunctive relief against Bidder's Edge for misappropriating its auction data. Along with a misappropriation claim, eBay brought eight other causes of action: trespass, false advertising, federal and state trademark dilution, computer fraud and abuse, unfair competition, interference with prospective economic advantage, and unjust enrichment. In an attempt to create its own "one-stop shop" auction website, Bidder's Edge was using robotic software to crawl the eBay site for the purpose of aggregating eBay data with data from other auction sites. Not surprisingly, this action was without eBay's consent and violated eBay's user agreement. The court preliminarily enjoined Bidder's Edge from accessing eBay's computer systems without eBay's written authorization, and it based its decision on a trespass to chattels theory. As is evident from the various claims listed above, a single infringing act may give rise to multiple causes of action depending upon the nature of the misappropriation.

PROBLEM 9.1

Jackson Sisk runs a website called "The Lead-Off" which reports on various happenings in the sports world, such as trades, game results, legal wranglings of various athletes, and general gossip. Instead of gathering the news himself, Jackson finds reports from other websites, some subscription-based and some free, and "re-reports" the news. He does, however, rewrite the information. Sometimes Jackson gives credit to the original reporting site, but sometimes he does not. He makes money through a combination of selling banner advertising space and subscriptions to his site.

(a) Assume that Sports Network, a subscription-based site, wishes to enjoin Jackson from using its information. Sports Network conducts original research for its stories at a considerable expense. Will it be able to successfully bring this suit? Should it matter if Jackson gives credit to Sports Network as the source of the information?

(b) Assuming that Sports Network is successful, what sort of injunctive relief should be imposed? *See Barclays Capital Inc. v. Theflyonthewall.com*, 700 F. Supp. 2d 310 (S.D.N.Y. 2010), *rev'd*, 650 F.3d 876 (2d Cir. 2011) (enjoining defendant from releasing information derived from research reports published while the market was closed until the later of thirty minutes after the close of the market or 10:00 a.m.).

(c) Contrary to the facts stated above, assume that Jackson does not run a for-profit website. Instead, he has a blog where he frequently comments on current happenings in sports. The blog is free to access and Jackson simply runs it as a hobby. How might this affect the outcome of a suit by Sports Network?

CHAPTER 10

TRADE SECRETS

■ ■ ■

A. TRADE SECRETS UNDER THE COMMON LAW

Trade secret law builds upon a theme developed in the previous Chapter that it is unfair, in some instances, for a competitor to reap where he has not sown. The law has protected trade secrets since the time of ancient Rome, and the legal principles have developed and evolved over the years. A business may create many different forms of intellectual property that could qualify under the term "trade secret." A new, more efficient process for manufacturing a product, for instance, may qualify as a trade secret, but so may a customer list, pricing information, market research, and marketing strategies. The choice to protect one's intellectual property via trade secret law may be due to a lack of alternative means of protection or may be a reasoned decision, weighing the benefits and detriments of seeking protection through federal copyright or patent law.

For example, assume that a business has developed a machine that makes door hinges twice as fast and at a greatly reduced cost. The business now faces a choice: it can seek to patent the machine under federal law, or resort to trade secret protection. In order to qualify for a patent, the business would have to overcome a number of hurdles, such as showing that the machine is novel and not obvious. Furthermore, even if granted, the protection offered by patent law only lasts for twenty years from the date of application. After that date, the machine's design is open for anyone to use. On the other hand, trade secret protection is governed by state common law and requires no registration. Such protection has no time limit and the subject matter of what qualifies for protection may be broader than what is available under patent law. Given such a choice, a business may very well decide to forgo the cost of registering a patent and simply rely upon the common law's protection of trade secrets.

While the above example demonstrates a reasoned choice by a business, sometimes the choice is made simply due to the subject matter. Take, for instance, a customer list. Such a collection of information will not qualify for protection under the Copyright Act (as discussed in the previous Chapter). Of course, it is unlikely that the business would want to make this information public anyway, as a customer list is no longer valuable if competitors have access to it. As such, the list is a perfect candidate for trade secret protection.

Taking advantage of trade secret law is not necessarily as easy as it sounds. As we will explore, not everything that a business keeps confidential qualifies as a trade secret, although secrecy is an important element. Furthermore, even when something qualifies as a trade secret, another's subsequent use of the secret may not qualify as a misappropriation. Before delving into the nuances of a trade secret claim, a brief discussion of the relevant sources of law is in order.

Trade secret law draws largely from state common law.[a] Section 757 of the First Restatement of Torts set forth some early principles of trade secret protection. In 1979, the National Conference of Commissioners on Uniform State Laws approved the Uniform Trade Secrets Act ("UTSA"), which was amended in 1985. Since its approval, 46 states and the District of Columbia have adopted it, although uniformity has been weakened somewhat by state legislatures that have "tweaked" the UTSA's standards. A few remaining states (including New York) continue to rely upon the First Restatement,[b] and courts look to the First Restatement for guidance even in states that have adopted the UTSA. The Third Restatement of Unfair Competition has also chosen to address trade secrets, although not as a substitute for the UTSA: "Except as otherwise noted, the principles of trade secret law described in this Restatement are applicable to actions under the [UTSA] as well as to actions at common law. The concept of trade secret as defined in this Section is intended to be consistent with the definition of 'trade secret' in § 1(4) of the [UTSA]." RESTATEMENT (THIRD) OF UNFAIR COMPETITION § 39 cmt. b (1995).

With so many sources, it may be tempting to conclude that there is no uniformity in trade secret principles. As we will explore, however, there are a number of generalities that can be made regarding trade secret law. We describe the various sources of law simply to put you on notice that courts have a number of resources to draw upon in making decisions. As we move through the material on trade secrets, we will reference these various sources so that you can see where they agree and where they differ.

B. ELEMENTS OF A TRADE SECRET CLAIM

There are two basic elements to a trade secret claim: (1) the subject of the suit must qualify as a trade secret, and (2) the secret must be misappropriated. This standard is deceptively simple. In fact, each

---

[a]   We say "largely" because federal law addresses trade secrets in some areas, such as in the international misappropriation of trade secrets and in certain criminal statutes.

[b]   Until recently, Texas was also a holdout. In 2013, the Texas legislature enacted the Texas Uniform Trade Secrets Act, which brought the state into the UTSA fold.

element involves a detailed inquiry into several matters, including the nature of the secret, what steps were taken to protect it, and how it fell into the hands of the alleged misappropriator.

1. QUALIFICATION AS A TRADE SECRET

Comment b to § 757 of the First Restatement of Torts defines a trade secret as "any formula, pattern, device or compilation of information which is used in one's business, and which gives him an opportunity to obtain an advantage over competitors who do not know or use it." It goes on to list six factors which may be used to determine whether something qualifies as a trade secret:

(1) the extent to which the information is known outside of his business;

(2) the extent to which it is known by employees and others involved in his business;

(3) the extent of measures taken by him to guard the secrecy of the information;

(4) the value of the information to him and to his competitors;

(5) the amount of effort or money expended by him in developing the information;

(6) the ease or difficulty with which the information could be properly acquired or duplicated by others.

Both the UTSA and the Third Restatement of Unfair Competition provide similar definitions of a trade secret. The UTSA provides that a trade secret is "information, including a formula, pattern, compilation, program device, method, technique, or process that: (i) derives independent economic value, actual or potential, from not being generally known to, and not being readily ascertained by proper means by, other persons who can obtain economic value from its disclosure or use, and (ii) is the subject of efforts that are reasonable under the circumstances to maintain its secrecy." UNIFORM TRADE SECRETS ACT § 1(4) (1985). The Third Restatement provides perhaps the most succinct definition of all: "A trade secret is any information that can be used in the operation of a business or other enterprise and that is sufficiently valuable and secret to afford an actual or potential economic advantage over others." RESTATEMENT (THIRD) OF UNFAIR COMPETITION § 39 (1995).

Although neither the UTSA nor the Third Restatement of Unfair Competition explicitly utilize the six-factor test of the First Restatement of Torts, the comments to both reference the First Restatement's elements, and courts in jurisdictions that have adopted the UTSA still look to those factors for guidance. The Third Restatement of Unfair

Competition, however, rejects the notion of any set test to establish a trade secret: "It is not possible to state precise criteria for determining the existence of a trade secret. The status of information claimed as a trade secret must be ascertained through a comparative evaluation of all the relevant factors, including the value, secrecy, and definiteness of the information as well as the nature of the defendant's misconduct." RESTATEMENT (THIRD) OF UNFAIR COMPETITION § 39 cmt. d. (1995)

Despite the lack of agreement on a single applicable test for the existence of a trade secret, all of the standards tend to include three common elements: (1) the trade secret must not be known by others; (2) the trade secret must be valuable; and (3) the plaintiff must have taken reasonable steps to maintain the secrecy.

a. Not Known by Others

Benjamin Franklin is widely credited as having said that "three can keep a secret, if two of them are dead." Luckily for trade secret plaintiffs, the law is not nearly as demanding. It may seem unnecessary to state that a trade secret, by its very nature, must not be known by others. The degree of secrecy required, however, can be quite confusing. As comment f to § 39 of the Third Restatement of Unfair Competition notes: "The secrecy, however, need not be absolute. The rule stated in this Section requires only secrecy sufficient to confer an actual or potential economic advantage on one who possesses the information." Revealing information to employees (who are agents of the business) usually does not destroy trade secret protection, but what about revealing the same information to potential customers who may wish to license a process? What about independent contractors who must have access to the trade secret to complete work? To what degree can a secret be divulged and still maintain its status as a secret? Consider these questions as you read the following case.

METALLURGICAL INDUS. INC. V. FOURTEK, INC.

790 F.2d 1195 (5th Cir. 1986)

GEE, CIRCUIT JUDGE:

Today's case requires us to review Texas law on the misappropriation of trade secrets. Having done so, we conclude that the district court misconceived the nature and elements of this cause of action, a misconception that led it to direct a verdict erroneously in favor of appellee Bielefeldt. We also conclude that the court abused its discretion in excluding certain evidence. Accordingly, we affirm in part, reverse in part, and remand the case for a new trial.

I. FACTS OF THE CASE

We commence with a brief description of the scientific process concerned. Tungsten carbide is a metallic compound of great value in certain industrial processes. Combined with the metal cobalt, it forms an extremely hard alloy known as "cemented tungsten carbide"[1] used in oil drills, tools for manufacturing metals, and wear-resistent coatings. Because of its great value, reclamation of carbide from scrap metals is feasible. For a long time, however, the alloy's extreme resistence to machining made reclamation difficult. In the late 1960's and early 1970's, a new solution—known as the zinc recovery process—was devised, a solution based on carbide's reaction with zinc at high temperatures. In the crucibles of a furnace, molten zinc will react with the cobalt in the carbide to cause swelling and cracking of the scrap metal. After this has occurred, the zinc is distilled from the crucible, leaving the scrap in a more brittle state. The carbide is then ground into a powder, usable in new products as an alternative to virgin carbide. This process is the generally recognized modern method of carbide reclamation.

Metallurgical Industries has been in the business of reclaiming carbide since 1967, using the more primitive "cold-stream process." In the mid-1970's, Metallurgical began to consider using the zinc recovery process. In that connection, it came to know appellee Irvin Bielefeldt, a representative of Therm-O-Vac Engineering & Manufacturing Company (Therm-O-Vac). Negotiations led to a contract authorizing Therm-O-Vac to design and construct two zinc recovery furnaces, the purchase order for the first being executed in July 1976.

The furnace arrived in April 1977. Dissatisfied with its performance, Metallurgical modified it extensively. First, it inserted chill plates in one part of the furnace to create a better temperature differential for distilling the zinc. Second, Metallurgical replaced the one large crucible then in place with several smaller crucibles to prevent the zinc from dispersing in the furnace. Third, it replaced segmented heating elements which had caused electrical arcing with unitary graphite heating elements. Last, it installed a filter in the furnace's vacuum-pumps, which zinc particles had continually clogged. These efforts proved successful and the modified furnace soon began commercial operation.

In the market for a second furnace in mid-1978, Metallurgical provided to Consarc, another furnace manufacturer, all its hard-won information about zinc-recovery furnace design. Apparently allowed to watch the first furnace operate, Consarc employees learned of its modifications. Because Consarc proved unwilling or unable to build what Metallurgical wanted, however, the agreement fell through, and Metallurgical returned to Therm-O-Vac for its second furnace. A purchase

---

[1] Hereafter referred to simply as "carbide."

order was signed in January 1979, and the furnace arrived that July. Further modifications again had to be made, but commercial production was allegedly achieved in January 1980.

In 1980, after Therm-O-Vac went bankrupt, Bielefeldt and three other former Therm-O-Vac employees—Norman Montesino, Gary Boehm, and Michael Sarvadi—formed Fourtek, Incorporated. Soon thereafter, Fourtek agreed to build a zinc recovery furnace for appellee Smith International, Incorporated (Smith). The furnace Fourtek provided incorporated the modifications Metallurgical had made in its furnaces; chilling systems, pump filters, multiple crucibles, and unitary heating elements. Smith has been unable to use this furnace commercially, however, because a current shortage of carbide scrap prevents its economically feasible operation.

Metallurgical nevertheless brought a diversity action against Smith, Bielefeldt, Montesino, Boehm, and Sarvadi in November 1981. In its complaint, Metallurgical charged the defendants with misappropriating its trade secrets. Other causes of action, not brought forward on appeal, were breach of contract, interference with business relations, conversion, and unfair competition. Trial began on June 4, 1984, and Metallurgical spent the next ten days presenting its case in chief. During this time, testimony indicated Metallurgical's frequent notices to Bielefeldt that the process was a secret and that the disclosures to him were made in confidence. Another witness recounted meetings in which the modifications were agreed to; Bielefeldt was allegedly unconvinced about the efficacy of these changes and contributed little to the discussion. Metallurgical also presented evidence that it had expended considerable time, effort, and money to modify the furnaces.

Such evidence apparently did not impress the trial court; at the close of Metallurgical's case, it granted the defendants' motions for directed verdicts. Ruling from the bench, the court provided an array of reasons for its order. The principal reason advanced was the court's conclusion that no trade secret is involved. At trial, Metallurgical acknowledged that the individual changes, by themselves, are not secrets; chill plates and pump filters, for example, are well-known. Metallurgical's position instead was that the process, taken as a whole, is a trade secret in the carbide business. The court, however, refused to recognize any protection Texas law provides to a modification process. It also concluded that the information Bielefeldt obtained from working with Metallurgical is too general to be legally protected. Finally, it ruled that "negative know-how"—the knowledge of what not to do—is unprotected. All these findings seem to have coalesced into a general conclusion by the court that this case involves no trade secret.

. . . .

III. DEFINING A "TRADE SECRET"

We begin by reviewing the legal definition of a trade secret. Of course, to qualify as one, the subject matter involved must, in fact, be a secret; "[m]atters of general knowledge in an industry cannot be appropriated by one as his secret." *Wissman v. Boucher,* 240 S.W.2d 278, 280 (1951); *see also Zoecon Industries v. American Stockman Tag Co.,* 713 F.2d 1174, 1179 (5th Cir.1983) ("a customer list of readily ascertainable names and addresses will not be protected as a trade secret"). Smith emphasizes the absence of any secret because the basic zinc recovery process has been publicized in the trade. Acknowledging the publicity of the zinc recovery process, however, we nevertheless conclude that Metallurgical's particular modification efforts can be as yet unknown to the industry. A general description of the zinc recovery process reveals nothing about the benefits unitary heating elements and vacuum pump filters can provide to that procedure. That the scientific principles involved are generally known does not necessarily refute Metallurgical's claim of trade secrets.

Metallurgical, furthermore, presented evidence to back up its claim. One of its main witnesses was Arnold Blum, a consultant very influential in the decisions to modify the furnaces. Blum testified as to his belief that Metallurgical's changes were unknown in the carbide reclamation industry. The evidence also shows Metallurgical's efforts to keep secret its modifications. Blum testified that he noted security measures taken to conceal the furnaces from all but authorized personnel. The furnaces were in areas hidden from public view, while signs warned all about restricted access. Company policy, moreover, required everyone authorized to see the furnace to sign a non-disclosure agreement. These measures constitute evidence probative of the existence of secrets. One's subjective belief of a secret's existence suggests that the secret exists. Security measures, after all, cost money; a manufacturer therefore presumably would not incur these costs if it believed its competitors already knew about the information involved. . . .

Smith argues, however, that Metallurgical's disclosure to other parties vitiated the secrecy required to obtain legal protection. As mentioned before, Metallurgical revealed its information to Consarc Corporation in 1978; it also disclosed information in 1980 to La Floridienne, its European licensee of carbide reclamation technology. Because both these disclosures occurred before Bielefeldt allegedly misappropriated the knowledge of modifications, others knew of the information when the Smith furnace was built. This being so, Smith argues, no trade secret in fact existed.

Although the law requires secrecy, it need not be absolute. Public revelation would, of course, dispel all secrecy, but the holder of a secret need not remain totally silent:

> He may, without losing his protection, communicate it to employees involved in its use. He may likewise communicate it to others pledged to secrecy. . . . Nevertheless, a substantial element of secrecy must exist, so that except by the use of improper means, there would be difficulty in acquiring the information.

Restatement of Torts, § 757 Comment b (1939). We conclude that a holder may divulge his information to a limited extent without destroying its status as a trade secret. To hold otherwise would greatly limit the holder's ability to profit from his secret. If disclosure to others is made to further the holder's economic interests, it should, in appropriate circumstances, be considered a limited disclosure that does not destroy the requisite secrecy. The only question is whether we are dealing with a limited disclosure here. . . .

Looking . . . to the policy considerations involved, we glean two reasons why Metallurgical's disclosures to others are limited and therefore insufficient to extinguish the secrecy Metallurgical's other evidence has suggested. First, the disclosures were not public announcements; rather, Metallurgical divulged its information to only two businesses with whom it was dealing. This case thus differs from *Luccous v. J.C. Kinley Co.,* 376 S.W.2d 336 (Tex.1964), in which the court concluded that the design of a device could not be a trade secret because it had been patented—and thus revealed to all the world—before any dealing between the parties. Second, the disclosures were made to further Metallurgical's economic interests. Disclosure to Consarc was made with the hope that Consarc could build the second furnace. A longstanding agreement gave La Floridienne the right, as a licensee, to the information in exchange for royalty payments. Metallurgical therefore revealed its discoveries as part of business transactions by which it expected to profit.

Metallurgical's case would have been stronger had it also presented evidence of confidential relationships with these two companies, but we are unwilling to regard this failure as conclusively disproving the limited nature of the disclosures. Smith correctly points out that Metallurgical bears the burden of showing the existence of confidential relationships. Contrary to Smith's assertion, however, confidentiality is not a requisite; it is only a factor to consider. Whether a disclosure is limited is an issue the resolution of which depends on weighing many facts. The inferences from those facts, construed favorably to Metallurgical, is that it wished only to profit from its secrets in its business dealings, not to reveal its secrets to the public. We therefore are unpersuaded by Smith's argument.

Existing law, however, emphasizes other requisites for legal recognition of a trade secret. In [*Hyde Corp. v. Huffines*, 314 S.W.2d 763 (Tex. 1958)], a seminal case of trade secret law, Texas adopted the widely-recognized pronouncements of the American Law Institute's Restatement of the Law. The Texas Supreme Court quoted the Restatement's definition of a trade secret:

> A trade secret may consist of any formula, pattern, device, or compilation of information which is used in one's business, and which gives him an opportunity to obtain an advantage over competitors who do not know it. It may be a chemical compound, a process of manufacturing, treating or preserving materials, a pattern for a machine or other device or a list of customers.

Id. at 776, *quoting* Restatement of Torts, § 757 Comment b (1939). From this the criterion of value to the holder of the alleged secret arises, a criterion we have noted before. In *Zoecon Industries*, 713 F.2d at 1179, we concluded that a customer list was a trade secret in part because the list gave to its owner an advantage "over competitors who did not have this information." *See also* [*University Computing Co. v. Lykes-Youngstown Corp.*, 504 F.2d 518, 535 (5th Cir. 1974)] ("[e]vidence was adduced at trial that [the product in question] had unique capabilities and features which made it a valuable competitive product").

Metallurgical met the burden of showing the value of its modifications. Lawrence Lorman, the company's vice president, testified that the zinc recovery process gave Metallurgical an advantage over its two competitors by aiding in the production of the highest quality reclaimed carbide powder. The quality of the powder, in fact, makes it an alternative to the more costly virgin carbide. Lorman testified that customers regarded Metallurgical's zinc reclaimed powder as a better product than that reclaimed by the coldstream process used by others. This evidence clearly indicates that the modifications that led to the commercial operation of the zinc recovery furnace provided a clear advantage over the competition.

Another requisite is the cost of developing the secret device or process. In *Huffines'* companion case, *K & G Oil, Tool & Service Co. v. G & G Fishing Tool Service*, 314 S.W.2d 782, 790 (1958), the court recognized the cost involved in developing the device in question; "[t]he record shows . . . that much work and ingenuity have been applied to the development of a practical and successful device." *See also Zoecon Industries*, 713 F.2d at 1179 ("even if the names and addresses were readily ascertainable through trade journals as the defendants allege, the other information could be compiled only at considerable expense"). No question exists that Metallurgical expended much time, effort, and money to make the necessary changes. It clearly has met the burden of demonstrating the effort involved in making a complex manufacturing process work.

That the cost of devising the secret and the value the secret provides are criteria in the legal formulation of a trade secret shows the equitable underpinnings of this area of the law. It seems only fair that one should be able to keep and enjoy the fruits of his labor. If a businessman has worked hard, has used his imagination, and has taken bold steps to gain an advantage over his competitors, he should be able to profit from his efforts. Because a commercial advantage can vanish once the competition learns of it, the law should protect the businessman's efforts to keep his achievements secret. As is discussed below, this is an area of law in which simple fairness still plays a large role.

We do not say, however, that all these factors need exist in every case. Because each case must turn on its own facts, no standard formula for weighing the factors can be devised. Secrecy is always required, of course, but beyond that there are no universal requirements. In a future case, for example, should the defendant's breach of confidence be particularly egregious, the injured party might still seek redress in court despite the possibility that the subject matter was discovered at little or no cost or that the object of secrecy is not of great value to him. The definition of "trade secret" will therefore be determined by weighing all equitable considerations. It is easy to recognize the possibility of a trade secret here, however, because Metallurgical presented evidence of all three factors discussed above.

Appellees posit two other reasons why Metallurgical's modification process cannot be defined as a trade secret. The first is premised on characterizing the process in question as the installation of various devices all well known to modern manufacturing. This being so, the argument runs, the process itself can be no secret, either. The technologies of chill plates, multiple crucibles, pump filters, and unitary graphite heating elements are all said to be public knowledge. This may well be so, but it does not prevent Metallurgical from seeking legal protection. *Ventura Manufacturing Co. v. Locke,* 454 S.W.2d 431 (Tex.Civ.App.1970), involved a process of finding and cleaning small yet valuable titanium scraps lost during the manufacturing of airplanes. Appellee Locke refined a previously unsuccessful process by implementing new procedures, none of which was innovative. The court nevertheless found that his efforts could constitute a trade secret:

> Obviously, the basic proposition involved in the cleaning of dirty parts by commercial detergents involves no trade secret. Also, the use of production line techniques as such must be considered as a matter of general knowledge. On the other hand, we cannot say that the details of the procedure followed in the cleaning of

these fasteners are matters of general knowledge. To the contrary, the record demonstrates that such details as the types and amounts of chemicals to be used and the times and temperatures for cleaning the fasteners were developed by Ventura through extensive trial and error and at considerable expense.

Id. at 434. Similarly, in [*Sikes v. McGraw Edison Co.,* 665 F.2d 731, 736 (5th Cir. 1982)], we quoted with approval the following passage from *Water Services, Inc. v. Tesco Chemicals,* 410 F.2d 163, 173 (5th Cir.1969).

It is clear that the theory of the Treat-A-Matic was not new to the industry. The court also found that the design was apparent from inspection, and that the system had been sold and advertised without restriction. These findings are supported by the evidence. But these findings are not conclusive. The trade secret here was the application of known techniques and the assembly of available components to create the first successful system in the industry. . . . As the Second Circuit stated in *Imperial Chemical, Ltd. v. National Distillers & Chemical Corp.* (2 Cir.1965) 342 F.2d 737, 742, "a trade secret can exist in a combination of characteristics and components each of which, by itself, is in the public domain, but the unified process, design and operation of which in unique combination, affords a competitive advantage and is a protectible secret."

We believe these cases cogently refute appellees' assertions to the contrary.

The second defense advances a supposed concept of "negative know how" in reliance on one sentence from *Hurst v. Hughes Tool Co.,* 634 F.2d 895 (5th Cir.) *cert. denied* 454 U.S. 829 (1981). The court there ruled that Hughes Tool Company did not really use the information Hurst provided; "Hurst's information, while of some benefit, provided only negative, 'what not to do,' input to Hughes." *Id.* at 899. Both the district court and Smith interpret this to mean that negative know-how cannot constitute a trade secret. The sentence in *Hurst,* however, has nothing to do with whether the information was a trade secret. It is not found in the section of the opinion dealing with the existence of a trade secret; rather, we were determining whether Hughes Tool Company could be found to have used commercially any secrets Hurst conveyed.

Regardless of this misreading, the argument that negative know-how is involved here is unpersuasive. We do not understand how the changes that we have described can be seen as only showing what not to do. Metallurgical's evidence shows that it encountered many problems with the furnaces Therm-O-Vac delivered. Striving to solve these problems, Metallurgical took several steps to modify the furnaces. Installing unitary heating elements, chill plates, multiple crucibles, and pump filters are all "positive" steps resulting from conclusions on what *to do*. These changes allegedly turned unusable furnaces into ones fit for commercial operation. One may say, of course, that these actions result from realizations of what not to do; but so does every human process: the selection of one action at a given moment involves the rejection of every other conceivable one that might have been chosen. Using multiple crucibles, for example, stems from the conclusion that a single large crucible should not be used. This characterization, however, can always describe the invention or modification of a device. Knowing what not to do often leads automatically to knowing what to do. Although we decline to hold that this distinction will always be unavailing, in this case at least we regard the distinction between "positive" and "negative" knowledge to be unintelligible. Because this final claim of Smith is unpersuasive, we conclude that the evidence which was presented at trial could have led a reasonable jury to believe a trade secret existed.

NOTES & QUESTIONS

(1) According to the court, what are the defining characteristics of a trade secret? What factors did the court consider in its analysis?

(2) Metallurgical admitted that there was nothing secret about the changes it made to the furnace. All of its techniques, such as using chill plates, were well known. Why then should its modifications qualify as a trade secret? *See* RESTATEMENT (THIRD) OF UNFAIR COMPETITION § 39 cmt. f (1995) ("Self-evident variations or modifications of known processes, procedures, or methods . . . lack the secrecy necessary for protection as a trade secret."). *But see Penalty Kick Mgmt. Ltd. v. Coca Cola Co.*, 318 F.3d 1284, 1291 (11th Cir. 2003) ("[E]ven if all of the information is publicly available, a unique combination of that information, which adds value to the information, also may qualify as a trade secret.").

(3) Prior to the alleged misappropriation, Metallurgical revealed its modifications to two parties, Consarc Corporation and La Floridienne. The defendants argued that, by revealing the modifications, Metallurgical had disclosed the secret and thus protection should no longer be available. Why was this argument unpersuasive? *See* RESTATEMENT (THIRD) OF UNFAIR COMPETITION § 39 cmt. f (1995). What role did confidentiality agreements (or lack thereof) play in the decision?

(4) Building on the previous question, what if Metallurgical had approached fifteen different parties to build the furnaces with the modifications? Should the number of parties to whom the secret is revealed play a role in the analysis? Would it make a difference if the parties were all potential licensees, such as La Floridienne, instead of manufacturers? *See INEOS Group, Ltd. v. Chevron Phillips Chem. Co.*, 312 S.W.3d 843, 852–54 (Tex. App. 2009) (upholding the grant of a preliminary injunction despite

evidence of disclosure to numerous licensees, some of whom were no longer bound by the terms of a written confidentiality agreement, and concluding that the plaintiff had established that the information was entitled to trade secret protection pending a trial on the merits); *Data General Corp. v. Digital Computer Controls, Inc.*, 297 A.2d 433, 436 (Del. Ch. 1971) (finding that giving design drawings of a computer to requesting customers, subject to an agreement not to disclose, did not defeat a trade secret claim).

(5) Assume that instead of acquiring the modified furnace from Fourtek, Smith acquired the very same furnace from Consarc. Consarc used the knowledge gained from its meetings with Metallurgical to make a furnace with the identical modifications. Should Smith be liable for trade secret misappropriation? What additional facts, if any, would you need to know? *See* RESTATEMENT (THIRD) OF UNFAIR COMPETITION §§ 39 cmt. f, 40, 41(b), 43 (1995); UTSA § 1(2).

(6) The plaintiff in a trade secret case bears the burden of establishing the existence of a trade secret. *See* RESTATEMENT (THIRD) OF UNFAIR COMPETITION § 39 cmt. d (1995) ("A person claiming rights in a trade secret bears the burden of defining the information for which protection is sought with sufficient definiteness to permit a court to apply the criteria for protection described in this Section and to determine the fact of an appropriation."). From a policy standpoint, why should the plaintiff bear this burden? *See id.* § 1 cmt. a.

(7) Given that the plaintiff must describe the secret with some particularity, can you think of practical reasons why a plaintiff might be reluctant to bring a claim for trade secret misappropriation? In answering this question, consider that the *Metallurgical* opinion is public record.

(8) The court briefly addressed "negative know how"—i.e., knowledge of what not to do. Because the court concluded that the dispute involved the alleged misappropriation of affirmative knowledge, the court did not squarely address the negative knowledge concept. It did hint, however, that the defendants were misreading *Hurst*. A common scenario in which negative knowledge becomes an issue is when a former employee goes to work for a competitor and helps the competitor avoid the mistakes made by the previous employer. We will return to this topic later, but for now you should be aware that the concept of imposing liability for the misappropriation of negative knowledge is controversial.

PROBLEM 10.1

Jill has started a high-end sunglasses retail business in Dallas, Texas selling ultra-expensive sunglasses to the rich and famous. As part of her marketing campaign, she accesses the on-line county real estate records of all single-family residences in the counties in and around the Dallas area. These records contain tax appraisal values, from which Jill selects addresses to receive her monthly mail-out advertisement. Keeping with her theme of servicing high-end clientele, she only sends the mailer out to addresses with an appraised value of $1 million or more.

Vincent is a manufacturer of high-end sunglasses. He is very selective about the retailers allowed to sell his products. Jill approaches Vincent to see if she can sell his latest product line. In response, Vincent asks to see Jill's marketing plan to ensure that she is targeting the type of clients that he wants wearing his product. Jill sends him a copy of her marketing plan in an email, including her list of addresses and the home values. In the email, Jill tells Vincent: "Please don't distribute this. I don't want this info falling into the hands of my competitors." Vincent ultimately decides not to use Jill and instead decides to market directly to the addresses on Jill's list. Jill learns of Vincent's plans and sues him for trade secret misappropriation.

Will Jill be able to establish the secrecy element of her claim? What facts will Vincent use to defend himself? *See* RESTATEMENT (THIRD) OF UNFAIR COMPETITION § 39 cmt. f (1995).

b. The Value of the Secret

As noted above, trade secret standards require the secret to be valuable. The fourth and fifth factors of the First Restatement of Torts address the value of the secret. The comments to the Restatement of Unfair Competition similarly observe: "A trade secret must be of sufficient value in the operation of a business or other enterprise to provide an actual or potential economic advantage over others who do not possess the information. The advantage, however, need not be great. It is sufficient if the secret provides an advantage that is more than trivial." RESTATEMENT (THIRD) OF UNFAIR COMPETITION § 39 cmt. e (1995). The UTSA also states that a trade secret "derives independent economic value, actual or potential, from not being generally known to, and not being readily ascertained by proper means by, other persons who can obtain economic value from its disclosure or use."

While each of these sources speaks to the value of the secret, none require the value to be significant. (Indeed, the comment to the Third Restatement requires only that the value be more than "trivial.") Furthermore, the UTSA speaks of value as it relates to "not being generally known" or "readily ascertained." This suggests that it is not enough for a secret to be valuable—its value must also derive from its secrecy.

NOTES & QUESTIONS

(1) Look back at the *Metallurgical* opinion. What role did the value of the secret play in that case? Why is value a useful factor to consider?

PROBLEM 10.2

United Technologies of San Antonio ("UTSA") is an engineering company that manufactures component parts for small electronic devices. During the course of production, one of the engineers accidentally discovers that two adhesive compounds used in the warehouse, when combined, create a super-strong adhesive—stronger than any other adhesive on the market. Unfortunately, the new adhesive is useless to UTSA as it is incompatible with electronics.

UTSA approaches A–1 Adhesives to license its discovery and reveals the combination (UTSA requires the A–1 representatives to sign a confidentiality agreement prior to the revelation). Upon learning the secret of the super-adhesive, A–1 begins making and marketing the product without paying UTSA.

Can UTSA claim trade secret protection for the new super-adhesive? Consider the approaches under the First Restatement of Torts, the Uniform Trade Secrets Act, and the Third Restatement of Unfair Competition. *See* RESTATEMENT (FIRST) OF TORTS § 757 cmt. b (1934); UTSA § 1 cmt.; RESTATEMENT (THIRD) OF UNFAIR COMPETITION § 39 cmt. e (1995); *see also* RESTATEMENT (FIRST) OF TORTS § 759 & cmt. b (1934); RESTATEMENT (THIRD) OF UNFAIR COMPETITION § 39 cmt. d.

c.   Reasonable Steps to Maintain Secrecy

Trade secret standards also consider the plaintiff's efforts to maintain the secrecy of the information. Let's use a fast-food chain's chicken-frying recipe as an example, and let's think of effort as a continuum. On one end, the plaintiff makes absolutely no effort to protect the recipe. It is emailed and shared frequently with employees and customers with no language, contractual or otherwise, that attempts to limit its dissemination. On the other end, the plaintiff takes significant steps to protect the recipe. It is kept in a lockbox at a remote location, and only high-level employees, bound by strict non-disclosure provisions in their employment contracts, can access it. Moreover, any accessing employee must first provide a retinal scan and thumbprint to enter the facility.

Obviously, neither of these extreme positions is likely for something the company values but still uses regularly. The first position leaves the "secret" open to so many people that it probably is no longer a secret. The second position is so strict that the company might not be able to efficiently utilize the recipe. Thus, a reasonable effort to maintain secrecy likely falls in between these two extremes, and courts must consider the issue based upon the facts of each case.

An oft-cited decision in this area is *Rockwell Graphic Systems, Inc. v. DEV Industries, Inc.*, 925 F.2d 174 (7th Cir. 1991). Rockwell was a printing press manufacturer who brought a trade secret misappropriation claim against DEV, a competing printing press manufacturer who had hired former employees of Rockwell. Rockwell alleged that DEV stole secret piece-part drawings which were used to create individual parts for the printing press. Rockwell subcontracted the production of replacement parts for its printing presses to various machine shops, called vendors, and supplied the vendors with the necessary piece-part drawings. DEV argued that the drawings did not qualify as trade secrets, in part because Rockwell did not take steps to maintain their confidentiality.

The district court granted DEV's motion for summary judgment, but the Seventh Circuit reversed. The court explained that Rockwell kept all of its engineering drawings in a vault. Moreover, access to the vault and the building containing the vault was limited to authorized employees who displayed identification (mainly engineers, of whom Rockwell employed two hundred). Rockwell also required employees to sign agreements promising not to disseminate the drawings or disclose their contents, other than as authorized by the company. Although some outsiders were permitted to have copies of the drawings (such as vendors), they too were required to sign confidentiality agreements. Finally, each drawing was stamped with a legend stating that it contained proprietary material. According to the court, the issue of reasonable efforts was more appropriate for a factfinder:

> [O]nly in an extreme case can what is a "reasonable" precaution be determined on a motion for summary judgment, because the answer depends on a balancing of costs and benefits that will vary from case to case and so require estimation and measurement by persons knowledgeable in the particular field of endeavor involved. On the one hand, the more the owner of the trade secret spends on preventing the secret from leaking out, the more he demonstrates that the secret has real value deserving of legal protection, that he really was hurt as a result of the misappropriation of it, and that there really was misappropriation. On the other hand, the more he spends, the higher his costs. The costs can be indirect as well as direct. The more Rockwell restricts access to its drawings, either by its engineers or by the vendors, the harder it will be for either group to do the work expected of it. . . .

> There are contested factual issues here, bearing in mind that what is reasonable is itself a fact for purposes of Rule 56 of the civil rules. Obviously Rockwell took some precautions, both physical . . . and contractual, to maintain the confidentiality of its piece part drawings. Obviously it could have taken more precautions. But at a cost, and the question is whether the additional benefit in security would have exceeded that cost.

Id. at 179–80.

The Third Restatement of Unfair Competition and the UTSA also emphasize the need to examine what is "reasonable under the circumstances to maintain secrecy." UTSA § 1(4)(ii); *see* RESTATEMENT (THIRD) OF UNFAIR COMPETITION § 39 cmt. f (1995). Furthermore, the precautions taken may inform whether the secret is known by others and whether the secret is valuable. *See* RESTATEMENT (THIRD) OF UNFAIR COMPETITION § 39 cmt. f (1995). As you read the next case, consider what efforts were taken to maintain secrecy and how this impacted the other inquiries.

LEARNING CURVE TOYS, INC. V. PLAYWOOD TOYS, INC.
342 F.3d 714 (2d Cir. 2003)

RIPPLE, CIRCUIT JUDGE.

PlayWood Toys, Inc. ("PlayWood") obtained a jury verdict against Learning Curve Toys, Inc. and its representatives, Roy Wilson, Harry Abraham and John Lee (collectively, "Learning Curve"), for misappropriation of a trade secret in a realistic looking and sounding toy railroad track under the Illinois Trade Secrets Act, 765 ILCS 1065/1 *et seq.* The jury awarded PlayWood a royalty of "8% for a license that would have been negotiated [absent the misappropriation] to last for the lifetime of the product." Although there was substantial evidence of misappropriation before the jury, the district court did not enter judgment on the jury's verdict. Instead, it granted judgment as a matter of law in favor of Learning Curve, holding that PlayWood did not have a protectable trade secret in the toy railroad track. PlayWood appealed. For the reasons set forth in the following opinion, we reverse the judgment of the district court and reinstate the jury's verdict. We further remand the case to the district court for a jury trial on exemplary damages and for consideration of PlayWood's request for attorneys' fees.

I

BACKGROUND

A. Facts

In 1992, Robert Clausi and his brother-in-law, Scott Moore, began creating prototypes of wooden toys under the name PlayWood Toys, Inc., a Canadian corporation. Clausi was the sole toy designer and Moore was the sole officer and director of PlayWood. Neither Clausi nor Moore had prior experience in the toy industry, but Clausi had "always been a bit of a doodler and designer," and the two men desired to "create high-quality hard-wood maple toys for the independent toy market." As a newly formed corporation, PlayWood did not own a facility in which it could produce toys. Instead, it worked in conjunction with Mario Borsato, who owned a wood-working facility. Subject to a written confidentiality agreement with PlayWood, Borsato manufactured prototypes for PlayWood based on Clausi's design specifications.

[While attending a toy fair in New York ("Toy Fair") to promote their toys, Clausi and Moore met Learning Curve representatives Roy Wilson, Harry Abraham and John Lee. Wilson identified himself as Learning Curve's toy designer and explained that his company had a license from the Britt Allcroft Company to develop Thomas the Tank Engine & Friends™ ("Thomas") trains and accessories. Wilson, Abraham, and Lee all commented positively on the quality of the prototypes on display and indicated that PlayWood might be a good candidate for a manufacturing contract with Learning Curve. During subsequent discussions with Learning Curve's representatives, Lee indicated that he would like two of his people, Abraham and Wilson, to visit PlayWood in Toronto in order to determine whether the two parties could work out a manufacturing arrangement for some or all of Learning Curve's wooden toys.] The parties ultimately agreed that Abraham and Wilson would visit PlayWood at Borsato's facility on February 18, 1993, four days after the conclusion of the Toy Fair. Clausi spent the next several days after the Toy Fair researching Learning Curve's products and considering how PlayWood could produce Learning Curve's trains and track.

On February 18, 1993, Abraham and Wilson visited PlayWood in Toronto as planned. The meeting began with a tour of Borsato's woodworking facility, where the prototypes on display at the Toy Fair had been made. After the tour, the parties went to the conference room at Borsato's facility. At this point, according to Clausi and Moore, the parties agreed to make their ensuing discussion confidential. Clausi testified:

> After we sat down in the board room, Harry [Abraham of Learning Curve] immediately said: "Look, we're going to disclose confidential information to you guys, and we're going to disclose some designs that Roy [Wilson of Learning Curve] has that are pretty confidential. If Brio [a competitor of Learning Curve] were to get their hands on them, then we wouldn't like that. And we're going to do it under the basis of a confidential understanding."

> And I said: "I also have some things, some ideas on how to produce the track and produce the trains now that I've had a chance to look at them for the last couple of days, and I think they're confidential as well. So if we're both okay with that, we should continue." So we did.

Moore testified to the existence of a similar conversation:

> It was at this point that Harry Abraham told us that they were going to disclose some confidential documents, drawings,

pricing, margins, and asked us if we would keep that information confidential.

* * * * * *

I believe it was Robert [Clausi] who said that, you know, absolutely, we would keep it confidential. In fact, we had some ideas that we felt would be confidential we would be disclosing to them, and would they keep it, you know, confidential? Would they reciprocate? And Harry [Abraham] said: "Absolutely." And then we proceeded to go along with the meeting.

Immediately after the parties agreed to keep their discussion confidential, Wilson, at Abraham's direction, showed Clausi and Moore drawings of various Thomas characters and provided information on the projected volume of each of the products. Clausi testified that he considered the documents disclosed by Learning Curve during the meeting confidential because they included information on products not yet released to the public, as well as Learning Curve's projected volumes, costs and profit margins for various products. After viewing Wilson's various drawings, the parties discussed PlayWood's ideas on how to manufacture Learning Curve's trains. Clausi suggested that they might use a CNC machine, which he defined as a computer numerically controlled drill that carves in three dimensions, to create Learning Curve's trains out of a single piece of wood (as opposed to piecing together separate pieces of wood).

The parties' discussion eventually moved away from train production and focused on track design. Wilson showed Clausi and Moore drawings of Learning Curve's track and provided samples of their current product. At this point, Abraham confided to Clausi and Moore that track had posed "a bit of a problem for Learning Curve." Abraham explained that sales were terrific for Learning Curve's Thomas trains, but that sales were abysmal for its track. Abraham attributed the lack of sales to the fact that Learning Curve's track was virtually identical to that of its competitor, Brio, which had the lion's share of the track market. Because there was "no differentiation" between the two brands of track, Learning Curve's track was not even displayed in many of the toy stores that carried Learning Curve's products. Learning Curve had worked unsuccessfully for several months attempting to differentiate its track from that of Brio.

After detailing the problems with Learning Curve's existing track, Abraham inquired of Clausi whether "there was a way to differentiate" its track from Brio's track. Clausi immediately responded that he "had had a chance to look at the track and get a feel for it [over] the last few days" and that his "thoughts were that if the track were more realistic and more functional, that kids would enjoy playing with it more and it would give the retailer a reason to carry the product, especially if it looked different than the Brio track." Clausi further explained that, if the track "made noise and [ ] looked like real train tracks, that the stores wouldn't have any problem, and the Thomas the Tank line, product line would have [ ] its own different track" and could "effectively compete with Brio." Abraham and Wilson indicated that they were "intrigued" by Clausi's idea and asked him what he meant by "making noise."

Clausi decided to show Abraham and Wilson exactly what he meant. Clausi took a piece of Learning Curve's existing track from the table, drew some lines across the track (about every three-quarters of an inch), and stated: "We can go ahead and machine grooves right across the upper section . . . , which would look like railway tracks, and down below machine little indentations as well so that it would look more like or sound more like real track. You would roll along and bumpity-bumpity as you go along." Clausi then called Borsato into the conference room and asked him to cut grooves into the wood "about a quarter of an inch deep from the top surface." Borsato left the room, complied with Clausi's request, and returned with the cut track three or four minutes later. Clausi ran a train back and forth over the cut piece of track. The track looked more realistic than before, but it did not make noise because the grooves were not deep enough. Accordingly, Clausi instructed Borsato to cut the grooves "just a little bit deeper so that they go through the rails." Borsato complied with Clausi's request once again and returned a few minutes later with the cut piece of track. Clausi proceeded to run a train back and forth over the track. This time the track made a "clickety-clack" sound, but the train did not run smoothly over the track because the grooves were cut "a little bit too deep." Based on the sound produced by the track, Clausi told Abraham and Moore that if PlayWood procured a contract with Learning Curve to produce the track, they could call it "Clickety-Clack Track."

Both Abraham and Wilson indicated that Clausi's concept of cutting grooves into the track to produce a clacking sound was a novel concept. Thereafter, Wilson and Clausi began to discuss how they could improve the idea to make the train run more smoothly on the track, but Abraham interrupted them and stated: "No, focus. You guys have to get the contract for the basic product first, and then we can talk about new products, because . . . it takes [our licensor] a long time to approve new products and new designs."

The meeting ended shortly thereafter without further discussion about Clausi's concept for the noise-producing track. Before he left, Wilson asked Clausi if he could take the piece of track that Borsato had cut with him while the parties continued their discussions. Clausi gave Wilson the piece of track without hesitation. The piece of track was the only item that Abraham and Wilson took from the meeting. Clausi and

Moore did not ask Wilson for a receipt for the cut track, nor did they seek a written confidentiality agreement to protect PlayWood's alleged trade secret. After the meeting, Clausi amended PlayWood's confidentiality agreement with Borsato to ensure that materials discussed during the meeting would remain confidential. Clausi also stamped many of the documents that he received from Learning Curve during the meeting as confidential because they included information on products not yet released to the public. PlayWood never disclosed the contents of Learning Curve's documents to anyone.

[During 1993, PlayWood and Learning Curve met on multiple occasions to discuss the possibility of PlayWood manufacturing Learning Curve's Thomas products. Twice Learning Curve requested that PlayWood submit a manufacturing proposal for the Thomas products. Learning Curve rejected both of PlayWood's proposals, first claiming that its licensor wanted the Thomas products to be made in the United States, and then later stating that its new business partner had decided to manufacture the product in China. Clausi and Moore continued to work on PlayWood's toy concepts throughout 1994.] During this time, Clausi and Moore made no attempt to license or sell the concept to other toy companies because they believed that PlayWood still had "an opportunity to get in the door" with Learning Curve if they could perfect the concept and also because they believed that they were bound by a confidentiality agreement.

In December of 1994, while shopping for additional track with which to experiment, Moore discovered that Learning Curve was selling noise-producing track under the name "Clickety-Clack Track." Like the piece of track that Clausi had Borsato cut during PlayWood's February 18, 1993, meeting with Learning Curve, Clickety-Clack Track™ has parallel grooves cut into the wood, which cause a "clacking" sound as train wheels roll over the grooves. Learning Curve was promoting the new track as

> the first significant innovation in track design since the inception of wooden train systems. . . . It is quite simply the newest and most exciting development to come along recently in the wooden train industry, and it's sure to cause a sensation in the marketplace. . . . [I]t brings that sound and feel of the real thing to a child's world of make-believe without bells, whistles, electronic sound chips or moving parts.

Moore was "stunned" when he saw the track because he believed that Learning Curve had stolen PlayWood's concept. He testified: "This was our idea. This is what we've been working on even up to that day to go back to [Learning Curve] as an opportunity to get in the door, and there it is on the shelf." Moore purchased a package of Clickety-Clack Track™ and showed it to Clausi. Clausi testified that he was disappointed when he saw the track because he believed that Learning Curve had taken PlayWood's name and design concept "almost exactly as per [their] conversation" on February 18, 1993.

PlayWood promptly wrote a cease and desist letter to Learning Curve. The letter accused Learning Curve of stealing PlayWood's concept for the noise-producing track that it disclosed to Learning Curve "in confidence in the context of a manufacturing proposal." Learning Curve responded by seeking a declaratory judgment that it owned the concept.

Previously, on March 16, 1994, Learning Curve had applied for a patent on the noise-producing track. The patent, which was obtained on October 3, 1995, claims the addition of parallel impressions or grooves in the rails, which cause a "clacking" sound to be emitted as train wheels roll over them. The patent identifies Roy Wilson of Learning Curve as the inventor.

Clickety-Clack Track™ provided an enormous boost to Learning Curve's sales. Learning Curve had $20 million in track sales by the first quarter of 2000, and $40 million for combined track and accessory sales.

B. District Court Proceedings

Learning Curve responded to PlayWood's cease and desist letter by seeking a declaratory judgment that it owned the concept for noise-producing toy railroad track, as embodied in Clickety-Clack Track.™ PlayWood counterclaimed against Learning Curve, as well as its representatives, Roy Wilson, Harry Abraham and John Lee. PlayWood asserted that it owned the concept and that Learning Curve had misappropriated its trade secret. Learning Curve voluntarily dismissed its complaint for declaratory relief, and PlayWood's claim for trade secret misappropriation proceeded to trial. The jury returned a verdict in favor of PlayWood. The trial court declined to enter judgment on the verdict and instead asked the parties to brief Learning Curve's Rule 50 motion on the issue of whether PlayWood had a protectable trade secret under the Illinois Trade Secrets Act, 765 ILCS 1065/1 *et seq.* The district court granted Learning Curve's motion and entered judgment in its favor on the ground that PlayWood presented insufficient evidence of a trade secret. Specifically, the court determined that PlayWood did not have a trade secret in its concept for noise-producing toy railroad track under Illinois law because: (1) PlayWood did not demonstrate that its concept was unknown in the industry; (2) PlayWood's concept could have been easily acquired or duplicated through proper means; (3) PlayWood failed to guard the secrecy of its concept; (4) PlayWood's concept had no economic value; and (5) PlayWood expended no time, effort or money to develop the concept.

II

DISCUSSION

A. Trade Secret Status

. . . .

The parties agree that their dispute is governed by the Illinois Trade Secrets Act ("Act"), 765 ILCS 1065/1 *et seq*. To prevail on a claim for misappropriation of a trade secret under the Act, the plaintiff must demonstrate that the information at issue was a trade secret, that it was misappropriated and that it was used in the defendant's business. The issue currently before us is whether there was legally sufficient evidence for the jury to find that PlayWood had a trade secret in its concept for the noise-producing toy railroad track that it revealed to Learning Curve on February 18, 1993.

The Act defines a trade secret as:

[I]nformation, including but not limited to, technical or non-technical data, a formula, pattern, compilation, program, device, method, technique, drawing, process, financial data, or list of actual or potential customers or suppliers, that:

(1) is sufficiently secret to derive economic value, actual or potential, from not being generally known to other persons who can obtain economic value from its disclosure or use; and

(2) is the subject of efforts that are reasonable under the circumstances to maintain its secrecy or confidentiality.

765 ILCS 1065/2(d). Both of the Act's statutory requirements focus fundamentally on the secrecy of the information sought to be protected. However, the requirements emphasize different aspects of secrecy. The first requirement, that the information be sufficiently secret to impart economic value because of its relative secrecy, "precludes trade secret protection for information generally known or understood within an industry even if not to the public at large." *Pope v. Alberto-Culver Co.*, 694 N.E.2d 615, 617 (Ill. App. 1998). The second requirement, that the plaintiff take reasonable efforts to maintain the secrecy of the information, prevents a plaintiff who takes no affirmative measures to prevent others from using its proprietary information from obtaining trade secret protection. *See Jackson v. Hammer*, 653 N.E.2d 809, 816 (Ill. App. 1995) ("[T]he Act requires a plaintiff to take 'affirmative measures' to prevent others from using information.").

Although the Act explicitly defines a trade secret in terms of these two requirements, Illinois courts frequently refer to six common law factors (which are derived from § 757 of the Restatement (First) of Torts) in determining whether a trade secret exists: (1) the extent to which the information is known outside of the plaintiff's business; (2) the extent to which the information is known by employees and others involved in the plaintiff's business; (3) the extent of measures taken by the plaintiff to guard the secrecy of the information; (4) the value of the information to the plaintiff's business and to its competitors; (5) the amount of time, effort and money expended by the plaintiff in developing the information; and (6) the ease or difficulty with which the information could be properly acquired or duplicated by others. In this respect, Illinois law is compatible with the approach in other states. Courts from other jurisdictions, as well as legal scholars, have noted that the Restatement factors are not to be applied as a list of requisite elements.

The existence of a trade secret ordinarily is a question of fact. As aptly observed by our colleagues on the Fifth Circuit, a trade secret "is one of the most elusive and difficult concepts in the law to define." *Lear Siegler, Inc. v. Ark-Ell Springs, Inc.*, 569 F.2d 286, 288 (5th Cir.1978). In many cases, the existence of a trade secret is not obvious; it requires an ad hoc evaluation of all the surrounding circumstances. For this reason, the question of whether certain information constitutes a trade secret ordinarily is best "resolved by a fact finder after full presentation of evidence from each side." *Id.* at 289. We do not believe that the district court was sufficiently mindful of these principles. The district court, in effect, treated the Restatement factors as requisite elements and substituted its judgment for that of the jury. PlayWood presented sufficient evidence for the jury reasonably to conclude that the Restatement factors weighed in PlayWood's favor.

1. Extent to which PlayWood's concept for noise-producing toy railroad track was known outside of PlayWood's business

PlayWood presented substantial evidence from which the jury could have determined that PlayWood's concept for noise-producing toy railroad track was not generally known outside of Playwood's business. It was undisputed at trial that no similar track was on the market until Learning Curve launched Clickety-Clack Track™ in late 1994, more than a year after PlayWood first conceived of the concept. Of course, as Learning Curve correctly points out, "[m]erely being the first or only one to use particular information does not in and of itself transform otherwise general knowledge into a trade secret." [*George S. May Int'l Co. v. Int'l Profit Assocs.*, 628 N.E.2d 647, 654 (Ill. App. Ct. 1993)]. "If it did, the first person to use the information, no matter how ordinary or well known, would be able to appropriate it to his own use under the guise of a trade secret." [*Serv. Ctrs. of Chicago, Inc. v. Minogue*, 535 N.E.2d 1132, 1137 (Ill. App. Ct. 1989)]. However, in this case, there was additional evidence from which the jury could have determined that PlayWood's concept was not generally known within the industry.

First, there was substantial testimony that Learning Curve had attempted to differentiate its track from that of its competitors for several months, but that it had been unable to do so successfully.

Furthermore, PlayWood's expert witness, Michael Kennedy, testified that PlayWood's concept, as embodied in Clickety-Clack Track™ was unique and permitted "its seller to differentiate itself from a host of competitors who [were] making a generic product." Kennedy explained that the look, sound and feel of the track made it distinct from other toy railroad track: "[W]hen a child runs a train across this track, he can feel it hitting those little impressions. And when you're talking about young children[,] having the idea that they can see something that they couldn't see before, feel something that they couldn't feel before, hear something that they couldn't hear before, that is what differentiates this toy from its other competitors."

Finally, PlayWood presented evidence that Learning Curve sought and obtained a patent on the noise-producing track. It goes without saying that the requirements for patent and trade secret protection are not synonymous. Unlike "a patentable invention, a trade secret need not be novel or unobvious." 2 Rudolf Callmann, *The Law of Unfair Competition, Trademarks and Monopolies* § 14.15, at 14–124 (4th ed.2003). "The idea need not be complicated; it may be intrinsically simple and nevertheless qualify as a secret, unless it is common knowledge and, therefore, within the public domain." *Forest Labs., Inc. v. Pillsbury Co.,* 452 F.2d 621, 624 (7th Cir.1971) (internal quotation marks omitted). However, it is commonly understood that "[i]f an invention has sufficient novelty to be entitled to patent protection, it may be said a *fortiori* to be entitled to protection as a trade secret." 1 Roger M. Milgrim, *Milgrim on Trade Secrets* § 1.08[1], at 1–353 (2002) (internal footnotes omitted). In light of this evidence, we cannot accept Learning Curve's argument that no rational jury could have found that PlayWood's concept was unknown outside of its business.

. . . .

3. Measures taken by PlayWood to guard the secrecy of its concept

There also was sufficient evidence for the jury to determine that PlayWood took reasonable precautions to guard the secrecy of its concept. The Act requires the trade secret owner to take actions that are "reasonable under the circumstances to maintain [the] secrecy or confidentiality" of its trade secret; it does not require perfection. 765 ILCS 1065/2(d)(2). Whether the measures taken by a trade secret owner are sufficient to satisfy the Act's reasonableness standard ordinarily is a question of fact for the jury. Indeed, we previously have recognized that "only in an extreme case can what is a 'reasonable' precaution be determined [as a matter of law], because the answer depends on a balancing of costs and benefits that will vary from case to case." *Rockwell Graphic Sys., Inc. v. DEV Indus., Inc.,* 925 F.2d 174, 179 (7th Cir.1991).

Here, the jury was instructed that it must find "by a preponderance of the evidence that PlayWood's trade secrets were given to Learning Curve as a result of a confidential relationship between the parties." By returning a verdict in favor of PlayWood, the jury necessarily found that Learning Curve was bound to PlayWood by a pledge of confidentiality. The jury's determination is amply supported by the evidence. Both Clausi and Moore testified that they entered into an oral confidentiality agreement with Abraham and Wilson before beginning their discussion on February 18, 1993. . . . In addition to this testimony, the jury heard that Learning Curve had disclosed substantial information to PlayWood during the February 18th meeting, including projected volumes, costs and profit margins for various products, as well as drawings for toys not yet released to the public. The jury could have inferred that Learning Curve would not have disclosed such information in the absence of a confidentiality agreement. Finally, the jury also heard (from several of Learning Curve's former business associates) that Learning Curve routinely entered into oral confidentiality agreements like the one with PlayWood.

PlayWood might have done more to protect its secret. As Learning Curve points out, PlayWood gave its only prototype of the noise-producing track to Wilson without first obtaining a receipt or written confidentiality agreement from Learning Curve—a decision that proved unwise in hindsight. Nevertheless, we believe that the jury was entitled to conclude that PlayWood's reliance on the oral confidentiality agreement was reasonable under the circumstances of this case.[4] First, it is well established that "[t]he formation of a confidential relationship imposes upon the disclosee the duty to maintain the information received in the utmost secrecy" and that "the unprivileged use or disclosure of another's trade secret becomes the basis for an action in tort." *Burten v. Milton Bradley Co.,* 763 F.2d 461, 463 (1st Cir.1985). Second, both Clausi and Moore testified that they believed PlayWood had a realistic chance to "get in the door" with Learning Curve and to produce the concept as part of Learning Curve's line of Thomas products. Clausi and Moore did not anticipate that Learning Curve would violate the oral confidentiality agreement and utilize PlayWood's concept without permission; rather, they believed in good faith that they "were going to do business one day again with Learning Curve with respect to the design concept." Finally,

---

[4] We iterate that the proper inquiry is not whether, in our independent judgment, we believe that PlayWood took reasonable precautions to maintain the secrecy of its concept; rather, the issue is whether PlayWood's "failure to do more was so plain a breach of the obligation of a trade secret owner to make reasonable efforts to maintain secrecy as to justify" overturning the jury verdict in its favor. *Rockwell,* 925 F.2d at 177.

we believe that, as part of the reasonableness inquiry, the jury could have considered the size and sophistication of the parties, as well as the relevant industry. Both PlayWood and Learning Curve were small toy companies, and PlayWood was the smaller and less experienced of the two. Viewing the evidence in the light most favorable to PlayWood, as we must, we conclude that there was sufficient evidence for the jury to determine that PlayWood took reasonable measures to protect the secrecy of its concept.

4. Value of the concept to PlayWood and to its competitors

There was substantial evidence from which the jury could have determined that PlayWood's concept had value both to PlayWood and to its competitors. It was undisputed at trial that Learning Curve's sales skyrocketed after it began to sell Clickety-Clack Track.™ In addition, PlayWood's expert witness, Michael Kennedy, testified that PlayWood's concept for noise-producing track had tremendous value. Kennedy testified that the "cross-cuts and changes in the [track's] surface" imparted value to its seller by causing the track to "look different, feel different and sound different than generic track." Kennedy further testified that, in his opinion, the track would have commanded a premium royalty under a negotiated license agreement because the "invention allows its seller to differentiate itself from a host of competitors who are making a generic product with whom it is competing in a way that is proprietary and exclusive, and it gives [the seller] a significant edge over [its] competition."

. . . .

It is irrelevant under Illinois law that PlayWood did not actually use the concept in its business. "[T]he proper criterion is not 'actual use' but whether the trade secret is 'of value' to the company." *Syntex Ophthalmics, Inc. v. Tsuetaki,* 701 F.2d 677, 683 (7th Cir.1983).[6] Kennedy's testimony was more than sufficient to permit the jury to conclude that the concept was "of value" to PlayWood. It is equally irrelevant that PlayWood did not seek to patent its concept. So long as the concept remains a secret, *i.e.,* outside of the public domain, there is no need for patent protection. Professor Milgrim makes this point well: "Since every inventor has the right to keep his invention secret, one who has made a patentable invention has the option to maintain it in secrecy, relying upon protection accorded to a trade secret rather than upon the rights which accrue by a patent grant." 1 Roger M. Milgrim, *Milgrim on Trade Secrets* § 1.08[1], at 1–353 (2002). It was up to PlayWood, not the

---

[6]   Both the Uniform Trade Secrets Act and the Restatement (Third) of Unfair Competition expressly reject prior use by the person asserting rights in the information as a prerequisite to trade secret protection.

district court, to determine when and how the concept should have been disclosed to the public.

5. Amount of time, effort and money expended by PlayWood in developing its concept

PlayWood expended very little time and money developing its concept; by Clausi's own account, the cost to PlayWood was less than one dollar and the time spent was less than one-half hour. The district court determined that "[s]uch an insignificant investment is . . . insufficient as a matter of Illinois law to establish the status of a 'trade secret.' " We believe that the district court gave too much weight to the time, effort and expense of developing the track.[7]

Although Illinois courts commonly look to the Restatement factors for guidance in determining whether a trade secret exists, as we have noted earlier, the requisite statutory inquiries under Illinois law are (1) whether the information "is sufficiently secret to derive economic value, actual or potential, from not being generally known to other persons who can obtain economic value from its disclosure or use;" and (2) whether the information "is the subject of efforts that are reasonable under the circumstances to maintain its secrecy or confidentiality." 765 ILCS 1065/2(d). A significant expenditure of time and/or money in the production of information may provide evidence of value, which is relevant to the first inquiry above. However, we do not understand Illinois law to require such an expenditure in all cases.

As pointed out by the district court, several Illinois cases have emphasized the importance of developmental costs. However, notably, none of those cases concerned the sort of innovative and creative concept that we have in this case. Indeed, several of the cases in Illinois that emphasize developmental costs concern compilations of data, such as customer lists.[8] In that context, it makes sense to require the expenditure of significant time and money because there is nothing original or creative about the alleged trade secret. Given enough time and money, we presume that the plaintiff's competitors could compile a similar list.

---

[7] Professor Milgrim, for one, rejects any per se requirement of developmental costs:

Where cost is referred to it is almost always invariably incidental to other, basic definitional elements, such as secrecy. Since it is established that a trade secret can be discovered fortuitously (ergo, without costly development), or result purely from the exercise of creative facilities, it would appear inconsistent to consider expense of development of a trade secret as an operative substantive element.

See 1 Roger M. Milgrim, *Milgrim on Trade Secrets* § 1.02[2], at 1–146 & 1–150 (2002) (internal footnotes omitted).

[8] *See, e.g., Delta Med. Sys. v. Mid-America Med. Sys., Inc.,* 772 N.E.2d 768, 781 (Ill. App. 2002) ("Delta presented no testimony at the hearing as to the amount of effort expended in acquiring its customer list."); *Strata Mktg., Inc. v. Murphy,* 740 N.E.2d 1166, 1177 (Ill. App. 2000) ("Strata's customer lists, which it alleged take considerable effort, time, and money to compile, could be deemed a trade secret.").

Here, by contrast, we are dealing with a new toy design that has been promoted as "the first significant innovation in track design since the inception of wooden train systems." Toy designers, like many artistic individuals, have intuitive flashes of creativity. Often, that intuitive flash is, in reality, the product of earlier thought and practice in an artistic craft. We fail to see how the value of PlayWood's concept would differ in any respect had Clausi spent several months and several thousand dollars creating the noise-producing track. Accordingly, we conclude that PlayWood's lack of proof on this factor does not preclude the existence of a trade secret.

6. Ease or difficulty with which PlayWood's concept could have been properly acquired or duplicated by others

Finally, we also believe that there was sufficient evidence for the jury to determine that PlayWood's concept could not have been easily acquired or duplicated through proper means. PlayWood's expert witness, Michael Kennedy, testified: "This is a fairly simple product if you look at it. But the truth is that because it delivers feeling and sound as well as appearance, it isn't so simple as it first appears. It's a little more elegant, actually, than you might think." In addition to Kennedy's testimony, the jury heard that Learning Curve had spent months attempting to differentiate its track from Brio's before Clausi disclosed PlayWood's concept of noise-producing track. From this evidence, the jury could have inferred that, if PlayWood's concept really was obvious, Learning Curve would have thought of it earlier.

Despite this evidence, the district court concluded that PlayWood's concept was not a trade secret because it could have been easily duplicated, stating that "[h]ad PlayWood succeeded in producing and marketing [the] notched track, the appearance of the track product itself would have fully revealed the concept PlayWood now claims as a secret." Of course, the district court was correct in one sense; PlayWood's own expert recognized that, in the absence of patent or copyright protection, the track could have been reverse engineered just by looking at it. However, the district court failed to appreciate the fact that PlayWood's concept was not publicly available. As Professor Milgrim states: "A potent distinction exists between a trade secret which *will be* disclosed if and when the product in which it is embodied is placed on sale, and a 'trade secret' embodied in a product which has been placed on sale, which product admits of discovery of the 'secret' upon inspection, analysis, or reverse engineering." 1 Roger M. Milgrim, *Milgrim on Trade Secrets* § 1.05[4], at 1–228 (2002). "Until disclosed by sale the trade secret should be entitled to protection." *Id.* Reverse engineering can defeat a trade secret claim, but only if the product could have been properly acquired by others, as is the case when the product is publicly sold. Here, PlayWood disclosed its concept to Learning Curve (and Learning Curve alone) in the context of a confidential relationship; Learning Curve had no legal authority to reverse engineer the prototype that it received in confidence. *See Laff v. John O. Butler Co.,* 381 N.E.2d 423, 433 (Ill. App. 1978) ("[A] trade secret is open to anyone, not bound by a confidential relationship or a contract with the secret's owner, who can discover the secret through lawful means."). Accordingly, we must conclude that the jury was entitled to determine that PlayWood's concept could not easily have been acquired or duplicated through proper means.

. . . .

Conclusion

For the foregoing reasons, the judgment of the district court is reversed, and the jury's verdict is reinstated. The case is remanded to the district court for a jury trial on exemplary damages and for consideration of attorneys' fees by the court. PlayWood may recover its costs in this court.

NOTES & QUESTIONS

(1)   Illinois has adopted the UTSA. Compare Illinois' version, quoted in the opinion, to the UTSA itself. Do you see any differences between the two versions? If so, are the differences significant?

(2)   Despite adopting its own version of the UTSA, the court looked to the six-factor test from the First Restatement of Torts. What impact did these factors have on the court's analysis?

(3)   We have noted that, in order to obtain trade secret protection, the secret must not be known by others. What facts did the court consider in making this determination? What role did the novelty of the concept play in the decision? *See* RESTATEMENT (THIRD) OF UNFAIR COMPETITION § 39, cmt. f.

(4)   The efforts taken to maintain secrecy require a factual inquiry into the circumstances. In perhaps a rather extreme example of what is reasonable under the circumstances, the Federal Circuit Court of Appeals held that a prisoner's invention (a device used to cut Kevlar), which he built in his cell was protected as a trade secret. *Lariscey v. United States,* 949 F.2d 1137, 1142–45 (Fed. Cir. 1991), *on* reh'g, 981 F.2d 1244 (Fed. Cir. 1993) (affirming by equally divided court). The prisoner, Earl Lariscey, was part of a federal prisoner work program working for UNICOR, a military manufacturer. Lariscey became aware of his employer's failed attempts to come-up with an affordable method of cutting Kevlar. Lariscey revealed his device to his employers but also expressed his intent to patent the device and his desire to profit from his invention. UNICOR subsequently replicated and used his invention without compensating him, and Lariscey brought suit. The government/employer defended that Lariscey's invention was no longer a trade secret because he revealed the device to others and could have made greater efforts to protect the secret, such as by only reducing the device to

writing rather than building it. The court of appeals rejected these arguments, stating:

> The construction in the prison environment and the demonstration of a working model by Lariscey to his employer and potential customer, under the circumstances that here prevailed, was not a dedication or waiver of property rights. It was not a dedication of the information and an abandonment of ownership. Even without giving weight to the exigencies of the prison environment insofar as it affected Lariscey's negotiating posture, the precautions to protect this information from public disclosure were reasonable under the circumstances that prevailed. When property rights are at issue, the common law weighs heavily against forfeiture by implication.

Id. at 1143.

Recall that the court held that Clausi and Moore had taken appropriate steps to maintain the secrecy of their design (or at least enough to uphold the jury's verdict). What steps did they take? Do you agree that they made reasonable efforts to maintain secrecy?

(5) If you were advising Clausi and Moore, would you advise them to do anything differently? Consider the following excerpt which describes the steps Coca-Cola takes to protect its secret formula for Coke, known as "Merchandise 7X":

> The written version of the secret formula is kept in a security vault at the Trust Company Bank in Atlanta, and that vault can only be opened by a resolution from the Company's Board of Directors. It is the Company's policy that only two persons in the Company shall know the formula at any one time, and that only those persons may oversee the actual preparation of Merchandise 7X. The Company refuses to allow the identity of those persons to be disclosed or to allow those persons to fly on the same airplane at the same time. The same precautions are taken regarding the secret formulae of the Company's other cola drinks—diet Coke, caffeine free diet Coke, TAB, caffeine free TAB, and caffeine free Coca-Cola. The secret formula for each drink is only known to three or four persons in the Company.

Coca-Cola Bottling Co. v. The Coca-Cola Co., 107 F.R.D. 288, 294 (D. Del. 1985). Should PlayWood have gone to such lengths to protect its prototype? What role does the value of the secret play in the reasonableness of the efforts? For instance, should PlayWood put the same amount of effort into protecting a list of potential licensees as it does into protecting its prototypes?

(6) The court also considered the value of the trade secret. What evidence of value was presented? In what way did the value analysis overlap with the secrecy of the design? *See* RESTATEMENT (THIRD) OF UNFAIR COMPETITION § 39, cmt. e.

(7)   Look back at the definition of a trade secret provided in § 39 of the Third Restatement of Unfair Competition. Compare it to the definitions found in § 757 comment b of the First Restatement of Torts and § 1(4) of the UTSA. Notice that the Third Restatement does not explicitly require reasonable efforts to maintain secrecy. It explains that "[p]recautions taken to maintain the secrecy of information are relevant in determining whether the information qualifies for protection as a trade secret," but it also states the following:

> Whether viewed as an independent requirement or as an element to be considered with other factors relevant to the existence of a trade secret, the owner's precautions should be evaluated in light of the other available evidence relating to the value and secrecy of the information. Thus, if the value and secrecy of the information are clear, evidence of specific precautions taken by the trade secret owner may be unnecessary.

RESTATEMENT (THIRD) OF UNFAIR COMPETITION § 39 cmt. g (1995).

Why might the Third Restatement have chosen to address this issue differently than the First Restatement of Torts and the UTSA? What purpose is served by having an independent inquiry into the owner's efforts to maintain secrecy? *See* RESTATEMENT (THIRD) OF UNFAIR COMPETITION § 39 cmt. g (1995) (noting that "[t]he precautions taken by the trade secret owner are also relevant to other potential issues in an action for the appropriation of a trade secret."). Do you agree with the Third Restatement's comment that if the value and secrecy of the information are clear, evidence of reasonable efforts to maintain secrecy may be unnecessary?

(8)   In *Learning Curve*, the district court observed that the design for the Clickety-Clack Track could have been easily replicated once the product was marketed. Why was that observation not fatal to the plaintiff's case?

(9)   The acquisition of a patent for the Clickety-Clack Track would defeat the secrecy requirement. The patent application must describe the invention in some detail, and the issued patents are available to the public. Does this notion of public disclosure suggest a defense for a trade secret misappropriator—i.e., publicly disclose the misappropriated secret, and then defend on the ground that the secret is now known by others? As you might expect, courts are not very sympathetic to this claim. In *Syntex Ophthalmics, Inc. v. Tsuetaki*, 701 F.2d 677 (7th Cir. 1983), a Syntex employee, Novicky, went to work for a competitor, Fused Kontacts of Chicago, Inc. Four days after leaving Syntex, Novicky prepared a patent disclosure statement revealing Syntex trade secrets. Syntex sued Novicky and his new employer for trade secret misappropriation. On appeal, the defendants argued that the disclosure statement defeated the secrecy element of the claim. The court rejected the argument:

> Appellants' second argument is that Novicky's wrongful patent application of Syntex's trade secrets deprives Syntex of its trade

secret protection and permits appellants to use those secrets. In support of their argument, they cite Sears *Roebuck & Co. v. Stiffel Co.*, 376 U.S. 225 (1964), and *Compco Corp. v. Day-Brite Lighting, Inc.*, 376 U.S. 234 (1964), which stand for the proposition that an owner of a trade secret who voluntarily discloses his trade secret makes an election to seek federal patent protection. That situation, though, is not present in the instant case. Here the holder of the trade secret did not make an election to obtain a patent, but instead it was appellants who had misappropriated the trade secrets and secured the patent. In 1936 we held in *Shellmar Products Co. v. Allen-Qually Co.*, 87 F.2d 104 (7th Cir.1936), that a wrongdoer who has made an unlawful disclosure of another's trade secrets cannot assert that publication to escape the protection of trade secret law. We believe that principle to be equally vital today. To hold otherwise in the instant case would be to permit appellants to profit from their own wrong.

Syntex, 701 F.2d at 683.

2.   MISAPPROPRIATION

As mentioned, a trade secret claim has two basic elements: (1) the subject of the suit must qualify as a trade secret, and (2) the trade secret must be misappropriated. A plaintiff can establish misappropriation by showing that the secret was acquired by "improper means," or by showing that the secret was disclosed or used in an unauthorized manner. *See* RESTATEMENT (THIRD) OF UNFAIR COMPETITION § 40 (1995); UTSA § 1(2). The First Restatement of Torts did not make the acquisition of a trade secret through improper means actionable without an accompanying use or disclosure; however, courts still granted relief if use or disclosure was likely.

a.   Acquisition by Improper Means

Section 40 of the Third Restatement of Unfair Competition makes actionable the acquisition of a trade secret by "means that are improper." What exactly are improper means? Section 43 provides some guidance:

> "Improper" means of acquiring another's trade secret under the rule stated in § 40 include theft, fraud, unauthorized interception of communications, inducement of or knowing participation in a breach of confidence, and other means either wrongful in themselves or wrongful under the circumstances of the case. Independent discovery and analysis of publicly available products or information are not improper means of acquisition.

The UTSA and comments to § 757 of the First Restatement of Torts also list similar activities as improper (adding espionage, wire-tapping, and eavesdropping). Criminal or independently tortious conduct will likely fall into the improper definition as well. The acquisition of a trade secret can be improper, however, even if the means of acquisition are not independently wrongful. As you read the next case, consider what was improper about the means utilized by the defendants.

E.I. DUPONT DENEMOURS & CO. V. CHRISTOPHER
431 F.2d 1012 (5th Cir. 1970)

GOLDBERG, CIRCUIT JUDGE:

This is a case of industrial espionage in which an airplane is the cloak and a camera the dagger. The defendants-appellants, Rolfe and Gary Christopher, are photographers in Beaumont, Texas. The Christophers were hired by an unknown third party to take aerial photographs of new construction at the Beaumont plant of E. I. duPont deNemours & Company, Inc. Sixteen photographs of the DuPont facility were taken from the air on March 19, 1969, and these photographs were later developed and delivered to the third party.

DuPont employees apparently noticed the airplane on March 19 and immediately began an investigation to determine why the craft was circling over the plant. By that afternoon the investigation had disclosed that the craft was involved in a photographic expedition and that the Christophers were the photographers. DuPont contacted the Christophers that same afternoon and asked them to reveal the name of the person or corporation requesting the photographs. The Christophers refused to disclose this information, giving as their reason the client's desire to remain anonymous.

Having reached a dead end in the investigation, DuPont subsequently filed suit against the Christophers, alleging that the Christophers had wrongfully obtained photographs revealing DuPont's trade secrets which they then sold to the undisclosed third party. DuPont contended that it had developed a highly secret but unpatented process for producing methanol, a process which gave DuPont a competitive advantage over other producers. This process, DuPont alleged, was a trade secret developed after much expensive and time-consuming research, and a secret which the company had taken special precautions to safeguard. The area photographed by the Christophers was the plant designed to produce methanol by this secret process, and because the plant was still under construction parts of the process were exposed to view from directly above the construction area. Photographs of that area, DuPont alleged, would enable a skilled person to deduce the secret process for making methanol. DuPont thus contended that the Christophers had wrongfully appropriated DuPont trade secrets by taking the photographs and delivering them to the undisclosed third party. In its suit DuPont asked for damages to cover the loss it had already sustained as a result of the wrongful disclosure of the trade secret and sought temporary and permanent injunctions prohibiting any further circulation of the photographs already taken and prohibiting any additional photographing of the methanol plant.

. . . .

On June 5, 1969, the trial court held a hearing on all pending motions and an additional motion by the Christophers for summary judgment. The court denied the Christophers' motions to dismiss for want of jurisdiction and failure to state a claim and also denied their motion for summary judgment. The court granted DuPont's motion to compel the Christophers to divulge the name of their client. Having made these rulings, the court then granted the Christophers' motion for an interlocutory appeal under 28 U.S.C.A. § 1292(b) to allow the Christophers to obtain immediate appellate review of the court's finding that DuPont had stated a claim upon which relief could be granted. Agreeing with the trial court's determination that DuPont had stated a valid claim, we affirm the decision of that court.

. . . . The only question involved in this interlocutory appeal is whether DuPont has asserted a claim upon which relief can be granted. The Christophers argued both at trial and before this court that they committed no "actionable wrong" in photographing the DuPont facility and passing these photographs on to their client because they conducted all of their activities in public airspace, violated no government aviation standard, did not breach any confidential relation, and did not engage in any fraudulent or illegal conduct. In short, the Christophers argue that for an appropriation of trade secrets to be wrongful there must be a trespass, other illegal conduct, or breach of a confidential relationship. We disagree.

It is true, as the Christophers assert, that the previous trade secret cases have contained one or more of these elements. However, we do not think that the Texas courts would limit the trade secret protection exclusively to these elements. On the contrary, in *Hyde Corporation v. Huffines*, 1958, 158 Tex. 566, 314 S.W.2d 763, the Texas Supreme Court specifically adopted the rule found in the Restatement of Torts which provides:

> One who discloses or uses another's trade secret, without a privilege to do so, is liable to the other if (a) he discovered the secret by improper means, or (b) his disclosure or use constitutes a breach of confidence reposed in him by the other in disclosing the secret to him * * *.

Restatement of Torts § 757 (1939).

Thus, although the previous cases have dealt with a breach of a confidential relationship, a trespass, or other illegal conduct, the rule is much broader than the cases heretofore encountered. Not limiting itself to specific wrongs, Texas adopted subsection (a) of the Restatement which recognizes a cause of action for the discovery of a trade secret by any "improper" means.

The defendants, however, read *Furr's Inc. v. United Specialty Advertising Co.*, Tex.Civ.App.1960, 338 S.W.2d 762, writ ref'd n.r.e., as limiting the Texas rule to breach of a confidential relationship. The court in *Furr's* did make the statement that "The use of someone else's idea is not automatically a violation of the law. It must be something that meets the requirements of a 'trade secret' and has been obtained through a breach of confidence in order to entitle the injured party to damages and/or injunction." 338 S.W.2d at 766.

We think, however, that the exclusive rule which defendants have extracted from this statement is unwarranted. In the first place, in *Furr's* the court specifically found that there was no trade secret involved because the entire advertising scheme claimed to be the trade secret had been completely divulged to the public. Secondly, the court found that the plaintiff in the course of selling the scheme to the defendant had voluntarily divulged the entire scheme. Thus the court was dealing only with a possible breach of confidence concerning a properly discovered secret; there was never a question of any impropriety in the discovery or any other improper conduct on the part of the defendant. The court merely held that under those circumstances the defendant had not acted improperly if no breach of confidence occurred. We do not read *Furr's* as limiting the trade secret protection to a breach of confidential relationship when the facts of the case do raise the issue of some other wrongful conduct on the part of one discovering the trade secrets of another. If breach of confidence were meant to encompass the entire panoply of commercial improprieties, subsection (a) of the Restatement would be either surplusage or persiflage, an interpretation abhorrent to the traditional precision of the Restatement. We therefore find meaning in subsection (a) and think that the Texas Supreme Court clearly indicated by its adoption that there is a cause of action for the discovery of a trade secret by any "improper means." *Hyde Corporation v. Huffines*, supra.

The question remaining, therefore, is whether aerial photography of plant construction is an improper means of obtaining another's trade secret. We conclude that it is and that the Texas courts would so hold. The Supreme Court of that state has declared that "the undoubted tendency of the law has been to recognize and enforce higher standards of commercial morality in the business world." *Hyde Corporation v. Huffines*, supra 314 S.W.2d at 773. That court has quoted with approval articles indicating that the proper means of gaining possession of a competitor's secret process is "through inspection and analysis" of the product in order to create a duplicate. *K & G Tool & Service Co. v. G & G Fishing Tool Service*, 1958, 158 Tex. 594, 314 S.W.2d 782, 783, 788. Later another Texas court explained:

> The means by which the discovery is made may be obvious, and the experimentation leading from known factors to presently unknown results may be simple and lying in the public domain. But these facts do not destroy the value of the discovery and will not advantage a competitor who by unfair means obtains the knowledge without paying the price expended by the discoverer.

Brown v. Fowler, Tex.Civ.App.1958, 316 S.W.2d 111, 114, writ ref'd n.r.e. (emphasis added).

We think, therefore, that the Texas rule is clear. One may use his competitor's secret process if he discovers the process by reverse engineering applied to the finished product; one may use a competitor's process if he discovers it by his own independent research; but one may not avoid these labors by taking the process from the discoverer without his permission at a time when he is taking reasonable precautions to maintain its secrecy. To obtain knowledge of a process without spending the time and money to discover it independently is improper unless the holder voluntarily discloses it or fails to take reasonable precautions to ensure its secrecy.

In the instant case the Christophers deliberately flew over the DuPont plant to get pictures of a process which DuPont had attempted to keep secret. The Christophers delivered their pictures to a third party who was certainly aware of the means by which they had been acquired and who may be planning to use the information contained therein to manufacture methanol by the DuPont process. The third party has a right to use this process only if he obtains this knowledge through his own research efforts, but thus far all information indicates that the third party has gained this knowledge solely by taking it from DuPont at a time when DuPont was making reasonable efforts to preserve its secrecy. In such a situation DuPont has a valid cause of action to prohibit the Christophers from improperly discovering its trade secret and to prohibit the undisclosed third party from using the improperly obtained information.

We note that this view is in perfect accord with the position taken by the authors of the Restatement. In commenting on improper means of discovery the savants of the Restatement said:

> f.   Improper means of discovery. The discovery of another's trade secret by improper means subjects the actor to liability independently of the harm to the interest in the secret. Thus, if one uses physical force to take a secret formula from another's

pocket, or breaks into another's office to steal the formula, his conduct is wrongful and subjects him to liability apart from the rule stated in this Section. Such conduct is also an improper means of procuring the secret under this rule. But means may be improper under this rule even though they do not cause any other harm than that to the interest in the trade secret. Examples of such means are fraudulent misrepresentations to induce disclosure, tapping of telephone wires, eavesdropping or other espionage. A complete catalogue of improper means is not possible. In general they are means which fall below the generally accepted standards of commercial morality and reasonable conduct.

Restatement of Torts § 757, comment f at 10 (1939).

In taking this position we realize that industrial espionage of the sort here perpetrated has become a popular sport in some segments of our industrial community. However, our devotion to free wheeling industrial competition must not force us into accepting the law of the jungle as the standard of morality expected in our commercial relations. Our tolerance of the espionage game must cease when the protections required to prevent another's spying cost so much that the spirit of inventiveness is dampened. Commercial privacy must be protected from espionage which could not have been reasonably anticipated or prevented. We do not mean to imply, however, that everything not in plain view is within the protected vale, nor that all information obtained through every extra optical extension is forbidden. Indeed, for our industrial competition to remain healthy there must be breathing room for observing a competing industrialist. A competitor can and must shop his competition for pricing and examine his products for quality, components, and methods of manufacture. Perhaps ordinary fences and roofs must be built to shut out incursive eyes, but we need not require the discoverer of a trade secret to guard against the unanticipated, the undetectable, or the unpreventable methods of espionage now available.

In the instant case DuPont was in the midst of constructing a plant. Although after construction the finished plant would have protected much of the process from view, during the period of construction the trade secret was exposed to view from the air. To require DuPont to put a roof over the unfinished plant to guard its secret would impose an enormous expense to prevent nothing more than a school boy's trick. We introduce here no new or radical ethic since our ethos has never given moral sanction to piracy. The market place must not deviate far from our mores. We should not require a person or corporation to take unreasonable precautions to prevent another from doing that which he ought not do in the first place. Reasonable precautions against predatory eyes we may require, but an impenetrable fortress is an unreasonable requirement, and we are not disposed to burden industrial inventors with such a duty in order to protect the fruits of their efforts. "Improper" will always be a word of many nuances, determined by time, place, and circumstances. We therefore need not proclaim a catalogue of commercial improprieties. Clearly, however, one of its commandments does say "thou shall not appropriate a trade secret through deviousness under circumstances in which countervailing defenses are not reasonably available."

Having concluded that aerial photography, from whatever altitude, is an improper method of discovering the trade secrets exposed during construction of the DuPont plant, we need not worry about whether the flight pattern chosen by the Christophers violated any federal aviation regulations. Regardless of whether the flight was legal or illegal in that sense, the espionage was an improper means of discovering DuPont's trade secret.

The decision of the trial court is affirmed and the case remanded to that court for proceedings on the merits.

NOTES & QUESTIONS

(1) The court cited to § 757 of the First Restatement of Torts (which Texas followed at the time). Suppose the Christophers had not yet given the pictures to their clandestine employer. Would DuPont have been able to maintain an action against the Christophers under § 757? Would it make a difference if, instead of hired photographers, the Christophers were simply out on a leisurely flight and took photos because they found the plant to be interesting? *See* RESTATEMENT (THIRD) OF UNFAIR COMPETITION § 40 cmt. b (1995).

(2) What are the justifications (economic or otherwise) for a rule that prohibits misappropriation by improper means? Consider what steps DuPont would have had to take if the rule did not exist.

(3) In thinking about the previous question, you may find it helpful to know that the U.S. Supreme Court has offered some insight into the justifications behind state laws that prohibit the misappropriation of trade secrets:

> Another problem that would arise if state trade secret protection were precluded is in the area of licensing others to exploit secret processes. The holder of a trade secret would not likely share his secret with a manufacturer who cannot be placed under binding legal obligation to pay a license fee or to protect the secret. The result would be to hoard rather than disseminate knowledge. Instead, then, of licensing others to use his invention and making the most efficient use of existing manufacturing and marketing structures within the industry, the trade secret holder would tend either to limit his utilization of the invention, thereby depriving the public of the maximum benefit of its use, or engage in the time-

consuming and economically wasteful enterprise of constructing duplicative manufacturing and marketing mechanisms for the exploitation of the invention. The detrimental misallocation of resources and economic waste that would thus take place if trade secret protection were abolished with respect to employees or licensees cannot be justified by reference to any policy that the federal patent law seeks to advance.

Nothing in the patent law requires that States refrain from action to prevent industrial espionage. In addition to the increased costs for protection from burglary, wire-tapping, bribery, and the other means used to misappropriate trade secrets, there is the inevitable cost to the basic decency of society when one firm steals from another. A most fundamental human right, that of privacy, is threatened when industrial espionage is condoned or is made profitable; the state interest in denying profit to such illegal ventures is unchallengeable.

Kewanee Oil Co. v. Bicron Corp., 416 U.S. 470, 486–87 (1974). Beyond the economics of recognizing trade secret protection, what other justifications does this quote articulate?

(4) The *DuPont* court seemed to believe that DuPont made reasonable efforts to maintain secrecy under the circumstances. The opinion, however, predated the widespread use and availability of satellite photography. Do you think a court would reach the same conclusion today? *See* RESTATEMENT (THIRD) OF UNFAIR COMPETITION §§ 39 cmt. f, 43 cmt. c (1995). If you think the result would change, is your reasoning based upon a lack of improper means or some other ground?

(5) Instead of flying over the plant, assume that the Christophers acquired the pictures from a subcontractor who was working on the construction of the plant. Assume further that the Christophers paid the subcontractor to take and deliver the pictures. Would the Christophers still be liable? *See id.* § 43 cmt. c.

PROBLEM 10.3

(a) Chad runs an engineering firm that designs farm machinery. The firm's engineering drawings depict designs that Chad considers secret and confidential, and they are kept on his office's computer network. The drawings are all marked confidential and access to the drawings is password-protected. Only high-level employees have passwords and all employees are bound by confidentiality agreements. Despite these steps, the firm's network security system is woefully out-of-date—a fact that Chad is aware of. Chad has been meaning to upgrade the system, but he has never gotten around to it. Al is a competitor of Chad's who hacks into Chad's computer network and downloads the confidential drawings. Can Chad maintain a suit against Al for misappropriation of trade secrets?

(b) Assume instead that Chad's network security system is up-to-date. Al is a high-level employee at Chad's firm who is planning to leave to start his own competing engineering firm. Prior to leaving, Al uses his authorized password to download the confidential drawings. After Al's departure, Chad learns of Al's actions. Can Chad maintain a suit against Al for misappropriation of trade secrets if Al has not yet used the drawings or disclosed them to anyone else? *See* UTSA § 2; RESTATEMENT (THIRD) OF UNFAIR COMPETITION §§ 40, 44 (1995).

b. Unauthorized Disclosure or Use

Along with improper means, § 40 of the Third Restatement of Unfair Competition provides that misappropriation can be established by showing that the secret was disclosed or used in an unauthorized manner:

§ 40 Appropriation of Trade Secrets

One is subject to liability for the appropriation of another's trade secret if:

. . . .

(b) the actor uses or discloses the other's trade secret without the other's consent and, at the time of the use or disclosure,

> (1) the actor knows or has reason to know that the information is a trade secret that the actor acquired under circumstances creating a duty of confidence owed by the actor to the other under the rule stated in § 41; or

> (2) the actor knows or has reason to know that the information is a trade secret that the actor acquired by means that are improper under the rule stated in § 43; or

> (3) the actor knows or has reason to know that the information is a trade secret that the actor acquired from or through a person who acquired it by means that are improper under the rule stated in § 43 or whose disclosure of the trade secret constituted a breach of a duty of confidence owed to the other under the rule stated in § 41; or

> (4) the actor knows or has reason to know that the information is a trade secret that the actor acquired through an accident or mistake, unless the acquisition was the result of the other's failure to take reasonable precautions to maintain the secrecy of the information.

Similar language is present in § 757 of the First Restatement of Torts and § 1(2) of the UTSA.

Notice that § 40 requires the actor to use or disclose the information. Mere possession, unless the possession is the equivalent of use, is not enough. Comment c to § 40 provides further guidance:

> There are no technical limitations on the nature of the conduct that constitutes "use" of a trade secret for purposes of the rules stated in Subsection (b). As a general matter, any exploitation of the trade secret that is likely to result in injury to the trade secret owner or enrichment to the defendant is a "use" under this Section. Thus, marketing goods that embody the trade secret, employing the trade secret in manufacturing or production, relying on the trade secret to assist or accelerate research or development, or soliciting customers through the use of information that is a trade secret (see § 42, Comment f) all constitute "use."

Can the use of negative knowledge—i.e., knowing what not to do—be actionable under § 40? Comment c is sufficiently broad to include the use of negative knowledge if it is employed in the manufacturing process or used to accelerate research. The comments to § 39 of the Third Restatement and to § 1 of the UTSA provide further support. *See* RESTATEMENT (THIRD) OF UNFAIR COMPETITION § 39 cmt. e (1995) ("Some early cases elevated use by the trade secret owner to independent significance by establishing such use as an element of the cause of action for the appropriation of a trade secret. Such a 'use' requirement, however, imposes unjustified limitations on the scope of trade secret protection . . . The requirement . . . places in doubt protection for so-called 'negative' information that teaches conduct to be avoided, such as knowledge that a particular process or technique is unsuitable for commercial use. Cases in many jurisdictions expressly renounce any requirement of use by the trade secret owner. . . . Use by the person asserting rights in the information is not a prerequisite to protection under the rule stated in this Section."); UTSA § 1 cmt. ("The definition includes information that has commercial value from a negative viewpoint, for example the results of lengthy and expensive research which proves that a certain process will **not** work could be of great value to a competitor."); *see also On-Line Technologies, Inc. v. Perkin-Elmer Corp.*, 253 F. Supp. 2d 313, 323 (D. Conn. 2003) (stating that "[n]egative knowledge is one form of 'using' trade secrets that is proscribed by [Connecticut's version of the UTSA] because one may 'use' a trade secret in ways other than direct manufacture and marketing").

Section 40 of the Third Restatement also requires the defendant to know or have reason to know that the information is a trade secret. You may be wondering how an actor could have possession of a trade secret and yet not have knowledge of that fact. To illustrate, assume that Company X, a manufacturer of cogs, hires A as a consultant on its manufacturing process. During the course of the engagement, A learns of X's secret process for manufacturing cogs in a manner that is twice as efficient as any other manufacturer. As part of A's engagement, he signs a confidentiality agreement that he will not reveal or disclose this information to anyone. A finishes his consulting job and goes to work for Company Y over a year later. A reveals the secret process to Y but claims that he developed the process himself. So long as Y has no reason to know that the process is actually someone else's trade secret, Y will not be liable to X for implementing and using the process (although A will surely be liable for his disclosure).[c]

The case of *Vantage Point, Inc. v. Parker Brothers, Inc.*, 529 F. Supp. 1204 (S.D.N.Y. 1981), offers a good illustration of the role that knowledge can play. Vantage had developed a board game based on oil exploration called "Wildcat." In July of 1972, Vantage sent the concept (photographs, rules, etc.) to Milton Bradley's ("MB") president for review. MB had a formal policy of not considering unsolicited submissions, and it returned the materials unexamined. Subsequently, Vantage sent letters to other companies urging them to review the game. Parker Brothers ("Parker") showed interest and Vantage sent a working version of the game so that Parker could further evaluate it. Ultimately, Parker decided that the costs of manufacturing the game were too high and returned the game to Vantage.

One of the Parker employees who had access to Wildcat during its evaluation was Robert Baron. Baron soon left Parker and joined two other men in a venture to create and sell toy ideas to game companies. The three men developed an oil exploration game called "Oil Baron" which they successfully marketed to MB. MB developed the game and renamed it "King Oil." In February of 1974, MB published the game at a toy fair and Vantage subsequently learned of the product, which was similar to Wildcat.

Vantage brought suit claiming that MB had misappropriated the Wildcat game concept by either: (1) using the materials Vantage had sent MB in July of 1972; or (2) using the concept when it knew or should have known that the idea was being disclosed to it in breach of a confidential relation (i.e., Baron breached a duty when he divulged the game idea). As for the first claim, the court found that there was insufficient evidence demonstrating that MB had reviewed the materials in question. As for the second ground, the court held that MB's lack of knowledge of the trade secret precluded liability:

---

[c] This does not necessarily mean that Y will be able to continue using the process in the future. Nevertheless, the relief available to X may be limited because of Y's good faith employment of A, and because of subsequent expenses incurred by Y in implementing the process. *See* RESTATEMENT (THIRD) OF UNFAIR COMPETITION §§ 44 cmt. b, 45 cmt. b (1995). We discuss remedies more fully in Section D.

Even if Baron misappropriated plaintiff's submission, no liability attaches because Milton Bradley did not have notice of any misconduct by Baron.... Furthermore, by the time defendant arguably was put on notice [of the possible misappropriation], it had changed its position by investing time and money in making Oil Baron into the marketable game King Oil. Under the theory plaintiff has used to support its second claim for relief, this change in position precludes liability.

Id. at 1214.

NOTES & QUESTIONS

(1) Apparently MB had a formal policy of returning unsolicited game concepts without reviewing them. Why might MB have instituted such a policy?

(2) Baron appeared to have taken the Wildcat concept from Parker to develop King Oil. As we will see, his subsequent use could have made him liable to Parker. Assume that Baron had tweaked the rules of the board game and instead developed it into a video game called Oil Barons. Could Baron successfully argue that he was not using the trade secret because the Oil Barons game is different from Wildcat? *See Mangren Res. & Dev. Corp. v. Nat'l Chem. Co.*, 87 F.3d 937, 944 (7th Cir. 1996) ("We have observed before, in fact, that if trade secret law were not flexible enough to encompass modified or even new products that are substantially derived from the trade secret of another, the protections that law provides would be hollow indeed."); RESTATEMENT (THIRD) OF UNFAIR COMPETITION § 40 cmt. c (1995).

(3) Assume that instead of returning Vantage's materials, MB reviewed them and ultimately developed them into King Oil. Could Vantage successfully claim that MB had misappropriated the concept? What additional facts would be useful in making your determination?

Image of the game ultimately produced by Milton Bradley.

i.   Breach of a Duty of Confidence

Section 40(b)(1), (3) of the Third Restatement of Unfair Competition speaks of use or disclosure that breaches a duty of confidence. Similarly, §§ (1)(1) and (1)(2)(ii)(B)(II)–(III) of the UTSA speak of a duty to maintain secrecy. Who owes such a duty? Certainly current employees, as we will soon explore, but what about third parties who are privy to trade secrets as part of a negotiation or licensing agreement? Recall that in *Learning Curve*, the parties had entered into an oral agreement to keep the information confidential. Such an express agreement is one of the two ways to establish a duty of confidence under the Third Restatement:

§ 41   Duty of Confidence

A person to whom a trade secret has been disclosed owes a duty of confidence to the owner of the trade secret for purposes of the rule stated in § 40 if:

(a) the person made an express promise of confidentiality prior to the disclosure of the trade secret; or

(b) the trade secret was disclosed to the person under circumstances in which the relationship between the parties to the disclosure or the other facts surrounding the disclosure justify the conclusions that, at the time of the disclosure,

(1) the person knew or had reason to know that the disclosure was intended to be in confidence, and

(2) the other party to the disclosure was reasonable in inferring that the person consented to an obligation of confidentiality.

Express agreements are covered under subsection (a). As subsection (b) makes clear, however, in the right circumstances a duty of confidence can arise even absent an express agreement.

PHILLIPS V. FREY
20 F.3d 623 (5th Cir. 1994)

REYNALDO G. GARZA, CIRCUIT JUDGE:

This is an appeal from a jury verdict in a trade secret misappropriation case. The jury found that the defendants had misappropriated a trade secret connected with the manufacture and/or marketing of the plaintiffs' hunting stand. For the following reasons, we AFFIRM.

STATEMENT OF FACTS

Plaintiffs-appellees, W.C. Phillips and his wife Mary Phillips, are owners and operators of Ambusher, Inc. Ambusher's main line of business is the manufacture and distribution of single pole deer stands to be used by hunters. Ambusher's stand is collapsible and consists of four main parts: the upper seat section and three ladder pole sections that enable the seat to be elevated approximately fourteen feet above the ground.[1] It has a unique design in that it has a single pole that a hunter can climb instead of having to climb the tree. For further safety and security, it locks to the tree from the ground before a hunter climbs into it.

W.C. Phillips began developing single pole tree stands in 1967. He worked on their design, off and on, for three years. He has developed a number of different models over the years culminating in the "V-Lok" tree stand which is the subject of this suit.[2] Ambusher also sold accessories to be used with the deer stands, including a gun/bow rest, a camo blind, a camo awning, a security cable, and an ATV "Piggy Back Bar." Ambusher and Buck Pro, Inc. are the only manufacturers of single pole tree stands

---

[1]   To assemble a single-pole deer stand, the ladder pole sections are connected together, the seat section is attached to the top of the poles, and the stand is secured against a tree with a rope. There are jaws on the back of the seat that dig into the tree to help hold the stand securely. The hunter may then climb steps built into the ladder pole sections to reach the seat for gun or bow hunting.

[2]   The previous models had double arms that locked around the tree, while the V-Lok has only one arm which gives the hunter the advantage of going around the tree twice with a rope making it even more secure.

in the United States. Buck Pro's tree stand is an exact copy of appellees' "V-Lok" tree stand.

Defendant John Collins[3] was a customer who had bought products from appellees for a number of years. The events which form the basis of this suit began in the summer of 1990, when Collins and Phillips had a telephone conversation wherein Phillips mentioned his desire to sell the business, including all equipment, jigs, logos, and the spec book, for $140,000.[4] Two weeks after that initial telephone call, Collins called Phillips back to inform him that he and two associates, Claude Frey and Gary Arnold, were interested in purchasing the business and wanted some information to look at. Collins informed Phillips that coming up with his asking price would not present a problem since he had $50,000 in savings, that Arnold already had a metal fabricating ship, and that Frey owned land. These facts led Phillips to believe that the defendants were legitimate prospective purchasers of Ambusher, Inc.

A couple of weeks later, on July 6, 1990, Phillips sent some information for Collins and his two associates to look over. This package included both a financial statement, and an inventory of his equipment and tools by make and model. He also included a video tape. Phillips wrote that he had a specification book that is referred to each time a component is made that is kept up to date and put away for safekeeping. He also stated that he had made a videotape of the component manufacturing the previous year, adding "[w]ithout the specs this information is no secret, and if you and your associate would like to view this for a detailed insight of the manufacturing procedures, I can send a copy to you. . . . This tape does not cover recent developments and the V-Lok stand." Because he felt the tape did not make sense without the "spec book," Phillips made a different tape on July 7, 1990 demonstrating Ambusher's manufacturing process for tree stands and accessories. The video tape gave appellants the knowledge necessary to manufacture tree stands, and was intended to bypass the spec book. Phillips did this in order to allow appellants to evaluate the business as prospective purchasers.

In the latter part of July 1990, Collins called to arrange a tour of appellees' shop in Texarkana. The tour lasted about three hours. During the tour, Phillips and his employee showed the defendants first hand how to manufacture the "V-Lok" deer stand.

Two weeks later, some time in August 1990, Collins and appellants returned to Texarkana for a second visit. Collins purchased seven V-Lok stands and returned to Louisiana. On September 10, 1990, Phillips sent a more recent financial statement and a copy of the current inventory.

---

[3]   Collins settled on the morning of the second day of trial.

[4]   The sales price included everything but Appellees' building in Texarkana.

Shortly thereafter, Collins informed Phillips that he and appellants were having problems securing financing. Collins then made a counteroffer for the business for $30,000 down, a $10 royalty per stand and that Phillips was to help set up shop in Wisner, Louisiana. On September 14, 1990, Phillips refused this counteroffer. On September 15, 1990, Phillips offered to sell the business for $45,000 down and $20,000 per year at 10% interest for seven years. On October 1, 1990, Collins informed Phillips that he and appellants would be unable to purchase the business.

Collins returned the information Phillips had sent him, except for the video. However, none of the information Collins sent to Frey or Arnold was returned. Moreover, it was later discovered that appellants never attempted to secure a loan for the purchase of Ambusher, despite having sufficient assets to do so.

By the end of March, 1991, appellants were manufacturing and marketing a tree stand known as the "BP91" under the name Buck-Pro, Inc. The tree stand and accessories were identical to plaintiffs' "V-Lok" tree stand and accessories. The plaintiffs filed an action against appellants and John Collins in district court alleging misappropriation of both the design of the product and Ambusher's manufacturing process; that the appellants deceived the Phillips into disclosing confidential trade secrets under the guise of purchasing the business. Appellants denied these allegations, stating that the BP91 deer stand was designed by permissible reverse engineering, and counterclaimed against appellees for malicious prosecution. The jury verdict awarded appellees $56,500.13 in actual damages, $75,000 in punitive damages, and $7,000 in attorneys' fees. The jury found against the appellants on the malicious prosecution claim. On the same day that the judgment was entered, the trial court signed a permanent injunction enjoining appellants from manufacturing, selling, or marketing deer stands and assorted accessories. Appellants have timely appealed.

DISCUSSION

The jury returned a verdict finding by a preponderance of the evidence that the defendants had misappropriated a trade secret of W.C. Phillips and Mary Phillips connected with the manufacture and/or marketing of a single pole V-Lok tree stand, T-Bar awning, or Piggy back bars for all terrain vehicles.

Trade secret misappropriation under Texas law is established by showing: (a) a trade secret existed; (b) the trade secret was acquired through a breach of a confidential relationship or discovered by improper means; and (c) use of the trade secret without authorization from the plaintiff.

The decisive component of our review of this case is the fact that the defendants failed to move for a judgment as a matter of law at the close of the evidence or after the verdict was returned. *See* Fed.R.Civ.P. 50. Consequently, these objections are being raised for the first time on appeal, and our review is therefore extremely limited: "It is the unwavering rule in this Circuit that issues raised for the first time on appeal are reviewed only for plain error," and we will reverse "only if the judgment complained of results in a 'manifest miscarriage of justice.'" *McCann v. Texas City Refining, Inc.,* 984 F.2d 667, 673 (5th Cir.1993) (quoting *Coughlin v. Capitol Cement Co.,* 571 F.2d 290, 297 (5th Cir.1978)). Therefore, the appellants have waived the right to appeal the sufficiency of the evidence, and may only complain of the legality of the verdict, i.e., whether there is *any* evidence to support the jury verdict. Even if there is no evidence in the record supporting the verdict, this Court lacks the power to enter judgment for the appellant. Our appellate relief is limited to ordering a new trial. *Id.*

It is the appellants' contention that there was no evidence to support the jury's verdict or the permanent injunction. Appellants' first argument is that no "trade secrets" were disclosed. Appellants assert that they acquired no information deserving protection under the trade secrets law. Alternatively, appellants claim that the plaintiffs are barred as a matter of law because the Buck-Pro BP91 was built exclusively through the use of permissible reverse engineering, that the Phillips failed in their affirmative duty to take reasonable steps to protect their secret, and finally, that no confidential relationship existed between the parties. Consequently, the jury's finding of misappropriation of trade secrets amounts to a "miscarriage of justice." We will examine each of these concerns independently, closely scrutinizing the record for any evidence to support the jury's verdict.

(1) Did a Trade Secret Exist?

Primarily, appellants assert that the only trade secret involved in this case was the specification book, and that was never given to the appellants. Any information other than the spec book would not rise to the specter of a "trade secret." Appellants point out that Phillips stated in his letter that "[w]ithout the specs this information is no secret...." Moreover, appellants claim that no admonitions against disclosure accompanied the videotape.

    . . . .

Appellees contend, and we find that the evidence supports, that it was Ambusher's manufacturing process that was the trade secret misappropriated, not the design of the tree stand.

The method of manufacturing must be a trade secret to be protected, in other words, it must give the owner a competitive advantage. The trade secret must possess at least that modicum of originality which will separate it from everyday knowledge. The record before us indicates that the Phillips's manufacturing process took years to develop and allowed Ambusher to manufacture the tree stands in a cost efficient manner, giving Ambusher a competitive advantage over anyone who would not know or use this method.[7] The manufacturing process itself was divulged in both the video tape and the personal tours given to appellants during the course of negotiations for purchase of the business.

Gary Arnold admitted at trial that prior to seeing the video tape sent to them by Phillips, he was unaware of how to mass produce deer stands. Additionally, the manufacturing equipment and tools used in Buck-Pro's manufacturing process were identical to those employed by Ambusher. This is some evidence that the manufacturing process came from improperly acquired trade secrets.

. . . .

In the same vein of argument, the appellants assert that they designed and manufactured their products by reverse engineering. Under Texas law, it is permissible to use a competitor's secret process if the process is discovered by reverse engineering applied to the finished product. *E.I. duPont deNemours & Co. v. Christopher,* 431 F.2d 1012, 1015 (5th Cir.1970), *cert. denied,* 400 U.S. 1024, 91 S.Ct. 581, 27 L.Ed.2d 637 (1971). Since they never had access to the spec book, it was necessary to compile their own specification for the deer stands and accessories. Appellants claim that Phillips admitted that they utilized reverse engineering to design their products when he testified:

A: They manufactured without my book, yes.

Q: And how did they do that?

A: They laid the stand down and measured it and copied it, and built some specs to match.

Q: Not from your book but from the stand itself?

A: From the stand itself, yes, sir.

Although it is likely appellants used reverse engineering for the design of the BP91, there was no evidence that the appellants used this method to acquire the manufacturing process employed by Ambusher. A process or device may be a trade secret even where others can gain knowledge of the process from studying the manufacturer's marketed product. *Ventura Manufacturing Co. v. Locke,* 454 S.W.2d 431, 433 (Tex.Civ.App.—San Antonio 1970, no writ). Although trade secret law

---

[7] When Phillips informed the appellants that his tree stand and accessories were not patented, Frey asked Phillips what he would do if someone started building them. Phillips replied that it would be cost prohibitive to do so without knowledge of his manufacturing process.

does not offer protection against discovery by fair and honest means such as independent invention, accidental disclosure, or "reverse engineering," protection will be awarded to a trade secret holder against the disclosure or unauthorized use by those to whom the secret has been confided under either express or implied restriction of nondisclosure or by one who has gained knowledge by improper means. Therefore, this argument does not further their position on appeal.

(2) Breach of Confidential Relationship and Improper Discovery

One is liable for disclosure of trade secrets if (a) he discovers the secret by improper means, or (b) his disclosure or use constitutes a breach of confidence reposed in one who is in a confidential relationship with another who discloses protected information to him.

The appellants assert that, even if the information disclosed was a trade secret, the information was not discovered through improper means. *E.I. duPont deNemours & Co. v. Christopher*, 431 F.2d 1012, 1014 (5th Cir.1970), involved trade secret misappropriation through aerial photography of the construction of a chemical plant. In condemning this action and explicitly finding misappropriation of trade secrets through improper means, this court noted that industrial espionage of this type "has become a popular sport in some segments of our industrial community. However, our devotion to free wheeling industrial competition must not force us into accepting the law of the jungle as the standard of morality expected in our commercial relations." *Id.* at 1016. We find that there is evidence to support the finding that appellants acquired the confidential information through improper means.

The facts before us indicate that Collins induced Phillips to reveal information by assuring him that accumulating the purchase price would be easy because providing collateral for a business loan would present no obstacle. Arnold testified that he owned a home, a business known as Arnold's Service Center which is a metal fabricating facility, and a 40 acre farm in Wisner, Louisiana. Frey testified that he owns farm land in both Mississippi and Louisiana. Frey also stated that they never made any effort to borrow money or even apply for a loan. In the face of such evidence, it does not amount to a miscarriage of justice for the jury to believe that the defendants improperly discovered the trade secret and breached their confidential relationship.

Appellants' next claim is that Phillips should not recover since he completely disregarded all prohibitions that would afford his legal protection on any trade secrets by voluntarily disclosing the manufacturing process through the videotape and the [on-site] tours. At no time did Phillips inform the appellants that the information was secret or in any way place them under a duty not to disclose.

It was this court that stated that it is not improper to obtain knowledge of a process where the holder of the alleged trade secret voluntarily discloses it or fails to take reasonable precautions to ensure its secrecy. *E.I. duPont deNemours & Co. v. Christopher,* 431 F.2d 1012, 1015 (5th Cir.1970). *See Interox America v. PPG Industries, Inc.,* 736 F.2d 194, 202 (5th Cir.1984) (one who voluntarily discloses information or fails to take reasonable precautions to insure its secrecy cannot claim that the information constituted a trade secret). However, an owner of a trade secret will not lose the secret by disclosure if he creates a duty in some manner and places that duty upon another not to disclose or use the secret. *Kewanee Oil Co. v. Bicron Corp.,* 416 U.S. 470, 474, 94 S.Ct. 1879, 1882–83 (1974) (holding necessary element of secrecy with respect to trade secret not lost if holder reveals it to another in confidence and under implied obligation not to use or disclose it). Therefore, while it is true that outside any confidential relationship, one who voluntarily discloses secret information or who fails to take reasonable precautions to secure its secrecy cannot properly claim that information constitutes a trade secret, creating such a duty upon the disclosee is a reasonable precaution, and a voluntary disclosure made within the periphery of a confidential relationship eliminates the need to take further precautions to secure the trade secret.

The record does contain evidence that Phillips did take steps to protect his secret by not disclosing the process to anyone until the sales negotiations commenced. By this precaution, Phillips disclosed within a confidence that placed the appellants under a duty to keep the secret.

However, appellants deny that there was ever any confidential relationship established that would prevent them from using the information given to them. Appellants assert that the fact that a sale of Ambusher was contemplated does not create a per se confidential relationship between the parties.

They cite to a 1st circuit case which holds that although a confidential relationship will typically be implied if the disclosure was made in a business relationship between a purchaser and supplier, the implied confidential relationship may be defeated if the disclosing party voluntarily conveys a trade secret to another without limitation upon its use. *Burten v. Milton Bradley Co.,* 763 F.2d 461, 463 (1st Cir.1985). Appellants find similarity in the instant case, where Phillips took no steps to protect himself and never indicated that he was giving confidential information to Collins or appellants.

In *Hyde Corp. v. Huffines,* 158 Tex. 566, 314 S.W.2d 763 (1958), the Supreme Court of Texas held that an express agreement was not necessary where the actions of the parties and the nature of their relationship, taken as a whole, established the existence of a confidential relationship.

> The chief example of a confidential relationship under this rule is the relationship of a principal and agent (See Restatement of Agency, Section 395 and 396). Such is also the relationship between partners or other joint adventurers. But this confidence may exist also in other situations. For example, A has a trade secret which he wishes to sell with or without his business. B is a prospective purchaser. In the course of negotiations, A discloses the secret to B solely for the purpose of enabling him to appraise its value. . . . In [that] case B is under a duty not to disclose the secret or use it adversely to A.

Hyde, 314 S.W.2d at 769. The injured party is not required to rely on an express agreement to hold the trade secret in confidence, nor is he to be denied relief where the offending party originally entered into the relationship without an improper motive. *Id.* at 770.

In *Smith v. Snap-On Tools Corp.,* 833 F.2d 578, 581 (5th Cir.1988), Basil Smith invented a ratchet by combining parts of two existing tools and submitted a tool suggestion form to Snap-On Tools' corporate headquarters. A short time later, Snap-On began manufacturing and selling the ratchet without paying any proceeds to Smith who brought a diversity action claiming trade secret misappropriation. *Id.* at 579. The district court found that Snap-On had misappropriated the trade secret. This court then reversed, holding that the record reflected that there was no confidential relationship existing at the time of disclosure between Smith and the corporation since Smith never explicitly requested that his disclosure be held in confidence, he had submitted the trade secret on his own initiative without any solicitation from Snap-On Tools, and disclosure was not intended as part of the business negotiations. *Id.* at 580. We cited to the Restatement of Torts § 757(b) (1939) which states, "[o]ne who discloses or uses another's trade secret, without a privilege to do so, is liable to the other if . . . his disclosure or use constitutes a breach of confidence reposed in him by the other in disclosing the secret to him." The proprietor of a trade secret may not unilaterally create a confidential relationship without the knowledge or consent of the party to whom he discloses the secret. *Snap-On Tools,* 833 F.2d at 579–80 (citing Restatement of Torts, comment j (1939)). However, no particular form of notice is needed; the question raised is whether the recipient of the information knew or should have known that the information was a trade secret and the disclosure was made in confidence. *Id.* at 580 (citing Restatement of Torts § 757 comment j (1939)).

The case before us is strikingly distinguishable. Even in *Snap-On* we implied that a manufacturer who has actively solicited disclosure from an inventor, and then used the disclosed material, would be liable for misappropriation of trade secrets even where the disclosure was made in the absence of any expressed understanding about confidentiality. *Id.* at 580. Although Phillips never explicitly requested that the secret of his manufacturing process, which gave him a competitive advantage over competitors, be held in confidence, both parties mutually came to the negotiation table, and the disclosure was made within the course of negotiations for the sale of a business. The jury could validly accept such evidence that the defendants knew or should have known that the information was a trade secret and the disclosure was made in confidence.

CONCLUSION

. . . .

The essence of this action is not infringement, but breach of faith, for it is clear that the plaintiffs could not assert a property right against one who would acquire the secret of their manufacturing process through reverse engineering of the plaintiffs' publicly marketed product . . . or any variety of permissible means including the limited access to a company's trade secrets obtained during the evaluation of a potential purchase. As Judge King points out in *Omnitech Intern., Inc. v. Clorox Co.,* 11 F.3d 1316, 1325 (5th Cir.1994),

> [t]o hold otherwise would lead to one of two unacceptable results: (i) every time a company entered into preliminary negotiations for a possible purchase of another company's assets in which the acquiring company was given limited access to the target's trade secrets, the acquiring party would effectively be precluded from evaluating other potential targets; or (ii) the acquiring company would, as a practical matter, be forced to make a purchase decision without the benefit of examination of the target company's most important assets—its trade secrets.

The fact is that they did not. Instead, the jury found, they gained it from the plaintiffs via their confidential relationship, and in so doing incurred a duty not to use it to plaintiffs' detriment. This duty they have breached. There was ample evidence available for the jury to conclude appellants were not sincere in their decision to buy the business, and procured the manufacturing process under the guise of purchasing the business. Moreover, the record supports the conclusion that the appellants acquired the manufacturing process through improper means.

. . . .

NOTES & QUESTIONS

(1) Why did Ambusher's process qualify as a trade secret? What evidence existed of secrecy? Value? Why wasn't the statement "without the specs this information is no secret" fatal to the trade secret claim?

(2) The appellants argued that they did not discover the information through improper means. Are they correct? Was it the acquisition of the trade secret that was improper? *Compare* RESTATEMENT (FIRST) OF TORTS § 757(a) (1939), *with id.* § 757(b), *and* RESTATEMENT (THIRD) OF UNFAIR COMPETITION § 40(b) (1995).

(3) What steps did Phillips take to maintain secrecy and how did this play into the court's analysis? *See* RESTATEMENT (THIRD) OF UNFAIR COMPETITION §§ 39 cmt. g, 40 cmt. d, 41 cmt. b (1995).

(4) What factors supported the finding that a confidential relationship existed between the parties? Do you agree that the *Snap-On* case is distinguishable?

(5) As *Phillips* demonstrates, a confidential relationship does not have to involve an express agreement. A number of other cases have found that, under the right circumstances, the absence of an express agreement of confidentiality does not defeat a trade secret claim. *See Hicklin Eng., L.C. v. Bartell*, 439 F.3d 346, 350 (7th Cir. 2006) (holding that an express agreement was unnecessary because the defendant understood that the information should have been kept confidential); *Speedry Chem. Prods., Inc. v. Carter's Ink Co.*, 306 F.2d 328 (2d Cir. 1962) ("It is true, as plaintiffs contend, that it is not necessary to show an express agreement to hold in confidence and not to use trade secrets obtained as the result of a confidence and not to use trade secrets obtained as the result of a confidential relationship."); *cf. Burten v. Milton Bradley Co.*, 768 F.2d 461, 463 (1st Cir. 1995) (finding that general and somewhat ambiguous language disclaiming a relationship between the parties was insufficient to disclaim a confidential relationship).

In some instances, the relationship itself indicates the existence of a confidential relationship, such as with fiduciaries or other close, personal relationships. *See Elm City Cheese Co. v. Federico*, 752 A.2d 1037 (Conn. 1999) (finding that a confidential relationship existed between an accountant and his client without a written agreement of confidentiality due partly to the nature of the relationship). In business relationships, the question of whether a confidential relationship exists can be much closer, and the absence of an express agreement may be fatal to the claim. *See Hoffman-LaRoche v. Yoder*, 950 F. Supp. 1348, 1354 (S.D. Ohio 1997) (rejecting a trade secret claim due to a lack of evidence indicating that the defendant was informed of the confidential nature of the information, including the absence of an express written or oral agreement to keep the information confidential); *Aerospace Am., Inc. v. Abatement Tech., Inc.*, 738 F. Supp. 1061, 1071 (E.D. Mich. 1990) (finding that without an express agreement of confidentiality, a confidential relationship did not exist because there is no implied confidential relationship between a manufacturer and a distributor). The unifying theme of all of these cases seems to be that courts will find a confidential relationship when a trade secret is revealed to facilitate a specific relationship and the receiving party knew, or should have known, that the information was secret.

PROBLEM 10.4

Assume that during the tour that Phillips was giving to the defendants, they came across a room with designs and prototypes of a duck call. Phillips, beaming with pride, tells the defendants: "This is why I am selling the business. I have a new venture that I am going to start—manufacturing my new duck calls." Phillips then proceeds to show the defendants his design, which has a sleek grip and is easier to use than other models on the market. Months later, the defendants start producing duck calls identical to the one Phillips showed them.

Phillips sues for trade secret misappropriation. Assuming that the duck call design qualifies as a trade secret, will Phillips be able to establish misappropriation? *See* RESTATEMENT (THIRD) OF UNFAIR COMPETITION § 41 cmt. b & illus. (1995).

ii. Breach of Duty by Current and Former Employees

The Third Restatement of Unfair Competition provides that current and former employees who disclose or use a trade secret in violation of a duty of confidence are liable for misappropriation. Employees are typically agents of their employers; thus, current employees generally owe a duty of confidence under basic principles of agency law. Section 387 of the Second Restatement of Agency provides that "[u]nless otherwise agreed, an agent is subject to a duty to his principal to act solely for the benefit of the principal in all matters connected with his agency."[d] This duty to act solely for the benefit of the principal includes a duty of confidentiality. Indeed, with regard to trade secrets, § 395 of the Second Restatement of Agency is particularly relevant:

§ 395   Using or Disclosing Confidential Information

Unless otherwise agreed, an agent is subject to a duty to the principal not to use or to communicate information confidentially given him by the principal or acquired by him during the course of or on account of his agency or in violation of his duties as agent, in competition with or to the injury of the principal, on his own account or on behalf of another, although such information

---

[d] The Third Restatement of Agency similarly provides that an agent owes a fiduciary duty to the principal. *See* RESTATEMENT (THIRD) OF AGENCY § 8.01 (2006).

does not relate to the transaction in which he is then employed, unless the information is a matter of general knowledge.[e]

Thus, with respect to current employees,[f] establishing a duty of confidence is rarely an issue. Such cases frequently turn more on whether what was disclosed qualified as a trade secret, or whether the owner of the trade secret sufficiently conveyed the confidential nature of the information to the current employee. *See, e.g., Omega Optical, Inc. v. Chroma Tech. Corp.*, 800 A.2d 1064, 1066 (Vt. 2002) (holding that the failure to put employees on explicit or implicit notice that the information being conveyed to them was confidential meant that the employees did not breach a duty of confidence, and were therefore not liable for misappropriating a trade secret).

Former employees pose a greater challenge to the trade secret plaintiff. Section 42 of the Third Restatement of Unfair Competition provides that former employees are to be treated the same as current employees. In addition, the Second Restatement of Agency imposes a duty upon former employees not to use or disclose trade secrets:

§ 396   Using Confidential Information after Termination of Agency

Unless otherwise agreed, after the termination of the agency, the agent:

(a)   has no duty not to compete with the principal;

(b)   has a duty to the principal not to use or to disclose to third persons, on his own account or on account of others, in competition with the principal or to his injury, trade secrets, written lists of names, or other similar confidential matters given to him only for the principal's use or acquired by the agent in violation of duty. The agent is entitled to use general information concerning the method of business of the principal and the names of the customers retained in his memory, if not acquired in violation of his duty as agent;

---

[e]   Section 8.05 of the Third Restatement of Agency is more succinct, but has the same meaning:

§ 8.05 Use of Principal's Property; Use of Confidential Information

An agent has a duty

(1) not to use property of the principal for the agent's own purposes or those of a third party; and

(2) not to use or communicate confidential information of the principal for the agent's own purposes or those of a third party.

[f]   Independent contractors can pose a problem with regard to a duty of confidence because not all independent contractors qualify as agents. *See* RESTATEMENT (SECOND) OF AGENCY §§ 2(3), 220 (1958). If an independent contractor is not an agent, then a different basis for a duty of confidence must be found under § 41 of the Third Restatement of Unfair Competition.

(c) has a duty to account for profits made by the sale or use of trade secrets and other confidential information, whether or not in competition with the principal;

(d) has a duty to the principal not to take advantage of a still subsisting confidential relation created during the prior agency relation.

Comment c to § 8.05 of the Third Restatement of Agency also provides that former employees are not free to use confidential information learned during their employment, but it makes an important clarification. While § 396(b) above suggests a possible defense for an employee who commits certain trade secrets to memory, the Third Restatement eliminates this possibility:

An agent is not free to use or disclose a principal's trade secrets or other confidential information whether the agent retains a physical record of them or retains them in the agent's memory. If information is otherwise a trade secret or confidential, the means by which an agent appropriates it for later use or disclosure should be irrelevant. Feats of human memory, however commendable and intriguing in many respects, should not be privileged as instruments of disloyal conduct.

While the rules governing former employees may seem rather straightforward, they are complicated by the tendency of former employees to go work for competitors. The rules stated above specifically disavow any duty not to compete with the principal (absent an agreement to the contrary), but many employers are understandably uncomfortable with the prospect of former employees, who have intimate knowledge of their inner workings and trade secrets, going to work for a competitor (or becoming competitors themselves). The employer may believe that the former employee will use a skill set against the employer—a skill set that the employee only gained after considerable investment by the employer. Moreover, the employer may be fearful that the employee will take clients when he leaves or try to convince other key employees to leave as well. Finally, the employer may simply not trust the former employee to keep the employer's trade secrets confidential.

To combat these fears, employers have developed a number of contractual provisions aimed at limiting a former employee's ability to compete with the employer. Listed below are a number of such provisions, which are collectively referred to as "restrictive covenants," and which are typically found in an employment agreement.

Covenant not to compete—A promise not to engage in the same type of business for a stated time in the same market as the buyer, partner, or employer.

Confidentiality agreement—A promise not to disclose trade secrets or other proprietary information learned in the course of the parties' relationship.

Nonsolicitation agreement—A promise to refrain from trying to lure customers away from the employer for a specified period of time.

"No-hire" or employee nonsolicitation agreement—A promise to refrain from enticing employees to leave the company for a specified period of time.

Another type of clause frequently found in employment agreements is a "trailer clause." As you will later learn, not all trade secrets developed during the employment relationship belong to the employer. Thus, many employers insert trailer clauses which require employees to assign their rights to inventions developed during the employment relationship to the employer. These clauses also frequently require the employees to assign their rights to inventions developed post-employment for a specified period of time. Trailer clauses are subject to the same limitations as the above restrictive covenants.

Restrictive covenants are creatures of contract law rather than trade secret law. In most jurisdictions, such covenants are subject to scrutiny due to their effect on commerce. While employers may well have a right to protect their legitimate business interests, former employees also have a right to work and ply their trades. Furthermore, such covenants may injure the public at large by denying it access to the full range of skills that former employees have to offer. For these reasons, restrictive covenants are typically subject to a reasonableness analysis by the courts which weigh the former employee's and employer's interests. Although such covenants can reach a broad range of conduct, the existence and possible use of trade secrets is often an issue in restrictive covenant disputes.

SIGMA CHEMICAL CO. V. HARRIS

794 F.2d 371 (8th Cir. 1986)

McMILLAN, CIRCUIT JUDGE.

Foster Harris appeals from a final judgment entered in the District Court for the Eastern District of Missouri enjoining him from employment for a two-year period with ICN Pharmaceuticals, Inc. (ICN), and from using and disclosing trade secrets. Sigma Chemical Company (Sigma) cross-appeals. For the reasons discussed below, we affirm in part and reverse in part . . . and remand for further proceedings. . . .

Briefly, the following is relevant to this appeal. Sigma sells 16,000 esoteric chemicals used in research, production, and analysis. Sigma purchases 10,000 of these chemicals from approximately 2,300 suppliers.

Sigma analyzes the purchased chemicals and packages them in smaller units for resale. For example, Sigma sells pure salt. Although common table salt can be purchased in a grocery store, Sigma expends time and effort to determine which supplier is capable of producing the requisite quality of pure salt for scientific research. The results of Sigma's chemical analyses are not made known to the supplier; Sigma does not inform the supplier of the reasons if it rejects the chemical.

Sigma maintains product and vendor files containing information about the chemicals purchased for resale. Sigma has developed these files over 40 years. A typical product file contains the name of the product, information regarding Sigma's source or sources for the product, quality control testing information, price and purchasing history information, and complaints, if any, from customers. A typical vendor file consists of the supplier's name, and price and quality information regarding products purchased from that vendor.

Harris was an experienced purchasing agent at Sigma. Although Harris had signed a restrictive covenant prohibiting him from working for a competitor of Sigma for a period of two years following his termination at Sigma and prohibit[ing] him from using or disclosing Sigma's trade secrets,[2] within two years of his termination at Sigma[,] Harris went to work as a purchasing agent for ICN, one of Sigma's top competitors.

The district court found that the information contained in Sigma's product and vendor files was protected trade secrets and that the restrictive covenant was reasonable as to time and geographic location and therefore enjoined Harris from working as a purchasing agent for ICN for the period of time covered by the covenant and from disclosing or using trade secrets.

[The court concluded that Missouri law applied to the diversity action and affirmed the district court's finding that the information at issue was a protectable trade secret.]

Harris next argues that the district court erred as a matter of law in enforcing the restrictive covenant because the covenant did not contain time and place restrictions. Under Missouri law, "[c]ovenants against

---

[2]   The covenant provided in pertinent part:

I shall not, directly or indirectly . . . for a period of two years following termination for any reason of my employment with the Company engage in or contribute my knowledge to any work or activity that involves a product, process, service or development which is then competitive with and the same as or similar to a product, process, service or development on which I worked or with respect to which I had access to Confidential Information while with the Company. . . .

. . . .

Following expiration of said two-year period, I shall continue to be obligated under the "Confidential Information" section of this Agreement not to use or to disclose Confidential Information so long as it shall remain proprietary or protectible as confidential or trade secret information.

competition ... must be reasonably limited in time and space." *Osage Glass, Inc. v. Donovan*, 693 S.W.2d 71, 74 (Mo. banc 1985).

Harris argues that the noncompetition covenant was unenforceable because it failed to contain a geographical restriction. He relies on *National Motor Club of Missouri, Inc. v. Noe*, 475 S.W.2d 16, 22 (Mo.1972), in which the state supreme court found that a noncompetition agreement was "void as against public policy because [it was] not reasonably limited to any territory of competition." The district court found that *National Motor Club of Missouri, Inc. v. Noe* was inapplicable to the instant case because, unlike the case before the court, there was no evidence of worldwide competition. The district court noted that "the test for the reasonableness of the geographic scope of a restrictive covenant is whether it is 'no greater than fairly required for protection,' " 605 F.Supp. at 1260, *citing Continental Research Corp. v. Scholz*, 595 S.W.2d 396, 400 (Mo.Ct.App.1980), and that in the instant case a worldwide restriction was reasonable because Sigma competed worldwide.

We need not decide whether Harris is correct in his assertion that under Missouri law the covenant was unenforceable because of a lack of a geographical restriction. In this case, the district court did not issue a worldwide injunction but only enforced the covenant to prohibit Harris' employment with ICN, clearly a reasonable restriction. Missouri courts "have decreed enforcement as against a defendant whose breach occurred within an area in which restriction would clearly be reasonable, even though the terms of the agreement imposed a larger and unreasonable restraint." *R.E. Harrington, Inc. v. Frick*, 428 S.W.2d 945, 951 (Mo.App.1968).

Harris also argues that the district court erred in enjoining disclosure of trade secrets because the nondisclosure covenant was unlimited as to time. The district court found that issuance of an injunction was proper because even in the absence of a nondisclosure covenant employees are under an "absolute, temporally unlimited duty not to disclose his/her employer's trade secrets." *Sigma Chemical Co. v. Harris*, 586 F.Supp. 704, 710 (E.D.Mo.1984) (memorandum opinion granting preliminary injunction). The district court, however, cited no Missouri case law in support but relied on *Nucor Corp. v. Tennessee Forging Steel Service, Inc.*, 476 F.2d 386, 392 (8th Cir.1973), in which this court applied Arkansas law.[4] Although Missouri law recognizes that employees are under an implied duty not to disclose trade secrets, the Missouri Supreme Court has stated that "in cases where the court has

---

[4] There has been a long-standing dispute among the federal circuits about whether a party misappropriating trade secrets should be enjoined permanently from using the information or whether the duration of the injunction should be limited to put the defendant in the position it would have been in absent the misappropriation. Although discussion of this issue often focuses on the disagreements between the circuits ... trade secret law is state law, and the federal appellate decisions are not necessarily the final word on these issues of state law.

granted injunctive relief based upon the misuse of actual trade secrets, the courts have limited the injunction to the time which would have been required to reproduce a copyable product." *National Rejectors, Inc. v. Trieman,* 409 S.W.2d 1, 43 (Mo. banc 1966).

We believe the statement from *National Rejectors, Inc. v. Trieman* is in conflict with the district court's holding that employees are under a "temporally unlimited" duty not to disclose trade secrets. *See also Carboline Co. v. Jarboe,* 454 S.W.2d 540, 552–53 (Mo.1970) (trade secret injunction should be limited to time in which products could be reproduced absent wrongful appropriation). In trade secret injunctions, "many . . . jurisdictions have used this 'independent development test.'" *Syntex Opthalmics, Inc. v. Novicky,* 745 F.2d 1423, 1435–36 n. 23 (Fed.Cir.1984) (*Syntex*), *vacated on other grounds,* 470 U.S. 1047 (1985). In *Syntex,* a case factually similar to the case at bar, the Federal Circuit Court of Appeals affirmed a district court's finding that under Illinois law a "set of processes and ingredients" used in the manufacture of contact lenses was entitled to trade secrets protection. *Id.* at 1433–34. The Federal Circuit, however, found that the durational scope of the injunction issued by the district court to prohibit disclosure of trade secrets was too broad under Illinois law. "Under Illinois law an injunction in a trade secret case must be limited to the approximate length of time necessary for the defendant to duplicate the trade secrets by lawful means." *Id.* at 1435.[5] The appellate court believed that the district court's error was important because extending the injunction beyond the time needed for independent development would give the employer " 'a windfall protection and would subvert the public interest in fostering competition and in allowing employees to make full use of their knowledge and ability.' " *Id.* (citations omitted).

We believe the part of the injunction prohibiting disclosure of trade secrets must be limited in duration and, accordingly, reverse in part and remand the case to the district court for consideration of the time it would take a "legitimate competitor" to independently reproduce the information contained in the product and vendor files. *See National Rejectors, Inc. v. Trieman,* 409 S.W.2d at 43, *citing Winston Research Corp. v. Minnesota Mining & Manufacturing Co.,* 350 F.2d 134, 142 (9th Cir.1965). On remand, the district court should also modify the language of the injunction to expressly state that Harris may use that information which is already in the public domain. *See Syntex,* 765 F.2d at 1437 ("because the misappropriated trade secrets consist of a compilation of reactions . . . [the] injunction should be modified to assure that appellant

---

[5]   The Federal Circuit found that the district court erred in extending the injunction for 20 years based on testimony that it took Syntex 20 years to develop the process. The court believed that it would not necessarily take the employee 20 years to recreate independently the trade secrets and remanded the case for further consideration of the time it would take for independent production of the trade secrets.

engineering design information contained herein is considered proprietary.

Though the testimony is disputed, the court found that after Henry made a preliminary commitment to purchase a Merrill dryer design, Bernier contacted Henry for a job, Bernier resigned from Merrill, Henry canceled the dryer order, and Bernier accepted a position at Henry. The court further found that when Bernier inquired about employment at Henry, he was informed that Henry's objectives included obtaining dryers at the lowest price. When Bernier interviewed with Henry, he told a Henry employee that he had his own dryer design. The offer of employment that Bernier accepted included bonuses for dryers built while he was at Henry. By the end of 1997, a new dryer was built at Henry under Bernier's supervision. The dryer built at Henry varied from the Merrill dryer design, although the parties dispute the degree of variation.

Merrill [alleged] breach of contract and misappropriation of trade secrets. The court held that Bernier did not violate the UTSA, but did breach his "contractual obligations under both paragraphs three and four of his contract." Finding that it was more likely than not that Henry would have ordered a dryer from Merrill if Bernier had not breached his employment contract, Merrill was awarded damages in the amount of Merrill's net profit from the construction and design of the dryer for Henry.

Bernier contends that the Superior Court erred in enforcing paragraph 3 (nondisclosure clause). First, Bernier contends that the nondisclosure clause is insufficient to protect information that is not protected by the UTSA. Second, Bernier contends that the nondisclosure clause is not reasonable.

An employer, under a proper restrictive agreement, can prevent a former employee from using his trade or business secrets, and other confidential knowledge gained in the course of the employment, and from enticing away old customers. The confidential knowledge or information protected by a restrictive covenant need not be limited to information that is protected as a trade secret by the UTSA. We have not previously read such limitations into restrictive covenants and do not do so now.

. . . .

Proper restrictive covenants cannot preclude former employees from following any trade or calling for which he is fitted and from which he may earn his livelihood or exercising the skill and general knowledge he has acquired or increased through experience or even instructions while in the employment. To be enforceable the agreement must impose no undue hardship upon the employee and be no wider in its scope than is reasonably necessary for the protection of the business of the employer.

The nondisclosure clause in the Bernier-Merrill employment contract is reasonable. We uphold the court's conclusion that paragraph 3 reasonably prohibits Bernier from using particularized, highly specialized proprietary protected original work that was custom designed for a particular prospect. In balancing Bernier's interest in securing employment and Merrill's interest in protecting the confidential information it created, we find that the agreement does not pose an undue hardship on Bernier, and it is not broader than necessary to protect Merrill's business. The nondisclosure clause does not prohibit Bernier from using the general skill and knowledge he acquired during his employment with Merrill. Instead, the nondisclosure clause protects the use of information that does not rise to the level of a trade secret but is more than general skill or knowledge. Thus, Paragraph 3 reasonably precluded Bernier from designing a dryer for Henry by using the "original work" he became privy to while developing Merrill's dryer proposal to Henry. In addition, we do not agree with Bernier's contention that the nondisclosure clause is unreasonable because it is not limited in duration. We do not find that durational limits are necessary in nondisclosure clauses, as they are in noncompete agreements, because the "imposition of geographic or durational limitations 'would defeat the entire purpose of restricting disclosure, since confidentiality knows no temporal or geographical boundaries.'" *Revere Transducers, Inc. v. Deere & Co.,* 595 N.W.2d 751, 761 (Iowa 1999) (citing 2 RUDOLF CALLMANN, THE LAW OF UNFAIR COMPETITION, TRADEMARKS & MONOPOLIES § 14.04, at 222–23 (Supp.1998)).

Next, we consider Bernier's contention that, even if the nondisclosure clause is enforceable, there is insufficient evidence to conclude that while employed at Henry, Bernier used or disclosed in the words of the Superior Court "particularized, highly specialized proprietary protected original work that was custom designed" for Henry by Merrill. Bernier contends that the components of Merrill's original work, including graph oil seals, staggered mirror image nozzles, welded wall panels, end enclosures and burners that were identified during the trial as being used by Bernier to develop the Henry dryer, are not "particularized, highly specialized proprietary protected original work." The Superior Court stated:

> [A]lthough there are differences between the original Merrill design and the ultimate dryer that was installed at Henry Molded Products, the timing of the negotiation and the hiring of Mr. Bernier and the timing of the Bernier design combined with the similarity of the Bernier design to the Merrill proposal led me to the inescapable conclusion that original work of Merrill was used.

Thus, the Superior Court made its determination based on a finding that the "original work" used by Bernier was the process and concept Merrill generated to create the Henry proposal, and not the separate components themselves.

. . . . We find that there is sufficient evidence that Bernier violated the nondisclosure clause by using "particularized, highly specialized proprietary protected original work" from Merrill. Whether Merrill's "original work" was used by Bernier to design the Henry dryer encompasses more than a component by component comparison. Bernier testified that while he was employed at Merrill, he assisted in preparing the Henry dryer proposal. The president of Merrill testified that the proposal contained the dryer description, including graph oil seals, tongue and groove walls, and the nozzle arrangement, and Bernier testified that the dryer he ultimately designed for Henry contained graph oil seals and mirror imaging nozzles. Bernier also testified that he was involved in observing and compiling the data that Merrill generated to create the Henry proposal. Furthermore, Bernier testified that he wrote an interoffice memorandum at the end of his first week at Henry that stated: "[t]he knowledge gained this week in conjunction with my previous knowledge of the project will allow me to move ahead with the dryer design next week." Thus, the combination of the common components, the specific knowledge gained while developing the Henry dryer proposal while employed at Merrill, and the process of designing the dryer for Henry are sufficient facts to find that Bernier breached his employment contract.

[The court stated that although Bernier violated the nondisclosure agreement, the district court's conclusion that the information did not rise to the level of a trade secret was not clearly erroneous. As a result, there was no independent cause of action under state trade secret law.]

NOTES & QUESTIONS

(1) What is the standard used by the court to review restrictive covenants? How does this standard compare to the *Sigma* case?

(2) The *Bernier* court affirmed the district court's conclusion that the product dryer information was not a trade secret, but nonetheless determined that the restrictive covenant may be enforced. Do you agree that information not rising to the level of a trade secret should be entitled to the same protection under a restrictive covenant as information that does rise to that level? Should the reasonableness of a covenant be judged, in part, by whether the information does in fact qualify as a trade secret? *See* RESTATEMENT (THIRD) OF UNFAIR COMPETITION § 41 cmt. d (1995). *But see Empire Farm Credit ACA v. Bailey*, 657 N.Y.S.2d 211, 212 (App. Div. 1997) (holding that restrictive covenants "will be enforced to the extent necessary to prevent the use of trade secrets *or confidential customer information*, but only so long as they are reasonable in time and area, not harmful to the general public and not unreasonably burdensome to the employee" (emphasis added)); *Lifetec,*

Inc. v. Edwards, 880 N.E.2d 188, 192 (Ill. App. Ct. 2007) ("In determining whether a restrictive covenant is enforceable, courts must determine whether the terms of the agreement are reasonable and necessary to protect a legitimate business interest of the plaintiff." (internal quotations omitted)).

(3) In *Sigma*, the court remanded the case to place a temporal (i.e., durational) limit on the injunction. The court did not decide whether the covenant was unenforceable because of a lack of a geographic restriction. In *Bernier*, the court addressed both the temporal and geographic limitations: "We do not find that durational limits are necessary in nondisclosure clauses, as they are in noncompete agreements, because the imposition of geographic or durational limitations would defeat the entire purpose of restricting disclosure, since confidentiality knows no temporal or geographical boundaries." Do you agree with the *Bernier* court that restrictive covenants on the disclosure and use of trade secrets do not need to be held to the same temporal and geographic standards as covenants not to compete?

(4) Contrary to the facts of the dispute, assume that Bernier did not work on or have access to the product dryer that was developed specifically for Henry. He nevertheless gained valuable engineering experience while at Merrill, which was the reason Henry hired him. Assume further that Bernier used this experience to help Henry develop its own product dryer. Would these facts have changed the result? *See* RESTATEMENT (THIRD) OF UNFAIR COMPETITION § 42 cmt. d (1995).

(5) Most states subject restrictive covenants to some form of reasonableness review. New York, for example, adopts a "prevailing standard of reasonableness." *See BDO Seidman v. Hirshberg*, 712 N.E.2d 1220, 1223 (N.Y. 1999) (explaining that a non-compete agreement is reasonable if it: "(1) is *no greater* than is required for the protection of the *legitimate interest* of the employer, (2) does not impose undue hardship on the employee, and (3) is not injurious to the public"). Similarly, Illinois examines the totality of the circumstances to determine if an employer's protectable interest is being advanced without unreasonably limiting competition. *See Lifetec, Inc. v. Edwards*, 880 N.E.2d 188, 192 (Ill. App. Ct. 2007) ("Because restrictive covenants in employment agreements are a form of restraint of trade, they are scrutinized carefully to ensure their intended effect is not to prevent competition *per se*."). Texas has adopted a statutory regime which focuses upon reasonableness. *See Marsh USA, Inc. v. Cook*, 354 S.W.3d 764, 777 (Tex. 2011) ("Rather, the statute's core inquiry is whether the covenant contains limitations as to time, geographical area, and scope of activity to be restrained that are reasonable and do not impose a greater restraint than is necessary to protect the goodwill or other business interest of the promisee." (internal quotations omitted)). Florida has also codified its law of restrictive covenants. Rather than rely purely on a general reasonableness analysis, Florida's statute provides a number of restrictive covenant "safe harbors" where reasonableness is presumed. *See* FLA. STAT. § 542.335.

California has notably broken from the traditional reasonableness analysis by viewing restrictive covenants as unlawful restraints of trade. *See* CAL. BUS. & PROF. CODE § 16600 ("[E]very contract by which anyone is restrained from engaging in a lawful profession, trade, or business of any kind is to that extent void."). This creates some conflict with trade secret law, however, as California has adopted the UTSA. To mitigate this conflict, California courts have created a "trade secret exception" to § 16600, which allows an employer to restrain a former employee who has knowledge of trade secrets from accepting work with a competitor. *See Whyte v. Schlage Lock Co.*, 125 Cal. Rptr. 2d 277, 293 (Cal. Ct. App. 2002) ("Nearly 40 years ago, the California Supreme Court recognized [that] covenants not to compete are enforceable notwithstanding Business and Professions Code section 16600 if 'necessary to protect the employer's trade secrets.' "). The scope of this exception has been called into doubt by recent decisions, but the ability to prevent disclosure of confidential information under the exception appears to be intact. *Compare Edwards v. Arthur Andersen LLP*, 189 P.3d 285, 288 (Cal. 2008) (stating that "[w]e conclude that section 16600 prohibits employee noncompetition agreements unless the agreement falls within a statutory exception"), *with id.* at 289 n.4 ("We do not here address the applicability of the so-called trade secret exception to section 16600, as Edwards does not dispute that portion of his agreement or contend that the provision of the noncompetition agreement prohibiting him from recruiting Andersen's employees violated section 16600."), *and Bank of America, N.A. v. Lee*, No. CV 08–5546, 2008 WL 4351348, at *6 (C.D. Cal. Sept. 22, 2008) ("The Court concludes that [the] trade secret exception to § 16600 still applies. Nothing in *Edwards* is to the contrary."). *But see Robinson v. U-Haul Co. of Calif.*, Nos. A124070, A124097, A124096, 2010 WL 4113578, at *10–11 (Cal. Ct. App. Oct. 20, 2010) (noting that "the so-called 'trade secrets' exception to Business and Professions Code section 16600 ... rests on shaky legal grounds," and observing that "[e]ven assuming the continued viability of this exception, it has no application here").

C. DEFENSES

1. REVERSE ENGINEERING AND INDEPENDENT DISCOVERY

Section 1(2) of the UTSA provides that misappropriation occurs when a trade secret is "acquired by improper means." The comments to § 1 clarify that proper means include reverse engineering and independent discovery. Section 43 of the Third Restatement of Unfair Competition similarly notes that "[i]ndependent discovery and analysis of publicly available products or information are not improper means of acquisition."

Under the comments to UTSA § 1, reverse engineering is defined as discovery "by starting with the known product and working backward to find the method by which it was developed." Thus, if a product is on the open market and a competitor purchases the item, takes it apart, and discovers how to manufacture it, the competitor is free to do so (absent protection under another theory, such as patent law). Of course, this assumes that the acquisition of the product itself was lawful. If a prototype was stolen from a competitor, for example, reverse engineering would not be a defense. *See* UTSA § 1 cmts.

Independent discovery is arguably further removed from the trade secret than reverse engineering, as it does not rely on copying or taking apart a competitor's process or product. For instance, assume that two competitors, A and B, are both trying to develop a new method of hydraulic fracturing (or "fracking" as it is often called) that conserves water.[g] A develops a method and begins to use it, but soon after, B discovers the same method and begins to use it. Assuming that none of A's employees had left to work for B, and absent a claim that B committed some form of corporate espionage, a suit by A would likely fail due to B's defense of independent discovery. In claiming independent discovery, the defendant is essentially saying there was no misappropriation.

The claims of reverse engineering and independent discovery are strongest when the defendant has not had any prior exposure to the trade secret. However, the defenses are much more questionable when the two parties shared information. Assume that B had approached A to develop a new method of hydraulic fracturing. The two shared some initial thoughts on the matter, but eventually B ended the negotiations. A and B subsequently develop very similar methods. Given that B has been exposed to A's ideas, can B successfully raise an independent discovery defense? What if B relied on A's concepts, but not in any substantial way? The following case considers these questions.

PENALTY KICK MANAGEMENT LTD. V. COCA COLA CO.
318 F.3d 1284 (11th Cir. 2003)

TJOFLAT, CIRCUIT JUDGE:

Penalty Kick Management Ltd. ("PKM") brought this lawsuit against the Coca-Cola Company ("Coca-Cola"), seeking legal and equitable relief under theories of conversion, misappropriation of a trade secret, breach of contract, breach of a confidential relationship and duty of good faith, unjust enrichment, and quantum meruit. The district court granted summary judgment in favor of Coca-Cola as to all claims, and PKM appeals. We affirm.

---

[g] Hydraulic fracturing is a method of oil and gas production whereby rock is fractured by a pressurized water compound.

I.

A.

In early 1995, PKM's Chief Executive Officer, Peter Glancy, conceived of a beverage label marketing and production process known as "Magic Windows." Magic Windows consisted of the following: a scrambled message on the inside of a beverage container label which could be decoded and read only after the beverage container was emptied. The message would be read through a colored filter printed on a label on the opposite side of the container, directly across from the coded message.

On November 2, 1995, Glancy and Charles Carter of PKM met with representatives of Coca-Cola to demonstrate Magic Windows. Glancy orally advised the Coca-Cola representatives that the information concerning Magic Windows was confidential, and the representatives regarded it as such. Glancy also advised the representatives that PKM was pursuing global patent protection on Magic Windows,[1] and thus would be in a position to provide Coca-Cola the exclusive rights to the Magic Windows marketing tool.

A few months after the meeting, in February of 1996, the parties executed a *Non-Disclosure Agreement* in which each agreed not to disclose to any third party any confidential information shared during discussions regarding Magic Windows. However, the agreement went on to provide:

[T]here is no obligation to maintain in confidence any information that:

(i)   at the time of disclosure is available to the public;

(ii) after disclosure, becomes available to the public by publication or otherwise;

(iii) is in [Coca-Cola's or its subsidiaries' or affiliates' possession], at the time of disclosure [ ];

(iv) is rightfully received from a third party; [or]

. . . .

(vi) [Coca-Cola] can establish was subsequently developed independently by [Coca-Cola or its subsidiaries or affiliates] independently of any disclosure hereunder.

After the execution of the agreement, PKM and Coca-Cola representatives met again to discuss the possibility of Coca-Cola licensing Magic Windows for its exclusive use. Following several months of

---

[1] Glancy applied for patents for Magic Windows in the United States and the United Kingdom. The U.S. patent application was rejected in July 1998 because Glancy's claims were anticipated by information in a 1993 international patent application filed by Virtual Image. After modifying the application, however, Glancy received a U.S. patent in 1999 covering some, but not all, aspects of Magic Windows.

discussions, on July 16, 1996, Coca-Cola drafted a *Development and License Agreement* in which, among other things, Coca-Cola proposed to pay PKM $1 million and a per label royalty for a global license giving Coca-Cola the exclusive right to use Magic Windows.

Concomitant with sending its proposed license agreement, however, Coca-Cola undertook an intellectual property review of PKM's patent applications to determine, inter alia, whether PKM could actually provide Coca-Cola with exclusivity over the concept embodied in Magic Windows. In the course of that review, Coca-Cola unearthed a copy of the Virtual Image patent application published in May of 1993, and sent a copy of the application to Glancy on October 7, 1996. The Virtual Image patent application revealed that the two main concepts of Magic Windows— using a colored filter to decode a disguised message and placing the filter on the side of a bottle label opposite the coded message, already existed in prior art. In view of the Virtual Image patent application, Coca-Cola concluded that the Magic Windows concept was in the public domain, and that PKM could not provide the patent exclusivity Coca-Cola was seeking. Accordingly, a month later, on November, 19, 1996, Coca-Cola informed PKM that it would " 'not pursue [an] exclusivity agreement' w[ith] them," and terminated all negotiations.

B.

PKM's presentation was not the first or only time that Coca-Cola had discussed window labels and decoder filters. Two other instances are particularly important in this case.[4] First, in November of 1995 (the same month PKM first met with Coca-Cola), Coca-Cola asked BrightHouse, an Atlanta-based ideation company, to create a promotion for the upcoming 1996 NFL season. One of the ideas presented by BrightHouse in December of 1995 was the creation of a bottle label with a scrambled message on the back inside of the label and a red decoder filter printed on the front side of the label. BrightHouse believed the concept would work, and proved its point with a graphic illustration and a bottle mock-up. Coca-Cola subsequently tested the BrightHouse concept with focus groups in order to gauge consumer reaction to a decoder bottle.

Second, in September of 1996 (while Coca-Cola was still negotiating with PKM), Coca-Cola met with Steve Everett, a salesman with ITW-Autosleeve ("ITW"), the regular printer for labels used on Coca-Cola's products in Argentina, to discuss a windows label promotion in Argentina. At this meeting, Coca-Cola representatives discussed the concept of the window label in general terms, showed Everett a mock-up of a bottle with a label, and asked if ITW was capable of manufacturing such a label. The label included a message that was printed off an ink-jet

---

[4] In addition to these two instances, Coca-Cola utilized color-encoded game pieces that were decoded by red filters in both 1981 and 1991.

or bubble-jet printer and was taped to the back side of the bottle; red litho paper was on the front side of the bottle. ITW informed Coca-Cola it could produce the label and set out to do so.

ITW's Graphic Arts Manager, Jeffrey Albaugh, was assigned the task. He was not given any instruction on how to create the sample label. Albaugh independently determined the type of printing press, inks, color sequences, and production processes needed. He alone did the following: constructed the scrambled text on the label; planned the print formula; selected the film to use as a substrate for the label; chose the color to use on the filter; figured how to block the scrambled message from being read from the outside; picked the weight and tone of the ink; established the printing setup; and decided whether to print on the surface or reverse print the label. Albaugh made these decisions based on his experience as a printer. He viewed the task as "simple, everyday printing" that did not require "anything new in technology." After approximately three weeks, Albaugh completed the bottle label. Coca-Cola subsequently used the label in an Argentinian marketing promotion.

In February of 1997, PKM learned of the Argentinian promotion. After viewing one of the Coca-Cola bottles, PKM was alarmed by (what it perceived to be) the striking similarity between its Magic Windows label and the bottle label developed by ITW. Glancy called Coca-Cola to determine whether Coca-Cola had used the information PKM had shared to help create the ITW label. When Coca-Cola denied any wrongdoing, PKM filed this suit.

C.

The complaint in this case is framed in six counts. Count I alleged that Coca-Cola converted PKM's Magic Label technology for its own use; Count II alleged that Coca-Cola misappropriated trade secrets when it divulged the disclosed information to ITW, who in turn, used that information to develop its label; Count III alleged that Coca-Cola breached the *Non-Disclosure Agreement* when it disclosed confidential information to ITW; Count IV alleged that Coca-Cola breached its confidential relationship and duty of good faith imposed by O.C.G.A. § 23–2–58; Count V alleged that Coca-Cola was unjustly enriched by utilizing PKM's design of, and production process for, the Magic Windows technology; finally, Count VI alleged that Coca-Cola failed to compensate PKM for the services and property provided to Coca-Cola.

Coca-Cola answered the complaint, denying liability on all counts. In short, Coca-Cola stated that the information revealed by PKM regarding Magic Windows was not a trade secret, was not disclosed to ITW or any other third party, and was not used by Coca-Cola. Additionally, Coca-Cola had complied with the *Non-Disclosure Agreement,* and did not owe any money to PKM because it did not provide Coca-Cola with any valuable services or property. Rather, the Magic Windows concept was rightfully received by Coca-Cola during the BrightHouse presentation, and any other allegedly misappropriated elements of Magic Windows were independently developed by ITW using well-known printing techniques.

As part of its defense, Coca-Cola served an interrogatory on PKM asking PKM to identify every element of the Magic Windows technology that PKM contended was misappropriated by Coca-Cola. Plaintiff responded, in pertinent part,

> PKM contends that Coke misappropriated a promotional concept referred to as "Magic Windows," "Clear View Windows," and "Rear View Windows" that requires purchasers of containers (in the case of Coke, a beverage container) to empty the contents of the container to receive a message or to determine whether they have won a prize which was incorporated in a commercially feasible beverage label printed on a gravure or comparable press with standard inks onto single-laminate, flexible plastic packaging material using a label production process and color sequences whereby up to eight colors can be utilized to print onto film, as a substrate, or reverse-printed, which leaves the plastic film facing forward and toward the viewer to create a beverage label with a non-embossed, two or three colored encrypted image or message on the inside or reverse side of the label that is visually incoherent which appears approximately opposite or approximately 180° from a colored window filter which is used as a viewing mechanism to decode the image or message in a visually coherent form.

From this response, Coca-Cola had an expert create a chart of the allegedly misappropriated elements. [The court produced a chart dividing PKM's claims into production and concept elements.]

> PKM's expert generally agreed with the chart. Additionally, the district court adopted the chart in a November 30, 2000 Order (in which the court limited PKM's trade secret claim to the elements listed in the chart). PKM did not object to the court's adoption of the chart.

Several months later, after extensive discovery and many depositions, the court, in a March 28, 2001 Order, granted Coca-Cola's motion for summary judgment on all counts of the complaint. As for the misappropriation of trade secrets claim, the court found as a matter of law that although Magic Windows was a trade secret, Coca-Cola had not misappropriated either the concept or the actual printing process of Magic Windows. The court also held that Coca-Cola had not breached the *Non-Disclosure Agreement,* finding as a matter of law that the Magic Windows concept was rightfully received from BrightHouse, and that ITW independently developed the labels from "simple, everyday printing" techniques. Finally, the court held that the remaining counts—conversion, breach of confidential relationship and duty of good faith, unjust enrichment, and quantum meruit—were superseded by Georgia's trade secret law. As a result of the court's rulings, judgment was entered for Coca-Cola and the case was closed.

PKM appeals each of the district court's rulings, contending that (1) there are genuine issues of material fact as to whether Coca-Cola misappropriated confidential information regarding Magic Windows and breached the *Non-Disclosure Agreement,* and (2) the district court improperly applied Georgia trade secret law regarding both misappropriation and supersession. For these reasons, PKM maintains the district court's judgment should be reversed.

Since the heart of this case involves the claim for the misappropriation of trade secrets, we begin our analysis of the district court's rulings on that issue.

II.

A.

Under the Georgia Trade Secrets Act ("GTSA"), O.C.G.A. § 10–1–760 *et seq.,* a claim for misappropriation of trade secrets requires a plaintiff to prove that (1) it had a trade secret and (2) the opposing party misappropriated the trade secret. Whether information constitutes a "trade secret" is a question of fact.

[The court concluded that under the GTSA, there was no legal error in the district court's finding that PKM's Magic Windows constituted a trade secret under Georgia law.]

B.

Having agreed with the district court that information regarding Magic Windows constitutes a trade secret, we must next determine whether Coca-Cola misappropriated PKM's trade secrets when it had ITW develop a label. A defendant misappropriates a trade secret when, among other things, it discloses or uses a trade secret of another, without express or implied consent, knowing that at the time of disclosure or use the trade secret was acquired under circumstances giving rise to a duty to maintain its secrecy or limit its use. In this case, the surrounding circumstances, namely the *Non-Disclosure Agreement,* clearly gave rise to a duty on the part of Coca-Cola to maintain the secrecy of any Magic Windows trade secrets. In fact, Coca-Cola does not dispute that it had a duty to maintain the secrecy of PKM's shared trade secrets. The issue of misappropriation, therefore, hinges on whether Coca-Cola actually disclosed or used PKM's trade secrets when it employed ITW to develop a label—an allegation Coca-Cola vigorously denies.

When the Supreme Court of Georgia recently addressed trade secrets under the GTSA, it relied heavily upon the *Restatement (Third) of Unfair Competition* (1995)—quoting and adopting two paragraphs from the *Restatement* to determine the meaning of "trade secret." We therefore think it prudent to consult the *Restatement* for guidance to determine what constitutes "disclosure" and "use" under the Act. Section 40 provides the answer:

> There are no technical limitations on the nature of the conduct that constitutes "use" of a trade secret. . . . As a general matter, any exploitation of the trade secret that is likely to result in injury to the trade secret owner or enrichment to the defendant is a "use". . . . Thus, marketing goods that embody the trade secret, employing the trade secret in manufacturing or production, [and] relying on the trade secret to assist or accelerate research or development . . . all constitute "use."

> The unauthorized use need not extend to every aspect or feature of the trade secret; use of any *substantial portion* of the secret is sufficient to subject the actor to liability. Similarly, the actor need not use the trade secret in its original form. Thus, an actor is liable for using the trade secret with independently created improvements or modifications if the result is *substantially derived* from the trade secret. . . . However, if the contribution made by the trade secret is *so slight* that the actor's product or process can be said to derive from other sources of information or from independent creation, the trade secret has not been "used" for purposes of imposing liability under the rules. . . .

> The owner of a trade secret may be injured by unauthorized disclosure of a trade secret as well as by unauthorized use. . . . Any conduct by the actor that enables another to learn the trade secret . . . is "disclosure" of the secret.

Restatement (Third) of Unfair Competition § 40 cmt. c (1995) (emphasis added).

To summarize, under the *Restatement,* a defendant is liable for the misappropriation of a trade secret only if the plaintiff can show that the defendant (1) disclosed information that enabled a third party to learn the trade secret or (2) used a "substantial portion" of the plaintiff's trade secret to create an improvement or modification that is "substantially derived" from the plaintiff's trade secret. On the other hand, if the defendant independently created the allegedly misappropriated item with only "slight" contribution from the plaintiff's trade secret, then the defendant is not liable for misappropriation. These standards suggest that for Coca-Cola to be liable for misappropriating Magic Windows, PKM must prove either that Coca-Cola disclosed information that enabled ITW to learn PKM's trade secret or that ITW's label was "substantially derived" from PKM's Magic Window label and not the result of independent creation.[8] We think that PKM has failed to prove either.

1.

PKM has presented no direct evidence that Coca-Cola disclosed PKM's trade secrets to ITW. Several Coca-Cola representatives testified that no PKM trade secrets were revealed to ITW. Moreover, employees from ITW, Steve Everett and Jeffrey Albaugh, both testified that ITW alone determined how to develop its bottle label and that they did not utilize any information from Coca-Cola or PKM in the production process.

Faced with a lack of direct evidence that Coca-Cola disclosed PKM's trade secrets, PKM resorts to relying on various forms of circumstantial evidence to prove [that] Coca-Cola actually disclosed its trade secrets to ITW. First, PKM highlights the fact that Coca-Cola cannot produce as evidence the label it provided to ITW, and argues Coca-Cola's inability to do so warrants a "negative inference" of misappropriation. We find no support in the law for such a proposition. In this circuit "an adverse inference is drawn from a party's failure to preserve evidence only when the absence of that evidence is predicated on bad faith." *Bashir v. Amtrak,* 119 F.3d 929, 931 (11th Cir.1997). There is no indication of bad faith in this case, so we decline to draw an adverse inference for the lost label.

Second, PKM points out that the "same [Coca-Cola] employees who received PKM's disclosures approached ITW to produce the Argentine label." It again suggests this fact warrants an inference of misappropriation. For the same reason, we decline to draw such an inference. Additionally, we note that it was the job of these Coca-Cola representatives to develop product and marketing promotions. This inevitably requires meeting with more than one entity.

Finally, PKM argues that notes written by Steve Everett, testimony by Jeffrey Albaugh, and a voice mail message left by a Coca-Cola representative who had met with both PKM and ITW all prove that Coca-Cola provided ITW with PKM's disclosed label and other trade secret information. We disagree. The testimony of Everett, Albaugh, and the Coke representative indicate that the label provided to ITW had red litho paper and was not of professional quality (as was PKM's). Additionally, that same testimony, especially Albaugh's, reveals that Coca-Cola did not disclose any information to ITW that belonged to PKM. The limited

---

[8] Courts applying Georgia's pre-GTSA trade secret law also indicate that the correct test for determining if a defendant has made unauthorized use of a trade secret is to figure out if the defendant's product is "substantially derived" from the plaintiff's product. *See Salsbury Labs., Inc. v. Merieux Labs., Inc.,* 908 F.2d 706, 712–13 (11th Cir.1990) (determining if the defendant's process "closely resembles" plaintiff's process and finding that defendant's process was "substantially derived" from plaintiff's process).

instructions given by Coca-Cola to ITW involved matters unrelated to elements that PKM claim as trade secrets.

In sum, we find that PKM has failed to provide evidence that Coca-Cola actually disclosed its trade secrets to ITW.

2.

We must next determine whether PKM has provided evidence that Coca-Cola and/or ITW actually used any Magic Windows trade secrets. To show unauthorized use, PKM must prove that the label developed by ITW was "substantially derived" from the Magic Windows label and not the product of independent development. Our inquiry requires us to compare and contrast the various elements of the two labels. For sake of analytical convenience we will discuss the Magic Windows elements along the two categories proposed by Coca-Cola's expert: concept and production.

a.

We begin with the five identified production processes, which the parties refer to as (1) printing press, (2) inks, (3) film material, (4) color sequencing, and (5) reverse printing:

Printing press

Magic Windows is printed on a gravure or comparable press. The evidence indicates that the ITW labels were created on flexographic presses.

Inks

Magic Windows is made with standard inks. The evidence provides that Albaugh, with the help of Sun Chemical, decided which inks to use and chose proprietary inks.

Film Material

Magic Windows is printed on a single-laminate, flexible plastic packaging material. The evidence shows that Albaugh alone decided which film to use as a substrate for the label and that he chose a single-ply film that was not laminated.

Color Sequencing

Magic windows uses a label production process and color sequences whereby up to eight colors can be utilized. The evidence indicates that Albaugh alone decided the label production process, including determining the numbers of colors to use and the color sequences. He chose both a different number of colors from Magic Windows (seven instead of eight) and used a different sequence than that used in Magic Windows.

Reverse printing

Magic Windows is printed on a film, as a substrate, or reverse-printed, which leaves the plastic film facing forward and toward the viewer. The evidence provides that Albaugh was responsible for determining whether to print on the surface or to reverse print on the label, and that he used forward printing.

The above comparisons show that none of the five production elements in ITW's label match those for Magic Windows. Moreover, the evidence also indicates that ITW employee Albaugh alone decided the various production processes. Accordingly, the conclusion is inevitable that the production processes of the ITW label were not derived, much less "substantially derived," from PKM's Magic Windows label.

b.

Having determined that Coca-Cola did not use PKM's production elements, we next consider whether Coca-Cola used PKM's Magic Windows concepts. A cursory analysis of the two labels indicates that the two labels share nearly identical concepts. On the surface it thus appears that Coca-Cola and ITW may have used PKM's concepts. Coca-Cola contends, however, that all of the concept elements listed in PKM's trade secret were presented to Coca-Cola by BrightHouse in late 1995, and as the lawful owner of the concepts presented by BrightHouse, Coca-Cola independently developed all of the concepts revealed by PKM's trade secret. Moreover, most of PKM's concepts were already part of the public domain, as revealed by the Virtual Image patent application. Coca-Cola argues, therefore, that any concept used to assist ITW with the making of labels belonged to or was legitimately used by Coca-Cola, and that no PKM's trade secret concept elements were used to make the ITW label. To assess Coca-Cola's argument, we compare the PKM concept elements with the concepts presented by BrightHouse.

As mentioned above, BrightHouse presented the idea of a bottle label with a scrambled message on the back side of the label and a red decoder filter—called the "Red Zone"—printed on the front of the label. BrightHouse's Chief Operating Officer, Roger Milks described the concept as follows:

> [T]he concept being that the bottle is—as the liquid is consumed and the level drops in the bottle, you could look through the Red Zone and you would see something on the opposite side of the bottle on the inside of the label, the purpose of that red device being to decode the message.
>
> . . . .
>
> If you weren't viewing it through the red [filter], all you would see is a blurred, illegible message. If you look at it through the

Red Zone—i.e., the prize is in the Red Zone—you would decode the message and you would either be an instant winner or not.

The color graphic shown to Coca-Cola by BrightHouse at the presentation stated: "Purchasers of 20oz bottle would look through the Coca-Cola Red Zone circle to reveal instant win prizes. The Red Zone is a clear plastic circle that allows consumer to look through the bottle, once the product is gone, to see [the] prize revealed on the inside of the label." The graphic also contained a label design with a "Red Zone" transparency that revealed a "You Win" message on the inside of the opposite side. The inside message contained three colors: red, white and black.

PKM has presented no evidence refuting this testimony. We find, as did the district court, that the BrightHouse presentation revealed all of PKM's concepts. Like PKM's Magic Windows, BrightHouse's idea is a (1) promotional concept (2) that requires purchasers of containers to empty the contents of a container (3) to determine if they have won a prize (4) from a commercially feasible beverage label (5) with a non-embossed (6) two or three colored (7) encrypted message (8) on the inside or reverse side of the label (9) that is visually incoherent (10) and located approximately 180° (11) from a colored window filter (12) used to view and decode the message (13) in a visually coherent form. Additionally, we agree with Coca-Cola that even if the BrightHouse concepts were not revealed to Coca-Cola, most of the concept elements at issue were part of the public domain and were not protectable as trade secrets.

PKM nonetheless argues that it is irrelevant whether the BrightHouse proposal is similar to the "concept" of PKM's Magic Windows because Coca-Cola relied on PKM's sample labels and not the BrightHouse drawing when it asked ITW to develop the labels. PKM contends that Coca-Cola's inability to demonstrate that it utilized the BrightHouse idea instead of the PKM concept when seeking ITW's assistance is "fatal to Coke's defense because it cannot prove that its alleged independent development was done 'in the absence of any misappropriation.'" We think, however, that PKM is improperly attempting to shift the burden of proof to the defendant; PKM, as the plaintiff, maintains the burden of proving misappropriation. PKM has simply not provided evidence to support its claim that Coca-Cola used the concepts from PKM.

In short, PKM has failed to demonstrate a fact issue as to whether the label developed by Coca-Cola via ITW was "substantially derived" from any PKM trade secrets.

. . . .

IV.

We have yet to address PKM's remaining count—the claim for breach of contract. PKM complains that Coca-Cola violated the *Non-Disclosure Agreement* by disclosing confidential information to ITW, which then used the information to make the Magic Windows labels. Coca-Cola responds by arguing that the agreement explicitly negated its obligation of confidence upon the occurrence of certain events. Specifically, Coca-Cola agrees with the ruling of the district court: Coca-Cola did not breach the *Non-Disclosure Agreement* because, pursuant to the Agreement's provision allowing it to disclose information that "at the time of disclosure, is available to the public" or "is rightfully received from a third party," Coca-Cola rightfully received the Magic Windows concept from BrightHouse and used bottle labels independently developed by ITW. The record clearly supports the district court's ruling.

. . . .

V.

For the foregoing reasons, the judgment of the district court is AFFIRMED.

NOTES & QUESTIONS

(1) Why might PKM have thought that Coca-Cola disclosed its trade secrets to ITW? What evidence existed to support this belief? What evidence did Coca-Cola offer in its defense?

(2) The court agreed that there was not enough evidence to demonstrate that Coca-Cola had disclosed PKM's trade secrets to ITW. Nevertheless, the court proceeded to address the use theory. Why? In other words, how could ITW (the party that ultimately developed the concept) have used the trade secret if it wasn't disclosed?

(3) With regard to the production elements, how did the court determine that ITW had developed its process independent of PKM's process? Is it possible that ITW could have used PKM's process as a starting point? If so, shouldn't this be enough to show use?

(4) The court found that "the BrightHouse presentation revealed all of PKM's concepts." Despite this finding, PKM claimed that "Coca-Cola relied on PKM's sample labels and not the BrightHouse drawing when it asked ITW to develop the labels." Is this a claim of concept misappropriation? Why did this claim fail?

(5) Is a claim of independent discovery or reverse engineering an affirmative defense, or is it simply evidence that rebuts the misappropriation element of the plaintiff's prima facie case? The courts have not clearly answered this question, but the answer implicates burden of proof issues. In

Moore v. Kulicke & Soffa Industries, Inc., 318 F.3d 561 (3d Cir. 2003), the court provided a helpful tutorial:

> At the risk of carrying coals to Newcastle, we discuss briefly the dual meaning of the term "burden of proof." We note that "[t]he two distinct concepts [embodied in the term 'burden of proof'] may be referred to as (1) the risk of nonpersuasion, sometimes called the 'burden of persuasion,' and (2) the duty of producing evidence (or the burden of production), sometimes called the burden of going forward with the evidence." FLEMING JAMES, JR. & GEOFFREY C. HAZARD, ET AL., CIVIL PROCEDURE § 7.12 (5th ed.2001). These two concepts can be distinguished by the fact that "[u]nlike the burden of persuasion, the burden of production can shift back and forth between parties during the trial." LARRY L. TEPLY & RALPH U. WHITTEN, CIVIL PROCEDURE 855 (2d ed.2000).
>
> At the outset of a trial, the plaintiff has both the burden of production and the burden of persuasion for each element of the prima facie case. Once the plaintiff has met this burden, the defendant may proceed with an affirmative defense. At this point, the defendant has both the burden of production and the burden of persuasion for the affirmative defense. Often, "courts have confused the ideas of affirmative defense and negation by affirmative proof." FLEMING JAMES, JR. & GEOFFREY C. HAZARD, ET AL., CIVIL PROCEDURE § 4.5 (5th ed.2001). A denial, as opposed to an affirmative defense, will simply shift the burden of production to the defendant to present evidence that would tend to rebut the plaintiff's case, while the burden of persuasion remains with the plaintiff. If the defendant cannot meet its burden of going forward by presenting some evidence, the plaintiff has met its burden of persuasion. But if the defendant presents some evidence to support the denial, the fact-finder weighs the evidence, bearing in mind that the plaintiff retains the ultimate burden of persuasion.

Id. at 569.

(6) Reverse engineering is a proper means of discovery under the law. Just because one person has discovered a trade secret through reverse engineering, however, does not mean that the secret has lost all legal protection. *See, e.g., Reingold v. Swiftships*, 126 F.3d 645, 652 (5th Cir. 1997) (rejecting defendant's argument that it could have reverse engineered chattel because "protection will be accorded to a trade secret holder against disclosure or unauthorized use gained by improper means, even if others might have discovered the trade secret by legitimate means"); *cf. Barr-Mullin, Inc. v. Browning*, 424 S.E.2d 226, 230 (N.C. Ct. App. 1993) ("A party asserting the existence of a trade secret does not have to establish the *impossibility* of reverse engineering. Plaintiff must merely show the alleged trade secret was not *readily ascertainable* through . . . reverse engineering.").

(7) Once a product is on the market, it is susceptible to reverse engineering. If the trade secret owner has not patented the device, this susceptibility is problematic, as competitors will be free to discover the trade secret and market the device themselves. To counteract this, can a trade secret owner turn to contract law for help? For instance, could the owner require the purchaser to agree not to reverse engineer the device as a condition of sale or as part of a license? *See Bowers v. Baystate Tech., Inc.*, 320 F.3d 1317, 1325 (Fed. Cir. 2003) (upholding a breach of contract determination that was based on a provision in the licensing agreement which prohibited reverse engineering). *But see Vault Corp. v. Quaid Software Ltd.*, 847 F.2d 255, 270 (5th Cir. 1988) (striking down a contract provision that banned reverse engineering and copying because the Copyright Act preempted the relevant sections of the Louisiana License Act which explicitly permitted such a provision).

2. SHOP RIGHTS

In general, when an employee is hired specifically to develop an invention, the invention is owned solely by the employer, regardless of whether the employee has agreed to assign trade secrets to the employer. Under the doctrine of "shop rights," when an employee not hired to specifically develop an invention does invent something during the hours of employment and using the employer's facilities, the employee retains ultimate ownership of the invention, but the employer is deemed to have a perpetual, non-exclusive license to use it. *See* RESTATEMENT (SECOND) OF AGENCY § 397 cmts. a, c (1958).[h] Although these concepts usually relate to patents, they have been applied to trade secrets as well. *See Avtec Sys., Inc. v. Peiffer*, 805 F. Supp. 1312, 1319–20 (E.D. Va. 1992) (concluding that an employer may acquire a trade secret in a "program's use for demonstration and marketing purposes in a similar manner as an employer may possess 'shop rights' to an employee's patented invention").

However, when an employee develops a trade secret on his or her own time—outside the scope of employment and without using the employer's facilities or information—the employee owns the trade secret and the employer acquires no license. Thus, employers may wish to have invention disclosure and assignment agreements with their employees (in addition to confidentiality and nondisclosure agreements). We referred to these agreements above as "trailer clauses" and they are subject to the same limitations as other restrictive covenants.

PROBLEM 10.5

(a) Walch Industries manufactures rubber stoppers for furniture (those things that you put on the feet of your couches to keep them from slipping on smooth surfaces, such as hardwood floors). While working for Walch, Ramona

---

[h] There is not an analogous provision in the Third Restatement of Agency.

develops a manufacturing process that increases efficiency by 25%. Ramona leaves Walch and goes to work for a competitor, Couchies Co., where she introduces her process. Discuss whether Walch can claim trade secret misappropriation in each of the factual scenarios below. *See* RESTATEMENT (SECOND) OF AGENCY § 397 cmt. a (1958).

(i)   Ramona was an engineer who was hired specifically to help Walch improve the efficiency of its manufacturing process. Ramona made extensive use of Walch's facilities in developing the new process and was paid a large bonus upon completion.

(ii)   Ramona was a low-level factory worker. Although she lacked a college education, she was mechanically inclined. Ramona often spent nights contemplating how to make the manufacturing process more efficient. In addition, she sometimes spent her working hours experimenting on the equipment with different processes rather than doing her assigned work.

(b)   Assume that Ramona was an engineer hired in part to improve the efficiency of Walch's manufacturing process, but she never successfully developed anything. Although Walch did not have her sign a covenant not to compete, it did have her sign a trailer clause assigning all rights to all inventions and processes that she might develop while employed at Walch and for six months after the end of her employment.

After working at Walch for eight years, Ramona quits to form her own competing company. Six months and one week later, Ramona opens shop utilizing a manufacturing process that is 25% more efficient than the one used at Walch. Can Walch bring a claim for trade secret misappropriation and breach of contract? *See General Signal Corp. v. Primary Flow Signal, Inc.*, Civ. A. No. 85–0471B, 1987 WL 147798, at *4 (D.R.I. 1987) (finding that the circumstances indicated a breach of contract where a former employee patented a device that must have existed in the employee's mind prior to the expiration of a non-compete agreement, despite the employee's claim that the device was conceived five days after the non-compete agreement expired).

3. PREEMPTION OF OTHER COMMON LAW CLAIMS

Section 7 of the UTSA preempts other civil remedies for trade secret misappropriation:

SECTION 7.   EFFECT ON OTHER LAW.

(a)   Except as provided in subsection (b), this [Act] displaces conflicting tort, restitutionary, and other law of this State providing civil remedies for misappropriation of a trade secret.

(b)   This [Act] does not affect:

(1)   contractual remedies, whether or not based upon misappropriation of a trade secret;

(2) other civil remedies that are not based upon misappropriation of a trade secret; or

(3) criminal remedies, whether or not based upon misappropriation of a trade secret.

Although this preemptive language is broad, notice that civil remedies not based upon misappropriation of a trade secret are still available. The Restatement (Third) of Unfair Competition § 40 similarly provides that, "[t]his section does not govern the imposition of liability for conduct that infringes other protected interests such as interference with contractual relations (see Restatement, Second, Torts §§ 766–774A (1979)), breach of the duty of loyalty owed by an employee or other agent (see Restatement, Second, Agency §§ 387–398 (1958)), or a breach of confidence not involving a trade secret (see § 41, Comment c)." In addition, contract-based claims are not preempted. Thus, the restrictive covenants discussed earlier are still governed by normal contract principles.

PENALTY KICK MANAGEMENT LTD. V. COCA COLA CO.

318 F.3d 1284 (11th Cir. 2003)

TJOFLAT, CIRCUIT JUDGE:

[The facts of this case are reprinted above.]

III.

In part II we held that the district court correctly determined that PKM's Magic Windows label was a trade secret within the meaning of the Georgia Trade Secrets Act. As a consequence of that ruling, we now must decide whether the district court rightly concluded that four of PKM's remaining claims—conversion, breach of confidential relationship and duty of good faith, unjust enrichment, and quantum meruit—must be dismissed because they are superseded by the Act.

Section 10–1–767(a) provides that the GTSA "supersede[s] conflicting tort, restitutionary, and other laws of [Georgia] providing civil remedies for misappropriation of a trade secret." Subpart (b) of that section goes on to state, however, that the statute does not affect (1) "contractual duties or remedies, whether or not based upon misappropriation of a trade secret"[9] or (2) "other civil remedies that are not based upon misappropriation of a trade secret." PKM contends that each of the above four claims falls under the second exception, and therefore they are not superseded by the GTSA. Coca-Cola, on the other hand, argues that the GTSA explicitly supersedes each of the four claims.

---

[9] PKM's Count III, Breach of Contract, clearly falls within this exception. The district court, accordingly, was correct to determine that this count was not superceded by the GTSA. . . .

Specifically, PKM argues that since claims of conversion, breach of confidential relationship and duty of good faith, unjust enrichment, and quantum meruit "are not dependent on the existence of a trade secret," each claim is not "based" upon the misappropriation of a trade secret, and therefore not preempted. Stated another way, PKM argues that conversion, breach of confidential relationship and duty of good faith, unjust enrichment, and quantum meruit are each distinct theories of civil remedies for the wrongful use of information not rising to the level of a trade secret,[10] and thus do not "conflict" with a misappropriation of a trade secret claim.[11] Although PKM's statements may be true under certain circumstances, we fail to recognize how they support its case here, given that the allegedly misused information actually does rise to the level of a trade secret.

In the lone Georgia appellate opinion to significantly address supersession under the GTSA, the court of appeals held that a claim of conversion is superseded by the GTSA "to the extent" the claim addresses a trade secret. *Tronitec, Inc. v. Shealy,* 249 Ga.App. 442, 547 S.E.2d 749, 755 (2001). Unlike the facts in *Tronitec,* which involved an allegation for the conversion of trade secret information and personal property, PKM's claims are wholly based upon a trade secret. Indeed, the *full* extent of each of PKM's claims, be it conversion, breach of confidential relationship and duty of good faith, unjust enrichment, quantum meruit, misappropriation of a trade secret, or breach of contract, is based upon a trade secret. So, even if PKM is correct that information outside the scope of a trade secret is not preempted under Georgia law, PKM's four claims at issue are clearly "based" upon a trade secret, and thus are superceded by the GTSA. *See Powell Products, Inc. v. Marks,* 948 F.Supp. 1469, 1474 (D.Colo.1996) (citing Roger M. Milgrim, *Milgrim on Trade Secrets,* § 1.01[4], at 1–68.14 (1996)) (noting that preemption is appropriate where "other claims are no more than a restatement of the same operative facts

---

[10] Some cases distinguish between trade secret information and confidential information, *see, e.g., Jensen Tools, Inc. v. Contact East, Inc.,* 1992 WL 245693 (D.Mass.1992), and hold that a claim (such as a breach of fiduciary duty) involving underlying information that does not qualify as a trade secret is not preempted. *See, e.g., Combined Metals of Chicago, Ltd. v. Airtek, Inc.,* 985 F.Supp. 827, 830 (N.D.Ill.1997); *see also Frantz v. Johnson,* 116 Nev. 455, 999 P.2d 351, 358 n. 3 (2000) ("There may be future instances where a plaintiff will be able to assert tort claims . . . that do not depend on the information at issue being deemed a trade secret, and [thus are not precluded] by the UTSA.")

[11] The GTSA only preempts common law claims that "conflict" with its provisions. O.C.G.A. § 10–1–767(a). Unfortunately, Georgia courts have not specifically defined what constitutes a conflict between the GTSA and the common law. Some non-Georgia courts, when addressing a particular state's version of the UTSA, have indicated that blanket preemption applies to all claims involving information that the plaintiff claims is a trade secret, *see Hutchison v. KFC Corp.,* 809 F.Supp. 68, 71 (D.Nev.1992), while other courts have held that claims are only preempted to the extent that they contain the same factual allegations as the claim for use or misappropriation of trade secrets. *See Micro Display Sys., Inc. v. Axtel, Inc.,* 699 F.Supp. 202, 204–05 (D.Minn.1988).

which would plainly and exclusively spell out only trade secret misappropriation").[14]

We therefore agree with the district court's holding that PKM's claims for conversion, breach of a confidential relationship and duty of good faith, unjust enrichment, and quantum meruit are superseded by the GTSA.

NOTES & QUESTIONS

(1) PKM argued that the additional claims were independent causes of action that did not require the existence of a trade secret. Why did the court reject this argument?

(2) In what way is the *Coca Cola* case distinguishable from the *Tronitec, Inc. v. Shealy* case cited by the court?

(3) In footnote 11, the court observed that some courts have "indicated that blanket preemption applies to all claims involving information that the plaintiff claims is a trade secret." Other courts "have held that claims are only preempted to the extent that they contain the same factual allegations as the claim for use or misappropriation of trade secrets." Does the *Coca Cola* court appear to agree with one of these views, or has it adopted a different approach altogether?

(4) Should the preemption provisions of the UTSA cover information that does not rise to the level of a trade secret? Courts appear to be of two views. A majority seems to adopt the "All Confidential Information" view, which applies to all causes of action where a party invokes state law to protect a secret, regardless of whether the secret qualifies as a trade secret under the UTSA. *See, e.g., BlueEarth Biofuels, LLC v. Hawaiian Elec. Co.*, 235 P.3d 310, 323 (Haw. 2010) ("[T]he [Hawaii UTSA] preempts non-contract, civil claims based on the improper acquisition, disclosure or use of confidential and/or commercially valuable information that does not rise to the level of a . . . trade secret."); *see also* Charles Tait Graves & Elizabeth Tippett, *UTSA Preemption and the Public Domain: How Courts Have Overlooked Patent Preemption of State Law Claims Alleging Employee Wrongdoing*, 65 RUTGERS L. REV. 59, 72–77 (2012) ("It appears that the majority of courts that have considered UTSA preemption—and certainly a substantial majority of state supreme courts to have addressed the question—have ruled that the UTSA displaces alternative state law tort claims that seek to hold the defendant liable for misusing the plaintiff's

---

[14] See also the *Restatement (Third) of Unfair Competition* . . . § 40 cmt. a (1995), which provides:

> The rules stated in this Section [addressing the appropriation of trade secrets] are applicable to common law actions in tort or restitution for the appropriation of another's trade secret, however denominated, including actions for "misappropriation," "infringement," or "conversion" of a trade secret, actions for "unjust enrichment" based upon the unauthorized use of a trade secret, and actions for "breach of confidence" in which the subject matter of the confidence is a trade secret.

information."); John T. Cross, *UTSA Displacement of Other State Law Claims*, 33 HAMLINE L. REV. 445, 452–54 (2010) ("Based upon those cases in which the court's view is clear or can be gleaned from the context, it appears a significant majority follows the All Confidential Information view.").

Other courts adopt a "Trade Secrets Only" view. Under this approach, if the information qualifies as a trade secret under the UTSA, the UTSA preempts other claims. If the information does not qualify as a trade secret, the plaintiff is free to seek a recovery under any cause of action. Graves & Tippett, *supra*, at 77–78; Cross, *supra*, at 452.

D. REMEDIES

Remedies for misappropriation of trade secrets are available under the UTSA and the common law. Specifically, the UTSA provides for injunctive relief, monetary damages (including, in appropriate circumstances, exemplary damages), attorney's fees, or any combination of these remedies. Other remedies, such as for breach of contract or for common law torts that are not preempted, may also be available.

1. INJUNCTIVE RELIEF

a. Preliminary and Permanent Injunctions

An injunction is a court order that generally prevents a person from engaging in specific conduct or commands a person to take certain actions (such as removing trade secrets from a publicly available website). UTSA § 2 specifically provides for injunctive relief:

SECTION 2. INJUNCTIVE RELIEF.

(a) Actual or threatened misappropriation may be enjoined. Upon application to the court, an injunction shall be terminated when the trade secret has ceased to exist, but the injunction may be continued for an additional reasonable period of time in order to eliminate commercial advantage that otherwise would be derived from the misappropriation.

See also RESTATEMENT (THIRD) OF UNFAIR COMPETITION § 44 (1995) (providing for injunctive relief).

Injunctive relief is an important remedy to the victim of trade secret misappropriation and can take many forms. It may prohibit a misappropriator from contacting a victim's clients, using a confidential manufacturing process, or even working for a competitor. It may also compel affirmative acts, such as destroying documents or giving back a prototype. *See* UTSA § 2(c). Notice that relief under the UTSA is available for "[a]ctual or threatened misappropriation." This means that former employees may be enjoined prospectively, even if they have not yet used or disclosed a trade secret.

Injunctive relief comes in two forms: preliminary and permanent. A preliminary injunction issues prior to a final determination on the merits. To obtain a preliminary injunction, a plaintiff must file a complaint which is usually accompanied by an ex parte application for a temporary restraining order (which will last until the preliminary injunction can be considered). The court will then hold a hearing on whether to order a preliminary injunction based upon four equitable criteria: (1) the likelihood of success on the merits; (2) the threat that the plaintiff will suffer irreparable harm if the injunction is denied; (3) a balance of the threat to the plaintiff with the harm to the nonmoving party; and (4) whether the public interest favors such relief. The moving party bears the burden of proof on each of these factors.

The issuance or denial of a preliminary injunction is a key component of subsequent settlement negotiations, as the granting of such an injunction suggests to the defendant that its position is not going to prevail. Conversely, the denial of such relief means the plaintiff must try the case, involving money and time, before relief will be granted. If a preliminary injunction is granted, it stays in place while a trial is held on the merits.

Upon the completion of the trial, a permanent injunction may be entered. The word "permanent," however, does not mean that the injunction will last forever. The length and type of injunctive relief will vary from case to case. With respect to length, the Third Restatement and the UTSA both indicate that an injunction should be long enough to eliminate the commercial advantage gained by the misappropriator, but should not be longer than necessary. *See, e.g.,* UTSA § 2 cmt. With respect to type, although the UTSA does not identify the factors that should be considered in determining the type of injunctive relief, § 44 of the Third Restatement of Unfair Competition provides a useful list:

(2) The appropriateness and scope of injunctive relief depend upon a comparative appraisal of all the factors of the case, including the following primary factors:

(a) the nature of the interest to be protected;

(b) the nature and extent of the appropriation;

(c) the relative adequacy to the plaintiff of an injunction and of other remedies;

(d) the relative harm likely to result to the legitimate interests of the defendant if an injunction is granted and to the legitimate interests of the plaintiff if an injunction is denied;

(e) the interests of third persons and of the public;

(f) any unreasonable delay by the plaintiff in bringing suit or otherwise asserting its rights;

(g) any related misconduct on the part of the plaintiff; and

(h) the practicality of framing and enforcing the injunction.

PROBLEM 10.6

Isaac's IT Innovations (III) is a computer troubleshooting and information technology support company in El Paso, Texas. The company is new and spends a good portion of its first year contacting various companies in town to see if they have computer systems that III might be able to service. III does this by cold-calling companies in the phone book and asking them basic questions about their computing and information technology needs. From these efforts, III has compiled a customer list (both actual and potential) which it uses to send out special promotions and offers.

Rene is a mid-level employee at III who leaves to start up his own competing company. Prior to leaving, Rene downloads a copy of the customer list to assist him in his new venture. III learns of Rene's actions and successfully sues to enjoin him from using the list.

(a) Assume that you are the trial court judge. Based upon these facts, what sort of injunctive relief would you grant to III? *See* UTSA § 2(a), (b) & cmt.; RESTATEMENT (THIRD) OF UNFAIR COMPETITION § 44(2), (3) & cmt. f (1995); *Sigma Chem. Co. v. Harris, supra.*

(b) Assume that while the case against Rene is pending, a different competitor uses the same methods as III and independently develops a substantially similar client list. Would this affect your decision on whether to grant an injunction?

b. Inevitable Disclosure

Perhaps one of the most powerful uses of injunctive relief is the ability to prohibit a former employee from working for a competitor under the "inevitable disclosure" doctrine. Recall that an injunction can issue under the UTSA for actual or threatened misappropriation. Based upon a threatened misappropriation, some courts will enjoin a departing employee who has possession of trade secrets from working for a competitor. This is to avoid the "inevitable disclosure" of those trade secrets to the new employer. The doctrine can be invoked even if the former employee is not in possession of confidential documents and even in the absence of a non-compete agreement.

An oft-cited decision discussing the inevitable disclosure doctrine is *PepsiCo, Inc. v. Redmond*, 54 F.3d 1262 (7th Cir.1995). In *PepsiCo*, William Redmond, a former high-ranking employee of PepsiCo, attempted to work in an executive capacity for Quaker Oats, a direct competitor in the beverage industry.[i] PepsiCo sought to enjoin Redmond from working for Quaker by claiming that Redmond had knowledge of PepsiCo's trade secrets, such as strategic plans for specific markets. Although Redmond had signed a confidentiality agreement and had not yet disclosed any secrets, the court found that "a plaintiff may prove a claim of trade secret misappropriation by demonstrating that defendant's new employment will inevitably lead him to rely on the plaintiff's trade secrets." *Id.* at 1269.

The court discussed three factors relevant to successfully invoking the inevitable disclosure doctrine. First, the employee must have "extensive and intimate knowledge"; in other words, the employee must possess knowledge of a trade secret. Second, the old and new positions must be so similar that the former employee would have to rely on the trade secrets to adequately perform in the new position. Third, the plaintiff must demonstrate proof of the employee's willingness to exploit the secrets, such as through a lack of candor by the former employee or the new employer. Under the circumstances of the *PepsiCo* case, the court found that an injunction was appropriate.

BIMBO BAKERIES USA, INC. v. BOTTICELLA

613 F.3d 102 (3d Cir. 2010)

GREENBERG, CIRCUIT JUDGE.

I. INTRODUCTION

This matter comes on before this Court on an interlocutory appeal from an order of the District Court dated February 9, 2010, and entered on February 12, 2010, granting appellee's motion for a preliminary injunction. The issue on appeal is whether the District Court erred in enjoining appellant Chris Botticella, formerly a senior executive at appellee Bimbo Bakeries USA, Inc. ("Bimbo"), from working for one of Bimbo's competitors until after the Court resolved the merits of Bimbo's misappropriation of trade secrets claim against Botticella. The Court intended that the preliminary injunction would last for about two months until the trial but, because of this appeal and a stay of the District Court proceedings following the filing of this appeal, the preliminary injunction has remained in effect. For the reasons we set forth below, we will affirm the order of the District Court.

II. BACKGROUND

A. *Botticella's Employment at Bimbo*

Bimbo, a Delaware corporation with its principal place of business in Pennsylvania, is one of the four largest companies in the United States

---

[i] Quaker Oats makes Gatorade and Snapple, in case you were wondering.

baking industry. Bimbo and its affiliates produce and distribute baked goods throughout the country under a number of popular brand names including Thomas', Entenmann's, Arnold, Oroweat, Mrs. Baird's, Stroehmann, and Boboli. Botticella, a California resident, who already had experience in the baking industry, began working for Bimbo in 2001 and was, until January 13, 2010, its Vice President of Operations for California. . . .

As one of Bimbo's senior executives, Botticella had access to and acquired a broad range of confidential information about Bimbo, its products, and its business strategy. For example, he was one of a select group of individuals with access to the code books containing the formulas and process parameters for all of Bimbo's products. He also regularly attended high-level meetings with other top Bimbo executives to discuss the company's national business strategy. Significantly, as Bimbo repeatedly has noted throughout these proceedings, Botticella was one of only seven people who possessed all of the knowledge necessary to replicate independently Bimbo's popular line of Thomas' English Muffins, including the secret behind the muffins' unique "nooks and crannies" texture. Thomas' English Muffins is the source of approximately half a billion dollars worth of Bimbo's annual sales income.

While employed at Bimbo, Botticella signed a "Confidentiality, Non-Solicitation and Invention Assignment Agreement" with Bimbo on March 13, 2009, in which he agreed not to compete directly with Bimbo during the term of his employment, not to use or disclose any of Bimbo's confidential or proprietary information during or after the term of his employment with Bimbo, and, upon ceasing employment [with] Bimbo, to return every document he received from Bimbo during the term of his employment. The agreement, however, did not include a covenant restricting where Botticella could work after the termination of his employment with Bimbo. The agreement contained a choice of law provision providing that Pennsylvania law would govern any dispute arising from the agreement. Moreover, the agreement provided that certain state and federal courts in Pennsylvania would have jurisdiction over litigation arising from the agreement and over the parties to that litigation. Thus, although this litigation seems only marginally related to Pennsylvania, Bimbo filed it in the United States District Court for the Eastern District of Pennsylvania, which has exercised jurisdiction.

B. *The Hostess Job Offer*

On September 28, 2009, one of Bimbo's primary competitors in the baking industry—Interstates Brand Corporation, which later changed its name to Hostess Brands, Inc. (collectively, "Hostess")—offered Botticella a position in Texas as Vice President of Bakery Operations for its eastern region. . . . On October 15, 2009, Botticella accepted the Hostess position and agreed to begin in January 2010. Botticella did not disclose his plans to Bimbo for several months, and he therefore continued to be engaged fully in his work at Bimbo and to have full access to Bimbo's confidential and proprietary information even after he accepted the Hostess position. Botticella maintains that he continued working for Bimbo notwithstanding his acceptance of the Hostess position in order to receive his 2009 year-end bonus and to complete two Bimbo projects for which he had responsibility.

After Botticella accepted the Hostess offer and while Bimbo still employed him, Hostess directed him to execute an "Acknowledgment and Representation Form," which essentially indicated that Hostess was not interested in any confidential information, trade secrets, or other proprietary information that Botticella had acquired from Bimbo, and that Botticella would not disclose such information to Hostess. Botticella signed the form on December 7, 2009.

Botticella informed his supervisor at Bimbo on January 4, 2010, that he was planning to leave Bimbo on January 15. But Botticella did not at that time indicate that he was leaving to work for a competitor. Moreover, there is no indication in the record that Bimbo asked him about his future employment plans. On January 12, Hostess announced that its Vice President of Bakery Operations for the eastern region was retiring and that Botticella would be replacing him, effective January 18. Bimbo personnel learned of the announcement and the next day, January 13, the company's Vice President for Human Relations requested that Botticella contact him. Botticella did so at approximately 10:00 a.m. PST and in the course of the ensuing telephone conversation disclosed his intention to work for Hostess. Bimbo directed Botticella to vacate its offices that day.

C.   *Botticella's Use of Confidential Information Following the Hostess Offer*

In the period between when Botticella accepted the Hostess offer on October 15, 2009, and when he ceased working for Bimbo on January 13, 2010, he continued to have all the access to Bimbo's confidential and proprietary information befitting a trusted senior executive. For instance, Botticella attended a meeting with Bimbo's president and other Bimbo officers in December 2009 at which the participants discussed confidential information regarding the company's strategic plan for California. Botticella concedes that if he had disclosed his intention to work for Hostess, Bimbo would have restricted his access to this and other types of information. Indeed, Botticella maintains that he no longer felt "comfortable" being privy to Bimbo's confidential information following his acceptance of the Hostess offer and that, accordingly, when he received emails and electronic documents containing confidential information, he deleted them, and that when he was exposed to confidential information during presentations at meetings, he "blocked it" out of his head.[4]

. . . .

Following Botticella's departure, Bimbo hired E. Brian Harris, a computer forensics expert, to investigate Botticella's use of his company laptop during December 2009 and January 2010. Harris's testing revealed that a user who logged in as Botticella had accessed a number of confidential documents during the final weeks of Botticella's employment at Bimbo. In particular, the testing revealed that the person logging in as Botticella had accessed twelve files within a span of thirteen seconds on January 13, 2010, Botticella's last day at Bimbo.[5] Significantly this access occurred minutes after the phone call in which Botticella finally disclosed to Bimbo his plans to work for Hostess and Bimbo told him to cease working for it.

There were several similar patterns of access in the weeks leading up to January 13. According to Harris, this type of activity—multiple files being accessed more or less simultaneously—was "inconsistent with an ordinary usage whereby individual files are opened and either read or edited." Harris concluded that the activity was, however, consistent with copying a group of files at the same time, but he could not determine conclusively whether the files Botticella had accessed had been copied and deleted or never copied at all. . . .

A number of the files accessed from Botticella's laptop during his final days at Bimbo were highly sensitive and their possession by a competitor would have been damaging to Bimbo. As described by the District Court, these documents include "Bimbo's cost-reduction strategies, product launch dates, anticipated plant and line closures, labor contract information, production strengths and weaknesses of many Bimbo bakeries, and the cost structure for individual products by brand." There were, however, more mundane documents such as a presentation titled "Safety Short-Wet Floors" included in these groups of files. In his video-taped deposition, portions of which were presented at the preliminary injunction hearing, Botticella admitted to copying files periodically from his laptop to external devices during his final weeks at Bimbo, but maintained that he had done so only to practice his computer skills in preparation for his new position at Hostess. Despite an earlier denial, he eventually admitted to conducting such "practice" exercises in January 2010. The District Court found that Botticella's explanation of his use of the laptop computer and the external devices was "confusing at best" and "not credible."

---

[4]   We are quite uncertain as to how an individual can block out information from his head for a human mind does not function like a computer from which, through an electronic process, materials may be deleted.

[5]   Botticella does not deny that he was the person logging in under his name.

D. *Procedural History*

After Botticella left Bimbo and joined Hostess, Bimbo brought this action seeking to protect its trade secrets and then promptly moved for preliminary injunctive relief.... The District Court granted Bimbo's motion and preliminarily enjoined Botticella from commencing employment with Hostess and from divulging to Hostess any confidential or proprietary information belonging to Bimbo. The Court further ordered Botticella to return to Bimbo any of the company's confidential or proprietary information in his possession. The Court issued the preliminary injunction on February 9, 2010, and ... Botticella appealed ... to this Court on February 16, 2010. The case remains untried and pending in the District Court as that Court on March 5, 2010, after a conference with the attorneys, postponed the trial and stayed all proceedings until its further order. We have expedited our consideration of this appeal.

. . . .

IV. DISCUSSION

In determining whether to grant a preliminary injunction, a court must consider whether the party seeking the injunction has satisfied four factors: "(1) a likelihood of success on the merits; (2) he or she will suffer irreparable harm if the injunction is denied; (3) granting relief will not result in even greater harm to the nonmoving party; and (4) the public interest favors such relief." [*Miller v. Mitchell,* 598 F.3d 139, 147 (3d Cir. 2010)]. We turn first to the question of whether Bimbo has demonstrated a likelihood of success on the merits, an inquiry that was the primary focus of the District Court, and, consequently, also is the primary focus of the parties on this appeal.

A. *Likelihood of Success on the Merits*

The District Court found that Bimbo was likely to prevail on the merits of its misappropriation of trade secrets claim. [The] Pennsylvania Uniform Trade Secrets Act ("PUTSA") ... is applicable in this case.... [The court reviewed the applicable standard for determining if a trade secret existed and concluded that Botticella had access to and acquired a number of Bimbo's trade secrets, including secret formulas and designs for, among other things, Thomas' English Muffins, strategic planning and financial information, and production methods.]

The District Court then determined that Bimbo likely would be able to prove at trial that Botticella would misappropriate these trade secrets if allowed to work at Hostess.

A person has misappropriated a trade secret under Pennsylvania law when he acquires knowledge of another's trade secret in circumstances giving rise to a duty to maintain its confidentiality and then discloses or uses that trade secret without the other's consent. 12 Pa. Cons.Stat. Ann. § 5302 (West 2004). A court may enjoin the actual or threatened misappropriation of a trade secret. *Id.* § 5303(a). After determining that Bimbo was seeking an injunction on the basis of threatened misappropriation, the District Court found there was "a substantial likelihood, if not an inevitability, that [Botticella] will disclose or use Bimbo's trade secrets in the course of his employment with Hostess." Accordingly, the Court concluded that Bimbo had demonstrated a likelihood of succeeding on the merits of its claim.

Botticella contends this conclusion was wrong as a matter of law because . . . such an injunction only can issue where it would be "virtually impossible" for the defendant to perform his new job without disclosing trade secrets[;] Bimbo did not present any evidence from which the District Court could conclude that Botticella's responsibilities at Hostess would lead him to disclose Bimbo's trade secrets; and . . . the District Court drew impermissible adverse inferences against Botticella in a way that effectively shifted the burden of proof from Bimbo to Botticella.

1.   *Air Products* and Inevitable Disclosure

The parties disagree about the circumstances that must be found to exist before a court can enjoin a defendant from beginning new employment. In its opinion granting the preliminary injunction, the District Court stated:

> When analyzing threatened misappropriation of trade secrets, Pennsylvania courts apply the 'inevitable disclosure doctrine.' That doctrine essentially posits that 'a person may be enjoined from engaging in employment or certain aspects of his employment where that employment is likely to result in the disclosure of information, held secret by a former employer, of which the employee gained knowledge as a result of his former employment situation.' The scope of the injunctive relief depends on the particular circumstances of the case.

In other words, the District Court concluded, albeit somewhat paradoxically, that Pennsylvania courts apply the "inevitable disclosure doctrine" to grant injunctions based not on a trade secret's *inevitable* disclosure but on its *likely* disclosure. *Cf. PepsiCo, Inc. v. Redmond,* 54 F.3d 1262, 1269 (7th Cir.1995) ("[a] plaintiff may prove a claim of trade secret misappropriation by demonstrating that defendant's new employment will *inevitably* lead him to rely on the plaintiff's trade secrets.") (emphasis added). While we agree with the District Court that Pennsylvania law empowers a court to enjoin the threatened disclosure of trade secrets without requiring a plaintiff to show that disclosure is inevitable, we do not consider that an injunction granted absent such a showing was issued pursuant to the "inevitable disclosure doctrine."

The leading Pennsylvania decision to discuss the inevitability of trade secret disclosure is *Air Products & Chemicals, Inc. v. Johnson.*[8] In that case Air Products, a manufacturer and distributor of industrial gas, sought an order enjoining Johnson, one of its former employees who primarily was responsible for selling on-site gas, from working in the on-site gas division of a competitor, Liquid Air, that lagged behind Air Products in the on-site gas market. [442 A.2d 1114, 1116–18 (Pa. Super. Ct. 1982)]. The trial court determined that Johnson, who had an engineering background, had acquired a number of technical and commercial trade secrets relevant to the operation and sale of on-site gas during his employment at Air Products, and that an injunction prohibiting Johnson from working in on-site sales at Liquid Air was necessary because "[i]t would be impossible [for Johnson] to perform his managerial functions in on-site work without drawing on the knowledge he possesses of Air Product[s]'s confidential information." *Id.* at 1122 (quoting trial court opinion).

On appeal, the Superior Court affirmed, agreeing with the trial court that Johnson possessed trade secrets belonging to Air Products that included technological innovations as well as commercial information such as "the status of negotiations with customers, proposed plant configurations and methods of delivery as well as analysis of market opportunities." *Id.* at 1121 (quoting trial court opinion). In reaching this conclusion, the Court emphasized that "trade secrets need not be technical in nature" to be protected under Pennsylvania law. *Id.* at 1124.

With respect to the probability of disclosure required to warrant an injunction, the Superior Court stated at the outset of its analysis that Pennsylvania law permits the issuance of an injunction where a defendant's new employment "is *likely* to result in the disclosure" of a former employer's trade secrets. *Id.* at 1120 (emphasis added). The Court then determined that it was reasonable for the trial court to issue an injunction based on the *inevitability* that Johnson would disclose trade secrets, but the Superior Court explicitly chose "not [to] adopt the reasoning of the trial court or its use of the term inevitable." *Id.* at 1124. Based on these statements it seems clear that the Superior Court believed that the trial court permissibly could have granted the injunction even if the disclosure of trade secrets was not inevitable.

. . . .

---

[8] While courts across the country have considered the applicability and scope of the inevitable disclosure doctrine, *see generally* Brandy L. Treadway, *An Overview of Individual States' Application of Inevitable Disclosure: Concrete Doctrine or Equitable Tool?*, 55 SMU L. Rev. 621, 626–49 (2002), our focus in this diversity action is on the decisions of the Pennsylvania courts.

4. Evidence of Botticella's Responsibilities at Hostess

Botticella next contends that the District Court erred by determining the probability that Botticella would disclose trade secrets while working at Hostess without requiring Bimbo to provide more detailed evidence of Botticella's anticipated responsibilities at Hostess. The record before the District Court contained little evidence in this regard apart from what could be inferred from Botticella's compensation package at Hostess and his title as the Vice President of Baking Operations for the eastern region.[14] Nevertheless the District Court concluded that Botticella's prospective position at Hostess was "substantially similar" to his former position at Bimbo, noting that the Hostess position was "an executive level position, with a salary comparable to his salary at Bimbo." We agree that the record supports the conclusion that in his new position at Hostess, Botticella would have broad oversight over bakery operations, just as he had at Bimbo. Accordingly, the District Court did not abuse its discretion by preliminarily determining that the Bimbo and Hostess positions were substantially similar.

5. Adverse Inference Based on Botticella's Failure to Testify

The District Court determined that Botticella's conduct following his acceptance of the Hostess job offer demonstrated his intention to use Bimbo's trade secrets during his employment with Hostess. The District Court bolstered this determination by drawing an adverse inference from Botticella's failure to testify at the preliminary injunction hearing. In so doing, the District Court relied on our decision in *SI Handling Systems, Inc. v. Heisley,* where we stated that because the misappropriation of a trade secret often must be proved by "construct[ing] a web of perhaps ambiguous circumstantial evidence" that outweighs the defendants' direct denial, the failure of defendants to testify in the face of a strong showing that a misappropriation or misuse occurred "justifies the inference that their testimony would be unfavorable to their cause." [753 F.2d 1244, 1261 (3d Cir. 1985) (internal citations omitted)]. On the other hand, Botticella contends that an adverse inference was inappropriate because he chose not to put forward any evidence at the preliminary injunction hearing. In support of this position he points to *Stowe Township v. Standard Life Ins. Co. of Indiana,* where we stated that "whatever inference might otherwise be available from the failure to call a witness is not permissible when a defendant chooses to put on no evidence at all, in apparent reliance on its determination that plaintiff has not met its burden." 507 F.2d 1332, 1338 (3d Cir.1975).

---

[14] The District Court also noted that in his position at Hostess, Botticella would report to Hostess's Senior Vice President for Bakery Operations. *Bimbo Bakeries,* 2010 WL 571774, at * 13.

Even assuming that the District Court erred by drawing an adverse inference from Botticella's failure to testify, the conclusion that Botticella intended to use Bimbo's trade secrets during his employment with Hostess rests on a solid evidentiary basis, namely, Botticella's "not disclosing to Bimbo his acceptance of a job offer from a direct competitor, remaining in a position to receive Bimbo's confidential information and, in fact, receiving such information after committing to the Hostess job, and copying Bimbo's trade secret information from his work laptop onto external storage devices." [*Bimbo Bakeries USA, Inc. v. Botticella,* Civ. A. No. 10–0194, 2010 WL 571774, at *13 (E.D. Pa. Feb. 9, 2010)]. Accordingly, the District Court did not abuse its discretion by determining that Bimbo demonstrated a likelihood of success on its misappropriation of trade secrets claim.

B. *Irreparable Harm*

The District Court concluded that Bimbo would suffer irreparable harm absent injunctive relief because the disclosure of its trade secrets to Hostess would put Bimbo at a competitive disadvantage that a legal remedy could not redress. On appeal, Botticella does not contest this finding apart from arguing that any harm Bimbo potentially might suffer from Botticella's employment at Hostess could be prevented by a narrow injunction—to which Botticella would stipulate—prohibiting Botticella only from disclosing Bimbo's trade secrets. We recognize that the evidence at trial may show that if Bimbo is entitled to relief that relief might be narrow yet adequate, just as Botticella suggests. Nevertheless, at this preliminary stage of the proceedings, the District Court did not abuse its discretion when, faced with evidence of Botticella's suspicious conduct during his final weeks at Bimbo, it determined that a stronger remedy was needed in the interim to protect Bimbo from imminent irreparable harm. *See* [*Den-Tal-Ez, Inc. v. Siemens Capital Corp.*, 566 A.2d 1214, 1232 (Pa. Super. Ct. 1989)] ("It is clear that under Pennsylvania law a court of equity may fashion a trade secrets injunction that is broad enough to ensure that the information is protected.") (quoting *SI Handling Sys.*, 753 F.2d at 1265) (internal alteration removed).

C. *Harm to Botticella Caused by Injunctive Relief*

The District Court concluded that the harm of Bimbo's trade secrets being disclosed to Hostess outweighed the harm to Botticella of not being able to commence employment at Hostess until the Court made a final determination of the merits following a trial, which it scheduled to start about two months from the date it issued the preliminary injunction.[15] The Court noted that Botticella would continue to receive compensation

---

[15] Botticella in effect extended the duration of the preliminary injunction by pursuing an interlocutory appeal for, as we indicated above, the District Court has stayed this case during this appeal.

for the eleven weeks of vacation time that he had accrued before leaving Bimbo. We agree with the District Court's determination. In so doing, however, we note that even a temporary injunction prohibiting someone from pursuing his livelihood in the manner he chooses operates as a severe restriction on him that a court should not impose lightly. Nevertheless, such a temporary restriction on his employment is warranted where, as here, the facts demonstrate that the restriction is necessary to prevent greater irreparable harm from befalling another party. Following a disposition on the merits which in the normal course of events will follow the disposition of this appeal and the remand of the case to the District Court, if the Court holds that Bimbo is entitled to relief, the Court should fashion a remedy appropriate to protect Bimbo's trade secrets without unduly imposing on Botticella's right to pursue his chosen occupation.

D. *The Public Interest*

We agree with the District Court's conclusion that granting the preliminary injunction was consistent with the public interest. There are several public interests at play in this case. As noted by the District Court, there is a generalized public interest in "upholding the inviolability of trade secrets and enforceability of confidentiality agreements." Additionally, there is a public interest in employers being free to hire whom they please and in employees being free to work for whom they please. Of these latter two interests, Pennsylvania courts consider the right of the employee to be the more significant. *See Renee Beauty Salons, Inc. v. Blose-Venable,* 652 A.2d 1345, 1347 (Pa.Super.Ct.1995) ("[T]he right of a business person to be protected against unfair competition stemming from the usurpation of his or her trade secrets must be balanced against the right of an individual to the unhampered pursuit of the occupations and livelihoods for which he or she is best suited.") (internal citation omitted). We are satisfied on the facts of this case that the public interest in preventing the misappropriation of Bimbo's trade secrets outweighs the temporary restriction on Botticella's choice of employment. *See SI Handling Sys.,* 753 F.2d at 1265 (finding unnecessary an "extended analysis of the public interest [because] extensive precedent supports an injunctive remedy where the elements of a trade secret claim are established").

V. CONCLUSION

For the reasons stated above, we will affirm the order of the District Court dated February 9, 2010, and entered on February 12, 2010, granting Bimbo's motion for a preliminary injunction and will remand the case to that Court for further proceedings.

NOTES & QUESTIONS

(1)   What is the standard for whether information will inevitably be disclosed? Why was it met in this case?

(2)   How would *Bimbo* have been decided under the three factors examined by the court in *PepsiCo* (described at the beginning of this Section)?

(3)   The district court in *Bimbo* stated that a "person may be enjoined from engaging in employment . . . where that employment is likely to result in the disclosure of information." If an employee has trade secret information and is planning to work for a competitor in the same or similar capacity, is that enough to show a likelihood of disclosure? Courts appear to be split on this question. On the one hand, the *PepsiCo* standard requires some showing of the employee's willingness to exploit secrets. *See also Les Concierges, Inc. v. Robeson*, No. C–09–1510, 2009 WL 1138561, at *2 (N.D. Cal. 2009) ("At the outset, the Court finds [that] a threat of misappropriation cannot, as a matter of California law, be inferred from the fact [that] Robeson, upon voluntarily terminating his employment with LC US, immediately began working for a direct competitor and appears to be performing for his new employer the same or similar job duties he performed while employed by LC US."); *Bayer Corp. v. Roche Molecular Sys., Inc.,* 72 F. Supp. 2d 1111, 1120 (N.D. Cal. 1999) ("A trade-secrets plaintiff must show an actual use or an actual threat."); *FLIR Sys., Inc. v. Parrish*, 95 Cal. Rptr. 3d 307, 316 (Ct. App. 2009) (stating that California law requires a plaintiff to show "a threat by a defendant to misuse trade secrets, manifested by words or conduct, where the evidence indicates imminent use").

On the other hand, some courts have granted relief without a showing of a willingness to exploit secrets when the defendant has intimate knowledge of the plaintiff's business. *See, e.g., Proctor & Gamble Co. v. Stoneham*, 747 N.E.2d 268, 279–80 (Ohio Ct. App. 2000) (finding a threat of inevitable disclosure when "an employee with detailed and comprehensive knowledge of an employer's trade secrets and confidential information has begun employment with a competitor of the former employer in a position that is substantially similar to the position held during the former employment").

(4)   In *Bimbo*, along with the likelihood of success, the court considered the interests of three entities: Bimbo, Botticella, and the public. The court ultimately determined that a preliminary injunction was warranted because the harm to Bimbo from the disclosure of its trade secrets outweighed the interests of Botticella and the public. After a trial on the merits, assume that Bimbo prevails. What sort of injunction should issue? *Cf. EarthWeb, Inc. v. Schlack*, 71 F. Supp. 2d 299, 310 (S.D.N.Y. 1999) ("[I]n its purest form, the inevitable disclosure doctrine treads an exceedingly narrow path through judicially disfavored territory. Absent evidence of actual misappropriation by an employee, the doctrine should be applied in only the rarest of cases.").

(5)   In answering the previous question, consider the practical effect of enjoining Botticella from working for Hostess. In essence, isn't this a

judicially imposed non-compete agreement to which Botticella never agreed? California courts certainly seem to think so. In *Whyte v. Schlage Lock Co.*, 125 Cal. Rptr. 2d 277 (Cal. Ct. App. 2002), the court made the following observations:

> The chief ill in the covenant not to compete imposed by the inevitable disclosure doctrine is its after-the-fact nature: The covenant is imposed after the employment contract is made and therefore alters the employment relationship without the employee's consent. When ... a confidentiality agreement is in place, the inevitable disclosure doctrine in effect converts the confidentiality agreement into such a covenant not to compete. . . . [A] court should not allow a plaintiff to use inevitable disclosure as an after-the-fact noncompete agreement to enjoin an employee from working for the employer of his or her choice. . . . As a result of the inevitable disclosure doctrine, the employer obtains the benefit of a contractual provision it did not pay for, while the employee is bound by a court-imposed contract provision with no opportunity to negotiate terms or consideration.

Id. at 293; *see also EarthWeb, Inc. v. Schlack*, 71 F. Supp. 2d 299, 310 (S.D.N.Y. 1999) ("However, in cases that do not involve the actual theft of trade secrets, the court is essentially asked to bind the employee to an implied-in-fact restrictive covenant based on a finding of inevitable disclosure. This runs counter to New York's strong public policy against such agreements and circumvents the strict judicial scrutiny they have traditionally required.").

2.   MONETARY DAMAGES

Both the UTSA and the Third Restatement of Unfair Competition provide for the possibility of monetary damages regardless of whether an injunction is also ordered. In relevant part, § 3 of the UTSA states the following:

> Damages can include both the actual loss caused by misappropriation and the unjust enrichment caused by misappropriation that is not taken into account in computing actual loss. In lieu of damages measured by any other methods, the damages caused by misappropriation may be measured by imposition of liability for a reasonable royalty for a misappropriator's unauthorized disclosure or use of a trade secret.

In essence, this statutory language provides for three categories of damages. The first is for compensatory damages based upon the owner's actual loss of the trade secret. The second is for unjust enrichment, which seeks to measure the advantage enjoyed by the defendant as a result of the misappropriation. The third is a provision for a reasonable royalty based upon the presumed market value of a license at the time of the misappropriation. The comments to UTSA § 3 provide that both compensatory and unjust enrichment damages may be available in the same case so long as there is no "double counting." Section 3 does not provide much guidance, however, as to when to award any particular category of damages.

Comment d to § 45 of the Third Restatement of Unfair Competition similarly recognizes the ability to recover compensatory damages and a reasonable royalty. It also identifies two other categories of damages, which may simply be different ways of measuring the unjust enrichment of the defendant. First, it provides for a measure of damages that awards the plaintiff the profits derived by the defendant from the misappropriation. Second, it allows the plaintiff to recover the savings enjoyed by the defendant that are attributable to the misappropriation.

The case of *University Computing Co. v. Lykes-Youngstown Corp.*, 504 F.2d 518 (5th Cir. 1974), provides a very useful discussion of the types of available damages and when they may be appropriate. University Computing Company ("UCC") entered into an agreement to form a joint corporation with Lykes-Youngstown Corporation ("LYC") for the purpose of offering computer services. After some initial steps toward forming the new company had been taken, the relationship between the parties broke down. LYC formed a wholly owned subsidiary, LYCSC, and transferred property from the UCC/LYC venture to LYCSC without UCC's consent. Among the property transferred by LYC was a computer system called AIMES III. LYCSC then competed with UCC and unsuccessfully tried to market the system. The court found that LYC had misappropriated the AIMES III system, which qualified as a protected trade secret. The court then discussed possible measures of damages:

> Once having determined that the jury finding that AIMES III was a trade secret wrongfully appropriated by the defendants was proper, the problem remains as to what is the appropriate measure of damages. It seems generally accepted that "the proper measure of damages in the case of a trade secret appropriation is to be determined by reference to the analogous line of cases involving patent infringement, just as patent infringement cases are used by analogy to determine the damages for copyright infringement." International Industries, Inc. v. Warren Petroleum Corp., 248 F.2d 696, 699 (3d Cir. 1957). The case law is thus plentiful, but the standard for measuring damages which emerges is very flexible.

> In some instances courts have attempted to measure the loss suffered by the plaintiff. While as a conceptual matter this seems to be a proper approach, in most cases the defendant has

utilized the secret to his advantage with no obvious effect on the plaintiff save for the relative differences in their subsequent competitive positions. Largely as a result of this practical dilemma, normally the value of the secret to the plaintiff is an appropriate measure of damages only when the defendant has in some way destroyed the value of the secret. The most obvious way this is done is through publication, so that no secret remains.[26] Where the plaintiff retains the use of the secret, as here, and where there has been no effective disclosure of the secret through publication the total value of the secret to the plaintiff is an inappropriate measure.

Further, unless some specific injury to the plaintiff can be established—such as lost sales—the loss to the plaintiff is not a particularly helpful approach in assessing damages.

The second approach is to measure the value of the secret to the defendant. This is usually the accepted approach where the secret has not been destroyed and where the plaintiff is unable to prove specific injury. In the case before us, then, the "appropriate measure of damages, by analogy to patent infringement, is not what plaintiff lost, but rather the benefits, profits, or advantages gained by the defendant in the use of the trade secret." International Industries, Inc. v. Warren Petroleum, *supra*, 248 F.2d at 699. The cases reveal, however, many variations in the way this benefit to the defendant can be measured.

Normally only the defendant's actual profits can be used as a measure of damages in cases where profits can be proved, and the defendant is normally not assessed damages on wholly speculative expectations of profits. Sheldon v. Metro-Goldwyn Pictures Corp., 309 U.S. 390 (1939). Had the defendants here been able to sell the AIMES III system at a profit, our task would be simplified. Because the defendants failed in their marketing efforts, no actual profits exist by which to value the worth to the defendants of what they misappropriated. However, the Supreme Court has held in a patent case that the lack of actual profits does not insulate the defendants from being obliged to pay for what they have wrongfully obtained in the mistaken belief their theft would benefit them. In re Cawood Patent, 94 U.S. 695 (1877).[29]

---

[26] *See, e.g.,* Precision Plating v. Martin Marietta, 435 F.2d 1262 (5th Cir. 1970), where public disclosure of a process was held to constitute a complete destruction of the value of the trade secret.

[29] Defendant's actual profits are now usually only one of a number of elements which can be considered in measuring damages for patent infringement. *See, e.g.,* Activated Sludge v. Sanitary

The rationale for this seems clearly to be that the risk of defendants' venture, using the misappropriated secret, should not be placed on the injured plaintiff, but rather the defendants must bear the risk of failure themselves. Accordingly the law looks to the time at which the misappropriation occurred to determine what the value of the misappropriated secret would be to a defendant who believes he can utilize it to his advantage, provided he does in fact put the idea to a commercial use.

This second technique frequently entails using what is called the "reasonable royalty" standard: While the parties to this action agree this is the appropriate standard, they are unable to agree on what the measure entails. Originally this measure was intended to deal with the situation where the misappropriated idea is used either to improve the defendant's manufacturing process, or is used as part of a larger manufactured product. In the early case of Egry Register Co. v. Standard Register Co., 23 F.2d 438 (6th Cir. 1928), a patent infringement case, the defendant manufactured and sold cash registers which in part used a device developed by the plaintiff to roll paper through the machine. The trial court had awarded the plaintiff the total profits the defendant had made on all sales of the machines using this device. The Sixth Circuit Court of Appeals held this measure of damages was inequitable, because the device was only a part of the larger product sold by the defendant. Because no actual apportionment of profits based on what percentage of the success of the marketing of the machines was due to the plaintiff's device could be shown, the court held the proper measure of damages would be a reasonable royalty on defendant's sales, thereby creating an apportionment of profits based on an approximation of the actual value of the infringed device to the defendant.

The Court explained its new measure in this way:

> "To adopt a reasonable royalty as the measure of damages is to adopt and interpret, as well as may be, the fiction that a license was to be granted at the time of beginning the infringement, and then to determine what the license price should have been. In effect, the court assumes the existence *ab initio* of, and declares the equitable terms of, a supposititious license, and does this *nunc pro tunc*; it creates and applies retrospectively a compulsory license. . . ."

District of Chicago, 64 F. Supp. 25 (N.D.Ill.1946), where the Court found no actual profits gained by the defendant, yet concluded "the law is not impotent in attempting precise valuation, even though no market value exists and no loss or impairment of sales can be proven." 64 F. Supp. at 27.

The Court further held the proper standard would be a willing buyer-willing seller test: ". . . the primary inquiry . . . is what the parties would have agreed upon, if both were reasonably trying to reach agreement." *Egry Register*, *supra*, at 443.

The language of the *Egry* decision has been often quoted, but the type of measure used by the Court, based on actual sales, has taken many different forms. As the term is presently understood, the "reasonable royalty" measure of damages is taken to mean more than simply a percentage of actual profits. The measure now, very simply, means "the actual value of what has been appropriated." Vitro Corporation of America v. Hall Chemical Co., 292 F.2d 678, 683 (6th Cir. 1961). When this is not subject to exact measurement, a reasonable estimate of value is used. Many different factors are now considered in arriving at the "reasonable royalty" in any given case:

> "As pointed out in many cases . . . in a case where no established royalty is shown it is for the Court to determine a reasonable royalty which represents the value of that which has been wrongfully taken by the infringer . . . [I]t is sufficient to point out that in making such determination many factors were taken into consideration. . . . In fact, the reasonable royalty was based upon the advantages which would have accrued to (the infringer) had it negotiated a license . . ."

Union Carbide Corp. v. Graver Tank and Manufacturing Co., 282 F.2d 653, 674–675 (7th Cir. 1960).

One other important variation on this "reasonable royalty" standard is the standard of comparison method, which also attempts to measure the value to the defendant to what he appropriated. As the Court in International Industries, Inc. v. Warren Petroleum Corp., 248 F.2d 696, 699 (3d Cir. 1957) explained this method, relating it to the facts of the case in which the defendant had misappropriated a method of converting dry cargo vessels into ones equipped to transport liquefied petroleum gas, and had actually used the technique to convert one vessel:

> "This method contemplates the comparison of the cost of transportation by means of the use of the trade secret with a method of accomplishing the same result which would have been open to defendant had he not appropriated the trade secret."

Occasionally this has been taken to mean the difference in costs to the defendant of developing the trade secret on his own, using the actual development costs of the plaintiff as the complete measure of damages. Servo Corp. v. General Electric Co., 342 F.2d 993 (4th Cir. 1965). This measure of damages simply uses the plaintiff's actual costs, and in our view is frequently inadequate in that it fails to take into account the commercial context in which the misappropriation occurred.

In certain cases, where the trade secret was used by the defendant in a limited number of situations, where the plaintiff was not in direct competition with the defendant, where the development of the secret did not require substantial improvements in existing trade practices but rather merely refined the existing practices, and where the defendant's use of the plaintiff's trade secret has ceased, such a limited measure might be appropriate. In the type of case which we now consider, when the parties were potentially in direct competition and the course of conduct of the defendant extended over a period of time and included a number of different uses of the plaintiff's trade secret, and where the process of developing a computer system was very difficult and required substantial technical and theoretical advances, we believe a broader measure of damages is needed.

This broader measure should take into consideration development costs, but as only one of a number of different factors. We believe this type of measure is appropriate despite the fact that the inclusion of other factors means the final damage figure "need not be as precise as if the actual development costs for the trade secret were itself the measure of damages." Forest Laboratories, Inc. v. Pillsbury Co., 452 F.2d 621, 628 (7th Cir. 1971).

Our review of the caselaw leads us to the conclusion that every case requires a flexible and imaginative approach to the problem of damages. We agree with the Court of Appeals for the Sixth Circuit that "each case is controlled by its own peculiar facts and circumstances," Enterprise Manufacturing Co. v. Shakespeare Co., 141 F.2d 916, 920 (6th Cir. 1944), and accordingly we believe that the cases reveal that most courts adjust the measure of damages to accord with the commercial setting of the injury, the likely future consequences of the misappropriation, and the nature and extent of the use the defendant put the trade secret to after misappropriation. Naturally in some cases the damages will be subject to exact measurement, either because the parties had previously agreed on a licensing price as in Vitro Corp. v. Hall Chemical Co., *supra*, or because some industry standard provides a clear measure.

Where the damages are uncertain, however, we do not feel that that uncertainty should preclude recovery; the plaintiff should be afforded every opportunity to prove damages once the misappropriation is shown.

Certain standards do emerge from the cases. The defendant must have actually put the trade secret to some commercial use. The law governing protection of trade secrets essentially is designed to regulate unfair business competition, and is not a substitute for criminal laws against theft or other civil remedies for conversion. If the defendant enjoyed actual profits, a type of restitutionary remedy can be afforded the plaintiff—either recovering the full total of defendant's profits or some apportioned amount designed to correspond to the actual contribution the plaintiff's trade secret made to the defendant's commercial success. Because the primary concern in most cases is to measure the value to the defendant of what he actually obtained from the plaintiff, the proper measure is to calculate what the parties would have agreed to as a fair price for licensing the defendant to put the trade secret to the use the defendant intended at the time the misappropriation took place.

In calculating what a fair licensing price would have been had the parties agreed, the trier of fact should consider such factors as the resulting and foreseeable changes in the parties' competitive posture; the prices past purchasers or licensees may have paid; the total value of the secret to the plaintiff, including the plaintiff's development costs and the importance of the secret to the plaintiff's business; the nature and extent of the use the defendant intended for the secret; and finally whatever other unique factors in the particular case which might have affected the parties' agreement, such as the ready availability of alternative processes. Hughes Tool Co. v. G. W. Murphy Industries, Inc., 491 F.2d 923, 931 (5th Cir. 1973).

University Computing Co. v. Lykes-Youngstown Corp., 504 F.2d 518, 535–39 (5th Cir. 1974).

NOTES & QUESTIONS

(1) The *University Computing* court discussed various measures of damages. According to the court, when is each measure appropriate, and what are the weaknesses of each? *See also* RESTATEMENT (THIRD) OF UNFAIR COMPETITION § 45 cmts. e–g (1995).

(2) Section 3 of the UTSA has a provision for exemplary damages. The decision to award exemplary damages is left to the court (rather than the jury), and the amount of such damages is limited to twice the amount of any

compensatory award. Exemplary damages under the UTSA require a showing of "willful and malicious misappropriation" by clear and convincing evidence. In jurisdictions that have not adopted the UTSA, punitive damages are permitted in similar circumstances. *See, e.g., Huschle v. Battelle*, 308 N.Y.S.2d 235, 236 (App. Div. 1970) (permitting punitive damages where the misconduct is accompanied by "malice, insult, reckless and willful disregard of the plaintiff's rights, or other proof showing the aggravated nature of the act"); RESTATEMENT (SECOND) OF TORTS § 908 (1977) ("Punitive damages may be awarded for conduct that is outrageous, because of the defendant's evil motive or his reckless indifference to the rights of others").

(3) Section 4 of the UTSA provides for attorney's fees under limited circumstances. It states that a court may award reasonable attorney's fees to the prevailing party if: "(i) a claim of misappropriation is made in bad faith; (ii) a motion to terminate an injunction is made or resisted in bad faith; or (iii) willful and malicious misappropriation exists." In jurisdictions that have not adopted the UTSA, a plaintiff wishing to recover attorney's fees would need to prevail on another cause of action that provides such fees and avoids preemption.

E. FEDERAL LAWS AFFECTING TRADE SECRETS

Although trade secret law is primarily left to the states, there are a number of federal laws in the area. Two noteworthy federal statutes are the Computer Fraud and Abuse Act ("CFAA") and the Economic Espionage Act of 1996 ("EEA").

The CFAA was passed in 1984 and was intended to protect classified financial and credit information on government and financial institution computers. Although it was a criminal statute initially, it was amended in 1994 to include civil remedies. The three most relevant provisions of the CFAA with respect to trade secret misappropriation are 18 U.S.C. § 1030(a)(2)(C), (a)(4), and (a)(5)(C).

Under § 1030(a)(2)(C), "[w]hoever . . . intentionally accesses a computer without authorization or exceeds authorized access, and thereby obtains . . . information from any protected computer if the conduct involved an interstate or foreign communication . . . shall be punished" as provided in the statute. In addition, § 1030(g) provides that "[a]ny person who suffers damage or loss by reason of a violation of this section may maintain a civil action against the violator to obtain compensatory damages and injunctive relief or other equitable relief." A "protected computer" means a computer "which is used in interstate or foreign commerce or communication." *Id.* § 1030(e)(2)(B). The term "exceeds authorized access" means "to access a computer with authorization and to use such access to obtain or alter information in the computer that the accesser is not entitled so to obtain or alter." *Id.* § 1030(e)(6).

A person violates § 1030(a)(4) if he or she:

> knowingly and with intent to defraud, accesses a protected computer without authorization, or exceeds authorized access, and by means of such conduct furthers the intended fraud and obtains anything of value, unless the object of the fraud and the thing obtained consists only of the use of the computer and the value of such use is not more than $5,000 in any 1-year period. . . .

The primary difference between this section and § 1030(a)(2)(C) is that § 1030(a)(4) requires an intent to defraud. Moreover, courts have indicated that the use of "fraud" in § 1030(a)(4) "simply means wrongdoing and not proof of the common law elements of fraud." *Shurgard Storage Centers, Inc. v. Safeguard Self Storage, Inc.*, 119 F. Supp. 2d 1121, 1126 (W.D. Wash. 2000).

Under § 1030(a)(5)(C), "[w]hoever . . . intentionally accesses a protected computer without authorization, and as a result of such conduct, causes damage" violates the CFAA. This provision requires the plaintiff to allege that "damage" occurred. Section 1030(e)(8) indicates that damage "means any impairment to the integrity or availability of data, a program, a system, or information." In *Shurgard*, the court held that allegations that the defendant infiltrated the plaintiff's computer network and collected and disseminated confidential information were enough to constitute damage under the statute. *See Shurgard*, 119 F. Supp. 2d at 1126–27.

Taken together, these CFAA provisions can serve as powerful weapons for employers to use against former employees who access computers without authorization. Importantly, CFAA claims do not require proof of a trade secret, but they do require proof of computer access. Given the amount of work that is done on computers, this requirement is typically not difficult to satisfy.

The EEA criminalizes trade secret misappropriation to combat espionage against private entities and threats to corporate security. The relevant portions of the Act make it a crime to knowingly convert a trade secret placed in interstate commerce. At one time the statute was limited to trade secrets that related to or were included in tangible products, but this limitation has been removed by the Theft of Trade Secrets Clarification Act of 2012. The EEA's definition of trade secrets mirrors the UTSA's, but its definition of misappropriation does not:

> § 1832.   Theft of trade secrets

> (a) Whoever, with intent to convert a trade secret, that is related to a product or service used in or intended for use in interstate or foreign commerce, to the economic benefit of anyone

other than the owner thereof, and intending or knowing that the offense will, injure any owner of that trade secret, knowingly—

(1) steals, or without authorization appropriates, takes, carries away, or conceals, or by fraud, artifice, or deception obtains such information;

(2) without authorization copies, duplicates, sketches, draws, photographs, downloads, uploads, alters, destroys, photocopies, replicates, transmits, delivers, sends, mails, communicates, or conveys such information;

(3) receives, buys, or possesses such information, knowing the same to have been stolen or appropriated, obtained, or converted without authorization. . . .

The Act is striking in that its definition of misappropriation, particularly under (2), is much broader than the UTSA's definition. Subsection (2) appears to prohibit reverse engineering given that such processes frequently involve copying, duplicating, or sketching the information. *See* James H.A. Pooley et al., *Understanding the Economic Espionage Act of 1996*, 5 TEX. INTELLECTUAL PROP. L.J. 177, 195 (1997). This is especially troubling when the potential penalties are considered. Although the EEA provides no civil remedy, an individual convicted of theft of a trade secret faces a maximum sentence of up to fifteen years in prison and a fine of up to $5,000,000 for foreign espionage, and up to ten years' imprisonment and a fine for domestic theft. *See* 18 U.S.C. §§ 1831(a), 1832(a). Corporations are subject to fines of up to $10,000,000 or three times the value of the stolen trade secret to the organization (whichever is greater) for foreign theft, and up to $5,000,000 for domestic theft. *See id.* §§ 1831(b), 1832(b).

CHAPTER 11

TRADEMARK INFRINGEMENT

■ ■ ■

A. THE PURPOSE OF TRADEMARK

Trademark law is concerned with the protection of goodwill established by a provider of goods or services. In this regard, trademark continues the theme developed in the previous two Chapters—namely, it is not fair to let others reap where they have not sown. Trademark law also serves another purpose that relates to a theme discussed in the deceptive marketing Chapter—preventing consumer confusion or deception. In that Chapter, one of the concepts discussed was the deceptive practice of "passing off," such as by substituting a seller's product for the requested item. If a customer asks for Coca-Cola and the restaurant instead serves its own house brand of soda without telling the consumer, it has passed-off its soda as Coca-Cola. This not only harms Coca-Cola, in that the restaurant is profiting from Coca-Cola's good name, but it also deceives the consumer. As previously explored, this conduct is prohibited under state unfair competition law as well as the Lanham Act.

In this Chapter, we will further consider these concepts as they relate to a business's trademarks. First, we discuss the requirements for trademark protection, both under the Lanham Act and at common law (it should come as no surprise that not every word or symbol used by a business is protected). We then describe the various types of marks, how marks are infringed, and the commonly raised defenses for trademark infringement. Finally, we conclude with a discussion of remedies.

B. REQUIREMENTS FOR PROTECTION

Trademark protection was recognized under state common law long before the federal government stepped in. In the late 1800s, however, the first federal act governing trademark protection was passed, and federal law in this area has expanded ever since. Today, the Lanham Act is the primary source of federal trademark law, but it has not displaced state common law; indeed, trademark rights can exist under both federal and state law.

The Lanham Act defines a trademark as:

any word, name, symbol, or device, or any combination thereof—

(1) used by a person, or

(2) which a person has a bona fide intention to use in commerce and applies to register on the principal register established by this chapter,

to identify and distinguish his or her goods, including a unique product, from those manufactured or sold by others and to indicate the source of the goods, even if that source is unknown.

15 U.S.C. § 1127.[a] To put this more succinctly, a trademark is a word or symbol used to identify a particular manufacturer's or seller's products and to distinguish them from the products of others. From this definition, two primary elements have been developed: (1) the mark must be either used in commerce (or there is a bona fide intention to do so); and (2) the mark must be distinctive. At one time, it was a prerequisite that the mark be used in commerce before protection could be obtained. The Lanham Act was amended, however, to provide that "intention to use" was sufficient to allow a party to obtain temporary preemptive rights to a mark that it intended in good faith to use in commerce. *See* 15 U.S.C. § 1051(b). Such a party must file a statement of use of the mark within six months of the issuance of a notice of allowance by the Patent and Trademark Office ("PTO").

While the use requirement can raise issues, particularly for unregistered trademarks, the distinctiveness requirement has received much more attention from the courts. As you read the following case, identify the types of categories that a mark can fall into and what protection such marks receive.

ZATARAINS, INC. v. OAK GROVE SMOKEHOUSE, INC.
698 F.2d 786 (5th Cir. 1983)

GOLDBERG, CIRCUIT JUDGE:

This appeal of a trademark dispute presents us with a menu of edible delights sure to tempt connoisseurs of fish and fowl alike. At issue is the alleged infringement of two trademarks, "Fish-Fri" and "Chick-Fri," held by appellant Zatarain's, Inc. ("Zatarain's"). The district court held that the alleged infringers had a "fair use" defense to any asserted

---

[a] The Restatement uses a similar definition: "A trademark is a word, name, symbol, device, or other designation, or a combination of such designations, that is distinctive of a person's goods or services and that is used in a manner that identifies those goods or services and distinguishes them from the goods or services of others." RESTATEMENT (THIRD) OF UNFAIR COMPETITION § 9 (1995).

infringement of the term "Fish-Fri" and that the registration of the term "Chick-Fri" should be cancelled. We affirm.

I.   FACTS AND PROCEEDINGS BELOW

A.   THE TALE OF THE TOWN FRIER

Zatarain's is the manufacturer and distributor of a line of over one hundred food products. Two of these products, "Fish-Fri" and "Chick-Fri," are coatings or batter mixes used to fry foods. These marks serve as the entreè in the present litigation.

Zatarain's "Fish-Fri" consists of 100% corn flour and is used to fry fish and other seafood. "Fish-Fri" is packaged in rectangular cardboard boxes containing twelve or twenty-four ounces of coating mix. The legend "Wonderful FISH-FRI®" is displayed prominently on the front panel, along with the block Z used to identify all Zatarain's products. The term "Fish-Fri" has been used by Zatarain's or its predecessor since 1950 and has been registered as a trademark since 1962.

Zatarain's "Chick-Fri" is a seasoned corn flour batter mix used for frying chicken and other foods. The "Chick-Fri" package, which is very similar to that used for "Fish-Fri," is a rectangular cardboard container labelled "Wonderful CHICK-FRI." Zatarain's began to use the term "Chick-Fri" in 1968 and registered the term as a trademark in 1976.

Zatarain's products are not alone in the marketplace. At least four other companies market coatings for fried foods that are denominated "fish fry" or "chicken fry." Two of these competing companies are the appellees here, and therein hangs this fish tale.

Appellee Oak Grove Smokehouse, Inc. ("Oak Grove") began marketing a "fish fry" and a "chicken fry" in March 1979. Both products are packaged in clear glassine packets that contain a quantity of coating mix sufficient to fry enough food for one meal. The packets are labelled with Oak Grove's name and emblem, along with the words "FISH FRY" [or] "CHICKEN FRY." Oak Grove's "FISH FRY" has a corn flour base seasoned with various spices; Oak Grove's "CHICKEN FRY" is a seasoned coating with a wheat flour base.

Appellee Visko's Fish Fry, Inc. ("Visko's") entered the batter mix market in March 1980 with its "fish fry." Visko's product is packed in a cylindrical eighteen-ounce container with a resealable plastic lid. The words "Visko's FISH FRY" appear on the label along with a photograph of a platter of fried fish. Visko's coating mix contains corn flour and added spices.

. . . .

B.   OUT OF THE FRYING PAN, INTO THE FIRE

Zatarain's first claimed foul play in its original complaint filed against Oak Grove on June 19, 1979, in the United States District Court for the Eastern District of Louisiana. The complaint alleged trademark infringement and unfair competition under the Lanham Act and La.Rev.Stat.Ann. § 51:1405(A) (West Supp.1982). Zatarain's later amended its complaint to add . . . Visko's as [a defendant]. . . . Oak Grove and Visko's . . . filed counterclaims against Zatarain's for cancellation of the trademarks "Fish-Fri" and "Chick-Fri" under section 37 of the Lanham Act, and for damages under section 38 of the Lanham Act.

. . . .

II.   ISSUES ON APPEAL

The district court found that Zatarain's trademark "Fish-Fri" was a descriptive term with an established secondary meaning, but held that Oak Grove and Visko's had a "fair use" defense to their asserted infringement of the mark. The court further found that Zatarain's trademark "Chick-Fri" was a descriptive term that lacked secondary meaning, and accordingly ordered the trademark registration cancelled. Additionally, the court concluded that Zatarain's had produced no evidence in support of its claims of unfair competition on the part of Oak Grove and Visko's. Finally, the court dismissed Oak Grove's and Visko's counterclaims. . . .

Battered, but not fried, Zatarain's appeals from the adverse judgment on several grounds. First, Zatarain's argues that its trademark "Fish-Fri" is a suggestive term and therefore not subject to the "fair use" defense. Second, Zatarain's asserts that even if the "fair use" defense is applicable in this case, appellees cannot invoke the doctrine because their use of Zatarain's trademarks is not a good faith attempt to describe their products. Third, Zatarain's urges that the district court erred in cancelling the trademark registration for the term "Chick-Fri" because Zatarain's presented sufficient evidence to establish a secondary meaning for the term. For these reasons, Zatarain's argues that the district court should be reversed.

. . . .

III.   THE TRADEMARK CLAIMS

A.   BASIC PRINCIPLES

1.   Classifications of Marks

The threshold issue in any action for trademark infringement is whether the word or phrase is initially registerable or protectable. Courts and commentators have traditionally divided potential trademarks into four categories. A potential trademark may be classified as (1) generic, (2) descriptive, (3) suggestive, or (4) arbitrary or fanciful. These categories, like the tones in a spectrum, tend to blur at the edges and merge together. The labels are more advisory than definitional, more like guidelines than pigeonholes. Not surprisingly, they are somewhat difficult to articulate and to apply.

A generic term is "the name of a particular genus or class of which an individual article or service is but a member." A generic term connotes the "basic nature of articles or services" rather than the more individualized characteristics of a particular product. Generic terms can never attain trademark protection. *William R. Warner & Co. v. Eli Lilly & Co.*, 265 U.S. 526, 528 (1924). Furthermore, if at any time a registered trademark becomes generic as to a particular product or service, the mark's registration is subject to cancellation. Lanham Act § 14, 15 U.S.C. § 1064(c) (1976). Such terms as aspirin and cellophane have been held generic and therefore unprotectable as trademarks. *See Bayer Co. v. United Drug Co.*, 272 F. 505 (S.D.N.Y.1921) (aspirin); *DuPont Cellophane Co. v. Waxed Products Co.*, 85 F.2d 75 (2d Cir.1936) (cellophane).

A descriptive term identifies a characteristic or quality of an article or service, such as its color, odor, function, dimensions, or ingredients. Descriptive terms ordinarily are not protectable as trademarks, Lanham Act § 2(e)(1), 15 U.S.C. § 1052(e)(1) (1976); they may become valid marks, however, by acquiring a secondary meaning in the minds of the consuming public. *See id.* § 2(f), 15 U.S.C. § 1052(f). Examples of descriptive marks would include "Alo" with reference to products containing gel of the aloe vera plant, *Aloe Creme Laboratories, Inc. v. Milsan, Inc.*, 423 F.2d 845 (5th Cir. 1970), and "Vision Center" in reference to a business offering optical goods and services, [*Vision Center v. Opticks, Inc.*, 596 F.2d 111, 117 (5th Cir. 1979)]. As this court has often noted, the distinction between descriptive and generic terms is one of degree. The distinction has important practical consequences, however; while a descriptive term may be elevated to trademark status with proof of secondary meaning, a generic term may never achieve trademark protection.

A suggestive term suggests, rather than describes, some particular characteristic of the goods or services to which it applies and requires the consumer to exercise the imagination in order to draw a conclusion as to the nature of the goods and services. A suggestive mark is protected without the necessity for proof of secondary meaning. The term "Coppertone" has been held suggestive in regard to sun tanning products. *See Douglas Laboratories Corp. v. Copper Tan, Inc.*, 210 F.2d 453 (2d Cir.1954).

Arbitrary or fanciful terms bear no relationship to the products or services to which they are applied. Like suggestive terms, arbitrary and fanciful marks are protectable without proof of secondary meaning. The term "Kodak" is properly classified as a fanciful term for photographic supplies, *see Eastman Kodak Co. v. Weil*, 243 N.Y.S. 319 (1930) ("Kodak"); "Ivory" is an arbitrary term as applied to soap. [*Abercrombie & Fitch Co. v. Hunting World, Inc.*, 537 F.2d 4, 9 n.6 (2d Cir. 1976)].

2.   Secondary Meaning

As noted earlier, descriptive terms are ordinarily not protectable as trademarks. They may be protected, however, if they have acquired a secondary meaning for the consuming public. The concept of secondary meaning recognizes that words with an ordinary and primary meaning of their own "may by long use with a particular product, come to be known by the public as specifically designating that product." *Volkswagenwerk Aktiengesellschaft v. Rickard*, 492 F.2d 474, 477 (5th Cir.1974). In order to establish a secondary meaning for a term, a plaintiff "must show that the primary significance of the term in the minds of the consuming public is not the product but the producer." *Kellogg Co. v. National Biscuit Co.*, 305 U.S. 111, 118 (1938). The burden of proof to establish secondary meaning rests at all times with the plaintiff; this burden is not an easy one to satisfy, for " '[a] high degree of proof is necessary to establish secondary meaning for a descriptive term.' " *Vision Center*, 596 F.2d at 118. Proof of secondary meaning is an issue only with respect to descriptive marks; suggestive and arbitrary or fanciful marks are automatically protected upon registration, and generic terms are unprotectible even if they have acquired secondary meaning.

3.   The "Fair Use" Defense

Even when a descriptive term has acquired a secondary meaning sufficient to warrant trademark protection, others may be entitled to use the mark without incurring liability for trademark infringement. When the allegedly infringing term is "used fairly and in good faith only to describe to users the goods or services of [a] party, or their geographic origin," Lanham Act § 33(b)(4), 15 U.S.C. § 1115(b)(4) (1976), a defendant in a trademark infringement action may assert the "fair use" defense. The defense is available only in actions involving descriptive terms and only when the term is used in its descriptive sense rather than its trademark sense. In essence, the fair use defense prevents a trademark registrant from appropriating a descriptive term for its own use to the exclusion of others, who may be prevented thereby from accurately describing their own goods. The holder of a protectable descriptive mark has no legal claim to an exclusive right in the primary, descriptive meaning of the term; consequently, anyone is free to use the term in its primary, descriptive sense so long as such use does not lead to customer confusion as to the source of the goods or services.

4. Cancellation of Trademarks

Section 37 of the Lanham Act, 15 U.S.C. § 1119 (1976), provides as follows:

> In any action involving a registered mark the court may determine the right to registration, order the cancelation of registrations, in whole or in part, restore canceled registrations, and otherwise rectify the register with respect to the registrations of any party to the action. Decrees and orders shall be certified by the court to the Commissioner, who shall make appropriate entry upon the records of the Patent Office, and shall be controlled thereby.

This circuit has held that when a court determines that a mark is either a generic term or a descriptive term lacking secondary meaning, the purposes of the Lanham Act are well served by an order cancelling the mark's registration.

We now turn to the facts of the instant case.

B. "FISH-FRI"[3]

1. Classification

Throughout this litigation, Zatarain's has maintained that the term "Fish-Fri" is a suggestive mark automatically protected from infringing uses by virtue of its registration in 1962. Oak Grove and Visko's assert that "fish fry" is a generic term identifying a class of foodstuffs used to fry fish; alternatively, Oak Grove and Visko's argue that "fish fry" is merely descriptive of the characteristics of the product. The district court found that "Fish-Fri" was a descriptive term identifying a function of the product being sold. Having reviewed this finding under the appropriate "clearly erroneous" standard, we affirm.

We are mindful that "[t]he concept of descriptiveness must be construed rather broadly." [3 R. Callman, *The Law of Unfair Competition, Trademarks and Monopolies* § 70.2 (3d ed. 1969)]. Whenever a word or phrase conveys an immediate idea of the qualities, characteristics, effect, purpose, or ingredients of a product or service, it is classified as descriptive and cannot be claimed as an exclusive trademark. Courts and commentators have formulated a number of tests to be used in classifying a mark as descriptive.

A suitable starting place is the dictionary, for the dictionary definition of the word is an appropriate and relevant indication of the ordinary significance and meaning of words to the public. *Webster's Third*

---

[3] We note at the outset that Zatarain's use of the phonetic equivalent of the words "fish fry"—that is, misspelling it—does not render the mark protectable. [*Soweco, Inc. v. Shell Oil Co.,* 617 F.2d 1178, 1186 n.24 (5th Cir. 1980)].

New International Dictionary 858 (1966) lists the following definitions for the term "fish fry": "1. a picnic at which fish are caught, fried, and eaten; . . . . 2. fried fish." Thus, the basic dictionary definitions of the term refer to the preparation and consumption of fried fish. This is at least preliminary evidence that the term "Fish-Fri" is descriptive of Zatarain's product in the sense that the words naturally direct attention to the purpose or function of the product.

The "imagination test" is a second standard used by the courts to identify descriptive terms. This test seeks to measure the relationship between the actual words of the mark and the product to which they are applied. If a term "requires imagination, thought and perception to reach a conclusion as to the nature of goods," [*Stix Prods., Inc. v. United Merchants and Mfrs., Inc.*, 295 F. Supp. 479, 488 (S.D.N.Y. 1968)], it is considered a suggestive term. Alternatively, a term is descriptive if standing alone it conveys information as to the characteristics of the product. In this case, mere observation compels the conclusion that a product branded "Fish-Fri" is a prepackaged coating or batter mix applied to fish prior to cooking. The connection between this merchandise and its identifying terminology is so close and direct that even a consumer unfamiliar with the product would doubtless have an idea of its purpose or function. It simply does not require an exercise of the imagination to deduce that "Fish-Fri" is used to fry fish. Accordingly, the term "Fish-Fri" must be considered descriptive when examined under the "imagination test."

A third test used by courts and commentators to classify descriptive marks is "whether competitors would be likely to need the terms used in the trademark in describing their products." *Union Carbide Corp. v. Ever-Ready, Inc.*, 531 F.2d 366, 379 (7th Cir.1976). A descriptive term generally relates so closely and directly to a product or service that other merchants marketing similar goods would find the term useful in identifying their own goods. Common sense indicates that in this case merchants other than Zatarain's might find the term "fish fry" useful in describing their own particular batter mixes. While Zatarain's has argued strenuously that Visko's and Oak Grove could have chosen from dozens of other possible terms in naming their coating mix, we find this position to be without merit. As this court has held, the fact that a term is not the only or even the most common name for a product is not determinative, for there is no legal foundation that a product can be described in only one fashion. There are many edible fish in the sea, and as many ways to prepare them as there are varieties to be prepared. Even piscatorial gastronomes would agree, however, that frying is a form of preparation accepted virtually around the world, at restaurants starred and unstarred. The paucity of synonyms for the words "fish" and "fry" suggests that a merchant whose batter mix is specially spiced for frying fish is likely to find "fish fry" a useful term for describing his product.

A final barometer of the descriptiveness of a particular term examines the extent to which a term actually has been used by others marketing a similar service or product. This final test is closely related to the question whether competitors are likely to find a mark useful in describing their products. As noted above, a number of companies other than Zatarain's have chosen the word combination "fish fry" to identify their batter mixes. Arnaud's product, "Oyster Shrimp and Fish Fry," has been in competition with Zatarain's "Fish-Fri" for some ten to twenty years. When companies from A to Z, from Arnaud to Zatarain's, select the same term to describe their similar products, the term in question is most likely a descriptive one.

. . . . The district court in this case found that Zatarain's trademark "Fish-Fri" was descriptive of the function of the product being sold. Having applied the four prevailing tests of descriptiveness to the term "Fish-Fri," we are convinced that the district court's judgment in this matter is not only not clearly erroneous, but clearly correct.[4]

---

[4] Oak Grove and Visko's argue in a conclusory manner that the term "fish fry" is a generic name for the class of substances used to coat fish prior to frying. We are unable to agree. No evidence in the record indicates that the term "fish fry" is the common, recognized name for any class of foodstuffs. The district court specifically rejected the contention that the term "Fish-Fri" was generic. This finding was not clearly erroneous and must be affirmed.

Zatarain's urges that its "Fish-Fri" mark is suggestive rather than descriptive, and our lengthy discussion in text addresses this contention fully. We pause here, however, to speak to Zatarain's argument that certain survey evidence introduced at trial proves the suggestive nature of the term "Fish-Fri." Just as the compleat angler exaggerates his favorite fish story, so Zatarain's overstates the results of its consumer survey. We consider the survey unpersuasive on the issue of suggestiveness for several reasons.

First, the survey was not intended to investigate the term's descriptiveness or suggestiveness. Rather, as expert witness Allen Rosenzweig testified, the survey was designed to explore two completely different issues: likelihood of confusion in the marketplace and secondary meaning. Furthermore, the district court prohibited Rosenzweig's testimony as to whether the survey data showed Zatarain's term to be suggestive or descriptive.

Second, a glance at the survey itself convinces us that, regardless of its purpose, the questions were not framed in a manner adequate to classify the mark properly. Respondents were asked the following questions: "2. If you planned to fry fish tonight, what would you buy at the grocery to use as a coating? 3. Are you familiar with any product on the market that is especially made for frying fish?" If these questions were to test the associational link between the mark "Fish-Fri" and Zatarain's product, they should have been devoid of such broad hints as the place of purchase ("grocery"), the nature of the product ("coating"), and the purpose or function of the product ("to fry fish"). Furthermore, we caution that survey samples such as these—100 women in each of four randomly selected cities—may not be adequate in size to prove much of anything.

Survey evidence is often critically important in the field of trademark law. We heartily embrace its use, so long as the survey design is relevant to the legal issues, open-ended in its construction, and neutral in its administration. Given the admitted purposes of this survey and its obvious design limitations, it is rather disingenuous of Zatarain's to assert that the survey provided conclusive evidence of suggestiveness. We therefore reject Zatarain's contention in this regard.

. . . .

2.   Secondary Meaning

Descriptive terms are not protectable by trademark absent a showing of secondary meaning in the minds of the consuming public. To prevail in its trademark infringement action, therefore, Zatarain's must prove that its mark "Fish-Fri" has acquired a secondary meaning and thus warrants trademark protection. The district court found that Zatarain's evidence established a secondary meaning for the term "Fish-Fri" in the New Orleans area. We affirm.

The existence of secondary meaning presents a question for the trier of fact, and a district court's finding on the issue will not be disturbed unless clearly erroneous. The burden of proof rests with the party seeking to establish legal protection for the mark—the plaintiff in an infringement suit. The evidentiary burden necessary to establish secondary meaning for a descriptive term is substantial.

In assessing a claim of secondary meaning, the major inquiry is the consumer's attitude toward the mark. The mark must denote to the consumer "a single thing coming from a single source," *Coca-Cola Co. v. Koke Co.*, 254 U.S. 143, 146 (1920), to support a finding of secondary meaning. Both direct and circumstantial evidence may be relevant and persuasive on the issue.

Factors such as amount and manner of advertising, volume of sales, and length and manner of use may serve as circumstantial evidence relevant to the issue of secondary meaning. While none of these factors alone will prove secondary meaning, in combination they may establish the necessary link in the minds of consumers between a product and its source. It must be remembered, however, that the question is not the extent of the promotional efforts, but their effectiveness in altering the meaning of the term to the consuming public.

Since 1950, Zatarain's and its predecessor have continuously used the term "Fish-Fri" to identify this particular batter mix. Through the expenditure of over $400,000 for advertising during the period from 1976 through 1981, Zatarain's has promoted its name and its product to the buying public. Sales of twelve-ounce boxes of "Fish-Fri" increased from 37,265 cases in 1969 to 59,439 cases in 1979. From 1964 through 1979, Zatarain's sold a total of 916,385 cases of "Fish-Fri." The district court considered this circumstantial evidence of secondary meaning to weigh heavily in Zatarain's favor.

In addition to these circumstantial factors, Zatarain's introduced at trial two surveys conducted by its expert witness, Allen Rosenzweig. In one survey, telephone interviewers questioned 100 women in the New Orleans area who fry fish or other seafood three or more times per month. Of the women surveyed, twenty-three percent specified Zatarain's "Fish-Fri" as a product they "would buy at the grocery to use as a coating" or a "product on the market that is especially made for frying fish." In a similar survey conducted in person at a New Orleans area mall, twenty-eight of the 100 respondents answered "Zatarain's 'Fish-Fri' " to the same questions.

The authorities are in agreement that survey evidence is the most direct and persuasive way of establishing secondary meaning. The district court believed that the survey evidence produced by Zatarain's, when coupled with the circumstantial evidence of advertising and usage, tipped the scales in favor of a finding of secondary meaning. Were we considering the question of secondary meaning de novo, we might reach a different conclusion than did the district court, for the issue is close. Mindful, however, that there is evidence in the record to support the finding below, we cannot say that the district court's conclusion was clearly erroneous. Accordingly, the finding of secondary meaning in the New Orleans area for Zatarain's descriptive term "Fish-Fri" must be affirmed.

3.   The "Fair Use" Defense

[Although the court agreed that Zatarain's "Fish-Fri" had acquired a secondary meaning in the New Orleans geographical area, it concluded that Oak Grove's and Visko's use of the phrase qualified under the fair use defense. The court upheld the district court's determination that Oak Grove's and Visko's use of the words "fish fry" was fair and in good faith. We return to the fair use defense later in this Chapter.]

C.   "CHICK-FRI"

1.   Classification

Most of what has been said about "Fish-Fri" applies with equal force to Zatarain's other culinary concoction, "Chick-Fri." "Chick-Fri" is at least as descriptive of the act of frying chicken as "Fish-Fri" is descriptive of frying fish. It takes no effort of the imagination to associate the term "Chick-Fri" with Southern fried chicken. Other merchants are likely to want to use the words "chicken fry" to describe similar products, and others have in fact done so. Sufficient evidence exists to support the district court's finding that "Chick-Fri" is a descriptive term; accordingly, we affirm.

2.   Secondary Meaning

The district court concluded that Zatarain's had failed to establish a secondary meaning for the term "Chick-Fri." We affirm this finding. The mark "Chick-Fri" has been in use only since 1968; it was registered even more recently, in 1976. In sharp contrast to its promotions with regard to "Fish-Fri," Zatarain's advertising expenditures for "Chick-Fri" were mere chickenfeed; in fact, Zatarain's conducted no direct advertising campaign to publicize the product. Thus the circumstantial evidence presented in support of a secondary meaning for the term "Chick-Fri" was paltry.

Allen Rosenzweig's survey evidence regarding a secondary meaning for "Chick-Fri" also "lays an egg." The initial survey question was a "qualifier:" "Approximately how many times in an average month do you, yourself, fry fish or other seafood?" Only if respondents replied "three or more times a month" were they asked to continue the survey. This qualifier, which may have been perfectly adequate for purposes of the "Fish-Fri" questions, seems highly unlikely to provide an adequate sample of potential consumers of "Chick-Fri." This survey provides us with nothing more than some data regarding fish friers' perceptions about products used for frying chicken. As such, it is entitled to little evidentiary weight.[10]

It is well settled that Zatarain's, the original plaintiff in this trademark infringement action, has the burden of proof to establish secondary meaning for its term. This it has failed to do. The district court's finding that the term "Chick-Fri" lacks secondary meaning is affirmed.

3. Cancellation

Having concluded that the district court was correct in its determination that Zatarain's mark "Chick-Fri" is a descriptive term lacking in secondary meaning, we turn to the issue of cancellation. The district court, invoking the courts' power over trademark registration as provided by section 37 of the Lanham Act, ordered that the registration of the term "Chick-Fri" should be cancelled. The district court's action was perfectly appropriate in light of its findings that "Chick-Fri" is a descriptive term without secondary meaning. We affirm.

. . . .

V. CONCLUSION

And so our tale of fish and fowl draws to a close. We need not tarry long, for our taster's choice yields but one result, and we have other fish to fry. Accordingly, the judgment of the district court is hereby and in all things

AFFIRMED.

---

[10] Even were we to accept the results of the survey as relevant, the result would not change. In the New Orleans area, only 11 of the 100 respondents in the telephone survey named "Chick-Fri," "chicken fry," or "Zatarain's 'Chick-Fri'" as a product used as a coating for frying chicken. Rosenzweig himself testified that this number was inconclusive for sampling purposes. Thus the survey evidence cannot be said to establish a secondary meaning for the term "Chick-Fri."

NOTES & QUESTIONS

(1)   The *Zatarain's* court designates a spectrum of categories that a mark can fall into. What are the categories and what effect do they have on a mark?

(2)   Although the *Zatarain's* decision is based on the Lanham Act, the common law has adopted a very similar categorical approach to distinctiveness. Review §§ 13–15 of the Restatement of Unfair Competition and comments b, c, and e to § 13. Do you see similar categories in those sections?

(3)   Zatarain's argued that its marks were suggestive while the defendants asserted that the marks were generic. How did the court ultimately decide that the marks were descriptive? Would the same result have been reached under the Restatement? *See* RESTATEMENT (THIRD) OF UNFAIR COMPETITION §§ 13 cmt. c, 14 cmt. b, 15 & cmt. a (1995).

(4)   How did Zatarain's establish secondary meaning for the term "Fish-Fri"? How does this compare with the methods discussed in comment e to § 13 of the Restatement?

PROBLEM 11.1

Archer's Fold is a nationwide hunting and camping store. It produces its own line of clothing, including hats and boots, that it labels as "Safari." Archer's has recently learned that a competitor, Hunter's World, has been marketing "Safari Hats" and boots "perfect for Safari." Archer's wishes to sue for trademark infringement. Using the tests set forth in *Zatarain's*, determine whether the term "Safari" is generic, descriptive, or suggestive. Do you reach the same conclusion for the hats and the boots?

C.   COMMON LAW MARKS AND FEDERAL REGISTRATION

1.   ADVANTAGES OF REGISTRATION

Once a mark has been used in interstate commerce and is distinctive, it is eligible for trademark protection under both the Lanham Act and the common law. *See* Lanham Act § 43(a) (15 U.S.C. § 1125(a)); RESTATEMENT (THIRD) OF UNFAIR COMPETITION § 9 (1995). Under the Lanham Act, trademark holders may also register trademarks in the Principal

Register[b] with the PTO. Unless a trademark is used in interstate commerce, however, it is ineligible to be registered.[c]

Given that protection exists regardless of registration, why bother registering a trademark? In short, registration offers a number of advantages, including the giving of constructive notice to other parties that the trademark is owned by the registrant. This is important as it eliminates a defense that a subsequent user might raise—namely, that he had adopted a mark in his geographic area in good faith and with lack of knowledge of the mark. By eliminating this defense of good faith and lack of knowledge, registration provides nationwide protection for marks regardless of the geographic area in which the registrant actually uses his mark.

Other advantages of registration on the Principal Register include:

- The Trademark Revision Act of 1988 changed the system from one based on use in commerce to a dual system based on use or bona fide "intent-to-use." This allows one to register before the mark is actually used in commerce, which provides the advantage of an earlier priority date.

- After a registered mark has been in continuous use for 5 consecutive years, the registrant's right to use the mark in commerce shall be incontestable, subject to certain exceptions, such as abandonment, fraudulent registration, or where the mark becomes the common generic name of the good or service.

- The certificate of registration constitutes prima facie evidence of the validity of the registration, the registrant's ownership of the mark, and the registrant's exclusive right to use the registered mark in commerce with respect to the goods or services described in the certificate.

- Registration confers the ability to bring an action concerning the mark in federal court.

- A federal registration in the United States facilitates registration in some foreign countries.

---

[b]   A Supplemental Register also exists for marks that are not yet eligible for protection, but that are capable of distinguishing the applicant's goods or services. This is sometimes used as an interim form of registration for marks that may eventually develop secondary meaning. Registration in the Supplemental Register does not confer the benefits of registration in the Principal Register, but it does allow U.S. applicants to satisfy certain home registration requirements that are necessary to obtain protection in some foreign trademark systems.

[c]   Even if ineligible to register under the Lanham Act, every state has enacted legislation providing for the registration and protection of trademarks. Many of these state registration systems are based upon the Model State Trademark Bill. *See* RESTATEMENT (THIRD) OF UNFAIR COMPETITION § 9 (1995) (Statutory Note).

- Registration may deter others from adopting the mark when they discover it in conducting a "right to use" search. This will avoid confrontation and legal expense at a later time.

2. MARKS PRECLUDED FROM REGISTRATION

Not all marks are eligible for registration. The PTO or a private party may raise substantive challenges to the registration of a mark under § 2(a)–(f) of the Lanham Act. *See* 15 U.S.C. § 1052. Some of these subsections simply incorporate common law concepts such as distinctiveness and likelihood of confusion. Others represent public policy restrictions, such as § 2(b), which forbids the use of a mark that "comprises the flag or coat of arms or other insignia of the United States, or of any State or municipality, or of any foreign nation, or any simulation thereof." Section 2(c) forbids the use of a person's name or likeness without the person's written consent.

One of the more interesting restrictions is found in § 2(a), which allows the PTO to deny registration for a mark that "[c]onsists of or comprises immoral, deceptive, or scandalous matter; or matter which may disparage or falsely suggest a connection with persons, living or dead, institutions, beliefs, or national symbols, or bring them into contempt, or disrepute." This provision can be broken down into at least three different types of restrictions: a deceptive restriction, a scandalous restriction, and a disparaging restriction.

With respect to the deceptive restriction, the Federal Circuit has articulated a three-part test for analyzing whether a mark is deceptive:

(1) Is the term misdescriptive of the character, quality, function, composition or use of the goods?

(2) If so, are prospective purchasers likely to believe that the misdescription actually describes the goods?

(3) If so, is the misdescription likely to affect the decision to purchase?

In re Budge Manufacturing Co., 857 F.2d 773, 775 (Fed. Cir. 1988). (Note that, much like the materials covered in the deceptive marketing Chapter, the focus here is the effect upon consumers. Scienter is not required.) In *Budge*, the court upheld the rejection of the mark LOVEE LAMB for automotive seat covers, as the covers were made wholly of synthetic materials. The court found that, under the three-part test, LAMB was misdescriptive and that "purchasers [were] likely to believe automobile seat covers denominated by the term LAMB or SHEEP [were] actually made from natural sheep or lamb skins."

Scandalous is perhaps the most amorphous of the three restrictions, as it turns on cultural mores and taboos in an ever-changing society. The

Trademark Trial and Appeal Board ("TTAB") articulated some of the concerns pertinent to the scandalous restriction in *In re Old Glory Condom Corp.*, 26 U.S.P.Q.2d 1216 (T.T.A.B. 1993):

> There is relatively little published precedent to guide us in deciding whether a mark is "scandalous" within the meaning of Section 2(a) of the Trademark Act. The examining attorney places principal reliance on *In re McGinley*, 211 U.S.P.Q 668 (CCPA 1981), the most recent decision in which the Board's reviewing court has interpreted the section of the Trademark Act here at issue. In *McGinley*, the Court was asked to decide the registrability of a mark comprising a photograph of a man and woman kissing and embracing in a manner appearing to expose the man's genitalia. In deciding whether the mark presented for registration was "scandalous" under Section 2(a), the Court first noted that whether a mark is scandalous is to be determined from the standpoint of a substantial composite of the general public. To define "scandalous," under Section 2(a), the Court looked to the "ordinary and common meaning" of the term, which meaning could be established, according to the Court, by reference to Court and Board decisions and to dictionary definitions. The Court went on to cite dictionary definitions of "scandalous" as "shocking to the sense of . . . propriety," "[that which gives] offense to the conscience or moral feelings" and "giving offense to the conscience or moral feelings; exciting reprobation, calling out condemnation . . . disgraceful to reputation. . . ." [Webster's New International Dictionary (2d ed. 1942)] and "shocking to the sense of truth, decency, or propriety; disgraceful, offensive; disreputable. . . ." [Funk & Wagnalls New Standard Dictionary (1945)]. In an attempt to put these provisions of Section 2(a) in context, the Court expressed its opinion that this section of the Trademark Act represents not ". . . an attempt to legislate morality, but, rather a judgment by the Congress that such marks not occupy the time, services, and use of funds of the federal government." Having set forth its opinion as to the underpinnings of this portion of Section 2(a) of the Trademark Act, the Court (one judge dissenting) concluded that the mark for which registration was sought (i.e., the pictorial representation of an embracing nude couple with exposed male genitalia) was scandalous and, therefore, unregistrable.

>   . . . .

> Although we have concentrated our attention on the more recent cases arising under Section 2(a), we are aware of several reported cases decided during the period 1938–1971 by the Court

of Customs and Patent Appeals, the Commissioner of Patents, or this Board, where marks were found scandalous and, therefore, unregistrable. We find the latter to be of little precedential value in deciding the case now before us. . . . Moreover, what was considered scandalous as a trademark or service mark twenty, thirty or fifty years ago may no longer be considered so, given the changes in societal attitudes. Marks once thought scandalous may now be thought merely humorous (or even quaint), as we suspect is the case with the marks held scandalous in *Ex parte Martha Maid Mfg. Co.*, 37 U.S.P.Q 156 (Comr.Pats.1938) ["QUEEN MARY" (and design) for women's underwear] and *In re Runsdorf*, 171 U.S.P.Q 443 (T.T.A.B. 1971) ["BUBBY TRAP" for brassieres]. The point to be made here is that, in deciding whether a mark is scandalous under Section 2(a), we must consider that mark in the context of contemporary attitudes.

In re Old Glory Condom Corp., 26 U.S.P.Q.2d at 1216, *2-4.

Recently, the scandalous and disparaging restrictions made headlines when a group of Native Americans sought to cancel the mark of the National Football League's Washington Redskins team. In *Harjo v. Pro-Football, Inc.*, 50 U.S.P.Q.2d 1705 (T.T.A.B. 1999), *rev'd*, 284 F. Supp. 2d 96 (D.D.C. 2003), the TTAB agreed that the mark was prohibited and formulated a two-part test for analyzing whether a mark is scandalous. First, the trier of fact must determine the meaning of the matter in question as it appears in the mark. Second, the trier of fact must decide if the meaning is one that would be scandalous to a substantial composite of the general public. Under the first step, the meaning must be derived not just from dictionary definitions, but also from the context within which the mark is used. Under the second step, the inquiry may draw upon surveys and other evidence from which it could be inferred that a substantial composite of the population would find the mark shocking to a sense of decency and propriety.

Although the two-part inquiry addresses scandalous marks, a similar inquiry is conducted for disparaging marks. First, the meaning of the mark must be determined. In the second step, however, the inquiry narrows. The question is not whether a substantial composite of the population would find the mark scandalous, but whether a substantial composite of the group allegedly referenced in the mark feels dishonored, slighted, deprecated, degraded, or injured by unjust comparison. In *Harjo*, the TTAB concluded that the term Redskins was disparaging. The ruling was reversed on appeal, however, based in part upon determinations that the evidence did not support a finding of disparagement and that many of the claims were barred on the grounds of laches.[d]

PROBLEM 11.2

Imagine that you are a member of the Trademark Trial and Appeal Board. Would you prohibit the below marks under § 2 of the Lanham Act? If so, how would you justify your decision? What additional information would you need, if any?

(a)   Use of the mark "BULLSHIT" for attaché cases, handbags, purses, belts, and wallets.

(b)   Use of the mark "BIG PECKER BRAND" for T-shirts, with the phrase used in conjunction with a bird design.

(c)   Use of a design consisting of the silhouette of a defecating dog, as a mark for polo shirts and T-shirts.

(d)   Use of the mark "MADONNA" in connection with the sale of wines.

(e)   Use of the mark "KORAN" in connection with the sale of wines.

D. TYPES OF MARKS

Thus far, we have primarily discussed marks that are written words associated with products. However, marks can also be verbal or image-based (the Nike "swoosh," for example, or the use of the color orange by Home Depot), and they can describe entire businesses or services. Although the distinctiveness spectrum sometimes applies to such marks, the spectrum is a poor fit in some instances. As a result, courts have developed alternative means for determining which marks are entitled to protection. We discuss the various types of marks below.

1.   SERVICE MARKS AND TRADE NAMES

A service mark is simply a trademark that is used in connection with services rather than goods. It qualifies for protection in the same way as a trademark for goods. As the Restatement of Unfair Competition explains:

> The Lanham Act . . . limit[s] the term "trademark" to marks used to identify the source of goods. A mark used to identify the source of services is denominated a "service mark." The substantive rules applicable to both types of marks are fundamentally identical, however, and the term "trademark" is generally understood to include marks used in the marketing of either goods or services. The definitions in this Section adopt this

---

[d]   The TTAB very recently cancelled the Redskins mark. *See Blackhorse v. Pro-Football, Inc.*, Cancellation No. 92046185, 2014 WL 2757516 (T.T.A.B. June 18, 2014). The Washington Redskins have appealed the decision.

convenient usage. The term "service mark" as defined here thus denotes a specific type of trademark.

RESTATEMENT (THIRD) OF UNFAIR COMPETITION § 9 cmt. f (1995).

A trade name, on the other hand, can sometimes cause confusion with a trademark. A trade name is simply a name used by a business that is not its legal name. A business may have a trade name and may register that name (called a "doing business as" (d/b/a) designation). However, this trade name registration is not the same as a trademark registration. While the same word or phrase may be used as a trade name and a trademark, the word or phrase only qualifies for trademark protection if it qualifies under the trademark standards (i.e., it must meet the use and distinctiveness requirements).

2. TRADE DRESS

Marks can be more than just words. As you are no doubt well-aware, many marks take the form of the shape or appearance of the product, or may even reflect the way the product is designed. Such marks are designated as "trade dress." Comment a to § 16 of the Restatement of Unfair Competition defines the concept:

> The term "trade dress" is often used to describe the overall appearance or image of goods or services as offered for sale in the marketplace. "Trade dress" traditionally includes the appearance of labels, wrappers, and containers used in packaging a product as well as displays and other materials used in presenting the product to prospective purchasers.

Section 16 provides that trade dress qualifies for protection if it is distinctive and non-functional. Both of these requirements present special issues for the party seeking protection.

The distinctiveness requirement for trade dress raises questions of how to apply the distinctiveness spectrum, such as whether trade dress can be inherently distinctive and whether secondary meaning must be established before the mark is entitled to protection. The U.S. Supreme Court addressed these questions in part in *Two Pesos, Inc. v. Taco Cabana, Inc.*, 505 U.S. 763 (1992). Taco Cabana, a Mexican restaurant chain located in Texas, brought suit against Two Pesos, another Mexican restaurant chain located in Texas, for infringing the unregistered trade dress of Taco Cabana, namely:

> [A] festive eating atmosphere having interior dining and patio areas decorated with artifacts, bright colors, paintings and murals. The patio includes interior and exterior areas with the interior patio capable of being sealed off from the outside patio by overhead garage doors. The stepped exterior of the building is

a festive and vivid color scheme using top border paint and neon stripes. Bright awnings and umbrellas continue the theme.

Id. at 765. A jury found that the trade dress was inherently distinctive and nonfunctional, but also found that it had not acquired secondary meaning. On appeal, the Fifth Circuit affirmed, holding that because the trade dress was inherently distinctive, there was no need to establish secondary meaning. This ruling conflicted with a Second Circuit opinion concluding that an unregistered trade dress required a showing of secondary meaning before protection would be granted. The Supreme Court accepted the case to resolve the split.

The Court ultimately agreed with the Fifth Circuit and held that inherently distinctive trade dress is protected without a showing that it has acquired secondary meaning. As the Court noted: "There is no persuasive reason to apply to trade dress a general requirement of secondary meaning that is at odds with the principles generally applicable to infringement suits under § 43(a)." *Id.* at 770. In *Two Pesos*, however, a jury had already found that the overall appearance was inherently distinctive, and the dress itself did not involve a product design. In 2000, the Court made clear that not all trade dress cases are to be treated the same.

WAL-MART STORES, INC. v. SAMARA BROTHERS, INC.
529 U.S. 205 (2000)

JUSTICE SCALIA delivered the opinion of the Court.

In this case, we decide under what circumstances a product's design is distinctive, and therefore protectible, in an action for infringement of unregistered trade dress under § 43(a) of the Trademark Act of 1946 (Lanham Act), 15 U.S.C. § 1125(a).

I

Respondent Samara Brothers, Inc., designs and manufactures children's clothing. Its primary product is a line of spring/summer one-piece seersucker outfits decorated with appliques of hearts, flowers, fruits, and the like. A number of chain stores, including JCPenney, sell this line of clothing under contract with Samara.

Petitioner Wal-Mart Stores, Inc., is one of the Nation's best known retailers, selling among other things children's clothing. In 1995, Wal-Mart contracted with one of its suppliers, Judy-Philippine, Inc., to manufacture a line of children's outfits for sale in the 1996 spring/summer season. Wal-Mart sent Judy-Philippine photographs of a number of garments from Samara's line, on which Judy-Philippine's garments were to be based; Judy-Philippine duly copied, with only minor modifications, 16 of Samara's garments, many of which contained copyrighted elements. In 1996, Wal-Mart briskly sold the so-called knockoffs, generating more than $1.15 million in gross profits.

In June 1996, a buyer for JCPenney called a representative at Samara to complain that she had seen Samara garments on sale at Wal-Mart for a lower price than JCPenney was allowed to charge under its contract with Samara. The Samara representative told the buyer that Samara did not supply its clothing to Wal-Mart. Their suspicions aroused, however, Samara officials launched an investigation, which disclosed that Wal-Mart and several other major retailers—Kmart, Caldor, Hills, and Goody's—were selling the knockoffs of Samara's outfits produced by Judy-Philippine.

After sending cease-and-desist letters, Samara brought this action in the United States District Court for the Southern District of New York against Wal-Mart, Judy-Philippine, Kmart, Caldor, Hills, and Goody's for copyright infringement under federal law, consumer fraud and unfair competition under New York law, and—most relevant for our purposes—infringement of unregistered trade dress under § 43(a) of the Lanham Act, 15 U.S.C. § 1125(a). All of the defendants except Wal-Mart settled before trial.

After a weeklong trial, the jury found in favor of Samara on all of its claims. Wal-Mart then renewed a motion for judgment as a matter of law, claiming, inter alia, that there was insufficient evidence to support a conclusion that Samara's clothing designs could be legally protected as distinctive trade dress for purposes of § 43(a). The District Court denied the motion, and awarded Samara damages, interest, costs, and fees totaling almost $1.6 million, together with injunctive relief. The Second Circuit affirmed the denial of the motion for judgment as a matter of law, and we granted certiorari.

II

The Lanham Act provides for the registration of trademarks, which it defines in § 45 to include "any word, name, symbol, or device, or any combination thereof [used or intended to be used] to identify and distinguish [a producer's] goods . . . from those manufactured or sold by others and to indicate the source of the goods. . . ." 15 U.S.C. § 1127. Registration of a mark under § 2 of the Lanham Act, 15 U.S.C. § 1052, enables the owner to sue an infringer under § 32, 15 U.S.C. § 1114; it also entitles the owner to a presumption that its mark is valid, see § 7(b), 15 U.S.C. § 1057(b), and ordinarily renders the registered mark incontestable after five years of continuous use, see § 15, 15 U.S.C. § 1065. In addition to protecting registered marks, the Lanham Act, in § 43(a), gives a producer a cause of action for the use by any person of "any word, term, name, symbol, or device, or any combination thereof . . . which . . . is likely to cause confusion . . . as to the origin, sponsorship, or approval of his or her goods. . . ." 15 U.S.C. § 1125(a). It is the latter provision that is at issue in this case.

The breadth of the definition of marks registrable under § 2, and of the confusion-producing elements recited as actionable by § 43(a), has been held to embrace not just word marks, such as "Nike," and symbol marks, such as Nike's "swoosh" symbol, but also "trade dress"—a category that originally included only the packaging, or "dressing," of a product, but in recent years has been expanded by many Courts of Appeals to encompass the design of a product. These courts have assumed, often without discussion, that trade dress constitutes a "symbol" or "device" for purposes of the relevant sections, and we conclude likewise. "Since human beings might use as a 'symbol' or 'device' almost anything at all that is capable of carrying meaning, this language, read literally, is not restrictive." *Qualitex Co. v. Jacobson Products Co.*, 514 U.S. 159, 162 (1995). This reading of § 2 and § 43(a) is buttressed by a recently added subsection of § 43(a), § 43(a)(3), which refers specifically to "civil action[s] for trade dress infringement under this chapter for trade dress not registered on the principal register." 15 U.S.C. § 1125(a)(3) (1994 ed., Supp. V).

The text of § 43(a) provides little guidance as to the circumstances under which unregistered trade dress may be protected. It does require that a producer show that the allegedly infringing feature is not "functional," see § 43(a)(3), and is likely to cause confusion with the product for which protection is sought, see § 43(a)(1)(A), 15 U.S.C. § 1125(a)(1)(A). Nothing in § 43(a) explicitly requires a producer to show that its trade dress is distinctive, but courts have universally imposed that requirement, since without distinctiveness the trade dress would not "cause confusion . . . as to the origin, sponsorship, or approval of [the] goods," as the section requires. Distinctiveness is, moreover, an explicit prerequisite for registration of trade dress under § 2, and "the general principles qualifying a mark for registration under § 2 of the Lanham Act are for the most part applicable in determining whether an unregistered mark is entitled to protection under § 43(a)." *Two Pesos, Inc. v. Taco Cabana, Inc.*, 505 U.S. 763, 768 (1992).

In evaluating the distinctiveness of a mark under § 2 (and therefore, by analogy, under § 43(a)), courts have held that a mark can be distinctive in one of two ways. First, a mark is inherently distinctive if "[its] intrinsic nature serves to identify a particular source." *Ibid.* In the context of word marks, courts have applied the now-classic test originally formulated by Judge Friendly, in which word marks that are "arbitrary" ("Camel" cigarettes), "fanciful" ("Kodak" film), or "suggestive" ("Tide" laundry detergent) are held to be inherently distinctive. *See Abercrombie & Fitch Co. v. Hunting World, Inc.*, 537 F.2d 4, 10–11 (2d Cir. 1976). Second, a mark has acquired distinctiveness, even if it is not inherently distinctive, if it has developed secondary meaning, which occurs when, "in the minds of the public, the primary significance of a [mark] is to identify the source of the product rather than the product itself." *Inwood Laboratories, Inc. v. Ives Laboratories, Inc.*, 456 U.S. 844, 851, n. 11 (1982).

The judicial differentiation between marks that are inherently distinctive and those that have developed secondary meaning has solid foundation in the statute itself. Section 2 requires that registration be granted to any trademark "by which the goods of the applicant may be distinguished from the goods of others"—subject to various limited exceptions. 15 U.S.C. § 1052. It also provides, again with limited exceptions, that "nothing in this chapter shall prevent the registration of a mark used by the applicant which has become distinctive of the applicant's goods in commerce"—that is, which is not inherently distinctive but has become so only through secondary meaning. § 2(f), 15 U.S.C. § 1052(f). Nothing in § 2, however, demands the conclusion that every category of mark necessarily includes some marks "by which the goods of the applicant may be distinguished from the goods of others" without secondary meaning—that in every category some marks are inherently distinctive.

Indeed, with respect to at least one category of mark—colors—we have held that no mark can ever be inherently distinctive. *See Qualitex, supra*, at 162–163. In *Qualitex*, petitioner manufactured and sold green-gold dry-cleaning press pads. After respondent began selling pads of a similar color, petitioner brought suit under § 43(a), then added a claim under § 32 after obtaining registration for the color of its pads. We held that a color could be protected as a trademark, but only upon a showing of secondary meaning. Reasoning by analogy to the *Abercrombie & Fitch* test developed for word marks, we noted that a product's color is unlike a "fanciful," "arbitrary," or "suggestive" mark, since it does not "almost automatically tell a customer that [it] refer[s] to a brand," 514 U.S., at 162–163, and does not "immediately . . . signal a brand or a product 'source,'" *id.*, at 163. However, we noted that, "over time, customers may come to treat a particular color on a product or its packaging . . . as signifying a brand." *Ibid.* Because a color, like a "descriptive" word mark, could eventually "come to indicate a product's origin," we concluded that it could be protected upon a showing of secondary meaning. *Ibid.*

It seems to us that design, like color, is not inherently distinctive. The attribution of inherent distinctiveness to certain categories of word marks and product packaging derives from the fact that the very purpose of attaching a particular word to a product, or encasing it in a distinctive packaging, is most often to identify the source of the product. Although the words and packaging can serve subsidiary functions—a suggestive word mark (such as "Tide" for laundry detergent), for instance, may invoke positive connotations in the consumer's mind, and a garish form of packaging (such as Tide's squat, brightly decorated plastic bottles for its liquid laundry detergent) may attract an otherwise indifferent consumer's attention on a crowded store shelf—their predominant function remains source identification. Consumers are therefore predisposed to regard those symbols as indication of the producer, which is why such symbols "almost automatically tell a customer that they refer to a brand," *id.* at 162–163, and "immediately . . . signal a brand or a product 'source,' " *id.* at 163. And where it is not reasonable to assume consumer predisposition to take an affixed word or packaging as indication of source—where, for example, the affixed word is descriptive of the product ("Tasty" bread) or of a geographic origin ("Georgia" peaches)—inherent distinctiveness will not be found. That is why the statute generally excludes, from those word marks that can be registered as inherently distinctive, words that are "merely descriptive" of the goods, § 2(e)(1), 15 U.S.C. § 1052(e)(1), or "primarily geographically descriptive of them," *see* § 2(e)(2), 15 U.S.C. § 1052(e)(2). In the case of product design, as in the case of color, we think consumer predisposition to equate the feature with the source does not exist. Consumers are aware of the reality that, almost invariably, even the most unusual of product designs—such as a cocktail shaker shaped like a penguin—is intended not to identify the source, but to render the product itself more useful or more appealing.

The fact that product design almost invariably serves purposes other than source identification not only renders inherent distinctiveness problematic; it also renders application of an inherent-distinctiveness principle more harmful to other consumer interests. Consumers should not be deprived of the benefits of competition with regard to the utilitarian and esthetic purposes that product design ordinarily serves by a rule of law that facilitates plausible threats of suit against new entrants based upon alleged inherent distinctiveness. How easy it is to mount a plausible suit depends, of course, upon the clarity of the test for inherent distinctiveness, and where product design is concerned we have little confidence that a reasonably clear test can be devised. Respondent and the United States as *amicus curiae* urge us to adopt for product design relevant portions of the test formulated by the Court of Customs and Patent Appeals for product packaging in *Seabrook Foods, Inc. v. Bar-Well Foods, Ltd.*, 568 F.2d 1342 (1977). That opinion, in determining the inherent distinctiveness of a product's packaging, considered, among other things, "whether it was a 'common' basic shape or design, whether it was unique or unusual in a particular field, [and] whether it was a mere refinement of a commonly-adopted and well-known form of ornamentation for a particular class of goods viewed by the public as a dress or ornamentation for the goods." *Id.*, at 1344 (footnotes omitted). Such a test would rarely provide the basis for summary disposition of an anticompetitive strike suit. Indeed, at oral argument, counsel for the

United States quite understandably would not give a definitive answer as to whether the test was met in this very case, saying only that "[t]his is a very difficult case for that purpose."

It is true, of course, that the person seeking to exclude new entrants would have to establish the nonfunctionality of the design feature, see § 43(a)(3), 15 U.S.C. § 1125(a)(3) (1994 ed., Supp. V)—a showing that may involve consideration of its esthetic appeal. Competition is deterred, however, not merely by successful suit but by the plausible threat of successful suit, and given the unlikelihood of inherently source-identifying design, the game of allowing suit based upon alleged inherent distinctiveness seems to us not worth the candle. That is especially so since the producer can ordinarily obtain protection for a design that is inherently source identifying (if any such exists), but that does not yet have secondary meaning, by securing a design patent or a copyright for the design—as, indeed, respondent did for certain elements of the designs in this case. The availability of these other protections greatly reduces any harm to the producer that might ensue from our conclusion that a product design cannot be protected under § 43(a) without a showing of secondary meaning.

Respondent contends that our decision in *Two Pesos* forecloses a conclusion that product-design trade dress can never be inherently distinctive. In that case, we held that the trade dress of a chain of Mexican restaurants, which the plaintiff described as "a festive eating atmosphere having interior dining and patio areas decorated with artifacts, bright colors, paintings and murals," 505 U.S., at 765 (internal quotation marks and citation omitted), could be protected under § 43(a) without a showing of secondary meaning, *see id.*, at 776. *Two Pesos* unquestionably establishes the legal principle that trade dress can be inherently distinctive, *see, e.g., id.*, at 773, but it does not establish that product-design trade dress can be. *Two Pesos* is inapposite to our holding here because the trade dress at issue, the decor of a restaurant, seems to us not to constitute product design. It was either product packaging— which, as we have discussed, normally is taken by the consumer to indicate origin—or else some *tertium quid* that is akin to product packaging and has no bearing on the present case.

Respondent replies that this manner of distinguishing *Two Pesos* will force courts to draw difficult lines between product-design and product-packaging trade dress. There will indeed be some hard cases at the margin: a classic glass Coca-Cola bottle, for instance, may constitute packaging for those consumers who drink the Coke and then discard the bottle, but may constitute the product itself for those consumers who are bottle collectors, or part of the product itself for those consumers who buy Coke in the classic glass bottle, rather than a can, because they think it more stylish to drink from the former. We believe, however, that the frequency and the difficulty of having to distinguish between product design and product packaging will be much less than the frequency and the difficulty of having to decide when a product design is inherently distinctive. To the extent there are close cases, we believe that courts should err on the side of caution and classify ambiguous trade dress as product design, thereby requiring secondary meaning. The very closeness will suggest the existence of relatively small utility in adopting an inherent-distinctiveness principle, and relatively great consumer benefit in requiring a demonstration of secondary meaning.

* * *

We hold that, in an action for infringement of unregistered trade dress under § 43(a) of the Lanham Act, a product's design is distinctive, and therefore protectible, only upon a showing of secondary meaning. The judgment of the Second Circuit is reversed, and the case is remanded for further proceedings consistent with this opinion.

NOTES & QUESTIONS

(1) The Court discusses the distinctiveness spectrum developed in the *Abercrombie & Fitch* case. Does the Court find the spectrum useful in determining whether trade dress is inherently distinctive? According to the Court, product design is analogous to what category on the spectrum?

(2) With regard to product design, the Court makes clear that trade dress can never be inherently distinctive and always requires a showing of secondary meaning. What then is the test for trade dress that is not a product design? How does one establish inherent distinctiveness in such cases? *See* RESTATEMENT (THIRD) OF UNFAIR COMPETITION § 16 cmt. b (1995).

(3) The Court distinguishes between product design and product packaging. Suppose a manufacturer of butterscotch hard candies wishes to claim trade dress in the light brown color it uses on its wrappers. Because the trade dress is not a product design, is it capable of being inherently distinctive?

(4) Under the *Abercrombie* distinctiveness spectrum (and under the Restatement), the category that is never protected is generic marks. Can trade dress ever be generic? *See Jeffrey Milstein, Inc. v. Greger, Lawlor, Roth, Inc.*, 58 F.3d 27 (2d Cir. 1995) ("Just as the first company to depict a heart and arrow on Valentine's cards or to produce cards depicting tabby cats could not seek protection for those designs because they are concepts, defined abstractly, so [plaintiff] cannot obtain protection for its general idea of creating cards out of die-cut photographs."); *Landscape Forms, Inc. v. Columbia Cascade Co.*, 113 F.3d 373 (2d Cir. 1997) ("While trademarking a generic term would create a monopoly in a necessary word or phrase, granting trade dress protection to an ordinary product shape would create a monopoly in the goods themselves.").

(5) What is the justification for requiring proof of secondary meaning for product design trade dress? What alternatives exist for the party seeking to protect a product design?

(6) The Court ultimately draws a distinction between trade dress involving product design and trade dress involving product packaging. How do you distinguish between product design and product packaging? What do you make of Justice Scalia's Coca-Cola bottle hypothetical? Do you agree that the bottle could be characterized as design as well as packaging?

As noted above, for trade dress to qualify for protection, it must be distinctive as well as non-functional. *See* RESTATEMENT (THIRD) OF UNFAIR COMPETITION § 16 (1995). Section 17 of the Restatement elaborates on when a design is functional:

> A design is "functional" for purposes of the rule stated in § 16 if the design affords benefits in the manufacturing, marketing, or use of the goods or services with which the design is used, apart from any benefits attributable to the design's significance as an indication of source, that are important to effective competition by others and that are not practically available through the use of alternative designs.

Id. at § 17. If a product's design is functional, it is more appropriate to seek the limited protection offered by the patent system. As the following case demonstrates, some parties want to have their cake and eat it too.

TRAFFIX DEVICES, INC. V. MARKETING DISPLAYS, INC.
532 U.S. 23 (2001)

JUSTICE KENNEDY delivered the opinion of the Court.

Temporary road signs with warnings like "Road Work Ahead" or "Left Shoulder Closed" must withstand strong gusts of wind. An inventor named Robert Sarkisian obtained two utility patents for a mechanism built upon two springs (the dual-spring design) to keep these and other outdoor signs upright despite adverse wind conditions. The holder of the now-expired Sarkisian patents, respondent Marketing Displays, Inc. (MDI), established a successful business in the manufacture and sale of sign stands incorporating the patented feature. MDI's stands for road signs were recognizable to buyers and users (it says) because the dual-spring design was visible near the base of the sign.

This litigation followed after the patents expired and a competitor, TrafFix Devices, Inc., sold sign stands with a visible spring mechanism that looked like MDI's. MDI and TrafFix products looked alike because they were. When TrafFix started in business, it sent an MDI product abroad to have it reverse engineered, that is to say copied. Complicating matters, TrafFix marketed its sign stands under a name similar to MDI's. MDI used the name "WindMaster," while TrafFix, its new competitor, used "WindBuster."

MDI brought suit under the Trademark Act of 1946 (Lanham Act), 60 Stat. 427, as amended, 15 U.S.C. § 1051 *et seq.,* against TrafFix for trademark infringement (based on the similar names), trade dress infringement (based on the copied dual-spring design), and unfair competition. TrafFix counterclaimed on antitrust theories. After the United States District Court for the Eastern District of Michigan considered cross-motions for summary judgment, MDI prevailed on its trademark claim for the confusing similarity of names and was held not liable on the antitrust counterclaim; and those two rulings, affirmed by the Court of Appeals, are not before us.

I

We are concerned with the trade dress question. The District Court ruled against MDI on its trade dress claim. 971 F.Supp. 262 (E.D.Mich.1997). After determining that the one element of MDI's trade dress at issue was the dual-spring design, *id.,* at 265, it held that "no reasonable trier of fact could determine that MDI has established secondary meaning" in its alleged trade dress, *id.,* at 269. In other words, consumers did not associate the look of the dual-spring design with MDI. As a second, independent reason to grant summary judgment in favor of TrafFix, the District Court determined the dual-spring design was functional. On this rationale secondary meaning is irrelevant because there can be no trade dress protection in any event. In ruling on the functional aspect of the design, the District Court noted that Sixth Circuit precedent indicated that the burden was on MDI to prove that its trade dress was nonfunctional, and not on TrafFix to show that it was functional (a rule since adopted by Congress, see 15 U.S.C. § 1125(a)(3) (1994 ed., Supp. V)), and then went on to consider MDI's arguments that the dual-spring design was subject to trade dress protection. Finding none of MDI's contentions persuasive, the District Court concluded MDI had not "proffered sufficient evidence which would enable a reasonable trier of fact to find that MDI's vertical dual-spring design is *non*-functional." 971 F.Supp., at 276. Summary judgment was entered against MDI on its trade dress claims.

The Court of Appeals for the Sixth Circuit reversed the trade dress ruling. 200 F.3d 929 (1999). The Court of Appeals held the District Court had erred in ruling MDI failed to show a genuine issue of material fact regarding whether it had secondary meaning in its alleged trade dress, *id.,* at 938, and had erred further in determining that MDI could not prevail in any event because the alleged trade dress was in fact a functional product configuration, *id.,* at 940. The Court of Appeals suggested the District Court committed legal error by looking only to the dual-spring design when evaluating MDI's trade dress. Basic to its reasoning was the Court of Appeals' observation that it took "little imagination to conceive of a hidden dual-spring mechanism or a tri or quad-spring mechanism that might avoid infringing [MDI's] trade dress." *Ibid.* The Court of Appeals explained that "[i]f TrafFix or another competitor chooses to use [MDI's] dual-spring design, then it will have to find *some other way* to set its sign apart to avoid infringing [MDI's] trade dress." *Ibid.* It was not sufficient, according to the Court of Appeals, that allowing exclusive use of a particular feature such as the dual-spring design in the guise of trade dress would "hinde[r] competition somewhat." Rather, "[e]xclusive use of a feature must 'put competitors at a *significant* non-reputation-related disadvantage'" before trade dress protection is denied on functionality grounds." *Ibid.* (quoting *Qualitex Co. v. Jacobson Products Co.,* 514 U.S. 159, 165 (1995)). In its criticism of the District Court's ruling on the trade dress question, the Court of Appeals took note of a split among Courts of Appeals in various other Circuits on the issue whether the existence of an expired utility patent forecloses the possibility of the patentee's claiming trade dress protection in the product's design. To resolve the conflict, we granted certiorari.

II

It is well established that trade dress can be protected under federal law. The design or packaging of a product may acquire a distinctiveness which serves to identify the product with its manufacturer or source; and a design or package which acquires this secondary meaning, assuming other requisites are met, is a trade dress which may not be used in a manner likely to cause confusion as to the origin, sponsorship, or approval of the goods. In these respects protection for trade dress exists to promote competition. As we explained just last Term, see *Wal-Mart Stores, Inc. v. Samara Brothers, Inc.,* 529 U.S. 205 (2000), various Courts of Appeals have allowed claims of trade dress infringement relying on the general provision of the Lanham Act which provides a cause of action to one who is injured when a person uses "any word, term, name, symbol, or device, or any combination thereof . . . which is likely to cause confusion . . . as to the origin, sponsorship, or approval of his or her goods." 15 U.S.C. § 1125(a)(1)(A). Congress confirmed this statutory protection for trade dress by amending the Lanham Act to recognize the concept. Title 15 U.S.C. § 1125(a)(3) (1994 ed., Supp. V) provides: "In a civil action for trade dress infringement under this chapter for trade dress not registered on the principal register, the person who asserts trade dress protection has the burden of proving that the matter sought to be protected is not functional." This burden of proof gives force to the well-established rule that trade dress protection may not be claimed for product features that are functional. *Qualitex, supra,* at 164–165; *Two Pesos, Inc. v. Taco Cabana, Inc.,* 505 U.S. 763 (1992). And in *Wal-Mart, supra,* we were careful to caution against misuse or overextension of trade dress. We noted that "product design almost invariably serves purposes other than source identification." *Id.,* at 213.

Trade dress protection must subsist with the recognition that in many instances there is no prohibition against copying goods and products. In general, unless an intellectual property right such as a patent or copyright protects an item, it will be subject to copying. As the Court has explained, copying is not always discouraged or disfavored by the laws which preserve our competitive economy. *Bonito Boats, Inc. v. Thunder Craft Boats, Inc.,* 489 U.S. 141, 160 (1989). Allowing competitors to copy will have salutary effects in many instances. "Reverse engineering of chemical and mechanical articles in the public domain often leads to significant advances in technology." *Ibid.*

The principal question in this case is the effect of an expired patent on a claim of trade dress infringement. A prior patent, we conclude, has vital significance in resolving the trade dress claim. A utility patent is strong evidence that the features therein claimed are functional. If trade dress protection is sought for those features the strong evidence of functionality based on the previous patent adds great weight to the statutory presumption that features are deemed functional until proved otherwise by the party seeking trade dress protection. Where the expired patent claimed the features in question, one who seeks to establish trade dress protection must carry the heavy burden of showing that the feature is not functional, for instance by showing that it is merely an ornamental, incidental, or arbitrary aspect of the device.

In the case before us, the central advance claimed in the expired utility patents (the Sarkisian patents) is the dual-spring design; and the dual-spring design is the essential feature of the trade dress MDI now seeks to establish and to protect. The rule we have explained bars the trade dress claim, for MDI did not, and cannot, carry the burden of overcoming the strong evidentiary inference of functionality based on the disclosure of the dual-spring design in the claims of the expired patents.

The dual springs shown in the Sarkisian patents were well apart (at either end of a frame for holding a rectangular sign when one full side is the base) while the dual springs at issue here are close together (in a frame designed to hold a sign by one of its corners). As the District Court recognized, this makes little difference. The point is that the springs are necessary to the operation of the device. The fact that the springs in this very different-looking device fall within the claims of the patents is illustrated by MDI's own position in earlier litigation. In the late 1970's, MDI engaged in a long-running intellectual property battle with a company known as Winn-Proof. Although the precise claims of the Sarkisian patents cover sign stands with springs "spaced apart," U.S. Patent No. 3,646,696, col. 4; U.S. Patent No. 3,662,482, col. 4, the Winn-Proof sign stands (with springs much like the sign stands at issue here) were found to infringe the patents by the United States District Court for the District of Oregon, and the Court of Appeals for the Ninth Circuit affirmed the judgment. *Sarkisian v. Winn-Proof Corp.*, 697 F.2d 1313 (1983). Although the Winn-Proof traffic sign stand (with dual springs close together) did not appear, then, to infringe the literal terms of the patent claims (which called for "spaced apart" springs), the Winn-Proof sign stand was found to infringe the patents under the doctrine of equivalents, which allows a finding of patent infringement even when the accused product does not fall within the literal terms of the claims. *Id.,* at 1321–1322; *see generally Warner-Jenkinson Co. v. Hilton Davis Chemical Co.,* 520 U.S. 17 (1997). In light of this past ruling—a ruling procured at MDI's own insistence—it must be concluded the products here at issue would have been covered by the claims of the expired patents.

The rationale for the rule that the disclosure of a feature in the claims of a utility patent constitutes strong evidence of functionality is well illustrated in this case. The dual-spring design serves the important purpose of keeping the sign upright even in heavy wind conditions; and, as confirmed by the statements in the expired patents, it does so in a unique and useful manner. As the specification of one of the patents recites, prior art "devices, in practice, will topple under the force of a strong wind." U.S. Patent No. 3,662,482, col. 1. The dual-spring design allows sign stands to resist toppling in strong winds. Using a dual-spring design rather than a single spring achieves important operational advantages. For example, the specifications of the patents note that the "use of a pair of springs . . . as opposed to the use of a single spring to support the frame structure prevents canting or twisting of the sign around a vertical axis," and that, if not prevented, twisting "may cause damage to the spring structure and may result in tipping of the device." U.S. Patent No. 3,646,696, col. 3. In the course of patent prosecution, it was said that "[t]he use of a pair of spring connections as opposed to a single spring connection . . . forms an important part of this combination" because it "forc[es] the sign frame to tip along the longitudinal axis of the elongated ground-engaging members." App. 218. The dual-spring design affects the cost of the device as well; it was acknowledged that the device "could use three springs but this would unnecessarily increase the cost of the device." *Id.,* at 217. These statements made in the patent applications and in the course of procuring the patents demonstrate the functionality of the design. MDI does not assert that any of these representations are mistaken or inaccurate, and this is further strong evidence of the functionality of the dual-spring design.

III

In finding for MDI on the trade dress issue the Court of Appeals gave insufficient recognition to the importance of the expired utility patents, and their evidentiary significance, in establishing the functionality of the device. The error likely was caused by its misinterpretation of trade dress principles in other respects. As we have noted, even if there has been no previous utility patent the party asserting trade dress has the burden to establish the nonfunctionality of alleged trade dress features. MDI could not meet this burden. Discussing trademarks, we have said " '[i]n general terms, a product feature is functional,' and cannot serve as a trademark, 'if it is essential to the use or purpose of the article or if it affects the cost or quality of the article.' " *Qualitex,* 514 U.S., at 165 (quoting *Inwood Laboratories, Inc. v. Ives Laboratories, Inc.,* 456 U.S. 844, 850, n. 10 (1982)). Expanding upon the meaning of this phrase, we have observed that a functional feature is one the "exclusive use of [which] would put competitors at a significant non-reputation-related disadvantage." 514 U.S., at 165, 115 S.Ct. 1300. The Court of Appeals in the instant case seemed to interpret this language to mean that a necessary test for functionality is "whether the particular product configuration is a competitive necessity." 200 F.3d, at 940. See also [*Vornado Air Circulation Sys., Inc. v. Duracraft Corp.,* 58 F.3d 1498, 1507 (10th Cir. 1995)] ("Functionality, by contrast, has been defined both by our circuit, and more recently by the Supreme Court, in terms of competitive need"). This was incorrect as a comprehensive definition. As explained in *Qualitex, supra,* and *Inwood, supra,* a feature is also functional when it is essential to the use or purpose of the device or when it affects the cost or quality of the device. The *Qualitex* decision did not purport to displace this traditional rule. Instead, it quoted the rule as *Inwood* had set it forth. It is proper to inquire into a "significant non-reputation-related disadvantage" in cases of esthetic functionality, the question involved in *Qualitex.* Where the design is functional under the *Inwood* formulation there is no need to proceed further to consider if there is a competitive necessity for the feature. In *Qualitex,* by contrast, esthetic functionality was the central question, there having been no indication that the green-gold color of the laundry press pad had any bearing on the use or purpose of the product or its cost or quality.

The Court has allowed trade dress protection to certain product features that are inherently distinctive. *Two Pesos,* 505 U.S., at 774. In *Two Pesos,* however, the Court at the outset made the explicit analytic assumption that the trade dress features in question (decorations and other features to evoke a Mexican theme in a restaurant) were not functional. *Id.,* at 767, n. 6. The trade dress in those cases did not bar competitors from copying functional product design features. In the instant case, beyond serving the purpose of informing consumers that the sign stands are made by MDI (assuming it does so), the dual-spring design provides a unique and useful mechanism to resist the force of the wind. Functionality having been established, whether MDI's dual-spring design has acquired secondary meaning need not be considered.

There is no need, furthermore, to engage, as did the Court of Appeals, in speculation about other design possibilities, such as using three or four springs which might serve the same purpose. 200 F.3d, at 940. Here, the functionality of the spring design means that competitors need not explore whether other spring juxtapositions might be used. The dual-spring design is not an arbitrary flourish in the configuration of MDI's product; it is the reason the device works. Other designs need not be attempted.

Because the dual-spring design is functional, it is unnecessary for competitors to explore designs to hide the springs, say, by using a box or framework to cover them, as suggested by the Court of Appeals. *Ibid.* The dual-spring design assures the user the device will work. If buyers are assured the product serves its purpose by seeing the operative mechanism that in itself serves an important market need. It would be at cross-purposes to those objectives, and something of a paradox, were we to require the manufacturer to conceal the very item the user seeks.

In a case where a manufacturer seeks to protect arbitrary, incidental, or ornamental aspects of features of a product found in the patent claims, such as arbitrary curves in the legs or an ornamental pattern painted on the springs, a different result might obtain. There the manufacturer could perhaps prove that those aspects do not serve a purpose within the terms of the utility patent. The inquiry into whether such features, asserted to be trade dress, are functional by reason of their inclusion in the claims of an expired utility patent could be aided by going beyond the claims and examining the patent and its prosecution history to see if the feature in question is shown as a useful part of the invention. No such claim is made here, however. MDI in essence seeks protection for the dual-spring design alone. The asserted trade dress consists simply of the dual-spring design, four legs, a base, an upright, and a sign. MDI has pointed to nothing arbitrary about the components of its device or the way they are assembled. The Lanham Act does not exist to reward manufacturers for their innovation in creating a particular device; that is the purpose of the patent law and its period of exclusivity. The Lanham Act, furthermore, does not protect trade dress in a functional design simply because an investment has been made to encourage the public to associate a particular functional feature with a single manufacturer or seller. The Court of Appeals erred in viewing MDI as possessing the right to exclude competitors from using a design identical to MDI's and to require those competitors to adopt a different design simply to avoid copying it. MDI cannot gain the exclusive right to produce sign stands using the dual-spring design by asserting that consumers associate it with the look of the invention itself. Whether a utility patent has expired or there has been no utility patent at all, a product design which has a particular appearance may be functional because it is "essential to the use or purpose of the article" or "affects the cost or quality of the article." *Inwood*, 456 U.S., at 850, n. 10.

TrafFix and some of its *amici* argue that the Patent Clause of the Constitution, Art. I, § 8, cl. 8, of its own force, prohibits the holder of an expired utility patent from claiming trade dress protection. Brief for Petitioner 33–36; Brief for Panduit Corp. as *Amicus Curiae* 3; Brief for Malla Pollack as *Amicus Curiae* 2. We need not resolve this question. If, despite the rule that functional features may not be the subject of trade dress protection, a case arises in which trade dress becomes the practical equivalent of an expired utility patent, that will be time enough to consider the matter. The judgment of the Court of Appeals is reversed, and the case is remanded for further proceedings consistent with this opinion.

NOTES & QUESTIONS

(1) What test does the Court articulate for determining functionality? How does this standard compare to § 17 of the Restatement? What was wrong with the Court of Appeals' standard for functionality?

(2) Why was the dual-spring design functional according to the Court? Why wasn't the Court persuaded by MDI's argument that competitors could simply hide the springs? Alternatively, why wasn't the Court persuaded by the argument that a competitor could simply use a three-spring design to achieve the same utility advantages as the dual-spring design?

(3) What role did the fact that the dual-spring design was claimed in a patent play in the Court's decision? Could a trade dress claimant ever be entitled to protection for a feature that it had previously described in a patent?

(4) The trial court found that there was no evidence of secondary meaning attached to the dual-spring design. Suppose MDI was able to establish secondary meaning—i.e., assume that consumers strongly associated the dual-spring design with MDI. Would that have changed the result?

(5) The *TrafFix* case dealt with the functional utility of a physical design. Could a product's design be aesthetically functional? For instance, could a manufacturer of chocolates claim trade dress protection in a heart-shaped box that it uses to sell its products around Valentine's Day? *See* RESTATEMENT (THIRD) OF UNFAIR COMPETITION § 17 cmt. c (1995); *E.R.B.E. Elektromedizin GmbH v. Candy Tech.*, LLC, 67 F.3d 1571, 1578–81 (Fed. Cir. 1995) (holding that the color blue was functional for purposes of use on certain medical devices). Doesn't recognition of such aesthetic functionality

have the potential to encompass a number of otherwise valid trade dresses? *See* Allison Midei, *Getting to Functional: Limiting the Applicability of the Trademark Aesthetic Functionality Doctrine*, 41 AIPLA Q.J. 467, 510 (2013) (criticizing aesthetic functionality jurisprudence and the Supreme Court for providing too little guidance on the matter, which has resulted in "some courts [that] apply the doctrine too liberally and inappropriately abrogate the right of a producer to provide identification of its mark, while other courts do not apply the doctrine at all and impinge on the competitors right to imitate useful product features").

3. COLORS AND NON-VISUAL MARKS

As previously suggested, trademarks can come in a number of media, including color. In the *Samara Bros. and TrafFix* opinions, however, you probably noted the references to the Supreme Court case of *Qualitex Co. v. Jacobson Products Co.*, 514 U.S. 159 (1995), in which the court held that color alone could not qualify for trademark protection without a showing of secondary meaning. *Qualitex* involved an alleged trademark in green-gold laundry press pads. The manufacturer of the press pads, Qualitex, obtained a registered trademark in the color and then sued a competitor for using a similarly colored press pad. Although Qualitex won at trial, the Ninth Circuit held that color alone could not be the subject of a trademark. The Supreme Court disagreed:

> The Lanham Act gives a seller or producer the exclusive right to "register" a trademark, 15 U.S.C. § 1052 (1988 ed. and Supp. V), and to prevent his or her competitors from using that trademark, § 1114(1). Both the language of the Act and the basic underlying principles of trademark law would seem to include color within the universe of things that can qualify as a trademark. The language of the Lanham Act describes that universe in the broadest of terms. It says that trademarks "includ[e] any word, name, symbol, or device, or any combination thereof." § 1127. Since human beings might use as a "symbol" or "device" almost anything at all that is capable of carrying meaning, this language, read literally, is not restrictive. The courts and the Patent and Trademark Office have authorized for use as a mark a particular shape (of a Coca-Cola bottle), a particular sound (of NBC's three chimes), and even a particular scent (of plumeria blossoms on sewing thread). If a shape, a sound, and a fragrance can act as symbols why, one might ask, can a color not do the same?

Id. at 162 (internal citations omitted). The Court went on to qualify its views by analogizing to the descriptive category of the distinctiveness spectrum:

True, a product's color is unlike "fanciful," "arbitrary," or "suggestive" words or designs, which almost automatically tell a customer that they refer to a brand. The imaginary word "Suntost," or the words "Suntost Marmalade," on a jar of orange jam immediately would signal a brand or a product "source"; the jam's orange color does not do so. But, over time, customers may come to treat a particular color on a product or its packaging (say, a color that in context seems unusual, such as pink on a firm's insulating material or red on the head of a large industrial bolt) as signifying a brand. And, if so, that color would have come to identify and distinguish the goods—i.e., "to indicate" their "source"—much in the way that descriptive words on a product (say, "Trim" on nail clippers or "Car-Freshener" on deodorizer) can come to indicate a product's origin. In this circumstance, trademark law says that the word (e.g., "Trim"), although not inherently distinctive, has developed "secondary meaning." Again, one might ask, if trademark law permits a descriptive word with secondary meaning to act as a mark, why would it not permit a color, under similar circumstances, to do the same?

We cannot find in the basic objectives of trademark law any obvious theoretical objection to the use of color alone as a trademark, where that color has attained "secondary meaning" and therefore identifies and distinguishes a particular brand (and thus indicates its "source"). In principle, trademark law, by preventing others from copying a source-identifying mark, "reduce[s] the customer's costs of shopping and making purchasing decisions," 1 J. MCCARTHY, MCCARTHY ON TRADEMARKS AND UNFAIR COMPETITION § 2.01[2], p. 2–3 (3d ed. 1994) (hereinafter McCarthy), for it quickly and easily assures a potential customer that this item—the item with this mark—is made by the same producer as other similarly marked items that he or she liked (or disliked) in the past. At the same time, the law helps assure a producer that it (and not an imitating competitor) will reap the financial, reputation-related rewards associated with a desirable product. The law thereby "encourage[s] the production of quality products," *ibid.*, and simultaneously discourages those who hope to sell inferior products by capitalizing on a consumer's inability quickly to evaluate the quality of an item offered for sale. It is the source-distinguishing ability of a mark—not its ontological status as color, shape, fragrance, word, or sign—that permits it to serve these basic purposes. And, for that reason, it is difficult to find, in basic trademark objectives, a reason to disqualify absolutely the use of a color as a mark.

Qualitex, 514 U.S. at 162–64 (internal citations omitted). Along with requiring secondary meaning, the Court later stated in the opinion that color would be subject to the functionality doctrine.

Based upon the *Qualitex* Court's reasoning, it would appear that any media—visual, audio, or even scent-based—could qualify for trademark protection so long as the claimed mark has inherent or acquired distinctiveness, is capable of distinguishing the source, and is not functional. Indeed, as mentioned in the *Qualitex* excerpt, scents (*see In re Clarke*, 17 U.S.P.Q.2d 1238 (T.T.A.B. 1990) ("[a] fresh, floral fragrance reminiscent of Plumeria blossoms")) and sounds (*see* Registration No. 916,522 (July 13, 1971) (NBC's chimes)) have been granted trademark registrations. *See also* Registration No. 75807526 (April 10, 2001) (involving the yodeling sound trademarked by Yahoo, Inc.).

4. COLLECTIVE MARKS AND CERTIFICATION MARKS

The Restatement of Unfair Competition describes two other types of marks, collective marks and certification marks, which are often confused. A collective mark is a mark used by members of a cooperative, association, or other collective group to identify the goods or services of such members or to indicate membership in the group. *See* Lanham Act § 45, 15 U.S.C.A. § 1127; RESTATEMENT (THIRD) OF UNFAIR COMPETITION § 10 (1995).[e] A collective mark indicates that goods or services originate from a member of the group, but not necessarily from a particular person within the group. (If the organization itself uses a mark to identify its own goods or services, this is not a collective mark but may simply be a trademark in its own right.) Examples of collective marks include the Professional Golfers Association, whose members use the "PGA" mark in providing services such as golf lessons, and the National Association of Realtors, whose members use the "REALTOR" mark in providing real estate services.[f]

Certification marks are defined in the Lanham Act as "any word, name, symbol, or device, or any combination thereof . . . used by a person other than its owner . . . to certify regional or other origin, material, mode of manufacture, quality, accuracy, or other characteristics of such person's goods or services or that the work or labor on the goods or services was performed by members of a union or other organization." Lanham Act § 45, 15 U.S.C.A. § 1127; *see also* RESTATEMENT (THIRD) OF UNFAIR COMPETITION § 11 (1995) (providing a similar definition). Unlike

---

    [e] The Restatement actually distinguishes between marks used to indicate that the goods or services originate from a member of a group, and marks used to indicate that a person or entity is a member of a group. The former are "collective marks" and the latter are "collective membership marks." RESTATEMENT (THIRD) OF UNFAIR COMPETITION § 10 cmt. a (1995).

    [f] For a discussion of collective marks, see 3 MCCARTHY ON TRADEMARKS AND UNFAIR COMPETITION § 19:99 (4th ed. 2015). McCarthy also cites an agricultural cooperative of sellers of farm produce as an example of a group that may use a collective mark.

collective marks, which indicate an association with a group, certification marks speak to an aspect of the good or service itself. An example of a certification mark is the "Good Housekeeping Seal of Approval." The Good Housekeeping Institute awards the Good Housekeeping Seal, which represents Good Housekeeping Magazine's limited warranty that if any product carrying the seal is found to be defective within two years from the date of purchase, Good Housekeeping will either replace the product or refund the purchase price up to $2,000.[g]

Distinguishing between a collective mark and a certification mark can be tricky, but it is useful to ask whether the mark is indicating that the seller is a member of a group (or that the product came from a seller who is a member of a group), or whether the mark speaks to a specific aspect of the good. The former indicates that it is a collective mark, whereas the latter indicates that it is a certification mark. This distinction can be meaningful, as certification marks are seen as more burdensome to register.[h] One thing both collective marks and certification marks have in common, however, is that someone other than the holder of the mark is using it.

E. INFRINGEMENT

In the previous Sections, we have primarily discussed how to establish trademark rights. If the holder of a mark wishes to bring suit, however, it is not enough to simply establish a protected trademark. The holder must also establish the most basic prerequisite to a trademark suit—i.e., prove that the infringing defendant's use is likely to confuse a purchaser as to the source. The infringer, of course, may attack the holder's right to the trademark (such as by alleging lack of secondary meaning or invoking the functionality doctrine), and may have a number of additional defenses available. We will explore all of these issues below.

1. LIKELIHOOD OF CONFUSION

Once a mark has been established, the holder can enjoin others from using it. This right, however, does not necessarily extend to every use of the mark. For instance, should Nike be able to prevent the use of a checkmark symbol, even for scholastic supplies that have nothing to do with sportswear, just because its "swoosh" symbol resembles a checkmark (or vice versa)? The answer is "no," as trademark law is only meant to protect the holder of a mark to the extent that a consumer would be

---

[g]   *See*   http://www.goodhousekeeping.com/institute/about-the-institute/a22148/about-good-housekeeping-seal/ (last visited Sept. 14, 2015).

[h]   *See* 3 MCCARTHY ON TRADEMARKS AND UNFAIR COMPETITION § 19:99 (4th ed. 2015) (citing the stricter requirements for registration of certification marks under the Lanham Act § 14(e) as a reason why some holders may opt to form groups with standards and to register collective marks instead).

confused as to the source. Determining when a consumer would be confused, however, is not always a simple inquiry.

POLAROID CORP. V. POLARAD ELECTRONICS CORP.
287 F.2d 492 (2d Cir. 1961)

FRIENDLY, CIRCUIT JUDGE.

Plaintiff, Polaroid Corporation, a Delaware corporation, owner of the trademark Polaroid and holder of 22 United States registrations thereof granted between 1936 and 1956 and of a New York registration granted in 1950, brought this action in the Eastern District of New York, alleging that defendant's use of the name Polarad as a trademark and as part of defendant's corporate title infringed plaintiff's Federal and state trademarks and constituted unfair competition. It sought a broad injunction and an accounting. Defendant's answer, in addition to denying the allegations of the complaint, sought a declaratory judgment establishing defendant's right to use Polarad in the business in which defendant was engaged, an injunction against plaintiff's use of Polaroid in the television and electronics fields, and other relief. Judge Rayfiel ... dismissed both the claim and the counterclaims, concluding that neither plaintiff nor defendant had made an adequate showing with respect to confusion and that both had been guilty of laches. Both parties appealed but defendant has withdrawn its cross-appeal. We find it unnecessary to pass upon Judge Rayfiel's conclusion that defendant's use of Polarad does not violate any of plaintiff's rights. For we agree that plaintiff's delay in proceeding against defendant bars plaintiff from relief so long as defendant's use of Polarad remains as far removed from plaintiff's primary fields of activity as it has been and still is.

The name Polaroid was first adopted by plaintiff's predecessor in 1935. It has been held to be a valid trademark as a coined or invented symbol and not to have lost its right to protection by becoming generic or descriptive. Polaroid had become a well known name as applied to sheet polarizing material and products made therefrom, as well as to optical desk lamps, stereoscopic viewers, etc., long before defendant was organized in 1944. During World War II, plaintiff's business greatly expanded, from $1,032,000 of gross sales in 1941 to $16,752,000 in 1945, due in large part to government contracts. Included in this government business were three sorts on which plaintiff particularly relies, the sale of Schmidt corrector plates, an optical lens used in television; research and development contracts for guided missiles and a machine gun trainer, both involving the application of electronics; and other research and development contracts for what plaintiff characterizes as "electro-optical devices employing electronic circuitry in combination with optical apparatus." In 1947 and 1948 plaintiff's sales declined to little more than their pre-war level; the tremendous expansion of plaintiff's business, reaching sales of $65,271,000 in 1958, came after the development of the Land camera in 1948.

Defendant was organized in December, 1944. Originally a partnership called Polarad Electronics Co., it was converted in 1948 into a New York corporation bearing the name Polarad Television Corp., which was changed a year later to Polarad Electronics Corp. Its principal business has been the sale of microwave generating, receiving and measuring devices and of television studio equipment. Defendant claimed it had arrived at the name Polarad by taking the first letters of the first and last names of its founder, Paul Odessey, and the first two letters of the first name of his friend and anticipated partner, Larry Jaffe, and adding the suffix "rad," intended to signify radio; however, Odessey admitted that at the time he had "some knowledge" of plaintiff's use of the name Polaroid, although only as applied to glasses and polarizing filters and not as to electronics. As early as November, 1945, plaintiff learned of defendant; it drew a credit report and had one of its attorneys visit defendant's quarters, then two small rooms; plaintiff made no protest. By June, 1946, defendant was advertising television equipment in "Electronics"—a trade journal. These advertisements and other notices with respect to defendant came to the attention of plaintiff's officers; still plaintiff did nothing. In 1950, a New York Attorney who represented plaintiff in foreign patent matters came upon a trade show display of defendant's television products under the name Polarad and informed plaintiff's house counsel; the latter advised plaintiff's president, Dr. Land, that "the time had come when he thought we ought to think seriously about the problem." However, nothing was done save to draw a further credit report on defendant, although defendant's sales had grown from a nominal amount to a rate of several hundred thousand dollars a year, and the report related, as had the previous one, that defendant was engaged "in developing and manufacturing equipment for radio, television and electronic manufacturers throughout the United States." In October, 1951, defendant, under its letterhead, forwarded to plaintiff a letter addressed to "Polarad Electronics Corp." at defendant's Brooklyn address, inquiring in regard to "polaroid material designed for night driving"; there was no protest by plaintiff. In 1953, defendant applied to the United States Patent Office for registration of its trademark Polarad for radio and television units and other electronic devices; in August, 1955, when this application was published in the Official Gazette of the Patent Office, plaintiff for the first time took action by filing a notice of opposition, which was overruled by the Examiner in April, 1957. Still plaintiff delayed bringing suit until late 1956. Through all this period defendant was expending considerable sums for advertising and its business was growing—employees increasing from eight in the calendar year 1945 to 530 in the year ended June 30, 1956, fixed assets from $2,300 to

$371,800, inventories from $3,000 to $1,547,400, and sales from $12,000 to $6,048,000.

Conceding that the bulk of its business is in optics and photography, lines not pursued by defendant, plaintiff nevertheless claims to be entitled to protection of its distinctive mark in at least certain portions of the large field of electronics. Plaintiff relies on its sales of Schmidt corrector plates, used in certain types of television systems, first under government contracts beginning in 1943 and to industry commencing in 1945; on its sale, since 1946, of polarizing television filters, which serve the same function as the color filters that defendant supplies as a part of the television apparatus sold by it; and, particularly, on the research and development contracts with the government referred to above. Plaintiff relies also on certain instances of confusion, predominantly communications intended for defendant but directed to plaintiff. Against this, defendant asserts that its business is the sale of complex electronics equipment to a relatively few customers; that this does not compete in any significant way with plaintiff's business, the bulk of which is now in articles destined for the ultimate consumer; that plaintiff's excursions into electronics are insignificant in the light of the size of the field; that the instances of confusion are minimal; that there is no evidence that plaintiff has suffered either through loss of customers or injury to reputation, since defendant has conducted its business with high standards; and that the very nature of defendant's business, sales to experienced industrial users and the government, precludes any substantial possibility of confusion. Defendant also asserts plaintiff's laches to be a bar.

The problem of determining how far a valid trademark shall be protected with respect to goods other than those to which its owner has applied it, has long been vexing and does not become easier of solution with the years. . . . Where the products are different, the prior owner's chance of success is a function of many variables: the strength of his mark, the degree of similarity between the two marks, the proximity of the products, the likelihood that the prior owner will bridge the gap, actual confusion, and the reciprocal of defendant's good faith in adopting its own mark, the quality of defendant's product, and the sophistication of the buyers. Even this extensive catalogue does not exhaust the possibilities—the court may have to take still other variables into account. Here plaintiff's mark is a strong one and the similarity between the two names is great, but the evidence of actual confusion, when analyzed, is not impressive. The filter seems to be the only case where defendant has sold, but not manufactured, a product serving a function similar to any of plaintiff's, and plaintiff's sales of this item have been highly irregular, varying, e.g., from $2,300 in 1953 to $303,000 in 1955, and $48,000 in 1956.[1]

If defendant's sole business were the manufacture and sale of microwave equipment, we should have little difficulty in approving the District Court's conclusion that there was no such likelihood of confusion as to bring into play either the Lanham Act, 15 U.S.C.A. § 1114(1), or New York General Business Law, § 368–b, or to make out a case of unfair competition under New York decisional law. What gives us some pause is defendant's heavy involvement in a phase of electronics that lies closer to plaintiff's business, namely, television. . . . [P]laintiff's normal business is "the interaction of light and matter." Yet, although television lies predominantly in the area of electronics, it begins and ends with light waves. The record tells us that certain television uses were among the factors that first stimulated Dr. Land's interest in polarization, plaintiff has manufactured and sold at least two products for use in television systems, and defendant's second counterclaim itself asserts likelihood of confusion in the television field. We are thus by no means sure that, under the views with respect to trademark protection announced by this Court . . . plaintiff would not have been entitled to at least some injunctive relief if it had moved with reasonable promptness. However, we are not required to decide this since we uphold the District Court's conclusion with respect to laches.

Plaintiff endeavors to answer that claim on three grounds: (1) That defendant is barred from advancing the claim because defendant sought affirmative relief; (2) that the doctrine of laches does not apply in trademark and unfair competition cases insofar as the complaint seeks an injunction rather than damages; and (3) that the defense is not made out on the facts. We find no merit in any of these contentions. [As to the first ground, rather than finding that defendant waived the laches defense by seeking cross-relief to which it was not entitled, the court held that both sides were barred because they failed to press their claims after gaining knowledge of the facts.]

For its second ground appellant relies on the statement in *Menendez v. Holt*, 1888, 128 U.S. 514, 523, that "Mere delay or acquiescence cannot defeat the remedy by injunction in support of the legal right, unless it has been continued so long, and under such circumstances, as to defeat the right itself." It contends that such defeat can come only from conduct, . . . giving a defendant justification for concluding that plaintiff had no

---

[1]   Even the high figure, in 1955, amounted to little more than 1% of plaintiff's business.

Plaintiff also cites defendant's sale of bicycle headlights and other consumer products and defendant's patents for a radio automatic vehicle guidance system and an electronic auto headlight dimmer. However, the former business, conducted through a separate division, has been abandoned, and exploitation of the patents has not been instituted. Our decision is not to be understood as dealing with plaintiff's rights if defendant should resume, or begin, activity along any of these lines.

objection to defendant's using its name. However, the portion of the opinion in *Saxlehner v. Eisner & Mendelson Co.*, 179 U.S. 19, 21, also relied on by appellant, which upheld the defense of laches with respect to the word "Hunyadi," indicated that *Menendez v. Holt* does not go so far as appellant claims, even when a portion of the marks and the products are identical. We need not explore just where the boundaries lie in such a case, for the . . . *Dwinell-Wright Co. v. White House Milk Co.*, 2 Cir., 1943, 132 F.2d 822, 824–825 [case and others show that] the doctrine has no such reach as claimed when, as here, the goods are different. The distinctions are developed in Judge Learned Hand's classic opinion in *Dwinell-Wright*, where he explained that the *Menendez* rule applies only when "a newcomer invades another's market by the use of the other's mark," since then "every sale is a separate wrong." "If however the question comes up, not when the newcomer is actually competing in the owner's market, but * * * is selling goods which the owner has never sold, though they are like enough to make people think him their source, the determining considerations are different. The owner's only interest in preventing such a use of his mark is because he may wish to preempt the market for later exploitation, or not to expose his reputation to the hazard of the newcomer's business practices, or both * * * Here, as often, equity does not seek for general principles, but weighs the opposed interests in the scales of conscience and fair dealing * * * The owner's rights in such appendant markets are easily lost; they must be asserted early, lest they be made the means of reaping a harvest which others have sown."

The previous summary of the facts shows how far plaintiff came from meeting this rigorous test. Plaintiff seeks to excuse its early inactivity on the ground that defendant's sales were small. But that is the very time when the owner of a mark ought forcefully to claim protection; "the scales of conscience and fair dealing" will tip far more readily for a plaintiff when a defendant will suffer little disadvantage by changing to another name. *See Valvoline Oil Co. v. Havoline Oil Co.*, D.C.S.D.N.Y.1913, 211 F. 189, 195. Moreover, even if plaintiff's inaction in 1945 and 1946 could be excused on the basis that defendant's activities were de minimis and that plaintiff might reasonably have expected defendant to fall by the wayside, an issue which we do not decide, the situation had surely changed by the year ended June 30, 1951, when defendant made $192,000 in catalog sales and $356,000 in sales under military contracts. Plaintiff would have us disregard the latter on the issue of its laches—just why we are not told—although it relies heavily on confusion by Federal purchasing agencies as part of its case on the merits. Plaintiff concedes that by 1952 defendant "had expanded its business from the design and construction of special apparatus on order, to include the manufacture and sale of television and other devices operable throughout the entire radio frequency band"; but plaintiff waited another four years before bringing suit. We find nothing to support plaintiff's assertion that defendant has further encroached on plaintiff's field since 1953; to be sure, defendant has trebled its business but not by moving away from its traditional area and into plaintiff's. As said in *Valvoline Oil Co. v. Havoline Oil Co., supra,* at page 195, "it cannot be equitable for a well-informed merchant with knowledge of a claimed invasion of right, to wait to see how successful his competitor will be and then destroy with the aid of a court decree, much that the competitor has striven for and accomplished—especially in a case where the most that can be said is that the trade-mark infringement is a genuinely debatable question." True, what the court regarded as debatable there was the confusing qualities of the names rather than, as here, the identity of the product; but the principle applies with at least the same force. If defendant should move into new territory more closely related to optics and photography, different considerations as to laches as well as on the merits will, of course, apply.

Judgment affirmed.

NOTES & QUESTIONS

(1) What factors does the court consider relevant in determining whether the use of a mark by an alleged infringer is likely to confuse a purchaser?

(2) The court ultimately upheld the district court's ruling on the grounds of laches. Absent laches, do you think Polaroid's suit would have been successful?

(3) In *Polaroid*, the court noted that the defendant's use of the mark was mostly in conjunction with different products. Should the same factors be relevant for similar (rather than different) products? In general, should certain factors be weighed more heavily than others?

(4) How do the *Polaroid* factors compare to the Restatement's standard for likelihood of confusion? *See* RESTATEMENT (THIRD) OF UNFAIR COMPETITION §§ 20–22 (1995).

(5) The *Polaroid* factors, or a variation of them, have been used by a number of courts. For instance, in *AMF Inc. v. Sleekcraft Boats*, 599 F.2d 341, 348–49 (9th Cir. 1979), the Ninth Circuit articulated the following list of factors: strength of mark, relatedness of goods, similarity between marks, actual confusion, marketing channels used, the degree of purchaser care, the alleged infringer's intent, and the likelihood of expansion of product lines. Most other circuits have similar tests. *See, e.g., Scott Paper Co. v. Scott's Liquid Gold, Inc.*, 589 F.2d 1225, 1229 (3d Cir. 1978); *Pizzeria Uno Corp. v. Temple*, 747 F.2d 1522, 1527 (4th Cir. 1984); *Frisch's Restaurants, Inc. v. Elby's Big Boy of Steubenville, Inc.* 670 F.2d 642, 648 (6th Cir. 1982); *SquirtCo v. Seven-Up Co.*, 628 F.2d 1086, 1091 (8th Cir. 1980).

(6) Similarity between marks is an important factor, but how can you tell if marks are similar? Most courts generally consider three types of

similarity: sight, sound, and meaning. *See* J. THOMAS MCCARTHY, 4 MCCARTHY ON TRADEMARKS AND UNFAIR COMPETITION § 23:21 (4th ed. 2015. Are sight, sound, and meaning reflected in the Restatement? *See* RESTATEMENT (THIRD) OF UNFAIR COMPETITION §§ 20–22 (1995).

(7)   The court ultimately found for Polarad on the equitable defense of laches. Federal courts are vested with the power to grant injunctions and to award profits and damages subject to the "principles of equity." Laches is included as a power granted to the courts under these principles. Why is it necessary to recognize laches rather than simply rely upon a statute of limitations? Consider whether there would have been anything inequitable in granting relief to the plaintiff in *Polaroid*.

PROBLEM 11.3

George Ogle owns Go Ogle Paint Company. The company has a specially patented process for applying a sealant to house paint that makes the paint last longer. It is labeled "Ogle Paint Sealant." His company operates mostly in the Phoenix, Arizona area, but recent marketing efforts have allowed him to expand statewide. His current logo is simply his company name in all caps which appears as "GO OGLE PAINT CO."

George recently received a cease and desist letter from Google, Inc. alleging that his logo is confusingly similar to its trademarked Google logo. George comes to you to ask whether this is worth fighting. "It's not like I run a software company—I just paint and seal houses. How can this be confusing to anyone?" George also points out to you, correctly, that on Google's own website it has a list of trademarked names, and Google Paint is not one of the listed trademarks.

Based on the *Polaroid* factors, analyze whether George's logo is confusingly similar to Google's. If you think more information is needed, explain what information you need and how you might get it.

2. DILUTION

As previously discussed, trademark infringement requires there to be a likelihood of confusion. Without proof of such likelihood, a mark holder may have no cause of action for a person's use of a similar mark to sell a totally different product. Does this make sense? After all, although an ordinary consumer may not be confused when a completely different product is at issue, isn't there some damage to the distinctive quality of the mark holder's brand name? This concern has led some holders to sue for mark dilution—a claim present in the following case.

MEAD DATA CENTRAL, INC. V. TOYOTA MOTOR SALES, U.S.A., INC.

875 F.2d 1026 (2d Cir. 1989)

VAN GRAAFEILAND, CIRCUIT JUDGE:

Toyota Motor Sales, U.S.A., Inc. and its parent, Toyota Motor Corporation, appeal from a judgment of the United States District Court for the Southern District of New York (Edelstein, J.) enjoining them from using LEXUS as the name of their new luxury automobile and the division that manufactures it. The district court held that, under New York's antidilution statute, N.Y.Gen.Bus.Law § 368–d, Toyota's use of LEXUS is likely to dilute the distinctive quality of LEXIS, the mark used by Mead Data Central, Inc. for its computerized legal research service.

THE STATUTE

Section 368–d of New York's General Business Law, which has counterparts in at least twenty other states, reads as follows:

> Likelihood of injury to business reputation or of dilution of the distinctive quality of a mark or trade name shall be a ground for injunctive relief in cases of infringement of a mark registered or not registered or in cases of unfair competition, notwithstanding the absence of competition between the parties or the absence of confusion as to the source of goods or services.

THE PARTIES AND THEIR MARKS

Mead and Lexis

. . . . Since 1972, Mead has provided a computerized legal research service under the trademark LEXIS. Mead introduced evidence that its president in 1972 "came up with the name LEXIS based on Lex which was Latin for law and I S for information systems." In fact, however, the word "lexis" is centuries old. It is found in the language of ancient Greece, where it had the meaning of "phrase," "word," "speaking" or "diction." PINKERTON, WORD FOR WORD, 179 (1982). [The court concludes that the word "lexis" had been incorporated into the English language and that numerous other companies had adopted "Lexis" in identifying their business or product.]

In sum, we reject Mead's argument that LEXIS is a coined mark which originated in the mind of its former president and, as such, is entitled per se to the greater protection that a unique mark such as "Kodak" would receive.

Nevertheless, through its extensive sales and advertising in the field of computerized legal research, Mead has made LEXIS a strong mark in that field, and the district court so found. In particular, the district court accepted studies proffered by both parties which revealed that 76 percent of attorneys associated LEXIS with specific attributes of the service provided by Mead. However, among the general adult population, LEXIS is recognized by only one percent of those surveyed, half of this one percent being attorneys or accountants. The district court therefore concluded that LEXIS is strong only within its own market.

As appears in the Addendum to this opinion, the LEXIS mark is printed in block letters with no accompanying logo.

Toyota and Lexus

Toyota Motor Corp. has for many years manufactured automobiles, which it markets in the United States through its subsidiary Toyota Motor Sales, U.S.A. On August 24, 1987 Toyota announced a new line of luxury automobiles to be called LEXUS. The cars will be manufactured by a separate LEXUS division of Toyota, and their marketing pitch will be directed to well-educated professional consumers with annual incomes in excess of $50,000. Toyota had planned to spend $18 million to $20 million for this purpose during the first nine months of 1989.

Before adopting the completely artificial name LEXUS for its new automobile, Toyota secured expert legal advice to the effect that "there is absolutely no conflict between 'LEXIS' and 'LEXUS.' " Accordingly, when Mead subsequently objected to Toyota's use of LEXUS, Toyota rejected Mead's complaints. The district court held correctly that Toyota acted without predatory intent in adopting the LEXUS mark.

. . . .

However, the district court erred in concluding that Toyota's refusal to acknowledge that its use of LEXUS might harm the LEXIS mark, deprived it of the argument that it acted in good faith. If, as we now hold, Toyota's mark did not dilute Mead's, it would be anomalous indeed to hold Toyota guilty of bad faith in proceeding in reliance on its attorney's correct advice to that effect. Indeed, even if the attorney's professional advice had been wrong, it does not follow that Toyota's reliance on that advice would have constituted bad faith.

The LEXUS mark is in stylized, almost script-like lettering and is accompanied by a rakish L logo.

THE LAW

The brief legislative history accompanying section 368–d describes the purpose of the statute as preventing "the whittling away of an established trade-mark's selling power and value through *its* unauthorized use by others upon dissimilar products." 1954 N.Y.Legis.Ann. 49 (emphasis supplied). If we were to interpret literally the italicized word "its," we would limit statutory violations to the unauthorized use of the identical established mark. . . . However, since the use of obvious simulations or markedly similar marks might have the same diluting effect as would an appropriation of the original mark, the concept of exact identity has been broadened to that of substantial similarity. Nevertheless, in keeping with the original intent of the statute, the similarity must be substantial before the doctrine of dilution may be applied.

Indeed, some courts have gone so far as to hold that, although violation of an antidilution statute does not require confusion of product or source, the marks in question must be sufficiently similar that confusion may be created as between the marks themselves. *See Holiday Inns, Inc. v. Holiday Out in America*, 481 F.2d 445, 450 (5th Cir.1973); *King Research, Inc. v. Shulton, Inc.*, 324 F.Supp. 631, 638 (S.D.N.Y.1971), *aff'd*, 454 F.2d 66 (2d Cir.1972). We need not go that far. We hold only that the marks must be "very" or "substantially" similar and that, absent such similarity, there can be no viable claim of dilution.

The district court's opinion was divided into two sections. The first section dealt with Toyota's alleged violation of the Lanham Act, and the second dealt with the alleged dilution of Mead's mark under New York's antidilution statute. The district court made several findings on the issue of similarity in its Lanham Act discussion; it made none in its discussion of section 368–d. Assuming that the district court's finding of lack of physical similarity in the former discussion was intended to carry over into the latter, we would find ourselves in complete accord with it since we would make the same finding. However, if the district court's statement in its Lanham Act discussion that "in everyday spoken English, LEXUS and LEXIS are virtually identical in pronunciation" was intended to be a finding of fact rather than a statement of opinion, we question both its accuracy and its relevance. The word LEXUS is not yet widely enough known that any definitive statement can be made concerning its pronunciation by the American public. However, the two members of this Court who concur in this opinion use "everyday spoken English," and we would not pronounce LEXUS as if it were spelled LEXIS. Although our colleague takes issue with us on this point, he does not contend that if LEXUS and LEXIS are pronounced correctly, they will sound the same. We liken LEXUS to such words as "census," "focus" and "locus," and differentiate it from such words as "axis," "aegis" and "iris."[2] If we were to substitute the letter "i" for the letter "u" in "census," we would not pronounce it as we now do. Likewise, if we were to substitute the letter "u" for the letter "i" in "axis," we would not pronounce it as we now do.

---

[2] Similarly, we liken LEXUS to NEXXUS, a nationally known shampoo, and LEXIS to NEXIS, Mead's trademark for its computerized news service. NEXXUS and NEXIS have co-existed in apparent tranquility for almost a decade.

In addition, we do not believe that "everyday spoken English" is the proper test to use in deciding the issue of similarity in the instant case. Under the Constitution, there is a " 'commonsense' distinction between speech proposing a commercial transaction, which occurs in an area traditionally subject to government regulation, and other varieties of speech." *Central Hudson Gas & Electric Corp. v. Public Service Comm'n*, 447 U.S. 557, 562 (1980). "The legitimate aim of the anti-dilution statute is to prohibit the unauthorized use of another's trademark in order to market incompatible products or services," and this constitutes a "legitimate regulation of commercial speech." *L.L. Bean, Inc. v. Drake Publishers, Inc.*, 811 F.2d 26, 32–33 (1st Cir.), cert. denied, 483 U.S. 1013 (1987). "Advertising is the primary means by which the connection between a name and a company is established . . . ," *Beneficial Corp. v. Beneficial Capital Corp.*, 529 F.Supp. 445, 448 (S.D.N.Y.1982), and oral advertising is done primarily on radio and television. When Mead's speech expert was asked whether there were instances in which LEXUS and LEXIS would be pronounced differently, he replied "Yes, although a deliberate attempt must be made to do so. . . . They can be pronounced distinctly but they are not when they are used in common parlance, in everyday language or speech." We take it as a given that television and radio announcers usually are more careful and precise in their diction than is the man on the street. Moreover, it is the rare television commercial that does not contain a visual reference to the mark and product, which in the instant case would be the LEXUS automobile. We conclude that in the field of commercial advertising, which is the field subject to regulation, there is no substantial similarity between Mead's mark and Toyota's.

There are additional factors that militate against a finding of dilution in the instant case. Such a finding must be based on two elements. First, plaintiff's mark must possess a distinctive quality capable of dilution. Second, plaintiff must show a likelihood of dilution. As section 368–d expressly states, a plaintiff need not show either competition between its product or service and that of the defendant or a likelihood of confusion as to the source of the goods or services.

Distinctiveness for dilution purposes often has been equated with the strength of a mark for infringement purposes. It also has been defined as uniqueness or as having acquired a secondary meaning. [*Allied Maintenance Corp. v. Allied Mechanical Trades, Inc.*, 369 N.E.2d 1162 (N.Y. 1977)]. A trademark has a secondary meaning if it "has become so associated in the mind of the public with that entity [Allied] or its product that it identifies the goods sold by that entity and distinguishes them from goods sold by others." Id. In sum, the statute protects a trademark's "selling power." *Sally Gee, Inc. v. Myra Hogan, Inc.*, [699 F.2d 621, 624–25 (2d Cir. 1983)]. However, the fact that a mark has selling power in a limited geographical or commercial area does not endow it with a secondary meaning for the public generally.

The strength and distinctiveness of LEXIS is limited to the market for its services—attorneys and accountants. Outside that market, LEXIS has very little selling power. Because only one percent of the general population associates LEXIS with the attributes of Mead's service, it cannot be said that LEXIS identifies that service to the general public and distinguishes it from others. Moreover, the bulk of Mead's advertising budget is devoted to reaching attorneys through professional journals.

This Court has defined dilution as either the blurring of a mark's product identification or the tarnishment of the affirmative associations a mark has come to convey. Mead does not claim that Toyota's use of LEXUS would tarnish affirmative associations engendered by LEXIS. The question that remains, therefore, is whether LEXIS is likely to be blurred by LEXUS.

Very little attention has been given to date to the distinction between the confusion necessary for a claim of infringement and the blurring necessary for a claim of dilution. Although the antidilution statute dispenses with the requirements of competition and confusion, it does not follow that every junior use of a similar mark will dilute the senior mark in the manner contemplated by the New York Legislature.

As already stated, the brief legislative history accompanying section 368–d described the purpose of the statute as preventing "the whittling away of an established trademark's selling power and value through its unauthorized use by others upon dissimilar products." The history disclosed a need for legislation to prevent such "hypothetical anomalies" as "Dupont shoes, Buick aspirin tablets, Schlitz varnish, Kodak pianos, Bulova gowns, and so forth," and cited cases involving similarly famous marks, *e.g.*, *Tiffany & Co. v. Tiffany Productions, Inc.*, 147 Misc. 679, 264 N.Y.S. 459 (1932), *aff'd*, 237 A.D. 801, *aff'd*, 188 N.E. 30 (1933); *Philadelphia Storage Battery Co. v. Mindlin*, 163 Misc. 52, 296 N.Y.S. 176 (1937). 1954 N.Y.Legis.Ann. 49–50.

It is apparent from these references that there must be some mental association between plaintiff's and defendant's marks.

> [I]f a reasonable buyer is not at all likely to link the two uses of the trademark in his or her own mind, even subtly or subliminally, then there can be no dilution. . . . [D]ilution theory presumes some kind of mental association in the reasonable buyer's mind between the two party's [sic] uses of the mark.

[2 J. MCCARTHY, *Trademarks and Unfair Competition* § 24.13, at 213–14 (2d ed. 1984)].

This mental association may be created where the plaintiff's mark is very famous and therefore has a distinctive quality for a significant percentage of the defendant's market. *Sally Gee, Inc. v. Myra Hogan, Inc.,* *supra,* 699 F.2d at 625. However, if a mark circulates only in a limited market, it is unlikely to be associated generally with the mark for a dissimilar product circulating elsewhere. *See, e.g., Estee Lauder, Inc. v. Cinnabar 2000 Haircutters, Inc.,* 218 U.S.P.Q. 191 (S.D.N.Y.), *aff'd,* 714 F.2d 112 (2d Cir.1982); *Markel v. Scovill Mfg. Co.,* 471 F.Supp. 1244 (W.D.N.Y.), *aff'd,* 610 F.2d 807 (2d Cir.1979). As discussed above, such distinctiveness as LEXIS possesses is limited to the narrow market of attorneys and accountants. Moreover, the process which LEXIS represents is widely disparate from the product represented by LEXUS. For the general public, LEXIS has no distinctive quality that LEXUS will dilute.

The possibility that someday LEXUS may become a famous mark in the mind of the general public has little relevance in the instant dilution analysis since it is quite apparent that the general public associates nothing with LEXIS. On the other hand, the recognized sophistication of attorneys, the principal users of the service, has substantial relevance. *See Sally Gee, Inc. v. Myra Hogan, Inc., supra,* 699 F.2d at 626. Because of this knowledgeable sophistication, it is unlikely that, even in the market where Mead principally operates, there will be any significant amount of blurring between the LEXIS and LEXUS marks.

For all the foregoing reasons, we hold that Toyota did not violate section 368–d. We see no need therefore to discuss Toyota's remaining arguments for reversal.

SWEET, DISTRICT JUDGE, concurring:

I concur, but write separately because I disagree with the majority's conclusion that LEXIS is not a strong mark capable of dilution and that LEXIS and LEXUS differ significantly in pronunciation, and I have a different view of the factors that are necessary to a finding of dilution.

It has become talismanic in the New York courts and in this Circuit that a cause of action under section 368–d involves two elements: 1) an extremely strong mark—either because of the mark's distinctive quality or because it has acquired secondary meaning—and 2) a likelihood of dilution. No showing of competition between the parties or confusion about the source of products is required.

Extremely Strong Trademark

The first element of a dilution cause of action requires the plaintiff to establish that it possesses an extremely strong mark—one "which is 'truly of distinctive quality' or which has 'acquired a secondary meaning in the mind of the public.'" *Sally Gee,* 699 F.2d at 625 (quoting *Allied,* 369

N.E.2d at 1166) (emphasis in original). A trademark has a distinctive quality if it is "distinctive, arbitrary, fanciful or coined" rather than "generic or descriptive." *Allied*, 369 N.E.2d at 1166. Courts have analyzed distinctiveness for antidilution purposes in much the same way they assess the strength of the mark when evaluating likelihood of confusion. . . .

The majority concludes that LEXIS is not a strong mark capable of dilution, noting that "the fact that a mark has selling power in a limited geographical or commercial area does not endow it with a secondary meaning for the public generally." . . .

This conclusion limits section 368–d's protection to nationally famous marks, because a strong mark capable of dilution is an element of a section 368–d cause of action and a plaintiff can lose on this ground alone.

However, "[t]he interest protected by § 368–d is . . . the selling power that a distinctive mark or name with favorable associations has engendered for a product in the mind of the consuming public." *Sally Gee, Inc. v. Myra Hogan, Inc.*, 699 F.2d 621, 624 (2d Cir.1983) (emphasis added). The LEXIS mark has "selling power" among its consuming public—attorneys and accountants. Its lack of selling power among the general public—i.e., the nonconsuming public—should not deprive the company of section 368–d's protection against dilution. *See Dreyfus Fund Inc. v. Royal Bank of Canada*, 525 F.Supp. 1108, 1125 (S.D.N.Y.1981) ("The statute should not be read to deprive marks from protection against dilution in limited areas of use, since otherwise it would afford protection only to the most notorious of all marks."); *Wedgwood Homes, Inc. v. Lund*, 659 P.2d 377, 381 (1983) ("We see no reason why marks of national renown should enjoy protection while local marks should not. A small local firm may expend efforts and money proportionately as great as those of a large firm in order to establish its mark's distinctive quality."). The renown of a senior mark is a factor a court should assess when evaluating the likelihood of dilution, not the strength of the mark.

Further, the district court as a matter of fact found LEXIS to be a very strong mark capable of dilution. Because imagination, thought, and perception are required to associate LEXIS with a computerized legal research service, the district court ruled that the mark is at least suggestive or arbitrary. . . . These findings cannot be set aside as arbitrary or capricious and amply support a conclusion that LEXIS is a strong mark capable of dilution.

Likelihood of Dilution

Several definitions of dilution exist. The legislative history defined the concept as "unlawful injury caused by the whittling away of an established trade-mark's selling power and value through its unauthorized use by others upon dissimilar products." 1954 N.Y.Leg.Ann. 49. The New York Court of Appeals offered the following definition:

> The harm that section [368–d] is designed to prevent is the gradual whittling away of a firm's distinctive trade-mark or name. It is not difficult to imagine the possible effect which the proliferation of various non-competitive businesses utilizing the name Tiffany's would have upon the public's association of the name Tiffany's solely with fine jewelry. The ultimate effect has been appropriately termed dilution.

Allied, 369 N.E.2d at 1165–66. In *Sally Gee*, this Court refined these general definitions by describing dilution as "an act which 'threatens two separable but related components of advertising value. Junior uses may blur a mark's product identification or they may tarnish the affirmative associations a mark has come to convey.'" 699 F.2d at 625 (quoting 3 R. CALLMAN, THE LAW OF UNFAIR COMPETITION, TRADEMARKS, AND MONOPOLIES § 84.2, at 954–55 (footnote omitted)).

. . . .

Applying *Sally Gee*'s definition, the majority finds little likelihood of dilution because LEXIS circulates in a limited market, the products covered by the LEXIS and LEXUS marks differ substantially, and Mead's principal consumers—attorneys—are sophisticated. Although I agree with these findings, I believe the majority has failed adequately to define the likelihood of dilution concept.

Defining likelihood of dilution as "tarnishing" is helpful because that principle can be applied in practice. "Blurring," however, offers practitioners and courts only marginally more guidance than "likelihood of dilution."

. . . .

Like likelihood of confusion, blurring sufficient to constitute dilution requires a case-by-case factual inquiry. A review of the anti-dilution cases in this Circuit indicates that courts have articulated the following factors in considering the likelihood of dilution caused by blurring:

1) similarity of the marks

2) similarity of the products covered by the marks

3) sophistication of consumers

4) predatory intent

5) renown of the senior mark

6) renown of the junior mark

The application of these factors here requires reversal of the decision below, although on a basis that I believe differs from that stated by the majority.

[JUDGE SWEET, applying each of the factors, concludes that a dilution claim should fail as there is not a likelihood of dilution].

NOTES & QUESTIONS

(1) According to the *Mead* majority, what are the two main elements of a dilution claim? On what element did Mead's claim fail?

(2) The majority made much of the supposed difference in pronunciation between LEXIS (with an "i") and LEXUS (with a "u"). Do you find this persuasive? Was this discussion even necessary given the rest of the opinion?

(3) The majority noted that a dilution claim involves either a blurring claim or a tarnishment claim. What type of dilution was alleged in the case? What is the difference between blurring and tarnishment? *See* RESTATEMENT (THIRD) OF UNFAIR COMPETITION § 25 & cmt. c (1995).

(4) Judge Sweet concurred in the judgment but not the reasoning. On what grounds did he differ from the majority?

(5) Consider Judge Sweet's factors for "likelihood of dilution." How do they compare to the "likelihood of confusion" factors from *Polaroid*?

(6) At the time the *Mead* case was decided, the Lanham Act did not include an anti-dilution provision. In 1995, Congress enacted the federal Trademark Dilution Act, which made dilution a matter of federal trademark law. For many years, however, the federal statute was interpreted to require actual dilution—not just a likelihood of dilution (the standard from the *Mead* decision). In 2006, Congress enacted the Trademark Dilution Revision Act, which replaced the actual dilution standard with a likelihood of dilution standard. The Revision Act also explicitly recognized dilution by tarnishment claims. *See* 15 U.S.C. § 1125(c)(1).

(7) Review 15 U.S.C. § 1125(c)(2)(A) & (B). With respect to how a dilution claim should be determined, has Congress sided with the *Mead* majority's view, the concurrence's view, or a little of both?

PROBLEM 11.4

Look back at Problem 11.3. Applying the Judge Sweet factors, consider whether Google, Inc. would likely succeed on a dilution claim.

3. GENERICIDE

Under the distinctiveness spectrum, generic terms are not entitled to trademark protection. Once a company registers a trademark under an arbitrary or fanciful name and uses it for some time, you might think that any concern over genericness would dissipate. However, sometimes a company is the victim of its own success.

KING-SEELEY THERMOS CO. V. ALADDIN INDUS., INC.
321 F.2d 577 (2d Cir. 1963)

L. MOORE, CIRCUIT JUDGE.

This action by brought by appellant King-Seeley Thermos Co. (King-Seeley) to enjoin the defendant, Aladdin Industries, Incorporated from threatened infringement of eight trademark registrations for the word 'Thermos' owned by appellant. Defendant answered, acknowledging its intention to sell its vacuum-insulated containers as 'thermos bottles,' asserted that the term 'thermos' or 'thermos bottle' is a generic term in the English language, asked that plaintiff's registrations of its trademark 'Thermos' be cancelled and that it be adjudicated that plaintiff have no trademark rights in the word 'thermos' on its vacuum bottles. The trial court held that plaintiff's registrations were valid but that the word 'thermos' had become a generic descriptive word in the English language as a synonym for 'vacuum insulated' container.

The facts are set out at great length in the comprehensive and well-reasoned opinion of the district court and will not be detailed here. In that opinion, the court reviewed King-Seeley's corporate history and its use of the trademark 'Thermos.' He found that from 1907 to 1923, King-Seeley undertook advertising and educational campaigns that tended to make 'thermos' a generic term descriptive of the product rather than of its origin. This consequence flowed from the corporation's attempt to popularize 'Thermos bottle' as the name of that product without including any of the generic terms then used, such as 'Thermos vacuum-insulated bottle.' The court found that by 1923 the word 'thermos' had acquired firm roots as a descriptive or generic word.

At about 1923, because of the suggestion in an opinion of a district court that 'Thermos' might be a descriptive word, King-Seeley adopted the use of the word 'vacuum' or 'vacuum bottle' with the word 'Thermos.' Although 'Thermos' was generally recognized in the trade as a trademark, the corporation did police the trade and notified those using 'thermos' in a descriptive sense that it was a trademark. It failed, however, to take affirmative action to seek out generic uses by non-trade publications and protested only those which happened to come to its attention. Between 1923 and the early 1950's the generic use of 'thermos' had grown to a marked extent in non-trade publications and by the end of this period there was wide-spread use by the unorganized public of 'thermos' as a synonym for 'vacuum insulated.' The court concluded that King-Seeley had failed to use due diligence to rescue 'Thermos' from becoming a descriptive or generic term.

Between 1954 and 1957, plaintiff showed awareness of the widespread generic use of 'thermos' and of the need to educate the public to the word's trademark significance. It diversified its products to include those not directly related to containers designed to keep their contents hot or cold. It changed its name from the American Thermos Bottle Company to The American Thermos Products Company and intensified its policing activities of trade and non-trade publications. The court found, however, that the generic use of 'thermos' had become so firmly impressed as a part of the everyday language of the American public that plaintiff's extraordinary efforts commencing in the mid-1950's came too late to keep 'thermos' from falling into the public domain. The court also held that appellant's trademarks are valid and because there is an appreciable, though minority, segment of the consumer public which knows and recognizes plaintiff's trademarks, it imposed certain restrictions and limitations on the use of the word 'thermos' by defendant.

We affirm the district court's decision that the major significance of the word 'thermos' is generic. No useful purpose would be served by repeating here what is fully documented in the opinion of the court below.

Appellant's primary protest on appeal is directed at the district court's finding that

> "The word 'thermos' became a part of the public domain because of the plaintiff's wide dissemination of the word 'thermos' used as a synonym for 'vacuum-insulated' and as an adjectival-noun, 'thermos,' through its educational and advertising campaigns and because of the plaintiff's lack of reasonable diligence in asserting and protecting its trademark rights in the word 'Thermos' among the members of the unorganized public, exclusive of those in the trade, from 1907 to the date of this action."

We are not convinced that the trademark's loss of distinctiveness was the result of some failure on plaintiff's part. Substantial efforts to preserve the trademark significance of the word were made by plaintiff, especially with respect to members of the trade. However, there was little they could do to prevent the public from using 'thermos' in a generic rather than a trademark sense. And whether the appropriation by the public was due to highly successful educational and advertising campaigns or to lack of diligence in policing or not is of no consequence; the fact is that the word 'thermos' had entered the public domain beyond recall. Even as early as 1910 plaintiff itself asserted that 'Thermos had become a household word.'

Judge Anderson found that although a substantial majority of the public knows and uses the word 'thermos,' only a small minority of the public knows that this word has trademark significance. He wrote:

The results of the survey (conducted at the behest of the defendant) were that about 75% of adults in the United States who were familiar with containers that keep the contents hot or cold, call such a container a 'thermos'; about 12% of the adult American public know that 'thermos' has a trade-mark significance, and about 11% use the term 'vacuum bottle.' This is generally corroborative of the court's conclusions drawn from the other evidence, except that such other evidence indicated that a somewhat larger minority than 12% was aware of the trade-mark meaning of 'thermos'; and a somewhat larger minority than 11% used the descriptive term 'vacuum' bottle or other container.

The record amply supports these findings.

Appellant argues that the court below misapplied the doctrine of the Aspirin[3] and Cellophane[4] cases. Its primary contention is that in those cases, there was no generic name, such as vacuum bottle, that was suitable for use by the general public. As a result, to protect the use of the only word the identified the product in the mind of the public would give the owners of the trademark an unfair competitive advantage. The rule of those cases, however, does not rest on this factor. Judge Learned Hand stated the sole issue in Aspirin to be: 'What do the buyers understand by the word for whose use the parties are contending? If they understand by it only the kind of goods sold, then, I take it, it makes no difference whatever what efforts the plaintiff has made to get them to understand more.' 272 F. at 509. Of course, it is obvious that the fact that there was no suitable descriptive word for either aspirin or cellophane made it difficult, if not impossible, for the original manufacturers to prevent their trademark from becoming generic. But the test is not what is available as an alternative to the public, but what the public's understanding is of the word that it uses. What has happened here is that the public had become accustomed to calling vacuum bottles by the word 'thermos.' If a buyer walked into a retail store asking for a thermos bottle, meaning any vacuum bottle and not specifically plaintiff's product, the fact that the appellation 'vacuum bottle' was available to him is of no significance. The two terms had become synonymous; in fact, defendant's survey showed that the public was far more inclined to use the word 'thermos' to describe a container that keeps its contents hot or cold than the phrase 'vacuum bottle.'

Appellant asserts that the courts in a number of cases have upheld the continued exclusive use of a dual functioning trademark, which both identifies the class of product as well as its source. *See, e.g., Standard*

---

[3] *Bayer Co. v. United Drug Co.*, 272 F. 505 (S.D.N.Y.1921).

[4] *DuPont Cellophane Co. v. Waxed Products Co.*, 85 F.2d 75 (2 Cir. 1936).

Brands v. Smidler, 151 F.2d 34 (2 Cir. 1945) ('V–8'); *Walgreen v. Obear-Nester*, 113 F.2d 956 (8 Cir.), cert. denied, 311 U.S. 708 (1940) ('Pyrex'); *Marks v. Polaroid Corp.*, 129 F.Supp. 243 (D.Mass. 1955), aff'd 237 F.2d 428 (1 Cir. 1956) ('Polaroid'); *Q-Tips v. Johnson & Johnson*, 108 F.Supp. 845 (D.N.J.1952), aff'd 206 F.2d 144 (3 Cir.), cert. denied, 346 U.S. 867 (1953) ('Q-Tips'); *Keebler Weyl Baking Co. v. J. S. Ivins' Son*, 7 F.Supp. 211 (E.D.Pa.1934) ('Club Crackers'); *Barnes v. Pierce*, 164 F. 213 (S.D.N.Y.1908) ('Argyrol'). As this court recently indicated:

> [A] mark is not generic merely because it has some significance to the public as an indication of the nature or class of an article. * * * In order to become generic the principal significance of the word must be its indication of the nature or class of an article, rather than an indication of its origin.

Feathercombs, Inc. v. Solo Products Corp., 306 F.2d 251, 256 (2 Cir.), cert. denied, 371 U.S. 910 (1962). *But see Marks v. Polaroid Corp., supra*, 129 F.Supp. at 270 ("a defendant alleging invalidity of a trademark for genericness must show that to the consuming public as a whole the word has lost all its trademark significance").

Since in this case, the primary significance to the public of the word 'thermos' is its indication of the nature and class of an article rather than as an indication of its source, whatever duality of meaning the word still holds for a minority of the public is of little consequence except as a consideration in the framing of a decree. Since the great majority of those members of the public who use the word 'thermos' are not aware of any trademark significance, there is not enough dual use to support King-Seeley's claims to monopoly of the word as a trademark.

No doubt, the Aspirin and Cellophane doctrine can be a harsh one for it places a penalty on the manufacturer who has made skillful use of advertising and has popularized his product. See 3 Callman, Unfair Competition and Trademarks 1149–50 (2d ed. 1950). However, King-Seeley has enjoyed a commercial monopoly of the word 'thermos' for over fifty years. During that period, despite its efforts to protect the trademark, the public has virtually expropriated it as its own. The word having become part of the public domain, it would be unfair to unduly restrict the right of a competitor of King-Seeley to use the word.

The court below, mindful of the fact that some members of the public and a substantial portion of the trade still recognize and use the word 'thermos' as a trademark, framed an eminently fair decree designed to afford King-Seeley as much future protection as was possible. The decree provides that defendant must invariably precede the use of the word 'thermos' by the possessive of the name 'Aladdin'; that the defendant must confine its use of 'thermos' to the lower-case 't'; and that it may never use the words 'original' or 'genuine' in describing its product. In addition, plaintiff is entitled to retain the exclusive right to all of its present forms of the trademark 'Thermos' without change. These conditions provide a sound and proper balancing of the competitive disadvantage to defendants arising out of plaintiff's exclusive use of the word 'thermos' and the risk that those who recognize 'Thermos' as a trademark will be deceived.

The courts should be ever alert, as the district court said, 'to eliminate confusion and the possibility of deceit.' The purchasing public is entitled to know the source of the article it desires to purchase. It is not within our province to speculate whether the dire predictions made by appellant in forceful appellate argument will come to pass. Certain it is that the district court made every endeavor in its judgment to give as much protection to plaintiff as possible. The use by defendant of the now generic word 'thermos' was substantially curtailed. Plaintiff's trademark 'thermos' was protected in every style of printing except the lower case 'thermos' and then the use of the word must be preceded by the possessive of defendant's name 'Aladdin' or the possessive of 'Aladdin' plus one of defendant's brand names. Any doubt about plaintiff's position in the field is removed by the prohibition against the use by defendant in labeling, advertising or publication of the words 'genuine' or 'original' in referring to the word 'thermos.' Furthermore, the district court has given both parties the opportunity to apply to it for such orders and directions as may be warranted in the light of changed circumstances and for the enforcement of compliance or for the punishment of violations. In our opinion the trial court has reached a most equitable solution which gives appropriate consideration to the law and the facts.

Affirmed.

NOTES & QUESTIONS

(1) What did King-Seeley do wrong in its advertising that contributed to the "genericide" of "thermos"?

(2) Once King-Seeley discovered that "thermos" was being used generically, what steps did it take to try and rectify the situation? Could it have done anything else?

(3) King-Seeley argued that "thermos" was different from products such as Aspirin and Cellophane because there was a generic term for "thermos"— i.e., "vacuum bottle." It also argued that "thermos" had a dual meaning in that it acted both to describe the product and to associate the source. Why was the court unpersuaded by these arguments?

(4) Trade dress is also susceptible to genericide. For instance, in *Sunrise Jewelry Manufacturing Corp. v. Fred S.A.*, 175 F.3d 1322, 1325–26 (Fed. Cir. 1999), the Federal Circuit reviewed Fred's registration of a mark described as a " 'metallic nautical rope design as an integral feature of the

goods,' which include[d] clocks, watches, and jewelry made of precious metal." Fred contended that a mark could only be cancelled for becoming generic if it was a name. The court disagreed and held that, despite the federal registration and the use of the phrase "mark name" in the Lanham Act, the mark could be challenged as having become generic:

> Our review of the Lanham Act and relevant case law persuades us that the term "generic name" as used in 15 U.S.C. § 1064(3), must be read expansively to encompass anything that has the potential but fails to serve as an indicator of source, such as names, words, symbols, devices, or trade dress. Any narrower interpretation of "generic name" would allow incontestable trademarks other than names that become generic to retain incontestable status despite their inability to serve as source designators. This would directly contravene the purpose of the Lanham Act.

Id. at 1326.

PROBLEM 11.5

George Ogle is back in your office with a new quandary. His Ogle Paint Co. (he changed the name after the Google fiasco) has taken off. He now has a nationwide brand and his company specializes in "Ogling" houses, which is the term his company uses for applying his patented sealant process. It turns out that the patent on the sealant process expired a few years ago, and it has recently come to George's attention that some competitors have been using the term "ogling" for applying the same process. He knows he can't sue for patent infringement anymore, but he wants to know if he can sue for trademark infringement. He registered "Ogle" and "Ogling" with the PTO many years ago before his company really took off.

What advice do you have for George about how to move forward with his suit? What advice do you have for George about how he should market "Ogling" in the future?

4.   FAIR USE DEFENSE

You may recall from the *Zatarain's* decision at the beginning of this Chapter that although "Fish-Fri" was held to be a descriptive term that had acquired secondary meaning, the court still found for the defendants under the "fair use" doctrine. As the court observed:

> Even when a descriptive term has acquired a secondary meaning sufficient to warrant trademark protection, others may be entitled to use the mark without incurring liability for trademark infringement. When the allegedly infringing term is "used fairly and in good faith only to describe to users the goods or services of [a] party, or their geographic origin," Lanham Act § 33(b)(4), 15 U.S.C. § 1115(b)(4) (1976), a defendant in a trademark infringement action may assert the "fair use" defense.

The defense is available only in actions involving descriptive terms and only when the term is used in its descriptive sense rather than its trademark sense. In essence, the fair use defense prevents a trademark registrant from appropriating a descriptive term for its own use to the exclusion of others, who may be prevented thereby from accurately describing their own goods. The holder of a protectable descriptive mark has no legal claim to an exclusive right in the primary, descriptive meaning of the term; consequently, anyone is free to use the term in its primary, descriptive sense so long as such use does not lead to customer confusion as to the source of the goods or services.

. . . .

Although Zatarain's term "Fish-Fri" has acquired a secondary meaning in the New Orleans geographical area, Zatarain's does not now prevail automatically on its trademark infringement claim, for it cannot prevent the fair use of the term by Oak Grove and Visko's. The "fair use" defense applies only to descriptive terms and requires that the term be "used fairly and in good faith only to describe to users the goods or services of such party, or their geographic origin." Lanham Act § 33(b), 15 U.S.C. § 1115(b)(4) (1976). The district court determined that Oak Grove and Visko's were entitled to fair use of the term "fish fry" to describe a characteristic of their goods; we affirm that conclusion.

Zatarain's term "Fish-Fri" is a descriptive term that has acquired a secondary meaning in the New Orleans area. Although the trademark is valid by virtue of having acquired a secondary meaning, only that penumbra or fringe of secondary meaning is given legal protection. Zatarain's has no legal claim to an exclusive right in the original, descriptive sense of the term; therefore, Oak Grove and Visko's are still free to use the words "fish fry" in their ordinary, descriptive sense, so long as such use will not tend to confuse customers as to the source of the goods.

The record contains ample evidence to support the district court's determination that Oak Grove's and Visko's use of the words "fish fry" was fair and in good faith. Testimony at trial indicated that the appellees did not intend to use the term in a trademark sense and had never attempted to register the words as a trademark. Oak Grove and Visko's apparently believed "fish fry" was a generic name for the type of coating mix they manufactured. In addition, Oak Grove and Visko's consciously packaged and labelled their products in such a way as to minimize any potential confusion in the minds of consumers. The dissimilar trade dress of these products prompted the district court to observe that confusion at the point of purchase—the grocery shelves—would be virtually impossible. Our review of the record convinces us that the district court's determinations are correct. We hold, therefore, that Oak Grove and Visko's are entitled to fair use of the term "fish fry" to describe their products; accordingly, Zatarain's claim of trademark infringement must fail.

As suggested above, the fair use defense applies only to marks which are descriptive and have acquired secondary meaning. The defense does not apply to suggestive marks or other marks which are inherently distinctive. The fair use defense is recognized in both the Restatement of Unfair Competition and the Lanham Act. Section 28 of the Restatement provides:

> In an action for infringement of a trademark, trade name, collective mark, or certification mark, it is a defense that the term used by the actor is descriptive or geographically descriptive of the actor's goods, services, or business, or is the personal name of the actor or a person connected with the actor, and the actor has used the term fairly and in good faith solely to describe the actor's goods, services, or business or to indicate a connection with the named person.

Similarly, the Lanham Act in 15 U.S.C. § 1115(b)(4) states that it is a defense to trademark infringement if the defendant can establish:

> That the use of the name, term, or device charged to be an infringement is a use, otherwise than as a mark, of the party's individual name in his own business, or of the individual name of anyone in privity with such party, or of a term or device which is descriptive of and used fairly and in good faith only to describe the goods or services of such party, or their geographic origin.

Essentially, these standards establish three elements that must be met for a trademark defendant to successfully claim fair use. First, the defendant must use the term other than as a mark. Second, the defendant must use the term fairly and in good faith. Finally, the defendant must use the term descriptively.

NOTES & QUESTIONS

(1) What is the policy justification for allowing a fair use defense against a descriptive mark with an established secondary meaning? If a descriptive term can still be used by other market participants, is there any value to a descriptive mark?

(2) An important advantage to the fair use defense is that the defendant need not disprove likelihood of confusion. In *KP Permanent Make-Up, Inc. v. Lasting Impression I, Inc.*, 543 U.S. 124 (2004), the U.S. Supreme Court stated that "defendant has no independent burden to negate the likelihood of any confusion in raising the affirmative defense that a term is used descriptively, not as a mark, fairly, and in good faith." The Court further noted that some likelihood of confusion will exist in many instances, but such likelihood is not relevant once the elements of the defense are established.

(3) Another type of fair use is "nominative fair use," in which a defendant uses the protected mark solely to describe or identify the product or service. For instance, in *New Kids on the Block v. New America Publishing, Inc.*, 971 F.2d 302 (9th Cir. 1992), the New Kids on the Block, a popular "boy band" from the late 1980s, sued two newspapers of national circulation who "conducted separate polls of their readers seeking an answer to a pressing question: Which one of the New Kids is the most popular?" The lawsuit asserted trademark infringement because the newspapers were using the trademarked name. *See id.* at 304–05. In rejecting the claim, the court described why such nominative use is not actionable under trademark law:

> Cases like these are best understood as involving a non-trademark use of a mark—a use to which the infringement laws simply do not apply, just as videotaping television shows for private home use does not implicate the copyright holder's exclusive right to reproduction. *See Sony Corp. v. Universal City Studios, Inc.*, 464 U.S. 417, 447–51 (1984). Indeed, we may generalize a class of cases where the use of the trademark does not attempt to capitalize on consumer confusion or to appropriate the cachet of one product for a different one. Such nominative use of a mark—where the only word reasonably available to describe a particular thing is pressed into service—lies outside the strictures of trademark law: Because it does not implicate the source-identification function that is the purpose of trademark, it does not constitute unfair competition; such use is fair because it does not imply sponsorship or endorsement by the trademark holder.

Id. at 307–08.

Not all circuits agree with the Ninth Circuit's approach, which appears to be a way of analyzing whether there is in fact a likelihood of confusion. *See* 4 MCCARTHY ON TRADEMARKS AND UNFAIR COMPETITION § 23:11 (4th ed. 2015). The Third Circuit, for example, has changed the Ninth Circuit's nominative fair use analysis into an affirmative defense to infringement:

> .... Once plaintiff has met its burden of proving that confusion is likely, the burden then shifts to defendant to show that its nominative use of plaintiff's mark is nonetheless fair. To demonstrate fairness, the defendant must satisfy a three-pronged nominative fair use test, derived to a great extent from the one articulated by the Court of Appeals for the Ninth Circuit. Under our

fairness test, a defendant must show: (1) that the use of plaintiff's mark is necessary to describe both the plaintiff's product or service and the defendant's product or service; (2) that the defendant uses only so much of the plaintiff's mark as is necessary to describe plaintiff's product; and (3) that the defendant's conduct or language reflect the true and accurate relationship between plaintiff and defendant's products or services.

Century 21 Real Estate Corp. v. Lendingtree, Inc., 425 F.3d 211, 222 (3d Cir. 2005). It should be noted that *Century 21* draws upon factors similar to those articulated in the *New Kids* case.

(4) The federal Trademark Dilution Revision Act expressly permits a fair use defense to claims of dilution. *See* 15 U.S.C. § 1125(c)(3).

F. REMEDIES

As you may recall, the remedies for deceptive marketing and trademark violations are the same.[i] Both the Restatement and the Lanham Act provide for injunctive relief and monetary damages in appropriate cases, but the primary remedy for trademark infringement (or dilution) is injunctive relief. Section 34 of the Lanham Act, 15 U.S.C. § 1116, grants courts the power to issue injunctive relief "according to the principle of equity and upon such terms as the court may deem reasonable, to prevent the violation of any right [of a mark holder]." As discussed in Chapter 7, Section D, fashioning an injunctive remedy can be a difficult task, and courts may consider a number of factors. (Many of the primary considerations are listed in § 35 of the Restatement of Unfair Competition.) As with deceptive marketing claims, courts can also order corrective advertising in appropriate disputes.

Section 35 of the Lanham Act provides for monetary damages in appropriate cases. It states, in part, the following:

(a) Profits; damages and costs; attorney fees

When a violation of any right of [a mark holder] shall have been established in any civil action arising under this chapter, the plaintiff shall be entitled, . . . subject to the principles of equity, to recover (1) defendant's profits, (2) any damages sustained by the plaintiff, and (3) the costs of the action. The court shall assess such profits and damages or cause the same to be assessed under its direction. In assessing profits the plaintiff shall be required to prove defendant's sales only; defendant must prove all elements of cost or deduction claimed. In assessing damages the court may enter judgment, according to the circumstances of the case, for any sum above the amount found

---

[i] You may find it useful to review the materials on remedies in deceptive marketing disputes. *See* Chapter 7, Section D.

as actual damages, not exceeding three times such amount. If the court shall find that the amount of the recovery based on profits is either inadequate or excessive the court may in its discretion enter judgment for such sum as the court shall find to be just, according to the circumstances of the case. Such sum in either of the above circumstances shall constitute compensation and not a penalty. The court in exceptional cases may award reasonable attorney fees to the prevailing party.

15 U.S.C. § 1117; *see also* RESTATEMENT (THIRD) OF UNFAIR COMPETITION §§ 36–37 (1995) (allowing plaintiff to recover its actual damages or the defendant's profits). Notice that § 35 of the Lanham Act provides three particular monetary remedies: (1) an award of the defendant's profits, (2) actual damages sustained by the plaintiff, and (3) costs of the action, which may include attorney's fees.

Before delving further into monetary damages, it should be noted that such awards are discretionary and subject to "principles of equity." This means that if a court deems an injunction adequate to protect the plaintiff's interests, it may decline to award damages. Although intent or willfulness is not required under the statute as a condition precedent to recovery, many courts find such intent to be a relevant factor in determining whether to award damages. The same is true for "actual confusion"—the statute does not require actual consumer confusion (recall that only a likelihood of confusion is necessary), but courts often look for actual confusion before awarding damages. *See* RESTATEMENT (THIRD) OF UNFAIR COMPETITION § 37(3) (1995) (listing relevant factors).

The first monetary remedy under § 35—an award of the defendant's profits—involves a two-step process. First, the plaintiff must establish the defendant's gross revenues. The burden then shifts to the defendant to demonstrate deductions (if any), such as by introducing evidence of expenses related to sales, or proving that certain profits are not attributable to the infringing acts. The award of profits does not require the plaintiff to show its own actual damages (indeed, if the plaintiff's actual damages are shown, the court may decide that those damages are a more appropriate remedy).

An award of the defendant's profits is a rather extraordinary remedy. Courts do not automatically grant it, and both courts and commentators have noted that it is a "rough" measure of damages. Courts will refuse to make the award (or limit it to only a percentage of the defendant's profits) if there is concern that the award will result in a windfall. In addition, most courts require the infringer's actions to be intentional or willful before making such an award.

The second monetary remedy under § 35 is the plaintiff's actual damages. As mentioned, the court has discretion to "enter judgment, according to the circumstances of the case, for any sum above the amount found as actual damages, not exceeding three times such amount." While an increased award is possible, courts generally grant it only in disputes involving intentional or willful conduct. Such an enhanced award is not meant as a penalty; indeed, plaintiffs are not entitled to punitive damages under the Lanham Act. Depending upon the jurisdiction, however, punitive damages may be recoverable under a state common law action. *See* J. THOMAS MCCARTHY, 5 MCCARTHY ON TRADEMARKS AND UNFAIR COMPETITION § 30:96 (4th ed. 2015) ("In jurisdictions where punitive damages are allowable in tort cases, they are equally allowable in cases of trademark infringement and unfair competition.").

Recovering the plaintiff's actual damages is subject to the usual requirements for damages—i.e., the plaintiff must prove both causation of harm and the amount of the damages (although courts are generally less demanding on the sufficiency of the evidence of amount once the fact of damages has been proven). Plaintiff's damages can be measured in a number of ways, such as by its own lost profits, injury to its goodwill and reputation, and costs incurred by the plaintiff when engaging in corrective advertising. *See* RESTATEMENT (THIRD) OF UNFAIR COMPETITION § 36(2) (1995). Generally speaking, a plaintiff cannot recover both the defendant's profits and the plaintiff's actual damages, as this would result in a double recovery. In some instances, however, courts have awarded both when the harm does not stem from the same lost sales. The comments to the Restatement clarify:

> In some cases courts have permitted the recovery of both damages under the rule stated in this Section and an accounting of the defendant's profits . . . , with the caveat that the plaintiff may not recover twice for the same loss. The prohibition against double recovery most clearly applies when the goods of the parties directly compete and the plaintiff seeks to recover both damages for losses attributable to diverted sales and the profits earned on sales made by the defendant. Although the two sums are not necessarily identical since the parties may have different profit margins and not all of the defendant's sales may represent sales diverted from the plaintiff, in the absence of contrary evidence the court may conclude that the defendant's profits adequately reflect the sales lost by the plaintiff. In such cases an award of both profits and damages is therefore prohibited under the rule precluding double recovery for the same loss. Recovery of both profits and damages is most clearly appropriate when the profits of the defendant are used as a measure of the loss attributable to sales diverted from the plaintiff, and the plaintiff in addition proves other losses such as harm to reputation.

Id. § 36 cmt. c.

The final remedy under § 35 of the Lanham Act is the "costs of the action," which may include an award of "reasonable attorney fees to the prevailing party" in exceptional cases. As with a recovery of the defendant's profits and an enhanced damages award, courts tend to reserve this remedy for instances of intentional or willful conduct.

CHAPTER 12

ANTITRUST

■ ■ ■

A. INTRODUCTION

Antitrust is too big of a topic to cover completely in just one chapter of a business torts and unfair competition text. However, its importance as an alternative claim and its relation to other unfair competition actions makes it worth exploring, even if just to cover some basics.

Antitrust law developed at the close of the nineteenth century in response to a growing distrust of the amount of power held by corporations. The growth of major corporations after the Civil War increased the long-held fear of monopoly by the public, particularly among farmers, workers, and small businessmen. In response to these fears, the Sherman Act was passed as a means of breaking up the so-called "trusts," which were viewed as restricting trade and competition.

Once upon a time, the anticompetitive nature of many unfair competition practices made them part of a prima facie antitrust claim under the *Pick-Barth* doctrine, at least in the First Circuit. This doctrine was based upon the First Circuit decision of *Albert Pick-Barth Co. v. Mitchell Woodbury Co.*, 57 F.2d 96, 102–03 (1st Cir. 1932), in which the court found that certain business practices were to be treated as unlawful per se under the antitrust laws because there was no pro-competitive justification for them. The First Circuit eventually disavowed the doctrine, however, and no other circuits appear to have adopted it. Today, acts of unfair competition may still raise the specter of an antitrust violation. Furthermore, it is not uncommon for claims such as misappropriation of trade secret, tortious interference with contract, and antitrust to all be alleged in the same lawsuit as independent causes of action.

There are a number of statutes that work together in the world of antitrust. The main ones are the Sherman Act and the Clayton Act (as amended by the Robinson-Patman Act). Section 1 of the Sherman Act prohibits two broad categories of business arrangements which restrain trade: horizontal arrangements between competitors and vertical arrangements between or among those in the supply chain (e.g., manufacturers, suppliers, distributors, and retailers). It is not unusual for both categories to be alleged in the same case. Courts also tend to view antitrust violations as either per se violations or violations of the "rule of reason"—a rule which takes into account the competitive and anticompetitive effects of the defendant's conduct, as well as the nature of the industry itself. Traditionally, activities such as price fixing and market and customer allocation were per se violations, but the Supreme Court has signaled a cautious approach to applying a per se rule (as we will explore).

Section 2 of the Sherman Act governs monopolistic behavior, which typically involves relationships between a single firm and its suppliers or customers. There are two primary elements to monopoly claims: (1) possession of monopoly power in the relevant market, and (2) willful acquisition or maintenance of that power. Intent is also required.

The Clayton Act prohibits tying arrangements and, more importantly for our discussion, grants private parties the ability to seek damages for economic injuries caused by antitrust violations. Plaintiffs can recover treble damages, attorney's fees, and equitable (injunctive) relief in appropriate cases. The ability to recover punitive damages in state unfair competition claims, however, may lead to an even greater recovery than what antitrust law can provide.

The Federal Trade Commission ("FTC") Act governs general unfair or deceptive practices and grants the FTC power to challenge them. The FTC also enforces the antitrust laws, but the FTC Act itself does not allow for private suits (which is why we have what are referred to as "little FTC" acts in many states).

The antitrust laws are enforced by the Antitrust Division of the U.S. Department of Justice, the FTC, and private parties. Violations of the Sherman Act can be investigated and prosecuted in civil or criminal proceedings. Government enforcers can seek imprisonment, criminal fines, and civil penalties. As mentioned, prevailing plaintiffs in civil antitrust actions brought by private parties under the Clayton Act are entitled to treble damages, attorney's fees, and equitable relief in appropriate cases. However, private parties have an additional burden in bringing an antitrust claim; they must show an "antitrust injury." For an injury to constitute an antitrust injury, it must be causally related to an antitrust violation, and the harm may not be indirect, consequential, or remote.

Before proceeding with the basics of an antitrust claim, an underlying theme should be stressed. The purpose of the antitrust laws is not to protect competitors from the effects of vigorous competition, but is instead to protect competition itself. Thus, conduct which may appear unsavory or downright unethical does not necessarily run afoul of the antitrust laws if it has no effect (or possibly even a positive effect) on competition. Such conduct may give rise to other causes of action, but antitrust law protects a unique interest which may not align with the interests of the plaintiff.

B. SHERMAN ACT § 1 VIOLATIONS

Section 1 of the Sherman Act (15 U.S.C. § 1) prohibits any agreement among competitors that unreasonably limits competition: "Every contract, combination . . . or conspiracy, in restraint of trade or commerce among the several States, or with foreign nations, is declared to be illegal. . . ." While the wording of § 1 is broad, the U.S. Supreme Court has held that "restraint of trade" actually means *unreasonable* restraint, as all contracts restrain trade in some manner. There are three elements to a § 1 violation: (1) an agreement that (2) unreasonably restrains trade, and (3) the restraint has an effect on interstate commerce. This third element is simply a recognition of the limits of congressional power under the Commerce Clause.

The essence of a § 1 claim is the agreement element, as there is no violation of § 1 for a unilateral attempt to restrain trade (although, depending upon the conduct, other causes of action may exist). As mentioned, restraints in trade have generally been divided into two types: horizontal and vertical. Horizontal restraints involve one or more competitors agreeing to restrain trade in some manner, such as by agreeing to charge a minimum price for their product, or dividing up territories to limit competition. Vertical restraints involve agreements between different levels of the supply chain, such as an agreement between a manufacturer and a retailer to resell merchandise at a specified price. We will explore both horizontal and vertical restraints below.

1. HORIZONTAL RESTRAINTS

a. Per Se Violations

As part of the inquiry into whether an alleged agreement unreasonably restrains trade, courts categorize potential antitrust violations. In *National Society of Professional Engineers v. U.S.*, 435 U.S. 679 (1978), the Supreme Court described these categories as follows:

> There are, thus, two complementary categories of antitrust analysis. In the first category are agreements whose nature and necessary effect are so plainly anticompetitive that no elaborate study of the industry is needed to establish their illegality—they are "illegal per se." In the second category are agreements whose competitive effect can only be evaluated by analyzing the facts peculiar to the business, the history of the restraint, and the reasons why it was imposed.

Id. at 692. As the next case explores, courts have found that certain conduct is per se illegal, despite what might appear to be a competitive intent.

UNITED STATES V. TOPCO ASSOCIATES, INC.

405 U.S. 596 (1972)

MARSHALL, J.

The United States brought this action for injunctive relief against alleged violation by Topco Associates, Inc. (Topco), of § 1 of the Sherman Act, 26 Stat. 209, as amended, 15 U.S.C. § 1. Jurisdiction was grounded in § 4 of the Act, 15 U.S.C. § 4. Following a trial on the merits, the United States District Court for the Northern District of Illinois entered judgment for Topco, and the United States appealed directly to this Court pursuant to § 2 of the Expediting Act, 32 Stat. 823, as amended, 15 U.S.C. § 29. We noted probable jurisdiction, and we now reverse the judgment of the District Court.

I

Topco is a cooperative association of approximately 25 small and medium-sized regional supermarket chains that operate stores in some 33 States.[1] Each of the member chains operates independently; there is no pooling of earnings, profits, capital, management, or advertising resources. No grocery business is conducted under the Topco name. Its basic function is to serve as a purchasing agent for its members.[2] In this capacity, it procures and distributes to the members more than 1,000 different food and related nonfood items, most of which are distributed under brand names owned by Topco. The association does not itself own any manufacturing, processing, or warehousing facilities, and the items that it procures for members are usually shipped directly from the packer or manufacturer to the members. Payment is made either to Topco or directly to the manufacturer at a cost that is virtually the same for the members as for Topco itself.

All of the stock in Topco is owned by the members, with the common stock, the only stock having voting rights, being equally distributed. The board of directors, which controls the operation of the association, is drawn from the members and is normally composed of high-ranking executive officers of member chains. It is the board that elects the association's officers and appoints committee members, and it is from the

---

[1] Topco, which is referred to at times in this opinion as the "association," is actually composed of 23 chains of supermarket retailers and two retailer-owned cooperative wholesalers.

[2] In addition to purchasing various items for its members, Topco performs other related functions: e.g., it insures that there is adequate quality control on the products that it purchases; it assists members in developing specifications on certain types of products (e.g., equipment and supplies); and it also aids the members in purchasing goods through other sources.

board that the principal executive officers of Topco must be drawn. Restrictions on the alienation of stock and the procedure for selecting all important officials of the association from within the ranks of its members give the members complete and unfettered control over the operations of the association.

Topco was founded in the 1940's by a group of small, local grocery chains, independently owned and operated, that desired to cooperate to obtain high quality merchandise under private labels in order to compete more effectively with larger national and regional chains.[3] With a line of canned, dairy, and other products, the association began. It added frozen foods in 1950, fresh produce in 1958, more general merchandise equipment and supplies in 1960, and a branded bacon and carcass beef selection program in 1966. By 1964, Topco's members had combined retail sales of more than $2 billion; by 1967, their sales totaled more than $2.3 billion, a figure exceeded by only three national grocery chains.[4]

Private-label products differ from other brand-name products in that they are sold at a limited number of easily ascertainable stores. A&P, for example, was a pioneer in developing a series of products that were sold under an A&P label and that were only available in A&P stores. It is obvious that by using private-label products, a chain can achieve significant cost economies in purchasing, transportation, warehousing, promotion, and advertising. These economies may afford the chain opportunities for offering private-label products at lower prices than other band-name products. This, in turn, provides many advantages of which some of the more important are: a store can offer national-brand products at the same price as other stores, while simultaneously offering a desirable, lower priced alternative; or, if the profit margin is sufficiently high on private-brand goods, national-brand products may be sold at reduced price. Other advantages include: enabling a chain to bargain more favorably with national-brand manufacturers by creating a broader supply base of manufacturers, thereby decreasing dependence on a few, large national-brand manufacturers; enabling a chain to create a "price-mix" whereby prices on special items can be lowered to attract customers while profits are maintained on other items; and creation of general goodwill by offering lower priced, higher quality goods.

Members of the association vary in the degree of market share that they possess in their respective areas. The range is from 1.5% to 16%, with the average being approximately 6%. While it is difficult to compare these figures with the market shares of larger regional and national chains because of the absence in the record of accurate statistics for these

---

[3] The founding members of Topco were having difficulty competing with larger chains. This difficulty was attributable in some degree to the fact that the larger chains were capable of developing their own private-label programs.

[4] The three largest chains are A&P, Safeway, and Kroger.

chains, there is much evidence in the record that Topco members are frequently in as strong a competitive position in their respective areas as any other chain. The strength of this competitive position is due, in some measure, to the success of Topco-brand products. Although only 10% of the total goods sold by Topco members bear the association's brand names, the profit on these goods is substantial and their very existence has improved the competitive potential of Topco members with respect to other large and powerful chains.

It is apparent that from meager beginnings approximately a quarter of a century ago, Topco has developed into a purchasing association wholly owned and operated by member chains, which possess much economic muscle, individually as well as cooperatively.

II

Section 1 of the Sherman Act provides, in relevant part:

"Every contract, combination in the form of trust or otherwise, or conspiracy, in restraint of trade or commerce among the several States, or with foreign nations, is declared to be illegal. . . ."

The United States charged that, beginning at least as early as 1960 and continuing up to the time that the complaint was filed, Topco had combined and conspired with its members to violate § 1 in two respects. First, the Government alleged that there existed:

"a continuing agreement, understanding and concert of action among the co-conspirator member firms acting through Topco, the substantial terms of which have been and are that each [co-conspirator] or member firm will sell Topco-controlled brands only within the marketing territory allocated to it, and will refrain from selling Topco-controlled brands outside such marketing territory."

The division of marketing territories to which the complaint refers consists of a number of practices by the association.

Article IX, § 2, of the Topco bylaws establishes three categories of territorial licenses that members may secure from the association:

"(a) Exclusive—An exclusive territory is one in which the member is licensed to sell all products bearing specified trademarks of the Association, to the exclusion of all other persons.

"(b) Non-exclusive—A non-exclusive territory is one in which a member is licensed to sell all products bearing specified trademarks of the Association, but not to the exclusion of others who may also be licensed to sell products bearing the same trademarks of the Association in the same territory.

"(c) Coextensive—A coextensive territory is one in which two (2) or more members are licensed to sell all products bearing specified trademarks of the Association to the exclusion of all other persons. . . ."

When applying for membership, a chain must designate the type of license that it desires. Membership must first be approved by the board of directors, and thereafter by an affirmative vote of 75% of the association's members. If, however, the member whose operations are closest to those of the applicant, or any member whose operations are located within 100 miles of the applicant, votes against approval, an affirmative vote of 85% of the members is required for approval. Bylaws, Art. I, § 5. Because, as indicated by the record, members cooperate in accommodating each other's wishes, the procedure for approval provides, in essence, that members have a veto of sorts over actual or potential competition in the territorial areas in which they are concerned.

Following approval, each new member signs an agreement with Topco designating the territory in which that member may sell Topco-brand products. No member may sell these products outside the territory in which it is licensed. Most licenses are exclusive, and even those denominated "coextensive" or "non-exclusive" prove to be de facto exclusive. Exclusive territorial areas are often allocated to members who do no actual business in those areas on the theory that they may wish to expand at some indefinite future time and that expansion would likely be in the direction of the allocated territory. When combined with each member's veto power over new members, provisions for exclusivity work effectively to insulate members from competition in Topco-brand goods. Should a member violate its license agreement and sell in areas other than those in which it is licensed, its membership can be terminated under Art. IV, §§ 2(a) and 2(b) of the bylaws. Once a territory is classified as exclusive, either formally or de facto, it is extremely unlikely that the classification will ever be changed. See Bylaws, Art. IX.

The Government maintains that this scheme of dividing markets violates the Sherman Act because it operates to prohibit competition in Topco-brand products among grocery chains engaged in retail operations. The Government also makes a subsidiary challenge to Topco's practices regarding licensing members to sell at wholesale. Under the bylaws, members are not permitted to sell any products supplied by the association at wholesale, whether trademarked or not, without first applying for and receiving special permission from the association to do so.[6] Before permission is granted, other licensees (usually retailers),

---

[6]   Article IX, § 8, of the bylaws provides, in relevant part:

"Unless a member's membership and licensing agreement provides that such member may sell at wholesale, a member may not wholesale products supplied by the Association. If a membership and licensing agreement permits a member to sell at

whose interests may potentially be affected by wholesale operations, are consulted as to their wishes in the matter. If permission is obtained, the member must agree to restrict the sale of Topco products to a specific geographic area and to sell under any conditions imposed by the association. Permission to wholesale has often been sought by members, only to be denied by the association. The Government contends that this amounts not only to a territorial restriction violative of the Sherman Act, but also to a restriction on customers that in itself is violative of the Act.

Shortly before trial, Topco amended this bylaw with an addition that permitted any member to wholesale in the exclusive territories in which it retailed. But the restriction remained the same in all other cases.

It is apparent that this bylaw on its face applies whether or not the products sold are trademarked by Topco. Despite the fact that Topco's general manager testified at trial that, in practice, the restriction is confined to Topco-branded products, the District Court found that the bylaw is applied as written. We find nothing clearly erroneous in this finding. Assuming, arguendo, however, that the restriction is confined to products trademarked by Topco, the result in this case would not change.

From the inception of this lawsuit, Topco accepted as true most of the Government's allegations regarding territorial divisions and restrictions on wholesaling, although it differed greatly with the Government on the conclusions, both factual and legal, to be drawn from these facts.

Topco's answer to the complaint is illustrative of its posture in the District Court and before this Court:

> "Private label merchandising is a way of economic life in the food retailing industry, and exclusivity is the essence of a private label program; without exclusivity, a private label would not be private. Each national and large regional chain has its own exclusive private label products in addition to the nationally advertised brands which all chains sell. Each such chain relies upon the exclusivity of its own private label line to differentiate its private label products from those of its competitors and to attract and retain the repeat business and loyalty of consumers. Smaller retail grocery stores and chains are unable to compete effectively with the national and large regional chains without also offering their own exclusive private label products.
>
> The only feasible method by which Topco can procure private label products and assure the exclusivity thereof is through trademark licenses specifying the territory in which each member may sell such trademarked products."

---

wholesale, such member shall control the resale of products bearing trademarks of the Association so that such sales are confined to the territories granted to the member, and the method of selling shall conform in all respects with the Association's policies."

Topco essentially maintains that it needs territorial divisions to compete with larger chains; that the association could not exist if the territorial divisions were anything but exclusive; and that by restricting competition in the sale of Topco brand goods, the association actually increases competition by enabling its members to compete successfully with larger regional and national chains.

The District Court, considering all these things relevant to its decision, agreed with Topco. It recognized that the panoply of restraints that Topco imposed on its members worked to prevent competition in Topco-brand products, but concluded that

> "(w)hatever anti-competitive effect these practices may have on competition in the sale of Topco private label brands is far outweighed by the increased ability of Topco members to compete both with the national chains and other supermarkets operating in their respective territories."

The court held that Topco's practices were procompetitive and, therefore, consistent with the purposes of the antitrust laws. But we conclude that the District Court used an improper analysis in reaching its result.

III

On its face, § 1 of the Sherman Act appears to bar any combination of entrepreneurs so long as it is "in restraint of trade." Theoretically, all manufacturers, distributors, merchants, sellers, and buyers could be considered as potential competitors of each other. Were § 1 to be read in the narrowest possible way, any commercial contract could be deemed to violate it. Chicago Board of Trade v. United States, 246 U.S. 231, 238 (1918) (Brandeis, J.). The history underlying the formulation of the antitrust laws led this Court to conclude, however, that Congress did not intend to prohibit all contracts, nor even all contracts that might in some insignificant degree or attenuated sense restrain trade or competition. In lieu of the narrowest possible reading of § 1, the Court adopted a "rule of reason" analysis for determining whether most business combinations or contracts violate the prohibitions of the Sherman Act. Standard Oil Co. v. United States, 221 U.S. 1 (1911). An analysis of the reasonableness of particular restraints includes consideration of the facts peculiar to the business in which the restraint is applied, the nature of the restraint and its effects, and the history of the restraint and the reasons for its adoption. *Chicago Board of Trade v. United States*, supra, 246 U.S., at 238.

While the Court has utilized the "rule of reason" in evaluating the legality of most restraints alleged to be violative of the Sherman Act, it has also developed the doctrine that certain business relationships are per se violations of the Act without regard to a consideration of their reasonableness. In *Northern Pacific R. Co. v. United States*, 356 U.S. 1, 5

(1958), Mr. Justice Black explained the appropriateness of, and the need for, per se rules:

> "(T)here are certain agreements or practices which because of their pernicious effect on competition and lack of any redeeming virtue are conclusively presumed to be unreasonable and therefore illegal without elaborate inquiry as to the precise harm they have caused or the business excuse for their use. This principle of per se unreasonableness not only makes the type of restraints which are proscribed by the Sherman Act more certain to the benefit of everyone concerned, but it also avoids the necessity for an incredibly complicated and prolonged economic investigation into the entire history of the industry involved, as well as related industries, in an effort to determine at large whether a particular restraint has been unreasonable—an inquiry so often wholly fruitless when undertaken."

It is only after considerable experience with certain business relationships that courts classify them as per se violations of the Sherman Act. One of the classic examples of a per se violation of § 1 is an agreement between competitors at the same level of the market structure to allocate territories in order to minimize competition. Such concerted action is usually termed a "horizontal" restraint, in contradistinction to combinations of persons at different levels of the market structure, e.g., manufacturers and distributors, which are termed "vertical" restraints. This Court has reiterated time and time again that "(h)orizontal territorial limitations . . . arc naked restraints of trade with no purpose except stifling of competition." White Motor Co. v. United States, 372 U.S. 253, 263 (1963). Such limitations are per se violations of the Sherman Act.

We think that it is clear that the restraint in this case is a horizontal one, and, therefore, a per se violation of § 1. The District Court failed to make any determination as to whether there were per se horizontal territorial restraints in this case and simply applied a rule of reason in reaching its conclusions that the restraints were not illegal. In so doing, the District Court erred.

United States v. Sealy, Inc., [388 U.S. 350 (1967)], is, in fact, on all fours with this case. Sealy licensed manufacturers of mattresses and bedding to make and sell products using the Sealy trademark. Like Topco, Sealy was a corporation owned almost entirely by its licensees, who elected the Board of Directors and controlled the business. Just as in this case, Sealy agreed with the licensees not to license other manufacturers or sellers to sell Sealy-brand products in a designated territory in exchange for the promise of the licensee who sold in that territory not to expand its sales beyond the area demarcated by Sealy.

The Court held that this was a horizontal territorial restraint, which was per se violative of the Sherman Act.

Whether or not we would decide this case the same way under the rule of reason used by the District Court is irrelevant to the issue before us. The fact is that courts are of limited utility in examining difficult economic problems. Our inability to weigh, in any meaningful sense, destruction of competition in one sector of the economy against promotion of competition in another sector is one important reason we have formulated per se rules.

Without the per se rules, businessmen would be left with little to aid them in predicting in any particular case what courts will find to be legal and illegal under the Sherman Act. Should Congress ultimately determine that predictability is unimportant in this area of the law, it can, of course, make per se rules inapplicable in some or all cases, and leave courts free to ramble through the wilds of economic theory in order to maintain a flexible approach.

In applying these rigid rules, the Court has consistently rejected the notion that naked restraints of trade are to be tolerated because they are well intended or because they are allegedly developed to increase competition.

Antitrust laws in general, and the Sherman Act in particular, are the Magna Carta of free enterprise. They are as important to the preservation of economic freedom and our free-enterprise system as the Bill of Rights is to the protection of our fundamental personal freedoms. And the freedom guaranteed each and every business, no matter how small, is the freedom to compete—to assert with vigor, imagination, devotion, and ingenuity whatever economic muscle it can muster. Implicit in such freedom is the notion that it cannot be foreclosed with respect to one sector of the economy because certain private citizens or groups believe that such foreclosure might promote greater competition in a more important sector of the economy.

The District Court determined that by limiting the freedom of its individual members to compete with each other, Topco was doing a greater good by fostering competition between members and other large supermarket chains. But, the fallacy in this is that Topco has no authority under the Sherman Act to determine the respective values of competition in various sectors of the economy. On the contrary, the Sherman Act gives to each Topco member and to each prospective member the right to ascertain for itself whether or not competition with other supermarket chains is more desirable than competition in the sale of Topco-brand products. Without territorial restrictions, Topco members may indeed "(cut) each other's throats." *Cf. White Motor Co.*, 372 U.S., at

278 (Clark, J. dissenting). But we have never found this possibility sufficient to warrant condoning horizontal restraints of trade.

The Court has previously noted with respect to price fixing, another per se violation of the Sherman Act, that:

> "The reasonable price fixed today may through economic and business changes become the unreasonable price of tomorrow. Once established, it may be maintained unchanged because of the absence of competition secured by the agreement for a price reasonable when fixed." *United States v. Trenton Potteries Co.*, 273 U.S. 392, 397 (1927).

A similar observation can be made with regard to territorial limitations. *White Motor Co.*, *supra*, 372 U.S., at 265 n. 2 (Brennan, J., concurring).

There have been tremendous departures from the notion of a free-enterprise system as it was originally conceived in this country. These departures have been the product of congressional action and the will of the people. If a decision is to be made to sacrifice competition in one portion of the economy for greater competition in another portion this too is a decision that must be made by Congress and not by private forces or by the courts. Private forces are too keenly aware of their own interests in making such decisions and courts are ill-equipped and ill-situated for such decision making. To analyze, interpret, and evaluate the myriad of competing interests and the endless data that would surely be brought to bear on such decisions, and to make the delicate judgment on the relative values to society of competitive areas of the economy, the judgment of the elected representatives of the people is required.

Just as the territorial restrictions on retailing Topco-brand products must fall, so must the territorial restrictions on wholesaling. The considerations are the same, and the Sherman Act requires identical results.

We also strike down Topco's other restrictions on the right of its members to wholesale goods. These restrictions amount to regulation of the customers to whom members of Topco may sell Topco-brand goods. Like territorial restrictions, limitations on customers are intended to limit intra-brand competition and to promote inter-brand competition. For the reasons previously discussed, the arena in which Topco members compete must be left to their unfettered choice absent a contrary congressional determination.

We reverse the judgment of the District Court and remand the case for entry of an appropriate decree.

NOTES & QUESTIONS

(1)   In what ways did Topco allegedly violate the Sherman Act? How did Topco defend its actions?

(2)   What approach did the district court take in finding for Topco? Why did the Supreme Court disagree with this approach?

(3)   In *Topco*, Justice Marshall gave a rather colorful description of the Sherman Act:

> Antitrust laws in general, and the Sherman Act in particular, are the Magna Carta of free enterprise. They are as important to the preservation of economic freedom and our free-enterprise system as the Bill of Rights is to the protection of our fundamental personal freedoms. And the freedom guaranteed each and every business, no matter how small, is the freedom to compete—to assert with vigor, imagination, devotion, and ingenuity whatever economic muscle it can muster. Implicit in such freedom is the notion that it cannot be foreclosed with respect to one sector of the economy because certain private citizens or groups believe that such foreclosure might promote greater competition in a more important sector of the economy.

Do you see anything inconsistent with this passage and the result in *Topco*?

(4)   *Topco* involved horizontal market allocation, a non-price form of horizontal restraint, which typically is treated as a per se violation. Other recognized non-price per se violations include certain group boycotts (which are typically horizontal restraints) and some tie-in arrangements (which are typically vertical restraints).

(5)   The term "group boycott" (or concerted refusal to deal) generally refers to an agreement among competitors not to deal with, or to deal only on certain terms with, other actors. It should be noted that nothing under § 1 prohibits unilateral refusals to deal with other parties. Such refusals are generally not thought to affect competition unless they are part of an effort to monopolize a relevant market. (Section 2 of the Sherman Act prohibits monopolization or attempted monopolization by a single firm.)

In *Klor's Inc. v. Broadway-Hale Stores, Inc.*, 359 U.S. 207 (1959), the Supreme Court established the per se illegality of concerted refusals to deal and offered a classic example of such an arrangement. Klor's, a retail store selling household goods and appliances in San Francisco, California, alleged that Broadway-Hale, a chain department store located right next to Klor's, had caused ten national manufacturers and their distributors to refuse to sell to Klor's (or to sell only at high prices and on unfavorable terms). Apparently, Broadway-Hale was able to effectuate this alleged boycott due to its superior buying power. Rather than dispute the allegations, the defendants (Broadway-Hale and the ten manufacturers and distributors) sought dismissal based on the fact that there were hundreds of other household appliance retailers in the area selling the same goods (including the defendants' goods), and therefore the consuming public was not injured.

The lower courts agreed with the defendants, but the Supreme Court reversed. The Court made clear that group boycotts could not be saved by lack of injury or any other sort of reasonableness defense:

> Group boycotts, or concerted refusals by traders to deal with other traders, have long been held to be in the forbidden category. They have not been saved by allegations that they were reasonable in the specific circumstances, nor by a failure to show that they fixed or regulated prices, parceled out or limited production, or brought about a deterioration in quality. Even when they operated to lower prices or temporarily to stimulate competition they were banned. For, as this Court said in *Kiefer-Stewart Co. v. Joseph E. Seagram & Sons*, 340 U.S. 211, 213, "such agreements, no less than those to fix minimum prices, cripple the freedom of traders and thereby restrain their ability to sell in accordance with their own judgment."

Klor's, 359 U.S. at 212.

In *Klor's*, you may have noticed that the agreement involved both a horizontal aspect (the agreement among competitors not to sell to Klor's) and a vertical aspect (Broadway-Hale was a retailer rather than a competitor of the suppliers). Purely vertical refusals to deal have not been characterized as per se illegal; however, courts have applied the per se characterization when there is a horizontal aspect to the conspiracy. *See, e.g., United States v. Gen. Motors Corp.*, 384 U.S. 127, 145 (1966) ("There can be no doubt that the effect of the combination or conspiracy here was to restrain trade and commerce within the meaning of the Sherman Act. Elimination, by joint collaborative action, of discounters from access to the market is a per se violation of the Act.").

ANHEUSER BUSCH, INC. V. GOODMAN

745 F. Supp. 1048 (M.D. Pa. 1990)

CALDWELL, DISTRICT JUDGE.

The parties have cross-moved for summary judgment pursuant to Fed. R. Civ. Pro. 56. Plaintiff, Anheuser-Busch, Inc., challenges certain Pennsylvania Liquor Control Board (LCB) regulations, set forth in 40 Pa.Code §§ 11.201 and 11.202, as precluding price competition between manufacturers in violation of the Sherman Act, 15 U.S.C. § 1 *et seq.* Plaintiff requests an injunction against enforcement of the regulations and a declaration that they are invalid. Defendants are the members of the Pennsylvania Liquor Control Board. . . .

Defendants' motion argues: (1) that the LCB is the sovereign for purposes of controlling beer sales in Pennsylvania and hence cannot be sued; (2) alternatively, the LCB was authorized by the sovereign to promulgate the contested regulations and its conduct was accordingly "state action" exempt from review by this Court; and (3) that this Court lacks subject matter jurisdiction over plaintiff's Sherman anti-trust claim because plaintiff failed to establish the requisite "substantial effect" of the regulation on interstate commerce.

I.   *Sovereign Immunity*

We begin our analysis of these matters with the "state action" issue. The state action defense holds the Sherman Act inapplicable "to the anti-competitive conduct of a state acting through its legislature." *Town of Hallie v. City of Eau Claire,* 471 U.S. 34, 38 (1985) (interpreting the so-called *Parker* immunity established in *Parker v. Brown,* 317 U.S. 341 (1943)). The defense must meet two conditions:

"First, the challenged restraint must be 'one clearly articulated and affirmatively expressed as State policy'; second, the policy must be 'actively supervised' by the State itself."

324 Liquor Corp. v. Duffy, 479 U.S. 335, 343 (1987).

Defendants contend that the LCB's conduct is action of the sovereign, the Commonwealth of Pennsylvania, because the LCB is the state agency empowered with the duty to regulate the sale of alcoholic beverages in accordance with express state law. Defendant relies exclusively on *Hoover v. Ronwin,* 466 U.S. 558 (1984) to support this position. However, *Hoover* is readily distinguishable in that it granted immunity to a state supreme court acting legislatively, rather than, as here, an agency acting administratively. The court stated:

> Closer analysis is required when the activity at issue is not directly that of the legislature or supreme court, but is carried out by others pursuant to state authorization. . . . In such cases, it becomes important to ensure that the anti-competitive conduct of the State's representative was contemplated by the State.

Hoover, 466 U.S. at 568. We find that for purposes of immunity the LCB was an agency, and not a legislature or sovereign body.

As defendants cannot claim immunity they argue alternatively that their enactment and enforcement of regulations was "state action" according to the two-tiered test, outlined in *324 Liquor Corp., supra.* We disagree with defendants' position, however, and find that the challenged regulations fail to be "affirmatively articulated" in state policy or "actively supervised" by the Commonwealth.

     . . . .

II.   *Interstate Commerce*

The second defense raised by defendants is that their pricing regulations have no substantial effect on interstate commerce, thereby precluding review by this Court due to lack of subject matter jurisdiction. Defendants contend that because the Sherman Act is derived from the Commerce Clause of the Constitution, the plaintiff must meet the "substantial effect" test in order to maintain its anti-trust claim in this forum.

All that is required to establish jurisdiction for a claim alleging a Sherman Act violation is that an "appreciable amount" of interstate commerce be involved in the business which is subject to the contested regulation. *McLain v. Real Estate Board of New Orleans, Inc.*, 444 U.S. 232 (1980). The activities being restricted in the present case need only take place in interstate commerce and there is no requirement for a showing that the challenged regulation itself substantially affects interstate commerce. *McLain*, 444 U.S. at 243, 245. It is undisputed that plaintiff's business is involved in interstate commerce—it is a Missouri corporation which sells beer nationwide, including beer sales in Pennsylvania which constitute approximately 26.7% of the Pennsylvania market. Based on these facts alone we have subject matter jurisdiction over plaintiff's anti-trust claim.

III. *Sherman Act Violation*

As we have rejected the defenses of sovereign immunity, "state action," and lack of jurisdiction, our analysis turns directly to the alleged Sherman Act violation. Section 1 of the Act prohibits unreasonable restraints of trade effected by agreements or conspiracies among private parties to fix prices. It has been long held that the maintenance of prices prevents competition among those who trade in competing goods. *Dr. Miles Medical Co. v. John D. Park & Sons*, 220 U.S. 373, 407 (1911).

The challenged regulations prohibit a manufacturer from increasing a price to distributors within a 180 day period after making any reduction in price. 40 Pa.Code § 11.201(b). This limit is also applicable any time a manufacturer introduces a new brand or package. 40 Pa.Code § 11.201(c). The initial reduction in price must be reflected throughout the chain of distribution (i.e. the importing distributor must charge the reduced price to the distributor, who must in turn charge the reduced price to the retailer, etc.). The regulations further provide that whenever the manufacturer reduces a price to any distributor it must reduce the price to all other distributors across Pennsylvania in an equal amount. 40 Pa.Code § 11.201(d). Upon review of the applicable law we conclude that the regulations are equivalent to private price-fixing and price-maintenance schemes which violate section 1 of the Sherman Act.

State liquor boards in the past have argued that when there is no agreement or concerted activity among manufacturers and wholesalers, the Sherman Act's proscription against price-fixing does not apply to liquor board regulations. They claim that when independent manufacturers individually comply with their regulations, the lack of concerted activity is considered "unilateral action" and is therefore immune from scrutiny under the Act.

However, the Supreme Court has consistently held that when price maintenance by individual parties is facilitated or compelled by state regulation competition is destroyed as effectively as if private parties formed an agreement not to compete. In other words, by forcing manufacturers to engage in price-fixing by threatening penalties, the state "compels activity that would otherwise be a *per se* violation of the Sherman Act," [*Miller v. Hedlund*, 813 F.2d 1344, 1349 (9th Cir. 1987)], and the regulation itself effectively impedes competition, thereby violating the Act. This point is expressed by the Supreme Court in *Rice,* as follows:

> A state statute, when considered in the abstract, may be condemned under the antitrust laws only if it mandates or authorizes conduct that necessarily constitutes a violation of the antitrust laws in all cases, or if it places irresistible pressure on a private party to violate the antitrust laws in order to comply with the statute.

[*Rice v. Norman Williams Co.*, 458 U.S. 654, 661 (1982)].

The LCB's threat to issue citations to private producers who refuse to adhere to its price maintenance scheme is a form of compulsion. The LCB's regulations effectively force private beer manufacturers to engage in price-fixing which is unlawful *per se*. The LCB's regulations *require* private manufacturers to maintain prices involuntarily and by doing so, the regulations, by their own terms, force agreements[9] to take place which violate anti-trust restrictions. The regulations themselves, therefore, violate the Sherman Act as they facilitate anti-competitive agreements.

Our conclusions are supported by *Miller*, in which regulations which parallel those at issue were declared violative of the Sherman Act. The Court stated:

> An agreement to adhere to previously announced prices and terms of sale is unlawful *per se* under the Sherman Act, "even though advance price announcements are perfectly lawful and even though the particular prices and terms *were not themselves fixed by private agreement*." *Catalano, Inc. v. Target Sales, Inc.,* 446 U.S. 643, 647 (1980) (*per curiam*), *discussing Sugar Institute v. United States*, 297 U.S. 553 (1936) (emphasis added).

---

[9] The challenged regulations require beer producers to fix prices which wholesalers must agree to before they, in turn, sell at that "agreed" price to distributors. This arrangement can be considered an anti-competitive "agreement" between the wholesaler and producer which was mandated by the state.

. . . .

While it is true that there is no agreement or concerted activity among the wholesalers, it cannot be ignored that the challenged regulations facilitate the exchange of price information and requires adherence to the publicly posted prices. In other words, the state compels activity that would otherwise be a *per se* violation of the Sherman Act.

. . . .

Schwegmann [*Bros. v. Calvert Distillers Corp.*, 341 U.S. 384 (1951)] demonstrates that a showing of concerted activity among the Oregon wholesalers is not necessary to establish an antitrust violation. The mere fact that each wholesaler complies unilaterally with the regulations does not save the impermissible pricing scheme from an antitrust challenge. In *Schwegmann,* non-contracting retailers were compelled to comply unilaterally with a state-authorized pricing scheme, but the absence of concerted activity among the retailers was not a bar to a finding of a Sherman Act violation.

Miller, 813 F.2d at 1349–51. The Court relied on the language in *Fisher v. City of Berkeley*, 475 U.S. 260 (1986) which stated:

Not all restraints imposed upon private actors by government units necessarily constitute unilateral action outside the purview of section 1. Certain restraints may be characterized as "hybrid," in that nonmarket mechanisms merely enforce private marketing decisions. . . . Where private actors are thus granted "a degree of private regulatory power," . . . the *regulatory scheme may be attacked under section 1.* Indeed, this Court has twice found such hybrid restraints to violate the Sherman Act.

Berkeley, 475 U.S. at 267–68.

Based on the above precedent we find that the LCB regulations are invalid under the Sherman Act. Any regulation tending to stabilize prices, insulate prices from the flexibility of the free market, or impede a manufacturer's ability to employ market strategies through short-term or geographically-based price promotions is counter to the broad thrust of the Sherman Act. The LCB's regulations intrude in all of these areas.

The challenged LCB regulations impose administrative penalties on manufacturers who fail to stabilize their prices accordingly, thereby compelling manufacturers to comply with the anti-competitive restrictions promulgated by the LCB. Manufacturers, like the plaintiff, are unable to engage in competitive short-term price reductions or "promotions" without courting a penalty from the LCB. Moreover, the LCB regulation requiring manufacturers to maintain the same price to all distributors in the state creates a bar to flexibility in geographic promotions, which are based on different markets and competition levels for various locations in Pennsylvania.

The Supreme Court in *Schwegmann* held invalid a statute which compelled a private manufacturer and other retailers to maintain the same prices throughout the chain of distribution. The Court stated, "When a state compels retailers to follow a parallel price policy, it *demands* private conduct which the Sherman Act forbids." *Id.*

. . . .

In [*California Retail Liquor Dealers Ass'n v. Midcal Aluminum, Inc.*, 445 U.S. 97 (1980)], a California statute compelled wholesalers to announce and maintain their price. The Court held that regardless of the absence of concerted activity among private parties, the statute required price maintenance inconsistent with the Sherman Act and therefore was invalid. The Court reasoned that a state's "vertical control" over individual manufacturers "*destroys horizontal competition* as effectively as if wholesalers formed a combination [conspiracy] and endeavored to establish the same restrictions by agreement with each other." *Id.* [at 102] (emphasis added).

The courts in *Miller*, *Schwegmann*, *Rice*, and *Midcal* held that regulations which force compliance with price maintenance schemes, like the LCB regulations, violate the Sherman Act. Defendants only discuss the *Miller* case and contend that it is inapplicable to the case at bar. Defendants, however, distinguish *Miller* based only on its "state action" findings, and we have already refuted the "state action" defense. Defendants fail to distinguish *Miller* on findings of Sherman Act violations, or establish that the 180-day price maintenance regulations in *Miller* were different than the LCB regulations.

Furthermore, defendants allege that the General Assembly of Pennsylvania intended their promulgation of anti-competitive regulations and that the LCB followed that authorization. In defendants' reply brief they state: "Undoubtedly, in Pennsylvania the General Assembly replaced manufacturer's competitive freedom with a complex, severely restrictive statutory and regulatory scheme." As noted, we have rejected defendants' claim that the LCB regulations are exempt from Sherman Act inquiry based on the "state action" doctrine. Thus, we treat defendants' argument as a concession that the regulations are in fact anti-competitive. Defendants rely strictly on defenses of immunity and jurisdiction and do not otherwise dispute that the regulations in fact conflict with the Sherman Act. We conclude, therefore, that no material issue of fact remains in dispute.

NOTES & QUESTIONS

(1) The regulation at issue had the effect of maintaining lower prices. How is this anti-competitive? Don't lower prices help consumers?

(2) Instead of concerted action by the individual manufacturers, this behavior was mandated by a regulation. According to the court, does that matter?

(3) *Goodman* involved what is known as a horizontal price restraint. These restraints are price-fixing agreements, and they have traditionally been subject to a per se analysis. The most obvious example of such an agreement is when a group of manufacturers agrees that its products will not be sold below a specified minimum price (or that a certain profit margin will be maintained). According to the Department of Justice, price-fixing agreements might also seek to do one or more of the following:

- establish or adhere to uniform price discounts;

- eliminate discounts;

- adopt a standard formula for the computation of selling prices;

- notify others prior to reducing prices;

- fix credit terms; or

- maintain predetermined price differentials between different quantities, types, or sizes of products.

U.S. DEP'T OF JUSTICE, AN ANTITRUST PRIMER FOR FEDERAL LAW ENFORCEMENT PERSONNEL (2005), *available at* http://www.justice.gov/atr/public/guidelines/209114.htm (last visited Oct. 1, 2015).

(4) Closely analogous to price fixing is the per se illegal practice of bid rigging. Bid rigging is a method of effectively raising prices where purchasers—often federal, state, or local governments—acquire goods or services by soliciting competing bids. The most typical arrangement is for competitors to agree in advance on who will submit the winning bid. For example, in *United States v. Portsmouth Paving Corp.*, 694 F.2d 312, 320 (4th Cir. 1982), paving contractors were alleged to have conspired with each other to withhold bids, or to submit artificially high "complimentary" bids, on certain scheduled and nonscheduled resurfacing projects in a number of cities in Virginia. Starting in 1963 and continuing until 1979, the contractors held annual secret meetings where project allocations were discussed. A jury found certain defendants guilty of violating § 1 of the Sherman Act. The Fourth Circuit upheld the convictions, explaining its per se approach as follows:

> Price fixing agreements are typical of those agreements per se violative of the Sherman Act. Even more egregiously contrary to vital competition among businesses, however, is the contract allocation agreement charged in the instant case. Such an accord eliminates not only price competition, but also competition in

service and product quality. Moreover, the collusive bid rigging dimension of the conspiracy charged makes the arrangement little less than a cartel, which is never legally nor economically justifiable. The undisputed effect is to force the contracting government entities to pay more for the goods and services sought than they would " 'had there been free competition in the open market.' " *United States ex rel. Marcus v. Hess*, 317 U.S. 537, 539 n. 1 (1943) (circuit court's description of "collusive bidding scheme" to defraud the United States); *see United States v. Bensinger Co.*, 430 F.2d 584, 589 (8th Cir.1970) (bid rigging agreement is "price-fixing agreement of the simplest kind"). As a result, we do not hesitate to conclude that the Government was not required to establish the unreasonableness of the conspiracy charged.

Portsmouth Paving Corp., 694 F.2d at 317–18.

(5) What is the justification for treating certain agreements as per se violations of the Sherman Act?

b. The Rule of Reason

We have discussed horizontal per se violations, but what of conduct that does not rise to the level of a per se violation? Courts have analyzed such cases under what has been termed the "rule of reason." In *DeLong Equipment Co. v. Washington Mills Abrasive Co.*, 887 F.2d 1499 (11th Cir. 1989), the court described the rule of reason as follows:

> It requires a weighing of the relevant circumstances of a case to decide whether a restrictive practice constitutes an unreasonable restraint on competition. Under the rule of reason, the factfinder weighs all of the circumstances of a case in deciding whether a restrictive practice should be prohibited as imposing an unreasonable restraint on competition. The burden of proving unreasonable effects on competition in a rule of reason case rests with the antitrust plaintiff. Among other things, this means that the plaintiff must allege and prove that the defendants' conduct had a significant anticompetitive effect in a defined product market.

Id. at 1507.

A rule of reason analysis essentially involves three steps. The first step consists of defining the relevant market affected by the agreement. The second step is determining whether the actors involved collectively have market power. The term "market power" is often synonymous with "monopoly power," and the terms generally refer to anticompetitive economic power that ultimately can compromise consumer welfare.[a] The

---

[a] For a discussion of the possible differences in meaning between "market power" and "monopoly power," see Thomas G. Krattenmaker, Robert H. Lande & Steven C. Salop, *Monopoly*

third step is a weighing of the competitive justifications against the anticompetitive effects. Under this step, a court must evaluate the defendant's actions to see if they are reasonably necessary to the accomplishment of legitimate goals and narrowly tailored to those ends.

For some time, courts examined antitrust claims using either a per se analysis or a rule of reason analysis (if the complained-of activity did not fit into one of the per se categories). As we will see in the following case, however, the Supreme Court has backed away from such a bright-line distinction.

NATIONAL COLLEGIATE ATHLETIC ASSOCIATION V. BOARD OF REGENTS OF THE UNIVERSITY OF OKLAHOMA
468 U.S. 85 (1984)

STEVENS, J.

The University of Oklahoma and the University of Georgia contend that the National Collegiate Athletic Association has unreasonably restrained trade in the televising of college football games. After an extended trial, the District Court found that the NCAA had violated § 1 of the Sherman Act and granted injunctive relief. The Court of Appeals agreed that the statute had been violated but modified the remedy in some respects. We granted certiorari, and now affirm.

[The NCAA had a television plan in place for college football games which limited the number of games that could be shown and the number of times a particular team's games could be shown. The plan was created in the 1950s due to a concern that televised games would affect the live attendance of games. From 1952–1977, an NCAA television committee developed these plans. The plans were then voted upon by the NCAA, of which there were 800 voting members (only 135 of whom were playing Division I football at the time). Once approved, these plans were the subject of negotiations with the television networks.

In 1977, the NCAA entered into a 4-year contract granting exclusive rights to ABC for the 1978–1981 seasons (ABC had held such rights since 1965). Another plan was issued for the 1982–1985 seasons which allowed two networks to show fourteen games each (ABC and CBS won the contracts). The contracts set forth a minimum aggregate compensation to be paid to participating schools in an amount that totaled $131,750,000. In effect, this fixed the price to be paid to the schools for showing their games. There were also restrictions on which teams the networks would

---

Power and Market Power in Antitrust Law, 76 GEO. L.J. 241, 246–49 (1987) ("We believe that market power and monopoly power are qualitatively identical concepts—both terms refer to anticompetitive economic power that ultimately can compromise consumer welfare. Courts should be less concerned with labeling the type of anticompetitive economic power exerted by a firm; rather, they should focus on the methods by which this power is achieved.").

televise (a minimum of 82 different schools were required to be shown) and limits on how often any one team could appear (no more than six times and only four national broadcasts).

A sub-group of NCAA schools formed the College Football Association ("CFA"), which was made up of the major football-playing schools. The CFA wanted a greater say in the television plan and entered into a preliminary agreement with NBC. The NCAA threatened sanctions against any member school that complied with the NBC agreement. The University of Oklahoma sought to obtain a preliminary injunction preventing the NCAA from initiating disciplinary proceedings and from interfering with the NBC agreement. Ultimately, however, the NCAA's threats worked and the NBC agreement was never consummated.]

Decision of the District Court

After a full trial, the District Court held that the controls exercised by the NCAA over the televising of college football games violated the Sherman Act. The District Court defined the relevant market as "live college football television" because it found that alternative programming has a significantly different and lesser audience appeal. The District Court then concluded that the NCAA controls over college football are those of a "classic cartel". . . .

The District Court found that competition in the relevant market had been restrained in three ways: (1) NCAA fixed the price for particular telecasts; (2) its exclusive network contracts were tantamount to a group boycott of all other potential broadcasters and its threat of sanctions against its own members constituted a threatened boycott of potential competitors; and (3) its plan placed an artificial limit on the production of televised college football.

In the District Court the NCAA offered two principal justifications for its television policies: that they protected the gate attendance of its members and that they tended to preserve a competitive balance among the football programs of the various schools. The District Court rejected the first justification because the evidence did not support the claim that college football television adversely affected gate attendance. With respect to the "competitive balance" argument, the District Court found that the evidence failed to show that the NCAA regulations on matters such as recruitment and the standards for preserving amateurism were not sufficient to maintain an appropriate balance.

Decision of the Court of Appeals

The Court of Appeals held that the NCAA television plan constituted illegal per se price fixing. It rejected each of the three arguments advanced by NCAA to establish the procompetitive character of its plan. First, the court rejected the argument that the television plan promoted live attendance, noting that since the plan involved a concomitant reduction in viewership [by restricting broadcast rights,] the plan did not result in a net increase in output and hence was not procompetitive. Second, the Court of Appeals rejected as illegitimate the NCAA's purpose of promoting athletically balanced competition. It held that such a consideration amounted to an argument that "competition will destroy the market"—a position inconsistent with the policy of the Sherman Act. Moreover, assuming arguendo that the justification was legitimate, the court agreed with the District Court's finding "that any contribution the plan made to athletic balance could be achieved by less restrictive means." Third, the Court of Appeals refused to view the NCAA plan as competitively justified by the need to compete effectively with other types of television programming, since it entirely eliminated competition between producers of football and hence was illegal per se.

Finally, the Court of Appeals concluded that even if the television plan were not per se illegal, its anticompetitive limitation on price and output was not offset by any procompetitive justification sufficient to save the plan even when the totality of the circumstances was examined. . . .

II

There can be no doubt that the challenged practices of the NCAA constitute a "restraint of trade" in the sense that they limit members' freedom to negotiate and enter into their own television contracts. In that sense, however, every contract is a restraint of trade, and as we have repeatedly recognized, the Sherman Act was intended to prohibit only unreasonable restraints of trade.

It is also undeniable that these practices share characteristics of restraints we have previously held unreasonable. The NCAA is an association of schools which compete against each other to attract television revenues, not to mention fans and athletes. As the District Court found, the policies of the NCAA with respect to television rights are ultimately controlled by the vote of member institutions. By participating in an association which prevents member institutions from competing against each other on the basis of price or kind of television rights that can be offered to broadcasters, the NCAA member institutions have created a horizontal restraint—an agreement among competitors on the way in which they will compete with one another. A restraint of this type has often been held to be unreasonable as a matter of law. Because it places a ceiling on the number of games member institutions may televise, the horizontal agreement places an artificial limit on the quantity of televised football that is available to broadcasters and consumers. By restraining the quantity of television rights available for sale, the challenged practices create a limitation on output; our cases have held that such limitations are unreasonable restraints of trade.[19] Moreover, the District Court found that the minimum aggregate price in fact operates to preclude any price negotiation between broadcasters and institutions, thereby constituting horizontal price fixing, perhaps the paradigm of an unreasonable restraint of trade.

Horizontal price fixing and output limitation are ordinarily condemned as a matter of law under an "illegal per se" approach because the probability that these practices are anticompetitive is so high; a per se rule is applied when "the practice facially appears to be one that would always or almost always tend to restrict competition and decrease output." *Broadcast Music, Inc. v. Columbia Broadcasting System, Inc.*, 441 U.S. 1, 19–20 (1979). In such circumstances a restraint is presumed unreasonable without inquiry into the particular market context in which it is found. Nevertheless, we have decided that it would be inappropriate to apply a per se rule to this case. This decision is not based on a lack of judicial experience with this type of arrangement,[21] on the fact that the NCAA is organized as a nonprofit entity,[22] or on our respect for the NCAA's historic role in the preservation and encouragement of intercollegiate amateur athletics.[23] Rather, what is critical is that this case involves an industry in which horizontal restraints on competition are essential if the product is to be available at all.

As Judge Bork has noted: "[S]ome activities can only be carried out jointly. Perhaps the leading example is league sports. When a league of professional lacrosse teams is formed, it would be pointless to declare their cooperation illegal on the ground that there are no other professional lacrosse teams." R. Bork, The Antitrust Paradox 278 (1978). What the NCAA and its member institutions market in this case is competition itself—contests between competing institutions. Of course, this would be completely ineffective if there were no rules on which the competitors agreed to create and define the competition to be marketed. A myriad of rules affecting such matters as the size of the field, the number of players on a team, and the extent to which physical violence is to be encouraged or proscribed, all must be agreed upon, and all restrain the manner in which institutions compete. Moreover, the NCAA seeks to

---

[19] *See, e.g., United States v. Topco Associates, Inc.*, [405 U.S. 596, 608–609 (1972)].

[21] While judicial inexperience with a particular arrangement counsels against extending the reach of per se rules, the likelihood that horizontal price and output restrictions are anticompetitive is generally sufficient to justify application of the per se rule without inquiry into the special characteristics of a particular industry.

[22] There is no doubt that the sweeping language of § 1 applies to nonprofit entities, and in the past we have imposed antitrust liability on nonprofit entities which have engaged in anticompetitive conduct. . . .

[23] While as the guardian of an important American tradition, the NCAA's motives must be accorded a respectful presumption of validity, it is nevertheless well settled that good motives will not validate an otherwise anticompetitive practice. See *United States v. Griffith*, 334 U.S. 100, 105–106 (1948).

market a particular brand of football—college football. The identification of this "product" with an academic tradition differentiates college football from and makes it more popular than professional sports to which it might otherwise be comparable, such as, for example, minor league baseball. In order to preserve the character and quality of the "product," athletes must not be paid, must be required to attend class, and the like. And the integrity of the "product" cannot be preserved except by mutual agreement; if an institution adopted such restrictions unilaterally, its effectiveness as a competitor on the playing field might soon be destroyed. Thus, the NCAA plays a vital role in enabling college football to preserve its character, and as a result enables a product to be marketed which might otherwise be unavailable. In performing this role, its actions widen consumer choice—not only the choices available to sports fans but also those available to athletes—and hence can be viewed as procompetitive.

Broadcast Music squarely holds that a joint selling arrangement may be so efficient that it will increase sellers' aggregate output and thus be procompetitive. Similarly, as we indicated in *Continental T.V., Inc. v. GTE Sylvania Inc.*, 433 U.S. 36, 51–57 (1977), a restraint in a limited aspect of a market may actually enhance marketwide competition. Respondents concede that the great majority of the NCAA's regulations enhance competition among member institutions. Thus, despite the fact that this case involves restraints on the ability of member institutions to compete in terms of price and output, a fair evaluation of their competitive character requires consideration of the NCAA's justifications for the restraints.

Our analysis of this case under the Rule of Reason, of course, does not change the ultimate focus of our inquiry. Both per se rules and the Rule of Reason are employed "to form a judgment about the competitive significance of the restraint." *National Society of Professional Engineers v. United States*, 435 U.S. 679, 692 (1978). A conclusion that a restraint of trade is unreasonable may be "based either (1) on the nature or character of the contracts, or (2) on surrounding circumstances giving rise to the inference or presumption that they were intended to restrain trade and enhance prices. Under either branch of the test, the inquiry is confined to a consideration of impact on competitive conditions." Id., at 690 (footnotes omitted).

Per se rules are invoked when surrounding circumstances make the likelihood of anticompetitive conduct so great as to render unjustified further examination of the challenged conduct. But whether the ultimate finding is the product of a presumption or actual market analysis, the essential inquiry remains the same—whether or not the challenged restraint enhances competition.[26] Under the Sherman Act the criterion to

---

[26] Indeed, there is often no bright line separating per se from Rule of Reason analysis. Per se rules may require considerable inquiry into market conditions before the evidence justifies a

be used in judging the validity of a restraint on trade is its impact on competition.

III

Because it restrains price and output, the NCAA's television plan has a significant potential for anticompetitive effects.[28] The findings of the District Court indicate that this potential has been realized. The District Court found that if member institutions were free to sell television rights, many more games would be shown on television, and that the NCAA's output restriction has the effect of raising the price the networks pay for television rights. Moreover, the court found that by fixing a price for television rights to all games, the NCAA creates a price structure that is unresponsive to viewer demand and unrelated to the prices that would prevail in a competitive market. And, of course, since as a practical matter all member institutions need NCAA approval, members have no real choice but to adhere to the NCAA's television controls.[31]

The anticompetitive consequences of this arrangement are apparent. Individual competitors lose their freedom to compete. Price is higher and output lower than they would otherwise be, and both are unresponsive to consumer preference.[33] This latter point is perhaps the most significant,

---

presumption of anticompetitive conduct. For example, while the Court has spoken of a "per se" rule against tying arrangements, it has also recognized that tying may have procompetitive justifications that make it inappropriate to condemn without considerable market analysis. See *Jefferson Parish Hospital Dist. No. 2 v. Hyde*, [466 U.S. 2, 11–12 (1984)].

[28] In this connection, it is not without significance that Congress felt the need to grant professional sports an exemption from the antitrust laws for joint marketing of television rights. See 15 U.S.C. §§ 1291–1295. The legislative history of this exemption demonstrates Congress' recognition that agreements among league members to sell television rights in a cooperative fashion could run afoul of the Sherman Act, and in particular reflects its awareness of the decision in *United States v. National Football League*, 116 F. Supp. 319 (ED Pa. 1953), which held that an agreement among the teams of the National Football League that each team would not permit stations to telecast its games within 75 miles of the home city of another team on a day when that team was not playing at home and was televising its game by use of a station within 75 miles of its home city, violated § 1 of the Sherman Act.

[31] Since, as the District Court found, NCAA approval is necessary for any institution that wishes to compete in intercollegiate sports, the NCAA has a potent tool at its disposal for restraining institutions which require its approval.

[33] "In this case the rule is violated by a price restraint that tends to provide the same economic rewards to all practitioners regardless of their skill, their experience, their training, or their willingness to employ innovative and difficult procedures." *Arizona v. Maricopa County Medical Society*, [457 U.S. 332, 348 (1982)]. The District Court provided a vivid example of this system in practice:

"A clear example of the failure of the rights fees paid to respond to market forces occurred in the fall of 1981. On one weekend of that year, Oklahoma was scheduled to play a football game with the University of Southern California. Both Oklahoma and USC have long had outstanding football programs, and indeed, both teams were ranked among the top five teams in the country by the wire service polls. ABC chose to televise the game along with several others on a regional basis. A game between two schools which are not well-known for their football programs, Citadel and Appalachian State, was carried on four of ABC's local affiliated stations. The USC-Oklahoma contest was carried on over 200 stations. Yet, incredibly, all four of these teams received exactly the same amount of money for the right to televise their games."

since "Congress designed the Sherman Act as a 'consumer welfare prescription.'" *Reiter v. Sonotone Corp.*, 442 U.S. 330, 343 (1979). A restraint that has the effect of reducing the importance of consumer preference in setting price and output is not consistent with this fundamental goal of antitrust law. Restrictions on price and output are the paradigmatic examples of restraints of trade that the Sherman Act was intended to prohibit. At the same time, the television plan eliminates competitors from the market, since only those broadcasters able to bid on television rights covering the entire NCAA can compete. Thus, as the District Court found, many telecasts that would occur in a competitive market are foreclosed by the NCAA's plan.[37]

Petitioner argues, however, that its television plan can have no significant anticompetitive effect since the record indicates that it has no market power—no ability to alter the interaction of supply and demand in the market.[38] We must reject this argument for two reasons, one legal, one factual.

As a matter of law, the absence of proof of market power does not justify a naked restriction on price or output. To the contrary, when there is an agreement not to compete in terms of price or output, "no elaborate industry analysis is required to demonstrate the anticompetitive character of such an agreement." *Professional Engineers*, 435 U.S., at 692. Petitioner does not quarrel with the District Court's finding that price and output are not responsive to demand. Thus the plan is inconsistent with the Sherman Act's command that price and supply be responsive to consumer preference.[40] We have never required proof of market power in such a case. This naked restraint on price and output requires some competitive justification even in the absence of a detailed market analysis.

As a factual matter, it is evident that petitioner does possess market power. The District Court employed the correct test for determining whether college football broadcasts constitute a separate market— whether there are other products that are reasonably substitutable for televised NCAA football games. Petitioner's argument that it cannot obtain supracompetitive prices from broadcasters since advertisers, and hence broadcasters, can switch from college football to other types of programming simply ignores the findings of the District Court. It found that intercollegiate football telecasts generate an audience uniquely

---

[37] One of respondents' economists illustrated the point:

"[I]t's my opinion that if a free market operated in the market for intercollegiate television of football, that there would be substantially more regional and even more local games being televised than there are currently. . . .

[38] Market power is the ability to raise prices above those that would be charged in a competitive market.

[40] Moreover, because under the plan member institutions may not compete in terms of price and output, it is manifest that significant forms of competition are eliminated.

attractive to advertisers and that competitors are unable to offer programming that can attract a similar audience. These findings amply support its conclusion that the NCAA possesses market power. Indeed, the District Court's subsidiary finding that advertisers will pay a premium price per viewer to reach audiences watching college football because of their demographic characteristics is vivid evidence of the uniqueness of this product. . . . It inexorably follows that if college football broadcasts be defined as a separate market—and we are convinced they are—then the NCAA's complete control over those broadcasts provides a solid basis for the District Court's conclusion that the NCAA possesses market power with respect to those broadcasts. "When a product is controlled by one interest, without substitutes available in the market, there is monopoly power." *United States v. E.I. du Pont de Nemours & Co.*, 351 U.S. 377, 394 (1956).

Thus, the NCAA television plan on its face constitutes a restraint upon the operation of a free market, and the findings of the District Court establish that it has operated to raise prices and reduce output. Under the Rule of Reason, these hallmarks of anticompetitive behavior place upon petitioner a heavy burden of establishing an affirmative defense which competitively justifies this apparent deviation from the operations of a free market. We turn now to the NCAA's proffered justifications.

IV

Relying on Broadcast Music, petitioner argues that its television plan constitutes a cooperative "joint venture" which assists in the marketing of broadcast rights and hence is procompetitive. While joint ventures have no immunity from the antitrust laws, as Broadcast Music indicates, a joint selling arrangement may "mak[e] possible a new product by reaping otherwise unattainable efficiencies." *Arizona v. Maricopa County Medical Society*, 457 U.S. 332, 365 (1982) (Powell, J., dissenting) (footnote omitted). The essential contribution made by the NCAA's arrangement is to define the number of games that may be televised, to establish the price for each exposure, and to define the basic terms of each contract between the network and a home team. The NCAA does not, however, act as a selling agent for any school or for any conference of schools. The selection of individual games, and the negotiation of particular agreements, are matters left to the networks and the individual schools. Thus, the effect of the network plan is not to eliminate individual sales of broadcasts, since these still occur, albeit subject to fixed prices and output limitations. Unlike *Broadcast Music*'s blanket license covering broadcast rights to a large number of individual compositions, here the same rights are still sold on an individual basis, only in a non-competitive market.

The District Court did not find that the NCAA's television plan produced any procompetitive efficiencies which enhanced the competitiveness of college football television rights; to the contrary it concluded that NCAA football could be marketed just as effectively without the television plan. There is therefore no predicate in the findings for petitioner's efficiency justification. Indeed, petitioner's argument is refuted by the District Court's finding concerning price and output. If the NCAA's television plan produced procompetitive efficiencies, the plan would increase output and reduce the price of televised games. The District Court's contrary findings accordingly undermine petitioner's position. In light of these findings, it cannot be said that "the agreement on price is necessary to market the product at all." *Broadcast Music*, 441 U.S., at 23. In *Broadcast Music*, the availability of a package product that no individual could offer enhanced the total volume of music that was sold. Unlike this case, there was no limit of any kind placed on the volume that might be sold in the entire market and each individual remained free to sell his own music without restraint. Here production has been limited, not enhanced. No individual school is free to televise its own games without restraint. The NCAA's efficiency justification is not supported by the record.

Neither is the NCAA's television plan necessary to enable the NCAA to penetrate the market through an attractive package sale. Since broadcasting rights to college football constitute a unique product for which there is no ready substitute, there is no need for collective action in order to enable the product to compete against its nonexistent competitors.[55] This is borne out by the District Court's finding that the NCAA's television plan reduces the volume of television rights sold.

V

Throughout the history of its regulation of intercollegiate football telecasts, the NCAA has indicated its concern with protecting live attendance. This concern, it should be noted, is not with protecting live attendance at games which are shown on television; that type of interest is not at issue in this case. Rather, the concern is that fan interest in a televised game may adversely affect ticket sales for games that will not appear on television.[56]

Although the [National Opinion Research Center's] studies in the 1950's provided some support for the thesis that live attendance would

---

[55] If the NCAA faced "interbrand" competition from available substitutes, then certain forms of collective action might be appropriate in order to enhance its ability to compete. Our conclusion concerning the availability of substitutes in Part III, *supra*, forecloses such a justification in this case, however.

[56] The NCAA's plan is not even arguably related to a desire to protect live attendance by ensuring that a game is not televised in the area where it is to be played. No cooperative action is necessary for that kind of "blackout." The home team can always refuse to sell the right to telecast its game to stations in the immediate area. The NCAA does not now and never has justified its television plan by an interest in assisting schools in "blacking out" their home games in the areas in which they are played.

suffer if unlimited television were permitted, the District Court found that there was no evidence to support that theory in today's market. Moreover, as the District Court found, the television plan has evolved in a manner inconsistent with its original design to protect gate attendance. Under the current plan, games are shown on television during all hours that college football games are played. The plan simply does not protect live attendance by ensuring that games will not be shown on television at the same time as live events.

There is, however, a more fundamental reason for rejecting this defense. The NCAA's argument that its television plan is necessary to protect live attendance is not based on a desire to maintain the integrity of college football as a distinct and attractive product, but rather on a fear that the product will not prove sufficiently attractive to draw live attendance when faced with competition from televised games. At bottom the NCAA's position is that ticket sales for most college games are unable to compete in a free market. The television plan protects ticket sales by limiting output—just as any monopolist increases revenues by reducing output. By seeking to insulate live ticket sales from the full spectrum of competition because of its assumption that the product itself is insufficiently attractive to consumers, petitioner forwards a justification that is inconsistent with the basic policy of the Sherman Act. "[T]he Rule of Reason does not support a defense based on the assumption that competition itself is unreasonable." *Professional Engineers*, 435 U.S., at 696.

VI

Petitioner argues that the interest in maintaining a competitive balance among amateur athletic teams is legitimate and important and that it justifies the regulations challenged in this case. We agree with the first part of the argument but not the second.

Our decision not to apply a per se rule to this case rests in large part on our recognition that a certain degree of cooperation is necessary if the type of competition that petitioner and its member institutions seek to market is to be preserved. It is reasonable to assume that most of the regulatory controls of the NCAA are justifiable means of fostering competition among amateur athletic teams and therefore procompetitive because they enhance public interest in intercollegiate athletics. The specific restraints on football telecasts that are challenged in this case do not, however, fit into the same mold as do rules defining the conditions of the contest, the eligibility of participants, or the manner in which members of a joint enterprise shall share the responsibilities and the benefits of the total venture.

The NCAA does not claim that its television plan has equalized or is intended to equalize competition within any one league. The plan is nationwide in scope and there is no single league or tournament in which all college football teams complete. There is no evidence of any intent to equalize the strength of teams in Division I–A with those in Division II or Division III, and not even a colorable basis for giving colleges that have no football program at all a voice in the management of the revenues generated by the football programs at other schools.[63] The interest in maintaining a competitive balance that is asserted by the NCAA as a justification for regulating all television of intercollegiate football is not related to any neutral standard or to any readily identifiable group of competitors.

The television plan is not even arguably tailored to serve such an interest. It does not regulate the amount of money that any college may spend on its football program, nor the way in which the colleges may use the revenues that are generated by their football programs, whether derived from the sale of television rights, the sale of tickets, or the sale of concessions or program advertising. The plan simply imposes a restriction on one source of revenue that is more important to some colleges than to others. There is no evidence that this restriction produces any greater measure of equality throughout the NCAA than would a restriction on alumni donations, tuition rates, or any other revenue-producing activity. At the same time, as the District Court found, the NCAA imposes a variety of other restrictions designed to preserve amateurism which are much better tailored to the goal of competitive balance than is the television plan, and which are "clearly sufficient" to preserve competitive balance to the extent it is within the NCAA's power to do so. And much more than speculation supported the District Court's findings on this score. No other NCAA sport employs a similar plan, and in particular the court found that in the most closely analogous sport, college basketball, competitive balance has been maintained without resort to a restrictive television plan.

Perhaps the most important reason for rejecting the argument that the interest in competitive balance is served by the television plan is the District Court's unambiguous and well-supported finding that many more games would be televised in a free market than under the NCAA plan. The hypothesis that legitimates the maintenance of competitive balance as a procompetitive justification under the Rule of Reason is that equal competition will maximize consumer demand for the product. The finding that consumption will materially increase if the controls are removed is a compelling demonstration that they do not in fact serve any such legitimate purpose.

---

[63] Indeed, the District Court found that the basic reason the television plan has endured is that the NCAA is in effect controlled by schools that are not restrained by the plan. . . .

VII

The NCAA plays a critical role in the maintenance of a revered tradition of amateurism in college sports. There can be no question but that it needs ample latitude to play that role, or that the preservation of the student-athlete in higher education adds richness and diversity to intercollegiate athletics and is entirely consistent with the goals of the Sherman Act. But consistent with the Sherman Act, the role of the NCAA must be to preserve a tradition that might otherwise die; rules that restrict output are hardly consistent with this role. Today we hold only that the record supports the District Court's conclusion that by curtailing output and blunting the ability of member institutions to respond to consumer preference, the NCAA has restricted rather than enhanced the place of intercollegiate athletics in the Nation's life. Accordingly, the judgment of the Court of Appeals is

Affirmed.

NOTES & QUESTIONS

(1) The NCAA's restrictions effectively meant that college football programs had banded together to control the prices charged to televise games and to limit the number of games shown. Are such limitations per se illegal? What justification did the Court give for departing from a per se analysis in this case?

(2) What is the underlying concern of courts when employing a per se analysis? A rule of reason analysis?

(3) Look back at the quoted language from *DeLong* describing the rule of reason. Does the *NCAA* Court's analysis under the rule of reason follow the standard articulated in *DeLong*?

(4) How did the NCAA defend its practices? Do you agree with the Court's conclusions regarding (a) the NCAA's market power, (b) the characterization of the NCAA's plan as a restraint of trade, and (c) the pro-competitive effects of the NCAA's plan?

(5) In *NCAA*, the Court found that a per se analysis was inappropriate, but it did not conduct a full-blown rule of reason examination. In response to *NCAA* and other Supreme Court decisions, some lower courts began to apply an intermediate form of examination, referred to as a "quick look" analysis. Under this approach, when a per se analysis is inappropriate, courts will apply a truncated review when "an observer with even a rudimentary understanding of economics could conclude that the arrangements in question would have an anticompetitive effect on customers and markets." *California Dental Assoc. v. FTC*, 526 U.S. 756, 770 (1999). Determining which type of analysis (i.e., per se, rule of reason, or quick look) is appropriate in a particular case, however, is not an easy task:

The truth is that our categories of analysis of anticompetitive effect are less fixed than terms like "*per se*," "quick look," and "rule of reason" tend to make them appear. We have recognized, for example, that "there is often no bright line separating *per se* from Rule of Reason analysis," since "considerable inquiry into market conditions" may be required before the application of any so-called "*per se*" condemnation is justified.

Id. at 779. The *California Dental* Court went on to discuss the circumstances that might justify a less-than-full-blown rule of reason analysis, observing that the critical question is whether the challenged restraint suppresses or enhances competition. The Court ultimately endorsed a flexible ad hoc analysis to be shaped by judicial experience with particular types of restraints. *See id.* at 779–81.

Understandably, lower courts have struggled with determining which type of analysis is appropriate in a particular dispute. A frequently cited decision which establishes a burden-shifting framework is *Polygram Holding Inc. v. FTC*, 416 F.3d 29 (D.C. Cir. 2005). In *Polygram*, the court approved a framework under which the plaintiff must first show that the complained-of conduct is inherently suspect due to its tendency to suppress competition. *See id.* at 35–36. Such inherently suspect conduct would include agreements that were previously found to be per se violations, or agreements that closely resembled such violations. *See id.* at 36–37. If this showing is made, the defendant then has the burden to demonstrate why the restraint is "unlikely to harm consumers or identify some competitive [offsetting] benefit." *Id.* at 36.

(6) In light of the later *NCAA* and *California Dental* decisions, how would a court decide *Topco* today?

2. VERTICAL RESTRAINTS

a. Resale Price Restraints

Vertical resale price restraints are typified by the situation where a manufacturer requires its retailers to abide by certain price restrictions. These restrictions can come in the form of minimum or maximum sale prices. At one time, under the Supreme Court case of *Dr. Miles Medical Co. v. Jon D. Park & Sons*, 220 U.S. 373 (1911), all resale price restraints were held to be per se violations of § 1 of the Sherman Act. In the century following *Dr. Miles*, the Court softened its approach to these restraints considerably—first, by deciding a series of cases which made the conspiracy element of a § 1 claim more difficult to meet, and second, by finally abandoning the per se approach altogether.

LEEGIN CREATIVE LEATHER PRODUCTS INC. V. PSKS, INC.

551 U.S. 877 (2007)

KENNEDY, J.

In *Dr. Miles Medical Co. v. John D. Park & Sons Co.*, 220 U.S. 373 (1911), the Court established the rule that it is *per se* illegal under § 1 of the Sherman Act, 15 U.S.C. § 1, for a manufacturer to agree with its distributor to set the minimum price the distributor can charge for the manufacturer's goods. The question presented by the instant case is whether the Court should overrule the *per se* rule and allow resale price maintenance agreements to be judged by the rule of reason, the usual standard applied to determine if there is a violation of § 1. The Court has abandoned the rule of *per se* illegality for other vertical restraints a manufacturer imposes on its distributors. Respected economic analysts, furthermore, conclude that vertical price restraints can have procompetitive effects. We now hold that *Dr. Miles* should be overruled and that vertical price restraints are to be judged by the rule of reason.

I

Petitioner, Leegin Creative Leather Products, Inc. (Leegin), designs, manufactures, and distributes leather goods and accessories. In 1991, Leegin began to sell belts under the brand name "Brighton." The Brighton brand has now expanded into a variety of women's fashion accessories. It is sold across the United States in over 5,000 retail establishments, for the most part independent, small boutiques and specialty stores. Leegin's president, Jerry Kohl, also has an interest in about 70 stores that sell Brighton products. Leegin asserts that, at least for its products, small retailers treat customers better, provide customers more services, and make their shopping experience more satisfactory than do larger, often impersonal retailers. Kohl explained: "[W]e want the consumers to get a different experience than they get in Sam's Club or in Wal-Mart. And you can't get that kind of experience or support or customer service from a store like Wal-Mart."

Respondent, PSKS, Inc. (PSKS), operates Kay's Kloset, a women's apparel store in Lewisville, Texas. Kay's Kloset buys from about 75 different manufacturers and at one time sold the Brighton brand. It first started purchasing Brighton goods from Leegin in 1995. Once it began selling the brand, the store promoted Brighton. For example, it ran Brighton advertisements and had Brighton days in the store. Kay's Kloset became the destination retailer in the area to buy Brighton products. Brighton was the store's most important brand and once accounted for 40 to 50 percent of its profits.

In 1997, Leegin instituted the "Brighton Retail Pricing and Promotion Policy." Following the policy, Leegin refused to sell to retailers that discounted Brighton goods below suggested prices. The policy contained an exception for products not selling well that the retailer did not plan on reordering. . . .

Leegin adopted the policy to give its retailers sufficient margins to provide customers the service central to its distribution strategy. It also expressed concern that discounting harmed Brighton's brand image and reputation.

A year after instituting the pricing policy Leegin introduced a marketing strategy known as the "Heart Store Program." It offered retailers incentives to become Heart Stores, and, in exchange, retailers pledged, among other things, to sell at Leegin's suggested prices. Kay's Kloset became a Heart Store soon after Leegin created the program. After a Leegin employee visited the store and found it unattractive, the parties appear to have agreed that Kay's Kloset would not be a Heart Store beyond 1998. Despite losing this status, Kay's Kloset continued to increase its Brighton sales.

In December 2002, Leegin discovered Kay's Kloset had been marking down Brighton's entire line by 20 percent. Kay's Kloset contended it placed Brighton products on sale to compete with nearby retailers who also were undercutting Leegin's suggested prices. Leegin, nonetheless, requested that Kay's Kloset cease discounting. Its request refused, Leegin stopped selling to the store. The loss of the Brighton brand had a considerable negative impact on the store's revenue from sales.

PSKS sued Leegin in the United States District Court for the Eastern District of Texas. It alleged, among other claims, that Leegin had violated the antitrust laws by "enter[ing] into agreements with retailers to charge only those prices fixed by Leegin." Leegin planned to introduce expert testimony describing the procompetitive effects of its pricing policy. The District Court excluded the testimony, relying on the *per se* rule established by *Dr. Miles.* At trial PSKS argued that the Heart Store program, among other things, demonstrated [that] Leegin and its retailers had agreed to fix prices. Leegin responded that it had established a unilateral pricing policy lawful under § 1, which applies only to concerted action. See *United States v. Colgate & Co.,* 250 U.S. 300, 307 (1919). The jury agreed with PSKS and awarded it $1.2 million. Pursuant to 15 U.S.C. § 15(a), the District Court trebled the damages and reimbursed PSKS for its attorney's fees and costs. It entered judgment against Leegin in the amount of $3,975,000.80.

The Court of Appeals for the Fifth Circuit affirmed. On appeal Leegin did not dispute that it had entered into vertical price-fixing agreements with its retailers. Rather, it contended that the rule of reason should have applied to those agreements. The Court of Appeals rejected this argument. It was correct to explain that it remained bound by *Dr. Miles* "[b]ecause [the Supreme] Court has consistently applied the *per se* rule to [vertical minimum price-fixing] agreements." On this premise the Court of Appeals held that the District Court did not abuse its discretion in excluding the testimony of Leegin's economic expert, for the *per se* rule rendered irrelevant any procompetitive justifications for Leegin's pricing policy. We granted certiorari to determine whether vertical minimum resale price maintenance agreements should continue to be treated as *per se* unlawful.

II

. . . .

The rule of reason is the accepted standard for testing whether a practice restrains trade in violation of § 1. "Under this rule, the factfinder weighs all of the circumstances of a case in deciding whether a restrictive practice should be prohibited as imposing an unreasonable restraint on competition." *Continental T. V., Inc. v. GTE Sylvania Inc.,* 433 U.S. 36, 49 (1977). Appropriate factors to take into account include "specific information about the relevant business" and "the restraint's history, nature, and effect." [*State Oil Co. v. Khan,* 522 U.S. 3, 10 (1997)]. Whether the businesses involved have market power is a further, significant consideration. *See, e.g., Copperweld Corp. v. Independence Tube Corp.,* 467 U.S. 752, 768 (1984) (equating the rule of reason with "an inquiry into market power and market structure designed to assess [a restraint's] actual effect"). In its design and function the rule distinguishes between restraints with anticompetitive effect that are harmful to the consumer and restraints stimulating competition that are in the consumer's best interest.

The rule of reason does not govern all restraints. Some types "are deemed unlawful *per se*." *Khan, supra,* at 10. The *per se* rule, treating categories of restraints as necessarily illegal, eliminates the need to study the reasonableness of an individual restraint in light of the real market forces at work, *Business Electronics Corp. v. Sharp Electronics Corp.,* 485 U.S. 717, 723 (1988); and, it must be acknowledged, the *per se* rule can give clear guidance for certain conduct. Restraints that are *per se* unlawful include horizontal agreements among competitors to fix prices, or to divide markets.

Resort to *per se* rules is confined to restraints, like those mentioned, "that would always or almost always tend to restrict competition and decrease output." *Business Electronics, supra,* at 723. To justify a *per se* prohibition a restraint must have "manifestly anticompetitive" effects, *GTE Sylvania, supra,* at 50, and "lack ... any redeeming virtue," *Northwest Wholesale Stationers, Inc. v. Pacific Stationery & Printing Co.,* 472 U.S. 284, 289 (1985).

As a consequence, the *per se* rule is appropriate only after courts have had considerable experience with the type of restraint at issue, and only if courts can predict with confidence that it would be invalidated in all or almost all instances under the rule of reason. It should come as no surprise, then, that "we have expressed reluctance to adopt *per se* rules with regard to restraints imposed in the context of business relationships where the economic impact of certain practices is not immediately obvious." *Khan, supra,* at 10; *see also White Motor Co. v. United States,* 372 U.S. 253, 263 (1963) (refusing to adopt a *per se* rule for a vertical nonprice restraint because of the uncertainty concerning whether this type of restraint satisfied the demanding standards necessary to apply a *per se* rule). And, as we have stated, a "departure from the rule-of-reason standard must be based upon demonstrable economic effect rather than . . . upon formalistic line drawing." *GTE Sylvania, supra,* at 58–59.

III

The Court has interpreted *Dr. Miles Medical Co. v. John D. Park & Sons Co.,* 220 U.S. 373, as establishing a *per se* rule against a vertical agreement between a manufacturer and its distributor to set minimum resale prices. In *Dr. Miles* the plaintiff, a manufacturer of medicines, sold its products only to distributors who agreed to resell them at set prices. The Court found the manufacturer's control of resale prices to be unlawful. It relied on the common-law rule that "a general restraint upon alienation is ordinarily invalid." 220 U.S., at 404–405. The Court then explained that the agreements would advantage the distributors, not the manufacturer, and were analogous to a combination among competing distributors, which the law treated as void. *Id.,* at 407–408.

The reasoning of the Court's more recent jurisprudence has rejected the rationales on which *Dr. Miles* was based. By relying on the common-law rule against restraints on alienation, the Court justified its decision based on "formalistic" legal doctrine rather than "demonstrable economic effect," *GTE Sylvania,* 433 U.S., at 58–59. The Court in *Dr. Miles* relied on a treatise published in 1628, but failed to discuss in detail the business reasons that would motivate a manufacturer situated in 1911 to make use of vertical price restraints. Yet the Sherman Act's use of "restraint of trade" "invokes the common law itself, . . . not merely the static content that the common law had assigned to the term in 1890." *Business Electronics, supra,* at 732. . . . We reaffirm that "the state of the common law 400 or even 100 years ago is irrelevant to the issue before us: the effect of the antitrust laws upon vertical distributional restraints in the American economy today." *GTE Sylvania, supra,* at 53, n. 21.

Dr. Miles, furthermore, treated vertical agreements [that] a manufacturer makes with its distributors as analogous to a horizontal combination among competing distributors. In later cases, however, the

Court rejected the approach of reliance on rules governing horizontal restraints when defining rules applicable to vertical ones. *See, e.g., Business Electronics, supra,* at 734 (disclaiming the "notion of equivalence between the scope of horizontal *per se* illegality and that of vertical *per se* illegality"); [*Arizona v. Maricopa County Medical Society,* 457 U.S. 332, 348 n.18 (1982)] (noting that "horizontal restraints are generally less defensible than vertical restraints"). Our recent cases formulate antitrust principles in accordance with the appreciated differences in economic effect between vertical and horizontal agreements, differences the *Dr. Miles* Court failed to consider.

The reasons upon which *Dr. Miles* relied do not justify a *per se* rule. As a consequence, it is necessary to examine, in the first instance, the economic effects of vertical agreements to fix minimum resale prices, and to determine whether the *per se* rule is nonetheless appropriate.

A

Though each side of the debate can find sources to support its position, it suffices to say here that economics literature is replete with procompetitive justifications for a manufacturer's use of resale price maintenance. Brief for United States as *Amicus Curiae* 9 ("[T]here is a widespread consensus that permitting a manufacturer to control the price at which its goods are sold may promote *inter*brand competition and consumer welfare in a variety of ways"); *see also* H. Hovenkamp, The Antitrust Enterprise: Principle and Execution 184–191 (2005); R. Bork, The Antitrust Paradox 288–291 (1978). Even those more skeptical of resale price maintenance acknowledge it can have procompetitive effects. *See, e.g.,* F. Scherer & D. Ross, Industrial Market Structure and Economic Performance 558 (3d ed.1990) (hereinafter Scherer & Ross) ("The overall balance between benefits and costs [of resale price maintenance] is probably close").

The few recent studies documenting the competitive effects of resale price maintenance also cast doubt on the conclusion that the practice meets the criteria for a *per se* rule. *See* Bureau of Economics Staff Report to the FTC, T. Overstreet, Resale Price Maintenance: Economic Theories and Empirical Evidence 170 (1983) (hereinafter Overstreet) (noting that "[e]fficient uses of [resale price maintenance] are evidently not unusual or rare"); *see also* Ippolito, Resale Price Maintenance: Empirical Evidence From Litigation, 34 J. Law & Econ. 263, 292–293 (1991) (hereinafter Ippolito).

The justifications for vertical price restraints are similar to those for other vertical restraints. Minimum resale price maintenance can stimulate interbrand competition—the competition among manufacturers selling different brands of the same type of product—by reducing intrabrand competition—the competition among retailers selling the same brand. The promotion of interbrand competition is important because "the primary purpose of the antitrust laws is to protect [this type of] competition." *Khan*, 522 U.S., at 15. A single manufacturer's use of vertical price restraints tends to eliminate intrabrand price competition; this in turn encourages retailers to invest in tangible or intangible services or promotional efforts that aid the manufacturer's position as against rival manufacturers. Resale price maintenance also has the potential to give consumers more options so that they can choose among low-price, low-service brands; high-price, high-service brands; and brands that fall in between.

Absent vertical price restraints, the retail services that enhance interbrand competition might be underprovided. This is because discounting retailers can free ride on retailers who furnish services and then capture some of the increased demand those services generate. *GTE Sylvania, supra*, at 55. Consumers might learn, for example, about the benefits of a manufacturer's product from a retailer that invests in fine showrooms, offers product demonstrations, or hires and trains knowledgeable employees. R. Posner, Antitrust Law 172–173 (2d ed. 2001) (hereinafter Posner). Or consumers might decide to buy the product because they see it in a retail establishment that has a reputation for selling high-quality merchandise. Marvel & McCafferty, Resale Price Maintenance and Quality Certification, 15 Rand J. Econ. 346, 347–349 (1984). If the consumer can then buy the product from a retailer that discounts because it has not spent capital providing services or developing a quality reputation, the high-service retailer will lose sales to the discounter, forcing it to cut back its services to a level lower than consumers would otherwise prefer. Minimum resale price maintenance alleviates the problem because it prevents the discounter from undercutting the service provider. With price competition decreased, the manufacturer's retailers compete among themselves over services.

Resale price maintenance, in addition, can increase interbrand competition by facilitating market entry for new firms and brands. "[N]ew manufacturers and manufacturers entering new markets can use the restrictions in order to induce competent and aggressive retailers to make the kind of investment of capital and labor that is often required in the distribution of products unknown to the consumer." *GTE Sylvania, supra,* at 55. New products and new brands are essential to a dynamic economy, and if markets can be penetrated by using resale price maintenance there is a procompetitive effect.

Resale price maintenance can also increase interbrand competition by encouraging retailer services that would not be provided even absent free riding. It may be difficult and inefficient for a manufacturer to make and enforce a contract with a retailer specifying the different services the retailer must perform. Offering the retailer a guaranteed margin and threatening termination if it does not live up to expectations may be the most efficient way to expand the manufacturer's market share by inducing the retailer's performance and allowing it to use its own initiative and experience in providing valuable services. See Mathewson & Winter, The Law and Economics of Resale Price Maintenance, 13 Rev. Indus. Org. 57, 74–75 (1998) (hereinafter Mathewson & Winter).

B

While vertical agreements setting minimum resale prices can have procompetitive justifications, they may have anticompetitive effects in other cases; and unlawful price fixing, designed solely to obtain monopoly profits, is an ever-present temptation. Resale price maintenance may, for example, facilitate a manufacturer cartel. An unlawful cartel will seek to discover if some manufacturers are undercutting the cartel's fixed prices. Resale price maintenance could assist the cartel in identifying price-cutting manufacturers who benefit from the lower prices they offer. Resale price maintenance, furthermore, could discourage a manufacturer from cutting prices to retailers with the concomitant benefit of cheaper prices to consumers.

Vertical price restraints also might be used to organize cartels at the retailer level. A group of retailers might collude to fix prices to consumers and then compel a manufacturer to aid the unlawful arrangement with resale price maintenance. In that instance the manufacturer does not establish the practice to stimulate services or to promote its brand but to give inefficient retailers higher profits. Retailers with better distribution systems and lower cost structures would be prevented from charging lower prices by the agreement.

A horizontal cartel among competing manufacturers or competing retailers that decreases output or reduces competition in order to increase price is, and ought to be, *per se* unlawful. *See* [*Texaco v. Dagher*, 547 U.S. 1, 5 (2006)]; *GTE Sylvania*, 433 U.S., at 58, n. 28. To the extent a vertical agreement setting minimum resale prices is entered upon to facilitate either type of cartel, it, too, would need to be held unlawful under the rule of reason. This type of agreement may also be useful evidence for a plaintiff attempting to prove the existence of a horizontal cartel.

Resale price maintenance, furthermore, can be abused by a powerful manufacturer or retailer. A dominant retailer, for example, might request resale price maintenance to forestall innovation in distribution that decreases costs. A manufacturer might consider it has little choice but to accommodate the retailer's demands for vertical price restraints if the manufacturer believes it needs access to the retailer's distribution network. *See* 8 P. Areeda & H. Hovenkamp, Antitrust Law 47 (2d ed.2004). A manufacturer with market power, by comparison, might use resale price maintenance to give retailers an incentive not to sell the products of smaller rivals or new entrants. As should be evident, the potential anticompetitive consequences of vertical price restraints must not be ignored or underestimated.

C

Notwithstanding the risks of unlawful conduct, it cannot be stated with any degree of confidence that resale price maintenance "always or almost always tend[s] to restrict competition and decrease output." *Business Electronics, supra*, at 723. Vertical agreements establishing minimum resale prices can have either procompetitive or anticompetitive effects, depending upon the circumstances in which they are formed. And although the empirical evidence on the topic is limited, it does not suggest efficient uses of the agreements are infrequent or hypothetical. As the rule would proscribe a significant amount of procompetitive conduct, these agreements appear ill suited for *per se* condemnation.

Respondent contends, nonetheless, that vertical price restraints should be *per se* unlawful because of the administrative convenience of *per se* rules. *See, e.g., GTE Sylvania, supra*, at 50, n. 16 (noting "*per se* rules tend to provide guidance to the business community and to minimize the burdens on litigants and the judicial system"). That argument suggests *per se* illegality is the rule rather than the exception. This misinterprets our antitrust law. *Per se* rules may decrease administrative costs, but that is only part of the equation. Those rules can be counterproductive. They can increase the total cost of the antitrust system by prohibiting procompetitive conduct the antitrust laws should encourage. *See* Easterbrook, Vertical Arrangements and the Rule of Reason, 53 Antitrust L.J. 135, 158 (1984) (hereinafter Easterbrook). They also may increase litigation costs by promoting frivolous suits against legitimate practices. The Court has thus explained that administrative "advantages are not sufficient in themselves to justify the creation of *per se* rules," *GTE Sylvania*, 433 U.S., at 50, n. 16, and has relegated their use to restraints that are "manifestly anticompetitive," *id.*, at 49–50. Were the Court now to conclude that vertical price restraints should be *per se* illegal based on administrative costs, we would undermine, if not overrule, the traditional "demanding standards" for adopting *per se* rules. *Id.*, at 50. Any possible reduction in administrative costs cannot alone justify the *Dr. Miles* rule.

Respondent also argues the *per se* rule is justified because a vertical price restraint can lead to higher prices for the manufacturer's goods. *See also* Overstreet 160 (noting that "price surveys indicate that [resale price maintenance] in most cases increased the prices of products sold"). Respondent is mistaken in relying on pricing effects absent a further showing of anticompetitive conduct. *Cf. id.*, at 106 (explaining that price surveys "do not necessarily tell us anything conclusive about the welfare effects of [resale price maintenance] because the results are generally consistent with both procompetitive and anticompetitive theories"). For, as has been indicated already, the antitrust laws are designed primarily to protect interbrand competition, from which lower prices can later result. *See Khan*, 522 U.S., at 15. The Court, moreover, has evaluated other vertical restraints under the rule of reason even though prices can be increased in the course of promoting procompetitive effects. And resale price maintenance may reduce prices if manufacturers have resorted to costlier alternatives of controlling resale prices that are not *per se* unlawful.

Respondent's argument, furthermore, overlooks that, in general, the interests of manufacturers and consumers are aligned with respect to retailer profit margins. The difference between the price a manufacturer charges retailers and the price retailers charge consumers represents part of the manufacturer's cost of distribution, which, like any other cost, the manufacturer usually desires to minimize. A manufacturer has no incentive to overcompensate retailers with unjustified margins. The retailers, not the manufacturer, gain from higher retail prices. The manufacturer often loses; interbrand competition reduces its competitiveness and market share because consumers will substitute a different brand of the same product. As a general matter, therefore, a single manufacturer will desire to set minimum resale prices only if the "increase in demand resulting from enhanced service . . . will more than offset a negative impact on demand of a higher retail price." Mathewson & Winter 67.

The implications of respondent's position are far reaching. Many decisions a manufacturer makes and carries out through concerted action can lead to higher prices. A manufacturer might, for example, contract with different suppliers to obtain better inputs that improve product quality. Or it might hire an advertising agency to promote awareness of its goods. Yet no one would think these actions violate the Sherman Act because they lead to higher prices. The antitrust laws do not require manufacturers to produce generic goods that consumers do not know about or want. The manufacturer strives to improve its product quality or to promote its brand because it believes this conduct will lead to increased demand despite higher prices. The same can hold true for resale price maintenance.

Resale price maintenance, it is true, does have economic dangers. If the rule of reason were to apply to vertical price restraints, courts would have to be diligent in eliminating their anticompetitive uses from the market. This is a realistic objective, and certain factors are relevant to the inquiry. For example, the number of manufacturers that make use of the practice in a given industry can provide important instruction. When only a few manufacturers lacking market power adopt the practice, there is little likelihood it is facilitating a manufacturer cartel, for a cartel then can be undercut by rival manufacturers. Likewise, a retailer cartel is unlikely when only a single manufacturer in a competitive market uses resale price maintenance. Interbrand competition would divert consumers to lower priced substitutes and eliminate any gains to retailers from their price-fixing agreement over a single brand. Resale price maintenance should be subject to more careful scrutiny, by contrast, if many competing manufacturers adopt the practice. *Cf.* Scherer & Ross 558 (noting that "except when [resale price maintenance] spreads to cover the bulk of an industry's output, depriving consumers of a meaningful choice between high-service and low-price outlets, most [resale price maintenance arrangements] are probably innocuous"); Easterbrook 162 (suggesting that "every one of the potentially-anticompetitive outcomes of vertical arrangements depends on the uniformity of the practice").

The source of the restraint may also be an important consideration. If there is evidence retailers were the impetus for a vertical price restraint, there is a greater likelihood that the restraint facilitates a retailer cartel or supports a dominant, inefficient retailer. If, by contrast, a manufacturer adopted the policy independent of retailer pressure, the restraint is less likely to promote anticompetitive conduct. *Cf.* Posner 177 ("It makes all the difference whether minimum retail prices are imposed by the manufacturer in order to evoke point-of-sale services or by the dealers in order to obtain monopoly profits."). A manufacturer also has an incentive to protest inefficient retailer-induced price restraints because they can harm its competitive position.

As a final matter, that a dominant manufacturer or retailer can abuse resale price maintenance for anticompetitive purposes may not be a serious concern unless the relevant entity has market power. If a retailer lacks market power, manufacturers likely can sell their goods through rival retailers. *See also Business Electronics, supra,* at 727, n. 2 (noting "[r]etail market power is rare, because of the usual presence of interbrand competition and other dealers"). And if a manufacturer lacks market power, there is less likelihood it can use the practice to keep competitors away from distribution outlets.

The rule of reason is designed and used to eliminate anticompetitive transactions from the market. This standard principle applies to vertical price restraints. A party alleging injury from a vertical agreement setting minimum resale prices will have, as a general matter, the information and resources available to show the existence of the agreement and its scope of operation. As courts gain experience considering the effects of these restraints by applying the rule of reason over the course of decisions, they can establish the litigation structure to ensure the rule operates to eliminate anticompetitive restraints from the market and to provide more guidance to businesses. Courts can, for example, devise rules over time for offering proof, or even presumptions where justified, to make the rule of reason a fair and efficient way to prohibit anticompetitive restraints and to promote procompetitive ones.

For all of the foregoing reasons, we think that were the Court considering the issue as an original matter, the rule of reason, not a *per se* rule of unlawfulness, would be the appropriate standard to judge vertical price restraints.

. . . .

The judgment of the Court of Appeals is reversed, and the case is remanded for proceedings consistent with this opinion.

NOTES & QUESTIONS

(1) Why did the Court believe that *Dr. Miles* was ripe for overturning? Was the case no longer relevant, or was it ill-conceived from the beginning?

(2) The Court stated that one of the pro-competitive effects of vertical price restraints is to increase interbrand competition by reducing intrabrand competition. What did the Court mean by this? What specific benefits to consumers are gained from a policy that keeps prices higher?

(3) In what ways can vertical price restraints be abused? In light of such possibilities, why did the Court decide to apply the rule of reason?

(4) According to the Court, what factors are relevant to a rule of reason inquiry into a vertical price restraint?

(5) Contrary to the facts, assume that Leegin did sell to large national retail outlets, but it did not initiate the minimum resale price policy. Instead, a group of large retail outlets approached Leegin and demanded that Leegin set a minimum resale price or they would no longer sell Leegin products. The retailers took this action due to a concern that small boutiques were undercutting their prices. Not wanting to lose the retail group's business, Leegin complied and PSKS brought suit for violations of § 1 of the Sherman Act. Under what standard should Leegin's conduct be reviewed?

(6) Prior to *Leegin*, manufacturers sought to circumvent the per se status of vertical price restraints by avoiding the concerted action requirement of § 1. An attempt to accomplish this involved selling goods on consignment. To distinguish between true consignments and mere creative labeling, courts looked to whether the consignment served a legitimate business purpose and examined which party bore the risk of loss. *See United States v. Gen. Elec. Co.*, 272 U.S. 476, 488 (1926) (finding that "genuine contracts of agency . . . however comprehensive as a mass or whole in their effect" are not violations of the Antitrust Act); *see also Simpson v. Union Oil Co. of California*, 377 U.S. 13, 16 (1964) ("If the 'consignment' agreement achieves resale price maintenance in violation of the Sherman Act, it and the lease are being used to injure interstate commerce by depriving independent

dealers of the exercise of free judgment whether to become consignees at all, or remain consignees, and, in any event, to sell at competitive prices.").

Another attempt to avoid concerted action was to simply suggest (rather than require) a retail price. This practice was upheld so long as the manufacturer did not explicitly make future sales contingent upon adherence to the suggestion; indeed, absent such a threat, the manufacturer could refuse to deal with retailers that did not abide by the suggestion. *See United States v. Parke, Davis & Co.*, 362 U.S. 29, 45–46 (1960) (observing that the suggested retail price would not "have violated the Sherman Act if its action thereunder was the simple refusal without more to deal with wholesalers"). *But see Dimidowich v. Bell & Howell*, 803 F.2d 1473, 1478 (9th Cir. 1986) (casting doubt on the *Parke, Davis & Co.* line of cases).

In light of *Leegin*, is there any reason for manufacturers to continue their attempts to avoid the appearance of concerted action?

(7) There is little left of per se treatment for vertical restraints. A type of vertical restraint that may still receive a per se analysis, however, is the tie-in arrangement. A tie-in arrangement is an agreement by a party to sell a product only if the buyer purchases a different product as well. For a tie-in arrangement to exist, there must be two distinct products involved. Where two products are so related that they cannot be disassociated from each other, no tying exists. For instance, if a franchisor requires a franchisee to purchase needed supplies from the franchisor (or from certain designated sources connected with the franchisor), this would likely constitute an illegal per se tie-in arrangement, as the franchisor is tying the franchise to the sale of separate products. However, if the franchise is related to a license to sell a certain product, then the franchise and the license will likely be considered so related that no tying will be involved. *See, e.g., In re Carvel Corp., FTC*, 55 Trademark Rep. 775, 778 (1965) ("Since Carvel's franchise for the sale of Carvel products and its license to use are part of a single package, we conclude that the examiner erred in holding that the Carvel franchise agreements were illegal tie-in arrangements.").

Tie-in arrangements are potentially problematic because they can lessen competition in the tied product and facilitate price discrimination. This gives a considerable amount of power to the seller, particularly a seller who has legitimately cornered the market on a specific good or service. As Judge Posner observed, "[t]he traditional antitrust concern with such an agreement is that if the seller of the tying product is a monopolist, the tie-in will force anyone who wants the monopolized product to buy the tied product from him as well, and the result will be a second monopoly." *Sheridan v. Marathon Petroleum Co.*, 530 F.3d 590, 592 (7th Cir. 2008).

(8) The Supreme Court does not subject all tie-in arrangements to a per se analysis. For such an arrangement to be per se illegal, the plaintiff must first establish that the seller has sufficient market power to force customers to purchase the unwanted second product. If the plaintiff cannot establish market power, then the case will be analyzed under the rule of reason, and

the plaintiff will need to prove that the challenged action adversely affected competition in the relevant market. *See Jefferson Parish Hosp. Dist. No. 2 v. Hyde*, 466 U.S. 2, 8 (1984); *Cnty. of Tuolumne v. Sonora Cmty. Hosp.*, 236 F.3d 1148, 1157 (9th Cir. 2001); *In re Visa Check/MasterMoney Antitrust Litig.*, 280 F.3d 124, 133 n.5 (2d Cir. 2001). In *Jefferson Parish*, the Supreme Court explained its rationale for not subjecting all tie-in arrangements to a per se approach:

> Certain types of contractual arrangements are deemed unreasonable as a matter of law. The character of the restraint produced by such an arrangement is considered a sufficient basis for presuming unreasonableness without the necessity of any analysis of the market context in which the arrangement may be found. A price fixing agreement between competitors is the classic example of such an arrangement. It is far too late in the history of our antitrust jurisprudence to question the proposition that certain tying arrangements pose an unacceptable risk of stifling competition and therefore are unreasonable "per se." The rule was first enunciated in *International Salt Co. v. United States*, 332 U.S. 392, 396 (1947), and has been endorsed by this Court many times since. . . . It is clear, however, that every refusal to sell two products separately cannot be said to restrain competition. If each of the products may be purchased separately in a competitive market, one seller's decision to sell the two in a single package imposes no unreasonable restraint on either market, particularly if competing suppliers are free to sell either the entire package or its several parts. For example, we have written that "if one of a dozen food stores in a community were to refuse to sell flour unless the buyer also took sugar it would hardly tend to restrain competition if its competitors were ready and able to sell flour by itself." *Northern Pac. R. Co. v. United States*, 356 U.S. 1, 7 (1958). Buyers often find package sales attractive; a seller's decision to offer such packages can merely be an attempt to compete effectively—conduct that is entirely consistent with the Sherman Act.
>
> Our cases have concluded that the essential characteristic of an invalid tying arrangement lies in the seller's exploitation of its control over the tying product to force the buyer into the purchase of a tied product that the buyer either did not want at all, or might have preferred to purchase elsewhere on different terms. When such "forcing" is present, competition on the merits in the market for the tied item is restrained and the Sherman Act is violated. . . . Accordingly, we have condemned tying arrangements when the seller has some special ability—usually called "market power"—to force a purchaser to do something that he would not do in a competitive market.

Jefferson Parish Hosp. Dist. No. 2 v. Hyde, 466 U.S. 2, 9–14 (1984).

(9) In *Jefferson Parish*, Justice Stevens provided what appeared to be a perfect example of market power—patents. If a seller holds a patent over a product, it is essentially a grant of monopoly power by the government. If the seller of the product chooses to tie it to a second product, this would seem to be an attempt to undermine competition that would call for a per se analysis. Congress, however, thought otherwise. In 1988, Congress amended the Patent Act to eliminate the market power presumption in patent misuse cases. *See* 35 U.S.C. § 271(d). In *Illinois Tool Works Inc. v. Independent Ink, Inc.*, 547 U.S. 28 (2006), the Court held that the mere fact that a tying product was patented did not support a presumption of market power in the patented product. *See id.* at 31.

b. The Rule of Reason

Territorial restraints and exclusive dealerships are vertical restraints that are typically subjected to a rule of reason analysis under § 1. A territorial restraint prevents a retailer from selling a manufacturer's product beyond certain geographic boundaries. An exclusive dealership (which is frequently utilized by franchisors) makes certain retailers the only ones authorized to sell a product in a given geographical area. Both territorial restraints and exclusive dealerships are meant to decrease intrabrand competition, but in different ways. Territorial restraints do not prevent other retailers from selling in the same geographical area, but exclusive dealerships do. Exclusive dealerships, however, do not prevent competing dealerships from delivering products outside of a geographical area, while territorial restraints do. Thus, it is not unusual to find a manufacturer utilizing both types of restraints to decrease intrabrand competition. Manufacturers are also generally free to sell to whomever they wish and are not obliged to sell to dealerships absent a contractual relationship. Nonetheless, refusing to sell to a dealer who has long enjoyed status as a distributor may irk the now-shunned dealer as demonstrated by the next case.

RUTMAN WINE COMPANY V. E. & J. GALLO WINERY
829 F.2d 729 (9th Cir. 1987)

STOTLER, DISTRICT JUDGE:

Rutman Wine Company ("Rutman") appeals from the district court's dismissal with prejudice of Counts 1–4 of its Second Amended Complaint. These counts charge appellee E. & J. Gallo Winery ("Gallo") and nonparty Wine Distributors, Inc. ("WDI") with nonprice-related violations of sections 1 and 2 of the Sherman Act, 15 U.S.C. §§ 1, 2 (1986). . . . Rutman seeks not less than $7 million in damages and injunctive relief requiring, *inter alia*, that Gallo reinstate Rutman as a distributor.

The Northern District of Ohio transferred the case on defendant's motion to the Eastern District of California in 1984. The district court dismissed the First Amended Complaint because plaintiff's allegations of injury to itself did not establish the required injury to competition. Although plaintiff amended, the court dismissed counts of the Second Amended Complaint due to the same deficiency. The court also concluded that defendant's alleged discrimination against Rutman in providing certain services did not show that plaintiff's ability to compete with favored purchasers of defendant's products was impaired. Plaintiff's requests to conduct discovery and amend anew were denied.

Since essential elements of claims under sections 1 and 2 of the Sherman Act and under section 2(e) of the Robinson-Patman Act are missing from appellant's third effort to state such claims, the district court's dismissal of Counts 1–4 is affirmed.

. . . .

II.

SUMMARY OF COMPLAINT

Rutman complains that Gallo terminated its distributorship agreement as part of a conspiracy or combination with WDI to restrain trade unreasonably and to effectuate Gallo's actual or attempted monopolization of the wine products market in Cuyahoga County, Ohio. In furtherance of this scheme, Gallo purportedly discriminated against appellant in favor of WDI. Count 1 alleges violations of both sections 1 and 2 of the Sherman Act; Count 3 contains the Robinson-Patman allegations; Counts 2 and 4 are based on the Ohio antitrust statute.

Appellant is an Ohio corporation engaged in the import and distribution of wines and beer in Cuyahoga County, Ohio. It distributes to approximately 1,500 retail outlets in and around Cleveland. The sale of wine products comprises at least 99% of Rutman's overall business. Approximately 95% of Rutman's products are purchased from out-of-state suppliers. It spends approximately $6 million per year for its wine products.

Gallo is a California corporation which manufactures relatively low-priced domestic wines. It possesses 25–33% of the wine sales market in the U.S. Rutman distributed Gallo wine for nearly forty years prior to its termination in August 1984. It was the largest wine vendor in the county and sold products of twenty-nine different wine manufacturers, Gallo's competitors among them. Rutman exclusively distributed Inglenook and Taylor California Cellar wines, Gallo's chief competitors in the county's retail wine market. Gallo products, however, constituted 25% of Rutman's sales for which appellant spent approximately $1.5 million per year.

In the early 1970's, Gallo established WDI as another wholesale distributor of wine products in Cuyahoga County. Gallo provided material assistance to WDI which was not provided to any of its competitors. On information and belief, appellant alleges that 1) Gallo obtained a warehouse facility for WDI's use and subleased it to WDI on favorable terms; 2) Gallo "took away" several products so that WDI could have the benefit of selling an established product without competition; 3) Gallo provided WDI with favorable financing options; 4) Gallo provided WDI with point-of-sale advertising and promotional materials not made available to Rutman; 5) Gallo provided advertising material to WDI which it refused to provide to Rutman, and 6) Gallo utilized advertisements of products sold by WDI and would not advocate products sold by Rutman.

The parties' relationship was governed by a 1977 non-exclusive Agreement of Distributorship. Gallo required Rutman to regularly report its sales level of wine products manufactured by Gallo's competitors. Thus, Gallo was able to monitor the level of appellant's sales of products, including those of Gallo's chief competitors in the county.

Gallo terminated Rutman via letter received June 18, 1984, effective sixty days thereafter. The letter allegedly resulted from a number of private or secret communications between Gallo and WDI representatives, and was issued with the purpose and effect of preventing, reducing, and unreasonably limiting competition in the market for the importation and the sale of wine products in Cuyahoga County. Such termination of appellant constituted an attempt to monopolize and/or to form a combination with WDI to monopolize the relevant market, all to the detriment of the public interest. The termination purportedly has injured and will continue to injure Rutman's ability to compete, to retain its customers, and to remain as a viable force in the business of wholesale wine distribution.

Appellant alleges that Gallo knows that the loss of the Gallo line in Cuyahoga County "could either drive Rutman totally out of business or force Rutman to implement severe cutbacks in personnel and resources so as to preclude or substantially diminish Rutman's ability to sell other brands of wine products competitive to Gallo" in that geographical market. Gallo's products purportedly serve as "door openers" or "call items" and facilitate Rutman's access to retail outlets. The loss of "door openers" has allegedly caused appellant to lose customers for the sale of wine products in the county and lessened competition in the sale of other product lines in the same geographical market by "frustrating" Rutman's ability to sell those other lines "through the cutbacks in personnel and services resulting from Gallo's wrongful termination of Rutman."

Rutman further alleges that with full knowledge that the elimination of Rutman as a distributor would hinder or eliminate competition in the sale of wine products competitive to Gallo in the county, appellee, WDI and unnamed co-conspirators engaged in an unlawful combination and conspiracy in unreasonable restraint of trade and commerce. This combination consisted in part of a continuing agreement, understanding and concert of action to engage in a group boycott of plaintiff, to willfully fail and refuse to provide plaintiff with products and supplies, including point-of-sale advertising and promotional materials, and to refrain from doing business with plaintiff.

III.

PER SE V. RULE OF REASON ANALYSIS

Appellant urges that a *per se* analytical standard is appropriate. Appellant relies on *Klor's, Inc. v. Broadway-Hale Stores,* 359 U.S. 207 (1959), for the proposition that dealer terminations resulting from group boycotts where manufacturers and distributors conspire to deprive a distributor of the goods he needs to compete, are *per se* violations of section 1 of the Sherman Act. *Klor's* concerned several manufacturers and distributors who conspired amongst themselves and with a major retailer, Broadway-Hale, either not to sell to Klor's or to sell to it only at discriminatory prices and highly unfavorable terms. *Klor's* is distinguishable in that it alleges a widespread horizontal and vertical combination. *Klor's* expressly stated: "This is not a case of a single trader refusing to deal with another, nor even of a manufacturer and a dealer agreeing to an exclusive distributorship." 359 U.S. at 212. The Court thus implied that the latter situations do not lend themselves to a *per se* standard of analysis.

Monsanto Co. v. Spray-Rite Service Corp., 465 U.S. 752, 761 (1984), reaffirmed that only vertical arrangements accompanying or implementing price-fixing schemes are to be considered *per se* violations of the antitrust laws;[b] other vertical arrangements are to be tested under the Rule of Reason. Though the Second Amended Complaint alleges that unnamed co-conspirators combined with Gallo and WDI in a concerted refusal to deal, appellant never alleges the existence of a horizontal or vertical arrangement which would trigger a *per se* analysis.

Gallo and WDI are not competitors. Appellant's claims of discrimination are vertical and nonprice-related. Any arrangement between them involving a group boycott or concerted refusal to deal with Rutman necessarily consists of a vertical arrangement to which the Rule of Reason applies.

---

[b] This is obviously no longer true, but this decision predates *Leegin*.

IV.

SECTION 1 OF THE SHERMAN ACT

Count 1 alleges that Gallo violated section 1 of the Sherman Act. . . . Rutman invokes section 4 of the Clayton Act, 15 U.S.C. § 15 (1986), which permits private civil actions to be brought by "any person who shall be injured in his business or property by reason of anything forbidden in the antitrust laws."

Indispensable to any section 1 claim is an allegation that *competition* has been injured rather than merely competitors. Appellant contends that because it is the exclusive dealer of two of Gallo's chief competitors, the injury to its own ability to compete in turn harms the public by substantially reducing or eliminating competition in the sale of wine products in Cuyahoga County. The loss of Gallo products also allegedly deprives appellant of "door openers" which facilitate Rutman's sale of Gallo's competitors' products. Rutman claims appellant's termination was a means employed by Gallo to reduce competition in the wine product industry in Cuyahoga County.

While appellant clearly pleads injury to itself, its conclusion that competition has been harmed thereby does not follow. Rutman charges that its termination was accomplished to prevent, reduce, and unreasonably limit competition in the market. Gallo responds that injury to appellant and injury to Gallo's competitors are not injury to competition. Appellee persuasively argues that appellant can prove no set of facts consistent with the allegations of its complaint which would entitle it to relief.

First, an agreement between a manufacturer and a distributor to establish an exclusive distributorship is not, standing alone, a violation of antitrust laws, and in most circumstances does not adversely affect competition in the market. *A.H. Cox & Co. v. Star Machinery,* 653 F.2d 1302, 1306–07 (9th Cir.1981). When a manufacturer and a distributor so agree, the termination of other distributors may necessarily result. No antitrust violation occurs unless the exclusive agreement is intended to or actually does harm competition in the relevant market.

> That one distributor will be hurt when another succeeds in taking its line will be axiomatic in some markets . . . but the intent to cause that result is not itself prohibited by the antitrust laws. The intent proscribed by the antitrust laws lies in the purpose to harm competition in the relevant market, not to harm a particular competitor.

Id. at 1307 (citation omitted). *Knutson v. Daily Review, Inc.,* 548 F.2d 795, 803 (9th Cir.1976) is in accord:

A termination is not unlawful because of some adverse effect on the distributor's business, even if the effect is the elimination of the distributor from the market. The complaining distributor must show that the refusal to deal was intended to or did bring about some restraint of trade beyond the loss of business suffered by the distributor or the market's loss of a distributor-competitor.

. . . . The mere fact of reduced sales of other brands by one wholesaler is not enough to establish an impact on competition.

The allegation of specific intent to terminate a distributor with the purposeful intent to bring about harm to competition is conclusory in the absence of anticompetitive conduct from which such specific intent may be inferred. As stated in *Hunt-Wesson Foods, Inc. v. Ragu Foods, Inc.,* 627 F.2d 919, 924 (9th Cir.1980), a court must ask whether plaintiff "could show any set of facts, consistent with the allegations of its complaint, that would constitute a violation of the antitrust laws." Gallo relies upon *Dunn & Mavis, Inc. v. Nu-Car Driveaway, Inc.,* 691 F.2d 241 (6th Cir.1982). Appellant Dunn & Mavis, a provider of auto transport services in Detroit, alleged that Nu-Car Driveaway, Inc., a competitor, conspired with Chrysler Motors to drive plaintiff out of business. Chrysler and Nu-Car conspired and made plans for the termination of Dunn & Mavis in order to eliminate existing competition in the relevant transportation market. The Court of Appeals affirmed the dismissal of claims under sections 1 and 2, indicating that "[t]he complaint states no set of facts which, if true, would constitute an antitrust offense, notwithstanding its conclusory language regarding the elimination of competition and improper purpose." *Id.* at 243.

Appellant alleges precisely what the appellant in *Dunn & Mavis* alleged: that a supplier and a distributor/competitor conspired to terminate it for the purpose of reducing or eliminating competition in the relevant geographical market. Termination of one distributor in order to establish an exclusive distributorship, even with the knowledge that harm to competition will ensue, does not create an inference that harm to competition is intended; a fortiori Rutman may not rest its allegation of purposeful conduct solely on such speculation. On these facts, the specific intent to harm competition is insufficiently pleaded. As stated in *Car Carriers:* "The pleader may not evade these requirements by merely alleging a bare legal conclusion; if the facts 'do not at least outline or adumbrate' a violation of the Sherman Act, the plaintiffs 'will get nowhere merely by dressing them up in the language of antitrust.'" 745 F.2d at 1106 (quoting *Sutliff, Inc. v. Donovan Companies,* 727 F.2d 648, 654 (7th Cir.1984)).

V.

SECTION 2 OF THE SHERMAN ACT

Count 1 also contains a claim under section 2 of the Sherman Act which provides in part:

> Every person who shall monopolize, or attempt to monopolize, or combine or conspire with any other person or persons, to monopolize any part of the trade or commerce among the several States, or with foreign nations, shall be deemed guilty of a felony, ...

The three requisite elements of a monopolization claim are: 1) possession of monopoly power in the relevant market, 2) willful acquisition or maintenance of that power, and 3) causal "antitrust" injury. *Hunt-Wesson,* 627 F.2d at 924.

A claim for attempted monopolization under section 2 also consists of three elements: 1) specific intent to control prices or destroy competition in the relevant market, 2) predatory or anticompetitive conduct directed to accomplishing the unlawful purpose, and 3) a dangerous probability of success. *Foremost Pro Color, Inc. v. Eastman Kodak Co.,* 703 F.2d 534, 543–44 (9th Cir.1983).

Monopoly power in the relevant geographical market of Cuyahoga County is an essential element for a monopolization claim. Appellant pleads that Gallo controls between 25–33% of the market for wine sales in the *United States.* However, appellant makes no statement as to Gallo's market share in Cuyahoga County. Appellant states that Gallo comprises 25% of Rutman's business, and that Rutman is the largest wine distributor in the county. Yet, appellant does not specify that Gallo comprises 25% of its business in Cuyahoga County. Even assuming the 25% refers to Gallo's share of Rutman's business in the county, Rutman thereby admits that three-quarters of its business is attributable to the twenty-eight other product lines it carries, among which are Inglenook and Taylor, Gallo's two largest competitors in the county. An allegation of monopoly power is an explicit element of actual monopolization and may be an implicit requirement of attempted monopolization's third prong relating to the dangerous probability of success. *California Computer Products, Inc. v. IBM Corp.,* 613 F.2d 727, 737 (9th Cir.1979) (dangerous probability of success may be inferred from direct proof of market power or from proof of specific intent and anticompetitive conduct). Appellant's section 2 claim cannot lie because it lacks an allegation that Gallo possesses monopoly power in the relevant geographical market.

Rutman's section 2 claim also fails because it does not sufficiently allege a specific intent to monopolize the wine market in Cuyahoga County and because Rutman fails to allege anticompetitive conduct. As addressed in the discussion regarding section 1, above, appellant's allegations of specific intent and anticompetitive conduct are insufficient to withstand a motion to dismiss. The absence of these elements in appellant's attempted monopolization claim leaves that aspect of Count 1 deficient as well.

. . . .

X.

CONCLUSION

The district court's dismissal of Counts 1 and 2 of the Second Amended Complaint are affirmed because plaintiff alleges no set of facts which could sustain its antitrust claims therein. Dismissal of Count 3 is affirmed because no allegation appears that Rutman's comparative ability to compete was damaged by Gallo's alleged discrimination. The Ohio state law claims also fail.

No abuse of discretion has occurred in denying further amendment, nor in denying discovery.

The judgment of the district court is therefore AFFIRMED.

NOTES & QUESTIONS

(1) Under what standard of analysis did the court view the alleged violation? Why was that standard chosen?

(2) What harm to competition did Rutman allege? Why was the court unpersuaded by Rutman's argument? Do you see any other flaws in Rutman's § 1 claim?

(3) Generally speaking, a manufacturer creating an exclusive dealership or simply ceasing to sell to all but one dealer in a given territory is protected conduct, provided that the conduct is independent (i.e., there is not a conspiracy between the manufacturer and other dealers). *See Monsanto Co. v. Spray-Rite Serv. Corp.*, 465 U.S. 752, 764, 768 (1984) (requiring direct or circumstantial evidence of a "conscious commitment to a common scheme designed to achieve an unlawful objective"); *Simpson v. Union Oil Co. of California*, 377 U.S. 13, 16 (1964) ("The fact that a retailer can refuse to deal does not give the supplier immunity if the arrangement is one of those schemes condemned by the antitrust laws."). However, if multiple dealers combine to pressure a manufacturer into terminating a cost-cutting competitor, a horizontal price-fixing case could be made. *See Denny's Marina, Inc. v. Renfro Prods., Inc.*, 8 F.3d 1217, 1220 (7th Cir. 1993) (finding that a conspiracy to exclude a marine dealer from boat shows by competitors and their trade association was horizontal price fixing).

3. PROVING CONCERTED ACTION

Section 1 of the Sherman Act requires a "contract, combination . . . or conspiracy . . . in restraint of trade." Thus, § 1 requires what is commonly referred to as "concerted action" by the defendants. This is not to say that all of the defendants must have the same motive, but rather that their agreed actions must have the necessary impact on competition.[c] Of course, it is rare for defendants to expressly agree to engage in antitrust violations such as price fixing. Frequently, an agreement must be inferred or implied from circumstantial evidence. Not surprisingly, the burden of proof to adduce sufficient evidence of an agreement rests with the plaintiff.

One way that a plaintiff can show an implied agreement is through "conscious parallelism." This is the theory that multiple competitors may be acting in concert, despite the lack of an explicit agreement, when the competitors have knowledge of each other's conduct and act in a like manner. The Supreme Court case of *Interstate Circuit v. United States*, 306 U.S. 208 (1939), demonstrates how such a theory works. Interstate Circuit and its affiliate, Consolidated Theaters, were movie theater operators with a significant share of the market in Texas. Interstate sent a letter to movie distributors (who had approximately 75% of the film market) asking them to exert control over admission prices and double-features if they wanted Interstate to continue to use them. The letters listed all of the addressees; thus, each distributor was aware that the others were receiving the same letter. Although there was no direct evidence that any of the distributors agreed to comply with Interstate's demands, each distributor did subsequently comply with at least some of the requests. The Court held that the circumstances justified the inference that the distributors acted in concert.

Despite this holding, concerted action requires more than showing a parallel act. Subsequent cases have held that conscious parallelism requires a plaintiff to demonstrate: (1) that defendants engaged in consciously parallel action,[d] and (2) that such action was contrary to their economic self-interest so as not to amount to good faith business judgment. *See Pan-Islamic Trade Corp. v. Exxon Corp.*, 632 F.2d 539, 559 (5th Cir. 1980). These elements derive from what have been termed "plus factors" drawn from the *Interstate* decision. Plus factors used to support an inference of concerted action have included: actions contrary to the defendants' economic interests; a motivation to enter into concerted

---

[c] As we have seen from the *Goodman* and *NCAA* cases, the concerted action can even be forced upon the actors by statute or coercion.

[d] This element is sometimes broken down into two components. The plaintiff must show (1) parallel action and (2) that the defendants were aware of each other's conduct, and this awareness was part of their decision-making process. *See Cosmetic Gallery, Inc. v. Schoeneman Corp.*, 495 F.3d 46, 53–54 (3d Cir. 2007).

action; attendance at meetings or discussions at which defendants had the opportunity to conspire; defendants engaged in parallel behavior that is economically irrational unless an agreement exists; and at least one participant expressly invited common action by the other. *See Petruzzi's IGA Supermarkets, Inc. v. Darling-Delaware Co.*, 998 F.2d 1224, 1242 (3d Cir. 1993) (citing WILLIAM C. HOLMES, 1992 ANTITRUST LAW HANDBOOK § 1.03[3], at 154).

Two areas of caution are worth mentioning before leaving the topic of conscious parallelism. First, some markets are by their nature oligopolic—i.e., characterized by only a few sellers. In such markets, it may be inevitable that sellers will act similarly. For example, if a seller is contemplating lowering its prices to capture a larger market share, it likely knows that its competitors will follow. The desired effect of capturing market share will not be realized, and instead, the seller will hurt its profits. Given this knowledge, the seller may choose not to lower prices, and neither will its competitors. On its face, this may appear to be conscious parallelism, but there is not necessarily any tacit agreement. Thus, courts consider the nature of the market involved and do not reach conclusions based merely on parallel conduct in an oligopolic industry. *See, e.g., Boise Cascade Corp. v. FTC*, 637 F.2d 573, 576–77 (9th Cir. 1980) ("It is important to stress that the weight of the case law and the Commission's own policy statement make it clear that we are looking for at least tacit agreement to use a formula which has the effect of fixing prices.").

Second, antitrust plaintiffs alleging an implied agreement based upon conscious parallelism face procedural hurdles, particularly the possibility of dismissal under Federal Rule of Civil Procedure 12(b)(6). The Supreme Court decision of *Bell Atlantic Corp. v. Twombly*, 550 U.S. 544 (2007), involved a class action lawsuit alleging a violation of § 1 of the Sherman Act. The plaintiffs alleged that incumbent local exchange carriers ("ILECs") engaged in parallel conduct by tacitly agreeing not to compete with one another. However, the complaint never alleged facts suggesting that the ILECs actually formed a contract, combination, or conspiracy to restrain trade by refusing to compete. The Supreme Court agreed with the dismissal of the claim under Rule 12(b)(6):

> The inadequacy of showing parallel conduct or interdependence, without more, mirrors the ambiguity of the behavior: consistent with conspiracy, but just as much in line with a wide swath of rational and competitive business strategy unilaterally prompted by common perceptions of the market. Accordingly, we have previously hedged against false inferences from identical behavior at a number of points in the trial sequence. An antitrust conspiracy plaintiff with evidence showing nothing beyond parallel conduct is not entitled to a directed verdict; proof

of a § 1 conspiracy must include evidence tending to exclude the possibility of independent action; and at the summary judgment stage a § 1 plaintiff's offer of conspiracy evidence must tend to rule out the possibility that the defendants were acting independently.

This case presents the antecedent question of what a plaintiff must plead in order to state a claim under § 1 of the Sherman Act. . . . While a complaint attacked by a Rule 12(b)(6) motion to dismiss does not need detailed factual allegations, a plaintiff's obligation to provide the grounds of his entitlement to relief requires more than labels and conclusions, and a formulaic recitation of the elements of a cause of action will not do.

In applying these general standards to a § 1 claim, we hold that stating such a claim requires a complaint with enough factual matter (taken as true) to suggest that an agreement was made. Asking for plausible grounds to infer an agreement does not impose a probability requirement at the pleading stage; it simply calls for enough fact[s] to raise a reasonable expectation that discovery will reveal evidence of [an] illegal agreement.

Id. at 554–57. After *Twombly*, it would appear that a plaintiff alleging an agreement under a conscious parallelism theory must allege facts consistent with the above-mentioned plus factors or risk dismissal at the pleading stage.

The plaintiff's burden to show concerted action can be complicated by another hurdle—the defendants may not be separate entities at all. For example, should conduct involving a wholly owned subsidiary and its parent company amount to concerted action? What about subsidiaries that are not wholly owned? Consider these questions as you read the following case.

AMERICAN NEEDLE, INC. V. NATIONAL FOOTBALL LEAGUE
560 U.S. 183 (2010)

STEVENS, J.

"Every contract, combination in the form of a trust or otherwise, or, conspiracy, in restraint of trade" is made illegal by § 1 of the Sherman Act, ch. 647, 26 Stat. 209, as amended, 15 U.S.C. § 1. The question whether an arrangement is a contract, combination, or conspiracy is different from and antecedent to the question whether it unreasonably restrains trade. This case raises that antecedent question about the business of the 32 teams in the National Football League (NFL) and a corporate entity that they formed to manage their intellectual property. We conclude that the NFL's licensing activities constitute concerted action that is not categorically beyond the coverage of § 1. The legality of that concerted action must be judged under the Rule of Reason.

I

Originally organized in 1920, the NFL is an unincorporated association that now includes 32 separately owned professional football teams. Each team has its own name, colors, and logo, and owns related intellectual property. Like each of the other teams in the league, the New Orleans Saints and the Indianapolis Colts, for example, have their own distinctive names, colors, and marks that are well known to millions of sports fans.

Prior to 1963, the teams made their own arrangements for licensing their intellectual property and marketing trademarked items such as caps and jerseys. In 1963, the teams formed National Football League Properties (NFLP) to develop, license, and market their intellectual property. Most, but not all, of the substantial revenues generated by NFLP have either been given to charity or shared equally among the teams. However, the teams are able to and have at times sought to withdraw from this arrangement.

Between 1963 and 2000, NFLP granted nonexclusive licenses to a number of vendors, permitting them to manufacture and sell apparel bearing team insignias. Petitioner, American Needle, Inc., was one of those licensees. In December 2000, the teams voted to authorize NFLP to grant exclusive licenses, and NFLP granted Reebok International Ltd. an exclusive 10-year license to manufacture and sell trademarked headwear for all 32 teams. It thereafter declined to renew American Needle's nonexclusive license.

American Needle filed this action in the Northern District of Illinois, alleging that the agreements between the NFL, its teams, NFLP, and Reebok violated §§ 1 and 2 of the Sherman Act. In their answer to the complaint, the defendants averred that the teams, NFL, and NFLP were incapable of conspiring within the meaning of § 1 "because they are a single economic enterprise, at least with respect to the conduct challenged." After limited discovery, the District Court granted summary judgment on the question "whether, with regard to the facet of their operations respecting exploitation of intellectual property rights, the NFL and its 32 teams are, in the jargon of antitrust law, acting as a single entity." *American Needle, Inc. v. New Orleans La. Saints,* 496 F. Supp. 2d 941, 943 (2007). The court concluded "that in that facet of their operations they have so integrated their operations that they should be deemed a single entity rather than joint ventures cooperating for a common purpose." *Ibid.*

The Court of Appeals for the Seventh Circuit affirmed. The panel observed that "in some contexts, a league seems more aptly described as a single entity immune from antitrust scrutiny, while in others a league appears to be a joint venture between independently owned teams that is subject to review under § 1." 538 F.3d, 736, 741 (2008). Relying on Circuit precedent, the court limited its inquiry to the particular conduct at issue, licensing of teams' intellectual property. The panel agreed with petitioner that "when making a single-entity determination, courts must examine whether the conduct in question deprives the marketplace of the independent sources of economic control that competition assumes." *Id.,* at 742. The court, however, discounted the significance of potential competition among the teams regarding the use of their intellectual property because the teams "can function only as one source of economic power when collectively producing NFL football." *Id.,* at 743. The court noted that football itself can only be carried out jointly. *See ibid.* ("Asserting that a single football team could produce a football game . . . is a Zen riddle: Who wins when a football team plays itself."). Moreover, "NFL teams share a vital economic interest in collectively promoting NFL football . . . [to] compet[e] with other forms of entertainment." *Ibid.* "It thus follows," the court found, "that only one source of economic power controls the promotion of NFL football," and "it makes little sense to assert that each individual team has the authority, if not the responsibility, to promote the jointly produced NFL football." *Ibid.* Recognizing that NFL teams have "license[d] their intellectual property collectively" since 1963, the court held that § 1 did not apply. *Id.,* at 744.

     We granted certiorari.

                                        II

     As the case comes to us, we have only a narrow issue to decide: whether the NFL respondents are capable of engaging in a "contract, combination . . . , or conspiracy" as defined by § 1 of the Sherman Act, 15 U.S.C. § 1, or, as we have sometimes phrased it, whether the alleged activity by the NFL respondents "must be viewed as that of a single enterprise for purposes of § 1." *Copperweld Corp. v. Independence Tube Corp.,* 467 U.S. 752, 771 (1984).

     Taken literally, the applicability of § 1 to "every contract, combination . . . or conspiracy" could be understood to cover every conceivable agreement, whether it be a group of competing firms fixing prices or a single firm's chief executive telling her subordinate how to price their company's product. But even though, "read literally," § 1 would address "the entire body of private contract," that is not what the statute means. *National Soc. of Professional Engineers v. United States,* 435 U.S. 679, 688 (1978). Not every instance of cooperation between two people is a potential "contract, combination . . . , or conspiracy, in restraint of trade." 15 U.S.C. § 1.

The meaning of the term "contract, combination . . . or conspiracy" is informed by the " 'basic distinction' " in the Sherman Act " 'between concerted and independent action' " that distinguishes § 1 of the Sherman Act from § 2. *Copperweld,* 467 U.S., at 767 (quoting *Monsanto Co. v. Spray-Rite Service Corp.,* 465 U.S. 752, 761 (1984)). Section 1 applies only to concerted action that restrains trade. Section 2, by contrast, covers both concerted and independent action, but only if that action "monopolize[s]," 15 U.S.C. § 2, or "threatens actual monopolization," *Copperweld,* 467 U.S., at 767, a category that is narrower than restraint of trade. Monopoly power may be equally harmful whether it is the product of joint action or individual action.

Congress used this distinction between concerted and independent action to deter anticompetitive conduct and compensate its victims, without chilling vigorous competition through ordinary business operations. The distinction also avoids judicial scrutiny of routine, internal business decisions.

Thus, in § 1 Congress "treated concerted behavior more strictly than unilateral behavior." *Id.,* at 768. This is so because unlike independent action, "[c]oncerted activity inherently is fraught with anticompetitive risk" insofar as it "deprives the marketplace of independent centers of decisionmaking that competition assumes and demands." *Id.,* at 768–769. And because concerted action is discrete and distinct, a limit on such activity leaves untouched a vast amount of business conduct. As a result, there is less risk of deterring a firm's necessary conduct; courts need only examine discrete agreements; and such conduct may be remedied simply through prohibition.[2] Concerted activity is thus "judged more sternly than unilateral activity under § 2," *Copperweld,* 467 U.S., at 768. For these reasons, § 1 prohibits any concerted action "in restraint of trade or commerce," even if the action does not "threate[n] monopolization," *Ibid.* And therefore, an arrangement must embody concerted action in order to be a "contract, combination . . . or conspiracy" under § 1.

III

We have long held that concerted action under § 1 does not turn simply on whether the parties involved are legally distinct entities. Instead, we have eschewed such formalistic distinctions in favor of a functional consideration of how the parties involved in the alleged anticompetitive conduct actually operate.

As a result, we have repeatedly found instances in which members of a legally single entity violated § 1 when the entity was controlled by a

---

[2]   If Congress prohibited independent action that merely restrains trade (even if it does not threaten monopolization), that prohibition could deter perfectly competitive conduct by firms that are fearful of litigation costs and judicial error. Moreover, if every unilateral action that restrained trade were subject to antitrust scrutiny, then courts would be forced to judge almost every internal business decision.

group of competitors and served, in essence, as a vehicle for ongoing concerted activity. In *United States v. Sealy, Inc.,* 388 U.S. 350 (1967), for example, a group of mattress manufacturers operated and controlled Sealy, Inc., a company that licensed the Sealy trademark to the manufacturers, and dictated that each operate within a specific geographic area. *Id.,* at 352–353. The Government alleged that the licensees and Sealy were conspiring in violation of § 1, and we agreed. *Id.,* at 352–354. We explained that "[w]e seek the central substance of the situation" and therefore "we are moved by the identity of the persons who act, rather than the label of their hats." *Id.,* at 353. We thus held that Sealy was not a "separate entity, but . . . an instrumentality of the individual manufacturers." *Id.,* at 356. In similar circumstances, we have found other formally distinct business organizations covered by § 1. *See, e.g., National Collegiate Athletic Assn. v. Board of Regents of Univ. of Okla.,* 468 U.S. 85 (1984) *(NCAA); United States v. Topco Associates, Inc.,* 405 U.S. 596, 609 (1972). We have similarly looked past the form of a legally "single entity" when competitors were part of professional organizations or trade groups.

Conversely, there is not necessarily concerted action simply because more than one legally distinct entity is involved. Although, under a now-defunct doctrine known as the "intraenterprise conspiracy doctrine," we once treated cooperation between legally separate entities as necessarily covered by § 1, we now embark on a more functional analysis.

The roots of this functional analysis can be found in the very decision that established the intraenterprise conspiracy doctrine. In *United States v. Yellow Cab Co.,* 332 U.S. 218 (1947), we observed that "corporate interrelationships . . . are not determinitive of the applicability of the Sherman Act" because the Act "is aimed at substance rather than form." *Id.,* at 227. We nonetheless held that cooperation between legally separate entities was necessarily covered by § 1 because an unreasonable restraint of trade "may result as readily from a conspiracy among those who are affiliated or integrated under common ownership as from a conspiracy among those who are otherwise independent." *Ibid.; see also Kiefer-Stewart Co. v. Joseph E. Seagram & Sons, Inc.,* 340 U.S. 211, 215 (1951).

The decline of the intraenterprise conspiracy doctrine began in *Sunkist Growers, Inc. v. Winckler & Smith Citrus Products Co.,* 370 U.S. 19 (1962). In that case, several agricultural cooperatives that were owned by the same farmers were sued for violations of § 1 of the Sherman Act. *Id.,* at 24–25. Applying a specific immunity provision for agricultural cooperatives, we held that the three cooperatives were "in practical effect" one "organization," even though the controlling farmers "have formally organized themselves into three separate legal entities." *Id.,* at 29. "To hold otherwise," we explained, "would be to impose grave legal consequences upon organizational distinctions that are of *de minimis* meaning and effect" insofar as "use of separate corporations had [no] economic significance." *Ibid.*

Next, in *United States v. Citizens & Southern Nat. Bank,* 422 U.S. 86 (1975), a large bank, Citizens and Southern (C & S), formed a holding company that operated *de facto* suburban branch banks in the Atlanta area through ownership of the maximum amount of stock in each local branch that was allowed by law, "ownership of much of the remaining stock by parties friendly to C & S, use by the suburban banks of the C & S logogram and all of C & S's banking services, and close C & S oversight of the operation and governance of the suburban banks." *Id.,* at 89, (footnote omitted). The Government challenged the cooperation between the banks. In our analysis, we observed that " 'corporate interrelationships . . . are not determinative,' " *id.,* at 116, "looked to economic substance," and observed that "because the sponsored banks were not set up to be competitors, § 1 did not compel them to compete."

We finally reexamined the intraenterprise conspiracy doctrine in *Copperweld Corp. v. Independence Tube Corp.,* 467 U.S. 752 (1984), and concluded that it was inconsistent with the " 'basic distinction between concerted and independent action.' " *Id.,* at 767. Considering it "perfectly plain that an internal agreement to implement a single, unitary firm's policies does not raise the antitrust dangers that § 1 was designed to police," *id.,* at 769, we held that a parent corporation and its wholly owned subsidiary "are incapable of conspiring with each other for purposes of § 1 of the Sherman Act," *id.,* at 777. We explained that although a parent corporation and its wholly owned subsidiary are "separate" for the purposes of incorporation or formal title, they are controlled by a single center of decisionmaking and they control a single aggregation of economic power. Joint conduct by two such entities does not "depriv[e] the marketplace of independent centers of decisionmaking," *id.,* at 769, and as a result, an agreement between them does not constitute a "contract, combination . . . or conspiracy" for the purposes of § 1.

IV

As *Copperweld* exemplifies, "substance, not form, should determine whether a[n] . . . entity is capable of conspiring under § 1." 467 U.S., at 773, n. 21. This inquiry is sometimes described as asking whether the alleged conspirators are a single entity. That is perhaps a misdescription, however, because the question is not whether the defendant is a legally single entity or has a single name; nor is the question whether the parties involved "seem" like one firm or multiple firms in any metaphysical sense. The key is whether the alleged "contract, combination . . . , or conspiracy" is concerted action—that is, whether it joins together separate decisionmakers. The relevant inquiry, therefore, is whether there is a "contract, combination . . . or conspiracy" amongst "separate economic actors pursuing separate economic interests," *id.*, at 769, such that the agreement "deprives the marketplace of independent centers of decisionmaking," *ibid.*, and therefore of "diversity of entrepreneurial interests," *Fraser v. Major League Soccer, L.L.C.*, 284 F.3d 47, 57 (C.A.1 2002) (Boudin, C.J.), and thus of actual or potential competition.

Thus, while the president and a vice president of a firm could (and regularly do) act in combination, their joint action generally is not the sort of "combination" that § 1 is intended to cover. Such agreements might be described as "really unilateral behavior flowing from decisions of a single enterprise." *Copperweld,* 467 U.S., at 767. Nor, for this reason, does § 1 cover "internally coordinated conduct of a corporation and one of its unincorporated divisions," *id.*, at 770, because "[a] division within a corporate structure pursues the common interests of the whole," *ibid.*, and therefore "coordination between a corporation and its division does not represent a sudden joining of two independent sources of economic power previously pursuing separate interests," *id.*, at 770–771. Nor, for the same reasons, is "the coordinated activity of a parent and its wholly owned subsidiary" covered. *See id.*, at 771. They "have a complete unity of interest" and thus "[w]ith or without a formal 'agreement,' the subsidiary acts for the benefit of the parent, its sole shareholder." *Ibid.*

Because the inquiry is one of competitive reality, it is not determinative that two parties to an alleged § 1 violation are legally distinct entities. Nor, however, is it determinative that two legally distinct entities have organized themselves under a single umbrella or into a structured joint venture. The question is whether the agreement joins together "independent centers of decisionmaking." *Id.*, at 769. If it does, the entities are capable of conspiring under § 1, and the court must decide whether the restraint of trade is an unreasonable and therefore illegal one.

V

The NFL teams do not possess either the unitary decisionmaking quality or the single aggregation of economic power characteristic of independent action. Each of the teams is a substantial, independently owned, and independently managed business. "[T]heir general corporate actions are guided or determined" by "separate corporate consciousnesses," and "[t]heir objectives are" not "common." *Copperweld,* 467 U.S., at 771. The teams compete with one another, not only on the playing field, but to attract fans, for gate receipts and for contracts with managerial and playing personnel.

Directly relevant to this case, the teams compete in the market for intellectual property. To a firm making hats, the Saints and the Colts are two potentially competing suppliers of valuable trademarks. When each NFL team licenses its intellectual property, it is not pursuing the "common interests of the whole" league but is instead pursuing interests of each "corporation itself," *Copperweld,* 467 U.S., at 770; teams are acting as "separate economic actors pursuing separate economic interests," and each team therefore is a potential "independent cente[r] of decisionmaking," *id.,* at 769. Decisions by NFL teams to license their separately owned trademarks collectively and to only one vendor are decisions that "depriv[e] the marketplace of independent centers of decisionmaking," *ibid.,* and therefore of actual or potential competition.

In defense, respondents argue that by forming NFLP, they have formed a single entity, akin to a merger, and market their NFL brands through a single outlet. But it is not dispositive that the teams have organized and own a legally separate entity that centralizes the management of their intellectual property. An ongoing § 1 violation cannot evade § 1 scrutiny simply by giving the ongoing violation a name and label. "Perhaps every agreement and combination in restraint of trade could be so labeled." *Timken Roller Bearing Co. v. United States,* 341 U.S. 593, 598 (1951).

The NFL respondents may be similar in some sense to a single enterprise that owns several pieces of intellectual property and licenses them jointly, but they are not similar in the relevant functional sense. Although NFL teams have common interests such as promoting the NFL brand, they are still separate, profit-maximizing entities, and their interests in licensing team trademarks are not necessarily aligned. Common interests in the NFL brand "*partially* unit[e] the economic interests of the parent firms," Broadley, *Joint Ventures and Antitrust Policy,* 95 Harv. L.Rev. 1521, 1526 (1982) (emphasis added), but the teams still have distinct, potentially competing interests.

It may be, as respondents argue, that NFLP "has served as the single driver of the teams' promotional vehicle, pursuing the common interests of the whole." But illegal restraints often are in the common interests of the parties to the restraint, at the expense of those who are not parties. It is true, as respondents describe, that they have for some time marketed their trademarks jointly. But a history of concerted activity does not immunize conduct from § 1 scrutiny. "Absence of actual competition may simply be a manifestation of the anticompetitive agreement itself." [*Freeman v. San Diego Ass'n of Realtors,* 322 F.3d 1133, 1149 (9th Cir. 2003)].

Respondents argue that nonetheless, as the Court of Appeals held, they constitute a single entity because without their cooperation, there would be no NFL football. It is true that "the clubs that make up a professional sports league are not completely independent economic competitors, as they depend upon a degree of cooperation for economic survival." [*Brown v. Pro Football, Inc.,* 518 U.S. 231, 248 (1996)]. But the Court of Appeals' reasoning is unpersuasive.

The justification for cooperation is not relevant to whether that cooperation is concerted or independent action.[6] A "contract, combination . . . or conspiracy," § 1, that is necessary or useful to a joint venture is still a "contract, combination . . . or conspiracy" if it "deprives the marketplace of independent centers of decisionmaking," *Copperweld,* 467 U.S., at 769. Any joint venture involves multiple sources of economic power cooperating to produce a product. And for many such ventures, the participation of others is necessary. But that does not mean that necessity of cooperation transforms concerted action into independent action; a nut and a bolt can only operate together, but an agreement between nut and bolt manufacturers is still subject to § 1 analysis. Nor does it mean that once a group of firms agree to produce a joint product, cooperation amongst those firms must be treated as independent conduct. The mere fact that the teams operate jointly in some sense does not mean that they are immune.

The question whether NFLP decisions can constitute concerted activity covered by § 1 is closer than whether decisions made directly by the 32 teams are covered by § 1. This is so both because NFLP is a separate corporation with its own management and because the record indicates that most of the revenues generated by NFLP are shared by the teams on an equal basis. Nevertheless we think it clear that for the same reasons the 32 teams' conduct is covered by § 1, NFLP's actions also are subject to § 1, at least with regards to its marketing of property owned by the separate teams. NFLP's licensing decisions are made by the 32 potential competitors, and each of them actually owns its share of the jointly managed assets. Cf. *Sealy,* 388 U.S., at 352–354. Apart from their agreement to cooperate in exploiting those assets, including their decisions as the NFLP, there would be nothing to prevent each of the teams from making its own market decisions relating to purchases of apparel and headwear, to the sale of such items, and to the granting of licenses to use its trademarks.

We generally treat agreements within a single firm as independent action on the presumption that the components of the firm will act to maximize the firm's profits. But in rare cases, that presumption does not hold. Agreements made within a firm can constitute concerted action covered by § 1 when the parties to the agreement act on interests separate from those of the firm itself, and the intrafirm agreements may

---

[6]   As discussed *infra,* necessity of cooperation is a factor relevant to whether the agreement is subject to the Rule of Reason. See *NCAA,* 468 U.S., at 101 (holding that NCAA restrictions on televising college football games are subject to Rule of Reason analysis for the "critical" reason that "horizontal restraints on competition are essential if the product is to be available at all").

simply be a formalistic shell for ongoing concerted action. *See, e.g., Topco Associates, Inc.,* 405 U.S., at 609; *Sealy,* 388 U.S., at 352–354.

For that reason, decisions by the NFLP regarding the teams' separately owned intellectual property constitute concerted action. Thirty-two teams operating independently through the vehicle of the NFLP are not like the components of a single firm that act to maximize the firm's profits. The teams remain separately controlled, potential competitors with economic interests that are distinct from NFLP's financial well-being. Unlike typical decisions by corporate shareholders, NFLP licensing decisions effectively require the assent of more than a mere majority of shareholders. And each team's decision reflects not only an interest in NFLP's profits but also an interest in the team's individual profits. The 32 teams capture individual economic benefits separate and apart from NFLP profits as a result of the decisions they make for the NFLP. NFLP's decisions thus affect each team's profits from licensing its own intellectual property. "Although the business interests of" the teams "will *often* coincide with those of the" NFLP "as an entity in itself, that commonality of interest exists in every cartel." *Los Angeles Memorial Coliseum Comm'n v. NFL,* 726 F.2d 1381, 1389 (C.A.9 1984) (emphasis added). In making the relevant licensing decisions, NFLP is therefore "an instrumentality" of the teams.

If the fact that potential competitors shared in profits or losses from a venture meant that the venture was immune from § 1, then any cartel "could evade the antitrust law simply by creating a 'joint venture' to serve as the exclusive seller of their competing products." *Major League Baseball Properties, Inc. v. Salvino, Inc.,* 542 F.3d 290, 335 (C.A.2 2008) (Sotomayor, J., concurring in judgment). "So long as no agreement," other than one made by the cartelists sitting on the board of the joint venture, "explicitly listed the prices to be charged, the companies could act as monopolies through the 'joint venture.'" *Ibid.* (Indeed, a joint venture with a single management structure is generally a better way to operate a cartel because it decreases the risks of a party to an illegal agreement defecting from that agreement). However, competitors "cannot simply get around" antitrust liability by acting "through a third-party intermediary or 'joint venture'." *Id.,* at 336.

VI

Football teams that need to cooperate are not trapped by antitrust law. "[T]he special characteristics of this industry may provide a justification" for many kinds of agreements. *Brown,* 518 U.S., at 252 (STEVENS, J., dissenting). The fact that NFL teams share an interest in making the entire league successful and profitable, and that they must cooperate in the production and scheduling of games, provides a perfectly sensible justification for making a host of collective decisions. But the conduct at issue in this case is still concerted activity under the Sherman Act that is subject to § 1 analysis.

When "restraints on competition are essential if the product is to be available at all," *per se* rules of illegality are inapplicable, and instead the restraint must be judged according to the flexible Rule of Reason. *NCAA,* 468 U.S., at 101; see *id.,* at 117 ("Our decision not to apply a *per se* rule to this case rests in large part on our recognition that a certain degree of cooperation is necessary if the type of competition that petitioner and its member institutions seek to market is to be preserved"). In such instances, the agreement is likely to survive the Rule of Reason. And depending upon the concerted activity in question, the Rule of Reason may not require a detailed analysis; it "can sometimes be applied in the twinkling of an eye." *NCAA,* 468 U.S., at 109, n. 39.

Other features of the NFL may also save agreements amongst the teams. We have recognized, for example, "that the interest in maintaining a competitive balance" among "athletic teams is legitimate and important," *NCAA,* 468 U.S., at 117. While that same interest applies to the teams in the NFL, it does not justify treating them as a single entity for § 1 purposes when it comes to the marketing of the teams' individually owned intellectual property. It is, however, unquestionably an interest that may well justify a variety of collective decisions made by the teams. What role it properly plays in applying the Rule of Reason to the allegations in this case is a matter to be considered on remand.

. . . .

Accordingly, the judgment of the Court of Appeals is reversed, and the case is remanded for further proceedings consistent with this opinion.

NOTES & QUESTIONS

(1)   Section 1 of the Sherman Act requires concerted action. According to the Court, why did Congress impose such a requirement?

(2)   In cases where multiple entities are acting under one umbrella organization, how should courts determine whether to treat them as separate firms or a single entity?

(3)   What is the "intraenterprise conspiracy doctrine" and why have courts moved away from it?

(4)   The Court concluded that the rule of reason should be used to determine whether the concerted action violated § 1. How do you think American Needle's claim will fare under the rule of reason?

(5)   Under the *Copperweld* rule, a parent company and its wholly owned subsidiary are considered to be a single entity for antitrust purposes. The rule is based upon a unity of interests between the parent and the subsidiary. This rule has been extended to other situations where a unity of interest can

be found. For example, in *Oksanen v. Page Memorial Hospital*, 945 F.2d 696 (4th Cir. 1991), the court held that the Board of Trustees and the medical staff of a hospital were not capable of conspiring to dismiss the plaintiff doctor through unfavorable peer reviews. The court noted, however, that only one other doctor on the staff was a true competitor to the plaintiff, and he had not taken part in the actions to dismiss. *See id.* at 705. *But see Nurse Midwifery Assocs. v. Hibbett*, 918 F.2d 605, 614–15 (6th Cir. 1990) (finding that three doctors who were competitors of the plaintiff were not agents of a hospital and thus could be co-conspirators).

(6) Although a wholly owned subsidiary may not conspire with its parent company, what about a subsidiary that is less than wholly owned? Should the percentage of ownership matter? *Compare Siegel Transfer, Inc. v. Carrier Express, Inc.*, 54 F.3d 1125, 1133 (3d Cir. 1995) (holding that 99.92% ownership is the same as 100% ownership for the purposes of applying *Copperweld*), *and Satellite Fin. Planning Corp. v. First Nat'l Bank of Wilmington*, 633 F. Supp. 386, 395 (D. Del. 1986) (finding that the de minimus difference between 99%-plus ownership and 100% ownership does not diminish *Copperweld's* applicability), *and Gov't Guarantee Fund of Republic of Finland v. Hyatt Corp.*, 955 F. Supp. 441, 458 (D.V.I. 1997) (finding that *Copperweld* was applicable where a parent company owned 52.9% of the total stock and 62.59% of the voting stock of its subsidiary, and stating that "the fact that [the parent] owns less than one hundred percent of [the subsidiary] does not change the economic reality that [the parent] controlled the economic affairs of [the subsidiary]"), *with Computer Identics Corp. v. S. Pac. Co.*, 756 F.2d 200, 204–05 (1st Cir. 1985) (upholding a jury charge where the jury was permitted to determine whether an 80%-owned subsidiary was an independent entity from its parent).

(7) In keeping with *Copperweld*, a number of cases have held that two wholly owned corporate subsidiaries of the same parent are incapable of conspiring with one another. *See Advanced Health-Care Servs., Inc. v. Radford Cmty. Hosp.*, 910 F.2d 139, 146 (4th Cir. 1990); *Directory Sales Mgmt. Corp. v. Ohio Bell Tel. Co.*, 833 F.2d 606, 611 (6th Cir. 1987); *Hood v. Tenneco Texas Life Ins. Co.*, 739 F.2d 1012, 1015 (5th Cir. 1984); *Greenwood Utils. v. Mississippi Power Co.*, 751 F.2d 1484, 1496–97 n.8 (5th Cir. 1985); *Weiss v. York Hosp.*, 745 F.2d 786, 814 n.48 (3d Cir. 1984); *see also Bell Atl. Bus. Sys. Servs. v. Hitachi Data Sys.*, 849 F. Supp. 702, 707 (N.D. Cal. 1994) (finding that subsidiary companies of the same parent could not conspire under § 1 of the Sherman Act, despite the fact that one of the sister companies was only 80% owned by the parent rather than 100% owned).

(8) Generally speaking, a corporation cannot conspire with its officers or other agents. This rule makes sense as officers and other agents are frequently viewed as mere extensions of the company (and because a company is not a natural person, it must always rely on officers and other agents to carry out its business). However, in some circumstances, courts have found that the independent interests of an officer or other agent justified treating that person as a separate actor from the corporation. A

conspiracy under § 1, therefore, could be found. For example, in *Greenville Publishing Co. v. Daily Reflector, Inc.*, 496 F.2d 391 (4th Cir. 1974), the court observed that an exception to the general rule "may be justified when the officer has an independent personal stake in achieving the corporation's illegal objective." *Id.* at 399. The court held that the president of the defendant company could conspire with it because he had a financial interest in another firm that competed with the plaintiff and would directly benefit if the plaintiff was eliminated as a competitor. *See id.* at 400. *But see Oksanen v. Page Mem'l Hosp.*, 945 F.2d 696, 705 (4th Cir. 1991) (declining to extend the personal stake exception where the economic implications of eliminating a competitor were unclear); *Nurse Midwifery Assocs. v. Hibbet*, 918 F.2d 605, 615 (6th Cir. 1990) (refusing to adopt the personal stake exception "in view of substantial policy reasons for not doing so").

(9) Not all concerted action is condemned despite a seemingly anticompetitive purpose. The primary example is concerted action to influence public officials, such as through lobbying, under the well-known *Noerr-Pennington* doctrine (which is named after a pair of Supreme Court cases, *Eastern Railroad Presidents Conference v. Noerr Motor Freight, Inc.*, 365 U.S. 127 (1961), and *United Mine Workers of America v. Pennington*, 381 U.S. 657 (1965)). In *Noerr*, a group of truckers alleged that the defendant railroads were conducting a publicity and lobbying campaign urging the passage of laws which would regulate the trucking industry. The truckers claimed that the campaign was concerted action designed to restrain trade in the long distance freight hauling business. The Supreme Court noted that there was a difference between agreements that petition for legislation to restrain trade and agreements that directly restrain trade. Given the First Amendment right to petition for government action, the Court also questioned the constitutionality of making such conduct a violation of the Sherman Act. *See Noerr*, 365 U.S. at 136–38.

In *Pennington*, the United Mine Workers petitioned the executive branch to induce the Tennessee Valley Authority, a government agency, to curtail spot market purchases and to increase the minimum wage. Relying upon its earlier decision in *Noerr*, the Court stated:

> *Noerr* shields from the Sherman Act a concerted effort to influence public officials regardless of intent or purpose. . . . Joint efforts to influence public officials do not violate the antitrust laws even though intended to eliminate competition. Such conduct is not illegal, either standing alone or as part of a broader scheme itself violative of the Sherman Act.

Pennington, 381 U.S. at 670.

Under the *Noerr-Pennington* doctrine, attempts to influence the legislative and executive branch are shielded from antitrust scrutiny. Lobbying judicial and other adjudicatory proceedings is also protected. *See California Motor Transp. Co. v. Trucking Unlimited*, 404 U.S. 508, 611–12 (1972) ("We conclude that it would be destructive of rights of association and of petition to hold that groups with common interests may not, without violating the antitrust laws, use the channels and procedures of state and federal agencies and courts to advocate their causes and points of view respecting resolution of their business and economic interests. . . ."). The doctrine has been found inapplicable, however, to lobbying private associations that are subsequently influential on rule-making bodies. *See Allied Tube & Conduit Corp. v. Indian Head, Inc.*, 486 U.S. 492, 509–10 (1988) (refusing to extend *Noerr* to an attempt by a group of manufacturers of steel conduit to influence a private fire protection association's revisions of its electrical code, which was typically adopted by a number of state and local governments). Furthermore, *Noerr-Pennington* does not protect so-called "sham" attempts to petition the government. Thus, in *California Motor*, the Court held that activities which resulted in a "pattern of baseless repetitive claims" as part of a concerted attempt to bar a party from government access were in fact a "sham" and not protected. *See California Motor*, 404 U.S. at 513. The Court has since clarified that the "sham exception" to *Noerr-Pennington* focuses on abusing the process of petitioning the government— such as by filing frivolous objections to impose expense or delay upon another party—rather than on the outcome of the petitioning. *See City of Columbia v. Omni Outdoor Adver., Inc.*, 499 U.S. 375, 380 (1991). Thus, legitimate attempts to seek favorable government action are still protected.

(10) Courts have extended the *Noerr-Pennington* doctrine into the broader business tort realm. Most notably, the doctrine has been held to apply to tortious interference with contract claims when the basis of the claim is a petition for government action. *See Sierra Club v. Butz*, 349 F. Supp. 934, 939 (N.D. Cal. 1972) (noting that application of the doctrine would be subject to the "sham" exception); *Oregon Natural Res. Council v. Mohla*, 944 F.2d 531, 533 (9th Cir. 1991); *Protect Our Mountain Env't, Inc. v. Dist. Court in and for Jefferson Cnty.*, 677 P.2d 1361, 1369 (Colo. 1984).

C. SHERMAN ACT § 2 VIOLATIONS

1. ELEMENTS OF A MONOPOLY CLAIM

Section 2 of the Sherman Act prohibits monopolistic behavior. Early on, questions arose as to whether the mere possession of monopoly power violated § 2 without any further conduct. The Supreme Court clarified this issue in *United States v. U.S. Steel Corp.*, 251 U.S. 417 (1920), by stating: "[T]he law does not make mere size an offense, or the existence of unexercised power an offense. It . . . requires overt acts." *Id.* at 451. However, the question of what further conduct was required for liability remained somewhat of a mystery. Judge Wyzanski famously laid out three possibilities for the type of conduct that violates § 2 in *United States v. United Shoe Machinery Corp.*, 110 F. Supp. 295 (D. Mass. 1953). Under the classic approach, a violation of § 2 occurs when the conduct would also violate § 1. Under the exclusionary approach, a violation would occur if the defendant obtained a monopoly by means of conduct that was predatory or exclusionary in purpose or effect. Finally, under the prima facie approach, the defendant is presumed to have engaged in monopolistic conduct if it took any steps, however benign, to attain power (the defendant would then have the burden of rebutting the presumption). *See id.* at 342.

The exclusionary approach appears to be the closest to current law. To establish a monopolization claim under the law today, the claimant must demonstrate: (1) monopolizing conduct coupled with (2) monopoly power in the relevant market. Monopolizing conduct is the "willful acquisition or maintenance . . . of monopoly power as distinguished from growth or development as a consequence of a superior product, business acumen, or historic accident." *United States v. Grinnell*, 384 U.S. 563, 570–71 (1966). Monopoly power is the possession of power to control prices or exclude competition. Before monopoly power may be assessed, the relevant geographic and product markets must be defined. Defendants frequently offer up pro-competitive justifications to counter claims that they are engaged in monopolistic behavior.

NOTES & QUESTIONS

(1) Why might courts have moved away from the classic and prima facie approaches to § 2 violations?

(2) Two other claims are related to a § 2 claim—attempted monopolization and conspiracy to monopolize. An attempted monopolization claim comprises three elements: (1) anticompetitive conduct; (2) intent to monopolize; and (3) a dangerous probability of obtaining monopoly power. A conspiracy to monopolize claim has two elements: (1) proof of a concerted action deliberately entered into with the specific intent to achieve an unlawful monopoly, and (2) the commission of an overt act in furtherance of the conspiracy.

How do these two claims differ from a monopolization claim? Are the elements easier or harder to meet?

2. TYPES OF MONOPOLIZATION CONDUCT

As mentioned, in *Grinnell*, the Supreme Court defined monopolistic conduct as the "willful acquisition or maintenance . . . of monopoly power as distinguished from growth or development as a consequence of a superior product, business acumen, or historic accident." Although this definition gives some guidance, it is still rather vague. Courts have examined various types of conduct for potential liability under Section 2.

a.   Mergers and Acquisitions

Businesses may seek to merge with or acquire other companies for a number of legitimate reasons, such as to reduce production costs or to efficiently move into a new market. However, mergers and acquisitions can also negatively affect competition, particularly in a market with few participants. Mergers and acquisitions can be horizontal, as between actual competitors, or vertical, as when a manufacturer decides to acquire a supplier to reduce costs. Such transactions can also occur between relatively unrelated entities—e.g., a company that buys a smaller business because it produces a product that the buyer does not. This last type of transaction, known as a conglomerate merger, often does not affect the competitive market because nothing has changed other than the ownership of the acquired company. As such, conglomerate mergers do not raise many antitrust concerns.

Vertical mergers do not appear to affect competition, as the same number of competitors remain in the market. However, vertical mergers may still affect competition through distribution efficiencies and reduced transaction costs. More obviously, the supplier, now owned by the manufacturer, could increase the cost of necessary materials to its competing manufacturers or simply refuse to deal with them. Such actions would raise antitrust concerns.

Horizontal mergers receive the highest level of scrutiny. Where there were once two competitors, there is now only one, which reduces competition and may result in price increases to consumers. However, not all horizontal mergers will have such effects. If the merger is between two relatively small competitors in a robust market, the effect may be minimal. In fact, in such a situation, the two small firms may now find themselves in a better position to compete with larger companies due to operating efficiencies and economies of scale. This may result in lower costs to consumers. Thus, even horizontal mergers must be examined with reference to the market that will be affected.

Early court decisions under § 2 of the Sherman Act, applying the rule of reason, seemed very permissive of mergers. In 1914, Congress passed § 7 of the Clayton Act, which proscribes mergers or acquisitions that have a reasonable probability of substantially lessening competition within a market. *See* 15 U.S.C. § 18. This statute requires a determination of the relevant market and a prediction of the effect that the merger will have on the market.

b.   Barriers to Entry

Businesses may prevent competition in a number of ways, including maintaining excess capacity of a needed resource (to deny a competitor access to that resource) and entering into exclusivity agreements with customers. The case of *American Professional Testing Service, Inc. v. Harcourt Brace Jovanovich Legal and Professional Publications, Inc.*, 108 F.3d 1147 (9th Cir. 1997), provides a colorful example of how this first type of conduct might violate § 2. American ran a bar preparation course called Barpassers that competed with Harcourt's BAR/BRI preparation course. A professor who had been teaching Constitutional Law for BAR/BRI was also to work for American, but Harcourt enticed the professor to work exclusively for its course. American sued, alleging that Harcourt had engaged in predatory hiring in violation of the Sherman Act. The court found that no violation occurs when the defendant hires away an employee for the purpose of utilizing the employee's skill:

> Most importantly, this court's decision in *Universal Analytics, Inc. v. MacNeal-Schwendler Corp.*, 914 F.2d 1256 (9th Cir.1990) is controlling on these facts. There, we reviewed whether there were any genuine issues of material fact with respect to Universal's claim that MacNeal's hiring of five of Universal's six key technical employees in 1986 and 1987 was predatory in violation of § 2. This was the first reported case of a claimed § 2 violation as a result of alleged employee raiding or predatory hiring. *Universal Analytics* held that an internal memo of the producer referring to "wounding" of a competitor by hiring key technical employees showed at most that a secondary motivation of the hirings was to disadvantage competition and was insufficient to show predatory conduct in violation of the Sherman Act. "Unlawful predatory hiring occurs when talent is acquired not for purposes of using that talent but for purposes of denying it to a competitor. Such cases can be proved by showing the hiring was made with such predatory intent, i.e. to harm the competition without helping the monopolist, or by showing a clear nonuse in fact." *Id.* at 1258. Absent either of those circumstances, the court agreed . . . that the hiring should not be held exclusionary.

American, 108 F.3d at 1153. Although the court did not agree that a Sherman Act violation had occurred, it did indicate that if Harcourt had hired the professor and not used him (i.e., hired him for the sole purpose of denying his services to American), a claim could be made. Similarly, if a manufacturer purchased excessive amounts of a needed resource for the sole purpose of denying a competitor access to the resource, a claim could be made. *See United States v. Aluminum Co. of Am.*, 148 F.2d 416, 429–30 (2d Cir. 1945) (holding that a producer of aluminum who controlled access to all of the ingot used to make aluminum violated § 2 of the Sherman Act by preventing competition). However, it should be noted that if a manufacturer can articulate a legitimate need for buying excessive amounts of the resource, a § 2 claim will likely fail.

Using exclusivity agreements to deter market entry has also been scrutinized by the courts. This can be accomplished through contractual devices, such as long-term leases with stiff penalties for breach. Future market entrants must price goods and services low enough to offset a potential buyer's penalties for breaching, which deters market entry and competition. In *United States v. United Shoe Machinery Corp.*, 110 F. Supp. 295 (D. Mass. 1953), the defendant held a monopoly in the production of shoe manufacturing equipment. Rather than sell the equipment, the defendant leased the equipment for a term of ten years. Lessees could return the equipment early for a fee, which was reduced if the lessee replaced the machine with another United Shoe machine. Judge Wyzanski found that the cumulative effect of United Shoe's practices was to restrain competition:

> In the relatively static shoe machinery market where there are no sudden changes in the style of machines or in the volume of demand, United has a network of long-term, complicated leases with over 90% of the shoe factories. These leases assure closer and more frequent contacts between United and its customers than would exist if United were a seller and its customers were buyers. Beyond this general quality, these leases are so drawn and so applied as to strengthen United's power to exclude competitors. Moreover, United offers a long line of machine types, while no competitor offers more than a short line. Since in some parts of its line United faces no important competition, United has the power to discriminate, by wide differentials and over long periods of time, in the rate of return it procures from different machine types. Furthermore, being by far the largest company in the field, with by far the largest resources in dollars, in patents, in facilities, and in knowledge, United has a marked capacity to attract offers of inventions, inventors' services, and shoe machinery businesses. And, finally, there is no substantial substitute competition from a vigorous secondhand market in shoe machinery.

> To combat United's market control, a competitor must be prepared with knowledge of shoemaking, engineering skill, capacity to invent around patents, and financial resources sufficient to bear the expense of long developmental and experimental processes. The competitor must be prepared for consumers' resistance founded on their long-term, satisfactory relations with United, and on the cost to them of surrendering United's leases. Also, the competitor must be prepared to give, or point to the source of, repair and other services, and to the source of supplies for machine parts, expendable parts, and the like. Indeed, perhaps a competitor who aims at any large scale

success must also be prepared to lease his machines. These considerations would all affect potential competition, and have not been without their effect on actual competition.

Not only does the evidence show [that] United has control of the market, but also the evidence does not show that the control is due entirely to excusable causes.... United's control does not rest solely on its original constitution, its ability, its research, or its economies of scale. There are other barriers to competition, and these barriers were erected by United's own business policies.... In one sense, the leasing system and the miscellaneous activities just referred to (except United's purchases in the secondhand market) were natural and normal, for they were ... honestly industrial. They are the sort of activities which would be engaged in by other honorable firms. And, to a large extent, the leasing practices conform to long-standing traditions in the shoe machinery business. Yet, they are not practices which can be properly described as the inevitable consequences of ability, natural forces, or law. They represent something more than the use of accessible resources, the process of invention and innovation, and the employment of those techniques of employment, financing, production, and distribution, which a competitive society must foster. They are contracts, arrangements, and policies which, instead of encouraging competition based on pure merit, further the dominance of a particular firm. In this sense, they are unnatural barriers; they unnecessarily exclude actual and potential competition; they restrict a free market. While the law allows many enterprises to use such practices, the Sherman Act is now construed by superior courts to forbid the continuance of effective market control based in part upon such practices.

Id. at 343–45.

c. Refusals to Deal

The idea that a business's refusal to deal with a competitor could violate the Sherman Act may seem odd. Antitrust law is aimed at encouraging competition, and it would seem that competition and cooperation are inconsistent. Indeed, § 1 of the Sherman Act looks suspiciously upon competitors who cooperate in a number of contexts. Nonetheless, there are a few limited situations where competitors may have to cooperate to encourage competition. One such situation involves what is known as the "essential facilities" doctrine. Under this doctrine, one in possession of a scarce resource is expected to deal with all parties in a nondiscriminatory manner. Thus, one who possesses monopoly power over a resource, even if the monopoly is lawful, will violate § 2 if it exploits the scarce resource in a way that arbitrarily disadvantages customers.

In *United States v. Terminal Railroad Association of St. Louis*, 224 U.S. 383 (1912), a number of railroad companies combined to form a terminal company with the express purpose of acquiring control of the city's railway facilities (which they accomplished). Once in control, the defendant railroad companies were able to discriminate against their competitors. The Court noted that, under the peculiar circumstances at issue, it was not feasible for the competitors to construct their own terminal facilities; thus, they were forced to pay whatever price was chosen by the defendants if they wanted to do business in St. Louis. Furthermore, it was insufficient to simply force the defendants to charge the same rate to competitors that defendants paid themselves, as the defendants could charge exorbitant rates with the knowledge that they would recoup the overages through the increased profits to the terminal company. As a result, the Court ordered the defendants to permit competitors to join the company. The Court also ordered that access to the terminals be made available to all railroad companies on a nondiscriminatory basis, regardless of whether they were owners of the company. Finally, the Court required that the rates charged for use of the railway facilities could not exceed reasonable amounts.

The facts that give rise to application of the essential facilities doctrine are rare and often involve some type of public utility. *See Hecht v. Pro-Football, Inc.*, 570 F.2d 982, 992–93 (D.C. Cir. 1977) (applying the essential facilities doctrine to a sports stadium); *United States v. AT&T Co.*, 524 F. Supp. 1336, 1352–53 (D.D.C. 1981) (breaking up AT&T's vertically integrated monopoly in the telecommunications industry). Closely related to the essential facilities doctrine is a monopolist's duty to deal on nondiscriminatory terms with a competitor. This duty extends beyond the essential facilities doctrine to situations where the cooperation of competitors leads to consumer welfare.

ASPEN SKIING COMPANY V. ASPEN HIGHLANDS SKIING CORPORATION

472 U.S. 585 (1985)

STEVENS, J.

In a private treble-damages action, the jury found that petitioner Aspen Skiing Company (Ski Co.) had monopolized the market for downhill skiing services in Aspen, Colorado. The question presented is whether that finding is erroneous as a matter of law because it rests on an assumption that a firm with monopoly power has a duty to cooperate with its smaller rivals in a marketing arrangement in order to avoid violating § 2 of the Sherman Act.

I

Aspen is a destination ski resort with a reputation for "super powder," "a wide range of runs," and an "active night life," including "some of the best restaurants in North America." Tr. 765–767. Between 1945 and 1960, private investors independently developed three major facilities for downhill skiing: Aspen Mountain (Ajax), Aspen Highlands (Highlands), and Buttermilk. A fourth mountain, Snowmass, opened in 1967.

The development of any major additional facilities is hindered by practical considerations and regulatory obstacles. The identification of appropriate topographical conditions for a new site and substantial financing are both essential. Most of the terrain in the vicinity of Aspen that is suitable for downhill skiing cannot be used for that purpose without the approval of the United States Forest Service. That approval is contingent, in part, on environmental concerns. Moreover, the county government must also approve the project, and in recent years it has followed a policy of limiting growth.

Between 1958 and 1964, three independent companies operated Ajax, Highlands, and Buttermilk. In the early years, each company offered its own day or half-day tickets for use of its mountain. In 1962, however, the three competitors also introduced an interchangeable ticket. The 6-day, all-Aspen ticket provided convenience to the vast majority of skiers who visited the resort for weekly periods, but preferred to remain flexible about what mountain they might ski each day during the visit. It also emphasized the unusual variety in ski mountains available in Aspen.

As initially designed, the all-Aspen ticket program consisted of booklets containing six coupons, each redeemable for a daily lift ticket at Ajax, Highlands, or Buttermilk. The price of the booklet was often discounted from the price of six daily tickets, but all six coupons had to be used within a limited period of time—seven days, for example. The revenues from the sale of the 3-area coupon books were distributed in accordance with the number of coupons collected at each mountain.

In 1964, Buttermilk was purchased by Ski Co., but the interchangeable ticket program continued. In most seasons after it acquired Buttermilk, Ski Co. offered 2-area, 6- or 7-day tickets featuring Ajax and Buttermilk in competition with the 3-area, 6-coupon booklet. Although it sold briskly, the all-Aspen ticket did not sell as well as Ski Co.'s multiarea ticket until Ski Co. opened Snowmass in 1967. Thereafter, the all-Aspen coupon booklet began to outsell Ski Co.'s ticket featuring only its mountains.

In the 1971–1972 season, the coupon booklets were discontinued and an "around the neck" all-Aspen ticket was developed. . . . Lift operators at Highlands monitored usage of the ticket in the 1971–1972 season by recording the ticket numbers of persons going onto the slopes of that mountain. Highlands officials periodically met with Ski Co. officials to review the figures recorded at Highlands, and to distribute revenues based on that count.

There was some concern that usage of the all-Aspen ticket should be monitored by a more scientific method than the one used in the 1971–1972 season. After a one-season absence, the 4-area ticket returned in the 1973–1974 season with a new method of allocating revenues based on usage. Like the 1971–1972 ticket, the 1973–1974 4-area ticket consisted of a badge worn around the skier's neck. Lift operators punched the ticket when the skier first sought access to the mountain each day. A random-sample survey was commissioned to determine how many skiers with the 4-area ticket used each mountain, and the parties allocated revenues from the ticket sales in accordance with the survey's results.

In the next four seasons, Ski Co. and Highlands used such surveys to allocate the revenues from the 4-area, 6-day ticket. Highlands' share of the revenues from the ticket was 17.5% in 1973–1974, 18.5% in 1974–1975, 16.8% in 1975–1976, and 13.2% in 1976–1977. During these four seasons, Ski Co. did not offer its own 3-area, multi-day ticket in competition with the all-Aspen ticket.[9] By 1977, multiarea tickets accounted for nearly 35% of the total market. Holders of multiarea passes also accounted for additional daily ticket sales to persons skiing with them.

Between 1962 and 1977, Ski Co. and Highlands had independently offered various mixes of 1-day, 3-day, and 6-day passes at their own mountains. In every season except one, however, they had also offered some form of all-Aspen, 6-day ticket, and divided the revenues from those sales on the basis of usage. Nevertheless, for the 1977–1978 season, Ski Co. offered to continue the all-Aspen ticket only if Highlands would accept a 13.2% fixed share of the ticket's revenues.

Although that had been Highlands' share of the ticket revenues in 1976–1977, Highlands contended that that season was an inaccurate measure of its market performance since it had been marked by unfavorable weather and an unusually low number of visiting skiers.[11] Moreover, Highlands wanted to continue to divide revenues on the basis

---

[9] In 1975, the Colorado Attorney General filed a complaint against Ski Co. and Highlands alleging, in part, that the negotiations over the 4-area ticket had provided them with a forum for price fixing in violation of § 1 of the Sherman Act and that they had attempted to monopolize the market for downhill skiing services in Aspen in violation of § 2. In 1977, the case was settled by a consent decree that permitted the parties to continue to offer the 4-area ticket provided that they set their own ticket prices unilaterally before negotiating its terms.

[11] The 1976–1977 season was "a no snow year." There were less than half as many skier visits (529,800) in that season as in either 1975–1976 (1,238,500) or 1977–1978 (1,273,400). In addition, Highlands opened earlier than Ski Co.'s mountains and its patrons skied off all the good snow. Ski Co. waited until January and had a better base for the rest of the season.

of actual usage, as that method of distribution allowed it to compete for the daily loyalties of the skiers who had purchased the tickets. Fearing that the alternative might be no interchangeable ticket at all, and hoping to persuade Ski Co. to reinstate the usage division of revenues, Highlands eventually accepted a fixed percentage of 15% for the 1977–1978 season. No survey was made during that season of actual usage of the 4-area ticket at the two competitors' mountains.

In the 1970's the management of Ski Co. increasingly expressed their dislike for the all-Aspen ticket. They complained that a coupon method of monitoring usage was administratively cumbersome. They doubted the accuracy of the survey and decried the "appearance, deportment, [and] attitude" of the college students who were conducting it. In addition, Ski Co.'s president had expressed the view that the 4-area ticket was siphoning off revenues that could be recaptured by Ski Co. if the ticket was discontinued. In fact, Ski Co. had reinstated its 3-area, 6-day ticket during the 1977–1978 season, but that ticket had been outsold by the 4-area, 6-day ticket nearly two to one.

In March 1978, the Ski Co. management recommended to the board of directors that the 4-area ticket be discontinued for the 1978–1979 season. The board decided to offer Highlands a 4-area ticket provided that Highlands would agree to receive a 12.5% fixed percentage of the revenue—considerably below Highlands' historical average based on usage. Later in the 1978–1979 season, a member of Ski Co.'s board of directors candidly informed a Highlands official that he had advocated making Highlands "an offer that [it] could not accept."

Finding the proposal unacceptable, Highlands suggested a distribution of the revenues based on usage to be monitored by coupons, electronic counting, or random sample surveys. If Ski Co. was concerned about who was to conduct the survey, Highlands proposed to hire disinterested ticket counters at its own expense—"somebody like Price Waterhouse"—to count or survey usage of the 4-area ticket at Highlands. Ski Co. refused to consider any counterproposals, and Highlands finally rejected the offer of the fixed percentage.

As far as Ski Co. was concerned, the all-Aspen ticket was dead. In its place Ski Co. offered the 3-area, 6-day ticket featuring only its mountains. In an effort to promote this ticket, Ski Co. embarked on a national advertising campaign that strongly implied to people who were unfamiliar with Aspen that Ajax, Buttermilk, and Snowmass were the only ski mountains in the area. For example, Ski Co. had a sign changed in the Aspen Airways waiting room at Stapleton Airport in Denver. The old sign had a picture of the four mountains in Aspen touting "Four Big

Mountains" whereas the new sign retained the picture but referred only to three.[12]

Ski Co. took additional actions that made it extremely difficult for Highlands to market its own multiarea package to replace the joint offering. Ski Co. discontinued the 3-day, 3-area pass for the 1978–1979 season,[13] and also refused to sell Highlands any lift tickets, either at the tour operator's discount or at retail.[14] Highlands finally developed an alternative product, the "Adventure Pack," which consisted of a 3-day pass at Highlands and three vouchers, each equal to the price of a daily lift ticket at a Ski Co. mountain. The vouchers were guaranteed by funds on deposit in an Aspen bank, and were redeemed by Aspen merchants at full value. Ski Co., however, refused to accept them.

Later, Highlands redesigned the Adventure Pack to contain American Express Traveler's Checks or money orders instead of vouchers. Ski Co. eventually accepted these negotiable instruments in exchange for daily lift tickets. Despite some strengths of the product, the Adventure Pack met considerable resistance from tour operators and consumers who had grown accustomed to the convenience and flexibility provided by the all-Aspen ticket.

Without a convenient all-Aspen ticket, Highlands basically becomes a day ski area in a destination resort. Highlands' share of the market for downhill skiing services in Aspen declined steadily after the 4-area ticket based on usage was abolished in 1977: from 20.5% in 1976–1977, to 15.7% in 1977–1978, to 13.1% in 1978–1979, to 12.5% in 1979–1980, to 11% in 1980–1981.[16] Highlands' revenues from associated skiing services like the

---

[12] Ski Co. circulated another advertisement to national magazines labeled "Aspen, More Mountains, More Fun." The advertisement depicted the four mountains of Aspen, but labeled only Ajax, Buttermilk, and Snowmass. Buttermilk's label is erroneously placed directly over Highlands Mountain.

[13] Highlands' owner explained that there was a key difference between the 3-day, 3-area ticket and the 6-day, 3-area ticket: "with the three day ticket, a person could ski on the . . . Aspen Skiing Corporation mountains for three days and then there would be three days in which he could ski on our mountain; but with the six-day ticket, we are absolutely locked out of those people." As a result of "tremendous consumer demand" for a 3-day ticket, Ski Co. reinstated it late in the 1978–1979 season, but without publicity or a discount off the daily rate.

[14] In the 1977–1978 negotiations, Ski Co. previously had refused to consider the sale of any tickets to Highlands, noting that it was "obviously not interested in helping sell" a package competitive with the 3-area ticket. Later, in the 1978–1979 negotiations, Ski Co.'s vice president of finance told a Highlands official that "[w]e will not have anything to do with a four-area ticket sponsored by the Aspen Highlands Skiing Corporation." When the Highlands official inquired why Ski Co. was taking this position considering that Highlands was willing to pay full retail value for the daily lift tickets, the Ski Co. official answered tersely: "we will not support our competition."

[16] In these seasons, Buttermilk Mountain, in particular, substantially increased its market share at the expense of Highlands.

ski school, ski rentals, amateur racing events, and restaurant facilities declined sharply as well.[17]

II

In 1979, Highlands filed a complaint in the United States District Court for the District of Colorado naming Ski Co. as a defendant. Among various claims,[18] the complaint alleged that Ski Co. had monopolized the market for downhill skiing services at Aspen in violation of § 2 of the Sherman Act, and prayed for treble damages. The case was tried to a jury which rendered a verdict finding Ski Co. guilty of the § 2 violation and calculating Highlands' actual damages at $2.5 million.

In her instructions to the jury, the District Judge explained that the offense of monopolization under § 2 of the Sherman Act has two elements: (1) the possession of monopoly power in a relevant market, and (2) the willful acquisition, maintenance, or use of that power by anticompetitive or exclusionary means or for anticompetitive or exclusionary purposes. Although the first element was vigorously disputed at the trial and in the Court of Appeals, in this Court Ski Co. does not challenge the jury's special verdict finding that it possessed monopoly power.[20] Nor does Ski Co. criticize the trial court's instructions to the jury concerning the second element of the § 2 offense.

On this element, the jury was instructed that it had to consider whether "Aspen Skiing Corporation willfully acquired, maintained, or used that power by anti-competitive or exclusionary means or for anti-competitive or exclusionary purposes." The instructions elaborated:

"In considering whether the means or purposes were anti-competitive or exclusionary, you must draw a distinction here between practices which tend to exclude or restrict competition on the one hand and the success of a business which reflects only a superior product, a well-run business, or luck, on the other. The line between legitimately gained monopoly, its proper use and maintenance, and improper conduct has been described in various ways. It has been said that obtaining or maintaining monopoly power cannot represent monopolization if the power was gained and maintained by conduct that was honestly industrial. Or it is said that monopoly power which is thrust

---

[17] Highlands' ski school had an outstanding reputation, and its share of the ski school market had always outperformed Highlands' share of the downhill skiing market. Even some Ski Co. officials had sent their children to ski school at Highlands.

[18] Highlands also alleged that Ski Co. had conspired with various third parties in violation of § 1 of the Sherman Act. The District Court allowed this claim to go to the jury which rendered a verdict in Ski Co.'s favor.

[20] The jury found that the relevant product market was "[d]ownhill skiing at destination ski resorts," that the "Aspen area" was a relevant geographic submarket, and that during the years 1977–1981, Ski Co. possessed monopoly power, defined as the power to control prices in the relevant market or to exclude competitors.

upon a firm due to its superior business ability and efficiency does not constitute monopolization.

"For example, a firm that has lawfully acquired a monopoly position is not barred from taking advantage of scale economies by constructing a large and efficient factory. These benefits are a consequence of size and not an exercise of monopoly power. Nor is a corporation which possesses monopoly power under a duty to cooperate with its business rivals. Also a company which possesses monopoly power and which refuses to enter into a joint operating agreement with a competitor or otherwise refuses to deal with a competitor in some manner does not violate Section 2 if valid business reasons exist for that refusal.

"In other words, if there were legitimate business reasons for the refusal, then the defendant, even if he is found to possess monopoly power in a relevant market, has not violated the law. We are concerned with conduct which unnecessarily excludes or handicaps competitors. This is conduct which does not benefit consumers by making a better product or service available—or in other ways—and instead has the effect of impairing competition.

"To sum up, you must determine whether Aspen Skiing Corporation gained, maintained, or used monopoly power in a relevant market by arrangements and policies which rather than being a consequence of a superior product, superior business sense, or historic element, were designed primarily to further any domination of the relevant market or sub-market."

The jury answered a specific interrogatory finding the second element of the offense as defined in these instructions.

Ski Co. filed a motion for judgment notwithstanding the verdict, contending that the evidence was insufficient to support a § 2 violation as a matter of law. In support of that motion, Ski Co. incorporated the arguments that it had advanced in support of its motion for a directed verdict, at which time it had primarily contested the sufficiency of the evidence on the issue of monopoly power. Counsel had, however, in the course of the argument at that time, stated: "Now, we also think, Judge, that there clearly cannot be a requirement of cooperation between competitors."[22] The District Court denied Ski Co.'s motion and entered a

---

[22] Counsel also appears to have argued that Ski Co. was under a legal obligation to refuse to participate in any joint marketing arrangement with Highlands:

> Aspen Skiing Corporation is required to compete. It is required to make independent decisions. It is required to price its own product. It is required to make its own determination of the ticket that it chooses to offer and the tickets that it chooses not to offer.

In this Court, Ski Co. does not question the validity of the joint marketing arrangement under § 1 of the Sherman Act. Thus, we have no occasion to consider the circumstances that might

judgment awarding Highlands treble damages of $7,500,000, costs and attorney's fees.[23]

The Court of Appeals affirmed in all respects. The court advanced two reasons for rejecting Ski Co.'s argument that "there was insufficient evidence to present a jury issue of monopolization because, as a matter of law, the conduct at issue was pro-competitive conduct that a monopolist could lawfully engage in." First, the Court of Appeals held that the multiday, multiarea ticket could be characterized as an "essential facility" that Ski Co. had a duty to market jointly with Highlands. Second, it held that there was sufficient evidence to support a finding that Ski Co.'s intent in refusing to market the 4-area ticket, "considered together with its other conduct," was to create or maintain a monopoly.

. . . .

III

In this Court, Ski Co. contends that even a firm with monopoly power has no duty to engage in joint marketing with a competitor, that a violation of § 2 cannot be established without evidence of substantial exclusionary conduct, and that none of its activities can be characterized as exclusionary. It also contends that the Court of Appeals incorrectly relied on the "essential facilities" doctrine and that an "anticompetitive intent" does not transform nonexclusionary conduct into monopolization. In response, Highlands submits that, given the evidence in the record, it is not necessary to rely on the "essential facilities" doctrine in order to affirm the judgment.

"The central message of the Sherman Act is that a business entity must find new customers and higher profits through internal expansion—that is, by competing successfully rather than by arranging treaties with its competitors." *United States v. Citizens & Southern National Bank,* 422 U.S. 86 (1975). Ski Co., therefore, is surely correct in submitting that even a firm with monopoly power has no general duty to engage in a joint marketing program with a competitor. Ski Co. is quite wrong, however, in suggesting that the judgment in this case rests on any such proposition of law. For the trial court unambiguously instructed the jury that a firm possessing monopoly power has no duty to cooperate with its business rivals.

---

permit such combinations in the skiing industry. See generally *National Collegiate Athletic Assn. v. Board of Regents of Univ. of Okla.,* 468 U.S. 85, 113–115 (1984).

[23] The District Court also entered an injunction requiring the parties to offer jointly a 4-area, 6-out-of-7-day coupon booklet substantially identical to the "Ski the Summit" booklet accepted by Ski Co. at its Breckenridge resort in Summit County, Colorado. The injunction was initially for a 3-year period, but was later extended through the 1984–1985 season by stipulation of the parties. Highlands represents that "it will not seek an extension of the injunction." No question is raised concerning the character of the injunctive relief ordered by the District Court.

The absence of an unqualified duty to cooperate does not mean that every time a firm declines to participate in a particular cooperative venture, that decision may not have evidentiary significance, or that it may not give rise to liability in certain circumstances. The absence of a duty to transact business with another firm is, in some respects, merely the counterpart of the independent businessman's cherished right to select his customers and his associates. The high value that we have placed on the right to refuse to deal with other firms does not mean that the right is unqualified.

In *Lorain Journal Co. v. United States,* 342 U.S. 143 (1951), we squarely held that this right was not unqualified. Between 1933 and 1948 the publisher of the Lorain Journal, a newspaper, was the only local business disseminating news and advertising in that Ohio town. In 1948, a small radio station was established in a nearby community. In an effort to destroy its small competitor, and thereby regain its "pre-1948 substantial monopoly over the mass dissemination of all news and advertising," the Journal refused to sell advertising to persons that patronized the radio station. *Id.,* at 153.

In holding that this conduct violated § 2 of the Sherman Act, the Court dispatched the same argument raised by the monopolist here:

> "The publisher claims a right as a private business concern to select its customers and to refuse to accept advertisements from whomever it pleases. We do not dispute that general right. 'But the word "right" is one of the most deceptive of pitfalls; it is so easy to slip from a qualified meaning in the premise to an unqualified one in the conclusion. Most rights are qualified.' *American Bank & Trust Co. v. Federal Bank,* 256 U.S. 350, 358. The right claimed by the publisher is neither absolute nor exempt from regulation. Its exercise as a purposeful means of monopolizing interstate commerce is prohibited by the Sherman Act. The operator of the radio station, equally with the publisher of the newspaper, is entitled to the protection of that Act. '*In the absence of any purpose to create or maintain a monopoly,* the act does not restrict the long recognized right of trader or manufacturer engaged in an entirely private business, freely to exercise his own independent discretion as to parties with whom he will deal.' (Emphasis supplied.) *United States v. Colgate & Co.,* 250 U.S. 300, 307."

The Court approved the entry of an injunction ordering the Journal to print the advertisements of the customers of its small competitor.

In *Lorain Journal,* the violation of § 2 was an "attempt to monopolize," rather than monopolization, but the question of intent is relevant to both offenses. In the former case it is necessary to prove a "specific intent" to accomplish the forbidden objective—as Judge Hand explained, "an intent which goes beyond the mere intent to do the act." *United States v. Aluminum Co. of America,* 148 F.2d 416, 432 (CA2 1945). In the latter case evidence of intent is merely relevant to the question whether the challenged conduct is fairly characterized as "exclusionary" or "anticompetitive"—to use the words in the trial court's instructions—or "predatory," to use a word that scholars seem to favor. Whichever label is used, there is agreement on the proposition that "no monopolist monopolizes unconscious of what he is doing." As Judge Bork stated more recently: "Improper exclusion (exclusion not the result of superior efficiency) is always deliberately intended."

The qualification on the right of a monopolist to deal with whom he pleases is not so narrow that it encompasses no more than the circumstances of *Lorain Journal.* In the actual case that we must decide, the monopolist did not merely reject a novel offer to participate in a cooperative venture that had been proposed by a competitor. Rather, the monopolist elected to make an important change in a pattern of distribution that had originated in a competitive market and had persisted for several years. The all-Aspen, 6-day ticket with revenues allocated on the basis of usage was first developed when three independent companies operated three different ski mountains in the Aspen area. It continued to provide a desirable option for skiers when the market was enlarged to include four mountains, and when the character of the market was changed by Ski Co.'s acquisition of monopoly power. Moreover, since the record discloses that interchangeable tickets are used in other multimountain areas which apparently are competitive,[30] it seems appropriate to infer that such tickets satisfy consumer demand in free competitive markets.

Ski Co.'s decision to terminate the all-Aspen ticket was thus a decision by a monopolist to make an important change in the character of the market. Such a decision is not necessarily anticompetitive, and Ski Co. contends that neither its decision, nor the conduct in which it engaged to implement that decision, can fairly be characterized as exclusionary in this case. It recognizes, however, that as the case is presented to us, we must interpret the entire record in the light most favorable to Highlands and give to it the benefit of all inferences which the evidence fairly supports, even though contrary inferences might reasonably be drawn. *Continental Ore Co. v. Union Carbide & Carbon Corp.,* 370 U.S. 690, 696 (1962).

Moreover, we must assume that the jury followed the court's instructions. The jury must, therefore, have drawn a distinction "between practices which tend to exclude or restrict competition on the one hand,

---

[30] Ski Co. itself participates in interchangeable ticket programs in at least two other markets.

and the success of a business which reflects only a superior product, a well-run business, or luck, on the other." Since the jury was unambiguously instructed that Ski Co.'s refusal to deal with Highlands "does not violate Section 2 if valid business reasons exist for that refusal," we must assume that the jury concluded that there were no valid business reasons for the refusal. The question then is whether that conclusion finds support in the record.

IV

The question whether Ski Co.'s conduct may properly be characterized as exclusionary cannot be answered by simply considering its effect on Highlands. In addition, it is relevant to consider its impact on consumers and whether it has impaired competition in an unnecessarily restrictive way.[32] If a firm has been attempting to exclude rivals on some basis other than efficiency, it is fair to characterize its behavior as predatory. It is, accordingly, appropriate to examine the effect of the challenged pattern of conduct on consumers, on Ski Co.'s smaller rival, and on Ski Co. itself.

Superior Quality of the All-Aspen Ticket

The average Aspen visitor "is a well-educated, relatively affluent, experienced skier who has skied a number of times in the past. . . ." Over 80% of the skiers visiting the resort each year have been there before— 40% of these repeat visitors have skied Aspen at least five times. Over the years, they developed a strong demand for the 6-day, all-Aspen ticket in its various refinements. Most experienced skiers quite logically prefer to purchase their tickets at once for the whole period that they will spend at the resort; they can then spend more time on the slopes and enjoying après-ski amenities and less time standing in ticket lines. The 4-area attribute of the ticket allowed the skier to purchase his 6-day ticket in advance while reserving the right to decide in his own time and for his own reasons which mountain he would ski on each day. It provided convenience and flexibility, and expanded the vistas and the number of challenging runs available to him during the week's vacation.

While the 3-area, 6-day ticket offered by Ski Co. possessed some of these attributes, the evidence supports a conclusion that consumers were adversely affected by the elimination of the 4-area ticket. In the first place, the actual record of competition between a 3-area ticket and the all-Aspen ticket in the years after 1967 indicated that skiers demonstrably preferred four mountains to three. Highlands' expert marketing witness testified that many of the skiers who come to Aspen want to ski the four mountains, and the abolition of the 4-area pass made it more difficult to

---

[32] "Thus, 'exclusionary' comprehends at the most behavior that not only (1) tends to impair the opportunities of rivals, but also (2) either does not further competition on the merits or does so in an unnecessarily restrictive way." 3 P. Areeda & D. Turner, Antitrust Law 78 (1978).

satisfy that ambition. A consumer survey undertaken in the 1979–1980 season indicated that 53.7% of the respondents wanted to ski Highlands, but would not; 39.9% said that they would not be skiing at the mountain of their choice because their ticket would not permit it.

Expert testimony and anecdotal evidence supported these statistical measures of consumer preference. A major wholesale tour operator asserted that he would not even consider marketing a 3-area ticket if a 4-area ticket were available. During the 1977–1978 and 1978–1979 seasons, people with Ski Co.'s 3-area ticket came to Highlands "on a very regular basis" and attempted to board the lifts or join the ski school. Highlands officials were left to explain to angry skiers that they could only ski at Highlands or join its ski school by paying for a 1-day lift ticket. Even for the affluent, this was an irritating situation because it left the skier the option of either wasting 1 day of the 6-day, 3-area pass or obtaining a refund which could take all morning and entailed the forfeit of the 6-day discount.[37] An active officer in the Atlanta Ski Club testified that the elimination of the 4-area pass "infuriated" him.

Highlands' Ability to Compete

The adverse impact of Ski Co.'s pattern of conduct on Highlands is not disputed in this Court. Expert testimony described the extent of its pecuniary injury. The evidence concerning its attempt to develop a substitute product either by buying Ski Co.'s daily tickets in bulk, or by marketing its own Adventure Pack, demonstrates that it tried to protect itself from the loss of its share of the patrons of the all-Aspen ticket. The development of a new distribution system for providing the experience that skiers had learned to expect in Aspen proved to be prohibitively expensive. As a result, Highlands' share of the relevant market steadily declined after the 4-area ticket was terminated. The size of the damages award also confirms the substantial character of the effect of Ski Co.'s conduct upon Highlands.[38]

Ski Co.'s Business Justification

Perhaps most significant, however, is the evidence relating to Ski Co. itself, for Ski Co. did not persuade the jury that its conduct was justified by any normal business purpose. Ski Co. was apparently willing to forgo daily ticket sales both to skiers who sought to exchange the coupons contained in Highlands' Adventure Pack, and to those who would have purchased Ski Co. daily lift tickets from Highlands if Highlands had been permitted to purchase them in bulk. The jury may well have concluded

---

[37] The refund policy was cumbersome, and poorly publicized.

[38] In considering the competitive effect of Ski Co.'s refusal to deal or cooperate with Highlands, it is not irrelevant to note that similar conduct carried out by the concerted action of three independent rivals with a similar share of the market would constitute a *per se* violation of § 1 of the Sherman Act.

that Ski Co. elected to forgo these short-run benefits because it was more interested in reducing competition in the Aspen market over the long run by harming its smaller competitor.

That conclusion is strongly supported by Ski Co.'s failure to offer any efficiency justification whatever for its pattern of conduct. In defending the decision to terminate the jointly offered ticket, Ski Co. claimed that usage could not be properly monitored. The evidence, however, established that Ski Co. itself monitored the use of the 3-area passes based on a count taken by lift operators, and distributed the revenues among its mountains on that basis. Ski Co. contended that coupons were administratively cumbersome, and that the survey takers had been disruptive and their work inaccurate. Coupons, however, were no more burdensome than the credit cards accepted at Ski Co. ticket windows. Moreover, in other markets Ski Co. itself participated in interchangeable lift tickets using coupons. As for the survey, its own manager testified that the problems were much overemphasized by Ski Co. officials, and were mostly resolved as they arose. Ski Co.'s explanation for the rejection of Highlands' offer to hire—at its own expense—a reputable national accounting firm to audit usage of the 4-area tickets at Highlands' mountain, was that there was no way to "control" the audit.

In the end, Ski Co. was pressed to justify its pattern of conduct on a desire to disassociate itself from—what it considered—the inferior skiing services offered at Highlands. The all-Aspen ticket based on usage, however, allowed consumers to make their own choice on these matters of quality. Ski Co.'s purported concern for the relative quality of Highlands' product was supported in the record by little more than vague insinuations, and was sharply contested by numerous witnesses. Moreover, Ski Co. admitted that it was willing to associate with what it considered to be inferior products in other markets.

Although Ski Co.'s pattern of conduct may not have been as "bold, relentless, and predatory" as the publisher's actions in *Lorain Journal,* the record in this case comfortably supports an inference that the monopolist made a deliberate effort to discourage its customers from doing business with its smaller rival. The sale of its 3-area, 6-day ticket, particularly when it was discounted below the daily ticket price, deterred the ticket holders from skiing at Highlands. The refusal to accept the Adventure Pack coupons in exchange for daily tickets was apparently motivated entirely by a decision to avoid providing any benefit to Highlands even though accepting the coupons would have entailed no cost to Ski Co. itself, would have provided it with immediate benefits, and would have satisfied its potential customers. Thus the evidence supports an inference that Ski Co. was not motivated by efficiency concerns and that it was willing to sacrifice short-run benefits and consumer goodwill in exchange for a perceived long-run impact on its smaller rival.

Because we are satisfied that the evidence in the record,[44] construed most favorably in support of Highlands' position, is adequate to support the verdict under the instructions given by the trial court, the judgment of the Court of Appeals is

Affirmed.

NOTES & QUESTIONS

(1) What actions did Ski Co. take that hindered Highland's ability to compete? Why did Ski Co. take such actions?

(2) What tension did the district court recognize in its jury instructions? How did the district court and the court of appeals resolve this tension?

(3) Ski Co. contended that it had no duty to cooperate with its competition. Did the Supreme Court agree with this contention? When, if ever, does a duty to cooperate exist?

(4) How was competition harmed by Ski Co.'s conduct?

(5) Ski Co. and Highlands had previously worked together successfully. What role did this fact play in the decision? Do you think the Court would have reached the same result if Highlands had been a new ski company with no prior history of offering ticket passes with its competitors?

D. PROVING AN ANTITRUST INJURY

Private litigants have standing to sue under § 4 of the Clayton Act (which also provides for treble damages); however, they must demonstrate that they have suffered an actual injury to their property or business and that the injury was caused by the defendant's conduct. In other words, to have standing, a plaintiff must be able to prove an "antitrust injury." This is not merely a showing that the plaintiff suffered harm as a result of the defendant's conduct. For instance, in *Brunswick Corp. v. Pueblo Bowl-O-Mat*, 429 U.S. 477 (1977), the owners of three bowling alleys sued Brunswick for buying competitors' alleys. The plaintiffs' theory was that if Brunswick had not purchased the alleys, the competitors would have closed, which would have provided the plaintiffs with a greater market share and higher profits. The Court, noting that plaintiffs could have suffered an identical loss had the competitors simply obtained refinancing and remained open, found that the injury was not the type contemplated under the antitrust laws:

---

[44] Given our conclusion that the evidence amply supports the verdict under the instructions as given by the trial court, we find it unnecessary to consider the possible relevance of the "essential facilities" doctrine, or the somewhat hypothetical question whether nonexclusionary conduct could ever constitute an abuse of monopoly power if motivated by an anticompetitive purpose. If, as we have assumed, no monopolist monopolizes unconscious of what he is doing, that case is unlikely to arise.

[For] the plaintiffs to recover . . . they must prove more than injury causally linked to an illegal presence in the market. Plaintiffs must prove antitrust injury, which is to say injury of the type the antitrust laws were intended to prevent and that flows from that which makes defendants' acts unlawful. The injury should reflect the anticompetitive effect either of the violation or of anticompetitive acts made possible by the violation. It should, in short, be "the type of loss that the claimed violations . . . would be likely to cause."

Id. at 489. This *Brunswick* approach involves two steps. First, plaintiffs must plead and prove that they were injured by a defendant's illegal conduct. Second, plaintiffs must show that their injuries were the type of injuries that the antitrust laws were intended to prevent. Thus, an injury caused by an increase in competition would not be compensable.

Similarly, in *Atlantic Richfield Co. v. USA Petroleum Co.*, 495 U.S. 328 (1990), a plaintiff was unable to recover from defendants involved in a vertical price-fixing scheme which set a maximum price. The plaintiff, a competitor, claimed that it was injured by the price-fixing agreement[e] under the theory that, absent the agreement, Atlantic Richfield (ARCO) dealers would have raised their prices, which would have improved the competitive position of the plaintiff's retailers. The Court found that, under the circumstances, the plaintiff-competitor was ill-suited for the role of antitrust protector:

Respondent's asserted injury as a competitor does not resemble any of the potential dangers described in [previous decisions]. For example, if a vertical agreement fixes maximum prices too low for the dealer to furnish services desired by consumers, or in such a way as to channel business to large distributors, then a firm dealing in a competing brand would not be harmed. Respondent was benefited rather than harmed if petitioner's pricing policies restricted ARCO sales to a few large dealers or prevented petitioner's dealers from offering services desired by consumers such as credit card sales. Even if the maximum-price agreement ultimately had acquired all of the attributes of a minimum-price-fixing scheme, respondent still would not have suffered antitrust injury because higher ARCO prices would have worked to USA's advantage. A competitor "may not complain of conspiracies that . . . set minimum prices at any level." Matsushita Electric Industrial Corp. v. Zenith Radio Corp., 475 U.S. 574, 585, n. 8 (1986). . . . In sum, respondent has not suffered "antitrust injury," since its losses do not flow from

---

[e]   At the time of this decision, recall that such arrangements were still per se violations.

the aspects of vertical, maximum price fixing that render it illegal.

Respondent argues that . . . it nonetheless suffered antitrust injury because of the low prices produced by the vertical restraint. We disagree. When a firm, or even a group of firms adhering to a vertical agreement, lowers prices but maintains them above predatory levels, the business lost by rivals cannot be viewed as an "anticompetitive" consequence of the claimed violation. A firm complaining about the harm it suffers from nonpredatory price competition "is really claiming that it [is] unable to raise prices." Blair & Harrison, Rethinking Antitrust Injury, 42 Vand.L.Rev. 1539, 1554 (1989). This is not antitrust injury; indeed, cutting prices in order to increase business often is the very essence of competition. The antitrust laws were enacted for "the protection of *competition*, not *competitors*." Brown Shoe Co. v. United States, 370 U.S. 294, 320, 82 S.Ct. 1502, 1521, 8 L.Ed.2d 510 (1962) (emphasis in original). . . .

. . . .

We decline to dilute the antitrust injury requirement here because we find that there is no need to encourage private enforcement by competitors of the rule against vertical, maximum price fixing. If such a scheme causes . . . anticompetitive consequences . . . consumers and the manufacturers' own dealers may bring suit. The existence of an identifiable class of persons whose self-interest would normally motivate them to vindicate the public interest in antitrust enforcement diminishes the justification for allowing a more remote party . . . to perform the office of a private attorney general.

Respondent's injury, moreover, is not "inextricably intertwined" with the antitrust injury that a dealer would suffer, and thus does not militate in favor of permitting respondent to sue on behalf of petitioner's dealers. A competitor is not injured by the anticompetitive effects of vertical, maximum price-fixing, and does not have any incentive to vindicate the legitimate interests of a rival's dealer. A competitor will not bring suit to protect the dealer against a maximum price that is set too low, inasmuch as the competitor would benefit from such a situation. Instead, a competitor will be motivated to bring suit only when the vertical restraint promotes interbrand competition between the competitor and the dealer subject to the restraint. In short, a competitor will be injured and hence motivated to sue only when a vertical, maximum-price-fixing arrangement has a procompetitive impact on the market. Therefore, providing the competitor a cause of action would not protect the rights of dealers and consumers under the antitrust laws.

Id. at 337–38, 345–46.

NOTES & QUESTIONS

(1) What justification might exist for requiring an "antitrust injury" above and beyond a mere showing of harm?

(2) Look back at the *NCAA* decision. What was the antitrust injury suffered in that dispute? Should it matter that the plaintiffs were part of the alleged conspiracy (albeit not voluntarily)?

(3) Antitrust injury is but one factor to be considered in assessing whether private plaintiffs have standing to sue under the antitrust laws. In *Associated General Contractors of California, Inc. v. California State Council of Carpenters*, 459 U.S. 519 (1983), the Supreme Court described other factors relevant to private plaintiff standing: the directness of the injury, whether the claim for damages is speculative, the existence of more direct victims, the potential for duplicative recovery, and the complexity of apportioning damages. *Id.* at 542–45. Thus, an injured party may be denied standing if it is not a direct competitor or consumer, *see SAS of Puerto Rico, Inc. v. Puerto Rico Telephone Co.*, 48 F.3d 39, 44–45 (1st Cir. 1995) (finding that a party lacked standing because its injuries were incidental to those suffered by customers and competitors in the alleged monopolized market), or if its injury is indirectly caused by the defendant's conduct. *See John Lenore & Co. v. Olympia Brewing Co.*, 550 F.2d 495, 499–500 (9th Cir. 1977) (stating that although the plaintiff had suffered an injury, it was not "directly and proximately caused by the challenged acquisition").

(4) Along with seeking damages, private parties are also empowered to seek injunctive relief. Section 16 of the Clayton Act authorizes private parties to seek injunctive relief to protect "against threatened loss or damage by a violation of the antitrust laws." 15 U.S.C. § 26. While the statute's text is broad, the Supreme Court has limited its reach to those plaintiffs who allege a threat of antitrust injury. *See Cargill, Inc. v. Monfort of Colorado, Inc.*, 479 U.S. 104, 113 (1986). However, many of the other standing factors referenced in *Associated General* are not relevant to a claim for injunctive relief. The standing inquiry under § 16 is therefore less demanding than under § 4 because factors such as the risk of duplicative recovery or the danger of complex apportionment are not at issue.

(5) The case of *Sprint Nextel Corp. v. AT&T Inc.*, 821 F. Supp. 2d 308 (D.D.C. 2011), provides a good example of how antitrust injury can affect standing in the context of injunctive relief. Sprint (the third-largest national provider of mobile wireless services) and a regional carrier sued to enjoin the proposed acquisition by AT&T (the second-largest national carrier) of T-Mobile (the fourth-largest national carrier). AT&T and T-Mobile moved to

dismiss the suit based upon the failure of the plaintiffs to allege an antitrust injury. The plaintiffs alleged that they would be harmed in the horizontal market of selling cellular services because "AT&T's acquisition of T-Mobile would affect an illegal concentration of market power and lead to higher retail wireless rates." *Id.* at 319. According to the plaintiffs, the end effect of this acquisition would be higher prices for consumers. The court dismissed the claim, noting that although prices may increase, this was not an injury to the plaintiffs because higher market-wide pricing would actually benefit competitors. "Alleging harm to consumers, while relevant to showing an antitrust violation, is not sufficient to demonstrate antitrust injury; harm to *consumers* by way of increased prices is the type of injury the antitrust laws were designed to prevent, but it is not an injury-in-fact that *competitors* suffer." *Id.*

Plaintiffs also alleged that the proposed merger would enable AT&T to foreclose plaintiffs from accessing "the most innovative handsets and raise their costs, such that [plaintiffs'] offers to [their] customers would be less attractive and [their] business would be injured." *Id.* at 320. Because the merged entity would control in excess of 40% of the national market, plaintiffs claimed that the merger would enable AT&T to leverage handset manufacturers into signing exclusive agreements that would prohibit the manufacturers from selling popular new phones, such as the iPhone, to the plaintiffs. The district court agreed that this alleged an antitrust injury, stating "[w]here a defendant, by means of anticompetitive conduct, restricts or forecloses a competitor plaintiff's access to a necessary input, courts have found that the resulting loss is injury of the type that the antitrust laws were designed to prevent." *Id.* The court further concluded that, given the past market, plaintiffs had sufficiently alleged a plausible threat. There was evidence that larger cellular service providers enjoyed preferences due to their ability to make higher-volume commitments to manufacturers, and that such providers also historically enjoyed exclusivity periods. *See id.* at 324–25.

CHAPTER 13

CIVIL RICO

■ ■ ■

A. INTRODUCTION

The Racketeer Influenced and Corrupt Organizations Act of 1970 ("RICO") was passed to combat organized crime and to curb the infiltration of legitimate business organizations by racketeers. Given these purposes, you may be asking yourself "what the heck does an act geared toward the mob have to do with unfair competition?" Believe it or not, a RICO claim can arise out of many business disputes. Congress intended RICO to be liberally construed and provided a private cause of action for RICO violations. The two statutory provisions most relevant to a civil RICO claim are 18 U.S.C. §§ 1964(c) and 1962. Section 1964(c) provides the following:

> (c)   Any person injured in his business or property by reason of a violation of section 1962 of this chapter may sue therefor in any appropriate United States district court and shall recover threefold the damages he sustains and the cost of the suit, including a reasonable attorney's fee, except that no person may rely upon any conduct that would have been actionable as fraud in the purchase or sale of securities to establish a violation of section 1962. The exception contained in the preceding sentence does not apply to an action against any person that is criminally convicted in connection with the fraud, in which case the statute of limitations shall start to run on the date on which the conviction becomes final.

Thus, to bring an action under § 1964, a plaintiff must show (1) injury to business or property caused by (2) a violation of § 1962.

Section 1962 describes four types of racketeering conduct that will support a cause of action:

- investment in an enterprise using racketeered money;

- acquisition of an enterprise using racketeering activities;

- participation in the conduct of the affairs of an enterprise through racketeering activity; or

- conspiracy to commit any of the previous three.[a]

The definition of "enterprise" is very broad and includes "any individual, partnership, corporation, association, or other legal entity, and any union or group of individuals associated in fact although not a legal entity." 18 U.S.C. § 1961(4). The definition of "racketeering activity" is also quite broad under the statute, including activities as sinister as sexual exploitation of children and bribery, as well as conduct that sounds more tort-like, such as mail and wire fraud, and trafficking in counterfeit goods and marks. If the conduct that is prohibited seems confusing at this early stage, don't worry—we will go into much more detail later.

A private plaintiff may bring a civil RICO action in state or federal court, and RICO permits recovery of treble damages and attorney's fees. These remedies make civil RICO claims very attractive to plaintiffs. For many years, lower courts attempted to curb civil RICO litigation by narrowly construing the statute, but the U.S. Supreme Court emphasized the breadth of RICO in the following case.

SEDIMA V. IMREX CO.
473 U.S. 479 (1985)

JUSTICE WHITE delivered the opinion of the Court.

The Racketeer Influenced and Corrupt Organizations Act (RICO), 18 U.S.C. §§ 1961–1968, provides a private civil action to recover treble damages for injury "by reason of a violation of" its substantive provisions. 18 U.S.C. § 1964(c). The initial dormancy of this provision and its recent greatly increased utilization are now familiar history. In response to what it perceived to be misuse of civil RICO by private plaintiffs, the court below construed § 1964(c) to permit private actions only against defendants who had been convicted on criminal charges, and only where there had occurred a "racketeering injury." While we understand the court's concern over the consequences of an unbridled reading of the statute, we reject both of its holdings.

I

RICO takes aim at "racketeering activity," which it defines as any act "chargeable" under several generically described state criminal laws, any act "indictable" under numerous specific federal criminal provisions, including mail and wire fraud, and any "offense" involving bankruptcy or securities fraud or drug-related activities that is "punishable" under federal law. § 1961(1). Section 1962, entitled "Prohibited Activities,"

---

[a] As we will later explore, a single racketeering activity is not enough for RICO liability; instead, the statute requires a pattern of racketeering activity. Liability may also be premised upon the "collection of an unlawful debt" under 18 U.S.C. § 1962 (a)–(c). This usually involves gambling and is rarely the basis for a civil RICO claim.

outlaws the use of income derived from a "pattern of racketeering activity" to acquire an interest in or establish an enterprise engaged in or affecting interstate commerce; the acquisition or maintenance of any interest in an enterprise "through" a pattern of racketeering activity; conducting or participating in the conduct of an enterprise through a pattern of racketeering activity; and conspiring to violate any of these provisions.

Congress provided criminal penalties of imprisonment, fines, and forfeiture for violation of these provisions. § 1963. In addition, it set out a far-reaching civil enforcement scheme, § 1964, including the following provision for private suits: "Any person injured in his business or property by reason of a violation of section 1962 of this chapter may sue therefor in any appropriate United States district court and shall recover threefold the damages he sustains and the cost of the suit, including a reasonable attorney's fee." § 1964(c).

In 1979, petitioner Sedima, a Belgian corporation, entered into a joint venture with respondent Imrex Co. to provide electronic components to a Belgian firm. The buyer was to order parts through Sedima; Imrex was to obtain the parts in this country and ship them to Europe. The agreement called for Sedima and Imrex to split the net proceeds. Imrex filled roughly $8 million in orders placed with it through Sedima. Sedima became convinced, however, that Imrex was presenting inflated bills, cheating Sedima out of a portion of its proceeds by collecting for nonexistent expenses.

In 1982, Sedima filed this action in the Federal District Court for the Eastern District of New York. The complaint set out common-law claims of unjust enrichment, conversion, and breach of contract, fiduciary duty, and a constructive trust. In addition, it asserted RICO claims under § 1964(c) against Imrex and two of its officers. Two counts alleged violations of § 1962(c), based on predicate acts of mail and wire fraud. See 18 U.S.C. §§ 1341, 1343, 1961(1)(B). A third count alleged a conspiracy to violate § 1962(c). Claiming injury of at least $175,000, the amount of the alleged overbilling, Sedima sought treble damages and attorney's fees.

The District Court held that for an injury to be "by reason of a violation of section 1962," as required by § 1964(c), it must be somehow different in kind from the direct injury resulting from the predicate acts of racketeering activity. While not choosing a precise formulation, the District Court held that a complaint must allege a "RICO-type injury," which was either some sort of distinct "racketeering injury," or a "competitive injury." It found "no allegation here of any injury apart from that which would result directly from the alleged predicate acts of mail fraud and wire fraud," and accordingly dismissed the RICO counts for failure to state a claim.

A divided panel of the Court of Appeals for the Second Circuit affirmed. After a lengthy review of the legislative history, it held that Sedima's complaint was defective in two ways. First, it failed to allege an injury "by reason of a violation of section 1962." In the court's view, this language was a limitation on standing, reflecting Congress' intent to compensate victims of "certain specific kinds of organized criminality," not to provide additional remedies for already compensable injuries. Analogizing to the Clayton Act, which had been the model for § 1964(c), the court concluded that just as an antitrust plaintiff must allege an "antitrust injury," so a RICO plaintiff must allege a "racketeering injury"—an injury "different in kind from that occurring as a result of the predicate acts themselves, or not simply caused by the predicate acts, but also caused by an activity which RICO was designed to deter." Sedima had failed to allege such an injury.

The Court of Appeals also found the complaint defective for not alleging that the defendants had already been criminally convicted of the predicate acts of mail and wire fraud, or of a RICO violation. This element of the civil cause of action was inferred from § 1964(c)'s reference to a "violation" of § 1962, the court also observing that its prior-conviction requirement would avoid serious constitutional difficulties, the danger of unfair stigmatization, and problems regarding the standard by which the predicate acts were to be proved.

The decision below was one episode in a recent proliferation of civil RICO litigation within the Second Circuit and in other Courts of Appeals. In light of the variety of approaches taken by the lower courts and the importance of the issues, we grant certiorari. We now reverse.

II

As a preliminary matter, it is worth briefly reviewing the legislative history of the private treble damages action. RICO formed Title IX of the Organized Crime Control Act of 1970. The civil remedies in the bill passed by the Senate, S. 30, were limited to injunctive actions by the United States and became §§ 1964(a), (b), and (d). Previous versions of the legislation, however, had provided for a private treble-damages action in exactly the terms ultimately adopted in § 1964(c).

During hearings on S. 30 before the House Judiciary Committee, Representative Steiger proposed the addition of a private treble-damages action "similar to the private damage remedy found in the anti-trust laws. . . . [T]hose who have been wronged by organized crime should at least be given access to a legal remedy. In addition, the availability of such a remedy would enhance the effectiveness of title IX's prohibitions." The American Bar Association also proposed an amendment "based upon the concept of Section 4 of the Clayton Act."

Over the dissent of three members, who feared the treble-damages provision would be used for malicious harassment of business competitors, the Committee approved the amendment. In summarizing the bill on the House floor, its sponsor described the treble-damages provision as "another example of the antitrust remedy being adapted for use against organized criminality." . . . The House then passed the bill, with the treble-damages provision in the form recommended by the Committee.

The Senate did not seek a conference and adopted the bill as amended in the House. The treble-damages provision had been drawn to its attention while the legislation was still in the House, and had received the endorsement of Senator McClellan, the sponsor of S. 30, who was of the view that the provision would be "a major new tool in extirpating the baneful influence of organized crime in our economic life."

III

The language of RICO gives no obvious indication that a civil action can proceed only after a criminal conviction. The word "conviction" does not appear in any relevant portion of the statute. See §§ 1961, 1962, 1964(c). To the contrary, the predicate acts involve conduct that is "chargeable" or "indictable," and "offense[s]" that are "punishable," under various criminal statutes. § 1961(1). As defined in the statute, racketeering activity consists not of acts for which the defendant has been convicted, but of acts for which he could be. See also S.Rep. No. 91–617, p. 158 (1969): "a racketeering activity . . . must be an act in itself *subject to* criminal sanction" (emphasis added). Thus, a prior conviction-requirement cannot be found in the definition of "racketeering activity." Nor can it be found in § 1962, which sets out the statute's substantive provisions. Indeed, if either § 1961 or § 1962 did contain such a requirement, a prior conviction would also be a prerequisite, nonsensically, for a criminal prosecution, or for a civil action by the Government to enjoin violations that had not yet occurred.

The Court of Appeals purported to discover its prior-conviction requirement in the term "violation" in § 1964(c). However, even if that term were read to refer to a criminal conviction, it would require a conviction under RICO, not of the predicate offenses. That aside, the term "violation" does not imply a criminal conviction. It refers only to a failure to adhere to legal requirements. This is its indisputable meaning elsewhere in the statute. Section 1962 renders certain conduct "unlawful"; § 1963 and § 1964 impose consequences, criminal and civil, for "violations" of § 1962. We should not lightly infer that Congress intended the term to have wholly different meanings in neighboring subsections.

The legislative history also undercuts the reading of the court below. The clearest current in that history is the reliance on the Clayton Act model, under which private and governmental actions are entirely distinct. *E.g., United States v. Borden Co.*, 347 U.S. 514 (1954). The only specific reference in the legislative history to prior convictions of which we are aware is an objection that the treble-damages provision is too broad precisely because "there need *not* be a conviction under any of these laws for it to be racketeering." 116 Cong.Rec. 35342 (1970) (emphasis added). The history is otherwise silent on this point and contains nothing to contradict the import of the language appearing in the statute. Had Congress intended to impose this novel requirement, there would have been at least some mention of it in the legislative history, even if not in the statute.

The Court of Appeals was of the view that its narrow construction of the statute was essential to avoid intolerable practical consequences.[9] First, without a prior conviction to rely on, the plaintiff would have to prove commission of the predicate acts beyond a reasonable doubt. This would require instructing the jury as to different standards of proof for different aspects of the case. To avoid this awkwardness, the court inferred that the criminality must already be established, so that the civil action could proceed smoothly under the usual preponderance standard.

We are not at all convinced that the predicate acts must be established beyond a reasonable doubt in a proceeding under § 1964(c). In a number of settings, conduct that can be punished as criminal only upon proof beyond a reasonable doubt will support civil sanctions under a preponderance standard. There is no indication that Congress sought to depart from this general principle here. That the offending conduct is described by reference to criminal statutes does not mean that its occurrence must be established by criminal standards or that the consequences of a finding of liability in a private civil action are identical to the consequences of a criminal conviction. But we need not decide the standard of proof issue today. For even if the stricter standard is applicable to a portion of the plaintiff's proof, the resulting logistical difficulties, which are accepted in other contexts, would not be so great as to require invention of a requirement that cannot be found in the statute

---

[9]   It is worth bearing in mind that the holding of the court below is not without problematic consequences of its own. It arbitrarily restricts the availability of private actions, for lawbreakers are often not apprehended and convicted. Even if a conviction has been obtained, it is unlikely that a private plaintiff will be able to recover for all of the acts constituting an extensive "pattern," or that multiple victims will all be able to obtain redress. This is because criminal convictions are often limited to a small portion of the actual or possible charges. The decision below would also create peculiar incentives for plea bargaining to non-predicate-act offenses so as to ensure immunity from a later civil suit. If nothing else, a criminal defendant might plead to a tiny fraction of counts, so as to limit future civil liability. In addition, the dependence of potential civil litigants on the initiation and success of a criminal prosecution could lead to unhealthy private pressures on prosecutors and to self-serving trial testimony, or at least accusations thereof. Problems would also arise if some or all of the convictions were reversed on appeal. Finally, the compelled wait for the completion of criminal proceedings would result in pursuit of stale claims, complex statute of limitations problems, or the wasteful splitting of actions, with resultant claim and issue preclusion complications.

and that Congress, as even the Court of Appeals had to concede, did not envision.

The court below also feared that any other construction would raise severe constitutional questions, as it "would provide civil remedies for offenses criminal in nature, stigmatize defendants with the appellation 'racketeer,' authorize the award of damages which are clearly punitive, including attorney's fees, and constitute a civil remedy aimed in part to avoid the constitutional protections of the criminal law." We do not view the statute as being so close to the constitutional edge. As noted above, the fact that conduct can result in both criminal liability and treble damages does not mean that there is not a bona fide civil action. The familiar provisions for both criminal liability and treble damages under the antitrust laws indicate as much. Nor are attorney's fees "clearly punitive." As for stigma, a civil RICO proceeding leaves no greater stain than do a number of other civil proceedings. Furthermore, requiring conviction of the predicate acts would not protect against an unfair imposition of the "racketeer" label. If there is a problem with thus stigmatizing a garden variety defrauder by means of a civil action, it is not reduced by making certain that the defendant is guilty of *fraud* beyond a reasonable doubt. Finally, to the extent an action under § 1964(c) might be considered quasi-criminal, requiring protections normally applicable only to criminal proceedings, the solution is to provide those protections, not to ensure that they were previously afforded by requiring prior convictions.

Finally, we note that a prior-conviction requirement would be inconsistent with Congress' underlying policy concerns. Such a rule would severely handicap potential plaintiffs. A guilty party may escape conviction for any number of reasons—not least among them the possibility that the Government itself may choose to pursue only civil remedies. Private attorney general provisions such as § 1964(c) are in part designed to fill prosecutorial gaps. This purpose would be largely defeated, and the need for treble damages as an incentive to litigate unjustified, if private suits could be maintained only against those already brought to justice. See also n. 9, *supra*.

In sum, we can find no support in the statute's history, its language, or considerations of policy for a requirement that a private treble-damages action under § 1964(c) can proceed only against a defendant who has already been criminally convicted. To the contrary, every indication is that no such requirement exists. Accordingly, the fact that Imrex and the individual defendants have not been convicted under RICO or the federal mail and wire fraud statutes does not bar Sedima's action.

IV

In considering the Court of Appeals' second prerequisite for a private civil RICO action—"injury . . . caused by an activity which RICO was designed to deter"—we are somewhat hampered by the vagueness of that concept. Apart from reliance on the general purposes of RICO and a reference to "mobsters," the court provided scant indication of what the requirement of racketeering injury means. It emphasized Congress' undeniable desire to strike at organized crime, but acknowledged and did not purport to overrule Second Circuit precedent rejecting a requirement of an organized crime nexus. The court also stopped short of adopting a "competitive injury" requirement; while insisting that the plaintiff show "the kind of economic injury which has an effect on competition," it did not require "actual anticompetitive effect."

The court's statement that the plaintiff must seek redress for an injury caused by conduct that RICO was designed to deter is unhelpfully tautological. Nor is clarity furnished by a negative statement of its rule: standing is not provided by the injury resulting from the predicate acts themselves. That statement is itself apparently inaccurate when applied to those predicate acts that unmistakably constitute the kind of conduct Congress sought to deter. The opinion does not explain how to distinguish such crimes from the other predicate acts Congress has lumped together in § 1961(1). The court below is not alone in struggling to define "racketeering injury," and the difficulty of that task itself cautions against imposing such a requirement.

We need not pinpoint the Second Circuit's precise holding, for we perceive no distinct "racketeering injury" requirement. Given that "racketeering activity" consists of no more and no less than commission of a predicate act, § 1961(1), we are initially doubtful about a requirement of a "racketeering injury" separate from the harm from the predicate acts. A reading of the statute belies any such requirement. Section 1964(c) authorizes a private suit by "[a]ny person injured in his business or property by reason of a violation of § 1962." Section 1962 in turn makes it unlawful for "any person"—not just mobsters—to use money derived from a pattern of racketeering activity to invest in an enterprise, to acquire control of an enterprise through a pattern of racketeering activity, or to conduct an enterprise through a pattern of racketeering activity. §§ 1962(a)–(c). If the defendant engages in a pattern of racketeering activity in a manner forbidden by these provisions, and the racketeering activities injure the plaintiff in his business or property, the plaintiff has a claim under § 1964(c). There is no room in the statutory language for an additional, amorphous "racketeering injury" requirement.

A violation of § 1962(c), the section on which Sedima relies, requires (1) conduct (2) of an enterprise (3) through a pattern[14] (4) of racketeering activity. The plaintiff must, of course, allege each of these elements to state a claim. Conducting an enterprise that affects interstate commerce is obviously not in itself a violation of § 1962, nor is mere commission of the predicate offenses. In addition, the plaintiff only has standing if, and can only recover to the extent that, he has been injured in his business or property by the conduct constituting the violation. As the Seventh Circuit has stated, "[a] defendant who violates section 1962 is not liable for treble damages to everyone he might have injured by other conduct, nor is the defendant liable to those who have not been injured." *Haroco, Inc. v. American National Bank & Trust Co. of Chicago,* 747 F.2d 384, 398 (1984), aff'd, 473 U.S. 606.

But the statute requires no more than this. Where the plaintiff alleges each element of the violation, the compensable injury necessarily is the harm caused by predicate acts sufficiently related to constitute a pattern, for the essence of the violation is the commission of those acts in connection with the conduct of an enterprise. Those acts are, when committed in the circumstances delineated in § 1962(c), "an activity which RICO was designed to deter." Any recoverable damages occurring by reason of a violation of § 1962(c) will flow from the commission of the predicate acts.

This less restrictive reading is amply supported by our prior cases and the general principles surrounding this statute. RICO is to be read broadly. This is the lesson not only of Congress' self-consciously expansive language and overall approach, but also of its express admonition that RICO is to "be liberally construed to effectuate its remedial purposes," Pub.L. 91–452, § 904(a), 84 Stat. 947. The statute's "remedial purposes" are nowhere more evident than in the provision of a private action for those injured by racketeering activity. Far from effectuating these purposes, the narrow readings offered by the dissenters and the court below would in effect eliminate § 1964(c) from the statute.

---

[14] As many commentators have pointed out, the definition of a "pattern of racketeering activity" differs from the other provisions in § 1961 in that it states that a pattern *"requires* at least two acts of racketeering activity," § 1961(5) (emphasis added), not that it "means" two such acts. The implication is that while two acts are necessary, they may not be sufficient. Indeed, in common parlance two of anything do not generally form a "pattern." The legislative history supports the view that two isolated acts of racketeering activity do not constitute a pattern. As the Senate Report explained: "The target of [RICO] is thus not sporadic activity. The infiltration of legitimate business normally requires more than one 'racketeering activity' and the threat of continuing activity to be effective. It is this factor of *continuity plus relationship* which combines to produce a pattern." S.Rep. No. 91–617, p. 158 (1969) (emphasis added). Similarly, the sponsor of the Senate bill, after quoting this portion of the Report, pointed out to his colleagues that "[t]he term 'pattern' itself requires the showing of a relationship. . . . So, therefore, proof of two acts of racketeering activity, without more, does not establish a pattern. . . ." 116 Cong.Rec. 18940 (1970) (statement of Sen. McClellan). . . .

RICO was an aggressive initiative to supplement old remedies and develop new methods for fighting crime. While few of the legislative statements about novel remedies and attacking crime on all fronts were made with direct reference to § 1964(c), it is in this spirit that all of the Act's provisions should be read. The specific references to § 1964(c) are consistent with this overall approach. . . .

Underlying the Court of Appeals' holding was its distress at the "extraordinary, if not outrageous," uses to which civil RICO has been put. Instead of being used against mobsters and organized criminals, it has become a tool for everyday fraud cases brought against "respected and legitimate 'enterprises.' " Yet Congress wanted to reach both "legitimate" and "illegitimate" enterprises. The former enjoy neither an inherent incapacity for criminal activity nor immunity from its consequences. The fact that § 1964(c) is used against respected businesses allegedly engaged in a pattern of specifically identified criminal conduct is hardly a sufficient reason for assuming that the provision is being misconstrued. Nor does it reveal the "ambiguity" discovered by the court below. "[T]he fact that RICO has been applied in situations not expressly anticipated by Congress does not demonstrate ambiguity. It demonstrates breadth." *Haroco, Inc. v. American National Bank & Trust Co. of Chicago, supra,* at 398.

It is true that private civil actions under the statute are being brought almost solely against such defendants, rather than against the archetypal, intimidating mobster. Yet this defect—if defect it is—is inherent in the statute as written, and its correction must lie with Congress. It is not for the judiciary to eliminate the private action in situations where Congress has provided it simply because plaintiffs are not taking advantage of it in its more difficult applications.

We nonetheless recognize that, in its private civil version, RICO is evolving into something quite different from the original conception of its enactors. Though sharing the doubts of the Court of Appeals about this increasing divergence, we cannot agree with either its diagnosis or its remedy. The "extraordinary" uses to which civil RICO has been put appear to be primarily the result of the breadth of the predicate offenses, in particular the inclusion of wire, mail, and securities fraud, and the failure of Congress and the courts to develop a meaningful concept of "pattern." We do not believe that the amorphous standing requirement imposed by the Second Circuit effectively responds to these problems, or that it is a form of statutory amendment appropriately undertaken by the courts.

V

Sedima may maintain this action if the defendants conducted the enterprise through a pattern of racketeering activity. The questions whether the defendants committed the requisite predicate acts, and whether the commission of those acts fell into a pattern, are not before us. The complaint is not deficient for failure to allege either an injury separate from the financial loss stemming from the alleged acts of mail and wire fraud, or prior convictions of the defendants. The judgment below is accordingly reversed, and the case is remanded for further proceedings consistent with this opinion.

NOTES & QUESTIONS

(1) How does the Supreme Court address the Second Circuit's position that there must be a conviction prior to using a racketeering activity as a predicate act? Does the legislative history support the Second Circuit's approach? What practical and public policy concerns does the approach raise?

(2) What is wrong with requiring "injury . . . caused by an activity which RICO was designed to deter"? Can you identify what such an injury would be?

(3) According to the Court, what must be alleged to sustain a RICO claim? Although the Court rejects the "RICO-type injury" approach, what level of proof is required for liability?

B. TYPES OF RICO CLAIMS

Let's elaborate further on what is necessary to bring a civil RICO claim. A plaintiff must prove that: (1) a "person" engaged (2) in a pattern of racketeering activity (3) in any of the four prohibited ways under § 1962(a)–(d) (4) that affected an "enterprise" engaged in interstate commerce and (5) resulted in injury to plaintiff's business or property. The term "person" is defined in § 1961(3) to mean "any individual or entity capable of holding a legal or beneficial interest in property." Thus, the term is broad enough to include partnerships, corporations, and other business organizations. As noted in the introduction, the term "enterprise" is broader than the definition of person in that it includes associations-in-fact which are not considered to be legal entities (think of the mafia). The injury requirement (which we will discuss later) excludes personal injuries by only covering injuries to the plaintiff's business or property. In this Section, we primarily discuss the third element and the ways in which a RICO violation can occur. Note, however, that all four subsections of § 1962 require a "racketeering activity" as a predicate act.

PROBLEM 13.1

Review the definition of "racketeering activity" in 18 U.S.C. § 1961(1) and determine which of the following activities would fall within the definition:

(a) A referee of a high school basketball game accepts money from an alumnus to influence the outcome of a state championship game. *See* 18 U.S.C. § 224.

(b) In need of quick cash, Billy, a college senior, sells his mother's credit card number (without her consent) to a classmate. *See* 18 U.S.C. § 1209.

(c) Jerry's friend Matt offers to pay for Jerry to attend a live concert of Matt's favorite band so long as Jerry tapes the performance and gives Matt a copy of the recording. *See* 18 U.S.C. § 2319A.

(d) Nancy lives in Texas, where the possession and sale of marijuana is illegal. She receives marijuana from various sources outside of Texas and resells it from her home in the suburbs. *See* 19 U.S.C. § 1981(1)(D).

(e) Ken is starting a new company for the stated purpose of trading energy on an online platform. Over the course of a year, he contacts multiple investors over the phone and internet and raises $10 million for his new venture. Unfortunately for the investors, Ken has been lying about the true nature of the business and has simply pocketed the invested money. In considering this scenario, would it be helpful to know whether Ken has already been convicted of securities fraud? *See* 18 U.S.C. § 1961(1)(D). *But see id.* § 1964(c).

1. CLAIMS UNDER § 1962(a) & (b)

Section 1962(a) prohibits a person from using or investing money received from a pattern of racketeering activity "in acquisition of any interest in, or the establishment or operation of, any enterprise." While this language would cover the mafia using money derived from an extortion ring to invest in a laundromat, the language can also reach less obvious activities. For example, in *Ideal Steel Supply Corp. v. Anza*, 652 F.3d 310 (2d Cir. 2011), the plaintiff, Ideal, alleged that the defendants caused it injury by establishing a competing business with money derived from mail and wire fraud—specifically from filing fraudulent tax returns which enabled the evasion of over $1 million in income taxes.

Similar to § 1962(a), § 1962(b) prohibits a person from acquiring or maintaining an interest in an enterprise through a pattern of racketeering activity. This provision reaches instances in which the racketeering activity itself is the vehicle which permits the acquisition or maintenance of an interest in an enterprise. A colorful illustration of how such a violation could occur is provided by *Abraham v. Singh*, 480 F.3d 351 (5th Cir. 2007). The plaintiffs were individuals from India who travelled to the U.S. to work for Falcon Steel Structures based upon promises of full-time employment and the opportunity to obtain permanent residence status. The defendants arranged for work visas at Falcon and the transportation of the plaintiffs, charging them between $7,000 and $20,000 for these services. Upon arriving in the U.S., the plaintiffs soon learned that the promises of employment were false. The defendants confiscated the plaintiffs' passports and housed the plaintiffs in poor conditions with little food. When plaintiffs were sent to work for others, they were charged arbitrary fees and their wages were skimmed. Plaintiffs who inquired about leaving were threatened with imprisonment and deportation. Plaintiffs eventually sued, alleging human trafficking, state law claims of breach of contract and fraudulent inducement, and RICO violations. The alleged racketeering acts included money laundering, peonage, visa fraud, immigration violations, Travel Act violations, and Hobbs Act extortion. These acts allegedly enabled the defendants to maintain an interest in the enterprise—i.e., Falcon.[b]

Civil claims under § 1962(a) and (b) are not common and rarely succeed. This is due, in large part, to the inability of plaintiffs to show that the complained-of violations caused harm. It is not enough that the underlying racketeering activities harmed the plaintiff—it must be the investment in (for § 1962(a)) or the acquiring or maintaining of (for § 1962(b)) an interest in the enterprise that causes the harm. Indeed, as sympathetic as the plaintiffs in *Abraham* were, their § 1962(a) and (b) claims were dismissed on this ground (although you may be relieved to know that their § 1962(c) and (d) claims survived). *See Abraham*, 480 F.3d at 357.

PROBLEM 13.2

Bill owns and operates a small coffee shop in Seattle, Washington. After the state of Washington legalized marijuana, a rival coffee shop, Tedz Buzz Shop, opens across the street from Bill. Tedz sells marijuana and uses the profits from the sale of the marijuana, which has a much higher mark-up than coffee, to undercut Bill's coffee prices. Bill is unwilling to sell marijuana on moral grounds, but also because it is still illegal federally and he does not wish to violate federal law. Bill has been consistently losing business ever since Tedz opened shop (even those who do not like the "atmosphere" at Tedz have been using the drive-thru for cheaper gourmet coffee). Assuming that Bill can show harm caused by the illegal marijuana sales, could Bill sue under § 1962 (a) or (b)?

2.   CLAIMS UNDER § 1962(c)

Section 1962(c) provides that it is "unlawful for any person employed by or associated with any enterprise . . . to conduct or participate, directly or indirectly, in the conduct of such enterprise's affairs through a pattern of racketeering activity or collection of unlawful debt." There are three components to this provision that require some explanation. First, the "person" who is violating § 1962(c) must be distinct from the enterprise

---

[b]   The plaintiffs also alleged violations of § 1962(a) because the defendants used the money they received to invest in the enterprise.

itself. Second, the person must be "employed by or associated with" the enterprise. Third, the person must "conduct or participate . . . in the conduct" of the enterprise's affairs.

a. The Person/Enterprise Distinction

The person/enterprise distinction is based upon the statutory language requiring a person to be associated with an enterprise, and the common sense proposition that you cannot associate with yourself. However, the requirement can be easily met. For instance, employees are distinct from the corporation they work for. A sole shareholder of a corporation is distinct from the corporation he owns. *See Cedric Kushner Promotions, Inc. v. King*, 533 U.S. 158, 163–64 (2001) ("[A] natural person is distinct from the corporation itself and is a legally different entity with different rights and responsibilities due to its different legal status."). Even without corporate status, an owner can be distinct from his sole proprietorship so long as the proprietorship is not a "one-man show." *See McCullough v. Suter*, 757 F.2d 142, 143–44 (7th Cir. 1985) ("There would be a problem if the sole proprietorship were strictly a one-man show. . . . But if the man has employees or associates, the enterprise is distinct from him, and it then makes no difference, so far as we can see, what legal form the enterprise takes."). While the idea that an owner can associate with his sole proprietorship may seem odd, it has its basis in the broad definition of "enterprise," which encompasses associations-in-fact even if they are not legal entities. Associations-in-fact can be loosely associated businesses, individuals, or unions, including illicit associations such as the mafia.

Based upon these principles, an employee who commits a predicate act as a defendant "person" may be liable because he is associated with an employer who qualifies as a separate entity (the "enterprise"). This is a common civil RICO fact pattern. Courts, however, have rejected claims that a company is a defendant "person" who has associated with an "enterprise" consisting of the company and its own employees. So while an employee as a defendant person is viewed as distinct from the entity he works for (the enterprise) under RICO, a company as a defendant person is not considered distinct from the employees that work for it (the alleged enterprise).

b. The "Employed by or Associated with" Requirement

It is not enough that the defendant person committed a predicate act. The person must also be employed by or associated with an enterprise whose affairs are conducted through a pattern of racketeering activity. Employees of a company clearly meet this standard. The "associated with" language is much broader, however, which raises the question of how attenuated the association can be. Doing business with an enterprise, or its employees, has been held to meet the "associated with" standard, even when doing so is detrimental to the enterprise. *See United States v. Yonan*, 800 F.2d 164 (7th Cir. 1986). The association, however, must involve the unlawful activities at issue. Simply conducting legitimate business with an enterprise is not enough.

c. The "Conduct or Participate . . . in the Conduct" of the Enterprise's Affairs Requirement

Showing that the defendant "conduct[ed] or participate[d], directly or indirectly, in the conduct of [the] enterprise's affairs" is one of the key obstacles faced by a plaintiff in a § 1962(c) claim. At one time, federal court interpretations of this phrase varied greatly. In the 1993 case of *Reves v. Ernst & Young*, 507 U.S. 170 (1993), the U.S. Supreme Court clarified the standard and concluded that the phrase required the defendant to be involved in the operation or management of the enterprise. *Id.* at 179. *Reves* involved RICO allegations brought against outside auditors by a trust. The *Reves* court described the relevant standard as follows:

> Once we understand the word "conduct" to require some degree of direction and the word "participate" to require some part in that direction, the meaning of § 1962(c) comes into focus. In order to "participate, directly or indirectly, in the conduct of such enterprise's affairs," one must have some part in directing those affairs. Of course, the word "participate" makes clear that RICO liability is not limited to those with primary responsibility for the enterprise's affairs, just as the phrase "directly or indirectly" makes clear that RICO liability is not limited to those with a formal position in the enterprise, but some part in directing the enterprise's affairs is required. The "operation or management" test expresses this requirement in a formulation that is easy to apply.

Id. at 179. The Court also noted that significant control is not required, and that control is not limited to upper-echelon employees. *Id.* at 184. Although the Court held that outside parties associated with an enterprise could meet the requisite level of control (such as through bribery), the drafting of financial statements for the enterprise did not rise to such a level. *See id.* at 184, 186.

The following case relies upon the *Reves* standard, but it also raises issues involving the person/enterprise distinction and what it means to associate with an enterprise. Consider all three requirements as you read the case.

ALLSTATE INSURANCE COMPANY V. ROZENBERG
590 F. Supp. 2d 384 (E.D.N.Y. 2008)

SPATT, DISTRICT JUDGE.

On February 12, 2008, the Plaintiffs (or "Allstate"), a group of nine insurers, commenced this action alleging that the numerous Defendants conspired to abuse New York's No-Fault Insurance regime, N.Y. Ins. Law § 5101 et seq., in order to obtain payment for medical services and diagnostic tests that were not medically necessary, or in some cases, never performed at all. The Plaintiffs assert common law claims for fraud and unjust enrichment, and seek damages for violations of N.Y. Gen. Bus. L. § 349, and violations of the Racketeer Influenced and Corrupt Organizations Act, 18 U.S.C. § 1961 et seq. ("RICO").

On April 30, 2008, Defendants Inna Polack, Alexander Polack, Natalya Shvartsman ("the Management Defendants"), and Mighty Management Group, Inc., Mighty Management LLC, and Blue Wave Management, Inc. ("the Management Companies") moved to dismiss Counts I, II, III, IV, V, and VIII of the Plaintiffs' complaint. On June 5, 2008, Defendants Dr. Alexander Rozenberg ("Rozenberg"), A.R. Medical Rehabilitation, P.C., A.R. Medical Art, P.C., and Yonkers Medical Art, P.C. ("the PC Defendants") moved to dismiss Counts I–V. For the sake of judicial economy, and because these separate motions raise the same arguments, the Court will address both motions together.

I. BACKGROUND

A. The Alleged Scheme

Pursuant to New York's No-Fault insurance regime, the Plaintiffs are required to provide benefits to eligible insured persons for medically necessary diagnostic tests. The insureds in turn may assign their rights to such benefits to their medical providers in order to reimburse them for services rendered. The Plaintiffs allege that Rozenberg, a licensed neurologist, is the straw owner of the PC Defendants. The PC Defendants are medical professional corporations that billed the Plaintiffs for consultations, neurological exams, and range of motion testing performed upon patients insured by Allstate. According to the Plaintiffs, Rozenberg played no role in the actual operation or management of the PC Defendants.

The Plaintiffs assert that the PC Defendants were in fact operated by the Management Companies; New York corporations that are owned and controlled by Inna Polack, Alexander Polack, and Yuliy Goldman. The Plaintiffs allege that the sole purpose of establishing the relationship between the PC Defendants and the Management Companies was to facilitate a scheme to defraud Allstate by creating and submitting, through the mail, fraudulent medical reports and invoices for medical services in support of hundreds of No-Fault insurance claims. In particular, the Plaintiffs aver that the Defendants submitted bills for services not rendered; charged excessive fees for unnecessary medical treatment; and induced Allstate and the other insurers to pay No-Fault insurance claims to professional medical corporations that were owned by non-licensed individuals.

The Plaintiffs allege that Inna Polack, Alexander Polack, and Rozenberg created the PC Defendants with different names, addresses, and taxpayer identification numbers to reduce the likelihood that insurers would uncover their scheme. The Plaintiffs further allege that, through the Management Companies, Inna Polack, Alexander Polack, and Goldman instructed non-medical personnel, including the Defendant Natalya Shvartsman, to implement pre-established treatment regimens that would maximize the PC Defendants' billing invoices.

The Plaintiffs contend that Rozenberg subjected their claimants to a battery of unnecessary tests and that the results of these examinations were often deliberately misrepresented or fabricated in order to justify further costly but unneeded treatments. The Plaintiff avers that, based upon these fabricated testing results, the Defendants submitted invoices to the Plaintiffs demanding payments for services that were not medically necessary or, in some cases, never rendered at all.

B.   The Indictment

On or about July 31, 2006, Rozenberg, Inna Polack, Natalya Shvartsman, Emmanuel Kucherovsky, Shaun Robinson, A.R. Medical, P.C., Mighty Management, LLC, and Mighty Management Group, Inc. ("the criminal Defendants") were indicted in Supreme Court, Kings County, in connection with a scheme to defraud No-Fault insurance carriers. According to the Indictment, the criminal Defendants controlled A.R. Medical. The Indictment alleges that the criminal Defendants paid a network of "steerers," such as Shaun Robinson, to stage automobile accidents and refer the victims to AR Medical for treatment. The Indictment alleges that AR Medical then defrauded insurance carriers by submitting fraudulent claims for health services.

The Indictment further alleges that although Rozenberg was the straw owner of AR Medical, it was in fact owned by Inna Polack. The Indictment alleges that Inna Polack established and enforced rules governing the solicitation of patients and the administration of patient treatment. According to the Indictment, the criminal Defendants fraudulently diagnosed patients with extensive injuries and submitted claims to insurance carriers for unnecessary treatment or, in some cases, treatment that was never provided at all. The Indictment also alleges that Inna Polack used the clinic's manager, Natalya Shvartsman, to carry out Polack's alleged scheme.

According to the Indictment, checks were drawn from the accounts of the Management Companies and made payable to corporations owned or controlled by Kucherovsky who, for a transaction fee, transferred these monies to Inna Polack. The Indictment alleges that during the period from January of 2005 until March of 2006, more than $2.3 million was deposited into the accounts of the Management Companies. According to the Plaintiffs, to date, Inna Polack, Shvartsman, Kucherovsky, and Robinson have all pled guilty to Insurance Fraud, Money Laundering, and Larceny.

C.   The Plaintiffs' Complaint

On February 12, 2008, the Plaintiffs commenced this lawsuit alleging that: (i) the Defendants violated RICO, 18 U.S.C. § 1962(c); (ii) the Defendants engaged in a RICO conspiracy in violation of 18 U.S.C. § 1962(d); (iii) the Defendants committed common law fraud and unjust enrichment; and (iv) the Defendants are liable under N.Y. Gen. Bus. L. § 349 for deceptive business practices.

II. DISCUSSION

. . . .

B.   The Defendants' Motions to Dismiss

The Defendants have filed separate motions to dismiss the complaint asserting that: (i) the Plaintiffs have failed to adequately set forth each Defendant's role in the alleged scheme; (ii) the Plaintiffs have failed to adequately plead that the Defendants carried on an "enterprise" within the meaning of RICO; [and] (iii) the Plaintiffs cannot show that there was a RICO conspiracy because they have failed to allege an underlying RICO violation. . . . The Court will review each of these arguments in turn.

1.   The Plaintiffs' Civil RICO Counts

The substantive RICO statute, 18 U.S.C. § 1962(c), makes it "unlawful for any person employed by or associated with any enterprise engaged in . . . interstate or foreign commerce, to conduct or participate, directly or indirectly, in the conduct of such enterprise's affairs through a pattern of racketeering activity . . ."

RICO defines "racketeering activity" to include certain predicate criminal acts including mail fraud. The Defendants argue, as a threshold matter, that the Plaintiffs have failed to set forth each Defendant's involvement in mail fraud—the alleged racketeering activity in this case. A plaintiff asserting a mail fraud claim must show: (1) the existence of a scheme to defraud, (2) defendant's knowing or intentional participation in the scheme, and (3) the use of interstate mails or transmission facilities in furtherance of the scheme.

[The court concluded that the Plaintiffs met their burden to show that each of the named Defendants committed mail fraud.]

a. Count I

The Defendants contend that the Plaintiffs have failed to allege the existence of an "enterprise" within the meaning of RICO. The statute provides that an "enterprise" includes "any individual, partnership, corporation, association, or other legal entity, and any union or group of individuals associated in fact although not a legal entity." 18 U.S.C. § 1961(4). However, under Section 1962(c), it is well-established that the alleged "enterprise" through which a pattern of racketeering activity is conducted must be distinct from those persons or entities who stand accused of conducting that racketeering activity. *See Riverwoods Chappaqua Corp. v. Marine Midland Bank, N.A.*, 30 F.3d 339, 344 (2d Cir.1994) (finding that the same corporate entity cannot be the RICO "person" and the RICO "enterprise" under section 1962(c)).

In Count I, the Plaintiffs have identified the PC Defendants and the Management Companies as the RICO enterprise, and Inna Polack, Alexander Polack, Rozenberg, Goldman, Shvartsman, Kucherovsky, and Robinson as the so-called RICO persons. The Defendants argue that the distinctiveness requirement is not met where a plaintiff alleges a conspiracy between a corporation and its own employees carrying on the affairs of the corporation. However, the Supreme Court has explicitly rejected such an exacting construction of the distinctiveness requirement.

In *Cedric Kushner Promotions, Ltd. v. King*, 533 U.S. 158 (2001), a corporate promoter of boxing matches sued boxing promoter Don King, the president and sole shareholder of Don King Productions ("DKP"), alleging that King had conducted a pattern of racketeering activity through DKP. The District Court dismissed the plaintiff's complaint finding that it failed to meet the distinctiveness requirement. The Second Circuit affirmed the dismissal holding that "King, in a legal sense, was part of, not separate from, the corporation," and that therefore "there was no 'person,' distinct from the 'enterprise,' who improperly conducted the 'enterprise's affairs.'" *Id.* [at 161].

The Supreme Court reversed the lower courts, holding that, in such circumstances, the distinctiveness requirement is met because a "corporate owner/employee ... is distinct from the corporation itself, a legally different entity with different rights and responsibilities due to its different legal status." *Id.* at 163. The Court was careful to distinguish the facts in Kushner from an earlier Second Circuit case, *Riverwoods Chappaqua Corp. v. Marine Midland Bank, N.A.*, 30 F.3d 339, 344 (2d Cir.1994), that the Defendants here rely upon.

In *Riverwoods*, the plaintiffs alleged that the defendant bank had fraudulently coerced them into restructuring loan agreements in violation of RICO. In their complaint, the plaintiffs alleged that the bank was the RICO person and the RICO enterprise was the bank along with its employees and agents. The Second Circuit found that the distinctiveness requirement could not be circumvented "by alleging a RICO enterprise that consists merely of a corporate defendant associated with its own employees or agents carrying on the regular affairs of the defendant . . ." *Id.* at 344.

However, here, as in *Kushner*, the Plaintiffs claim that the corporate officers and employees are the RICO persons while the corporations are the RICO enterprise. The legal distinction between the RICO enterprise (the PC and Management Company Defendants) and the RICO persons (the officers and employees of those corporations) is sufficient to satisfy the distinctiveness requirement. *See Kushner*, 533 U.S. at 164 (noting that such a construction of the distinctiveness requirement comports with the statute's aim to protect "the public from those who would unlawfully use an 'enterprise' (whether legitimate or illegitimate) as a 'vehicle' through which 'unlawful . . . activity is committed.' ").

Having determined that the Plaintiffs have alleged a valid RICO enterprise, the Court must analyze whether each of the Defendants conducted or participated, directly or indirectly, in the conduct of the enterprise's affairs. 18 U.S.C. § 1962(c). The Supreme Court has held that "to conduct or participate, directly or indirectly, in the conduct" of an enterprise's affairs "one must participate in the operation or management of the enterprise itself." *Reves v. Ernst & Young*, 507 U.S. 170, 185 (1993). The Supreme Court teaches that "the word 'participate' makes clear that RICO liability is not limited to those with primary responsibility, just as the phrase 'directly or indirectly' makes clear that RICO liability is not limited to those with a formal position in the enterprise . . ." *Id.* at 179.

At the pleading stage, the Plaintiffs have offered allegations sufficient to show that all of the individual Defendants participated in the alleged enterprise. Here, Inna Polack, Alexander Polack, and Yuliy Goldman are alleged to have been the true owners of the enterprise. The Plaintiffs allege that Rozenberg conducted the enterprise's affairs by misdiagnosing patients and performing the unnecessary treatments that drove the fraud. The Plaintiffs further allege that Shvartsman directed the enterprise's affairs by implementing the treatment regimens established by Inna Polack. The Plaintiffs also aver that Kucherovsky participated in the enterprise by laundering the fraudulent proceeds of the alleged scheme. Finally, although the allegations that Robinson participated in the conduct of the enterprise are more tenuous, they are sufficient to state a RICO claim against him because he managed a crucial part of the alleged scheme—steering patients to the PC Defendants.

The Plaintiffs having established all of the requisite elements of a civil RICO claim, the Defendants' motions to dismiss Count I of the complaint are denied.

b.   Count II—The "Innocent Victim Enterprise" Theory

In Count II, the Plaintiffs argue that Allstate—the alleged victim of the racketeering activity—is actually the RICO enterprise. The Supreme Court has observed that "the enterprise in subsection (c) [of § 1962] connotes generally the vehicle through which the unlawful pattern of racketeering activity is committed, rather than the victim of that activity." [*Nat'l Org. for Women, Inc. v. Scheidler*, 510 U.S. 249, 259 (1994)]. Although this conception of a RICO enterprise is rarely invoked, the Supreme Court has not foreclosed the possibility that, under certain circumstances, the victim of racketeering activity could also serve as the RICO enterprise. *See Com-Tech Assoc. v. Computer Assoc. Int'l*, 753 F.Supp. 1078, 1088 (E.D.N.Y.1990) ("Even though the plaintiffs themselves are also the 'enterprise,' it is permissible for the victimized enterprise to sue for damages under RICO, so long as it is alleged that the defendants conducted the enterprise through a pattern of racketeering activity.") (emphasis added).

To analyze this theory of RICO liability, the Court must again turn to the operation and management test. The Plaintiffs appear to claim that the Defendants conducted or participated in the Plaintiffs' affairs by submitting allegedly fictitious insurance claims that affected the insurance companies' claim-paying process. In the absence of any Second Circuit authority supporting the proposition that such conduct is sufficient to satisfy the "operation and management test," the Plaintiffs lean heavily on the First Circuit's decision in *Aetna Cas. Sur. Co. v. P & B Autobody*, 43 F.3d 1546 (1st Cir.1994). In *Aetna*, the First Circuit upheld a jury verdict for an insurer under § 1962(c) against five automobile body shops, their owners, and several Aetna claims adjusters who had engaged in a scheme to submit fraudulent insurance claims.

One of the issues on appeal was whether Aetna, the victim of the fraud, was an enterprise for RICO purposes. The appellants argued that Aetna could not properly be regarded as a RICO enterprise because, among other things, the appellants did not participate in Aetna's operation or management. The First Circuit disagreed finding that "[b]y acting with purpose to cause Aetna to make payments on false claims, appellants were participating in the 'operation' of Aetna." *Id.* at 1559. Crucial to the First Circuit's decision was the fact that several of the named defendants were Aetna claims adjusters who were bribed by their co-defendants into submitting false claims. *Id.* at 1559–60. The First Circuit's reasoning in Aetna has not been well received by courts within the Second Circuit. *See Allstate Ins. Co. v. Seigel*, 312 F.Supp.2d 260

(D.Conn.2004); In re *SmithKline Beecham Clinical Lab., Inc. Lab. Test Billing Practices Litig.*, 108 F.Supp.2d 84 (D.Conn.1999).

In *Seigel*, the plaintiff alleged that a doctor and a medical corporation owned by that doctor created fraudulent invoices and medical reports for the purpose of inducing the plaintiff to pay for medical treatments that were never performed. The plaintiff alleged a variety of RICO violations, and contended that it met the distinctiveness requirement because Allstate, and not the named defendant medical corporation, was the relevant RICO enterprise for the purposes of the plaintiff's 1962(c) claim. Although the Court declined to dismiss the plaintiff's RICO claim at the pleading stage, the Court observed that the First Circuit's construction would effectively undermine the operation and management test because "any time a company is defrauded by the conduct of a defendant, one could say that the defendant 'controlled' the company's operations, since absent the fraud, the company would not have done what it did or acted in the manner in which it did." *Seigel*, 312 F.Supp.2d at 275. The Court also noted that "[s]uch a free-wheeling interpretation," of the test was inconsistent with "the more rigorous approach to the operation and management requirement that district courts in the Second Circuit have adopted." See [*id.*] (collecting cases).

In *SmithKline*, healthcare insurers and other parties brought suit against a chain of medical laboratories alleging, among other things, that the defendant violated 1962(c) by engaging in a fraudulent billing scheme. 108 F.Supp.2d 84. The plaintiffs argued that one of the RICO enterprises was the hospitals and physicians' offices through which the defendant laboratories sent their allegedly fraudulent bills. The defendant countered that these entities could not serve as the RICO enterprise because none of the defendants actually participated in or conducted these entities' affairs. The Court agreed with the defendants and dismissed the plaintiffs' claim finding that "although [the defendant's] alleged fraudulent billing practices may have victimized the physicians' offices, hospitals, and laboratories, that does not suffice to establish that [the defendant] 'operated or managed' the affairs of each of these alleged enterprises." *Id.* at 100.

With due respect, the Court finds the First Circuit's construction of the "operation and management" test to be unpersuasive. However, even if the Court did apply this less stringent version of the test, *Aetna* is clearly distinguishable from the instant case. Significantly, unlike in *Aetna*, here the Plaintiffs do not allege that any of their employees conspired with the Defendants in the alleged scheme. As noted above, the fact that Aetna's claims adjusters were named as defendants for accepting bribes was the linchpin of the First Circuit's finding that the defendants conducted Aetna's affairs in such a way as to make Aetna an enterprise within the meaning of the statute.

Nevertheless, the Plaintiffs contend that Rozenberg and the PC Defendants occupied a unique position of trust as medical providers that gave them an operational or management role in Plaintiffs' decisions regarding the payment of claims. However, it is difficult to see how this position of trust goes to the salient question of whether the Defendants directed the Plaintiffs' affairs. *See Reves*, 507 U.S. at 185 (noting that 1962(c) "cannot be interpreted to reach complete 'outsiders' because liability depends on showing that the defendants conducted or participated in the conduct of the 'enterprise's affairs,' not just their own affairs."); *Redtail Leasing, Inc. v. Bellezza*, 1997 WL 603496, at *4 (S.D.N.Y. Sept. 30, 1997) (observing that the operation and management test is not easily satisfied because "[t]here is a 'substantial difference' between actual control over an enterprise and association with an enterprise in ways that do not involve control; [and] only the former is sufficient under *Reves*."). Accordingly, Count II is dismissed because the Plaintiffs have failed to show, under the facts at bar, that Allstate may serve as a RICO enterprise.

. . . .

III. CONCLUSION

Based on the foregoing, it is hereby

ORDERED, that the Defendants' motions to dismiss Count II are GRANTED, and it is further

ORDERED, that the Defendants' motions to dismiss Counts I, III, IV, V, and VIII are DENIED.

NOTES & QUESTIONS

(1)   Who exactly are the RICO defendants in this case under Count I? Were these defendants distinct from the alleged enterprise?

(2)   According to the court, why is the Second Circuit's *Riverwoods* decision distinguishable from the dispute at issue? Do you agree with the distinction? Why should a defendant employee be considered distinct from the corporation he works for, but a defendant corporation is not considered distinct from the employees that work for it? Should it matter whether the defendant person is an owner rather than an employee or agent?

(3)   Under Count I, the court agreed that the plaintiffs had adequately pled that the defendants conducted the enterprise's affairs. Do you agree with this conclusion? *See United States v. Viola*, 35 F.3d 37, 41 (2d Cir. 1994) ("Since *Reves*, it is plain that the simple taking of directions and performance of tasks that are 'necessary or helpful' to the enterprise, without more, is insufficient to bring a defendant within the scope of § 1962(c)."); *Redtail Leasing, Inc. v. Bellezza*, No. 95 Civ. 5191, 1997 WL 603496, at *5 (S.D.N.Y. 1997) (dismissing a RICO claim where the amended complaint alleged facts

tending to show that the defendants participated in the enterprise's affairs by passing along inside information, but was "devoid of allegations suggesting that [they] had some part in directing the enterprise's affairs").

(4) Under Count II, Allstate claimed that it was the RICO enterprise. Why might it have made such an allegation given that Count I alleged an enterprise consisting of the various companies of the individual defendants?

(5) The court rejected Allstate's "Innocent Victim Enterprise" theory (the theory of Count II). What was the basis for the court's rejection of Allstate as the enterprise? Can you imagine a set of circumstances under which Allstate could have succeeded on this theory?

(6) Should the "operation and management" test be different as applied to outsiders versus insiders, such as employees and officers? Even if the test is the same, are there any additional difficulties for a plaintiff alleging that an outside defendant qualifies under § 1962(c)?

(7) The defendants in this case included numerous companies. Could Allstate have alleged that each company was a defendant person for RICO purposes and that the enterprise was the association-in-fact of these companies? (Hint: see the next note.) Would it matter if the companies were all subsidiaries of a larger company that was also named as a defendant? *Compare Discon, Inc. v. NYNEX Corp.*, 93 F.3d 1055, 1064 (2d Cir. 1996) (finding that the distinctiveness requirement was not met, despite the involvement of three legally separate entities, because the affiliates "operate[d] within a unified corporate structure" and were "guided by a single corporate consciousness"), *and Fogie v. THORN Americas, Inc.*, 190 F.3d 889, 898 (8th Cir. 1999) ("[T]here must be a greater showing that the parent and subsidiary are distinct than the mere fact that they are separate legal entities."), *with* Pamela Bucy Pierson, *RICO, Corruption and White-Collar Crime*, 85 TEMPLE L. REV. 523, 552–55 (2013) (arguing that the cases finding no distinctiveness between parents and subsidiaries are inconsistent with *Cedric Kushner*, and observing that the case law in this area "is a bungled mess").

(8) In considering the questions in the above note, some background on the Supreme Court's jurisprudence in this area may be useful. In *United States v. Turkette*, 452 U.S. 576 (1981), the Court held that for an enterprise to be found, there must be "evidence of an on-going organization, formal or informal, and ... evidence that the various associates function as a continuing unit." *Id.* at 583. The Court noted, however, that "[t]he 'enterprise' is not the 'pattern of racketeering activity'; it is an entity separate and apart from the pattern of activity in which it engages." *Id.* This language led to some confusion among the lower courts with regard to associations-in-fact that were only associated by virtue of the racketeering activity. Some courts held that, under *Turkette*, a plaintiff must present evidence establishing an enterprise that is distinct from the evidence establishing the pattern of racketeering activity. *See, e.g., First Capital Asset Mgmt., Inc. v. Satinwood*, 385 F.3d 159, 173 (2d Cir. 2004); *United States v. Bledsoe*, 674 F.2d 647 (8th

Cir. 1982). In effect, these courts required some sort of ascertainable structure beyond the criminal enterprise being alleged. Other courts, however, took a more liberal view, requiring only that both an enterprise and a pattern of racketeering activity be shown—regardless of whether the evidence overlapped. *See, e.g., United States v. Salerno*, 108 F.3d 730, 739 (7th Cir. 1997); *United States v. Pelullo*, 964 F.2d 193, 212 (3d Cir. 1992); *United States v. Perholtz*, 842 F.2d 343, 363 (D.C. Cir. 1988); *United States v. Qaoud*, 777 F.2d 1105, 1115 (6th Cir. 1985); *United States v. Hewes*, 729 F.2d 1302, 1310–11 (11th Cir. 1984); *United States v. Mazzei*, 700 F.2d 85, 88–89 (2d Cir. 1983).

In *Boyle v. United States*, 556 U.S. 938 (2009), the issue was resolved in favor of a more liberal reading of the enterprise requirement. *Boyle* involved a group of bank robbers, some of whom argued that the informal group lacked any ascertainable structure and therefore failed to constitute a RICO enterprise. The Court rejected such a strict reading and instead adopted a more liberal definition:

> We agree with petitioner that an association-in-fact enterprise must have a structure. In the sense relevant here, the term "structure" means "[t]he way in which parts are arranged or put together to form a whole" and "[t]he interrelation or arrangement of parts in a complex entity." American Heritage Dictionary 1718 (4th ed.2000).

> From the terms of RICO, it is apparent that an association-in-fact enterprise must have at least three structural features: a purpose, relationships among those associated with the enterprise, and longevity sufficient to permit these associates to pursue the enterprise's purpose. As we succinctly put it in *Turkette*, an association-in-fact enterprise is "a group of persons associated together for a common purpose of engaging in a course of conduct." 452 U.S., at 583.

> That an "enterprise" must have a purpose is apparent from [the] meaning of the term in ordinary usage, i.e., a "venture," "undertaking," or "project." Webster's Third New International Dictionary 757 (1976). The concept of "associat[ion]" requires both interpersonal relationships and a common interest. Section 1962(c) reinforces this conclusion and also shows that an "enterprise" must have some longevity, since the offense proscribed by that provision demands proof that the enterprise had "affairs" of sufficient duration to permit an associate to "participate" in those affairs through "a pattern of racketeering activity."

> . . . .

> *"Beyond that inherent in the pattern of racketeering activity."* This phrase may be interpreted in least two different ways, and its correctness depends on the particular sense in which the phrase is used. If the phrase is interpreted to mean that the existence of an

enterprise is a separate element that must be proved, it is of course correct. As we explained in *Turkette*, the existence of an enterprise is an element distinct from the pattern of racketeering activity and "proof of one does not necessarily establish the other." 452 U.S., at 583.

On the other hand, if the phrase is used to mean that the existence of an enterprise may never be inferred from the evidence showing that persons associated with the enterprise engaged in a pattern of racketeering activity, it is incorrect. We recognized in *Turkette* that the evidence used to prove the pattern of racketeering activity and the evidence establishing an enterprise "may in particular cases coalesce." *Ibid.*

Boyle, 556 U.S. at 945–47. The end result of the Court's analysis is that an enterprise can be proven by the same evidence used to establish the pattern of racketeering activity. Moreover, a structure need only have three features to qualify as an enterprise: (1) purpose; (2) relationships; and (3) longevity sufficient to achieve the purpose.

PROBLEM 13.3

(a) Venture Industries, Inc. ("VI") manufactures medical devices including the Mach V Pacemaker. The Mach V has come under intense media scrutiny for its propensity to fail, which causes harm to its recipients. Rusty is an outside attorney who helped VI navigate its way through the various governmental approvals that were necessary to get the Mach V to market. Currently, a class of plaintiffs is suing certain VI employees and Rusty under § 1962(c) claiming that evidence of the Mach V's deficiencies was knowingly hidden to help expedite the approval process. The suit lists Rusty as a defendant "person" and VI as the "enterprise."

Rusty would like to have the suit against him dismissed. Considering the elements of a § 1962(c) claim, is dismissal of the suit likely? What additional information might you need? *See Handeen v. Lemaire*, 112 F.3d 1339 (8th Cir. 1997) ("Furnishing a client with ordinary professional assistance, even when the client happens to be a RICO enterprise, will not normally rise to the level of participation sufficient to satisfy . . . *Reves*."); *Goren v. New Vision Int'l Inc.*, 156 F.3d 721, 728 (7th Cir. 1998) ("[S]imply performing services for an enterprise, even with knowledge of the enterprise's illicit nature, is not enough to subject an individual to RICO liability under § 1962(c); instead, the individual must have participated in the operation and management of the enterprise itself.").

(b) Assume that Rusty directed that evidence of the Mach V's shortcomings be destroyed to help expedite the approval process. This fact is later discovered, but Rusty and the culpable employees are now bankrupt. Could the plaintiffs allege that VI is the defendant person and that the enterprise is the association-in-fact of VI and Rusty? *Compare Florida Evergreen Foliage v. E.I. Dupont de Nemours & Co.*, 336 F. Supp. 2d 1239,

1268 (S.D. Fla. 2004) (dismissing a claim by a plaintiff against a company and its attorney for failure to show distinctness as an enterprise), *and Palmas Y Bambu, S.A. v. E.I. Dupont de Nemours & Co., Inc.*, 881 So. 2d 565, 575–77 (Fla. Dist. Ct. App. 2004) (same), *with Living Designs, Inc. v. E.I. DuPont de Nemours & Co.*, 431 F.3d 353, 362 (9th Cir. 2005) (alleging an enterprise consisting of an attorney and the attorney's client (a company), and concluding that the attorney and the client were distinct).

3.   CLAIMS UNDER § 1962(d)

Section 1962(d) makes it a RICO violation to conspire to commit a § 1962(a), (b), or (c) violation. Thus, if a plaintiff cannot establish a substantive claim under (a), (b), or (c) the conspiracy claim may still prove viable. It is not necessary to allege or prove that (a), (b), or (c) have been violated to succeed under (d) or that the defendant even knows of all the other co-conspirators and their roles.

SALINAS V. UNITED STATES
522 U.S. 52 (1997)

JUSTICE KENNEDY delivered the opinion of the Court.

The case before us presents [the following question:] does the conspiracy prohibition contained in the Racketeer Influenced and Corrupt Organizations Act (RICO) apply only when the conspirator agrees to commit two of the predicate acts RICO forbids? Ruling against the petitioner on [this issue], we affirm the judgment of the Court of Appeals for the Fifth Circuit.

I

This federal prosecution arose from a bribery scheme operated by Brigido Marmolejo, the Sheriff of Hidalgo County, Texas, and petitioner Mario Salinas, one of his principal deputies. In 1984, the United States Marshals Service and Hidalgo County entered into agreements under which the county would take custody of federal prisoners. In exchange, the Federal Government agreed to make a grant to the county for improving its jail and also agreed to pay the county a specific amount per day for each federal prisoner housed. Based on the estimated number of federal prisoners to be maintained, payments to the county were projected to be $915,785 per year. . . .

Homero Beltran-Aguirre was one of the federal prisoners housed in the jail under the arrangement negotiated between the Marshals Service and the county. He was incarcerated there for two intervals, first for 10 months and then for 5 months. During both custody periods, Beltran paid Marmolejo a series of bribes in exchange for so-called "contact visits" in which he remained alone with his wife or, on other occasions, his girlfriend. Beltran paid Marmolejo a fixed rate of $6,000 per month and $1,000 for each contact visit, which occurred twice a week. Petitioner Salinas was the chief deputy responsible for managing the jail and supervising custody of the prisoners. When Marmolejo was not available, Salinas arranged for the contact visits and on occasion stood watch outside the room where the visits took place. In return for his assistance with the scheme, Salinas received from Beltran a pair of designer watches and a pickup truck.

Salinas and Marmolejo were indicted and tried together, but only Salinas' convictions are before us. Salinas was charged with one count of violating RICO, 18 U.S.C. § 1962(c), one count of conspiracy to violate RICO, § 1962(d), and two counts of bribery in violation of § 666(a)(1)(B). The jury acquitted Salinas on the substantive RICO count, but convicted him on the RICO conspiracy count and the bribery counts. A divided panel of the Court of Appeals for the Fifth Circuit affirmed, and we granted certiorari. . . .

. . . .

III

Salinas directs his . . . challenge to his conviction for conspiracy to violate RICO. There could be no conspiracy offense, he says, unless he himself committed or agreed to commit the two predicate acts requisite for a substantive RICO offense under § 1962(c). Salinas identifies a conflict among the Courts of Appeals on the point. Decisions of the First, Second, and Tenth Circuits require that, under the RICO conspiracy provision, the defendant must himself commit or agree to commit two or more predicate acts. Eight other Courts of Appeals, including the Fifth Circuit in this case, take a contrary view.

Before turning to RICO's conspiracy provision, we note the substantive RICO offense, which was the goal of the conspiracy alleged in the indictment. It provides: "It shall be unlawful for any person employed by or associated with any enterprise engaged in, or the activities of which affect, interstate or foreign commerce, to conduct or participate, directly or indirectly, in the conduct of such enterprise's affairs through a pattern of racketeering activity or collection of unlawful debt." 18 U.S.C. § 1962(c).

The elements predominant in a subsection (c) violation are: (1) the conduct (2) of an enterprise (3) through a pattern of racketeering activity. *See Sedima, S.P.R.L. v. Imrex Co.*, 473 U.S. 479, 496 (1985). "Pattern of racketeering activity" is a defined term and requires at least two acts of "racketeering activity," the so-called predicate acts central to our discussion. 18 U.S.C. § 1961(5). "Racketeering activity," in turn, is defined to include "any act . . . involving . . . bribery . . . which is chargeable under State law and punishable by imprisonment for more than one year."

§ 1961(1)(A). The Government's theory was that Salinas himself committed a substantive § 1962(c) RICO violation by conducting the enterprise's affairs through a pattern of racketeering activity that included acceptance of two or more bribes, felonies punishable in Texas by more than one year in prison. The jury acquitted on the substantive count. Salinas was convicted of conspiracy, however, and he challenges the conviction because the jury was not instructed that he must have committed or agreed to commit two predicate acts himself. His interpretation of the conspiracy statute is wrong.

The RICO conspiracy statute, simple in formulation, provides: "It shall be unlawful for any person to conspire to violate any of the provisions of subsection (a), (b), or (c) of this section." 18 U.S.C. § 1962(d). There is no requirement of some overt act or specific act in the statute before us, unlike the general conspiracy provision applicable to federal crimes, which requires that at least one of the conspirators have committed an "act to effect the object of the conspiracy." § 371. The RICO conspiracy provision, then, is even more comprehensive than the general conspiracy offense in § 371.

In interpreting the provisions of § 1962(d), we adhere to a general rule: When Congress uses well-settled terminology of criminal law, its words are presumed to have their ordinary meaning and definition. The relevant statutory phrase in § 1962(d) is "to conspire." We presume Congress intended to use the term in its conventional sense, and certain well-established principles follow.

A conspiracy may exist even if a conspirator does not agree to commit or facilitate each and every part of the substantive offense. The partners in the criminal plan must agree to pursue the same criminal objective and may divide up the work, yet each is responsible for the acts of each other. *See Pinkerton v. United States*, 328 U.S. 640, 646 (1946) ("And so long as the partnership in crime continues, the partners act for each other in carrying it forward"). If conspirators have a plan which calls for some conspirators to perpetrate the crime and others to provide support, the supporters are as guilty as the perpetrators. As Justice Holmes observed: "[P]lainly a person may conspire for the commission of a crime by a third person." *United States v. Holte*, 236 U.S. 140, 144 (1915). A person, moreover, may be liable for conspiracy even though he was incapable of committing the substantive offense. *United States v. Rabinowich*, 238 U.S. 78, 86 (1915).

The point Salinas tries to make is in opposition to these principles, and is refuted by *Bannon v. United States*, 156 U.S. 464 (1895). There the defendants were charged with conspiring to violate the general conspiracy statute, *id.*, at 464, which requires proof of an overt act. One defendant objected to the indictment because it did not allege he had committed an overt act. We rejected the argument because it would erode the common-law principle that, so long as they share a common purpose, conspirators are liable for the acts of their co-conspirators. We observed in *Bannon*: "To require an overt act to be proven against every member of the conspiracy, or a distinct act connecting him with the combination to be alleged, would not only be an innovation upon established principles, but would render most prosecutions for the offence nugatory." 156 U.S., at 469. The RICO conspiracy statute, § 1962(d), broadened conspiracy coverage by omitting the requirement of an overt act; it did not, at the same time, work the radical change of requiring the Government to prove each conspirator agreed that he would be the one to commit two predicate acts.

Our recitation of conspiracy law comports with contemporary understanding. When Congress passed RICO in 1970, the American Law Institute's Model Penal Code permitted a person to be convicted of conspiracy so long as he "agrees with such other person or persons that they or one or more of them will engage in conduct that constitutes such crime." Model Penal Code § 5.03(1)(a) (1962). As the drafters emphasized, "so long as the purpose of the agreement is to facilitate commission of a crime, the actor need not agree 'to commit' the crime." American Law Institute, Model Penal Code, Tent. Draft No. 10, p. 117 (1960). The Model Penal Code still uses this formulation. See Model Penal Code § 5.03(1)(a), 10 U.L.A. 501 (1974).

A conspirator must intend to further an endeavor which, if completed, would satisfy all of the elements of a substantive criminal offense, but it suffices that he adopt the goal of furthering or facilitating the criminal endeavor. He may do so in any number of ways short of agreeing to undertake all of the acts necessary for the crime's completion. One can be a conspirator by agreeing to facilitate only some of the acts leading to the substantive offense. It is elementary that a conspiracy may exist and be punished whether or not the substantive crime ensues, for the conspiracy is a distinct evil, dangerous to the public, and so punishable in itself.

It makes no difference that the substantive offense under § 1962(c) requires two or more predicate acts. The interplay between subsections (c) and (d) does not permit us to excuse from the reach of the conspiracy provision an actor who does not himself commit or agree to commit the two or more predicate acts requisite to the underlying offense. True, though an "enterprise" under § 1962(c) can exist with only one actor to conduct it, in most instances it will be conducted by more than one person or entity; and this in turn may make it somewhat difficult to determine just where the enterprise ends and the conspiracy begins, or, on the other hand, whether the two crimes are coincident in their factual circumstances. In some cases the connection the defendant had to the alleged enterprise or to the conspiracy to further it may be tenuous enough so that his own commission of two predicate acts may become an important part of the Government's case. Perhaps these were the considerations leading some of the Circuits to require in conspiracy cases that each conspirator himself commit or agree to commit two or more predicate acts. Nevertheless, that proposition cannot be sustained as a definition of the conspiracy offense, for it is contrary to the principles we have discussed.

In the case before us, even if Salinas did not accept or agree to accept two bribes, there was ample evidence that he conspired to violate subsection (c). The evidence showed that Marmolejo committed at least two acts of racketeering activity when he accepted numerous bribes and that Salinas knew about and agreed to facilitate the scheme. This is sufficient to support a conviction under § 1962(d).

. . . .

NOTES & QUESTIONS

(1) According to the Court, what was wrong with Salinas's view of conspiracy? Would Salinas have fared better if he was charged under the general conspiracy statute applicable to federal crimes rather than under § 1962(d) for conspiracy to commit a RICO violation? See Bannon v. United States, 156 U.S. 464 (1895) (cited by the Salinas Court).

(2) As a practical matter, what is the appeal of the approach advocated by Salinas? What is the downside of such an approach?

(3) Recall that in Reves, the U.S. Supreme Court stated that a § 1962(c) violation required the defendant person to participate in the operation or management of the enterprise. Although no overt act is required under § 1962(d), must the defendant conspire to operate or manage the enterprise, or must the defendant simply conspire to violate § 1962(c) without considering the operation or management test? See United States v. Quintanilla, 2 F.3d 1469, 1484–85 (7th Cir. 1993) ("[T]o require the government to show that all of the alleged coconspirators conducted, or participated in the conduct of, the affairs of the racketeering enterprise to the extent mandated by § 1962(c) or other substantive RICO offense would entail a degree of involvement in the affairs of the conspiracy that is not required in any other type of conspiracy, where agreeing to a prescribed objective is sufficient."); Jones v. Meridian Towers Apartments, Inc., 816 F. Supp. 762, 773 (D.D.C. 1993) ("To hold that under § 1962(d) a plaintiff must show that an alleged coconspirator was capable of violating the substantive offense under § 1962(c), that is, that he participated to the extent required by Reves, would add an element to RICO conspiracy that Congress did not direct.").

(4) Salinas stands for the proposition that a RICO conspiracy claim need not involve a substantive violation of § 1962(a), (b), or (c). Nevertheless, for standing in a civil suit, there must be an injury to the plaintiff. This

raises the question of whether the injurious action must itself be a violation of a predicate act for liability under § 1962(d) to attach. The Supreme Court addressed this issue in *Beck v. Prupis*, 529 U.S. 494 (2000). The Court held that, in order to show that an injury was proximately caused by a RICO conspiracy, the plaintiff had to demonstrate that the injury stemmed from the commission of an overt act listed in § 1961(1).

C. ESTABLISHING A PATTERN OF RACKETEETING ACTIVITY

Recall that to bring a civil RICO claim, a plaintiff must prove that: (1) a "person" engaged (2) in a pattern of racketeering activity (3) in any of the four prohibited ways under § 1962(a)–(d) (4) that affected an "enterprise" engaged in interstate commerce and (5) resulted in injury to plaintiff's business or property. We have previously discussed the four prohibited ways under § 1962(a)–(d) with little discussion of the racketeering activities themselves. In this Section, we tackle that topic by focusing on the thorny issue of when a person has engaged in a "pattern of racketeering activity."

1. WHAT QUALIFIES AS A "RACKETEERING ACTIVITY"?

We touched upon the breadth of the "racketeering activity" definition in Problem 13.1. We return to the subject here to emphasize two particular types of racketeering activities that frequently serve as the basis of RICO claims—mail and wire fraud.

Under the mail fraud statute, it is a violation for any person to use the mail (or similar private carrier service like UPS or FedEx) "for the purpose of executing" any "scheme or artifice to defraud." 18 U.S.C. § 1341.[c] The wire fraud statute (which was modeled after the mail fraud statute) covers schemes to defraud that make use of wire, radio, or television communications. *See* 18 U.S.C. § 1343. Given that both of these statutes involve fraud, you might wonder about the relationship of the statutes to the common law elements of fraud. In *Neder v. United States*, 527 U.S. 1 (1999), the Supreme Court discussed the relationship and explained that although the "common law elements of 'justifiable reliance' and 'damages' . . . have no place in the federal fraud statutes . . . materiality of falsehood is an element of the federal mail [and] wire fraud . . . statutes." *Id.* at 24–25. In addition, the federal fraud statutes also require intent to deceive or reckless disregard for the truth.

---

[c] In civil RICO cases, it is not enough that a mailing was made if it was incidental to an essential part of the fraudulent scheme. The pattern of mail fraud violations must cause the plaintiff's injury to business or property.

Can mail or wire fraud serve as the basis of a RICO claim when the fraud also involves a statute not listed under the definition of "racketeering activity"? For instance, tax fraud is not a predicate act under § 1961(1), but such fraud will frequently (if not always) involve mail or wire fraud. The absence of tax fraud as a predicate offense could be viewed as evidence of congressional intent to leave such conduct solely to the tax fraud statute. Tax fraud is not the only area where this issue arises; indeed, fraud allegations that violate the Fair Labor Standards Act, the National Labor Standards Act, and the McCarran-Ferguson Act (dealing with insurance) have also raised this question. *See, e.g., Humana, Inc. v. Forsyth*, 525 U.S. 299, 313–14 (1999) (resolving the question with respect to the McCarran-Ferguson Act by concluding that the Act did not preclude the application of RICO: "RICO's private right of action and treble damages provision . . . compliment statutory and common-law claims for relief.").

2. WHAT QUALIFIES AS A "PATTERN" OF RACKETEERING ACTIVITY?

H.J. INC. V. NORTHWESTERN BELL TELEPHONE CO.
492 U.S. 229 (1989)

JUSTICE BRENNAN delivered the opinion of the Court.

[RICO] imposes criminal and civil liability upon those who engage in certain "prohibited activities." Each prohibited activity is defined in 18 U.S.C. § 1962 to include, as one necessary element, proof either of "a pattern of racketeering activity" or of "collection of an unlawful debt." "Racketeering activity" is defined in RICO . . . but of the term "pattern" the statute says only that it "requires at least two acts of racketeering activity" within a 10-year period, 18 U.S.C. § 1961(5). We are called upon in this civil case to consider what conduct meets RICO's pattern requirement

I

. . . .

Petitioners, customers of respondent Northwestern Bell Telephone Co., filed this putative class action in 1986 in the District Court for the District of Minnesota. Petitioners alleged violations of §§ 1962(a), (b), (c), and (d) by Northwestern Bell and the other respondents—some of the telephone company's officers and employees, various members of the Minnesota Public Utilities Commission (MPUC), and other unnamed individuals and corporations—and sought an injunction and treble damages under RICO's civil liability provisions, §§ 1964(a) and (c).

The MPUC is the state body responsible for determining the rates that Northwestern Bell may charge. Petitioners' five-count complaint alleged that between 1980 and 1986 Northwestern Bell sought to influence members of the MPUC in the performance of their duties—and in fact caused them to approve rates for the company in excess of a fair and reasonable amount—by making cash payments to commissioners, negotiating with them regarding future employment, and paying for parties and meals, for tickets to sporting events and the like, and for airline tickets. Based upon these factual allegations, petitioners . . . raised four separate claims under § 1962 of RICO. Count II alleged that, in violation of § 1962(a), Northwestern Bell derived income from a pattern of racketeering activity involving predicate acts of bribery and used this income to engage in its business as an interstate "enterprise." Count III claimed a violation of § 1962(b), in that, through this same pattern of racketeering activity, respondents acquired an interest in or control of the MPUC, which was also an interstate "enterprise." In Count IV, petitioners asserted that respondents participated in the conduct and affairs of the MPUC through this pattern of racketeering activity, contrary to § 1962(c). Finally, Count V alleged that respondents conspired together to violate §§ 1962(a), (b), and (c), thereby contravening § 1962(d).

The District Court granted respondents' Federal Rule of Civil Procedure 12(b)(6) motion, dismissing the complaint for failure to state a claim upon which relief could be granted. The court found that "[e]ach of the fraudulent acts alleged by [petitioners] was committed in furtherance of a single scheme to influence MPUC commissioners to the detriment of Northwestern Bell's ratepayers." It held that dismissal was therefore mandated [under Eight Circuit precedent]. The Court of Appeals for the Eighth Circuit affirmed the dismissal of petitioners' complaint, confirming that under Eighth Circuit precedent "[a] single fraudulent effort or scheme is insufficient" to establish a pattern of racketeering activity, and agreeing with the District Court that petitioners' complaint alleged only a single scheme. . . . Most Courts of Appeals have rejected the Eighth Circuit's interpretation of RICO's pattern concept to require an allegation and proof of multiple schemes, and we granted certiorari to resolve this conflict. We now reverse.

II

In *Sedima, S.P.R.L. v. Imrex Co.,* 473 U.S. 479 (1985), this Court rejected a restrictive interpretation of § 1964(c). . . . In doing so, we acknowledged concern in some quarters over civil RICO's use against "legitimate" businesses, as well as "mobsters and organized criminals". . . . But we suggested that RICO's expansive uses "appear to be primarily the result of the breadth of the predicate offenses, in particular the inclusion of wire, mail, and securities fraud, and the failure of Congress and the courts to develop a meaningful concept of 'pattern' "—

both factors that apply to criminal as well as civil applications of the Act. Congress has done nothing in the interim further to illuminate RICO's key requirement of a pattern of racketeering; and as the plethora of different views expressed by the Courts of Appeals since *Sedima* demonstrates, developing a meaningful concept of "pattern" within the existing statutory framework has proved to be no easy task.

. . . .

A

We begin, of course, with RICO's text, in which Congress followed a pattern of utilizing terms and concepts of breadth. As we remarked in *Sedima*, the section of the statute headed "definitions," 18 U.S.C. § 1961, does not so much define a pattern of racketeering activity as state a minimum necessary condition for the existence of such a pattern. Unlike other provisions in § 1961 that tell us what various concepts used in the Act "mean," 18 U.S.C. § 1961(5) says of the phrase "pattern of racketeering activity" only that it "requires at least two acts of racketeering activity, one of which occurred after [October 15, 1970,] and the last of which occurred within ten years (excluding any period of imprisonment) after the commission of a prior act of racketeering activity." It thus places an outer limit on the concept of a pattern of racketeering activity that is broad indeed.

Section 1961(5) does indicate that Congress envisioned circumstances in which no more than two predicates would be necessary to establish a pattern of racketeering—otherwise it would have drawn a narrower boundary to RICO liability, requiring proof of a greater number of predicates. But, at the same time, the statement that a pattern "requires at least" two predicates implies "that while two acts are necessary, they may not be sufficient." *Sedima*, 473 U.S., at 496, n. 14. Section 1961(5) concerns only the minimum *number* of predicates necessary to establish a pattern; and it assumes that there is something to a RICO pattern *beyond* simply the number of predicate acts involved. The legislative history bears out this interpretation, for the principal sponsor of the Senate bill expressly indicated that "proof of two acts of racketeering activity, without more, does not establish a pattern." 116 Cong.Rec. 18940 (1970) (statement of Sen. McClellan). Section § 1961(5) does not identify, though, these additional prerequisites for establishing the existence of a RICO pattern.

In addition to § 1961(5), there is the key phrase "pattern of racketeering activity" itself, from § 1962, and we must start with the assumption that the legislative purpose is expressed by the ordinary meaning of the words used. In normal usage, the word "pattern" here would be taken to require more than just a multiplicity of racketeering predicates. A "pattern" is an "arrangement or order of things or activity,"

11 Oxford English Dictionary 357 (2d ed. 1989), and the mere fact that there are a number of predicates is no guarantee that they fall into any arrangement or order. It is not the number of predicates but the relationship that they bear to each other or to some external organizing principle that renders them "ordered" or "arranged." The text of RICO conspicuously fails anywhere to identify, however, forms of relationship or external principles to be used in determining whether racketeering activity falls into a pattern for purposes of the Act.

It is reasonable to infer, from this absence of any textual identification of sorts of pattern[s] that would satisfy § 1962's requirement, in combination with the very relaxed limits to the pattern concept fixed in § 1961(5), that Congress intended to take a flexible approach, and envisaged that a pattern might be demonstrated by reference to a range of different ordering principles or relationships between predicates, within the expansive bounds set. For any more specific guidance as to the meaning of "pattern," we must look past the text to RICO's legislative history, as we have done in prior cases construing the Act.

The legislative history, which we discussed in *Sedima*, shows that Congress indeed had a fairly flexible concept of a pattern in mind. A pattern is not formed by "sporadic activity," S.Rep. No. 91–617, p. 158 (1969), and a person cannot "be subjected to the sanctions of title IX simply for committing two widely separated and isolated criminal offenses," 116 Cong. Rec., at 18940 (1970) (Sen. McClellan). Instead, "[t]he term 'pattern' itself requires the showing of a relationship" between the predicates, and of " 'the threat of continuing activity,' " *ibid.*, quoting S.Rep. No. 91–617, at 158. "It is this factor of *continuity plus relationship* which combines to produce a pattern." *Ibid.* (emphasis added). RICO's legislative history reveals Congress' intent that to prove a pattern of racketeering activity a plaintiff or prosecutor must show that the racketeering predicates are related, *and* that they amount to or pose a threat of continued criminal activity.

B

For analytic purposes these two constituents of RICO's pattern requirement must be stated separately, though in practice their proof will often overlap. The element of relatedness is the easier to define, for we may take guidance from a provision elsewhere in the Organized Crime Control Act of 1970 (OCCA), of which RICO formed Title IX. OCCA included as Title X the Dangerous Special Offender Sentencing Act, 18 U.S.C. § 3575 *et seq.* (now partially repealed). Title X provided for enhanced sentences where, among other things, the defendant had committed a prior felony as part of a pattern of criminal conduct or in furtherance of a conspiracy to engage in a pattern of criminal conduct. As we noted in *Sedima*, Congress defined Title X's pattern requirement solely in terms of the *relationship* of the defendant's criminal acts one to another: "[C]riminal conduct forms a pattern if it embraces criminal acts that have the same or similar purposes, results, participants, victims, or methods of commission, or otherwise are interrelated by distinguishing characteristics and are not isolated events." § 3575(e). We have no reason to suppose that Congress had in mind for RICO's pattern of racketeering component any more constrained a notion of the relationships between predicates that would suffice.

RICO's legislative history tells us, however, that the relatedness of racketeering activities is not alone enough to satisfy § 1962's pattern element. To establish a RICO pattern it must also be shown that the predicates themselves amount to, or that they otherwise constitute a threat of, *continuing* racketeering activity. As to this continuity requirement, § 3575(e) is of no assistance. It is this aspect of RICO's pattern element that has spawned the "multiple scheme" test adopted by some lower courts, including the Court of Appeals in this case. See 829 F.2d, at 650 ("In order to demonstrate the necessary continuity appellants must allege that Northwestern Bell 'had engaged in similar endeavors in the past or that [it was] engaged in other criminal activities.' . . . A single fraudulent effort or scheme is insufficient"). But although proof that a RICO defendant has been involved in multiple criminal schemes would certainly be highly relevant to the inquiry into the continuity of the defendant's racketeering activity, it is implausible to suppose that Congress thought continuity might be shown *only* by proof of multiple schemes. The Eighth Circuit's test brings a rigidity to the available methods of proving a pattern that simply is not present in the idea of "continuity" itself; and it does so, moreover, by introducing a concept—the "scheme"—that appears nowhere in the language or legislative history of the Act.[3] We adopt a less inflexible approach that seems to us to derive from a commonsense, everyday understanding of RICO's language and Congress' gloss on it. What a plaintiff or prosecutor must prove is continuity of racketeering activity, or its threat, *simpliciter*. This may be done in a variety of ways, thus making it difficult to formulate in the abstract any general test for continuity. We can, however, begin to delineate the requirement.

"Continuity" is both a closed- and open-ended concept, referring either to a closed period of repeated conduct, or to past conduct that by its

---

[3] Nor does the multiple scheme approach to identifying continuing criminal conduct have the advantage of lessening the uncertainty inherent in RICO's pattern component, for "scheme" is hardly a self-defining term. . . . Though the definitional problems that arise in interpreting RICO's pattern requirement inevitably lead to uncertainty regarding the statute's scope— whatever approach is adopted—we prefer to confront these problems directly, not by introducing a new and perhaps more amorphous concept into the analysis that has no basis in text or legislative history.

nature projects into the future with a threat of repetition. It is, in either case, centrally a temporal concept—and particularly so in the RICO context, where *what* must be continuous, RICO's predicate acts or offenses, and the *relationship* these predicates must bear one to another, are distinct requirements. A party alleging a RICO violation may demonstrate continuity over a closed period by proving a series of related predicates extending over a substantial period of time. Predicate acts extending over a few weeks or months and threatening no future criminal conduct do not satisfy this requirement: Congress was concerned in RICO with long-term criminal conduct. Often a RICO action will be brought before continuity can be established in this way. In such cases, liability depends on whether the *threat* of continuity is demonstrated.

Whether the predicates proved establish a threat of continued racketeering activity depends on the specific facts of each case. Without making any claim to cover the field of possibilities—preferring to deal with this issue in the context of concrete factual situations presented for decision—we offer some examples of how this element might be satisfied. A RICO pattern may surely be established if the related predicates themselves involve a distinct threat of long-term racketeering activity, either implicit or explicit. Suppose a hoodlum were to sell "insurance" to a neighborhood's storekeepers to cover them against breakage of their windows, telling his victims he would be reappearing each month to collect the "premium" that would continue their "coverage." Though the number of related predicates involved may be small and they may occur close together in time, the racketeering acts themselves include a specific threat of repetition extending indefinitely into the future, and thus supply the requisite threat of continuity. In other cases, the threat of continuity may be established by showing that the predicate acts or offenses are part of an ongoing entity's regular way of doing business. Thus, the threat of continuity is sufficiently established where the predicates can be attributed to a defendant operating as part of a long-term association that exists for criminal purposes. Such associations include, but extend well beyond, those traditionally grouped under the phrase "organized crime." The continuity requirement is likewise satisfied where it is shown that the predicates are a regular way of conducting defendant's ongoing legitimate business (in the sense that it is not a business that exists for criminal purposes), or of conducting or participating in an ongoing and legitimate RICO "enterprise."[4]

---

[4] Insofar as the concurrence seems to suggest, that very short periods of criminal activity that do *not* in any way carry a threat of continued criminal activity constitute "obvious racketeer[ing]" to which Congress intended RICO, with its enhanced penalties, to apply, we have concluded that it is mistaken, and that when Congress said predicates must demonstrate "continuity" before they may form a RICO pattern, it expressed an intent that RICO reach activities that amount to or threaten long-term criminal activity.

The limits of the relationship and continuity concepts that combine to define a RICO pattern, and the precise methods by which relatedness and continuity or its threat may be proved, cannot be fixed in advance with such clarity that it will always be apparent whether in a particular case a "pattern of racketeering activity" exists. The development of these concepts must await future cases, absent a decision by Congress to revisit RICO to provide clearer guidance as to the Act's intended scope.

. . . .

IV

We turn now to the application of our analysis of RICO's pattern requirement. Because respondents prevailed on a motion under Federal Rule of Civil Procedure 12(b)(6), we read the facts alleged in the complaint in the light most favorable to petitioners. And we may only affirm the dismissal of the complaint if "it is clear that no relief could be granted under any set of facts that could be proved consistent with the allegations." *Hishon v. King & Spalding*, 467 U.S. 69, 73 (1984).

Petitioners' complaint alleges that at different times over the course of at least a 6-year period the noncommissioner respondents gave five members of the MPUC numerous bribes, in several different forms, with the objective—in which they were allegedly successful—of causing these commissioners to approve unfair and unreasonable rates for Northwestern Bell. RICO defines bribery as a "racketeering activity," 18 U.S.C. § 1961(1), so petitioners have alleged multiple predicate acts.

Under the analysis we have set forth above, and consistent with the allegations in their complaint, petitioners may be able to prove that the multiple predicates alleged constitute "a pattern of racketeering activity," in that they satisfy the requirements of relationship and continuity. The acts of bribery alleged are said to be related by a common purpose, to influence commissioners in carrying out their duties in order to win approval of unfairly and unreasonably high rates for Northwestern Bell. Furthermore, petitioners claim that the racketeering predicates occurred with some frequency over at least a 6-year period, which may be sufficient to satisfy the continuity requirement. Alternatively, a threat of continuity of racketeering activity might be established at trial by showing that the alleged bribes were a regular way of conducting Northwestern Bell's ongoing business, or a regular way of conducting or participating in the conduct of the alleged and ongoing RICO enterprise, the MPUC.

The Court of Appeals thus erred in affirming the District Court's dismissal of petitioners' complaint for failure to plead "a pattern of racketeering activity." The judgment is reversed, and the case is remanded for further proceedings consistent with this opinion.

JUSTICE SCALIA, with whom THE CHIEF JUSTICE, JUSTICE O'CONNOR, and JUSTICE KENNEDY join, concurring in the judgment.

Four Terms ago, in *Sedima, S.P.R.L. v. Imrex Co.*, we gave lower courts the following four clues concerning the meaning of the enigmatic term "pattern of racketeering activity" in [RICO]. First, we stated that the statutory definition of the term in 18 U.S.C. § 1961(5) implies "that while two acts are necessary, they may not be sufficient." *Sedima*, 473 U.S., at 496, n. 14. Second, we pointed out that "two isolated acts of racketeering activity," "sporadic activity," and "proof of two acts of racketeering activity, without more" would not be enough to constitute a pattern. *Ibid.* Third, we quoted a snippet from the legislative history stating "[i]t is this factor of *continuity plus relationship* which combines to produce a pattern." *Ibid.* Finally, we directed lower courts' attention to 18 U.S.C. § 3575(e), which defined the term "pattern of conduct which was criminal" used in a different title of the same Act, and instructed them that "[t]his language may be useful in interpreting other sections of the Act," 473 U.S., at 496, n. 14. Thus enlightened, the District Courts and Courts of Appeals set out "to develop a meaningful concept of 'pattern,'" *id.*, at 500, and promptly produced the widest and most persistent Circuit split on an issue of federal law in recent memory. Today, four years and countless millions in damages and attorney's fees later (not to mention prison sentences under the criminal provisions of RICO), the Court does little more than repromulgate those hints as to what RICO means, though with the caveat that Congress intended that they be applied using a "flexible approach." *Ante*, at 2900.

Elevating to the level of statutory text a phrase taken from the legislative history, the Court counsels the lower courts: " 'continuity plus relationship.' " *Ante*, at 2900 (emphasis deleted). This seems to me about as helpful to the conduct of their affairs as "life is a fountain." Of the two parts of this talismanic phrase, the relatedness requirement is said to be the "easier to define," yet here is the Court's definition, *in toto:* " '[C]riminal conduct forms a pattern if it embraces criminal acts that have the same or similar purposes, results, participants, victims, or methods of commission, or otherwise are interrelated by distinguishing characteristics and are not isolated events.' " This definition has the feel of being solidly rooted in law, since it is a direct quotation of 18 U.S.C. § 3575(e). Unfortunately, if normal (and sensible) rules of statutory construction were followed, the existence of § 3575(e) . . . suggests that *whatever* "pattern" might mean in RICO, it assuredly *does not* mean that. "[W]here Congress includes particular language in one section of a statute but omits it in another section of the same Act, it is generally presumed that Congress acts intentionally and purposely in the disparate inclusion or exclusion." *Russello v. United States,* 464 U.S. 16, 23 (1983). But that does not really matter, since § 3575(e) is utterly uninformative anyway. It hardly closes in on the target to know that "relatedness" refers to acts that are related by "purposes, results, participants, victims, . . . methods of commission, *or* [just in case that is not vague enough] *otherwise*." Is the fact that the victims of both predicate acts were women enough? Or that both acts had the purpose of enriching the defendant? Or that the different coparticipants of the defendant in both acts were his coemployees? I doubt that the lower courts will find the Court's instructions much more helpful than telling them to look for a "pattern"— which is what the statute already says.

The Court finds "continuity" more difficult to define precisely. "Continuity," it says, "is both a closed- and open-ended concept, referring either to a closed period of repeated conduct, or to past conduct that by its nature projects into the future with a threat of repetition." I have no idea what this concept of a "closed period of repeated conduct" means. Virtually all allegations of racketeering activity, in both civil and criminal suits, will relate to past periods that are "closed" (unless one expects plaintiff or the prosecutor to establish that the defendant not only committed the crimes he did, but is still committing them), and all of them *must* relate to conduct that is "repeated," because of RICO's multiple-act requirement. I had thought, initially, that the Court was seeking to draw a distinction between, on the one hand, past repeated conduct (multiple racketeering acts) that is "closed-ended" in the sense that, in its totality, it constitutes only one criminal "scheme" or "episode"—which would not fall within RICO unless in its nature (for one or more of the reasons later described by the Court) it threatened future criminal endeavors as well—and, on the other hand, past repeated conduct (multiple racketeering acts) that constitutes several separate schemes—which is alone enough to invoke RICO. But of course that cannot be what it means, since the Court rejects the "multiple scheme" concept, not merely as the *exclusive* touchstone of RICO liability, but in all its applications, since it "introduc[es] a concept . . . that appears nowhere in the language or legislative history of the Act," and is so vague and "amorphous" as to exist only in the eye of the beholder. Moreover, the Court tells us that predicate acts extending, not over a "substantial period of time," but only over a "few weeks or months and threatening no future criminal conduct" do not satisfy the continuity requirement. Since the Court has rejected the concept of separate criminal "schemes" or "episodes" as a criterion of "threatening future criminal conduct," I think it must be saying that at least a few months of racketeering activity (and who knows how much more?) is generally for free, as far as RICO is concerned. The "closed period" concept is a sort of safe harbor for racketeering activity that does not last *too* long, no matter how many different crimes and different schemes are involved, so long as it does not otherwise "establish a threat of continued racketeering activity." A gang of hoodlums that commits one act of extortion on Monday in New York, a second in Chicago on Tuesday, a third in San Francisco on Wednesday, and so on through an entire week, and then finally and completely disbands, cannot be reached under RICO. I am sure that is not what the statute intends, but I cannot imagine what else the Court's murky discussion can possibly mean.

Of course it cannot be said that the Court's opinion operates only in the direction of letting some obvious racketeers get out of RICO. It also makes it clear that a hitherto dubious category is included, by establishing the rule that the "multiple scheme" test applied by the Court of Appeals here is not only nonexclusive but indeed nonexistent. This is, as far as I can discern, the Court's only substantive contribution to our prior guidance—and it is a contribution that makes it *more* rather than *less* difficult for a potential defendant to know whether his conduct is covered by RICO. Even if he is only involved in a single scheme, he may still be covered if there is present whatever is needed to establish a "threat of continuity." The Court gives us a nonexclusive list of three things that do so. Two of those presumably polar examples seem to me extremely difficult to apply—whether "the predicates can be attributed to a defendant operating as part of a long-term association that exists for criminal purposes," *ante,* at 2902, and whether "the predicates are a regular way of conducting defendant's ongoing legitimate business," *ibid.* What is included beyond these examples is vaguer still.

It is, however, unfair to be so critical of the Court's effort, because I would be unable to provide an interpretation of RICO that gives significantly more guidance concerning its application. It is clear to me from the prologue of the statute, which describes a relatively narrow focus upon "organized crime," that the word "pattern" in the phrase "pattern of racketeering activity" was meant to import some requirement beyond the mere existence of multiple predicate acts. Thus, when § 1961(5) says that a pattern "requires at least two acts of racketeering activity" it is describing what is needful but not sufficient. . . . But what that something more is, is beyond me. As I have suggested, it is also beyond the Court. Today's opinion has added nothing to improve our prior guidance, which has created a kaleidoscope of Circuit positions, except to clarify that RICO may in addition be violated when there is a "threat of continuity." It seems to me this increases rather than removes the vagueness. There is no reason to believe that the Courts of Appeals will be any more unified in the future, than they have in the past, regarding the content of this law.

. . . .

However unhelpful its guidance may be, however, I think the Court is correct in saying that nothing in the statute supports the proposition that predicate acts constituting part of a single scheme (or single episode) can never support a cause of action under RICO. Since the Court of Appeals here rested its decision on the contrary proposition, I concur in the judgment of the Court reversing the decision below.

NOTES & QUESTIONS

(1) What is the test developed by the Court to determine if there is a pattern, and how does the test relate to the description found in § 1961? Why didn't the Court simply adopt the Eight Circuit's separate scheme approach?

(2) The Court stated that there were two types of continuity: closed- and open-ended. What is the time frame for closed-ended continuity? Are two weeks of racketeering activity enough?

(3) As to open-ended continuity, the Court stated that there must be a continuing threat of racketeering activity. What is the Court's rule for determining when there is a continuing threat?

(4) Why did the Court believe that the relationship and continuity prongs were both met in this case?

(5) Justice Scalia is quite critical of the majority, despite the fact that he ultimately concurs. What is Scalia's main problem with the majority's approach?

(6) As a practical matter, the relatedness prong has not been a major obstacle for plaintiffs. The Court quoted 18 U.S.C. § 3575(e) in noting that acts are related if they "have the same or similar purposes, results, participants, victims, or methods of commission, or otherwise are interrelated by distinguishing characteristics and are not isolated events." These criteria are generously construed. For instance, acts may be related by nothing more than a common method, such as defrauding customers. *See Bank v. Wolk*, 918 F.2d 418, 422 (3d Cir. 1990) (stating that a narrow interpretation of the relatedness prong should be avoided by the courts when a plaintiff alleges predicate offenses in furtherance of multiple schemes, and observing that "the relatedness requirement should not insulate defendants who merely vary the methods by which they defraud their victims").

(7) Some courts have described relatedness in terms of horizontal and vertical relatedness. Horizontal relatedness is simply the relationship that the racketeering acts have to each other, while vertical relatedness describes the relationship of the acts to the enterprise. These terms are simply ways of describing relatedness, however, and they do not alter the broad definition given by the Court in *Northwestern Bell*. *See United States v. Minicone*, 960 F.2d 1099, 1106 (2d Cir. 1992); *United States v. Long*, 917 F.2d 691, 697 (2d Cir. 1990).

(8) The lower courts have not consistently applied the continuity prong discussed in *Northwestern Bell*. A closed-ended time period must be for a "substantial period of time," but what amount of time is "substantial"? Courts tend to agree that the determination must be made on a case-by-case basis.

As a consequence, judicial conclusions often vary, although some trends can be seen in the minimum length of time required. *See, e.g., Fresh Meadow Food Serv., LLC v. RB 175 Corp.*, 282 Fed. Appx. 94, 99 (2d Cir. 2008) (declining repeatedly to find that closed-ended continuity has been met in any case shorter than two years); *Hughes v. Consol-Pennsylvania Coal Co.*, 945 F.2d 594, 611 (3d Cir. 1991) (deciding, as a matter of law, that one year is not long enough for closed-ended continuity: "[W]e hold that twelve months is not a substantial period of time.").

(9) Unlike closed-ended schemes, open-ended schemes may be very brief so long as the predicate acts project a threat of continuing misconduct. In determining whether a continuing threat exists, some courts look to the nature of the predicate acts and find that inherently illegal activities, such as murder or drug trafficking, constitute a continuing threat, while crimes such as fraud are less likely to meet the standard without more evidence. As the Court suggested in *Northwestern Bell*, one way to show a continuing threat is to prove that the predicate acts "are part of an ongoing entity's regular way of doing business." Although a sustained period of time is not required, the frequency of the predicate acts over a period of time may help to demonstrate that the acts are part of the entity's regular way of doing business.

PROBLEM 13.4

Look back at Problem 13.1 and review the scenarios that meet the definition of "racketeering activity." Which of those scenarios also meet the "pattern" requirement?

D. COLLECTION OF AN UNLAWFUL DEBT

As an alternative to engaging in a pattern of racketeering activity, a defendant can be found liable under § 1962 "through collection of an unlawful debt." Section 1961(6) defines "unlawful debt" as follows:

> [A] debt (A) incurred or contracted in gambling activity which was in violation of the law . . . or which is unenforceable under State or Federal law in whole or in part as to principal or interest because of the laws relating to usury, and (B) which was incurred in connection with the business of gambling in violation of the law . . . or the business of lending money or a thing of value at a rate usurious under State or Federal law, where the usurious rate is at least twice the enforceable rate.

This definition essentially divides unlawful debts into two categories: those generated by illegal gambling and those involving usurious rates (i.e., loan-sharking). Both categories may require reference to state law to determine whether the gambling activity is illegal or the lending rate is usurious. Unlike a pattern of racketeering activity, multiple predicate acts are not required for the collection of an unlawful debt; instead, a single collection will suffice. You might think, therefore, that allegations involving the collection of an unlawful debt would be a more fruitful ground for civil RICO plaintiffs. In practice, however, this has not been the case, as collection of an unlawful debt is infrequently alleged in civil RICO claims. This may be due to the difficulty of establishing such a claim. For instance, a usurious lending claim requires proof of all of the following elements:

> [1] the debt was unenforceable in whole or in part because of state or federal laws relating to usury, [2] the debt was incurred in connection with the "business of lending money . . . at a [usurious] rate," . . . [3] the usurious rate was at least twice the enforceable rate . . . [4] as a result of the above confluence of factors, [the plaintiff] was injured in its business or property.

Durante Bros. and Sons, Inc. v. Flushing Nat. Bank, 755 F.2d 239, 248 (2d Cir. 1985). It should be clear from these elements that the RICO provisions governing lending are concerned not simply with high interest rates, but with more sinister lending activities that are uncommon among legitimate banking institutions.

E. DEMONSTRATING AN INJURY

To have standing to sue under RICO, a civil claimant must show injury to his business or property. This means that physical and emotional injuries caused by RICO violations are not recoverable, nor are economic injuries that flow from such physical and emotional injuries (e.g., a loss of earnings due to a physical injury). As the *Sedima* Court held, there is no "racketeering injury" requirement separate and apart from the injury caused by the predicate acts: "the compensable injury necessarily is the harm caused by predicate acts sufficiently related to constitute a pattern." The injury must still be direct, however, as indirect or attenuated injuries are not recoverable.

This directness requirement likely derives from the "by reason of" language in § 1964(c), which imposes a proximate cause requirement on the plaintiff. In other words, a RICO plaintiff must show that the § 1962 violation proximately caused the injury to the plaintiff's business or property. As demonstrated below, this can result in a complex inquiry by the courts.

COMMERCIAL CLEANING SERVICES, L.L.C. v. COLIN SERVICE SYSTEMS, INC.
271 F.3d 374 (2d Cir. 2001)

LEVAL, CIRCUIT JUDGE.

Plaintiff-appellant Commercial Cleaning Services, L.L.C. (Commercial) appeals from the dismissal of its suit. Commercial brought this putative class-action suit for damages against a business competitor, defendant-appellee Colin Service Systems, Inc. (Colin), under the Racketeer Influenced and Corrupt Organizations statute (RICO), 18 U.S.C. § 1964(c) (2000). The complaint alleges that Colin engaged in a pattern of racketeering activity by hiring undocumented aliens for profit in violation of Section 274 of the Immigration and Nationality Act (INA), 8 U.S.C. § 1324(a), a RICO predicate offense. According to the complaint, Colin's illegal hiring practices enabled it to lower its variable costs and thereby underbid competing firms, which consequently lost contracts and customers to Colin. Colin moved to dismiss the complaint pursuant to Fed.R.Civ.P. 12(b)(6) for failure to state a claim upon which relief can be granted. The district court granted Colin's motion and dismissed the complaint without leave to amend, granting judgment in Colin's favor, on the grounds that (i) Commercial had no standing to sue because it did not allege a direct injury proximately caused by Colin's illegal hiring, and (ii) Commercial failed to provide a sufficiently detailed RICO case statement as required by the Connecticut district court's Standing Order in Civil RICO Cases (Standing Order).

We agree with Commercial's contentions that its allegations satisfy the proximate cause requirement for civil RICO cases and that the deficiencies in its RICO case statement filed pursuant to the district court's Standing Order did not justify the grant of judgment in defendant's favor. We therefore vacate the judgment.

BACKGROUND

A. The Complaint

For the purposes of reviewing the grant of Colin's motion to dismiss, we take as true the factual allegations of Commercial's complaint, as supplemented by the RICO case statement submitted pursuant to the district court's Standing Order.

1. *The Parties*

Commercial and Colin each provide janitorial services for commercial buildings. According to the complaint, Commercial is a small company that has bid against Colin for competitively awarded janitorial service contracts in the Hartford area. Colin operates throughout the Eastern seaboard and is described in the complaint as one of the nation's largest corporations engaged in the business of cleaning commercial facilities. The complaint was filed as a national class action on behalf of Colin's competitors.

2. *The "Illegal Immigrant Hiring Scheme"*

The complaint alleges that Commercial and the members of the plaintiff class are victims of Colin's pattern of racketeering activity in violation of 18 U.S.C. § 1962(c), referred to as "the illegal immigrant hiring scheme." The theory of the case, succinctly stated, is that Colin obtained a significant business advantage over other firms in the "highly competitive" and price-sensitive cleaning services industry by knowingly hiring "hundreds of illegal immigrants at low wages." Colin's illegal immigrant hiring scheme allows it to employ large numbers of workers at lower costs than its competitors must bear when operating lawfully. Colin allegedly pays undocumented workers less than the prevailing wage, and does not withhold or pay their federal and state payroll taxes, or workers' compensation insurance fees. The complaint refers to Colin's prosecution in 1996 by the United States Department of Justice for, among other things, hiring at least 150 undocumented workers, continuing to employ aliens after their work authorizations had expired, and failing to prepare, complete, and update employment documents.

The allegations assert that Colin is part of an enterprise composed of entities associated-in-fact that includes employment placement services, labor contractors, newspapers in which Colin advertises for laborers, and "various immigrant networks that assist fellow illegal immigrants in obtaining employment, housing and illegal work permits." The complaint neither describes how the undocumented workers allegedly hired by Colin entered the country, nor claims that Colin had knowledge of how those workers came to the United States. It alleges that Colin's participation in the affairs of the enterprise through the illegal immigrant hiring scheme violates 8 U.S.C. § 1324(a), which prohibits hiring certain undocumented aliens, and which is a RICO predicate offense if committed for financial gain. *See* 18 U.S.C. § 1961(1)(F).

3. *The Pratt & Whitney Contracts*

What apparently led to this lawsuit was Commercial's loss of lucrative cleaning contracts to Colin. In 1994, Commercial obtained a contract to clean Pratt & Whitney's facility at Southington, Connecticut. After successfully performing on that contract for approximately one year, however, Commercial was underbid by Colin for cleaning contracts at other Pratt & Whitney facilities in the area. The complaint alleges that, through the illegal immigrant hiring scheme, Colin could offer Pratt & Whitney and other potential customers access to "a virtually limitless pool of workers on short notice" at significantly lower prices than other firms could offer by operating lawfully. As a result, Pratt & Whitney and other large contractors for cleaning services accepted Colin's lower bids over Commercial's.

B. Proceedings Below

Commercial's complaint requests class certification, an award of treble damages, and injunctive relief. Commercial submitted a RICO case statement with its complaint, as required by the District of Connecticut's Standing Order in Civil RICO Cases. Colin moved pursuant to

Fed.R.Civ.P. 12(b)(6) to dismiss the complaint for failure to state a claim. Before ruling on Commercial's request for class certification, the district court granted Colin's motion. The court dismissed the complaint primarily on the ground that Commercial had no standing to bring suit because its injury did not bear a "direct relation" to Colin's racketeering activity as required by *Holmes v. Securities Investor Protection Corp.,* 503 U.S. 258, 268 (1992). The district court believed the perceived deficiency in Commercial's standing to bring suit was not curable. It therefore dismissed the complaint without leave to amend. The court also asserted, as an alternative justification for dismissal without leave to amend, that Commercial's RICO case statement, filed pursuant to the Standing Order, was so insufficiently detailed as to violate the intended purpose of giving the defendant basic factual information underlying the RICO claim.

This appeal followed.

DISCUSSION

I.   Civil RICO Standing

. . . .

B.   Proximate Cause

RICO grants standing to pursue a civil damages remedy to "[a]ny person injured in his business or property by reason of a violation of [18 U.S.C. § 1962]." 18 U.S.C. § 1964(c). In order to bring suit under § 1964(c), a plaintiff must plead (1) the defendant's violation of § 1962, (2) an injury to the plaintiff's business or property, and (3) causation of the injury by the defendant's violation. *See First Nationwide Bank v. Gelt Funding Corp.,* 27 F.3d 763, 767 (2d Cir.1994). Commercial's appeal turns in part on whether its complaint satisfies the causation requirement.

RICO's use of the clause "by reason of" has been held to limit standing to those plaintiffs who allege that the asserted RICO violation was the legal, or proximate, cause of their injury, as well as a logical, or "but for," cause. *See Holmes,* 503 U.S. at 268; *see also Hecht v. Commerce Clearing House, Inc.,* 897 F.2d 21, 23 (2d Cir.1990) ("By itself, factual causation . . . is not sufficient."). The requirement that a defendant's actions be the proximate cause of a plaintiff's harm represents a policy choice premised on recognition of the impracticality of asserting liability based on the almost infinite expanse of actions that are in some sense causally related to an injury. In marking that boundary, the Supreme Court has emphasized that a plaintiff cannot complain of harm so remotely caused by a defendant's actions that imposing legal liability would transgress our "ideas of what justice demands, or of what is administratively possible and convenient." *Holmes,* 503 U.S. at 268 (internal quotation marks omitted) (quoting W. Page Keeton et al., *Prosser and Keeton on the Law of Torts* § 41, at 264 (5th ed.1984)).

C. "Direct Relation" Test

Colin contends that the chain of causation between its alleged hiring of undocumented workers and Pratt & Whitney's decision to award cleaning contracts to Colin instead of Commercial is too long and tenuous to meet the proximate cause test of *Holmes*. The defendants in *Holmes* were alleged to have participated in a conspiracy to manipulate the value of the stock of several companies. *See Holmes*, 503 U.S. at 262. Two broker-dealers who dealt in large amounts of the manipulated stock were put into liquidation when they experienced financial difficulties after the fraud was disclosed and the value of the manipulated stock precipitously declined. The Securities Investor Protection Corporation (SIPC) alleged that the defendants' securities and wire-fraud offenses amounted to a pattern of racketeering activity within the meaning of the RICO statute. It brought suit, based on a subrogation theory, on behalf of certain of the injured broker-dealer firms' customers who became unsecured creditors of the firms when the firms became insolvent. *See id.* at 270.

The *Holmes* Court applied a proximate cause test requiring a "direct relation between the injury asserted and the injurious conduct alleged." *Id.* at 268. The "direct relation" requirement generally precludes recovery by a "plaintiff who complain[s] of harm flowing merely from the misfortunes visited upon a third person by the defendant's acts." *Id.; see also Laborers Local 17 Health & Benefit Fund v. Philip Morris, Inc.,* 191 F.3d 229, 235–36 (2d Cir.1999) ("[T]he other traditional rules requiring that defendant's acts were a substantial cause of the injury, and that plaintiff's injury was reasonably foreseeable, are *additional elements*, not substitutes for alleging (and ultimately, showing) a direct injury."). The Court found that the link between the customers' losses SIPC sought to recover and the defendants' stock manipulation was too remote to satisfy the direct relation test. It explained that "[t]he broker-dealers simply cannot pay their bills, and only that intervening insolvency connects the conspirators' acts to the losses suffered by the . . . customers." *Holmes,* 503 U.S. at 271. The Court noted in contrast that the liquidating trustees suing directly on behalf of the defunct broker-dealers would have been the proper plaintiffs. *Id.* at 273.

The Court stressed the difficulty of achieving precision in fashioning a test for determining whether a plaintiff's injury was sufficiently "direct" to permit standing under RICO. *Id.* at 272 n. 20 ("[T]he infinite variety of claims that may arise make it virtually impossible to announce a black-letter rule that will dictate the result in every case." (internal quotation marks omitted)). It expressly warned against applying a mechanical test detached from the policy considerations associated with the proximate cause analysis at play in the case. *See id.* ("[O]ur use of the term 'direct' should merely be understood as a reference to the proximate-cause enquiry that is informed by the [policy] concerns set out in the [opinion]."). We have accordingly turned to those policy considerations explained in *Holmes* to guide any application of the Court's direct relation test.

D. Evaluation of Plaintiff's Claim in Relation to the Proximate Cause Test

We conclude that Commercial's complaint, when evaluated in light of these considerations, adequately states a direct proximate relationship between its injury and Colin's pattern of racketeering activity. The *Holmes* Court gave three policy reasons for limiting RICO's civil damages action only to those plaintiffs who could allege a direct injury. First, the less direct an injury is, the more difficult it becomes to determine what portion of the damages are attributable to the RICO violation as distinct from other, independent, factors. *Holmes*, 503 U.S. at 269, 273 (discussing the difficulty of determining whether customers' inability to collect from broker-dealers was the result of the defendants' stock manipulation as opposed to the broker-dealers' "poor business practices or their failures to anticipate developments in the financial markets"). Second, if recovery by indirectly injured plaintiffs were not barred, courts would be forced, in order to prevent multiple recovery, to develop complicated rules apportioning damages among groups of plaintiffs depending on how far each group was removed from the defendant's underlying RICO violation. *Id.* at 273. Third, there was no need to permit indirectly injured plaintiffs to sue, as directly injured victims could be counted on to vindicate the aims of the RICO statute, and their recovery would fix the injury to those harmed as the result of the injury they suffered. *Id.*

1. *Difficulty of Determining Damages Attributable to the RICO Violation*

The district court found plaintiff's claim deficient on the first *Holmes* factor, because a fact finder would be required to determine whether Commercial's lost business to Colin was the result of the illegal immigrant hiring scheme as opposed to independent business reasons, such as the comparative quality of the companies' services, their comparative business reputations, the fluctuations in demand for their services, or other reasons customers might have for selecting one cleaning company over another. The district court concluded that, even if a fact finder could make such a determination, the calculation of damages attributable to the illegal immigrant hiring scheme would be "daunting, if not impossible."

The difficulty of proof identified in *Holmes,* however, was quite different from the circumstances of this case. Here, the plaintiffs bid against the defendant as direct competitors. The complaint asserts that Pratt & Whitney chose Colin because Colin submitted "significantly lower" bids in a "highly competitive" price-sensitive market. According to the complaint, Colin was able to underbid its competitors because its scheme to hire illegal immigrant workers permitted it to pay well below the prevailing wage for legal workers. Although we do not deny that there may be disputes as to whether the plaintiff class lost business because of defendant's violation of § 1324(a) or for other reasons, the plaintiff class was no less directly injured than the insolvent broker-dealers in *Holmes*, whose trustees, the Court indicated, would be proper plaintiffs. *See Holmes*, 503 U.S. at 273. If plaintiffs can substantiate their claims, the plaintiffs may well show that they lost contracts directly because of the cost savings defendant realized through its scheme to employ illegal workers.

This theory fits our suggestion in [*Sperber v. Boesky*, 849 F.2d 60, 65 (2d Cir. 1988)], where we affirmed the dismissal on proximate causation grounds of a civil RICO complaint by investors whose share values declined in the wake of the defendant's guilty plea to insider trading. Although we found the causation chain offered by plaintiffs too remote, we distinguished a circumstance where a plaintiff was a direct competitor against a defendant. *See id.* We stated that the RICO statute would grant standing if plaintiff were a "head-to-head bidder against [defendant] who lost because of [defendant's] illegally-enhanced reputation or economic power." *Id.* Where, as here, the parties have bid against each other, the difference between the lowest and second lowest bid[3] is readily discoverable. If Commercial can prove that but for Colin's lower wage costs attributable to its illegal hiring scheme, Commercial would have won the contract and would have earned a profit on it, it will have shown a proximately caused injury, compensable under RICO.

Colin objects that any reduced labor costs were due to its alleged underpayment of workers and failure to pay other employment-related costs of doing business, not its participation in the illegal immigrant hiring scheme. In other words, Colin claims that Commercial complains of an injury caused by the low wages paid to Colin's workers—and not by their immigration status. Of course, paying workers less than the prevailing wage and failing to withhold payroll taxes are not RICO predicate acts. Nonetheless, the purpose of the alleged violation of 8 U.S.C. § 1324(a), the hiring of illegal alien workers, was to take advantage of their diminished bargaining position, so as to employ a cheaper labor force and compete unfairly on the basis of lower costs. By illegally hiring undocumented alien labor, Colin was able to hire cheaper labor and compete unfairly. The violation of § 1324(a) alleged by the complaint was a proximate cause of Colin's ability to underbid the plaintiffs and take business from them.

---

[3]   Commercial asserted at oral argument that it was the second bidder to Colin on at least one contract.

2. *Difficulty of Apportioning Damages Among Injured Parties*

The *Holmes* Court warned that if courts did not limit recovery to injuries directly related to the RICO violation, they would be forced to devise complicated rules apportioning damages among plaintiffs at different degrees of separation from the violative acts alleged. *See Holmes*, 503 U.S. at 273. The Court noted the difficulty of apportioning damages between the broker-dealers and customers who suffered losses when the broker-dealers became insolvent. Colin contends that its business competitors are not the only aggrieved parties who could recover under Commercial's theory and that the difficulty of apportioning damages among potential plaintiffs will be severe. Colin's response misses the point. The point made in *Holmes* was that, if damages are paid both to first tier plaintiffs—those directly injured by defendant's alleged acts—and to second tier plaintiffs—those injured by the injury to the first tier plaintiffs—then the payment of damages to the first tier plaintiffs would cure the harm to the second tier plaintiffs, and the payment of damages to the latter category would involve double compensation. Colin's answer is no answer to this point. If a defendant's illegal acts caused direct injury to more than one category of plaintiffs, the defendant may well be obligated to compensate different plaintiffs for different injuries. It does not follow that any plaintiff will have been twice benefitted, which was the concern in *Holmes*.

Unlike the situation in *Holmes*, Commercial and its fellow class members are not alleging an injury that was derivative of injury to others. Commercial does not seek to recover based on "the misfortunes visited upon a third person by the defendant's acts." *Holmes*, 503 U.S. at 268. It claims to have lost profits directly as the result of Colin's underbidding, which it achieved through its violation of § 1324(a). *See Terminate Control Corp. v. Horowitz*, 28 F.3d 1335, 1343 (2d Cir.1994) (holding that the value of business opportunities lost due to defendant's RICO violations is compensable); *Mid Atlantic Telecom Inc. v. Long Distance Servs., Inc.*, 18 F.3d 260, 264 (4th Cir.1994) (noting that plaintiff was not seeking to vindicate claims of customers who accepted defendant's fraudulent, ostensibly lower rates, but rather alleged "distinct and independent injuries: lost customers and lost revenues"). We have stated a plaintiff has standing where the plaintiff is the direct target of the RICO violation. *See Abrahams v. Young & Rubicam Inc.*, 79 F.3d 234, 238 (2d Cir.1996); [*In re American Express Co. S'Holder Litig.*, 39 F.3d 395, 400 (2d Cir. 1994)] (targets of RICO violations were competitive rivals not shareholders harmed by decrease in stock value upon exposure of scheme). As discussed above, the theory of Commercial's claim is that Colin undertook the illegal immigrant hiring scheme in order to undercut its business rivals, thus qualifying them as direct targets of the RICO violation.

Colin raises the specter of a proliferation of civil RICO suits that would be permitted under Commercial's theory. It argues that a finding in Commercial's favor would mean that a dance club that failed to pay license fees on recordings it played, thereby decreasing its overhead costs and thereby allowing it to decrease its admission charge, would be liable not only to the copyright holder but to all the infringer's business competitors. We do not find this hypothetical problematic. First, the hypothetical competitors would still be required to overcome the hurdle of showing that their loss of business was proximately caused by the infringer's decrease in admission fees. But more importantly, once again, the concern of *Holmes* was that a violator might be obligated to pay double compensation if required to compensate those directly injured and those injured by the injury to those directly injured. It was not that a violator might be obligated to compensate two or more different classes of plaintiffs, each of which suffered a different concrete injury, proximately caused by the violation. In Colin's hypothetical, the competitors and the copyright owners would have suffered entirely separate injuries. Although there may well be other reasons such plaintiffs would lack standing, they would not be barred from bringing a RICO action because of a concern for multiple recoveries. Compensating both would not overcompensate any plaintiff.

3. *Ability of Other Parties to Vindicate Aims of the Statute*

In relation to the third *Holmes* policy factor, the Supreme Court has observed that "[t]he existence of an identifiable class of persons whose self-interest would normally motivate them to vindicate the public interest in [RICO] enforcement diminishes the justification for allowing a more remote party . . . to perform the office of a private attorney general." *Associated Gen. Contractors of California, Inc. v. California State Council of Carpenters,* 459 U.S. 519, 542 (1983), *cited in Holmes,* 503 U.S. at 270. Colin argues that this factor weighs against Commercial's standing, because other parties, such as state and federal authorities charged with collecting unpaid taxes and workers' compensation fees, may sue to vindicate the statute. Moreover, the INS, which enforces § 1324(a), has already obtained Colin's agreement to pay $1 million for violations of the immigration laws.

Once again, Colin misses the point. If the existence of a public authority that could prosecute a claim against putative RICO defendants meant that the plaintiff is too remote under *Holmes,* then no private cause of action could ever be maintained, for every RICO predicate offense, as well as the RICO enterprise itself, is separately prosecutable by the government. In *Holmes,* those directly injured could be expected to sue, and their recovery would redound to the benefit of the plaintiffs suing for indirect injury. Here, in contrast, suits by governmental authorities to recover lost taxes and fees would do nothing to alleviate the plaintiffs' loss of profits. There is no class of potential plaintiffs who have been more directly injured by the alleged RICO conspiracy than the defendant's business competitors, who have a greater incentive to ensure that a RICO violation does not go undetected or unremedied, and whose recovery would indirectly cure the loss suffered by these plaintiffs.

. . . .

III. Pleading the Elements of the Predicate Offense

We agree with Colin that Commercial's complaint was deficient in one respect. While alleging that Colin has committed "well over 100 acts of knowingly hiring illegal aliens," it failed to allege an essential element of § 1324(a)—that Colin had actual knowledge that the illegal aliens it hired were brought into the country in violation of the statute.

Although Commercial's complaint fails to allege an essential element of the RICO predicate offense, the flaw is not fatal, and can be cured by repleading.[5]

CONCLUSION

The judgment of the district court is vacated, and the case is remanded for further proceedings consistent with this opinion.

NOTES & QUESTIONS

(1) What is the correct causation standard for civil RICO claims and how should courts determine if the standard has been met?

(2) The district court found that Commercial was unable to establish that it lost contracts due to Colin's RICO violations. Why did the Second Circuit disagree? How could Commercial show that the RICO violation was the proximate cause of its injury?

(3) Colin argued that where a suit involves multiple victims, liability should be limited under the direct relation test because it will be difficult to apportion damages accurately. Why was the Second Circuit unpersuaded by this argument? How is the Commercial-Colin dispute different from *Holmes*?

(4) Colin also argued for the dismissal of Commercial's claim because other parties, such as state and federal authorities, could sue to vindicate the rights of those harmed (such as Commercial). Why was the Second Circuit unpersuaded by this argument? *See 4 K & D Corp. v. Concierge Auctions, LLC*, 2 F.Supp.3d 525 (S.D.N.Y. 2014) (noting that a real estate auction house could not allege a RICO violation against another competitor because the auction house only suffered an indirect injury, which was derivative of injury to the property sellers, and the property sellers were capable of bringing suit).

---

[5] At oral argument, Commercial asserted that it can allege Colin's knowledge of how the workers in question were brought into the country and that they were brought into the country in violation of § 1324(a).

(5)   "But for" causation is not enough to succeed on a civil RICO claim; proximate cause is also required. This typically means showing both that the RICO violation was a substantial factor in causing the plaintiff's injury, and that the injury was foreseeable. *See Baisch v. Gallina*, 346 F.3d 366, 373–74 (2d Cir. 2003) ("[T]he plaintiff must have suffered a direct injury that was foreseeable: Central to the notion of proximate cause [under RICO] is the idea that a person is not liable to all those who may have been injured by his conduct, but only to those with respect to whom his acts were a substantial factor in the sequence of responsible causation, and whose injury was reasonably foreseeable or anticipated as a natural consequence.").

(6)   Deciding what RICO violations qualify as the proximate cause of an injury is not always clear. In *Anza v. Ideal Steel Supply Corp.*, 547 U.S. 451 (2006), the plaintiff claimed that its competitor had defrauded the state by failing to pay sales taxes on products that it sold, which enabled the competitor to sell the products at a lower price. The Supreme Court held that the direct victim of the scheme was the state, and it similarly concluded that the injury suffered by the plaintiffs was not shown to be directly caused by the RICO violations. The Court stated that the defendant "could have lowered its prices for any number of reasons unconnected to the asserted pattern of fraud." *Id.* at 458. Although the Court acknowledged that there was no risk of duplicative recoveries (a factor considered in *Holmes*), it nonetheless concluded that the cause of the injury before the Court was too speculative in nature to allow the claim to proceed. *Id.* at 459.

In contrast to *Anza*, consider *Bridge v. Phoenix Bond & Indemnity Co.*, 553 U.S. 639 (2008). *Bridge* involved a rather complicated tax lien bidding process where bidders purchased tax liens on property from the county. The property owners could redeem their respective properties by paying the amount of the delinquent taxes plus a penalty to the winning bidder. Instead of bidding money, the winning bidders were those who agreed to accept the lowest percentage penalty from the owners, which resulted in multiple bids of zero percent. The county set up a rotational system where the zero percent bidders would purchase the liens in turn, and it established a corresponding rule that no bidder could use agents or other related parties to create bids (as that would effectively give the bidder another position in the rotation). One bidder violated this rule by fraudulently claiming to be different entities, and the plaintiffs sued based upon the smaller number of liens that they were able to obtain. The defendants argued that the plaintiffs did not meet the *Holmes* direct-relation requirement and thus could not establish injury under RICO. The Court disagreed, finding that the plaintiffs were the only parties who could show harm from the scheme.[d] *See id.* at 654–55.

Why were the plaintiffs able to succeed in *Bridge*, but not in *Anza* and *Holmes*? In light of the later *Anza* and *Bridge* decisions, do you think that *Commercial Cleaning* would be decided the same way today?

---

[d]   The defendants also claimed that the plaintiffs could not recover because they did not rely on the fraud. The Court clarified that, as far as a civil RICO claim was concerned, only proximately caused injury was required to be shown by the plaintiffs—not direct reliance.

PROBLEM 13.5

(a) Look back at Problem 13.2 and recall that Bill saw a decline in business seemingly due to Tedz' marijuana sales, which made it possible for Tedz to offer coffee at lower prices. Assume that Bill is able to show through customer surveys that he is in fact losing business to Tedz based on the lower coffee prices. Under the reasoning of *Holmes, Commercial Cleaning, Anza,* and *Bridge*, should Bill be able to recover?

(b) Assume that right next to Tedz is Grimm's Laundromat. Like Bill, the laundromat has seen a significant drop in business since Tedz opened. Grimm's believes that many of its customers no longer feel comfortable patronizing its business due to the clientele of Tedz next door. Assuming that Grimm's can show a loss in business since Tedz opened, should Grimm's be able to recover under the reasoning of the above-cited cases?

F. AVAILABLE REMEDIES

Section 1964(c) provides that an injured party "shall recover threefold the damages he sustains and the cost of the suit, including a reasonable attorney's fee." Damages are usually measured in the form of out-of-pocket loss, and they can include lost profits and even future damages to the extent the plaintiff can establish the amount with a reasonable degree of certainty. The measure of damages is subject to the single-satisfaction rule, which means that any amount paid in settlement by co-defendants is deducted from the total award at trial. Importantly, this reduction comes from the tripled amount of damages—i.e., the total damages are tripled and then the deduction is made.

The availability of punitive damages and equitable relief under RICO is not clear—largely because § 1964(c) is silent on the issues. A number of judicial opinions have concluded that the remedies listed in the statute are exclusive and that punitive damages are therefore unavailable. Similarly, courts have held that injunctive relief, as well as the equitable remedy of disgorgement, are also unavailable under § 1964.

The attorney's fee provision is an exception to the "American Rule" that parties must bear their own costs. The provision is a mandatory, one-way fee-shifting clause that benefits any plaintiff who obtains a judgment on the merits. This means, of course, that attorney's fees are unavailable to plaintiffs who settle or who simply achieve interim success on motions followed by settlement. Courts have generally held that the attorney's fee provision does not require proportionality to the actual award. It is therefore possible for the plaintiff to receive more in attorney's fees than in damages. *See, e.g., Northeast Women's Center v. McMonagle,* 889 F.2d 466, 471–74 (3d Cir. 1989) (approving an award of approximately $65,000 in attorney's fees and costs even though the tripled damages award was less than $2,700).

G. PRACTICAL CONCERNS FOR A CIVIL RICO CLAIM

Given the availability of treble damages and attorney's fees, it is no wonder that a civil RICO claim is attractive to many plaintiffs. However, there are a number of practical concerns that should be weighed before deciding to bring a claim. First, not all plaintiffs want their lawsuits heard in federal court, which may have more stringent pleading requirements than state court. Second, as is likely clear to you by now, civil RICO claims are difficult to plead and prove, and they may be harder for juries to understand than more garden-variety claims (such as fraud). Third, civil RICO claims involving intentional conduct may be excluded from the coverage of directors and officers liability insurance. This means that any collection from director or officer defendants will be dependent upon their individual ability to pay (and will also be subject to the prospect of individual bankruptcy). Finally, the stigma of being labeled as a racketeer may make settlement less likely in particular cases, as some defendants may believe that a favorable judicial outcome is the only way to avoid such a "taint." While these concerns do not necessarily suggest that civil RICO claims should be avoided, they are considerations that plaintiffs should weigh in deciding whether a particular RICO claim makes sense.

INDEX

References are to Pages